HANDBOOK OF DEVELOPMENT ECONOMICS
VOLUME 4

HANDBOOKS IN ECONOMICS

9

Series Editors

KENNETH J. ARROW
MICHAEL D. INTRILIGATOR

AMSTERDAM • BOSTON • HEIDELBERG • LONDON
NEW YORK • OXFORD • PARIS • SAN DIEGO
SAN FRANCISCO • SINGAPORE • SYDNEY • TOKYO

HANDBOOK OF DEVELOPMENT ECONOMICS

VOLUME 4

Edited by

T. PAUL SCHULTZ

Malcolm K. Brachman Professor of Economics, Yale University, CT, USA

and

JOHN STRAUSS

Professor of Economics, University of Southern California, USA

AMSTERDAM · BOSTON · HEIDELBERG · LONDON
NEW YORK · OXFORD · PARIS · SAN DIEGO
SAN FRANCISCO · SINGAPORE · SYDNEY · TOKYO

ELSEVIER

North-Holland is an imprint of Elsevier
Radarweg 29, PO Box 211, 1000 AE Amsterdam, The Netherlands
Linacre House, Jordan Hill, Oxford OX2 8DP, UK

First edition 2008

Library of Congress Cataloging-in-Publication Data
A catalog record for this book is available from the Library of Congress

British Library Cataloguing in Publication Data
A catalogue record for this book is available from the British Library

ISBN: 978-0-444-53100-1

ISSN: 0169-7218 (Handbooks in Economics series)
ISSN: 1573-4471 (Handbook of Development Economics series)

For information on all North-Holland publications
visit our website at books.elsevier.com

Printed and bound in the UK

08 09 10 11 12   10 9 8 7 6 5 4 3 2 1

INTRODUCTION TO THE SERIES

The aim of the *Handbooks in Economics* series is to produce Handbooks for various branches of economics, each of which is a definitive source, reference, and teaching supplement for use by professional researchers and advanced graduate students. Each Handbook provides self-contained surveys of the current state of a branch of economics in the form of chapters prepared by leading specialists on various aspects of this branch of economics. These surveys summarize not only received results but also newer developments, from recent journal articles and discussion papers. Some original material is also included, but the main goal is to provide comprehensive and accessible surveys The Handbooks are intended to provide not only useful reference volumes for professional collections but also possible supplementary readings for advanced courses for graduate students in economics.

KENNETH J. ARROW and MICHAEL D. INTRILIGATOR

CONTENTS OF THE HANDBOOK

VOLUME 1

INTRODUCTION

The field of development economics has evolved since Volume 3 of the Handbook was published more than a decade ago. Volume 4 takes stock of some of the newer trends and their implications for research in the field and our understanding of economic development. First, the micro-economic orientation of the field is increasingly evident, and is reflected here. Economic behavior is traced from the individual to family, and in some cases to the local schools or communities and labor markets. Because most people in poor countries continue to work in agriculture, the focus is often on the family farm and includes household production, following the early leads of Gary Becker (1981), as well as the emphasis assigned to human capital as a constraint on development by T.W. Schultz (1964, 1974). A second emerging feature of the field is an interest in explaining how institutions develop and operate in low-income countries, or political economy. A third change in the field is the vast improvement in data, primarily in the form of household surveys and censuses combined with local community modules which facilitate the identification of causal effects from outside of the household, in terms of environmental factors, relative prices, local policies and facilities, in which the response of individuals, families, and communities to policies may be heterogeneous. A variety of econometric methods have become commonplace, relying on improved panel and community data which allow the introduction of fixed effects and provide more credible instruments for program treatment when randomized designs are not feasible, and have arguably attenuated or eliminated some of the more obvious sources of estimation bias. A fourth development is the alternative strategies adopted to evaluate the effects of policy initiatives, including the selection of who participates in the policy programs from among those who are eligible to participate. The different methods for program evaluation are founded in classical statistics and econometrics, but ultimately rely on different identification strategies for estimating key parameters, such as the response or outcome changes attributable to program treatment. Behavioral mechanisms can be structurally modeled with layers of more or less attractive working assumptions, or summarized by a reduced-form approximation subsuming technical/biological/behavioral structural components but still estimating the sum of direct and indirect effect of the program on policy objectives. When these structural or reduced form approaches to evaluation do not credibly identify the critical program effects, organizing specific social experiments have been designed and implemented with increasing frequency, where the policy treatments are administered randomly at the individual, family, or community level.

The handbook is divided into four sections (Parts 10–13), of which the first (Part 10) deals with agricultural and rural development. In the first article (Chapter 47) Andrew

Foster and Mark Rosenzweig, challenge, for rural India, some of the oldest views regarding the role of agriculture in fostering industrial development. They review the literature on the linkages between non-farm employment and agriculture, demonstrating that in India at least, that it was capital movement across rural areas, from high wage to low wage areas, that was the spark for rural non-farm employment. Migration of labor is less important.

Kaivan Munshi, in Chapter 48, surveys the relatively new area of development economics that is concerned with networks of people, and their impacts on factors such as the diffusion of production technology, as for example, agricultural and contraceptive technologies. This literature is focused on the role of networks in spreading information, and adds to the pioneering work of Griliches (1957), who pointed out that it was profitability that was ultimately responsible for the adoption or not of new technologies. However, the speed of that diffusion may be a function, in addition to underlying potential profits, to the degree of information flows which are affected by social networks. Networks may be interpreted as indigenous institutions that operate alongside market institutions, possibly correcting market failures and under some conditions improving the efficiency and equity of development, or the reverse.

The second section (Part 11) is concerned with developments in the theory and evidence regarding public goods and political economy. Abhijit Banerjee, Lakshmi Iyer and Rohini Somanathan review developments in the theories explaining when public action in rural areas gets harnessed politically to ensure provision of appropriate kinds, quality and levels of public goods. They focus on collective action and its interaction with various "top down processes." This chapter, which focuses on the supply side of public goods, is closely related to the chapters of the third section (Part 12), which discuss household demand for public goods in the social service sectors of family planning, education, health.

Rohini Pande, in Chapter 50, examines the recent political economy literature related to the issue of corruption in low income countries. She focuses here on the underlying factors that give rise to corruption in the first instance, including the political processes from which corruption emerges, and the economic incentives giving rise to opportunities for corrupt behavior.

The third section (Part 12) of this Volume is focused on the behavior of households and individuals regarding various aspects of human capital investments, in the face of the various constraints that they face, particularly market incentives and public goods. This is the longest section of the Volume, reflecting in part, the enormous amount of research which has continued to extend the frontiers of the field since Volumes 3A and 3B of the Handbook. In Chapter 51, Marcel Fafchamps and Agnes Quisumbing look at the processes behind formation of households in rural areas. They are quite general, examining the reasons why people might want to form households, then discussing marriage, divorce, the reasons for single-parent households, as well as more general reasons why people move into and out of households, and what determines dowries, child fostering, and old age support. Income generating opportunities for women are viewed as changing the bargaining power of women, a development underlying many of the noted changes in the family.

T. Paul Schultz takes up the issue of fertility and discusses the evidence, or lack of it, on how exogenous changes in fertility prices, such as contraception or the availability of new family planning programs, affect fertility and thereby a variety of outcomes related to the woman's welfare and that of her family including children, in the long-run. Evidence for many of the interesting questions having to do with the child "quantity–quality tradeoff" is examined, based on instruments such as twins, sex composition of children, or exposure to program treatments. The potentially unbiased estimates of the effects of declines in fertility on women's health, market labor supply, and child survival and schooling are positive, but tend to be smaller than estimates that simply treat fertility as exogenous and fail to control for the various problems of omitted variables, selection, and non-random program placement.

Germano Mwabu takes up health in Chapter 53. He reviews the extensive economics literature on health from industrial countries and asks what is relevant in poor countries. He notes that many topics that have consumed the attention of health economists have been largely left out of economic development, such as the literature on health insurance, moral hazard and adverse selection, and the bias in estimates of health production functions arising because health inputs are correlated with the errors in the health production function. He reviews studies of income and health, noting the difficulties of identification, and surveys causal studies documenting health impacts on income and labor market outcomes.

John Strauss and Duncan Thomas, in Chapter 54, extend their earlier work on the linkages between health and development. They review both static and dynamic economic models of health and the connections between health and other outcomes such as wages. They discuss measurement issues, providing some basic facts regarding some correlations between health and development at both the country and individual levels, and bringing to bear recent developments in the measurement of health. They then discuss the literature relating health events in early life or even in utero on health and productivity outcomes across the life cycle. They argue that economists have much to learn from the growing knowledge of biological processes, and the accumulating evidence linking schooling attainment to early health status. Finally, they summarize what has been learned from the empirical literature on the impacts of HIV/AIDS on development, through its effects on child schooling, family labor supply, household incomes, expenditures and assets.

Investments in schooling are taken up in Chapter 55 by Peter Orazem and Elizabeth King. They provide a framework within which to analyze the private demand for schooling, and the school supply of educational services. Their model focuses first on the critical behavioral and technical parameters that help to explain empirical regularities in schooling attainment and cognitive achievement, as well as differences between females and males, and rural and urban populations in low-income countries. They then present static and dynamic models of the demand for school choice, focusing on the role of government policies underlying supply. Although increasing refinement in the estimation of wage functions yield similar private returns to schooling, the efforts to estimate school production functions have not been as successful, probably because of the difficulty of identifying models with endogenous school inputs. Measurement of schooling outcomes and inputs is discussed in closing.

In Chapter 56 Edward Miguel and Paul Glewwe take up the specific question of how better health and nutrition of young children impact schooling. This pathway from better early child health and nutrition to cognitive achievement has long been hypothesized to be important, but only in the last ten years has there been considerable progress by economists on this issue, and the literature is surveyed by Miguel and Glewwe. They distinguish between cross-sectional and panel data studies. The early studies in this literature tended to be cross-sectional and required extremely strong and untested assumptions to obtain unbiased estimates. Some of the panel data studies have improved this situation, but more recent experimental studies have provided the best evidence to date.

The topic of child labor, which is of course closely related to child schooling, is taken up in Chapter 57 by Eric Edmonds. He reviews the evidence of characteristics of children who work and what types of work is normally performed by children. Data problems are discussed extensively, for it is not easy to document child labor since much of it occurs within the household or as unpaid labor in family self employment activities. Some models of child work are presented and the growing literature on children's work is surveyed. The chapter ends with a detailed discussion of different policy options to discourage child work and the evidence on the connections between schooling and work of children.

Finally in Chapter 58, Donald Cox and Marcel Fafchamps discuss extended families and kin networks. They focus on the interrelationships between public transfers such as social security, and family transfers, and whether public programs crowd out private transfers. As part of this, they review the large literature on intergenerational transfers between parents and their adult children, and the related issues of risk sharing and public and private transfers. At the end of the chapter they discuss the relevance of the recent evolutionary biology literature on the family to understanding economic behavior of the family.

Since Volumes 3A and 3B appeared in 1995, increased attention has been directed to program evaluation by development economists. This involves evaluation, largely of benefits, of different investments or programs, like a child de-worming program or a conditional cash transfer program to motivate parents to invest in their children's human capital. The fourth section (Part 13) contains papers that describe the different methods now available, both experimental and non-experimental, to conduct program evaluations, as well as describing papers that implement these methods.

Martin Ravallion, in Chapter 59, reviews non-experimental methods that are increasingly used to mimic social experiments. He discusses methods using panel data, such as difference in difference, but also methods such as propensity score matching that stress the construction of treatment and control populations to simulate the implicit counterfactual outcomes used in evaluation when social experiments are not possible. The assumptions that are required for each method are set out and practical problems and the applicability of these methods in different settings are considered. He reviews in depth many recent studies that have used these methods, particularly to evaluate anti-poverty programs, and argues that no one method dominates the others. The best method is context dependent.

Petra Todd, in Chapter 60, sets out the econometric theory behind non-experimental program evaluation. There is complementarity between her chapter and Ravallion's with Todd focusing somewhat more on the theoretical background. She reviews regression-based estimators, matching estimators, control function estimators, instrumental variables estimators and regression discontinuity design estimators, detailing the assumptions and potential biases of each. She then discusses some practical issues of implementation.

Social experiments are extensively discussed in Chapter 61 by Esther Duflo, Rachel Glennerster and Michael Kremer. Randomization is a tool that is relatively new in development economics, and being used increasingly. It can, when used well, overcome problems of omitted variables bias and selection bias that are prominent with non-experimental data. On the other hand, other non-experimental problems can arise, notably non-random attrition, which may effectively undo the randomization. Carefully thought though experiments are one tool amongst many. It can be very useful and influential as in the built-in evaluation of the Progresa welfare program in rural Mexico.

Susan Parker, Luis Rubalcava and Graciela Teruel review in Chapter 62 this well-known experimental program evaluation, that of the Mexican Progresa, which offered, starting in 1998, cash transfers to poor mothers, conditional on their children receiving basic health care and attending school regularly. Starting in 1997 with surveys of 500 poor rural villages, two thirds of the village began receiving the program in the fall of 1998 whereas the remaining third entered the program two years later in 2000, allowing a two year window during which to follow the treatment and control households. Many papers have been written using these public data from the Progresa rural social experiment, and papers are starting to emerge analyzing the urban extension of the program named Oportunidades. Progresa relied on a randomized design of treatment and control at the village level because of the relatively remote location of the poor communities, whereas the Oportunidades in poor urban settings was designed to compare a matched set of urban communities, with and without the program, relying also on propensity score matching of eligibles. The difficulties of implementing and analyzing these types of data from social welfare programs are summarized in this final chapter. The authors also survey the expanding number of countries where similar conditional cash transfer programs have since been implemented in Latin American and their emergence elsewhere in the developing world.

Acknowledgements

We appreciate the prolonged efforts of the authors to develop their papers for this Handbook, and their prompt responses to the suggestions of their colleagues, reviewers and editors. We are grateful for the support provided by the Rockefeller Foundation's Bellagio Conference Center in Italy for their hospitality in coordinating the conference at which drafts of these papers were first presented and critically evaluated on May 2–6, 2005. The special setting offered by Bellagio contributed to our work in difficult to evaluate ways, but the Villa's reputation undoubtedly helped attendance when some were still balancing teaching at their home institutions. The planning and participation at the conference was financed by a Rockefeller Foundation grant to the Economic Growth Center of Yale University for training and research program on the family in low-income countries, and some authors were affected by this program at an earlier stage in their careers. We thank Kathryn Toensmeier who made travel arrangements.

References

Becker, G.S. (1981). A Treatise on the Family. Harvard Univ. Press, Cambridge, MA.
Griliches, Z. (1957). "Hybrid corn: An exploration in the economics of technological change". Econometrica 25 (4), 501–522.
Schultz, T.W. (1964). Transforming Traditional Agriculture. Yale Univ. Press, New Haven, CT.
Schultz, T.W. (1974). Economics of the Family: Marriage, Children and Human Capital. Univ. of Chicago Press, Chicago.

T. PAUL SCHULTZ
JOHN STRAUSS

CONTENTS OF VOLUME 4

PART 11: PUBLIC GOODS AND POLITICAL ECONOMY: THEORY AND
EVIDENCE

Chapter 49
Public Action for Public Goods

Chapter 50
Understanding Political Corruption in Low Income Countries

Chapter 60
Evaluating Social Programs with Endogenous Program Placement and Selection
of the Treated

Chapter 61
Using Randomization in Development Economics Research: A Toolkit
ESTHER DUFLO, RACHEL GLENNERSTER AND MICHAEL KREMER

PART 10

NEW INSIGHTS INTO RURAL AND AGRICULTURAL DEVELOPMENT

Chapter 47

ECONOMIC DEVELOPMENT AND THE DECLINE OF AGRICULTURAL EMPLOYMENT*

ANDREW D. FOSTER

Economics Department, Brown University, Box B, 64 Waterman Street, Providence, RI 02912, USA

MARK R. ROSENZWEIG

Economic Growth Center, Yale University, PO Box 208269, New Haven, CT 06520-8269, USA

Contents

* The research for this paper supported in part by grants NIH HD30907, NIH HD28687, and NSF SBR93-0405.

Handbook of Development Economics, Volume 4
DOI: 10.1016/S1573-4471(07)04047-8

Abstract

This chapter considers the linkages between agricultural development and rural non-farm activities. The chapter is motivated by growing evidence that non-farm activities provide an increasingly important share of rural incomes in many low-income questions, questions about whether increasing agricultural productivity is a necessary precondition for raising incomes and reducing poverty in rural areas, and increased evidence of factor and commodity flows between rural and urban areas. Unfortunately, the existing literature is sparse and has not been sufficiently attentive to the underlying structures and mechanisms that drive the relationship between agricultural productivity and rural non-farm change. A particular weakness of this literature is the lack of attention given to the importance of flows of both capital and labor. The reason for this is in part due to the limitations of existing data. An assessment of the strengths and weaknesses of existing data sets is thus also provided, with particular attention to panel data sets that might be useful for assessing the extent of geographic mobility. In order to clarify the relevant issues the Chapter presents a model of the rural economy that permits examination of the linkages between agricultural development and non-farm employment under different regimes distinguished by the mobility of capita and labor. Basic features of the model are then tested using newly available data from South Asia. The Chapter concludes with suggestions for future data collection efforts as well as the development of more sophisticated models of the rural economy.

Keywords

non-farm, rural, migration, development

JEL classification: O13, O14, O15, O18

1. Introduction

Among the most pervasive features of the process of economic development is the shift of labor out of the agricultural sector into other such sectors as manufacturing and services. This pattern is thought to be a necessary component of the process of sustained macroeconomic growth because of two significant facts: that per capita demand for agricultural goods is relatively price- and income-inelastic at high levels of income and that the presence of a dominant fixed factor in agricultural production (land) limits the ability of the agricultural sector to absorb labor in the face of growing population levels. Surprisingly, however, while there is a substantial theoretical and empirical macroeconomic literature describing this transformation (see e.g. Syrquin, 1988), the microeconomic foundations of the transition from an agriculture-based economy to a diversified industrial economy are poorly understood.

Two important aspects of the exit from agriculture that are even less studied are the spatial dimension and the selectivity of the process in terms of the human capital of those who leave the agricultural sector. With respect to the former, for example, it is unclear what conditions must be in place for the movement of labor from agriculture to non-farm activities to reflect changes in the locus of economic activity as opposed to changes in the nature of economic activity at any given point. That is, it is unclear when the reduction in agricultural activities is accompanied by rural to urban migration and when it is not. To the extent that there is a change in the nature of economic activity at a particular place, little is also known about how this process is affected by local conditions such as local rates of agricultural productivity growth, the presence of physical infrastructure that links local and regional markets, and opportunities for investment in levels of human capital. With respect to the selectivity of the exit of people from agriculture, although the reduction in the size of the population engaged in agriculture is generally thought to be selective in terms of the types of people who are most likely to shift to non-agricultural employment, the nature of this selection and the extent to which the benefits of this transformation accrue primarily to those who undertake these new activities versus the population as a whole are also not well understood.

The significance of these issues is perhaps most clearly seen in terms of the debates about the necessity of agricultural productivity growth for achieving sustained economic growth. Agricultural development is seen by many researchers (e.g., Mellor, 2000; Johnson, 2000) as critical for economic development. Advances in agricultural productivity improve welfare by lowering the cost of food and by freeing up persons to engage in non-farm activities that produce goods and services that enrich lives. From a global perspective, the proposition that agricultural development is necessary for economic development is clear. What is less understood is the relationship between agricultural development and non-farm activities within rural areas in which agricultural development occurs. Knowledge about the linkage between agricultural productivity and rural non-farm employment is important because most of the world's poor is located in rural areas and engaged in agriculture and the lowest-income countries are primarily agricultural. Indeed, billions of dollars are spent in developing higher-productivity crops that can be grown in even the least suitable agricultural areas of the world, where many poor reside, based on the idea that agricultural development is a necessary component of a development policy everywhere.

In this Chapter we examine the linkages between agricultural development and rural non-farm activities. We first review in Section 2 the literature on the agriculture-non-agriculture nexus in rural areas. This literature is sparse, and has a major failing – it does not consider how the impact of agricultural development on the *local* rural economy, which is the focus of this literature, may be mediated by the spatial mobility of goods, capital and labor. We also review the literature on out-migration from rural areas, a literature that is even more sparse. Both literatures, which are in principle related, suffer from a lack of data as well as a suitable framework. Hence we discuss data issues; including the principal failings of existing data sets, how some existing data can be used to better understand migration, and what kinds of new data are needed; and the need to develop a more comprehensive simple general-equilibrium model of a rural economy incorporating factor flows. Information on salient features of migration from a number of countries with appropriate data are also shown. In Section 3 we present the rural economy model, which is used to examine the linkages between agricultural development and non-farm employment under different regimes characterized by the mobility of capital and labor. In Section 4 we use the model to examine newly-available data to assess the propositions in the literature about the relationships between agricultural productivity improvements and local non-farm activities in South Asia. Section 5 uses the same data to assess the relationships between agricultural development and the magnitude and selectivity of rural out-migration.

2. Literature

2.1. Rural non-farm activities, rural poverty and agricultural development

Although much of the empirical literature on non-farm activities in rural areas of developing countries is of recent vintage, there is an older literature that examines from a more theoretical perspective whether the rural non-farm sector is likely to survive a process of sustained economic development. These models were developed to explain the apparent decline in rural nonagricultural activities in developing countries during the colonial era (Hymer and Resnick, 1969). The idea is that most traditional non-farm production in rural areas represents subsistence production of goods used by rural households such as clothing, cutlery and furniture. These goods are unlikely to be able to compete on grounds of cost or quality with mass-produced items that become available through the intervention of colonial powers. More generally, it seems plausible that the process of increased specialization and trade that is fundamental to the process of economic development should reallocate production activities in rural households away from the generation of these types of goods and toward the production of cash crops that can be used to finance the purchase of modern consumer goods.

It is clear, however, that this argument rests heavily on a specific characterization of non-farm activity. Ranis and Stewart (1973) note that despite the predictions made in the earlier literature the non-farm sector in many rural villages has remained quite active. To justify these apparent patterns they propose a more sophisticated characterization of the rural non-farm sector that includes both traditional processes as described above and modern-influenced activities such as metal-working and machinery repair shops. While traditional activities such as household rice milling or hand-looming may will be crowded out through the process of market integration, there are non-farm activities that may reasonably be set in rural areas, although the organization of such activities is likely to be quite different from that characterizing traditional non-farm products. More significantly, whether non-farm activities can be retained will depend importantly on the structure and distribution of economic activity and even macroeconomic policy. The structure of consumer demand which may, for example, be influenced in their model through inequality (large plantations are less likely to generate local demand for non-farm products than smaller family farms), plays a particularly important role in their model. As an example, they present descriptive statistics from Taiwan and the Philippines that, consistent with their argument, suggest that substantially higher levels of land inequality in the Philippines are responsible for its low growth in non-farm employment over the 1970s and 1980s (8.4 percentage points) relative to Taiwan (27.8 percentage points).

More recent data clearly support the proposition that non-farm activity remains an important share of the rural economy. Lanjouw and Lanjouw (2001), in a useful survey article describe some of the relevant data from a variety of different countries. It notes that the percentage employed in the non-farm rural sector is quite consistent across the major continents, with most figures being in the range of 20–40% for both men and women. While there are very few studies that permit a direct comparison over time using comparable measures of non-farm employment, these figures are sufficiently high that it would seem reasonable to conclude that the process of development has *not* substantially diminished the non-farm sector.

A second major and long-standing issue has to do with whether agricultural development is a necessary precondition for growth in the rural non-farm sector (see, e.g., Binswanger, 1983). This is not only a significant question intellectually in terms of what it says about the process of growth, but it is also one that has considerable policy importance. In particular, if non-farm growth is dependent on agricultural development to take place than there would seem to be a particularly high return to investments in agricultural technology. While there is little question that modifications to agricultural seeds and processes have had a major impact on yields and therefore food output in the world's most productive land, a considerable share of investment in agricultural technology has been in terms of trying to find more robust technologies that may be used on less productive land. If growth in the non-farm sector is dependent on growth in agricultural activity than this investment is critical in terms of raising standards of living in impoverished rural villages at least in the absence of migration, which will be discussed in detail below. But if it is possible to have considerable non-farm growth without agricultural technology then policy makers are faced with another possible alternative: finding ways to improve non-farm employment in those areas not well-suited to agriculture.

There are a couple of arguments for the importance of agricultural productivity in generating rural non-farm employment. The most significant linkage stems from the fact that agricultural productivity growth raises incomes and thus increases the demand for non-farm products (see Mellor and Johnston, 1984). This point is central to Ranis and Stewart's (1973) argument as to why the development process, at least given a reasonably equitable distribution, can lead to expansion of the non-farm sector. An important caveat is readily apparent here however – whether demand effects will importantly drive non-farm activity depends on whether these goods can be efficiently produced and supplied at the local level, in the rural areas where agricultural productivity growth occurs. Thus an evaluation of this argument depends critically on the composition of demand. A key distinction is thus between non-traded non-farm goods and services (that is those that must be consumed and produced locally) and goods that can be efficiently supplied from elsewhere. Agricultural development may also clearly serve as an engine of growth in the rural non-farm sector through its effect on value added processing of agricultural products. Arguably, it is often efficient to undertake such tasks as rice milling or paper production in reasonable proximity to the sources of these products so as not to be transporting relatively low-value high-volume products across space.

It is also thought that agricultural productivity growth may be an important source of non-farm activity through the process of generating savings or releasing labor that can then be utilized in non-farm production. The basic point here is that agricultural productivity increases will, at least at a global level, permit farmers to produce the same levels of output with fewer workers. This in turn should put downward pressure on the wage, causing workers to look for other opportunities. Similarly with respect to savings, higher agricultural profits (through greater productivity and lower wages) may in part be used to finance capital investment for non-farm activities. While this argument has a certain appeal, it is also clear that it is only true at the global level or at least at the level in which trade in agricultural goods is reasonably fluid. From a local perspective and given the opportunity to sell agricultural commodities to other villages, a local increase in technology is likely to result in an expansion of agricultural activity and rising rural wages. What is overlooked in the literature is that the rise in labor costs associated with increased agricultural productivity that is not inherently labor-saving will serve as a damper on certain types of non-farm investment in those areas experiencing the agricultural productivity gains.

A third question that has emerged in the literature is whether growth in the rural non-farm sector has important effects on poverty or income distribution (e.g., Kijima and Lanjouw, 2004; Mellor, 2000; Haggblade et al., 2002). This literature is concerned about the poverty impacts of agricultural development because most rural poor are landless. Thus, agricultural productivity growth, while clearly providing some benefits to the poor, may not be particularly progressive in terms of its distributional effects. However, given low capital and land requirements it seems possible that non-farm activities may be potentially more open to the poor than agricultural activities.

While the issue of how agricultural development affects poverty has received relatively little theoretical attention there is a growing body of empirical papers that address this issue. Perhaps the strongest evidence to date on the effects of sources of growth on rural poverty and inequality has been compiled by Ravallion and Datt (1996, 1999) using a state-level data set from India that combines multiple national-level cross-sectional household surveys with state-level aggregate data on sectoral income. These authors find evidence that agricultural growth decreases rural poverty but provide a more mixed picture of the effects of non-agricultural growth, with overall effects depending, among other things, on initial conditions. As they acknowledge, however, an important limitation of their data is that non-farm income is not available from their data sources separately for rural and urban areas. Because the impacts of urban and rural non-farm growth on rural poverty may be different from each other and even of opposite sign, it is difficult to know what Ravallion and Datt's results tell us about the extent to which rural growth in the farm and non-farm sectors is likely to be more successful in reducing rural poverty. Moreover, it is also not possible with such data to assess the more fundamental policy or institutional determinants of sectoral income growth.

Other empirical tests of whether non-farm activity tends to be pro-poor have focused on the question of whether the poor are particularly concentrated in the non-farm sector. Much of the relevant literature (see Kijima and Lanjouw, 2004) suggests that in fact better-off households are disproportionately represented in the non-farm sector in the sense that the share of income from non-farm sources is typically higher among better-off households than it is among poor households. As Foster and Rosenzweig (2002) point out, however, this exercise, even if carried out conclusively in terms of issues of causal inference, is problematic to the extent that labor markets are reasonably competitive. Unless there are particular rigidities in the market, the primary determinant of poverty is the level of the unskilled wage rate, which is typically approximated by the agricultural wage. As such the question of whether the non-farm sector raises the well being of the poor is primarily a question of whether the unskilled wage is affected by the presence of the non-farm sector, not whether the poor are differentially likely to work in the non-farm sector which has typically been what has been tested.

2.2. Rural out-migration

The literature on the relationship between agricultural development and non-farm activities focuses on rural areas and presumes that populations are stationary. However, the geographic movement of people is a potential response to agricultural development, and indeed migration from rural areas marked US agricultural development in the 19th century. For the study of the consequences of rural development out-migration is of potential importance for three reasons. First, migration may both be an important consequences of rural development, or its lack and may hinder or promote economic development through reducing population densities and or through transfers. Second, to comprehensively assess the consequences of rural development on a given population over time, it is necessary to include all members of the population, some of whom may have migrated out. For example, a large proportion of those who shift from agricultural activities to non-agricultural activities may be out-migrants from rural areas. If these are excluded from the analysis of rural development (by focusing only on rural areas), the shifts out of agriculture will be understated and inferences about the determinants of moving out of agriculture may be biased. Third, if the focus is on the effects of agricultural development in rural areas, not taking into account heterogeneity of the rural population and the possibility of non-random out-migration or in-migration may lead to incorrect predictions.

The literature on internal migration in developing countries was reviewed by Robert Lucas (1997) in the 1997 *Handbook of Population Economics Family*, and thus need not be covered extensively here. Two points are worthy of note, however. First, an important limitation of that review is that it did not consider the importance of growth in the rural non-farm sector as an alternative mechanism for achieving a substantial transformation in the sectoral allocation of labor. As is clear from the non-farm literature, the growth in non-farm income in rural areas has been substantial and thus an attempt to understand internal migration without reference to this sector may be quite misleading in terms of, for example, implications for policy. There is a clear need to develop a framework for simultaneously considering both processes.

Second, there have been remarkably few important additions to the literature on rural migration since the time that the Lucas review was published. It seems unlikely that the slow pace of this literature reflects a lack of importance of the issue. There is growing evidence that internal migration in developing countries is increasing and this pattern has raised new concerns about consequences for both sending and receiving areas of this process. This growth is particularly evident in two of the world's largest and fastest growing economies, India and China largely as a consequence of reductions in economic and residential restrictions (Deshingkar, 2006). Instead, as is argued below, progress in this area seem to have primarily been limited by the availability of appropriate data.

Information even on the amount of rural out-migration is scarce. Census and other cross-sectional data sets provide information that identifies migrants at destination, either with information on the birthplace of a person or residence at some fixed interval prior to the survey or census. Cross-sectional data at one point in time thus do not permit the construction of appropriate migration rates – the proportion of the origin population that exits. Rather, such data only permit construction of in-migration rates. Indeed, even specialized migration surveys are surveys of migrants at destination. For example, The Migration Survey of Thailand, a biannual national survey of migrants in Thailand carried out by the National Statistical Office, identifies the district of origin and migration histories of in-migrants and thus cannot directly be used to compute out-migration rates from rural areas. However, these data could possibly be combined with the annual Labor Force Survey (see below).

It is possible to use temporally adjacent cross-sectional data from censuses or surveys to construct out-migration rates from rural areas to urban areas, assuming such data provide temporally consistent information on rural and urban location, with information on survival rates by age. The probability of a rural person age x at time t migrating to an urban area in y years $\rho_{\text{C}t}$ is given by

$$\left[P_{ux+y}^{t+y} - \left(P_{ux}^{t+y}\right)(l_{x+y}/l_x)\right]/P_{rx}^{t}, \tag{1}$$

where $t = $ year, $x = $ age group, $y = $ census interval, $u = $ urban, $r = $ rural, $P = $ population, $l_{x+y}/l_x = $ survival rate for age group x in y years. Expression (1) uses the cohort method for constructing the migration rate, and is accurate if the economy is closed and death rates are similar for migrants and non-migrants.

We can compare the cohort migration out-migration rate with the in-migration rate for rural-origin migrants at an urban destination from one cross section, taken in year $t + y$, assuming that information is given on the location of residents of the urban area y years ago. The rural–urban in-migration rate $\rho_{\text{CS}t}$, that is, the proportion of rural–urban migrants in the urban population aged $x + y$ at time $t + y$, is given by

$$\left[P_{ux+y}^{t+y} - \left(P_{ux}^{t+y}\right)(l_{x+y}/l_x)\right]/P_{ux+y}^{t+y}. \tag{2}$$

The ratio of the two rates gives the bias in the cross-sectional rate:

$$\rho_{\text{CS}t}/\rho_{\text{C}t} = P_{rx}^{t}/P_{ux+y}^{t+y}. \tag{3}$$

Expression (3) shows that the cross-sectional rural–urban in-migration rate overstates the out-migration rate from rural areas in countries in which rural populations are greater than urban populations, which is the case in most low-income countries. Moreover, because the upward bias will be smaller (the denominator containing the new urban population will be bigger) when rural–urban migration is higher, changes in the cross-sectional in-migration rate over time will understate the increase in rural–urban migration.

Figure 1 provides the cohort rates of rural out-migration to urban areas for males aged 15–24 at the beginning of each decade from the 1961, 1971, 1981, 1991, and 2001 Indian Censuses and the corresponding cross-sectional urban in-migration rates for 1961–1991 that we have computed using the formulas given by (1) and (2). The (appropriate) cohort rates indicate (i) out-migration rates from rural areas to urban areas in India are low – at a maximum of 5.4% in the peak 1961–1971 period and as low as 2% in the 1981–1991 period and (ii) in the post-reform decade, 1991–2001, out-migration rates from rural areas in India were higher than they were in the preceding decade (3.4% versus 2%), but this rate is lower than the rate in the 1971–1981 period and only slightly higher than that in the 1961–1971 decade. The movements in the cross-sectional urban in-migration rates are similar to the out-migration rates, but they overstate the rates of out-migration considerably. Dev and Evenson (2003) compute urban in-migration rates from the Indian National Social Surveys (NSS), national surveys of the Indian population, and also find an increase in migration during the "reform" period, but it is a smaller increase than indicated by the cohort rates in Fig. 1. Exit from rural areas to urban areas does not appear to be a major consequence of the more open Indian economy. Nevertheless, developments in specific rural areas may have importantly affected those areas

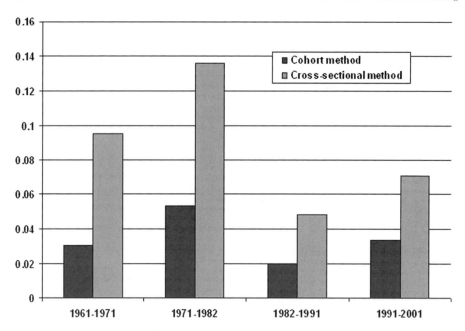

Figure 1. Decadal rural–urban migration rates for males aged 15–24, by decade, computed using two methods from adjacent censuses, 1961–2001.

via the out-migration of rural residents, and migration could be very selective, as we investigate below.

The cohort method to quantify rural–urban migration can also be applied to data from periodic surveys in a country that have consistent sample frames and geographic identifiers. For example, the annual Labor Force Survey (LFS) of Thailand has been undertaken by the National Statistical Office (NSO) since 1963 and provides information on individuals and households, with province of residence identified. Another annual large-scale survey is the Indonesian Socio-economic Survey (SUSENAS), which has been collected since 1963 and covers all provinces of Indonesia (Surbakti, 1995). But the cohort method of assessing migration cannot be applied to all regularly-collected "national" data sets. First, the method requires that the data come from a survey or Census covering the entire population. Second, as noted, the definitions of rural and urban must stay the same over time. In many survey-based data sets coverage is not geographically comprehensive and the rural–urban divide is not stable. For example, the well-known, large-scale (approximately 100,000 households) Brazilian *Pesquisa Nacional por Amostra de Domicilios* (PNAD), also known as the National Household Sample Survey (NHSS), is an annual survey of the Brazilian population. But the survey excludes rural areas in the Northern region of the country. This is a small proportion of the total population but a relatively large proportion of the agricultural workforce. Moreover, in that survey the definition of urban is based on the individual definitions of municipalities, and changes over time. Thus, rural "out-migration" occurs across rounds of these data even when no households move.

The cohort method does not permit analyses of the determinants of out-migration or provide information on migration selectivity – who leaves within an age cohort in terms of their human capital. Moreover, some of the persons who migrate from rural to urban areas were not engaged in agricultural activities in the rural areas, and not everyone who migrates from rural areas and out of agriculture migrates to urban areas. Thus, the low rural-to-urban migration rates are not very informative about the exit from agriculture. For such analyses, panel data on individuals is required.

Existing panel data sets also have serious deficiencies with respect to their ability to shed light on migration. Most panel surveys in low-income countries exclude persons or households that move or suffer from attrition associated with the geographic mobility of respondents and thus are not well-suited for studying either the determinants of out-migration or especially the consequences of local developments if out-migration is high. For example, the Indian Village Level Studies of the International Crop Research Institute of the Semi-Arid Tropics (ICRISAT), which followed households in six villages starting in 1975 for ten years (Walker and Ryan, 1984) and provided valuable information for understanding risk-coping (e.g., Townsend, 1994), dropped from the survey the 14% of households that divided (by 1999, half of the original ICRISAT households had split). Similarly, the 1982 national Rural Economic Development Survey (REDS) of Indian households (Vashishtha, 1989) excluded the one-third of 1971 baseline households that had divided by 1982. Moreover, the design of the World Bank Living Standards Measurement Surveys (LSMS) includes in the panel component of each survey only those members of sampled residences that have not left the original residence (Glewwe and Grosh, 1999). Hill (2004) reviews the attrition history of 13 panel studies of at least two years duration in developing countries and concludes that attrition is mostly due to moves. Longitudinal studies without tracking had attrition rates of 9 to 21 percent *per year*.

It is important to distinguish between two types of sample attrition, that caused solely by respondent behavior and that caused by a combination of survey design and respondent behavior. In surveys whose aim is to follow all *individual* respondents from an original sample, such as the US Panel Survey of Income Dynamics and the National Longitudinal Survey of Youth, attrition is of the first type. Attrition occurs due to either respondent non-cooperation or the inability of survey personnel to track down respondents. Thus spatial mobility is an important component of attrition even in surveys designed to follow individuals – movers are disproportionally represented among attritors. Attrition is in fact high in the US surveys – approximately half of original respondents are not represented in the PSID panel 17 years after the initial sample.

For most if not all panel surveys undertaken in low-income countries, loss of respondents is due to spatially- and residence-limited sampling by design, and results in panels that purposely exclude either all those persons who leave the originally-sampled household or those who leave a geographic location, such as a village or a surveillance area (e.g., Matlab). There are three types of design-based attrition characterizing panel surveys undertaken in low-income countries. The first, typified by the Living Standards Measurement Surveys carried out by the World Bank in many countries of the world, includes in panels households defined by addresses. Any member of an original household who leaves is not followed, and if the entire family inhabiting the sampled address moves out, none are reinterviewed. A more severe variant of this was employed in the design of the ICRISAT panel surveys – all members of a household in which any male left the household were dropped from the sample. Either household division or migration thus leads to attrition.

A second type of panel survey includes all of the members of the initially-sampled households who stay in a pre-defined geographic area, including those persons who leave (split from) the original household but stay in the area. Examples include the MHSS Survey in Matlab, Bangladesh (which did include a sub-sample of out-migrants), the 1982 NCAER-REDS survey, and the Palanpur Survey, a panel survey of all households in one village. A third survey design attempts to include in a subsequent round all *households*, but considers a household as included in a round if any member of that household is resurveyed. This definition of a household panel is used by the Indonesia Family Life Survey (IFLS).

Eliminating the spatially restrictive design features that results in most attrition in developing country panels is widely presumed to be costly. Two well-known studies which attempt to follow households who move are the KwaZulu-Natal Income Dynamic Study (KIDS) and the Indonesian Family Life Surveys (IFLS). In both cases, however, a household that moved from the original study region was considered to be found if at least one member of the original household was reinterviewed. Reports of low attrition rates thus are based on this household definition; attrition rates at the individual level, relevant to the study of mobility and long-term effects of local interventions or developments, are considerably higher. The baseline KIDS survey of 2003 was a random sample of inhabited physical dwellings. Maluccio (2004) reports that 80.8 percent of the rural dwellings had at least one inhabitant who also was found living in the dwelling in the 1998 re-survey. These "households" are considered non-attritors. Tracking at least one member of the 1993 survey to a new location reduced rural attrition from 19.2 percent to 16.6 percent. Even with this tracking, he concludes that attrition in the sample is related to observed household characteristics, among other things, household size and community and household-level resources. A Heckman-type model of selection correction, with a set of variables for the quality of the 1993 interview used as identifying instruments, reveals statistically significant attrition bias in the estimation of household expenditure functions.

Tracking was instituted in the 1997 wave of the Indonesian Family Life Survey. As noted above, Thomas et al. (2001) define a household as being reinterviewed if at least one person from the original 1993 household was located and a roster which listed the current whereabouts of all original household members was completed. Households with split-offs in 1997 are treated as a single household that was found. There was no attempt to track households that moved outside of one of the 13 IFLS provinces. They succeeded in re-interviewing 93.5 percent of the IFLS households; excluding households where all members died, the reinterview rate was 94.4 percent. Without tracking, the reinterview rate would have been 84 percent. Refusal rates were less than 1 percent. Multinomial models of attrition lead the authors to conclude that, in terms of observable characteristics, households that were found in the tracking exercise share much in common with households that did not change locations, and locally tracked households have more in common with stayers than with movers who were not located. However, using the metric of individual attrition, it appears that 15% of originally-included surviving persons were not reinterviewed in the survey round that took place only seven years after the initial survey, mostly because of geographic mobility.

Alderman et al. (2001) consider the extent and implications of attrition for three longitudinal household surveys from Bolivia (Bolivian Pre-School Program Evaluation Household Survey Data (PIDI)), Kenya (Kenyan Ideation Change Survey (KDICP)), and the KwaZulu-Natal Income Dynamics Study (KIDS) referenced above. They conduct tests of attrition as they relate to observable variables in the data using the tests presented in Fitzgerald, Gottschalk and Moffit (1998). In the Bolivian PIDI and South African KIDS surveys, attrition is at the level of the household. In the Kenyan KDICP survey, based upon a sample of ever-married women of childbearing age and their husbands, attrition is at the individual level. The Bolivian survey experienced 35 percent attrition over two years, the Kenyan survey experienced 33, 28 and 41 percent attrition for men, women, and couples, respectively, over about two years, and the KIDS attrition was 16 percent for the combined (rural and urban) sample over five years, including the tracking noted above. The paper concludes that neither family background variables or outcome variables measured in the first round of each survey predicted attrition well, and that attrition did not significantly affect the estimates of the association between family background variables and outcome variables.

The finding of minimal attrition bias by Alderman et al. has limited applicability for the study of economic mobility over a period of a decade or more. First, the panel data they analyze cover much shorter periods of time, only two years for the Bolivian and Kenyan surveys. Second, like the IFLS, retention in two of the three surveys is not defined at the level of the individual but at the level of the household. In the Kenya KDICP survey, the original sample is ever-married women and their husbands, a demographic group that is quite unlike the 0–15 year-old children that form the core demographic group in studying economic mobility over much longer periods of time. Finally, the attrition tests of Alderman et al. are tests of *selection on observables* and provide no direct evidence on whether migration-based attrition truncates the distribution of unobserved heterogeneity. Maluccio (2004) finds strong evidence of selection on unobservables with the same South African KIDS data set for which Alderman et al. find no evidence of selection on observables, although these inferences are based on unverified identification restrictions. It is thus unclear how the relatively high rates of mobility-based attrition existing in almost all panel data sets from surveys in low-income countries affect inferences about the long-term consequences of rural development.

Two long-term panel data sets characterizing rural South Asian populations and that were designed to capture information on individual out-migrants are the 1982–2002

Bangladesh Nutrition Survey and the 1982–1999 NCAER Rural Economic Development Survey. The latter survey was based on a stratified probability sample of households residing in 250 villages in 16 major states of India in 1982 (excluding Assam). All original households in the 1982 survey and split-off households still residing in the village were interviewed in 1999. In addition, information was elicited on all of the immediate relatives of the household head in 1982 who had left the households, including the head's brothers, sisters, sons and daughters. Information on when they left the household; their schooling attainment; and their current age, marital status and location was provided. Thus, there is information on all individuals residing in the villages in 1982 regardless of their location in 1999 as long as any of their fellow household members was living in the original village at the time of the 1999 survey. No migrant's household, however, was included in the survey. For details, see Foster and Rosenzweig (2002).

The 2002 Bangladesh Nutrition Survey was designed to include all individuals who were residing in the households included in the 1982 Bangladesh Nutrition Survey, a stratified random sample of households 375 residing in 15 randomly-chosen villages from all areas of rural Bangladesh. Ninety-seven percent of the households of all individuals alive in 2002 and residing in Bangladesh who had been in the 1982 households were included in the 2002 survey, with proxy information obtained on those living abroad or who were not located for a household interview. Details of the survey are discussed in Pitt, Rosenzweig and Hassan (2005). Rosenzweig (2003) used preliminary data from the panel survey to assess the accuracy of proxy information, as the Bangladesh survey also obtained information on departed household members from members of the original households still residing in the initial 15 villages. Thus there is information that is both self-reported and proxy-reported for migrants. The results suggested that proxy-based information on schooling was reasonably accurate and unbiased, but information on occupation was not very precise. The 1999 REDS collected by proxy schooling information on migrants but did not attempt to collect proxy information on migrant occupations.

Table 1 reports the proportion of persons aged 10 through 24 in 1982, by gender, who had left the original sampled villages at the time of the next survey round – 17 years

Table 1
Percent of individuals migrating from their village, by gender:
Persons aged 10–24 in 1982 migrating between 1982 and 1999 (India) and 2002 (Bangladesh)

Gender	Bangladesh[a]	India[b]
Male	21.2	23.7
Female	56.3	86.9

[a]Source: Bangladesh Nutrition Surveys of 1982 and 2002.

[b]Source: NCAER REDS 1999.

later for India and 20 years later for Bangladesh. Both populations display migration patterns consistent with patrilocal exogamy that characterizes South Asian population, with men typically staying in the same household or village and the women marrying persons residing outside the village. Rates of out-migration for men are substantially lower than for women in both populations. In both India and Bangladesh, about 23 percent of the men had left the village after 17–20 years, while 56 (87) percent of the women had left their villages in Bangladesh (India).

Figures 2 and 3 indicate that out-migration for men (aged 10–24 in 1982) is selective with respect to schooling attainment in both populations. In Bangladesh, years of schooling are higher overall for the migrants who leave the village compared with those who stay (3.5 versus 2.9 years), with schooling attainment higher the more distant are the migrants from the origin village among those who remain in the country. The average schooling level of migrants who are abroad, however, is lower than those who remained in the village. These migrants are likely temporary migrants, as they all are in either Malaysia or a Middle Eastern country. In India too schooling attainment is higher for migrants than for non-migrants (6.2 versus 5.5 years) for men in the same age group, and among migrants schooling is also positively correlated with distance from the origin villages, including those who migrated outside the country. However, schooling for migrants who stay in the same district is lower than schooling for stayers.

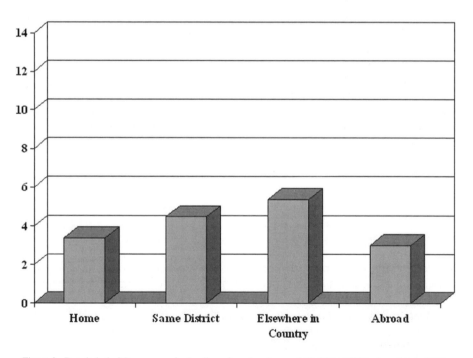

Figure 2. Bangladesh: Mean years of schooling of rural males aged 15–24 in 1982 by location in 2002.

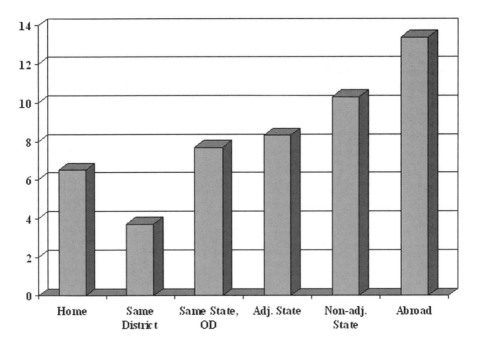

Figure 3. India: Mean years of schooling of rural males aged 15–24 in 1982 by location in 1999.

Finally, as expected, migrants are significantly less likely to be engaged in an agricultural occupation than those who remain in the villages – the Bangladesh survey, which provides self-reported occupation for both migrants and non-migrants, indicates that among the men aged 10 through 24 in 1982, almost 90 percent of those who had migrated from the villages were working outside the agricultural sector in 2002, compared with 37% of the men in the same age group who remained in the villages. To assess how strongly out-migration is associated with leaving agriculture, however, requires information as well on who leaves – whether migrants tend to be from non-farm households.

3. Theory

In order to establish a framework for how the effects of agricultural development affect sectoral employment and incomes in a local area, or in a country, we develop a simple general equilibrium model of the "village" economy. A key feature of the model is that the effects of agricultural development are mediated by factor flows in the form of migration and non-farm capital, so that the degree of economic "openness" is an important factor in understanding the consequences of advances in agricultural technologies. The model builds and modifies that in Foster and Rosenzweig (2002). We start with a quite general characterization and then consider a series of more restricted versions that permit the derivation of testable comparative statics. In particular, it is assumed that there are three sectors, an agricultural sector, a factory goods sector, and a local non-traded sector. Agricultural goods are produced using land and labor, non-traded goods are produced using labor, and factory goods are produced using externally-provided capital and labor. The economy consists of a representative landless household with labor endowment l^N and a representative landed household with land A and labor endowment l^A. Let total labor be $l = l^A + l^N$. It is assumed that labor moves freely within sectors of the village. In the most general model both labor and capital move across villages (or between villages and urban centers).

Household utility for both landed and landless households

$$u(c_z, c_g, c_f) \tag{4}$$

is determined by the consumption of a non-tradable good c_z, the consumption c_g of agricultural goods, and the consumption of factory produced goods c_f. We assume that agricultural and factory goods are traded at world prices p_g and p_f, respectively, with agricultural goods serving as the numeraire ($p_g = 1$). Agricultural production is undertaken by landed households according to a CRS production function in agricultural labor l_g and land net of labor costs and produces agricultural profits

$$y_g = \theta A g(l_g/A) - w l_g \tag{5}$$

where θ denotes the level of technology, $g()$ is the per-land unit production function, w denotes the wage, and $\rho \geqslant 1$ reflects the cost of working capital. We also assume, without loss of generality, that non-traded good production may be undertaken only by landed households and is produced according to a CRS production function in labor l_z net of labor costs

$$y_z = p_z l_z - w l_z \tag{6}$$

where p_z is the local price of the non-traded good. The assumption that the local traded good depends only on labor captures a key distinction between the non-traded and agricultural sector, namely that land is an important fixed input in the latter but not the former and credit plays a crucial role in agriculture, given the temporal nature of farm production. It also is consistent with patterns in rural India where non-tradable services are small-scale enterprises such as tailors and bakers with low intensity of capital and land.

Factory production is assumed to be undertaken by external entrepreneurs with access to capital who can introduce factory good production. We assume that the agents in the factory sector are located outside the local economy, face a constant cost of capital r, employ a constant returns to scale technology, and experience labor costs that are increasing in labor utilization. Factory income for the representative entrepreneur is thus

$$y_f = l_f f(k_f/l_f) - \left(w + \frac{l_f}{\delta}\right) l_f - r k_f. \tag{7}$$

Increasing average costs of may be thought of as arising from labor regulation that differentially applies to large employers or to greater likelihood of collective labor action.[1] The assumption that this effect is present in the factory sector but not the other sectors seems justified given that, as will be shown below, the non-traded and agricultural sectors are almost exclusively family businesses with few employees while factories are large employers and frequently employ workers from outside the village in which they are located.[2]

A fraction of workers from each type of households migrates from the rural area to the urban area. Letting x^A and x^N be the landed and landless share of individuals that remain in the village, and τ^A and τ^N the per-migrant transfers from these migrants relative to the wage, respectively, the household budget constraint for landed households is

$$p_z c_z^A + p_f c_f^A + p_g c_g^A = y_g + y_z + w x^A l^A + \left(1 - x^A\right) l^A \tau^A w \tag{8}$$

and for landless households is

$$p_z c_z^N + p_f c_f^N + p_g c_g^N = w x^N l^N + \left(1 - x^N\right) l^N \tau^N w. \tag{9}$$

Workers are assumed to migrate if the wage they would receive in the urban area given their endowment of human capital exceeds their local income.[3] This implies, in particular, that migrants give up claims on agricultural profits in the event that they leave. Migrants also may make transfers to the local area. Letting ξ denote the urban return to human capital, and h^A and h^N the landed and landless levels of human capital, which we take as given, then the equilibrium migration conditions for landed and landless migration, respectively, will be

$$\xi h^A = y_g / \left(x^A l^A\right) + w + \left(1 - x^A\right) \tau^A w / x^A \tag{10}$$

and

$$\xi h^N = w + (1 - x_N) \tau^N w / x^N. \tag{11}$$

Clearing of the labor market, given the exit of migrants, then requires

$$x^A l^A + x^N l^N = l_g + l_z + l_f. \tag{12}$$

---

[1] National governmental rules for lay-offs in India only apply to establishments employing more than 300 workers. Some states impose different (lower) employment thresholds.

[2] In the factories located in our sample of villages in 1999, described below, on average 63% of factory workers were hired from outside the villages. Note that as specified, an increase in δ represents a decrease in the costs of labor regulation.

[3] A potential shortcoming of this model is that it does not explicitly incorporate the relative cost of living in urban and rural areas.

3.1. The closed economy

We first consider the effects of agricultural technology on employment by sector when the economy is closed – no capital inflows and no possibility of laborers migrating out or in. Thus there is neither factory employment nor migration in response to low wages. While it is natural to expect that in this context factor-neutral increases in agricultural technology will tend to increase employment in agriculture, this result does not necessarily obtain due to the presence of the non-traded (non-farm) good. Assume, for example, that demand for the non-traded good may be written

$$c_z(y, p_z) = y/(p_z \pi(p_z)), \tag{13}$$

a specification that is consistent for some function $\pi(z)$, for example, with CES preferences. Assuming that landed households maximize profits and that the market for the non-traded good clears so that

$$c_z^A + c_z^N = l_z \tag{14}$$

and implicitly differentiating it may be established that

$$\frac{dl_g}{d\theta} = -\frac{\pi'(w)\alpha w l_g l_z}{\theta(\alpha(1-\alpha)wl_z \pi'(w) + (1 - \alpha + \pi(w)\alpha)l_g)}. \tag{15}$$

That is, agricultural employment may be increasing or decreasing in agricultural technology depending on the sign of $\pi'(w)$. In the special case of Cobb–Douglas, $\pi(w) = 1/v$ for the non-traded share parameter v, agricultural income will be invariant with respect to agricultural technology. The reason is that agricultural technology change increases total incomes which, in turn, pushes up the demand for the non-traded good and thus its price. Under the Cobb–Douglas assumption the price will grow at precisely the same rate as technology so there is no reallocation of labor. If, on the other hand, non-traded goods are complementary with other goods it may be established that agricultural labor will actually decline with agricultural technology as more and more labor will need to be shifted to the non-farm sector to accommodate the demand for the non-traded good.

To address the effects of agricultural technology change on total agricultural income or the non-farm income share is more complicated. Not surprisingly an increase in agricultural technology tends to increase the equilibrium wage.

$$\frac{dw}{d\theta} = -\frac{wl_g(1 - \alpha + \alpha\pi(w))}{\theta(\alpha(1-\alpha)wl_z \pi'(w) + (1 - \alpha + \pi(w)\alpha)l_g)}. \tag{16}$$

But whether this results in higher or lower agricultural income will depend on whether agricultural labor is increasing or decreasing in θ.

3.2. Entry of factory capital

Opening up the local economy to external entrepreneurs with access to capital who can introduce factory good production sharply alters the conclusions of the closed-economy general-equilibrium model. In particular, non-farm activities are of two types, with distinct responses to external change because labor demand in the non-farm sector is no longer linked to local demand as is the case for the non-tradable sector. Moreover, the share of agricultural income or activities in the economy will depend on the external source of growth.

Given the specification (7), it is clear from a partial equilibrium perspective that the decision of the external capitalists is driven by two key factors, the degree of convexity in the cost of labor and the local wage. Thus

$$l_f = l_f^*(w, \delta) \tag{17}$$

where

$$\frac{\partial l_f^*}{\partial w} = -\frac{\delta}{2} < 0 \tag{18}$$

and

$$\frac{\partial l_f^*}{\partial \delta} = \frac{l_f}{\delta} > 0. \tag{19}$$

Restricting attention to the case of Cobb–Douglas preferences with non-traded good share v, it follows that

$$\frac{dl_g}{d\theta} = \frac{((1 - \alpha)l_g + \alpha l)wl_g(\partial l_f^*/\partial w)}{((1 - \alpha)^2 wl_g + \alpha(1 - \alpha)wl(\partial l_f^*/\partial w) + (l - (1 - \alpha)l_f)l_g)\theta} > 0. \tag{20}$$

Thus under this scenario non-farm employment (the converse in this case of agricultural employment) is decreasing with advances in agricultural technology, a result that contrasts markedly with the corresponding case when there is no factory capital.

Interestingly, however, the overall reduction in non-farm employment obscures the fact that there are opposite trends with respect to the two components of non-farm employment. In particular, because the wage is increasing in agricultural technology,

$$\frac{dw}{d\theta} = \frac{(l + (1 - \alpha)l_f)wl_g}{((1 - \alpha)^2 wl_g + \alpha(1 - \alpha)wl(\partial l_f^*/\partial w) + (l - (1 - \alpha)l_f)l_g)\theta} > 0. \tag{21}$$

Eq. (18) implies that factory employment is decreasing in technology. On the other hand,

$$\frac{dl_z}{d\theta} = \frac{(1 - \alpha)l_z wl_g}{((1 - \alpha)^2 wl_g + \alpha(1 - \alpha)wl(\partial l_f^*/\partial w) + (l - (1 - \alpha)l_f)l_g)\theta} > 0 \tag{22}$$

so the non-traded part of the non-farm employment sector is increasing in agricultural technology.

3.3. Migration

While in principle inflows of capital and outflows of labor are just opposite sides of the same coin in terms of their implications for the overall balance of agricultural and non-agricultural employment, the implications of these two types of flows for the village itself can be quite different. In particular, although capital flows into the village result in increased economic activity and increased demand for local non-tradables at the level of the village, labor outflows result in a shift of economic activity and may have important compositional effects. In particular, given migrant outflows there is no longer a direct relationship between increases in agricultural employment and decreases in the non-farm sector.

It is straightforward to establish that, like capital flows, migration tends to dampen the effects of agricultural change on the wage. For example, if we rule out transfers and assume, again, Cobb–Douglas preferences, the local wage is unaffected by agricultural technical change:

$$\frac{dw}{d\theta} = 0. \tag{23}$$

Moreover, while, as might be anticipated, an increase in agricultural productivity results in an increase in village employment in agriculture

$$\frac{dl_g}{d\theta} = \frac{l_g}{\theta(1-\alpha)} > 0, \tag{24}$$

the effects on non-agricultural employment within the village are less clear. In particular, an increase in local agricultural productivity induced by technological improvements increases the share of both landed and landless households that remain in the village,

$$\frac{dx^A}{d\theta} = \frac{x^A}{(1-\alpha)\theta} > 0, \tag{25}$$

$$\frac{dx^N}{d\theta} = \frac{x^N}{(1-\alpha)\theta} > 0, \tag{26}$$

and as it turns out this effect dominates the increased agricultural employment so that non-farm employment also increases

$$\frac{dl_z}{d\theta} = \frac{l_z}{\theta(1-\alpha)}, \tag{27}$$

with the overall share of agricultural employment staying fixed.

There are also significant compositional effects associated with technical change. In particular, given the proportionate growth in the shares of the landed and landless households remaining in the village it is straightforward to see that the composition of migrants will increasingly shift toward the group with the lower initial levels. In particular let

$$\varphi = \frac{l^N(1 - x^N) - l^A(1 - x^A)}{l^A(1 - x^A)} \tag{28}$$

be the percentage excess of landless relative to landed migrants. Then the model implies that

$$\frac{d\varphi}{d\theta} = \frac{l^N(x^A - x^N)}{\theta(1 - \alpha)l^A(1 - x^A)^2}. \tag{29}$$

Thus if the share of the landed who migrate is less than the share of the landless who migrate, then the landless share among migrants is increasing in agricultural technology. Whether this latter condition is met depends on two factors – on the relative gap in schooling between landed and landless which, given higher schooling levels for the landed, provides the landless with a higher incentive to migrate and on the fact that migration is more costly for the landed because they give up a share of their agricultural profits by assumption.

There are also important compositional effects associated with a rise in the return to schooling in destination areas. Increases in these returns will lead to an increase in migration for both landed and landless households

$$\frac{dl^A}{d\xi} = -\frac{x^A}{\xi(1 - \alpha)} < 0, \tag{30}$$

$$\frac{dl^A}{d\xi} = -\frac{x^A}{\xi(1 - \alpha)} < 0, \tag{31}$$

but the relative effects will be determined by difference in migrant shares

$$\frac{d\varphi}{d\xi} = -\frac{l^N(x^A - x^N)}{\xi(1 - \alpha)l^A(1 - x^A)^2}, \tag{32}$$

that is, the landless share among migrants is decreasing in destination returns to schooling whenever it is increasing in technology.

3.4. Identifying the relative contributions to wage growth of agricultural technical change, factory employment creation and out-migration

It is possible to use the model to examine directly the relative importance of technical change in agriculture, factory employment, and migration on wages and, in particular, to distinguish the effects of migration that operates through population declines and those that may operate through transfers. The approach involves substitution of the equilibrium condition for agricultural labor force into the marginal product equation yielding an equation of the form

$$w = w^*\left(\theta, A, l_x, l_f, x^A, x^N\right) \tag{33}$$

where

$$l_x = x^A l^A + x^N l^N \tag{34}$$

is the size of the remaining population. The comparative statics from this equation are quite straightforward – increases in both agricultural technology and factory employment increase the local wage and increases in the size of the labor force l_f decrease the wage. However, changes in the stock of out-migrants may also affect the local wage, given the size of the local labor force depending on whether migrants remit back to their origin households. In particular,

$$\frac{\partial w^*}{\partial x^A} = \theta g''(l_g/A) \frac{\alpha v l^A \tau^A}{x^A (\alpha + v - \alpha v) A}, \tag{35}$$

which will be negative in the presence of transfers from landed out-migrants but zero in the absence of such transfers. Intuitively, this expression arises because transfers from out-migrants increase local incomes net of the population and land endowments and thus push up demand for the non-traded good. An analogous expression may be derived for the effect of the landless share of migrants.

4. Empirical findings: Rural non-farm employment and agricultural development in India

The ARIS REDS panel data from rural India described above have been used by Foster and Rosenzweig (2002) to assess the various prediction of the model of non-farm growth presented above and, in so doing, to shed light on how the effects of changes in agricultural technology on the local economy are mediated by the non-farm sector. These data are perhaps uniquely suited to the study of the consequences of agricultural change given that they contain rich modules of income and employment from different sectors and span a space (rural India) and time frame (1968–1999) over which there is considerable variance in rates of agricultural productivity growth.

The basic results from this body of work can be summarized with a few simple tables. In particular, Tables 2, 3 and 4 examine data over time on non-farm activity in five-different categories of villages based on productivity growth over the 1974–1999 period. As seen in Table 2, yield growth is only weakly related to the proportion of men primarily in the non-agricultural wage sector in 1971. By 1999, however, the overall non-farm share is particularly high in the lowest growth area. These results clearly indicate that growth in non-agricultural wage work is highest in those areas with the lowest productivity growth as predicted by the model above if non-agricultural employment is equated with factory employment. Moreover, it is evident that this growth in non-agricultural wage work is closely associated with the proportion of villages with a factory. In particular, as shown in Table 3, there is a 42 point increase in the fraction of low growth villages with a factory but a 7.7 point *decline* in the in the fraction of high growth villages. Finally,

Table 2
Proportion of men aged 25–44 whose primary activity is nonagricultural:
Wage work by year and HYV yield growth

Category of yield growth	1971	1982	1999
161.3	0.169	0.224	0.510
527.3	0.089	0.248	0.347
733.9	0.089	0.206	0.287
955.0	0.086	0.094	0.356
1098.1	0.089	0.110	0.320

Table 3
Proportion of villages with at least one factory by year and HYV yield growth

Category of yield growth	1971	1982	1999
161.3	0.12	0.14	0.53
527.3	0.12	0.25	0.49
733.9	0.07	0.16	0.11
955.0	0.05	0.18	0.10
1098.1	0.20	0.06	0.12

Table 4
Number of local service enterprises by year and HYV yield growth

Category of yield growth	1971	1982	1999
161.30	–	60.29	51.39
527.30	–	53.68	34.64
733.90	–	22.99	30.06
955.00	–	25.64	30.03
1098.10	–	20.54	25.67

it is evident as predicted by the model that the number of local service on net in-creases more in the high than low growth areas over the 1982–1999 period. This result is expected given the model because these local services are largely driven by local demand conditions and is further supported in the multivariate analysis. In-deed, the multivariate analysis is instructive in that it shows significant effects of productivity growth on the two components of non-farm activity that are of opposite sign.

While there is no real alternative to using the ARIS-REDS panel to analyze the effects of changes over time in agricultural productivity, it is possible to compare at least in part

Table 5
Comparison of the NSS and REDS household survey indicators of rural industrialization in 1999

Household-based indicator of rural industrialization	% Workers in non-agricultural wage or salary activities		% Wage income non-agricultural	
Source:	NSS 1999	REDS 1999	NSS 1999	REDS 1999
Statistic:	17.4	32.5	53.7	72.9
Cross-state regression coefficient	0.887		1.02	
(standard error)	(0.202)		(0.352)	
Number of states	15		15	
Regression R^2	0.60		0.39	
Test $\beta = 1$ $F(1, 13)$	0.31		0.85	

Sources: 55th Round of the NSS and 1999 REDS.

the estimates from this panel with the 55th round of an another nationally representative sample of rural India, the NSS, which has detailed non-farm information. These comparisons are presented in Table 5. While differences in the exact nature of the questions being asked in the two surveys are sufficiently large that one would not expect an exact match, the differences do seem surprisingly large. It is particularly striking that the percentage of non-agricultural wage and salary workers for the REDS panel is almost twice that for the NSS. Fortunately, it appears that at least across states these two measures are highly correlated with each other, suggesting that the coefficient effects in the non-farm employment may be robust to this difference. However, there is also a significant point to be made: it seems likely that although the set of villages chosen in 1968 for the ARIS-REDS panel were a representative sample of villages at the time – this representativeness may not necessarily be preserved over time given village births and deaths. Indeed, one would expect that the ARIS panel villages are older and more established on average than the NSS panel villages. It is thus, perhaps, not surprising to see higher levels of non-farm usage in the 1999 cross section of the REDS relative to NSS.

In addition to finding that there is a significant negative relationship between productivity growth in agriculture and growth in non-farm activity, the multivariate model permits an assessment of other village and individual attributes that may impact non-farm growth. Interestingly we find very little evidence that financial intermediaries or access play an important role in non-farm growth. This is consistent with the fact that there are few capital assets associated with the non-farm self-employment sector which produces the non-traded goods and that the large amounts of capital needed for the construction of factories are provided from external (to the village) sources.

Similarly, there is little evidence in the ARIS-REDS data that schools or education importantly determine entry of the factory sector and which workers end up being employed in the non-farm sector. This result does, however, seem a bit at odds with conclusions based on other data sets such as the NSS, which report a high concentration of non-farm employment among better off individuals (e.g., Kijima and Lanjouw, 2004). It

Table 6
Do rural factories employ educated workers? Results from the NSS and REDS:
Determinants of the log-odds of having a manufacturing job, rural individuals aged 25–44 in 1999

Sample:	All		In villages with manufacturing jobs			
Estimation procedure:	Logit		Logit		Fixed-effects logit	
	NSS	REDS	NSS	REDS	NSS	REDS
Secondary school	0.272	0.273	−0.0300	0.0964	−0.143	−0.217
graduate	(0.078)[a]	(0.152)	(0.0780)	(0.230)	(0.0804)	(0.240)
Female	−1.72	−0.940	−1.86	−0.862	−1.96	−0.695
	(0.0940)	(0.114)	(0.0954)	(0.183)	(0.0986)	(0.209)
Age	−0.0106	−0.0133	−0.0140	−0.0191	−0.0144	−0.277
	(0.00604)	(0.00814)	(0.00613)	(0.121)	(0.00622)	(0.0171)
Constant	−1.77	0.965	0.417	1.45	–	–
	(0.245)	(0.353)	(0.243)	(0.526)		
N	100,124	3095	17,537	1075	12,584	901

Sources: 55th round of the NSS and 1999 REDS.
[a] Absolute value of asymptotic standard error in parentheses.

appears, however, that at least part of the discrepancy arises from a failure to distinguish between cross-village differences that create a correlation between non-farm employment and village-educational attainment and individual differences in the propensity to work in the non-farm sector within villages. Table 6, in particular, shows that the NSS and REDS data sets yield similar strong results in terms of the effects of secondary education on the probability of working in the non-farm sector at a cross-village level. However, when conditioning on village fixed-effects or even simply whether there is a factory in the village at all this effect goes away in both data sets. Thus, although cross-sectionally, factories do seem to be more common if there are high average levels of schooling, more educated individuals, within the village, are no more likely to be found in the non-farm sector than less educated individuals.

5. Empirical findings: Rural out-migration in South Asia

5.1. Determinants of the magnitude and composition of out-migrant flows

Table 7 reports estimates of the determinants of leaving the village for males aged 10–24 in 1982 from the Bangladesh and Indian panel data sets described in Section 2.2 in terms of the characteristics of their households in 1982. The results suggest that migrants in fact do give up at least some of agricultural profits when they leave, as in both populations increases in landholding decrease the probability of exiting the village. Given the strong correlation between parental education and children's education observed in these populations, the fact that children with fathers who have more schooling (primary

Table 7
Determinants of village out-migration between 1982 and 1999 (India) and 2002 (Bangladesh):
Men aged 10–24 in 1982

Variable	Bangladesh[a]	India[b]
Owned land (acres $\times 10^3$) in 1982	−0.119	−0.0582
	(1.75)[c]	(2.88)
Head in 1982 has primary schooling	0.0984	0.0382
	(1.70)	(1.99)
Household size in 1982	0.00764	0.00438
	(0.70)	(1.59)
Age in 1982	0.0941	0.0198
	(1.89)	(1.66)
Age squared in 1982	−0.00281	−0.000591
	(1.80)	(1.68)
N	219	5861

[a]Specification also includes whether household is Muslim. *Source*: Bangladesh Nutrition Survey, 2002.

[b]Specification also includes whether household is Muslim, whether lower caste, the log of village HYV yields on irrigated land in 1982, the Besley–Burgess state industry regulation index in 1982, and mean state per-child expenditures on tertiary education in 1982. *Source*: NCAER REDS 1999.

[c]Absolute value of robust *t*-statistics in parentheses.

schooling) are more likely to exit is consistent with schooling having payoffs elsewhere or (not incorporated in the model) education facilitating migration, for given migration returns.

The REDS Indian panel data permit, as noted, estimates of the relationship between out-migration, agricultural technology and industry regulation. In addition we can look at the effects of governmental education expenditures on migration. Data are available on state-level expenditures for tertiary education in 1991, which we deflated using census information on potential students in 1981 – children age 8–12. Column (1) in Table 8 reports estimates of the relationship between the probability of out-migration over the period 1982–1999 for men aged 10–24 in 1982 and the log of the index of HYV yields on irrigated lands in the origin village in 1982, the Besley–Burgess state-level index of industry regulation in that year, and the tertiary school expenditure variable. The specification also includes all of the household-level variables reported in Table 7. The estimates conform to the general framework – higher agricultural productivity and more onerous regulation of industry, which evidently increases local rural factory employment, lower out-migration from the village, while public spending on higher education increases out-migration. The former two results imply that estimates of the effects of local agricultural technical change and local factory employment on local wages and employment understate the effect of these for the country as a whole, to the extent that out-migration from a country is relatively small.

Table 8
Determinants of the probability and selectivity of village out-migration in India:
The migration of men aged 10–24 in 1982 between 1982 and 1999

Variable	Migrated by 1999[a] (1)	If primary schooling[a] (2)
Log of village HYV yield on irrigated land in 1982	−0.0405 (3.12)[b]	0.0671 (5.07)
Log of village HYV yield on irrigated land in 1982 × out-migrant	–	−0.0762 (3.62)
Besley–Burgess regulation index in 1982	−0.00494 (2.25)	0.00199 (0.06)
Besley–Burgess regulation index in 1982 × out-migrant	–	−0.00555 (1.40)
Per-child state expenditures on tertiary education in 1982	328.0 (6.82)	2.76 (0.06)
Per-child state expenditures on tertiary education in 1982 × out-migrant	–	397.6 (4.43)
Out-migrant	–	0.291 (2.48)
N	5861	5861

[a]Specification also includes whether household is Muslim, whether lower caste, and the variables listed in Table 7.
[b]Absolute value of robust t-statistics in parentheses.

To assess the selectivity of out-migration with respect to schooling we estimate the determinants of whether the males aged 10–24 in 1982 attained primary schooling and assess whether the probability differed across out-migrants and stayers depending on the level of agricultural productivity, on the determinants of local factory presence, and on state school expenditures. Column (2) of Table 8 reports the estimates. These confirm that on average out-migrants are more likely to have completed primary schooling, consistent with the finding in Table 7 that migrants are more likely to come from households with primary-schooled heads and with Fig. 3. More interestingly, the estimates also show that higher agricultural productivity significantly increases schooling but also lowers the differential in schooling between out-migrants and stayers. The latter effect is the compositional effect implied in the model and by the estimates in columns (2) and (3) – increases in agricultural productivity lower out-migration from households with greater landholdings. Given the higher levels of schooling in households with more land (confirmed in the data), this lowers the average education level of migrants. These results imply that the local effect of improvements in agricultural technology on schooling attainment overstate the effect at the national level, for which the potential for out-migration is relatively small.

5.2. Migrant remittances

We have seen that local agricultural development in part affects local employment and schooling by affecting the size and composition of the labor force due to out-migration. Out-migration also may affect the local economy via remittances, which alter demand for local products. How important are remittances in South Asian economies? Table 9 presents average net and gross transfers from four data sets characterizing populations in three South Asian countries.[4] Column (1) reports transfer for rural households from the IFPRI Pakistan Food Security Survey, which provides information in twelve rounds for a sample of 926 households residing in 52 villages in three major wheat-growing provinces of Pakistan – Punjab, Sind and the Northwest Frontier Province – followed over the period July 1986 through September 1989. In this population, households are clearly net recipients of remittances, mostly from male migrants, with net transfer income representing just over 10 percent of agricultural income. In rural Pakistan, migration evidently mediates the effects of local development both by altering the size and composition of the local labor force and also by directly affecting incomes, given the size of the local labor force.

Columns 2 and (3) are from Indian surveys – the NCAER ARIS survey based on a nationally representative sample of 4118 rural households interviewed in the crop years 1968–1969, 1969–1960, 1970–1971 and the ICRISAT Village Level Survey, a sample of 40 households in 6 rural villages covering the period 1976–1984. Both of these surveys indicate that on average rural households in India, at least in these time periods, are neither net recipients nor providers of transfers, reflecting the small incidence of male migration. The incidence of transfers in the ICRISAT villages are high, but they balance over time, suggestive of their role in insuring consumption in the face of fluctuating incomes, a role in which female marital migration is of importance (Rosenzweig and Stark, 1989). These statistics imply that in the Indian context the role of male migration in affecting local incomes is confined to labor-force size and composition effects.

Finally, column (4) in Table 9 reports transfers for households in the Matlab area of Bangladesh based on the Matlab Health and Socio-economic Survey of 1996, a sample of 4657 households. The data indicate that, as in Pakistan but unlike in India, the Matlab area households are net recipients of transfers, with net transfers 23 percent of total income. Clearly, South Asia is not homogeneous with respect to the contribution of migration to local rural economies.

The equilibrium model suggests that if transfers are unimportant in augmenting incomes on average, such as in India, the number of migrants from a community will not affect local wages, given the size of the local labor force and net of changes in local agricultural productivity and non-farm labor demand. In Foster and Rosenzweig (2002), a conditional wage function was estimated based on the model excluding direct endogenous migration effects. Estimates were obtained of the effects of changes in

---

[4] Columns (1), (2) and (3) of Table 9 are from Foster and Rosenzweig (2002).

Table 9
Descriptive statistics on transfers from four South Asian longitudinal household data sets

	Pakistan 1985–1988 (IFPRI) Rs (1)	India 1968–1971 (NCAER) Rs (2)	India 1976–1984 (ICRISAT) Rs (3)	Bangladesh 1996 (MHSS) Tk (4)
Average annual net transfers out by partner	−3180 (9188)	−29.8 (756.5)	46.8 (2638)	−7932 (43863)
Average transfers in[a]	7758 (14542)	906.8 (2946)	644.3 (2785)	15251 (46671)
Average transfers out[b]	2742 (5049)	1364 (8429)	496.7 (1582)	4621 (26741)
Percent of households with transfers[c]	84.1	7.8	100.0	89.4
Average annual income[d]	31498 (26738)	2284 (3354)	3429 (6232)	34486 (56049)

[a] Standard deviations in parentheses.

[b] Average transfers in and out and percent for NCAER sample are based on annual net transfers while those for Pakistan, ICRISAT and Bangladesh are based on gross transfers. Average transfers in and out exclude zeros.

[c] Percent of household with transfers is over three years for Pakistan and India data sets and one year for Bangladesh data set.

[d] Income is agricultural for Pakistan and India sets and total for Bangladesh.

HYV yields and factory employment using a combination of an instrumental-variables approach and fixed effects. In particular, the difference in the village-level log of male agricultural wages from 1982 to 1999 was regressed against the differences over the same period in the log of the HYV yield variable, the log of the number of village workers employed in factories and the log of the village population, and some control variables, using as instruments for the first two variables 1971 HYV yield measures and changes in state industry regulations between 1982 and 1999. The estimates are reported in column (1) of Table 10, from which it can be seen that increases in agricultural productivity and factory employment push up wages, while increases in population decrease wages. To this specification we add the number of male migrants who left the villages after 1982, treated as an endogenous variable (out-migration is affected by the local wage) using as an additional instrument the 1991 state tertiary expenditure variable, which we have seen significantly affects village out-migration. The estimates of the augmented specification are provided in column (2) of Table 10. Consistent with the evident lack of importance of net remittances to local incomes in India, variation in the stock of migrants from a village has no effect on its local wage net of the size of the population. Population decreases, induced by migration or any other demographic change, however, significantly increase the local wage net of migration outflows.

Table 10
FE-TV estimates: Determinants of the log village male agricultural wage in India, 1982–1999

Variable	(1)[a]	(2)
Log of village HYV yield on irrigated land in 1982	0.439 (2.39)[b]	0.226 (1.75)
Log of number of village factory workers	0.0981 (1.67)	0.0619 (1.76)
Log of village population size	−0.0197 (1.72)	−0.0240 (1.95)
Number of out-migrants	–	−0.000161 (0.94)
Number of villages	222	222

[a]Estimates from Foster and Rosenzweig, 2002. Specification also includes whether a commercial bank is located in the village and rainfall variables. Instruments include the Besley–Burgess state regulation index, per-child state expenditures on tertiary education, HYV yields in 1971, population in 1982, bank presence in 1971.
[b]Absolute value of robust *t*-statistics in parentheses.

6. Conclusion

The movement of people across sectors and across areas is a hallmark of economic development. Yet these processes are not well-integrated in economic models, and current data collection designs for the most part are ill-suited to studying spatial mobility and the allocation of labor across sectors in rural areas. In this Chapter we set out a framework that seeks to integrate the processes and we presented some findings from data sets that provide most of the requisite information. There are a number of important limitations of this framework that need to be addressed in the future.

First, the framework is essentially static and deterministic. Processes such as migration of individuals, the location of factories, and even the setting up of a small family business may have fixed cost elements and these processes may have important effects. For example, due to these fixed costs gaps between rural and urban incomes are likely to persist and the young are likely to be the most mobile because they will have a longer time to accrue a return. In addition, uncertainty may play an important role in the process of decisions about labor-force allocation either as a source of diversification given the variability of agricultural incomes or through reentry into the agricultural labor market in cases when a migrant or non-farm worker is unable to find stable employment.

Second, careful consideration needs to be given to the extent to which migrant households lose their claim on local assets when they migrate. The above model focused on land as an asset and assumed that the rents from that land accrued only to those household members who remained in place. But migrants may be able to claim a considerable share of these rents and this, in turn, will make migration more attractive for the individual than it would be otherwise. There are other forms of capital that a migrant may give up in the process of migration. Munshi and Rosenzweig (2005), for example, show that locally-based caste networks that are important source of income insurance and credit play an important role as a constraint to migration in rural India.

Third, sectoral choices may not involve simply a choice based on a comparison of earnings capacity in the different sectors. Urban amenities may play an important role in terms of the differential migration of educated individuals to urban areas. There also may be benefits to rural residence such as that it provides a healthier and safer environment in which to raise children (de Laat, 2005). Changes in technology such as mechanization in agriculture may affect the perceived costs and benefits of agricultural work relative to non-farm employment. Changes in communication technology may also affect the relative importance of migration and rural non-farm activity as destinations for labor that leaves the agricultural sector. At some level these changes may be added with relative ease to the existing framework. The primary difficulty is in finding appropriate ways to measure and test for the presence of such effects.

Fourth, the above framework does not make a distinction between individuals and households. Migration or the decision to undertake non-farm employment may involve migration of single household member or an entire household as part of an overall household decision. But these processes may be quite different and there is a need to develop models that explicitly recognize these distinctions. Moreover, once one recognizes that sectoral allocation decisions are made in the context of the household it becomes clear that there is a potential value to modeling collective household decision making. Two recent papers, de Laat (2005) and Chen (2006), provide instructive examples of this approach. In particular, de Laat (2005) provides evidence that absentee migrant husbands invest considerable effort in monitoring technologies in order to influence the behavior of their rural spouses. Chen (2006) shows that there are important differences in terms of child outcomes that are readily monitored and those that are not in cases of absentee husbands. Analogously, collective models may also shed light on the effects of sectoral allocation decisions that allow individuals who were formerly involved in family production to control (and hide) their effort and earnings from other household members.

References

Alderman, H.B., Behrman, J.R., Kohler, H., Maluccio, J.A., Watkins, S.C. (2001). "Attrition in longitudinal household survey data". Demographic Research 5 (4), 79–124.
Binswanger, H.P. (1983). "Agricultural growth and rural non-farm activities". Finance and Development (June), 38–40.
Fitzgerald, J., Gottschalk, P., Moffit, R. (1998). "An analysis of sample attrition in panel data: The Michigan Panel Study of income dynamics". Journal of Human Resources 33 (2), 251–299.
Chen, J. (2006). "Migration and imperfect monitoring: Implications for Intra-household allocation". American Economic Review: Papers and Proceedings 96 (2), 227–231.
Deshingkar, P. (2006). "Internal migration, poverty and development in Asia". Manuscript. Institute of Development Studies, Sussex.

Dev, S.M., Evenson, R.E. (2003). "Rural development in India: Agriculture, non-farm and migration". Mimeo. Yale University.

de Laat, J. (2005). "Moral hazard and costly monitoring; The case of split migrants in Kenya". Manuscript. Brown University.

Foster, A.D., Rosenzweig, M.R. (2002). "Household division and rural economic growth". Review of Economic Studies 69 (4), 839–870.

Glewwe, P., Grosh, M. (1999). Designing Household Survey Questionnaires for Developing Countries: Lesson from 10 Years of LSMS Experience. World Bank, Washington, DC.

Haggblade, S., Hazell, P., Reardon, T. (2002). "Strategies for stimulating poverty-alleviating growth in the rural non-farm economy in developing countries". Mimeo. International Food Policy Research Institute, Washington, DC.

Hill, Z. (2004). "Reducing attrition in panel studies in developing countries". International Journal of Epidemiology 33, 493–498.

Hymer, S., Resnick, B.F. (1969). "A model of an agrarian economy". American Economic Review 59 (4), 493–506.

Johnson, D.G. (2000). "Population, food, and knowledge". American Economic Review 90 (1), 1–14.

Kijima, Y., Lanjouw, P. (2004). "Agricultural wages, non-farm employment and poverty in rural India". World Bank. Washington, DC. Processed.

Lanjouw, J.O., Lanjouw, P. (2001). "The rural non-farm sector: Issues and evidence from developing countries". Agricultural Economics 26 (1), 1–23.

Lucas, R. (1997). "Internal migration in developing countries". Chapter 13 in: Rosenzweig, M., Stark, O. (Eds.), Handbook of Population and Family Economics. Elsevier Science.

Maluccio, J.A. (2004). "Using quality of interview information to assess nonrandom attrition bias in developing-country panel data". Review of Development Economics 8 (1), 91–100.

Mellor, J.W. (2000). "Faster more equitable growth: The relation between growth in agriculture and poverty reduction". Consulting Assistance on Economic Reform II. Discussion paper No. 70, Cambridge, MA.

Mellor, J.W., Johnston, B.F. (1984). "The world food equation: Interrelations among development, employment, and food consumption". Journal of Economic Literature 22, 531–574.

Munshi, K., Rosenzweig, M.R. (2005). "Why is mobility in India so low? Social insurance inequality and growth. Manuscript.

Pitt, M.M., Rosenzweig, M.R., Hassan, M.N. (2005). "Sharing the burden of disease: Gender, the household division of labor and the health effects of indoor air pollution. Mimeo. Harvard University.

Ranis, G., Stewart, B.F. (1973). "Rural nonagricultural activities in development: Theory and application". Journal of Development Economics 40, 75–101.

Ravallion, M., Datt, G. (1996). "How important to India's poor is the sectoral composition of economic growth?" World Bank Economic Review 10 (1), 1–25.

Ravallion, M., Datt, G. (1999). "When is growth pro-poor? Evidence from the diverse experiences of India's states". Working paper 2263, World Bank Policy Research.

Rosenzweig, M.R. (2003). "Payoffs from panels in low-income countries: Economic development and economic mobility". American Economic Review 93 (2), 112–117 (May).

Rosenzweig, M.R., Stark, O. (1989). "Consumption smoothing, migration and marriage: Evidence from rural India". Journal of Political Economy 97, 905–926.

Surbakti, P. (1995). Indonesia's National Socio-economic Survey, A Continual Data Source for Analysis on Welfare Development, second ed. Central Bureau of Statistics, Indonesia.

Syrquin, M. (1988). "Patterns of structural change, in Chenery". In: Srinivasan, H.T.N. (Ed.), Handbook of Development Economics, vol. 1. Elsevier Science.

Thomas, D., Frankenberg, E., Smith, J.P. (2001). "Lost but not forgotten: Attrition and follow-up in the Indonesia family life". Journal of Human Resources 36 (3), 556–592.

Townsend, R.M. (1994). "Risk and insurance in village India". Econometrica 62 (3), 533–591.

Vashishtha, P.S. (1989). "Changes in structure of investments in rural households, 1970–1971 to 1981–1982". Journal of Income and Wealth 10 (2), 21–45.

Walker, T., Ryan, J. (1984). Village and Household Economies in India's Semi-arid Tropics. The Johns Hopkins Univ. Press, Baltimore.

Chapter 48

INFORMATION NETWORKS IN DYNAMIC AGRARIAN ECONOMIES

KAIVAN MUNSHI

Department of Economics, Box B, Brown University, 64 Waterman Street, Providence, RI 02912, USA

and

NBER, USA

Contents

Handbook of Development Economics, Volume 4
© 2008 Elsevier B.V.   *All rights reserved*
DOI: 10.1016/S1573-4471(07)04048-X

Abstract

Over the past 50 years, people living in developing countries have gained access to technologies, such as high yielding agricultural seed varieties and modern medicine, that have the potential to dramatically alter the quality of their lives. Although the adoption of these technologies has increased wealth and lowered mortality in many parts of the world, their uptake has been uneven. The traditional explanation for the observed differences in the response to new opportunities, across and within countries, is based on heterogeneity in the population. An alternative explanation, which has grown in popularity in recent years is based on the idea that individuals are often uncertain about the returns from a new technology. For example, farmers might not know the (expected) yield that will be obtained from a new and uncertain technology and young mothers might be concerned about the side effects from a new contraceptive. In these circumstances, a neighbor's decision to use a new technology indicates that she must have received a favorable signal about its quality and her subsequent experience with it serves as an additional source of information. Because information must flow sequentially from one neighbor to the next, social learning provides a natural explanation for the gradual diffusion of new technology even in a homogeneous population. Social learning can also explain the wide variation in the response to external interventions across otherwise identical communities, simply as a consequence of the randomness in the information signals that they received. Recent research described in this chapter indicates that social learning can play an important role in the adoption of new agricultural technology, the fertility transition, and investments in health and education in developing countries.

Keywords

social learning, technology adoption

JEL classification: D80, O30

1. Introduction

The post-colonial era has witnessed many dramatic technological changes in the developing world. The introduction of high yielding varieties of wheat and rice in the 1960s dramatically increased farm incomes. Mass immunization programs and the availability of modern medicines led to a sharp decline in mortality. These changes in mortality and incomes, together with aggressive family planning initiatives, saw many countries enter the fertility transition.

While this change is very encouraging, it masks substantial variation in the response to new opportunities across and within countries. Countries at similar levels of economic development have been observed to display very different patterns of fertility behavior. Entire communities sometimes stubbornly oppose the use of modern medicine or contraceptives. And while new agricultural technology might have spread widely, it took as long as two decades in some cases for the new technology to be adopted.

One explanation for these commonly observed patterns of behavior is that heterogeneity in the population, in terms of wealth, education, or individual ability, sometimes leads different groups to respond to new opportunities at different rates. Persistent patterns of behavior might arise due to liquidity constraints or because traditional institutions, such as community-based networks, hold their members back. Starting from the early 1990s, however, an alternative information-based explanation has been proposed for the patterns of behavior described above. The seminal contributions to this "social learning" literature are Banerjee (1992) and Bikhchandani, Hirshleifer, and Welch (1992), and the basic idea behind this line of research is that individuals are often uncertain about the returns from the new opportunities that are available to them. For example, farmers might not know the (expected) yield that will be obtained from a new and uncertain technology and young mothers might be concerned about the side-effects from a new contraceptive. In these circumstances, neighbors' decisions and experiences can be extremely valuable. A neighbor's decision to use the new technology indicates that she must have received a favorable signal about its quality and her subsequent experience with it serves as an additional source of information.

Since information must flow sequentially from one neighbor to the next and since there is typically a lag between the adoption decision and the subsequent outcome, social learning provides a natural explanation for the gradual diffusion of new technology even in a homogeneous population. Furthermore, it can be shown that the entire population could end up choosing the wrong investment, when multiple options are available, if the signals received by neighbors about the new technology cannot be completely backed out from their decisions. Social learning can thus explain the wide variation in the response to external interventions across otherwise identical communities, simply as a consequence of the randomness in the information signals that they received.

The early work on social learning gave rise to an enormous theoretical literature (see Bramoulle and Kranton, 2004 for an excellent summary). This chapter, however, is concerned with a smaller empirical literature on social learning in dynamic agrarian economies that has emerged in recent years. The initial contributions to this literature focussed on the adoption of new agricultural technology. Agriculture provides a natural setting in which to test for social learning since agricultural production occurs at fixed frequency and is a relatively simple and well-understood process. The domain of the information network is also conveniently defined as the village, at least for the case of Indian agriculture which is the setting for these early studies.

Subsequent research has extended this work to the fertility transition, investment in education, and the adoption of new health technology. It is reasonable to assume that farmers operate in competitive input and output markets and that there are no social restrictions on the adoption of new crops. In contrast, may traditional societies had norms in place that prohibited fertility regulation. The availability of modern contraceptives would have made fertility regulation more attractive and encouraged some women to deviate from the norm, opening up the possibility for multiple reproductive equilibria. The object of interest in this case might not be the performance of the new contraceptive, but the nature of the social equilibrium that the community ultimately ends up in. Women gradually learn about this equilibrium over time as they interact with each other and so social change, and the gradual weakening of traditional restrictions in some communities, can also be characterized by a process of social learning.

Learning about health technology differs from agricultural adoption due to the externality that accompanies the individual's decision to participate in a public health program, for example. More information about the new technology becomes available as more members of the information network vaccinate themselves, but the immunity to the rest of the community that this provides implies that the benefit to the individual from vaccination will decline as well. If the group-immunity is sufficiently large, an increase in adoption within the network could actually lower the individual's propensity to adopt the technology.

Despite these important differences across the applications that we consider in this chapter, the characterization of social learning as a signal extraction process remains the same and we will see that the same basic framework can be used, with some modification, to test for the presence of social learning in each case. The chapter is organized in five sections. The second section lays out a theoretical framework for social learning, due to Banerjee (1992), and then proceeds to apply this framework to the adoption of new agricultural technology. The third and fourth sections extend this framework and the empirical tests that are proposed to the fertility transition, investment in education, and the adoption of new health technology. Section five concludes.

2. The adoption of new agricultural technology

This section describes the role played by information networks in the adoption of new agricultural technology. The past five decades have witnessed tremendous technological progress in agricultural production throughout the developing world, starting with the Green Revolution in the 1960s. The Green Revolution is associated with the introduction of high-yielding varieties (HYVs) of wheat and rice. These dwarf varieties have a high grain-to-straw ratio and thus provide much higher average yields than the traditional varieties. However, their performance is relatively sensitive to expensive inputs such as fertilizer and irrigation and is generally associated with greater uncertainty than the traditional varieties.

The HYVs did ultimately spread widely, but this diffusion process was not entirely smooth. There were long lags in adoption for some crops and the rate of diffusion varied widely with geography and by crop. Such delays have been observed historically in US agriculture as well; for example, Ryan and Gross (1943), in an influential study that spawned an enormous literature in rural sociology estimate that it took 14 years before hybrid seed corn was completely adopted in two Iowa communities. The traditional explanation for this lag focussed on heterogeneity in the population (Griliches, 1957; Mansfield, 1968). The idea here is that some people may be more receptive to new ideas and innovations (Rogers, 1962) or, alternatively, that individuals face different economic opportunities which lead them to adopt at different speeds (Griliches, 1957). An alternative explanation, which has grown in popularity in recent years, is based on the idea that farmers will learn from their neighbors' experiences (their previous decisions and outcomes) about a new and uncertain technology. Since the individual's information network—the set of neighbors that he learns from—is limited, this social learning process generates natural lags in adoption even in a homogeneous population. Moreover, we will show below that otherwise identical communities can end up at very different long-run adoption levels, depending on the (random) pattern of information signals that their neighbors receive.

This section begins with a theoretical framework, due to Banerjee (1992), that characterizes the social learning process. Subsequently, we describe social learning and the adoption of new agricultural technology in a number of different settings. This section concludes with a discussion on the identification of social learning in agriculture.

2.1. A simple theoretical framework

All individuals are identical and risk neutral in Banerjee's model. They must choose an asset from a set of assets indexed by numbers in [0, 1]. Only one asset i^* yields a positive return, while all other choices in the unit interval yield zero return. Thus, everyone wants to invest in i^*, but no one knows which asset it corresponds to. Individuals have uniform priors on [0, 1] and so there is no likely candidate for i^*. However, a positive fraction of the population receive an information signal informing them about the value of i^*. Signal quality does not vary across those individuals who receive a signal, with a positive fraction receiving the correct signal. When a signal is false, it is uniformly distributed on [0, 1] and so is completely uninformative.

Banerjee makes the following assumptions to rule out ties:

A1: Whenever an individual has no signal and everyone else has chosen $i = 0$, he always chooses $i = 0$.

A2: When individuals are indifferent between following their own signal and following someone else's choice, they always follow their own signal.

A3: When an individual is indifferent between following more than one of the previous decision makers, he chooses the one with the highest i.

Notice that these assumptions, particularly A2, are chosen deliberately to minimize the potential for herding, which we will see below could nevertheless easily occur in this set up.

The equilibrium decision rule is straightforward to derive in this framework. Assume that individuals make choices sequentially. The first individual will choose $i = 0$ if he has no signal. If he has a signal, he will certainly follow it. If the second individual has no signal, he will certainly follow the first individual. If he has a signal and the first individual made a choice that was inconsistent with that signal (including $i = 0$), he will follow his own signal from assumption A2.

The decision rule for the third individual is more complicated since in general one of four cases could occur:

CASE 1. *The first and second individual chose $i = 0$.*

In this case, the third individual will follow his own signal if he received one, else he will choose $i = 0$.

CASE 2. *One of the two chose $i = 0$.*

The third individual will follow the individual that chose $i \neq 0$ from assumption A3 if he did not receive a signal. If he did receive a signal and it does not match the previous decision maker with $i \neq 0$, he will follow his own signal from assumption A2. If the two signals match, then there is no inconsistency and the third individual will of course follow his own signal.

CASE 3. *The first and second individuals both disagreed and chose some $i \neq 0$.*

If the third individual did not receive a signal, he should follow the higher i from assumption A3. If he did receive a signal, he will follow it regardless of whether or not it coincides with either of the choices made previously.

CASE 4. *The first and second individuals both agreed and chose some $i \neq 0$.*

If the third individual did not receive a signal, he will of course follow the first two individuals. If he did receive a signal and it coincides with the previous choices, then there is no ambiguity and he can simply follow his own (correct) signal. The more interesting situation, which is key to herding, arises when the third individual's signal does not coincide with the previous choices. If the third individual knew with certainty that the second individual did not receive a signal, then he would be indifferent between the first individual's signal and his own signal; from assumption A3 he would then follow his own signal. However, as long as there is even a small probability that the second individual received a signal, the balance will shift in favor of the first two choices since two signals could only have coincided if they were correct.[1]

Since there is indeed a positive probability that the second individual received a signal, the third individual will abandon his own signal and follow the first two choices. Using the same reasoning, all the individuals that follow will do likewise, regardless of whether or not they receive a signal. Such herding can lead the entire community to the incorrect choice if the first individual received a false signal and the second individual received no signal. Herding can also occur with the more general case in which the first n individuals choose different options. If the next decision maker does not have a signal, he will choose the highest i among those that have already been chosen, and all the individuals that follow will do the same unless they receive a signal and it happens to match one of the first n options that were chosen (two signals can only match if they are correct and so the individual would certainly follow his own signal in that case).

The basic reason for the herding described above is that the unobserved signals that individuals receive cannot be backed out from the decision that they subsequently make. In contrast, the empirical literature on social learning and the adoption of new agricultural technology has assumed that the decision function is invertible; the population always ends up at the correct choice in the long run and the only issue is how long it takes before convergence occurs. While this assumption might be appropriate in the specific contexts that have been studied, it rules out the pathological outcomes that make the theoretical framework so interesting and I will return to this point in Section 5.

2.2. Empirical applications

Following Munshi (2004), consider a simple model of agricultural investment in which there are two technologies: a new risky HYV technology and a safe traditional technology. The traditional technology provides a certain yield y_{TV}, where the yield is defined as the profit per unit of land. The yield from the new HYV technology for grower i in period t is specified as

$$y_{it} = y(Z_i) + \eta_{it} \tag{1}$$

where $y(Z_i)$ is the yield under normal growing conditions and Z_i is a vector of soil characteristics and prices. η_{it} is a mean-zero serially independent disturbance term with variance λ_i^2. η_{it} is determined by a combination of rainfall, temperature and other growing conditions. While the farmer may be aware of some of the individual factors that contribute to the growing conditions in a given year, their net effect on the yield and, hence, η_{it} cannot be observed.

The grower arrives at his (optimal) expected utility maximizing acreage A_i^* immediately when the expected yield $y(Z_i)$ is known with certainty. Under reasonable conditions, A_i^* will be increasing in $y(Z_i) - y_{TV}$ and decreasing in λ_i. A role for social

---

[1] Recall that false signals are uniformally distributed on the unit interval.

learning does arise, however, when the grower has incomplete knowledge of the new technology. Specifically, assume now that the expected yield $y(Z_i)$ is no longer known to the grower with certainty. The acreage function can then be expressed as

$$A_{it} = A(\hat{y}_{it} - y_{TV}, \lambda_i, \sigma_{it}) \tag{2}$$

where $\hat{y}_{it}$ is the grower's best estimate of the expected yield in period t and σ_{it}^2 is the variance of the grower's expected yield estimate. For the risk averse grower, the chosen acreage A_{it} is increasing in $\hat{y}_{it} - y_{TV}$ and decreasing in λ_i, σ_{it}. We will see below that $\hat{y}_{it}$ slowly converges to $y(Z_i)$ as the grower receives more information over time, accompanied by a corresponding convergence in A_{it} to A_i^*.

The risk-averse grower is always interested in minimizing the uncertainty in $y(Z_i)$ since his expected utility is declining in σ_{it}. He will thus utilize all the information about $y(Z_i)$ that is available to him to arrive at his best estimate $\hat{y}_{it}$ in each period. Three sources of information are available to the grower. First, he receives an exogenous information-signal, perhaps from the local extension agent, about the value of his expected yield in each period. We assume that this signal provides an unbiased estimate of the yield that the grower should expect on his own land. We also assume that all growers in the village receive signals of equal precision. Second, he can use his neighbors' decisions to infer the signals that they received. Third, he can learn directly from his own and his neighbors' yield realizations.

The timing of receipt of the alternative sources of information is as follows. At the beginning of a period the grower receives his private information-signal. In a Bayesian setting, the grower combines that signal with his prior at the beginning of the period to compute the best-estimate of his expected yield. This in turn determines the acreage that he allocates to HYV in that period. Subsequently, he observes his neighbors' acreage decisions, which reveal the signals that they received, as well as all the yields that are realized in the village. With social learning the new information from neighbors' decisions as well as their yield realizations is used to update the grower's prior about the value of his expected yield for the next period.

To begin with, assume that expected yields are constant across growers in the village so neighbors' information-signals and yield realizations provide an unbiased estimate of the grower's own yield, y. The information-signals that arrive in the village in a given period and the yields that are subsequently realized are pooled together by each grower and applied to update his prior in the next period. All growers in the village begin with a common prior $\hat{y}_0$ in period 0. Since they utilize the same information to update their priors in each period, all growers have a common prior in subsequent periods as well. Over time these beliefs converge to the true yield y.[2]

Following the timing of various information-sources outlined above, each grower combines the common prior at the beginning of period t, $\hat{y}_t$, with the private

---

[2] σ_{it} declines over the course of this convergence process, which explains the increase in acreage allocated to the new technology A_{it} over time that is commonly observed.

information-signal that he receives at the beginning of that period, u_{it}, to arrive at his best-estimate of the expected yield on his land. Beliefs at the time of planting thus vary across growers in the village in each period. When η_{it}, u_{it} are normally distributed, $\hat{y}_{it}$ will be a weighted average of $\hat{y}_t$ and u_{it} in a Bayesian setting:

$$\hat{y}_{it} = \alpha \hat{y}_t + (1 - \alpha)u_{it}. \tag{3}$$

The next step in describing the learning process is to study how $\hat{y}_t$ is determined. For this we need to go back one period in time. After all the growers in the village have made their decision in period $t - 1$, the mean information-signal that they received in that period $\bar{u}_{t-1}$ can be extracted from their decisions when the acreage function is invertible. Since no one is systematically misinformed, the mean-signal provides more information about the expected yield than any individual signal. Thus $\bar{u}_{t-1}$ supersedes u_{it-1} when it becomes available at the end of period $t - 1$ and so is used to compute each grower's prior for the next period $\hat{y}_t$. Of course, growers subsequent yield realizations also appear as an additional source of information by the end of period $t - 1$. Applying Bayes' Rule once more, the expression for $\hat{y}_t$ is consequently obtained as

$$\hat{y}_t = (1 - \beta - \gamma)\hat{y}_{t-1} + \beta \bar{u}_{t-1} + \gamma \bar{y}_{t-1} \tag{4}$$

where $\hat{y}_{t-1}$ captures all of the information about the expected yield that was received in the village up to the beginning of period $t - 1$ in Eq. (4). The village-means, $\bar{u}_{t-1}$, $\bar{y}_{t-1}$, represent the new information that became available in that period.[3]

Two important variables that characterize the learning process, $\hat{y}_{t-1}$, $\bar{u}_{t-1}$ are not directly observed by the econometrician. Assuming that A_{it} is an additively separable function of $\hat{y}_{it}$ in Eq. (2), Munshi proceeds to derive A_{it} as a function of observed characteristics using Eqs. (3) and (4):

$$A_{it} = \pi_0 + \pi_1 A_{it-1} + \pi_2 \bar{A}_{t-1} + \pi_3 \bar{y}_{t-1} + \epsilon_{it}, \tag{5}$$

with π_1, π_2, π_3 derived in terms of α, β, γ. The specification for the acreage function described above is very intuitive. When information is pooled efficiently within the village, A_{it-1} contains all the information about the expected yield that was available at the beginning of period $t - 1$; specifically the entire history of information-signals and yield realizations up to that time. Conditional on A_{it-1}, $\bar{A}_{t-1}$ represents the new information that was received by the village in period $t - 1$ through the exogenous signals. Similarly, $\bar{y}_{t-1}$ represents the information that was obtained from the yield realizations in that period. Note that the grower's own lagged yield y_{it-1} does not enter independently in Eq. (5) since it is superseded by the mean-yield in the village $\bar{y}_{t-1}$.

The previous scenario that we discussed was the most suitable for social learning. Neighbors' signals and yields provide an unbiased estimate of the grower's own expected yield and so can be utilized without modification. In fact, information from a

---

[3] The grower will actually place more weight on his prior as he grows more confident about the yield level on his land. Thus, α will be increasing, while β, γ are decreasing, over time. We ignore the time subscripts on α, β, γ to simplify the exposition.

neighbor is as useful as the information that the grower receives himself. However, the expected yield will more generally depend on the farmer's characteristics; the fact that the technology worked well for a neighbor does not necessarily imply that it will work well for you. Ellison and Fudenberg (1993) use this argument to justify simple rules of thumb where individuals learn from similar neighbors only, slowing down the rate of diffusion, but the grower could in principle do better than that by conditioning for differences between his own and his neighbors' observed characteristics when learning from them. However, the prospects for social learning decline immediately once we allow for the possibility that some of these characteristics may be unobserved, or imperfectly observed.

The grower may be prepared to accept transitory errors in his yield estimates; associated with the η disturbance term in Eq. (1) or noise in the exogenous information-signals. However, mistakes that arise because he is unable to control for differences between his own and his neighbors' characteristics when learning from their yields are persistent, and therefore more serious. Take the case where all the neighbors' characteristics are unobserved by the grower. He now has two choices. He could rely on his own information-signals and yield realizations, ignoring information from his neighbors. Consistent but inefficient estimates of the expected yield would be obtained with such *individual* learning. Alternatively, he could continue to utilize information from his neighbors, measured by the mean-acreage and the mean-yield, as before. The efficiency of his estimates increases with *social* learning since more information is being utilized, but some bias will inevitably be introduced since the grower cannot control for variation in the underlying determinants of the yield when learning from his neighbors. The grower will ultimately choose between individual learning and social learning on the basis of the trade-off between bias and efficiency. The testable prediction in this case is that the grower will choose individual learning if the population is heterogeneous and the yield with the new agricultural technology (crop) is sufficiently sensitive to unobserved characteristics, otherwise he will prefer to learn from his neighbors.

While Munshi (2004) and Besley and Case (1994) assume that the yield (or profit) $y(Z_i)$ is exogenous and uncertain, Foster and Rosenzweig (1995) and Conley and Udry (2005) assume that the grower's objective is to learn his optimal (profit-maximizing) input use Z_i. The point of departure for their work is the target-input model of Jovanovic and Nyarko (1996), but we will see that the signal extraction aspect and, hence, the basic structure of the learning process remains the same across these different models of learning.

With a slight change of notation, Foster and Rosenzweig assume that the grower attempts to learn the optimal or target input use on his land θ^*,

$$\tilde{\theta}_{ijt} = \theta^* + u_{ijt} \tag{6}$$

where $\tilde{\theta}_{ijt}$ is the optimal input use on plot i for farmer j in period t, u_{ijt} is an i.i.d. random variable with a (known) variance σ_u^2, and the farmer's prior on θ^* is $N(\hat{\theta}_{j0}, \hat{\sigma}_{\theta j0}^2)$. Notice the similarity with Eq. (1), where the grower's objective was to learn the value of the (expected) yield $y(Z_i)$. Previously he was seen to collect information on $y(Z_i)$ from various sources to finally arrive at the optimal acreage. In the current set up, the grower collects information on θ^* from various sources to arrive at his profit-maximizing input level.

The yield (or profit) per plot from HYV on the ith most suitable plot for HYV for a farmer with A_j plots is

$$\eta_a + \eta_h - \eta_{ha}\frac{i}{A_j} - \left(\theta_{ijt} - \tilde{\theta}_{ijt}\right)^2$$

where η_a is the yield from traditional varieties, η_h is the maximum yield from HYV on the plot most suitable for the new technology, and η_{ha} represents the loss from using land less suitable for HYV. $\left(\theta_{ijt} - \tilde{\theta}_{ijt}\right)^2$ is the loss due to sub-optimal input use, which declines over time with social learning.

Based on the expression above, the profit from all the farmer's plots can be specified as,

$$\sum_{i=1}^{H_{jt}}\left(\eta_a + \eta_h - \eta_{ha}\frac{i}{A_j} - \left(\theta_{ijt} - \tilde{\theta}_{ijt}\right)^2\right) + (A_j - H_{jt})\eta_a$$

where H_{jt} is the number of plots allocated to HYV. The profit expression can be simplified further as

$$\eta_h H_{jt} - \frac{\eta_{ha}}{A_j}\frac{H_{jt}^2}{2} + A_j\eta_a - \sum_{i=1}^{H_{jt}}\left(\theta_{ijt} - \tilde{\theta}_{ijt}\right)^2.$$

Taking expectations, the grower's expected profit can finally be expressed as,

$$\pi_{jt} = \left[\eta_h - \frac{\eta_{ha}}{A_j}\frac{H_{jt}}{2} - \sigma_{\tilde{\theta}jt}^2 - \sigma_u^2\right]H_{jt} + \eta_a A_j. \tag{7}$$

The term in square brackets above represents the yield from HYV, which is declining in $\sigma_{\tilde{\theta}jt}^2$ and σ_u^2. σ_u^2, which corresponds to λ^2 in Munshi's model, is a source of (natural) uncertainty that the grower cannot avoid. However, $\sigma_{\tilde{\theta}jt}^2$, which corresponds to $\sigma_{\theta it}^2$ in Munshi's framework, will go to zero as the grower learns the value of θ^* from his own and his neighbors' experiences, and so the HYV yield will increase over time with social learning. The next step in the analysis is consequently to characterize this change in $\sigma_{\tilde{\theta}jt}^2$ over time.

Foster and Rosenzweig assume that the optimal input on each plot $\tilde{\theta}_{ijt}$ is revealed to the farmer at the end of each year. The farmer also learns from his neighbors' input decisions and profit realizations, although the signals received from neighbors' plots are assumed to be less precise than the signals received from the grower's own plots. Under the normality assumption, the variance of θ^* can be expressed in a Bayesian setting as,

$$\sigma_{\tilde{\theta}jt}^2 = \frac{1}{\rho + \rho_0 S_{jt} + \rho_v \bar{S}_{-jt}} \tag{8}$$

where S_{jt} is the cumulative experience on the grower's own land and $\bar{S}_{-jt}$ is the average of the cumulative experience of the neighbors. As experience with the new technology grows, mistakes in input use and hence the variance in θ^* get smaller, which increases profits from Eq. (7) and Eq. (8).

While Munshi shows that the effect of neighbors' past decisions and experiences on the grower's current decision will vary across crops, depending on growing conditions and the technology, Foster and Rosenzweig derive predictions for changes in the pattern of learning over time.

$$\frac{\partial \pi_{jt}/\partial S_{jt}}{\partial \pi_{jt}/\partial \bar{S}_{-jt}} = \frac{\rho_0}{\rho_v}$$

and so own and neighbors' acreage effects change at the same pace over time.

Let $y_{jt+1} = \pi_{jt+1}/H_{jt+1}$ and $y_{jt} = \pi_{jt}/H_{jt}$ be the profit per unit of HYV acreage in period $t + 1$ and t, respectively. Then it is easy to verify that

$$\frac{\partial y_{jt+1}/\partial S_{jt+1}}{\partial y_{jt}/\partial S_{jt}} = \frac{(\rho + \rho_0 S_{jt} + \rho_v \bar{S}_{-jt})^2}{(\rho + \rho_0 S_{jt+1} + \rho_v \bar{S}_{-jt+1})^2} < 1$$

and so returns per hectare from own experience are decreasing over time. By a similar calculation, it can be shown that returns per hectare from neighbors' experience are also decreasing in the same fashion.

The grower's objective, in Munshi's framework, is to learn the value of the expected yield y, which we take to be constant across all farmers in the simplest case. Each neighbor's expected yield estimate in period $t - 1$ can be backed out from his acreage decision in that period, assuming that the acreage function is invertible, while his accompanying yield realization provides an additional estimate of y. Foster and Rosenzweig's learning problem is more challenging since the grower is presumed to infer the optimal input on each plot in each period for himself and his neighbors. This seems to be a difficult task with a single observation per plot-period and at best we might imagine that the grower obtains an unbiased estimate of $\tilde{\theta}_{ijt}$; I suspect that the implications of Foster and Rosenzweig's model would in fact go through in this case as well. However, obtaining even an unbiased estimate of the optimal input with a single observation might sometimes be a difficult task. A paper by Conley and Udry (2005) consequently proceeds to relax this assumption.

To understand Conley and Udry's model of learning it is convenient to ignore idiosyncratic variation in the optimal input use u_{ijt} and assume instead a common and constant optimal level θ^* on all plots and in all periods. The grower observes the input level and the associated profit on his own and his neighbors' plots in each period. With "parametric" learning, the grower could specify a particular functional relationship between profits and inputs and then estimate these parameters with the data obtained from his own and his neighbors' experiences. Assuming that the profit function is correctly specified, the estimated parameters would converge over time to the true parameters and the grower would arrive at the optimal level of input use. Conley and Udry assume instead that the grower learns "nonparametrically"; profits observed at a particular input level provide no information about the profit-input relationship at any other level. Nonparametric learning avoids potential misspecification in the profit function, but convergence will now occur relatively slowly. The grower will trade off efficiency and potential bias when choosing between parametric and nonparametric learning, and this choice will in practice be motivated by growing conditions and the nature of the crop technology (as in Munshi, 2004). While they do not provide such a motivation, Conley and Udry's nonparametric learning model nevertheless yields a number of testable implications for the relationship between the grower's input (fertilizer) use and his neighbors' past use.

First, suppose that a neighbor uses the same level of input as the grower's current level, which is presumably his best estimate of the optimal level. If the neighbor's profit exceeds the grower's expected profit at that input level, then this will only reinforce the grower's belief that he is at the optimal level and there will be no change in inputs in the future. If the neighbor's profit is below the grower's expected level, then this increases the probability that the grower will shift to a new level in the future. Second, suppose that a neighbor uses a different level of input than the grower. If his profit exceeds the grower's prior belief about the profit at that level, then this increases the probability that the grower will switch to his neighbor's input level in the future. If the neighbor's profit is below what the grower expected, then this only reinforces his prior that it is a sub-optimal input level and there will be no response in the future.

Munshi generates predictions for differences in the pattern of learning across crops. Foster and Rosenzweig place restrictions on the pattern of learning over time. Conley and Udry's learning model distinguishes between the response to input use at the grower's own level and at other levels. We will see below that these testable predictions play an important role in the identification of social learning.

2.3. Identifying social learning

The simplest test of social learning in agriculture, following Eq. (5), is to see whether the grower's current acreage is determined by his neighbors' past acreage decisions and yield realizations. We thus estimate regressions of the form

$$A_{it} = \Pi_0 + \Pi_1 A_{it-1} + \Pi_2 \bar{A}_{t-1} + \Pi_3 \bar{y}_{t-1} + \epsilon_{it}$$

where A_{it} is the acreage allocated to the new technology by grower i in period t, A_{it-1} is the acreage allocated in the previous period, $\bar{A}_{t-1}$ is the average HYV acreage in the village in that period, and $\bar{y}_{t-1}$ is the corresponding average yield. As discussed earlier, A_{it-1} collects all the information about the new technology that was available in the village up to the beginning of period $t - 1$, $\bar{A}_{t-1}$ represents the new information that became available through the external signals ($\bar{u}_{t-1}$) in period $t - 1$, and $\bar{y}_{t-1}$ represents the new information obtained from yield realizations in the village in that period.

The acreage decision in period t depends on the grower's best estimate of the HYV yield $\hat{y}_{it}$, which is determined in turn by his prior $\hat{y}_t$ and the new information signal u_{it}. The prior $\hat{y}_t$ is represented by the A_{it-1}, $\bar{A}_{t-1}$, $\bar{y}_{t-1}$ terms and u_{it} is included in ϵ_{it}. As long as information signals are correlated over time and across growers in the village,

$\bar{A}_{t-1}$ will be correlated with ϵ_{it} and learning from neighbors' signals cannot be distinguished from learning from own signals.[4] Unlike Banerjee (1992), Munshi assumes that growers are never systematically misinformed, $E(u_{it}) = y$, and so $\bar{y}_{t-1}$ and ϵ_{it} will be correlated as well.

One solution to this problem would be to difference $\bar{y}_{t-2}$ from $\bar{y}_{t-1}$, leaving us with $\bar{\eta}_{t-1} - \bar{\eta}_{t-2}$ from Eq. (1). Under the assumptions of the model, $\bar{\eta}_{t-1}$, $\bar{\eta}_{t-2}$ measure unobserved (to the grower) deviations from normal growing conditions, which will be uncorrelated with the information signals. However, this differencing procedure leaves an additional $\pi_3 \bar{y}_{t-2}$ term in the residual of the acreage regression, which is negatively correlated with $\bar{\eta}_{t-1} - \bar{\eta}_{t-2}$ by construction and so will generate conservative estimates of the yield effect. A potentially more serious problem is that changes in village yield over time could be due to factors other than serially independent deviations from normal growing conditions. By specifying yield to be the sum of a constant term $y(Z_i)$ and an idiosyncratic shock η_{it} we are implicitly assuming that input markets function smoothly and that input and output prices do not change over time. In practice, changes in the yield from period $t - 2$ to $t - 1$ could reflect changes in prices or access to scarce resources that are unobserved by the econometrician but directly determine the grower's period-t acreage decision. A spurious yield effect could in that case be obtained.

We could control to some extent for unobserved determinants of current acreage by including prices and access to seeds, fertilizer, and irrigation, as well as the grower's wealth.[5] An alternative solution takes advantage of the distinction between parametric and nonparametric learning described above. Social learning will be weaker in a heterogeneous population, particularly when the performance of the new technology is sensitive to neighbors' unobserved characteristics. The rice growing areas of Peninsular India are characterized by wide variation in soil characteristics. In contrast, conditions are fairly uniform in the Northern Plains, where wheat is grown traditionally. The early rice varieties were also quite sensitive to soil characteristics such as salinity, as well as to managerial inputs, which are difficult to observe. The rice grower would thus have found it difficult to control for differences between his own and his neighbors' characteristics when learning from their experiences. Consistent with this view, Munshi (2004) using farm-level data over a three-year period at the onset of the Green Revolution finds that HYV acreage responds to lagged yield shocks in the village with wheat but not rice. While the acreage effects are more difficult to interpret, the coefficient on own lagged acreage is larger for rice than for wheat, whereas the pattern across crops is reversed for the coefficient on lagged mean HYV acreage in the village, consistent with the view once again that social learning was stronger for wheat than for rice.

---

[4] Following Manski (1993), neighbors' past acreage allocations will be correlated with the grower's current acreage decision if any unobserved determinant of the acreage decision is correlated across neighbors and over time.

[5] Along the same lines, we could include the grower's own lagged yield-shock in the acreage regression to distinguish social learning from individual learning.

If access to credit and other scarce inputs varied systematically across the wheat- and rice-growing areas of the country, then the observed differences in the yield effect across crops could still be explained without appealing to differences in underlying social learning. Munshi responds to this potential concern by testing for social learning at the district level, which reflects underlying learning at the farm level, using districts that grow both wheat and rice. The set of neighbors is now defined by the set of geographically contiguous districts and the acreage regressions are estimated over the 1969–1985 period. The estimated pattern of acreage and yield coefficients across crops, with district fixed effects, matches the patterns described above at the farm level, providing independent support for the presence of social learning in the adoption of new agricultural technology.

Munshi's test of social learning is based on the relationship between the grower's current HYV acreage and his neighbors' lagged HYV yields. In contrast, Foster and Rosenzweig derive implications for the relationship between the grower's profit (yield) with HYV and cumulative experience with the new technology:

$$\pi_{jt} = \left(\eta_h + \beta_{ot} S_{jt} + \beta_{vt} \bar{S}_{-jt}\right) H_{jt} + \eta_a A_{jt} + \xi_{jt}$$

where the term in parentheses represents the profit (yield) from HYV, which is increasing in the cumulative experience with the new technology on own land S_{jt} and neighbors' land S_{-jt}. H_{jt}, A_{jt} measure acreage allocation in period t to the new technology and the traditional technology, and π_{jt} measures crop profits. The potential sources of spurious correlation that arise in Munshi's analysis evidently apply here as well. To begin with, fixed grower characteristics could jointly determine HYV yields and acreage allocations. Since farm level data are available over a three-year period, grower fixed effects can be included in the profit regression. However, unobserved time-varying changes in growing conditions or access to scarce resources, which would affect both the current HYV yield as well as S_{jt}, $\bar{S}_{-jt}$, would not be accounted for by the fixed effects. Foster and Rosenzweig use inherited wealth and lagged values of S_{jt}, $\bar{S}_{-jt}$ as instruments for S_{jt}, $\bar{S}_{-jt}$, but these instruments will only be valid if the unobserved determinants of the yield are serially uncorrelated, which may not be the case in practice.

Once again it is possible to appeal to the restrictions from the theory to provide additional support for the presence of social learning. Foster and Rosenzweig's learning model generates the predictions that (i) β_{ot}, β_{vt} will be declining over time, and (ii) $\frac{\beta_{ot}}{\beta_{vt}} = \frac{\beta_{ot+1}}{\beta_{vt+1}}$. These predictions are successfully tested, consistent with the presence of social learning. Conley and Udry take a similar approach, testing the restrictions placed on the relationship between the grower's input use and his neighbors' lagged input use. They find that farmers are more likely to change their fertilizer use when members of their information network using similar levels of fertilizer achieve unexpectedly low profits. Farmers also increase (decrease) fertilizer use when their neighbors using more (less) fertilizer than them do unexpectedly well, as predicted.

Finally, differences in patterns of experimentation across farmers or crops generate additional testable restrictions that can be taken to the data. All the studies discussed in this section allow for experimentation on the grower's own plot, as well as for strategic adoption, when deriving testable predictions for social learning. Munshi, in particular, generates predictions for patterns of experimentation across crops to support his argument that social learning was stronger for wheat than for rice. If the view that rice growers were informationally disadvantaged is correct, then we would expect such growers to have compensated for their lack of information by experimenting on their own land. Munshi shows that rice growers who do adopt HYV allocate a greater amount of land to the new technology than comparable wheat growers. This is despite the fact that farms are smaller in the rice growing areas of the country and the likelihood of HYV adoption is significantly higher for wheat growers.

Along the same lines, Bandiera and Rasul (2006) use strategic delays to explain the inverted U-shaped relationship between the number of neighbors that adopt and the individual's own decision to adopt a new agricultural technology in Mozambique. On the one hand, an increase in the number of adopters in the individual's information network increases the amount of (social) information that is made available, increasing his propensity to adopt. On the other hand, having many adopters in the network increases the individual's incentive to delay adoption and free-ride on the information that is made available by his neighbors. Bandiera and Rasul show that the second effect dominates once the adoption level within the network grows beyond a cut off point.[6]

While the early studies on social learning in agriculture such as Besley and Case (1994), Foster and Rosenzweig (1995), and Munshi (2004), treat the village as the exogenous domain of the information network, recent studies such as Conley and Udry (2005) and Bandiera and Rasul (2006) use a self-reported list of social contacts to construct the network. All plots are clustered together in India and so all decisions and experiences in the village are readily observable. In contrast, agriculture is more spatially dispersed in sub-Saharan Africa and so information will flow less smoothly within the village. The advantage of using the actual (self-reported) network links as opposed to the potential (village-wide) links is that tests of social learning will have more power. The potential cost of using a self-reported network is that the omitted variable problems discussed above could be worsened. This point will be discussed in greater detail in Section 3 in the context of the identification of social learning in the fertility transition.

3. The fertility transition

Declining mortality, together with rising incomes and access to modern contraceptives throughout the developing world have led to a substantial decline in fertility over the

---

[6] Bandiera and Rasul depart from the set up in previous studies by analyzing the relationship between the grower's decision to adopt the new technology and the proportion of his self-reported network that adopts *contemporaneously*. The interesting predictions that they derive are based on the grower's response to exogenous variation in his neighbors' adoption. With cross-sectional data, what they identify instead is the equilibrium correlation between the individual's adoption and his neighbors' adoption, which is difficult to interpret.

past decades. However, long delays and wide differentials in the response to family planning programs have been frequently observed, both across countries and within countries (Bulatao, 1998; Cleland et al., 1994; NRC, 1993). One explanation for such slow adoption is based on the idea that individuals may be uncertain about the efficacy of the new contraceptive technology or, perhaps more importantly, they may be concerned about its potential side-effects. Such concerns are very relevant given the long-term nature and potential medical risks of contraceptives such as IUD and injectables that are typically distributed in developing countries. In these circumstances, a neighbor's decision to adopt the new contraceptive technology indicates that she must have received favorable information about its performance. Her subsequent experience with the new technology serves as an additional source of information.

The social learning just described is conceptually no different from the learning about new agricultural technology that was discussed in some detail in the previous section. The performance of the new contraceptive technology is likely to be relatively insensitive to the individual's socio-economic characteristics and so learning from a neighbor's experience with the new technology, at the very least, should proceed without any need to condition for differences in characteristics across individuals. What slows down the fertility transition is not the nature of the technology, as in the agricultural case, but the restrictions on fertility regulation put in place in most traditional societies. While such social regulation may have had advantages of its own historically, the drawback is that it may prevent individuals from responding immediately to the new opportunities associated with the availability of modern contraceptives. Social learning will be seen in a moment to play an important role in the gradual weakening of these restrictions as well.

Social norms are seen to emerge in environments characterized by multiple equilibria to keep the community in a preferred equilibrium (Kandori, 1992). Changes in the economic environment, such as the unexpected availability of modern contraceptives, could reopen the possibility for such multiple equilibria. The point of departure for Munshi and Myaux's (2006) model of the fertility transition is a social uncertainty following the introduction of a family planning program: the individual does not know the reproductive equilibrium that her community will ultimately converge to. This uncertainty is gradually resolved as individuals interact sequentially with each other over time. There are only two types of individuals in their simple model, which is constructed so that only two possible equilibria can emerge in the long-run. No one regulates fertility prior to the intervention. While this remains a potential equilibrium, a new equilibrium in which a sufficient fraction of the community regulates fertility is also shown to emerge. The discussion that follows describes the social learning process that leads some communities from the traditional equilibrium to the modern equilibrium, while others remain where they were. Testable implications will subsequently be derived and empirical results discussed from a particular setting, as we did in the previous section with the adoption of agricultural technology.

3.1. Social norms and social learning in the fertility transition

Each community consists of a continuum of individuals. Each individual chooses from two actions at the beginning of every period: the traditional (t) action corresponding to unchecked fertility and the modern (m) action, which refers to fertility control. Subsequently she is randomly matched with a member of the community. When reproductive behavior is socially regulated, the individual's payoff from a particular action depends not only on the intrinsic utility that she derives from that action, but also on the social pressure or sanctions that go with it. Following Kandori's (1992) characterization of social norms, the individual's payoff depends on her own action, as well as her partner's action, which determines the social sanction that she will face in that period.

Since there are two possible actions, and the individual matches with a single partner in each period, payoffs corresponding to four combinations of actions must be considered:

$$V_i(m, m) = U_i,$$
$$V_i(m, t) = U_i - l,$$
$$V_i(t, t) = 0,$$
$$V_i(t, m) = g.$$

V_i is individual i's payoff at the end of the period, where the first term in parentheses refers to the individual's own action, and the second term refers to her partner's action. U_i is the intrinsic utility that the individual derives from the modern action. There are two types of individuals in this simple model, conformists and reformists, with reformists comprising a fraction P of the community. Conformists are assumed to have internalized the opposition to reproductive control that is built into the social norm. Thus they derive lower intrinsic utility from the m action than the reformists; $U_i = v$ for the conformists and $U_i = w > v$ for the reformists.

l and g refer to the punishment and rewards that have been put in place to regulate reproductive behavior. When a woman who chooses the modern action meets another woman who continues to follow the traditional action, she faces some sort of social censure. The reward g may be associated with enhanced social standing, possibly within a very restricted peer group, for having punished a deviator. Notice that there are no social sanctions when two deviators meet each other.

Munshi and Myaux impose the following conditions on the payoffs prior to the external intervention: $v > 0$, $w - l < 0$, $w < g$. Under these conditions it is easy to verify that a unique equilibrium is obtained in each period, in which both conformists and reformists choose the t action. Subsequently they allow for the availability of modern contraceptives, which reduces the inconvenience associated with fertility control, increasing the individual's intrinsic utility from the m action by an amount S. The conditions on payoffs in the new regime are the same as what we described above, with one important exception: $v + S > 0$, $w + S - l < 0$, $w + S > g > v + S$.

It is easy to verify that the traditional equilibrium, without fertility control, continues to be sustainable in the new regime. A new modern equilibrium can also be sustained if the proportion of reformists in the community P is sufficiently large. In this equilibrium all the reformists choose m and all the conformists choose t. A reformist will not deviate from this equilibrium if the expected payoff from choosing m exceeds the expected payoff from choosing t

$$P(w + S) + (1 - P)(w + S - l) \geqslant Pg. \tag{9}$$

Simplifying the expression above, a necessary condition to sustain the modern equilibrium is obtained as $P \geqslant P^* = \frac{l - (w + S)}{l - g}$. Communities with $P \geqslant P^*$ must choose between two equilibria, while only the traditional equilibrium can be supported in communities with $P < P^*$.

The basic source of uncertainty in Munshi and Myaux's model is that the proportion of reformists P is not known to begin with, since each individual's type is private information and both conformists and reformists chose the same traditional action prior to the intervention. To simplify the equilibrium dynamics they assume that there are two types of communities: stable communities with $\underline{P} < P^*$ reformists and unstable communities with $\bar{P} > P^*$ reformists. We will see in a moment that information about P is gradually revealed over time as individuals interact with each other, with unstable communities moving to the modern equilibrium while stable communities remain where they were.

All communities continue to remain in the traditional equilibrium following the introduction of the family planning program. Since the program has increased the payoff from the m action by an amount S, it is evidently interested in making sure that the reformists in the unstable communities take advantage of the new opportunities that are available. Most family planning programs employ health workers to persuade women to adopt the new contraceptive technology. In our context, these workers play a critical role in initiating the transition from the traditional equilibrium to the modern equilibrium in the unstable communities, just as extension workers must provide the exogenous information signals to initiate the adoption of new agricultural technology. The health worker visits a fraction θ of the community, drawn at random, in each period and persuades any reformist that she meets to switch to the m action, but for a single period only. Since there is a continuum of individuals in each community, this implies that a constant fraction θP of the community, where $P = \bar{P}$ in unstable communities and $P = \underline{P}$ in stable communities, deviates *exogenously* in each period. We will see that this exogenous deviation provides the seed for subsequent *endogenous* deviation in the unstable communities, which ultimately moves them to the new social equilibrium.

Let $\alpha_t \in [0, 1]$ be the individual's belief about the state of the world, the probability that $P = \bar{P}$, in period t. Begin with a degenerate distribution of beliefs α_0 in period 0, in both stable and unstable communities, such that no reformist deviates endogenously. This leaves only exogenous deviation in the first few periods: a proportion $\theta \bar{P}$ of the individuals in the unstable communities and a corresponding proportion $\theta \underline{P}$

of the individuals in the stable communities choose the m action in each period.[7] While contraceptive prevalence might be constant in these early periods, the distribution of beliefs within each community will spread out over time as different individuals are faced with a different sequence of matches. To derive the evolution of individual beliefs during these early periods without endogenous deviation apply Bayes' Rule to an individual with belief α_t in period t who matches with an m in that period. Her belief α_{t+1} in the subsequent period is then expressed as:

$$\alpha_{t+1} = \Pr\left(P = \bar{P} \mid m\right) = \frac{\alpha_t(\theta\bar{P})}{\alpha_t(\theta\bar{P}) + (1-\alpha_t)(\theta\underline{P})}. \tag{10}$$

θ is common knowledge, and while the individual might not know the type of community that she belongs to, she does know the values of $\bar{P}$, $\underline{P}$. Since the term in the denominator of Eq. (10) is a weighted average of $\theta\bar{P}$ and $\theta\underline{P}$, it is easy to verify that $\alpha_{t+1}/\alpha_t > 1$. As the individual matches with m's in the community, her belief that $P = \bar{P}$ grows. The right-hand support of the distribution in any period t is thus defined by the beliefs of the individuals in the community who have matched with a continuous sequence of m's up to that period, and so will shift steadily over time.

A reformist will choose the m action in any period, without persuasion from the health worker, if the expected probability of matching with an m exceeds P^* (from Eq. (9)). The expected probability of matching with an m in these early periods is simply $\alpha(\theta\bar{P}) + (1-\alpha)(\theta\underline{P})$, where α is the individual's belief that $P = \bar{P}$. This expected probability is evidently increasing in α. As long as $\theta\bar{P} > P^*$, there exists a threshold belief α^*, for which the individual is indifferent between the t and the m action, satisfying the following condition:

$$\alpha^*\left(\theta\bar{P}\right) + (1-\alpha^*)(\theta\underline{P}) = P^*. \tag{11}$$

If the individual's belief that $P = \bar{P}$ exceeds α^*, then the expected probability of matching with an m will exceed P^*, and she will deviate endogenously. If not, she will only choose m when she meets the health worker. Following the discussion above, the support of the belief distribution will shift steadily over time in the early periods until ultimately the right-hand support reaches α^*. The first wave of endogenous deviators will now appear, at the same time in both stable and unstable communities.

To describe actions in the community after the first wave of endogenous deviators appears, Munshi and Myaux begin by showing that the distribution of beliefs in the unstable communities shifts steadily to the right over time, whereas the distribution shifts in the opposite direction in the stable communities. In every period following the emergence of the first endogenous deviators there exists an α_t^* such that all individuals with

---

[7] If the health worker observes all the individual decisions, then P would be revealed to the external agency in the first period itself. Immediate withdrawal by the external agency would signal in turn whether a community was stable or unstable. Programatic constraints would typically rule out such early withdrawal by the external agency from a subset of communities.

beliefs to the right of this threshold belief will choose the m action. Given the change in the distribution of beliefs described above, this implies that contraceptive prevalence in the unstable communities will increase steadily over time until all the reformists ultimately switch to the m action. In contrast, contraceptive prevalence in the stable communities will decline after some initial endogenous deviation and ultimately these communities will end up where they were to begin with, in the traditional equilibrium.[8]

The simple model just described can explain two stylized facts that are commonly observed in the fertility transition; relatively slow rates of change and wide variation in the response across communities to the same external intervention.[9] The model can also be extended to derive the individual's decision rule over the course of the transition.

The individual's decision in period t is determined by her belief, relative to the threshold belief α_t^*. If her belief lies to the right (left) of α_t^* she will choose the $m(t)$ action. The individual's belief in period t is in turn determined by her belief in period $t-1$, augmented by the change in this belief through the social interaction in that period. It is easy to see that matching with an m will shift her belief to the right by returning to Eq. (10) and replacing $\theta \bar{P}$, $\theta \underline{P}$ with $\bar{x}_{t-1}$, $\underline{x}_{t-1}$, the contraceptive prevalence in unstable and stable communities in period $t-1$. The transition dynamics described above indicate that $\bar{x}_{t-1} > \underline{x}_{t-1}$, which implies from the equation that $\alpha_t / \alpha_{t-1} > 1$ when the individual matches with an m. Munshi and Myaux map these changes in beliefs into changes in actions to derive the individual's decision rule: the probability that the individual chooses the m action in period t is specified to be the weighted average of her decision in period $t-1$ and the probability that she matched with an m in that period. With random matching, this last probability is in turn measured by the proportion of m's in the community in period $t-1$.

Notice that we have arrived at precisely the specification derived by Munshi (2004) in the context of agricultural technology adoption. This is not entirely surprising, since the fertility transition model would have yielded the same decision rule if the uncertainty

---

[8] This process of social learning is conceptually similar to Banerjee's (1993) characterization of a rumor process. In his model, the delay before individual's meet reveals the state of the world. In our case, individuals match every period; it is the sequence of partners' decisions that ultimately reveals the type of community that the individual belongs to.

[9] While we focus on uncertainty about social fundamentals (the underlying social structure of the community), a model based on strategic uncertainty could also generate some of the stylized facts observed in the data. Suppose, for example, that all the communities are unstable, with $\bar{P} > P^*$. We are still left with a coordination problem, since both the traditional and the modern equilibrium can be sustained in these communities. The standard approach to model this coordination problem would be to perturb the system by exogenously switching a fraction of the community to the m-action in period 0. If we assume that individuals mimic their partner's action (in the next period) with a fixed probability, then we are essentially describing the beginning of a contagion. It is well known that if the initial perturbation is sufficiently large, then the community will "tip over" to the modern equilibrium, if not it will return to the traditional equilibrium after a temporary deviation. While the contagion model can explain the gradual change in reproductive behavior that is commonly observed, it cannot explain the wide variation in the response across communities to the *same* external intervention.

revolved around the performance of the contraceptive technology S rather than the composition of the community P. Munshi and Myaux's characterization of changing social norms as a learning process, however, provides an additional testable implication that is absent with technology adoption. Social norms are organized at the level of the social group, defined by religion, caste, ethnicity, or some other group characteristic. Thus, contraceptive prevalence within the individual's social group alone should determine her own contraception decision. In contrast, contraceptive prevalence outside the narrow social group should also provide useful information if the objective is to learn about a new contraceptive technology.

3.2. Identifying social learning

Demographers have recognized that the fertility transition is a relatively slow diffusion process for many decades. Early studies on this diffusion process concentrated on spatial patterns of fertility change, in some cases identifying remarkably strong ethnic and linguistic aspects to these spatial patterns, as in the case of the European demographic transition (see, for example, Lesthaeghe, 1977; Livi-Bacci, 1971, 1977). As discussed in the context of agricultural technology adoption, alternative explanations for such spatial patterns that do not rely on underlying social interactions are readily available, the simplest one being that the economic change or mortality decline that gave rise to the fertility transition occurred along ethnic or linguistic lines as well.

Recently there have been some attempts using micro-data to test directly for the role of social interactions in the fertility transition. Montgomery and Casterline (1993) is an early contribution to this literature, which has been followed by Entwistle et al. (1996) and Behrman, Kohler, and Watkins (2002), among other studies. A common approach in these studies is to ask individuals whom they talk to in general, or more specifically about health and contraception. An attempt is then made to establish a statistical link between the individual's contraceptive use and the level of contraceptive use in the self-reported reference group. As discussed earlier, the basic problem with this approach is that contraceptive prevalence in the reference group could proxy for any unobserved determinant of individual contraceptive use, to the extent that it is correlated among the members of the group. Replacing current prevalence with lagged prevalence does not solve the problem when the unobserved determinants of contraceptive use are serially correlated. This is why lagged HYV acreage in the village was seen to be less useful than lagged yield (shocks) in identifying social learning in agriculture. Individuals will generally tend to interact with those that are similar to them and so the problem with correlated unobservables is exacerbated when a self-reported endogenous reference group is used to define the social unit, as in the demographic studies, instead of an exogenous group that the individual is born into such as the village, caste, or clan. Behrman, Kohler, and Watkins (2002) control to some extent for the omitted variable problem by using individual fixed effects, but this approach does not account for changes in the individual determinants of the contraception decision over time.

The model of the fertility transition as a process of changing social norms laid out in the previous section allows us to place additional restrictions on the relationship between the individual's contraception decision and lagged contraceptive prevalence in the local area. In particular, we expect that social effects will be restricted to the narrow social group within which norms restricting fertility were traditionally enforced. Contraceptive prevalence outside that social group should have no effect on the individual's contraception decision.

Munshi and Myaux (2006) test these predictions using data from rural Bangladesh. The International Centre for Diarrhoeal Disease Research, Bangladesh (ICDDR,B) launched a Maternal Child Health—Family Planning (MCH-FP) project in 1978, covering 70 villages in Matlab *thana*, Comilla district. Contraceptive use information for all married women of reproductive age (15–49) and capable of conceiving in the 70 villages is available at six-monthly intervals over the 1983–1993 period. The MCH-FP project is quite possibly the most intensive family planning program ever put in place: all households in the *intervention area* have been visited by a Community Health Worker (CHW) once every two weeks since the inception of the project in 1978, and contraceptives are provided to them free of cost. Not surprisingly, contraceptive prevalence increased substantially over the sample period, from 40% in 1983 to 63% in 1993, with an accompanying decline in the total fertility rate from 4.5 children per woman to 2.9 children over that period. Munshi and Myaux's objective is to study the relationship between individual contraception decisions and lagged contraceptive prevalence within well defined exogenous social groups over the course of this transition.

Recall from the model of the fertility transition that the individual's contraception decision is determined by her own lagged decision and lagged contraceptive prevalence in the social group when norms are breaking down. In rural Bangladesh, the traditional norm was characterized by early and universal marriage, followed by immediate and continuous child-bearing. Religious authority provided legitimacy and enforced the rules that sustained this equilibrium. Changes in social norms should then have occurred independently within religious groups within the village. The two major religious groups in rural Bangladesh are Hindus, who constitute 18% of the sample, and Muslims who account for the remainder of the sample. Munshi and Myaux thus estimate regressions of the form:

$$C_{ijt} = \alpha C_{ijt-1} + \beta_I \bar{C}_{jt-1} + \beta_O \bar{C}_{-jt-1} + X_{ijt}\gamma + \omega_{jt} \qquad (12)$$

where $C_{ijt} = 1$ if individual i belonging to religion j uses contraceptives in period t, $C_{ijt} = 0$ if she does not. C_{ijt-1} is her decision in the previous period, $\bar{C}_{jt-1}$ measures contraceptive prevalence in her own religious group within the village in that period, and $\bar{C}_{-jt-1}$ represents the corresponding statistic outside the religious group. X_{ijt} is a vector of individual characteristics that includes age, age-squared, and in some specifications, individual fixed effects and time-period dummies. ω_{jt} collects all unobserved determinants of the contraception decision at the level of the religious group within the village in period t. Taking expectations across individuals within the religious group in Eq. (12), and then lagging the expression that is obtained by one period, it is evident that $\bar{C}_{jt-1}$ will be correlated with ω_{jt-1} and, hence, with ω_{jt} when the unobserved term is serially uncorrelated.

The model of changing social norms, however, places additional restrictions on the coefficients in Eq. (12): $\beta_I > 0$, $\beta_O = 0$. While a positive within-religion effect ($\beta_I > 0$) could be easily obtained, as discussed above, Munshi and Myaux show that positive within-religion effects and zero cross-religion effects ($\beta_I > 0$, $\beta_O = 0$) could only be spuriously generated if the unobserved ω_{jt}, ω_{-jt} terms are uncorrelated. The intuition for this result is that $\bar{C}_{jt-1}$ cannot completely proxy for ω_{jt} once additional controls, C_{ijt-1}, X_{ijt}, are included in the contraception regression. $\bar{C}_{-jt-1}$ then provides information about ω_{jt} unless it is uncorrelated with that unobserved term, which can only be the case if ω_{jt}, ω_{-jt} are uncorrelated.

Munshi and Myaux estimate Eq. (12) separately for Hindus and Muslims. They find that $\hat{\beta}_I > 0$, $\hat{\beta}_O = 0$ in each case. This result is obtained with and without fixed effects and time-period dummies, with six-monthly and annual data, as well as with restricted samples in which villages that are dominated by a single religion are excluded. In contrast, when they partition the village using age or education, positive and significant cross-group effects are consistently obtained. It is only when the village is partitioned by religion that cross-group effects are completely absent.

Munshi and Myaux use the absence of cross-religion effects to rule out alternative interpretations of these results, based on changing program effects, economic development, and learning about new contraceptive technology. They argue that while these unobserved determinants of the contraception decision might be correlated across individuals in the village, it is difficult to imagine that they would be uncorrelated across religious groups within the village, which is necessary to spuriously generate $\hat{\beta}_I > 0$, $\hat{\beta}_O = 0$. For example, program inputs are provided by the same health worker to all households in the village, and while she might have a differential impact on women from different groups, her influence will not be uncorrelated across these groups. Occupations are not segregated by religion within these villages and so once again economic change cannot explain the absence of cross-religion effects. Finally, while female mobility is severely restricted in rural Bangladesh and so social interactions will typically occur within the religious group, we would still expect information about the new contraceptive technology to ultimately cross religious boundaries within the village. It is only the norm-based motivation for the fertility transition that can easily explain the striking within-religion and cross-religion patterns that are obtained, since information flows across religious boundaries are irrelevant in this case.

4. Health and education

Technological change increases farm profits and the returns to schooling, as established for example by Foster and Rosenzweig (1996) in the context of the Indian Green Revolution. Just as the grower was seen to be uncertain about the yield from the new HYVs, we would also expect him to be uncertain about the returns to schooling in this new economic environment. And just as the grower's neighbors were seen to provide information about the new crop technology above, we would expect them to provide information about the returns to schooling as well.

A recent paper (Yamauchi, 2007) studies social learning and investment in education with the same three-year farm panel at the onset of the Indian Green Revolution that was used by Foster and Rosenzweig (1995) and Munshi (2004). Schooling levels among the growers in the sample were determined long before the unexpected availability of the new HYV technology and so the returns to schooling can be estimated directly at the level of the village using realized incomes. A positive relationship between schooling enrollment among the children and the returns to schooling in the previous generation is then seen to be indicative of social learning.

One potential problem with this empirical strategy is that a spurious role for neighbors' returns to schooling could be obtained. Suppose that the returns to schooling are correlated across households in the village and over time and that there is no uncertainty. Returns to education in the previous generation could still proxy for the corresponding returns in the current generation, which determine school enrollment. The implicit assumption in Yamauchi's analysis is that the returns to schooling were essentially constant across villages prior to the Green Revolution, or that these returns were uncorrelated with the returns in the post-Green Revolution period. Under these conditions, the returns in the new economic environment can be consistently estimated using growers' previously determined schooling levels. A second potential problem is that learning could occur at the level of the household rather than the village; if returns to schooling are spatially correlated then these alternative learning channels cannot be easily disentangled.

Yamauchi's solution to the problems discussed above is to derive testable predictions from the theory that provide additional support for the presence of social learning at the level of the village. He shows formally that social learning will be faster when the income-variance is lower and when there is *greater* heterogeneity in educational attainment in the village. This last prediction is particularly interesting, but not inconsistent with Munshi's observation that social learning will be slower in heterogeneous populations where neighbors' characteristics are unobserved or imperfectly observed. Schooling is an easily observed characteristic and Yamauchi's insight is that more variance in this characteristic leads to more precise estimates of the returns to schooling. Matching these predictions from the theory, schooling enrollment among the children is increasing in the returns to schooling in the village in the previous generation and, more importantly, is increasing in the interaction of the returns and the variance in educational attainment in the village.

In parallel with the introduction of new production technologies, vaccines and other medical treatments for infectious diseases have dramatically lowered morbidity and mortality throughout the developing world. However, the introduction of modern medicines has often met with community resistance and public health programs have sometimes been seen to collapse after an initial period of success. Recent research on a deworming program in Western Kenya by Kremer and Miguel (2007) applies social learning to understand these dynamics.

The program that they evaluate covered 75 primary schools in Busia district, with over 30,000 enrolled students aged 6–18. The schools were randomly divided into three groups: Group 1 schools participated in the deworming program over the 1998–2001 period, Group 2 schools participated 1999–2001, and Group 3 schools began participating in 2001. A representative sample of parents of children in Group 2 and Group 3 schools were interviewed in 2001. The respondents were asked to list their closest social links: the five friends they speak with most frequently, the five relatives they speak with most frequently, additional social contacts whose children attend local primary schools, and individuals with whom they discuss child health issues. The listed individuals define the respondent's set of social links.

Kremer and Miguel study the effect of access to "early" links, in Group 1 and Group 2 schools, on the individual's participation in the program. The total number of reported links could reflect unobserved parental characteristics, such as how sociable they are, which could be correlated in turn with other characteristics that directly determine the choices that are made for the child. Conditional on the total number of links, however, the number of early links is determined by the random assignment of schools to different groups. Kremer and Miguel find that an exogenous increase in the number of early treatment links leads to a significant decline in the probability that the individual will participate in the program.

One explanation for this negative effect is based on the group-immunity externality that accompanies these early links. Previous research by Kremer and Miguel in the same setting indicates that deworming programs significantly reduce infection rates and increase attendance in both participating schools as well as neighboring schools. We might expect such externalities to be even stronger within the individual's own social group, although the empirical results appear to indicate otherwise. An increase in program participation within the social group would then lower the benefit to the individual from deworming, since the child is less likely to get infected. If the group-immunity externality dominates the information externality that accompanies links' participation in the program, as in Bandiera and Rasul, then the negative effect that is observed could be obtained.

Kremer and Miguel, in contrast, favor an alternative explanation based on the idea that members of the community were systematically misinformed about the private benefit from the deworming medicine. They argue that the agency providing this medicine might have described what is effectively the social benefit, inclusive of the group-immunity externality that is provided by participation, as opposed to the private benefit. This explanation is also consistent with the estimated negative social effect, with individuals gradually learning the true private value of the new technology over time and downgrading their priors. While Kremer and Miguel do not consider such a possibility, I suspect that there may exist conditions under which it is optimal for the external agency to inflate the benefit from the treatment, in response to the group-immunity externality which fails to be internalized by the individual. The inflated priors will ultimately come in line with the true private value of the new technology, but in the short to medium term, at least, participation rates may be brought closer to the socially optimal level.

The deworming program also provides a convenient setting in which to compare non-experimental estimates with the experimental results described above. Kremer and Miguel study the relationship between the participation rate in the individual's school and the individual's own decision and find a positive association, in contrast with the negative experimental results that are obtained. While these differences between the experimental results and the non-experimental results are instructive, they do not undermine previous studies on social learning. Most of the non-experimental studies described in this chapter use panel data to estimate the effect of neighbors' *lagged* decisions and outcomes on the individual's current decision. Individual fixed effects, and even the individual's lagged decision, are used in some applications to control for unobserved characteristics that may be correlated within the social group. Recognizing the inherent difficulties in identifying social learning from neighbors' lagged decisions, many studies of agricultural adoption have concentrated on the grower's response to neighbors' yield shocks rather than decisions. It is not obvious that Kremer and Miguel's spurious non-experimental results would hold up with all of these controls. Furthermore, previous non-experimental studies explicitly acknowledge the potential for omitted variable bias and so have used restrictions from the theory to rule out alternatives to social learning. For example, Munshi and Myaux use the context-specific result that cross-religion effects are completely absent in rural Bangladesh to rule out alternatives. The result that within-group effects are larger than cross-group effects in the non-experimental regressions, as reported by Kremer and Miguel, is not as useful in ruling out alternatives.

5. Conclusion

It has now been 10 years since the first empirical papers on social learning in developing countries were published. While the theoretical literature on this topic has grown rapidly over this period, the empirical literature has not generated a similar surge of research papers. As the discussion in this chapter suggests, the identification of social learning is a challenging problem, and while previous studies have made some progress along this dimension, their overall lack of success might have discouraged new entrants to the field. Here the use of randomized experiments, as in Kremer and Miguel's work in Kenya, seems to be a promising direction for future research.

The empirical literature has also been unable to come up with hypotheses that go beyond straightforward tests of social learning, albeit in different contexts. What makes the theoretical literature so interesting is that rational individuals can end up making choices that lead the entire community to the wrong outcome. Whether such pathologies are widespread or not is an important empirical question, which the learning literature has not attempted to answer. More recent moves towards alternatives to the classical model, as in Kremer and Miguel's argument that the external agency provides exaggerated signals of the quality of the new technology, takes the literature in a new direction. But once again, it is not clear that such misinformation is empirically relevant.

Ultimately how important is social learning in the development process? Foster and Rosenzweig report results from a simulation exercise based on the estimated parameters from their learning model, which compares profits without learning, with learning from own experience, and with learning from own and neighbors' experience. Profitability from the new HYV was lower than profitability from the traditional variety to begin with, but HYV profits exceed traditional profits after four years of experience without learning. With social learning, this point is reached one year earlier. Similarly, Yamauchi's simulations indicate that an increase in schooling inequality within the village could increase enrollment levels by nearly 10 percent. Access to social information appears to be readily available in many practical applications, particularly since there is little cost to the individual from providing information to his neighbors. Thus, the value of interventions that provide the seed for the subsequent spread of such information could be quite high. Understanding how best to design such interventions would seem to be an important area for future research.

Acknowledgements

I thank Abhijit Banerjee, Esther Duflo, George Mailath, and Jack Porter for many discussions that have shaped my thinking on this topic. Rohini Pande and participants at the May 2005 Bellagio Conference provided helpful comments. I am responsible for any errors that may remain.

References

Bandiera, O., Rasul, I. (2006). "Social networks and technology adoption in northern Mozambique". Economic Journal 116.

Banerjee, A.V. (1992). "A simple model of herd behavior". Quarterly Journal of Economics 117 (3).

Banerjee, A.V. (1993). "The economics of rumours". Review of Economic Studies 60.

Behrman, J., Kohler, H.-P., Watkins, S.C. (2002). "Social networks and changes in contraceptive use over time: Evidence from a longitudinal study in rural Kenya". Demography 39 (4).

Besley, T., Case, A. (1994). "Diffusion as a learning process: Evidence from HYV cotton". Discussion paper #174. Princeton University, RPDS.

Bikhchandani, S., Hirshleifer, D., Welch, I. (1992). "A theory of fads, fashion, custom, and cultural change as informational cascades". Journal of Political Economy 100 (5).

Bramoulle, J., Kranton, R. (2004). "Public goods in social networks: How networks can shape social learning and innovation". Working paper. University of Maryland.

Bulatao, R. (1998). The Value of Family Planning Programs in Developing Countries. RAND, Santa Monica, CA.

Cleland, J., Phillips, J., Amin, S., Kamal, G.M. (1994). The Determinants of Reproductive Change in Bangladesh. The World Bank, Washington, DC.

Conley, T., Udry, C. (2005). "Learning about a new technology: Pineapple in Ghana." Mimeo.

Ellison, G., Fudenberg, D. (1993). "Rules of thumb for social learning". Journal of Political Economy 101 (4).

Entwistle, B., Rindfuss, R.R., Guilkey, D.K., Chamratrithirong, A., Curran, S.R., Sawangdee, Y. (1996). "Community and contraceptive choice in rural Thailand: A case study of Nang Rong". Demography 33 (1).

Foster, A.D., Rosenzweig, M.R. (1995). "Learning by doing and learning from others: Human capital and technical change in agriculture". Journal of Political Economy 103 (6).

Foster, A.D., Rosenzweig, M.R. (1996). "Technical change and human capital returns and investments: Evidence from the green revolution". American Economic Review 86, 931–953.

Griliches, Z. (1957). "Hybrid corn: An exploration in the economics of technological change". Econometrica 25 (4).

Jovanovic, B., Nyarko, Y. (1996). "Learning by doing and the choice of technology". Econometrica 64 (6).

Kandori, M. (1992). "Social norms and community enforcement". Review of Economic Studies 59.

Kremer, M., Miguel, E. (2007). "The illusion of sustainability". Quarterly Journal of Economics 122 (3), 1007–1065.

Lesthaeghe, R. (1977). The Decline of Belgian Fertility, 1800–1870. Princeton Univ. Press, Princeton.

Livi-Bacci, M. (1971). A Century of Portuguese Fertility. Princeton Univ. Press, Princeton.

Livi-Bacci, M. (1977). A History of Italian Fertility During the Last Two Centuries. Princeton Univ. Press, Princeton.

Mansfield, E. (1968). The Economics of Technological Change. W.W. Norton and Company, Inc., New York.

Manski, C.F. (1993). "Identification of endogenous social effects: The reflection problem". Review of Economic Studies 60.

Montgomery, M., Casterline, J. (1993). "The diffusion of fertility control in Taiwan: Evidence from pooled cross section time-series models". Population Studies 47.

Munshi, K. (2004). "Social learning in a heterogeneous population: Technology diffusion in the Indian green revolution". Journal of Development Economics 73 (1).

Munshi, K., Myaux, J. (2006). "Social norms and the fertility transition". Journal of Development Economics 60.

National Research Council (NRC) (1993). Factors Affecting Contraceptive Use in Sub-Saharan Africa. National Academy Press, Washington, DC.

Rogers, E.M. (1962). Diffusion of Innovations. The Free Press, New York.

Ryan, B., Gross, N.C. (1943). "The diffusion of hybrid seed corn in two iowa communities". Rural Sociology 8.

Yamauchi, F. (2007). "Social learning, neighborhood effects, and investment in human capital: Evidence from green-revolution India". Journal of Development Economics 83.

PART 11

PUBLIC GOODS AND POLITICAL ECONOMY:
THEORY AND EVIDENCE

Chapter 49

PUBLIC ACTION FOR PUBLIC GOODS

ABHIJIT BANERJEE

MIT Department of Economics E52-252d, 50 Memorial drive, Cambridge, MA 02142-1347, USA

LAKSHMI IYER

Harvard Business School, Soldiers Field, Boston, MA 02163, USA

ROHINI SOMANATHAN

Department of Economics, Delhi School of Economics, University of Delhi, Delhi 110007, India

Contents

Handbook of Development Economics, Volume 4
© *2008 Elsevier B.V.   All rights reserved*
DOI: 10.1016/S1573-4471(07)04049-1

Abstract

This paper focuses on the relationship between public action and access to public goods. It begins by developing a simple model to capture the various mechanisms that are discussed in the theoretical literature on collective action. We use the model to illustrate the special assumptions embedded in many popular theories of collective action and show how their apparently conflicting predictions can be reconciled in a more general framework. This is followed by a review of empirical research on collective action and public goods. These studies, while broadly consistent with the theoretical literature, account for a small part of the observed variation in provision. Access to public goods is often better explained by "top-down" interventions rather than the "bottom-up" processes highlighted in the collective action literature. We conclude with a discussion of some historically important interventions of this type.

Keywords

public goods, collective action

JEL classification: H41, 012

1. Introduction

Public goods in poor rural communities are remarkably scarce. Basic health and education have long been regarded as fundamental rights, yet constitutional and political commitments towards them remain largely unmet. Over a quarter of adults in developing countries are illiterate, at least a quarter of all children are not immunized, twenty percent of the population is without access to clean water and more than half live without adequate sanitation.[1]

Within this picture of overall inadequacy there is considerable variation, both across countries and inside national boundaries. Table 1 documents access to public goods and associated outcomes for a small set of countries for which secondary data are readily available at the sub-national level.[2] Even keeping in mind the difficulties of cross-country comparisons of this type arising from the way regions and public goods are defined, these numbers are striking. In Nepal, access to schools is ten times better in the best districts compared to the worst. For Kenyan provinces, this ratio is 8:1; it is more than 2:1 for both Indian states and Russian regions and slightly over 1.5:1 for Chinese provinces. In contrast, regional differences are small in Mexico and Thailand and negligible in Vietnam.

While it is true that the largest gaps in access are typically found in the poorest countries, it is not clear how we are to explain the considerable variation that remains after we take account of differences in income levels. For example, public goods do not seem to arrive in any particular order as countries get richer. Nor do different types of public goods generally move together. Health and education services are especially scarce and unequal in South Asia but this is less true of other types of physical infrastructure such as roads, electricity and transport facilities.[3] Vietnam has sizable gaps in physical infrastructure, but equal access to health and education. Economic reforms and prosperity have been accompanied by considerable convergence in access to education in India but by growing inequalities in China.[4]

Physical access to facilities is, of course, just one aspect of provision. Recent surveys show that existing facilities are often dysfunctional: A study in which enumerators made surprise visits to primary schools and health clinics in Bangladesh, Ecuador, India, Indonesia, Peru, and Uganda concluded, "Averaging across the countries, about 19 percent of teachers and 35 percent of health workers were absent." Even when physically present, many of these providers were not working: In India, only half of primary school

---

[1] UNDP (2005, Tables 1, 6, and 7, pp. 222–243).

[2] Data sources are described in the notes accompanying Table 1. We present data at the largest sub-national level for which they are customarily reported.

[3] UNDP (2006).

[4] Zhang and Kanbur (2003) show sharp increases in the Gini coefficient of illiteracy rates for Chinese provinces after 1985 even though corresponding changes in income inequality across provinces were relatively small. In contrast, school availability during the nineties increased fastest in the backward states of Central and East India (Office of the Registrar General of India, 2001).

Table 1
Access to public goods across sub-national regions

Country	Year	% population with access to												Access to schools		
		Clean water			Health facilities			Sanitation			Electricity					
		Overall	Highest region	Lowest region	Overall	Highest region	Lowest region	Overall	Highest region	Lowest region	Overall	Highest region	Lowest region	Overall	Highest region	Lowest region
Brazil	2003	94.30	98.30	76.30				94.10	98.10	89.70	99.50	99.90	97.80	97.20	98.90	93.70
Bulgaria	2001	96.30	100.00	74.72		99.50	61.11								100.00	82.80
China	1999														100.60	57.79
Egypt	2002	91.30	99.80	72.10	3.80[a]	16.10	1.80	93.60	99.90	73.00	98.70	99.90	75.40	72.10	79.70	56.50
India*	2001	33.70	99.00	2.00	3.20	61.00	0.00				76.00	100.00	36.00	78.00	98.00	39.00
Indonesia	2002	55.20	72.20	21.50	76.90	97.10	49.90	75.00	100.00	43.70				96.10	99.00	83.50
Kenya	2000	54.90	93.90	37.20	49.00	55.00	11.00							50.70	76.70	9.50
Mexico	2002	87.45	97.77	67.06	50.84	79.77	22.70	72.31	96.80	38.47				63.14	75.46	58.82
Nepal	2001	44.80	82.00	12.00	0.30[b]	2.24	0.00	43.72	93.25	11.18	32.15	97.38	5.89	1.35	4.85	0.44
Pakistan	1998													71.00	75.00	64.00
Russia	2001													69.80	100.80	43.80
South Africa	2001	72.80	90.50	50.50	66.10	79.00	49.70	90.80	98.70	70.90	71.70	88.10	46.80	83.90	90.30	72.60
Thailand	2001	98.90	99.80	97.10				98.90	100.00	96.60	98.30	99.90	97.20	73.80	63.40	88.60
Vietnam	2001				99.00	100.00	97.20				79.30	98.90	50.50	99.90	100.00	99.30

Access to schools is measured by primary school enrollment rates for Brazil, Indonesia and Pakistan; combined primary, secondary and high school enrollment for Bulgaria, China, Egypt, Kenya and Russia; % of villages having any educational institution in India; number of schools per 1000 population in Nepal; lower secondary enrollment in Thailand; % of population living within 2 km of a primary school for South Africa; and % of communes with access to a primary school in Vietnam.

Sources: Authors' calculations from Indian census 2001 data, Institute Brasiliero de Geografia e Estatistica (2004), Ministry of Agriculture and Rural Development (2002), Rimal, Rimal and Rimal (2002), UNDP (2003a, 2003b, 2003c, 2003d, 2004a, 2004b), UNDP, and Institute for Development Studies University of Nairobi (2004), UNDP, and the Institute for National Planning (2004), UNDP, and the Stockholm Environment Institute (2002), UNDP, BPS-Statistics Indonesia, and BAPPENAS (2004).

The relevant sub-national units are regions for Brazil, Bulgaria, Russia, South Africa and Thailand; provinces for China, Indonesia, Kenya, Pakistan and Vietnam; governorates for Egypt; states for India and Mexico; and districts for Nepal.

[a] Number of health units per 100,000 population.
[b] Number of health centers per 1000 population.
* All numbers for India refer to the % of villages with access to specified public goods.

teachers present were actually teaching when the enumerators arrived (Chaudhury et al., 2004). In a survey of a hundred hamlets in the Indian state of Rajasthan, enumerators found that most hamlets had a government health sub-center, but repeated visits revealed that some of these are almost never open, while others are open most of the time (Banerjee, Deaton, and Duflo, 2004). These measures of public good quality are often correlated with physical access.[5] In such cases, regional disparities are likely to be even larger than those suggested by the distribution of facilities.

It is implausible these very large differences in access to education, better hygiene, health and longevity could be entirely explained by differences in what people want. The National Election Survey in India, carried out by the Center for the Study of Developing Societies in 1996, asked 10,000 voters an open-ended question: "What are the three main problems people like you face today?" Poverty was the most popular response and was ranked first by about a quarter of all respondents, but public goods came in a close second. Nearly a fifth of those surveyed listed problems associated with different types of public amenities (education, drinking water, electricity, transport and communication) as their "main problem."[6] Voting behavior seems to reflect these preferences, with numerous instances of incumbent politicians being voted out of office when their tenure is associated with poorly functioning public services.[7]

Motivated by observations like these, a recent literature has focused on the role of collective action by communities in improving their access to public goods. In this approach, the distribution of public goods is determined by what we call *bottom-up processes* in which communities compete, in various ways, to lay claim to limited public resources. In Section 2, we lay out a framework within which the theoretical research in this area can be understood and outline conditions under which these models provide clear predictions for the relationship between community characteristics and the strength of collective action. We also discuss the many cases where the theory is ambiguous.

Section 3 surveys the empirical research related to these models of collective action. The broad patterns do suggest that public action by communities brings them public goods. However, an exclusive focus on these bottom-up mechanisms leaves important questions unanswered and a great deal of the observed variation in public goods unexplained. Important historical expansions in public goods often served communities that were economically and politically weak. For instance, elementary schools in Indonesia in the 1970s, and programs to augment classroom facilities in India in the 1980s,

---

[5] The PROBE Team (1999, Chapter 4), documents this for public schools in India.

[6] See Center for the Study of Developing Societies (1996) for survey questionnaires. Tabulated data for this question were provided to us by their Data Unit.

[7] The incumbent Congress Party in the Indian state of Madhya Pradesh was defeated in the Assembly elections in 2003; the landslide victory of the Bharatiya Janata Party is often attributed to their slogan of "bijli, sadak, pani" (electricity, roads and water). A majority of voters surveyed at that time felt that there had been a deterioration in the quality of public infrastructure in Madhya Pradesh during the term of the incumbent government (*The Hindu*, 2003).

were both concentrated in regions with the worst outcomes. In Europe, North America and Japan in the early twentieth century, schools reached the most marginal members of these societies.[8] During the colonial era in India, the autonomously ruled princely states of Cochin and Travancore invested heavily in education and health in the absence of any political imperatives, and the unusually high social outcomes in the present-day Kerala state are, in part, "an example of princely autonomy having widespread, long-term effects."[9]

We conclude that the distribution of public goods is the outcome of interactions between the forces of collective action and various *top-down processes*. These processes may be fueled by changes in the technology of providing public goods, the compulsions of the state, or the private objectives of its agents. What they have in common is that they are largely unrelated to what is happening on the ground *in the specific area* where the public goods get supplied. We end the chapter with a few historically significant examples of these types of interventions.

2. Theories of collective action

The premise of this approach is that an individual's benefit from a public good depends on the group he is a part of, but his costs of participating in group activities are privately incurred. The early literature on public goods and collective action is concerned with questions relating to the provision of locally financed schools and the sustainability of common property resources managed by local communities. More recently, the focus has shifted to incorporate a much broader set of public goods and a variety of different mechanisms that influence their provision.

The change in focus has resulted in part from efforts to explain access to public goods in poor countries with centralized fiscal systems. Local infrastructure in such cases is not locally financed and often depends on decisions taken by politicians and bureaucrats living outside the communities that receive it. Community action in such cases includes writing to state officials, entertaining them, making private contributions for the good and a range of other influence activities. It could also include voting and investing in learning more about potential candidates, in order to elect those who would best serve their interests. In such cases, the collective action game would need to incorporate the kinds of non-convexities typical in most voting models.

Most models of collective action and public goods share a common underlying structure. Individuals, acting non-cooperatively, choose effort levels based on the costs and returns from such investments. In the case of local provision, group benefits depend

---

[8] Lindert (2004, Chapter 5), and Benavot and Riddle (1988) present cross-national figures for primary school enrollments in the late nineteenth and early twentieth centuries. Goldin (1998) documents the rapid expansion in secondary school enrollment rates in North America in the inter-war period. Sen (2001) briefly describes the spectacular growth in literacy in Japan during the first decade of the twentieth century.

[9] Jeffrey (1993, p. 56).

directly on the public goods technology. Under central financing, they are the result of some more complex political process. Either way, since returns depend on the collective behavior of different groups, the equilibrium allocation of public goods will be determined by the distribution of group characteristics. We start by summarizing this basic logic in a simple model and then proceed to various extensions. We will often use the language of political competition in describing the results in this section, although the framework is more general and could be used to study collective action in many different contexts.

Imagine m groups in society with $n_1, \ldots, n_m$ members. Think of these as m, perhaps spatially distinct, homogeneous communities. We will subsequently introduce subgroups to capture within-community heterogeneity. Groups compete to extract public goods from the state; we are interested in how the nature of this competition and the ultimate allocation of public goods varies with group characteristics: their political visibility, their tastes, their size, their potential benefits from public goods, and other social factors that influence their ability to act together.

Denote by a_{ij} the effort put into the collective enterprise by member i of group j. We will sometimes use A_j to denote total effort by members of group j and A for the aggregate effort of all groups. Benefits from the public good for member i of group j are denoted by $b_{ij}(n_j)$. The dependence on n_j allows for possible congestion effects which might reduce the per-member value of the public good as a group gets larger.

The probability that group j will succeed in extracting the public good from the state depends on the effort expended by the group, as well as the total effort expended by all other groups in society. This probability is given by

$$f_j \left(\sum_{k=1}^{m} \sum_{i=1}^{n_k} a_{ik}, \sum_{i=1}^{n_j} a_{ij} \right).$$

We assume that this probability is increasing in the second argument and decreasing in the first ($f_{1j} < 0$, $f_{2j} > 0$) and that $f_{1j} + f_{2j} > 0$. These conditions imply that the probability of receiving the good always increases when a group puts in more effort, keeping constant the effort of other groups. In addition, we assume that $f_{11j} > 0$ and $f_{22j} < 0$ for all j. We do not require that $\sum f_j = 1$. We therefore allow higher aggregate effort to generate higher aggregate provision and, in particular, for the possibility that none of the groups may get the good. These convexity assumptions rule out a conventional, first-past-the-post voting model, but can accommodate proportional representation or probabilistic voting.

Suppose that the cost of the effort is given by a_{ij}^β, $\beta > 1$. The payoff to agent i in group j is

$$b_{ij}(n_j) f_j \left(\sum_{k=1}^{m} \sum_{i=1}^{n_k} a_{ik}, \sum_{i=1}^{n_j} a_{ij} \right) - a_{ij}^\beta. \tag{1}$$

We assume that agents choose a_{ij} to maximize their private benefits and focus on the Nash Equilibrium of the political competition game that results from these non-cooperative decisions. The first order condition for the equilibrium effort level is:

$$b_{ij}(n_j)\left[f_{1j}\left(\sum_{k=1}^{m}\sum_{i=1}^{n_k}a_{ik},\sum_{i=1}^{n_j}a_{ij}\right)+f_{2j}\left(\sum_{k=1}^{m}\sum_{i=1}^{n_k}a_{ik},\sum_{i=1}^{n_j}a_{ij}\right)\right]=\beta a_{ij}^{\beta-1}. \quad (2)$$

The second order condition, $f_{11j}+2f_{12j}+f_{22j}<0$, is assumed to hold everywhere and for all j.[10]

Notice that we do not allow effort decisions to be coordinated at the group level. If they were, each member's effort would be chosen so as to maximize

$$\sum_{i=1}^{n_j}\left[b_{ij}(n_j)f_j\left(\sum_{k=1}^{m}\sum_{i=1}^{n_k}a_{ik},\sum_{i=1}^{n_j}a_{ij}\right)-a_{ij}^{\beta}\right]$$

and the corresponding first-order condition would be

$$\sum_{i=1}^{n_j}b_{ij}(n_j)\left[f_{1j}\left(\sum_{k=1}^{m}\sum_{i=1}^{n_k}a_{ik},\sum_{i=1}^{n_j}a_{ij}\right)+f_{2j}\left(\sum_{k=1}^{m}\sum_{i=1}^{n_k}a_{ik},\sum_{i=1}^{n_j}a_{ij}\right)\right]=\beta a_{ij}^{\beta-1}.$$

$$(3)$$

For any fixed choice of effort by the other groups, each member in group j would now choose a higher level of effort. Aggregate effort (assuming that the groups play a Nash Equilibrium in effort choice) would also be higher. This is the well-known free-rider problem in collective action; each member tends to undervalue the spillover benefits of his own effort on other members and puts in less effort than would be optimal for the group as a whole.

Even though the structure of this game implies that free-riding always hurts the group, there is no presumption that it makes everyone worse off. Groups that are especially active inflict costs on other groups and could reduce social welfare through wasteful competition. There is nothing surprising here; we may be grateful for the disunity within social groups that makes it harder for them to go to war with each other! We will come back to this point later in our discussion of the empirical evidence. What remains true is that groups which are more subject to free-riding are likely to be less successful. We are then left with questions about how such free-riding is influenced by community characteristics.

By focusing on non-cooperative equilibria, we do not allow for actions explicitly aimed at improving group cooperation. In other words, there is no scope for leadership, sanctions or any other type of organization in our model. Some of these devices have been shown to be empirically important in mitigating free-rider problems in public goods settings and our main reason for staying clear of them here is that strong enough coordination mechanisms can make almost any group outcome implementable. We be-

---

[10] This condition holds, for example, if $f_j = [A_j/A]^{\alpha}$, $\alpha \in (0, 1]$. We will frequently return to this particular specification.

lieve a micro-founded theory of such coordination is required to make this approach interesting and sharpen its predictive power. In its absence, it is hard to incorporate these coordination mechanisms into the type of analysis presented here.

Returning to our particular model, it can be shown that if $f_{11j} + f_{12j} < 0$ for all j, the game where each agent chooses his or her a_{ij} non-cooperatively will have a unique equilibrium.[11] For future reference, define $a_{ij}^*(n_j; \mathbf{n}_{-j})$ to be the optimal choice of a_{ij} in the unique equilibrium of the political competition game when there are n_j people in group j and $\mathbf{n}_{-j}$ people in the other groups,[12] and let the corresponding payoff be $U_{ij}^*(n_j; \mathbf{n}_{-j})$. The uniqueness of the equilibrium, which makes it easier to think about the comparative statics, is something of an artifact of the way we set up the game. The simple and plausible modification of the model considered below introduces the possibility of multiple equilibria even when $f_{11j} + f_{12j} < 0$.

Suppose it was possible to buy the "public" good on the market at a price p, yielding a net payoff of $b_{ij} - p$ to the buyer.[13] There would now be a trade-off between paying what is presumably a higher price and getting the good for sure, and the gamble of trying to get it from the public system. If $b_{ij}(n_j) = b_j$ for all j, the solution to the first-order condition (2) takes the form $a_{ij} = a_j$ and can be rewritten as

$$b_j \left[f_{1j}\left(\sum_{k=1}^{m} A_k, A_j \right) + f_{2j}\left(\sum_{k=1}^{m} A_k, A_j \right) \right] = \beta \left(\frac{A_j}{n_j} \right)^{\beta-1} \qquad (4)$$

where $A_j = n_j a_j$.

Now suppose some members of group j defect to the market so that n_j goes down but $\mathbf{n}_{-j}$ remains the same. The right-hand side of Eq. (4) is declining in n_j and the left-hand side is declining in A_j (by the second order condition for individual maximization) so with no change in the behavior of other groups, the fall in n_j must be accompanied by a fall in A_j to restore equality in (4). This however corresponds to a change in the aggregate effort level A and causes other groups to increase their effort (since $f_{11k} + f_{12k} < 0$ for any group k). Both the fall in A_j and the rise in $\mathbf{A}_{-j}$ will make group j worse off, the former because the group was putting in too little effort to start with (as a result of free-riding) and the latter because it is less likely to succeed in receiving public goods when its share of total effort declines.

If the corresponding decline in the utility of the $\tilde{n}_j$ members remaining in group j is large enough, we may have $b_j - p > U_j^*(\tilde{n}_j; \mathbf{n}_{-j})$. Now everyone else in group j would also want to defect, leading to a new equilibrium with group j entirely in the

---

[11] This condition may often be violated. For example, in the case where $f_j = [A_j/A]^\alpha$, $(\alpha \in (0, 1])$, it only holds when A_j is small relative to A for all j and α is not too close to zero. On the other hand, the condition is sufficient but hardly necessary.

[12] $\mathbf{n}_{-j}$ represents the vector $(n_1, \dots, n_{j-1}, n_{j+1}, \dots, n_m)$.

[13] Such "exit" from the public market is plausible for certain services such as education, individual medical care and electricity. It is likely to be much more costly for services such as roads, public health or law and order.

private market. A sufficient condition for there being two equilibria is

$$U_j^*(n_j; n_{-j}) > b_j - p,$$
$$U_j^*(0; n_{-j}) < b_j - p$$

for some $n_j > 0$.[14]

The multiplicity here is entirely natural and captures the idea that there is no point in trying to get things from the public system if all your compatriots have deserted you. For the rest of this section we will ignore the possibility of such multiplicity in order to better focus on questions of comparative statics. We discuss, in turn, the various characteristics of communities that determine their ability to collectively invest in activities that bring them public goods.

2.1. Power or influence

For a variety of historical, sociological and economic reasons, some groups in society hold power disproportionate to their size and their control over economic or social hierarchies influences the functioning of democratic institutions in their favor. Obvious examples are whites in South Africa in the Apartheid years, high castes in India through most of its history, large landowners in Brazil, capitalists of the robber baron years in the United States and party apparatchiks in China in the recent past. Group membership is sometimes by birth and sometimes circumstance. The existence of such groups is often associated with autocratic regimes, although democracy per se does not rule out their salience.

In terms of our model, an increase in power is captured by a shift in the $f_j(.,.)$ function. As long as this shift is not accompanied by a sharp fall in the productivity of effort, we would expect a higher probability of success for more powerful groups. This is easy to see in the case where $f_j(.,.) = \theta_j f(.,.)$, and effort costs are independent of θ.

The institutional histories of nation-states are dotted with instances of dramatically changed power equations that allow a careful study of how such power influences public goods. For instance, the extension of the franchise in the West was clearly aimed at reallocating power towards the working classes and resulted in dramatic changes in the composition of government spending. In India, the reservation of seats in local and national legislatures for women and selected minorities was also intended to shift the balance of power in those specific directions. Our discussion of the evidence on public goods allocations suggests that these institutional changes often had important effects.

---

[14] There is a third, "unstable" equilibrium in between these two, in which all the members of group j are indifferent between trying to get the good through collective action and purchasing it from the market.

2.2. Tastes

Tastes for public goods in our model are captured by the parameters b_{ij}. To rank groups by their preference for a public good would involve comparisons of the distributions of these benefits across groups. In the special case where all members of a group enjoy the same benefit, groups with higher values of b_j would put in more effort and face a higher probability of receiving the public good. In the more general case where there is within-group inequality in benefits, we could define group j as placing a higher value on the public good than another group k if benefits for all members of group j are higher than those for members of group k. This is perhaps overly restrictive and would in general provide only a partial ordering of group preferences, but would once again generate the positive association between higher benefits from public goods and their greater availability.

The notion that differences in preferences can be used to explain the distribution of public goods has a long and hallowed tradition in public economics, going back to the work of Tiebout (1956). At the core of this approach is the idea that geographical differentiation in tastes emerges as an equilibrium outcome of a sorting process in which households select residential areas based on the public goods they offer. With well-functioning housing and credit markets, those that care most about public goods get the best provision.

The important insight of the Tiebout approach was that for local public goods, as for private goods, there was a "mechanism to force the consumer-voter to state his true preferences."[15] It also showed that, under certain conditions, the equilibrium allocation of public goods is efficient. Models of this type have been widely used to explain the response of local government budgets to the demographic characteristics of city populations. Subsequent work in this tradition has however shown that the link between preferences and public good allocations can be fairly tenuous. Benabou (1993) shows that spillover effects in the benefits from public goods can result in variations in quality across neighborhoods even with no individual heterogeneity, and that such variations are often inefficient. Such spillovers are certainly important in many practical cases. They allow, for example, the possibility that a school will function better if the average child in it is highly motivated.

Much of the recent literature on public goods in developing countries has ignored household mobility and has focused instead on the processes of collective decision-making that translate the characteristics of heterogeneous communities into policy choices. This seems appropriate for most developing countries where land markets are often dysfunctional and residential mobility is very limited. While 40 percent of the US population reside in a state which is different from the one in which they were born,[16] it is unusual for entire families in developing countries to relocate from one community

---

[15] Tiebout (1956, p. 417).
[16] US Census (2000).

to another; this would involve leaving social networks that have been central to their lives for many generations and creating space for themselves in established hierarchies elsewhere. We find that stark differences in public good access in many poor countries have not resulted in much permanent migration across rural communities.

2.3. Group size

The question of how the size of a group affects its political leverage is an old and controversial one. As Mancur Olson argued in a very influential essay, "the larger the group, the less it will be able to favor its common interests" (Olson, 1965). Problems of free-riding are more serious in larger groups. On the other hand, in our earlier discussion of the multiple equilibrium issue we showed that total group effort in our model (and hence its probability of getting the good) is *increasing* in group size, echoing a point made by Esteban and Ray (2001). The effect of group size on access to public goods is thus theoretically ambiguous.

In the special case when $b_{ij}(n_j) = b_j$ for all i in group j, and

$$f_j\left(\sum_{k=1}^{m}\sum_{i=1}^{n_k} a_{ik}, \sum_{i=1}^{n_j} a_{ij}\right) = \theta\left[\frac{\sum_{i=1}^{n_j} a_{ij}}{\sum_{k=1}^{m}\sum_{i=1}^{n_k} a_{ik}}\right]^{\alpha} \tag{5}$$

where θ is some positive constant, it is easy to check that group effort increases in group size, even though total equilibrium effort as a fraction of first-best effort for the group goes to zero as the group size becomes very large. Free-riding, in this case, does not outweigh the natural advantage of larger groups.

The free-rider problem becomes much more serious when the benefits per head go down as the group gets larger. The assumption of constant benefits is a reasonable description of the situation when the group is trying to get a school or a health center or a road. It is much less so when the group wants a well or an irrigation canal, where the total off-take is limited and crowding more likely. In such cases benefits might take the form

$$b_{ij}(n_j) = b_0 + \frac{b_1}{n_j}.$$

Assuming the form of the f function given in (5), a group member will now maximize

$$\theta\left(b_0 + \frac{b_1}{n_j}\right)\left[\frac{\sum_{i=1}^{n_j} a_{ij}}{\sum_{k=1}^{m}\sum_{i=1}^{n_k} a_{ik}}\right]^{\alpha} - a_{ij}^{\beta},$$

from which it follows that in equilibrium

$$\alpha\theta\left(b_0 + \frac{b_1}{n_j}\right)n_j^{\beta-1} = \beta(A)^{\alpha}(A_j)^{\beta-\alpha}\left[1 - \frac{A_j}{A}\right]^{-1}.$$

The right-hand side of this equation is increasing in A_j. Therefore, comparing two groups in this equilibrium, the bigger group is more likely to get the good if and only if the left-hand side is increasing in n_j. But increasing n_j increases congestion on the one hand (thereby reducing benefits to each member) and raises the ability of the group to put in more effort on the other. As long as $\beta < 2$, the net effect can go either way. In particular, if $\beta < 2$ and the purely public component $b_0 = 0$, smaller groups will do better, while if $b_1 = 0$ (no congestion effects), bigger groups will do better.

2.4. The distribution of group benefits

Olson (1965) argued that groups could be more effective in articulating their demands if most of the benefits from public goods are captured by a small number of group members, because the strong stake of these members would encourage them to invest in group activities. In our model, this is just one possibility. In general, group inequality has ambiguous effects and can increase or decrease collective effort depending on the shape of the effort cost function.

To show this, assume that f is given by (5), $\beta < 2$ and the total benefit that the group can get from the public good is fixed at b_1. As discussed above, this is the case where the Olson group-size effect dominates and smaller groups do better in the absence of within-group inequality.

What if members of the same community receive different shares of total benefits? Schools benefit those with young children, roads are most useful to those who commute out of the village, and benefits from irrigation water may be proportional to the amount of land owned. Denote by γ_{ij} the share of the benefits going to member i in group j, so that $\sum_{i=1}^{n_j} \gamma_{ij} = 1$. Each group member chooses an action that maximizes

$$\gamma_{ij} b_1 \theta \left[\frac{\sum_{i=1}^{n_j} a_{ij}}{\sum_{k=1}^{m} \sum_{i=1}^{n_k} a_{ik}} \right]^{\alpha} - a_{ij}^{\beta}$$

and effort as a function of γ_{ij} is therefore given by

$$a_{ij} = (\gamma_{ij})^{\frac{1}{\beta-1}} \left[\frac{\alpha b_1 \theta}{A^{\alpha} \beta} (A_j)^{\alpha-1} \left(1 - \frac{A_j}{A} \right) \right]^{\frac{1}{\beta-1}}.$$

It follows that in equilibrium

$$A_j = \sum_{i=1}^{n_j} a_{ij} = \left[\frac{\alpha b_1 \theta (A_j)^{\alpha-1}}{A^{\alpha} \beta} \left(1 - \frac{A_j}{A} \right) \right]^{\frac{1}{\beta-1}} \left[\sum_{i=1}^{n_j} \gamma_{ij}^{\frac{1}{\beta-1}} \right]$$

or

$$\frac{A_j}{\left[\frac{\alpha b_1 \theta (A_j)^{\alpha-1}}{A^{\alpha} \beta} \left(1 - \frac{A_j}{A} \right) \right]^{\frac{1}{\beta-1}}} = \left[\sum_{i=1}^{n_j} \gamma_{ij}^{\frac{1}{\beta-1}} \right].$$

The left-hand side of this expression is increasing in A_j so group effort and the equilibrium probability of success is increasing in $\left[\sum_{i=1}^{n_j} \gamma_{ij}^{\frac{1}{\beta-1}} \right]$. As long as $\beta < 2$, this expression is convex in γ and success is most likely when group benefits are concentrated with $\gamma_{ij} = 0$ or 1. This is the Olson case.

When $\beta > 2$, $\sum_{i=1}^{n_j} \gamma_{ij}^{\frac{1}{\beta-1}}$ becomes concave in γ_{ij} and diluted benefits are an advantage because costs are rising steeply. Spreading total benefits across many group members elicits higher aggregate group effort in this case. This is the case emphasized in Baland, Dagnelie, and Ray (2006).

Khwaja (2004) proposes an interesting combination of these two cases where the convexity of individual cost functions decreases after a certain threshold because large farmers use hired labor rather than their own at the margin. This can result in a U-shaped relationship between inequality and total effort: Effort falls when we first move away from equal benefits because the cost of effort function is convex, but eventually the person who gets the greater share of the benefits will start employing outside labor. Further increases in inequality beyond this point actually increase total effort. Bardhan, Ghatak, and Karaivanov (2006) consider a cost function that permits corner optima. They focus on equilibria where some people put in zero effort but enjoy the public good nonetheless. The effects of increased inequality in the sharing of benefits now depends on whether inequality hurts those with positive contributions or just those putting in zero effort.

The effects of unequal benefits are further complicated if we introduce the possibility of exiting from the system into the private market, along the lines suggested at the beginning of this section. If the individuals with the highest benefits are the ones most likely to exit from the system, inequality reduces the probability that those who stay behind get the public good; a small increase in inequality can then cause the entire group to switch to the market.[17]

2.5. Cohesion

It seems intuitive that more cohesive groups will be able to organize themselves more effectively to secure the public goods they want. This may happen because individuals in a community want different types of goods, but only one of these goods can be provided in equilibrium (Alesina, Baqir, and Easterly, 1999). Alternatively, people may be socially minded, but such altruism may only extend to those whom they consider similar to themselves (Vigdor, 2004). If this set of people is large, each person would invest in the collective effort whereas if perceived differences among individuals are large, they may all shirk even if they all have the same preferences for the public good.

Miguel and Gugerty (2005) suggest an alternative reason why the lack of cohesion may influence provision even if there is no disagreement about the ideal public good. They envision a scenario where free-riding is observable but not necessarily contractible. For instance, villagers can identify those who attend village meetings but it is

---

[17] We are assuming here that the exit by some does not increase the absolute amount of benefits that would go to those who remain, if they were to get the public good.

just too costly to exclude non-attendees from using public goods. In such settings, social networks help sanction those who free-ride and it is easier to impose these sanctions when everyone is a part of the same network.

These models all share the prediction that a community consisting of n equal-sized subgroups will be better at getting the public goods they want than one with $n + 1$ groups. There are however other plausible contexts in which this may not hold. Consider a simple extension of our previous model in which group j consists of n_{jq} equal-sized subgroups, $s_1, \ldots, s_k$. Suppose that the public good has a purely public component b_0 as well as a subgroup-specific component b_1 which reaches only one of the subgroups. The probability that subgroup s_k will get the subgroup specific component, conditional on the public good being built in the village, is assumed to be given by

$$\frac{\sum_{i \in s_k} a_{ij}}{\sum_{i=1}^{n_j} a_{ij}}.$$

An example would be a road that connects the village to the highway. All the groups in the village want the road (this is the b_0) but only one of them will have it start in their neighborhood (the value of a road in the neighborhood is b_1). A member i of subgroup s_k will maximize

$$\theta \left(b_0 + b_1 \frac{\sum_{i \in s_k} a_{ij}}{\sum_{i=1}^{n_j} a_{ij}} \right) \left[\frac{\sum_{i=1}^{n_j} a_{ij}}{\sum_{k=1}^{m} \sum_{i=1}^{n_k} a_{ik}} \right]^{\alpha} - a_{ij}^{\beta}.$$

At the optimum

$$\alpha \theta \left(b_0 + b_1 \frac{\sum_{i \in s_k} a_{ij}}{A_j} \right) \left(\frac{A_j}{A} \right)^{\alpha - 1} \left(\frac{A - A_j}{A^2} \right)$$

$$+ \theta b_1 \left(\frac{A_j - \sum_{i \in s_k} a_{ij}}{A_j^2} \right) \left(\frac{A_j}{A} \right)^{\alpha} = \beta a_{ij}^{\beta - 1}$$

which can be rewritten as

$$\left[\alpha \left(b_0 + b_1 \frac{\sum_{i \in s_k} a_{ij}}{A_j} \right) \left(1 - \frac{A_j}{A} \right) + b_1 \left(1 - \frac{\sum_{i \in s_k} a_{ij}}{A_j} \right) \right] (A_j)^{\alpha - 1}$$

$$= \frac{\beta}{\theta} a_{ij}^{\beta - 1} A^{\alpha}.$$

Using the fact that everyone in group j faces the same problem and will make the same choice, we get

$$\alpha \left(b_0 + b_1 \frac{1}{n_{jq}} \right) \left(1 - \frac{A_j}{A} \right) + b_1 \left(1 - \frac{1}{n_{jq}} \right) = \frac{\beta}{\theta} (A_j)^{\beta - \alpha} (n_j)^{\beta - 1} A^{\alpha}$$

or

$$\alpha b_0 \left(1 - \frac{A_j}{A} \right) + b_1 \left(1 - \frac{1}{n_{jq}} \left[1 - \alpha \left(1 - \frac{A_j}{A} \right) \right] \right) = \frac{\beta}{\theta} (A_j)^{\beta - \alpha} (n_j)^{\beta - 1} A^{\alpha}. \quad (6)$$

It is clear that increasing n_{jq}, keeping n_j fixed, makes the group more divided, and raises the left-hand side of the above expression. On the other hand, increasing A_j increases the right-hand side but lowers the left-hand side. It follows that if we compare two groups with the same n_j, the group with the higher n_{jq} will put in greater effort. Heterogeneity helps! This apparently surprising result is a direct implication of the Olson group size effect. Smaller groups are less subject to failures of collective action and a community with many such tiny groups does better than a conglomerate of a few large groups. In the special case when $\alpha = 1$ and $\frac{A_j}{A} \approx 0$, the fact that others are working does not make you want to work less. There is therefore no Olson group size effect and, as is evident from Eq. (6), sub-dividing the group neither helps nor hurts.

Esteban and Ray (1999) consider a variant of this setup in which groups can impose a certain effort level on their members. Heterogeneity in this case can be shown to dampen collective action. Let ξ_j be the share of group j in the entire population. Let a_j be the action chosen by everyone in group j. Assuming that $\beta = 2$ and $b_0 = 0$ (the purely public component is absent), the choice of a_j will maximize

$$b_1 \left[\frac{\xi_j a_j}{\sum_{k=1}^m \xi_k a_k} \right] - a_j^2.$$

The first order condition for this maximization can be written in the form

$$b_1 \xi_j^2 \left[1 - \frac{\xi_j a_j}{C} \right] = 2 C a_j \xi_j$$

where $C = \sum_{k=1}^m \xi_k a_k$. Adding across groups gives us

$$b_1 \sum_{k=1}^m \xi_k^2 \left[1 - \frac{\xi_k a_k}{C} \right] = 2C^2.$$

In an equilibrium with m equal and identical groups we must have $\frac{\xi_j a_j}{C} = \frac{1}{m}$. We can now rewrite the above expression as

$$b_1 \frac{1}{m} \left[1 - \frac{1}{m} \right] = 2C^2. \tag{7}$$

Effort C is decreasing in m for $m > 2$. Bigger groups in this case have a bigger stake in the success of their group and since there is no free-riding, get their groups to put in more effort.

These results on heterogeneity and collective action should be interpreted with caution. One can certainly think of settings where, intuitively, it seems more precarious to have two large and more or less equal-sized groups that are opposed to each other than a hundred tiny squabbling groups.[18] As discussed earlier, group activities in a game of

---

[18] As Voltaire once said, "If there were one religion ..., its despotism would be terrible; if there were only two, they would destroy each other; but there are 30, and therefore they live in peace and happiness."

political competition could be quite wasteful. This is seen in Esteban and Ray (1999). They use a model very similar to the one above with the key difference that group effort directly reduces the quality of the public good. Effort is interpreted as more lobbying, and lobbying is assumed to reduce the net resources spent on the public good. For example, the group might allow the bureaucrat to steal some part of the public goods budget as long as he builds the public good that the group desires. Social divisions could therefore result in better public goods: having no divisions is ideal but having two equal-sized groups is the worst possible outcome.

Before we discuss the empirical evidence on public good allocations, it is useful to reflect briefly on some plausible empirical hypotheses that emerge from the theoretical analysis in this section. In the absence of coordinated behavior by individuals, we always get under-provision of effort from the perspective of the group but the extent, and even the presence, of social under-provision depends on the nature of collective action. If most group activities take the form of lobbying for relatively fixed aggregate allocations, group characteristics that reduce collective action could be welfare-improving and would have little effect on the overall availability of public goods. In contrast, in countries with rapidly expanding economies and government budgets, aggregate allocations may be quite responsive to the effort citizens put in to extracting public goods from the state, and free-riding is more likely to lead to overall under-provision. We've seen that allocations of public goods depend in a relatively straightforward manner on group preferences and group influence. Group size, within-group inequality in benefits and group fragmentation have more nuanced predictions and their net effects are hard to sign without additional information on the structure of individual costs of investing in group activity and the benefits from public goods. Careful empirical studies are therefore especially useful in understanding the nature of these effects.

3. Evidence on public good provision

Testing theories with nuanced predictions is always a challenge. In our setting, there are three main obstacles to empirical research. The most important problem is that public action is almost never directly observed except in experimental settings that are designed for this purpose. We review some of these studies in Section 3.3. Observational studies must search for empirical patterns between the availability of public goods and the characteristics of communities that influence collective action. However, many community characteristics that influence collective action also determine the ease with which public goods can be supplied. Large villages, for example, are often located close to urban areas and such proximity makes it easier and cheaper to provide them with public goods (their roads, communication and power lines are closer to existing networks, bus services involve relatively short diversions from major routes and it is cheaper to transport school and medical supplies). To isolate the group-size effect on public goods that operates through collective action we would have to somehow control for these differences in the cost of supplying public goods.

Second, public good quality varies enormously, but these quality differences are notoriously difficult to measure. Most studies rely on public good expenditures or on the physical location of facilities. In the presence of widespread bureaucratic corruption and agency problems that plague the public sector, the link between these outcome measures and actual provision can be fairly weak. Third, community characteristics may respond to the availability of public goods, as in the Tiebout framework, making it hard to identify the causal effects of these characteristics.

These problems are now well-recognized in the empirical literature on public goods and empirical strategies have tried to address them with varying degrees of success. Unfortunately, except in a few specific instances, establishing causality remains an issue and the conclusions drawn in most studies continue to be based on suggestive correlations that are woven into a plausible story.

3.1. Empirical methods

The typical empirical relationship that is estimated in this literature takes the form

$$y_{jkt} = f(\mathbf{p}_{jt}, \mathbf{x}_{jt}). \tag{8}$$

The dependent variable y_{jkt} is a measure of access or quality of public good k in community j at time t, $\mathbf{p}_{jt}$ is a set of population characteristics of the community in year t and $\mathbf{x}_{jt}$ is a vector representing various geographical and historical features of the area in which the community is located. The population characteristics $\mathbf{p}_{jt}$ are of principal interest because they are directly related to the various mechanisms explored in the theoretical literature on collective action. These typically include the shares of various population groups in the community (to capture differences in preferences or power), measures of social heterogeneity (as proxies for social cohesion), and measures of income or asset inequality that reflect the distribution of benefits from public goods. The variables $\mathbf{x}_{jt}$ might include population density, village size, terrain, climate and other features of an area which might influence the demand for different public goods and the costs of providing them.

There is no universally accepted measure of the cohesion of a given group or population. It is most common to represent social heterogeneity by the index of ethnolinguistic fragmentation,

$$h_f = 1 - \sum_{i=1}^{n} \xi_i^2 \tag{9}$$

where ξ_i refers to the population share of the ith group. This is a measure that is maximized when there is a large number of very small groups. An alternative is to use the measure of polarization proposed by Esteban and Ray (1994) which formalizes the idea that two big groups may have a harder time working together than many small groups.

Their measure takes the form

$$h_p = A \sum_{i=1}^{n} \sum_{j \neq i} \xi_i^{1+\alpha} \xi_j \delta_{ij}, \quad \alpha \geqslant 0,$$

where δ_{ij} denotes the *social distance* between group i and group j. Assuming that δ_{ij} is a constant (normalized to 1) for i not equal to j (and δ_{ii} is zero) this reduces to

$$h_p = A \sum_{i=1}^{n} \xi_i^{1+\alpha} (1 - \xi_i).$$

Notice that for the case where all the $\xi_i = \frac{1}{m}$ and $\alpha = 1$, this expression is exactly the one on the left-hand side of equation (7) derived in the previous section. There is therefore at least one model for which an index of polarization corresponds exactly to a measure of (the lack of) social cohesion. In fact, as pointed out by Montalvo and Reynal-Querol (2005), there is a close relationship between this specific class of models of public action and the specific measure of polarization where $\alpha = 1$, that goes beyond the special case of equal group sizes.

Different measures work well in different settings: Using data for 138 countries between 1960 and 1999, Montalvo and Reynal-Querol (2005) find that polarization measures are important predictors of civil wars while fractionalization measures have no statistically significant effect. In contrast, Alesina et al. (2003) find that fractionalization performs better than polarization in explaining long-run growth across countries and that the explanatory power of fractionalization measures improves significantly when coarse classifications of ethnic divisions are replaced by finer ones. However, it is not clear that either of these measures is particularly effective in capturing the many aspects of social distance that are relevant to collective action: the fact that one works better than the other in certain cases might be largely fortuitous.

3.2. The role of group characteristics

3.2.1. Group tastes and group influence

Group preferences are not directly observable and evidence linking public goods to preferences is therefore fairly limited. Group influence on the other hand can be more easily linked to legislative and institutional changes, and the literature here is therefore more substantial. In fact, as we will see below, changes in group influence, and the resulting changes in the composition of public goods, can often reveal information about differences in preferences across groups.

One approach to testing whether the availability of public goods responds to group preferences is to identify variables that determine the economic returns to public goods and examine whether the availability of these goods responds to changes in these returns. Foster and Rosenzweig (2000) use data from a panel of 245 villages in India and find that between 1971 and 1982, secondary school enrollments and school construction both responded to the rapid growth in agricultural yields. Investments in schooling were found to be greatest in areas with a high fraction of landed relative to landless households. They argue that technological changes and the corresponding rise in yields made education more valuable and that the investments in public schools are therefore responses to the increased demand for schooling. They link the land distribution to public goods by emphasizing that it is the landed who make decisions on technology adoption and benefit most from schooling during a period of rapid technological change. The demand for schooling among the landless may actually fall as the withdrawal of children of landed households from the labor market increases agricultural wages and therefore the opportunity costs of sending children to school rather than to work. Their story is plausible, but the data are also consistent with other explanations. For instance, schools (and other public goods) expanded rapidly through the Indian countryside in the 1970s as part of the government's Minimum Needs Program, and it may be that the political leverage of the landed relative to the landless allowed them to appropriate a large share of these newly provided public goods. To be more convincing, one would have to show that it was precisely those public goods that farmers would want in times of substantial technological change that became more widely available to them and that the structural changes in the economy that accompanied technological change did not commensurately raise the returns to education for the landless.

Cultural norms and religious beliefs can sometimes provide us with information on group preferences. In the caste-based social hierarchy of rural India, Brahmans are the elite priestly caste. Banerjee and Somanathan (2007) use data for Indian parliamentary constituencies and find that in the early 1970s, the population share of Brahmans in a constituency is positively correlated with access to primary, middle and secondary schools, to post offices and to piped water. These are precisely the goods we would expect them to value given their traditional role as the repositories of written knowledge and the norms of ritual purity which prevent them sharing wells and other common water sources. Brahman concentrations are not associated with more of other public goods such as electricity connections, health centers, roads or transport services. Preferences for this latter set of goods are more likely to be similar across the different castes.

Some studies have used exogenous changes in the political voice of particular groups to understand both the nature of a social group's preferences and their effects on public good provision. The idea is that these political shocks translate into demand shocks for public goods. An interesting example of this approach is Acemoglu, Johnson, and Robinson (2001), which observes that the early mortality rates of European settlers had a strong influence on settlement patterns in the European colonies of the eighteenth and nineteenth centuries. Places where the early settlers did relatively well attracted more Europeans settlers and as a result, these areas ended up with institutions and public goods which the Europeans demanded.

Another instance of a change in political power which influenced public goods was brought about by the 73rd Amendment to the Indian Constitution (passed in 1992), by which a certain fraction of the positions of the heads of village governments were reserved for women. The reserved villages are chosen randomly at each election.

Chattopadhyay and Duflo (2004) find that political reservation for women in local government resulted in greater provision of goods which women value, such as drinking water and roads.

Changing political voice may not be a simple matter of passing appropriate legislation, as shown by the experiences of the Scheduled Tribes and the Scheduled Castes in India.[19] Both groups have long been recognized as disadvantaged, and affirmative action policies were put in place to increase their representation in politics and within the bureaucracy. Pande (2003) finds that reserving electoral constituencies for Scheduled Caste candidates resulted in higher job quotas and greater welfare spending for that group while similar policies for the Scheduled Tribes did not lead to the same benefits. Similarly, Banerjee and Somanathan (2007) find that, between 1971 and 1991, areas with Scheduled Caste concentrations experienced a rapid expansion in public goods while the Scheduled Tribes continued to lag behind. This asymmetry across the two groups is also seen in their political behavior. The Scheduled Castes began to mobilize effectively in the 1970s and a major political party representing their interests came to power in the North Indian state of Uttar Pradesh in the 1980s. Scheduled Tribes on the other hand remained isolated, both geographically and politically.[20] While one cannot rule out the possibility that these relationships are partly driven by omitted variables (perhaps Scheduled Tribes live in remote areas that are harder to reach with public goods), patterns of provision do appear to mirror changing political equations.

3.2.2. Distribution of benefits

In general it is not easy to separate the effects of inequality in the distribution of benefits from that of inequality in the underlying asset distribution, for the simple reason that inequality of benefits is often a result of inequality in assets. Khwaja (2002) tries to deal with this by separately measuring assets and benefits. Even after controlling for inequality in the land distribution, inequality in benefits has a significant U-shaped effect. Increases in inequality at low levels of inequality hurt the maintenance of public projects, but further increases at higher levels of inequality actually lead to greater maintenance. As noted in the theory section, Khwaja also suggests a reason for why he finds a U-shaped relationship.

Gaspart et al. (1998) study the role of inequality in benefits on labor contributions in building draining canals in rural Ethiopia, while Gaspart and Platteau (2002) study voluntary restraints on fishing by Senegalese fishermen. Individual contributions in both these cases are shown to increase significantly in the benefits derived from the public good. These studies also show that part of the effect of inequality on public goods

---

[19] The Scheduled Castes have historically been at the bottom of the Hindu caste hierarchy and the Scheduled Tribes in India are groups outside the Hindu caste system.

[20] Chandra (2004) documents the rise of the Scheduled Castes in Indian politics and speculates on reasons for the poor mobilization of the Scheduled Tribes.

comes about because richer households enjoy the leadership and prestige that comes with coordinating collective activities.

Foster and Rosenzweig (1995) provide an interesting example of the Olson effect, though in a context that is slightly removed from our main concern here. They consider knowledge about new agricultural technologies as the public good. Since those who have the most land have the biggest stake in experimentation, big farmers will experiment the most and as a result a small farmer who lives next to a big farmer will experiment less than a small farmer who is next to another small farmer. Using data from the introduction of high-yielding varieties (HYV) of cereals in India, they find that those who have more assets do adopt HYV sooner, but those whose neighbors have more assets adopt late.[21]

3.2.3. Cohesion

Much of the empirical work on public good provision focuses on the relationship with social and economic heterogeneity. Alesina, Baqir, and Easterly (1999) pioneered this literature by analyzing data on public expenditures from a cross-section of US cities in 1990. They regress the share of expenditures on specific public goods on per capita income, city size, average educational attainments, income inequality, age structure and a measure of ethnic fragmentation (based on a five-way classification of ethnicity). They find that more fragmented cities spend proportionally less on schooling, roads and trash pickup but more on health and police, even after controlling for the population shares of specific ethnic groups and whether the city is majority African-American.

This, and other related research, is subject to three major caveats. First, the welfare implications of these types of results are unclear. Can we be sure that heterogeneous communities are not simply substituting other, equally useful, public goods for the ones that they are under-supplying? It is not clear, for instance, that the increased spending on health and police is less useful than spending on schools or roads. Second, do the results indicate that there is less collective action when there are more groups (as Alesina et al. believe), or is it the case that multiple groups actually generate more collective action, but that the collective action is wasteful, as Esteban and Ray (1999) suggest?

Finally, and perhaps most importantly, it is difficult to establish the exogeneity of the heterogeneity measure. A number of factors that can affect heterogeneity (such as urbanization, being in a border area, being near a major road or waterway, being next to a region where there was a war and therefore a large exodus) can also directly influence other economic outcomes, including the demand for and the supply of public goods. There may also be reverse causality, with the poor, for example, converging to areas that effectively implement anti-poverty programs, making these areas much more homogeneous than they would otherwise be. Because the measures of heterogeneity used

---

[21] The chapter by Munshi in this Handbook surveys several other instances where the public good in question is information about new technologies.

in the literature are often contemporaneous with the measures of public good availability, this is likely to be a serious problem, especially in high mobility environments.

Alesina et al. (1999) try to address the endogeneity issue by using community fixed effects, but once they include fixed effects and all their controls, the effect of heterogeneity becomes insignificant or even positive. Their results do however get some support from a companion paper on heterogeneity and school district consolidation in the United States: One natural implication of the view that heterogeneity makes it harder to provide public goods is that people will want to separate into smaller jurisdictions. The constraint is that there are increasing returns to scale in urban agglomerations, which makes it costly to have very tiny jurisdictions. Over the 20th century the number of jurisdictions (school districts) in the United States has decreased by a factor of 12. Alesina, Baqir, and Hoxby (2004) find that this process of consolidation was significantly slower in areas where racial heterogeneity increased: Areas where racial heterogeneity went up by 2 standard deviations between 1960 and 1990 lost 6 fewer jurisdictions over the same period.

Several subsequent papers have looked at the same question in a developing country context. Overall, the results indicate a negative relationship between heterogeneity measures and access to public goods, but, once again, it is not fully clear whether these results can be interpreted in a causal sense.

Banerjee and Somanathan (2007) limit the substitution problem mentioned above by using data on the location of public goods (where a particular community can do better along all dimensions) rather than expenditure shares, where some substitution is inevitable. They also consider a range of public goods: various types of schools, health centers, water, power, communication and transport facilities. Their measure of social heterogeneity uses data on population shares of non-Hindu religions as well as 185 distinct Hindu caste groups. In 1971, when most public goods were extremely scarce, they find that the standard measure of ethnolinguistic fragmentation applied to caste and religious divisions was negatively related to access to several public goods. Land inequality on the other hand had a positive association with provision, reflecting perhaps the political weight of large landowners in India at that time. They also estimate a differenced model based on changes in provision and a set of explanatory variables between 1971 and 1991 and find much weaker effects of both social heterogeneity and land inequality on public goods. These two decades experienced rapid expansions in rural access to public goods as well as realignments in the balance of political power. While it is certainly plausible the role of these measures of social and economic heterogeneity declined over this period, it is not possible to convincingly establish this because of differences in the extent to which these two specifications deal with measurement error and omitted constituency-level variables.

Miguel and Gugerty (2005) look at the effect of ethnic heterogeneity on school spending in western Kenya. In Kenya, a significant part of school expenses are financed by parents through their *Harambee* contributions. Least squares estimates of school spending on school-level heterogeneity suggest an insignificant or slightly positive effect of heterogeneity. School heterogeneity is however likely to be endogenous with good schools being chosen by committed parents from all social groups. When they use the regional ethnic composition as an instrument for school-level heterogeneity, they find a negative effect of heterogeneity on school spending, maintenance and the per pupil availability of desks and textbooks. Going from a perfectly homogeneous school to one with the average level of diversity reduces school spending by 20 percent. It is of course possible that a region that is more open to outside influences is both more heterogeneous and more serious about education and this would cast doubt on the use of regional social composition as a valid instrument.

There are a number of other interesting papers that look at the correlation between heterogeneity and public good outcomes. Khwaja (2002) finds that village-level social heterogeneity (based on religious and political differences as well as clan divisions) in the Baltistan area of northern Pakistan adversely affected the maintenance of public infrastructure. Baland and Platteau (1998) and Dayton-Johnson (2000) also find a negative relationship between heterogeneity and maintenance of the commons. Somanathan, Prabhakar, and Mehta (2006) find no relationship of heterogeneity on forest conservation in the Indian Himalayas. Baland et al. (2003) look at firewood collection in Nepal and find that social heterogeneity increases firewood collection (implying worse maintenance of the commons). Both these papers find that economic inequality improves conservation for certain types of forests, perhaps because the benefits are more concentrated, as discussed above.

Banerjee et al. (2001) model a very specific public good setting; the productivity of a sugar farmers' cooperative, which jointly runs a sugar crusher. They begin from the observation that the productivity of the cooperative depends on paying attractive prices to the sugar growers. On the other hand, a cooperative that pays lower-than-optimal prices makes profits, which can be skimmed by the farmers who control the cooperative. When small farmers are in an overwhelming majority, they make sure that high prices are maintained. When the large farmers dominate, low prices are much more likely unless large farmers are so numerous that the distortion caused by the low price hurts them more than they can gain by capturing the profits of the cooperative. The model leads to the prediction that cooperatives with a very low or a very high share of large farmers will have high prices. They test for this U-shaped relationship using data from sugar cooperatives in the state of Maharashtra in India and find that there is indeed such a relationship between the share of small farmers in the area around the cooperative and the price of sugar. To control for unobserved differences in the productivity of different areas, they used a fixed-effects specification. They also show that the participation of the larger farmers in the area moves in the opposite direction to the price of sugar-cane while the participation of the smaller farmers mirrors the price: if the movements in the price were driven by unobserved differences in productivity, one would have expected the participation of the small and the large farmers to move together.

An alternative way to circumvent the problem of endogenous heterogeneity measures is to focus on the effect of specific shocks that radically alter social structure. Engerman and Sokoloff (2000, 2002) observe that among the European colonies in the Americas, those suitable for the cultivation of sugar (Brazil, Haiti) or for extractive industries (Mexico, Peru) have less egalitarian institutions than areas with no such possibilities (United States, Canada). Engerman and Sokoloff argue that the presence of these highly profitable but labor intensive industries made it very important for these economies to have a large and docile labor supply which came about by either importing slaves or enslaving the local population. This created a society with high inequality and consequently much less cohesion. Also, the elites controlling these states were not particularly interested in investing in education for the masses, since this was likely to make labor more expensive. As a result, these colonies had much lower literacy than the United States and Canada.

In a similar vein, Banerjee and Iyer (2005) study the long-term impact of being assigned a particular land revenue collection system by the British colonial rulers in India. They distinguish between areas with landlord-based systems, where the landlord was assigned the primary responsibility for collecting land revenue on behalf of the British, and a non-landlord system where the taxes were collected directly from the peasant. They argue that the landlord-based system introduced a class of powerful intermediaries between the rulers and the ruled, and this class was perceived (probably rightly) to be exploitative by the peasant population. While the landlord-based system was abolished (along with all land revenue collection systems) in the early 1950s, this history of class conflict made rural society in the ex-landlord areas less cohesive and therefore less effective in getting public goods. Using district-level data from the 1981 Indian census, they find that formerly landlord-controlled areas indeed lag behind other areas in the provision of schools and health centers, and consequently have lower literacy rates and higher infant mortality rates. Some indication of the different social climate is provided by the fact that rates of violent crimes (such as murders) are much higher in ex-landlord areas. The potential endogeneity of the land revenue system is dealt with by exploiting changes in British land revenue policy over the 19th century to construct instrumental variables estimates.[22]

The impact of historical landlord control persists in the 1991 census data: Banerjee, Iyer and Somanathan (2005) extend the analysis to 25 different public goods, and they also control for caste and religious fractionalization and a dummy for being directly ruled by the British in the past. As in Banerjee and Somanathan (2007), they include a wide range of geographic and population characteristics as controls. The OLS estimates of the non-landlord effect are positive and significant for 13 of the 25 goods and negative and significant for three. In related work, Pandey (2005) compares one landlord area (Oudh) with the area surrounding it (which was non-landlord) and finds that while both areas have the same level of access to primary schools in 2002, teacher attendance is 17% higher in the non-landlord area schools and teacher activity is 32% higher.

Overall, these results suggest that where heterogeneity is highly salient because of historical circumstances, it can be a major constraint on public action. In other cases,

---

[22] Specifically, Banerjee and Iyer (2005) use the fact of being conquered by the British in the period 1820–1856 as an instrument for being non-landlord. The paper contains detailed discussions of the validity of this instrument.

the estimates of commonly used measures of heterogeneity on public goods are more mixed.

3.3. Public goods experiments

A serious concern with the observational studies discussed above is that collective action choices are inferred from public goods outcomes. It is possible that, at least some of the time, we are spuriously attributing empirical patterns to the mechanisms contained in our models. Experiments allow us to observe the actual choices made by individuals under varying conditions and therefore address some of these doubts.

There have been a large number of laboratory experiments on *Voluntary Contribution Mechanisms*. In the simplest experiment of this type, subjects are divided into groups and given a fixed endowment of tokens. They are asked to choose the fraction of their endowment that they would like to contribute to a group project or public good. The group members decide, simultaneously and independently, on their contributions. The experimenter totals group contributions, doubles them (or multiplies them by some other constant) and divides this amount between the subjects in each group. Each member's payoff consists of an equal share of the group return plus the amount the member decided not to invest in the project. These experiments are typically set up such that the first-best outcome involves some level of positive contributions by all members and Nash equilibria are characterized by under-provision of the public good.

A survey of the results from such experiments is found in Ledyard (1995). A common finding in this literature is that subjects generally contribute more to the public good than predicted by Nash-equilibrium strategies. In one-shot trials, contributions are usually positive and total to about 40–60% of the socially optimal level. With repeated trials, most studies find that contributions tend to decline towards Nash-equilibrium levels.

These results are similar in flavor to those obtained from experiments on ultimatum bargaining games. There has been some debate about whether the positive contributions reflect altruism and cooperative behavior or whether they are just mistakes made by agents who would like to maximize their own payoff but do not fully understand the structure of the game. To distinguish between these possibilities, experiments have been set up to ensure that both the Nash equilibrium outcome and the social optimum are interior so that mistakes can be made in both directions (by contributing both too little and too much), while altruism would always result in contributing too much. The results obtained suggest that a sizable fraction of subjects do seem to behave selfishly but a sizable fraction do not, which raises questions about the modeling of collective action in the theoretical literature summarized above.

The effects of group size on public goods have also been studied in an experimental setting. Issac and Walker (1988) perform experiments with groups of two different sizes and find that larger groups exhibit more free-riding, but mainly because marginal returns fall as the group size increases. To isolate the "pure numbers-in-the-group" effect from the effect of declining marginal returns, they increase the return from investing in the public good for larger groups in a manner that keeps the marginal return roughly constant. They find that most of the group-size effect can be attributed to differences in marginal returns from the group activity. Once this is controlled for, individuals in larger groups do not contribute less.

A variety of approaches have been used to test the role of inequality or heterogeneity within the group on public goods. Cardenas, Stanlund and Willis (2002) conduct experiments in rural Colombia in which subjects allocate a fixed time endowment between collecting firewood and a market activity. To examine the role of heterogeneity, they contrast the results of two treatments: One in which the return from the private activity is the same across agents and another where the return is unequal. They find that public goods levels are higher (firewood extraction lower) when returns are unequal. This happens because increases in private returns lead to lower extraction levels, while decreases do not increase extraction very much (theoretically, this could go either way as shown in Section 2.4). Anderson, Mellor and Milyo (2004) introduce heterogeneity into the voluntary contributions game by varying the distribution of payments for participation rather than changing payoffs within the game. In experiments with college students, they find that heterogeneous show-up costs lower public good contributions if the distribution of these costs is publicly observed. Cardenas (2003) also finds that awareness of payoff asymmetries lowers contributions in heterogeneous groups. It appears that some of the effects of heterogeneity on public goods may stem from psychological effects of heterogeneity on perceived status.

Of special interest are experiments that estimate the importance of group monitoring and communication on the size of contributions. Monitoring in these games means that group members are informed about the value of total group contributions between successive trials of the experiment. Communication refers to allowing subjects a few minutes to converse before they decide on contributions. There are usually no restrictions on the nature of this conversation and subjects can use this to coordinate their actions or just to get to know each other. This communication is strictly *cheap talk* in the sense that it is not allowed to directly influence payoffs. Cason and Khan (1999) contrast outcomes from alternative versions of this type of experiment to understand how interactions between communication and monitoring determined contributions. In the perfect monitoring case, subjects are informed about total contributions after each round, while in the imperfect monitoring case, this information is available after every six rounds. Their results on communication are particularly striking: They find that in the absence of communication, contributions with both types of monitoring are fairly similar and decline over time. In the presence of communication, overall contributions are much higher (about 80 percent of the tokens were invested in the group activity as opposed to a high of 40 percent in the no-communication case) and did not decline in later rounds. Monitoring thus improved contributions only when it was combined with communication. This favorable effect of communication on contributions in public goods experiments is observed more generally under many different experimental designs (Ostrom, 2000).

The communication effects described above can be used to justify measures of heterogeneity such as the ethnolinguistic fractionalization index. If it is true that most communication takes place within groups, and that communication favorably influences contributions to group activity, then we would expect an index that is correlated with the frequency of within-group interactions to explain the provision of public goods. In a recent experimental study in Uganda, Habyarimana et al. (2006) find that successful public goods provision in homogeneous ethnic communities can be attributed to the fact that co-ethnics are more closely linked through social networks, and hence may be able to sustain cooperation through the threat of social sanction.

3.4. The welfare costs of public good misallocation

The empirical research that we have discussed in Section 3.2 attempts to isolate the causes of variation in the availability of public goods. It demonstrates that the uneven political leverage of social groups and their various other characteristics can skew the allocation of public goods in favor of some groups and against others. In this section we briefly discuss some recent approaches to measuring the aggregate welfare costs associated with the misallocation of public facilities.

There has been a very rapidly expanding computer science literature on *facility location* that deals with spatial optimization problems. A common problem in this class is one in which there is a given (arbitrary) distribution of the population across a finite set of locations and a fixed number of facilities are to be allocated to a subset of these locations. In a typical developing country, we can think of the locations as villages and facilities as centrally financed public goods (schools, health centers, post offices). Suppose that social welfare is decreasing in the aggregate distance traveled by the population. For small numbers of citizens and facilities, the total number of possible spatial configurations of facilities remains small and one can simply compute the allocation of facilities that minimizes distance traveled. A measure of the cost of misallocation is then the difference between the distance traveled under the actual and the optimal allocations. As the number of villages increases, the number of computations involved increases exponentially and this optimization problem becomes intractable. A variety of optimization algorithms have been recently developed which provide approximate solutions. The difference between the actual distance traveled and the distance corresponding to the algorithmic solution is then a lower bound on the welfare cost of public good misallocation.

Athreya and Somanathan (2007) adapt an algorithm in the facility location literature and apply it to the allocation of post offices in a region of South India. Between 1981 and 1991, there was a 23% increase in the number of villages with post offices in the area studied. They find that aggregate travel costs corresponding to the observed allocation of post offices in 1991 are 21% higher than the costs associated with the (near)-optimal allocation of the additional post offices. Rahman and Smith (1999) study the location of Health and Family Welfare Centres in an administrative region of Bangladesh, and find that relocating a set of seven centers can reduce the mean distance traveled by 43%. These papers, in themselves, do not offer any clues to the reasons for misallocation. Given, however, that they both deal with fairly small geographical areas (an administrative block in South India and a Bangladeshi *Thana*, each with less than a quarter of a million people), the social composition of villages does not vary very much. Bureaucratic mistakes could thus be a large part of the explanation, given the difficulty in computing optimal allocations.

The types of problems that have been studied so far in this literature are still fairly specific and little is known about the optimality of available algorithms when applied to non-linear travel costs and multi-period settings. The field is however expanding rapidly. As spatial data become widely available, this approach might well become very valuable in improving the delivery of public goods.

4. Some top-down interventions

Much of the evidence summarized in the previous section points to the importance of local population characteristics in determining access to public goods. There are two major reasons to look for explanations beyond those provided by these results. The first is that population variables, even when they exhibit systematic effects on the availability of public goods and on associated outcomes, leave much of the observed variation in these variables unexplained. The *World Development Report* [World Bank (2006)], for instance, reports significant differences in educational attainment between urban and rural populations and between males and females; yet, the share of inequality attributable to location and gender on average is only 6 percent and 2 percent respectively. Among the papers cited in the previous section, the explanatory variables in Miguel and Gugerty (2005) account for less than 25 percent of the variation in school funding across schools and those in Banerjee and Iyer (2005) account for about 30 percent of the variation in public good outcomes. This brings us to our second point: If public good access were determined primarily by local population characteristics, we would rarely see rapid changes in such access, since many of these characteristics (religion, caste, ethnicity) change very slowly over time. It would also be difficult to explain the convergence of under-provided areas with those that have been historically advantaged. In this section, we discuss the role of *top-down* interventions in bringing about these changes.

It is worth emphasizing that we are not claiming that top-down interventions are more effective than bottom-up interventions, nor that they explain more of the observed variation in the data. We mainly want to highlight that there are several cases where they have been central to the process of public good expansion and it is worth trying to understand them better.

Much of the historical expansion in public schooling took place under colonial or autocratic regimes. In the late 19th century and early 20th century, large parts of the presently developing world were ruled by colonial powers. One might expect the compulsions of these powers to be roughly similar with regard to the provision of public goods, yet the differences in provision across the colonies were very large. In 1930, the mean primary enrollment rate for British colonies was 35 percent, the corresponding figure for French colonies was about half of this (Benavot and Riddle, 1988). Dutch colonies were somewhere in between, and Belgian and Portuguese colonies had the worst outcomes. More recently, in Indonesia, in the five years between 1973–1974 and 1978–1979, more than 61,000 primary schools were built under the Sekolah Dakar IN-PRES program; this more than doubled the number of schools in the country [Duflo (2001)]. While the autocratic Suharto regime probably had a specific political purpose behind this intervention, the fact that it was based on a rule that explicitly targeted under-served areas and that this rule was largely followed suggests that there was very little local influence on the decision to build the schools.

The history of public good provision in India is dotted with a series of top-down interventions. The erstwhile princely states of India provide us with interesting cases of autocratic rulers providing public goods even with limited political incentives to do so. These princely states were parts of India that had accepted the overall suzerainty of the British and, in return, were allowed to retain a large measure of internal autonomy. The presence of the British army guaranteed that the power of these rulers was unchallenged within their domains, and they could afford to ignore the wishes of their people.[23]

Despite the limited pressure to deliver, some rulers did invest heavily in public goods and the high social outcomes observed in some areas today are arguably a legacy of these investments. The Travancore state in present-day Kerala is particularly well known for its long tradition of enlightened rulers. In 1817, the Regent Gauri Parvathi Bai declared, "The state should defray the entire cost of the education of its people in order that there might be no backwardness in the spread of enlightenment among them, that by diffusion of education they might become better subjects and public servants and that the reputation of the state might be enhanced thereby." This remarkable announcement was said to be heavily influenced by the Diwan (prime minister) James Munro, and it set an important precedent for state action in education. In particular, the reign of Swati Tirunal (1829–1847) was regarded as a "golden age" for the state. An English school was opened in Trivandrum in 1834, and schools were established in each district as well. His successors were all committed rulers who continued the process of reforms in various branches of the government; Mulam Tirunal Rama Varma (1885–1924) introduced an Education Code, opened the schools to children of untouchable communities and even set up a Popular Assembly consisting of elected representatives of the people. The contribution of the Travancore rulers to education in the state went well beyond expanding enrollments. The *Travancore Administrative Report* (State of Travancore, 1901) records 809 students in the Maharaja's High School of whom 800 had received vaccinations. The students came from both the priestly Brahman caste and the lower castes and from a wide range of occupational groups. This was quite remarkable given the numerous accounts of bitter caste conflicts in the state at that time.

We see a similar pattern in nearby Cochin, where Munro again acted as Diwan. In both Travancore and Cochin, he reorganized the administration of the states along the

---

[23] British administrative intervention in these kingdoms was limited to posting a British Political Agent or a British Resident in these states. The Resident's reports of misrule could result in a ruler being deposed by the British and another being set up in his place. This was relatively rare.

lines of the system in British India and played a large role in eradicating corruption. He was also instrumental in setting up vernacular schools in every village of Cochin state. Future Diwans of Cochin continued on the path of progressive reforms, introducing western medicine and English schools, and expanding access to education for all sections of society. We should note that while some public investments might be motivated by the desire to expand the tax base, it is unclear that setting up an English school was such a case at that time. After all, the British colonial state, never shy to make investments that expanded the tax base, set up the first English school in British Malabar (northern region of modern Kerala state) only in 1848.

Another dynamic ruler was Sayajirao III of Baroda in present-day Gujarat state, who declared that education was "absolutely necessary for the realization of my ambitions and wishes for the future of my people." The state ordered that schools be provided in all villages which could produce 16 children willing to attend; Sayajirao was also the first to introduce compulsory education in certain areas in 1892. It took the British more than twenty years to introduce a similar law in the neighboring Central Provinces.

In more recent times, the Indian state has made important commitments to public good provision. These first appeared in the late 1960s. In 1968, the ruling Congress Party brought out the National Policy on Education, which made a commitment to universal primary education. The Minimum Needs Program of 1974–1975 set down explicit norms about access to public goods in rural areas: a primary school and safe water within a mile of every village, paved roads to villages with populations over 1000, electricity to at least 40 percent of villages in every state, and a multi-tiered health system. Indira Gandhi made the removal of poverty (*Garibi Hatao*) the cornerstone of her successful election campaign in 1971. This rhetoric was accompanied by concrete results. Between 1971 and 1991, the fraction of villages with primary schools went up by about a third, those with high schools doubled and access to piped water increased ninefold. Many of these changes were specifically targeted at bringing about equality of access. Banerjee and Somanathan (2007) find that for 12 out of 15 public goods, higher access in 1971 was associated with significantly slower growth in the subsequent period. This is by no means a mechanical *mean reversion* effect; many of these facilities were available in less than 5 percent of Indian villages in 1971 and in less than 10 percent of villages in 1991.

There have been a variety of other nationally mandated programs which have been shown to improve health and educational outcomes in India over the last two decades. In education, *Operation Blackboard* significantly increased the availability of teachers and infrastructure in areas with poor educational outcomes.[24] The program of Integrated Child Development Services (ICDS), introduced in 1975, is a good example of how top-down interventions interact with local characteristics. The program, funded by the government and various donor agencies, expanded very rapidly in the 1990s and now covers over 7 million mothers and 34 million children below the age of 6.[25]

---

[24] Chin (2005) contains an evaluation study of *Operation Blackboard*, which began in 1987.

[25] http://www.unicef.org/india/nutrition_1556.htm.

Although the program is envisioned to have universal coverage, current coverage still varies widely across states and survey evidence shows that the functioning of ICDS units and workers is strongly influenced by the degree to which mothers are involved in the program.[26]

Top-down interventions do not need to be initiated by governments or political actors. For instance, an NGO is one of the biggest suppliers of primary schooling in Bangladesh: BRAC's Non-Formal Primary Education Program (which covers the same competencies as the government schools) had grown from 22 one-room schools in 1985 to 49,000 schools in 2004, accounting for about 11% of the primary school children in Bangladesh.[27] BRAC also has large health-care and microfinance programs, and has recently expanded its activities into Afghanistan and Sri Lanka. Singh (2006) describes how a group of committed bureaucrats created the innovative *Lok Jumbish* program in Rajasthan, with the goal of promoting primary schooling.

A recent innovation in top-down interventions is the trend towards explicit experimentation, as a way to find ways to improve the effectiveness of public good delivery. A number of them focus on corruption and governance issues. In one such experiment, conducted on behalf of the Indonesian government, Olken (2005) finds that corruption in road construction in Indonesia was substantially reduced (and road quality improved) when an auditing program was introduced. Duflo and Hanna (2005) describe another experiment, conducted on behalf of an NGO in India, which shows that using cameras to monitor teacher attendance reduces absenteeism and improves test scores in rural primary schools. Other experiments look at the benefits of providing additional resources: for example, Glewwe, Kremer and Moulin (1997) and Glewwe et al. (2004) find that providing more textbooks or flip charts to schools in Kenya at best improves the test scores of the top quintile of students, without much improvement in the overall level of learning.

Miguel (2004) illustrates how top-down actors can influence the allocation of public goods by manipulating the conditions under which the bottom-up processes operate. He describes the contrast between Kenya and Tanzania, which shared many common characteristics during the colonial period. After independence, the Kenyan leadership played up tribal loyalties for political reasons and little effort was put into building a Kenyan identity; in contrast, the Tanzanian leadership put a lot of emphasis on creating a single Tanzanian identity. This seems to have implications for public good provision: in the Busia region of Kenya, ethnic heterogeneity at the local level is negatively correlated with the quality of public goods (mainly schools), while in the nearby Meatu region of Tanzania, they are slightly positively correlated.

Taken together, these examples make a number of useful points. First, it seems clear that an agency with sufficient political will, be it a dictatorial state or a local NGO, can

---

[26] State coverage figures are available at http://wcd.nic.in. Dreze (2006) contains data from the FOCUS survey of ICDS units and participating households across seven Indian states.

[27] http://www.brac.net/history.htm.

improve access to public goods, irrespective of local conditions. Second, there might be important interactions between top-down and bottom-up processes that are not captured in the current literature. In the case of Kerala, after the initial set of initiatives led by the local kings, the next stage in the expansion of access to public schools was actually much more bottom up – the result of lower caste social movements in the late nineteenth and early twentieth centuries ([Singh (2006)] and [Ramachandran (1997)]). The fact that Gujarat, which started out as the other early leader in education in India (see the discussion of Baroda state above), is now much like the average Indian state, while Kerala is almost 100 percent literate, may be a result of differences between them at this later bottom-up stage.

We are still far from understanding the systematic patterns behind the success or failure of top-down interventions, compared to bottom-up processes. Bardhan and Mookherjee (2000, 2006a, 2006b) and Bardhan (2002) ask whether local government elections are more subject to capture than elections to the national (more top-down) government. They suggest that national elections may indeed be less subject to capture, partly because the national elite tends to be more divided and also because national elections tend to be more competitive (perhaps because more is at stake). Weighing against this, however, is the fact that it might be cheaper to "buy" the national election because the lobby group can focus on a smaller set of pivotal constituencies. Their model also shows that local capture is more likely in high inequality districts. It is not clear whether these results would extend easily to other types of collective action that do not operate through the electoral process but these papers point to the need for more theoretical and empirical work in this direction.

5. Conclusion

We began this chapter by documenting the enormous spatial variation that is commonly observed in the availability of public goods. We proceeded to survey the now substantial literature that links this variation to the characteristics of groups and the ability of their members to act collectively to promote group interests. Theoretical approaches in this area explain the under-provision of public goods in terms of individual incentives to free-ride in collective endeavors. Group characteristics influence these incentives and they can therefore be linked to variations in public good access. Empirical research on group characteristics and public good provision finds that while these characteristics do matter, the social composition of communities is able to explain only a fraction of the total variation in provision. The experimental evidence is also not entirely conclusive: Experiments on voluntary contribution mechanisms find that group contributions are generally below socially optimum levels but often above those corresponding to Nash equilibrium strategies. Moreover, these experiments find that communication between members can be important in achieving group cooperation, even if it is not directly linked to payoffs. This suggests that group identities can be created by communication, something our models currently do not allow.

   More generally, the research on group characteristics and collective action surveyed
here suggests that there are many missing pieces to the public goods puzzle. Access to
many basic public goods is likely to converge in the coming years. Some areas that have
had historically poor access are currently in the midst of major economic expansions
accompanied by rapid increases in public good coverage. As this happens, we will need
to shift our attention to quality differences, where both the theoretical and empirical
literature is in its infancy. There are several challenges to delivering quality rather than
access. First, quality is much harder to evaluate than access – anyone can see that there
is no school building in the neighborhood, but judging whether the children are learning
as much as they should can be quite a challenge. This makes it harder both to demand
quality and to deliver it. Second, the incentives of the government bureaucrats may be
very different in delivering access versus quality. For instance, they may favor school
construction and even hiring new teachers for venal personal reasons (such as being able
to give contracts to favored parties), but they clearly have no financial stake in getting
the teachers to work.
   Another major deficiency in this literature is the absence of a body of knowledge
on the technology of delivering public services. Even in the absence of political competition and rent-seeking by different communities, the efficient allocation of public
goods requires the ability to compute optimal allocations and provide bureaucrats with
the incentives to implement them. This is not a trivial exercise. The field of spatial optimization techniques has been expanding rapidly and shows that optimal allocations can,
at best, be computed quite approximately. We still know relatively little about the extent
to which misallocation results from these types of information gaps. This is likely to be
a fruitful area of future research.
   The problem of providing the right incentives to government agents is related to
the question of the appropriate level of political and administrative decentralization.[28]
The World Development Report on Making Services Work for the Poor [World Bank
(2004)], comes out in favor of giving local communities greater control over the delivery of public goods as a way of improving quality. While those who consume public
goods are presumably the ones with the greatest stake in making sure that they work
well, factors determining the effectiveness of local control need to be better understood.
Such control may depend on collective community effort, as we saw in the first part
of this paper, on the nature of political capture (as discussed in the previous section)
and also on whether decentralized monitors have the information necessary to evaluate
public services. Can a patient really judge whether he is getting the right medicines?
Will remote village level governments know whether building contractors are using the
stated materials, or whether teachers are properly covering the grade-appropriate course
syllabus? The field experiment by Olken (2005) suggests that the task of monitoring
may indeed be quite difficult for the village community: While centralized auditing reduces corruption in his data, greater monitoring by villagers has no detectable impact

---

[28] Oates (1999) provides a review of the literature on the vertical structure of the public sector.

on the level of corruption. Perhaps decentralized delivery works well only with simple project designs, as Khwaja (2002) seems to suggest.

Even if one opts for decentralization, there are many more decisions that have to be taken. Is it enough to give the local community the right to hire and fire the teacher? Or do they also need information about how well the teacher is doing (from standardized tests, for example)? If allowing them to hire and fire is politically infeasible, is it still worth giving them information about the teacher's performance? If, instead, we opt for centralization, so that hiring and firing teachers is in the hands of some higher level government, how can we make sure that the government finds out when the teacher is absent, or when the money for books is stolen before it reaches the school? The recent empirical work mentioned at the end of the previous section has made a start in answering these important policy questions, but there is clearly much more work to be done.

References

Acemoglu, D., Johnson, S., Robinson, J.A. (2001). "The colonial origins of comparative development: An empirical investigation". American Economic Review 91 (5), 1369–1401.

Alesina, A., Baqir, R., Easterly, W. (1999). "Public goods and ethnic divisions". Quarterly Journal of Economics 114 (4), 1243–1284.

Alesina, A., Baqir, R., Hoxby, C. (2004). "Political jurisdictions in heterogeneous communities". Journal of Political Economy 112, 348–396.

Alesina, A., Devleeschauwer, A., Easterly, W., Kurlat, S., Wacziarg, R. (2003). "Fractionalization". Journal of Economic Growth 8, 155–194.

Anderson, L., Mellor, J., Milyo, J. (2004). "Inequality and public good provision: An experimental analysis". Working paper.

Athreya, S., Somanathan, R. (2007). "Quantifying spatial misallocation in centrally provided public goods". Economics Letters, in press.

Baland, J.M., Dagnelie, O., Ray, D. (2006). "Inequality and inefficiency in joint projects". Economic Journal, in press.

Baland, J.M., Platteau, J.P. (1998). "Wealth inequality and efficiency on the commons part II: The regulated case". Oxford Economic Papers 50, 1–22.

Baland, J.M., Bardhan, P., Das, S., Mookherjee, D., Sarkar, R. (2003). "The environmental impact of poverty: Evidence from firewood collection in rural Nepal". Working paper.

Banerjee, A., Deaton, A., Duflo, E. (2004). "Wealth, health, and health services in rural Rajasthan". American Economic Review 94 (2), 326–330.

Banerjee, A., Iyer, L. (2005). "History, institutions and economic performance: The legacy of colonial land tenure systems in India". American Economic Review 95 (4), 1190–1213.

Banerjee, A., Iyer, L., Somanathan, R. (2005). "History, social divisions and public goods in rural India". Journal of the European Economic Association 3 (2–3), 639–647.

Banerjee, A., Somanathan, R. (2007). "The political economy of public goods: Some evidence from India". Journal of Development Economics 82 (2), 287–314.

Banerjee, A., Mookherjee, D., Munshi, K., Ray, D. (2001). "Inequality, control rights and rent seeking: Sugar cooperatives in Maharashtra". Journal of Political Economy 109 (1), 138–190.

Bardhan, P. (2002). "Decentralization of governance and development". Journal of Economic Perspectives 16 (4), 185–205.

Bardhan, P., Ghatak, M., Karaivanov, A. (2006). "Wealth inequality and collective action". Working paper.

Bardhan, P., Mookherjee, D. (2000). "Capture and governance at local and national levels". American Economic Review 90 (2), 135–139.

Bardhan, P., Mookherjee, D. (2006a). "Corruption and decentralization of infrastructure delivery in developing countries". Economic Journal 116, 101–127.

Bardhan, P., Mookherjee, D. (2006b). "Decentralization, corruption and government accountability: An overview". In: Rose-Ackerman, S. (Ed.), Handbook of Economic Corruption. Edward Elgar.

Benabou, R. (1993). "Workings of a city". Quarterly Journal of Economics 108 (3), 619–652.

Benavot, A., Riddle, P. (1988). "The expansion of primary education 1870–1940: Trends and issues". Sociology of Education 61 (3), 191–210.

Cardenas, J.C. (2003). "Real wealth and experimental cooperation". Journal of Development Economics 70 (2), 263–289.

Cardenas, J.C., Stanlund, J., Willis, C. (2002). "Economic inequality and burden-sharing in the provision of local environmental quality". Ecological Economics 40 (3), 379–395.

Cason, T.N., Khan, F.U. (1999). "A laboratory study of voluntary public goods provision with imperfect monitoring and communication". Journal of Development Economics 58, 533–552.

Center for the Study of Developing Societies (1996). National Election Studies, New Delhi. http://www.lokniti.org/dataunit.htm.

Chandra, K. (2004). Why Ethnic Parties Succeed: Patronage and Ethnic Head Counts in India. Cambridge Univ. Press.

Chattopadhyay, R., Duflo, E. (2004). "Women as policy makers: Evidence from a randomized policy experiment in India". Econometrica 72 (5), 1409–1443.

Chaudhury, N., Hammer, J., Kremer, M., Rogers, F.H. (2004). "Teacher and health care provider absenteeism: A multi-country study". Working paper.

Chin, A. (2005). "Can redistributing teachers across schools raise educational attainment? Evidence from Operation Blackboard in India". Journal of Development Economics 78, 384–405.

Dayton-Johnson, J. (2000). "The determinants of collective action on the local commons: A model with evidence from Mexico". Journal of Development Economics 62 (1), 181–208.

Dreze, J. (2006). "Universalisation with quality: ICDS in a rights perspective". Economic and Political Weekly, 3706–3715.

Duflo, E. (2001). "Schooling and labor market consequences of school construction in Indonesia: Evidence from an unusual policy experiment". American Economic Review 91 (4), 795–813.

Duflo, E., Hanna, R. (2005). "Monitoring works: Getting teachers to come to school". Working paper. MIT.

Engerman, S.L., Sokoloff, K.L. (2000). "Institutions, factor endowments, and paths of development in the New World". Journal of Economic Perspectives 14 (3), 217–232.

Engerman, S.L., Sokoloff, K.L. (2002). "Factor endowments, inequality, and paths of institutional and economic development among New World economies". Working paper 9259. NBER.

Esteban, J., Ray, D. (1994). "On the measurement of polarization". Econometrica 62 (4), 819–851.

Esteban, J., Ray, D. (1999). "Conflict and distribution". Journal of Economic Theory 87, 379–415.

Esteban, J., Ray, D. (2001). "Free riding and the group size paradox". American Political Science Review 95, 663–672.

Foster, A., Rosenzweig, M. (1995). "Learning by doing and learning from others: Human capital and technical change in agriculture". Journal of Political Economy 103 (6), 1176–1209.

Foster, A., Rosenzweig, M. (2000). "Technological change and the distribution of schooling: Evidence from Green-Revolution India". Working paper.

Gaspart, F., Platteau, J.P. (2002). "Heterogeneity and collective action for effort regulation: Lessons from the Senegalese small-scale fisheries". Working paper.

Gaspart, F., Jabbar, M., Melard, C., Platteau, J.P. (1998). "Participation in the construction of a local public good with indivisibilities: An application to watershed development in Ethiopia". Journal of African Economies 7 (2), 157–184.

Glewwe, P., Kremer, M., Moulin, S. (1997). "Textbooks and test scores: evidence from a prospective evaluation in Kenya". Working paper.

Glewwe, P., Kremer, M., Moulin, S., Zitzewitz, E. (2004). "Retrospective vs. prospective analyses of school inputs: The case of flip charts in Kenya". Journal of Development Economics 74 (1), 251–268.

Goldin, C. (1998). "America's graduation from high school: The evolution and spread of secondary schooling in the twentieth century". Journal of Economic History 58, 345–374.

Habyarimana, J., Humphreys, M., Posner, D., Weinstein, J. (2006). "Why does ethnic diversity undermine public goods provision?" IZA Discussion paper 2272.

Institute Brasiliero de Geografia e Estatistica (2004). "Sintese de Indicadores Sociais". Rio de Janeiro.

Issac, M.R., Walker, J.M. (1988). "Group size effects in public goods provision: The voluntary contributions mechanism". Quarterly Journal of Economics 103 (1), 179–199.

Jeffrey, R. (1993). Politics, Women and Well Being: How Kerala Became "A Model". Oxford Univ. Press, New Delhi.

Khwaja, A.I. (2002). "Can good projects succeed in bad communities? Collective action in public good provision". Working paper.

Khwaja, A.I. (2004). "Is increasing community participation always a good thing?". Journal of the European Economic Association 2 (2–3), 427–436.

Ledyard, J. (1995). "Public goods: A survey of experimental research". In: Kagel, J.H., Roth, A. (Eds.), The Handbook of Experimental Economics. Princeton Univ. Press, pp. 205–356.

Lindert, P. (2004). Growing Public. Cambridge Univ. Press, Cambridge.

Miguel, E. (2004). "Tribe or nation? Nation-building and public goods in Kenya versus Tanzania". World Politics 56 (3), 327–362.

Miguel, E., Gugerty, M.K. (2005). "Ethnic diversity, social sanctions and public goods in Kenya". Journal of Public Economics 89 (11–12), 2325–2368.

Ministry of Agriculture and Rural Development (2002). Statistics of Agriculture and Rural Development 1996–2000. Agricultural Publishing House, Hanoi.

Montalvo, J.G., Reynal-Querol, M. (2005). "Ethnic polarization, potential conflict and civil wars". American Economic Review 95 (3), 796–816.

Oates, W.E. (1999). "An essay on fiscal federalism". Journal of Economic Literature 37, 1120–1149.

Office of the Registrar General of India (2001). Census of India 2001: Village Directory Data. Electronic Data Files, New Delhi.

Olken, B. (2005). "Monitoring corruption: Evidence from a field experiment in Indonesia". Working paper.

Olson, M. (1965). The Logic of Collective Action: Public Goods and the Theory of Groups. Harvard Univ. Press, Cambridge, MA.

Ostrom, E. (2000). "Collective action and the evolution of social norms". Journal of Economic Perspectives 14 (3), 137–158.

Pande, R. (2003). "Minority representation and policy choices: The significance of legislator identity". American Economic Review 93 (4), 1132–1151.

Pandey, P. (2005). "Service delivery and capture in public schools: How does history matter and can mandated political representation reverse the effects of history?" Working paper.

PROBE Team (1999). Public Report on Basic Education in India. Oxford Univ. Press, New Delhi.

Rahman, S.U., Smith, D.K. (1999). "Deployment of rural health facilities in a developing country". Journal of the Operational Research Society 50 (9), 892–902.

Ramachandran, V.K. (1997). "On Kerala's development achievements". In: Dreze, J., Sen, A. (Eds.), Indian Development: Selected Regional Perspectives. Oxford Univ. Press, pp. 205–356.

Rimal, G., Rimal, S., Rimal, R. (2002). Nepal District Profile: A Districtwise Socioeconomic Profile along with a Comprehensive Ntional Profile. National Development Institute, Kathmandu.

Sen, A. (2001). "Economic development and capability expansion in historical perspective". Pacific Economic Review 6 (2), 179–191.

Singh, P. (2006). "Understanding Rajasthan's educational achievements in the 1990s or the tale of two projects". Working paper.

Somanathan, E., Prabhakar, R., Mehta, B.S. (2006). "Collective action for forest conservation: Does heterogeneity matter?" In: Baland, J.-M., Bardhan, P., Bowles, S. (Eds.), Inequality, Cooperation, and Environmental Sustainability. Princeton Univ. Press.

State of Travancore (1901). Travancore Administrative Report.

The Hindu (2003). "Behind the election outcomes". Editorial, December 13.

Tiebout, C.M. (1956). "A pure theory of local expenditures". Journal of Political Economy 64 (5), 416–424.

UNDP (2003a). Bulgaria National Human Development Report. Rural Regions: Overcoming Development Disparities. UNDP, Bulgaria.

UNDP (2003b). Pakistan National Human Development Report: Poverty, Growth and Governance. Oxford Univ. Press.

UNDP (2003c). South Africa Human Development Report. The Challenge of Sustainable Development: Unlocking People's Creativity. Oxford Univ. Press.

UNDP (2003d). Thailand Human Development Report 2003.

UNDP (2004a). Human Development Report Russian Federation: Towards a Knowledge-Based Society. VES MIR Publishers, Moscow.

UNDP (2004b). Informe Sobre Desarrollo Humano Mexico 2004.

UNDP (2005). Human Development Report 2005: International Cooperation at a Crossroads: Aid, Trade and Security in an Unequal World. United Nations Development Programme, New York.

UNDP (2006). Asia-Pacific Human Development Report: Trade on Human Terms. MacMillan India.

UNDP, and Institute for Development Studies University of Nairobi (2004). Third Kenya Human Development Report: Participatory Governance for Human Development.

UNDP, and the Institute for National Planning (2004). Egypt Human Development Report: Choosing Decentralization for Good Governance. Commercial Press, Egypt.

UNDP, and the Stockholm Environment Institute (2002). China Human Development Report: Making Green Development a Choice. Oxford Univ. Press.

UNDP, BPS-Statistics Indonesia, and BAPPENAS (2004). "The economics of democracy: Financing human development in Indonesia". Indonesia Human Development Report 2004.

US Census (2000). Table PHC-T-38: State of Residence in 2000 by State of Birth in 2000.

Vigdor, J.L. (2004). "Community composition and collective action: Analyzing initial mail response to the 2000 census". Review of Economics and Statistics 86 (1), 303–312.

World Bank (2004). World Development Report 2004: Making Services Work for Poor People. The World Bank and Oxford Univ. Press, Washington, DC.

World Bank (2006). World Development Report 2006: Equity and Development. The World Bank and Oxford Univ. Press, Washington, DC.

Zhang, X., Kanbur, R. (2003). "Spatial inequality in education and health care in China". Working paper.

Chapter 50

UNDERSTANDING POLITICAL CORRUPTION IN LOW INCOME COUNTRIES[*]

ROHINI PANDE

Kennedy School of Government, Harvard University, Mailbox 46, 79 JFK Street, Cambridge, MA 02138-5801, USA

Contents

[*] Thanks to Daniel Fetter for excellent research assistance and Abhijit Banerjee, Marcel Fafchamps, Asim Khwaja and, especially, Dominic Leggett for discussion.

Handbook of Development Economics, Volume 4
DOI: 10.1016/S1573-4471(07)04050-8

Abstract

Building on the large and growing empirical literature on the political behavior of individuals in low income countries, this Chapter seeks to understand corruption through the lens of political economy – particularly in terms of the political and economic differences between rich and poor countries. Our focus is on the political behavior of individuals exposed to democratic political institutions. We review the existing literature on the determinants of individual political behavior to ask whether we can understand the choice of political actors to be corrupt and, importantly, of other individuals to permit it, as a rational response to the social or the economic environment they inhabit. We also discuss the implications of this view of corruption for anti-corruption policies.

Keywords

political corruption, political participation in low income countries, public allocation of resources, democratic institutions, gender preferences, determinants of political behavior, electoral competition, politician's identity

JEL classification: O12, O20, H30

1. Introduction

A growing body of evidence suggests that corruption in low income countries is a significant constraint on economic performance (see, for instance, Mauro, 1995 and Treisman, 2000).[1] The most common definition of corruption in the economics literature is the misuse of public office for private gain. While private gain is typically interpreted in terms of monetary benefit, it can potentially include non-monetary benefits such as improved chances of reelection and helping friends or members of their social or ethnic networks obtain public resources. The usual interpretation of misuse is the use of office for illegal purposes, but it is occasionally construed more broadly as the misallocation of public resources in ways that enhance the official's private returns.

Recent years have also seen an explosion of empirical research on corruption measurement. This research, which has developed and used both subjective indices which are based on perceptions of corruption and objective measures of either illegal activity by politicians or the extent of theft of public resources,[2] typically finds a relatively high incidence of corruption in low income countries (Svensson, 2005).

A common explanation for this observation is that corruption is a social norm/habit that is much more pervasive in low income countries. That is, on average citizens in low income countries are relatively more willing to condone corruption and less likely to want to use their electoral power to vote out the corrupt. The presumption is that this has, in turn, reduced economic growth in these countries. Fisman and Miguel (2006) use data on diplomatic parking ticket violations in New York city to suggest that highly corrupt countries are, on average, countries with a widespread acceptance of corrupt practices. They exploit the fact that diplomatic immunity in New York city meant essentially zero legal enforcement of diplomatic parking violations to show that the incidence of parking violations by diplomats from a country is strongly positively correlated with other country corruption measures. This relationship is robust to conditioning on region fixed effects, country income, and a wide range of other controls (including government employee salary measures). In a similar vein, Barr and Serra (2006), in an experiment at Oxford University, show that a participant's willingness to offer bribes in a laboratory setting is correlated with the corruption record in his/her home country. Both papers interpret their findings as suggesting that social norms are important in explaining the incidence of corruption. This would suggest that corruption would require a change in ideology rather than a change in institutions or economic conditions.[3]

---

[1] Mauro (1995) estimates a one standard deviation reduction in corruption would raise investment rates by almost 5 percentage points, and annual GDP growth by half a percentage point. Some of the likely channels of influence include (i) corruption, by acting as an additional tax, may lower individual work incentives, and (ii) rent seeking which leads to a misallocation of labor.

[2] The most well-known and widely-used indices from Transparency International and the World Bank mix both types, but are dominated by expert surveys.

[3] However, the findings of both papers remain consistent with an alternative explanation. That is, corruption in a low income country may be caused by a small set of opportunistic individuals who are able to succeed in

The notion that a high incidence of corruption in a society reflects, in part, social acceptance of corrupt practices (and individuals) has been influential in policy circles. The US government and the World Bank, for instance, are strong proponents of the view that support for development aid should be made conditional on the extent to which a country succeeds in reducing corruption.[4] This view would seem to assume that a country's ability to reduce corruption is independent of its economic status (Pande, 2006).

This view stands in contrast to the idea that corrupt behavior is a choice made by specific individuals who make or implement policies and is at least partly a rational response to the structure of the political or economic environment. In this environment citizens' choice to vote for the corrupt may reflect the economic constraints they face rather than a willingness to condone corruption. In this chapter we develop this approach. Building on the large and growing empirical literature on the political behavior of individuals in low income countries we try to understand corruption through the lens of political economy – particularly in terms of the political and economic differences between rich and poor countries. Individual political behavior and political outcomes in any society are constrained by its political institutions (Persson and Tabellini, 2003).[5] Political institutions provide the structure for collective decision-making, and define the context for resource redistribution and public good provision by governments. An important potential constraint on corruption is the democratic political process which gives voters the opportunity to dismiss corrupt politicians and to support laws that constrain corruption.

Our focus is on the political behavior of individuals exposed to democratic political institutions and its implications for corruption. We review the existing literature on the determinants of individual political behavior to ask whether we can understand the choice of political actors to be corrupt and, importantly, of other individuals to permit it, as a rational response to the social or the economic environment they inhabit.

We argue that many factors that affect the extent of corruption vary with economic development. These include the personal motivation of those who enter politics and their subsequent remuneration, the opportunities for corruption, the relative strength of institutions to identify and prevent corruption, the extent to which bureaucrats are accountable to elected officials, and how individuals trade-off politician quality against the policies and transfers associated with different politicians. For instance, a higher incidence of poverty in a country, combined with imperfect credit markets, may create popular pressure to allocate resources through the political process. If this, in turn,

the existing politico-economic system and are also the ones able to get coveted diplomatic jobs in New York and/or send their family members to prestigious universities abroad.

[4] Since 2005 concerns of corruption have caused the World Bank to delay a 800 million dollar loan for health related services to India, cut debt relief to the Republic of Congo Brazzaville, suspend 261 million dollars of aid to Kenya and withhold 124 million dollars of disbursement to Chad.

[5] In this chapter we do not examine the direct implications of institutional form for political corruption (for a more general discussion of how institutional form affects policy outcomes see, for instance, Acemoglu, Johnson, and Robinson, 2005 and Pande and Udry, 2005).

is accompanied by increased regulation of the allocation process then opportunities for corruption may increase. In addition, if voters have preferences over both politician honesty and his/her ability to target resources towards their group then increased resource allocation through the political process may reduce the extent to which the electoral process constrains corruption.

In Section 2 we describe the relevant political economy literature, and identify the likely links between the political process and politician corruption. In Section 3 we identify how the economic organization of low income countries may affect the allocation of political power, and its implications for the incidence of corruption. Section 4 concludes.

2. Politician's identity and political corruption

In what ways can an individual in a position of political power exploit that position to further his private ends, and what constrains his actions?

First, he may steal resources, either by directly plundering public coffers or by exploiting his position as a regulator of economic activities and taking bribes (Gehlbach and Sonin, 2004). The classic example of this is the use of red tape, i.e. complex rules and regulations associated with transferring resources to particular individuals that gives the political actor a pretext to extract bribes (Banerjee, 1997). While the literature has typically focused on bureaucratic red tape, evidence suggests that in many countries politicians deal directly with situations involving red tape.

Second, a politician may engage in corruption of the electoral process by vote buying or, more indirectly, by exploiting her control over the media and limiting the information available to citizens. For instance, Besley and Prat (2006) use data from 90 countries in 1999 to show that corruption is positively correlated with political longevity, and press freedom is negatively correlated with political longevity. Further, the share of state ownership of newspapers is positively correlated with corruption, negatively correlated with print freedom and positively correlated with political longevity.

Finally, a politician may misallocate public resources by, for instance, choosing to target resources towards specific groups of citizens, such as her own ethnic group. Whether such pork barrel politics constitutes illegal practice varies across countries and contexts.

How does the political process potentially constrain opportunistic behavior by elected officials?

The most immediate answer, and the one explicitly related to the political system, is by voting the corrupt out of office. Ferraz and Finan (2006) provide evidence of this mechanism at work in Brazil. Starting in April 2003, the federal government in Brazil began to randomly audit municipal governments for the misappropriation of federal funds, and any other irregularity associated with a federally-sponsored project or public work. To promote transparency, the results of these audits were disseminated publicly to both the municipality and general media. The order in which municipalities were audited was determined by a lottery. Ferraz and Finan (2006) exploit the resulting random variation in whether a municipal government was audited before or after the municipal election to estimate the effect of the disclosure of local government corruption on the reelection success of incumbent mayors in municipal elections. They find that disclosure of audit results had a significant impact on the reelection rates of mayors found to be corrupt.[6]

Other constraints on political corruption may involve prosecution of corrupt officials and social sanctions such as editorials in newspapers. It is very likely that the outcome of these processes, such as an official's legal record, also affect citizens' voting behavior.

The ways in which these constraints are likely to affect politician behavior while in office depends on how we understand their motivations. If electoral gains alone motivate politicians' behavior and politicians commit absolutely to policies prior to the election, then in a democratic setting the incidence of political corruption in a society will reflect voters' willingness to condone such behavior, not politicians' willingness or ability to engage in corrupt behavior (Downs, 1957). That is, electoral competition should cause candidates to implement the policies preferred by the median voter. If citizens oppose corrupt practices, and this is reflected in their voting decisions, then as long as voters observe politicians' activities politicians will choose not to engage in corrupt activities.

However, the Downsian assumption that candidate behavior is purely office-motivated is both theoretically and empirically unsatisfactory. Since citizens are presumed to have policy preferences it is unclear why candidates (who are also citizens) will not. Most existing evidence suggests systematic differences in the policy preferences espoused by different parties (see, for instance, Lee, Moretti, and Butler, 2004).

An alternative view of politicians, and one in which a politician's identity (and policy preferences) matters, is provided by the citizen candidate approach to political selection (Besley and Coate, 1997 and Osborne and Slivinski, 1996). This approach assumes that candidates have no flexibility in platform selection – their policy positions reflect their personal policy preferences. That is, once elected, a candidate has no incentive to implement his announced platform of policies if it diverges from his preferred policies. The assumption is strong but has proven useful in understanding why candidate characteristics, such as party identity, ethnic identity and gender, tend to predict policy outcomes.

A growing body of evidence suggests that, as predicted by the citizen candidate model, the identity of elected representatives can help explain the subsequent choice of public policies by these representatives, and often overall economic performance. Jones and Olken (2005), for instance, exploit unexpected deaths of national leaders in office to isolate exogenous variation in leader identity. They ask whether leader identity matters and find that unexpected changes in the identity of a leader are associated with changes in growth outcomes – a one standard deviation increase in leader quality is associated with a growth change of 1.5% points per year. Similarly, Besley, Persson, and

---

[6] A one standard deviation increase in reported corruption reduced the incumbent's likelihood of reelection by 25 percent.

Sturm (2006) find evidence that individual governor identity is a significant determinant of a US state's economic performance.[7]

How a candidate's policy preferences affect her electability and subsequent performance also has implications for the likelihood of political corruption.[8] If politicians differ in their honesty then in a Downsian model where citizens have a preference for honest politicians the least corrupt politician should be elected (since other policy preferences of the politician are irrelevant for her performance).

In contrast, in a citizen candidate model voters care about both the honesty of a politician and his/her policy preferences. Myerson (1993) shows that if voters choose candidates on the basis of candidate policy preferences then a coordination failure across voters may imply that the least corrupt candidate is not selected. Voters continue to vote for the relatively corrupt candidate as they are concerned that if they vote differently then the least preferred candidate may win. This result relies on citizens being strategic in their voting decisions. Banerjee and Pande (2006) consider the case of sincere voting by citizens, and demonstrate that with multi-dimensional preferences the least corrupt candidate may not be selected if his/her policy preferences do not match those of the majority population group. For instance, politicians belonging to historically socio-economically disadvantaged groups are likely to favor transfers to the poor but, being poor themselves, are also more likely to use office to enrich themselves (especially if politician salaries are low). If the intensity of citizens' policy preferences on dimensions such as redistribution differs across rich and poor countries then citizens' trade-off between politicians' policy preferences and corruption records is also likely to vary with economic development.

Caselli and Morelli (2004) consider a citizen candidate model of politics and analyze the factors which affect the supply of bad politicians in situations characterized by incomplete information. In our context bad politicians can be interpreted as politicians who are relatively more corrupt, and no better than honest politicians on other dimensions. They suggest two reasons why bad politicians, in general, will have greater incentives to pursue elective office. First, the opportunity cost of being in politics is likely to be lower for bad politicians (since their market wages will be lower than those of honest politicians). Second, a greater willingness to misuse their office implies that bad politicians reap higher returns from holding office.

Caselli and Morelli (2004) also demonstrate that political outcomes may be characterized by multiple equilibria – countries can find themselves stuck in bad equilibria such that honest citizens avoid public office because other honest citizens do so too. Multiple equilibria may arise if an elected representative's productivity depends on that of other elected representatives (this may be particularly important if decision-making is often

---

[7] Other papers that provide evidence on the importance of a politician's identity for policy outcomes include Lee, Moretti, and Butler (2004) and Levitt (1996) for the US and Pande (2003) and Chattopadhyay and Duflo (2004a) for India.

[8] A politician's overall quality and corruptness are often assumed to be negatively correlated. However, it remains possible that more corrupt individuals are also more effective at getting things done.

done within committees). Another cause of multiplicity is the existence of ego rents, that is politicians care about how politics is perceived by citizens. Honest politicians get less ego rents, and are less likely to enter, if politics is perceived as full of crooks. Multiplicity of equilibria is also likely if politicians' after-office earnings opportunities depend on the average quality of the political class (this, of course, relies on voters' being able to observe quality. Otherwise low quality candidates will have an incentive to enter even if all other candidates are high quality).

3. The political organization of low income countries and its consequences for corruption

3.1. The economic environment and politics

An important feature of the process of development is increased industrialization and a greater reliance on markets for economic transactions. Relative to rich countries, a high fraction of the population in low income countries is rural and dependent on agriculture for its livelihood. In addition, low income countries in general, and Subsaharan Africa in particular, are characterized by high levels of ethnic diversity.[9] Limited factor mobility in poor countries implies that initial asset ownership is a significant determinant of an individual's lifetime wealth, and imperfect credit and insurance markets increase credit constraints at the individual level. In addition, a larger fraction of economic activity in these countries occurs in non-market settings through networks, particularly ethnic ones.[10] Many low income countries are also post-colonial states. Using electoral data from 34 African countries between 1980 and 2000, Mozaffar, Scarritt, and Galaich (2003) argue that colonial institutions, and in particular the policy of divide and rule, provided the initial incentives for politicizing ethnic divisions and the rise of ethnic party competition. More generally, colonization in many countries increased the economic and political organization along ethnic lines and this is reflected in the present day political salience of ethnicity in these countries.

In this section we argue that these facts have a number of implications for the political organization of low income countries.

---

[9] The average country has five ethnic groups larger than 1 percent of the population. In roughly 70 percent of the countries a single ethnic group forms a population majority. Subsaharan Africa is the main exception to the rule (Fearon, 2003). According to a commonly used ethnic diversity measure printed in the 1964 Atlas Narodov Mira (Atlas of Peoples of the World), fourteen out of the fifteen most ethnically heterogeneous societies in the world are in Africa; eight countries classified as high-income-countries by the World Bank Development Report are among the most ethnically homogeneous and no rich countries are among the top-15 most ethnically diverse countries.

[10] Typically, membership of an ethnic group is usually defined by a descent rule, where members of a typical ethnic group share some but not necessarily all of a common language, religion, customs, sense of a homeland, and relatively dense social networks (Fearon, 2003).

Politicians in low income countries are typically richer than the average citizen. Meyer (1969) provides evidence that in the two decades after Independence Indian politics was dominated by rich landowners, and Besley, Pande, and Rao (2005b) show that this is still true of rural politics in India – relative to other villagers, politicians in South Indian villages own significantly more land. Baland and Robinson (2005) show that prior to the introduction of the secret ballot in 1957 this was also true in Chile.

Other correlates of economic wealth have also been shown to be important for entry in politics and selection to political office. For Uttar Pradesh, India's most populous state, Banerjee and Pande (2006) find evidence of increased entry by politicians from wealthier backgrounds and by businessmen and contractors (they compare the backgrounds of elected politicians in 1969, 1980 and 1996). For South East Asia, as early as the 1970s, Scott noted the rise of business classes in politics. Laothamatos (1988) provides evidence that in Thailand 'business tycoons' have dominated politics ever since democratic elections became widespread in the late 1970s. Shatkin (2004) argues that, in Thailand and Philippines, the increasing entry of businessmen in local and national politics is related to increased affluence of the economy and greater state investment in sectors such as construction.[11]

The rise of business interests in the politics of low income countries has often been said to resemble 19th-century United States, which had a high representation of the business elite among urban mayors and aldermen (see, for instance, Dahl, 1961; Kipp, 1977) and some railroad presidents directly entered politics (Crandall, 1950).

The relative affluence of politicians that occurred in urban politics of the United States in the 19th century, of course, is also true of rich countries today. It is usually explained by the fact that entering and winning elections in any country requires substantial financial resources. It may also reflect the relatively high returns to a political career.[12] That said, there are important reasons why the economic organization of low income countries may increase the political advantage enjoyed by the elite in these countries.

Factor market imperfections in poor countries often translate into a relatively unequal distribution of land wherein a small fraction of the rural population controls a large share of total land. One consequence is the widespread use of wage contracts whereby the landless poor work for landowners. In environments where agricultural production exhibits significant variation in output, these contracts often take the form of efficiency

---

[11] He provides a case-study of the province Chonburi in the Eastern Seaboard in Thailand which benefitted from large-scale state investment in the late 1980s and 1990s. Between 1980 and 2000 manufacturing sector jobs grew from 31,000 to 121,000. Shatkin argues that this spurt in economic activity led to the rise of a local political boss, Somchai Khunpleum, who both dominates political activity in the Eastern Seaboard and heads a business empire which includes interests in mining, real estate, retail, hotel, ports, transportation, shipping and construction.

[12] Daniel Diermeier and Merlo (2005), for instance, use data from United States to show that congressional experience significantly increases post-congressional wages, both in the private and public sectors. They also find that the non-pecuniary rewards from being in Congress are rather large (especially in the Senate). These rewards may be generated by the utility politicians derive from affecting policy outcomes, or from additional perks and benefits enjoyed by the members of Congress.

wages (Bardhan and Udry, 1999). Baland and Robinson (2005) develop a model to show that the resulting economic rents in the wage contracts may provide landowners with a source of political power over workers. In particular, when the workers receive rents employers can control the political behavior of their workers by threatening to withdraw these rents.

At the individual level, imperfect credit and insurance markets in low income countries imply that social networks, especially ethnic networks, are an important source of insurance for network members (Lucas and Stark, 1985). Ferrara (2002), for instance, reports that in production cooperatives in the informal settlements of Nairobi, members who share the same ethnicity as the chairperson were 20 to 25 percentage points more likely to borrow from the group or from other members. This means that network members with greater access to resources or less volatile incomes are particularly important members of the network. Like the landlords in Baland and Robinson (2005), these individuals can potentially leverage their economic power within the network to obtain political support from other network members. So networks become a means through which political activity is organized. Again, there are similarities to the dominance of political machines in many US cities in the late 19th and early 20th century. These machines were typified by the existence of a political boss, a patronage hierarchy and vote buying. Immigrants in these cities provided political support to other members of their ethnic group in return for help in finding jobs and insurance. Scott (1969) provides evidence of the emergence of ethnicity based political networks, which look very similar to these urban political machines, in a number of newly independent low income countries. He describes this as exemplifying patron client relations where "an individual of higher socio-economic status (patron) uses his own influence and resources to provide protection or benefits, or both, for a person of lower status who, for his part, reciprocates by offering general support and assistance" (Scott, 1972). On a related note Horowitz (1985) documents the rise of ethnic parties in a number of low income countries, and argues that the organization of political competition along ethnic lines is significantly more pronounced in low income countries.[13]

In addition to affecting the political entry and selection process, factor market imperfections in low income countries may also affect the scope of public policy. For instance, Banerjee (1997) suggests that high levels of poverty combined with imperfect credit markets will increase the demand for political allocation of resources. Along similar lines Johnson and Mitton (2006) suggest that the economic organization of low income countries also implies that they are more likely to use public policy to regulate economic activity, for instance by imposing capital controls.[14] Limited labor mobility

---

[13] In the political science literature an ethnic party is typically seen as a "party that overtly represents itself to the voters as the champion of the interests of one ethnic group or a set of groups to the exclusion of another or others, and makes such a representation central to its mobilizing strategy" (Chandra, 2004).

[14] Until the late 1970s, capital controls were widely used to restrict the free flow of finance in low income countries. This was seen as an effective way of stabilizing the economy if it had faced major financial crisis and also as a means of preventing speculative attacks.

in low income countries may also affect the scope of public policy – free trade, for instance, may be associated with more negative distributional consequences (Topalova, 2005).

A further factor which may affect the political organization of low income countries differentially is gender discrimination. Women are significantly less likely than men to enter politics in both high and low income countries.[15] However, to the extent gender inequality is often greater among the poor, both within and across countries we may expect the barriers faced by women seeking access to politics to be particularly high in the rural areas of low income countries. Chattopadhyay and Duflo (2004b) examine mandated political representation for women in Indian villages, and report that women only stand for election in jurisdictions reserved for them. In Section 3.3.2 we describe how such discrimination appears to have translated into lower female participation in politics.

3.2. Implications for opportunities for corruption

3.2.1. Power and networks

The nature of land relations, and the widespread existence of a network economy, lead to a greater inter-linkage of economic and political relations in low income countries. In such a setting a relatively corrupt politician who controls a large network of voters may be more likely to both succeed electorally and to remain in power. For US cities Menes (2001) describes the widespread misuse of political power for personal gain (both electoral and monetary) by the bosses of urban political machines. Baland and Robinson (2005) suggest that landowners in Chile misused their economic leverage over laborers to force them to vote in line with landowner interests. They examine how political outcomes in rural areas of Chile were affected by the introduction of the secret ballot. The introduction of the secret ballot, which limited the extent to which landlords could monitor the political behavior of workers, was associated with a significant reduction in the electoral support for the right-wing parties. The right-wing parties in Chile had traditionally favored the economic interests of landlords. It may also be the case that the inter-linkage of economic and political relations affords politicians greater opportunities for private gain. Goldstein and Udry (2005) describe how leaders in Ghanaian villages exploit their political power for economic purposes. In these villages land is held by the *abusua*, which is defined by matrilineal descent, on the authority of the paramount chief (or *stool*). The leadership of the matrilineage is locally-based and is responsible for allocating use rights within a village to members of the matrilineage. Land allocation is, thus, a political process that operates at the level of the local matrilineage. Goldstein and

---

[15] While measures to enforce women's access to political positions through quotas have been instituted in 81 countries, women constitute just 15.9 percent of the members of lower and upper houses of parliaments (United Nations, 2005).

Udry (2005) show that individuals in a position of political power enjoy more secure property rights on their land, and this translates into greater agricultural profits. They find that this is because the land of political leaders is less likely to be redistributed to meet the needs of villagers.

3.2.2. Ethnicity and gender

A number of papers suggest that ethnic diversity of low income countries is also an important predictor of corruption levels. Easterly and Levine (1997) use cross-country data to suggest that an important channel through which ethnic diversity reduces growth is increased corruption. More micro-evidence is provided by Olken (2006). He uses data from the Indonesian redistribution program to show that more ethnically fragmented villages lose more rice to corruption.

Chandra's (2004) analysis of ethnic politics in India suggests that the scope of public policy can affect the political salience of ethnicity. She argues that patronage politics, typified by the use of affirmative action policies in favor of low castes in India, has made ethnicity relevant for the allocation of state resources. If identity-based targeting of resources is also a form of politics which are more susceptible to corruption, or to regulation as discussed below, then we may expect ethnification of politics, patronage politics and increased corruption to be positively correlated.

Banerjee and Pande (2006) identify a different channel through which greater organization of political competition along ethnic lines can increase political corruption. In a world with incomplete policy commitment, if individuals care about both the ethnic identity of a candidate and her corruption record, then increased polarization of voters' ethnic preferences can increase corruption. The reason is that more extreme ethnic candidates are more likely to succeed, and this will tend to favor parties with access to such candidates, even if they are, on average, of lower quality. Banerjee and Pande (2006) provide supportive evidence from India's most populous state, Uttar Pradesh. This state has both seen a significant rise in ethnic politics and increased political corruption, both as measured by voter perceptions of candidates and candidates' criminal records.

While low income countries are characterized by relatively high levels of political competition along ethnic lines, political representation afforded to women in these countries remains low. Azfar et al. (2001) and Dollar, Fisman, and Gatti (1999) provide cross-country evidence that female under-representation in politics is correlated with higher levels of corruption. Further evidence from India is provided by Duflo and Topalova (2004a). They analyze a village-level data set from India with both objective and subjective information about women's actions as policymakers. The objective data comes from technical audits of the number and quality of public goods available in the villages, and it shows that women provide more public goods and at better quality than men do. Moreover, on average, women take significantly fewer bribes than men. In addition, villagers are 1.5 percentage points less likely to pay bribes for obtaining service or to the police when the village leader is a woman.[16]

3.2.3. Public allocation of resources and regulation

A third set of reasons for extended opportunities for corruption relates to the type of public goods that are needed in low income countries. If officials' ability to extract bribes, and their amount, varies with the type of public good, then differences in the types of public goods being provided across high and low income countries may be associated with differences in the extent of corruption.

Banerjee (1997) develops a model of red tape and corruption in low income countries. He argues that welfare-minded governments in low income countries will seek to provide public goods to the most needy. They will introduce regulation to improve resource allocation to the poor, but elected officials can exploit these regulations to extract resources from the public while ensuring that they are not caught by higher authorities for resource misallocation. Alternatively, regulation can be designed and used as red tape, i.e. non-monetary socially unproductive activities which may be used to ration public goods, or to extract resources from the public. Banerjee (1997) suggests that if the economic or political characteristics of low income countries lend themselves to greater regulation and regulation provides opportunities for corruption then this suggests one reason for higher corruption in poor countries.

In a recent paper, Bertrand et al. (2006) provide evidence of the misuse of regulation by corrupt officials. They examine corruption in the driving license process in India. To do so they follow a sample of 822 applicants through the process of obtaining a driver's license in New Delhi, India. Participants were randomly assigned to one of three groups: bonus, lesson, and comparison groups. Participants in the bonus group were offered a financial reward if they could obtain their license fast; participants in the lesson group were offered free driving lessons. They find that regulations associated with obtaining a driving license are exploited for rent-seeking – members of the bonus group obtained a driving license 40% faster and at a 20% higher rate. They also provide evidence that the driving test is used *not* to screen unsafe from safe drivers, but rather that, irrespective of their ability to drive, officials arbitrarily fail drivers at a high rate. To overcome this, individuals pay informal agents to bribe the bureaucrat and avoid taking the exam altogether. Their results suggest that bureaucrats raise red tape to extract bribes and that this corruption undermines the very purpose of regulation.

In a related empirical study Hunt (2006) uses cross-country and Peruvian data to document the fact that for individuals in low-income countries with limited access to

---

[16] Why women are less corrupt than men has received limited attention in the literature. As Azfar et al. (2001) state, 'gender differences we observe may be attributable to socialization, or to differences in access to networks of corruption, or in knowledge of how to engage in corrupt practices, or to other factors.' It may also be the case that women tend not to work in sectors such as road contracting or business, and therefore derive less rents from politics.

insurance, negative income or health shocks, increase an individual's demand for public services and her propensity to bribe certain officials in order to use them, possibly
because victims are desperate, vulnerable, or demanding services particularly prone to
corruption.

High returns to political connections and strong incentives for businessmen to enter
politics in low income countries may also be a consequence of the possibility of misuse
of regulations.

Such returns are not limited to poor countries – Jayachandran (2006), for instance,
exploits the unanticipated resignation of Senator Jeffords from the Republican party
in the US to identify corporate returns to political connections and Faccio (2006) uses
data from 47 countries to show that corporate political connections are relatively widespread – there is at least one connected firm in 35 of the 47 countries she considers.
However, the presumption in the literature seems to be that the level of corruption associated with political connections is higher in low income countries. Faccio (2006) for
instance shows a strong correlation between subjective measures of corruption and the
extent of political connections in the country.

Again, this may be explained by the fact that poor countries tend to be more regulated,
and more regulations raise the returns to exploiting these connections for economic
gain. That is, if, on average, exploiting economic regulations in low income countries
provides greater rents for, say, businessmen then, relative to their counterparts in richer
countries, these individuals may be more likely to enter politics. Another possibility
is that the cost of using political connections in a highly networked economy may be
relatively low.

Some evidence in support of this view comes from Gehlbach and Sonin (2004). They
argue that the economic organization of low income and transition economies can both
explain the increased entry into politics by those with business interests and the extent
of political corruption. Specifically, they interpret the entry of economic elites, such
as businessmen, for political office as an alternative to lobbying for influence. They
illustrate their argument by the experience of a recent gubernatorial election in a large
Siberian region dominated by two industrial interests, with the winner of the election
the former general director of one of the two firms. This, they argue, exemplifies a more
general trend in Russian politics. It is also likely that the entry of such individuals is to
be accompanied by a misallocation of resources in favor of politician owned firms.

Johnson and Mitton (2006) examine the use of capital controls by Malaysian politicians to support the financing of particular firms. They label as 'connected' firms whose
officers or major shareholders have close relationships with key government officials
(primarily Mahathir, Daim, and Anwar). If political connections, combined with capital controls, are a source of corruption then politically connected individuals and firms
should suffer more when a macroeconomic shock reduces the government's ability to
provide privileges and subsidies, and benefit more when the imposition of capital controls allows a higher level of privileges. Johnson and Mitton (2006) show that after
capital controls were reimposed in Malaysia in September 1998, of the estimated five

billion dollar gain in market value for firms connected to Prime Minister Mahathir, about 32% can be attributed to the increase in the value of their connections.

In addition to Johnson and Mitton (2006), a number of other recent papers suggest significant returns to political connections in developing countries. Khwaja and Mian (2005), for instance, estimate that in Pakistan politically connected firms borrow 45 percent more and have 50 percent higher default rates. They estimate the economy wide annual costs of the rents identified as 0.3–1.9 percent of GDP. Fisman (2001) concludes that in Indonesia a sizeable percentage of the value of well-connected firms comes from political connections. He compares returns across firms with differing degrees of political exposure at the time of rumors of the Indonesian President Suharto's worsening health. Around that time, stock prices of firms closely connected with Suharto dropped more than the prices of less well connected firms, and the stock price reactions were more severe when the news was more negative.

3.2.4. Information

Another source of market incompleteness which is likely to contribute to corruption is insufficient information. If individuals in low income countries are less likely to have access to the media or other sources of information about politician quality/performance, or are less educated, then their ability to identify and electorally punish corrupt politicians will also be more limited. A number of recent papers suggest that information problems may indeed be an important reason for the persistence of corruption. Ferraz and Finan (2006), for instance, find that electoral punishment for corruption in Brazilian municipalities is positively correlated with the extent of information provision in the municipality (on this, also see Section 2). Along similar lines, Reinikka and Svensson (2004) compare the capture of public funds in schools in Uganda with and without access to newspapers before and after a large anti-corruption campaign. Schools with newspaper access received, on average, 13 percent more of their entitlement.

3.3. Implications for willingness to tolerate corruption

How does the economic, ethnic and gender identity of a citizen in low income countries affect her exposure to corruption and her willingness to tolerate it?

3.3.1.   Redistributive preferences

The average individual in a low income country is poorer and less educated than her counterpart in a rich country, and political economy models suggest that this should affect her demand for income redistribution (see, for instance, Meltzer and Richard, 1981 and Roberts, 1977) and also for public goods.[17]

---

[17] Specifically, if individual utility is increasing in income then at the aggregate level the demand for income redistribution should be increasing in the gap between the median and mean income – arguably, this gap,

Unfortunately, for low income countries, there are very few micro-data based studies which examine how income and education affect redistributive preferences.[18] In Table 1 we provide some suggestive evidence using data from World Values Surveys. The reported regressions rely on within-country variation in individual characteristics. In line with the existing literature, we observe that richer individuals are, on average, less likely to favor the political left or equality of incomes. In contrast, the correlation between redistributive preferences and education is insignificant. We do not observe any significant differences in redistributive preferences across rich and poor countries. However, there is a growing literature in development economics that examines how the demand for public goods varies with economic development. Foster and Rosenzweig (1996), for instance, use the green revolution in India as a partially exogenous source of increase in returns to education to estimate how expected growth and higher returns to schooling affects the demand for education. Compared to average growth areas, the enrollment rates of children of farmers in areas with yield growth rates one standard deviation above the mean are 16 percentage points higher.[19] In addition, Foster and Rosenzweig (2004b) find this translated into increased provision of schools, suggesting that the demand for some public goods (such as school infrastructure) is potentially increasing in income.

Another way of examining how individual wealth affects political preferences is by studying the correlation between the population shares of different economic groups and public good outcomes. Land ownership is a good proxy for household wealth in the rural areas of low income countries. Foster and Rosenzweig (2004a) exploit time-series variation in the introduction of local elected governments across Indian states and show that the allocation of public goods across villages varied with the population shares of landed and landless households.

Another dimension of individual identity which may be important in shaping redistributive and public good preferences is ethnicity. A number of recent papers suggest that there is a greater tendency for the demand for public goods in low income countries to be organized along ethnic lines, either because ethnicity defines which groups are historically disadvantaged or because individuals of the same ethnicity tend to live in the same areas. Geographic proximity would be important if preferences for public goods may vary geographically, or if it is easier to organize public action among individuals

---

and therefore the demand for income redistribution, is higher in poorer countries. How the differences in the income distribution across rich and poor countries should affect the demand for public goods is, theoretically, less clear.

[18] Bratton et al. (2005) use data from the Afrobarometer surveys to examine support for liberalizing economic reforms (an additive index of support for policies such as user free (e.g. for schooling), market pricing for consumer goods, privatization and retrenchment of civil service jobs) and find that support for the reforms is increasing in income for every survey country, and in a regression on the full sample, it increases with both education and income.

[19] Foster and Rosenzweig (2004b) find that increased schooling attainment does not improve the productivity of workers engaged exclusively in menial tasks. Increases in schooling among landed households goes hand in hand with reduced schooling in landless households. The authors interpret this as suggestive of substitution of child labor from landless households.

Table 1

Interest in government and redistributive preferences: World Values Survey

	Income equality	Government does too little	Left	Discuss politics	Importance of politics	Interest in politics
	(1)	(2)	(3)	(4)	(5)	(6)
Female	0.0137	0.0086	-0.0281***	-0.0651***	-0.0445***	-0.1197***
	(0.0030)***	(0.0017)***	(0.0062)	(0.0054)	(0.0059)	(0.0096)
Female* Low income country	-0.0129	-0.0108	0.0037	-0.0175*	-0.0436***	0.0035
	(0.0067)*	(0.0056)*	(0.0092)	(0.0099)	(0.0121)	(0.0178)
Income below 50th decile	0.0804***	0.0039	0.0164***	-0.0275***	0.0140	-0.0518***
	(0.0085)	(0.0053)	(0.0060)	(0.0052)	(0.0155)	(0.0103)
Income below 50th decile* Low income country	-0.0147	0.0120	-0.0045	-0.0046	-0.0244	0.0389*
	(0.0212)	(0.0134)	(0.0081)	(0.0126)	(0.0206)	(0.0209)
Primary education or less	0.0263	-0.0011	-0.0047	-0.1006***	-0.2120***	-0.2034***
	(0.0249)	(0.0344)	(0.0128)	(0.0159)	(0.0383)	(0.0395)
Primary education* Low income country	0.0213	-0.0585	0.0083	0.0465**	0.1590***	0.0843
	(0.0266)	(0.0469)	(0.0288)	(0.0195)	(0.0452)	(0.0706)
Fixed effect	Country	Country	Country	Country	Country	Country
N	142923	142923	142923	142923	142923	142923
R-squared	0.09	0.58	0.04	0.06	0.09	0.13

Notes: 1. Standard errors, clustered by country, in parentheses.

2. Data are from World Values Surveys (see Data Appendix for more details). *Left* is a measure of political ideology on a scale from left to right, where 1 = completely to the left, 10 = completely to the right. We define *Left* as a dummy variable = 1 if ideology is from 1 to 3. *Importance of politics*: How important is politics in your life? Scale from 1 to 3. *Interest in politics*: How interested would you say you are in politics? Scale from 1 to 4: 1 = very interested, 2 = somewhat interested, 3 = not very interested, 4 = not at all interested.

3. Regressions also include age dummy and its interaction with low income, dummies for being married, divorced, separated and widowed, and year and country fixed effects.

*Significant at 10%. **Significant at 5%. ***Significant at 1%.

who live nearby. It is also the case that infrastructure investments are place-specific. Bates (1974) has, in the context of Africa, stressed the role of geography in making ethnic identity an important predictor of observed public good preferences. He argues that the geographic clustering of members of an ethnic group causes the struggle for access to at least some goods to be organized on an ethnic basis. A different channel is suggested by Pande (2003). She suggests that voters belonging to minority ethnic groups will favor targeting on ethnic lines over more general income redistribution as they receive a higher per capita transfer in the former case.

A few recent papers seek to provide direct evidence on the extent of ethnic preferences, i.e. individuals' attributing positive utility to the well being of members of their own group, and negative utility to that of members of other groups. Miguel and Gugerty (2005) studies neighboring areas along the Tanzanian–Kenyan border and argues that processes of political socialization affects the salience of ethnic identity. Western areas of Kenya and Tanzania were similar along key dimensions in the 1960s. However, after independence Tanzania adopted arguably the most serious nation-building program in sub-Saharan Africa. This, he argues, has implied a much more limited role for ethnicity in predicting preferences in Tanzania than in Kenya.

James Habyarimana, Mccartan Humphreys, and Weinstein (2006) approach this question in a different way. They run a series of experimental games in order to examine the importance of ethnicity in shaping preferences. Their sample consists of 300 subjects from adjacent neighborhoods in Kampala, Uganda that combined high levels of ethnic diversity with low levels of public goods provision. They do not find any evidence in favor of preference-based explanations – the games suggest that co-ethnics are not more altruistic toward one another nor do they have different preferences over outcomes. They do, however, find evidence that social sanctions are easier to impose on members of one's own ethnic group.

Another set of papers shows that the ethnic identity of leaders predicts policy outcomes, and interpret this as evidence of ethnic policy preferences. Pande (2003), for instance, exploits variation over time and across states in the incidence of mandated political representation for lower castes and tribal groups in India to isolate the effect of a legislator's identity on public policy. She finds that the extent to which state resources are targeted towards lower caste and tribal groups is increasing in the share of low caste legislators in the state assembly. Besley, Pande, and Rao (2004) examine within village allocation of resources, and find that low caste villagers are more likely to receive transfers from the state when the village leader belongs to their caste.

Another important predictor of political behavior is gender. A number of studies suggest that men and women have different preferences – compared to income or assets in the hands of men, income or assets in the hands of women raises spending on education, health, nutrition and other expenditures benefiting women and children (Lundberg, Pollak, and Wales, 1997; Thomas, 1997 and Duflo, 2003). Increasing women's income also leads to higher survival rates for children and larger improvements in child health (Thomas, 1990).

Studies, mainly based on the data for rich countries, suggest significant gender differences in policy preferences with women more likely to support liberal policies, in particular spending on child care and other child related expenses (Lott and Kenny, 1999 and Edlund and Pande, 2002). There is also evidence of a strong time trend in women's political preferences in rich countries. Relative to men, women in these countries have become significantly more left-wing over the last three decades. Edlund and Pande (2002) and Edlund, Haider, and Pande (2005) interpret the growth of the political gender gap as reflecting an increasing divergence in men and women's economic well-being, and trace this divergence to the rise in non-marriage.[20] This trend, however, seems to be largely absent in low income countries. One explanation for this may be that the smaller decline in marriage in low income countries. Other explanations would include greater religiosity, and the fact that lower female labor force participation rates implies that women are less exposed to labor market institutions such as unions which often espouse the cause of increased redistribution.

In a world with incomplete policy commitment differences in the policy preferences of citizens (of the kind outlined above) will translate into differences in the identity of the politicians they prefer (on this, see Section 2). Specifically, it will affect how citizens trade-off a politician's corruption record versus her ability to implement the policy preferences of different ethnic groups (Banerjee and Pande, 2006). This suggests one way in which an individual's redistributive preferences may affect the extent of corruption. The existence of such a channel would, for instance, provide an explicitly political underpinning to the observed negative correlation between ethnic diversity and public good outcomes. For the United States, Alesina, Baqir, and Easterly (1999) show that in more fragmented cities the provision of productive public goods (roads, hospitals, schools, etc.) is lower while the types of expenditures that more closely resembles transfers targeted to ethnic and racial groups are larger. Miguel and Gugerty (2005) exploit historic differences in geographic location of different ethnic groups to show that increased ethnic diversity in a region of Kenya reduced school funding.

It could also explain the fact that political competition is often organized on ethnic lines. Competition along ethnic lines would be accentuated if ethnic coalitions are more stable than coalitions formed along other dimensions, such as class (Esteban and Ray, 2006).

3.3.2. Participation

Another important aspect is political participation. The extent of political participation in a country directly affects its citizens' ability to use the electoral process to punish politician misbehavior. A commonly used measure of citizen participation in politics is voter turnout – i.e. the fraction of eligible voters who show up to vote. The recent

---

[20] Specifically, if men and women only share resources within marriage and men, on average, earn more than women then increasing non-marriage would be associated with the emergence of a political gender gap.

literature on social capital has also emphasized participation in civic and political associations.[21]

There is evidence that since the 1950s turnout has fallen in some rich countries – the extent of this decline varies from slight in some Western European countries to significant in the United States (for evidence on the decline of voter turnout see Miller and Shanks, 1996 for the US and Topf, 1995 for Europe). Putnam (2000) provides evidence of a similar decline in civic mobilization in America since the 1960s and 1970s. This includes declines in attendance at political rallies or speeches, party work and membership in civic organizations. However, Topf (1995) finds that forms of political activism other than voting have increased in Western Europe over the same time period. However, the implications of this decline for the quality of governance remains understudied.

In low income countries, political participation does not appear to have fallen over time. According to Norris (2002), electoral participation in developing countries has steadily increased during the last fifty years, a pattern most evident in Latin America (see IDEA, 1997 and Ochoa, 1987). This pattern holds for both the newer democracies that emerged from the early 1970s onwards, as well as elections held by semi-democracies and by non-democratic regimes.[22]

One possible explanation for the difference in participation trends across rich and poor countries relates to differences in the costs and private benefits of participation.[23] It may also be the case that the cost of corrupting the electoral process by, for instance, buying votes varies with economic development. Below we examine the evidence on how individual characteristics, which are likely to affect the costs and benefits of participation, affect political participation across rich and poor countries and discuss its implications for the incidence of corruption in these countries.

In some rich countries, especially the United States, income and education are positive predictors of turnout – though the correlation appears weak for many Western European countries. Income and education are similarly related to other forms of participation, e.g., volunteering in campaigns, contacting officials, demonstrating/protesting, working with others to solve community problems and attending meetings of a board/organizations regularly (Verba, Scholzman, and Brady, 1995 discuss these findings for the United States and Blais, 2000 for nine middle income countries).[24] Verba, Scholzman, and Brady (1995) embed income and education in a more general model of resources, engagement and political mobilization. They emphasize the importance of

---

[21] A common definition of social capital is "the collective value of all 'social networks' and the inclinations that arise from these networks to do things for each other" (Putnam, 1993).

[22] This evidence is often cited as consistent with modernization theories which argue that the process of economic development induces greater political participation (Norris, 2002).

[23] The *Calculus of Voting* model suggests that in a two candidate election an individual will vote if $pB+d \geqslant c$ where p is the probability that the individual's vote will swing the election; B is the individual's benefit from his preferred candidate winning; d is the individual's benefit from doing his civic duty; and c is the cost of voting.

[24] He uses the Comparative Study of Electoral Systems Survey which includes survey data from nine countries (Australia, Britain, Czech Republic, Israel, Poland, Romania, Spain, Taiwan, the US) in 1996–1997.

having time, money, and the civic skills to participate, and note that, for example, those more likely to acquire civic skills in their workplace are those with higher income and education.

A basic problem with a causal interpretation of these findings remains the fact that a higher income is likely to be correlated with other determinants of political participation. These potentially range from better access to polling booths in richer neighborhoods to greater exposure to political news via the media. Causal interpretations of the correlation between education and propensity to vote face similar problems. To address this problem Milligan, Moretti, and Oreopoulos (2004) use compulsory schooling laws to get exogenous variation in education levels across subsequent cohorts. They find a strong and robust impact of education on participation in US, but not in UK. In a similar vein Dee (2004) uses proximity to 2-year colleges and child labor laws as instruments, and find that education increases probability of voting as well as civic engagement in the US.

Unfortunately, studies which are able to disentangle the causal impact of income and education on participation are absent for low income countries. That said, a number of papers do identify the correlation between individual income and education and political participation. A common finding in this literature is an insignificant correlation of the decision to vote or participate in political events with either education or income. Norris (2002), for instance, looks at data from twenty-two countries and finds that income and education are only significant in roughly half the sample of countries. These are mainly the richer countries. Most micro-studies also find mixed or no evidence in favor of income and education increasing participation in low income countries. Kuenzi and Lambright (2005) use individual-level attitudinal survey data for 10 sub-Saharan countries and find no significant correlation of voting with education or income. Bratton and Logan (2006) consider participation in Zambian data and find insignificant correlations of education with most measures of political participation. Krishna (2002) examines political participation by Indian villagers and finds no effect of wealth on participation, though education positively predicts participation. In Table 2 we provide some evidence using data from World Values Surveys. We estimate individual level regressions where we include country fixed effects. The results suggest that the positive correlation between education and participation is more muted in low income countries.

One possible explanation is if the cost associated with voting (mainly measured as the opportunity cost of time) is increasing in income and education at a relatively high rate in low income countries. The absence of evidence on the relative costs of voting in rich and poor countries (and how that changes along the income distribution), however, limits our ability to judge the worth of this theory.

Another explanation relates to differences in the benefits from voting for poor and less educated individuals in rich and poor countries. Social safety nets in developing countries are far smaller than in developed economies. According to Chetty and Looney (2006) in 1996, the average expenditure on social insurance as a fraction of GDP in countries with below-median per capita income was 6.8 percent while the corresponding figure in above-median countries was 18.5 percent. In the absence of institutionalized

Table 2
Overall political participation and involvement with parties and labor unions

	Political participation (1)	Active party member (2)	Active labor union member (3)	Sign petition (4)	Join boycott (5)	Lawful demonstrat (6)	Unofficial strike (7)
Income below 50th decile	-0.0192 (0.0041)***	-0.0087 (0.0022)***	-0.0057 (0.0025)**	-0.0449 (0.0075)***	-0.0128 (0.0049)**	-0.0193 (0.0055)***	-0.0041 (0.0022)*
Income below 50th decile* Low income country	0.0073 (0.0076)	0.0044 (0.0037)	-0.0001 (0.0053)	-0.0028 (0.0186)	0.0114 (0.0103)	0.0027 (0.0112)	0.0022 (0.0053)
Primary education or less	-0.0983 (0.0126)***	-0.0247 (0.0137)*	-0.0334 (0.0083)***	-0.1390 (0.0164)***	-0.0562 (0.0142)***	-0.0700 (0.0150)***	-0.0276 (0.0123)**
Primary education or less* Low income country	0.0470 (0.0180)**	0.0265 (0.0168)	0.0277 (0.0099)***	0.0999 (0.0286)***	0.0290 (0.0184)	0.0386 (0.0266)	0.0150 (0.0110)
Female	-0.0533 (0.0038)***	-0.0174 (0.0022)***	-0.0177 (0.0026)***	-0.0326 (0.0088)***	-0.0238 (0.0041)***	-0.0651 (0.0064)***	-0.0320 (0.0036)***
Female* Low income country	-0.0087 (0.0073)	-0.0134 (0.0053)**	0.0042 (0.0050)	-0.0069 (0.0127)	-0.0158 (0.0103)	0.0096 (0.0118)	0.0033 (0.0067)
Fixed effect	Country	Country	Country	Country	Country	Country	Country
N	142923	142923	142923	142923	142923	142923	142923
R-squared	0.15	0.03	0.03	0.20	0.04	0.05	0.03

Notes: 1. Standard errors, clustered by country, in parentheses.

2. Political participation is an index, valued between 0 and 1, weighted by answers to several questions about political participation. Active party member is an indicator variable = 1 if respondent is an active member of a political party. Active labor union member is an indicator variable = 1 if respondent is an active member of a labor union. Sign petition is an indicator variable = 1 if respondent has ever signed a petition. Join boycott is an indicator variable = 1 if respondent has ever joined a boycott. Lawful demonstration is an indicator variable = 1 if respondent has ever been involved in a lawful demonstration. Unofficial strike is an indicator variable = 1 if respondent has ever joined an unofficial strike.

3. Regressions also include age dummy and its interaction with low income, dummies for being married, divorced, separated and widowed, and year and country fixed effects.

*Significant at 10%. **Significant at 5%. ***Significant at 1%.

social safety nets the form and extent of redistribution available to individuals is much more likely to vary with changes in the elected government. This provides one argument for why the benefits of political participation may be higher for the poor and less educated in low income countries. Some supportive evidence is offered by Besley, Pande, and Rao (2005a). They examine participation in village meetings in South India and find that members of socially and economically disadvantaged groups, specifically landless and low caste individuals, are both more likely to attend these meetings and be chosen as beneficiaries in villages which have village meetings.

While increased political participation by voters is likely to enhance the electoral punishment for engaging in corrupt behavior, the impact of changes in the mix of who participates is less clear. One may be concerned that the poor and less educated are less able to report corrupt behavior to higher authorities and punish politicians. On the other hand, if they are the main beneficiaries of government programs then they may be better informed of illegal activities undertaken by politicians.

A different approach to identifying the link between voter identity and participation is taken by Banerjee and Iyer (2005) (on this, also see the chapter by Banerjee et al.). They show that public good provision is more limited in areas which under colonial rule were exposed to political structures that created antagonistic classes (landowners and landless). They interpret this as being related to more limited collective action in these areas, and provide suggestive evidence that crime rates in these areas are higher. To the extent citizens' ability to punish corrupt behavior is more limited in situations where participation rates are low, this suggests one channel through which colonial institutions may affect current political outcomes, and the extent of corruption.

Ethnic diversity may also affect the extent of political participation by different groups.[25] For low income countries the existing evidence suggests that increased ethnic diversity lowers participation in community projects and therefore public good provision (see the chapter by Banerjee et al. for further discussion of these issues). For instance, Okten and Osili (2004) use household data from Indonesia and find that ethnic diversity has a negative, significant effect on monetary giving. In addition, the share of ethnic group in community has an insignificant effect on financial contributions by an individual but a positive and significant impact on time contributions. Similarly, for Pakistan Khwaja (2006) finds that 'social' heterogeneity, measured as the fragmentation into different clans, political and religious groups, is negatively associated with project maintenance. Sokoloff and Engerman (2003) explicitly examine political participation

---

[25] For high-income countries, most studies are unable to disentangle whether ethnicity (usually defined as race), over and above socio-economic status, has an independent effect on participation. Verba and Nie (1972), for instance, find that controlling for socio-economic status, blacks in the United States participate as much, maybe more than Anglo-whites. There is, however, some recent evidence that ethnic group size affects participation by members of the ethnic group. Oberholzer-Gee and Waldfogel (2005) use data from the 1994, 1996, 1998 Current Population Surveys and find that for blacks the probability of voting is increasing in the size of their district's black population. They argue that much of this is due to increased group targeting by the media when group size is large.

by members of different social groups in South Indian villages. They find that members of historically disadvantaged lower castes show relatively high levels of political participation. They interpret this as reflecting the fact that, due to affirmative action, members of these groups are the intended beneficiaries of many public programs.

Differential levels of political participation across or within ethnic groups suggest another explanation for the observed positive correlation between ethnic diversity and political corruption. Miguel and Gugerty (2005) suggest that members of a group may be better able to impose social sanctions against members of their own ethnic group and therefore increased ethnic diversity may worsen voters' collective ability to monitor elected officials.

Most low income countries implemented universal franchise at the end of colonization, or when democratic elections were instituted, and the set of countries which explicitly restrict women's voting rights is relatively small.[26] However, most studies report a significant gender gap for low income countries with women less likely to participate. Using general indices of participation constructed from survey data for fifteen African countries (Bratton and Logan, 2006) shows that women are less likely to participate than men, even after controlling for multiple individual characteristics. Similar findings are reported by Bratton (1999) for Zambia and Krishna (2002) for India.

In Table 2, where we use data from World Values surveys, we observe significant gender differences in participation across countries and some weak evidence that these gender differences are accentuated in poorer countries.

A first explanation for lower female participation in low income countries is discrimination. Women may be explicitly prevented from participating, or not listened to at public forums, leading them to reduce their participation. Some evidence on this issue comes from Duflo and Topolova (2004b). Since 1993, one third of the seats and presidencies of the rural village councils in India have been reserved for women. Duflo and Topolova (2004b) analyze a data set with both objective and subjective information about the women's actions as policymakers. Technical audits of the number and quality of public goods available in the villages show that women provide more public goods and at better quality than men do. However, villagers are less satisfied with the performance of female presidents in providing all services. Overall, villagers are two percentage points less satisfied with public goods when the president is a woman. They interpret this as evidence that there is a significant cultural barrier to recognizing women as competent policy makers.

In related work Beaman et al. (2006) find that female attendance and participation in village meetings is relatively higher when the village chief is a woman. Women are significantly more likely to ask a question or raise an issue at a village meeting (by 13 percentage points) when the chief is a woman. On the other hand, if a woman speaks on an issue during a village meeting conducted by a male leader she is significantly more

---

[26] As of 2005, this set included Saudi Arabia and United Arab Emirates. In Lebanon women have partial suffrage and in Bhutan each household has a single vote.

likely to get a negative response. This gender difference in type of response is absent in the village meeting, she is much more likely to receive a bad response from the Panchayat than a man raising the same issue. A woman speaking during the meeting is 14 percentage points more likely to receive a negative response on average. In unreserved villages, this likelihood increases to 25 percentage points. However, in villages reserved for a woman, men and women seem to be treated equally when they raise issues in front of the general assembly. Finally, women may participate at lower rates if they benefit less from public transfers. This would be true if, for instance, public transfers are targeted at households and typically collected by the husband.[27]

To the extent men were more likely to condone (and potentially exhibit) corrupt behavior (Azfar et al., 2001), one cost of lower female participation is in terms of political corruption.

3.3.3. Monitoring

An individual's income and educational attainment might also affect her ability to monitor/punish those who are corrupt. One may argue that the relatively rich and educated are better able to punish politicians by, for instance going to court, and therefore should pay fewer bribes. In addition, the rich may be less dependent on public services and so should be better placed to avoid interactions with corrupt individuals. On the other hand, if individuals engaged in corrupt practices undertake price discrimination then the rich should, on average, pay higher bribes. Finally, if corruption is rife in business activities which are regulated (rather than in public service delivery) then the rich and more educated may actually be more exposed to corruption.

The empirical evidence on how income and education are correlated with corruption is mixed. Hunt and Lazslo (2006) use data from Uganda and Peru to find that bribery for public services works like a flat tax i.e. its incidence does not change across the income distribution. In contrast, a recent study of Ugandan firms suggests that corrupt officials are more likely to engage in price discrimination and larger firms are more likely to give bribes (Svensson, 2003). Olken (2006) finds relatively weak evidence that richer areas in Indonesia have less corruption (as measured by the difference between the amount of rice received by different Indonesian regions to the amount intended for distribution).

Besley, Pande, and Rao (2005b) provide evidence that increased education among the voter population reduces the extent of political corruption. The main mechanism appears to be improved monitoring of elected officials, both at village meetings and via greater access to the media.

---

[27] It would be interesting to check whether women remain as disaffected from politics when they are the direct beneficiaries of the public distribution system.

4. Conclusion

In this chapter we have argued that differences in the economic environment faced by citizens in rich and poor countries can suggest important reasons why corruption is often higher in poor countries. Interventions which address some of the market imperfections which encourage corruption might pay rich dividends in terms of reduced corruption. These could include improving the information available to citizens through, for instance, voter awareness campaigns and breaking down existing power structures which discriminate against certain population groups (for instance, by introducing mandated political reservation for women). In addition, improving formal returns from politics and limiting the political role of ethnic parties are potential candidates for anti-corruption policies.

Overall, the evidence presented in this paper suggests that investment in specific mechanisms which alter individual incentives to engage in corrupt practices may succeed in reducing levels of corruption (one such mechanism which has received some attention in the literature is auditing – see Olken, 2006). This would suggest that the policy emphasis should be on identifying features of the economic environment which increase the incidence of corruption, not simply identifying individuals who are corrupt.

Data Appendix

The World Value regressions use data from the "World Values Survey and European Values Surveys, 1990–1993, and 1995–1997" (ICPSR 2790). Adults aged 18 and over were sampled from more than fifty countries. The surveys focus on the values and beliefs of those surveyed and contain much individual demographic information. Approximately 1500 people were surveyed in each country in each wave of the survey, although the exact numbers vary from country to country.

We interact our explanatory variables by a low income dummy. This dummy equals one if the country is lower income or lower middle income as classified by the World Bank's 2004 World Development Indicators. All other variables are defined in the tables.

References

Acemoglu, D., Johnson, S., Robinson, J.A. (2005). "Institutions as the fundamental cause of long-run growth". In: Aghion, P., Durlauf, S. (Eds.), Handbook of Economic Growth, vol. 1A. Elsevier, pp. 385–472.
Alesina, A., Baqir, R., Easterly, W. (1999). "Public goods and ethnic divisions". Quarterly Journal of Economics 114 (4), 1243–1284.
Azfar, O., Knack, S., Lee, Y., Swamy, A. (2001). "Gender and corruption". Journal of Development Economics 64, 25–55.
Baland, J.M., Robinson, J. (2005). "Land and power". Mimeo.
Banerjee, A.V. (1997). "A theory of misgovernance". Quarterly Journal of Economics 112 (4), 1289–1332.
Banerjee, A., Iyer, L. (2005) . American Economic Review 95 (4), 1190–1213.
Banerjee, A., Pande, R. (2006). "Parochial politics: Ethnic preferences and politician corruption". Mimeo.

Bardhan, P., Udry, C. (1999). Development Microeconomics. Oxford Univ. Press, Oxford.

Barr, A., Serra, D. (2006). "Culture and corruption". Mimeo.

Bates, R. (1974). "Ethnic competition and modernization in contemporary Africa". Comparative Political Studies 6, 457–484.

Beaman, L., Duflo, E., Pande, R., Topolova, P. (2006). "Women policy-makers, child outcomes and gender bias in Indian villages". Background paper. State of World's Children Report UNICEF.

Bertrand, M., Djankov, S., Hanna, R., Mullainathan, S. (2006). "Does corruption produce unsafe drivers?" Working paper series No. w12274. NBER.

Besley, T., Coate, S. (1997). "An economic model of representative democracy". Quarterly Journal of Economics 112 (1), 85–114.

Besley, T., Pande, R., Rao, V. (2004). "The politics of public good provision: Evidence from Indian local governments". Journal of European Economic Association 2 (2-3), 416–426.

Besley, T., Pande, R., Rao, V. (2005a). "Participatory democracy in action: Survey evidence from India". Journal of European Economic Association 3 (2-3), 648–657. April–May.

Besley, T., Pande, R., Rao, V. (2005b). "Political selection and the quality of government: Evidence from south India." Working paper 921, Economic Growth Center, July.

Besley, T., Persson, T., Sturm, D. (2006). "Political competition and economic performance: Theory and evidence from the United States". Working paper No. 11484. NBER.

Besley, T., Prat, A. (2006). "Handcuffs for the grabbing hand? The role of the media in political accountability". American Economic Review.

Blais, A. (2000). To Vote or Not to Vote: The Merits and Limits of Rational Choice Theory. University of Pittsburgh Press, Pittsburgh.

Bratton, M. (1999). "Political participation in a new democracy: Institutional considerations from Zambia". Comparative Political Studies 32 (5), 549–588.

Bratton, M., Logan, C. (2006). "The political gender gap in Africa: Similar attitudes, different behaviors". Afro Barometer working paper No. 58.

Bratton et al. (2005). "Public opinion, democracy, and market reform in Africa". Mimeo.

Caselli, F., Morelli, , M. (2004). "Bad politicians". Journal of Public Economics 88 (3-4), 759–782.

Chandra, K. (2004). Why Ethnic Parties Succeed. Patronage and Ethnic Head Counts in India. Cambridge Univ. Press, Cambridge.

Chattopadhyay, R., Duflo, E. (2004a). "Women as policy-makers: Evidence from an India-wide randomized experiment". Econometrica 72 (5), 1409–1443.

Chattopadhyay, R., Duflo, E. (2004b). "Women's leadership and policy decisions: Evidence from a nationwide randomized experiment in India". 72 (5), 1409–1443.

Chetty, R., Looney, A. (2006). Income Risk and the Benefits of Social Insurance: Evidence from Indonesia and the United States. Fiscal Policy and Management: East Asia Seminar on Economics. University of Chicago Press, Chicago.

Crandall, R. (1950). "American railroad presidents in the 1870s: Their background and careers". Explorations in Entrepreneurial History 2, 282–296.

Dahl, R. (1961). Who Governs? Democracy and Power in an American City. Yale Univ. Press, New Haven.

Daniel Diermeier, M.K., Merlo, A. (2005). "A political economy model of congressional careers". American Economic Review 95 (1), 347–373.

Dee, T. (2004). "Are there civic returns to education?" Journal of Public Economics 88, 1697–1720.

Dollar, D., Fisman, R., Gatti, R. (1999). "Are women really the fairer sex? Corruption and women in government". Journal of Economic Behavior and Organization 46, 423–429.

Downs, A. (1957). An Economic Theory of Democracy. Harper Collins, New York.

Duflo, E. (2003). "Grandmothers and granddaughters: Old age pension and intra-household allocation in South Africa". World Bank Economic Review 17 (1), 1–25.

Duflo, E., Topolova, P. (2004a). "Unappreciated service: Female politicians in India". Mimeo, MIT.

Duflo, E., Topolova, P. (2004b). "Unappreciated service: Performance, perceptions, and women leaders in India". Mimeo, MIT.

Easterly, W., Levine, R. (1997). "Africa's growth tragedy: Policies and ethnic divisions". Quarterly Journal of Economics 112 (4), 1203–1250.

Edlund, L., Haider, L., Pande, R. (2005). "Unmarried parenthood and redistributive politics". Journal of European Economic Association 3 (1), 95–119.

Edlund, L., Pande, R. (2002). "Why have women become left-wing? The political gender gap and the decline in marriage". Quarterly Journal of Economics 117 (3), 917–961.

Esteban, J., Ray, D. (2006). "On the salience of ethnic conflict". Mimeo.

Faccio, M. (2006). "Politically connected firms". American Economic Review 96 (1), 369–386.

Fearon, J. (2003). "Ethnic and cultural diversity by country". Journal of Economic Growth 8, 195–222.

Ferrara, E.L. (2002). "Self-help groups and income generation in the informal settlements of Nairobi". Journal of African Economies 11 (1), 61–89.

Ferraz, C., Finan, F. (2006). "Exposing corrupt politicians: The effect of Brazil's publicly released audits on electoral outcomes". Mimeo, UC Berkeley.

Fisman, R. (2001). "Estimating the value of political connections". American Economic Review 91 (4), 1095–1102.

Fisman, R., Miguel, E. (2006). "Cultures of corruption: Evidence from diplomatic parking tickets". Mimeo.

Foster, A., Rosenzweig, M. (1996). "Technical change and human capital returns and investments: Evidence from the green revolution". American Economic Review 86 (4), 931–953.

Foster, A., Rosenzweig, M. (2004a). "Democratization, decentralization and the distribution of local public goods in a poor rural economy". Mimeo.

Foster, A., Rosenzweig, M. (2004b). "Technological change and the distribution of schooling: Evidence from green-revolution India". Journal of Development Economics 74 (1), 87–111.

Gehlbach, S., Sonin, K. (2004). "Businessman candidates: Special-interest politics in weakly institutionalized environments". Working paper No. 733, William Davidson Institute.

Goldstein, M., Udry, C. (2005). "The profits of power: Land rights and agricultural investment in Ghana." Mimeo, Yale University.

Horowitz, D.L. (1985). Ethnic Groups in Conflict. Univ. of California Press, Berkeley.

Hunt, J. (2006). "How corruption hits people when they are down". Working paper, NBER.

Hunt, J., Lazslo, S. (2006). "Bribery: Who pays, who refuses, what are the payoffs?" McGill University, Department of Economics in its series *Departmental Working Papers*.

IDEA (1997). Voter Turnout from 1945 to 1998: A Global Report. International IDEA, Stockholm.

Habyarimana, J., Humphreys, M., Posner, D.N., Weinstein, J. (2006). "Why does ethnic diversity undermine public goods provision? An experimental approach". Mimeo.

Jayachandran, S. (2006). "The Jeffords effect". Journal of Law and Economics 49 (2), 397–425. October.

Johnson, S., Mitton, T. (2006). "Cronyism and capital controls: Evidence from Malaysia". Mimeo, SSRN.

Jones, B., Olken, B. (2005). "Do leaders matter? National leadership and economic growth since World War II". Quarterly Journal of Economics 120 (3), 835–864.

Khwaja, A.I. (2006). "Can good projects succeed in bad communities? Collective action in the Himalayas." Working paper.

Khwaja, A.I., Mian, A. (2005). "Do lenders favor politically connected firms? Rent provision in an emerging financial market". Quarterly Journal of Economics 120 (4).

Kipp, S.M. (1977). "Old notables and newcomers: The economic and political elite of Greensboro, North Carolina, 1880–1920". Journal of Southern History 43 (3), 373–394.

Krishna, A. (2002). "Enhancing political participation in democracies – What is the role of social capital?" Comparative Political Studies 35 (4), 437–460.

Kuenzi, M., Lambright, G. (2005). "Who votes in Africa? An examination of electoral turnout in 10 African countries." Afro Barometer working paper #51.

Laothamatos, A. (1988). "Business and politics in Thailand: New patterns of influence". Asian Survey.

Lee, D.S., Moretti, E., Butler, M. (2004). "Do voters affect or elect policies? Evidence from the US house". Quarterly Journal of Economics 119 (3), 807–860.

Levitt, S. (1996). "How do senators vote? Disentangling the role of voter preferences, party affiliation and senate ideology". American Economic Review 86 (3), 425–441.

Lott, J.R., Kenny, L.W. (1999). "Did women's suffrage change the size and scope of government?" Journal of Political Economy CVI, 1163–1198.

Lucas, R.E., Stark, O. (1985). "Motivations to remit: Evidence from Botswana". Journal of Political Economy 93 (5), 901–918.

Lundberg, S., Pollak, R.A., Wales, T.J. (1997). "Do husbands and wives pool their resources? Evidence from the UK child benefit". Journal of Human Resources 32 (3), 463–480.

Mauro, P. (1995). "Corruption and growth". Quarterly Journal of Economics 110, 681–712.

Meltzer, A.H., Richard, S.F. (1981). "A rational theory of the size of government". Journal of Political Economy LXXXIX, 914–927.

Menes, R. (2001). "Corruption in cities: Graft and politics in American cities at the turn of the twentieth century". Mimeo.

Meyer, R. (1969). "The political elite in an underdeveloped society". PhD dissertation, University of Pennsylvania.

Miguel, E., Gugerty, M.K. (2005). "Ethnic divisions, social sanctions, and public goods in Kenya". Journal of Public Economics 89 (11-12), 2325–2368.

Miller, W., Shanks, J.M. (1996). The New American Voter. Harvard Univ. Press, Cambridge, MA.

Milligan, K., Moretti, E., Oreopoulos, P. (2004). "Does education improve citizenship? Evidence from the United States and the United Kingdom". Journal of Public Economics 88 (9-10), 1667–1695.

Mozaffar, S., Scarritt, J., Galaich, G. (2003). "Electoral institutions, ethnopolitical cleavages, and party systems in Africa". American Political Science Review 97 (3), 379–390.

Myerson, R. (1993). "Effectiveness of electoral systems for reducing government corruption: A game theoretic analysis". Games and Economic Behavior 5, 118–132.

Norris, P. (2002). Democratic Phoenix: Reinventing Political Activism. Cambridge Univ. Press, New York.

Oberholzer-Gee, F., Waldfogel, J. (2005). "Strength in numbers: Group size and political mobilization". Journal of Law and Economics 48, 73–91.

Ochoa, E. (1987). The Rapid Expansion of Voter Participation in Latin America: Presidential Elections 1845–1986. Statistical Abstract of Latin America, vol. 25. Stanford Univ. Press. UCLA Latin American Center Publication.

Okten, C., Osili, U. (2004). "Contributions in heterogeneous communities: Evidence from Indonesia". Journal of Population Economics 14, 603–626.

Olken, B. (2006). "Corruption and the costs of redistribution: Micro evidence from Indonesia". Journal of Public Economics 90, 853–870.

Osborne, M., Slivinski, A. (1996). "A model of political competition with citizen-candidates". Quarterly Journal of Economics 111 (1), 65–96.

Pande, R. (2003). "Can mandated political representation provide disadvantaged minorities policy influence? Theory and evidence from India". American Economic Review 93 (4), 1132–1151.

Pande, R. (2006). "Why aren't we achieving the millennium development goals? Book review for the proceedings of annual World Bank conference in development economics. Journal of Economic Literature.

Pande, R., Udry, C. (2005). "Institutions and development: A view from below". Mimeo.

Persson, T., Tabellini, G. (2003). The Economic Effects of Constitutions: What Do the Data Say? MIT Press, Cambridge.

Putnam, R. (1993). Making Democracy Work. Civic Traditions in Modern Italy. Princeton Univ. Press, Princeton.

Putnam, R. (2000). Bowling Alone. The Collapse and Revival of American Community. Simon and Schuster, New York.

Reinikka, R., Svensson, J. (2004). "The power of information: Evidence from a newspaper campaign to reduce capture of public funds". Mimeo, IIES.

Roberts, K. (1977). "Voting over income tax schedules". Journal of Public Economics 8 (3), 329–340.

Scott, J. (1969). "Corruption, machine politics and political change". American Political Science Review 63, 1142–1158.

Scott, J.C. (1972). "Patron–client politics and political change in Southeast Asia". American Political Science Review 66.

Shatkin, G. (2004). "Globalization and local leadership: Growth, power and politics in Thailand's eastern seaboard". International Journal of Urban and Regional Research 28.

Sokoloff, K., Engerman, S. (2003). "Institutions, factor endowments, and paths of development in the new world". Journal of Economic Perspectives 14 (3), 217–232.

Svensson, J. (2003). "Who must pay bribes and how much? Evidence from a cross section of firms". Quarterly Journal of Economics 118, 207–230.

Svensson, J. (2005). "Eight questions about corruption". Journal of Economic Perspectives 19, 19–42.

Thomas, D. (1990). "Intra-household resource allocation: an inferential approach". Journal of Human Resources 25 (4), 635–664.

Thomas, D. (1997). "Incomes, expenditures and health outcomes: Evidence on intra-household resource allocation". In: Haddad, L., Hoddinott, J., Alderman, H. (Eds.), Intra-Household Resource Allocation in Developing Countries: Models, Methods, and Policy. Johns Hopkins Press, Baltimore, pp. 142–164.

Topalova, P. (2005). "Trade liberalization, poverty, and inequality: Evidence from Indian districts". Working paper No. 11614, NBER.

Topf, R. (1995). Beyond Electoral Participation, Citizens and the State. Oxford Univ. Press, Oxford.

Treisman, D. (2000). "The causes of corruption: A cross-national study". Journal of Public Economics 76 (3), 399–457.

Verba, S., Nie, N. (1972). Participation in America: Social Equality and Political Democracy. Harper and Row, New York.

Verba, S., Scholzman, K.L., Brady, H.E. (1995). Voice and Equality: Civic Voluntarism in American Politics. Harvard Univ. Press, Cambridge, MA.

PART 12

HUMAN RESOURCES AND HOUSEHOLD RESPONSES
TO MARKET INCENTIVES AND PUBLIC GOODS

.

Chapter 51

HOUSEHOLD FORMATION AND MARRIAGE MARKETS IN RURAL AREAS

MARCEL FAFCHAMPS

Department of Economics, University of Oxford, Manor Road, Oxford OX1 3UQ, UK

AGNES R. QUISUMBING

International Food Policy Research Institute, 2033 K Street, NW Washington, DC 20006-1002, USA

Contents

Handbook of Development Economics, Volume 4
© *2008 Elsevier B.V. All rights reserved*
DOI: 10.1016/S1573-4471(07)04051-X

Abstract

This chapter surveys the voluminous literature on household formation and marriage markets in developing countries. We begin by discussing the many social and economic factors that incite individuals to live together in households. Many of these factors are particularly important in poor countries, especially in a rural setting. We then focus on marriage, which is the process by which the main building block of most households is formed. After discussing assortative matching and polygyny, we introduce bargaining and strategic bequest and discuss their implication for the equilibrium of the marriage market. We end the chapter with a discussion of marriage dissolution and other changes in household structure. Fertility decisions are not discussed here as they have already been covered elsewhere.

Keywords

marriage market, intrahousehold allocation, household size, child fostering, divorce, dowry, assortative matching

JEL classification: D13, J12, O12

1. Introduction

The purpose of this chapter is to review the economic literature on household formation, focusing on rural areas of developing countries. Since the seminal work of Becker (1981), economists have devoted an increasing amount of attention to issues surrounding the household. This is true in advanced economies as well as in developing countries. The volumes edited by Haddad, Hoddinott and Alderman (1997) and Quisumbing (2003), for instance, are representative of the intrahousehold literature in developing countries. Household formation in developed countries is discussed, inter alia, in Bergstrom (1997) and Grossbard-Shechtman (2003).

Our ultimate objective is not to review the entire literature on intrahousehold issues, which is now extremely voluminous. Rather we seek to organize the abundant theoretical and empirical material into a coherent whole that can serve as starting point for analyzing issues of household structure and family formation in developing countries. The conceptual framework proposed here is intended to be sufficiently general to encompass many specific models and ideas found in the literature, while remaining internally consistent. We use it to guide the reader through part of the literature and to provide a basis for evaluating the abundant empirical evidence.

Households are important. They fulfill many critical functions – from production and reproduction to consumption, saving, insurance, and human capital accumulation. Changes in their function help explain changes in their size and shape over time and across societies. At the heart of many households is a couple. The matching process by which couples are formed has deep implications regarding intergenerational mobility and long-term equity. This is particularly true in agrarian societies that still characterize much of the developing world today. Households can also dissolve, shed members, or gain new ones. Economic theory of household formation and marriage markets provide a framework for thinking about changes in household structure over time.

Each section of this Chapter combines a presentation of the empirical evidence with a conceptual discussion focusing on testable predictions and testing strategies. Section 2 focuses on the reasons for household formation. Marriage markets are discussed in Section 3. Marriage dissolution is covered in Section 4 while Section 5 discusses the circumstances leading to single-parent or single-adult households. The last section contains a brief discussion of other issues pertaining to household structure, such as the factors affecting the decision to leave or join an existing household.

2. Household formation

Throughout this chapter the term "household" is used to designate a group of individuals living together. It is distinct from the term "family," which designates a group of individuals related by marriage and consanguinity. In general, households are composed of family members.[1] But they can also include unrelated individuals (servants, visitors, fostered children). Families typically consist of multiple households forming a network of kith and kin, related by blood or marriage but not necessarily living together. Family and kinship networks are the object of a separate chapter in this volume.

2.1. Coercion and free will

Households are facts of life, so much so that we normally take them for granted. Yet economic theory is couched in terms of individual agents. As economists, we may wonder why people live in households. One possibility is that they do not have the choice. Minor children, for instance, are normally not allowed to leave their parents until they come of age. If they run away from home, they can be compelled to return, by force if necessary. The same is true in some societies for wives and other adult female dependents.

This begs the question of why society would force people to live together. In the case of minor children, most people would probably agree that society has the welfare of children at heart. Since children are vulnerable, society may calculate that the abuse they would endure while living on their own is in all likelihood worse than the abuse to which they could be subjected at home. While there certainly are exceptions to this principle, it is safe to assume that it holds on average. The welfare of young children is thus probably an important motivation for the formation of households, a point that we revisit below.

Feminists have sometimes argued that households are nothing but a device for adult males to extract forced labor from women and children: a male dominated society improves male welfare, the story goes, by coercing wives, children, and dependent adult females to remain in the household (Folbre, 1997).[2] Domestic violence and the indoctrination of women are the weapons by which such enslavement is accomplished. In the popular psyche, this is best illustrated by the cliche of the good-for-nothing husband who drinks his income away while his wife and kids labor at home. We do not dispute that such men exist. We also do not dispute that women's agency is highly restricted in some societies where the law equates them to minor children and where ostracism rewards those who challenge women's socially assigned role. We do not have much to say about these practices here, except that they are abhorrent and should be eliminated.

Our focus is elsewhere. If households were solely the result of coercion, they would disappear once women's freedom of choice was guaranteed. Yet they do not: all countries have households, whether or not their legal code and social mores recognize women's free will. This means that households have to be explained. Living together

---

[1] We follow the common practice of omitting from the definition of a household all formal institutions in which generally unrelated individuals share room and board. Examples of such institutions include boarding schools, retirement homes, monasteries, army barracks, ship crews, and prisons.

[2] Ironically, recent research suggests instead that in developed economies men would do better financially by staying single (e.g. Jarvis and Jenkins, 1999; Bourreau-Dubois, Jeandidier and Berger, 2003).

typically puts constraints on individual choice. Why then do people form groups that, de facto, restrict their freedom of choice? Answering this question is the focus of the first part of this Chapter.

If free individuals decide to form a household, it must be that living together yields higher personal welfare than living alone. This fundamental intuition is the organizing principle behind the economic analysis of household formation. Gains from household formation also help sustain households in the presence of coercion, and probably play a central role even in societies that do not recognize women's free will. Even when legal and customary rules prohibit individuals from leaving a household, enforcing these rules may be problematic given that running away from home always remains an option, albeit perhaps not an attractive one. Gains from household formation make the rules easier to enforce because leaving the household means losing many of the benefits it provides. When gains from household membership are sufficiently large, these rules can even become self-enforcing in the sense that individuals find it in their interest to follow them.[3] Furthermore, if the household head is a dictator at home, he can decide to shed members. For the household to be sustainable, it must be in the interest of the head to keep all its members. Gains from household formation, especially if they are captured by the household head, make shedding members less likely.

With these few words of introduction, we are ready to delve into the economic literature on household formation. To represent household formation formally, let vector A_i denote the endowments and characteristics of individual i, such as assets, education, health status, etc. Let $W_i(A_i)$ be the utility individual i can achieve on his or her own. Consider another individual j with assets A_j and autarchy payoff $W_j(A_j)$. Let the utility they achieve by living together be denoted $V_i(A_i, A_j)$ and $V_j(A_i, A_j)$ which, for now, we take as exogenously determined. It is in the joint interest of i and j to form a household if and only if[4]:

$$V_i(A_i, A_j) \geqslant W_i(A_i),$$
$$V_j(A_i, A_j) \geqslant W_j(A_j).$$

The same approach naturally extends to groups of more than two individuals.[5]

To understand household formation in a free society, we must therefore understand the origin of the welfare gains generated by living together. Our first insight into the source of these welfare gains comes from the definition of a household. Its defining

---

[3] This abstracts from the welfare gain that individuals may derive from agency itself, that is, from making their own decisions.

[4] Of course, it is conceivable that i and j nominally form a household but continue to live in exactly the same way as before, in which case $V_i(A_i, A_j) = W_i(A_i)$ and $V_j(A_i, A_j) = W_j(A_i)$. To rule out such uninteresting cases, we require that at least one of the above inequalities be strict. Alternatively, we may assume that some transaction cost must be incurred in order to form a household.

[5] The formalism of the model can be extended to households in which membership is coerced by recognizing that members can run away but incur a penalty (psychological, physical, or financial) for doing so. The stronger the penalty, the more constrained choices are. We discuss constrained choices later in the Chapter.

characteristic is the sharing of resources and activities. Coresidence is usually regarded as a necessary condition for a group of people to be regarded as a household. This excludes children living separately from their parents, for instance. Coresidence is seldom sufficient, however. Tenants in an apartment building live under the same roof but form separate households. For this reason, a household is often defined as a group of people 'eating from the same pot,' that is, sharing the same food budget or cooked meals (e.g. Grosh and Glewwe, 2000; Deaton, 2000). The advantage of this definition is that it is factual and does not depend on legal categories, such as whether people are married or related.

Sharing resources is only one of many possible gains generated by household formation. In this Section, we briefly discuss various potential gains from living together as a household and, whenever possible, present empirical evidence relative to the evidence and strength of these effects. The form and strength of these gains may also help us understand the optimal size and composition of households.

2.2. Companionship and reproduction

The first welfare gain from living together is emotional. Human beings are social animals. They enjoy companionship. Living alone often is a source of anxiety and depression. Based on this observation alone, we would expect human beings to live in large groups, not small household units. There must therefore exist a countervailing force that discourages the formation of very large groups and incite human societies to organize in groups of a few individuals only. Part of this negative externality probably has to do with freedom of choice: because individual preferences are heterogeneous, sharing resources and activities often means doing things that are not optimal from a purely individual point of view. The larger the group, the stronger the loss of autonomy.

If the sole purpose of households is to fight loneliness, companionship can a priori be achieved by any arbitrary grouping, not necessarily couples or parents with children. The fact that most households are made of couples with or without children suggests that sex and reproduction play an important role in household formation. Although sex can be sought outside a couple, coresidence cuts down on transactions cost and facilitates regular sexual interaction, making it an important dimension of companionship for many couples. Furthermore, sex often fosters strong emotions that can bind people together. Since sexual activity tends to decrease with age, as couples age together companionship probably takes on a more important role. As we all know, however, mutual sexual attraction need not last forever and can change in unexpected ways. This introduces an element of unpredictability in household formation and dissolution.

Many social phenomena cannot be understood without realizing that sexual interaction need not take place within households. For instance, because of financial or legal reasons, migrant husbands are often unable to bring their wife to their place of work. As a result they often seek sexual encounters outside marriage. Wealthier men may also indulge in their craving for sexual diversity by having extra-marital affairs. This creates a demand for prostitution services, a topic we will revisit later when we discuss exit options open to married women dissatisfied with their fate. Prostitution in turn has an important role in the dissemination of diseases, most notably HIV-AIDS and tuberculosis. How adequately households satisfy sexual needs can therefore have far-reaching repercussions on society.

Casual empiricism suggests that reproduction is another important function of households. Young children cannot support themselves. For them, autarchy is not a viable option. For many years, they have to be cared for by adults. Fortunately, human beings have been genetically programmed to care about children, especially their own (Buss, 2005). The altruism most parents feel towards their progeny encourages them to look after young children, which is most easily achieved if they reside together.

This simple process undoubtedly plays a major role in household formation. But it is important to recognize that both reproduction and child care can be achieved outside households. By adopting or fostering children, adults can obtain offspring without being their biological parents (e.g. Akresh, 2004b; Castle, 1996). There are, however, differences in outcomes across genetic versus adoptive offspring. Careful analysis of US and South African data shows that, controlling for household size, age composition, and income, food expenditures are less in households in which a child is raised by an adoptive, step, or foster mother (Case, Lin and McLanahan, 2000). Daly and Wilson (1987) provide evidence that child abuse and child homicide are significantly correlated with the presence of a stepparent; abusive stepparents abuse only stepchildren while sparing their natural offspring within the same household.

The urge to have children is quite strong, so much so that many couples are willing to spend much money and effort to adopt children or to seek fertility care. This urge also explains why, in certain societies, men repudiate or divorce women unable to bear them children. In societies where repudiation is not permitted and divorce frowned upon, husbands may even be tempted to kill an infertile wife, as occurs for instance with wife burning in South Asia.[6]

Although the desire to have children is strong in many societies, enormous differences in fertility rates have been observed between countries or within countries over time. Very high fertility rates have been found in societies expanding the frontier of human settlement. In contrast, low fertility levels are now prevalent in many rich countries, and a fertility decline has been observed in most countries in the latter part of the last century. These dramatic changes in the number of children per woman affect household formation in profound ways. When having children no longer is a primary objective of couples, marriage is less necessary and can be replaced by cohabitation, which is more flexible. Marriage also occurs later and unions may be less durable. Adult children may choose to remain with their parents longer. In Japan, for instance, demographers have noted that many adult men and women in their 30s now live with their parents. This

---

[6] Failure to pay the dowry in full is also a contributing factor in bride burning. But if the wife has a child, especially a son, bride burning is likely to be met with extreme disapproval even by those who condone it in other circumstances.

new phenomenon has been explained in part by fertility decline and in part by the cost of real estate, which makes setting up an independent household more expensive. We revisit the latter point below.

It is possible for a single man or woman to obtain a biological offspring without forming a household with the other parent. In fact, this is usually what happens upon divorce. It is also possible for a parent to care for a child without being in the same household, as when a divorced parent pays child support for a child residing with his or her former spouse. Finally, it is possible for children to be raised in institutions. The AIDS epidemic in Africa has created millions of orphans, many of whom are taken care of by other relatives or by institutions (Evans, 2004b). Children who are not absorbed into households or institutions typically end up as street children. What little we know about their welfare is sufficiently disturbing to justify emphasizing the child care role of households.

Altruism towards children is a major driving force behind the formation of households. Altruism towards parents is also present, and often explains why adult children coreside with elderly parents in order to care for them, an issue to which we return later in this chapter. Altruism alone, however, does not explain household formation: parents who care for children or children who care for parents could demonstrate their altruism simply by paying for their children or parents to be taken care of by others, say, a boarding school or a retirement home. Coresidence is not an automatic consequence of altruism. Other forces are at work as well. To these we now turn.

2.3. Consumption

Households are the locus where most consumption takes place. Many consumption goods are non-rival in the sense that consumption by one does not reduce (by much) consumption by others. This is true for instance for housing, numerous household electronics, and many forms of family entertainment. Consumption items enjoyed by one household member can be passed on to others, such as books or children's clothes. Non-rival consumption goods are often referred to as household public goods in the literature (e.g. Bergstrom, 1997; Browning and Chiappori, 1998; Lechene and Preston, 2005). By pooling consumption expenditures, household members reduce duplication of household public goods and achieve higher utility. In some cases, joint consumption can even raise individual utility, such as taking a meal together.

Formally, consider a symmetric model in which $U(C_i)$ is utility and C_i is the consumption vector of individual i. We partition C_i into rival C_i^r and non-rival goods C_i^n with $C_i = \{C_i^r, C_i^n\}$. Let X denote consumption expenditures per person, which for simplicity we assume identical across individuals. We wish to show that individual utility increases with household size. Since all household members consume the same non-rival goods, $C_i^n = C^n$ for all i. We have:

$$\max_{\{C_i\}} \sum_{i=1}^{N} U\left(C_i^r, C^n\right) \quad \text{subject to} \quad NX = Np^r C_i^r + p^n C^n$$

which, by symmetry, can be rewritten as:

$$V\left(X, p^r, \frac{p^n}{N}\right) = \max_{\{C\}} U\left(C^r, C^n\right) \quad \text{subject to} \quad X = p^r C^r + \frac{p^n}{N} C^n.$$

Since $\frac{\partial V}{\partial p} < 0$ for consumed goods, it immediately follows that $\frac{\partial V}{\partial N} > 0$: thanks to non-rival consumption, utility increases in household size.

The above model ignores the fact that, beyond a certain household size, congestion sets in and consumption goods are no longer non-rival. How quickly congestion sets in determines optimal household size N^* from a consumption maximization point of view. If, as is likely, congestion sets in faster for certain goods than for others, N^* depends on individual tastes. For instance, people who love to play sports together probably have a larger optimal household size than people who like to read. By the same reasoning, optimal household size may also vary with income level. If the rich have more individual forms of consumption, they will have smaller households, and vice versa. Technological change can affect N^* by changing the type of consumption goods available and the extent of non-rivalry in consumption. For instance, a TV can be watched by several people while a walkman is, by design, individual. A shift towards smaller, more individualized consumer durables encourages – or at least assists – the formation of smaller households.[7]

Utility gains from pooling non-rival consumption goods can also be achieved outside the household, for instance by engaging in sports with friends or by watching a football match in a bar. As emphasized before, the existence of substitutes outside the household is also likely to affect optimal household size. Whether outside options are good substitutes for consumption within the household depends on transactions costs – e.g., coordinating a game with friends, going to the bar. Higher population density in urban areas tends to reduce such transactions costs – it is easier to find people with similar tastes, distance to the bar is on average smaller. It is also likely to increase the range of consumption substitutes outside the household. For these reasons, we expect household size to be smaller in urban areas.

The literature has looked for evidence of economies of scale in consumption, typically using household size as the scale variable. Lanjouw and Ravallion (1995) investigate the relationship between household size and food consumption. The starting point of their inquiry is the empirical negative relationship between household size and consumption per head. The authors note that it would be erroneous to interpret this relationship as necessarily implying that welfare is lower in large households. The reason is the possible existence of economies of scale due to household public goods. They note the crucial importance of these issues when it comes to poverty targeting. Their approach focuses on an equivalence scale parameter θ such that welfare depends on x/n^θ, where x is household consumption expenditures and n is the number of household members. If $\theta = 1$, individual welfare is proportional to consumption per head;

---

[7] It is also conceivable that the reduction in household size induces technological innovation towards rival consumption goods, such as single user consumer electronics.

if $\theta < 1$, there are economies of size. If welfare levels are, on average, the same in large and small households, x/n^θ should on average be the same across households of different sizes. Using household data from Pakistan, they find that a value of θ around 0.5 or 0.6 would yield no relationship between x/n^θ and household size.

Lanjouw and Ravallion then use an Engel approach to estimate θ from household data. Their idea is that a decrease in the food share as household size increases can be interpreted as indicating the presence of positive economies of scale. If the estimated $\hat{\theta}$ is larger than 0.6, this would also indicate that smaller households are better off in terms of food consumption per equivalent person. To obtain an estimate of θ the authors regress the food share ω on the logs of total expenditures and household size:

$$\omega_i = \alpha + \beta \log x_i - \beta\theta \log n_i + \gamma z_i + u_i$$

where the z_i are various controls. Taking the ratios of the two coefficients, the authors obtain $\hat{\theta} = 0.59$, which is indicative of strong returns to household size.

The application of Engel equivalent scales to welfare comparisons between households of different sizes is severely criticized by Deaton and Paxson (1998), who argue that it 'makes no sense'. Deaton and Paxson point out that, because the food share ω_i is per capita food expenditure divided by total per capita expenditure, a decline in ω_i keeping total per capita expenditure constant can occur only if there is a decline in food expenditure per capita. Because food is a rival good, they argue, a decline in individual food consumption cannot be a welfare improvement. This argument ignores the possibility of scale economies in the transformation of purchased food products into consumed food, a point we revisit in the next section.

Using household level data from a series of developed and developing countries, Deaton and Paxson propose an alternative methodology to test for the existence of economies of scale driven by explicitly distinguishing between exclusive goods – such as food – and household public goods. The basis for their test is the observation that, if people pool resources, they save on household public goods and can afford to spend more on rival goods. This should be particularly true for food, which is not easily substitutable. This leads to the prediction that, at constant per capita expenditure, demand for food should increase in household size. Furthermore this effect should be stronger in poor countries because, at low levels of income, food is a more important determinant of individual welfare – and thus should increase more as households economize on household public goods. Using data from seven countries (three developed and four developing), the authors instead find a negative relationship between household size and food shares, controlling for per capital expenditures. Moreover, this negative relationship is stronger in poor countries. These results contradict the economies of scale hypothesis.[8] The authors are unable to explain their paradoxical findings.

---

[8] The literature has sometimes given a different interpretation to such findings. According to Engel's second law, a lower food share is taken to indicate higher welfare. Consequently, a decrease in food share as household size increases has sometimes been interpreted as indicating the presence of positive economies of scale (Lanjouw and Ravallion, 1995). Deaton and Paxson (1998) argue that such inference is misguided.

A resolution is proposed by Gan and Vernon (2003). Revisiting the Deaton and Paxson data and methodology, these authors show that, as predicted by theory, the share of food in consumption expenditures on food and goods known to be more public than food (e.g., housing) increases with household size. They also analyze the share of food in expenditures on food and a good known to be more private than food and find this share to be decreasing with family size. Consumption of food away from home also decreases with family size. Finally, instead of comparing across countries, the authors compare the elasticity of food share with respect to household size across expenditure quartiles within countries. They find this elasticity to be larger among poor households. These results suggest that the economies of size hypothesis may hold but that careful data analysis is required.

This debate illustrates some of the issues regarding the use of household size, arguably an endogenous variable, in establishing the existence of economies of scale. To some extent, one could argue that observed household size, being endogenous, already reflects adjustments by households to achieve optimum scale economies. The existence of scale economies also seems to depend on the existence of household public goods, which are probably very context-specific (fewer public goods in more industrialized settings, more public good consumption in rural areas). Thus, it is very difficult to generalize or extrapolate the existence of economies of scale to other settings. Household size may not also take into account the different needs or contributions of different types of household members. To some extent, the use of adult equivalent scales attempts to address the first issue. But if equivalent scales are derived from actual consumption data that may reflect societal preferences for allocations towards specific household members – rather than biological needs – adjustments using equivalent scales are only partial. Lastly, the household size variable treats all types of household members as the same. We return to the difficulties of making comparisons across household types – even with household size equal – when we discuss the issue of female-headed vs. male-headed households. Nevertheless, it is safe to say that much more work is needed in this area.

2.4. Production

As first modeled by Becker (1965), Nakajima (1965) and Sen (1966), households are a locus where much production occurs. Household production takes many different forms and is not restricted to poor farmers in developing countries. As Becker (1965) pointed out, all household chores – such as preparing a meal, cleaning the house, or fetching firewood – can be regarded as part of a household production function whereby household endowments $A = \{A_1, \ldots, A_N\}$ and purchased commodities $Z = \{Z^1, \ldots, Z^K\}$ are transformed into individual flows of consumption services $C_i = \{C_i^1, \ldots, C_i^M\}$ where M is the number of consumption services. Total consumption of good j is denoted C^j. The household maximization problem can be written in fairly general terms as:

$$\max_{\{C_i, Z\}} \sum_{i=1}^{N} \omega_i U_i(C_i) \quad \text{subject to}$$

$$0 \geqslant G(C^j, Z, A) \quad \text{(production function)}$$

$$\sum_{i=1}^{N} X_i = \sum_{k=1}^{K} p^k Z^k \quad \text{(budget constraint)}$$

$$C^r = \sum_i C_i^r \quad \text{(rival goods)}$$

$$C^n = C_i^n \quad \text{(non-rival goods)}$$

where X_i is the monetary income brought by individual i and the ω_i's denote arbitrary welfare weights. For now, both are taken as exogenous.

We have written the production technology $G(C^j, Z, A)$ in the broadest possible way to allow for economies of scope, fixed costs, and the like. One common example of economies of scope is child care and house-based chores: many chores can be completed while at the same time attending to a child. The production function can of course be simplified to suit modeling purposes. For instance, if certain purchased goods are consumed without transformation, we have $C^j = Z^j$. The notation can also be expanded to allow for the fact that households consume what is left of an endowment – say time – after it has been partly used for household production.

2.4.1. Gains from specialization

A detailed analysis of such models is beyond the scope of this chapter and can be found, for instance, in Singh, Squire and Strauss (1986) and de Janvry, Fafchamps and Sadoulet (1991). What interests us here is what insights this model generates about household formation. Our first insight is about household production of non-rival consumption goods. Many household chores have this quality. For instance, cleaning the house benefits all household members. A closely related insight is that many household production activities have fixed costs or local increasing returns. For instance, cooking for three does not take much more time than cooking for two. Both effects – non-rival consumption goods and increasing returns in household production – generate returns to scale in household size (e.g. Deaton and Paxson, 1998; Lanjouw and Ravallion, 1995; Fafchamps and Quisumbing, 2003). The stronger these returns to scale, the larger is the optimal household size N^*. This probably explains why household size tends to be larger in places where much consumption is home produced. This is typically the case in poor rural economies where households self-provide much of what they consume – i.e., not only agricultural produce but also house construction, animal husbandry, food processing, fuel, water, child care, elderly care, crafts, and entertainment.

Considering the household as a production unit enables us to borrow further insights from the theory of the firm. These insights are particularly useful to understand who joins the household and how tasks and responsibilities are shared among members. Becker (1981) was among the first to point out that if there are gains from specialization in household production, members should specialize.

Gains from specialization may be static. This happens whenever two separate tasks are better taken care of (e.g., more cheaply) if they are undertaken by two distinct individuals. To see why, think of driving a car and reading the map: these two tasks are best performed if one person drives while the other reads the map, not if both try to do both at the same time. In order to achieve this kind of task specialization, some coordination mechanism is required. We also need to provide incentives for individual members to perform the task adequately. Borrowing from the theory of the firm, one possible way of solving such coordination and incentive problems is to opt for a hierarchical structure that allocates tasks to individual members and holds them responsible for that task. Some evidence to this effect can be found, for instance, in Fafchamps and Quisumbing (2003).

For certain tasks, allocation among members is arbitrary: all members could perform the task equally well. In this case each household may decide to allocate tasks differently and to change task allocation over time, if only to relieve boredom. Coordinating task allocation may be time consuming even if allocation is arbitrary. It may also lead to haggling if certain tasks are more pleasant than others. In this case, social norms or focal points may be used to minimize the need for coordination – and the risk of disagreement. Gender casting, for instance, is common in many societies whereby certain tasks are reserved for women while others are reserved for men. Social roles may also be assigned to children, or to daughters-in-law, etc.

Gender casting has strong implications for household formation. If, for instance, men are not supposed to cook, it will be difficult for a man to live alone. By making men and women complementary in the tasks reserved to them, societies may seek not only to reduce haggling but also to make men and women necessary to each other – and thus to reduce the risk of divorce.

Many tasks require specific skills. Sometimes these skills are innate. For instance, tasks that require physical strength are better entrusted to healthy adult males who, on average, are stronger than children or women. Other times, skills are acquired, either through schooling or through learning by doing. Tasks that require literacy, for instance, are best entrusted to educated household members. Cooking is best entrusted to someone who knows how to cook. Consequently, household members who have acquired certain skills are more likely to undertake tasks that require those skills.

As pointed out by Becker (1981), differences in skills may also determine which household members work outside the home and which take care of most household chores. For instance, consider a household with two tasks: working outside the home for a wage, and taking care of household chores. Suppose that both are equally skilled at household chores but that the husband is better educated and that wages are higher for educated people. Comparative advantage dictates that the husband should work outside the home while the wife does household chores.

This begs the question of why the husband is better educated in the first place. Becker (1981) argues that parents may seek to orient the future allocation of tasks for their children by imparting them task-specific skills, e.g., by teaching girls to cook and boys to read. Parental investment in skills for their offspring may also respond to social norms and gender casting: if wives are supposed to cook, then parents should teach daughters to cook. Gender-specific skills learned during childhood play the same role as gender casting in making husband and wife complementary.

These issues are examined in detail by Fafchamps and Quisumbing (2003) using data from Pakistan. In that paper, we begin by testing the presence of returns to scale in household production. To this effect, we regress total time L_{ij} devoted in household i to chore j on household size n_i. Controls are included to capture wealth effects and household composition. We find evidence of economies of scale in household chores. For certain chores such as fetching firewood, collecting water, and visiting the market, the coefficient of n_i is non-significant, suggesting that the amount of time spent on these chores does not vary with household size: these activities appear to represent fixed household costs. Cooking, washing clothes, and cleaning the house increase less than proportionally with household size, indicating economies of scale there as well. Only livestock herding appears to increase faster than household size, but the coefficient of n_i is not precisely estimated so that we cannot rule out constant or decreasing returns to scale.

We then test whether differences in task allocation between household members reflect comparative advantage. This is accomplished by regressing the share $S_{ij}^k = L_{ij}^k / L_{ij}$ of each task j performed by household member k in household i on characteristics of individual k such as education, age, gender, and height. Results indicate that, as predicted by Becker (1981), human capital plays an important in determining who does what. We find that better educated individuals are more likely to work off-farm and less likely to tend the livestock, work as casual workers, or perform household chores – except visit the market. Education also raises leisure time, suggesting that better educated household members have a higher welfare weight. Age and height also matter. Activities reserved for youngsters are essentially home-based chores such as cooking, washing, knitting, and cleaning the house. Older household members focus on activities that require travel outside the house. Intrahousehold task allocation thus responds to differences in skills and education, providing some evidence in support of Becker's comparative advantage hypothesis.

Human capital differences, however, do not explain everything. There are large systematic differences by gender and status within the family. Males focus on market oriented work while females focus on self-subsistence activities and household chores. We also observe large differences in leisure consumption, with all male categories consuming more leisure than females. Family status also matters. The head of household and his wife do most of the work. Other adults of similar age and gender work less. The only exception is that daughters-in-law work much harder than daughters of similar age and education level – and work even harder than the head's wife. They are also less likely to participate in activities that involve traveling outside the household and earning an independent income. From this we conclude that gender casting and social roles explain a major proportion of intrahousehold task allocation.

Finally, we examine the data for evidence of returns to specialization and learning by doing. We find overwhelming evidence of specialization in the sense that individuals tend to be exclusively responsible for certain tasks. To find out whether this special-ization is the result of learning-by-doing, we examine whether individuals change tasks over time. Indeed, if tasks take time to learn, we would expect household members to keep doing the same task over time. Except for activities such as farming and off-farm employment, we find instead that household members swap tasks frequently, thereby suggesting that learning-by-doing does not lock individuals into specific tasks. Returns to specialization thus appear to result from incentive and coordination concerns.

While there may appear to be gains from specialization, it is possible that some household members will be worse off, in the long run, if some household members are consistently allocated tasks that interfere with their health or those of future gener-ations. Pitt, Rosenzweig and Hassan (2005) analyze the allocation of cooking time to females in rural Bangladesh, a society where a rigid division along gender lines exists. Because biomass fuel contributes significantly to indoor air pollution, but provides more than 90 percent of household energy, women who cook and the children they supervise are likely to be adversely affected. Using a 2000–2003 survey of 1638 rural households in Bangladesh, the authors find that more cooking time is allocated to individuals with lower endowed health, who have lower opportunity costs in terms of working outside the household, while women with very young children are less exposed, presumably to protect the health of young children. An extension of this analysis using longitudi-nal data on Indian children (Pitt, Rosenzweig and Hassan, 2007) shows that mothers' exposure to indoor smoke in the first two years after a child's conception significantly increases the incidence of respiratory symptoms when the child is aged 5–9. This sug-gests that the allocation of cooking chores to women in their childbearing years in these societies, while appearing to maximize current household income, may in fact maximize long-term damage to the lung capacities of the next generation.

2.4.2. *Technology and markets*

In the long run, the organization of tasks within the household is affected by technology. The development of household appliances such as the stove and microwave oven has reduced the importance of food preparation skills: while cooking a meal in clay pots on an open fire requires quite a bit of skill and practice, everyone, including a child, is capable of heating a simple meal in a microwave oven. This has had far reaching effects in developed countries (Goldin, 1992). The time freed by these appliances has enabled women either to join the labor force or to focus on other chores such as child care. Because less skill is required to perform house chores, it is easier to reallocate these chores among household members as needed. This has enabled women to challenge roles assigned to them by tradition. Similar processes can be observed in poor countries, although around different technologies. The introduction of food processing technology such as corn mills and fuel-efficient stoves in African villages frees up women's time to do other things.

In households where many production activities are undertaken simultaneously, deci-sions are largely decentralized, one household member being responsible for an activity.

Technology may also dictate whether farm activities are organized in a decentralized or hierarchical way. Boserup (1965) observed, for instance, that hoe agriculture such as it is still practiced in much of Africa does not generate any returns to scale or economies of scope in farming. In this context, decentralized field management is usually optimal. Once animal draft power is introduced, however, economies of scope arise because of complementarities between animal husbandry and crop production. With animal draft power the centralization of power in the hands of the household head is often beneficial because it facilitates integrated management of a more complex organization of production (Binswanger and McIntire, 1987).

This contrast between hoe agriculture, where fields are managed by individual household members, and plough agriculture, where production decisions are centralized, further suggests that when returns to coordination are low enough, households naturally gravitate towards autonomy of decision. This suggests that autonomy surfaces whenever the cost of decentralized decision making is low enough.

Decentralization may reduce efficiency, however, because it reduces the scope for the pooling of resources. This point is made most clearly by Udry (1996) using detailed plot-level data from Burkina Faso. The author finds, in contrast, that plots controlled by women are farmed much less intensively and receive less manure than similar plots within the household controlled by men. The estimates imply that about 6 percent of output is lost because of inefficient factor allocation within the household.

Other forms of technological innovations can also affect the internal organization of work within the household. A good example is the introduction of rice irrigation in the Gambia discussed by von Braun and Webb (1989). The authors document how the introduction of irrigation in rice cultivation dramatically affected the division of labor between men and women. Until irrigation was introduced, the cultivation of rice along the banks of the Gambia river was exclusively a female activity. Once irrigation was introduced, however, returns to rice cultivation rose considerably and control over the crop shifted rapidly into male hands. This resulted in a concentration of control over labor resources in the hands of the household head, thereby affecting the division of labor and balance of power within the household.

2.4.3. Household formation

The above issues are important in their own right but they have an immediate relevance for household formation. First, gains from specialization, whether static or dynamic, generate economies of scale in household size – at least over a certain range. Gains from specialization are thus essential to understand optimal household size.

Second, essential tasks often can only be performed by certain categories of people because of acquired skills or social norms – for instance, women for food preparation or children for tending livestock. This implies that in order for a household to be an effective production unit, all these categories of people must be present. In the Ethiopian highlands, for instance, a man who enters the kitchen is laughed at. In these conditions, at least one woman has to be present in the household in order to prepare meals. By the same token, in livestock producing areas, children and young adults often play a major role in tending animals. The presence of children in the household is then essential to enable livestock production. Of course, one could "purchase" livestock tending services by hiring children from other households, but at higher transactions costs and possible risk of moral hazard. This simple observation may explain why school enrollment is often lower and fertility higher in livestock producing countries. The need for specific skills and the magnitude of returns to household size may also explain why young males marry later or stay with parents after marriage (Binswanger and McIntire, 1987). In rural communities, parents can effectively delay the age of marriage of their sons by failing to provide start-up capital and access to lineage land.

We have discussed how markets can substitute for home consumption and thus enable small households to reap the benefits of non-rival consumption goods. A similar observation can be made regarding household production. If markets are perfect and complete, household size and composition no longer matter; production decisions only depend on market prices. Missing skills are hired from the market and non-produced goods are secured outside the household. This is the standard separability result for household models (e.g. Singh, Squire and Strauss, 1986; de Janvry, Fafchamps and Sadoulet, 1991). It follows that production considerations affect household formation only when some markets are missing. Because of population density, markets are usually best developed in and around cities. This enables households to be smaller. Fafchamps and Shilpi (2005), for instance, show that households living in urban areas are much more specialized in their production pattern than those living in remote rural areas. Fafchamps and Wahba (2006) similarly find that children living in and around urban centers work less on the household farm or doing house chores, and spend more time in school.

In practice, it is very common for certain markets either to be missing entirely or to be unattractive because of transactions costs. For instance, eating out enables the household to avoid cooking its own food, but it means going out and waiting for food once at the restaurant. Take-away food reduces some of the transactions cost but still implies some transportation. When markets exist but are subject to transactions costs, some households typically choose to self-provide while others rely on the market either as sellers or as buyers (Key, Sadoulet and de Janvry, 2000).

To economize on transactions costs, households may aim to be just large enough so as to self-provide most of their needs. If this cannot be achieved, they may hire domestic servants, a practice that is widespread in developing countries. Hybrid cases also exist. For instance, in the Ethiopian highlands there exists an ancient marriage contract stipulating that a woman joins a man 'as a servant and a wife'. In case of marriage dissolution, the woman does not share household assets but is paid a compensation equal to the wage she would have earned as a servant over the time she was married. This was a kind of prenuptial agreement used by rich husbands – usually older men – unwilling to share their wealth with their bride. This ancient practice illustrates well the dual purpose of this kind of marriage.

In this context, technological innovation in home production can have dramatic consequences on household formation. In developed economies, the introduction of household appliances over the last fifty years, combined with a wider availability of goods through the market, have sharply reduced returns to household size and enabled households to shrink Deaton and Paxson (1998). Nowadays, there are many single person households, especially in large urban centers. A similar phenomenon can be found in the cities of developing countries, where many migrants live in single person households. In contrast, rural households often are quite large and produce a very diversified range of consumption goods and services. The fact that human beings often choose to live on their own when the economic penalty for doing so is reduced suggests that many value consumption autonomy, a force we discussed at the beginning of this section but that is usually ignored in the literature.

2.5. Insurance

A discussion of the reasons for household formation would be incomplete without bringing out their role as risk coping mechanisms (Fafchamps, 2003). It has long been recognized that one of the primary functions of the family is to protect its members against shocks. This is best exemplified by the traditional wording of the wedding ceremony which emphasizes risk sharing (e.g., "in sickness and in health"). One of the purposes of household formation is to pool resources for risk purposes: the able can look after the sick, the more fortunate can share with the less fortunate (Fafchamps, 1992).

The need for old age support is largely predictable and is not, strictly speaking, an insurance problem. It nevertheless has an important insurance component because it is difficult to predict the exact time at which support will be needed – and the precise nature of the required support. Integrating an elderly parent into one's household can in principle be done at the time when the need arises. But it can also be anticipated through coresidency.

The insurance role of the household is so much taken for granted that much of the literature on this issue has focused on pathological cases in which household members fail to pool resources. The literature on famines, for instance, has described situations in which households break apart under pressure because members better able to feed themselves find it impossible to provide for their spouse, parents, or children (e.g. Sen, 1981; Alamgir, 1980; Greenough, 1982). Anthropological accounts of the bushmen tell of households abandoning elderly members who can no longer walk. In a paper focusing on North-East Tanzania, Miguel (2003) shows that the practice of 'witch' killings covers mostly the physical elimination of elderly people (principally women) in times of duress. Put differently, accusations of witchcraft are brought disproportionately upon the elderly precisely at a time when their family finds it difficult to support them.

Absence of risk-sharing is not confined to pathological cases. Evidence from West Africa suggests that husbands and wives do not necessarily pool risk (e.g. Doss, 2001; Goldstein, 2000; Duflo and Udry, 2004). In their paper on risk sharing between spouses,

Dercon and Krishnan (2000) come to the more upbeat conclusion that in most of the Ethiopian highlands, risk is shared efficiently. They do, however, find significant deviations from risk sharing in parts of the country. This is also the part of the country where the status of women is the weakest (e.g. Pankhurst, 1992; The World Bank, 1998; Fafchamps and Quisumbing, 2002).

The nature of risk can have a profound effect on household formation. It is well known that, other things being equal, better risk pooling can be achieved in a larger group. Risk pooling thus militates in favor of large household size or larger kin networks that may be spatially diversified. In their discussion of agrarian institutions in land abundant economies, Binswanger and McIntire (1987) for instance point out that it is in environments characterized by a lot of risk that we mostly observe households that are integrated vertically (parents living with married children) and horizontally (married brothers living together). In troubled times (e.g., war, economic crisis), it is common to observe people putting more emphasis on family ties. This can be seen as a natural response to the heightened salience of risk in people's lives. The marginal gain from adding members to the group falls with group size, however. If the marginal cost of household size is constant or increasing, it follows that the household size that is optimal from a risk sharing point of view is finite.

Households can also realize gains from risk-sharing through spatial diversification, and may even choose household members' location and occupation to insure against spatially covariant risk. Rosenzweig and Stark (1989), for instance, find that Indian farm households with more variable profits tend to engage in longer distance marriage-cum-migration. In contrast, wealthier families, which are better able to self-insure, are less likely to engage in such long-distance insurance schemes. In the Dominican Sierra, female migrants play the role of insurers; men insure parents only if there is no other migrant in the household (de la Briere et al., 2002). Migrant family members who have not established independent households are also likely to have regular salaries or incomes that are not highly covariant with their household of origin. In the Philippines, the family's short run need for a stable source of income motivates unmarried female migrants to seek wage-earning jobs, despite their lack of long-term stability, since parents expect remittances to decrease after daughters marry and have their own familial obligations (Lauby and Stark, 1988).

Dercon and Krishnan (2000) test the risk sharing role of the household using data from rural Ethiopia. They point out that, irrespective of the internal decision structure of the household – e.g., whether unitary or collective – efficient allocation of resources between risk averse individuals within the household requires that individual shocks be pooled. Building on a framework developed by Altonji, Hayashi and Kotlikoff (1992), Mace (1991), and Cochrane (1991) and first applied in a developing context by Townsend (1994), they test whether individual illness shocks affect the evolution of an individual nutrition index, controlling for a variety of confounding factors. To correct for possible endogeneity of illness shocks, the regression is estimated in a dynamic framework using a GMM estimator developed by Arellano and Bond (1991). The authors cannot reject the null hypothesis of efficient risk pooling within households, except for poor women in the Southern part of the country. They use their results to estimate the relative welfare weights of men and women in the household. They find that a wife's relative position is better if customary laws on settlement at divorce a favorable or if she comes from a relatively wealthy background. Poor Southern women have lower Pareto weights in allocation, confirming the relative deprivation of these women.

This point is revisited more in detail by Duflo and Udry (2004) who reject the hypothesis of complete insurance within households, even with respect to publicly observable weather shocks. Different sources of income are allocated to different uses depending upon both the identity of the income earner and upon the origin of the income. Using data from Cote d'Ivoire the authors find that conditional on overall levels of expenditure, the composition of household expenditure is sensitive to the gender of the recipient of a rainfall shock. For example, rainfall shocks associated with high yields of women's crops shift expenditure towards food. In the studied country, strong social norms constrain the use of profits from yam cultivation, which is carried out almost exclusively by men. In line with these norms, Duflo and Udry find that rainfall-induced fluctuations in income from yams are transmitted to expenditures on education and food, not to expenditures on private goods (like alcohol and tobacco). Income pooling between coresident sons and fathers is also rejected by Kochar (2000) in rural Pakistan. She finds instead that sons contribute to household public goods, such as consumer durables and ceremonies, thereby enabling their father to work less.

Optimal household size also depends on the risk coping strategies open to individuals. In developed economies, many of the risks people face in their everyday life are insured. In some developing countries this is achieved primarily via government social programmes such as national health insurance, disability provisions, and redistributive pension schemes. In others, this is achieved largely through private markets. Whatever the precise means by which social insurance is achieved, what matters to us is that it eliminates or dramatically reduces one of the gains from household formation. This effect, combined with the other factors discussed earlier, might explain why households in countries with social insurance are smaller than households in countries without it. It certainly can explain why elderly parents seldom live with their children: they are taken care of by their retirement pension and the health insurance system. This process can also explain why groups with restricted access to social insurance (e.g., migrants) put more emphasis on family – either by sending remittances to relatives elsewhere, or by having more children (e.g. Rosenzweig and Stark, 1989; Stark and Lucas, 1988).

Exclusive reliance on public and private insurance programs can be mistaken, however. A sizeable proportion of the poor and destitute seem to be people from broken families – runaway children, single parents, and lone individuals who, for various reasons, have severed all ties with their relatives. This appears to be true everywhere, even in middle income or developed economies. What this suggests is that, even in richer economies, the household continues to play an important insurance role.

2.6. Saving, investment and capital accumulation

So far we have focused primarily on static gains from household formation. There are dynamic gains as well. One possible gain is in joint saving. By pooling their precautionary savings together, household members can better smooth risk. Pooling savings also enables them to better diversify their asset holdings, either because there are non-divisibilities (e.g., house, livestock) or because there is a minimum threshold to acquire a more remunerative financial asset. One good illustration of this idea is when couples jointly purchase a home in which they intend to retire. If one of them passes away, the other still has the benefit of a larger home.

Households are also the locus in which start-up capital can be accumulated for the creation of a new household unit. This is particularly true in farming communities. In order to set up an independent farm, a son needs land and equipment. The same is true for any other business. In many countries, much of the land, equipment, and working capital of newly formed households originates from parental transfers. In some cases, parents transfer (or 'lend') the money required to purchase the necessary capital. In other cases, they transfer the land and equipment in kind. Evidence of this is provided for Pakistan by Kochar (2004) who finds that households save in anticipation of the ill-health of young adult males, but also reduce investment in productive assets. The reason is that the expected return on productive assets is lower due to the poor health of young adults. Put differently, this means that in households where young adult males are in good health, parents accumulate productive assets for them. Parents may also use their contacts and social capital to access productive resources for their children – as when parents lobby the chief or peasant association for common land for their offspring.

A corollary of the above is that parents have some control over the time at which their children leave the household: children have to wait for parents to authorize their leaving the household. In practice, this often means that children must negotiate with their parents the right to marry and form their own household. Children who leave the household without authorization or who choose to elope run the risk of not receiving parental transfers. This may explain why, in agrarian societies, many young adults continue to live with their parents well into their late twenties and early thirties.

Inter vivos transfers at marriage are not the only form of transfer from parents to children. In most human societies, human capital formation takes place primarily in the household. By taking good care of their children, parents endow them with a good health and nutritional status. Children who have been malnourished early in life often are stunted and have poorer health. Parents impart a number of vocational and social skills to their offspring. The overwhelming majority of farmers, for instance, learn to farm with their parents. Many other skills are imparted in the same manner, that is, through learning-by-doing. The desire to transmit skills to children may affect household formation and composition, for instance when parents place one of their offspring as apprentice. Depending on circumstances, this may require that the child move to another household. In the case of land inheritance, both the physical asset and specific experience in using land are transmitted from parent to child (e.g. Rosenzweig and Wolpin, 1985; Fafchamps and Wahba, 2006).

Most parents also help their children attend school by paying for school expenses and by providing them with encouragement and intellectual support. Since this issue is covered in detail in other chapters, we do not discuss it further, except to say that school attendance may require that the child leaves the household, at least for part of the year. It is common, for instance, for children to move in with relatives in order to attend secondary school elsewhere. Children may also go to boarding school. Because of the lack of financial independence that it implies, attending school may also induce the child or young adult to remain with his or her parents.

When capital and labor markets are imperfect, parents may find themselves forced to ration available funds and time between their children. One consequence is that children become rivals for household resources. In economies with pro-male bias, sibling rivalry yields gains to having relatively more sisters than brothers. Garg and Morduch (1998), for instance, find that on average if Ghanaian children had all sisters (and no brothers) they would do roughly 25–40% better on measured health indicators than if they had all brothers (and no sisters). Using Indian data, Rose (1999) provides an extreme example of sibling rivalry. She shows that female children are more likely to die following an income shock, suggesting that severely constrained parents choose to neglect girls relative to boys. More work is needed in this area.

2.7. Centrifugal forces

In this section we have reviewed various sources of mutual gains from household formation. This presentation would nevertheless remain incomplete without a discussion of the forces that operate against household formation. We have already briefly mentioned some of them in passing. Here we discuss them more fully.

The first factor militating against household expansion is congestion: household public goods that are non-rival when the household is small often become rival as it expands. This is true for instance of housing and consumption durables. This implies, for instance, that the housing stock has an influence on household size: if houses are small and cannot accommodate large families, this should discourage parents from having more children, for instance. To the extent that real estate prices are higher in town than in the countryside, rural-urban migrations may favor a decline in fertility simply because parents cannot find large enough houses. By the same reasoning, the size of cars or consumption durables offered on the market may affect fertility as well.

Of course, the size of houses and cars is partly determined by demand: if parents demand larger houses, the market should accommodate them. There are reasons to suspect that this need not always be the case. First, regulation and zoning restrictions may limit the size of dwellings. In countries where large families are found mostly among immigrant populations, many city councils may seek to keep immigrants away by favoring development schemes that emphasize small dwellings. Second, in the presence of fixed product development or production costs, producers may optimally choose not to serve certain segments of the market, such as parents with large families, focusing instead on the median household size. This would restrict the range of goods available to large households, thereby creating congestion in consumption for them.

Congestion may also arise on the production side of the household. It is common for family enterprises to benefit from increasing returns to scale over a narrow range. These increasing returns may originate from non-divisibilities in production – e.g., a pair of oxen or a shop – that are underemployed when the family business is too small. They may also originate from non-traded factors of production – e.g., lineage land, entrepreneurial acumen, specific skill – that cannot reach their full potential if the size of operation is not large enough. Once the minimal size of operation has been achieved, returns to scale become constant or even decreasing (Fafchamps, 1994). This is particularly true of managerial capability: many entrepreneurs can only handle a small firm and get overwhelmed once the business expands beyond a certain size, for instance in poor countries where many of them are illiterate or poorly educated. This observation suggests one reason why more entrepreneurial individuals may choose to have a larger household: they can keep everyone productively occupied.

Loss of autonomy is another limit to household size. As we have argued earlier, pooling household resources often increases average consumption because of non-rival goods. But it is also likely to result in a lower adequacy between consumption and individual preferences; household members must compromise in order to achieve the gains from household formation. It follows that factors influencing individuals' willingness to compromise affect household formation. Age, for instance, may induce young adults to become more assertive and to seek a consumption pattern that better reflects their tastes. It should therefore come as no surprise that it is young adults who often leave the household to create a separate consumption unit.

Restricted autonomy in production decisions may also affect optimal household size. This occurs because of moral hazard: it is often difficult to mobilize the energy and initiative of household members in a given household production activity when they are not residual claimants nor responsible for that activity. Determining the precise reason for this state of affairs is beyond the scope of this chapter, but it probably due to a combination of moral considerations, material and psychological incentives, and coordination failure. It is therefore common for households to decentralize activities by making specific members responsible for a given task, field, or business (e.g. von Braun and Webb, 1989; Fafchamps and Quisumbing, 2003; Goldstein, 2000; Duflo and Udry, 2004). As we have explained earlier, doing so is not always possible. To the extent that the household head – or the central couple in the household – remains the residual claimant of household resources and can redistribute gains across members, decentralizing may fail to resolve all adverse incentive problems. In such cases, it becomes more efficient to 'spin off' part of the household production activities as a distinct production unit or household.

From a theoretical point of view, many incentive problems arising within the household – whether moral hazard or loss of autonomy – could be solved via long-term contracting. In our earlier example, the father could motivate his son by promising a reward at harvest time. The problem is that contracts between households members are surprisingly difficult to enforce. From a legal point of view, this arises because of rules regarding the joint ownership of assets between spouses. This creates an essential fungibility that nullifies attempts to modify claims on household resources. Legal and traditional norms regarding the control of resources within the household also put limits on what can credibly be promised. Of course, a repeated game argument could be invoked to solve these commitment problems. But as we know well, repeated games no longer work when household members anticipate that the household will break apart. Broken promises are indeed often invoked to justify leaving the household – whether between spouses or between parents and children.

Finally, one should not forget that household members often have the option to leave the household. This is true for spouses, who can divorce or separate. This is also true of children after they have come of age. Minor children, in contrast, can be constrained, by law, to live with their parents. But many choose to escape the law by running away from home. Individuals can also be lured away from their household by an outsider, for instance to elope. Outside bidding is at the core of Becker's theory of marriage, to which we turn in the next section.

It is reasonable to assume that, in general, people choose to remain in a household if it provides a better life for them than what they could achieve by leaving. In many cases, this is indeed the case. It is been shown that the wealth and income of spouses fall after a divorce, especially for women and children (see Jarvis and Jenkins, 1999; Bourreau-Dubois, Jeandidier and Berger, 2003 and the references cited therein). This fall is due not only to legal costs, but also to duplication of a house, car, appliances, etc. Children who run away from home often face a very bleak future living on the streets of a anonymous city, at the mercy of various criminals. Understanding the gains achieved through household formation can thus help us understand the process by which households are formed and broken. To this we turn in the next section, starting with a discussion of the marriage market and continuing with other entry and exit processes.

2.8. Summary

Many of the factors that affect household formation are amenable to economic analysis. Optimal household size can be seen as resulting from a trade-off between the multiple gains from living, consuming, accumulating, and producing together and the associated costs in terms of loss of autonomy, incentive problems, and congestion. Marginal gains from household formation are all declining beyond a certain household size while marginal costs increase. This implies that optimal household size is always finite.

From our discussion, it appears that certain factors influencing the returns and costs of household formation affect entire societies: technology change in household appliances, social insurance. Other factors operate at a more disaggregated level, i.e., at the local (e.g., market availability) or individual level (e.g., entrepreneurial talent). Although societal factors are quite salient for most of us – by comparing how our parents were living and how we live – they are difficult to test formally without long-term panel data. More work is required in this area.

Local effects are easier to analyze empirically, either by examining the behavior of migrants over time, or even by cross section analysis. Individual factors are in principle the easiest to test, although many of the forces we have emphasized in the preceding pages are difficult to measure or instrument – e.g., entrepreneurial talent, altruism, taste for large families, preference for autonomy. Again, more work is needed in this area.

Given the focus of this Handbook, we want to emphasize again how important the issues raised here are for farming households. Most farms anywhere are family operated. This means that the farming enterprise is managed by a household, relying heavily on the manpower, expertise, assets, and managerial capability of the household. The farm enterprise is virtually indistinguishable from the household. The immediate corollary is that household formation is extremely important for the success or failure of individual farm enterprises: the loss of a single member can cripple the enterprise, while the addition of extra hands can enable it to prosper. It is therefore no surprise if farming households the world over put a lot of emphasis on marriage and children: marriage marks the creation of a new enterprise, and without children this enterprise cannot reach its full potential.

Other factors reinforce this even further. Farming households normally reside close to the land they farm. This implies that they are scattered over a large territory, often far from urban centers. As we have argued, geographical isolation raises transactions costs in consumption and thus incites households to be more self-reliant. This is certainly true in consumption, many farming households self-providing much of what they consume. It is also true in coping with risk: geographical isolation makes it difficult if not impossible to rely on others (ambulance, fire brigade, police) in case of trouble. Farmers must be able to respond to many emergencies themselves. These observations probably explain the strong sense of individualism that is often associated with farming.

Households also play a central role in the gestation process of new farming enterprises. There is no better place to learn farming than on a farm. Unlike nearly all other occupations, learning-by-doing remains essential to farming. Much of the knowledge about the land, the animals, and the complex decision process is imparted from parents to children. This is true not only of the human capital needed to be a successful farmer, but also of the physical capital required – i.e., land, machinery, and working capital. Parents often play a crucial role in accumulating the assets required for a new farm to be created for their children. Depending on the existence of economies of scale, indivisible assets, returns to specific experience, or superior managerial talent of the household head, the transmission of assets can take place either inter vivos at the time of marriage, or at the time of death. The latter case arises in particular when married children choose to remain on the farm and to take over the farm once their father dies or retires. In the rural Philippines, for example, where rice farming does not involve much economies of scale, parents typically bestow a son with a portion of land upon marriage, forming part of the male "land dowry" (Quisumbing, 1994). In contrast, in India and Bangladesh, married brothers typically jointly farm land owned by their father; land is divided typically only after the father's death (e.g. Foster and Rosenzweig, 2001; Joshi, 2004) The bottom line is that enterprise formation and household formation are deeply intertwined as far as farming is concerned.

3. Marriage

In the preceding section we have discussed various reasons for the existence of households. Now we discuss the process by which households are formed. We begin with marriage, which often marks the creation of a new household. Like Becker (1981), we do not distinguish between legal marriage and common-law unions although being married may confer additional benefits not available to common-law partners. Edlund (2000) argues, for example, that while sex, children, and cohabitation are increasingly more frequently available outside marriage, only marriage automatically confers paternity: a husband is considered the father of a child borne by his wife. Enforcing claims to children and establishing clear inheritance rights may be one of the more important functions of marriage as an institution, at least in the Western World. Things are less clear-cut in rural areas of developing countries, where many marriages – or unions – follow customary rather than statutory law, and where allegiance to an extended family may be more important than establishing paternity.[9]

3.1. Assortative matching

To the best of our knowledge, the phrase 'marriage market' was first coined by Becker (1981). This terminology often is misleading to the neophyte because the word 'market' conjures up concepts of supply, demand, and price – seemingly suggesting that marriage is a process by which, say, husbands buy wives. This is not the intended mental association. The correct analogy is that of the labor market, the function of which is to match employees and employers. In a well functioning labor market, employees suited for bread making should work in a bakery while those suited for management should be CEOs. The labor market can thus be seen as a sorting process by which workers are allocated to the job that best suits them, and by which employers hire the workers best suited for the position they need to fill. This process is called assortative matching.

Becker's fundamental insight is that for a match to constitute an equilibrium of any assortative matching process, an employer must not be able to lure an employee from his or her current match, and vice versa. To illustrate this, suppose that there are N workers. Workers differ only in one dimension, say λ_i, $i \in N$. For simplicity we suppose that there are no ties, that is, no two workers with the same talent λ. Let us sort workers according to λ_i so that workers with the lowest index have the highest talent λ. There

---

[9] In matrilineal areas of Ghana, for example, inheritance follows the uterine line (Awusabo-Asare, 1990), and prior to the promulgation of the Intestate Succession Law in 1984, a man's children may be left with nothing if he dies intestate, his property reverting to the matriclan.

are N jobs which vary in their return to talent λ. Let the return to talent for firm j be denoted $g_j(\lambda)$ with $g'_j(\lambda) > 0$ for all $j \in N$. We sort jobs such that jobs with the highest return have the lowest index. Further assume that

$$g'_j(\lambda) > g'_k(\lambda) \quad \text{for all } \lambda \text{ and all } j < k.$$

It immediately follows that the efficient match is that which gives the job with the highest marginal return to talent to the most talented worker, the second highest job to the second highest worker, and so on. Put differently, workers and jobs of equal rank should be matched together.

It turns out that this assignment is also the only stable equilibrium of a matching game in which workers and employers can bid for jobs and employees. To see why, consider an assignment in which a less talented worker $i > m$ has been matched with job m and, at the same time, worker m has been matched with less demanding job i. Worker m can credibly offer to perform job m better than worker i while at the same time employer m can credibly offer a higher wage to worker m than what employer m can offer. Put differently, employer m and worker m can mutually deviate from any allocation in which worker m is matched with an inferior job. Of course, employer i and worker i prefer the status quo but, as long as contracting is voluntary, they cannot make an offer equivalent to what worker m and employer m can make. This simple but powerful reasoning is the basis for the assortative matching argument.

Assortative matching applies to a wide variety of situations, from academic jobs to medical interns (e.g. Gale and Shapley, 1962; Roth and Sotomayor, 1990). It also applies to marriage because the decision to form a particular union depends not only on the specific merits of a particular match, but also on the whole range of opportunities available to each partner. Since individuals in any society have many potential partners, this situation resembles a matching problem.

To see this formally, consider a population of suitable grooms and brides. We assume that polygyny (multiple wives) and polyandry (multiple husbands) are not allowed. Let W denote the discounted future utility from marriage. The welfare W of the newlyweds depends upon what they bring to marriage, namely physical wealth A_m and A_f and human capital H_m and H_f, where m stands for groom and f stands for bride. Thanks to the various gains from household formation discussed in the previous section, we assume that gains from household formation permit newlyweds to both achieve a welfare level higher than autarchy. We have:

$$W = W(A_m + A_f, H_m, H_f; Z) \tag{3.1}$$

where $W(.)$ captures all the gains from household formation discussed in Section 2 and Z represents a vector of location or time-specific factors that exogenously affect the utility from marriage. We assume that $\frac{\partial W}{\partial A} > 0$, $\frac{\partial W}{\partial H_m} > 0$, and $\frac{\partial W}{\partial H_f} > 0$: the utility from marriage increases with assets and human capital.

An interesting special case is when human capital is only valued for its income generating potential and there are no externalities from one spouse's human capital to the other's. In this case, the utility from marriage can be written:

$$W = W(A_m + A_f + \gamma_m H_m + \gamma_f H_f; Z) \tag{3.2}$$

where γ_m and γ_f denote life-time returns from human capital, with $\gamma_m > 0$, and $\gamma_f > 0$. In this special case, brides and grooms can be unambiguously ranked: all brides prefer grooms with high $A_m + \gamma_m H_m$ and all grooms prefer brides with high $A_f + \gamma_f H_f$.

We now move to the marriage market proper. There are M potential grooms and F potential brides in the economy, each with an endowment of assets A_i and human capital H_i. If Eq. (3.2) holds, then without loss of generality, potential grooms and brides can be indexed according to their physical and human capital such that:

$$A_m^1 + \gamma_m H_m^1 > A_m^2 + \gamma_m H_m^2 > \cdots > A_m^M + \gamma_m H_m^M,$$
$$A_f^1 + \gamma_f H_f^1 > A_f^2 + \gamma_f H_f^2 > \cdots > A_f^F + \gamma_f H_f^F.$$

For simplicity, assume that there are no ties so that each of the above inequalities is strict. Following Becker (1981), a assignment of potential brides and grooms is *not* a marriage market equilibrium if a groom (bride) wishes to attract another bride (groom) and this bride (groom) prefers to marry this groom (bride) than her (his) currently allotted partner. An assignment is stable if (1) there is no married person who would rather be single; and (2) there are no two persons who both prefer to form a new union with each other. Given our assumptions, we have:

PROPOSITION 1 *(Assortative Matching). If Eq. (3.2) holds, the marriage market equilibrium is unique. In this equilibrium, the top ranked groom marries the top ranked bride, the second ranked groom marries the second ranked bride, etc. In the absence of polygyny and polyandry, supernumerary brides (if $M < F$) or grooms (if $M > F$) do not marry.*

PROOF. See Becker (1981).   □

Assortative matching implies that we should observe a correlation between the combined physical and human capital of all brides and grooms in a given marriage pool. Competition between individuals for the best match means that, on average, the rich and educated marry the rich and educated.

In practice, other factors affect rankings so that a perfect correlation is not observed. Some of these factors are perfect substitutes for wealth but are not observable (e.g., business acumen). Other factors are ranked differently by different individuals. For instance, it is possible that farming grooms value brides with farm experience while other grooms do not. In this case, the ranking of brides differs across grooms. Assignments can also be influenced by external factors or chance events (e.g., kinship and family ties, personal traits, geographical proximity, similar interests). A detailed discussion of such cases is beyond the scope of this chapter. Recent theoretical papers on assortative matching are given by Legros and Newman (2004) and Hoppe, Moldovanu and Sela (2005).

There is ample empirical evidence in support of the assortative matching hypothesis (Montgomery and Trussell, 1986). Boulier and Rosenzweig (1984) is an early example from a developing country. Empirical findings from the Philippines support the hypothesis that schooling, marital search, and spouse selection are endogenous variables influenced directly or indirectly by the total resources of parents, endowed traits of offspring, the cost of schooling, and marriage-market conditions. Instrumental variable techniques confirm that there are payoffs to spouse search and positive assortative mating with respect to schooling, even if female labor force participation is low. The results also suggest that while additional schooling attracts a higher-value spouse, it lowers the gains from marrying. Consequently, women with more schooling and less attractive women tend to marry later than other women. The results also reject the hypotheses that more educated women in the Philippines have lower fertility because of a higher value of time and lower preferences for children. Instead, the observed female education-fertility association in the Philippines reflects the optimal search and mating behavior of agents with heterogeneous marriage market traits that are substitutes for children in household consumption. Fafchamps and Quisumbing (2005b) show that the formation of new couples in rural Ethiopia is characterized by assortative matching. Parental background variables, particularly parental land, strongly predict what individuals bring to marriage, particularly the first marriage. Combined with high inequality in assets brought to marriage, their results suggest that the pairing of prospective brides and grooms favors the reproduction of rural inequality over time, consistent with studies of earnings inequality elsewhere (e.g. Hyslop, 2001 for the United States).

With very few exceptions, empirical modeling of marriage markets has been stymied by the absence of data on all potential matches. There are few studies that have been able to link longitudinal data on marriages to censuses to model potential matches, as in Foster's (1998) study of marriage selection in Bangladesh. Proxies for potential opportunities – whether in the marriage or labor markets – have been used in certain studies, such as that of Rao (1993). By and large, differences in the level of aggregation of available data determine the degree of aggregation – and therefore relevance – of such proxy measures. Given the typical age difference between husbands and wives in rural India, Rao uses the district sex ratio of marriageable females (females 10–19) to marriageable males (males 20–29), to proxy the "marriage squeeze". Quisumbing and Hallman (2003), in their study of assets brought to marriage by husbands and wives in six countries, define the sex ratio as the ratio of females in the age category corresponding to the mean marriage age of females to that of males in the corresponding mean marriage age category, and was obtained from United Nations country-level population statistics. Although it would have been desirable to have district- or village-level sex ratios corresponding to the marriage year, historical data at this level of disaggregation for each study site were not available, and the authors used the countrylevel figures instead. Because this variable is defined at the country level, it masks the possibility that some areas within the same country (e.g., rural areas with high rates of male outmigration) may have a relative surplus of marriageable wives, while other areas may have a deficit. It also does not capture possible differences in the supply of marriageable individuals of a specific caste or race, if interracial or intercaste marriages are rare. Thus, the coefficients on the sex ratio variable in most of these studies should be interpreted with caution because it is a highly imperfect measure of the "marriage squeeze."

Empirical evidence suggests that assortative matching on human capital attributes has increased relative to sorting based on parental wealth and physical capital. Quisumbing and Hallman (2003) examine the family background, education, and assets brought to marriage by husbands and wives in six countries. They find that correlations between personal characteristics (e.g. schooling) have increased through time, while correlations based on parental characteristics (parental wealth) have decreased. A secular trend indicating increased sorting on human capital is also evident in marriages of young Guatemalan adults (Quisumbing et al., 2005). We also find this trend (at least, in our Ethiopia data) as the number of marriages increases (subsequent marriages seem to sort more on personal rather than parental characteristics) but the evidence also shows that this is a secular trend Fafchamps and Quisumbing, 2005b.

Assortative matching is an important factor to consider in assessing the impact of spousal attributes on child outcomes. Perhaps the most often cited link is that between mother's schooling and child health and nutrition. It has been argued that the magnitude of this link is overstated. If men who preferred to have fewer and better educated children married wives who are better educated and who prefer to have fewer and better educated children, mother's schooling – or better educated women's preferences for fewer, better quality children – cannot be solely responsible for better schooling outcomes. Rather, better educated children could be due to the higher home productivity of the mother's schooling, the preferences of women for higher quality children, or an outcome of the marriage matching process and men's and women's preferences (Schultz, 2001). Studies from Bangladesh (Foster, 2002) and India (Behrman, Birdsall and Deolalikar, 1995) suggest that part of the correlation between women's schooling and their children's schooling is due to assortative matching, and thus can be attributed to men's preferences rather than to women's differential productivity in educating their children.

Assortative matching is also of interest to policymakers because of its effect on inequality, both within and among households. Fafchamps and Quisumbing (2005b) find that, to a large extent, the formation of new couples in rural Ethiopia is characterized by assortative matching, with sorting based on human capital becoming more important through time. There is also substantial inequality in assets brought to marriage, with a Gini coefficient for all combined assets of 0.621. We also observe extreme inequality in assets brought to marriage by brides: most brides bring nothing while a few bring a lot. Gini coefficients for individual assets are higher than for total assets combined, the highest being for land, reflective of the high inequality in parental landholdings. They also find that the correlation between parental wealth and wealth at marriage is high, thereby suggesting relatively low intergenerational mobility. However, the correlation between assets at marriage and current assets is lower, indicating either that couples continue to accumulate assets over their married life, that bequests counteract some of the initial asset inequality at marriage, or that public redistribution policies (particularly the redistribution of land by Peasant Associations) have had an impact on current inequality. Combined with high inequality in assets brought to marriage, the pairing of prospective brides and grooms based on human capital favors the reproduction of rural inequality over time. This result is consistent with studies of earnings inequality elsewhere: Hyslop (2001), for instance, shows that in the United States assortative matching contributes over one-quarter of the level of permanent inequality, and 23 percent of the increase in inequality between 1979 and 1985.

3.2. Polygyny and polyandry

Many societies practice polygyny, whereby one man can marry several women at the same time.[10] Becker argues that, other things being equal, polygamy should improve the welfare of women. The basic intuition is that if marriage is voluntary, polygamy cannot hurt women: if a woman is satisfied with a proposed monogamous match, there is no reason for her to agree to switch to a polygamous marriage. Polygamy can therefore only arise when women prefer to enter in a polygamous union than remain in a monogamous marriage with a lower ranked groom.

Let us illustrate with a simple example that a rich groom can attract several wives because he can guarantee them a higher level of welfare than the next richest groom can provide. For simplicity, assume utility is monotonically increasing in the sum of all assets divided by the number of people.[11] Suppose men like having several wives, either because they derive satisfaction from multiple regular sexual partners, or because they value the added manpower and children that multiple wives bring. The assets of brides do not matter in this example, so without loss of generality we assume they have nothing. Payoffs to grooms m and brides f can be written:

$$W_m \left[\frac{A_m}{1+B}, B \right],$$

$$W_f \left[\frac{A_m}{1+B} \right]$$

where B is the number of wives and A_m is the assets of the groom.

Consider the simplest possible case: two grooms and two brides. If one bride marries the top ranked groom and the other marries the lower ranked groom, their utility is:

$$W_m^2 \left[\frac{A_m^2}{2}, 1 \right], \qquad W_f^2 \left[\frac{A_m^2}{2} \right] \quad \text{in the first marriage,}$$

$$W_m^1 \left[\frac{A_m^1}{2}, 1 \right], \qquad W_f^1 \left[\frac{A_m^1}{2} \right] \quad \text{in the second marriage.}$$

In contrast, if both brides marry the top groom, utilities are:

$$W_m^2 \left[\frac{A_m^2}{3}, 2 \right], \qquad W_f^2 \left[\frac{A_m^2}{3} \right], \qquad W_f^1 \left[\frac{A_m^2}{3} \right] \quad \text{in the polygamous marriage,}$$

---

[10] Polyandry is when one woman is married to several men; it is a rare phenomenon (e.g., the Naxi). Both can be modeled in the same way.

[11] This is a conservative assumption. As we discussed in the previous section, with economies of scale, utility falls more slowly with the addition of new members to the household.

$$W_m^1 \left[\frac{A_m^1}{1}, 0 \right] \quad \text{for the unmarried groom.}$$

To capture the idea that men prefer multiple wives, we assume that:

$$W_m^2 \left[\frac{A_m^2}{3}, 2 \right] > W_m^2 \left[\frac{A_m^2}{2}, 1 \right].$$

This implies that the highest ranked groom prefers the polygamous union. Furthermore, he can lure the second bride provided that the second bride prefers to be the second wife of the rich groom than be the first wife of the poor groom, i.e., if:

$$W_f^1 \left[\frac{A_m^2}{3} \right] > W_f^1 \left[\frac{A_m^1}{2} \right] \quad \text{that is, if}$$

$$A_m^2 > 1.5 A_m^1. \tag{3.3}$$

Since both brides are identical, the first bride also prefers to remain in the polygamous union than marry the low ranked groom. It follows that both brides prefer the polygamous union because it guarantees them a higher welfare than marrying the poor groom. This illustrates the idea that, since marriage is voluntary, women only enter in a polygamous union when it is in their interest. For this reason, Becker (1981) argues that polygyny is in the interest of women but against the interest of poorer men who remain unmarried.

As it turns out, the condition for women to prefer polygamy ex ante is more stringent than (3.3), a point that is not always recognized. To show this, let's compare the expected utility that the two (identical) brides can achieve in a monogamous society with what they can achieve in a polygamous society. For women to prefer polygamy ex ante, it must guarantee them a higher expected utility:

$$\frac{1}{2} W_f \left[\frac{A_m^1}{2} \right] + \frac{1}{2} W_f \left[\frac{A_m^2}{2} \right] < W_f \left[\frac{A_m^2}{3} \right].$$

Joint sufficient conditions are that $A_m^2 > 3 A_m^1$ and that $W_f[]$ is not risk loving.[12] Note that A_m^2 has to be quite a bit bigger than $1.5 A_m^1$ for women to prefer polygamy ex ante. This is because in a monogamous system, one bride would have achieved the higher utility level $W_f[\frac{A_m^2}{2}]$.

This tension is reflected if marriages are sequential instead of simultaneous. The first wife does not like her husband to take a second wife if her utility falls with the second

---

[12] Proof: Say $U_f(.)$ is linear. In this case, the inequality is satisfied only if:

$$\frac{1}{2} \frac{A_m^1}{2} + \frac{1}{2} \frac{k A_m^1}{2} \leqslant \frac{k A_m^1}{3},$$

$$3 \leqslant k.$$

By Jensen's inequality, if brides are risk averse, they prefer polygamy for lower values of k.

marriage. In order to convince the first wife to accept a second one, the husband has to alter the welfare distribution between wives so that the first wife keeps the same utility as in a monogamous marriage but the second wife receives less. To illustrate this point, continue to assume that all consumption is rival and further assume that the husband needs $\frac{A_m^2}{3}$ (the same level as before) to prefer polygamy. What the husband can offer to the second wife is:

$$A_m^2 - \frac{A_m^2}{2} \text{ (for first wife)} - \frac{A_m^2}{3} \text{ (for himself)} = \frac{A_m^2}{6}.$$

For the second wife to prefer this to marrying the poor groom, it must be that:

$$\frac{A_m^2}{6} > \frac{A_m^1}{2},$$
$$A_m^2 > 3A_m^1$$

which is the same as the sufficient condition for women to prefer polygamy ex ante. This may explain why many polygamous societies require the first wife to give her assent to further marriages (e.g., Kenya).

Does the above reasoning imply that the welfare of women is higher in polygamous societies? Not necessarily. Monogamous and polygamous societies differ in many respects. For instance, it is very common for polygamous societies to limit the legal rights of women and to restrict female inheritance, thereby reducing their bargaining power within the household. The net effect on female welfare may thus be negative.

Empirical work on polygyny is scarce; what exists is focused on Sub-Saharan Africa. Because women play an important role in agriculture in Sub-Saharan Africa, attempts have been made to link the demand for wives to women's productivity in agriculture. Anthropologists such as Goody (1976), using highly aggregate ethnographic data, have found that the incidence of polygyny across societies is associated with the extent of female involvement in agriculture. Grossbard (1976), using an urban sample, indicates that wealthier men take more wives, but the effect of greater male wealth cannot be separated from that of greater female home productivity. Singh's (1988) empirical analysis of about 60 agricultural households in Burkina Faso finds that farmers with greater landholdings have more wives, interpreting this as a shadow price effect.

Jacoby (1995) criticizes Singh's (1988) approach as unsuccessful in controlling for farm size and farm income simultaneously. He also calls attention to the assumption that land and other farm assets are exogenous variables, which is questionable given that wives themselves are partially viewed as farm assets. Jacoby (1995) uses a large scale household survey conducted in Cote d'Ivoire to estimate the productivity of female labor in farm households and then relates it to the number of wives of the household head, controlling for differences in wealth and other male characteristics. Empirical results support Becker's emphasis on inequality across men within a marriage market in explaining polygamy. First, men with greater wealth have more wives. This positive wealth effect means that wealthier men are able, and willing to, compete wives away from less wealthy men. Second, conditional on wealth, men with more productive farms have more wives; that is, wives are attracted to husbands on whose farms their labor is more productive. This finding substantiates the role of male inequality, but also suggests that the productive contribution of women is important. Third, taller men have more wives, a finding that is interpreted as capturing a number of traits, whether physical attractiveness, ability to support his wives, or other unobserved characteristics.

Jacoby (1995) explicitly relates his findings to Boserup's hypothesis linking polygyny to women's role in agricultural production. He finds that women's productivity is relatively high in regions with a large proportion of land devoted to certain food crops – particularly yams, peanuts, rice, and plantains – compared to regions growing mainly cocoa and coffee. In these areas where female labor contributes a larger share to agricultural income, men have more wives. Jacoby (1995) hypothesizes that the modest decline in rural polygyny in Cote d'Ivoire in the 1960s and the 1970s may be related to the increase in cocoa and coffee production for export, two crops where women's productivity is lower. If the expansion of export crops diminished the role of women in agriculture, wives may have become dearer, leading to less polygyny.[13]

3.3. Parental involvement

So far we have assumed that the bride and groom act in isolation when deciding who to marry. In practice, parents often get involved. As we have discussed in the previous section, this is particularly true in agrarian societies where parents transfer capital to children at the time of marriage. Since assets brought to marriage in large part come from the parents of the bride and groom, bequest considerations come into play as well. It is also common for parents to be involved in the choice of a suitable spouse. They can do so either directly or via match makers. In this case, parents act on the behalf of their children.[14]

The bequest choice facing altruistic parents marrying off their children can thus be represented as:

$$\max_{A_m, A_f, H_m, H_f} U\left(S - \sum_b A_m - \sum_g A_f - \sum_b sH_m - \sum_g sH_f; Z\right)$$
$$+ \sum_b \omega_b W_m\left(A_m + \overline{A}_f + \gamma_m H_m + \gamma_f \overline{H}_f; Z\right)$$
$$+ \sum_g \omega_g W_f\left(\overline{A}_m + A_f + \gamma_m \overline{H}_m + \gamma_f H_f; Z\right)$$

---

[13] Wives may also have become dearer through other mechanisms. In Western Ghana, the expansion of cocoa cultivation led to increased private property rights for women, as husbands had to grant women stronger property rights on land to cocoa, in return for labor in weeding and taking care of trees while the trees were still young. Women were able to accomplish this task because food crops and cocoa trees are typically intercropped while the trees are not yet mature Quisumbing et al. (2001). Because men had to give wives "gifts" of land to assure their labor input, women's labor became relatively more expensive.

[14] In some cases, children are not even involved in the choice of a spouse.

where the b and g subscripts denote boys and girls, respectively, $U(.)$ is the utility of parents, S is their wealth, s is the cost of human capital (e.g., school fee), and the ω's are welfare weights for sons and daughters. Variables A_m and A_f denote the assets given to sons and daughters as they marry; H_m and H_f denote their level of human capital. Variables $\bar{A}_m$, $\bar{A}_f$, $\bar{H}_m$, and $\bar{H}_f$ represent the assets and human capital of the people sons and daughters marry. In the above model, we have assumed symmetry among sons and among daughters.[15] We also assume that $W'' < 0$, so that parents have an incentive to equalize the welfare of their children.

The solution to the parents' choice can be characterized as follows:

1. Given symmetry, all sons and all daughters are treated equally.
2. Sons and daughters receive more if their welfare weight is larger, parents are wealthier, or they have fewer siblings.
3. Parents invest more in human capital relative to assets if the cost of human capital s is lower or the return to human capital γ_i is higher.

The empirical evidence strongly indicates that sons and daughters are not treated equally (e.g. Strauss and Thomas, 1995; Behrman, 1997). The extent of gender inequality nevertheless varies across cultures, depending on patrilineal, matrilineal, or bilateral forms of kinship and inheritance (Quisumbing, Estudillo and Otsuka, 2004). A series of studies in the Philippines, Sumatra, and Ghana explores the allocation of land and schooling across siblings. In the Philippines, where kinship is bilateral, analysis of a rice farming households who have completed inheritance decisions finds that daughters are not disadvantaged in schooling, but receive significantly less land and total inheritance, with partial compensation through receiving greater non-land assets (Quisumbing, 1994). A follow-up study of the same households finds that, in the younger generation, girls receive significantly more schooling, but less land; however, this does not translate to significant differences in lifetime incomes for sons and daughters, owing to women's higher participation in non-agricultural labor markets where returns to schooling are higher (Estudillo, Quisumbing and Otsuka, 2001).

In Sumatra, a traditionally matrilineal society, the inheritance system is evolving from a strictly matrilineal system to a more egalitarian system in which sons and daughters inherit the type of land which is more intensive in their own work effort. That is, daughters receive large areas of paddy land, since rice is more intensive in female labor, while sons inherit bush-fallow land, consistent with the requirement of men's labor for future development of such land (Quisumbing and Otsuka, 2001). There is also evidence of sibling rivalry: more sisters decrease one's inheritance of paddy land, while more brothers decrease receipts of agroforestry and bush-fallow areas. This is consistent with the differences in comparative advantages in lowland and upland farming between daughters and sons. In Western Ghana, while daughters are disadvantaged in both schooling and land inheritance, the allocation of land and schooling is biased against daughters.

---

[15] For a discussion of asymmetric bequest norms such as primogeniture, see for instance Platteau and Baland (2001) and Chu (1991).

However, the bias against daughters in both land and schooling is decreasing in the generation of the respondents' children (Quisumbing, Estudillo and Otsuka, 2004). This is consistent with the strengthening of women's land rights associated with the adoption of cocoa cultivation (Quisumbing et al., 2001).

Sibling rivalry can affect the assets received from parents, although the effect may depend on the timing of transfers. In Ethiopia, for example, the groom's number of brothers has strong negative effects on both total and land inheritance, but an insignificant effect on assets at marriage (Fafchamps and Quisumbing, 2005b). Possibly because sons do not all marry at the same time, or because new couples are allocated land from the Peasant Association, siblings do not compete for parents' land resources at the same time, unlike in the case of inheritance, when an estate is typically divided among all eligible heirs at the same time. With sisters, competition is much less pronounced since women inherit less in general. This results is consistent with other findings on sibling rivalry in Africa (e.g. Garg and Morduch, 1998; Morduch, 2000).

Extreme cases of sibling rivalry can also be found when some children are sacrificed to the welfare of their siblings. In our model, this corresponds to cases in which $W'' > 0$, that is, welfare is convex. In this case, parental welfare is maximized by sacrificing some children in order to raise the utility of others. Examples of such situations include children who do not marry and remain to care for elderly or sick parents. More extreme cases have been documented in which children are sold to landlords or sweatshops or even to prostitution in order to raise the funds required to educate their siblings. The extent to which some children are sacrificed to the welfare of others remains an under-researched area.

3.4. Dowry and bride-price

So far we have reasoned in terms of the assets the bride and groom bring to marriage, recognizing that many of these assets are transmitted to them by their parents (e.g., education, land, start-up capital). In many societies, marriage is also the occasion for large transfers of wealth between the family of the bride and that of the groom. Bride-price refers to the case when assets are transferred from the groom's family to the bride's; when assets flow from the bride's family to the groom's, it is called a dowry. Others define dowry as a large transfer made to the daughter at the time of her marriage, regardless of whether it is controlled by her or by the groom's family Botticini and Siow (2003). The world can in general be divided into dowry and bride-price countries. Asia is generally dowry-based while Sub-Saharan Africa generally follows a bride-price system.[16]

---

[16] There may also be other kinds of transfers, such as contributions to the cost of the wedding ceremony itself. These are relatively small compared to the value of assets ultimately transferred to the bride and groom. They are not discussed separately here, except to say that money is fungible. What matters is net transfers.

There are several explanations for the presence of dowry and bride-price.[17] One explanation posits that dowries (or bride-price) are pecuniary transfers used to clear the marriage market. The model has two predictions. When grooms are relatively scarce, brides pay dowries to grooms; when brides are relatively scarce, grooms pay bride-prices to brides. Moreover, since a dowry is a component of bridal wealth, when other components of bridal wealth become more important, the dowry is predicted to disappear and may be replaced by bride-price. In support of the first prediction, Rao (1993) attributes the rise of dowries in South Asia to a "marriage squeeze" caused by population growth, resulting in larger younger cohorts and a surplus of women in the marriage market. The prices of brides and grooms in the marriage market have been shown to be determined by spousal attributes – both individual and family characteristics. Consistent with South Asia's arranged marriage system, Deolalikar and Rao (1998) for instance find that grooms and brides in six villages in South Central India are matched by both individual and household characteristics, and that household characteristics are more valued in the marriage market.

Rao's (1993) specification uses trait differences, defined as female – male, to eliminate sources of measurement error common to husband and wife. He also argues that because assortative mating is very high, across all spousal traits, a specification using traits of both spouses as explanatory variables, without differencing them, could be potentially affected by multicollinearity. Thus, his specification focuses on the impact of relative differences between the traits and the spouses. The analysis of Rao (1993) has been criticized by Edlund (2000). She argues that regressing dowries on differences between spousal attributes imposes the restriction that attributes influence dowries in a symmetrical fashion. Using the same data, she finds that regressing dowry on individual traits instead of differences improves model fit considerably. She also fails to replicate Rao's result that the ratio of women aged 10–19 to men aged 20–29 contributes significantly to increasing dowries, casting doubt on the marriage squeeze hypothesis. Edlund (2000) argues that calculating dowry as the net difference between bride and groom families' transfers to the couple at the time of marriage is likely to overstate the relative contribution of the bride's family to the new couple, especially among wealthy families. If dowries are premortem inheritances for daughters, the larger the bequest component of the dowry (which would be the case for wealthier families), the larger the difference between the bride and groom families' transfers at the time of marriage. If parental bequests increased over the studied period, dowry thus computed could also increase without necessarily indicating a "rising price of husbands."

In his rejoinder, Rao (2000) points out that differences in his and Edlund's decisions on how to construct a consistent series of the marriage ratio variable have resulted in significantly different versions of that variable. While Rao was unable to replicate his earlier results using a linear specification, the later results using a quadratic definition of the marriage squeeze variable (as well as the non-differenced specification preferred

---

[17] See Botticini and Siow (2003) for a review of these explanations.

by Edlund) yield very similar substantive interpretations. Rao also points out that it is unlikely that parents transferred larger premortem bequests to daughters. First, evidence from the villages does not indicate that wealth has significantly increased (Walker and Ryan, 1990). Second, he cites recent anthropological evidence from India (e.g. Raheja, 1995; Kapadia, 1996) that shows that contemporary dowries are not bequests but involuntary payments often coercively extracted by the groom's family. Nevertheless, Rao's study is subject to the same criticism as other studies of marriage markets that use district-level averages to proxy conditions of the marriage markets. At best, these are only proxies for the supply of brides and grooms, and may be inadequate characterizations of the marriage market in societies where there may be significant barriers, even within the same geographical area and appropriate age cohorts, for persons of different castes, religions, and social classes to intermarry.

One of the main ideas in the economic literature on dowry and bride-price is that these represent prices paid for future services.[18] Married women join their husband's family, bringing with them their manpower, human capital, and reproductive potential. The bride-price is seen as compensation to the bride's family for letting go one of its female members. According to this reasoning, the bride-price is expected to rise if the value of what women bring to marriage increases. For instance, if the value of female farm labor rises, so should the bride-price.

By joining the husband's family, the bride also gains access to a certain lifestyle. Parents keen to ensure their daughter a good life may be willing to pay something in order for her to marry a wealthy groom. This is the rationale for a dowry system. Following this reasoning, the dowry is predicted to rise the wealthier the groom's family is.

Putting the two together gives a theory of dowry and bride-price that depends on the relative values of the groom's family assets and the bride's human and reproductive capital. Intuitively, the lower the value of female labor and the higher the groom's assets, the higher the dowry – or the lower the bride-price. Seen in this light, dowry and bride-price are nothing but advanced inheritance transfers by which parents seek to manipulate the marriage market outcomes of their progeny. In a society where women are free to work outside the home, devoted parents may choose to purchase their daughter a top education; in a society where women are more or less confined to the home, devoted parents choose instead to help their daughter marry the wealthiest possible groom. The rationale is the same: altruism towards children. Only the method differs.

Botticini and Siow (2003) argue that the market clearing explanation does not fully explain the existence of dowries. If the main purpose of dowries is to clear the marriage market, how do marriage markets clear in societies without dowry or bride-price? Moreover, the traditional theory of dowries does not explain why the timing of intergenerational transfers is gender-specific, with dowries given to daughters at marriage and bequests to sons. Botticini and Siow (2003) develop a model that is consistent with historical evidence ranging from ancient Near Eastern civilizations to modern times.

---

[18] On this point the classic contribution in the anthropological literature is Goody (1973).

They suggest that in virilocal (mostly agricultural) societies, parents provide dowries for daughters and bequests for sons in order to mitigate a free riding problem between their married sons and daughters. Since married sons live with their parents, they have a comparative advantage in working with the family assets relative to their sisters. If daughters leave home to marry, it will be difficult for them to claim parental assets upon their parents' death. The authors also argue that dowries will disappear as labor markets develop and children become less dependent on their family's assets for their livelihoods. As the demand for different types of occupations grows, parents will invest more in general rather than family-specific human capital. Instead of the dowry, parents will transfer wealth to both sons and daughters as human capital investments and bequests.

Expectations and strategic considerations are present even when large transfers between the bride and groom's family do not take place. Parents' bequest decisions may depend on their expectations regarding marriage market outcomes. For instance, if parents expect husbands to bring lots of assets to marriage, i.e., if $\bar{A}_m$ is large and $\bar{A}_f$ is small, they may compensate by giving less to daughters and more to sons, themselves contributing to the observed pattern of bequeathing more to sons.

Parents may also seek to strategically manipulate marriage market outcomes by increasing what they give to their child. For instance, parents may raise what they give to their daughter if doing so enables her to marry a higher ranked groom. Bidding for grooms can thus raise bequest from parents to children. Fafchamps and Quisumbing (2005a) find some evidence of strategic bidding in rural Ethiopia. While parents do not transfer wealth to children in ways that compensate for marriage market outcomes, certain parents give more assets to daughters whenever doing so increases the chances of marrying a wealthy groom.

Dowries and bride-prices serve other functions besides market clearing and bequests. They can be used to increase the bargaining power of the bride in the allocation of resources in the new household, thereby raising her welfare and protecting her from ill treatment by in-laws (Zhang and Chan, 1999). Indeed, Bloch and Rao (2002) find that noncompliance with dowry agreements increases the incidence of domestic violence. Dowry can also be used to guarantee sexual fidelity, although the effect can be asymmetric. In Uganda, being in a union in which a bride-price was paid reduces the probability that a woman reports engaging in an extramarital liaison by 20 percent (Bishai, Pariyo and Hill, 2003). Interestingly, men who report paying a bride-price have roughly twice the odds of reporting extramarital relations. Men may thus be substituting cash payments for their own fidelity to secure wives who provide marital fidelity.

Lastly, the timing of payment of bridewealth can serve a risk-smoothing function. In Zimbabwe, bride wealth is paid in installments rather than a lump sum on the date of marriage. Bridewealth is demanded by the bride's parents when the household experiences a loss in cattle possessions or has a low wealth status. Payment of an installment takes place when a household has high wealth status and the transfer of cattle does not endanger the cattle possessions of the debtor. In this environment where rural insurance markets are absent, flexibility in both the timing and type of bride wealth payment enhances household security beyond what is feasible through income pooling between relatives related through marriage (Dekker and Hoogeveen, 2002). The additional security results from the creation of a large pool of contingent, enforceable claims on assets (usually livestock) that are valuable for income generation and consumption smoothing purposes.

This issue is revisited by Hoogeveen, van der Klaauw and van Lommel (2003) who focus on the timing of marriage itself. Zimbabwean marriages are associated with bride wealth payments, which are transfers from (the family of) the groom to the bride's family. Unmarried daughters could therefore be considered assets who, at time of need, can be cashed in. The authors investigate to what extent the timing of a marriage of a daughter is affected by the economic conditions of the household from which she originates. They distinguish household-specific wealth levels and two types of shocks-correlated (weather) shocks and idiosyncratic shocks. The authors estimate a duration model using a unique panel survey of Zimbabwean smallholder farmers. The estimation results support the hypothesis that the timing of marriage is affected by household characteristics: girls from households that experience a negative (idiosyncratic) shock in their assets are more likely to marry.

3.5. Bargaining, threats and prenuptial agreements

So far we have assumed that the discounted future utility from marriage W is an exogenously given function. We now seek to endogenize it. We begin by noting that, as emphasized in the previous section, marriage generates welfare gains. The question then is how are these welfare gains divided between spouses.

A good starting point for understanding intrahousehold bargaining is the model by McElroy and Horney (1981). The authors posit that spouses derive utility from consuming rival and non-rival goods. Children are regarded as non-rival public goods since both parents derive satisfaction from their children's achievements. Spouses could live on their own, in which case their utility would be the outcome:

$$V_m\left(p_m, I_m^d\right) \equiv \max_{x_0, x_1, x_3} U_m(x_0, x_1, x_3)$$

$$\text{subject to} \quad p_0 x_o + p_1 x_1 = p_3(T - x_3) + I_m^d,$$

$$V_f\left(p_f, I_f^d\right) \equiv \max_{x_0, x_2, x_4} U_f(x_0, x_2, x_4)$$

$$\text{subject to} \quad p_0 x_o + p_2 x_2 = p_4(T - x_4) + I_f^d$$

where x_0 denotes the public good, x_1 the male good, x_2 the female good, x_3 male leisure, x_4 female leisure, T is time endowment, I_m^d the unearned income of the husband upon marriage dissolution, and I_f^d is the unearned income of the wife upon marriage dissolution. The indirect utility functions $V_m(p_m, I_m^d)$ and $V_f(p_f, I_f^d)$ represent the utility husband and wife could guarantee to themselves upon marriage dissolution. This is regarded by McElroy and Horney as setting up their respective threat points in a bargaining game modeled as a cooperative Nash equilibrium:

$$\max_x \left[W_m(x) - V_m(p_m, I_m^d) \right] \left[W_f(x) - V_f(p_f, I_f^d) \right]$$

$$\text{subject to} \quad p_0 x_0 + p_1 x_1 + p_2 x_2 + p_3 x_3 + p_4 x_4 = T(p_3 + p_4) + I_m + I_f$$

where I_m and I_f are the income of each spouse during marriage. In the paper, the authors make the strong assumption that $I_m = I_m^d$ and $I_f = I_f^d$. In practice, this is unwarranted because the income spouses would earn upon marriage dissolution depends on many factors such as alimony and child support, the division of household assets upon divorce, possibly influenced by a prenuptial agreement, and the capacity to combine work and child care.

Lundberg and Pollak (1993) revisit the bargaining model and argue that in most cases the threat of divorce is too strong to be credible because leaving the household means losing the gains from household formation. They propose an alternative model where threat points come from non-cooperation within the household. The equilibrium concept they propose is the non-cooperative (Cournot) equilibrium where each spouse takes the consumption level of the other as given and chooses his or her own independently. Formally, we have:

$$x^m(p, I_m, x_{0f}) \equiv \arg \max_{x_{0m}, x_1, x_3} U_m(x_{0m} + x_{0f}, x_1, x_3)$$

$$\text{subject to} \quad p_0 x_{om} + p_1 x_1 = p_3(T - x_3) + I_m,$$

$$x^f(p, I_f, x_{0m}) \equiv \arg \max_{x_{0f}, x_2, x_4} U_f(x_{om} + x_{0f}, x_2, x_4)$$

$$\text{subject to} \quad p_0 x_{of} + p_2 x_2 = p_4(T - x_4) + I_f.$$

The non-cooperative Nash equilibrium is the vector $\{x_{0m}, x_{0f}\}$ such that in which $x_{0m} = x_0^m(p, I_m, x_{0f})$ and $x_{0f} = x_0^f(p, I_f, x_{0m})$. Let the utility values associated with this equilibrium be denoted $V_m^*(p_m, I_m)$ and $V_f^*(p_f, I_f)$, respectively. The rest of the model is solved as in the cooperative Nash bargaining model of McElroy and Horney, replacing threat points $V_m(p_m, I_m^d)$ and $V_f(p_f, I_f^d)$ with $V_m^*(p_m, I_m)$ and $V_f^*(p_f, I_f)$, respectively. Lundberg and Pollak implicitly assume that, in a non-cooperative household, spouses would have full control over their individual income.

Formally, the main difference between the two models is that in the Lundberg and Pollak model, if spouses stop cooperating, they continue to share household public good x_0 since they remain together but they no longer coordinate their contribution to it. As a result, one would expect under-supply of labor and under-provision of non-rival goods in non-cooperative marriages. Drawing on the public finance literature, Bergstrom (1997) provides an excellent review of the issues surrounding the provision of public goods in non-cooperative households.

Fafchamps (2001) points out that the threat of divorce and the threat of non-cooperation within marriage are not independent from each other. To see this, suppose that:

$$V_m^*(p_m, I_m) < V_m(p_m, I_m^d),$$
$$V_f^*(p_f, I_f) > V_f(p_f, I_f^d).$$

This means that the wife prefers to threaten non-cooperation within marriage while the husband prefers divorce – perhaps because the law favors husbands in case of marriage dissolution. In this case, non-cooperation by the wife is met with divorce by the husband. Consequently, the credible threat points are $V_m(p_m, I_m^d)$ and $V_f(p_f, I_f^d)$. Spouses may also use violence as bargaining tool (Fafchamps, 2001). As shown by Bloch and Rao (2002), domestic violence is unfortunately predominant in many countries.

These different kinds of threat points have very different implications in terms of empirical applications. If divorce is the relevant threat, what matters most is the income spouses would earn after divorce, the assets they would keep, and possible alimony and child support transfers.[19] In poor countries, alimony payments are rare. Wife and child support are typically organized through the distribution of assets. Land, for instance, may be given to the wife for her to support herself and her children (Fafchamps and Quisumbing, 2002).

In contrast, if the relevant threat is non-cooperation within marriage, what matters most is control over household finances and sources of independent income. In many societies, households hold a common purse, but who actually is in charge of consumption expenditures varies considerably from place to place. Moreover, some expenditures are dictated by norms and customs. For instance, in many African societies, the husband is supposed to provide food and shelter for the household. Failure to provide would be interpreted as breach of contract and could trigger divorce proceedings and asset transfers (Fafchamps and Quisumbing, 2002). In many instances, spouses retain areas of independent control over 'pocket money' which they can spend as they wish. Some societies (e.g., West African coast), in contrast, hold separate finances for both spouses, each having a separate source of income and distinct responsibilities regarding common household expenditures (e.g. Goldstein, 2000; Duflo and Udry, 2004). We know of very few empirical attempts to distinguish between divorce and "separate spheres" models of exit options in developing countries. As discussed above, theory predicts that bargaining power within marriage depends on the division of assets upon divorce (exit options) and on control over assets during marriage (separate spheres). Using detailed household data from rural Ethiopia, Fafchamps and Quisumbing (2002) show that assets brought to marriage, ownership of assets, control within marriage, and disposition upon death or divorce are only partly related. Control over productive resources tends to be centralized into the hands of the household head, be it a man or a woman, irrespective of ownership of assets at or after marriage. Disposition upon death or divorce only loosely depends on

---

[19] The level of such transfers is a function of laws and customs and may involve court action. Divorced spouses may also seek to elude their obligations, in which case the likelihood of legal transfers being made enters the calculation of threat points.

individual ownership during marriage but control is associated with larger claims upon divorce. Assets brought into marriage have little impact on disposition upon death, but matter in case of divorce. The study did not test which type of threat point had a greater impact on intrahousehold allocation.

These issues are discussed in greater detail in the chapter devoted to intrahousehold issues. What we would like to emphasize here is that the bride and groom (and their parents) may seek to anticipate future bargaining in the household by manipulating threat points. This can be achieved at the individual level. The bride and groom, for instance, may sign a prenuptial agreement that shapes the distribution of assets upon divorce. They may also negotiate their 'rights' and 'duties' during marriage, e.g., the right for the wife to work or to have an independent income.

In most countries, laws and customs impose strong restrictions on individual negotiations. In some countries, for instance, it is illegal for women to work. Until recently, many European countries had restrictions on the kind of work women were allowed to undertake, restrictions inherited from an earlier era in which trade unions had sought to protect women from unsafe and arduous work. In some countries, women are not allowed to hold an individual bank account or are not eligible for a bank loan. In agrarian societies, it is common for women to be excluded from any freehold ownership on lineage land. The purpose is admittedly to keep land within the patriarchal lineage, thereby ensuring the future of the blood line. Social norms may also play a role. For instance, it is customary for Japanese and Filipino wives to hold the household purse and to look after household finances. In contrast, Ethiopian husbands control most household expenditures.

Economic conditions also influence what spouses can negotiate. For reasons that are beyond the scope of this Chapter, female workers in most countries get paid less than men for equal jobs (Altonji and Blank, 1999). This undoubtedly affects spouses' outside options. As Becker (1981) pointed out a long time ago, it may also influence how they choose to allocate work among themselves. More work is needed on these issues.

4. Marriage dissolution

Marriage dissolution is largely the mirror image of marriage formation: the same factors that affect the formation of a new couple affect its dissolution.

4.1. The causes of marriage dissolution

The starting point of the economic theory of marriage dissolution is the marriage market. Suppose grooms and brides are paired with each other in a way that violates assortative matching. Because the pairing is not an equilibrium, it is unstable: better grooms are able to reject a lesser bride to attract a better bride from a lesser groom. This process of bidding and counter-bidding resembles what happens in the academic job markets for PhD economists: between the job interviews at the ASSA meetings in early January and the end of the fly-outs, several weeks unfold during which tentative matches are made, only to be unmade when a candidate receives a better offer from another department.

Transposed to the marriage market, this mutual search process may take prior to marriage but some of it may take place afterwards as well. According to this view, extra-marital affairs can be seen as a search process by which one or both spouses continues to search for a better match. Of course, in such a union, the other spouse is likely to question the philandering partner's commitment to the couple.

Imperfect information may also play a role. Some characteristics of the bride and groom are not perfectly observable. Each has an incentive to misrepresent his or her own traits to achieve a better match. As information is revealed after marriage, one of the spouses may discover that he or she can achieve a better match elsewhere. Time, for instance, may reveal that one spouse has a proclivity for domestic violence, crime, or gambling. Infertility may also motivate husband and wife to seek another partner with whom to have children. These considerations can explain why a high proportion of divorces occur relatively shortly after marriage.

Individual traits change over time. Some people may develop an addiction to alcohol or drugs, or succumb to depression. People's priorities and behavior often change after child birth in ways that are seldom fully anticipated by their spouse (or themselves). External shocks may affect the gains spouses derive from a particular marriage. For instance, individual assets can be destroyed by events (drought, fire, warfare, natural disaster). Human capital can change, as when people earn a new degree or suffer a disability. Looks obviously change over time in ways that cannot be fully anticipated. Changes in traits and external shocks would alter rankings and destabilize existing pairings.

Empirical evidence suggests that the likelihood of marriage dissolution is influenced by changing conditions. It has been noted, for instance, that famines trigger divorce and separation (e.g. Sen, 1981; Alamgir, 1980; Greenough, 1982). The same is true for warfare. Drug and alcohol addiction are often associated with divorce. So is depression.

Marriage dissolution may result from mistakes. While bargaining over the distribution of gains from household formation, spouses may escalate their threats and counter-threats in ways that eventually lead to divorce. We have seen in the previous section that escalation is likely to arise whenever one spouse – say the wife – can credibly threaten non-cooperation within marriage but the other – say the husband – can retaliate by threatening to leave the household. In such situations, miscalculation by one or both parties may result in divorce even though no external forces are at play.

Government programs can affect the probability of marital dissolution by affecting women's options outside marriage, the subject of a large literature on the effects of welfare payments in developed countries, e.g. Schultz (1994) for the United States. In Mexico, for example, PROGRESA, a national conditional cash transfer program designed to improve children's education and health outcomes, targeted cash transfers to women conditional on children's enrollment and visits to health clinics. Bobonis (2004) finds that families that were eligible for the transfer experience a significant increase in separation rates, with most of the effect concentrated among indigenous households. While the absolute size of the effect is modest (0.7 percentage points), it is large relative to the underlying separation rate in the control group of households that were not eligible for the transfer.

4.2. The probability of divorce

So far we have discussed the factors that are likely to influence the likelihood of marriage dissolution in a specific couple. Theory also makes predictions about the unconditional probability of divorce in different societies. If the gains from household formation are very substantial, divorcing someone to search for a better match is extremely costly. This serves as a strong disincentive to divorce. In contrast, when the gains from household formation are limited, spouses may be more easily tempted to leave their current partner in the hope of finding better elsewhere. This, for instance, would predict that couples without children are more likely to divorce while farming households, who are more dependent on their children's labor, are less likely to.

Society may also seek to limit marriage dissolution, either by banning it entirely, or by discouraging search. Most human societies, for instance, disapprove of adultery, which is an effective way of making search for a new partner difficult. In some societies, adultery is even considered a crime and punished severely, especially female adultery. Laws and social norms may also seek to limit the exit option of one gender only, e.g., women. By making it extremely difficult for women to live independently, these laws and norms make it unlikely that a women would initiate marriage dissolution. The problem of course is that this also weakens the bargaining power of women within marriage. In some societies, the situation is partially redressed by other norms that compel husbands to provide for their wives and to treat them well.

It follows from the above that there is a strong relationship between exit options, stability of marriage, and what happens to divorced women. The world can be grossly divided into three groups: those countries that regard all women as dependent; those countries that regard all women as independent; and those that are somewhere in between.[20]

In the first group of countries, women must be taken care of by a man. Consequently, they have no access to factors of production, except in special circumstances when they need to take care of small children on their own (e.g., widowhood). To eliminate the latter circumstance, some societies go as far as banning divorce entirely and requiring that a man marry his dead brother's wife (levirate). This approach is well exemplified by Sharia law, but also by the Napoleonic code of law as practiced in continental Europe in the early 19th century. In this system, women typically do not inherit land. Much of the rural areas of the developing world fall in this category.

---

[20] In some societies, it is men who are considered as dependent. In Sumatra, for instance, land ownership is in the hands of women. Polyandry societies usually fall into this category. Because such societies are numerically very rare, we do not discuss them further here.

In the second group of countries, women and men are both regarded as independent adults. Since women have the right to live independently, they must be put in a position to take care of themselves. Hence, they have more or less equal access to factors of production. This means, for instance, that they inherit land and that they have a right to half of farm assets upon divorce. Much of the Western world falls in this category today, although this is a relatively recent development.

In the third category, we find many societies in transition, caught half-way between the two systems. This is the case, for instance, of many middle income countries, especially in urban areas. As discussed for land tenure by Andre and Platteau (1998) in Rwanda and by Otsuka and Quisumbing (2001) in Ghana, the weakening of a female dependency system need not result into female independence but rather in a muddle where social norms of support for women are weakened but land ownership remains largely inaccessible to them.

4.3. Female headship

In this section, we delve more deeply into the issue of female headship. Policy makers are concerned about female headship owing to its possible impact on child outcomes and on the welfare of women themselves. Most comparisons of this issue have been between male-headed and female-headed households, motivated by the assertion that female-headed households are overrepresented among the poor. The evidence behind this assertion, however, is mixed. Buvinic and Gupta (1997), for example, review 61 studies on headship and poverty and find that female-headed households are disproportionately represented among the poor. In contrast, Quisumbing, Haddad and Peña (2001), using stochastic dominance techniques, find that the relationship between female headship and poverty is strong only in two out of ten countries in their sample, Ghana and Bangladesh. Dreze and Srinivasan (1997) also find that, using standard poverty indices based on household per capita expenditure, there is no evidence that widows in India are disproportionately concentrated in poor households, or of female-headed households being poorer than male-headed households. However, poverty incidences are quite sensitive to the level of economies of scale. Even relatively small economies of scale imply that the incidence of poverty among single widows, widows living with unmarried children, and female households heads (who tend to live in smaller households) is higher than in the population as a whole.

These comparisons can be misleading for a number of reasons. First, in many comparisons male-headed households are composed primarily of households in which both spouses are present, while female-headed households are made up mostly of households in which a husband is not present. This is because, in nearly all societies, if both husband and wife are present, the husband is listed as head of household. As we have discussed in Section 2, living together generates many benefits. Due to returns to specialization, gender casting, and differentiated access to factors of production, households in which only a woman is present fail to capture all the benefits achieved by a household with a man and woman. It follows that female-headed and male-headed households are not directly comparable, even if they are of the same size. A more appropriate comparison would be between single-parent households headed by males and single-parent households headed by females, or between single women and single men living alone.

Secondly, comparisons between male-headed and female-headed households pay little attention to the endogeneity of female headship. Female headed households are a highly heterogeneous category. Female headship could result from women not marrying at all (as in many Western societies), to marriage postponement, to widowhood, or to temporary female-headedness due to migration, war, etc. The factors influencing the likelihood of a woman being selected into one of these various categories are likely to differ markedly across categories. Furthermore, as emphasized by the literature, we need to distinguish between *de jure* female headed households (headed by divorced or widowed women) and *de facto* female headed households (in which the husband is absent, but may contribute to – or even control – household finances). The consequences of female headship may differ quite markedly depending on the process by which a household becomes female-headed (Joshi, 2004).

A substantial literature exists examining the impact of female headship on child outcomes. This literature is vulnerable to selection bias. Indeed, if household formation decisions are correlated with preferences regarding children, conventional OLS estimates of the effect of headship on child outcomes will be biased. For instance, if women who care less about their children are more likely to live separately from the children's father, this will result in a negative correlation between female headship and child welfare.

Heterogeneity and endogeneity of female headship have policy implications. Since not all female-headed households are poor, the heterogeneity of female heads should be considered in designing policies that aim to improve child outcomes. Moreover, neglecting the endogeneity of female headship structure may result in unanticipated results, for instance by encouraging women to leave their husband. While this may be in the interest of the women concerned, it need not serve the interest of the children that the policy maker seeks to assist.

Examples of studies that examine the impact of female headship on child outcomes, controlling for the endogeneity of female headship, are from Jamaica and Bangladesh. The prevalence of female-headedness in Jamaica (42 percent) is one of the highest incidences in the world. Handa (1996a), citing work by anthropologists, claims that mating and residential patterns of adult women in Jamaica is a response to local economic conditions. The poor economic conditions in the region and the high rate of male unemployment make reliance on a male partner an uncertain proposition. At the same time, the presence of an unemployed male in the household restricts a woman from receiving support from her relatives and other male partners. Thus, female headship emerges as a survival strategy chosen by women to secure their own and their children's welfare, particularly in the lower socioeconomic classes.

Handa (1996a) estimates a structural probit model that examines whether outside opportunities, or threat points, affect the decision to become a female head. An increase in the expected level of adult women's consumption and their children's welfare, associated with being a female head, significantly increases the probability of becoming a head. Labor market work also increases the welfare of women and is an important determinant of the decision to head one's household. In another paper, Handa (1996b) finds that sex and union status of the household head have a significant influence of household expenditure behavior. While the presence of a female decision maker generally increases the share of the household budget allocated to child and family goods, female-headed households also spend more on adult wear and less on health. However, lower health expenditures are partially offset by the differential use of other health inputs in female-headed households In this study, Handa also takes into account the endogeneity of female headship.

The situation surrounding female headship in Bangladesh is quite different. Most female-headed households fall into two groups: widows, and married women, most of whom are wives of migrants. Joshi (2004) examines the impact of female headship on children's outcomes using a two-stage least squares procedure that controls for the endogeneity of both types of female headship. She finds that these two types of female heads differ not only in their income, asset ownership, and children's outcomes, but also their socioeconomic backgrounds prior to marriage. Compared to wives of male heads, widows are less likely to have brought dowries to their husbands' families, more likely to have lost a parent before their marriage, had fewer brothers, and come from poorer families than the families they married into. The situation of married wives of male heads is almost the exact opposite. She finds that residing in a household headed by a widow increases the likelihood of working outside the home by 93%, but has no statistically significant impact on any measure of children's schooling. However, children residing in a household headed by married women are 12% less likely to work outside the home, 19% more likely to have ever attended school, 8% more likely to be currently enrolled in school, and 41% more likely to have finished at least two or more years of school. In most cases, the hypothesis of exogeneity of female headship is rejected.

Structural estimation of the effects of headship on other household outcomes can be stymied by the difficulty of identifying the headship variable, as illustrated by Handa's study (Handa, 1996a) on the effects of female headship on household expenditure decisions. This study uses three types of identifying restrictions: (1) unearned remittance income (from friends and relatives); (2) a dummy variable indicating whether the household is eligible for food stamps; and (3) nonlinearities in the reduced-form probit. However, it is doubtful that remittance income affects the probability of headship without directly affecting expenditure decisions. In many developing countries, such transfers may be earmarked for particular expenditures, for example, a child's schooling or health expenditures, or investments in assets. Regarding the second identifying variable, Handa argues that the small size of the income transferred through food stamps makes it highly unlikely that households would alter their structure simply to become eligible for the program. However, the criteria for eligibility are closely linked with household demographic structure, which could exert its own independent effects on household demand patterns. The difficulty in identifying appropriate instruments continues to be a challenge in this literature, one that can potentially be overcome if one has longitudinal or retrospective data on family background or conditions at the time of marriage. Joshi (2004), for example, uses information on family background (whether the mother's father was alive at the time of her marriage), weather (the average level of rainfall when the mother was between the ages of 11 and 15), the fraction of the village with siblings residing in other thanas of Bangladesh (excluding Dhaka city or abroad), and the fraction of the village that has siblings residing in either Dhaka city or outside the country. The first two variables are thought to be correlated with the probability that the woman is a widow, while the latter two instruments have strong explanatory power in explaining a parent's decision to migrate away from the village.

5. Changes in household structure

Changes in household structure can be explained as the result of many of the same forces as those driving marriage formation and dissolution. Families are residentially extended when the gains from being extended (public goods, etc.) outweigh the gains of being nuclear (privacy, etc.). We can expand this to look at, for example, migration decisions and other changes in family structure such as child fostering. While our framework suggests that household structure is endogenous, in empirical work household structure is typically treated as an exogenous, or given, characteristic – usually because of the absence of data to control for selection bias.

The emerging literature suggests that an improved understanding of household formation or dissolution is useful for evaluating the impact of government policies, particularly those that are targeted on demographic characteristics (Edmonds, Mammen and Miller, 2005), dealing with the potential selectivity of panel designs that drop dividing households (Foster and Rosenzweig, 2001), and for studying household behavior and income change more generally.

Households can adjust their composition by sending or receiving household members. Because households can adjust their structure in response to government programs, it is critical for policy makers to recognize that changes in household structure may counteract some of the intended objectives of government programs. In this section we examine two phenomena clustered at two ends of the age distribution: child fostering and old age living arrangements. We also briefly discuss household division.

5.1. Child fostering

Child fostering is an institution by children live in a household other than that of their biological parents. Child fostering is particularly widespread in Sub-Saharan Africa where the percentage of households with foster children ranges from 15 percent in Ghana to 37 percent in Namibia (Vandermeersch, 1997). Factors affecting child fostering include risk-coping (Evans, 2004b), the quality of social networks (Akresh, 2004b), and imbalances in household demographics vis-à-vis the requirements of household production (e.g. Ainsworth, 1990, 1996). In recent years this institution has attracted increasing attention as researchers seek to understand how poor households deal with the AIDS epidemic.

The role of child fostering as a risk coping strategy has best been documented by Akresh (2004b). In a remarkable study on child fostering in Burkina Faso that uses data on sending and receiving households, he finds that households are more likely to send out a child if they experience a negative income shock, have better quality social networks, or have additional children in a given age and gender class. Increases of one standard deviation in a household's agricultural shock, percentage of good members in its network, or number of older girls would increase the probability of sending a child above the current level of fostering by 29.1, 30.0, and 34.5 percent, respectively.

Concern about the welfare of non-biological children in households (e.g., fostered children and orphans, especially in the context of the HIV/AIDs epidemic) has stimulated proposals from international development organizations trying to prevent children from growing up away from their biological parents. There is indeed ample evidence about the poorer outcomes of orphans in Africa. Orphans are equally less likely to be enrolled in school relative to both non-orphans as a group and to the non-orphans with whom they reside (Case, Paxson and Ableidinger, 2003). Children living in households headed by non-parental relatives fare systematically worse than those living with parental heads, and those living in households headed by non-relatives fare even worse. Case, Paxson and Ableidinger (2003) find that much of the gap between the schooling of orphans and non-orphans is explained by the greater tendency of orphans to live with more distant relatives or unrelated caregivers. The difference persists across income groups, but does not seem to differ by gender, although gender could potentially matter in cases of abuse.

Despite the growing evidence that fostered children may be treated differently from biological offspring, cross-country studies for Latin America, the Caribbean and Africa – such as that by Filmer and Ainsworth (2002) on orphans and school enrollment – suggest that the extent to which orphans are disadvantaged is country-specific. Ainsworth (1996) and Harper, Marcus and Moore (2003) note that a number of West African studies, including those from Mali (e.g. Castle, 1996; Engle, Castle and Menon, 1996) and Sierra Leone (Bledsoe, 1990), show that the reason for fosterage – whether it reflects a desire to strengthen ties between families, childlessness on the part of the household fostering-in, or resulting from death, divorce or migration of the biological parents – affects the support a fostered child receives.[21] Cross-sectional studies, however, shed only a limited light on the good – or ill – caused by child fostering arrangements. The problem is that cross-sectional studies comparing fostered to non-fostered children, or orphans to non-orphans, do not provide the appropriate counterfactual: that is, what would the welfare of a fostered child be, if he or she were not fostered? The ideal

---

[21] Other studies include Haddad and Hoddinott (1994), Lloyd and Blanc (1996) and Strauss and Mehra (1989).

comparison should be for orphans with or without fostering arrangements, not between orphans and non-orphans. Longitudinal studies of children that capture changes in fostering arrangements, allowing double-difference estimates, are the appropriate tool for studying the impact of this arrangement. In a particularly good study, Akresh (2004a) finds that fostered children are *not* negatively affected (in terms of school enrollment) in either the short or long run by living away from their biological parents (see also Evans, 2004a). If child fostering insulates households from adverse shocks, provides them access to the benefits of extended family networks, and moves children to households where they are more productive, then restricting the movement of children as a policy prescription needs to be reevaluated.

Similar to living arrangements of children, residential status of the elderly is a household decision variable. Edmonds, Mammen and Miller (2005) study the impact of an old-age income support program on the living arrangements of elder black women in South Africa. Social pension income for these women depends primarily on age-eligibility: women become eligible for the pension at age 60. Edmonds, Mammen and Miller (2005) identify the impacts of pension income on elderly living arrangements, overcoming the problem that pension income is age dependent, by exploiting the discontinuous nature of the age eligibility rule in the pension eligibility formula. Allowing for flexible smooth trends in age, the authors look for discontinuous changes in household composition that occur at the age of pension eligibility. In contrast to the results for developed countries, the authors do not find that the additional pension income leads to an increased propensity to live alone. Rather, at the age of pension eligibility, prime working age women depart, and the presence of children under 5 and young women of child bearing age increase. These shifts in coresidence patterns are consistent with a setting where prime age women have comparative advantage in work away from the extended family relative to younger women,who may be less productive in market work owing to child care obligations and less labor market experience. Moreover, the grandmother may help with the child care of young children, thereby improving the ability of young mothers to work in addition to their household production activities. The additional income from old age support then enables the household to allocate labor more optimally by moving young women in and prime age women out.

The fluidity of household structure in response to government programs emphasizes the need to pay attention to the endogeneity of household structure. In addition to the usual distortions imposed by government transfer programs such as the one studied by Edmonds, Mammen and Miller (2005), a policy that is conditioned on household composition may introduce additional distortions because it interferes with households' optimal responses to income changes. For example, targeting cash transfers to children but varying transfers with household size or limiting transfers to households with single parents may prevent individuals from adjusting their living arrangements in response to income fluctuations. In South Africa, the extension of a retirement insurance scheme to the poor has been shown to be associated with a massive change in the family structure of the elderly (Case and Deaton, 1998).

The changes in family structure as a result of pension arrangements leads one to question findings of studies that assume that family structures remain unchanged after an income transfer program is implemented. For example, Duflo (2003) takes advantage of the 1993 extension of the South African social pension program to the black population to investigate the effect of grandmother altruism on child nutritional status. Her estimates suggest that pensions received by women had a large impact on the anthropometric status (weight for height and height for age) of girls but little effect on that of boys, while no similar effect is found for pensions received by men. However, a key assumption is that pension income has no impact on unmeasured characteristics of those people who coreside with pension recipients. Hamoudi and Thomas (2005) find that adjustments in household composition as a result of the old age pension occur not only in terms of residents' standard measured characteristics (like age and gender, which can be controlled for), but are also related to measured and unmeasured individual characteristics which are themselves related to individuals' bargaining power, their tastes, and therefore, potentially, to a broad array of outcomes. Hamoudi and Thomas find that pension-eligible adults are more likely to coreside with other adults who have lower levels of human capital as measured by height and education. Since height and education are fixed for adults, this cannot be an effect of the pension income but rather reflects the selection of adults who coreside with older adults when they become eligible for the pension. The authors then explore the importance of treating living arrangements as endogenous in (re)interpreting the results on the impact of the pension in the literature, and highlight the potential value of moving beyond a spatially determined definition of the household to a more inclusive definition of the family as a decisionmaking unit.

5.2. Old age support

The literature has identified several reasons for coresidence with elderly family members. Supporting elderly people may reflect social norms of reciprocity: parents supported you when you were a child, you have to support them when they can no longer support themselves. Altruism is also likely to affect one's willingness to support the elderly. As argued in the Chapter devoted to extended family and kinship networks, altruism is affected by genes. It is therefore widely believed that, in developing countries, elderly men and women are taken care of by their children.

Kochar (2000) investigates this issue in Pakistan. She examines the negative correlation between the days of work reported by fathers in rural Pakistani households and the incomes earned by their coresident adult sons. She finds that the decline in fathers' days of work that accompanies increases in sons' incomes primarily results because such income is used to finance expenditures on household public goods, such as consumer durables and ceremonies. Empirical tests reject most alternative explanations of the benefits of coresidence, including the belief that sons contribute to fathers' wealth.

What is true for leisure need not be true for health care. In another article also on Pakistan, Kochar (1999) documents a robust correlation between a sharp decline in individual wage with age and a reduction in medical expenditures for the elderly. She argues that this constitutes evidence that the intergenerational old age support is unable to meet the higher health care needs of the elderly.

Another reason for old age support is that elderly people are still useful in spite of their age. They can assist with light chores such as child care, thereby enabling younger members of the household to work outside the home. They are the repository of much valuable experience and social history. By recalling past events, they can provide useful insights regarding rare occurrences. Their farming and business experience may also be quite useful (Datta and Nugent, 1984). Note that these benefits can in principle be obtained from many elderly persons, not necessarily from relatives – unless relatives have household-specific experience that is of value, such as experience with a given plot of land or a given business. Evidence for India is provided by Rosenzweig and Wolpin (1985) who test and calculate the contribution to agricultural profits of the farm experience embodied in coresident elderly kin.

Old age support need not imply coresidence. In many developed countries, elderly people are increasingly taken care of through the market – e.g., they join a retirement home or community. Children may remain involved, for instance by assisting financially. But coresidence is no longer considered a requirement of old age support. It is interesting to note that this development in developed countries arises at a time when elderly people are less useful in the home (fewer children, more household appliances) and when experience is less relevant, either because children are in another line of business or because technology has changed so much that the experience of the elderly is not longer valued. As developing countries urbanize, we can expect similar forces to reshape the way in which the elderly are taken care of – or not.

5.3. Household division

The above discussion has focused on incremental changes to household structure. Households may also undergo more radical changes, such as household partition. The basis for extended family structures is similar to the rationale for household formation: households can be extended if the gains from extension outweigh those from being nuclear. Conversely, if the gains from being an extended family are less than the gains from being nuclear, the family will split.

While the collective model of the household has usually been applied to the analysis of intrahousehold allocation, it can also be used to examine household division. Foster and Rosenzweig (2001) formulate a collective model of household division in which individuals are assumed to optimize subject to a set of predefined entitlement rules (inheritance laws) and intrahousehold allocations are efficient. Gains from coresidence arise from cost-sharing a household-specific public good and lower barriers to information-sharing on farming techniques. Whether such gains are sufficient to make coresidence desirable depends on the existence of scale economies or diseconomies in production and on how household structure affects risk-sharing. In the Indian data studied by the authors, most splits occur at the death of the household head. In the context of the model, the death of the household head would lead to division if the head has above average preferences for the public good, or if the head has superior knowledge about agricultural practices. The authors test the model using panel data from India starting from the onset of the Green Revolution in the late 1960s through 1982. As predicted by the model, within- household inequality in schooling, marriages, and risk increase the probability of household division. In particular, households that eventually divided resided in slightly riskier areas and had on average a greater number of daughters of the household head who had left the household, presumably for marriage, and a greater number of married claimants (sons) initially residing within the household compared with households that remained intact.

The authors argue that taking into account the process of household division is essential to understanding the effects of technical change on inequality. Due to the importance of human capital externalities in production, combined with greater within-household schooling inequality in richer households, and the presence of decreasing returns to scale in production under the Green Revolution technology, technical change that occurred during the first decade of the Green Revolution tended to differentially reduce household division among households with more land resources per capita. Because of these reductions, the average effect of technical change on income growth for members of these richer households was weaker than the effects on less wealthy households at the beginning of the period. Thus, without taking into account the possible consequences of technical change on household division, it is possible to overestimate the extent to which better-off households benefited from technical change relative to poorer ones.

6. Conclusions

Through this very incomplete survey of the literature, we hope to have convinced the reader that economics has much to say about family formation. Many empirical patterns regarding marriage, dowries, child fostering, or old age support can be explained using simple economic concepts.

The economic literature on family formation and marriage is important not only for is positive content, but also because of its far-reaching policy implications. Laws regarding marriage, divorce, and child support shape incentives in profound ways, leading to – or at least accompanying – massive social changes, such as the dramatic rise of out-of-wedlock birth in France where it now represents half of all newborns.[22]

Laws and social customs regarding female wages and labor market participation shape the bargaining power of women within and outside marriage. Restricting women's access to income generating opportunities may be a way of cementing marriage by reducing the exit options of women. But it does so largely at the expense of women's welfare. This is particularly true in societies where traditional safeguards protecting

---

[22] Edlund (2006) mentions that more than one third of children are born to unmarried mothers in the US, Canada, the UK, Ireland, France, and the Nordic countries.

women have been eroded, but market opportunities for women have not increased enough to compensate for this erosion. No matter how strongly society seeks to discourage marriage dissolution, it is a fact of life that some couples are ill-suited and that separation is inevitable. This means that some women will find themselves without the protection of a husband or father. When these women do not have adequate access to employment or business income, they may be forced into unhealthy or demeaning activities, such as begging or prostitution (Cohen, 1969). The rise of HIV/AIDS has made prostitution a particularly dangerous way of generating income. Based on the analysis presented here, we suspect that this has worsened the bargaining position of women, particularly those for whom prostitution is the only viable exit option.

As shown most vividly in the case of South Africa (Case and Deaton, 1998), welfare programs such as retirement and widowhood insurance can have a dramatic impact on household formation. In some countries such as the UK, social programs such as child care benefits have been amended to favor women. Lundberg, Pollak and Wales (1997) have shown that this change has led to a significant – albeit small – increase in household expenditures earmarked for female consumption.

As illustrated by a growing literature (e.g. Haddad and Kanbur, 1990; Behrman, 1997), much inequality exists within households. Economists and policymakers alike need to better understand the ways that marriage markets contribute to perpetuating inequality both within and across households, given the evidence that marriage markets and assortative mating provide a powerful engine for sustaining, if not widening, the inter-household inequalities in most societies. The impact of assortative mating on human capital on inequality is likely to increase, especially as human capital endowments become more important both in the overall output of societies and as attributes that individuals value in future spouses. The literature presented here gives us ways to think about the various factors affecting this inequality while at the same time suggesting policy levers through which intrahousehold inequality can be alleviated.

References

Ainsworth, M. (1990). "The demand for children in Cote d'Ivoire: Economic aspects of fertility and child fostering". Unpublished PhD dissertation. Department of Economics, Yale University, New Haven.

Ainsworth, M. (1996). "Economic aspects of child fostering in Cote d'Ivoire". In: Schultz, T.P. (Ed.), In: Research in Population Economics, vol. 8. JAI Press, Greenwich CT, pp. 25–62.

Akresh, R. (2004a). "Adjusting household structure: School enrollment impacts of child fostering in Burkina Faso". Technical report. Working paper No. 89, BREAD, Washington DC.

Akresh, R. (2004b). "Risk, network quality, and family structure: Child fostering decisions in Burkina Faso". Mimeo.

Alamgir, M. (1980). Famine in South Asia: Political Economy of Mass Starvation. Oelgeschlager, Gunn and Hain Publ., Cambridge, MA.

Altonji, J.G., Blank, R.M. (1999). "Race and gender in the labor market". In: Ashenfelter, O., Card, D. (Eds.), In: Handbook of Labor Economics, vol. 3. Elsevier, New York, pp. 3143–3258.

Altonji, J.G., Hayashi, F., Kotlikoff, L.J. (1992). "Is the extended family altruistically linked? Direct tests using micro data". American Economic Review 82 (5), 1177–1198.

Andre, C., Platteau, J.-P. (1998). "Land relations under unbearable stress: Rwanda caught in the Malthusian trap". Journal of Economic Behavior and Organization 34 (1), 1–47.

Arellano, M., Bond, S.R. (1991). "Some tests of specification for panel data: Monte Carlo evidence and an application to employment equations". Review of Economic Studies 58, 277–297.

Awusabo-Asare, K. (1990). "Matriliny and the new intestate succession law of Ghana". Canadian Journal of African Studies 24 (1), 1–16.

Becker, G.S. (1965). "A theory of the allocation of time". Economic Journal 75 (299), 493–517.

Becker, G.S. (1981). A Treatise on the Family. Harvard U.P., Cambridge, MA.

Behrman, J.R. (1997). "Intrahousehold distribution and the family". In: Rosenzweig, M.R., Stark, O. (Eds.), Handbook of Population and Family Economics. North-Holland, Amsterdam, pp. 125–187.

Behrman, J.R., Birdsall, N., Deolalikar, A. (1995). "Marriage markets, labor markets and unobserved human capital: An empirical exploration for South-Central India". Economic Development and Cultural Change 43 (3), 585–601.

Bergstrom, T.C. (1997). "A survey of theories of the family". In: Rosenzweig, M.R., Stark, O. (Eds.), Handbook of Population and Family Economics. North-Holland, Amsterdam, pp. 21–79.

Binswanger, H.P., McIntire, J. (1987). "Behavioral and material determinants of production relations in land-abundant tropical agriculture". Economic Development and Cultural Change 36 (1), 73–99.

Bishai, D., Pariyo, G., Hill, K. (2003). "Far above rubies: The association between bride price and extramarital liaisons in Uganda". Mimeo.

Bledsoe, C. (1990). "No success without struggle: Social mobility and hardship for foster children in Sierra Leone". Man 25, 70–88.

Bloch, F., Rao, V. (2002). "Terror as a bargaining instrument: A case study of dowry violence in rural India". American Economic Review 92 (4), 1029–1043.

Bobonis, G. (2004). "Income transfers, marital dissolution and intrahousehold resource allocation: Evidence from rural Mexico". Mimeo.

Boserup, E. (1965). The Conditions of Agricultural Growth. Aldine Publishing Company, Chicago.

Botticini, M., Siow, A. (2003). "Why dowries?" American Economic Review 93 (4), 1385–1398.

Boulier, B.L., Rosenzweig, M.R. (1984). "Schooling, search, and spouse selection: Testing economic theories of marriage and household behavior". Journal of Political Economy 92 (4), 712–732.

Bourreau-Dubois, C., Jeandidier, B., Berger, F. (2003). "Poverty dynamics, family events, labour market events in Europe: Are there any differences between women and men?" Mimeo.

Browning, M., Chiappori, P. (1998). "Efficient intrahousehold allocation: A general characterization and empirical test". Econometrica 66 (6), 1241–1278.

Buss, D.M. (2005). The Handbook of Evolutionary Psychology. Wiley, Hoboken.

Buvinic, M., Gupta, G.R. (1997). "Female-headed households and female-maintained families: Are they worth targeting to reduce poverty in developing countries?" Economic Development and Cultural Change 45 (2), 259–280.

Case, A., Deaton, A. (1998). "Large cash transfers to the elderly in South Africa". Economic Journal 108 (450), 1330–1361.

Case, A., Lin, I.F., McLanahan, S. (2000). "How hungry is the selfish gene?" Economic Journal 110 (466), 781–804.

Case, A., Paxson, C., Ableidinger, J. (2003). "The education of African orphans". Mimeo.

Castle, S. (1996). "The current and intergenerational impact of child fostering on children's nutritional status in rural Mali". Human Organization 55 (2), 193–205.

Chu, C.Y. (1991). "Primogeniture". Journal of Political Economy 99, 78–99.

Cochrane, J.H. (1991). "A simple test of consumption insurance". Journal Political Economy 99 (5), 957–976.

Cohen, A. (1969). Custom and Politics in Urban Africa: A Study of Hausa Migrants in Yoruba Towns. Univ. of California Press, Berkeley.

Daly, M., Wilson, M. (1987). "The Darwinian psychology of discriminative parental solicitude". Nebraska Symposium on Motivation 35, 91–144.

Datta, S.K., Nugent, J.B. (1984). "Are old-age security and the utility of children in rural India really unimportant?" Population Studies 38, 507–509.

de Janvry, A., Fafchamps, M., Sadoulet, E. (1991). "Peasant household behavior with missing markets: Some paradoxes explained". Economic Journal 101 (409), 1400–1417.

de la Briere, B., de Janvry, A., Lambert, S., Sadoulet, E. (2002). "The roles of destination, gender, and household composition in explaining remittances: An analysis for the Dominican Sierra". Journal of Development Economics 68 (2), 309–328.

Deaton, A. (2000). The Analysis of Household Surveys. The World Bank, Washington, DC.

Deaton, A., Paxson, C.H. (1998). "Economies of scale, household size and the demand for food". Journal of Political Economy 106 (5), 897–930.

Dekker, M., Hoogeveen, H. (2002). "Bride wealth and household security in rural Zimbabwe". Journal of African Economies 11 (1), 114–145.

Deolalikar, A., Rao, V. (1998). "The demand for dowries and bride characteristics in marriage: Empirical estimates for rural South-Central India". In: Krishnaraj, M., Sudarshan, R.M., Shariff, A. (Eds.), Gender, Population and Development. Oxford Univ. Press, Delhi, Oxford and New York, pp. 122–140.

Dercon, S., Krishnan, P. (2000). "In sickness and in health: Risk-sharing within households in rural Ethiopia". Journal of Political Economy 108 (4), 688–727.

Doss, C. (2001). "Is risk fully pooled within the household? Evidence from Ghana". Economic Development and Cultural Change 50 (1), 101–130.

Dreze, J., Srinivasan, P. (1997). "Widowhood and poverty in rural India: Some inferences from household survey data". Journal of Development Economics 54 (2), 217–234.

Duflo, E. (2003). "Grandmothers and granddaughters: Old-age pensions and intrahousehold allocation in South Africa". World Bank Economic Review 17 (1), 1–25.

Duflo, E., Udry, C. (2004). "Intrahousehold resource allocation in Cote d'Ivoire: Social norms, separate accounts, and consumption choices". Working paper 10498. National Bureau of Economic Research.

Edlund, L. (2000). "The marriage squeeze interpretation of dowry inflation: A critique". Journal of Political Economy 108 (6), 1327–1333.

Edlund, L. (2006). "Marriage: Past, present, future?" Economic Studies 52 (4), 621–639.

Edmonds, E., Mammen, K., Miller, D.L. (2005). "Rearranging the family? Income support and elderly living arrangements in a low income country". Journal of Human Resources 40 (1), 186–207.

Engle, P., Castle, S., Menon, P. (1996). "Child development: Vulnerability and resilience". Technical report. Discussion Paper 12, FCND, International Food Policy Research Institute, Washington, DC.

Estudillo, J.P., Quisumbing, A.R., Otsuka, K. (2001). "Gender differences in land inheritance, schooling and lifetime income: Evidence from the rural Philippines". Journal of Development Studies 37 (4), 23–48.

Evans, D. (2004a). "Orphans and schooling in Africa: A longitudinal analysis". Mimeo.

Evans, D. (2004b). "The spillover impacts of Africa's orphan crisis". Mimeo.

Fafchamps, M. (1992). "Solidarity networks in pre-industrial societies: Rational peasants with a moral economy". Economic Development and Cultural Change 41 (1), 147–174.

Fafchamps, M. (1994). "Industrial structure and microenterprises in Africa". Journal of Developing Areas 29 (1), 1–30.

Fafchamps, M. (2001). "Intrahousehold access to land and sources of inefficiency: Theory and concepts". In: de Janvry, A., Gordillo, G., Platteau, J.-P., Sadoulet, E. (Eds.), Access to Land, Rural Poverty, and Public Action. Oxford Univ. Press, Oxford and New York. UNU-WIDER Studies in Development Economics.

Fafchamps, M. (2003). Rural Poverty, Risk and Development. Edward Elgar Publishing, Cheltenham, UK.

Fafchamps, M., Quisumbing, A.R. (2002). "Control and ownership of assets within rural Ethiopian households". Journal of Development Studies 38 (2), 47–82.

Fafchamps, M., Quisumbing, A.R. (2003). "Social roles, human capital, and the intrahousehold division of labor: Evidence from Pakistan". Oxford Economic Papers 55 (1), 36–80.

Fafchamps, M., Quisumbing, A.R. (2005a). "Assets at marriage in rural Ethiopia". Journal of Development Economics 77 (1), 1–25.

Fafchamps, M., Quisumbing, A.R. (2005b). "Marriage, bequest, and assortative matching in rural Ethiopia". Economic Development and Cultural Change 53 (2), 347–380.

Fafchamps, M., Shilpi, F. (2005). "Cities and specialization: Evidence from South Asia". Economic Journal 115 (503), 477–504.

Fafchamps, M., Wahba, J. (2006). "Child labor, urban proximity, and household composition". Journal of Development Economics 79 (2), 374–397.

Filmer, D., Ainsworth, M. (2002). "Poverty, AIDS, and children's schooling: A targeting dilemma". Technical report. Policy Research Working Paper Series 2885, The World Bank.

Folbre, N.R. (1997). "Gender coalitions: Extrafamily influences on intrafamily inequality". In: Haddad, L., Hoddinott, J., Alderman, H. (Eds.), Intrahousehold Resource Allocation in Developing Countries: Methods, Models and Policy. Johns Hopkins Univ. Press, Baltimore.

Foster, A.D. (1998). "Marriage market selection and human capital allocations in rural Bangladesh". Mimeo.

Foster, A.D. (2002). "Altruism, household coresidence and women's health investments in rural Bangladesh". Mimeo.

Foster, A.D., Rosenzweig, M.R. (2001). "Imperfect commitment, altruism and the family: Evidence from transfer behavior in low-income rural areas". Review of Economics and Statistics 83 (3), 389–407.

Gale, D., Shapley, L. (1962). "College admissions and the stability of marriage". American Mathematical Monthly 69, 9–15.

Gan, L., Vernon, V. (2003). "Testing the Barten model of economies of scale in household consumption: Toward resolving a paradox of Deaton and Paxson". Journal of Political Economy 111 (6), 1361–1377.

Garg, A., Morduch, J. (1998). "Sibling rivalry and the gender gap: Evidence from child health outcomes in Ghana". Journal of Population Economics 11, 471–493.

Goldin, C. (1992). Understanding the Gender Gap: An Economic History of American Women. Oxford Univ. Press, Oxford.

Goldstein, M. (2000). "Chop time no friends: Intrahousehold and individual insurance mechanisms in Southern Ghana". Mimeo.

Goody, J.R. (1973). "Bridewealth and dowry in Asia and Eurasia". In: Goody, J., Tambiah, S.J. (Eds.), Bridewealth and Dowry. Cambridge Univ. Press, Cambridge.

Goody, J.R. (1976). Production and Reproduction: A Comparative Study of the Domestic Sphere. Cambridge Univ. Press, Cambridge.

Greenough, P.R. (1982). Prosperity and Misery in Modern Bengal. Oxford Univ. Press, New York.

Grosh, M., Glewwe, P. (2000). Designing Household Survey Questionnaires for Developing Countries: Lessons from Fifteen Years of the Living Standards Measurement Study. The World Bank, Washington, DC.

Grossbard, A. (1976). "An economic analysis of polygyny: The case of Maiduguri". Current Anthropology 17, 701–707.

Grossbard-Shechtman, S.A. (2003). Marriage and the Economy: Theory and Evidence from Advanced Industrial Societies. Cambridge Univ. Press, Cambridge.

Haddad, L., Hoddinott, J. (1994). "Household resource allocation in the Côte d'Ivoire: Inferences from expenditure data". In: Lloyd, T.A., Morrissey, W.O. (Eds.), Poverty, Inequality and Rural Development. MacMillan, London.

Haddad, L., Hoddinott, J., Alderman, H. (1997). Intrahousehold Resource Allocation in Developing Countries: Models, Methods, and Policy. Johns Hopkins Univ. Press, Baltimore.

Haddad, L., Kanbur, R. (1990). "How serious is the neglect of intra-household inequality?" Economic Journal 100, 866–881.

Hamoudi, A., Thomas, D. (2005). "Pension income and the well-being of children and grandchildren: New evidence from South Africa". Unpublished paper. Department of Economics, University of California, Los Angeles.

Handa, S. (1996a). "The determinants of female headship in Jamaica: Results from a structural model". Economic Development and Cultural Change 44 (4), 793–815.

Handa, S. (1996b). "Expenditure behavior and children's welfare: An analysis of female headed households in Jamaica". Journal of Development Economics 50 (1), 165–187.

Harper, C., Marcus, R., Moore, K. (2003). "Enduring poverty and the conditions of childhood: Lifecourse and intergenerational poverty transmissions". World Development 31 (3), 535–554.

Hoogeveen, H., van der Klaauw, B., van Lommel, G. (2003). "On the timing of marriage, cattle, and weather shocks in rural Zimbabwe". Technical report. Policy Research Working Paper Series 3112, The World Bank.

Hoppe, H., Moldovanu, B., Sela, A. (2005). "The theory of assortative matching based on costly signals". Mimeo.

Hyslop, D. (2001). "Rising US earnings inequality and family labor supply: The covariance structure of intrafamily earnings". American Economic Review 91 (4), 755–777.

Jacoby, H. (1995). "The economics of polygyny in sub-Saharan Africa: Female productivity and the demand for wives in Cote d'Ivoire". Journal of Political Economy 103 (5), 938–971.

Jarvis, S., Jenkins, S.P. (1999). "Marital splits and income changes: Evidence from the British household panel survey". Population Studies 53 (2), 237–254.

Joshi, S. (2004). "Female household-headship in rural Bangladesh: Incidence, determinants, and impact on children's schooling". Technical report. Discussion paper No. 894. Economic Growth Center, Yale University, New Haven, CT.

Kapadia, K. (1996). Siva and Her Sisters: Gender, Caste, and Class in Rural South India. Oxford Univ. Press, Delhi.

Key, N., Sadoulet, E., de Janvry, A. (2000). "Transactions costs and agricultural household supply response". American Journal of Agricultural Economics 82 (2), 245–259.

Kochar, A. (1999). "Evaluating familial support for the elderly: The intrahousehold allocation of medical expenditures in rural Pakistan". Economic Development and Cultural Change 47 (3), 620–656.

Kochar, A. (2000). "Parental benefits from intergenerational coresidence: Empirical evidence from rural Pakistan". Journal of Political Economy 108 (6), 1184–1209.

Kochar, A. (2004). "Ill-health, savings and portfolio choices in developing economies". Journal of Development Economics 73 (1), 257–285.

Lanjouw, P., Ravallion, M. (1995). "Poverty and household size". Economic Journal 105, 1415–1434.

Lauby, J., Stark, O. (1988). "Individual migration as a family strategy: Young women in the Philippines". Population Studies 42, 473–486.

Lechene, V., Preston, I. (2005). "Household Nash equilibrium with voluntarily contributed public goods". Mimeo.

Legros, P., Newman, A.F. (2004). "Beauty is a beast, frog is a prince: Assortative matching with nontransferabilities". Mimeo.

Lloyd, C.B., Blanc, A.K. (1996). "Children's schooling in sub-Saharan Africa: The role of fathers, mothers and others". Population and Development Review 22 (2), 265–298.

Lundberg, S.J., Pollak, R.A., Wales, T.J. (1997). "Do husbands and wives pool their resources? Evidence from the United Kingdom child benefit". Journal of Human Resources 32 (3), 463–480.

Lundberg, S., Pollak, R.A. (1993). "Separate spheres bargaining and the marriage market". Journal of Political Economy 101 (6), 988–1010.

Mace, B.J. (1991). "Full insurance in the presence of aggregate uncertainty". Journal of Political Economy 99 (5), 928–956.

McElroy, M.B., Horney, M.J. (1981). "Nash-bargained household decisions: Toward a generalization of the theory of demand". International Economic Review 22 (2), 333–349.

Miguel, E. (2003). "Poverty and witch killing". Technical report. Working paper No. 41. Department of Economics, BREAD, UC Berkeley, Berkeley.

Montgomery, M., Trussell, J. (1986). "Models of marital status and childbearing". In: Handbook in Labor Economics, vol. 1. Elsevier Science, pp. 205–271.

Morduch, J. (2000). "Sibling rivalry in Africa". American Economic Review 90, 405–409.

Nakajima, C. (1965). "Subsistence and commercial family farms: Some theoretical models of subjective equilibrium". In: Wharton (Ed.), Subsistence Agriculture and Economic Development. Aldine Publishers, Chicago.

Otsuka, K., Quisumbing, A.R. (2001). "Land rights and natural resource management in the transition to individual ownership: Case studies from Ghana and Indonesia". In: de Janvry, A., Gordillo, G., Platteau, J.-P., Sadoulet, E. (Eds.), Access to Land, Rural Poverty, and Public Action. Oxford Univ. Press, Oxford.

Pankhurst, H. (1992). "Gender, Development, and Identity: An Ethiopian Study". Zed Books Ltd., London and Atlantic Highlands, NJ.

Pitt, M.M., Rosenzweig, M.R., Hassan, M.N. (2005). "Sharing the burden of disease: Gender, the household division of labor and the health effects of indoor air pollution". Technical report. Working paper No. 119. Center for International Development, Harvard University.

Pitt, M.M., Rosenzweig, M.R., Hassan, M.N. (2007). "Short- and long-term health effects of burning biomass in the home in low-income countries". Unpublished paper. Department of Economics, Yale University.

Platteau, J.-P., Baland, J.-M. (2001). "Impartible inheritance versus equal division: A comparative perspective centered on Europe and sub-Saharan Africa". In: de Janvry, A., Gordillo, G., Platteau, J.-P., Sadoulet, E. (Eds.), Access to Land, Rural Poverty, and Public Action. Oxford Univ. Press, Oxford, pp. 27–67.

Quisumbing, A., Behrman, J., Maluccio, J., Murphy, A., Yount, K. (2005). "Levels, correlates, and differences in human, physical, and financial assets brought into marriages by young Guatemalan adults". Food and Nutrition Bulletin 26 (2), 55–67. Supplement 1.

Quisumbing, A.R. (1994). "Intergenerational transfers in Philippine rice villages: Gender differences in traditional inheritance customs". Journal of Development Economics 43 (2), 167–195.

Quisumbing, A.R. (2003). Household Decisions, Gender, and Development: A Synthesis of Recent Research. International Food Policy Research Institute, Washington, DC.

Quisumbing, A.R., Estudillo, J.P., Otsuka, K. (2004). Land and schooling: Transferring wealth across generations. Johns Hopkins Univ. Press for the International Food Policy Research Institute, Baltimore, MD.

Quisumbing, A.R., Haddad, L., Peña, C. (2001). "Are women over-represented among the poor? An analysis of poverty in ten developing countries". Journal of Development Economics 66 (1), 225–269.

Quisumbing, A.R., Hallman, K.-K. (2003). "Marriage in transition: Evidence on age, education, and assets from six developing countries". Technical report No. 121. Working paper No. 183, The Population Council, New York. Policy Research Division.

Quisumbing, A.R., Otsuka, K. (2001). "Land, trees, and women: Evolution of land tenure institutions in Western Ghana and Sumatra". Research report No. 121. International Food Policy Research Institute, Washington, DC.

Quisumbing, A.R., Payongayong, E., Aidoo, J.B., Otsuka, K. (2001). "Women's land rights in the transition to individualized ownership: Implications for the management of tree resources in Western Ghana". Economic Development and Cultural Change 50 (1), 157–182.

Raheja, G. (1995). "Crying when she's born and crying when she goes away: Marriage and the idiom of the gift in Pahansu song performance". In: Harlan, L., Courtright, P.B. (Eds.), From the Margins of Hindu Marriage: Essays on Gender, Religion, and Culture. Oxford Univ. Press, Oxford.

Rao, V. (1993). "The rising price of husbands: A hedonic analysis of dowry increases in rural India". Journal of Political Economy 101 (4), 666–677.

Rao, V. (2000). "The marriage squeeze interpretation of dowry inflation: Response". Journal of Political Economy 108 (6), 1334–1335.

Rose, E. (1999). "Consumption smoothing and excess female mortality in rural India". Review of Economics and Statistics 81 (1), 41–49.

Rosenzweig, M.R., Stark, O. (1989). "Consumption smoothing, migration, and marriage: Evidence from rural India". Journal of Political Economy 97 (4), 905–926.

Rosenzweig, M.R., Wolpin, K.I. (1985). "Specific experience, household structure, and intergenerational transfers: Farm family land and labor arrangements in developing countries". Quarterly Journal of Economics 100, 961–987. Supplement.

Roth, A., Sotomayor, M. (1990). "Two-Sided Matching". Cambridge Univ. Press, Cambridge.

Schultz, T. (1994). "Marital status and fertility in the United States: Welfare and labor market effects". Journal of Human Resources 29 (2), 637–669.

Schultz, T.P. (2001). "Women's roles in the agricultural household: Bargaining and human capital investments". In: Gardner, B., Rausser, G. (Eds.), Agricultural and Resource Economics Handbook. North-Holland, Amsterdam.

Sen, A. (1966). "Peasants and dualism with or without surplus labor". Journal of Political Economy 74 (5), 425–450.

Sen, A. (1981). Poverty and Famines. Clarendon Press, Oxford.

Singh, I., Squire, L., Strauss, J. (1986). Agricultural Household Models: Extensions, Applications and Policy. World Bank, Washington, DC.

Singh, R.D. (1988). Economics of the Family and Farming Systems in Sub-Saharan Africa: Development Perspectives. Westview Press, Boulder, CO.

Stark, O., Lucas, R.E. (1988). "Migration, remittances, and the family". Economic Development and Cultural Change 36 (3), 465–481.

Strauss, J., Mehra, K. (1989). "Child anthropometry in Cote d'Ivoire: Estimates from two surveys, 1985 and 1986". Technical report. Working paper No. 51, Living Standards Measurement Study, World Bank, Washington, DC.

Strauss, J., Thomas, D. (1995). "Human resources: Empirical modeling of household and family decisions". In: Behrman, J., Srinivasan, T.N. (Eds.), In: Handbook of Development Economics, vol. 3A. North-Holland, Amsterdam, New York and Oxford, pp. 1883–2023.

The World Bank, O. (1998). Implementing the Ethiopian National Policy for Women: Institutional and Regulatory Issues. The World Bank and The Women's, Washington, DC. Affairs Office, Federal Democratic Republic of Ethiopia.

Townsend, R.M. (1994). "Risk and insurance in village India". Econometrica 62 (3), 539–591.

Udry, C. (1996). "Gender, agricultural production and the theory of the household". Journal of Political Economy 104 (5), 1010–1046.

Vandermeersch, C. (1997). "Les Enfants Confiés au Sénégal, Colloque Jeune Chercheurs". INED. May 12–14 (cited in Akresh, 2004b).

von Braun, J., Webb, P.J. (1989). "The impact of new crop technology on the agricultural division of labor in a West African setting". Economic Development and Cultural Change 37 (3), 513–534.

Walker, T.S., Ryan, J. (1990). "Village and Household Economics in India's Semi-Arid Tropics". John Hopkins Univ. Press, Baltimore.

Zhang, J., Chan, W. (1999). "Dowry and wife's welfare: A theoretical and empirical analysis". Journal of Political Economy 107 (4), 786–808.

Chapter 52

POPULATION POLICIES, FERTILITY, WOMEN'S HUMAN CAPITAL, AND CHILD QUALITY*

T. PAUL SCHULTZ

Economics Department, Box 208269, Yale University, New Haven, CT 06520-8269, USA

Contents

  * Support of the MacArthur and Rockefeller Foundations are acknowledged, and the comments of Eric Edmonds, John Strauss and other participants at the Conference on Economic Development, at the Bellagio Center, Italy, May 2–6, 2005 and the editorial comments of Sarah Cattan are appreciated.

Handbook of Development Economics, Volume 4
DOI: 10.1016/S1573-4471(07)04052-1

Abstract

Population policies are defined here as voluntary programs which help people control their fertility and expect to improve their lives. There are few studies of the long-run effects of policy-induced changes in fertility on the welfare of women, such as policies that subsidize the diffusion and use of best practice birth control technologies. Evaluation of the consequences of such family planning programs almost never assess their long-run consequences, such as on labor supply, savings, or investment in the human capital of children, although they occasionally estimate the short-run association with the adoption of contraception or age-specific fertility. The dearth of long-run family planning experiments has led economists to consider instrumental variables as a substitute for policy interventions which not only determine variation in fertility but are arguably independent of the reproductive preferences of parents or unobserved constraints that might influence family life cycle behaviors. Using these instrumental variables to estimate the effect of this exogenous variation in fertility on family outcomes, economists discover these "cross effects" of fertility on family welfare outcomes tend to be substantially smaller in absolute magnitude than the OLS estimates of partial correlations referred to in the literature as evidence of the beneficial social externalities associated with the policies that reduce fertility. The paper summarizes critically the empirical literature on fertility and development and proposes an agenda for research on the topic.

Keywords

consequences of fertility decline, child quality, evaluation of population policies

JEL classification: J13, J24, O15

1. Introduction – Why are economists interested in fertility?

The relationship of fertility to economic development is a controversial subject, which is viewed differently by various schools of economists. Malthus (1798) relies on the classical economics concept of diminishing returns to labor applied to a fixed supply of natural resources, such as agricultural land. If fertility contributes to population growth, it diminishes in the long run the marginal product of labor and thereby reduces wage rates, holding the supply of agricultural land constant. In Malthus' framework fertility is assumed to cause a negative 'externality' or impose a social cost on society, because private individuals ignore these social consequences of their decisions to marry earlier and have more children. Malthus implicitly assumes an aggregate production framework to link higher levels of fertility to reduced workers' welfare, and completes the feedback mechanism by allowing falling wages to discourage early (i.e. improvident) marriage and reduce the number of births women have, on average. This model of macroeconomic-demographic equilibrium accounts for some key aspects of the pre-industrial European experience (Lee, 1973; Schultz, 1981, 2002; Guinanne, 1997; Bengtsson, 2004), but does not explain the events that followed the industrial revolution when population growth paralleled economic growth in per capita terms.

In the two decades following the Second World War, high levels of fertility emerged as a potential constraint on economic development, at least in low-income countries. Population growth increased in these poor countries from 0.5 percent per year in 1900, to 1.2 percent by 1940, and doubled again to 2.5 percent by 1960 (Kuznets, 1966; United Nations, 2003). This increase in the rate of population growth, although due to improvements in health which reduced mortality rather than increased fertility, seemed likely to overwhelm the capacity to accumulate capital in these developing countries to employ productively their rapidly growing populations. If fertility in low-income countries declined as slowly and with as long a lag after mortality declined as in Europe and areas of European settlement, this Malthusian framework implied a demographic poverty trap could arise which would prevent economic development (Coale and Hoover, 1958; National Academy of Sciences, 1971). With further study, however, the evidence linking rapid population growth to slower economic development was not confirmed to be a major impediment to modern economic growth, except where it was very rapid and discouraged investments in health and schooling (National Research Council, 1986; Johnson, 1999). This conclusion does not contradict classical diminishing returns to population growth, but only suggests that technical change and behavioral responses are able to outweigh these Malthusian constraints on economic growth, as illustrated by the successes in Asia and Latin America.

A second macro framework economists use to assess the implications of the fertility decline in the demographic transition focuses on the consequences of resulting changes in the age composition of a national population, that occurs because of the demographic transition. Modigliani and Brumburg (1954) assume that in each period the marginal utility from consumption diminishes with increasing levels of consumption, and adults maximize a lifetime utility function which is the separable sum of each adult's discounted utility. These widely accepted assumptions imply that adults would save a larger proportion of their earnings during their most productive years, between say age 35 to 55, in order to raise their consumption opportunities during their less productive old age. If birth cohorts follow this hypothesized life cycle consumption-smoothing savings behavior, changes in the age composition of nations would affect national savings rates, in the absence of secular growth in economic productivity. Higgins and Williamson (1997), among others, have argued that the increase in the proportion of the population age 35 and 55 in the East Asian countries after fertility began to decline from 1960 to 1980 explains the rise in their national savings rates from 1970 to 1990. Although savings rates increased in the wake of the demographic transition in many East and South-East Asian countries, savings rates have also increased in countries where the demographic transition has been more gradual and thus the age composition has changed much less, such as India. Conversely, savings rates have stagnated in other regions, such as Latin America, which experienced a relatively rapid early demographic transition similar to that experienced in East Asia. Even the within country variation in Asia does not suggest a robust statistical relationship between the age composition and savings rates within countries (Schultz, 2004a). Moreover, studies of household surveys do not generally find the pronounced humped shaped life-cycle variation in savings rates in either high- or low-income countries, as plausibly postulated by Modigliani (Deaton and Paxson, 1997).

With these two macro economic frameworks attributing social benefits to a decline in fertility, micro economists have sought to understand the determinants and consequences of fertility as a family decision process. Data from household sample surveys are analyzed to test the implications of household consumption and production models (Becker, 1960, 1981; Mincer, 1963; T.W. Schultz, 1974; Schultz, 1981, 1997; Hotz, Klerman and Willis, 1997). If fertility and family resource allocations are determined jointly and simultaneously within a lifetime household decision making framework, it is expected that unobserved economic constraints on the household and preferences of couples would impact fertility and other lifetime household behaviors. The correlations between fertility and these family lifetime outcomes would therefore represent biased estimates of any causal effects or externalities that might follow if population programs were to reduce the cost of birth control and thus reduce fertility voluntarily. Empirical evidence has accumulated to substantiate the view that fertility is subject to choice in most settings and is determined simultaneously with other lifetime family behaviors (Rosenzweig and Wolpin, 1980a, 1980b; Schultz, 1981; Moffitt, 2005).

The challenge is to estimate how exogenous shocks to fertility, such as might be produced by a population program, would impact other household coordinated choices, such as the allocation of women's time and other lifetime resources among activities which parents view as complements to, or substitutes for, having more children. On this list of coordinated household behaviors is, of course, the mother's supply of time to the labor market (Mincer, 1963), life cycle savings for old age support, as well as the expenditures of parents on a variety of activities that increase the lifetime productivity of their children, or child human capital (Becker and Lewis, 1974). Nutrition, health care, schooling, and migration of children are the most salient and readily quantified of these family outcomes, and many of these investments in children are publicly subsidized and encouraged, because they are viewed as benefitting society. It is often hypothesized that children customarily provide parents with support and consumption insurance in old age, and parents might view these child services as a substitute for savings in the form of physical assets (e.g. Samuelson, 1958). Within a lifetime household demand and savings framework, the problem is to disentangle the effects of exogenous variation in fertility on other long term family outcomes and to identify and estimate these effects. To estimate these effects of fertility variation on family resource allocations, retrospective life cycle histories or panel household surveys would be useful, which describe families for a sufficient time to infer long term equilibrium consequences of fertility change. Moreover, the researcher must specify a credible "exclusion restriction," which typically takes the form of an observed instrumental variable representing an exogenous "treatment" that affects to a significant extent fertility, and has no other effect on the family's welfare outcome of interest, such as the woman's health, productivity, labor supply, and asset accumulations, and her children's human capital.

There are relatively few empirical studies, reviewed later in this paper, which assess how fertility declines that can be attributed to population policy treatments or other forces outside of the family's control, have contributed to the formation of more human capital in women and in children, or augmented family physical savings, and thereby reduced poverty in the current and future generations of the family and contributed to economic development. Without credible evidence at the household level of these "cross effects" of population programs on fertility and long term family welfare, some skepticism is understandable when causal interpretations are offered for empirical associations between fertility, age compositions, and family welfare across populations at the aggregate level. Cross-country regressions are notoriously difficult to interpret as causal relationships in this context, because mortality and fertility tend to be dominated by secular trends (Moffitt, 2005; Schultz, 2004b), and this paper will therefore focus only on empirical evidence derived from analyses of household level data.

Although fertility may not be confidently linked as a causal factor driving national savings or growth, there is a persistent cross-country inverse relationship between real income per adult (i.e. GDP in Purchasing Power Parity per potential worker) and the total fertility rate (TFR is defined as the sum of age-specific birth rates for women summed across all reproductive ages, 15 to 49, in one time period). This inverse relationship has remained quite stable between 1960 and 2000 (as plotted in Fig. 1), during which time the average TFR in this sample of 95 countries decreased by 39 percent while real income per adult increased by 88 percent.[1] Does this empirical regularity imply that

---

[1] The slope of the linear fit of log GDP per adult and TFR is not significantly different in the two years at the 5 percent confidence level, but TFR has fallen more slowly than the log of GDP per adult, suggesting that the level of a fitted linear function has shifted upwards slightly. This shift in intercept is also not significantly different from zero. The stability of this empirical regularity should not be interpreted as an indication that the relationship is causal and constant over time, but rather is a surprising outcome possibly caused by different changes in both fertility supply and demand (Rosenzweig and Schultz, 1985; Schultz, 1995).

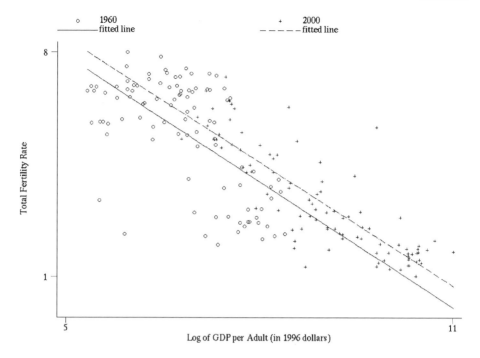

Figure 1. Total fertility rates by adult productivity in 1960 and 2000.

Source: United Nations (2003), World Bank development data base. Income per person age 15 or over in 1996 US real dollars, converted to purchasing power parity. Maximum sample of the same 95 countries for which data are available in both years.

fertility declines cause income to increase, or does causation operate in the opposite direction from economic growth to fertility decline? There is as yet no consensus on the answer to this question. However, promising directions for research are reviewed below, in which individuals and households in cross-sectional and panel surveys are analyzed to recover insights from special situations where exogenous environmental variables, including the exposure of individuals to population policies, account for some of the variation in fertility. Opportunities for this research include well-designed social experiments, quasi-experiments stimulated by nature or human institutions, and carefully evaluated instrumental variable strategies that are shown to have both power and validity. The second stage in this research methodology is then to link this "exogenous" variation in fertility to long term "cross effects" in the household of these women and their families. These cross effects may eventually provide a more precise assessment of the spillover effects on development of specific population programs, such as family planning, child health and reproductive health programs, as well as provide a basis for explaining how the economic and social structure of development affects fertility.[2]

In this Chapter, Section 2 describes the potential consequences of fertility and health changes for individual and family well being. Section 3 outlines the policies which may change fertility and mortality and thereby contribute to the demographic transition. Section 4 summarizes a household life cycle demand model to illustrate how reduced form equations might be conceptually derived, and how identification is achieved to estimate structural relationships, such as the "cross effects" of policy-induced changes in fertility on long-term family outcomes. Empirical studies which have estimated the effects of specific exogenous sources of variation in fertility or population programs on family outcomes are surveyed in Section 5, concluding with a discussion of evaluations of the Matlab family planning program in rural Bangladesh, for which an experimental program has been followed for two decades. Section 6 draws some tentative generalizations from this survey, and reviews an agenda for further research.

2. Long term effects of fertility for individuals and families: A micro perspective

There are many potential mechanisms at the family level which could link the declines in mortality and fertility associated with the demographic transition to household resource reallocations and improvements in the welfare of women, children, and men. These linkages between production and consumption in the extended family unfold over an extended period of time, during which children are a long term responsibility of parents, after which children may customarily become care-givers for their elderly parents. Table 1 outlines how fertility may exert an influence over long term family choices and living arrangements, and thus categorizes the many "cross effects" from fertility that one could imagine estimating.

One hypothesis is that human capital formation is affected by changes in fertility and mortality. Maternal mortality per birth is many times higher in many low-income countries in Africa and South Asia than it is in middle and high income countries. The decline in fertility would thus be associated in these low income regions with fewer risks of maternal mortality. Acute and chronic health problems of women may also be reduced, especially if birth control substitutes for unsanitary and high risk abortion, and achieves a healthier spacing of births for the mother. However, correlations between

---

[2] The "cross effects" of fertility on family life cycle decisions and outcomes that are emphasized in this paper are not viewed as conditional demand effects, of for example, inflexible allocation shocks to the quantity of children on child quality. Conditional demand functions assume separable utility and are useful for interpreting short-run consumer behavior where "fixed commitments prevent instantaneous adjustment to the long run equilibrium and to the study of consumer behavior under rationing" (Pollak, 1969). In this paper the goal is to estimate the long-run equilibrium family response to changing prices of birth control (family planning programs) and fertility, although there are relatively few examples of such research.

Table 1
Family behaviors and outcomes likely to be affected by exogenous decline in fertility

I. Human capital formation
    A. Mother's health improves with fewer and better-timed births, especially in her later years
    B. Mother's market wage rises as her training through experience in the labor market increases
    C. Child's health improvements may eventually be documented along many dimensions
        (i)   Infant survival and survival until age five increases
        (ii)   Weight at birth by sex increases
        (iii) Height for age and sex increases, especially under
               age 5
        (iv)   Weight-for-height (Body Mass Index) by age and sex
               increases
        (v)   Age of menarche decreases
        (vi)   Inputs to produce health increase, such as
               expenditures on preventive health
    D. Child's schooling increases along many dimensions
        (i)   Age of entry into school system
        (ii)   Repetition of school years reduced because of failure
               to matriculate
        (iii) Current enrollment, given age and sex
        (iv)   Graduated from specific levels of the school system
        (v)   Final year of schooling completed among older
               children
        (vi)   Children's years of schooling completed at younger
               ages, normalized as a Z score by the population
               distribution of schooling by age and sex
        (vii) Inputs to produce education increase, such as
               expenditures, student time on homework, or parent
               home time facilitating child education
    E. Child's migration from parent residential community
        (i)   To find better employment
        (ii)   To marry and reside with spouse's family in order to
               reduce extended family risks
    F. Delay of child's age at marriage

II. Family labor supply or time allocation
    A. Mother's market labor supply within and outside of the family increases
    B. Children's labor supply may decrease
    C. Father's labor supply may respond positively in short run and may later decrease with wealth gains

III. Saving rate of parents increase to accumulate physical wealth for production and retirement
    A. Because savings is measured only at the household level, it is difficult to attribute
        savings between generations in a multi-generational household or even extended family
    B. Sample selection bias in estimating savings for young and old, concealing life cycle variation

IV. Transfers of cash, goods, and time to and from household members
    A. From parents to their children
    B. From children to their parents
    C. Among other relatives in extended family or clan
    D. From the state to support the vulnerable: young, old and disabled

(continued on next page)

Table 1
(*continued*)

V. Household living arrangements
   A. Household formation
      (i) Marriage or cohabitation or visiting relationships
      (ii) Partition as sons and daughters and brothers of household head leave to establish own household or join the family of their spouse
      (iii) Migration to improve economic opportunities and reduce family pooled risks
   B. Household partition because of death or ill health of head, e.g. placement of orphans
   C. Female heads of household
      (i) Because of widowhood
      (ii) Because of divorce or permanent separation
      (iii) Because of temporary migration of husband who transfers support and remains de facto head

---

fertility and family outcomes such as women's health, do not denote causation, without developing a compelling strategy for identification of this "cross effect" within the family.

Adolescent and young women may be able to stay in school longer because they do not become pregnant, and programs which inform youth of contraceptive options and the likely consequences of their behavior may delay childbearing. Once they leave school, women who have fewer children may accumulate more training and vocational experience outside of the home, which may be associated with increased productivity in the market labor force and enhanced wages over their remaining lives, as well as the ability to bargain more effectively over the allocation of household resources (Lloyd, 2005). However, few studies show how population programs lower fertility and thereby affect the vocational experience of women which would raise their wages (Table 1, I B).

Some instrumental variable (IV) studies reviewed later provide a basis for conjecturing the magnitude of such a mechanism from exogenous fertility change to women's accumulation of human capital and earnings capacity in later life. However, these IV studies are not yet an adequate basis for generalization, because the scope for women to work in the labor force and outside of their family varies greatly across cultures and over time. Women who are relieved of the responsibility of bearing and rearing more unwanted children may be more likely to engage in self-employment activities which add to family resources and increase the opportunity value of women's time to other household activities. Women released from child care responsibilities may also increase their participation in women's groups, including microfinance organizations, and thus acquire productive assets to enhance their business opportunities. Decision making in the community and participation in local government may also evolve as women gain the capacity to regulate the timing and number of their births.

The effect of fertility decline may also take the form of intergenerational transfers, associated most often with child human capital in nutrition and health (Table 1, I C), schooling (I D), migration (I E) and perhaps delay of a daughter's marriage (I F) (Field and Ambrus, 2005). To these studies should be added investigations of inter vivos gifts and bequests from parents to children to complete the accounting of intergenerational transfers (Becker, 1981). These various forms of child human capital and financial transfers may also have reinforcing returns, at least in some settings (Schultz, 2001). The link of fertility to child migration is perhaps the least well studied, and most analyses of inter-generational effects of fertility on child human capital treat fertility as not being a choice variable which embody the multiple effects of preferences and unobserved heterogeneity. Therefore, the associations reported in the literature are generally incorrectly viewed as causal effects of the number of siblings (parent fertility) on human capital and economic performance, and only rarely is fertility treated more appropriately as endogenous and identified by an valid instrument (Black, Devereux and Salvanes 2005a, 2005b).

In a growing number of low income countries legislated transfer programs are being introduced which are conditional on investments being made in child human capital. In Bangladesh a conditional transfer program made payments to a girl's bank account, if she enrolled in secondary school and did not get married before the legal age of 18 (Arends-Kuenning and Amin, 2004). Although increasing women's schooling appears to increase her wage opportunities, a delay in her marriage may be privately costly for her parents. Field and Ambrus (2005) find in rural Bangladesh that delaying a daughters marriage beyond the age of menarche when she commands the best prospects in the marriage market contributes to an increase in the dowry the parents are required to pay, even if the daughter who is now older has completed more schooling. It is also unclear whether the wage returns a daughter might potentially earn due to attending more school are recovered by her parents, even if she takes a job before marriage (Quisumbing and Maluccio, 2003). As noted later, an experimental family planning program in Matlab Bangladesh reduced fertility, but was not associated with increasing the age when women exposed to the program had their first birth, although the woman's sons tend to eventually receive more schooling and have fewer siblings (Joshi and Schultz, 2007).

The second broad area of family resource allocation which is likely to be sensitive to fertility is the family's allocation of time, and specifically the woman's supply of time to work outside of the family (Table 1, II A). When they reduce their fertility, women tend to allocate more of their time to activities other than child care, and if the employment opportunities outside of the family are more attractive than those within the family, a program induced decline in fertility is likely to be associated with an increase in labor force participation and an increase in hours worked. If the market employment opportunities for women were unattractive, she may allocate more time to home production and self-employment activities. But as emphasized before, these correlations of fertility with different allocations of labor within the family are not a reliable measure of a causal effect, nor should it be assumed that by women working in any specific set of activities women's welfare will necessarily improve.

The probability that children will work in the labor force and the number of hours they so work could also be impacted by a policy-induced decline in their mother's fertility (II B). One might hypothesize that mothers who have reduced their fertility are more likely to send their children to school, and this may reduce the time available for the children to work. Yet, the connection between the increase in school enrollment induced by a random village allocation of the Mexican Progresa Program's conditional cash transfers for enrollment had a relatively small effect of reducing the reported level of child labor (Schultz, 2004a).[3]

Models in which the labor supply of all family members are potentially coordinated find the expected interdependency of the time allocation of all family members, not only within the nuclear and intergenerational family, but also within the household and perhaps the residential compounds of the extended family e.g. the Bari in Bangladesh. In high income countries, the effect on the market labor supply of the husband of an increase in his wife's wage tends to be negative (uncompensated for the implicit income effect) but generally small and imprecisely estimated. In contrast, the effect on the wife's labor supply of an increase in her husband's wage tends to be negative and relatively large in most studies of family labor supply (Killingsworth, 1983; Schultz, 1981).

The life cycle model of savings assumes that children do not influence wealth accumulation, and the ratio of savings out of disposable income follows a regular profile with respect to the adult's age. Individuals accumulate sufficient wealth to smooth their consumption during their old age when their productivity declines (Modigliani and Brumburg, 1954). It is perhaps more plausible to assume parents are motivated to have children in part by the expectation that their children would support and care for them in old age (Samuelson, 1958). A policy-induced reduction in fertility could motivate parents to substitute more of their resources into savings to replace the support they had previously expected to receive from children. Although national accounts define savings as only the accumulation of nonhuman capital, parents may also increase their children's human capital as an alternative form of life cycle savings. Few studies report the association between conventional savings and fertility of parents (Hammer, 1986), and I could not find a single study estimating the savings effects of a policy-induced change in fertility. As with the Rosenzweig–Wolpin (1980b) model of fertility and female labor supply, I would expect parent relative preferences for childbearing as a means to smooth life-cycle consumption might be inversely related to the preferences for other forms of their physical savings, across a population with heterogeneous preferences. Estimates of fertility "cross effects" on savings based on exogenous shocks to fertility might then be expected to be smaller in absolute value than those implied by OLS estimates from a cross section in which fertility is assumed to be determined outside of the model and to affect life cycle savings as an exogenous factor.

It is hypothesized that parents in reducing their fertility increase their transfers to each child in the form of gifts as well as human capital, motivated possibly by an increase in the returns for their support of schooling, health, and migration investments

---

[3] It should be stressed that child labor is not easily measured in a household survey in a low-income country, because children generally work with their parents, without receiving formal payment, and are therefore not customarily viewed by parents as "workers" despite their contribution to family income. Work and schooling do not exhaust the time of children, and children are able to work without apparently reducing their schooling or subsequent earnings, although this is likely to depend on many other factors. See E. Edmonds' (2008) chapter of this volume.

(e.g. Becker, 1981; Quisumbing and Maluccio, 2003). If physical savings, child human capital investments, and parent to child transfers are all substitutes for numbers of children, empirical studies are needed to document the degree of substitutability, and how they vary across cultural and institutional settings (Quisumbing, Estudillo and Otsuka, 2004). The responsiveness of parents in this regard could be an important social rationale for population policies which achieve a voluntary reduction in fertility.

But the magnitude of such within family transfer relationships to the mother would be mediated by family structures and the customary obligations of children to their elderly parents, and weakened by the state's provision of pensions or medical care for the old and infirm. If the woman who has fewer children improves her own earnings capacities and she accumulates more over her life in physical assets through personal savings, she may have less need for income transfers from her offspring in old age. Whether inter-generational investments in child human capital lead to reciprocation in the form of child-to-parent transfers has not been extensively studied, where the source of variation in fertility is arguably exogenous. Because panel surveys rarely collect wealth, income, or consumption data from all related family units, currently it is hard to assess whether a transfer between parents and children is motivated by family altruism, strategic behavior, or family wealth maximization.

A final consequence of fertility decline is on family living arrangements (Table 1, V). Since the 19th century economists have studied the determinants of household expenditures and sought to control for the needs of the different households as summarized by their demographic composition, or the number of household members in various age and sex categories (Deaton, 1997). In studies of economic and demographic behavior, such as the family lifetime outcomes listed in Table 1, it is not plausible to assume that household composition and living arrangements are independent of changes in fertility, or that they are exogenous to human capital investments, time allocation, savings and transfers. These tenuous working assumptions underlying many studies of behavioral and productive relationships centered on the family are likely to distort estimates of cause and effect relationships. Households form, divide, grow through births and in-migration, and decline through deaths and out-migration, partly in response to the key income, price and technology variables that are expected to account for household behavioral demands (Rosenzweig and Wolpin, 1985; Foster, 1998; Maluccio, Thomas and Haddad, 2003; Hamoudi and Thomas, 2005). Thus, household composition should be treated as endogenous to studies of individual outcomes. The long standing convention in studies of family welfare of conditioning on household composition should thus be approached with caution, or at a minimum evaluated critically as a potential source of model mis-specification. If household composition adjusts to the opportunities created by a family planning program, which reduces the cost of birth control, then data on the extended family unit may need to be collected, and initial conditions should be specified to help explain the evolving composition of families (e.g. Akresh, 2004; Joshi, 2004; Hamoudi and Thomas, 2005; Ksoll, 2007).

3. Policy interventions in family planning, child and reproductive health?

Public policy interventions to promote the decline in mortality, morbidity, and fertility, are expected to benefit women and their families. Table 2 outlines five overlapping ways policy could contribute to declines in fertility. Because each may operate by different behavioral mechanisms and influence different groups, each is likely to cause different "cross effects" on other forms of family behavior and outcomes as listed in Table 1.

Table 2

Mechanisms by which population policy may influence family behavior and fertility

I.		Subsidize home productive inputs or activities
	A.	Subsidize the diffusion of knowledge or best practice reproductive technological opportunities, through sex education in schools, family planning in health clinics and outreach programs, STD clinics, HIV testing and counseling
	B.	Subsidize the cost of adoption of new technology, i.e. new methods of family planning
	C.	Subsidize the continuing use of family planning by lowering user monetary and time costs
	D.	Provide lower cost and lower risk options for male and female sterilization
	E.	Increase access to emergency contraception, menstrual regulation, and safer and lower cost abortion
II.		Provide local public health care for preventive and curative purposes
	A.	Prenatal care and tetanus vaccination of mother
	B.	Assistance with child birth
	C.	Monitoring early child growth and provide oral dehydration therapy for diarrhea
	D.	Childhood vaccinations
	E.	Protocols to identify health crises and securing appropriate treatment
III.		Cash transfers to families conditional on their investments in child human capital
	A.	Food and nutritional supplements targeted to the poor and malnourished
	B.	School enrollment of girls and boys at critical transitions in school system
	C.	Discourage early marriage among girls
	D.	Discourage child labor in unhealthy and dangerous occupations
IV.		Strengthen the property rights and bargaining empowerment of women
	A.	Define and enforce property rights of women in productive assets and wealth
	B.	Establish and enforce rights to inheritance of women
	C.	Codify settlement patterns for women in divorce and regarding child custody
	D.	Facilitate information and legal protection for migrants to change residences
	E.	Discourage dowries or secure mechanisms whereby dowries become the property of the woman, in the event that the marriage ends or husband dies
	F.	Discourage polygyny
V.		Rationing of births as in China's one-child policy: involuntary population policy
	A.	No compensating subsidy payment made to encourage fertility compliance, and penalties for out-of-plan births often regressive
	B.	With uniform rations for children, the costs of compliance are born primarily by those who want the most children, e.g. poorly educated, rural women
	C.	Reproductively rationed women confront incentives to consume more substitutes for children, for which the cross-price effects are positive, although wealth effects are negative

3.1. Public subsidies to accelerate diffusion of beneficial innovations

First, public policies can subsidize sex education, information regarding best practice birth control methods, related supplies and medical services, and reproductive health programs with testing and treatment of various health problems including sexually transmitted diseases. Subsidies could directly reduce the cost of birth control, provided by either the private sector or by public delivery systems. The choice between private and public sector distribution could be determined in part to minimize social costs (psychic and monetary) and also to achieve a more equitable distribution of the private benefits of the program.

The initial adoption of birth control techniques may occur slowly, despite the existence of demand for reduced fertility. Heterogeneity in individual capacity to evaluate new opportunities may lead to behavioral lags which can be reduced by subsidies for related information, education, and supplies. Targeting the subsidies might be based on expected benefits, which could be approximated by the effectiveness of a subsidy to reduce birth rates. Alternatively, the subsidy could be targeted to achieve other distributional goals, such as reducing unsafe abortion or decreasing childbearing among teen-agers, or serving poor rural communities in which health and schooling services are otherwise sparse.

Subsidies may be allotted so as to also be cost-effective in promoting voluntary adoption of new birth control techniques. Once adoption and use of modern birth control becomes widespread, general subsidies for their continued use may become a lower priority. By targeting the subsidy to those groups whose fertility continues to respond most strongly to a given price subsidy, the program can strive to maximize its effect on birth rates. Other program objectives could justify targeting specific segments of the population, such as lower income rural households, or teenagers, are other groups for which the health risks of unwanted childbearing are relatively high, assuming "unwantedness" can be suitably measured.

3.2. Redistribution of benefits within and between families

A second argument for public expenditures is to spread the voluntary use of birth control involves the consequences of improved birth control on the personal distribution of welfare *within families*, and specifically improvements in lifetime opportunities for women and their children. Intra-family distributional effects of population policies may be important and deserve more study using collective or bargaining models of the family (McElroy and Horney, 1981; Chiappori, 1992; Haddad, Hoddinott and Alderman, 1997; Browning and Chiappori, 1998). The major initial technological innovations in birth control occurred in the 1960s with the refinement of the intra uterine device (IUD-Ota ring) and the discovery of the oral steroid (pill), which separated the practice of birth control from the act of sexual intercourse, and gave women a more independent role in the adoption and practice of birth control. Although it is not empirically well established, it is reasonable to presume that women are able to exercise greater control of their reproductive lives due to these new birth control technologies, and subsequent advances in birth control — injections, implants, copper wrapped or drug coated IUDs, female condoms, laproscopic sterilization procedures, "menstrual regulation," abortion, and pills for pregnancy termination – have further added to options for *women* to control their reproduction.

These changes in birth control technology reduce uncertainties regarding when children are born and allow women to plan more confidently for their own education and careers, and thus optimize their lifetime productive opportunities, working either in the home or in the labor force. Society should gain from this wider access to "best practice" methods of birth control, which allows women to invest more efficiently in their market-oriented human capital. Women with an additional year of schooling receive wages which are proportionately higher than their less educated peers, and these private wage returns to schooling tend to be as high or higher for women as for men (Schultz, 1995). The diffusion and continued use of best practice birth control techniques should, therefore, motivate women to complete more schooling *relative* to men, other things being equal. These new birth control technologies may redistribute control of resources within families, and according to some empirical studies guided by the bargaining or collective models of the family, this should increase household expenditures on the nutrition, schooling, and health of children (Thomas, 1990, 1994; Browning, 1992; Haddad, Hoddinott and Alderman, 1997; Lam and Duryea, 1999; Schultz, 2001; Quisumbing and Maluccio, 2003).

"Change in production technology has also been viewed as an exogenous development which raises the returns to human capital, and thereby leads parents to substitute investments in their children's human capital for having additional children, contributing to economic growth. A family planning program which reduced the cost of fertility control, thereby facilitates the downward adjustment in fertility and increases investment in human capital induced by exogenous technical change" (Rosenzweig, 1990).

When should health programs, such as family planning and reproductive health, be publicly subsidized, and for whom and by how much, raise distributional issues that cannot be dealt with in this paper. Evidence is accumulating to suggest that better early childhood nutrition and the prevention of inflammatory childhood diseases can increase childhood survival in the short run, and in the long run improve the children's health status as adults, as measured by reduced chronic illnesses and degenerative diseases and fewer functional limitations and disabilities (Barker, 2001; Finch and Crimmins, 2004; Fogel, 2004; Gluckman and Hanson, 2006).

3.3. Conditional transfers

A third form of public intervention, noted earlier, involves conditional transfers to families, if families engage in high-return investments, typically in human capital. For example, Bangladesh introduced a secondary school scholarship program for girls, contingent on their not marrying before age 18. Mexico made transfers to poor mothers in rural marginalized areas (the Progresa program), if their children enroll in school and family members receive recommended vaccinations and preventive health care (Schultz, 2004a; Parker, Rubalcava and Teruel, 2008 in this volume). These targeted public subsidies require methodical planning, design of appropriate incentives, and careful monitoring to achieve their objectives. These conditional transfer programs offer a promising mechanism to alleviate poverty in the short run while encouraging longer run investments in the nutrition, health and schooling of poor children (Morley and Coady, 2003). Combined with effective targeting to the poor, conditional transfer programs may be more efficient in stimulating investment demand for human capital among the poor than conventional policies which increase public supply of expenditures, such as on education by constructing more schools, reducing class size, or paying higher teacher salaries.

3.4. Women's property rights and access to credit

Women's property rights to productive assets, inheritances, pensions, divorce and child custody are hypothesized to enhance both the welfare of women and possibly their children. If women are provided more bargaining power in the family, do their human capital capabilities increase, and does this enhanced economic value of women's time cause them to have fewer children and invest a greater amount in each child's human capital, holding constant the family's full income (Schultz, 2001; Quisumbing and Maluccio, 2003)? Where marketable title to land and other assets are insecure for women, and their land is vested in the hands of their husbands, women have greater difficulty borrowing to invest in their own enterprises. When they head their own households, they may be restricted to engage in home production activities, because of the need to protect their property rights (Field, 2003).

An objective of many micro finance programs is to help women overcome their traditional disadvantages in the credit market due to their lack of loan collateral and the customary interpretation of their property rights. Group joint liability arrangements for borrowing, encourage others in the group to monitor and enforce repayment of loans, in order for each participant to benefit in the future by access to the revolving credit. One prototype of this micro credit organization is the Grameen Bank of Bangladesh (Pitt and Khandkar, 1998). The design of legal systems and the practice of customary arrangements at the time of marriage may also affect bride prices and dowries, and may influence who actually controls the transfers at the time of marriage within the families, and who has custody of the children of that union, if it dissolves (Quisumbing, Estudillo and Otsuka, 2004; Joshi, 2004; Field and Ambrus, 2005; Edlund and Lagerlof, 2006). Does the increased control of reproduction achieve for women greater economic independence outside of the family, and thereby contribute to their participation in the economy?

3.5. Involuntary population policies which set birth quotas

Population policies can either change the incentives and opportunities which lead people to voluntarily change their fertility, or it can set administrative limits on fertility, without compensating those who are then prevented from realizing their desired family size. Many of the welfare programs emphasized above which subsidize birth control, increase women's human capital, or strengthen their control of resources in the family. They are thus designed to affect fertility by changing the balance of private costs and benefits of having children, in other words, the income of women and men and the relative prices of children and other lifetime activities which are complements and substitutes for children.

China is alone in adopting a birth quota to reduce fertility and slow population growth. The costs of this policy differs across individuals, though it is difficult to identify who is disadvantaged and thus suffers a welfare loss because of the quota restriction. It is arguably the least educated, rural women (and men) who are most likely to be penalized by the quota, who tend to have the largest families in other similarly poor countries. Moreover, when fines are imposed for an "out-of-plan" birth, they appear to be fixed in monetary terms in China at the community level, and are therefore less of a disincentive to the rich than to the poor (Schultz, 2004c). Rationing theory implies that the magnitude of the "cross effect" from the rationed good to substitute goods will be larger (in the vicinity of the equilibrium amounts demanded) under the rationing regime than under a voluntary (family planning) regime where choice is affected only by subsidies and taxes (Tobin and Houthakker, 1950–1951; Pollak, 1969). Thus, if child schooling and physical life cycle savings are substitutes for children, cross effects of a population policy would be greater on these family outcomes with a birth quota than with a voluntary family planning regime which had equivalent effects on fertility. Thus, voluntary versus mandatory population policies, which might lead to the same decline in fertility, could theoretically have a different effect on other family outcomes and on the distribution of welfare losses and gains.

4. A conceptual framework for family lifetime fertility and coordinated decisions

How do families respond to a reduction in the cost of birth control or an increase in access to more cost-effective forms of birth control? The avoidance of "unwanted births" increases the family's resources available for other activities, in other words it causes a lifetime gain in wealth. If the other activities are thought of as substitutes for the services children otherwise provide their parents, these substitute activities would receive a disproportionately larger share of these augmented family resources, and may improve the status of women and children and facilitate economic development. A simple economic framework may illustrate this idea.

Assume parents maximizes a separable two-period lifetime utility function, V, that is the sum of the utility from their periods of (1) working adulthood and (2) retirement, in which the arguments in their unified family utility function are consumption in both period, C_1, C_2, leisure in the first period, L, number of children, N, human capital per child or child quality, Q, and assets inherited in the first period, A. Parents may add savings in the first period (or draw down inherited assets) and thereby increase (or diminish) their consumption in the second period, when parents are unable to work. Parents could value A, N, and Q in the second period in part because they expect these selected variables to yield them a "return" as would an investment, r_a, r_n, r_q, respectively, while N and Q may also be enjoyed by parents as a form of pure consumption.

$$V = U_1(C_1, L, N, Q) + (1/(1 + \delta))U_2(C_2, N, Q),$$

where δ is a discount rate for the second period of the life cycle. Parents have a fixed amount of time in the first period, T, to allocate between working H hours for wage w or leisure (household production), L, and income in the first period is exhausted by consumption and savings, S:

$$Y = Hw + r_a A = C_1 + S,$$

where expenditures on children, $P_n N$, and expenditures on child human capital, $P_q QN$, are expressed in terms of the market prices of a child and child human capital, P_n and P_q, respectively. Consumption in the terminal period, C_2, is then the sum of returns on the three forms of assets parents can accumulate over their working period for their consumption during retirement: physical assets, children, and child human capital:

$$C_2 = r_a(A + S) + r_n P_n N + r_q P_q QN.$$

Ideally, empirical estimates would be identified of the "cross effects" of exogenous variation in fertility on the family's demand for child quality, savings, and leisure (or market labor supply): Q, S, and L (or H). Hypotheses are advanced regarding the sign of the cross derivatives of the effects of prices on various demands, holding income constant (i.e. income-compensated cross-effects are denoted here by *):

   (1) children and child quality (i.e. human capital) are widely hypothesized to be substitutes for parents, in which case $(dV^2/dN\, dQ)^* < 0$, and
   (2) a parallel hypothesis is that children and physical savings over the life cycle are also substitutes, i.e. $(dV^2/dN\, dS)^* < 0$, and finally
   (3) that non-market time or leisure and home production of the mother is a complement with the number of children she has, at least this is expected when children are young and in the household, $(dV^2/dN\, dL)^* > 0$.

The cross derivatives of an exogenous change in price of fertility caused by exposure to the experimental family planning program on the demand for a commodity is negative if parents view children and that commodity as complements, or positive if children and that commodity are substitutes (Tobin and Houthakker, 1950–1951; Rosenzweig and Wolpin, 1980a). Some assets may be more productive when parents have more children, as for example complementarity between child labor and farmland. Other types of assets such as a tube-well for drinking water in the homestead might function as a substitutes for child labor as well as women's labor in the family.

Statistical evidence is now needed on how the household portfolio of different types of assets adjusts to lower cost of birth control, which reduces fertility, and thereby exerts what is generally expected to be a positive substitution effect on the family's life cycle demand for physical assets and especially on those types of assets whose marginal product does not increase with child labor. There will also be a positive income effect due to the avoidance of unwanted and ill-timed births which raises the demand for all normal goods, which will include second period consumption as supported by the accumulation of household physical assets. The income effect will also tend to increase the demand for child quality (presumably a normal good). This positive income effect on quality of avoiding unwanted births could be erroneously interpreted as implying that the income-compensated cross-substitution effect is positive, and that child quantity and quality are substitutes.

Child mortality, although less readily controlled by the family's resource allocation decisions and technology than fertility, may also be affected by the family's behavioral responses to its preferences and constraints, although child mortality is in this context often assumed to be exogenous (Schultz, 1981). The family's formation of child human capital, Q, in the form of nutrition and health care, may influence child mortality, as well as respond to the local availability of public and private health services, the general disease environment, and the child's genetic frailty. When a community public health program reduces the cost of birth control and introduces effective child and maternal health inputs, it may be difficult to recover from an empirical evaluation of the program's effects whether the consequence are of *only* the birth control subsidy component of the program, or a consequence of *only* the (child and maternal) health component of the program, or both. The theoretical implications of child survival for fertility are also more complex in a dynamic behavioral model with uncertainty, features of the life cycle decision making process which are neglected here (Ben Porath, 1976; Wolpin, 1997).

Reduced-form equations may be estimated for N, Q, S, and H in terms of all the exogenous variables in the model: A, w, the prices of N and Q, and the financial returns in the market to A, N, and Q. Unfortunately, many surveys provide little data on Q, S, H, or returns on the three forms of family assets. The statistical errors in these reduced-form equations will tend to also be intercorrelated because they are jointly determined by unobserved parent preferences, family endowments, prices, or technological opportunities, and errors in optimization.

A key issue for empirical analysis is the specification and measurement of an instrumental variable which impacts fertility and yet is unrelated to the preferences or unobserved endowments and constraints affecting the family's other demands. In other words, the researcher must assume that an instrumental variable is uncorrelated with the errors in the reduced-form equations for the other family outcomes? [4]

The review of the empirical literature below in Section 5 finds a variety of instrumental variables that researchers have treated are exogenous to the family lifetime decision making process, and that thus provide the critical basis for identifying and estimating

---

[4] Various instrumental variables for fertility, such as the family planning program, could lead to different estimates of "cross effects" of a fertility decline in different circumstances. Our estimates are therefore not presented as a general pattern of response to this type of policy intervention, but as local average-estimates of the treatment effect (or intension to treat at say the village level) for a specified population (Imbens and Angrist, 1994).

the "cross effects" or the structural impacts of exogenous changes in fertility on another family outcome. A secondary issue is how widely the estimated "cross effect" would apply to represent the effect of different policy treatments, and to different changes in other family outcomes. The response to a decline in the price of birth control may in a stylized model be equated to the response of having twins, with the sign reversed (Rosenzweig and Wolpin, 1980a, 2000). But more realistically, the effect of a population program or exogenous event is likely to depend on the mechanism by which it impacts fertility, and to which subgroups in the population are influenced by the treatment. There is some reason to expect that the same instrumental variable could lead to different estimates of "cross effects" of a program-induced fertility decline in different circumstances, and a goal of the paper is to assess whether existing regularities in the empirical literature are consistent with any generalizations (Imbens and Angrist, 1994).

5. Empirical studies of fertility and the consequences for families

This Chapter does not review the extensive interdisciplinary literature reporting the direct associations between fertility and family outcomes (e.g. Becker, 1981; Blake, 1989; Hanushek, 1992; Lloyd, 1994; Desai, 1995). I concentrate instead on studies which estimate an explicitly causal model for fertility and another family outcome, in which both outcomes are allowed to be jointly and simultaneously determined. These investigations often report both the direct (OLS or Probit) associations as well as an instrumental variable (IV) estimate consistent with their hypothesized causal framework and identification strategy.[5]

5.1. Early investigations of the allocation of women's time and their fertility

Women's labor supply in the United States differs depending on their marital status, number of children under age 18, and in particular the number of their pre-school-aged children (e.g. Mincer, 1962). Early investigations tried to infer from these empirical regularities in the United States how changes in marital status and fertility might have contributed to the increases in female market labor supply in the 20th century. Goldin (1990), for example, treats marriage and number of children as exogenous factors in her US simulation of the gender wage gap, and concludes that the decline in fertility contributed to the increase in women's labor force participation, which reduced the pay gap between women and men. The mechanism is intuitively clear that with fewer children, the productive value of a mother's time at home for child care diminishes,

---

[5] The Hausman specification test provides a basis for assessing the severity of the statistical bias due to neglecting the simultaneity or heterogeneity problem. If the statistical discrepancy between the OLS and IV estimates is empirically unimportant, the specification test is likely to not reject the null hypothesis that fertility is exogenous with respect to the relevant family outcome variable. In this case, the OLS estimate may be preferred, because it does not appear significantly biased and it is likely to be more precisely estimated than the IV estimate.

encouraging her to work outside of the family in activities which can not be readily combined with her customary child care responsibilities (Heckman, 1974).

But fertility and female labor supply are both decisions over which women exercise some choice; it is plausible to imagine that variables unobserved by the researcher, such as parent preferences for children and working in the home covary positively, in which case the negative association observed between fertility and mother's market labor supply is likely to overstate the causal relationship. Rosenzweig and Wolpin (1980b) postulate that heterogeneity in women's preferences for childbearing and for work in the labor market are systematically related, and I would propose that they are generally inversely related. This proposed pattern of preference heterogeneity would lead to a larger negative correlation between fertility and female market labor supply than would be observed if fertility declined due to an exogenous decline in the price of birth control, for example.

The market wage of women may be initially assumed to be exogenous to family lifetime decisions, but in response to an exogenous decline in fertility, wage offers for women might be expected to first decrease as women have fewer children women and seek alternative work, but as they then invest more in market oriented vocational experiences which enhanced their market productivity, their rising market wages will reinforce the substitution of their time away from home production and further into the market. This possible scenario is not empirically documented in a convincing manner, although the long term study of Matlab, Bangladesh may provide some estimates of these effects of family planning on women's human capital accumulation, but they are evident only among the better educated.

Reallocating women's time from home work to market work does not necessarily entail any additional private gain or social benefit. It may occur because the woman's household is more impoverished due to her husband's bad health or death, or because the market wage rates available to the women increase. Push and pull factors may both be relevant to women's labor supply behavior, making the time allocation of women, and for that matter the time allocation of children, an interesting dependent variable, but not a unambiguous indicator of the welfare of the private individual, their family, or society.

5.2. Coordination of reproduction, production, and consumption

The empirical strategy follows from the conceptual framework outlined in Section 4 in which lifetime decisions of couples, including fertility, labor supply, human capital investments in children, and physical savings, are determined jointly and simultaneously over a lifetime. Research can then proceed to either estimate a reduced-form or a structural model of these family choices or coordinated behaviors.

A *reduced-form equation* can be approximated in which each family choice variable is expressed as a function of all observed environmentally fixed constraints on the family, thereby excluding from the list of explanatory variables those which are thought to involve any element of lifetime choice for the family. These reduced-form estimates

may provide a basis for evaluating policy, if the policy is administered as a randomized social experiment, such that the differences in treatment are not correlated with
unobserved determinants of family behavior. Even if the policies are exogenous to the
family's preferences and constraints, the reduced form does not indicate the pathways
by which the policy works to influence family outcomes. But this need not be a critical
limitation for many reasons.

   Reduced form estimates, because they are not dependent on a potentially controversial choice of an "exclusion restriction" can be estimated side-by-side for fertility and
other observed family outcomes. Insight into the system of household behaviors may be
gleaned from comparing this series of reduced form equations. Hypotheses can be proposed to account for how parents treat different outcomes, as *substitutes* for children, or
as *complements*. Reduced form studies have examined data from India (Duraisamy and
Malathy, 1981; Rosenzweig and Wolpin, 1982), Colombia (Rosenzweig and Schultz,
1982), Bangladesh (Hussein, 1989), Cote d'Ivoire and Ghana (Benefo and Schultz,
1996), for example.[6] Some evaluations of family planning programs estimate the fertility effect of local expenditures or field staff time per woman of childbearing age, as
in Taiwan and Thailand (Schultz, 1973, 1992), while controlling for household characteristics which are assumed to be exogenous determinants of fertility demands. In
other investigations, repeated cross sections are pooled and fixed effects are included
for regions, and the effect of the family planning program is identified from variation in
the intensity of treatments over time within program administrative regions (Gertler and
Molyneaux, 1994; Schultz, 1973, 1981). However, the local variation in family planning program treatment may not be independent of the local population's preferences
or unobserved characteristics, because governments may systematically allocate program resources to where they believe the program services are most needed. Individuals
will also tend to migrate, other things equal, to reside where local services appeal most
strongly to their preferences (Rosenzweig and Wolpin, 1986). Thus, even with the inclusion of community fixed effects, the within community changes and trends in program
activity may be correlated with changing unobserved parent preferences (via migration)
or demand determinants (such as changes in local factory employment opportunities
for women). Miller (2004) extends this approach in his study of the Colombian family
planning program, in which he allows for regional fixed effects and distinct regional

---

[6] A study of the Colombian 1973 Census sample began by estimating reduced form equations for children-
ever-born and child mortality rates of women by age cohorts separately for rural and urban residents, and
found across 900 municipalities that more local expenditures on family planning and more clinics per capita
are associated negatively with fertility and child mortality, controlling for the woman's characteristics and
the community climate and infrastructure (Rosenzweig and Schultz, 1982). Subsequent research reported to
USAID exploited information on malaria prevalence to identify the cross effect of child mortality on fertility,
by assuming that malaria affects only child mortality, whereas fertility is only affected by family planning
expenditures. These conditional demand estimates of fertility on child mortality were small and never statistically significant, whereas the child mortality effects on fertility were large and significant in all six urban age
groups of women, but not among rural women for whom fertility is still very high at older ages.

trends, while evaluating the family planning program effects on fertility and women's subsequent labor supply and the schooling of local children.

Rosenzweig and Evenson (1977) estimate a system of reduced form equations across Indian 1961 Census districts to account for a relatively comprehensive set of family outcomes, including fertility, labor supply, and school enrollments for boys and girls. But to prescribe even the sign of the partial effects of exogenous constraints such as the wages of children on child schooling and child work decisions, the researchers had to assume additional structural assumptions such as which family outcomes were substitutes and complements for each other, and when price effects dominate income effects. Reduced-form estimations may thus be informative regarding the effect of exogenous policy variation, but not always be very helpful in testing restrictions implied by economic theory of household choice.

The alternative to estimating a reduced form is to assume fertility affects specific other family choices or outcomes, and then to estimate this *structural equation* which includes the parameter of interest. This estimate of the "cross effect" of fertility on say child quality, then requires an identification restriction. The conventional simultaneous equations approach to estimating such a structural relationship is to propose an "exclusion restriction" which typically specifies a variable that affects fertility but does not affect the other family outcome, except through its mediated impact on fertility.

5.3. Structural estimates of the "cross effects" of fertility on family outcomes

To assess fertility as an independent factor in development, and a lever on which policy interventions may operate, estimates are needed of the "cross effects" of policy-induced changes in fertility, which thereby modify other aspects of family welfare or other social outcomes that society values positively or negatively. Estimating the economic cross effects of policy-induced declines in fertility on women's productivity and on child human capital formation are therefore central objectives of this paper. But the empirical literature that recognizes the joint and simultaneous determination of fertility and family lifetime outcomes is sparse, probably because there is little consensus on what variables are valid exclusion restrictions for the purposes of estimating how fertility causes these changes in family outcomes. In addition, it would seem likely that the estimated cross effects of fertility will depend on the choice of identifying instrument for a particular policy mechanism, because of the heterogeneity in the population's response to any specific treatment approximated by different instruments. In other words, the effect estimated from variation in a policy variable represents a *specific* "local average treatment effect" (LATE) of modifying the fertility of certain groups in the population (Imbens and Angrist, 1994; Heckman, 1997; Moffitt, 2005). With this interpretation of what instrumental variable (IV) estimates are measuring, it is reasonable to select the instrument to predict fertility so as to replicate the effect of policies governments or non-profit organizations view as feasible and cost-effective. Then the LATE estimates will represent the likely consequences of this policy treatment.

There are few long-term studies to document how randomly assigned treatments of a population to family planning or reproductive health programs have impacted fertility and other family outcomes. I return later to the case in Matlab Bangladesh. Lacking situations where instruments arguably represent a random treatment, most empirical research on the causal effects of fertility has gravitated toward the use of two instruments which capture variation in fertility which is arguably exogenous to parent demand for births: (1) twins or multiple births by parity, and (2) the sex outcomes of early births. These instruments explain only a small share of the variation in fertility, but this explained share is arguably independent of the demand for children and thus uncorrelated with preferences and constraints. Twins are more readily interpreted across cultures as an instrument, because they represent a "treatment" of a woman to an unanticipated "shock" or increase in her biological supply of births, irregardless of the sex of those children. But twins have the disadvantage of occurring infrequently, in the sense that they normally affect less than one percent of pregnancies, and therefore a large sample is required to obtain precise estimates from this instrument of the cross effect of fertility and they depend on the parity of the twin and the definition of the counterfactual or control group.[7]

5.4. Twins as an exogenous instrument for fertility and labor supply

Rosenzweig and Wolpin (1980b) analyzed twins as a rationing device which allocates number of births per woman more or less randomly, as well as modifies the timing of births. They propose a two-period model of fertility and mother's labor supply to illustrate that the cross effect of a "twin on first birth" on the mother's labor supply would be larger in the first period than in a second period. They also postulate preference heterogeneity on the part of couples, by which they mean those with stronger than average preferences for numbers of children also tend to have different preferences for women working in the market labor force. I would propose that this preference heterogeneity would bias the directly observed cross effect (estimated by ordinary least squares-OLS) of fertility on labor supply to be a larger (absolute value) negative effect than if this

---

[7] Rosenzweig and Wolpin (1980b, 2000) emphasize that parents have a goal in terms of the number and timing of births, and the effect of a birth on the mother's labor supply will differ depending on when the labor supply is measured, e.g. the year after the birth or twenty years thereafter. A "twin on first birth" may provide parents with the time to adopt contraception and avoid having more births than they want over their lifetime, if they wanted two or more. But the parents still have to accommodate the unwanted timing of their first two births. A contraceptive failure leading to an unwanted or mistimed birth could have different implications, if it occurred before marriage or after, or if it occurred on the first or after the last intended birth. Models dedicated to explaining the timing of births have not been widely replicated, perhaps because the theory of demand for timing of births has not derived novel and testable implications which are distinct from those implied by the static lifetime model (Willis, 1974; Becker, 1981; Wolpin, 1984, 1997; Heckman and Walker, 1991). Twins are also different from singleton births; on average they are lighter and less healthy, and twins may require different reallocations of family lifetime resources than mistimed singleton births (Behrman and Rosenzweig, 2002).

cross effect were estimated on the basis of an exogenous shock of a "twin on first birth." They also argue the need to control for age at first birth in their model to deal with the timing of births within the biologically fixed reproductive span of the couple. Conditioning their labor supply estimates on the age at first birth, which they recognize is an endogenous decision variable, complicates the interpretation of their estimates as long run equilibrium responses (Rosenzweig and Wolpin, 2000). They analyze the 1965 and 1973 US National Fertility Surveys from which they obtain samples of about 4000 women who had a first birth before age 25 or after age 24. Their estimates based on 87 twins are imprecise but generally consistent with their framework.

This approach to using twins as an instrument for exogenous variation in fertility has been employed in a growing number of studies, which although they were initially mostly in high-income countries, have helped to clarify the conceptual framework as it is extended to low income countries. Bronars and Groggers (1994) rely on the 1970 and 1980 US Census public-use-microdata-samples to obtain a much larger number of twins. Angrist and Evans (1998) use "twins-on-second-birth" or "sex outcome of the first two births," or both, to estimate by instrumental variables how fertility exerts a "cross effect" on several dimensions of the mother's labor supply. Both studies find women with twins have higher fertility and diminished labor supply. Of importance for this paper, the IV estimate based on twins on second birth as an instrument are about half as large in absolute value as the OLS direct estimates, and Hausman-type specification test suggest fertility can be rejected as exogenous in the labor supply equation of the mother. The smaller IV estimate is thus preferred as an unbiased measure of the cross-effect of fertility on the mother's market labor supply. Hypothesis (3) in Section 4 was that the non-market time or leisure of mothers appears to be a complement with numbers of children, and this prediction is consistent with these studies, in which case the neglected compensating income effect associated with the extra birth would presumably decrease the demand for a mother's leisure or non-market time, and thus understate any complementary cross effect of fertility on demand for non-market time.

5.5. Twins as an instrument for fertility and the demand for child human capital

Another within-family consequence of fertility could arise if the number of siblings affects the consumption, productivity, and welfare of a child. In other words, it has been hypothesized that parents who have more children commit less of their time and resources to each of their children (e.g. Becker, 1960; Becker and Lewis, 1974; T.W. Schultz, 1974; Becker and Tomes, 1976; Zajonc, 1976; Blake, 1989).[8] This inverse relationship between what is called the "quantity of children" and the "quality of children" suggests that parents who are subsidized to have fewer children may also invest

---

[8] Becker (1960, p. 217) conjectured: "Because (child) quality seems like a relatively close substitute for quantity, families with excess children would spend less on each child than other families with equal income and tastes. Accordingly, an increase in contraceptive knowledge would raise the quality of children as well as reduce their quantity."

more, on average, in the human capital of their children, and thereby improve the health, education, migration and lifetime consumption opportunities of each of their children on average. This view of the trade-off for parents between having more offspring and allocating more resources to each child, given their resources, is also a central idea in sociobiology and psychology (Zajonc, 1976; Dawkins, 1976; Becker, 1981). Because society often intervenes to subsidize or organize social services to improve childhood nutrition, public health, and schooling, the magnitude of this causal quantity–quality trade-off could be a motivation for society to assist couples to avoid unwanted births, or to subsidize birth control.[9] These empirical regularities would appear to be consistent with hypothesis (1) in Section 4 that exogenous changes in the number of births affect inversely the per child levels of human capital, holding constant the family's income, or that child quantity and quality are substitutes. But it should be obvious that these empirical regularities do not test this hypothesis, because they are not based on exogenous variation in fertility that is independent of heterogeneous parent preferences or unobserved economic constraints, and these regularities do not compensate for the gain in income associated with a policy intervention, such as a birth control subsidy, which could also explain why a population policy contributes to child quality.

Cross tabulations of census, administrative, and survey data show that the number of siblings an individual has tends to be inversely related their schooling or their success in the labor market (Becker, 1960; Blake, 1989). But even this direct empirical correlation is not observed in all rural low-income populations where education levels are low. For example, Maralani (2004) documents in the Indonesian Family Life Survey collected in 1993 and 1997 that a woman's completed fertility and the schooling of her children are not inversely related in rural areas. Among women residing in urban areas, the "modern" quantity–quality trade-off is significantly different from zero only for the youngest women age 20–29.[10] Montgomery, Kouame and Oliver (1995) analyze Living Standard Measurement Surveys from Cote d'Ivoire and Ghana collected in the late 1980s and find little evidence that schooling of children is lower for women who have

---

[9] In those states which first legalized abortion in the United States, the frequency of crime two decades later appears to have diminished significantly. A study has explored many aspects of these data and argues that the increased access to abortion, as a means for avoiding unwanted children among the poor, led to a reduction in youth from disadvantaged backgrounds in those states, which was the cause for the decline in crime (Donohue and Levitt, 2001). One interpretation of their instrumental variable estimates of the determinants of crime is that policy which reduces unwanted childbearing (i.e. legal access to abortion) helps not only poor women and their children, but also relieves society of the external social costs of crime. Indicators of child welfare and living conditions are also shown to improve for children whose parent had access to legal abortion (Gruber, Levine and Staiger, 1999).

[10] I would conjecture that at the low levels of schooling attained by the children of older rural Indonesian women, schooling was not a major cost of childbearing, and wealthier rural parents sought more children and provided them with more schooling because their existing land allowed them to employ more complementary child labor, adding to their traditional incentives for more children. In the urban sector where today the average child receives some secondary schooling, and children are a less important source of family income, the modern trade-off is clearly evident in the cross section. However, this does not mean that family planning programs have increased the schooling of children. But the hypothesis warrants more study.

higher fertility. But even when the conventional inverse empirical regularity between these family choice variables is present, it does not imply that an exogenous increase in fertility would necessarily depress the school attainment of a woman's children, or vice versa. To test the quantity–quality hypothesis, the researcher requires variation in quantity (e.g. completed fertility or number of siblings) which is caused by an exogenous variable – one which is arguably uncorrelated with desired, demanded, or preferred fertility or otherwise affected by the lifetime wealth of families and relative prices.

Based on the Additional Rural Income Survey of 1969–1971 from India, Rosenzweig and Wolpin (1980a) use the frequency of twins per completed pregnancy as an exogenous determinant of the woman's completed fertility. This approximately random instrument is then shown to be significantly associated with lower levels of completed schooling of the woman's other (non-twin) children, based on 25 twins in 1633 families. If one assumes that the rate of twining is independent of other determinants of schooling, income, etc., fertility is increased by about 0.8 births by a twin, and this exogenous shock to fertility induces the family to substitute away from schooling per child. In a rationed consumer demand framework where the allocation of twins is an exogenous shock to fertility, the negative cross-effect of fertility on schooling per child suggests that parents treat their number of children and the human capital per child as substitutes, neglecting the negative income effect that would also reduce the demand for schooling.

The occurrence of twins on a specific parity has been used to instrument for the total number of children in a family (sibling number) in order to explain various measures of human capital of children born before the twin, or other life course events, such as the child's age at marriage in the case of daughters. The OLS estimates of the effect of child quantity on indicators of child quality tend to yield strong negative relationships, but the IV estimate identified by twins tends to be smaller in absolute value, and sometimes insignificant and even positive in sign in some cases (e.g. Angrist, Lavy and Schlosser, 2006, in Israel; Qian, 2006, in China). Does this imply that quantity and quality are not substitutes and that population policies which achieve a voluntary reduction in fertility would not induce an increase in child human capital?

Rosenzweig and Zhang (2006) consider the possibility that parents might allocate their resources in children to compensate (or reinforce) endowments differences among their children (Becker and Tomes, 1976). However, twins themselves may have below-average endowments, as clearly is the case for their birthweight. The question is then how parents compensate across their children for the below-average twins, and will this behavioral process affect the estimated "cross-effect" of twin induced fertility variation on child quality which will combine a negative wealth effect of the involuntary fertility shock and mistimed spacing of births, as well as the compensation effect among their children. In their framework Rosenzweig and Zhang (2006) show that if parents reinforce endowment differences among children, as they empirically observe in their sample of twins from Yunnan Province in China, the twin effect on twins' quality is a lower bound (more negative) estimate of the true average effect, whereas the twin effect on the quality of a younger non-twin is an upper bound (more positive) estimate of the average cross effect. They conclude, therefore, that the results from estimating twin effects on non-twins, as commonly reported in the literature, is an upper-bound estimate and hence positively biased toward rejecting substitution between quantity and quality which implies a negative cross effect. This does not however, modify the implications of the empirical regularity emphasized in this paper that using twins as an instrument for fertility generally reduces in absolute value the estimated fertility effect on child quality and on the mother's labor supply.[11]

5.6. *Fecundity approximated by the residual from a fertility production function*

Another way to distinguish exogenous variation in fertility is to recover a measure of biological heterogeneity or a couple's fecundity by assuming more structure for the reproductive process and predicting the choice of contraceptive practice during each reproductive cycle. In other words, contraceptive practice and the conception rate of a couple are used to infer the couple's latent reproductive endowment or biological fecundity.[12] Based on the 1976 Malaysian Family Life Survey this measure of fecundity is estimated from reproductive calendars from 1971–1976 (Rosenzweig and Schultz, 1987). This residual is a continuous variable approximating a couple's reproductive "endowment," given their predicted contraceptive behavior, and is roughly analogous to the effect of a twin. Controlling for her education, age, and husband's earnings, this fecundity variable is associated with more children ever born, use of more effective contraception ($n = 816$), lower birth weight for her children, and less schooling per child (Rosenzweig and Schultz, 1985, 1987). All of these IV estimates of the effects of exogenous residual fertility on child quality outcomes are smaller in absolute value

---

[11] One final example of twin-instrumented fertility variation investigates birth order-specific effects of twins on schooling of earlier births in Norway, a high-income low fertility setting. Using data for all persons, Black, Devereux and Salvanes (2005a) rely on twins on a second or subsequent birth as an instrument to predict the completed schooling of a woman's children (currently age 25 or more) born before the arrival of the twins. The twin-induced variation in the mother's fertility is not a statistically significant determinant of the children's schooling, based on the IV estimate, with or without controls for birth order. The conventional OLS relationship, however, is strongly negative (Black, Devereux and Salvanes, 2005a, Table 6). Their evidence is consistent with heterogeneity in women's preferences for going to school and for reduced childbearing (or another unobservable variables such as ability) which contributes to the spurious inverse direct OLS relationship. Norwegian mothers may be able to compensate for the effect on the "quality" of earlier children of having a later twin because of the egalitarian welfare and schooling systems in Norway, which would not be present in a low income country.

[12] Desired family size and accumulating knowledge by the couple of their reproductive endowment is expected to influence whether they use a contraceptive in each period, and the effectiveness of the method they choose. The technical effectiveness of various contraceptives to reduce fertility is first estimated in the form of a two-stage fertility production function, in which local prices and household characteristics affect the couple's demand for contraception. Then this estimated model and the actual contraceptive practice are used to recover the residual variation in a couple's latent rate of conception (Rosenzweig and Schultz, 1985). The couple's unexplained variation in fertility is then interpreted as a noisy measure of the couple's fecundity.

than if they are estimated as the direct partial association between actual fertility and the indicator of child quality.[13]

Fertility and child health outcomes are analyzed as joint choices in the Kenyan Welfare Monitoring Surveys of 1994 and 1997 ($n = 4921, 3206$), in which the rate of twinning per completed pregnancy is employed as an instrument for children ever born among women over age 35, controlling for age, region, etc. The negative partial correlation (OLS) between fertility and child health is significant, but this association becomes smaller and less statistically significant when the mother's fertility's effect on child health is estimated using the rate of twinning as the instrumental variable (Schultz and Mwabu, 2003).[14]

Kim and Aassve (2006) estimate the determinants of conception rates from the 1989 and 1992 from the Indonesian Family Life Survey ($n = 4548$) including endogenous choices of birth control by type, with community fixed effects, identified by the couples' education and Muslim religion. Persistent and transitory exogenous measures of individual fecundity are then defined from this estimated model, predicted inputs, and fertility, following Rosenzweig and Schultz (1987). The permanent component of fecundity for a couple accounts for a significantly lower level of mother's labor supply in 1993 estimated as a Tobit model. When this estimated impact of exogenous fecundity is rescaled to be in units of births, it is about one third of the magnitude as the coefficient obtained by alternatively including the couple's actual number of births from 1989 to 1992 in the log labor supply equation for women. Thus, the OLS estimate which treats fertility is exogenous is substantially larger in absolute value, or -0.220 a birth on log weekly hours, than the IV derived estimate which -0.069. Moreover, this anticipated female labor supply effect of fecundity is statistically significant and substantial only among rural residents in 1993. In addition, Kim and Aassve estimate the parallel specification of their model for the husband's labor supply as affected by permanent and transitory fecundity, and find that the husband's labor supply (ln weekly hours) increases by 0.024 in the rural areas due to a birth according to the IV estimate, and by 0.062 according to the OLS estimate, and does not respond significantly in the urban areas. The implication is that women's and men's labor supply responses to fertility are

---

[13] The Demographic Health Surveys distinguish if a woman's births were mistimed or unwanted ever. Montgomery and Lloyd (1999) find the schooling of a woman's children is not uniformly associated with mistimed and unwanted births in the last five years in four low-income countries. Rosenzweig and Schultz (1987) find that their residual estimate of fecundity of couples in Malaysia is significantly correlated with the couple's reporting their last birth unwanted or mistimed. The respondent's classification of a birth as mistimed or unwanted is, however, arguably subjective and endogenous itself, invalidating it as an exogenous instrument for latent fecundity, or even as a basis for checking the reasonableness of the fertility production function estimates.

[14] The health of children under age five is summarized by height-for-age and sex, and weight-for-height by age and sex, expressed as standardized Z scores, which is defined as the child's deviation from the median child of the same age and sex as observed in a well nourished (US) population, expressed in units of standard deviations for each age and sex group. The findings are robust to constructing the Z scores around Kenyan median anthropometric growth curves for children rather than those derived from US population figures.

offsetting to a degree, but these plausible family specialized labor supply effects are evident only in the rural economic setting of Indonesia.

Because multiple births occur naturally infrequently, twins may not be an ideal instrument for fertility unless large census samples are available and the reporting of twins is very accurate. On the other hand, estimating fertility production functions in order to "back out" an exogenous measure of fecundity requires extensive and complete information on birth control behavior and its environmental determinants. Other biological markers for fecundity may also be directly observed in a household survey, although they may not be measured without systematic error. An alternative instrument for fertility (or conceptually fecundity) may be a woman's experience of miscarriage. Xia Li (2005) analyzes whether a woman on her first pregnancy experiences a miscarriage (and on subsequent pregnancies for later birth orders). Miscarriages are reported in roughly 11 percent of first births in the 1988, 1995, and 2002 in the US National Survey of Family Growth ($n = 12,000$).[15] Using a miscarriage on first pregnancy to identify exogenous variation in fertility, she finds the probability of miscarriage is negatively and significantly related to children ever born, suggesting the instrument proxies subfecundity or a discouragement effect of miscarriage on the demand for childbearing.[16] The associated IV estimate of the cross-effect of fertility on a mother's labor force participation and hours worked is negative, and about one half the absolute magnitude of the directly estimated (OLS or Probit) associations.

5.7. Sex composition of births as an instrument for fertility and labor supply in high-income countries

A second instrument proposed to identify independent variation in US fertility is the sex of the first two births, where the sex composition is hypothesized to be independent of preferences for numbers of children or of unobserved variables affecting female labor supply (Angrist and Evans, 1998). In the case of sex composition, the power of the instrument(s) to predict fertility depends on parents having a distinct reproductive response to different combinations of boys and girls, and the direction of the OLS bias will depend on how this gender preference is related to preferences motivating women's labor supply or demand for child quality. This is more complex than in the case of twins which is a plausible surrogate for fertility without regard to gender preference. Angrist and Evans (1998) reports that a US couple is about 15 percent more likely to continue to have a third birth (0.46 versus 0.40 in the 1980 Census) if their first two births are

[15] Although miscarriages occur much more frequently than twins, the overall explanatory power of miscarriages as an IV for fertility is not much higher than twins in these US surveys.

[16] If all women are not equally aware of an early miscarriage, or some fail to report this event, this instrument could be measured with error, and if reporting error is related to the demand for children, it could undermine its validity for an exogenous instrument for fertility. The main limitation of miscarriage as an instrument is that its reporting could be subject to systematic errors of measurement and recall, especially if it includes some induced abortion.

either both boys or both girls. In other words, parents prefer to have at least one boy and one girl. When having a third birth is predicted on the basis of the sex outcome of the first two births, the IV estimate of fertility's effect reducing the mother's labor supply is again much smaller in absolute magnitude than the OLS estimate.[17]

Jacobsen, Pearce and Rosenbloom (1999) also examine the 1970 and 1980 US Censuses and use as their instrument for fertility "the sex of the first two births" and obtain negative IV estimates of the cross effect on labor supply which are significantly smaller in absolute value than the OLS estimates. Sampling from the same birth cohort of women represented in the 1970 Census and among those ten years older in the 1980 Census, they show that the labor supply IV effects of fertility on mother's labor supply diminished as the cohort ages, consistent with the birth timing framework as proposed by Rosenzweig and Wolpin for the study of the behavioral effects of twins (1980b).

The sex of the first two births and whether the second birth is a twin are analyzed by Iacovou (2001) as instruments for predicting the probability of women continuing to have a third birth in the United Kingdom, and the resulting effect of this IV variation in fertility on the mother's labor supply. Estimates are for women with two or more births in the National Child Development Study which includes a cohort born in a week in 1958 and followed through 1991 ($n = 3188$), and a British Household Panel Study from 1991–1992 ($n = 1374$). According to the direct partial association (OLS), a third birth is significantly negatively associated with the woman participating in the labor force and her hours of work. But when the effect of the third birth on labor supply is estimated by IV methods, the cross effect on labor supply is no longer statistically different from zero in either sample, and indeed its sign becomes positive. The inverse OLS association between fertility and female labor supply in the UK is apparently not the same as these IV estimates of the impact of an exogenous birth. Heterogeneity in preferences for children and women's work, or other unobservables correlated with fertility and female labor supply in opposite directions, could explain these findings from the UK.

5.8. Sex composition of births as an instrument for fertility in labor supply in low-income countries

Parent preferences for the sex of their offspring may differ widely across cultures, and could also change with economic development. There are, however, at this time relatively few studies in low-income countries from which to generalize. In some settings

---

[17] Angrist and Evans (1998) also report evidence across age groups suggesting that the labor supply effect of the twin on second birth or same sex outcomes are larger (negatively) for younger women for whom the marginal birth may be a more recent event, consistent with the Rosenzweig–Wolpin (1980b) timing model. The OLS estimates of fertility's effect on the mothers labor supply in 1980 are consistently larger in absolute value than the IV estimates across different dimensions of her work and its value: (1) working for pay (OLS from −0.18 to IV −0.12), (2) for hours per week (−6.7 to −4.6), (3) weeks per year (−9.0 to −5.7), and (4) in terms of total annual labor income of the mother (−$3768.0 to −1961.0). Their estimates from the 1990 Census are similar. Clearly, this estimate only pertains to the self-selected sample of the population who have two or more children.

there is a strong preference for male offspring, as distinct from the preference for having a child of both sexes as described by Angrist and Evans and observed in the US and UK. There would appear to be substantial effects of sex composition of children on the lifetime wealth of a family in some areas of Asia, perhaps because parents must provide a daughter with a dowry, whereas they can expect to benefit from a dowry paid to their sons, when they marry (Rose, 2000). Thus, the sex composition of births in such an Asian context can involve not only a potential effect on fertility, but also on family wealth and relative prices which affect other family members. Sex composition of births as an instrument for fertility is therefore invalid, because it will not approximate the "cross effect" of a supply shift of fertility on family outcomes, as it will be inseparable from potentially large changes in family wealth, which may also be a complex function of class or caste in which customs surrounding marriage and dowries differ.

Chun and Oh (2002) use the sex of the *first* child in Korea as an instrument in the first stage regression for fertility, before estimating in the second stage for the women's labor force participation as a function of fertility. They analyze the 1996 wave of the Korean National Survey of Family Income and Expenditures ($n = 3997$). Having a male on first birth is associated with a woman having 0.15 fewer children at the time of the survey; Korean parents appear to be more likely to stop bearing children after having a male birth than a female birth, and the effect of a second male birth is to reduce further the likelihood of continuing to a third birth. Estimates of fertility's effect on female labor force participation based on this IV strategy implies participation is -0.28 for each child, whereas the OLS estimate is also statistically significant but smaller in absolute magnitude, -0.06. This is an unusual case in this paper where the IV estimate of the cross effect of fertility on a family outcome is larger in absolute magnitude than the OLS estimate of the same parameter. This pattern is consistent with there being an income effect associated with having a male offspring that encourages a mother to engage in more home production or leisure, or due to the hypothesized (3) cross-substitution effect. This empirical regularity suggests that the local average treatment effect (LATE) of a male on first birth is to decrease the woman's labor supply by a greater amount than is the case for all fertility which includes girls (Imbens and Angrist, 1994). Apparently in Korea, women whose fertility is most affected by their preference to have a male child are also as a consequence less likely than the average to work in the labor force, perhaps because they regard themselves as wealthier with a male offspring to rear. And because the boy is valued more highly, it might be expected that the mother would allocate more of her time to the care of the son than to a daughter, even though gender differences in schooling and health across siblings may diminish with increasing household income (Schultz, 2001). Heterogeneity in traditional values toward the sex of offspring could explain why Korean parents who have a relatively stronger preference for their offspring to be male, tend to also have a relatively stronger preference for mothers to *not* work outside of the home, or at least to dedicate more of her time to the task of rearing the son.

It should be noted that technological developments may also undermine the validity of these two instruments for measuring exogenous variation in fertility. Techniques to test for the sex of the fetus early in a pregnancy (e.g. by means of ultrasound, amniocentesis, or chorionic villus sampling) allow parents who have a sufficiently strong preference for the gender of their child to abort a fetus of the unwanted sex. If this occurs, the sex composition of children may become correlated with the couples' preferences for women to work (and other family choice outcomes), and sex of the child cease to be a valid instrument for estimating the cross-effect of fertility. The increasing number of male to female births at each successively higher parity in countries such as Korea, China, and portions of India reflects probably a strong preference for male offspring.[18]

Since about 1980 in high-income countries, twins are also becoming an unsatisfactory instrument for exogenous fertility variation, because drugs administered to assist parents to conceive also increase the probability of having a multiple births. Because parents with multiple births are increasingly likely to have used fertility enhancing drugs, twinning will be correlated with subfecundity, on the one hand, and also with relatively strong preferences on the part of parents for additional children. It can no longer be confidently assumed that twins or multiple births are uncorrelated with the preferences of parents for childbearing or for women working in the market labor force, or for that matter unrelated to income, since the infertility treatments tend to be privately costly in most countries.

5.9. Sex composition of births as an instrument for fertility and child human capital

Other studies estimating the effect of exogenous variation in fertility on child quality have used the sex composition of births. It should be reemphasized that these instruments have explanatory power to predict fertility among parents who have a strong preference between having boys and girls, and are selected in a culture-specific manner. In some settings they will also capture substantial income and other price effects that could change long run family outcome variables and therefore do not necessarily predict how population policies would affect behavior (Rose, 2000; Deolalikar and Rose, 1998).

Lee (2004) analyzes the determinants of fertility and child educational investments in Korea. He examines the Korean Household Panel Study from 1993 to 1998 ($n = 5180$), and finds that if a woman's first child is a girl, the woman is more likely to have a second birth, and the time to the second birth is also shorter, according to a fitted hazard model.

---

[18] By 1989 the ratio of male to female births in Korea increased from a normal value of 1.06 for first births, to 2.17 for fourth-order births (Schultz, 1997, Table 4). Models of fertility estimated from Chinese data for women with at least one birth also reveal the strength of traditional male preference, in which the share of male births reduces the likelihood a Chinese woman will have an additional birth at all estimated parities (Schultz and Zeng, 1995). However, it has been observed that the sex ratio of births may be affected by the prevalence of Hepatitis B Virus, which may offer a supplemental biological mechanism for exogenously modifying the regional pattern of sex ratios at birth in East Asia where the prevalence of hepatitis is substantial and regionally varies (Oster, 2005).

The same is true for continuing to a third birth, if the first and/or second births is a girl. Relying on whether the first birth is a girl as an instrument for completed fertility, Lee finds the direct (OLS) estimate of the elasticity of educational investment per child with respect to fertility is −0.5, whereas the instrumental variable estimate of this elasticity is −0.3. The observed relationship between women's fertility and the education of their children is thus weakened when identified from variation in fertility induced by the sex composition of a couple's births.

Jensen (2005) hypothesizes that in India son preference is combined with a rule to stop bearing children only if the woman has a sufficient number of living sons. This he argues would lead girls to have more siblings than boys, on average, and thus receive less education in a larger family. In a 2001 Survey of Aging in Rural areas of five Indian states ($n = 2693$ households) Jensen reports that girls have 0.47 more siblings if the first child in their family is a girl and 0.76 more siblings if the first two births are girls (Table 5). Dividing his sample into those couples who indicate a son preference and a desire to educate sons more than daughters (51%), the OLS estimated effect of an additional sibling is −1.2 years of schooling, whereas the estimated effect of siblings instrumented by the sex of the first two births is −0.69. The quantity–quality trade-off is still present, but diminished by about half when it is based on the response of couples to the sex outcomes of their first two birth.

The role of sex of offspring as an instrument for fertility or other family behaviors depends on the researcher to interpret cultural and economic repercussions of the sex composition, not just its impact of number of children born (Deolalikar and Rose, 1998; Rose, 2000). The sex composition of children can represent a random treatment, but its outcome on fertility is likely to depend on marriage customs and gender inequality in a specific society, as well as the couple's individual preferences for a wide variety of family lifetime outcomes. It is therefore not a valid instrument for fertility as an objective of population policy, in order to estimate the cross effects of fertility on long run family outcomes, which is a central motivation of this paper.

China after introducing the one-child quota policy in 1979, relaxed this policy after about 1984 in some regions and permitted rural couples with a girl as their first born to have a second child. Qian (2006) analyzes a sample of 28,771 households from the 1990 Census, drawn from 21 rural counties in four provinces for which she relies on the 1989 China Health Nutrition Survey to document the local timing of this relaxation in the birth quota policy. First-born girls born in 1976–1981, who are resident in counties which relaxed their one-child rule, are shown to have 0.25 more siblings on average than first-born girls born in the earlier period of 1973–1976, whose parents would have been more likely to be constrained by the one-child policy. Qian concludes from two-stage least squares estimates of school enrollment conditioned on the local policy-induced change in number of siblings, that a one sibling increase due to the local government's relaxed policy is associated with an 18 percent increase in first-born girl's probability of being enrolled in school according to the 1990 Census. The census data, however, does not report education on children who have left the home, and migration which is increasing in this period could introduce a serious selection bias.

The ordinary least squares estimate of the partial association of sibling number on girl's enrollment is significantly negative, as typically observed in the descriptive literature on child quality(schooling)–quantity(sibling number). If this policy-induced change in number of siblings is uncorrelated with unobserved factors determining differences in the parent's demand for male and female children's schooling, Qian's IV estimated cross-effect of *increases* in siblings increases the schooling of the first born girls, but not of boys. Thus, increasing the quantity of children from the first to second birth order does not appear to elicit the anticipated negative substitution response in her sample. She regards this as evidence that the quantity–quality relationships is non-monotonic.[19]

One alternative interpretation for Qian's findings is that the relaxation of the one-child policy represents a large lifetime gain in wealth or welfare for families with a first-born girl. In many studies family income effects on the enrollment of girls tend to be larger than the income effects on the enrollment of boys (Schultz, 1995). If these income effects favoring girls schooling dominate any possible negative cross-substitution effect from quantity to quality, the policy relaxation could favor increased fertility and girls schooling. However, Quin does not find evidence for a positive income effect on fertility in her data.[20]

5.10. Estimates of population program effects on fertility and other family outcomes

If the private cost of birth control is reduced by a population program, fertility is expected to decline.[21] Table 1 proposed other family outcomes which might be affected during a family's lifetime by a program-induced decline in fertility. As stressed in this paper, many of these potentially important mechanisms have not been empirically studied, but could be analyzed by studying social experiments, matching studies, or well-designed instrumental variables to identify the effect of exogenous variation in fertility on these lifetime developments.

Many forms of social welfare policy, including family planning and reproductive health programs, could be viewed as a possible program instruments affecting fertility, and variation in access to these programs could be candidates for exogenous program

---

[19] The author's assumption that a four year interval between births was uniformly enforced in all counties of China does not seem realistic. One might also expect the local relaxation of the one-child policy would have been affected by the local demands of parents for additional births and not imposed for some exogenous reason. Although in one set of estimates controls are included for mother's schooling and household income, father's income is not included, and household income is not derived from a series of questions on expenditures or income sources, which are generally believed to produce a more reliable value for household income.

[20] As already noted, Rosenzweig and Zhang (2006) offer another explanation for her estimates of the cross substitution effect being biased in a positive direction.

[21] A reduction in the price of birth control would raise the cost of children but also add slightly to income. The implicit assumption is that the price effect of population programs dominate the income effect, where children are presumed to be "normal" economic good exhibiting a positive income elasticity when relative prices are unchanged.

treatments, as outlined in Table 2. The random occurrence of twins and the reduction in the private cost of birth control due to a family planning program could influence fertility in opposite directions, but otherwise can be thought of as having an analogous exogenous effects on fertility, neglecting for the moment any consequences for income and biology on child quality. Heterogeneity in the individual's response to the policy treatment may also be important and can complicate simple differences in before-and-after evaluations which often assume for simplicity homogeneity in the response of the treated.[22]

The welfare consequences for different individuals of a supply shock to fecundity or a randomized exposure to a family planning programs will differ according to a couple's reproductive goals, their current number of surviving children, age, and fecundity. The private cost of a twin on first birth will be smaller for a couple who wants many children, than for a couple who wants only one birth. The private benefit of a policy-induced decline in the price of birth control is correspondingly smaller for the couple who wants many more children, than for the couple who wants no more children, other things being equal. The policy treatment provided by the independent family planning program and the twin on first birth yield instrumental variable (IV) estimates which identify a local average treatment effect (LATE). Adding to the model explanatory variables defined as the interaction of the program treatment intensity and the exogenous characteristics of individuals treated can help to assess whether heterogeneity in response to the program is substantively important, and how it is distributed across groups in the population (Schultz, 1992).

A key issue for social policy is whether a subsidy for family planning will not only reduce fertility, but also improve child quality and family welfare? Studies evaluating the success of family planning programs often stop with an evaluation of how contraceptive knowledge, attitudes and practices change following a program intervention. Even when the intervention treatment is designed as a randomized experiment across local residential areas, the common focus on short run adoption of modern means of birth control tends to overlook the longer run consequences (cf. Taichung City Experiment in 1963, Taiwan, documented by Freedman and Takeshita, 1969). Program evaluations should assess how *completed* fertility is impacted by the program, as well as the timing of births. Traditional means of birth control, such as prolonged breast-feeding, postpartum delay of intercourse, and even induced abortion, may diminish in the aftermath of a modern family planning program, implying that the uptake of modern contraceptives in the program will overstate the program's impact on fertility, as well as possibly overlook other welfare gains (Schultz, 1992). Even changes in fertility in the first few years after a program starts tend to overstate the longer run consequences on lifetime fertility, because initially the program achieves a better timing of births which may increase intervals between births and thereby cause a transitory dip in period-specific birth rates that will be less pronounced in final number of children-ever-born across a series of birth cohorts.

---

[22] See chapter in this volume by Duflo, Glennerster and Kremer (2008).

What can one learn from study of a family planning program's regional expansion about its long run consequences on family welfare outcomes? Miller (2004) estimates the relationship in Colombia between the timing of a woman's local exposure to the family planning program in the 1970s and her fertility in 1993. He then estimates the relationship between this exposure to the family planning program and a variety of indicators of her welfare and that of local matches for her children. Miller interprets these associations as unbiased reduced-form estimates of the consequences of the family planning program. This reduced form approach has the attraction that it captures the effects of family planning that may influence a variety of family outcomes, some of which may operate through fertility decline, while other program effects may empower women and foster changes in community social organizations, etc. Earlier exposure to family planning is shown to be positively related to the woman's years of education, work in the formal sector, and negatively associated with current cohabitation in 1993, but is surprisingly insignificantly related to the survival of her children. The household data cannot match the individual woman to her own children, and moreover those children who are enumerated in the mother's household can also be an unrepresentative sample of children, because the age of leaving home tends to be related to the child's schooling and the household's poverty. Miller reports evidence that "statistical mothers" with longer community exposure to family planning programs are associated with children who are more likely to be attending school, have completed more years of education, are less likely to work in the formal sector, and are less likely to have already had a child of their own by the time of the census. In sum, the study concludes that exposure of a woman to family planning from age 15 to 44 is associated with a reduction in cumulative fertility of 10–12 percent in urban areas, improvements in her educational attainment of 0.3 years, and an increase in her formal employment, an inter-generational increase in her children's schooling of 0.1 years, and a delay in a child's first birth (Tables 5, 9, 10). Similar patterns have also been estimated based on the earlier 1973 Census of Colombia where the focus is only on fertility and child mortality (Rosenzweig and Schultz, 1982).

A limitation of Miller's study is that the Colombian family planning program started in the late 1960s in the major metropolitan areas, and then expanded in the 1970s and 1980s to serve smaller towns and eventually to reach rural municipalities. Those communities first served by the family planning program are thus unrepresentative of the Colombian population. Women in the metropolitan areas who were first exposed to the family planning program may already have had stronger demands for birth control than the average woman of that age within all urban or rural areas. The variable representing exposure to family planning for women of different cohorts within a region may therefore also capture the effect of unobserved changing characteristics of these neighborhoods which influenced fertility, etc. If these characteristics are not adequately controlled for by including, as Miller (2004) does, dummies for municipality and linear municipality trends, the estimates of the family planning program effect are potentially biased.

Miller tests his identifying assumption of exogenous program placement by comparing changes in fertility between women of different ages in the five years before a family planning program started in a region, and finds no pre-program relation to fertility or to the other welfare indicators (Table 7). The analysis also considers separately women in urban and rural areas, but may nonetheless need to deal with sample selection bias due to intersectoral migration. Excluding migrants and rural residents from one specification of the model begins to address this problem. Interregional migration is frequent in Colombia, especially from rural to urban areas, and already by 1973 migration is strongly related to women's fertility, child mortality, and children's education, conditional on the woman age, education, and region of birthplace (Rosenzweig and Wolpin, 1986; Schultz, 1988). Nonetheless, Miller's (2004) study illustrates how historical data can be used to evaluate the longer term welfare consequences of family planning. This general methodology might be used to evaluate family planning and reproductive health programs in other countries where they were introduced in a staggered regional fashion, even when the program's implementation does not follow an experimental design. But the burden of proof is upon the researcher to show that the program expansion did not follow other socioeconomic features of the population that are likely to influence economic and demographic behavior (cf. Colombia by Rosenzweig and Schultz, 1982; Indonesia by Gertler and Molyneaux, 1994; and Taiwan and Thailand, Schultz, 1973, 1981, 1992).

5.11. A family planning-health services project in Matlab, Bangladesh: 1977–1996

Social experiments randomly designed to document the efficacy of family planning programs to reduce lifetime fertility and to improve the long-run welfare of women and their families are rare. One widely cited example occurred in a relatively remote rural district of Matlab, Bangladesh where the population has been followed since 1966 with a Demographic Surveillance System (DSS). In this relatively homogeneous poor tidal delta region, an outreach family planning and health services project (FPMCH) was introduced in October of 1977 and maintained for two decades. The program trained local female field workers to visit all reproductive-aged married women approximately every two weeks. The field workers provided not only information regarding birth control methods, they also reduced the private time and perhaps psychic costs of obtaining birth control from government community clinics by offering in the woman's household a range of methods and instructions on their use, including the more popular injectables. In 70 of the 149 villages of the surveillance system this family planning program was initiated (Fauveau, 1994, Chapter 6). Nineteen years later in 1996 a comprehensive Matlab Health and Socioeconomic Survey (MHSS) interviewed 4363 households in 70 treatment and 71 control villages (Rahman et al., 1999).

Sinha (2005) estimates from the MHSS the relationship between residing in a treatment village and women's fertility and indicators of child welfare. Reduced-form equations evaluate the effect of the family planning outreach intervention on fertility. Residential exposure to this experimental program ($n = 4124$) is significantly associated with women reporting 14 percent fewer children ever born in the 1996 MHSS. Phillips et al. (1982) found after two years (1978–1979) of program's operation, it was associated with a 25 percent reduction in the general fertility rate. As observed earlier, a program's estimated effect on period fertility may be larger in the short run, than on cumulative fertility in the long run, if during the initial transition to use the new technologies, contraception is used extensively to increase inter-birth intervals (Phillips et al., 1988; Koenig et al., 1992).[23]

However, Sinha (2005) did not find greater school enrollment among boys or girls in the treatment villages compared with the children in the control communities, holding constant for the child's age, the parents religion, mother's age and education, and father's education, farmland, and distance to district headquarters (cf. Table 7, $n = 1335, 1165$). Residence in the villages exposed to the program is a significant instrument for predicting the woman's fertility, but the second stage IV estimate of the child's mother's fertility cross-effect on the school enrollment among either girls or boys separately (or together) is insignificant and small in magnitude (Table 9). Her findings do not support Becker's (1960, 1981) hypothesis that parents substitute quality (schooling) for quantity, when the price of birth control is reduced.[24]

Sinha also analyzes whether the program-induced decline in fertility contributed to a reduction in child labor, and finds no effect for girls and a statistically significant small effect of the family planning program treatment *increasing* the market labor supply by boys (Table 7). Thus, this program evaluation study of a long-term experimentally designed family planning and health project concludes that the program achieved a major decline in fertility. But the anticipated increase in children's school enrollment or decrease in child labor was not evident. In other words, the cross-effects of the fertility decline on child quality which may be viewed as an beneficial consequence justifying subsidies for family planning and child and maternal health programs in low income rural populations are absent.[25]

---

[23] In Taiwan, analyzing the partial association of family planning program activity per woman across 361 districts, the apparent effect of the program on age-specific birth rates was larger in the first few years of the program than after five years, when the program's effect on fertility could no longer be precisely estimated from the cross-sectional variation. Including regional fixed effects and estimating first differences did not change the results appreciably. The reductions in births related to an increased application of program staff per woman of reproductive age implies nonlinear effects, with diminishing returns to scale of effort (Schultz, 1973). A similar pattern of diminishing returns to scale is observed in Thailand's public family planning program as of 1970 (Schultz, 1992).

[24] Foster and Roy (1997) analyzed a 1990 Survey of the Matlab region and estimate the program's impact on fertility and its cross-effect on child schooling by the sex composition of the mother's children. Simulation of their estimated model suggests the program reduced fertility by 31 percent. Children born to women who first received program services at a young age are estimated to obtain 32 percent more schooling than similar children whose mothers did not receive program services at all (p. 20).

[25] Two limitations of analyses of the 1996 MHSS are that the comparability of the treatment and control villages before the program started had not been extensively analyzed in the literature and migration into and out of the villages could be affected by the program, potentially biasing the inferences based on the sample of persons who remained in Matlab in 1996. Joshi and Schultz (2007) link the censuses of 1974, 1978, and 1982 to the treatment and control villages and find no significant differences in child-woman ratios (proxy for surviving fertility) in 1974 before the program started. The potential bias due to migration from and into

The Family Planning and Child Maternal Health program in Matlab offers an unusual opportunity to evaluate the long-term effects of an experimentally designed population program on both fertility and other life cycle consequences for women and their families. Joshi and Schultz (2007) explore these questions with several sources of data over time. A primary issue is whether the 71 treated and 70 comparison villages in the Matlab are comparable in terms of fertility and other economic development conditions before the program was started in 1977. With the 141 villages as observations, the first Census of the area in 1974 indicates no significant differences between the treatment and comparison villages in surviving fertility, approximated by the ratio of children age 0–4 to women age 15–49. By 1982 a Census shows surviving fertility in the treatment areas is significantly lower than in comparison villages by 18 percent, and this relative gap in surviving fertility remains 16 percent lower in the 1996 survey.[26] Using a double difference methodology that controls for initial village levels of surviving fertility, the authors find the program appears to exert a large and persistent effect on surviving fertility. Although the 1974 Census does not include much socioeconomic information, education levels of adults and children are not significantly different between the treatment and comparison populations in this pre-program period.

From the reproductive histories of individual women in the 1996 MHSS ($n = 5379$) the average program treatment effect on fertility is found to be significantly negative for all age groups of women less than 55 in 1996, women who in 1977 when the program started were less than age 37 and hence still likely to have more children. The program's effects on fertility are clearly not homogeneous across woman of different birth cohorts, and interactions between 11 age dummies and treatment are therefore included in the reduced-form estimates of the program's effect on fertility and also in estimating the program effects on other family life-cycle outcomes. This heterogeneity in response to the program by mother's age may explain why Sinha's (2005) estimates of program cross effects differ from this subsequent study, and her focus on current enrollment rather than years of schooling completed may explain the lack of quantity–quality trade-off.

Including controls in the reduced form fertility model for exogenous characteristics of the woman, her husband, household, and community infrastructure, the program treatment and interaction effects on the number of children ever born by women age 25 to 55 in 1996 are approximately one fewer child. The mother's health and nutrition,

---

the Matlab demographic registration area was also estimated from the 1996 survey and was never statistically significant. This form of potential attrition bias in panel surveys warrants more study (Fitzgerald, Gottschalk, and Moffitt, 1998).

[26] By 1996 the total fertility rate had declined by half in the comparison areas from 6 to 7 children per woman to about 3.5 children. The lack of convergence in fertility between the treatment and comparison areas after nearly two decades of program operation suggests the program provides more than a one-time improvement in information about new birth control and health technologies. Modest amounts of diffusion in the effective use of birth control techniques is documented in comparison villages which have boundaries with the treatment villages but this diffusion does not extend to use of preventive health inputs or other family life cycle consequences (Joshi and Schultz, 2007). See also Munshi and Myaux (2006).

measured by her body mass index, is one unit higher in the treatment than in comparison areas. Her wage earnings or total income are significantly greater in the treatment areas among better educated women, even though the program's effect reducing fertility does not differ between women of different education levels. Access to drinking and bathing/cleaning water sources within the extended family compound is greater in treatment areas by 1996, which should save women's time who are customarily responsible for fetching water, preparing food, and attending to family hygiene. The households of older and better educated women have higher total value of assets, specifically assets in the form of farmland, housing, ponds and orchards, jewelry and savings, if they reside in a program areas. This pattern is consistent with hypothesis 2 in Section 4 that life cycle savings in the form of physical assets is a substitute for children, and consequently the program's effect reducing fertility facilitates household to accumulate more household assets by 1996.

Finally, intergenerational effects of the outreach population program in Matlab are estimated. Child mortality before age 5 is a quarter less in program areas, but Z scores of the height and weight of children do not appear to improve, although the body mass index for daughters age 1 to 14 is greater in the treatment areas. Years of schooling of the woman's children, measured as a age-normalized Z score, are significantly greater for sons age 9–14 and 15–29, but the effects are smaller in magnitude for daughters and not statistically significant. [27]

The cumulative effect of the Matlab program's outreach effort to subsidize the adoption and use of birth control and child and maternal health inputs is associated with relatively large declines in fertility and child mortality, improvements in the health and nutrition of women and daughters, and educational gains for children, but these are only significant for boys. A puzzle in these findings is why the program's long-term effects on women's earnings and household assets are concentrated among better educated women. The avoidance of an unwanted birth contribute to women's market productivity and asset positions, but only among the better educated strata of society. Why would the welfare gains of reduced childbearing not translate into economic benefit for the less educated women as well? The limited labor market opportunities for less educated women is one possible explanations for this puzzle, due to the structure of development increasing the local demand for only better educated female labor. Alternatively, cultural restrictions on married women's geographic mobility imposed by purdah in this traditional Muslim rural area of Bangladesh is another possible explanation, arising from

---

[27] Second-stage estimates of fertility cross effects on these various family outcomes are reported under the strong assumption that the program induced changes in fertility transmit all of the program effects on other family outcomes (Joshi and Schultz, 2007, Table 11). Were this valid, the reported IV estimates of fertility's effect identified by these program treatment variables provide additional evidence on the cross effects of exogenous fertility changes on family outcomes which are consistent with the reduced forms reported for mother's BMI, household assets and water sources, and son's schooling. The program started as a focused family planning program, but grew over time to extend child and maternal health services, and thus the IV estimates are also likely to capture the program effect of parallel improvements in child and maternal health.

the household supply side. The study does not determine the reason for why the Matlab program should be associated after roughly two decades with increased economic inequality by educational strata.

Half a century of experience with implementing family planning programs throughout the world has produced few experimental evaluation studies which document the long-term consequences of family planning programs on family welfare. Estimating even the effect of programs on *completed* fertility of cohorts are rare and instead comparisons of adoption rates of new contraceptive methods or short run period birth rates are reported, few of which are experimentally designed, or statistically matched using propensity score methods or other satisfactory evaluation methods.

Other economic and demographic conditions that are hypothesized to have contributed to the transition decline in fertility include (1) improved child health and survival and diminished child malnutrition which are associated with increased supplies of calories per capita (Schultz, 1997) and improved public health programs for children and mothers; (2) increased educational attainment of females relative to males; and (3) improved employment opportunities for women, especially those outside of the family, which may empower women and are less readily combined with a mother's performance of child care (Schultz, 1995, 1997, 2002). In the following Sections 5.12 and 5.13, a few studies are reviewed that estimate how public policies or instrumental variables account for variation in child health and parent education, respectively, and may thereby indirectly account for the reduction in fertility and the welfare gains of woman and their families.

5.12. Health effects on fertility and family well being

Improvements in health that reduce child mortality have benefitted families and the benefit can be viewed as a reduction in price of surviving children which would, other things equal, increase the demand for children. The many-fold increase in world population since the onset of the Industrial Revolution is a result of the decline in age-specific mortality rates that has led to a doubling of the expectation of life at birth. This increase in survival rates occurred slowly at all ages until the end of the 19th century, when survival rates increased more for infants and young children than at later ages. After the Second World War improvements in drugs and public health methods diffused rapidly to many low-income countries and very high levels of child mortality declined sharply (Schultz, 1969). If parents defined their reproductive goals in terms of having a specific number of *surviving* children to work with parents as adolescents and to care for elderly parents, and child loss was large fraction of the cost of parents producing a surviving child, price inelastic demand of parents for surviving children could account for birth rates declining in response to the drop in child mortality, and possibly to a homeostatic adjustment of fertility by parents to mortality which would dampen or prevent an acceleration in population growth.[28]

---

[28] Studies of household surveys have generally documented the positive association between a woman's child mortality rate and her fertility rate (e.g. Schultz, 1969, 1973, 1981). But this empirical regularity should be

Early child mortality and health of pregnant women, often proxied by the birthweight of their child, are correlated in clinical and epidemiological samples with the incidence of chronic illnesses and death in middle and late age, often related to cardiovascular and lung diseases (Barker, 2001). Historical samples (Fogel, 2004) also link in a wide range of settings improvements in nutrition and health of the mother and her community around the time of birth, childhood nutrition, and reduced exposure of early infectious diseases to improved adult health status, reduced chronic health problems after a individual reaches age 50, and increased years of disability-free life in old age, controlling in some cases for later socioeconomic status (Kannisto et al., 1994; Finch and Crimmins, 2004; Gluckman and Hanson, 2006). Conditions that achieved the reduction in child mortality and improvement in early child nutrition may have also physically and cognitively facilitated the child's achievement in school and enhanced their productivity as adult workers, and some evidence indicates the returns to early childhood investments exceed what can be attributed to forms of observable human capital acquired later in life (Glewwe, Jacoby and King, 2001; Schultz, 2001; Cunha and Heckman, 2007). As in the case of evaluating family planning, however, researchers have rarely been able to identify with confidence the contribution to this general advance in child health of specific public health policy interventions. Without knowing the consequences of providing particular health interventions for specific groups, the general allocation of public resources to public health may be inefficient and fail to achieve economic and social development or improve social welfare.

The impact of fertility on family members requires careful empirical assessment. This paper has surveyed the evidence on exogenous sources of fertility to assess the likely impact of exogenous population policy on long run family outcomes. Although I have only outlined the conditions under which these estimates are satisfactory, more formal models characterize how estimates differ.[29] Because the behavioral and biological mechanisms involved cut across disciplines, research in demography, sociology, public health, psychology and clinical sciences may all be relevant. Additional research is undoubtedly relevant and omitted here due to my lack of familiarity with these allied fields. Different forms of survey and experimental data, including qualitative research, may contribute to the generation of new hypotheses. One factor common to most efforts to understand fertility and health outcomes is parent education. Education may

---

interpreted with caution as evidence of a replacement response of parents to their experience of child loss, because other factors are probably contributing to both the decline in child mortality and fertility. Lacking a valid exogenous basis for identifying this cross-effect of child mortality on fertility, only reduced-form equations can be estimated for both fertility and child mortality rates. Where there exists a clear empirical basis for identifying cross-effects, they may be tentatively estimated, and they suggest substantial positive responses of fertility to child survival in low income countries (Rosenzweig and Schultz, 1982; Schultz, 1969, 1997; Benefo and Schultz, 1996).

[29] See Rosenzweig and Wolpin (2000) and especially their last section which discusses estimates of the effect of fertility on mother's labor supply, of Cunha and Heckman (2007) where dynamic complementarities in various early childhood inputs to skill formation and labor productivity is hypothesized in various scientific disciplines analyzing child development.

affect their productivity and hence the shadow price of their time in family production activities such as child training as well as in market production activities. Capacity to innovate and to use more efficiently new production techniques may also be linked to adult education, including their adoption and effective use of health care inputs and birth control (Schultz, 1992). Mother's health and education may also transfer inter-generational advantages to her children, and parents may be matched through marriage on these advantageous characteristics to their spouse, making more difficult any attri-bution of causal effects (Behrman and Rosenzweig, 2002; Behrman, Foster and Rosen-zweig, 1997). Therefore, parents education is being reappraised in some studies as an endogenous determinant of child development, potentially associated with unobserved characteristics of the marriage match, genetic ability, transmitted from parent to child genetically as well as through the family's socioeconomic status and economic wealth and marriage markets (e.g. Scarr, 1978; Plug, 2004).

5.13. Effects of women's education on fertility and family well being

The effects of female and male education on fertility and child health are critical for understanding the demographic transition, just as they are for explaining changes in health and birth control practices (Schultz, 1981, 1997). Instrumental variable meth-ods may be useful in exploring whether the associations between parents education and health and fertility are causal, or biased by unobserved heterogeneity, such as due to preferences or innate abilities that affect many facets of family behavior. As with the in-strumental variable estimates of fertility, research on this topic is currently concentrated in high-income countries, although it may be extended to low-income countries where the expansion of education has been more rapid and now measured in periodic cen-suses and surveys. A key question is whether policy-induced changes in the education of women exerts less of an effect on fertility and on family health outcomes than im-plied by the cross-sectional correlation estimates, which assumes the education of men and women is exogenous to factors affecting fertility and health, or there is no bias due to omitted variables. The consequences of schooling on labor productivity have been analyzed for fifty years by social scientists who were initially skeptical that the correla-tion between schooling and wages is entirely a causal effect. The choice to go to school is a family and individual decision, possibly affected by many unobserved abilities, ed-ucational opportunities, and policies which could benefit different sub-populations and potentially bias the directly estimated relationships between parent education, fertility and other family outcomes.

Currie and Moretti (2003) report for the United States that if a junior college opens in the county in which a woman is born, this extra local educational opportunity is positively associated with her probability of attending college which appears to cause these 'treated' women on average to have improved health outcomes for themselves and their children.

The educational attainment of Indonesian and women as observed in 1995 is related to a 1974 primary school-building program (INPRES) which may have occurred in the individual's birthplace (Duflo, 2001). Two decades later in 1995, the school-building-induced gain in education is associated with wage returns of the potential beneficiaries born in those regions. Breierova and Duflo (2004) extend the analysis to assess the program's impact on fertility and child mortality of parents who are better educated due to the program. They account first for the average of wife and husband schooling and then for the schooling difference between wife and husband, using as instruments the school building program in birthplace and the Indonesian difference in age of husbands and wives, and the interactions between the program and age differences between husband and wife. These predicted average and gender differences in education are then employed to account for the women's fertility and child mortality as of 1995. The probability of having a child by age 15 is significantly reduced by the gender difference in education, whether estimated by OLS or IV methods. Where women's education is predicted to be greater relative to men, child mortality is lower, other things equal. But the number of children ever born by age 25 is not associated with the IV gender difference in education, possibly because the better educated women will have fewer children than their less educated peers after age 25. Although the 1995 survey is not able to assess how the program's effects on gender differences in schooling affected completed fertility, the empirical strategy may be more informative when implemented with later surveys picking up the program affected women at a later point in their life-cycle.

Osili and Long (2004) analyze the 1999 Nigerian Demographic Health Survey (DHS) and estimate the effect of female education on fertility (by age 25) due to an Universal Primary Education(UPE) program implemented for the non-Western regions of Nigeria during the petroleum boom of 1976–1981. Women born in 1970–1975 and currently residing in a UPE area report 1.1 to 1.3 more years of schooling than did women of other cohorts and living in other areas (Table 2). For these women, exposure to the UPE program is associated with them having 0.91 to 0.83 fewer children before the age of 25, controlling for initial female enrollment rates in their area (Table 3). According to their difference in difference method by birth cohort and region, and by instrumental variables based on the same identifying variation in program exposure, they conclude that the UPE increased female schooling and thereby decreased fertility by age 25 by 0.11 and 0.24 births, for each additional year of female completed schooling. These estimates of the program's effect on fertility through its effect on schooling are larger than those estimated by regressing fertility on female schooling using ordinary least squares. The study notes that the IV estimate of education's effect on fertility by age 25, when freed of omitted "ability" bias are larger than the OLS estimates, which is contrary to their expectation. One recognized limitation of the study is that without information in the DHS on where a woman lived when she was eligible to attend primary school, the estimates are based on a restricted sample of two-thirds of the women who report they have never moved (Appendix 1), introducing potentially a sample selection bias.[30]

---

[30] If out-migrants are on average better educated than those who stayed in their birthplace (as widely observed cf. Schultz, 1981), the estimation sample of non-movers will under-represent better educated women in the

Using educational program expansions to estimate the effect of both parents' education on family outcomes allows one to assess how policies affect the levels of education by gender and how this development works through the marriage market to affect couples over their life. It has been hypothesized that women who are better educated may be sought as wives by men because of their greater capacity to produce high quality children, among other reasons. The correlation between women's schooling and child quality could therefore reflect in part men's preferences for lower fertility and higher child quality (Behrman, Foster and Rosenzweig, 1997). The outcome of the marriage market and bargaining process cannot, to my knowledge, be forecasted without making further assumptions. A limitation of the instrumental variable approach designed to isolate how regional educational expansions impact household decision making is that the *gender difference* in schooling is likely to be related to the gender differences in age at marriage, and in fertility.[31] IV estimation techniques may validly identify the effects of men's and women's program-induced education on fertility and on investments in child quality, only if the regional implementation of the program is independent of other factors determining these household behaviors (Rosenzweig and Wolpin, 1986).

6. Tentative conclusions and an agenda for research on fertility and development

Fertility is thought to be an important determinant of the welfare of women, children, and men. Policies that help individuals reduce unwanted fertility are expected to improve the well being of their families and society. But there is relatively little empirical evidence of these connections from fertility to family well-being and to intergenerational welfare gains, traced out by distinct policy interventions. Associations do not clarify the underlying causal relationships which should be the foundation for program evaluations (Moffitt, 2005). It is difficult to evaluate the consequences of social welfare programs, such as family planning, which change complex forms of lifetime behavior with ramifications for many other family outcomes and arrangements over many years.

---

same birth cohort from a region. The omitted out-migrants may also be expected to have fewer children than women from the same birthplace with the same education who did not migrate, because the cost of migration would tend to be larger for women with more children. The selection of the Nigerian estimation sample is likely to bias toward zero the estimated effect of the UPE on female education and on fertility, but additional information is needed to assess how the sample selection bias would affect the IV estimates of the effect of female schooling on fertility.

[31] A final example is noted from Norway, where the compulsory length of education increased during the 1960s, but the timing of the reforms was left to be determined by the municipal school districts (Black, Devereux and Salvanes 2005a, 2005b). In this case, the IV estimates imply that policy induced changes in compulsory education of mothers are less likely to improve the schooling or "quality" of offspring, compared with the direct OLS association between mother's and child's schooling. The study does not instrument for the gender difference in schooling of the parents, probably because it is a weak instrument and the age gap between husbands and wives in Norway is smaller than in Indonesia.

First, population policies tend to be national in scope, and they may respond in politically subtle ways to evolving private demands by the population for the program's services, as well as to the public's priorities. Therefore, program treatments vary across a population in a manner that is likely to be nonrandom, and complicate what would otherwise be a more straightforward statistical evaluation of the association between a random program's treatment and outcome (Rosenzweig and Wolpin, 1986). The interpretation of non-experimental program expansions across regions and over time, as illustrated by Miller's (2004) study of Colombia, should be interpreted with caution, because the program expansions are likely to be targeted to populations with distinct private demands for the public service.

Second, different groups in society may respond differently to the same social welfare program treatment, and this implies that the spillover effects on family outcomes of a certain program-induced change in fertility may benefit different groups in society only "locally". The instrumental variable (IV) empirical strategy used to identify the causal effect of a policy on completed fertility is interpreted here as estimating Local Average Treatment Effects (LATE) (Imbens and Angrist, 1994). These IV LATE estimates may not be readily generalized, because of program and population heterogeneity (Heckman, 1997; Moffitt, 2005).

Third, the responsiveness of individual well-being to a policy-induced change in fertility of a specified magnitude will depend on how the policy is implemented (e.g. voluntary family planning or birth quotas) and on what "activities" are available to substitute for having fewer children, including investment in productive assets such as land, self employment opportunities, credit, and schooling. More specifically, do parents benefitting from a program and having fewer children decide (1) the mother who had been responsible for child care is now able to reallocate more of her time to more productive activities outside of the family, (2) their children now are able to obtain more schooling and get better nutrition and health care, and (3) to save more of their lifetime income in the form of physical capital to provide for their support in old age?

Based on the limited empirical studies reviewed in this paper, some answers begin to emerge. It should be emphasized, however, that many of the studies are not yet based on rural communities in low-income countries because of a shortage of data and a lack of consensus on how to model fertility and family decision making:

(1) About half of the direct association between fertility and a mother's market labor supply appears to be due to the causal effect of fertility as it is affected by observable exogenous variables, such as twins. Although maximizing women's productive opportunities is a social goal, there are too few studies assessing the productivity of women in the home and market to confirm whether women with fewer children are indeed more productive and inclined to allocate more of their time to the market labor force in poor agricultural economies.

(2) The trade-off between the quantity of children a woman bears and the quality of those children is viewed by many as a stylized fact, but this behavioral regularity may be more common in high-income urban societies than elsewhere. This inverse relationship between fertility and the average child human capital could be caused by unobserved

heterogeneity in people's preferences and constraints, and may not indicate the theoretically hypothesized positive cross-substitution effect (Rosenzweig and Wolpin, 1980b). Therefore, fertility-reducing programs in predominantly rural low-income countries should be evaluated with the goal of assessing whether particular policies that help women control their reproduction and improve their health contribute to the welfare of their children. Joshi and Schultz's (2007) study of the Matlab, Bangladesh reconfirmed Sinha's (2005) finding that this long term experiment in family planning reduced fertility by about one child. Joshi and Schultz (2007) find gains associated with the village family planning and health program in child survival and male schooling as well.

(3) The hypothesis that policy-induced fertility declines have contributed to increases in family savings rates is intuitively plausible, as is the life-cycle savings hypothesis. No studies were found, however, to show exogenous sources of fertility decline have actually increased family life cycle savings and added over time to the accumulation of physical assets. The Matlab family planning program was implemented experimentally, and the program has clearly contributed to a decline in fertility. After 19 years, household assets in villages provided the program are larger than in comparison villages, a finding which is consistent with the hypothesis that parent savings and children are substitutes. It is difficult to prove, however, that household assets and growth potential did not differ between program and control villages before the program was initiated in 1977. Nor is it transparent why households with better educated women were those which accumulate more assets in the program villages.

Most of the studies reviewed in this paper find that exogenous sources of fertility variation exert an absolutely smaller effect on a mother's market labor supply and on her children's health and schooling than is observed in raw cross-sectional data. Instrumental variable estimates based on quasi-natural experiments are not a perfect substitute for a well-run policy experiment, such as implemented in Matlab. But well specified IV estimates can provide an initial approximation of the magnitude of the long-term consequences of population programs on female labor supply and investments in the human capital of children, two important sources of modern economic growth (Young, 1995). In the single case study where the impact of an intensive family planning program involving frequent home visits in a rural low-income community can be followed for 20 years, the accumulating evidence suggests that the program had a substantial and persistent effect reducing fertility by one child, reducing child mortality by a quarter, and raising schooling (Joshi and Schultz, 2007).

The challenge is to extend rigorous assessments of which population programs reduce fertility and improve family outcomes in a cost-effective way and distribute their benefits toward the least advantaged individuals, generally the rural poor. Program objectives should be defined in terms of long run family outcomes associated initially with declines in fertility and child mortality. With the passage of time, migration and adult earnings capacities of the mother may be expected to increase in response to the program, and difficult to measure improvements in health may emerge clearly for the mother and her children. To assess the effect of population policies on household savings will probably require better asset data from household panel surveys than are available currently, which will involve measuring before and after a program's implementation how all forms of marketable wealth change, including homes, consumer durables, land, business capital, financial assets, and jewelry. Moreover, these outcomes are likely to have a bearing on the way in which individuals form families and combine themselves into households. Normalizing the income or wealth of households for composition of members may introduce other sources of misleading bias because they are endogenous, as in studies of orphans in Africa. Households also share resources with extended family members and strategically rely on kinship networks, thus sustaining these private institutions to manage risk, provide insurance, and create what might be called social capital. Dealing appropriately with these complex behavioral issues opens an extensive agenda for microeconomic research on the family. The research will progress more rapidly if researchers share a common conceptual framework for analyzing these questions and translate that shared framework into a consistent statistical approach for describing how policies change family behavior and thereby achieve desired economic and social development. This framework at a minimum must recognize fertility as a family choice variable, and thus incorporate fertility and its long run consequences into behavioral models. To progress in this research household panel surveys will be especially valuable, and need to be designed to evaluate the role of population programs in the poorer parts of the world where today access to birth control and child and maternal health services are most limited.

References

Akresh, R. (2004). "Adjusting household structures: School enrollment impacts of child fostering in Burkina Faso". Discussion paper 897. Economic Growth Center, Yale University, New Haven, CT, November.

Angrist, J., Evans, W. (1998). "Children and their parent's labor supply: Evidence from exogenous variation in family size". American Economic Review 88 (3), 450–477.

Angrist, J., Lavy, V., Schlosser, A. (2006). "Multiple experiments for the causal link between the quantity and quality of children". Working paper 06-26. MIT, Cambridge, MA.

Arends-Kuenning, M., Amin, S. (2004). "School incentive programs and children's activities: The case of Bangladesh". Comparative Education Review 48 (3), 295–317.

Barker, D.J.P. (Ed.) (2001). Fetal Origins of Cardiovascular and Lung Disease. Dekker, New York.

Becker, G.S. (1960). "An economic analysis of fertility". In: Demographic and Economic Change in Developed Countries. National Bureau of Economic Research, Princeton, NJ.

Becker, G.S. (1981). A Treatise on The Family. Harvard Univ. Press, Cambridge.

Becker, G.S., Lewis, H.G. (1974). "Interaction between quantity and quality of children". In: Schultz, T.W. (Ed.), The Economics of the Family. Univ. of Chicago Press, Chicago.

Becker, G.S., Tomes, N. (1976). "Child endowments and quantity and quality of children". 84 (2) S143–S162.

Behrman, J.B., Foster, A., Rosenzweig, M.R. (1997). "Women's schooling, home teaching and economic growth". Journal of Political Economy 107, 632–714.

Behrman, J.B., Rosenzweig, M.R. (2002). "Does increasing women's schooling raise the schooling of the next generation?" American Economic Review 92 (2), 323–334.

Ben Porath, Y. (1976). "Fertility response to child mortality: Micro data from Israel". Journal of Political Economy 84 (4-2), S163–S178.

Benefo, K., Schultz, T.P. (1996). "Fertility and child mortality in Cote d'Ivoire and Ghana". World Bank Economic Review 10 (1), 123–158.

Bengtsson, T., et al. (2004). Life under Pressure: Mortality and Living Standards in Europe and Asia, 1700–1900. MIT Press, Cambridge, MA.

Blake, J. (1989). Family Size and Achievement. Univ. of California Press, Berkeley and Los Angeles.

Black, S.E., Devereux, P., Salvanes, K. (2005a). "Why the apple doesn't fall far: Understanding intergenerational transmission of human capital". American Economic Review 95 (1), 437–449.

Black, S.E., Devereux, P., Salvanes, K. (2005b). "The more the merrier? The effect of family composition on children's education". Quarterly Journal of Economics 120 (2), 669–700.

Breierova, L., Duflo E. (2004). "The impact of education on fertility and child mortality: Do father's really matter less than mothers?" Working paper No. 10513. National Bureau of Economic Research, Cambridge, MA.

Bronars, S.G., Groggers, J. (1994). "The economic consequences of unwed motherhood: Using twin births as a natural experiment". American Economic Review 84 (6), 1141–1156.

Browning, M. (1992). "Children and household economic behavior". Journal of Economic Literature 30 (3), 1434–1475.

Browning, M., Chiappori, P.A. (1998). "Efficient intrahousehold allocations: A generalized characterization and empirical test". Econometrica 66 (6), 1241–1278.

Chiappori, P.A. (1992). "Collective labor supply and welfare". Journal of Political Economy 100 (3), 437–467.

Chun, H., Oh, J. (2002). "An instrument variable estimate of the effect of fertility on the labor force participation of married women". Applied Economics Letters 9 (10), 631–634.

Coale, A., Hoover, E. (1958). Population Growth and Economic Development in Low Income Countries. Princeton Univ. Press, Princeton, NJ.

Cunha, F., Heckman, J.J. (2007). "The technology of skill formation". Discussion paper No. 2350. IZA, Institute for Study of Labor, Bonn, Germany.

Currie, J., Moretti, E. (2003). "Mother's education and the intergenerational transmission of human capital: Evidence from college openings". Quarterly Journal of Economics 118 (4), 1495–1532.

Dawkins, R. (1976). The Selfish Gene. Oxford Univ. Press, Oxford, UK.

Deaton, A. (1997). The Analysis of Household Surveys. John's Hopkins Univ. Press, Baltimore, MD.

Deaton, A., Paxson, C.H. (1997). "The effects of economic and population growth on national savings and inequality". Demography 34 (1), 97–114.

Deolalikar, A., Rose, E. (1998). "Gender and savings in rural India". Journal of Population Economics 11 (4), 453–470.

Desai, S. (1995). "When are children from large families disadvantaged? Evidence from cross-national analyses". Population Studies 49 (2), 195–210.

Donohue, J.J., Levitt, S.D. (2001). "Legalized abortion and crime". Quarterly Journal of Economics 116 (2), 379–420.

Duflo, E. (2001). "Schooling and labor market consequences of school construction in Indonesia". American Economic Review 91 (4), 795–813.

Duflo, E., Glennerster, R., Kremer, M. (2008). "Using randomization in development economics research: A toolkit". Chapter 61 in this volume.

Duraisamy, P., Malathy, R. (1981). "Impact of public programs on fertility and gender specific investments in human capital of children in rural India". In: Schultz, T.P. (Ed.), Research in Population Economics, vol. 7. JAI Press, Greenwich, CT.

Edlund, L., Lagerlof, N.-P. (2006). "Individual vs. parental consent in marriage: Implications for intra household resource allocation and growth". American Economic Review 96 (2), 542–551.

Edmonds, E.V. (2008). "Child labor". Chapter 57 in this volume.

Fauveau, V. (Ed.) (1994). Women, Children and Health. International Centre for Diarrhoeal Disease Research, Bangladesh, Dhaka. Special Publication No. 35, ICDDR B.

Field, E. (2003). "Fertility response to urban land titling programs: The role of ownership security and the distribution of household assets". Unpublished paper, Harvard University.

Field, E., Ambrus, A. (2005). "Early marriage and female education in Bangladesh". Unpublished paper, Harvard.

Finch, C.E., Crimmins, E.M. (2004). "Inflammatory exposure and historical changes in human life-spans". Science 305, 1736–1739.

Fitzgerald, J., Gottschalk, P., Moffitt, R. (1998). "An analysis of sample attrition in panel data". Journal of Human Resources 33 (2), 251–299.

Fogel, R.W. (2004). The Escape from Hunger and Premature Death, 1700–2100. Cambridge Univ. Press, New York.

Foster, A.D. (1998). "Altruism, household coresidence, and women's health investments in Bangladesh". Unpublished. Brown University, Providence, RI.

Foster, A.D., Roy, N. (1997). "The dynamics of education and fertility: Evidence from a family planning experiment". Processed. Brown University, Providence, RI.

Freedman, R., Takeshita, J.Y. (1969). Family Planning in Taiwan: An Experiment in Social Change. Princeton Univ. Press, Princeton, NJ.

Gertler, P.J., Molyneaux, J.W. (1994). "How economic development and family planning programs combined to reduce Indonesian fertility". Demography 31 (1), 33–63.

Glewwe, P., Jacoby, H.G., King, E.M. (2001). "Early childhood nutrition and academic achievement: A longitudinal analysis". Journal of Public Economics 81, 345–368.

Gluckman, P., Hanson, M. (Eds.) (2006). Developmental Origins of Health and Disease. Cambridge Univ. Press, Cambridge, UK.

Goldin, C. (1990). Understanding the Gender Gap. Oxford Univ. Press, New York.

Guinanne, T.W. (1997). The Vanishing Irish: Household Migration and the rural Economy in Ireland, 1850–1914. Princeton Univ. Press, Princeton, NJ.

Gruber, J., Levine, P.B., Staiger, D. (1999). "Abortion legalization and child living circumstances: Who is the marginal child". Quarterly Journal of Economics 114 (1), 263–291.

Haddad, L., Hoddinott, J., Alderman, H. (1997). Intra-Household Resource Allocation in Developing Countries. Johns Hopkins Univ. Press, Baltimore, MD.

Hammer, J.S. (1986). "Children and savings in less developed countries". Journal of Development Economics 23, 107–118.

Hamoudi, A., Thomas, D. (2005). "Pension income and the well being of children and grandchildren: New evidence from South Africa". Economics Department, UCLA.

Hanushek, E.A. (1992). "The trade-off between child quantity and quality". Journal of Political Economy 100 (1), 84–117.

Heckman, J.J. (1974). "Shadow prices, market wages and labor supply". Econometrica 42 (1), 679–694.

Heckman, J.J. (1997). "Instrumental variables: A study of implicit behavioral assumptions used in making program evaluations". Journal of Human Resources 32 (2), 441–462.

Heckman, J.J., Walker, J.R. (1991). "Economic models of fertility dynamics: A study of Swedish fertility". In: Schultz, T.P. (Ed.), In: Research in Population Economics, vol. 7. JAI Press, Greenwich, CT.

Higgins, M., Williamson, J.G. (1997). "Age structure dynamics in Asia and dependence on foreign capital". Population and Development Review 23 (2), 261–293.

Hotz, V.J., Klerman, J.A., Willis, R.J. (1997). "The economics of fertility in developed countries". In: Rosenzweig, M.R., Stark, O. (Eds.), Handbook of Population and Family Economics. North-Holland, Amsterdam.

Hussein, S. (1989). "Effect of public programs on family size, child education, and health". Journal of Development Economic 30, 145–158.

Iacovou, M. (2001). "Fertility and female labour force participation". Discussion paper. IS, University of Essex, Colchester, UK.

Imbens, G.W., Angrist, J.D. (1994). "Identification and estimation of local average treatment effects". Econometrica 62 (2), 467–476.

Jacobsen, J.P., Pearce III, J.W., Rosenbloom, J. (1999). "The effects of childbearing on married women's labor supply and earnings". Journal of Human Resources 34 (3), 449–474.

Jensen, R. (2005). "Equal treatment, unequal outcomes? Generating gender inequality through fertility behavior". J.F. Kennedy School of Government, Harvard University, Cambridge, MA.

Johnson, D.G. (1999). "Population and development". China Economic Review 10 (1), 1–16.

Joshi, S. (2004). "Female household-headship in rural Bangladesh: Incidence, determinants, and impact of children's schooling". Discussion paper No. 894. Economic Growth Center, Yale University, New Haven, CT, September.

Joshi, S., Schultz, T.P. (2007). "Family planning as an investment in development: Evaluation of a program's consequences in Matlab, Bangladesh". Discussion paper 951. Economic Growth Center, Yale University, New Haven, CT.

Kannisto, V., Lauritsen, J., Thatcher, A.R., Vaupel, J.W. (1994). "Reductions in mortality at advanced ages". Population and Development Review 20 (4), 793–810.

Killingsworth, M. (1983). Labor Supply. Cambridge Univ. Press, Cambridge.

Kim, J., Aassve, A. (2006). "Fertility and its consequences on family labour supply". Discussion paper No. 2162. IZA, Bonn, Germany.

Koenig, M.A., Rob, U., Kahn, M.A., Chakraborty, J., Fauveau, V. (1992). "Contraceptive use in Matlab. Bangladesh in 1990: Levels, trends and explanations". Studies in Family Planning 23 (6), 352–364.

Ksoll, C. (2007). "Family networks and orphan caretaking in Tanzania". Unpublished paper, Yale University.

Kuznets, S. (1966). Modern Economic Growth: Rate, Structure and Spread. Yale Univ. Press, New Haven, CT.

Lam, D., Duryea, S. (1999). "Effects of schooling on fertility, labor supply and investment in children, with evidence from Brazil". Journal of Human Resources 34 (1), 160–192.

Lee, J. (2004). "Sibling size and investment in children's education: An Asian instrument". Discussion paper 1323. IZA, Bonn, Germany.

Lee, R.D. (1973). "Population in preindustrial England: An econometric analysis". Quarterly Journal of Economics 84 (4), 581–607.

Li, X. (2005). "Impact of childbearing on women's labor market outcome: Using new data and methods". Unpublished, PhD draft. Yale University, New Haven, CT.

Lloyd, C.B. (1994). "Investing in the next generation: The implications of high fertility at the level of the family". In: Cassan, R. (Ed.), Population and Development: Old Debate, New Conclusions. Overseas Development Council, Washington, DC.

Lloyd, C.B. (Ed.) (2005). Growing up Global: The Changing Transitions to Adulthood in Developing Countries. National Academies Press, Washington, DC. National Research Council and Institutes of Medicine.

Malthus, T. (1798). An Essay on the Principle of Population. St Paul's Church Yard, London. http://www.esp.org/books/malthus/population/malthus.pdf.

Maluccio, J., Thomas, D., Haddad, L. (2003). "Household structure and child well-being: Evidence from KwalaZulu-Natal". In: Quisumbing, A. (Ed.), Household Decisions, Gender, and Development: A Synthesis of Recent Research. IFPRI and Johns Hopkins Univ. Press, Baltimore, MD, pp. 130–131.

Maralani, V. (2004). "Family size and educational attainment in Indonesia: A cohort perspective". Paper presented at The Population Association of America meetings. UCLA, Boston, MA, April 1–3.

McElroy, M., Horney, M.J. (1981). "Nash-bargained household decisions: Toward a generalization of the theory of demand". International Economic Review 22 (2), 333–350.

Miller, G. (2004). "Contraception as development? New evidence from family planning in Colombia". Graduate student working paper. Harvard University, November, Cambridge, MA.

Mincer, J. (1962). "Labor force participation of married women". In: Lewis, H.G. (Ed.), Aspects of Labor Economics. Princeton Univ. Press, Princeton, NJ. Universities National Bureau Conference for No. 14.

Mincer, J. (1963). "Market prices, opportunity costs and income effects". In: Christ, C. (Ed.), Measurement in Economics. Stanford Univ. Press, Stanford, CA.

Modigliani, F., Brumburg, R. (1954). "Utility analysis and the consumption function". Chapter 15 in: Kurihara, K.K. (Ed.), Post-Keynesian Economics. Rutgers Univ. Press, New Brunswick, NJ, pp. 388–436.

Moffitt, R. (2005). "Remarks on the analysis of causal relationships in population research". Demography 42 (1), 91–108.

Montgomery, M.R., Kouame, A., Oliver, R. (1995). "The tradeoff between number of children and child schooling". Working paper No. 112. Living Standards Measurement Study, The World Bank, Washington, DC.

Montgomery, M.R., Lloyd, C.B. (1999). "Excess fertility, unintended births, and children's schooling". In: Bledsoe, C., Casterline, J.B., Johnson-Kuhn, J.G., Haaga, J.A. (Eds.), Critical Perspectives on Schooling and Fertility in the Developing World. National Academies Press, Washington, DC. National Research Council.

Morley, S., Coady, D. (2003). "From social assistance to social development: Targeted educational subsidies in developing countries". Center for Global Development, Washington, DC.

Munshi, K., Myaux, J. (2006). "Norms and the fertility transition". Journal of Development Economics 80, 1–38.

National Academy of Sciences (1971). Rapid Population Growth. John Hopkins Univ. Press, Baltimore, MD.

National Research Council (1986). Population Growth and Economic Development: Policy Questions. National Academy Press, Washington, DC.

Osili, U.O., Long, B.T. (2004). "Does female schooling reduce fertility? Evidence from Nigeria". Indiana University Purdue-Indianapolis, Indianapolis, IN.

Oster, E. (2005). "Hepatitis B and the case of the missing women". Journal of Political Economy 113 (6), 1163–1216.

Parker, S.W., Rubalcava, L., Teruel, G. (2008). "Evaluating conditional schooling and health programs: The case of Progresa". Chapter 62 in this volume.

Phillips, J.F., Stinson, W., Bhatia, S., Rahman, M., Chakraborty, J. (1982). "The demographic impact of family planning – Health services project in Matlab, Bangladesh". Studies in Family Planning 13 (5), 131–140.

Phillips, J.F., Simmons, R., Koenig, M.A., Chakraborty, J. (1988). "Determinants of reproductive change in a traditional society: Evidence from Matlab, Bangladesh". Studies in Family Planning 19 (6), 313–334.

Pitt, M., Khandkar, S. (1998). "The impact of group based credit programs on poor households in Bangladesh. Does the gender of participants matter?" Journal of Political Economy 106 (5), 958–996.

Plug, E. (2004). "Estimating the effects of mother's schooling on children's schooling using a sample of adoptees". American Economic Review 94 (1), 358–368.

Pollak, R.A. (1969). "Conditional demand functions and consumption theory". Quarterly Journal of Economics 83 (1), 60–78.

Qian, N. (2006). "Quantity–quality: The positive effect of family size on school enrollment in China". Economics Department, Brown University, Providence, RI.

Quisumbing, A.R., Estudillo, J.P., Otsuka, K. (2004). Land and Schooling: Transferring Wealth Across Generations. Johns Hopkins Univ. Press, Baltimore, MD.

Quisumbing, A.R., Maluccio, J.A. (2003). "Resources at marriage and intrahousehold allocation: Evidence from Bangladesh, Ethiopia, Indonesia, and South Africa". Oxford Bulletin of Economics and Statistics 65 (3), 283–323.

Rahman, O., Menken, J., Foster, A., Gertler, P. (1999), "Matlab [Bangladesh] health and socioeconomic survey (MHSS), 1996". Inter-University Consortium for Political and Social Research, Ann Arbor, MI (ICPSR 2705).

Rose, E. (2000). "Gender bias, credit constraint and time allocation in rural India". Economic Journal 110 (465), 738–758.

Rosenzweig, M.R. (1990). "Population growth and human capital investments: Theory and evidence". Journal of Political Economy 98 (5), S38–S70.

Rosenzweig, M.R., Evenson, R.E. (1977). "Fertility, schooling and the economic contribution of children in rural India". Econometrica 45 (5), 1065–1079.

Rosenzweig, M.R., Schultz, T.P. (1982). "Child mortality and fertility in Colombia". Health Policy and Education 2, 305–348.

Rosenzweig, M.R., Schultz, T.P. (1985). "The demand and supply of births: Fertility and it's life-cycle consequences". American Economic Review 75 (5), 992–1015.

Rosenzweig, M.R., Schultz, T.P. (1987). "Fertility and investment in human capital in Malaysia". Journal of Econometrics 36, 163–184.

Rosenzweig, M.R., Wolpin, K. (1980a). "Testing the quantity–quality fertility model". Econometrica 48 (1), 227–240.

Rosenzweig, M.R., Wolpin, K.I. (1980b). "Life cycle labor supply and fertility: Causal inferences from household models". Journal of Political Economy 88 (2), 328–348.

Rosenzweig, M.R., Wolpin, K.I. (1982). "Government interventions and household behavior in a developing country". Journal of Development Economics 10, 209–226.

Rosenzweig, M.R., Wolpin, K. (1985). "Specific experience, household structure and intergenerational transfers: Farm family land and labor arrangements in developing countries". Quarterly Journal of Economics 100 (Supplement), 961–987.

Rosenzweig, M.R., Wolpin, K. (1986). "Evaluating the effects of optimally distributed public programs: Child health and family planning interventions". American Economic Review 76 (3), 470–482.

Rosenzweig, M.R., Wolpin, K.I. (2000). "Natural 'natural experiments' in economics". Journal of Economic Literature 38, 827–874.

Rosenzweig, M.R., Zhang, J. (2006). "Do population control policy induce more human capital investment? Twins, birthweight and China's one-child policy". Discussion paper 933. Economic Growth Center, Yale University, New Haven, CT.

Samuelson, P.A. (1958). "An exact consumption loan model of interest with or without the contrivance of money". Journal of Political Economy 66 (6), 467–482.

Scarr, S. (1978). "The influence of "family background" on intellectual attainment". American Sociological Review 43 (5), 674–692.

Schultz, T.P. (1969). "An economic model of family planning and fertility". Journal of Political Economy 77 (2), 153–180.

Schultz, T.P. (1973). "Explanations of birth rate changes over space and time: A study of Taiwan". Journal of Political Economy 81 (2-II), 238–274.

Schultz, T.P. (1981). Economics of Population. Addison-Wesley, Reading, MA.

Schultz, T.P. (1988). "Heterogeneous preferences and migration: Self-selection, regional prices and programs, and the behavior of migrants in Colombia". In: Research in Population Economics, vol. 6. JAI Press, Greenwich, CT.

Schultz, T.P. (1992). "Assessing family planning cost-effectiveness". In: Phillips, J.F., Press, J.A. (Eds.), Family Planning Programmes and Fertility. Oxford Univ. Press, New York, pp. 78–105.

Schultz, T.P. (Ed.) (1995). Investment in Women's Human Capital. Univ. of Chicago Press, Chicago.

Schultz, T.P. (1997). "The demand for children in low-income countries". Chapter 8 in: Rosenzweig, M.R., Stark, O. (Eds.), In: Handbook of Population and Family Economics, vol. 1. North-Holland, Amsterdam.

Schultz, T.P. (2001). "Women's roles in the agricultural household: Bargaining and human capital investments". In: Gardner, B., Rausser, G. (Eds.), Agricultural and Resource Economics Handbook. Elsevier, Amsterdam.

Schultz, T.P. (2002). "Fertility transition: Economic explanations". In: Smelser, N.J., Baltes, P.B. (Eds.), International Encyclopedia of the Social and Behavioral Sciences. Pergamon, Oxford, pp. 5578–5584.

Schultz, T.P. (2004a). "School subsidies for the poor: Evaluating the Mexican Progresa poverty program". Journal of Development Economics 74, 199–250.

Schultz, T.P. (2004b). "Demographic determinants of savings: Estimating and interpreting aggregate associations in Asia". Discussion paper No. 1479. Presented at 10th Anniversary Conference of The China Center for Economic Research. Beijing, September 16–17.

Schultz, T.P. (2004c). "Human resources in China: The birth quota, returns to education and migration". Pacific Economic Review 93 (3), 245–267.

Schultz, T.P., Mwabu, G. (2003). "The causes and consequences of fertility in contemporary Kenya". Unpublished paper. Economic Growth Center, Yale University, New Haven, CT.

Schultz, T.P., Zeng, Y. (1995). "Fertility in rural China". Journal of Population Economics 8, 329–350.

Schultz, T.W. (1974). Economics of the family. Univ. of Chicago Press, Chicago.

Sinha, N. (2005). "Fertility, child work, and schooling consequences of family planning programs". Economic Development and Cultural Change 54 (1), 97–128.

Thomas, D. (1990). "Intra-household resource allocation: An inferential approach". Journal of Human Resources 25 (4), 635–664.

Thomas, D. (1994). "Like father, like son: Like mother, like daughter". Journal of Human Resources 29 (4), 950–989.

Tobin, J., Houthakker, H.S. (1950–1951). "The effects of rationing on demand elasticities". Review of Economic Studies 18, 140–153.

United Nations, O. (2003). World Population Prospects: The 2002 Revision, vol. 1. United Nations, New York. Dept of Economic and Social Affairs, Population Division.

Willis, R.J. (1974). "A new approach to the economic theory of fertility". In: Schultz, T.W. (Ed.), Economics of the Family. Univ. of Chicago Press, Chicago.

Wolpin, K.I. (1984). "An estimable dynamic stochastic model of fertility and child mortality". Journal of Political Economy 92, 852–974.

Wolpin, K.I. (1997). "Determinants and consequences of the mortality and health of infants and children". In: Rosenzweig, M.R., Stark, O. (Eds.), Handbook of Population and Family Economics. North-Holland, Amsterdam.

Young, A. (1995). "The tyranny of numbers: Confronting the statistical realities of the east Asian growth experience". Quarterly Journal of Economics 110 (3), 641–680.

Zajonc, R.B. (1976). "Family configuration and intelligence". Science 192 (4236), 227–236.

Chapter 53

HEALTH ECONOMICS FOR LOW-INCOME COUNTRIES*

GERMANO MWABU

Department of Economics, University of Nairobi, PO Box 30197, Nairobi, Kenya

Contents

* I am very grateful to T. Paul Schultz for guidance in the preparation of this chapter. I thank T. N. Srinivasan for providing me with valuable references and Robert Evenson, Christopher Ksoll and John Strauss for helpful comments. Discussions with Tekabe Ayalew, Christopher Ksoll, Tavneet Suri, Harsha Thirumurthy and Firman Witoelar clarified my thoughts on several issues. I gratefully acknowledge financial support from the Rockefeller Foundation grant to Economic Growth Center at Yale University for research and training in the economics of the family in low-income countries. However, I retain sole responsibility for any errors in the manuscript.

Handbook of Development Economics, Volume 4
© 2008 Elsevier B.V. All rights reserved
DOI: 10.1016/S1573-4471(07)04053-3

Abstract

Good health is a determinant of economic growth and a component of the well-being of the population. This chapter discusses and synthesizes economic models of individual and household behavior, showing how the models may be used to illuminate health policy making in low-income countries. The models presented could help address questions such as: How can the health of the poor be improved, and what are the economic consequences of better health? What policies would improve intra-household distribution of health outcomes?

It is argued that health economics research can provide information of relevance to health policies in low-income countries, if it were to take into account specific institutional contexts in which economic agents in these countries operate. Although institutions are universal, their type and extent of development differ across countries, and differ as well, in their effects on economic behavior. An important mechanism by which institutions affect health is through their effects on demand for health production inputs. Cooperative and noncooperative household models for analyzing intra-family allocations of health production inputs are reviewed, stressing the role institutions play in accounting for differences in levels of health and health care among individuals and across countries.

Next, examples of application of nonexperimental and experimental approaches to estimation of economic and social impacts of better health in low-income countries are presented. Two main results emerge from the examples. First, health in low-income countries can be improved through implementation of simple interventions, such as provision of communities with basic social services, supplementation of normal household diets with micronutrients, deworming of school children, and cash transfers to families conditional on illness prevention and health promotion behaviors. Second, there are large returns to health investments. However, since placement and utilization of health interventions may not be random with respect to health status (clinics for instance may be constructed in high morbidity villages and then used more intensively by educated people with fewer health problems than illiterate individuals), estimated direct impacts of better health may be contaminated by indirect effects of other factors. The chapter shows how IV regression methods and randomized experiments have been used to resolve this endogeneity problem.

Since its emergence as a disease in 1981, HIV/AIDS has become a major health problem in low-income countries, especially in Africa. The chapter illustrates how information generated by demand for HIV counseling and testing can be used to control the disease through mechanisms such as: treating pregnant women to reduce the risk of transmitting the virus from mother to child, targeting preventive measures and messages to individuals according to their HIV status, and timely treatment of AIDS-patients. Issues of industrial organization of health care, such as public provision of treatment, managed care, and national health insurance are briefly considered. The chapter concludes with a discussion of policy options for improving health in low-income countries.

Keywords

health production, health care markets, household production and intra-household allocation, health economics, low-income countries

JEL classification: I12, I11, D13, O12

1. Introduction

Good health is a determinant of economic growth and a component of the well-being of the population. This chapter presents and synthesizes economic models that can be used to analyze dominant health policy issues in developing countries and thus provide information that policy makers can use to improve the health of the population. The models may be used to investigate the following sorts of questions.

Who produces health and how? An answer to this question is important in helping policy makers plan for health production, or provide incentives for its production. Knowledge of human biology, epidemiology and household technologies of producing market and non-market goods are important in answering this question (Becker, 1965, 1981; Ben-Porath, 1967; Grossman, 1972a, 1972b). What are the channels through which health inputs affect health, and how can their effects be correctly measured? Models that endogenize health inputs are required to answer this question (Rosenzweig and Schultz, 1983). To what extent is demand for health inputs responsive to variables that can be changed by public policy, such as household income and time and money prices? Data from household surveys (Acton, 1975; Gertler, Locay, and Sanderson, 1987) can be used to address these issues.

What are the causal effects of health on labor market outcomes such as wages and labor force participation? Randomized experiments such as provision of micronutrients to workers (e.g., Thomas et al., 2006) may be used to estimate these effects. IV methods can also be used to analyze effects of health on labor market outcomes (Strauss and Thomas, 1998). What determines the distribution of health outcomes and consumption of health care within a household? Collective models of the family are appropriate for addressing this question (see e.g., Alderman et al., 1995; Udry, 1996; Browning and Chiappori, 1998; and Strauss, Mwabu, and Beegle, 2000).

What health policies would increase growth and reduce poverty? Macroeconomic models that analyze effects of diseases on growth could be used to identify such policies (see Bloom and Sachs, 1998; Commission on Macroeconomics and Health, 2001). What pattern of industrial organization of health care exists in developing countries? Agency models of physician-patient relationship, monopolistic competition and managed care models (Culyer and Newhouse, 2000) can provide insights into this issue, but their application to date has been limited mainly to high-income countries. What are the demographic and economic implications of HIV/AIDS in low-income countries in light of the unfolding technologies for preventing, testing and treating this disease? (WHO, 2004; Lopez-Casasnovas, Rivera, and Currais, 2005; Thirumurthy, Zivin, and Goldstein, 2005).

Each of the above issues is important in its own right. For example, a good understanding of the effect of health on labor market outcomes is not only a prerequisite for enhancing labor productivity through better health, but may also be the basis for designing better education and nutrition policies. Together the foregoing issues constitute the core questions to be answered before organizing health systems and programs for promoting adult health and for further reducing infant mortality in low-income countries.

Health economics can undoubtedly be used to shed light on other health concerns apart from the issues highlighted above. Nonetheless, the above listing depicts examples of the issues that economic analysis can help clarify, and thus empower policy makers to design and implement effective health interventions.

The remainder of the chapter is structured as follows. An overview of health economics is presented in Section 2, with a special focus on its distinctiveness as a sub-discipline. Section 3 describes the main features of health economics for low-income countries. Section 4 reviews specific economic models and techniques for analyzing some of the health policy issues highlighted in this introduction. Section 5 concludes.

2. Health economics

The issues in Section 1 fit well into standard categories of economic theory. For example, they fall under topics of demand, consumer choice, production technology, supply, markets, industrial organization, economics of information, incentive structure and social welfare. However, the standard economic analysis as conducted under these categories often fails to provide adequate understanding of health and health care phenomena (Culyer and Newhouse, 2000). The special characteristics of health and health care are the sources of this failure. For example, consumer theory cannot successfully be used to analyze health care demand under the usual assumption that income and money prices are the main factors affecting health care decisions because the effects of information and time prices are also quite important.

Health economics is concerned with the formal analysis of costs, benefits, management, and consequences of health and health care. Often, health economics is used synonymously with medical economics, the branch of economics concerned with the application of economic theory to phenomena and problems associated with health and health care (see Zweifel and Breyer, 1997; Mills, 1998; Feldstein, 1999; Jack, 1999). A notable feature of this application is the concern for equity in health outcomes and health care provision. The equity concern in health outcomes arises because health is universally accepted as a merit good, a minimum of which each individual is entitled regardless of ability to pay (WHO, 1948). In health care markets, the equity issue is manifested by widespread public subsidization or direct provision of health care. The case for health subsidies is particularly strong because evidently, an individual needs some minimum amount of health human capital to survive (see Fogel, 1997; Grossman, 2000).

Health economics has progressed rapidly from an infant state in the 1960s to a distinct sub-discipline of economics today. It draws its disciplinary inspiration from the fields of finance, insurance, industrial organization, econometrics, labor economics, public finance and development studies (Culyer and Newhouse, 2000). Arrow's (1963) article gave health economics its present form as a separate field of study, with its parallel development in human capital theory (T.W. Schultz, 1960, 1961; and Becker, 1964). The field has substantively contributed to mainstream economics in many areas, including human capital theory, the principal agent theory, econometric methods, the methodology of cost-effectiveness analysis, and the theory of supplier-induced demand (Newhouse, 1987; Culyer and Newhouse, 2000).

In the *Handbook of Health Economics*, Culyer and Newhouse (2000) provide a comprehensive discussion of the main components of health economics, originally proposed by Williams (1987). The components include the meaning and scope of health economics; determinants of health; demand for health and health care; supply of health care; health care markets; the relationship between economic growth and health; health sector budgeting and planning; national health systems; equity in health outcomes and in health care; and international health, under which topic, diseases such as HIV/AIDS, and bird flu may be analyzed. Jack (1999) looks at some of these components in the context of low-income countries.

The present chapter covers only a few of the topics mentioned above to illustrate the type of models and methods that can be used to analyze the topics in the context of developing countries. The motivation of the chapter is to show the type of knowledge that health economics research needs to generate to assist health policy-making in low-income countries. For example, although accumulation of health human capital is a key determinant of economic growth (Barro and Sala-i-Martin, 1995; Lopez-Casasnovas, Rivera, and Currais, 2005), little is known about health production technologies and the institutional contexts in which health improvements occur (Fuchs, 2004). This knowledge gap is acute in low-income countries, where health policies are urgently needed to reverse declining health indicators due to disease epidemics of which HIV/AIDS is the leading example (see WHO, 2004).

3. Health economics for low-income countries

A conspicuous fact about the body of knowledge encompassed by health economics is that this knowledge has so far been applied vigorously in developed economies. Indeed, the recent and the only handbook of health economics to date was designed to cover material relevant to service sectors of high-income countries (Culyer and Newhouse, 2000; Aaron, 2001; Grossman, 2004).

As indicated in Section 2, the basic principles of health economics for low-income countries are the same as the core principles of the parent discipline. Thus, health economics for low-income countries may be viewed as an adaptation of health economic principles and methods to institutional conditions of developing and transitional economies. Examples of institutions include (a) formal rules such as regulatory and legal structures, property rights, insurance laws, and constitutions; (b) informal rules such as customs, traditions and social values and beliefs; and (c) social networks and civil society organizations (North, 1990; Williamson, 2000). Despite their ubiquitous nature, institutions are country- and time-specific. Thus, the welfare outcomes of interventions based on the same theory can differ substantially across countries and over time (Oliver,

Mossialos, and Maynard, 2005). Further, such interventions may not work at all if key institutions are absent or function imperfectly.

Indeed, even in the United States, managed care became a dominant feature of the health sector only after the 1980s, when institutional environment favorable to its development emerged (Newhouse, 1996; Glied, 2000). In particular, after the 1980s health care providers and health insurance companies began to form networks as cooperative mechanisms for cutting costs of health care provision and financing. Participation in these network by insurers was motivated by their desire to deal with the moral hazard problem (excessive benefit claims by the insured), whereas participation of providers was prompted by a desire to cut costs of care to attract more patients.

Issues of industrial organization of health care, such as the preceding ones, are quite different in low-income countries, where formal health insurance schemes are limited to tiny fractions of the population in urban areas. The moral hazard problem, for example, is of little interest to policy-makers in low-income countries because the bulk of health care is financed through taxation or out of direct payments made by patients. The main health policy issues in such a setting, concern identification of the poor for "free" or subsidized care at government health facilities and design of incentives for motivating doctors to work in public rather than in private clinics. Moreover, because health care markets in low-income countries are much more imperfect than in industrialized countries or are missing altogether, the practice of free or subsidized service provision by the state is quite common. Policy concerns in such contexts often revolve around issues of service access and quality rather than around the moral hazard problem. Indeed, in many rural and slum settings, where the majority of the population in low-income countries reside, time and transport costs of using free health care at public clinics are substantial; so problems of moral hazard and frivolous demand should be rare.

Apart from unique features of the industrial organization of health care in low-income countries, disease burdens in poor countries are quite different from the burdens prevailing in industrialized countries. Therefore, policy-relevant research on issues such as cost-effective health care technologies, health care financing mechanisms, and training requirements for health professionals in low-income countries cannot be the same as the research conducted in industrialized countries on similar issues. It can thus be seen that a focus on health economics for low-income countries provides an opportunity to generate research information that policy-makers there can use directly to improve health or to enhance performance of their health care systems.

Because of country differences in institutions, behavioral parameters such as demand elasticities in high-income countries may not be applicable to low-income countries. For example, although price elasticities of demand from the Rand Health Insurance Experiment in the United States (that average around −0.2) "have become the standard in the literature" and are "among the most definitive" (Cutler and Zeckhauser, 2000, p. 584; Contoyannis et al., 2005, p. 2), they are nonetheless not very informative of how user fees affect health service utilization in developing countries because households there operate under very different institutional contexts. Obviously, price elasticities of demand for health care such as those from the Rand Health Insurance Experiment in the United States (Manning et al., 1987; Cutler and Zeckhauser, 2000) could be used to conduct an exploratory analysis of how high-income households in developing countries would respond to changes in user fees for hospital services. However, since such analysis would apply only to a small section of the population, its policy value would be limited.

Potential applications of Grossman's (1972a, 1972b) theory of demand for health and health care in developing countries is in Schultz (2004). Schultz shows how concepts of health production and demand for behavioral and market inputs can be used to design policies for promoting preventive measures in the fight against HIV/AIDS in developing countries. Studies that demonstrate the economic burdens of malaria (see, e.g., Bloom and Sachs, 1998; Commission on Macroeconomics and Health, 2001) provide the basis for urgency in the design and implementation of policies to fight this deadly disease. The foregoing studies are good examples of health economics for low-income countries because interest in research on diseases such as HIV/AIDS and malaria is strongest in poor countries where these epidemics continue to have a large toll on economies and human lives.

4. Review of the literature

This section provides a detailed review of analytical frameworks that can be used to analyze the policy issues listed in Section 1.

4.1. Special characteristics of health and health care

4.1.1. Health

Health is a component of human capital, which in some recent literature is referred to as *health* human capital to distinguish it from *education* human capital (see Schultz, 1999; Lopez-Casasnovas, Rivera, and Currais, 2005). This is in contrast to other literatures (see e.g., Mankiw, Romer, and Weil, 1992; Barro and Sala-i-Martin, 1995), where the term human capital is used to mean education.[1]

Human capital is part and parcel of human beings and is not easily measurable (T.W. Schultz, 1961; Mushkin, 1962; Becker, 1964; Lucas, 1988). The World Health Organization's definition of health clearly illustrates the conceptual nature of health, and the implied difficulty involved in measuring it: "health is a state of complete physical and mental well-being and not merely the absence of disease or infirmity" (WHO, 1948).

A further characteristic of health human capital is that it is positively correlated with other forms of human capital. Healthy individuals, for instance, are on average better nourished and better educated than individuals in poor health (Fuchs, 1996, 2004). However, although both health and education increase labor productivity, health has

---

[1] Since human capital encompasses more than just education, human capital models that are conditioned on education as the only form of human capital are mis-specified. The term "human capital" has been in use for a long time (Mincer, 1958; Weisbrod, 1961; Kiker, 1969). However, the theory of human capital was shaped into its modern form in the 1960s by T.W. Schultz (1960, 1961) and Becker (1964).

the additional feature that by reducing the time spent in sickness, it increases the total amount of time available to produce money earnings and commodities, as well as the time available for leisure (Grossman, 1972a, 1972b).

As an asset, health is accumulated at the individual or household level. To paraphrase Grossman (1972a, 1972b; 2000), individuals must use their own time and transportation services to seek health maintenance care. The same idea has been echoed elsewhere: "Health is produced by households not doctors or hospitals" (Dowie, 1975, p. 4). However, this does not deny the importance of hospitals and doctors as inputs into health production, as serious illnesses cannot be effectively treated without these inputs. The quotation emphasizes the role of individuals in choosing hospitals and doctors for treatment or in complying with treatment regimen (Jacobson, 2000). Moreover, households and doctors may, and often emphasize different dimensions of health. Many variables are used to summarize health status of households (Strauss and Thomas, 1998), and each captures only some facets of health and ignores others, and they generally measure even these emphasized facets with error and possible bias, adding to the econometrician's problems of estimating the effects of health capital on worker productivity or on consumer benefits.

4.1.2. Health care

The most important difference between health and health care is that health care is tradable in markets while health is not. However, health care markets are highly imperfect. The imperfection arises from the special characteristics of health care. These characteristics were introduced into the health economics literature by Mushkin (1962), Arrow (1963). In the opening part of his paper, Arrow stressed that its subject matter was health care and not health. "It should be noted that the subject is the *medical-care industry*, not *health*" (Arrow, 1963, p. 94; emphasis in the original). The distinction is important because in the real world only markets for health care are observed. Although individuals trade health against other commodities over time (Claxton et al., 2006), there are no markets in which sellers and buyers can exchange health.[2]

Although individually, the health care attributes discussed below are not unique to health care markets, when "taken together, they establish a special place for health care in economic analysis" (Arrow, 1963, p. 948). Following Arrow (1963), we illustratively discuss these characteristics with respect to a few categories of economic theory, as they relate to health care, namely: demand and supply, uncertainty, information asymmetry, and health care pricing practices.

A. The nature of demand for health care

Health care demand is distinct from the demand for other commodities because illness incidence, the reason for medical care, is irregular and unpredictable. Consumption

---

[2] There exists a large variety of health care services that are not tradable. For example, physical exercise, which is an important input into health production is not tradable. Although facilities for exercise are tradable, the exercise itself is not. More generally, health inputs that are related to behavioral change are not tradable.

of health care, particularly preventive care, is often associated with positive externalities. For example, treatment of a patient with a infectious illness does not only benefit the person treated, but also other persons because they are protected from exposure to infection. Similarly, immunization of an individual against a communicable disease protects other people from the disease. An individual therefore would typically understate the full value of such forms of health care, which is one reason for its subsidization in virtually all countries. In low-income countries, health care is typically provided by the state free of charge or at nominal cost, whereas in industrialized countries it is paid for through insurance.

B. Expected behavior of health care providers

An intrinsic technological attribute of medical care is that it belongs to the category of commodities for which the product (treatment) and the activity of production are identical (Arrow, 1963). Thus, unlike other commodities, the quality of medical care cannot be assessed before consumption. Consequently, in providing care, a physician is expected to act in the best interest of the patient, rather than in his own financial interest. This agency relationship creates the opportunity for health care providers to induce health care demand (Fuchs, 2004). The relationship is conducive to observed inefficiencies in health care provision and consumption (e.g., unnecessary medical tests, injections, surgeries and drug prescriptions).

C. Product uncertainty and information asymmetry

The quality or outcome of medical care is uncertain to patients as well as to providers. Neither the patient nor the provider can predict the outcome of treatment with certainty partly due to unobservable aspects of treatment and partly because the treatment itself can have unpredictable adverse effects. This information uncertainty, as to treatment quality, is asymmetrically distributed. The asymmetry is double-sided in the sense that both patients and providers have advantages and disadvantages in observing some aspects of inputs into health production (Leonard, 2003; Leonard and Zivin, 2005). Specifically, providers are well informed about their own treatment effort, but about which patients are ignorant. Similarly, patients know their treatment compliance effort, of which providers are ill-informed. Because the patient is uninformed about treatment, the provider must decide for him the quantity of medical care to buy. Contrary to other market transactions, the buyer here does not entirely decide the quantity demanded.

D. Supply conditions and pricing practices

Medical care is too complicated to be fully understood by patients or persons without medical training. Therefore, there is the risk that patients will buy or receive ineffective or harmful treatment. Society deals with this risk by restricting entry into the medical profession through the licensing of care givers. In contrast to other markets, where licensing is partly meant to raise government revenue, the purpose of licensing in medical care markets is almost exclusively to ensure that patients receive good quality care. However, licensing also restricts competition. Thus, the standard competitive model is not a suitable tool for analyzing health care markets. McGuire (1983, 2000) presents monopolistic models that may be appropriate for this purpose.

An important characteristic of health care is that it is not retradable (McGuire, 2000), which makes it an ideal target for price discrimination (Kessel, 1958).

4.2. Health production functions and health input demand functions

Health is an individual-specific phenomenon. Individuals accumulate this asset in the context of a family or household. While issues related to family formation (Becker, 1973, 1981) are not considered here, issues related to household-level decision making are analyzed in Section 4.3. The present section describes health production by individuals using a structural model due to Rosenzweig and Schultz (1983). In the model, individuals choose health inputs. The fact that health inputs are choice variables introduces heterogeneity in the health of individuals. The heterogeneity arises from unobserved preferences and health endowments of individuals that influence their choice of health inputs. The model also recognizes heterogeneity in health status arising from unobservable influences of biological processes on health production technology. The heterogeneity of health human capital in the population is due to both unobserved behavior and technology. A procedure for dealing with these sources of heterogeneity (biology, preferences, and technology) when empirically analyzing health accumulation is one of the novelties of the Rosenzweig–Schultz model.

The model is chosen for exposition because of its generality. It incorporates key insights from models of household production and consumption (Becker, 1965), health production (Ben-Porath, 1967; Auster, Leverson, and Saracheck, 1969), and models of demand for health and health care (Grossman, 1972a, 1982 and Acton, 1975). It further illustrates procedures for consistent estimation of parameters of any economic model when the behavior of agents is conditioned on unobserved variables.

Although some of the studies reviewed in this section were completed over two to four decades ago, they form the basis for modern research in health production and demand for health and health care, and provide the necessary concepts and techniques for further developments in the field. Some of these concepts and methods have not been incorporated into the current health economics literature, especially as it relates to developing countries (see Grossman, 2004). It is hoped that the review will help rectify this situation.

4.2.1. Health production and input demand functions

Following Rosenzweig and Schultz (1983), and adopting their notation, we assume that a household's preference ordering over health, H, n X-goods, and $m - n$ Y-goods that affect health can be characterized by a utility function of the form

$$U = U(X_i, Y_j, H), \quad i = 1, \ldots, n; \; j = n + 1, \ldots, m. \tag{1}$$

Let the production of health by a household be described by the function

$$H = \Gamma(Y_j, I_k, \mu), \quad k = m + 1, \ldots, r \tag{2}$$

where, the $r - m$ I_k are health inputs which do not enter the utility function except through their effects on H (e.g, health care); Y_j is a subset of Y (e.g., smoking or physical exercise) that both affects health and contributes to utility directly; X_i is good i (e.g., clothing) that contributes only to utility; and μ represents unobservable household-specific health endowments known to the household but not controlled by it, e.g., genetic traits of its members or environmental factors. It should be noted that both Y_j, and I_k in (2) are subsets of Y, i.e., all the inputs that enter health production function.

The budget constraint for the household in terms of the r purchased goods is

$$F = \sum_t Z_t p_t, \quad t = 1, \ldots, r \tag{3}$$

where F is the exogenous money income, the p_t are exogenous prices, and Z_t is a vector of all purchased goods, i.e., all the subsets of X, Y, and I that are obtained from the market. Needless to say Eq. (3) can easily be modified to incorporate non-market goods with a full income constraint.

The household's reduced-form demand functions for r goods, including the $r - n$ health inputs, derived from the maximization of Eq. (1) subject to Eqs. (2) and (3), are

$$Z_t = S_t(p, F, \mu) \quad t = 1, \ldots, r. \tag{4}$$

Similarly, the reduced-form demand function for health outcome may be expressed as

$$H = \psi(p, F, \mu). \tag{5}$$

Notice that in Eqs. (4) and (5), the subscript t for p is suppressed because consistent with demand theory, the entire set of prices enters the demand function for each and every good. Since demand equations (4) and (5) contain unobserved health production technology, this fact should be taken into account when estimating the equations.

Yet empirical investigations of health care and health production have concentrated mainly on estimating health input functions such as (4) or health human capital demand equations such as (5). See Acton (1975), Manning, Newhouse, and Ware (1982), Cameron et al. (1988), and Deri (2005) for an implementation of (4) and (5) in developed economy contexts. There is a large literature on health care demand from developing countries that is consistent with (4), but examples consistent with (5) are rare (Leonard, 2003). See for example Akin et al. (1986, 1998), Bolduc, Lacroix, and Muller (1996), Gertler, Locay, and Sanderson (1987), Heller (1982), Lindelow (2005), Mocan and Tekin (2004), Mwabu (1989), Sahn, Younger, and Genicot (2003), Sauerbon, Nougtara, and Latimer (1994), and Schneider and Hanson (2006) for applications of various versions of Eq. (4) in developing country contexts.

Although these models are useful in providing policy relevant parameters for health care demand and for its prediction, they fail to take policy making to the next stage of connecting causally the usage of health inputs to health capital production. In developing countries where health status is low, and is in dire need of improvement, this is a major failing of the models.

4.2.2. Hybrid health production and health demand functions

4.2.2.1. Motivation In an attempt to causally connect usage of health inputs to changes in health status, a hybrid health production model that combines Eqs. (2), (4) and (5) is often estimated (Rosenzweig and Schultz, 1983). The hybrid form of the theoretical model is

$$H = \theta(Y_m, p_l, F, \mu), \quad l = 1, \ldots, m - 1, m + 1, \ldots, r \tag{6}$$

where H, Y, F and μ are defined as before, i.e., H is health status, Y_m is a health input of type m such as medical care, F is exogenous income, μ is unobservable health endowment specific to each household, while p_l is a vector of prices of type m health inputs. In contrast to (2), Y in (6) incorporates health inputs of all types. Moreover, the health input, Y_m, is endogenous because it depends on health status, H, the initial health status before Y_m is demanded. Thus, in estimating this equation the endogeneity of Y_m and the unobservability of μ should be taken into account. Several other key features of Eq. (6) are worth emphasizing.

First, Eq. (6) may be interpreted as a form of demand for *health* (Engel curve for health) since it is conditioned on exogenous income, F, with other covariates in the function being treated as shift factors. If the price of health were available in (6), the expression can be viewed as a Marshallian demand for health. However, as shown in Section 4.2, the shadow price of health is endogenous, an issue that would need to be considered when estimating the demand for health.

Second, Eq. (6) may be interpreted as a form of a health production function, with F being treated as a proxy for health inputs other than medical care, and with prices of health inputs, p_l, serving as background variables. Explicit specification of input prices in Eq. (6) allows it to be interpreted as a meta production function as in Evenson (2001) and Bindlish and Evenson (1993, 1997). A meta-production function is an envelope of output response curves, each curve representing different degrees of changes in output due to an input response to price variation (see Hayami, 1969, p. 1298). The concept is useful here because it helps focus attention on changes in health input prices in an analysis of health production and health input demands, thereby showing the extent to which input prices can be used as instruments for improving health.

Furthermore, looking at Eqs. (1) and (6) together, it can be seen that even if the health input Y_m is a source of disutility, such as tooth extraction (see Eq. (1)), it may still be demanded because it enhances health (Eq. (6)). In the same vein, even if a health-related input such as smoking is harmful to health, it may still be consumed as long as its marginal utility is positive. It is evident from Eq. (6) that to evaluate the health effects of input prices, information is needed on marginal products of health inputs whose prices have changed.

Third, Eq. (6) states that an individual's health status is influenced by a total of r pur-chased health inputs, of which m are of medical care variety, and $r - m$ belong to other types, such as food, shelter, and *behavioral* health production inputs such as smoking, recreation and alcohol consumption. These types of inputs may be extended to include non-market behavioral inputs such as the timing of marriage or the first birth. The dis-tinction between derived demand for "behavioral health inputs" and derived demand for "commodity or market health inputs" is important because it helps separate out poli-cies that promote desired behavioral changes in the production of health from those that alter consumption levels of health-enhancing commodities. The distinction greatly widens the scope of the concept of demand in the analysis of policies that individuals and society may use to enhance health. Treatment of health-improving behaviors as de-rived non-market demands, helps stress the fact that these behaviors are choices that households make and that policy can be used to modify them.

Fourth, Eq. (6) states that the price vector, p_l, comprises l prices, one for each of the $m - 1$ inputs of type m, with the price of the mth input being omitted because it is a numeraire. Further, the prices of $r - m$ inputs are omitted because, for simplicity, only the health effects of m inputs are being considered. Fifth, it further states that health status depends on medical care, the exogenous prices of other health inputs (i.e., $m - 1$), exogenous income, and unobservable household-specific health endowment term, μ.

Sixth, the conditioning variable of direct interest, Y_m, represents either a continuous choice or a discrete choice demand for medical care. If demand is discrete, Y_m, rep-resents consumption of medical care by households or individuals, with the estimated coefficients being interpreted as responses of demand to its determinants at the exten-sive margin. In the event of continuous choice, Y_m represents the intensity of health care usage, conditional on up-take, so that the estimated parameters are demand responses at the intensive margin. Rosenzweig and Schultz (1983) illustrate the shortcomings of the hybrid model under the assumption that Y_m is a continuous variable. Dow (1999), Gertler and van der Gaag (1990) are notable examples of discrete choice models of medical care demand in developing countries while Jones (2000) contains a summary of the literature in this area.

Since medical care is a choice variable, the health effect of medical care in Eq. (6) is biased if estimated by ordinary least squares. Further, even if medical care is randomly provided to a particular region, the OLS estimate of its coefficient would still be biased due to unobervability of μ, apart from any omitted variables bias. Rosenzweig and Schultz (1983, p. 728) show analytically that the sign and size of the overall bias here depends on (i) the properties of the utility function, (ii) the marginal products of all health inputs, (iii) how μ affects health directly, and (iv) how μ affects the marginal products of the controllable health inputs. A statistical discussion of these issues is taken up after a further elaboration of Eq. (6).

4.2.2.2. Demand for health Equation (6) is consistent with Grossman's (1972a, 1972b) formulation of the demand for health human capital. In his pure investment model, H is a factor of production, whereas in the pure consumption model, it is a consumer good; in his general model, H is simultaneously a producer as well as a consumer good.

Two desirable properties of Grossman's model are not captured in Eqs. (4)–(6). First, the shadow price of health (which is nontradable), is not explicitly shown in any of the equations. Second, the overall benefit of health capital (both as a producer and as a consumer good) is not derived. These contributions can be illustrated with a one period version of the utility function in Eq. (1), expressed in Grossman's (1972a, 1972b) notation. The utility is maximized subject to the household income and production technology.

$$\text{Max } U = U(\varphi_i H_i, Z_i) \tag{7a}$$

subject to

$$P_i M_i + V_i X_i + W_i(T L_i + T H_i + T_i) = W_i \Omega + A_i = R, \tag{7b}$$

$$I_i = I_i(M_i, T H_i; E_i), \tag{7c}$$

$$I_i = (H_i - H_0) + \delta H_i,$$

$$Z_i = Z(X_i, T_i; E_i), \tag{7d}$$

where:
H_i is the stock of health in period i (time period $i = 1$ for all variables);
φ_i is the flow of services per unit of health stock so that $h_i = \varphi_i H_i$ is the total quantity of health services available for consumption in period i, measured in this case by the number of healthy days;
H_0 is inherited stock of health capital, and δ_i is its depreciation rate in period i;
P_i and V_i are prices of medical care (M_i) and other goods (X_i) respectively;
W_i is the wage rate in the labor market;
I_i is gross investment in health;
Z_i is an aggregate of all commodities besides health;
$T H_i$ and T_i are time inputs associated with the production of I_i and Z_i;
$T L_i$ is the time lost from market and non-market activities due to illness;
E_i is level of education;
A_i is non-labor income;
Ω is the total amount of time available in any period;
R is full income, the monetary value of assets plus the earnings an individual would obtain if he spent all of his time working.

Equation (7b) is the full household income constraint, where

$$\Omega = T W_i + T L_i + T H_i + T_i,$$

where $T W_i$ is hours of work. The inclusion of $T L_i$ in (7b) modifies Becker's (1965) time budget constraint, so that it can fully exhaust the total time available in any period (Grossman, 1972a, 1972b). Part of the 'full income,' R, a concept coined by Becker

(1965), is spent on market goods, part of it is spent on nonmarket production, and the remaining part is lost due to illness.

Equations (7c) and (7d) are production functions for health and a composite non-health commodity respectively.

The Lagrangian Function to be maximized is

$$\mathcal{L} = U(\varphi_i H_i, Z_i) + \lambda\big(R - (C_i + C_{1i} + W_i T L_i)\big) \tag{8}$$

where:
$C_i = P_i M_i + W_i T H_i$ (total cost of medical care);
$C_{1i} = V_i X_i + W_i T_i$ (cost of non-medical commodities);
$H_i - H_0 = I_i$ (gross investment in health, with its arguments M and TH suppressed) and with depreciation rate δ_i set equal to zero.

The optimal quantity of health capital demanded, H, is found by differentiating Eq. (8) with respect to gross investment (I) and setting the partial derivatives equal to zero to obtain the first order condition, which after manipulation yields the equilibrium condition

$$U_{hi} \bullet (\partial h_i/\partial H_i) \bullet (\partial H_i/\partial I_i) = \lambda\big\{(dC_i/dI_i) + W_i(\partial T L_i/\partial H_i) \bullet (\partial H/\partial I_i)\big\} \tag{9A}$$

where,

(a) $U_{hi} = \partial U/\partial h_i$ (is the marginal utility of healthy days, h_i);

(b) $\partial h_i/\partial H_i = G_i$ (a unit increase in health capital, H_i, increases the number of healthy days, h_i, by G_i, which is the marginal product of health capital in the production of healthy days);

(c) $\partial H_i/\partial I_i = 1$ (a unit increase in gross investment raises health human capital, H_i, by 1 unit);

(d) λ (is the marginal utility of income, since from (8), $\partial\mathcal{L}/\partial R = \lambda$);

(e) $dC_i/dI_i = \pi_i$ (the marginal cost of gross investment, the *shadow* price of health, which depends on opportunity costs of purchased health inputs, M, and non-purchased inputs, TH);

(f) $\partial T L_i/\partial H_i = -G_i$ (reduction in the number of healthy days lost to illness arising from a unit increase in health capital, H, which is the reverse of (b) above).

Expression (9A), where the effect of health on wages or income is ignored, can now be rewritten as

$$U_{hi} \bullet G_i = \lambda(\pi_i - W_i \bullet G_i). \tag{9B}$$

The left-hand side of (9B) is the marginal benefit of investing in an extra unit of health human capital, expressed in utility terms while the right-hand side is the associated marginal cost, also stated in utility terms. Lambda (λ), the marginal utility of income, converts the monetary cost $(\pi_i - W_i \bullet G_i)$ on the right-hand side of (9B) into a utility magnitude. Thus, the net marginal cost of producing a unit of health capital is $(\lambda\pi_i - \lambda_i W_i \bullet G_i)$. In equilibrium, the marginal benefit, $U_{hi} \bullet G_i$, must be equal to the net marginal cost, $(\lambda\pi_i - \lambda_i W_i \bullet G_i)$.

Dividing both sides of (9B) by lambda (λ) to convert utilities into monetary magnitudes and rearranging the expression slightly, one obtains

$$\pi_i = W_i \bullet G_i + (U_{hi} \bullet G_i) \bullet (1/\lambda)$$

or

$$\pi_i = G_i\big(W_i + U_{hi} \bullet (1/\lambda)\big) \tag{9C}$$

where

π_i = marginal cost of producing a unit of health capital, in monetary terms;

$W_i \bullet G_i$ = the value of the marginal product of health capital (extra healthy time resulting from successful treatment of an illness);

$(U_{hi} \bullet G_i) \bullet (1/\lambda)$ = the monetary equivalent of an increase in utility due to a unit increase in health capital (i.e., a unit increase in healthy time).

Equation (9C) shows that at equilibrium, the *shadow* price of health is equal to its marginal benefit, which in this non-separable household production model, consists of two distinct parts. One part ($W_i \bullet G_i$) reflects the monetary value of the marginal product of an extra unit of 'healthy time' in market and non-market activities, while the other part ($U_{hi} \bullet G_i) \bullet (1/\lambda)$ represents the monetary equivalent of the additional utility derived from that unit.[3]

Expression (9C) provides two insights into health human capital. The first insight is that health is jointly valued as a producer and as a consumer good, but these two distinct elements of the benefits are impossible to disentangle because the utility element is not observed. The only way to separate out these benefits is to arbitrarily assume that health human capital is either a producer or a consumer good. In that case, the equilibrium shadow price of health would be equal to one or the other of the two benefit magnitudes in (9C). The second insight from (9C) is that the shadow price of health human capital encompasses more than just the price of medical care. As can be seen from (8), the shadow price of health depends on the price of medical care and on the wage rate.

The wage rates and the medical care prices are determined in labor markets and in medical care markets respectively. An individual takes these prices as given in making health care decisions. However, even when the wage rates and medical care prices are exogenously given to an individual, the shadow price of health human capital is endogenous, because this price depends on health, which is a choice variable in the health production function. Once the shadow price of health is given, the demand for health follows directly from the theory of consumer behavior, but this price should not be taken as exogenous when estimating a model of demand for health.

A key point that is worth repeating is that health is not traded in the marketplace. Thus, at a shadow price, of say π_i, one must produce and supply health capital to one

---

[3] Equations (8)–(9) are derived under the assumption that a unit of health human capital lasts for one period only and does not depreciate. It is straightforward to introduce concepts of durable health capital, depreciation, inter-temporal utility and interest rate, r, into the analysis (see Grossman, 1972a, pp. 228–230).

self. If π_i is constant, the individual is willing to supply to self an infinite amount of health. At that price, the quantity he "buys" depends on his health demand schedule. If the demand schedule is downward sloping, a finite optimal quantity of health capital would be demanded. If the demand curve were flat, no such quantity would exist.

In Grossman's health demand model, health is endogenous, in the uncontroversial sense that individuals choose the optimal amount of it that they need so as to produce "healthy days." In other words, health status is governed by health investment and consumption activities of individuals. This is a major contribution of the model to policy making because it links health status to health maintenance activities of households and society.

However, unnecessary controversy has arisen in the literature over this feature of the model (Grossman, 1998, 2000) because the optimal quantity of health capital is associated with a particular length of life or time of death. The controversy is rooted in Grossman's (1972a, 1972b) assessment of his own model. "Death is said to occur when the stock falls below a certain level, and one of the novel features of the model is that individuals "choose" their length of life" (Grossman, 1972a, p. 225; 1972b, p. 1). In Grossman's model, individuals choose the optimal number of healthy days, rather than the length of life itself. The number of healthy days, can be zero without death occurring. Indeed, people can live for years in a constant state of illness. Furthermore, at the individual level, illness is a random event, which cannot be anticipated or insured against. Thus, the health capital accumulated by successful treatment of an illness in a previous period can be wiped out by a random illness in the next period, so that death can occur during a period of good health. However, this need not be so if in reducing mortality, health interventions are complementary across time periods. Specifically, if inter-temporal complementarity exists, an intervention undertaken against a specific risk to health in a prior period would reduce another risk in a future period (Dow, Philipson, and Sala-i-Martin, 1999).

In Grossman's model, three outputs are produced sequentially. The first output is health capital, which is produced using two inputs, namely, medical care and personal time. The accumulated health capital is then used to produce the second output, namely, healthy days. The healthy days are finally used to produce market and nonmarket commodities.

The second production activity above seems unnecessary (Muurinen, 1982). Once accumulated, health capital can be used directly as a producer or a consumer good. Healthy days are simply units for measuring health. Alternative measures of health at the individual level include height, weight, body mass index, and indicators of activities of daily living. It should also be noted that in determining the optimal length of life, it is the marginal utility of an extra day of life (not of an extra healthy day) that is relevant.[4]

---

[4] See Cropper (1977), Ried (1998), and Ehrlich and Chuma (1990). The time of death in these models is exogenous due to unpredictability of illness. Even after receiving medical treatment, recovery is uncertain."Recovery from illness is as unpredictable as is its incidence" (Arrow, 1963, p. 951). Although an individual contributes to his longevity at each age, the actual length of life he lives is outside his control.

The above are but minor criticisms of Grossman's model. The model's result that people contribute to their longevity through health maintenance activities is quite intuitive. It is also intuitive that the additions that people make to their longevity are limited by resource availability and by the technology available to produce health.

A serious shortcoming of Grossman's model is that estimation of both the health production function and demand functions relies on restrictive functional forms. Grossman's identification strategy (Grossman, 1972b) that uses per capita income as an instrument for medical care can be improved. The next section discusses better methods for estimating health production and health input demand functions.

4.2.3. Functional forms for health production

4.2.3.1. Specification issues Ideally, the health effects of input demands depicted in Eqs. (6) and (7c) should be estimated using a functional form that imposes a minimum of restrictions on the way the inputs are combined to produce health. The transcendental logarithmic health production technology has certain attractive properties, one of which is a second-order approximation in log form, to any production technology. The translog health production function may be stated as in Eq. (10); for derivations and details see Diewert (1971) and Fuss and McFadden (1978).

$$\ln(H) = \gamma + \frac{1}{2} \sum_i \sum_j \beta_{ij} \bullet \ln(Y_i) \ln(Y_j) + \sum_i \beta_i \cdot \ln(Y_i) + \delta \cdot Z + \mu + \varepsilon \quad (10)$$

where, ln is a natural log operator; γ, δ, β_i, and β_{ij} are technological parameters to be estimated; Y_i is health input i, with $i \neq j$; Z is a vector of other control variables such as socioeconomic characteristics of households; ε is a random error term. As before, the term, μ, represents unobservable household-specific health endowments known to the household but not controlled by it, e.g., genetic traits of its members.

The constant term, $\frac{1}{2}$, in the translog specification of the health production function comes from the local second-order approximation to any production function using the Taylor series expansion.[5] That is, *any* function of unknown form is approximated by a second degree polynomial function (see Diewert, 1971).

---

[5] The following generalized linear health production function can also be specified as $H = \sum_i \sum_j \alpha_{ij} \bullet (Y_i)^{1/2} \bullet (Y_j)^{1/2}$, where α_{ij} are the health effects of the interaction terms (see Diewert, 1971, p. 505). In the case of four health inputs, the model to be estimated would have sixteen interaction coefficients (including the parameters on squared terms). However, symmetry restrictions, i.e., $\alpha_{ij} = \alpha_{ji}$, considerably reduce the number of the parameters that are actually estimated. As in the case of the translog function, the generalized linear and Leontief specifications are very useful in providing second-order approximations to an arbitrary function at a given vector of covariates using only a minimal number of parameters, i.e., the coefficients of the interaction terms (Diewert, 1971, pp. 497–506; Rosenzweig and Schultz, 1982, pp. 67–81). Examples of other functional forms for continuous choice health care demands are in Deaton (1997) and Hunt-McCool, Kiker, and Ng (1994), while examples for discrete choice demands are in Dow (1999) and Sahn, Younger, and Genicot (2003).

Since μ is unobserved, the composite error term in Eq. (10) is the sum of ε and μ, which is likely to be correlated with Y_is so that the OLS estimates of β_i and β_{ij} parameters may be inconsistent, a situation that calls for the testing of exogeneity of Y_is.

The translog production function has two desirable properties. First, it is flexible in the sense that it allows the data to help determine the correct mathematical form of the production technology to a second-order approximation. If for example, the estimated β_{ij}s are equal to zero, Eq. (7) takes the form of a Cobb–Douglas production technology. Second, the symmetry restriction, $\beta_{ij} = \beta_{ji}$, can be used to reduce the number of β_{ij} parameters to be estimated, thus conserving the degrees of freedom. The generalized Leontief–Diewert specification has the same advantages as the translog function (see Diewert, 1971, p. 505).

4.2.3.2. Estimation strategies and some results   Because of the problems of endogeneity of health inputs and heterogeneity of patients, the OLS parameter estimates in Eq. (10) are biased. If longitudinal data are available, fixed and random effects methods can be used to solve the time invariant heterogeneity problem. However, since the health inputs are chosen by households, the endogeneity problem would still remain. Thus, IV estimation methods should be used irrespective of whether or not the available data are longitudinal or cross-sectional.

The challenge in using the IV methods is to find valid instruments for the endogenous health inputs. In general, local commodity prices and measures of community level infrastructure can be used as instruments for health inputs (Strauss, 1986; Strauss and Thomas, 1995; Wooldridge, 2002). Instruments for medical care in Eq. (10) would include user fees at local clinics, distances and travel time to clinics, prices of staple foods, alcohol and cigarettes, distances to market centers, and to social infrastructure such as roads, schools and clinics. These factors are assumed to influence the demand for medical care, while exerting no independent effect on health.

Once valid instruments for the endogenous health inputs are available, IV parameter estimates of a health production function can be estimated consistently. Rosenzweig and Schultz (1983) illustrate with data from the United States how to deal with the problem of endogeneity of health inputs in the estimation of a health production function, when birth weight is used as a measure of health status of newborns. Using the 2SLS method, they showed large child-health effects of behavioral inputs, such as the timing of prenatal care, smoking, and mother's age at first birth. In particular, educated women and women from high-income families sought prenatal care earlier, but women from low socioeconomic background postponed such care. A mother's delay in seeking prenatal care reduced both the birth weight and the gestation period. A delay of six months in seeking prenatal care lowered birth weight by 45 grams and reduced gestation period by 1.6 weeks. Availability of family planning programs did not always affect the timing of births. In contrast to these findings, biased OLS estimates showed that delay in receiving prenatal care had no effect on the weight of the new born, confirming that estimation method matters.

The econometric methodology proposed by Rosenzweig and Schultz (1983) can be used to generate information that policy-makers need to design and implement programs for increasing utilization of prenatal and immunization services by mothers. Effects of prenatal care programs on child health (as measured for example, by birth weight or survival probabilities at birth) can be quantified using this methodology and thus be the basis for rationalizing resource allocation in the fight against childhood diseases. This is a substantial contribution of the model because mortality and morbidity of children are some of the most pressing health problems in low-income countries. However, the severe data requirements that must be met to properly estimate health production functions must be noted. First, many household surveys do not collect information on community-level variables such as prices and social infrastructure so that instruments for endogenous health inputs like medical care and immunizations are very difficult to find. Second, even when community-level information is available, one is often restricted to using cross-section data because few national statistical offices in developing countries (the main sources of household surveys) rarely collect panel data. On the same vein, the national statistical offices take time to release data to researchers so that estimation of health production functions on current data is often infeasible. Moreover, substantial effort is required to clean survey data sets and to ensure that they are internally consistent.

4.3. Household production, consumption and health

4.3.1. Background

The household provides the environment in which individuals produce and consume health and other commodities. Becker (1965, p. 496) described this environment as follows; "a household is truly a 'small factory': it combines capital goods, raw materials, and labor to clean, feed, procreate and otherwise produce useful commodities." Becker's comparison of a household with a factory is not exact, however. As he is fully aware, there is more to a household than its production role. Another key role of the household is the distribution of intermediate and final goods such as leisure time, health care services, food and clothing among its members. This role is important because it determines the health and other welfare dimensions of each household member. In Becker's model – the unitary model, the intra-household distribution of commodities occurs automatically. The model predicts that in a household with a caring head, all members are motivated to pursue a common goal. Becker (1974, p. 1080) stresses this point (his Rotten Kid Theorem), as follows: "Put still differently, sufficient 'love' by one member guarantees that all members act as if they loved other members as much as themselves. As it were, the amount of 'love' required in a family is economized: sufficient 'love' by one member leads all other members by 'an invisible hand' to act as if they too loved everyone."

In this idealized setting, even a selfish family member would willingly make transfers to other members, to avoid the risk of being sanctioned by the head, the only person in the family with sufficient love and resources. In this model, the Rotten Kid Theorem ensures that the household head would never actually have to intervene to enforce intra-household allocations. Any intra-household transfers are voluntarily done (see Bergstrom, 1989, pp. 1139–1140).

Becker's model, predicts that household members pool their resources and that the welfare of members is unaffected by the identity of the person controlling resource allocation.[6] Since these predictions hardly find support in the data (Strauss and Thomas, 1995), intra-household distributional issues should receive priority in policies aimed at improving health, especially the health of the vulnerable household members such as women and children (Dercon and Krishnan, 2000).

Intra-household distribution issues in the area of human capital are complicated. For example, in contrast to the usual case of income redistribution within a household, where income transfers are made from one person to another, health human capital itself cannot be so redistributed. Once human capital has been accumulated by an individual, part of it cannot be transferred to another. However, some categories of health inputs, such as medical care expenditures, nutrients and insecticide-impregnated bed-nets can be redistributed, but behavioral health inputs such as dietary habits, personal hygiene and sexual practices cannot be reallocated from one individual to another.

The non-transferability of health from one person to another, including an important set of its determinants (behavioral health inputs), poses a serious problem to the unitary model as a framework for understanding health effects of public policies within households. This problem arises because of missing markets. There are no markets for health or for behavioral health inputs, both of which are self-produced. For example, an individual learns methods of personal hygiene and uses them to prevent illnesses, i.e., to produce health. The individual in this context cannot use an income transfer from the caring head, or from another family member to buy personal hygiene, but can use the income to purchase inputs that help produce personal hygiene. Other things equal, intra-household income transfers would not improve health if key inputs to health production are self-produced. Briefly, it is virtually impossible to predict a priori how health of individuals within a household will be affected by re-distributive policies, without making strong assumptions about markets for health and heath care, as well as about health production technologies. Because there are no markets for health and for key health inputs, separation of health consumption and production processes is not possible, a situation that fully undermines the predictive power of reduced-form health demand functions. For precise formulation of this argument see (Pitt and Rosenzweig, 1986).

---

[6] Alderman et al. (1995) call the Beckerian model of the household "unitary" because all household members are assumed to act as one person, all pursuing a common goal, to distinguish it from "collective" models, where individuals who constitute a household act separately. In their model labeling, Alderman et al. (1995) follow the terminology in Chiappori (1988) and Browning et al. (1994). The term "collective" in these models stresses the analysis of many individualistic behaviors of members of a group (a household), in contrast to one-person model under the same setting. Recent summaries and discussion of the large literature on household models is in Strauss, Mwabu, and Beegle (2000), and Vermeulen (2002). Earlier formulations and analyses of these models are in Udry (1996), Behrman (1997) and Bergstrom (1997), while a synthesis of agricultural household models is in Singh, Squire, and Strauss (1986).

4.3.2. The collective model

The collective model (Alderman et al., 1995; Haddad, Hoddinott, and Alderman, 1997) is appropriate for analyzing health capital formation within a household because it can address distributional issues related to both tradable and non-tradable commodities. The various versions of the collective model that exist in the literature share one feature: they all attempt to explain intra-household allocations.

Following Thomas (2000), the welfare maximization problem of the household can be expressed as

$$\text{Max } W = \sum_m \tau_m U_m(L, X; A, e), \quad m = 1, \dots, N \tag{14A}$$

subject to

$$pX = \sum_m \left(w_m (T_m - L_m) + Y_m \right) \tag{14B}$$

where:
W = Welfare derived from total household consumption;
$\tau_m U_m(.)$ is an individual utility function, weighted by τ_m, the index of bargaining power of individual m in the allocation of consumption within the household;
p is a vector of commodity prices;
w is a vector of wages for all household members;
T is total household time;
Y is total non-labor income;
X is a vector of goods consumed by all household members, including *medical care* so that commodity expenditure, pX is equal to total labor and non-labor income;
L is a vector of leisure time for all household members;
A is a vector of household-level demographics such as household size, composition, and personal characteristics such as age, gender, health status and education of all household members[7];
e is a vector of unobserved heterogeneity in the household, such as attitudes and ability of members or more generally, efficiency parameters (Manser and Brown, 1980, p. 35).

Notice that since $\sum_m \tau_m$ is equal to 1, if the bargaining weights for all m except $m - 1$ are equal to zero, consumption allocation within the household is determined by one person, and expression (14A) simplifies to a unitary model.[8] The bargaining power index, τ, is variously known in the literature as a Pareto weight (Dercon and

---

[7] Some of the variables here, such as household size and composition, and health status are endogenous and would require instrumentation to properly estimate the model.

[8] Notice that Eq. (14A) is a generalization of the following two-person expression

$$\text{Max } W = (1 - \tau)\left[U_m(L, X; A, e) \right] + \tau \left[U_m(L, X; A, e) \right], \quad m = 1, 2.$$

Krishnan, 2000; Browning et al., 2004; Duflo and Udry, 2004) and as a distribution of power index (Browning et al., 1994). The Pareto weight indicates the influence that individual m has on household market demands. It is a welfare weight, meaning that it shows the importance attached to each individual's utility when aggregating the utilities of household members.

The Pareto weight is conceptually different from the resource sharing rule (Browning et al., 2004). The sharing rule is a mechanism for *decentralizing* decision making within a houschold, while the Pareto weight is a utility *aggregating* device. The sharing rule specifies the share of individual m in total household income. The rule depends on individuals' options outside the household and on demographic characteristics or the preference shifters (Browning et al., 2004). Although preference shifters influence the Pareto weight, they enter it through the budget constraint. The Pareto weight (bargaining power index), τ_m, in Eq. (14A) amounts to the share of individual m in total household welfare. The Pareto weight and the sharing rule can be expressed as (a) $\tau_m = \tau_m(\rho_m(\theta); y, p, w)$ and (b) $\rho_m = \rho_m(\theta; y, p, w, d)$, respectively, where d is a vector of demographics and θ is a vector of extra-household environmental parameters, including any alimony rights mandated by government (Rangel, 2006). As just noted, the demographics, d, enter the Pareto weight, τ, through the sharing rule, ρ.

The key feature of the extra-household environmental variables, θ, e.g., non-earned income, assets brought into the family through marriage, sex ratios within the village, and family law is that they influence the decision making process within the household (by altering the resource sharing rule, ρ) but do not affect an individual's preference over commodities and are thus exogenous to demand functions. As expected, the sharing rule is also affected by total household expenditure, y, the commodity prices p, the wage rates, w and demographics, d. Browning et al. (2004) provide examples of general functional forms for Pareto weight, and the corresponding forms for the sharing rule. Although Browning et al. indicate that in empirical applications, interest is usually in the sharing rule, Dercon and Krishnan (2000) focus on Pareto weights in their Ethiopian study.

Subsuming e in τ and solving Eq. (14A) yields a set of commodity and leisure demand functions so that the demand for commodity g (such as medical care) by an individual m in a household can be expressed as

$$X_g = g\bigl(p, w, y; A, \tau\bigl(\rho(\theta)\bigr)\bigr). \tag{15A}$$

The term $\tau(\rho(\theta))$ in Eq. (15A) captures both the rule for intra-household allocations, ρ, and the weight, τ, for utility aggregation within a household. As expected, the resource sharing rule influences intra-household distribution of commodities. For example, holding total household income constant, modification of the rule governing intra-household allocation of commodity g (medical care) to m, will change the quantity of g demanded by m as well as $m's$ Pareto weight.

Thomas (2000) discusses how expression (15A) can be used to test the assumptions underlying unitary and collective models, e.g., income pooling and Pareto efficiency.

Since the Pareto weight in Eq. (15A) is unobservable, and in any case, since its magnitude can be inferred once the sharing rule is determined, it can be suppressed for convenience of notation. Accordingly, in a two-person-two commodity case (see Quisumbing and Maluccio, 2003), the test for income pooling and for Pareto efficiency can be expressed as

$$(\partial X_1/\partial\theta_h)/(\partial X_1/\partial\theta_w) = (\partial\rho_h/\partial\theta_h)/(\partial\rho_w/\partial\theta_w) = (\partial X_2/\partial\theta_h)/(\partial X_2/\partial\theta_w)$$
(15B)

where

$$\partial X_g/\partial/\theta_m = (\partial X_g/\partial\rho_m)(\partial\rho_m/\partial\theta_m), \quad m = h, w; \ g = 1, 2.$$

The first and last terms in Eq. (15B) are ratios of the effects of bargaining power of any two household members, say h and w on demands for commodities 1 and 2. The middle term captures the idea that a change in bargaining power of either household member changes the individuals' shares in total household income. If there is income pooling, the changes in budget shares experienced by the two individuals will be the same, irrespective of whether it is the bargaining power of h or w that has changed, so that the ratio of the two magnitudes is equal to one. Since the middle term is common, the test for income pooling or for Pareto efficiency on the consumption side of the household model involves a comparison of the first and the second terms. If both ratios are the same across the two commodities, Pareto efficiency cannot be rejected. The constancy of the ratios across the two commodities is an indication that there is no gain from the re-allocation of the commodities, i.e, the existing intra-household allocation is Pareto optimal. Equation (15B), an expression for the test of Pareto efficiency using the consumption side of the household model, is easily generalizable to a multiple commodity case.

In expression (14A), the household maximizes the weighted sum of utilities that its members derive from individual consumption, given the Pareto weights, τ_m. The equation represents only one of the ways of modeling the welfare of the household in collective decision making contexts, with a focus on consumption. The key assumptions underlying the model are that the outcome of resource allocation within the household is Pareto efficient, and that the household has a functioning resource sharing rule.

Chiappori (1988) and Browning et al. (1994) propose collective models in which Pareto efficiency is the only assumption needed, arguing that it implies the existence of intra-household resource sharing rule. In these general collective models, each household member maximizes the unweighted version of Eq. (14A) subject to his own budget constraint, provided that total consumption expenditure of all members does not exceed the full household income (see Browning et al., 1994, p. 1074). The assumption that the outcome of resource allocation decisions of individuals within a household is Pareto efficient implies that for a given a resource sharing rule, welfare gains from intra-household redistribution have been exhausted.

Udry (1996) develops a general collective model capable of analyzing both consumption and production decisions of households, and uses it to test the Pareto efficiency assumption with data from Burkina Faso.[9] He finds large production inefficiencies within households, contrary to the Pareto assumption of efficiency. In particular, crop output per acre in plots managed by women was found to be 30% lower than the output on similar plots controlled by men planted with the same crop in the same year.

In African agrarian contexts, a woman's plot serves as a school as well as a farm (Udry, 1996, p. 1034). Thus, apart from allocative inefficiency, due for example to transactions costs, an alternative reason why crop output per acre on a woman's plot might be lower than on a man's plot within the same household, is that the woman's plot is being used to teach children how to farm, i.e., to produce farm-specific human capital for the household. If this were so, women's plots would have higher intensities of child labor than men's plots. Since this was not the case in Burkina Faso, Udry rejected the Pareto efficiency assumption. The assumption has also been rejected by Dercon and Krishnan (2000) with a consumption-based test applied to Ethiopian data. However, Quisumbing and Maluccio (2003) fail to reject Pareto efficiency assumption. To date, the Pareto efficiency hypothesis has been rejected only with evidence from African countries.

Udry's model can easily be adapted to analyze health production and health care utilization activities within a household. A woman's plot is not only a farm as well as a school, but also a clinic. Since a primary activity of women in agrarian communities is child rearing, small children in these settings would typically be found on women's plot. In the event of illness, the children would receive initial treatment on this plot, and if treated outside the plot, return to the same unit for subsequent care. Women may farm their plots less intensively than men, not only because they use some of their time to teach children about farming, but also to meet the health and nutrition needs of children. Thus, although women's crop output per acre on a plot may be lower than on a similar plot controlled by men, women's contribution to child health on their plot would likely exceed that on men's plot, a situation that could then be consistent with Pareto efficiency. These health human capital considerations greatly complicate the testing of Pareto efficiency within a household. Pareto efficiency failures in contexts of health production within a household, may be more severe than in agricultural production contexts studied by Udry, because information about health technology is likely to be asymmetrically held among household members. For example, information about treatment of childhood diseases such as diarrhea or malaria may differ significantly between wife and husband. This information asymmetry could account for any observed differences in child health outcomes by the gender of the parent providing non-earned income for

---

[9] In contrast to expression (15B), the test was implemented using a productivity equation of the form: $Q_{\mathrm{htci}} = X_{\mathrm{htci}}\beta + \gamma G_{\mathrm{htci}} + \lambda_{\mathrm{htc}} + \varepsilon_{\mathrm{htci}}$ where, X_{htci} is a vector of characteristics of plot i planted with crop c at time t by a member of household h (X_{htci} includes, along with other information, the area of the plot); Q_{htci} is the yield on the plot; G_{htci} is gender of the individual who controls the plot; λ_{htc} is the household-year-crop fixed effect that restricts attention to the variation in yields across plots planted to the same crop within a single household in a year; and $\varepsilon_{\mathrm{htci}}$ is an error term that summarizes the effects of unobserved plot quality variation and plot-specific production shocks on yields; see Udry (1996, pp. 1013–1015) for the complete model; notice that Pareto efficiency implies that $\gamma = 0$.

medical treatment or giving home remedies for an illness. In the case of adult health, Pitt and Rosenzweig (1985, 1986) could not reject the hypothesis that a reduced-form health production technology of the head of a farm-household in Indonesian was different from that of his wife, a finding that is consistent with asymmetry of information regarding prevention and treatment of illnesses among household members.

In general collective models (see, e.g., Chiappori, 1988; Browning et al., 1994; and Udry, 1996), independent resource allocation decisions of household members are beneficial to the whole household. This aggregate, Pareto efficiency outcome of allocation decisions of self-interested household members is reflected by the linearity of the household-level welfare function as in Eq. (14A). In this framework, household members advance their collective well-being without coordinating their individual decisions. However, the fact that the household members live together and interact repeatedly, may enable them to learn the household-level needs to which each is obliged to contribute. Indeed, individuals who live together cannot succeed in some vital production and consumption activities without cooperative behavior that coordinates self-interests. In general collective models (see Chiappori, 1988; Browning, 2000), cooperative behavior is implied by the assumption that the outcomes of individual decisions within a household are Pareto optimal. This formulation of general models is in stark contrast to parallel bargaining models of household behavior where explicit cooperation among household members in their individual activities is modeled, and is key to the advancement of household welfare.

Manser and Brown (1980) and McElroy and Horney (1981) propose bargaining household models in which cooperation among household members is required for existence of a household-level welfare function. In contrast to Eq. (14A), where a household maximizes the weighted sum of personal utilities, in cooperative bargaining models, the household maximizes the *product* of net personal utilities of its members; see Manser and Brown (1980, p. 38), McElroy (1997, p. 57). The household-level utility is zero whenever one of the personal utilities is zero (due for example to non-cooperation, which may be motivated by options outside the household). This was the starting point of Nash (1950, p. 155) in his analysis of the bargaining problem: "A two-person bargaining situation involves two individuals who have the opportunity to collaborate for mutual benefit in more than one way. In the simple case, which is considered in this paper, no action taken by one of the individuals without the consent of the other can affect the well-being of the other one."

Cooperation within a household facilitates production and consumption of health and health care. In cooperative household models, as in other collective models, the amount of health care consumed by an individual, and thus the health status of that individual, depends on his bargaining power within the household. The household bargaining models have fruitfully been used to analyze intra-household distribution of health care and health outcomes in developing countries (see Rosenzweig, 1986; Strauss and Thomas, 1995). However, this model has the shortcoming that it ignores conflicts among household members even in the absence of outside options that would otherwise motivate the conflicts.

Chen and Woolley (2001) propose a non-cooperative household model in which individuals act strategically within a household to maximize self-interest, taking as given the behavior of other members. In this model, an individual cooperates with other household members if the utility from cooperation exceeds that from his selfish behavior within the household. Chen and Woolley (2001, p. 732) use the concept of Cournot–Nash equilibrium to analyze this conditional cooperation. A threshold level utility from strategic behavior is modeled as a threat-point to cooperation, where the threat is about a return to a non-cooperative behavior in a separate sphere of a household (see Lundberg and Pollak, 1993, 1994, 1996; Duflo and Udry, 2004), rather than about quitting the household as in the cooperative bargaining models of Manser and Brown (1980) and McElroy and Horney (1981).

McElroy (1997, p. 61) uses a diagrammatic scheme to classify household models into two main overlapping groups: the bargaining models and the Pareto-optimal models. The Nash bargaining models and the unitary models (the family utility models) are depicted as special cases of the subset of the Pareto-efficient models encompassed within the bargaining models. McElroy's diagrammatic scheme is quite useful as it illustrates the relationships among the dominant household models, all of which are designed for partial-equilibrium analysis of production, consumption, saving and other activities of households.

The non-cooperative bargaining model is quite appealing if individuals are assumed to intuitively know their personal utilities in separate spheres of the household, and then use that information to change their bargaining power. These models can be used to analyze health capital formation within households where public goods serve as inputs into health and health care production. Examples of household public goods include, housing, sanitation services, the caring for chronically ill-members of the family, and other vulnerable members such as orphans and the elderly, and treatment and prevention of communicable diseases.

The collective model of the household has major advantages over the unitary model in an analysis of human capital effects of public policy and other relevant variables within a household. First, the model focuses on an individual as a unit of analysis, and thus is able to address the conflicting interests of household members. Second, in a collective model, the person controlling household resources is identified, thus allowing an analysis of direct health effects of placing resources in the hands of different household members, e.g., women with young children (Lundberg, Pollak, and Wales, 1997). Third, the collective model permits the testing of the assumptions of the unitary model, e.g., altruism, income pooling and the Pareto efficiency outcome of resource allocation decisions. Fourth, although both models are able to explain intra-household differences in incomes and human capital outcomes (Strauss and Thomas, 1995), the unitary model relies on unrealistic assumptions. For example, the unitary model assumes that unobservable factors such as "invisible hand" and "love" account for the observed intra-household allocations. In contrast, collective models explain intra-household allocations using the concept of bargaining power, which is determined by observable factors, such as unearned income, demographics, violence or threat of violence, and career or marriage options outside the household (McElroy, 1990).

The collective models that address conflicts, cooperation, and other interactions within a household through a bargaining process, are better suited to analyzing intra-household allocations of health care in low-income countries than the parallel collective models that posit Pareto efficiency as the sole mechanism through which household members achieve their individual and common goals. Because of imperfection and incompleteness of health care markets in developing countries, the outcome of resource allocation based on such markets is unlikely to be Pareto efficient.

4.4. Income and health

The relationship between income and health at the micro- and macro-levels is widely studied (see, e.g., Audibert, 1986; Summers, 1992; Pritchett and Summers, 1996; Schultz and Tansel, 1997; and Strauss and Thomas, 1998). Interest in a two-way relationship between health and income, especially in developing countries, arises from the need to design policies based on this relationship to improve living standards (Strauss and Thomas, 1995, 1998; Alderman, Behrman, and Hoddinott, 2005).

There is an established literature on theoretical models of nutrition-based efficiency wages, showing strong non-linearities between calorie intake and labor productivity (Bliss and Stern, 1978a,1978b; Strauss, 1986; Dasgupta, 1993). Workers who consume more calories are more productive. These models imply that employers have an incentive to raise wages to give workers incomes that would enable them to consume productivity-enhancing amount of calories. At the same time, the employers have an incentive to exclude the poorest and malnourished workers from wage employment because such workers are too expensive to hire. This latter type of incentive works against poverty reduction policies of governments in low-income countries, where expansion of labor market participation rates is the main strategy used to fight poverty. However, despite this important policy implication of the efficiency wage models, little credible empirical work exists on effects of nutrition on labor productivity in low-income countries (Srinivasan, 1994).

The functional consequences of malnutrition and illnesses during childhood are felt throughout the life-cycle Deaton, 2006; Fogel, 2004; Fogel and Costa, 1997; Strauss and Thomas, 2008). Thus, prevention of childhood diseases and malnutrition would substantially increase health and economic growth in low-income countries. Child nutrition investment, especially those that promote school feeding programs can supplement the nutrients children receive at home.

Since income has a strong impact on health (the so-called "wealthier is healthier hypothesis"), there is a need to know how health benefits of growth are distributed in the population (Pritchett and Summers, 1996; Case and Deaton, 2005). If economic growth benefits a few, its impact on health will also be limited to a few. As demonstrated in Section 4.3, such an inequality can only be corrected in the long-run because it is the distribution of health inputs, rather than of health per se, that has to be changed.

Information on effects of income on health across social groups can help design health policies that promote equity in health outcomes in the population (Gakidou, Murray, and Frenk, 2000). The ensuing subsections survey the literature that clarifies the above issues in the context of developing countries.

4.4.1. Measurement of health

Health is multidimensional and thus has a variety of measures, each of which is likely to have a different effect on productivity and labor market outcomes such as wages, nature, and duration of employment (see, e.g., Strauss and Thomas, 1995; Ahlburg, 1998). As pointed out by Fuchs (1982), "there is no one measure of health status (or even one summary measure) that is best for all purposes" (p. 11). Several types of measures of health are identified and discussed below.

1. The first measure relates to indicators of general health, typically derived from household surveys. Individuals in a probability survey are asked to report on their health status. An individual is typically asked to indicate whether his health status is excellent, good, fair or poor. The responses are then averaged to determine the proportions of the populations that correspond to each of the above discrete categories. This measure has the disadvantage that people may perceive health differently so that good health might not mean the same thing to all people. Furthermore, if health perceptions are systematically correlated with socioeconomic characteristics such as income and exposure to health care systems, self-assessed health status can be misleading. For example, sick individuals in a poor disease endemic area, with limited opportunities for medical treatment may report being in good health because some illnesses such as blindness, ringworms or malaria may be perceived as normal phenomena due to their prolonged, widespread occurrence in the area. Such people might be adapted to the sickness that they experience (Banerjee, Deaton, and Duflo, 2004).

Other self-reported measures of general health include illness restricted activity days, and disease symptoms, which are also subjective. A less subjective measure is self-reported or externally observed performance in activities of daily living (ADLs). The ADLs are used mainly to measure the health status of the elderly rather than of the youth or prime-age adults (Strauss and Thomas, 1995; Schultz, 1999). The most commonly used measures of general health include mortality and morbidity rates, life expectancy at birth and various indicators of disease burdens, e.g., disability adjusted life years and quality adjusted life years (Culyer and Newhouse, 2000). However, these measures can be constructed only for large populations (not individuals) and then only if vital events in the populations are well recorded.

2. Ability to move out of birthplace to take advantage of health care services elsewhere, to avoid disease endemic areas, or to find employment may be a proxy for health status. However, this form of health status is difficult to measure. For example, a migration dummy, that takes a value of one if a person migrated from his birthplace and zero otherwise, could capture a non-health attribute such as ed-

ucational attainment. However, if information is available about types of diseases prevalent in a particular area, a migration dummy to the healthy location could be interpreted as a measure of health status. In particular cases of river blindness and malaria, persons migrating to cities from rural areas endemic to these diseases are likely to be healthier in cities than their rural counterparts. Thus, migration status needs to be combined with specific health information both about the birthplace and current area of residence to serve as a measure of health status.

3. Biomedical evidence suggests that calorie intake is correlated with increases in oxygen uptake (Strauss and Thomas, 1998). Measures of calorie consumption include daily per capita calorie availability or intake. The availability measure has the obvious disadvantage that the available quantity of calories may not be consumed due to wastage and other reasons, while the intake measure is prohibitively expensive to obtain because it requires an intrusive household survey. The most common approach to obtaining calorie intakes of household members is to ask them to recall ingredients that went into meals consumed, usually over the previous 24 hours. This is a time intensive but feasible method. The calorie intake is a measure of the quantity of nutritional inputs used to produce health. The outcomes of these inputs, expressed in terms of anthropometrics, such as height, weight, arm circumference, and body mass index (the ratio of weight in kilograms to height in meters squared) are other accumulative nutrition-based measures of health (Currie, 2000). However, caution should be exercised in using calorie consumption data from short time intervals to make conclusions about nutrition and health status because energy intake of an individual can vary within a homeostatic range without impairing health and without changes in body mass (see Srinivasan, 1992).

4. Hemoglobin levels of individuals can be measured through household surveys to provide information about prevalence of anemia in children and adults. Anemia occurs when the blood does not have enough hemoglobin, a red pigment in red blood cells that helps carry oxygen from lungs to all parts of the body. Anemia might be caused by iron deficiency, malnutrition, worm infestation and other health problems. The hemoglobin level in the blood can easily be measured by paramedical personnel. Typically, 11–13 grams per deciliter (g/dl) are used as the cutoff points for adequate levels of hemoglobin in the blood (see Banerjee, Deaton, and Duflo, 2004; Gertler, 2004; Thomas et al., 2006). Persons with hemoglobin levels below the thresholds indicated above are likely to suffer from fatigue, low body temperature, rapid heartbeat, shortness of breath, chest pain, dizziness, headache, irritability, numbness and cold in the hands and feet, conditions that can cause death or interfere with schooling or work performance.

5. The type of disease (e.g., acute or chronic) is a good indicator of health status of an individual. A long-term disability such as diabetes does not have the same effect on health as an acute condition such as an injury. Disease categories constitute notable measures of community and personal health, and are suggestive of clinical and other interventions that are required to improve health at various

levels of society (Jamison et al., 2006). However, since diseases are diagnosed after individuals have had contacts with health care system, they reflect health care treatment choices of individuals and households. Thus, disease types cannot be treated as exogenous in the measurement of economic effects of health, a caution that also applies to health measures indicated in parts 1–4 above.

4.4.2. Health and labor market outcomes

What regularities exist between health and labor market outcomes such as wages and labor force participation? Strauss and Thomas (1998) show a strong and positive correlation between adult height and hourly wages in the United States and Brazil in the 1970s. Taller men in both countries earn more, especially in Brazil. In Brazil, a 1% increase in men's height is associated with about 8% increase in hourly wages. However, with controls for other dimensions of health human capital, the height elasticity of Brazilian wages declines to about 4% (Thomas and Strauss, 1997).

In a more recent study, in which wage effects of height are corrected for endogeneity, Schultz (2002) reports large differences in effects of height on wages between United States and two low-income countries (Brazil and Ghana). At the margin, wage returns to height in Brazil and Ghana are about three times larger than the returns in the United States. A centimeter increase in height in Brazil and Ghana is associated with 8–10% increase in wages for both men and women, i.e., a 1% increase in height raises wages by 13–17%, a large increment, compared with the earlier upper bound estimate of 8% reported by Strauss and Thomas (1998).

The differences in wage returns to nutrition between developed and low-income countries reflect nutrition levels, as well as the types of work available in the two societies. The mean height in the United States is higher than in Brazil and Ghana. Thus, because of diminishing returns to nutrition, the wage effects of height are lower in the United States. The larger share of white collar jobs in the United States may also contributes to lower returns to height there, because height may not be a good proxy for the type of human capital required to perform white collar jobs.

Strauss and Thomas (1998) show a persistent correlation between the fraction of urban men who are not working and their nutritional status. In urban Brazil, short men earn less than tall men, and are less likely to be working (see also Rivera and Currais, 2005). A similar profile emerges from the same data that combines height and weight. The probability that a man is not working decreases until his BMI reaches around 24, at which point the employment probability becomes essentially flat. In other words, in Brazilian urban areas, overweight and obesity are negatively correlated with men's chances of finding employment. However, in rural areas where malnutrition is still prevalent, overweight and obesity may not be a problem. These results suggest different returns to nutrition (as proxied by height and body mass index) in Brazil and the United States.

4.4.2.1. Wage effects of health Is health the source of the observed variation in wages among workers? This is a difficult question to answer because health is endogenous to wages. To help answer this question, Strauss and Thomas (1998) specify the following wage function

$$w = w(H; A, S, B, I, \alpha, e_w) \tag{20}$$

where,

w is an individual's log of real wage;
H is an array of measured health human capital;
A is a vector of demographic characteristics;
S is education human capital;
B is family background of the individual, which includes education human capital of parents;
I is local community infrastructure such as electrification or road density;
α is an array of unobservables such as ability;
e_w is measurement error.

In estimating Eq. (20), problems of simultaneity, heterogeneity, measurement errors, and omitted variables must be addressed (Haddad and Hoddinott, 1994). The problem in Eq. (20) is to isolate the effect of health on wages. The α-variables play a major role in the estimation of Eq. (20). Some of these variables include time-invariant natural ability, while others may include the social network of individuals, which varies over time. If available, panel data can be used to deal with the individual-specific, time-invariant α-variables. However, the time-varying αs would continue to be a source of heterogeneity in wages. Strauss and Thomas (1998, p. 778) suggest that local community infrastructure, the disease environment, prices of food and prices of health inputs can be used as valid instruments for health. Although these factors would normally affect health status without directly influencing labor productivity, there may be some important exceptions. For example, low-productivity workers might migrate to locations with high densities of roads and clinics or such facilities may be selectively placed to serve low wage workers. In either case, local densities of roads or clinics would be weak instruments for the health of workers. Moreover, which variable is used as an instrument for health depends on how health is measured. If health indicators are nutrition-based, food prices as well as fees for medical care services would be potential instruments for health (see Strauss, 1986).

4.4.2.2. Effects of health on labor supply The next issue concerning the relationship between health and labor market outcomes is whether better health increases labor force participation and labor supply. The welfare effects of health manifest themselves through labor force participation. To analyze labor supply (and participation) effects of health, Strauss and Thomas (1998, p. 780) specify the following model of labor supply, conditioning it on health and wages:

$$L = L\big(H, pc, w\{H; S, A, B, I, \alpha, e_w\}, S, A, B, V, \xi\big) \tag{21}$$

where,

L is labor supply or labor market participation;

pc is a vector of prices for consumer goods;

$w\{.\}$ is the real wage;

V is non-labor income;

ξ is the taste parameter, with the other variables being defined as in Eq. (20).

Estimation of Eq. (21) permits the separation of the labor supply effect of health, H, from the effect of preferences, ξ. Apart from the problem posed by the joint determination of wages and labor supply, isolating the role of health and preferences in the labor supply is complicated, because preferences are unobserved, and health is measured with error, and its identification based on local infrastructure is subject to debate. The measurement error in health forces one to use IV for H, i.e., to look for instruments for health. There are other factors complicating the estimation of (21). As can be seen from Eq. (21), health status influences labor supply and labor market participation by changing wages, inducing both income and substitution effects that may bear opposite signs. In addition, the workers' preferences for leisure and goods affect labor supply directly, as well as indirectly through the substitution effect induced by wages. As in Eq. (20), local social infrastructure and prices can be used as instruments for health. The instruments should be designed to purge the covariance between health status and the error term of the labor supply equation.

In addition to the above individual-level labor supply effects of health, household-level effects may also be important. Thirumurthy, Zivin, and Goldstein (2005) show that the effect of an individual's health on his own labor supply can be quite different from its effect on the labor supply at the household level. An improvement in BMI and in the CD4 count of AIDS patients receiving ARV therapy in Western Kenya, led to an increase in individual labor supply, but to a reduction in the labor supply of other household members at the household level, notably among adult women and young boys.

4.4.2.3. Effects of health on self-employment profits   Equations (20) and (21) focus on effects of health on labor market outcomes. The same equations can be modified to investigate effects of health on profits generated from self-employment as well as the number of hours worked. Local prices and infrastructure remain valid instruments for health.

However, if labor and credit markets exist, health has no effect on self-employment output or profits because sick family labor can be replaced by market labor (Pitt and Rosenzweig, 1986). Pitt and Rosenzweig showed that although illness reduced the farm-labor supply of males in Indonesia, it had no effect on farm profits because ill farm-workers could be replaced by hired labor. Strauss (1986) showed in the case of rural Sierra Leone that the marginal product of family labor was practically the same as the marginal product of hired labor. In such a setting, profit or output from self-employment can be written as

$$\pi = \pi(pf, pm, wh, wf, I, F, S, \varphi, e_\pi) \tag{22}$$

where,

π is profit from self-employment;

pf is the price of output, say, food;

pm is the price of non-labor input;

wh is the wage of hired labor;

wf is the wage of family labor;

I is local infrastructure;

F is a vector of fixed factors;

φ is a vector of unobserved factors affecting the production of self-employment output;

e_π is measurement error in profits.

The essential point in Eq. (22) is that health is not a determinant of profits or output when labor supply and production decisions are separable. However, if a well-functioning labor market does not exist, or if family and hired labor are not perfect substitutes, profits and outputs generated from self-employment activities will depend on health status. Equation (22) illustrates that the nature of local labor markets is important in specifying the role of health in self-employment production functions. In the above setting, separability of a household's decisions in production and consumption is assumed. "That is, the household acts as though its decisions can be divided into two steps: first, maximize self-employment profits subject to the available technology, and second, maximize utility subject to the budget constraint augmented by the value of profits" (Strauss and Thomas, 1998, p. 782). See Singh, Squire, and Strauss (1986) for an analysis of separability of consumption, production and labor supply decisions of farm households.

Separability in farm household models means that production decisions can be made independently of decisions as to consumption of goods and leisure, but the reverse is not true. That is, consumption decisions must involve production decisions, because consumption is constrained by income. Production decisions are independent of consumption here because all the production inputs required are obtainable from labor and credit markets, which are assumed to exist (see Singh, Squire, and Strauss, 1986).

4.4.2.4. Productivity effects of health in subsistence agriculture In farm environments without the separability feature, Strauss (1986) in Sierra Leone, and Audibert (1986) in Cameroon find substantial effects of health on farm productivity. In Cameroon, a reduction in the incidence of bilharziasis increased rice production, but a reduction in malaria prevalence had no output effect. However, these results were not corrected for endogeneity of health status. In Sierra Leone, where instruments for health were used, calorie intake was found to have large effect on productivity. The instruments for calories (proxy for health) included local infrastructure and food prices. Dercon and Krishnan (2000) cite evidence that body mass index (Quetelet index) is positively correlated with ability to perform strenuous work and with farm productivity of women.

However, there is need to recognize that the relationship between nutrition and productivity is not a simple one because "energy intake could vary in the short-term within a homeostatic range without affecting the health and work capacity" (Srinivasan, 1994,

p. 1851). Srinivasan (1994, pp. 1848–1849) explains the non-linearities between nutrition and farm productivity as follows: "The efficiency wage is based on the relationship between nutritional status and productivity of the laborer. In this relationship the requirement of energy for maintaining basic metabolic processes (and for performing activities other than agricultural work) serves as a threshold: if food intakes do not provide enough energy to exceed this threshold, it is impossible (physiologically) for the laborer to engage in agricultural work."

Taken together, the above two ideas indicate that for well-nourished workers, energy intake can vary up or down within some range without affecting farm productivity, while for severely malnourished laborers an increase in energy intake would not affect their productivity, if the amount of energy consumed remains below the threshold that an individual needs to engage in farm work.

4.4.2.5. Effect of income on health   The macro level effect of income on health (the wealthier is healthier hypothesis) is documented in Pritchett and Summers (1996) and analyzed by Sala-i-Martin (2005). There is strong micro level evidence that income affects health. In Brazil, Thomas (1990) estimates large effects of mother's non-earned income on child health. In Sierra Leone, Strauss (1984) finds significant effects of income on nutritional status. Subramanian and Deaton (1996) report similar findings for South India. Despite the controversy surrounding the calorie-income relationship (Behrman and Deolalikar, 1987), the micro level evidence shows that increases in incomes raise caloric consumption, especially at low levels of income (see Strauss and Thomas, 1995). However, the elasticity of calories with respect to income is less than unity. Pitt, Rosenzweig, and Hassan (1990) show that the income calorie elasticity in Pakistan is low during harvest time.

4.5. Identifying causal effects of better health: Examples

Measurement of effects of health on income, and vice versa, is complicated by endogeneity of both health and income in the estimated equations, and by the externalities of health human capital.[10] The instrumental variables methods, and experimental treatment designs, are two approaches that have been developed to deal with this problem. A study by Schultz (2003) in West Africa (Cote d'Ivoire and Ghana) is used to illustrate the IV approach, while studies by Thomas et al. (2006) in East Asia (Indonesia), Miguel and Kremer (2004) in East Africa (Kenya) and Gertler (2004) in Central America (Mexico) illustrate the experimental treatment approaches.

---

[10] Duflo (2004) has shown that while education increased the wages of the workers who were exposed to a large school construction program in Indonesia, the wages of unexposed workers fell or increased less rapidly. Thus, the aggregate effect of education expansion can be negative, if for example, a complementary factor of production such as infrastructure cannot be adjusted. Similarly, although a malaria control program may increase farm yields per hour in a particular area, its economy-wide effect may be negative if market inputs remain fixed as health human capital increases and the marginal product of labor declines.

The IV methods and the randomized designs are employed to solve differently the same problem, namely, identification and estimation of a causal effect. The causal effect in both approaches is identified through a two-stage process. In the first stage, variation of the hypothesized causal factor is made exogenous; in the second stage, the impact of the causal factor on outcome of interest is measured. The studies illustrated in this section attempt to answer the question: what is the effect of better health on economic or social prosperity?

In solving this problem, the first stage in the IV method is to find exogenous variables that affect health without influencing the outcome of interest (e.g., wage income). Similarly, in the experimental approach, the first stage involves organizing a field experiment that varies health exogenously without affecting the outcome variable of interest, i.e., wage income. The factor that causes health to vary exogenously is called an instrumental variable in the IV approach, while in the experimental approach, it is known as treatment assignment mechanism (see Todd, 2008). In the IV approach, estimation of a causal effect is through regression methods, whereas in randomized experiments, simple differencing of values of the outcome variable across treatment and control groups may suffice (see Duflo, Glennerster, and Kremer, 2008).

There are important caveats about the two approaches which need to be stated: the results from experimental designs are not easily generalizable, and the experimental designs themselves may not meet strict criteria of randomness (Rosenzweig and Wolpin, 2000; Harrison and List, 2004). In the same vein, the IVs results may not apply outside the study site, and the IVs themselves may be weak and correlated with the outcomes of interest.

To overcome the problem of specification bias associated with the IVs, Rosenzweig and Wolpin (2000, p. 828) recommend the use of "naturally random events as instrumental variables" whenever possible, and provide five examples of such instruments, linking them to particular studies, namely: twin births, monozygotic twins, birth date, gender, and weather shocks.

The problem of experimental designs in field settings not meeting criteria of randomness, usually due to selection bias, may be overcome by advance planning of field activities and by working closely with local communities to ensure that study subjects comply with experimental designs (see Thomas et al., 2006; Parker, Rubalcava, and Teruel, 2008).

The four cases below illustrate the use of IV methods and randomized experimental designs in the estimation of causal effects of better health. The approaches themselves are generic even though they are drawn from applications in specific countries.

4.5.1. The IV methods

Schultz (2003) uses the IV regression method to estimate the income effect of health in Ghana and Ivory Coast using survey data. In the first stage regression, instruments for major forms of human capital (not just health capital) are identified; see also Thomas and Strauss (1997). In the second stage regression, the coefficients on endogenized hu-

man capital variables (see Mincer, 1974), with a focus on health, are estimated. The first
step is accomplished by estimating the following input demand equations:

$$I_{ij} = \alpha_j \bullet Y_i + \beta_j \bullet X_i + \varepsilon_{ij}, \quad j = H, E, B, M; \ i = 1, \dots, n \tag{23}$$

where,

I_{ij} is human capital investment of type j embedded in individual i;
H = Adult height, a dimension of health human capital that indicates childhood nutritional status;
E = Years of schooling (a measure of education human capital);
B = Body mass index, an indicator of adult nutritional status and current health;
M = Migration status (whether the individual has migrated from region of birth), an
indicator of combined elements of education and health;
Y = a vector of variables that affect the demand for human capital partly through its
impact on wage structures and through other channels;
X = a vector of variables that affects the demand for human capital without modifying
the wage structure;
ε_{ij} = the i.i.d. error term.

In the second stage, the predicted values of the various forms of human capital (I_{ij}^*)
are used to estimate the wage or productivity equation of the form:

$$w_i = \sum_j \gamma_j \bullet I_{ij}^* + \delta Y_i + v_i, \quad j = H, E, B, M \tag{24}$$

where

w_i = the logarithm of the wage rate for individual i;
Y_i = a vector of variables that belong to the wage function for individual i;
γ_j = the effect of human capital j on log wage;
δ = log wage effects of covariates, Y.

Equation (24) conveys the key idea that when estimating the wage effect of one form
of health human capital, e.g., body mass index, the effects of all the other forms of
human capital must be held constant. Failure to do this results in a mis-specification
of the wage function, because the omitted human capital variables are relegated to the
error term, thus biasing the wage effect of health. For example, to estimate the impact
of BMI on the wage rate using Eq. (24), controls are needed for education, migration,
and height.

Because all forms of human capital must be included in the wage function, and not
just the health status variable of interest, a generic set of instruments for human capital
has been identified in the literature (see Strauss, 1986). Since this set of instruments has
become standard, an example from Schultz (2003) is presented in Table 1a. (The results
for Ivory Coast and for female sub-samples are omitted.)

The human capital variables shown in Table 1a are for adults at the time of the survey
collection, while the family background variables refer to earlier periods when human
capital of the adults was being formed. The instrumental variables in Table 1a affect
demands for human capital inputs in the direction predicted by theory. For example,

Table 1a

Instruments for endogenous human capital variables in a wage function (selected results from the first stage regression for the male sub-sample, absolute t-statistics in parentheses), Ghana

Instrumental variables	Various forms of human capital			
	Education[b]	Migration[b]	Body mass index[b]	Height[b]
Mother's years of	0.779	−0.0007	−0.0300	0.0006
education	(2.13*)	(0.27)	(1.45)	(1.03)
Father's years of	0.122*	0.0025	0.0452*	0.0000
education	(5.63)	(1.72)	(3.67)	(0.15)
Father's education	0.687	−0.0147	−0.684	0.0215
unknown (= 1)	(0.81)	(0.26)	(1.41)	(1.66)
Mother employed in	−0.725*	−0.0774*	−0.605*	−0.0216*
agriculture (= 1)	(3.97)	(6.24)	(5.81)	(4.54)
Father employed in	−0.424*	−0.0014	0.108	−0.0019
Agriculture (= 1)	(2.03)	(1.10)	(0.91)	(0.60)
Rural resident[a] (= 1)	0.101	0.921*	0.165	0.0069*
	(0.46)	(61.4)	(1.32)	(2.09)
Rainfall[a] (annual mm)	0.0063	−0.0059	0.0153	−0.0003
	(0.46)	(6.32)*	(1.96)*	(1.68)
Malaria (= 1)	−0.7690*	−0.0647*	−0.339	−0.0143*
	(2.47)	(3.06)	(1.92)	(3.03)
Diarrhea (= 1)	−0.204	−0.137	0.117	−0.0000
	(0.78)	(7.62)	(0.79)	(0.01)
Measles (= 1)	0.506	−0.141*	−0.239	0.0065
	(1.70)	(6.96)	(1.41)	(1.43)
Sanitation and water	0.274	0.142*	0.0397	−0.0031
problem (= 1)	(1.00)	(7.62)	(0.26)	(0.76)
Immunization campaign	−0.231	−0.0922*	−0.180	−0.0019
in last 5 years (= 1)	(0.64)	(3.74)	(0.88)	(0.35)
Distance to nurse or	0.0282	−0.0021	0.0131	0.0005
doctor (km/miles)	(1.22)	(1.37)	(1.00)	(1.32)
Distance to permanent	0.0069	−0.0106*	−0.0031	0.0002
market (km/miles)	(0.38)	(8.65)	(0.37)	(0.79)
Distance to primary	−0.198	−0.0503*	−0.0031	0.0002
school (km/miles)	(1.69)	(6.32)	(0.37)	(0.79)
Distance to middle	−0.199*	−0.0373*	−0.0399	0.0007
school (km/miles)	(3.85)	(10.6)	(1.36)	(0.87)
Distance to secondary	−0.283*	−0.0076*	0.0011	0.0005*
school (km/miles)	(2.49)	(9.86)	(0.16)	(2.66)

Source: Extracted with minor changes from Schultz (2003, Table A.2).

[a]These variables are also in the wage function, and thus do not belong to the set of the identifying instrumental variables, i.e., they are in Y but not in X in Eq. (23).

[b]Other control variables include 4 age dummies (in Y), 6 ethnic groups (in Y), 10 regions (in Y), 10 local food prices (in X), state level per capita expenditure on curative and preventive health programs in 1987 (in X), and malaria campaigns in the last 5 years (in X).

*Statistically significant.

distances to social facilities are negatively associated with measures of human capital. Employment in agriculture is negatively correlated with household demands for human capital, a result that may be attributed to low incomes in agriculture. Although a number of coefficients on instrumental variables are statistically insignificant, the hypothesis that the joint effect of all the instrumental variables is non-zero cannot be rejected (see Schultz, 2003, Table 5), a finding that enhances the validity of the instruments (Bound, Jaeger, and Baker, 1995).

The diagnostic results that must be reported include the first stage F-statistics and incremental R-squareds on exclusion restrictions. Following the first stage regression, exogeneity and overidentification tests should also be carried out and their results reported (see Schultz, 2003, pp. 347–348). The stata estimation command, *ivreg2*, has two options (*ivendog* and *overid*) that may be specified to carry out these otherwise computationally burdensome tests.

The IV estimates of the effects of human capital variables on wages for male workers in Ghana are shown in Table 1b; the OLS estimates are reported for comparison purposes. The results are from a linear wage function (estimates from non-linear specifications have been omitted). It should be noted that if Eq. (24) is estimated with endogenized human capital inputs as the regressors, the standard errors of regression coefficients must be adjusted (see Wooldridge, 2002, p. 568).

As can be seen from the table, the IV estimates (column (2)) are substantially larger than those obtained via OLS (column (1)). Focusing on the IV estimates, it is evident that there are large returns from better health: a unit increase in mean BMI raises the log wage by 0.079, whereas an extra meter above the mean height increases the log wage

Table 1b

Wage effects of four human capital inputs in Ghana: Dependent variable is log hourly wage for adult males (absolute t-statistics in parentheses)

Variables	Estimation method ($N = 3414$)		Sample Means (3)
	OLS (1)	IV (2)	
Education (years of schooling completed)	0.0437*	0.0445*	7.13
	(9.86)	(2.46)	(5.47)
Migration (moved from birthplace = 1)	0.348*	0.218*	0.333
	(6.75)	(2.26)	(0.471)
BMI (body mass index (kg/m^2)	0.0530*	0.0793*	20.9
	(6.80)	(1.95)	(2.52)
Height (meters)	1.48*	5.69*	1.69
	(5.02)	(3.45)	(0.066)
Mean of dependent variable (St. Dev.)			5.77 (1.38)

Note: Controls in all the regressions include region of birth, ethnicity, age group, and season of interview.
Source: Constructed from Schultz (2003, Tables 2 and 4).
*Statistically significant.

by 5.69. In other words, a unit increase in BMI in Ghana increases male wages by 7.9%, while a male worker whose height is 1 cm taller than the mean height earns about 1.3% higher wage than a worker of average height. Height also effects labor productivity through its effects on choice of occupation (see Fogel, 1986).

The effects of other human capital variables on wages are also large, and statistically significant. The IV results show that a year of schooling increases male wage rate by 4.45% while migration increases it by 21.8% above the mean wage at the place of birth. It is important to emphasize that without controls for education and migration, estimates of returns to health investments would be biased. The stocks of human capital in Ghana in the 1980s are shown in the last column of Table 1b (see Schultz, 2003, Table 2). Although the BMI for males in the 1980s was within the normal range of 18.5 to 25 (see Fogel, 2004), the mean education level at around 7 years was quite low. The migration dummy shows that one third of male workers had moved from their birthplace prior to the household survey. The estimated coefficients on human capital variables in columns (1) and (2) of Table 1b show the response of the mean log-wage to marginal changes in the sample means of these variables (column (3)). Thus, descriptive statistics are an essential part of estimation results and should always be reported.

4.5.2. Randomized experimental studies

4.5.2.1. Indonesian study Thomas et al. (2006) present a randomized field experiment on how consumption of nutrients affects nutritional status, and how better nutrition in turn, affects labor earnings, employment, leisure, physical health, and psycho-social health. WISE (Work and Iron Status Evaluation) is the name of the field experiment, implemented in Java, Indonesia, over the period October 2001 to December 2004. The experiment randomly assigned iron tables and placebos to households, with the households that received placebos serving as the control group. Differences in the outcome of the experiment between the control and the treatment groups was then evaluated. The results presented below relate to the outcome of the experiment over the first 12 months. A brief account of the experiment may be helpful in interpreting the results, which are also highlighted elsewhere (see Todd, 2008).

The health input studied was supplementation of the normal household diet with iron tablets. In September 2001, a screener study was carried out to select the households and obtain baseline information for the study sample. Over 37,000 individuals in 9500 households were screened for hemoglobin deficiency by pricking their fingers to obtain the blood required for the test. All screened persons, i.e., those for whom hemoglobin levels were established, were pooled and an experimental sample randomly drawn from them. Since benefits of iron supplementation accrue mainly to iron-deficient persons, males age 25–75 and females age 40–75 with low hemoglobin levels were over-sampled, generating sample of over 17,500 persons living in 4300 households.

Once an individual was selected, his or her entire household was included in the sample so that randomization to treatment and control groups was at the household level. Adults in treatment households received 120 mg of purple-colored iron tablets and children age 5 years or less received orange flavored syrups while counterpart individuals in control households received placebos of the same appearance. These tablets and placebos were taken once a week, over a period of one year. Randomization at the household level averted the sharing of tablets among members of the same household, and avoided the necessity of keeping records of who in the household took what tablets. Randomly assigning a study sample (which need not be random) to treatment and control groups is the decisive step in a field experiment (see Duflo, Glennerster, and Kremer, 2008).

The pre-baseline survey was conducted between January and April 2002, four months before the baseline study in May 2002. Subsequently, households were interviewed every four months to record changes in socio-demographics, health status, work and leisure activities. The intervention commenced in August 2002 and ended in December 2003, but the four-month interviews continued through December 2004, with the final interview for all households taking place in 2005. Attrition from the study sample was minimal, and compliance with treatment instructions was high. See Thomas et al. (2006, pp. 12–15) for details of the experiment.

Table 2a shows the effect of treatment on health status, measured by the difference in hemoglobin level between the treatments and controls, 12 months into the intervention. The table shows the intent-to-treat-effects, i.e., it compares hemoglobin levels among individuals assigned to the treatment group relative to hemoglobin levels among persons assigned to the control group. Focus is on effect of intent-to-treat because it represents the outcome of the experiment when everyone fully complies with treatment instructions.

In this study, compliance rate for treatment group as well as for the control group was 92 percent. Division of the intent-to-treat effect (obtained via differencing) with the compliance rate for the treatment group yields the average effect of treatment on the treated (see Ravallion, 2008). If the compliance rate is equal to one, the intent-to-treat effect is the same as the average effect of treatment on the treated (TT). If experimental data are available, the TT, the average treatment effect (ATE), the local average treatment effect (LATE) and the marginal treatment effect (MTE) can all be derived using local IV regression methods and the control function approach (see Wooldridge, 1997; Heckman and Vytlacil, 2000; Card, 2001; Todd, 2008). Tables 2a and 2b illustrate the simplicity of computing TT when implementation of a randomized experiment is almost ideal, as in Thomas et al. (2006).

In the first panel of Table 2a, columns (1) and (2) report Hb at eight months into the study for treatment and control groups, respectively. The difference in hemoglobin levels between these two groups is in column (3), while column (4) reports the baseline difference, i.e., the pre-existing difference, prior to the start of the intervention. Column (5) presents the Hb difference-in-difference between the treatments and the controls after the intervention, i.e, the Hb difference at eighth month of the intervention between the two groups, minus the corresponding difference at baseline. In column (6) the estimates are adjusted for differences in ages of the subjects.

Column (6) shows that prior to the intervention, the hemoglobin levels for the treatments and the controls were about the same for males (diff $= -0.059$; se $= 0.059$),

Table 2a

Selected results for hemoglobin status: Intent to treat effects (standard errors in brackets), Indonesia

Indicator	Sample	Status at 8 months		Diff. (T−C)	Diff. at baseline, (4 months before T) (T−C)	8 Months *minus* baseline (DinD)	Adj. DinD
		Treatm. (T)	Cont. (C)				
		(1)	(2)	(3)	(4)	(5)	(6)
Hemoglobin	Male	13.250*	13.127*	0.123*	−0.059	0.183*	0.181*
		[0.040]	[0.040]	[0.057]	[0.059]	[0.057]	[0.057]
	Female	11.974*	11.819*	0.156*	0.040*	0.116*	0.117*
		[0.033]	[0.033]	[0.046]	[0.048]	[0.048]	[0.048]
Hemoglobin	Male	0.179*	0.206*	−0.027*	−0.004	−0.023	−0.023
(<12 g/dl)		[0.009]	[0.009]	[0.013]	[0.014]	[0.015]	[0.015]
(proportion)	Female	0.461*	0.499*	−0.038*	−0.024	−0.014	−0.014
		[0.011]	[0.011]	[0.016]	[0.016]	[0.019]	(0.014]
Sample size	Male	1804	1759	3563	3563	3563	3563
	Female	2021	2042	4063	4063	4063	4063

Note: Column (3) = (1) − (2); (5) = (3) − (4); (6) adjusts for age effects.
Source: Thomas et al. (2006, Table 3).
*Statistically significant.

which is as it should be, because the two groups had been randomly selected from the screened population, and randomly assigned to receive iron-tablets or placebos. Column (3) shows that by the eighth month into the intervention, hemoglobin level of the treatment group among males exceeded that of the control group by 0.123 g/dl, a difference that was statistically significant (se = 0.057). This is the first glimpse of evidence that the iron tables were effective in fighting anemia.

However, this is not yet the intent-to-treat effect of the intervention, because the pre-existing differences among subjects have not been taken into account. Column (5) does this by subtracting the difference in Hb levels for the two groups at the start of the intervention (column (4)) from the difference in Hb levels at the eighth month (column (3)) to yield an intent-to-treat effect of 0.183 g/dl for males, which is statistically significant (se = 0.057). In other words, since the Hb for the treatments (*T*) was 0.059 g/dl lower than that for the controls (*C*) at baseline, this amount must be added to 0.123 g/dl (the excess of Hb for *T* over *C* at the eighth month) to obtain the full amount by which iron tablets increased hemoglobin in the male sub-sample. Similarly, in the female sub-sample, where the reverse situation prevailed at baseline, 0.040 g/dl (column (4)) is subtracted from 0.156 g/dl (column (3)) to yield 0.116 g/dl (se = 0.048). In column (6) an adjustment for age differences in Hb response to treatment leaves the estimate in column (5) practically unchanged for both sub-samples.

Biomedical evidence suggests that subjects with low HB levels would gain most from consumption of iron tablets (Thomas et al., 2006). If this is so, the intent-to-treat effects shown in columns (5) and (6) for both sexes are understated. This hypothesis can be tested by subtracting from column (3), the difference in column (4) for subjects with low Hb prior to the start of the intervention (i.e., Hb < 12 g/dl at the baseline survey). For this group, Thomas et al. (2006, Table 3) report large Hb gains for both sexes (0.4 g/dl for males and 0.2 g/dl for females). The conclusion from the first panel of Table 2b is that the iron-supplementation increased Hb levels in the study sample, with males gaining substantially more than females.

The second panel of Table 2a depicts the effects of the intervention among iron-deficient subjects (i.e., those with HB < 12 g/dl at baseline). The results show that 20% of males and 50% of females (column (2)) were iron-deficient at the start of the intervention. Eight months into the intervention, the prevalence of iron-deficiency among males had dropped by 2.7% compared with a drop of 3.8% among females (column (3)). However, the adjustment for pre-existing differences between treatment and control groups shows that by the eighth month of the intervention, the prevalence of iron-deficiency in the study sample had not changed (columns (5) and (6)). That is, although the hemoglobin level of the sample had increased, it was still below the cut-off point of 12 g/dl for both sexes.

Table 2b shows the intent-to-treat effects of better health (improvement in Hb level) on selected measures of economic prosperity after eight months of iron-supplementation. Columns (1) and (2) of Table 2b parallel columns (5) and (6) of Table 2a. Specifically, column (1) reports the change in each labor market outcome for the treatment group between the eighth month of the intervention and the time prior to the start of the intervention (the baseline), relative to the change in the same outcome for the control group. The effects computed were mainly generated during the first four months of the intervention because hemoglobin levels take time to build up. Moreover, the intent-to-treat effects are calculated for subjects with low Hb levels at baseline (Hb < 12.5 g/dl), under the assumption that the subjects were the ones most likely to benefit from iron-supplemented diets. Similarly, column (2) reports effects for persons with high Hb levels at baseline (Hb > 12.5 g/dl), which are mostly negligible, as expected. Panel 1 shows that among low Hb persons, probability of working during the eighth month of the intervention had increased by 3.6% for males, with the increase for females being smaller and statistically insignificant (column (1)). As expected, working probabilities for persons with baseline Hb levels greater than 21.5 g/dl did not change (column (2)).

Panels 2 through 5 report similar effects for wage earnings, hours spent working, hourly earnings, and earnings from self-employment. The striking findings here relate to effects of better health on hours worked and on hourly earnings. The number of hours worked remained the same for both sexes (because the changes shown in panel 1 are statistically insignificant). Thus, the increase in total earnings for males shown in panel 2, is due to the increase in earnings per hour (panel 4). Although the females experienced an increase in total earnings, the increase in their hourly wage is statistically insignificant. Increases in male earnings among the self-employed substantially dominate the increases in female earnings (see Thomas et al., 2006).

Table 2b
Intent-to-treat effects on work, earnings and hours worked by hemoglobin status at baseline (standard errors in brackets), Indonesia

Indicator	Sample	Change in outcome for treatment group *minus* change in outcome for control group	
		If low Hb at baseline (DinD) (1)	If high Hb at baseline (DinD) (2)
1. Pr(not working in month of survey interview)	Male	−0.036* [0.012]	−0.003 [0.007]
	Female	−0.020* [0.014]	0.029 [0.020]
2. Quartic root earnings (Rp 000) last 4 months	Male	0.576 [0.299]	−0.012 [0.173]
	Female	0.163 [0.091]	0.033 [0.127]
3. Hours spent working last 4 months	Male	−12.968 [36.368]	−144.185 [21.027]
	Female	9.644 [15.264]	30.137 [21.425]
4. Quartic root hourly earnings (Rp 000) last 4 months	Male	0.126* [0.066]	0.007 [0.038]
	Female	0.034 [0.025]	−0.009 [0.035]
5. Quartic earnings (Rp 000) if self-employed last 4 months	Male	0.113* [0.040]	−0.006 [0.040]
	Female	0.056 [0.026]	−0.21 [0.037]

Source: Thomas et al. (2006, Table 5).
*Statistically significant.

4.5.2.2. Kenyan study   Miguel and Kremer (2004) report on results of a field experiment, conducted in Kenya to investigate effects of deworming on pupils' health, school attendance and test scores. Their findings show that deworming increased school attendance through better health, but had no effect on pupils' test scores.

The experiment, known as the Primary School Deworming Project (PSDP), was implemented in western Kenya between 1997 and 2001 in an area with high prevalence of helminth infections – Hookworms, Roundworms, Whipworms and Schistosomiasis. Practically all primary schools in the project site (75 schools), with a total enrollment of about 30,000 pupils were sampled. The seventy-five PSDP schools were randomly divided into three groups of 25 schools each, and randomly assigned to a treatment or control status, with randomization taking place all at one time. The schools were first stratified by geographic zone, then listed alphabetically, and then counted off 25 times in the order 1–2–3, 1–2–3, etc. The "1"s became the Group 1 schools, the "2"s became the

Group 2 schools, and the "3"s became Group 3 schools. Group 1 schools were treated in 1998 while Group 2 schools were treated in 1999.[11]

Thus in 1998, Group 1 schools were the treatment group, and Groups 2 and 3 were the comparison schools. In 1999, when Group 2 schools were phased into treatment, Groups 1 and 2 schools became the treatment group, and Group 3 schools, which did not begin treatment until 2001, were the control group. This experimental design had the advantage of exposing the whole population of schools to treatment over time in a random fashion.

The consent of the community and parents was sought before children were given deworming drugs. It is important to stress that although treatment was at the individual level, randomization was at the school level. That is, the unit of observation was a school rather than a pupil. Randomization at the school level permitted estimation of the following direct and indirect effects of treatment: (a) the direct effect of deworming on infection rate among treated and untreated children within a school; (b) the cross effect of the schools treated in 1998 on the infection rate among children in untreated schools in 1999; (c) the cross effect of treated schools on infection rate among children in the nearby schools; (d) the direct effect of treated pupils on their own infection rates within a school in subsequent periods.

In addition to receiving drug treatment, the children and teachers were taught how to prevent worm infections. However, no worm prevention behaviors were observed among children in either the treatment or control schools. As a result, Miguel and Kremer (2004, p. 175) concluded that the health effects of the PSDP were through helminthic drugs rather than through health education.

Table 3a shows the status of infections, pupils' health, and worm prevention behaviors in treatment and control schools after one year of program activities. As can be seen from Panel A, worm infection rates were lower in the treatment group than in the control group, indicating that the program was generally effective against helminths. The differences in infection rates between treatment and control schools were statistically significant (last column of Table 3a). The prevalence of moderate-to-heavy infections in treatment schools (0.27) was 25% lower than the prevalence in comparison schools (0.52). Panel B shows that pupils' in treatment schools had better measures of general health than pupils in comparison schools. In particular, self-reported cases of sickness were 3–4% lower in treatment than in comparison schools.

Panel C shows that there was no difference between the treatment and control schools in behaviors associated with helminth-infection prevention, such as wearing shoes and general cleanliness. This finding shows that the health education messages given to children were not effective in inducing behavioral changes necessary to prevent worm infections, and is suggestive of the need to explore alternative mechanisms for doing so. One obvious reason for children not wearing shoes despite the associated benefits

---

[11] I am very grateful to Edward Miguel for clarifying, in an email communication, the randomization of schools into treatment and control groups.

Table 3a

Health and health behavior differences between treatment and comparison schools (standard errors of differences in parentheses)

Variables	Treatment schools (Group1)	Comparison schools (Group 2)	Treatment *minus* comparison
Panel A: Helminth Infection Rates			
Any moderate-heavy infection, January–March 1998 (baseline)	0.38	–	–
Any moderate-heavy infection, 1999	0.27	0.52	−0.25*
			(0.06)
Hookworm moderate-heavy infection, 1999	0.06	0.22	−0.16*
			(0.03)
Roundworm moderate-heavy infection, 1999	0.09	0.24	−0.15*
			(0.04)
Schistosomiasis moderate-heavy infection, 1999	0.08	0.18	−0.10
			(0.06)
Whipworm moderate-heavy infection, 1999	0.13	0.17	−0.04
			(0.05)
Panel B: Other Nutrition and Health Outcomes			
Sick in the past week (self-reported), 1999	0.41	0.45	−0.04*
			(0.02)
Sick often (self-reported)	0.12	0.15	−0.03*
			(0.01)
Hemoglobin concentration (g/L)	124.8	123.2	1.6
			(1.4)
Proportion anemic (Hb < 100 g/L), 1999	0.02	0.04	−0.02*
			(0.01)
Panel C: Worm Prevention Behaviors			
Clean (observed by field worker), 1999	0.59	0.60	−0.01
			(0.02)
Wears shoes (observed by field worker), 1999	0.24	0.26	−0.02
			(0.03)
Days contact with fresh water in past week (self-reported), 1999	2.4	2.2	0.2
			(0.3)

Sample size information: Parasitological Results: 2328 (862 Treatment Group, 1467 Comparison Group); Hemoglobin Results: 778 (292 Treatment Group, 486 Comparison Group); Pupil Questionnaire Health Outcomes: 9102 (3562 Treatment Group, 5540 Comparison Group).

Notes: Moderate-to-heavy infection thresholds for the various intestinal helminths are: 250 egp for *S. Mansoni*, 5000 for Roundworm; 750 epg for Hookworm; and 400 epg for Whipworm.
Source: Miguel and Kremer (2004, Table V).
*Statistically significant.

stressed by health education messages is that their parents could not afford to buy them shoes.

Table 3b shows the effect of deworming on school attendance between the treatment and comparison schools over the period May 1998 and March 1999, approximately

Table 3b
Effects of deworming (via better health) on school participation, school level data

Variables	Group 1 (25 schools)	Group 2 (25 schools)	Group 3 (25 schools)	Differences	
	Treatment	Comparison	Comparison	Group 1 – (Groups 2 & 3)	Group 2 – Group 3
First Year Post-Treatment (May 1998 to March 1999)					
Girls < 13 years, and all boys	0.841	0.731	0.767	0.093* (0.031)	−0.037 (0.036)
Females	0.855	0.771	0.789	0.076* (0.027)	−0.018 (0.032)
Males	0.844	0.736	0.780	0.088* (0.031)	−0.044 (0.037)
Girls ⩾ 13 years	0.864	0.803	0.811	0.057* (0.029)	−0.008 (0.034)

Source: Miguel and Kremer (2004, Table VIII, Panel A).
*Statistically significant.

one year into the intervention. As is clear from the table, school attendance increased significantly in treatment schools relative to comparison schools. Among young girls and all boys, school attendance in treatment schools exceeded the comparison schools by 9.3% $[0.841 - (0.731 + 0.767)/2]$ in the first phase of the project. Moreover, gains in school participation among the treated pupils were larger among boys than girls (8.8% and 7.6%, respectively).

The smaller gain in school participation (5.7%) among teenage girls is consistent with the fact that a small proportion of these girls received helminthic drugs (Miguel and Kremer, 2004, p. 190), and is indicative of a causal effect of deworming on school attendance. The causal effect of deworming on school participation is confirmed in the last column of Table 3b, which shows that the difference in attendance rates in the two control schools (Groups 2 and 3) was not significantly different from zero at the 5% level.

Next, Miguel and Kremer (2004) investigate the effect of deworming on pupils' test scores in school examinations. Deworming was hypothesized to improve tests scores by increasing the total amount of time spent in school and by improving learning while pupils are in school. However, the study's hypothesis – that better health resulting from a reduction in parasitic infections would increase test scores was not supported by the data (Miguel and Kremer, 2004, Table X). Citing Strauss and Thomas (1998), Miguel and Kremer (p. 202) claim that there is an analogous result in the labor market literature where the impact of poor health on labor productivity is inconclusive. However, these two findings are not comparable because the labor market result, where it exists (see Section 4.4), relies on separability of production and labor supply (Singh, Squire, and Strauss, 1986) so that the work of sick family members can effectively be done by hired labor. In the present context of a test score (an approximate indicator of the output of an education production function, where child health is an exogenously varied input) this is not the case. That is, labor supply (school participation) is not separable from acquisition of cognitive skills (production of education human capital). The most likely reason for the reported test score result is that the experimentally induced change in school participation rate was not large enough to produce an effect, or it was not well measured – issues that Miguel and Kremer discuss in detail.

The differences in health status (Table 3a) and in school attendance rates (Table 3b) between the treatment and control schools exclude the externalities and long-run effects of deworming. Miguel and Kremer illustrate the strength of combining experimental designs with regression methods in their identification of within-school externalities. "Although randomization across schools makes it possible to experimentally identify both the overall program effect and the cross-school externalities, we must rely on non-experimental methods to decompose the effect on treated schools into a direct effect and within-school externality effect" (Miguel and Kremer, 2004, p. 175).

In addition to using the regression method as a decomposition tool, Miguel and Kremer also use it to estimate direct and externality effects of deworming on health and school participation controlling for school and pupil characteristics. As to externality effects, each one thousand pupils in treatment schools that were 3 kilometers away from untreated schools reduced moderate to-heavy infections in the untreated schools by 26%. Similar externality effects were calculated for school participation rates (see Miguel and Kremer, 2004, Tables VII and IX). Todd (2008) presents econometric methods for estimating causal effects when data from randomized experiments are not available, or when such data suffers from sample selection, attrition and other problems.

4.5.2.3. Mexican study   An evaluation of health effects of a large, nationally representative experiment in Mexico, known as *Progresa*, is presented in Gertler (2000, 2004). Like the Kenyan and Indonesian experiments above, Progresa was demand-oriented. That is, it provided subsidies which were administratively targeted to particular groups (the poor) within communities. This is in contrast to supply-driven approaches, that transfer increased amounts of resources to communities, e.g. in form of clinics.

The program was started in 1997 by the Government of Mexico to address the problem of extreme poverty in rural communities. Within three years of implementation, Progresa extended benefits to about 2.6 families in 50,000 villages, comprising 40% of rural families. However, the villages were phased into the program randomly due to budgetary and logistical constraints as in the Kenyan study above. The government chose 320 treatment and 186 control villages, a total of 506 study villages, during the first phase of the program. The treatment villages began receiving benefits in August 1998, while the eligible households in the control villages waited for two years before receiving benefits. Although Progresa benefits were targeted to households, the program was randomized at the village level. The structure, objectives and implementation of *Progresa*, i.e., a program on education, health and nutrition (see Ravallion, 2008) and similar programs in Latin America are described in Parker, Rubalcava, and Teruel (2008).

In an effort to improve health in rural communities, Progresa made cash transfers worth 20–30% of family income every two months to mothers of participating families in treatment villages if one or more of the following conditions held (see Gertler, 2004, pp. 336–337).

   (i) Children of age 0–23 visited immunization and nutrition monitoring clinics;

  (ii) Children age 24–60 months attended nutrition monitoring clinics;

 (iii) Pregnant women visited clinics to obtain prenatal care;

 (iv) Lactating women visited clinics to obtain postpartum care, nutrition supplements and education about health, nutrition and hygiene;

  (v) Other family members visited clinics for physical check-ups;

 (vi) Adult family members participated in regular meetings at which health, hygiene, and nutrition issues and best practices were discussed.

Gertler (2004) evaluated consequences of Progresa on child health by comparing health status of children between the treatment and control villages. The technical problem was the estimation a child health production function, the market inputs of which included immunizations, nutrition supplements, medical care, and a set of behavioral inputs such as breast feeding and other best practices, e.g., avoidance of alcohol consumption and smoking during pregnancy (see Rosenzweig and Schultz, 1983). Items (i)–(vi) above provide a flavor of the types of inputs that belong in a child health production function; the inputs however, are endogenous to child health.

The inputs into child health were varied exogenously by randomization of Progresa's benefits across treatment and control villages. This was the first stage in the evaluation, accomplished by the Mexican Government at the design and start of Progresa. It is worthwhile to contrast the Mexican study with the Indonesian and Kenyan studies, where researchers had to implement their own randomized designs to permit identification of impacts.

The second stage in the evaluation of the impact of Progresa on child health is the measurement of the change in health status of children following implementation of the program, which can be accomplished through a simple calculation. "The randomization and the fact the control and treatment samples are well balanced in characteristics imply that a simple comparison of mean outcomes post-intervention will likely provide an unbiased estimate of program impacts" (Gertler, 2004, p. 338). However, to better account for effects of heterogeneity among households, regression methods were used. The post-intervention data were collected through a household survey from a subset of the original 506 experimental communities (320 treatment villages and 186 control villages).

The dependent variables in the regressions were (a) illness (whether child was reported ill four weeks prior to the household survey); (b) stunting (defined as being two or more standard deviations below the age–sex standardized height of a health reference population); and anemia (defined as hemoglobin less than 11 g/dl). The controls in the regressions included family background variables and village dummies (Gertler, 2004, pp. 338–339).

The evaluation results are in Tables 4a and 4b, which show, respectively, the baseline descriptive statistics, and the effect of *Progresa* on the odds ratio of illness (probability of being ill if in treatment villages, divided by probability of being ill if in control villages) in a sample of children. Since the sample is random, the results from the experiment apply to all rural children in Mexico.

The last column of Table 4a shows that at baseline, all of the characteristics of children were statistically indistinguishable between treatment and control villages. Also notable, is the fact that at baseline in 1997, the parents of children had very low levels of education, 3–4 years of schooling. However, both the control and treatment villages seem to have had good access to social infrastructure at baseline because about 70% of households in which the children lived had electricity.

Table 4b reports estimates of the impact of Progresa on the odds ratio of illness in a combined sample of children from treatment and control villages. The odds ratio of an illness is equal to 1, if the probability of illness in treatment villages is equal to probability of illness in control villages. Thus, if the odds ratio is equal to 1, the program has no effect on probability of being ill.

The first two columns of Table 4b show the estimated odds ratio from logistic regression estimates of the coefficients on dummy variables indicating whether the child was in a treatment village and also eligible to receive Progresa benefits. The third column reports results for the effect of length of time that the child could have been in Progresa

Table 4a

Pre-intervention descriptive statistics for sample of children, age 0–35 months at baseline, 1997

Variable	Treatment	Control	*p*-value for difference
Child was ill in the last 4 weeks (= 1)	0.330	0.323	0.771
Age (months)	1.625	1.612	0.914
Male (= 1)	0.511	0.491	0.091
Father's years of education	3.803	3.840	0.980
Mother's years of education	3.495	3.829	0.062
Father speaks Spanish (= 1)	0.942	0.929	0.276
Mother speaks Spanish (= 1)	0.935	0.917	0.443
Own house (= 1)	0.93	0.917	0.465
House has electricity (= 1)	0.644	0.711	0.091
Hectares of land owned	0.809	0.791	0.553
Male daily wage rate (pesos)	30.483	31.219	0.370
Female daily wage rate (pesos)	27.258	27.844	0.493
Sample size	4519	3306	

Source: Gertler (2004, p. 339, Table 1).

Table 4b

Estimates of health impacts of *Progresa*: Dependent variable is children's odds ratio of illness (the *p*-value for the test of the hypothesis that the estimated odds ratio is equal to 1 is in parentheses)

Variable	Newborns	Child age 0–35 months at baseline	
		Model 1	Model 2
Progresa eligible (= 1)	0.747	0.777	
	(0.013)	(0.000)	
Progresa eligible for 2 months (= 1)			0.940
			(0.240)
Progresa eligible for 8 months (= 1)			0.749
			(0.000)
Progresa eligible for 14 months (= 1)			0.836
			(0.005)
Progresa eligible for 20 months (= 1)			0.605
			(0.000)

Note: Control variables include the socioeconomic variables reported in Table 41a, measured at baseline prior to intervention.
Source: Gertler (2004, Table 2).

on odds ratio. The results strongly reject the hypothesis that Progresa had no effect on illness probabilities in treatment villages.

The estimates indicate that the newborns in treatment villages were 25.3% less likely than their counterparts in the control villages to be reported as being ill in the previous month (odds ratio = 0.747, *p*-value = 013).[12] Similarly, the second column of the table shows that the 0–3 year-olds in treatment villages were 22.3% less likely to be ill compared with the same age-group in control villages. The third column reports results for effects of duration of exposure to the program on odds ratio of illness. Two months into the program, illness probabilities were not different in treatment and control villages (odds ratio = 0.940, *p*-value = 0.240). That is, children in treatment villages were 6% less likely to be reported ill, relative to those in the control villages, but this difference was not statistically significant. However, 20 months into the program, the probability of illness in treatment villages was 39.5% lower than in comparison villages. A similar analysis shows that children in program areas were less likely to be stunted or anemic relative to children in control villages (see Gertler, 2004, Table 3, p. 340). In particular, treatment children were 25.3% less likely to be anemic and grew about a centimeter taller during the first year of the program.

---

[12] Gertler (2004, p. 339) uses the term log-odds to refer to the estimates presented in Table 4b (his Table 2). Instead, we use the term odds ratio because an estimate such as 0.747 is simply the ratio of the probability of illness in treatment villages divided by probability of illness in control villages; however, the logarithm of 0.747 is the log-odds ratio, which is not required here.

4.5.2.4. Summary and discussion The four studies above illustrate structural (IV) and experimental approaches to the measurement of benefits from health improvements, focusing on advantages of a particular approach in specific contexts. Glewwe and Miguel (2008) provide a detailed account of strengths and weaknesses of using IVs and randomized experiments to measure the impact of child health on education in low-income countries; see also Ravallion (2008).

Schultz's study in Ghana and Ivory Coast shows how IV methods can be applied to survey data to provide consistent estimates of returns to health investments. Miguel and Kremer 's study in Kenya illustrates how a deworming program, randomized at the school level, can be used to evaluate the impact of children's health on school attendance and on test scores in the presence of treatment externalities. The study by Thomas et al. in Indonesia shows how supplementation of household normal diet with iron tablets (randomized at the household level to avoid the sharing of tablets among treatment and control subjects from the same household), can be used as a source of exogenous variation in health, thus permitting measurement of its impact on earnings, productivity, and leisure. Gertler's study exploits exogenous variation in utilization of health care services across village (due to *Progresa*), to estimate the impact of the services on child health using regression methods. Progresa was randomized at the village level because of the broader geographic nature of some program benefits, such as improvements in local health facilities, and because it was perceived that randomization within a village would be politically difficult (see Behrman, Sengupta, and Todd, 2005).

The outcomes of randomized social programs are dependent on compliance with various program requirements, and in this regard, Progresa's conditionality of cash transfer is noteworthy. The government transferred cash to families only after they had used the services availed by program, such as immunizations, health education and prenatal care. Becker's (1965) and Grossman's (1972a, 1972b) models show that the opportunity cost of the time spent to seek health care can be a major deterrent to health care utilization, even when the money price of care is fully subsidized. Paying families to use basic health care, as in Progresa, recognizes this fact, and amounts to reimbursing families for the time cost of seeking care, which the very poor can hardly afford. Indeed, even without treatment externalities of the type documented by Miguel and Kremer (2004), such payment is justified on grounds of the opportunity cost of the time individuals must incur to seek and use health care. There is a strong case for extending subsidies to the poor to cover health care costs beyond the money cost of care.

4.6. HIV/AIDS and development

4.6.1. Introduction

The relationship between HIV/AIDS and development is a special case of the interdependence between income and health (Section 4.4). The methods and concepts discussed in Section 4.4 can be applied to investigate the relationship between HIV/AIDS and development. The term development encompasses more than economic growth. It also includes progress in reducing inequality and poverty and increasing the expected length of life.

HIV/AIDS has characteristics that distinguish it from many others diseases. It is pandemic, chronic, fatal, and highly stigmatized. A virus called HIV (human immunod-eficiency virus) causes AIDS (acquired immune-deficiency syndrome) when it destroys white blood cells that are essential to the disease fighting ability of the body (the immune system). In most low-income countries, HIV among adults is heterosexually transmitted. After transmission, infected individuals enter a clinical latent stage dur-ing which health status declines gradually without signs of disease symptoms. In east Africa, the median time from infection to AIDS is 9.4 years (Thirumurthy, Zivin, and Goldstein, 2005). Over time, the immune systems of almost all infected individuals become too weakened to fight diseases. This period of immune deficiency is associated with substantial weight loss, and opportunistic diseases such as cancers, pneumonia and tuberculosis. In resource poor countries, individuals usually die within one year after progression to AIDS (Thirumurthy, Zivin, and Goldstein, 2005). ARV (antiretroviral) therapy can reduce the likelihood of opportunistic diseases and prolong life (WHO, 2004, 2005). However, to implement ARV therapies, information is needed on health care demand behavior of individuals. Also important in the context of HIV/AIDS con-trol, is information on demand for VCT (voluntary counseling and testing) services (see Glick and Sahn, 2006). Use of VCT services allows early detection of AIDS, so that ARV therapy can be initiated before the HIV substantially weakens the immune system. The results of VCT may also motivate behavioral change to prevent further transmission of the virus. Individuals who know their HIV status have an incentive to change sexual behavior to avoid infection or exposure of others to the virus.

4.6.2. The world profile of HIV/AIDS

Since the reporting of the first five cases of HIV/AIDS on June 5, 1981 in Los Angeles 25 years ago, the disease has reached virtually every corner of the globe, infecting more than 65 million people, of whom 25 million have died (Fauci, 2006). The world profile of HIV/AIDS (Bloom and Sachs, 1998; World Bank, 2005) shows that the poorest re-gions in the world have the highest incidence of HIV/AIDS. Africa for example bears the burden of two-thirds of AIDS deaths worldwide, and about three quarters of new HIV/AIDS infections. Furthermore, for every 8 people living with HIV/AIDS world-wide 5 are in Africa (Table 5).

Although the social and economic losses associated with HIV/AIDS have so far been limited mainly to Africa, the epidemic is in a nascent stage in other developing regions of the world, notably Asia (World Bank, 2005). If policy measures are not taken to stop the spread of HIV/AIDS in Asia, the worldwide regional HIV/AIDS profile will, within several decades, mimic the current world poverty profile (World Bank, 2000). That is, the highest incidence of HIV/AIDS will continue to be in Africa, but the largest number of HIV/AIDS deaths and infections will occur in Asia because of that continent's large share in the world population. Thus, while implementation of extensive prevention and treatment programs are required in Africa to control HIV/AIDS, widespread prevention measures and focused treatment campaigns are required in Asia to stop the emergence of the epidemic there on the scale observed in Africa.

4.6.3. Effects of HIV/AIDS on growth

The evidence in Table 5 that poor regions in the world have high HIV/AIDS prevalence can be interpreted to mean that HIV/AIDS causes poverty as intuition suggests. There is a large literature that examines the causal effects of HIV/AIDS on macroeconomic growth (Kambou, Devarajan, and Over, 1992; Cuddington, 1993; Bloom and Mahal, 1997; Arndt and Lewis, 2000). Many macroeconomic studies find small negative effects of HIV/AIDS on growth (see, e.g., Bloom and Mahal, 1997), while a few report large negative effects (see McDonald and Roberts, 2006; Roe and Smith, 2006). A positive long-run growth effect of HIV/AIDS has been simulated for South African economy (Young, 2005).

HIV/AIDS reduces growth by increasing depreciation of health capital and therefore reducing life expectancy (Grossman, 1972a). This foreshortening of life expectancy undermines individuals' incentives to accumulate education human capital. Thus, HIV/AIDS may cause poverty by reducing both the health and education human capital, the two key determinants of income (Couderc and Ventelou, 2005). However, the positive relationship from poverty to HIV/AIDS is not causal, because a virus is the reason for the disease. The positive relationship from poverty to AIDS reflects the correlation between poverty and a cluster of behavioral patterns that put individuals at high risks of infection by human immunodeficiency viruses. For instance, since use of condoms among the poor is limited, the virus and the associated sexually transmitted diseases spread rapidly among the poor.

Table 5
Estimates of HIV infections and AIDS mortality by region as of December 2004

Region	Persons living with HIV/AIDS	Number of new infections in 2004	Number of AIDS deaths in 2004
Sub-Saharan Africa	25.4 million	3.1 million	2.3 million
South and Southeast Asia	7.1 million	890,000	490,000
Latin America and Caribbean	2.1 million	293,000	131,000
Eastern Europe and Central Asia	1.4 million	210,000	60,000
East Asia	1.1 million	290,000	51,000
Middle East and North Africa	0.5 million	92,000	28,000
North America, Western Europe and Oceania	1.6 million	70,000	23,200
Total	39.4 million	4.9 million	3.1 million

Source: World Bank (2005, p. 5).

4.6.4. Policies to control HIV/AIDS

To design effective AIDS prevention strategies, a good understanding of the dominant modes through which HIV is transmitted is needed (Feachem and Jamison, 1991; World Bank, 1997). Globally, HIV is spread through (a) unprotected sex with an infected partner, (b) the sharing of infected injection equipment, (c) childbirth and breast-feeding (mother-to-child transmission), (d) transfusion of contaminated blood and blood products and through (e) health facilities that do not take precautions to protect their patients and staff against HIV (World Bank, 2005, p. 5). Since all these correlates of AIDS are behavioral in nature, information on demand for behavioral health inputs is critical in the design of policies to prevent the epidemic and treat the infected persons.

Acquisition of information about own HIV status can help slow down transmission of HIV by motivating infected individuals to seek early antiretroviral (ARV) treatment. Early uptake of ARV considerably reduces the intensity of HIV infection. The effectiveness of ARV therapy when received before the CD4 count drops below a threshold level has recently been demonstrated in Kenya. AIDS patients who received ARV therapy when their CD4 count was too low (below 35) had small survival probabilities but those who began treatment earlier experienced rapid recovery (Thirumurthy, Zivin, and Goldstein, 2005).

Provision of formal and informal education could increase VCT for expectant mothers and increase the uptake of ARVs that reduce the mother-to-child transmission rate. Nevirapine, a relatively low cost ARV drug, can be briefly administered to a mother at the onset of labor and to her child at the time of delivery to reduce the likelihood of transmission of HIV from mother to child by a substantial amount (see Canning, 2006). But to achieve this low-cost reduction in transmission, a pregnant woman must undergo VCT and decide to have this locally provided therapy. Without information on her HIV infection status, a woman may not consider the pros and cons of this intervention. In the last few years, Nevirapine has become more widely available in Africa and elsewhere. But the results of routine testing for HIV at prenatal clinics and birthing hospitals have been treated as confidential information, and the results of testing are provided only to women who request them. Many women are not informed of the likely benefits which they could obtain for their child and their own future health if the test determined they were infected by HIV. With the recent decline in the cost of ARV drugs and the growing capacity of health care systems to dispense them, it is important to design new educational programs which publicized the private benefits of testing and of timely treatment of HIV/AIDS, and evaluate the effects of these programs on prevention behavior and on transmission of the epidemic.

A desired change in demand for behavioral health inputs can be achieved through public subsidization of such inputs. In particular, demand for VCT services can be increased through subsidization of VCT visits or health education programs. However, even when services at voluntary counseling and testing centers (VCT) are provided free of charge, time cost and lack of appropriate information can be a major barrier to using them (see Gersovitz, 2005). Thus, in addition to reducing financial and time costs of making VCT visits, information about the value of such visits need to be generated and disseminated widely. Policies for controlling HIV/AIDS in low-income countries should include making basic education widely available to the youth, age 15–19. Ainsworth, Beegle, and Nyamete (1996) show that schooling is positively correlated with demand for contraceptives in Africa, behavior that is likely to be negatively correlated with the risk of exposure to HIV. There is some evidence that educated persons are more likely to be tested for HIV than persons without any schooling (Gersovitz, 2005).

Support for fighting HIV/AIDS should be given to projects that have the greatest potential for reducing the scale and effect of the epidemic, relying on locally generated information to design, implement and manage them (World Bank, 2005). The material in this sub-section complements this view because it shows the types of health inputs that can be made available by the projects to reduce the transmission of HIV/AIDS and to mitigate its health and economic impacts within the infected population. Supporting community-based organizations and the health ministries to deliver cost-effective treatment, preventive, counseling and testing services to populations, as suggested by the above evaluation, would go along way in effectively attacking the epidemic. However, as emphasized in this chapter, care should be taken to design projects that address demand-side as well as the supply-side barriers to health care utilization, paying attention to the linkage between utilization and health outcomes. At the policy level, the link between health outcomes and the services for HIV/AIDS prevention, treatment, and for the care and support of the persons living with HIV/AIDS, can be made by periodic monitoring and evaluation of the effectiveness of the projects, especially in improving the health status of the poor.

4.7. Industrial organization of health care

The nature of health care industry determines the cost of medical care, its quality and accessibility by the population.[13] In developed countries, private methods of health service financing and provision include employer-based health insurance schemes, medical group practices, and a variety of not-for-profit health care providers, commonly known as health maintenance organizations. The essential feature of these privately organized health care entities is that they operate mainly through a variety of markets. Prominent among these, are markets for health care, pharmaceuticals, drugs, and medical supplies and equipment. Industrial networks of health care firms (health care providers and payers for the services provided) are supported by an elaborate system of social institutions such as the laws relating to medical insurance, public health, contracts, patents, development of pharmaceutical products, and training of health professionals.

---

[13] An analysis of industrial organization "focuses on individual, imperfectly competitive markets and seeks to understand the behavior of firms that compose them and the resulting efficiency, i.e., performance of those markets" (Dranove and Satterthwaite, 2000, p. 1095).

In contrast to the above case, health care in low-income countries is directly provided to the population with financing from general taxation. In a few countries, government-provided health insurance exists for certain categories of public sector employees. However, efforts to implement large-scale, national health insurance programs in low-income countries, especially in Africa, have met with great difficulties (see World Bank, 1993).

The industrial organization of health care in developed countries is analyzed in parts 5 and 6 of the *Handbook of Health Economics* (Culyer and Newhouse, 2000). In their study of industrial organization of health care in the United States, Dranove and Satterthwaite (2000) limit themselves to topics such as agency, decision-making under uncertainty, non-price competition, market entry and exit, and product differentiation. The *Handbook of Industrial Organization* (Schmalensee and Willig, 1989) provides examples of the range of similar and parallel topics that are usually studied under the general subject of industrial organization. These topics include determinants of firm and market organization, transactions costs, collective bargaining, price discrimination, politics of regulation, and the environment.

Dranove and Satterthwaite (2000) note that health care markets fail to satisfy the key requirements of a perfect market, namely, large numbers of consumers and firms; free entry and exit; marketability of all goods and services including risk; symmetric information with zero search costs; and no increasing returns, externalities or collusion. Thus, while the perfect market model, may still serve as benchmark for optimal performance of health care markets, it cannot be used to illuminate how these markets actually function. Instead, a monopolistically competitive model has been recommended for that purpose (Stiglitz, 1989; McGuire, 2000). Dranove and Satterthwaite analyze health care market structures (provision and financing of health services) in contexts of independent and regulated physicians and under managed care insurance plans. They show that health care quantity, quality, price, and outcome vary across different market structures and industrial organizations (see also Risso, 2005). For example, health care prices are lower under managed care health insurance plans (where large groups of health care payers negotiate price discounts for treatments on behalf of their clients) than under settings of independent hospitals or physicians (where patients undertake such price negotiations individually). In the United States, managed care has become a dominant mode of organizational form of health care because it offers payers and providers alike an incentive to be cost conscious (Glied, 2000; Cuellar and Gertler, 2006). Managed care health insurance plans (health care payers such as a network of insurance firms) have an incentive to reduce the costs that patients pay for health care to limit the insurance benefits paid out, while health care providers (hospitals, physicians or health maintenance organizations) have an incentive to reduce health care costs to attract more patients. However, there is evidence that in United States, health care providers such as hospitals and physicians have formed consortia to neutralize the price reducing power of managed care (Cuellar and Gertler, 2006).

In industrialized countries, government is one of the payers for health care that patients obtain from the market (Chalkley and Malcomson, 2000). Thus, types of contracts that ensure that patients get quality health care is a major concern in the industrial organization of health care in such countries. In low-income countries, the government simply provides health care directly to patients free of charge or at a nominal fee, although in many settings private patients make side payments to providers to receive services and drugs or to avoid waiting; or to receive better quality care (see Banerjee, Deaton, and Duflo, 2004). In these countries, private health insurance is limited, and the national health insurance has not taken root. However, fragmentary schemes of community-based health insurance exist (Schneider and Hanson, 2006).

The industrial organization of health care in low-income countries is in formative stages because the social institutions conducive to its emergence and growth are lacking. However, since developing countries are globalizing at a rapid rate, the policymakers in these economies may soon face issues of managed care in private health sectors. Already, managed care is a notable feature of the private health sector in South Africa (Van den Heever, 1998). Readers interested in managed care and related issues may consult Culyer and Newhouse (2000), McGuire and Riordan (1994) or the general industrial organization literature (Schmalensee and Willig, 1989).

5. Conclusion

This chapter has reviewed a large literature on economic methods and concepts that can be used to effectively address health policy issues in low-income countries. Health policy-making in developing countries can be strengthened through a better understanding of five issues:

(A) How can the health of the population, especially of the poor be improved?
(B) What are the economic effects of investments in health and how do investments that increase income from various sources affect different dimensions of health?
(C) What are the effects on health of demand for behavioral inputs such as smoking and personal hygiene and of demand for market inputs such as food, medical care, nutrition, and vaccinations?
(D) How important are the intra-household allocations in influencing these demands?
(E) What analytical work exists on HIV/AIDS that could be used to inform prevention and treatment of this disease in low-income economies?

A. Improving health outcomes

The review finds that developing country literature is largely silent on policies to improve health. This is because in this literature, health production is not properly linked to patterns of demand for market inputs and to behavioral changes. An integrated conceptual and empirical framework for analyzing policies that can be implemented to improve health (Rosenzweig and Schultz, 1983) has been presented in this chapter and linked to related literatures. Despite estimation challenges, the framework can still be used with available data to illuminate health policy issues in low-income countries. In applying the framework, it is important to recognize that the inputs that go into health production are choices of economic agents, and thus the estimated effects of the inputs are likely to be biased by preferences, and by unobserved components of health endowments and household constraints.

B. Economic effects of better health

The chapter shows how health improvements affect wages, labor supply (number of hours worked and whether or not individuals enter the labor force), farm productivity (yields per hour) and fertility. The empirical evidence thus provided can guide investment of scarce resources in ways that best improve the economic well-being of the population through improvements in health. However, to avoid misguided policies, it is important to also consider the effect on income of health of individuals *not* exposed to health-improving interventions. See Duflo (2001, 2004) for examples of effects of education on wages and employment in Indonesia that go beyond the individuals exposed to schooling opportunities.

More generally, caution should be exercised in extrapolating micro level findings to the macro level because general equilibrium adjustments can undo the findings derived from a localized experiment. Increases in health human capital may not be accompanied by economic growth due to bad macro policies or corruption that misallocate or dissipate the additional capital.

C. Behavioral changes as health inputs

A behavioral change such as quitting smoking, changing a sexual practice or overcoming addiction to drugs, alcohol, or diet is associated with better health, just as is the use of market inputs such as medical care and vaccinations. Thus, a behavioral change serves as an input into health production. Indeed, health effects of changing behavioral inputs may be as important as effects of altering market inputs of medical care.

In the United States, approximately 50% of deaths in 1990 could be attributed to behavior-related health problems (McGinnis and Foege, 1993; Cutler and Glaeser, 2005). The low-income countries also suffer many diseases that are rooted in behavioral choices, and in psycho-social problems as in the US case analyzed by McGinnis and Foege. The chapter has highlighted structural models and statistical methods for estimating without bias, the effects of behavioral changes and market inputs on health outcomes.

D. Intra-household distribution of health inputs

Equity in health outcomes is an important consideration in health care at the household and national levels. Health outcomes such as height, longevity, or the number of healthy days (Grossman, 1972a, 1972b) cannot be redistributed from one individual to another. However, market inputs into health production, such as medical services, drugs, vaccinations, food, housing, and clothing can be re-allocated to change the existing distribution of health outcomes. Society can improve equity in health outcomes by designing policies directed at changing the distribution of health inputs within households in a particular way. For example, policies that give control of child care resources to mothers can be implemented with good outcomes. An instance of this in the education sector, is a family law in Brazil that extended alimony rights to women living in informal marriages, with the consequence that the schooling of their children increased without altering the amount of family resources (Rangel, 2006). Specifically, the schooling of first born-daughters of less educated women in informal marriages (whose bargaining power was strengthened the most by the law) increased compared with that of first-born daughters of mothers in formal marriages.

The chapter has reviewed unitary and collective household models that may be used to evaluate such policies. If for example, the key assumption of the unitary model (income pooling) is valid, it is not necessary to place child care resources in the hands of mothers to improve child health. Effort instead, should go into increasing household income, without regard to the identity of the person controlling the additional income. However, if the main assumptions of collective models are accepted (Pareto efficiency or bargaining), and the unitary model is not maintained, policies that promote control of resources by particular household members may be needed to improve equity in health outcomes within households.

The main problem in choosing between the above alternative health policy designs is that unitary and collective models are empirically difficult to distinguish one from another. For example, a unitary household may still distribute a market input (e.g., food) like a collective household. In a unitary household, a healthy individual might get greater allocation of calories than an unhealthy individual on efficiency grounds (Pitt, Rosenzweig, and Hassan, 1990). The same allocation pattern may also be observed in a collective household, because the assumption of Pareto efficient outcome of individualistic behavior guarantees that everyone in the household is better-off when greater allocations go to a healthy person.

The assumption that resource allocation decisions are Pareto efficient may be too strong for health care markets. The income pooling assumption is even stronger. The collective household models with a bargaining element do not rely on either the pooling or the efficiency assumption. They are more suited than the unitary or the general collective models to the analysis of intra-household distribution of a non-market outcome such as health status. Within a household, the bargained resource sharing rule seems to play the role of an internal market mechanism.

E. HIV/AIDS and development

Previous research on this topic in developing countries has focused on effects of HIV/AIDS on macroeconomic performance. This line of research needs to be complemented by studies at the household level that provide information on demand for both behavioral and market inputs and their consequences. Behavioral changes can dramatically affect risks of exposure to HIV infection. Information on preventive behavior is critical to designing policies directed at the root cause of HIV transmission. In particular, information derived from demand for VCT services can be used to improve the timing of ARV therapies, to target prevention measures to individuals according to their

HIV status, make treatment more effective in increasing the longevity and productivity of those living with AIDS.

Increasing longevity of HIV-parents, has the additional social benefit of reducing the number of AIDS orphans. A decline in the number of orphans in countries suffering from AIDS pandemic would reduce household and government expenditures on orphans and likely increase saving. Since life-prolonging ARVs are still unaffordable in many low-income countries, a dilemma may arise as to whether, in a program designed to reduce the number of AIDS-related orphans, ARVs should be targeted to mothers or fathers. Although information on the impact of ARVs on survival probabilities by gender may help illuminate the efficiency issue involved here, it would not resolve the ethical dilemma. This example brings to light an instance of the limit of economic analysis in health care policy making.

References

Aaron, H.J. (2001). "Book review: Handbook of health economics". Journal of Health Economics 20 (5), 847–854.

Acton, J.P. (1975). "Nonmonetary factors in the demand for medical services: Some empirical evidence". Journal of Political Economy 83 (3), 595–614.

Ahlburg, D. (1998). "Intergenerational transmission of health". American Economic Review 88 (2), 265–270.

Ainsworth, M., Beegle, K., Nyamete, A. (1996). "The impact of women's schooling on fertility and contraceptive use: A study of 14 sub-Saharan countries". World Bank Economic Review 10 (1), 85–122.

Akin, J., Griffin, C., Guilkey, D.K., Popkin, B.M. (1986). "The demand for primary health care services in the Bicol region of the Philippines". Economic Development and Cultural Change 34 (4), 755–782.

Akin, J., Guilkey, D.K., Hutchinson, P., McIntosh, M. (1998). "Price elasticities of the demand for curative health care with control for sample selectivity and endogenous illness: An analysis for Sri Lanka". Health Economics 7 (6), 509–531.

Alderman, H., Behrman, J.R., Hoddinott, J. (2005). "Nutrition, malnutrition, and economic growth". In: Lopez-Casasnovas, G., Rivera, B., Currais, L. (Eds.), Health and Economic Growth: Findings and Policy Implications. MIT Press, Cambridge, pp. 169–194.

Alderman, H., Chiappori, P.-A., Haddad, L., Hoddinott, J., Kanbur, R. (1995). "Unitary versus collective models of the household: Is it time to shift the burden of proof?" World Bank Research Observer 10 (1), 1–19.

Arndt, C., Lewis, J.D. (2000). "The macroeconomic implications of HIV/AIDS in South Africa: A preliminary assessment". South African Journal of Economics 68 (5), 856–887.

Arrow, K.J. (1963). "Uncertainty and the welfare economics of medical care". American Economic Review 53 (5), 941–973.

Audibert, M. (1986). "Agricultural non-wage production and health status: A case study in tropical environment". Journal of Development Economics 24 (2), 275–291.

Auster, R., Leverson, I., Saracheck, D. (1969). "The production of health, an exploratory study". Journal of Human Resources 4 (4), 411–436.

Banerjee, A., Deaton, A., Duflo, E. (2004). "Wealth, health, and health services in rural Rajasthan". American Economic Review 94 (2), 326–330.

Barro, R.J., Sala-i-Martin, X. (1995). Economic Growth. McGraw–Hill, New York.

Becker, G.S. (1964). Human Capital. Columbia Univ. Press, New York.

Becker, G.S. (1965). "A theory of the allocation of time". Economic Journal 75 (299), 493–517.

Becker, G.S. (1973). "A theory of marriage: Part I". Journal of Political Economy 81 (4), 813–846.

Becker, G.S. (1974). "A theory of social interactions". Journal of Political Economy 82 (6), 1063–1093.

Becker, G.S. (1981). A Treatise on the Family. Harvard Univ. Press, Cambridge, MA.

Behrman, J.R. (1997). "Intrahousehold distribution and the family". In: Rosenzweig, M.R., Stark, O. (Eds.), Handbook of Population and Family Economics. North-Holland, Amsterdam, pp. 125–187.

Behrman, J.R., Deolalikar, A.B. (1987). "Will developing country nutrition improve with income?" Journal of Political Economy 95 (3), 108–138.

Behrman, J.R., Sengupta, P., Todd, P.E. (2005). "Progressing through Progresa: An assessment of a school subsidy experiment in Mexico". Economic Development and Cultural Change 54 (1), 237–275.

Ben-Porath, Y. (1967). "The production of human capital and the life cycle of earnings". Journal of Political Economy 75 (4), 352–365.

Bergstrom, T.C. (1989). "A fresh look at the rotten kid theorem – And other household mysteries". Journal of Political Economy 97 (5), 1138–1159.

Bergstrom, T.C. (1997). "A survey of theories of the family". In: Rosenzweig, M.R., Stark, O. (Eds.), Handbook of Population and Family Economics. North-Holland, Amsterdam, pp. 21–79.

Bindlish, V., Evenson, R. (1993). "Evaluation of the performance of T&V extension in Kenya." Technical paper 208. The World Bank, Washington, DC.

Bindlish, V., Evenson, R. (1997). " The impact of T&V extension in Africa: The experience of Kenya and Burkina Faso". World Bank Research Observer 12 (2), 183–201.

Bliss, C., Stern, N.H. (1978a). "Productivity, wages, and nutrition, Part I: The theory". Journal of Development Economics 5 (4), 331–362.

Bliss, C., Stern, N.H. (1978b). "Productivity, wages, and nutrition, Part II: Some observations". Journal of Development Economics 5 (4), 363–398.

Bloom, D., Mahal, A.S. (1997). "Does the AIDS epidemic threaten economic growth?" Journal of Econometrics 77 (1), 105–124.

Bloom, D., Sachs, J. (1998). "Geography, demography, and economic growth in Africa". Brookings Papers on Economic Activity 1998 (2), 207–295.

Bolduc, D., Lacroix, G., Muller, C. (1996). "The choice of medical providers in rural Benin: A comparison of discrete choice models". Journal of Health Economics 15 (4), 477–498.

Bound, J., Jaeger, D., Baker, R. (1995). "Problems with instrumental variables estimation when the correlation between the instruments and the endogenous explanatory variables is weak". Journal of the American Statistical Association 90 (430), 443–450.

Browning, M. (2000). "The saving behavior of a two-person household". Scandinavian Journal of Economics 10 (2), 236–251.

Browning, M., Chiappori, P.A. (1998). "Efficient intra-household allocations: a general characterization and empirical tests". Econometrica 66, 1241–1278.

Browning, M., Bourguignon, F., Chiappori, P.-A., Lechene, V. (1994). "Incomes and outcomes: A structural model of intrahousehold allocations". Journal of Political Economy 102 (6), 1067–1096.

Browning, M., Bourguignon, F., Chiappori, P.-A., Lechene, V. (2004). "Collective and unitary models: A clarification." Working paper, University of Copenhagen.

Cameron, A.C., Trivedi, P.K., Milne, F., Piggott, J. (1988). "A microeconometric model of demand for health care and health insurance in Australia". Review of Economic Studies 55 (1), 55–106.

Canning, D. (2006). "The economics of HIV/AIDS in low-income countries: The case for prevention". Journal of Economic Perspectives 20 (2), 169–190.

Card, D. (2001). "Estimating the return to schooling: Progress on some persistent econometric problems". Econometrica 69 (5), 1127–1160.

Case, A., Deaton, A. (2005). "Health and wealth among the poor: India and South Africa compared". American Economic Review 95 (2), 229–233.

Chalkley, M., Malcomson, J.M. (2000). "Government purchasing of health services". In: Culyer, A.J., Newhouse, J. (Eds.), Handbook of Health Economics, vols. 1A and 1B. North-Holland, Amsterdam, pp. 847–890.

Chen, Z., Woolley, F. (2001). "A Cournot–Nash model of family decision making". Economic Journal 111 (474), 722–748.

Chiappori, P.-A. (1988). "Rational household labor supply". Econometrica 56 (1), 63–90.

Claxton, K., Sculpher, M., Culyer, A., McCabe, C., Briggs, A., Akehurst, R., Buxton, M., Brazer, J. (2006). "Discounting and cost-effectiveness in NICE". Health Economics 15 (1), 1–4.

Commission on Macroeconomics and Health (2001). Macroeconomic and Health: Investing in Health for Economic Development. Geneva, World Health Organization.

Contoyannis, P., Hurley, J., Grootendorst, P., Jeon, S.-H., Tamblyn, R. (2005). "Estimating the price elasticity of expenditure for prescription drugs in the presence of non-linear schedules: An illustration from Quebec Canada". Health Economics 14 (September), 909–923.

Couderc, N., Ventelou, B. (2005). "AIDS, economic growth and the epidemic trap in Africa". Oxford Development Studies 33 (3–4), 417–426.

Cuddington, J.T. (1993). "Modeling the macroeconomic effects of AIDS with an application to Tanzania". World Bank Economic Review 7 (2), 173–189.

Cuellar, A.E., Gertler, P.J. (2006). "Strategic integration of hospitals and physicians". Journal of Health Economics 25 (1), 1–28.

Culyer, A.J., Newhouse, J. (Eds.) (2000). Handbook of Health Economics, vols. 1A and 1B. North-Holland, Amsterdam.

Currie, J. (2000). "Child health in developed countries". In: Culyer, A.J., Newhouse, J.P. (Eds.), Handbook of Health Economics. North-Holland, Amsterdam, pp. 1053–1090.

Cutler, D.M., Glaeser, E. (2005). "What explains differences in smoking, drinking, and health-related behaviors". American Economic Review 95 (2), 238–242.

Cutler, D.M., Zeckhauser, R.J. (2000). "The anatomy of health insurance". In: Culyer, A.J., Newhouse, J. (Eds.), Handbook of Health Economics, vols. 1A and 1B. North-Holland, Amsterdam, pp. 563–643.

Cropper, M.L. (1977). "Health, investment in health, and occupational choice". Journal of Political Economy 85 (6), 1273–1294.

Dasgupta, P. (1993). An Inquiry into Well-being and Destitution. Oxford Univ. Press, Oxford.

Dercon, S., Krishnan, P. (2000). "In sickness and in health: Risk sharing within households in Ethiopia". Journal of Political Economy 108 (4), 688–727.

Deaton, A. (1997). The Analysis of Household Surveys: A Microeconometric Approach to Development Policy. Johns Hopkins Univ. Press, Baltimore.

Deaton, A. (2006). "The great escape: A review of Robert Fogel's 'The Escape from Hunger and Premature Death', 1700–2100". Journal of Economic Literature 44 (1), 106–144.

Deri, C. (2005). "Social networks and health service utilization". Journal of Health Economics 24 (6), 1076–1107.

Diewert, W.E. (1971). "An application of the Shephard duality theorem: A generalized Leontief production function". Journal of Political Economy 79 (3), 481–507.

Dow, W.H. (1999). "Flexible discrete choice demand models consistent with utility maximization: An application to health care demand". American Journal of Agricultural Economics 81 (3), 680–685.

Dow, W.H., Philipson, T.J., Sala-i-Martin, X. (1999). "Longevity complementaries under competing risks". American Economic Review 89 (5), 1358–1371.

Dowie, J. (1975). "The portfolio approach to health behavior". Social Science and Medicine 9 (11–12), 619–631.

Dranove, D., Satterthwaite, M. (2000). "The industrial organization of health care markets". In: Culyer, A.J., Newhouse, J. (Eds.), In: Handbook of Health Economics, vols. 1A and 1B. North-Holland, pp. 1094–1135.

Duflo, E. (2001). "Schooling and labor market consequences of school construction in Indonesia: Evidence from an unusual policy experiment". American Economic Review 91 (4), 795–813.

Duflo, E. (2004). "The medium-run effects of education expansion: Evidence from a large school construction in Indonesia". Journal of Development Economics 74 (1), 163–197.

Duflo, E., Glennerster, R., Kremer, M. (2008). "Using randomization in development economics research: A toolkit". In: Schultz, T.P., Strauss, J. (Eds.), Handbook of Development Economics, vol. 4. Elsevier/North-Holland, Amsterdam. (Chapter 61 in this book.)

Duflo, E., Udry, C. (2004). "Intrahousehold resource allocation in Cote d'Ivoire: Social norms, separate accounts and consumption choices." Working paper No. 857. Economic Growth Center, Yale University, New Haven.

Ehrlich, I., Chuma, H. (1990). "A model of the demand for longevity and the value of life extension". Journal of Political Economy 98 (4), 761–782.

Evenson, R.E. (2001). "Economic impacts of agricultural research and extension". In: Gardner, B.L., Rausser, G.C. (Eds.), Handbook of Agricultural Economics. North-Holland, Amsterdam, pp. 573–628.

Fauci, A.S. (2006). "Twenty-five years of HIV/AIDS". Science 313 (28 July), 409.

Feachem, R.G., Jamison, D.T. (Eds.) (1991). Disease and Mortality in Sub-Saharan Africa. Oxford Univ. Press, Oxford.

Feldstein, P.J. (1999). Health Care Economics, fifth ed. Delmar, Albany, NY.

Fogel, R.W. (1986). "Physical growth as a measure of the economic well-being of populations: The eighteenth and nineteenth centuries". In: Falkner, F., Tanner, J.M. (Eds.), Human Growth: A Comprehensive Treatise, vol. 3, second ed. Plenum Press, New York, pp. 263–281.

Fogel, R.W. (1997). "New findings on secular trend in nutrition and mortality: Some implications for population theory". In: Rosenzweig, M.R., Stark, O. (Eds.), Handbook of Population and Family Economics, vol. IA. North-Holland, Amsterdam, pp. 433–481.

Fogel, R.W. (2004). The Escape from Hunger and Premature Death: Europe, America and the Third World, 1700–2100. Cambridge Univ. Press, New York.

Fogel, R.W., Costa, D.L. (1997). "A theory of technophysio evolution, with some implications for forecasting population, health care costs, and pension costs". Demography 34 (1), 49–66.

Fuchs, V.R. (Ed.) (1982). Economic Aspects of Health. Univ. of Chicago Press, Chicago.

Fuchs, V.R. (1996). "Economics, values, and health care reform". American Economic Review 86 (1), 1–24.

Fuchs, V.R. (2004). "Reflections on the socioeconomic correlates of health". Journal of Health Economics 23 (4), 653–661.

Fuss, M., McFadden, D. (1978). Production Economics: A Dual Approach to Theory and Applications, vol. 1. North-Holland, Amsterdam.

Gakidou, E.E., Murray, C.J.L., Frenk, J. (2000). "Defining and measuring health inequality: An approach based on the distribution of health expectancy". Bulletin of the World Health Organization 78 (1), 42–54.

Gersovitz, M. (2005). "The HIV epidemic in four African countries seen through the demographic and health surveys". Journal of African Economies 14 (2), 191–246.

Gertler, P. (2000). "Final report: The impact of Progresa on health." Mimeo. International Food Policy Institute, Washington, DC.

Gertler, P. (2004). "Do conditional cash transfers improve child health? Evidence from PROGRESA's controlled randomized experiment". American Economic Review 94 (2), 336–341.

Gertler, P., Locay, L., Sanderson, W. (1987). "Are user fees regressive? The welfare implications of health care financing proposals in Peru". Journal of Econometrics 36 (supp), 67–88.

Gertler, P., van der Gaag, L. (1990). Health Care Financing in Developing Countries. Johns Hopkins Univ. Press, Baltimore.

Glewwe, P., Miguel, E. (2008). "The impact of child health and nutrition on education in less developed countries". In: Schultz, T.P., Strauss, J. (Eds.), Handbook of Development Economics, vol. 4. Elsevier/North-Holland, Amsterdam. (Chapter 56 in this book.)

Glick, P., Sahn, D.E. (2006). "Changes in HIV/AIDS knowledge and testing behavior in Africa: How much and for whom?" Journal of Population Economics, in press.

Glied, S. (2000). "Managed care". In: Culyer, A.J., Newhouse, J. (Eds.), Handbook of Health Economics, vols. 1A and 1B. North-Holland, Amsterdam, pp. 705–753.

Grossman, M. (1972a). "On the concept of health capital and the demand for health". Journal of Political Economy 80 (2), 223–255.

Grossman, M. (1972b). The Demand for Health: A Theoretical and Empirical Investigation. Columbia Univ. Press, New York for the National Bureau of Economic Research.

Grossman, M. (1982). "The demand for health after a decade". Journal of Health Economics 1 (1), 1–3.

Grossman, M. (1998). "On optimal length of life". Journal of Health Economics 17 (4), 499–509.

Grossman, M. (2000). "The human capital model". In: Culyer, A.J., Newhouse, J. (Eds.), Handbook of Health Economics, vols. 1A and 1B. North-Holland, Amsterdam, pp. 347–408.

Grossman, M. (2004). "The demand for health, 30 years later: A very personal retrospective and prospective reflection". Journal of Health Economics 23 (4), 629–636.

Haddad, L., Hoddinott, J. (1994). "Women's income and boy–girl anthropometric status in Cote d'Ivoire". World Development 22 (4), 543–553.

Haddad, L., Hoddinott, J., Alderman, H. (Eds.) (1997). Intrahousehold Resources and Allocation in Developing Countries. Johns Hopkins Univ. Press, Baltimore.

Harrison, G., List, J. (2004). "Field experiments". Journal of Economic Literature 42 (4), 1009–1055.

Hayami, Y. (1969). "Resource endowments and technological change in agriculture: US and Japanese experiences in international perspective". American Journal of Agricultural Economics 51 (5), 1293–1303.

Heckman, J.J., Vytlacil, E.J. (2000). "Local instrumental variables." Technical working paper No. 252, National Bureau of Economic Research.

Heller, P.S. (1982). "A model of the demand for medical and health services in peninsular Malaysia". Social Science and Medicine 16 (3), 267–284.

Hunt-McCool, J., Kiker, B.F., Ng, Y.C. (1994). "Estimates of the demand for medical care under different functional forms". Journal of Applied Econometrics 9 (2), 201–218.

Jack, W.G. (1999). Principles of Health Economics for Developing Countries. The World Bank, World Bank Institute, Washington, DC.

Jacobson, L. (2000). "The family as producer of health – An extended Grossman model". Journal of Health Economics 19 (5), 611–637.

Jamison, D.T., Breman, J.G., Measham, A.R., Alleyne, G., Claeson, M., Evans, D.B., Jha, P., Mills, A., Musgrove, P. (Eds.) (2006). Disease Control Priorities in Developing Countries, second ed. Oxford Univ. Press, New York.

Jones, A.M. (2000). "Health econometrics". In: Culyer, A.J., Newhouse, J. (Eds.), Handbook of Health Economics, vols. 1A and 1B. North-Holland, Amsterdam, pp. 265–344.

Kambou, G., Devarajan, S., Over, M. (1992). "The economic impact of AIDS in an African country: Simulations with a general equilibrium model for Cameroon". Journal of African Economies 1 (1), 109–130.

Kessel, R.A. (1958). "Price discrimination in medicine". Journal of Law and Economics 1 (October), 20–53.

Kiker, B.F. (1969). "The historical roots of the concept of human capital". Journal of Political Economy 74 (5), 481–499.

Leonard, K.L. (2003). "African traditional healers and outcome-contingent contracts for health care". Journal of Development Economics 71 (1), 1–22.

Leonard, K.L., Zivin, J.G. (2005). "Outcome versus service based payments in health care: Lessons from African traditional healers". Health Economics 14 (6), 575–593.

Lindelow, M. (2005). "The utilization of curative health care in Mozambique: Does income matter?" Journal of African Economies 14 (3), 435–482.

Lopez-Casasnovas, G., Rivera, B., Currais, L. (Eds.) (2005). Health and Economic Growth: Findings and Policy Implications. MIT Press, Cambridge.

Lucas, R.E. (1988). "On the mechanics of economic development". Journal of Monetary Economics 22 (1), 3–42.

Lundberg, S., Pollak, R.A. (1993). "Separate spheres bargaining models of marriage". Journal of Political Economy 106 (6), 988–1010.

Lundberg, S., Pollak, R.A. (1994). "Non-cooperative bargaining models of marriage". American Economic Review 84 (2), 132–137.

Lundberg, S., Pollak, R.A. (1996). "Bargaining and distribution in marriage". Journal of Economic Perspectives 10 (4), 139–158.

Lundberg, S., Pollak, R., Wales, T.J. (1997). "Do husbands and wives pool their resources? Evidence from the UK child benefit". Journal of Human Resources 34 (6), 23–67.

Manning, G.W., Newhouse, J.P., Ware, J.E. (1982). "The status of health in demand estimation; Or, beyond excellent, good, fair and poor". In: Fuchs, V.R. (Ed.), Economic Aspects of Health. Univ. of Chicago Press, Chicago, pp. 433–484.

Manning, W.G., Newhouse, J.P., Duan, N., Keeler, E.B., Leibowitz, A. (1987). "Health insurance and the demand for medical care: Evidence from a randomized experiment". American Economic Review 77 (3), 251–277.

Manser, M., Brown, M. (1980). "Marriage and household-making: A bargaining analysis". International Economic Review 21 (1), 31–44.

Mankiw, G., Romer, D., Weil, D. (1992). "A contribution to the empirics of economic growth". Quarterly Journal of Economics 107 (2), 407–437.

McDonald, S., Roberts, J. (2006). "AIDS and economic growth: A human capital approach." Journal of Development Economics, in press.

McElroy, M.B. (1990). "The empirical content of Nash–Bargained household behavior". Journal of Human Resources 25 (4), 559–583.

McElroy, M.B. (1997). "The policy implications of family bargaining and marriage markets". In: Haddad, L., Hoddinott, J., Alderman, H. (Eds.), Intrahousehold Resources and Allocation in Developing Countries. Johns Hopkins Univ. Press, Baltimore, pp. 53–74.

McElroy, M.B., Horney, M.J. (1981). "Nash-bargained decisions: Towards a generalization of the theory of demand". International Economic Review 22 (2), 333–349.

McGinnis, J.M., Foege, W.H. (1993). "Actual causes of death in the United States". Journal of the American Medical Association 270 (18), 2207–2212.

McGuire, T.G. (1983). "Patients' trust and the quality of physicians". Economic Enquiry 21 (2), 203–222.

McGuire, T.G. (2000). "Physician agency". In: Culyer, A.J., Newhouse, J.P. (Eds.), Handbook of Health Economics. North-Holland, Amsterdam, pp. 461–531.

McGuire, T.G., Riordan, M.H. (1994). "Introduction: The industrial organization of health care". Journal of Economics and Management Strategy 3 (1), 1–6.

Miguel, E., Kremer, M. (2004). "Worms: identifying impacts on education and health in the presence of treatment externalities". Econometrica 72, 159–217.

Mills, A. (1998). "Book review: 'An Introduction to Health Economics for Eastern Europe and the Former Soviet Union'. Chincester: John Wiley and Sons, 1997 (by Witter, S. and Ensor, T.)". Health Economics 7 (2), 183.

Mincer, J. (1958). "Investment in human capital and personal distribution of income". Journal of Political Economy 66 (4), 281–302.

Mincer, J. (1974). Schooling, Experience and Earnings. Columbia Univ. Press, New York.

Mocan, H., Tekin, E. (2004). "The demand for medical care in urban China". World Development 32 (2), 289–304.

Mushkin, S.J. (1962). "Health as an investment". Journal of Political Economy 70 (5), 129–157.

Muurinen, J.-M. (1982). "Demand for health: A generalized Grossman model". Journal of Health Economics 1 (1), 5–28.

Mwabu, G. (1989). "Nonmonetary factors in the household choice of health facilities". Economic Development and Cultural Change 37 (2), 383–392.

Nash, J. (1950). "The bargaining problem". Econometrica 18 (2), 155–162.

Newhouse, J.P. (1987). "Health economics and econometrics". American Economic Review 77 (2), 269–274.

Newhouse, J.P. (1996). "Reimbursing health plans and health providers: Production versus selection". Journal of Economic Literature 34 (3), 1236–1263.

North, D.C. (1990). Institutions, Institutional Change and Economic Performance. Cambridge Univ. Press, New York.

Oliver, A., Mossialos, E., Maynard, A. (2005). "The contestable nature of health policy analysis". Health Economics 14 (September), S3–S6.

Parker, S.W., Rubalcava, L., Teruel, G. (2008). "Evaluating conditional schooling-health transfer programs". In: Schultz, T.P., Strauss, J. (Eds.), Handbook of Development Economics, vol. 4. Elsevier/North-Holland, Amsterdam. (Chapter 62 in this book.)

Pitt, M.M., Rosenzweig, M.R. (1985). "Health and nutrition consumption across and within farm households". Review of Economics and Statistics 67 (2), 212–223.

Pitt, M.M., Rosenzweig, M.R. (1986). "Agricultural prices, food consumption, and the health and productivity of Indonesian farmers". In: Singh, I.J., Squire, L., Strauss, J. (Eds.), Agricultural Household Models: Extension, Application and Policy. Johns Hopkins Univ. Press, Baltimore, MD, pp. 153–182.

Pitt, M.M., Rosenzweig, M.R., Hassan, M.N. (1990). "Productivity, health, and inequality in the intrahousehold distribution of food in low-income countries". American Economic Review 80 (5), 1139–1156.

Pritchett, L., Summers, L.H. (1996). "Wealthier is healthier". Journal of Human Resources 31 (4), 841–868.

Quisumbing, A., Maluccio, J. (2003). "Resources at marriage and intrahousehold allocation: Evidence from Bangladesh, Ethiopia, Indonesia, and South Africa". Oxford Bulletin of Economics and Statistics 65 (3), 283–327.

Rangel, M. (2006). "Alimony rights and intrahousehold allocation of resources: Evidence from Brazil". Economic Journal 116 (513), 627–658.

Ravallion, M. (2008). "Evaluating anti-poverty programs". In: Schultz, T.P., Strauss, J. (Eds.), Handbook of Development Economics, vol. 4. Elsevier/North-Holland, Amsterdam. (Chapter 59 in this book.)

Ried, W. (1998). "Comparative dynamic analysis of the full Grossman model". Journal of Health Economics 17 (4), 383–425.

Risso, J. (2005). "Are HMOs bad for health maintenance?" Health Economics 14 (1), 1117–1131.

Rivera, B., Currais, L. (2005). "Individual returns to health in Brazil: A quantile regression analysis". In: Lopez-Casasnovas, G., Rivera, B., Currais, L. (Eds.), Health and Economic Growth: Findings and Policy Implications. MIT Press, Cambridge, pp. 287–311.

Roe, T.L., Smith, R.B.W. (2006). "Disease dynamics and economic growth." Mimeo, University of Minnesota.

Rosenzweig, M.R. (1986). "Program interventions, intrahousehold distribution and the welfare of individuals". World Development 14 (2), 233–243.

Rosenzweig, M.R., Schultz, T.P. (1982). "The behavior of mothers as inputs to child health: The determinants of birth weight, gestation, and the rate of fetal growth". In: Fuchs, V.R. (Ed.), Economic Aspects of Health. Univ. of Chicago Press, Chicago, pp. 53–92.

Rosenzweig, M.R., Schultz, T.P. (1983). "Estimating a household production function: Heterogeneity, the demand for health inputs, and their effects on birth weight". Journal of Political Economy 91 (5), 723–746.

Rosenzweig, M.R., Wolpin, K.I. (2000). "Natural 'natural' experiments in economics". Journal of Economic Literature 38 (4), 827–874.

Sahn, D.E., Younger, S.D., Genicot, G. (2003). "The demand for health care services in rural Tanzania". Oxford Bulletin of Economics and Statistics 65 (2), 241–259.

Sala-i-Martin, X. (2005). "On the Health Poverty Trap". In: Lopez-Casasnovas, G., Rivera, B., Currais, L. (Eds.), Health and Economic Growth: Findings and Policy Implications. MIT Press, Cambridge, pp. 95–114.

Sauerbon, R.A., Nougtara, A., Latimer, E. (1994). "The price elasticity of the demand for health care in Burkina Faso: Differences across age and income groups". Health Policy and Planning 9 (2), 185–192.

Schmalensee, R., Willig, R. (Eds.) (1989). Handbook of Industrial Organization. North-Holland, Amsterdam.

Schneider, P., Hanson, K. (2006). "Horizontal equity in utilization of care and fairness of health financing: A comparison of micro-health insurance and user fees in Rwanda". Health Economics 15 (1), 19–31.

Schultz, T.P. (1999). "Health and schooling in Africa". Journal of Economic Perspectives 13 (3), 67–88.

Schultz, T.P. (2002). "Wage gains associated with height as a form of human capital". American Economic Review 92 (2), 349–353.

Schultz, T.P. (2003). "Wage rentals for reproducible human capital: Evidence from Ghana and the Ivory Coast". Economics and Human Biology 1 (3), 331–366.

Schultz, T.P. (2004). "Health economics and applications in developing countries". Journal of Health Economics 23 (4), 637–641.

Schultz, T.P., Tansel, A. (1997). "Wage and labor supply effects of illness in Côte d'Ivoire and Ghana: Instrumental variable estimates for days disabled". Journal of Development Economics 53 (2), 251–286.

Schultz, T.W. (1960). "Capital formation by education". Journal of Political Economy 68 (6), 571–583.

Schultz, T.W. (1961). "Investments in human capital". American Economic Review 51 (1), 1–17.

Singh, I.J., Squire, L., Strauss, J. (Eds.) (1986). Agricultural Household models: Extension, Application and Policy. Johns Hopkins University Press, Baltimore, MD.

Stiglitz, J.E. (1989). "Imperfect information in the product market". In: Schmalensee, R., Willig, R. (Eds.), Handbook of Industrial Organization. North-Holland, Amsterdam, pp. 769–847.

Strauss, J. (1984). "Joint determination of food consumption and production in rural Sierra Leone: Estimates of a household firm model". Journal of Development Economics 14 (1), 77–103.

Strauss, J. (1986). "Does better nutrition raise farm productivity?" Journal of Political Economy 94 (2), 297–320.

Strauss, J., Mwabu, G., Beegle, K. (2000). "Intrahousehold allocations: A review of theories and empirical evidence". Journal of African Economies 9, 83–143.

Strauss, J., Thomas, D. (1995). "Human resources: Empirical modeling of household and family decisions". In: Behrman, J., Srinivasan, T.N. (Eds.), Handbook of Development Economics, vol. 3A. North-Holland, Amsterdam, pp. 1883–2023.

Strauss, J., Thomas, D. (1998). "Health, nutrition, and economic development". Journal of Economic Literature 36 (2), 766–817.

Strauss, J., Thomas, D. (2008). "Health over the lifecourse". In: Schultz, T.P., Strauss, J. (Eds.), Handbook of Development Economics, vol. 4. Elsevier/North-Holland, Amsterdam. (Chapter 54 in this book.)

Srinivasan, T.N. (1992). "Undernutrition: Concepts, Measurements, and Policy Implications". In: Osmani, S.R. (Ed.), Nutrition and Poverty. Oxford Univ. Press, Oxford, pp. 95–120.

Srinivasan, T.N. (1994). "Destitution: A discourse". Journal of Economic Literature 32 (4), 1842–1855.

Subramanian, S., Deaton, A. (1996). "The demand for food and calories". Journal of Political Economy 104 (1), 133–162.

Summers, L.H. (1992). "Investing in all the people." Working paper WPS 905. Policy Research, The World Bank, Washington, DC.

Thirumurthy, H., Zivin, J.G., Goldstein, M. (2005). "The economic impact of AIDS treatment: Labor supply in Western Kenya." Working paper. Economic Growth Center, Yale University, and National Bureau of Economic Research (NBER).

Thomas, D. (1990). "Intrahousehold resource allocation: An inferential approach". Journal of Human Resources 25 (4), 635–664.

Thomas, D. (2000). "Comments on 'intrahousehold allocations'". Journal of African Economies 9, 144–149.

Thomas, D., Strauss, J. (1997). "Health and wages: Evidence on men and women in Brazil". Journal of Econometrics 77 (1), 159–185.

Thomas, D., Frankenberg, E., Friedman, J., Habicht, J.-P., Hakimi, M., Ingwersen, N., Jones, N., McKelvey, C., Pelto, G., Sikoki, B., Seeman, T., Smith, J.P., Sumantri, C., Suriastini, W., Wilopo, S. (2006). "Causal effect of health on labor market outcomes: Experimental evidence." Mimeo. University of California, Los Angeles.

Todd, P. (2008). "Evaluating social programs with endogenous program placement and selection of the treated". In: Schultz, T.P., Strauss, J. (Eds.), Handbook of Development Economics, vol. 4. Elsevier/North-Holland, Amsterdam. (Chapter 60 in this book.)

Udry, C. (1996). "Gender, agricultural production and, and the theory of the householder". Journal of Political Economy 104 (5), 1010–1046.

Van den Heever, A.M. (1998). "Private sector health reform in South Africa". Health Economics 7 (4), 281–289.

Vermeulen, F. (2002). "Collective household models: Principles and main results". Journal of Economic Surveys 16 (4), 533–564.

Weisbrod, B.A. (1961). "The valuation of human capital". Journal of Political Economy 69 (5), 425–436.

Williams, A. (1987). "Health economics: The cheerful face of the dismal science?" In: Williams, A. (Ed.), Health Economics. Oxford Univ. Press, New York.

Williamson, O. (2000). "The new institutional economics: Taking stock, looking ahead". Journal of Economic Literature 38 (3), 595–613.

Wooldridge, J.M. (1997). "On two-stage least squares estimation of the average treatment effect in a random coefficient model". Economics Letters 56, 129–133.

Wooldridge, J.M. (2002). Econometric Analysis of Cross Section and Panel Data. MIT Press, Cambridge, MA.

World Bank (1993). World Development Report 1993: Investing in Health. Oxford Univ. Press, New York.

World Bank (1997). Confronting AIDS: Public Priorities, in a Global Epidemic. Oxford Univ. Press, New York.

World Bank (2000). World Development Report. Oxford Univ. Press, Oxford.

World Bank (2005). Committing to Results: Improving the Effectiveness of HIV/AIDS Assistance. The World Bank, Washington, DC.

World Health Organization (WHO) (1948). Constitution of the World Health Organization. United Nations, New York.

World Health Organization (WHO) (2004). World Health Report 2004. World Health Organization, Geneva.

World Health Organization (WHO) (2005). World Health Report 2005. World Health Organization, Geneva.

Young, A. (2005). "The gift of the dying: The tragedy of AIDS and the wealth of future African generations". Quarterly Journal of Economics 120 (2), 423–466.

Zweifel, P., Breyer, F. (1997). Health Economics. Oxford Univ. Press, New York.

Chapter 54

HEALTH OVER THE LIFE COURSE*

JOHN STRAUSS

Department of Economics, University of Southern California, 3620 South Vermont Avenue, 306A Kaprielian Hall, Los Angeles, CA 90089-0253, USA

DUNCAN THOMAS

Department of Economics, Duke University, Box 90097, Durham, NC 27708, USA

Contents

* The authors thank Facundo Cuevas for research assistance, Sheila Evans and Eileen Miech for editorial assistance and Jere Behrman, Amar Hamoudi, Chris Ksoll, Doug McKee, Jenna Nobles, Tristan Reed, and T. Paul Schultz for very helpful comments. This research was supported, in part, by NIH grants AG020905, HD047522, HD049766 and HD050452.

Handbook of Development Economics, Volume 4
© 2008 Elsevier B.V.   All rights reserved
DOI: 10.1016/S1573-4471(07)04054-5

Abstract

In recent years, significant advances have been made in better understanding the complex relationships between health and development. This reflects the combined effects of methodological innovations at both the theoretical and empirical level, the integration of insights from the biological and health sciences into economic analyses as well as improvements in the quantity and quality of data on population health and socio-economic status. To provide a foundation for discussing these advances, we describe static and dynamic models of the evolution of health over the life course in conjunction with the inter-relationships between health, other human capital outcomes and economic prosperity. Facts about health and development at both the aggregate and individual levels are presented along with a discussion of the importance of measurement. We proceed to review the empirical literature with a goal of highlighting emerging lines of scientific inquiry that are likely to have an important impact on the field. We begin with recent work that relates health events in early life, including in utero, to health, human capital and economic success in later life. We then turn to adult health and its relationship with socio-economic success, exploring the impact of health on economic outcomes and *vice versa* as well as the links between health and consumption smoothing. Recent evidence from the empirical literature on the micro-level impacts of HIV/AIDS on development is summarized. We conclude that developments on the horizon suggest a very exciting future for scientific research in this area.

Keywords

health, economic development

JEL classification: O12, I1, D13

1. Introduction

This chapter provides a review of recent advances in microeconomic research on health over the life course, emphasizing empirical findings in developing country contexts. The literature in this field has made substantial progress on many fronts in recent years. This is a reflection of several factors. First, innovative research designs have been used very creatively to shed new light on important and, at least until recently, unresolved questions. The most influential of these designs have a strong foundation in economic theory and, in many cases, also integrate insights from biology. Second, clever ways have been used to isolate causal pathways in studies that use observational or quasi-experimental methods and, increasingly, random assignment treatment-control designs. Third, and closely related, is the fact that studies have exploited new sources of data that contain a rich and improving array of measures of health and socio-economic success, often with repeated measures for the same individual over time.

The relationship between health and development is, and promises to continue to be, an extremely active line of inquiry not only in economics but also in the population and health sciences. By way of examples, recent and on-going research includes studies that highlight the complex dynamics underlying the joint evolution of different domains of health and socio-economic success over the life course. Other work seeks to isolate some of the causal pathways through which different dimensions of health might affect indicators of socio-economic status (SES) and, in turn, how individual, family and community resources affect health. Studies have highlighted the ways in which early life health, including fetal health, potentially influence health and well being over the entire life course. Those studies underscore the importance of understanding the evolution of health from conception to the end of life. This, and other work, indicates the key role played by genes, and their interaction with the environment, in influencing health outcomes throughout life. This emerging body of research promises to yield important new insights that will contribute to better understanding the relationships between population health and economic development.

Our primary goal is to assess the current state of scientific knowledge regarding the dynamic inter-linkages between health and economic prosperity at the micro level. We do not focus on the policy implications of this research or on the allocation of resources to health or other sectors, health care financing or the production and distribution of health services. These and other issues are discussed in considerable detail in Jamison et al. (2006). The Copenhagen Consensus brought together leading economists to rank the global challenges in terms of their impact on human well-being. They concluded that three of the top four priorities relate to health – controlling HIV/AIDS, providing micronutrients and controlling malaria. See Lomborg (2004, 2006) for a discussion of the costs and benefits associated with such interventions.[1]

---

[1] Of particular relevance here are Behrman, Alderman and Hoddinott (2004) who discuss the costs and benefits of nutrition-related interventions and Mills and Shillcutt (2004) who discuss communicable diseases.

The next section discusses some key conceptual and methodological issues in the literature, highlighting the dynamics of health over the life course. It is followed by a brief description of some basic facts on health and development in which we pay special attention to concerns about interpretation of different health indicators. Those sections set the stage for a critical assessment of the evidence. We begin with a review of the literature on the long arm of childhood health reaching into the health and economic well-being of adults. The relationships between childhood health and other dimensions of human capital are discussed. We then turn to adult health and its relationship with socio-economic success, exploring the impact of health on economic outcomes and *vice versa*. This is followed by a discussion of health and consumption smoothing. We end with a brief discussion of HIV/AIDS, concentrating on recent studies that examine the impacts of HIV/AIDS on socio-economic outcomes.

2. Conceptual framework and methods

The empirical literature on health is replete with correlations relating measures of resources at the individual or family level, such as income, wealth or education, to many domains of individual health including mortality, other indicators of health status, health behaviors and inputs into the production of health. How these correlations should be interpreted has played a central role in the literature for at least two decades and while substantial progress has been made in understanding the links between health and economic prosperity, many questions remain unresolved.

There are at least three sets of issues that have been stumbling blocks in this literature. First, health varies over the life course and there is limited understanding of the complex dynamics underlying relationships between health, health behaviors and other factors that influence the well-being of individuals; there is even less understanding of how these relationships evolve over the life course. Second, poor health likely affects economic well-being while limited economic resources presumably affect health investments and outcomes, and there are quite likely to be feedbacks between health and resources. It has been extremely difficult to establish causality, which likely operates in both directions. Interpretation of evidence is further complicated by unobserved heterogeneity that affects both health and material well-being. Third, health is multidimensional and hard to measure. Not only do many health markers fluctuate randomly over time but, potentially more pernicious for interpretation, some widely-used indicators of health and health behaviors are likely to be measured with errors that are systematically related to characteristics of interest in many models such as age, education or income.

This section discusses a series of simple economic models of decisions regarding investment in health and health outcomes that provide a starting place to shed light on these issues. To fix ideas, we begin with static models and then proceed to discuss dynamic models of the evolution of health over the life course. The section ends with a discussion of the implications of the models for research design and empirical methods.

2.1. Static models of health investments and health outcomes

2.1.1. Health production functions

Models of the production of health in a static context, and the implications of those models for interpreting relationships between health and development, have been discussed extensively (see for example, Schultz, 1984, 2005; Strauss, 1986, 1993; Behrman and Deolalikar, 1988; Behrman, 1996; Strauss and Thomas, 1995, 1998; Smith, 1999). We briefly review some key models and important conceptual issues to provide a foundation for discussion of some of the dynamic concerns that have received less attention.

We are concerned with health across the entire life course from conception to death. Parents are assumed to make key health decisions for children whereas an adult is assumed to make his or her own decisions. It is important to distinguish health outcomes, such as height, body mass, disease incidence or physical functioning, from health inputs and health behaviors which might include nutrient intakes, exercise, smoking, and utilization of preventive or curative health care.[2]

Assume there is a static health production function for an individual:

$$H = H(N; A, B_H, D, \mu) \tag{1}$$

where H represents an array of measured health outcomes. They depend on a vector of health inputs and behaviors, N. These include, for example, use of health care services, nutrient intake, energy output and time allocated directly or indirectly to the production of health. Examples of behaviors that might contribute to health outcomes include smoking, risky or very stressful lifestyles. The inputs, N, are under the control of the individual. The technology, or shape of the underlying health production function is likely to vary over the life course and so varies with age and, possibly, with other socio-demographic characteristics, A, such as gender. The technology may also vary with dimensions of family background that affect health, B_H, such as parental health and genetic endowment. Technology will likely vary with environmental factors, D, such as the disease environment, public health infrastructure and treatment practices or standards of care.

There are two classes of unobserved characteristics, μ, in the health production function. First, there are unobserved factors that are assumed to be known to the individual but are not known to the econometrician; such as innate healthiness. Second, μ reflects the fact that health and its determinants are potentially measured with error. In some cases, these errors will be random (the "classical" measurement error case) but in some cases the errors may be systematically related to observed or unobserved factors that affect health.

---

[2] The distinction is not always clean since some health outputs may also be intermediate inputs into other outputs. For example, disease incidence might affect body mass and *vice versa*. We abstract from these complications. Note also that some health outputs may be produced jointly, while others may be produced solely.

The health production function, which is analogous to an agricultural or manufacturing production function, represents the technological and biological constraints that determine how inputs are converted into outputs. In the agricultural economics literature, Nelson (1964) and Hayami and Ruttan (1971) suggested that the available set of technologies is not likely to be the same over time, across countries or even within countries and will depend on the rate of adoption of new technology, the diffusion of technology and the adaption of technology to local settings. Hayami and Ruttan (1971) called the envelope of feasible technological relationships a meta-production function and argued that a farmer at a point in time is likely to face the opportunities on only part of the meta-production function. The same concept probably applies to the production function of health which depends on the development, diffusion, adaption and availability of new technologies (see Cutler, 2004, for an insightful discussion). Moreover, in the case of health, the part of the meta-production function that an individual faces may be a function of his or her own previous choices or the choices of others living in the community. For instance, a person who is HIV positive may be on a different part of the meta-production function than someone who is HIV negative. This substantially complicates identification and estimation of a health production function as it is no longer a technical relationship but incorporates behavioral choices.

2.1.2. Modeling behavioral choices

More generally, behavioral choices play a central role in the conceptual framework. Assume that an individual's welfare depends on labor supply, L, and consumption of purchased goods, C. Utility, U, is assumed to depend on health outputs, H, as well as observed characteristics such as socio-demographic characteristics, A, non-health human capital (including schooling) and family background, B_U:

$$U = U(C, L; H, A, B_U, \xi). \tag{2}$$

The unobserved characteristics, ξ, include heterogeneity in tastes which may be related to unobserved characteristics that affect the production of health (1), preferences, for example, may themselves depend on innate healthiness.

Resource allocations are constrained by budget and time constraints in addition to the health production function (1). Suppose that the individual earns wage, w, for each unit of labor supplied and that asset or nonlabor income is V. The budget constraint is:

$$p_c C^* + p_n N^C = wL + V. \tag{3}$$

For expositional simplicity, the vector of consumption, C, has been decomposed into two elements: consumption that is not related to the production of health, C^*, with prices, p_c, and a vector of purchased health inputs, N^C, with prices, p_n. In practice, the division between these groups is not always clear and not all health inputs may be valued directly in the utility function. Time allocated to the production of health, N^T, leisure and labor supply, L, is equal to the individual's total time endowment. Note that the vector of inputs in the health production, N, includes not only N^C and N^T but also non-purchased inputs that are not valued directly in the utility function.

Solving the system (1) through (3) yields a function for each health input and output which will depend on prices of consumption and health inputs along with the observed and unobserved characteristics that affect health and utility including demography, human capital and background, nonlabor income and the disease environment. In addition, each function depends on wages, which are the outcome of choices made by the individual and so it is necessary to specify a wage function in order to substitute for wages and specify a reduced form demand function for health inputs and outputs. We turn, therefore, to the determination of wages.

2.1.3. Wages and health

Assume that an individual's real wage is equal to his marginal product. A person's wage, w, varies with health outputs, H, socio-demographic characteristics, A, as well as own and family background characteristics, B_w, such as schooling, other non-health human capital, parents' schooling and health:

$$w = w(H; A, B_w, I, \alpha). \tag{4}$$

As discussed below, health outputs (such as height or body mass) may affect wages through better physical or mental health as well as through strength and endurance. Local community infrastructure, I, such as electrification or road density, may be related to labor demand, or to various work characteristics which are valued separately from wages. Wages will also be influenced by unobserved factors, α. These might include ability, effort and school quality (which appear in A if they are measured) along with tastes like ambition and competitiveness that might affect economic productivity as well as tastes for investment in human capital. Note that some of these unobserved characteristics are shared with μ in the health production function (1) and tastes, ξ, that condition welfare in (2). In addition, variation in wages due to measurement error will be reflected in α.

As is the case in the interpretation of schooling in estimated wage functions (Card, 1999), interpretation of health covariates in the wage function (4) is plagued by potential bias due to unobserved heterogeneity that is correlated with both wages and health. For example, unobserved factors that affect wages, α, may well be correlated with health measures, either directly, or through being correlated with unobserved innate healthiness or tastes for investments in human capital, μ. For instance, nutrition as an infant and young child affects height as an adult; moreover the literature indicates that early childhood nutrition is correlated with cognitive development (Pollitt et al., 1993, among numerous others), which may well affect productivity at work. Many empirical wage functions have reported a positive relationship between wages and height. This might be driven by the fact that wages are affected by cognitive achievement which is not observed but is correlated with height because both cognition and height are driven by early childhood investments.

In models of health and wages, there are at least two additional substantively important sources of unobserved heterogeneity. First, the biological and social science literatures suggest there may be contemporaneous feedbacks between health and economic productivity. This will arise, for example, if increases in income caused by improvements in health are spent, at least in part, in ways that further improve health. Specifically, say improvements in the health of a worker cause his or her wages to be higher and that results in higher earnings. There will be a feedback effect if the worker spends some of the additional income on inputs into the health production function (1), such as improved diet (perhaps more food and hence more calories or higher valued foods, that have more protein, iron, vitamin A, or some other micronutrients), improved sanitation and living conditions or improved health care. Feedbacks will arise if greater consumption of these inputs results in improved health. These issues are taken up in more detail below.

As noted above, a second potentially important source of unobserved heterogeneity in models of wages and health revolves around measurement of health. We defer a fuller discussion to the next section.

2.1.4. Reduced form demand for health investments and outcomes

Solving the optimization program (1), (2), (3) and (4) for an adult, letting λ be the marginal utility of income and assuming interior solutions,[3] the first-order condition with respect to consumption of the jth health input, N_j, is:

$$\frac{\partial U}{\partial N_j} + \frac{\partial U}{\partial H}\frac{\partial H}{\partial N_j} = \lambda \left(p_{n_j} - L\left[\frac{\partial w}{\partial H}\frac{\partial H}{\partial N_j}\right] - w\left[\frac{\partial L}{\partial H}\frac{\partial H}{\partial N_j}\right] \right) \tag{5}$$

where the first element is zero if N_j is not valued in and of itself (is not an element of C in (2)).

This first-order condition highlights an important substantive point. If health inputs raise wages or labor supply through improving health outcomes, then there will be a decline in the shadow price of inputs that affect health, inducing greater use of those inputs (assuming the usual regularity conditions). In the model, it is possible that the rate of change of health input shadow prices will depend on the level of health, H. Indeed, biomedical evidence suggests that, in some instances, links between health inputs and outputs are not linear. For example, when levels of iron in the blood fall below a threshold (say hemoglobin levels below 13 g/dl), work capacity is reduced; however, additional iron above this threshold has no impact on work capacity. This has been demonstrated in rigorous clinical trials with humans and animals, and the mechanisms underlying the non-linear relationship are well-understood right down to the cell level (Haas and Brownlie, 2001).

---

[3] Corner solutions complicate the exposition. Under the assumptions of the model, an individual will work if the wage exceeds the shadow value of time and, in that case, the quantity of time allocated to labor supply will equate the wage to the shadow value of time.

There is a reduced form demand function for each element of the vector of health inputs, N, and each of the health outputs, H, which we collect into the vector θ:

$$\theta = \theta(p_n, p_c, A, B, V, D, I, \varepsilon). \tag{6}$$

Each demand function depends on health input prices, p_n, consumption prices, p_c, demographic characteristics, A, non-health human capital and family background, B (which encompasses those dimensions of background that affect the production of health, B_h, productivity in the labor market, B_w, and preferences, B_U), nonlabor income, V, the disease and health environment, D, and non-health determinants of wages, I. All of these characteristics are assumed to be exogenous to the individual's decisions about behaviors and investments related to health, time allocation and resource allocation. In addition, they are all, by definition, observed. There are also factors which influence demand for each of the health inputs and outputs that are not observed, ε. These encompass not only tastes, ξ, but also innate healthiness, μ, and characteristics such as ability and effort, α, which affect wages.

2.1.5. Estimation of the relationship between health and economic prosperity

Under the assumptions we have made, it is clear that health is potentially affected by earnings and that earnings may depend on health. There is a vast literature documenting a strong positive correlation between health and different markers of socio-economic status (SES) across the globe. Identifying the causal pathways underlying this correlation – and the extent to which it is driven by unobserved heterogeneity in a particular empirical model – is not straightforward. We provide a brief discussion of models that examine the impact of health on wages or economic productivity and then turn to models that explore the effect of SES on health.

Inspection of (4) and (6) illustrates one of the difficulties associated with disentangling the causal effect of health on wages and *vice versa*. Specifically, there are unobserved factors that affect both wages and utility as indicated by α appearing in the wage function, (5), and also being an element of ε in the health demand function, (6). Intuitively, this may be because unobserved dimensions of ability which affect wages also impact utility because, for example, more able people transform the same inputs into a different level of utility than less able people. Common unobserved heterogeneity may also reflect dimensions of tastes, such as inter-temporal preferences, that affect both wages and utility. These are examples of contemporaneous feedbacks discussed above. An analogous argument applies to disentangling the causal effect of health on labor supply.

Comparing the functions (4) and (6) also suggests potential instruments to identify the causal effect of health on economic productivity. Conditional on health outcomes, H, and levels of local infrastructure, I, productivity should not be affected by health input prices, p_n, or the disease environment, E. For example, the accessibility, price and quality of health services available to an individual, along with the epidemiological environment in which he or she is living, are potential instruments to the extent they affect health but have no direct impact on wages in (4). The same characteristics are also potential instruments for inputs into the health production function (1). Similarly, factors, I, that affect wages and hours of work, such as local labor demand conditions and levels of economic infrastructure, are potential instruments for earnings and other indicators of SES in conditional demand functions that relate health to SES. Note that if the health services available to an individual are the outcome of choices – such as decisions about where to live or occupational choice – then they are not appropriate instruments. The same issue applies to prices of local health inputs, the local disease environment and local labor market conditions.

Many studies examine how health covaries with schooling or some other dimension of background, B, or with nonlabor income, V. These estimates can be interpreted in the context of the static reduced form model (6) although, as we shall see below, moving to dynamic framework complicates interpretation. Moreover, there is substantial interest in estimating the demand for health conditional on an individual's earnings or total income. Earnings is the product of wages, w, and labor supply, L, both of which are choices that are likely correlated with unobserved characteristics that affect health in even this simple model. Thus, wages, labor supply and earnings should be treated as endogenous in these conditional demand for health functions. The same principle applies to demand functions that are conditioned on total household income or total expenditure which are potentially more complicated if household living arrangements are associated with unobserved characteristics that affect individual health. The key point is that consistent estimation of these conditional demand for health functions will take the joint determination of health and SES into account.

2.2. Dynamic models of health investments and health outcomes

Health evolves over the life course. For at least some health behaviors and health outcomes, health at one point in the life course affects health in later life, and emerging evidence suggests that even health *in utero* is predictive of health as an adult. Incorporating dynamics into models of health not only builds more realism into the models but also yields important theoretical insights as well as useful implications for the implementation and interpretation of empirical applications. Building on the foundation laid in the previous subsection, we turn now to sketching out some of these implications.

2.2.1. Dynamic health production function

It is natural to start with a dynamic health production function in which current health status, H_t, depends on all current and prior health inputs, $N_\sigma, \sigma = 0, \ldots, t$, the disease or public health environment, D_σ (Grossman, 1972), current and prior demographic characteristics such as age, A_σ, which are time-varying and other demographic and background characteristics, B_H, which are time invariant.

$$H_t = H(N_t, N_{t-1}, \ldots, N_0, D_t, D_{t-1}, \ldots, D_0, A_t, A_{t-1}, \ldots, A_0, B_H,$$

$$\mu, \mu_t, \mu_{t-1}, \ldots, \mu_0). \tag{7}$$

Time is treated as discrete and all characteristics are measured at the end of the time period. We have assumed that the unobserved, individual-level health endowment comprises two components: one that is time-invariant, μ, and is known to the individual, and another that varies over time, $\mu_\sigma, \sigma = 0, \ldots, t$. In principle, all past realizations of μ may be known to an individual although this knowledge may come at a cost (such as testing) and the implications of these innovations may not be fully absorbed.

2.2.2. Allocating resources over the life course

At each point over the life course, t, an individual will choose consumption, C, and labor supply, L, to maximize the present discounted value of life-time welfare, Ψ, conditional on health outcomes, H, demographic characteristics, A, background, B_U, and tastes, ξ, a component of which is time invariant and a component which may vary over time:

$$\Psi_\tau = \Psi \left\{ E_\tau \delta_t^{t-1} U_t(C_t, L_t; H_t, A_t, B_U, \xi, \xi_t) \right\} \quad t = \tau, \tau + 1, \ldots, T. \tag{8}$$

Welfare in any period, τ, is updated depending on realizations of unobserved characteristics at that point. The individual's discount rate δ_t is allowed to vary over the life course. We have made no assumptions about separability of preferences over time and so welfare may depend on prior health and demographic characteristics as well as predictions about their trajectory in the future.

Choices are constrained by the period-specific technology of health production, a period-by-period time budget constraint which limits the sum of hours of leisure, work and time spent on investment in health in that period and a lifetime budget constraint:

$$V_T = \prod_{t=1}^{T}(1+r_t)V_0 + \sum_{t=1}^{T} \left(\prod_{\tau=t}^{T}(1+r_\tau) \right) \left\{ w_t L_t - \left(p_{ct}C_t^* + p_{nt}N_t^c \right) \right\}. \tag{9}$$

V_T is assets at the end of life which may be positive (bequests), zero or negative (debts). V_0 is assets at the beginning of life (inheritances) and r_t is the interest rate so the first term on the right-hand side of (9) is the present discounted value of initial assets. Asset accumulation in each period $t = 1, \ldots, T$ is the value of the difference between earnings and expenditure that period. Earnings is the product of working L_t hours at wage w_t. Expenditure is given by spending on consumption goods C_t^* and inputs into the health production function N_{ct} valued at prices p_{ct} and p_{nt} respectively. The second term in (9) is the sum of the present discounted value of additions to assets in each period. The extent to which total assets in any period can be negative is limited by whatever constraints exist on borrowing. They are straightforward to include but are not explicitly specified in this general framework.

2.2.3. Economic productivity and health over the life course

To derive dynamic demand functions for health inputs and outcomes, we need to specify the determinants of wages and labor supply. Taking as given that some dimensions of health contain both a stock and a flow component, labor productivity, w, will likely depend not only on current health, but also prior health investments, N, and health outcomes, H. For example, the former will occur if an investment in health in early adulthood (say exercise) affects productivity (because of elevated endurance) over and above the impact of health outcomes on productivity. An example of the latter might arise if being overweight at a point in time affects productivity later in life, conditional on current weight. As above, we collect health inputs and outcomes in the vector θ.

Current labor productivity will also vary with time-invariant background characteristics that affect labor market outcomes, B_w, as well as current and prior demographic characteristics, A, that do vary with time. Wages will also depend on variation in economic infrastructure and labor demand over time, I:

$$w_t = w(\theta_t, \theta_{t-1}, \ldots, \theta_0; B_w, A_t, \ldots, A_0, I_t, \ldots, I_0; \alpha, \alpha_t). \tag{10}$$

There are at least three sources of unobserved heterogeneity, each of which may be correlated with current or prior θ. First, time-invariant unobserved ability, α, may be correlated with health if some people are inherently better able to manage health risks or disease insults. For example, Goldman and Smith (2002) demonstrate that the better educated are better at self-managing health problems by adhering more closely to treatment protocols. Second, time-varying unobserved ability, α_t, may depend, in part, on prior health outcomes. This will arise, for example, if early childhood health affects cognitive development or performance in school (Pollitt et al., 1993; Behrman, 1996). Third, part of α_t reflects measurement error in wages which may be related to current effort that is affected by health status.

Note that the model (10) is specified in a sufficiently general form so that levels of health and changes in health may interact in their influence on productivity and hours of work. For example, the effect of a loss in body mass due to a crippling bout of diarrhea is likely to differ depending on the initial level of body mass of the individual. It is worth emphasizing that the multi-dimensionality of health inputs and outcomes underscores the importance of taking care in specifying non-linearities in relationships between health and economic success. For example, there may be non-linear relationships between wages and body mass as seen in the U-shaped association between BMI and mortality. However, it is also possible that there are important interactions between dimensions of health – and other controls – and those can provide insights into the complementarities and substitutability between different health domains. Crimmins and Finch (2006) provide an example. They argue that part of the dramatic increases in life expectancy in the 19th and 20th century can be attributed to the complementary effects of improved nutrition and reduced inflammation because of lower rates of infection and trauma. Since inflammation and BMI tend to be positively correlated (Crimmins et al.,

2007), a non-linear relationship between BMI and wages might be a reflection of a complementary effect of inflammation.

As in the static case, there is an analogous relationship between labor supply and health, controlling demographics, schooling, background and infrastructure. The same issues that arise with estimation of the wage function (10) also apply in the labor supply case. In addition, labor force participation and hours of work in the current period might be influenced by expectations about future health. One way to mitigate the negative consequences of poor health in the future (or to pay for future health inputs) might be to work more now and take more leisure in the future. This inter-temporal trade will depend on substitutability between leisure and work in good and poor health and, also, on liquidity and credit constraints. If effort expended at work, and hence effective labor supply, is influenced by future health, then the labor supply function will depend not only on current and prior health but also expected future health inputs and outputs. Similar arguments apply for expectations about future demographic characteristics, the disease environment and infrastructure.

2.2.4. Dynamic conditional demand for health

Solving the life cycle optimization program (7)–(10) yields a series of dynamic demand for health functions, θ, one for each health input, N, and outcome, H, which are conditional on health in other periods:

$$\theta_t = \theta\left(\theta_\sigma, m_t(\theta_\tau), p_{nr}, p_{cs}, A_s, B, V_0, D_s, I_s, \varepsilon, \varepsilon_s\right) \qquad (11)$$

where

$$\theta_\sigma = \theta_{t-1}, \theta_{t-2}, \ldots, \theta_0; \qquad m_t(\theta_\tau) = m_t(\theta_{t+1}), m_t(\theta_{t+2}), \ldots, m_t(\theta_T),$$

$$Z_s = Z_0, \ldots, Z_{t-1}, Z_t, m_t(Z_{t+1}), \ldots, m_t(Z_T) \quad \text{for } Z = p_c, A, I \text{ and } \varepsilon$$

$$\text{and} \quad Z_r = Z_t, m_t(Z_{t+1}), \ldots, m_t(Z_T) \quad \text{for } Z = p_n \text{ and } D.$$

Each element of the vector of current health inputs and outcomes, θ_{jt}, depends on a vector of lagged health inputs and outcomes which date back to birth (or *in utero*), $\theta_\sigma = \theta_{t-1}, \theta_{t-2}, \ldots, \theta_0$. Since current health depends on prior health inputs, a forward looking person will choose inputs this period in an anticipation of future health inputs and outcomes. In general, therefore, demand for health in the current period, t, will depend on expectations at time t about future health $E_t \theta_\tau$ for each future period from $\tau = t + 1$ until $\tau = T$ which is the (expected) end of life. Since future health is uncertain, it is not only the expected value of future health that will enter (11) but the entire distribution of predicted future health that potentially affects current health and health investments. We denote that distribution evaluated at time t by $m_t(.)$. Obviously expected end of life is endogenous in this model as is the actual end of life since longevity will depend on health investments and resource allocations through the life course.

Current health inputs and outcomes also depend on current health input and consumption prices, p_n and p_c respectively, as well as all expectations about future prices. Prior prices of inputs into the health production function, p_{nt}, should affect θ_t only through lagged health and so do not belong in the dynamic conditional demand function (11). However, prior prices of all consumption goods (and any inputs that enter directly into the utility function (8) belong in (11). To ease notation, we use the subscript s to denote these past, present and the distribution of predicted future values and subscript r denotes current and expected future values.

The conditional demand for health in any period is dependent on time-varying demographic characteristics, A_s, non-health human capital and background, B, which are time invariant; assets at birth, V_0, as well as local labor demand and infrastructure, I_s. Again, the subscript s denotes all prior, current and predicted future values of time-varying demographic characteristics and infrastructure. As is the case for prices of health inputs, demand for health depends on current and future expectations about the disease and health services environment, D_r. (If there are any elements of D that overlap with infrastructure, I, then their state in prior periods will affect demand.) Without loss of generality, all dimensions of background and human capital that are time-varying are captured in A_s. Time invariant background characteristics, B, include all the factors that affect the production of health, B_H, tastes, B_U, and wages, B_W.

Unobserved heterogeneity, ε, encompasses innate healthiness, μ, in the health production function, innate ability, α, in the wage function, tastes that influence resource allocation in any period, ξ, as well as inter-temporal preferences, δ. Since each of μ, α, and ξ has a time-invariant and time-varying component, unobserved heterogeneity in the conditional demand for health function is also separated into a time invariant, ε, and time-varying component, ε_s. The time-invariant component includes, for example, genetic endowment, ability and those tastes that do not change over the life course. At any point in the life course, the entire history of innovations in unobserved factors $\varepsilon_0, \ldots, \varepsilon_t$ affects demand for health in the current period as do expectations about the future evolution of those factors, $\varepsilon_{t+1}, \ldots, \varepsilon_T$.[4] Future innovations can be ignored if it is only their first moments that affect demand for health, assuming $\varepsilon \sim f(0, \sigma^2)$. In general, higher order moments of innovations will play a role in decisions about health if, for example, the possibility of large negative (or positive) innovations in unobserved dimensions of healthiness affect decisions today perhaps because of risk aversion.

2.2.5. Dynamic reduced form demand for health

Before discussing estimation of the life cycle models of health and productivity, it is useful to derive the reduced form demand for health inputs and outcomes at time t by substituting all endogenous variables in (11) with their determinants. These potentially endogenous variables include all prior levels of health $\theta_{t-1}, \theta_{t-2}, \ldots, \theta_0$, expectations about future health $m_t(\theta_{t+1}), m_t(\theta_{t+2}), \ldots, m_t(\theta_T)$, and predictions about the evolution of socio-demographics, A, the disease environment, D, and infrastructure, I. The

---

[4] Note that prior innovations in innate healthiness, μ, play no role in ε.

determinants of these potentially endogenous variables are prices and the information set that governs predictions about the future:

$$\theta_t = \theta(p_{n\sigma}, p_{c\sigma}, A_\sigma, B, V_0, D_\sigma, I_\sigma, \upsilon, \upsilon_\sigma)$$

$$\text{where} \quad Z_\sigma = Z_0, \ldots, Z_{t-1}, Z_t \quad \text{for } Z = p_n, p_c, A, D, I \text{ and } \upsilon. \tag{12}$$

It is important to note that all dimensions of A, D and I that are potentially correlated with unobserved characteristics that affect health do not belong in the reduced form demand function. These will include, for example, the local disease or infrastructure environment if the individual chooses to live in a particular location because of their impact on health either directly (through reduced infection) or indirectly (through improved earnings opportunities).

2.2.6. Estimation of dynamic demand for health functions

In principle, estimation and interpretation of dynamic reduced form demand for health inputs and outcomes, (12), is straightforward. However, the data demands are beyond the reach of current population survey data resources since the model calls for knowledge of all prices of health inputs and consumption goods in the current period and in every period back to conception along with a complete demographic and environmental history for each respondent.

Estimation of the dynamic conditional health function is even more demanding of data. Not only does current health depend on the complete health history, price, demographic and environmental history but also on expectations about all of these processes including the evolution of future health.

In the absence of such data, it is necessary to place restrictions on the model and reduce the dimensionality of the estimation problem. We describe three separability assumptions that are commonly made, often only implicitly, in this literature.

First, few empirical studies of health demand functions examine more than one or a small number of domains of health at any time. These studies assume that the specific markers capture all domains of health or that other health inputs and outcomes have no direct impact on the health markers of interest.

Second, if health in the previous period is a sufficient statistic for all health prior to that period, then the conditional demand function simplifies to:

$$\theta_t = \theta\left(\theta_{t-1}, m_t(\theta_{t+1}), p_{nr}, p_{cs}, A_s, B, V_0, D_r, I_s, \varepsilon, \varepsilon_s\right)$$

$$\text{where} \quad Z_r = Z_t, m_t(Z_{t+1}) \quad \text{for } Z = p_n \text{ and } D$$

$$\text{and} \quad Z_s = Z_0, \ldots, Z_{t-1}, Z_t, m_t(Z_{t+1}), \ldots, m_t(Z_T) \quad \text{for } Z = p_c, A, I \text{ and } \varepsilon. \tag{13}$$

The conditional demand model can be estimated with knowledge of health and health input prices in only three periods: the prior period, current period and expectations about the next period. However, all other control variables (p_c, A and I) continue to enter the demand function in all past, current and future periods.

The third assumption, which is often invoked in models of life cycle consumption and labor supply, requires that preferences are additively (or strongly) separable over time:

$$\Psi = E \sum_{t=1}^{T} \delta_t^{t-1} U_t(C_t, L_t; H_t, A_t, B_U, \xi, \xi_t) \tag{14}$$

which places restrictions on the way that out-of-period characteristics affect current period decisions. Specifically, the marginal utility of income (or its inverse, the price of utility) is fixed over time and so, given that price, decisions in any one period can be made without regard for any prices or other characteristics in any other period, conditional on the price of utility.

Combining these assumptions the conditional dynamic demand function simplifies dramatically to:

$$\theta_t = \theta\left(\theta_{t-1}, m_t(\theta_{t+1}), p_{nr}, p_{cs}, A_s, B, V_0, D_r, I_s, \varepsilon, \varepsilon_s\right)$$
$$\text{where} \quad Z_s = Z_{t-1}, Z_t, m_t(Z_{t+1}) \quad \text{for } Z = p_n, p_c, A, I \text{ and } \varepsilon$$
$$\text{and} \quad Z_r = Z_t, m_t(Z_{t+1}) \quad \text{for } Z = p_n \text{ and } D. \tag{15}$$

Taken together, these are very powerful assumptions. The conditional demand model can be estimated with knowledge of not only health but also all control variables in only three periods: the prior period, current period and expectations about the future. This contrasts with (13) which depends on all past, current and future values of the control variables. Note also that these assumptions have no effect on the reduced form which continues to depend on all prior values of all covariates.

The assumption of inter-temporal separability of preferences in combination with assuming that θ_{t-1} is a sufficient statistic for health prior to that date is not only powerful. These are also very strong assumptions. The credibility of additive separability will depend on the completeness of financial markets. The credibility of assuming previous period health is a sufficient statistic for all prior health will vary depending on the specific measure of health and whether prior health problems are likely to have long-lived effects on later health.

An increasing amount of non-experimental evidence has accumulated that establishes an association between health *in utero* or in very early childhood and later life health and non-health outcomes (see Barker, 1994, and Godfrey and Barker, 2000 for instance). It seems that it would be profitable to draw on insights from the biological and biomedical literatures on the persistence of changes in specific domains of health to aid the selection of plausible exclusion restrictions for the model. Depending on the data available, it may be possible to allow health in a limited number of other periods to affect current health. Alternatively, the exclusion restrictions can be subjected to testing by determining whether health and the control variables measured in other periods have a direct impact on current health (appropriately taking account of unobserved heterogeneity).

Some surveys collect information about expectations regarding the future, including future health. In the absence of that information, it will be necessary to specify a model of expectation formation in order to estimate the dynamic conditional demand functions (11) or (15).

There are at least two additional challenges to estimation of the functions. First, it is likely that unobserved heterogeneity, ε, is correlated with one or more of the observed characteristics in the model. Consider, first, the component of unobserved heterogeneity that is time-invariant. This includes genetic endowments and innate healthiness, ability and tastes that do not change over the life course. These are likely to be correlated with health in any period as well as family background such as parental health and schooling. This suggests including an individual-specific fixed effect in the model. This raises two concerns. First, the fixed effect will also absorb all observed characteristics that are fixed, such as height, that enter the model in a linear and additive way. This is unfortunate since the relationship between these observed characteristics and health are often of substantive interest. Second, while convenient, the assumption that all time-invariant observed and unobserved characteristics enter the model in a linear and additive way is typically *ad hoc* and may not be innocuous. For example, as noted above, it is possible that height or innate healthiness, ability or completed education might interact with other time-varying covariates that are included in the model; in that case, the fixed effects estimates will be biased.

The second challenge to the estimation of the dynamic conditional demand function is that prior health and expectations about future health will also be correlated with unobserved heterogeneity that is time-varying. For example, unobserved factors, μ_{t-1}, that affect the production of health outcomes, H_{t-1}, and possibly inputs into that production, N_{t-1}, will be correlated with θ_{t-1}. This suggests an instrumental variables approach to estimation, possibly in combination with fixed effects. In the general form of (11), there are no obvious instruments. However, given some exclusion restrictions on the lags and leads of θ included in the model, all covariates from all other periods are potential instruments. For example, imposing the assumptions underlying (15), all prices, demographics, disease environment and infrastructure from $t = 0$ through $t - 2$ and all expectations of those characteristics from $t = t + 2$ through T are candidate instruments. Health inputs and outcomes from the same periods are also potential instruments.

2.2.7. Estimation of dynamic health production functions

As with the other models, estimation of the dynamic health production functions (7) is very demanding of data. Invoking the same separability assumptions used above, rewrite the production function with health in the previous period serving as a sufficient statistic for all health inputs and outcomes for all other prior periods:

$$H_t = H(H_{t-1}, N_t, L_t; D_t, A_t, B, \mu, \mu_{t-1}). \tag{16}$$

Subtracting H_{t-1} from both sides, the specification can be interpreted as relating changes in health (such as growth in child height or changes in weight) to health in prior periods and other contemporaneous inputs into the production function. The assumption that H_{t-1} is a sufficient statistic for all prior health reduces the empirical problem to explaining flows in health and not the evolution of the stock of health over the entire life course. Estimation needs to take into account the fact that prior health, H_{t-1} and contemporaneous inputs, N_t, are likely correlated with time invariant innate healthiness, μ, and time-varying unobserved variation in healthiness, μ_{t-1}. An individual fixed effect will absorb the impact of μ if its influence is approximately linear and additive. Prices of inputs and earlier period characteristics in the production function are potential instruments for prior health and contemporaneous inputs. Again, it may be profitable to combine a fixed effects and instrumental variables approach and it is straightforward to assess the validity of the assumptions underlying the specification using over-identification tests.

The instrumental variables approach was adopted in an important paper by the Cebu Study Team (1992) which used extremely rich data to estimate a complicated dynamic weight function for children every two months from birth to 24 months of age in Cebu, Philippines. The study assumes that weight in any period depends on inputs that period and weight in the prior period; weight and inputs in other periods do not influence current weight except through previous-period weight.

2.2.8. Estimation of dynamic relationships between health and economic prosperity

Examination of the dynamics underlying the relationship between health, labor market prosperity and socio-economic success provides several additional substantive insights and empirical challenges. We begin with models of the effect of health on economic prosperity and then examine dynamic demand for health conditional on indicators of SES.

As above, it is necessary to impose exclusion restrictions to yield an empirically tractable model. The simplest model treats current health as a sufficient statistic for all past and future health inputs and outcomes

$$w_t = w(\theta_t; B_w, A_t, I_t, \alpha, \alpha_t). \tag{17}$$

Dynamics are embedded in time-invariant unobserved heterogeneity, α, which, in a pioneering paper, Deolalikar (1988) treated as a fixed effect. This amounts to examining the effect of changes in health on changes in wages.

Consistent estimation of (17) requires that differences in the time-varying errors, $(\alpha_t - \alpha_{t-1})$, be uncorrelated with differences in time-varying health characteristics, $(\mu_t - \mu_{t-1})$. This is plausible if the time-varying errors only contain random measurement error. The assumption is less appealing if the errors also comprise omitted characteristics which affect wages since part of these wage shocks may be invested in health. This will arise, for example, if a worker experiences a surprisingly good year and spends some of the unanticipated income on health-augmenting inputs (perhaps by eating more nutritious foods). In that case, it makes sense to combine the fixed effect with an instrumental variables approach. The prices of health inputs in prior periods and expected prices in future periods are potential instruments. Prices of consumption goods in periods other than t are also potential instruments as long as they have no direct effect on wages. This precludes, for example, the prices of crops produced by a farmer. In this specification, prior realizations and future expectations about demographics and infrastructure are also instruments if they do not have a direct impact on wages.

Returning to the assumption that previous period health is a sufficient statistic for all prior health, the conditional wage function becomes:

$$w_t = w(\theta_t, \theta_{t-1}, E_t\theta_{t+1}; B_w, A_t, A_{t-1}, E_t A_{t+1}, I_t, I_{t-1};$$
$$E_t I_{t+1}, \alpha, \alpha_t, \alpha_{t-1}, E_t\alpha_{t+1}) \tag{18}$$

where the moments, $m(.)$, are replaced with expectations, $E_t(.)$, to facilitate exposition. As in our earlier notation for moments, $m(.)$, expectations, $E_t(.)$, are taken over all future periods, from $t+1$ onwards. The model in (18) can be estimated using a fixed effects instrumental variables approach (with instruments drawn from observed characteristics in periods not included in the model). Separating θ_t into a part that is anticipated at time $t-1$, $E_{t-1}\theta_t$, and a part that is not, $\theta_t - E_{t-1}\theta_t$, highlights the differences between the effect of anticipated changes in health and health shocks. Prior health, demographics and infrastructure can also be separated into a component that is anticipated and a component that is not.

This extended model provides opportunities to address several important questions about the relationship between prior health, changes in health, current health and labor outcomes. For example, to what extent do current episodes of ill-health, especially unforeseen health shocks, affect labor market outcomes now and in the future? Does it matter whether ill-health episodes are expected or unexpected, as in principle it should? How important is previous health, conditional on current health, in determining labor market outcomes and health itself, over the life course? What types of health shocks have permanent effects on health, what types of shocks can be overcome by later periods of good health, and what types of shocks can be ameliorated by positive health interventions? By allowing for separate effects of current and past health on wages in (18), it is possible to examine the impact of *changes* in health status, or of the joint effects of levels and changes in health, on labor market, health and schooling outcomes. To date, there is only limited evidence on these types of questions.

Note also that the same conceptual framework described for wages in (10), (17) and (18) can be applied to explore the relationship between health and other labor outcomes such as labor force participation, sectoral choice and hours of work although identification in those models is more complicated. First, it is likely that demographics and infrastructure will have a direct impact on labor supply choices. For example, if labor demand is expected to fall in the future, an individual may choose to work more hours in this period. Second, prices of any goods that affect the real shadow price of time are not valid instruments for health.

As in the static model, there is substantial interest in the reverse relationship: the demand for health conditional on economic prosperity. The reduced form, (12), provides a basis for interpreting the impact on the evolution of health over the life course of schooling, any other background indicator included in B, and assets at birth, V_0. Models of health conditional on earnings or total income are more difficult to interpret. Substituting for prior and future health in the conditional demand function (11), health in the current period depends on wages, w, and labor supply, L, as well as wealth, V, input and consumption prices, p, demographics, A, background, B, and the disease environment, E. All current and prior realizations of these control variables along with predictions about how they will evolve in the future belong in the model:

$$\theta_t = \theta(w_s, L_s, V_s, p_{ns}, p_{cs}, A_s, B, D_s, \varsigma, \varsigma_s)$$

where $\quad Z_s = Z_0, \ldots, Z_{t-1}, Z_t, m_t(Z_{t+1}), \ldots, m_t(Z_T)$

for $Z = w, L, V, p_n, p_c, A, D$ and ς. $\hfill (19)$

As above, it is useful to separate prior realizations of each covariate into a part that is predicted and a part that is not anticipated. Estimation of (19) is a challenge. If a fixed effect is included in the model to absorb time-invariant unobserved heterogeneity, ς, then, as long as individuals are able to transfer resources across periods, it is only unanticipated components of realized wages, hours of work, wealth and all other covariates that will affect current health status. The longevity of unanticipated fluctuations in these covariates is an empirical question and will depend on both the extent to which the measure of health reflects the role of a stock or flow and the specific covariate.

2.3. Health, the individual, the household and the family

The discussion thus far has focused on decisions about health investments, resource and time allocation made by an individual. Many of these decisions are made within the context of decisions made by other household or family members and take into account their health and well-being. For example, if one member of a family falls ill, other members might respond by reallocating time and goods to provide care to that person, to avoid other members also falling sick and to offset transitory fluctuations in income or expenditures associated with the illness. Reactions by family members will likely be different if the illness is expected to be persistent, or if the person dies, and there is a permanent reduction in family resources.

The extent to which household and family members are able to smooth fluctuations due to anticipated and unanticipated variation in health of a family member is of substantial interest. In addition, there are important questions about how the burden of poor health is distributed within the family. There is a substantial literature on the allocation of resources among children with different endowments. (See, for example, Behrman, Pollak and Taubman, 1982.) On the one hand, from the perspective of maximizing family resources, it may be optimal for a family to invest most in the child with the greatest endowment of innate healthiness. On the other hand, families may allocate resources to offset these innate differences (Pitt, Rosenzweig and Hassan, 1990).

More generally, how family members with different economic opportunities, endowments and preferences co-ordinate decisions and allocate resources is an active area of research. Incorporating insights from those models into the conceptual framework described above is beyond the scope of this chapter. Browning, Chiappori and Weiss (2007) provide an excellent review of the literature; see also Behrman (1997), Pitt (1997) and Mwabu (2008). We will explore some of the empirical evidence on these issues below. For example, we will discuss the impact of illness and death in areas which HIV/AIDS is prevalent on adults and children; we will also discuss evidence on how the impact of income shocks on health is distributed within families.

The discussion of conceptual models thus far has highlighted at least two issues that are important for the design of research on health and development: the likely contributions of longitudinal studies and the potential value of studies designed to pin down causal mechanisms. We take up those issues next.

2.4. Longitudinal study designs

As discussed in the previous section, studies of the relationships between health and other life outcomes that rely exclusively on contemporaneous associations substantially limit the scope for understanding the complexities underlying these relationships. Dynamic models of behavior call for measurement of health and life outcomes over the life course. Investments in high-quality longitudinal data sets have had substantial payoffs in terms of their contributions to the field. The recent literature on the long arm of early childhood health and its impact on later life outcomes suggests that it may be profitable to develop long-term longitudinal studies which follow individuals from the fetal period through to death and, arguably, studies that follow the children of those respondents. While this is an expensive endeavor, it is not impossible as evidenced by several high-quality cohort studies which have followed individuals from conception through adolescence into adulthood. These include, for example, five British cohorts, the Cebu study conducted by Popkin, Adair and associates, and the Birth to Twenty cohort in South Africa (Barbarin and Richter, 2001).

Attrition is the Achilles heel of longitudinal surveys. In telephone and web-based surveys, participant refusal drives much of the attrition. Refusal rates are typically very low in developing country studies. Most of those surveys involve face-to-face interviews and attrition is primarily due to migration away from the study sites since movers are the hardest and most expensive to follow-up. Until recently, many panel surveys were designed to exclude migrants from follow-up.

Migration is typically positively correlated with human capital and so is likely to be associated with some dimensions of health. The extent to which attrition is correlated with observed characteristics that affect health inputs and outcomes will complicate interpretation of the models discussed in the previous section. Attrition that is correlated with unobserved characteristics in the models poses substantially greater empirical challenges. At the very least, it will be prudent to assess the extent to which attrition is correlated with observed characteristics that are included in the models of interest and take those results into account in the interpretation. To the extent possible, it would also be worth relating attrition to observed characteristics, which are not included in the model, but are likely to be correlated with unobserved factors in the model of interest. The choice of characteristics will be model-dependent but might include the example of migration above, the value of time, performance on cognitive tests and so on.

It is possible to model attrition drawing, say, on characteristics of the survey itself and the enumerators as predictors of survey quality that are not related to the health behaviors of respondents. (See, for example, Thomas, Frankenberg and Smith, 2001.) It is also possible that judiciously combining longitudinal surveys with data collected on health status and health inputs retrospectively will yield useful resources for the research community. (See, for example, Schultz and Tansel, 1997; Smith, 2004.) Of course, none of these is a substitute for spending resources on surveys that are well-designed and maintain high retention rates across waves.

2.5.   Studies designed to identify causal effects

The second issue highlighted by the discussion of the conceptual models is that identi-fying causal effects is far from straightforward. This is not a new insight. However, in recent years, there has been greater emphasis on designing studies that have the poten-tial to disentangle causal pathways and those studies promise to provide important new evidence. It is useful to identify three classes of studies: randomized experiments, quasi-experiments and other non-experimental methods. See Duflo, Glennerster and Kremer (2008) for an extensive discussion of the theory and practice of randomization in de-velopment economics. Angrist and Krueger (1999) provide an excellent overview of non-experimental methods.

2.5.1.   Experimental designs

Experimental studies are designed to randomly assign respondents into treatment and control groups. In principle, a comparison of changes in behavior between the groups after the treatment provides evidence on the causal effect of the treatment. Examples of treatment-control designs include providing nutritional supplements (as in the INCAP study or the Mexican Oportunidades program); providing drugs to treat a health problem (such as drugs to treat HIV/AIDS, schistomasias or worms, Miguel and Kremer, 2004), changing the epidemiological environment (by draining rivers and canals or providing bed nets in areas where malaria is endemic, Watson, 1953) or changing the prices of health services (as in the RAND Health Insurance Experiment, Newhouse, 1996) or the availability, quality and thus effective price of health services (by providing incentives for health service providers to attend clinics, Banerjee, Deaton and Duflo, 2004).

It is estimated that nearly 2 billion people suffer from iron deficiency anemia (IDA) with prevalence rates being highest in Asia. While rigorous clinical studies on animals and humans have demonstrated that IDA reduces work capacity,[5] there is little evidence on the impact of iron deficiency on wages, time allocation and other economic choices. The Indonesian Work and Iron Status Evaluation (WISE) was specifically designed to provide evidence on the extent to which there is a causal effect of health on economic prosperity. About half the 17,000 subjects were assigned to receive a weekly iron supplement. The other half received an identical-looking placebo. Take up of the supplement was monitored very closely. Subjects were interviewed every four months – for a year before supplementation, the year of supplementation and for two years after supplementation. The impact of supplementation on iron in the blood was measured at each interview along with a rich array of economic and social indicators. It is thus possible to trace out the impact over time of improved nutritional status by contrasting changes in the lives of the treatments relative to the controls (Thomas et al., 2006).

In practice, treatment-control design experiments can be difficult to implement successfully. For example, if the treatment is effective then respondents in control groups are likely to observe others who are benefiting from the treatment and respond by seeking out the treatment. In order to minimize this effect, several experiments randomize at the level of the village or school so that all peers receive the same treatment. This complicates interpretation of evidence at any other level (such as the individual) and thus dissipates some of the key benefits of the experimental design. More generally, subjects are likely to change their behavior in response to the experiment and these behavioral responses further contaminate interpretation of experimental evidence.

Moreover, experimental designs are often expensive to implement and there are many key questions about health which are either difficult or impossible to address using experimental designs. For example, it is difficult to prospectively randomize *in utero* development to measure the causal impact of fetal deprivation on outcomes in later life. Because most experiments are conducted on specific sub-populations for a limited period of time or, if the experiment is long-lived, there is often substantial attrition from the sample and the degree to which attrition is different between treatments and controls is likely to be related to the perceived net benefits of the treatment. This substantially contaminates interpretation of results from experiments. More broadly, it is often difficult in social experiments to establish the generalizability of results, assess the longevity of impacts or provide insights into likely general equilibrium effects.

With all of these concerns in mind, and as discussed in more detail below, randomization has been, and promises to continue to be, an extremely valuable tool in this literature. It seems likely that combining the exogenous variation provided by randomization with non-experimental methods that take into account behavioral responses is likely to be a very productive approach to addressing some of the most pressing unresolved questions in the literature. We turn, therefore, to a discussion of non-experimental methods to pin down causal effects.

---

[5] The biochemical literature has established the key role that iron plays in transporting oxygen through the blood and the mechanisms underlying the causal effect of iron on VO_2max, say, are well-understood right down to the cell level.

2.5.2. *Quasi-experimental designs*

Many important studies have used a quasi-experimental design exploiting variation in the social, economic or health environment surrounding individuals. To the extent that this variation is outside of the control of the individual (or is uncorrelated with observed and unobserved characteristics that affect the outcome of interest in the empirical model), it provides plausibly exogenous variation which is exploited to pin down causal effects. For example, studies have exploited variation in weather, variation due to natural disasters, unanticipated changes in the epidemiological environment, the introduction of new drugs and changes in health services, as well as changes in public policies associated with the provision of health, education, income or some other type of support.

Studies of the 1944 Dutch Winter Famine provide an example of a quasi-experimental design that has proved to be very powerful (Stein et al., 1975; Ravelli et al., 1998 and Roseboom et al., 2001b, for example). In the winter of 1944/1945, western Holland was under Nazi occupation and, as punishment for resistance activities, the Germans gave each person a very small daily ration of between 400 and 800 calories. Children who were *in utero* during this period have been weighed and measured from birth throughout their lives. Their children have also been followed to investigate the inter-generational consequences of deprivation during the fetal period.

In practice, it is often difficult to identify a "treatment effect" by comparing health inputs, outcomes or behaviors of the same group of people before and after some "treatment" because at least part of the observed differences may be due to secular change. To control for this, many studies compare differences over time among the treated group with differences over the same period among a control group and attribute the difference-in-difference to the causal effect of the 'treatment.' A key issue is selection of control groups that mimic the treatment group.

Spatial or temporal variation in the introduction of new programs, policies or health services is often exploited to measure the effect of the change. In some cases, this variation can be treated as randomly assigned, say, because the new program is introduced in a phased way and the phasing is unrelated to observed or unobserved characteristics in the model of interest. However, in many cases, programs are targeted to place where the need is greatest or where implementation is easiest because of the existence of other, complementary infrastructure. In these cases, the difference-in-difference estimates will be misleading unless the differences are fully controlled. That said, arguably, developing countries are an especially good context for studies that exploit a quasi-experimental design precisely because of the many rich sources of variation they provide both across time and space which can be treated as randomly assigned.

Several studies have exploited changes in the environment in combination with insights from the biological literature to develop quasi-experimental designs. As an example, under the assumption that child length, conditional on age, is little affected by health and nutrition inputs after age 3 or 4 years (Habicht, Martorell and Rivera, 1995), it is possible to measure the impact of health interventions, school feeding programs and public support programs, *inter alia*, by comparing the length of children exposed with those not exposed to the program. Such studies include examination of the impact of the old age pension program in South Africa (Case and Deaton, 1998; Duflo, 2000; Hamoudi and Thomas, 2005) and the introduction of midwives to villages in Indonesia (Frankenberg, Suriastini and Thomas, 2005).

To be sure, not all observed variation is "natural" and it is imperative that the first step in any quasi-experimental design is to demonstrate that the sources of variation that are being exploited can be treated as exogenous. See, for example, Rosenzweig and Wolpin (2000) for an insightful discussion.

2.5.3. Other non-experimental methods

Non-experimental data are the workhorse of empirical research in development. In reduced form models, estimates of causal effects are provided by ordinary least squares (OLS) or matching methods. Matching, be it on covariates or through estimation of propensity scores (Rosenbaum and Rubin, 1983), seeks to replicate the advantages of a treatment-control design. Importantly, matching places fewer parametric restrictions on the relationships of interest relative to OLS which assumes the model is linear and additive in unobserved characteristics. It is also straightforward to estimate the distribution of the effects of characteristics in these models using non-parametric methods (Hardle, 1992). All of these methods assume selection is only on observed characteristics.

Estimation of causal effects in production functions and conditional demand functions is more complicated because selection is likely to be on unobserved characteristics that are correlated with covariates in the model. The biases caused by these unobserved characteristics will affect OLS and matching method estimators. To the extent that these unobserved characteristics are fixed for an individual and affect the outcome in a linear and additive way, they can be absorbed by including a fixed effect in the model. As noted above, a drawback of a fixed effect is that it absorbs all characteristics that are fixed, such as height or education, and enter the model in a linear and additive form. In addition, it is well known that the inclusion of a fixed effect exacerbates problems associated with classical measurement error in covariates – an issue that is of considerable import when estimating relationships between health and indicators of SES (Griliches and Hausman, 1985).

In general, it will be necessary to identify instruments that are not correlated with the unobserved characteristics in the model but are correlated with the "endogenous" covariates or "treatments." Instrumental variable (IV) methods are well established in the literature but involve strong parametric assumptions. If the unobserved characteristics that affect the "treatments" are additively separable from the observed and unobserved characteristics affecting the outcome of main interest, then IV will identify the local average treatment effect (LATE). Notice this rules out the possibility of heterogeneity of treatment effects across the distribution of unobserved characteristics. This is a potentially important restriction in the health and development literature. Not only is the distribution of "effects" of paramount interest in some cases, but the biological literature suggests that at least for some health indicators such as glucose, cholesterol, inflammation and stress markers, there may be heterogeneous "treatment effects" on, say, economic productivity across characteristics that are not usually observed. The latter might include genetic endowment, prior and concurrent health and related behaviors.

Greater flexibility can be achieved with control function methods, pioneered by Heckman (Heckman, 1978; Heckman and Robb, 1985), or local instrumental variable methods (Heckman and Vytlacil, 2006). For example, control function methods include controls for unobserved heterogeneity that is correlated with covariates in the model of interest (the so-called "λ-method") and these controls can be estimated nonparametrically. (See Blundell and Powell, 2003, and Heckman and Navarro-Lozano, 2004, for excellent discussions of these methods.)

Studies have attempted to exploit the temporal ordering of variation in health and economic status to isolate "Granger" causality (Granger, 1969). Using longitudinal data on older Americans from Asset and Health Dynamics among the Oldest Old (AHEAD), Adams et al. (2003) relate the incidence of new health conditions to prior health conditions and SES in the previous period (which is two years earlier). Finding that SES does not predict future health problems (except for mental health), they conclude that SES does not have a causal impact on physical health in this sample. Conversely, controlling prior wealth, prior health does predict current wealth and so causality from health to wealth cannot be ruled out.

Inspection of the dynamic model (7)–(12) above highlights one of the difficulties with this approach. In general, the evolution of both health and SES are the outcomes of choices made over the entire life course and the relationship between health and SES in a short window may not be informative about the causal mechanisms that underlie their association over the life span. This concern is likely to be particularly germane in early life (when SES amounts to parental resources) and later life (when health and SES reflect the cumulation of decisions made earlier in life).

In addition, all the issues discussed above regarding identification of the causal effect of health on SES and *vice versa* are relevant in tests of Granger causality and they are not easy to address. These include concerns regarding correlations between covariates included in the empirical models and unobserved characteristics. For example, wealth in any period is a function of prior spending and savings decisions as well as portfolio allocations; those choices are likely to have affected prior health and possibly will affect health in the future over and above the value of wealth in the prior period. More generally, innate healthiness and preferences, which are typically not observed, are likely to be correlated with prior health and SES, and estimation strategies that fail to take into account correlations between covariates and unobserved heterogeneity will not be consistent. These and other issues are discussed in detail in Adams et al. (2003) and related commentaries (Adda, Chandola and Marmot, 2003; Hausman, 2003; and Heckman, 2003, *inter alia*).

An important feature of the estimation approaches discussed thus far is that it is not necessary to fully specify the health production function (7) or preferences (8). An alternative approach specifies functional forms for these relationships and makes stronger assumptions about the stochastic components of the models and then, using dynamic programming methods, solves the lifetime optimization problem from end of life back to birth, at least in principle. There are at least two advantages to this approach. First, spelling out the full lifetime optimization program clarifies what assumptions are necessary to pin down relationships of interest and imposes greater discipline on the interplay between relationships of interest. Second, it is possible to recover parameters of interest which can then be used for out-of-sample predictions. What would happen if there was a significant increase in health investments or if an epidemic swept through a population? The cost, of course, is that the estimates are only as valid as the assumptions and data that underlie them. See, for example, Eckstein and Wolpin (1989) for a discussion of the approach and McKee (2006) for a recent application to labor supply and health in a developing country context.

2.5.4. *Measurement of potential instruments to identify causal effects*

The discussion about models, in the previous section, and methods, in this section, highlights the importance of designing studies that include data on characteristics that can serve as instruments that address concerns about unobserved heterogeneity in the models of interest. Prices of health inputs are one set of potential instruments that were noted several times in the previous subsection. Yet, relatively few surveys allocate significant resources to the design and collection of high-quality data on prices of health inputs. There are a large number of potential health inputs that might be important: they include health services, drugs, nutrients, and the epidemiological environment. Moreover, prices should be interpreted broadly to include the availability of inputs (or the time costs associated with obtaining the input) and the quality of the inputs. On the one hand, this further complicates the study design but, on the other hand, it also provides potentially exogenous and possibly important variation that can be exploited in empirical models.

There are potentially substantial payoffs to integrating individual-level survey data with community-level surveys or administrative records. For example, virtually every country collects detailed data on prices in multiple markets; and many countries track the availability and quality of public health services. With the increasing prevalence of data on precise locations of markets, service providers and respondents in surveys (through, for example, GPS measurements), it is in principle straightforward to significantly enrich individual-level survey data by integrating them with community-level information on the local environment (including prices and historical rainfall). This becomes especially important when studies use retrospective measures of health (or health indicators that do not change during prime ages, such as height) as long as the survey data also provides a residential location history (or at least birth place) for each respondent and the residential histories can be linked to administrative or survey records.

3. Meaning of health

The discussion of health thus far has been largely abstract. Defining and measuring health is far from easy. This section takes up these issues from the perspective of empirical research in economics and provides a context for our exploration of the literature in the next sections.

It is widely recognized that health is multi-dimensional and reflects the combination of an array of factors that include physical, mental and social well-being, genotype and phenotype influences as well as expectations and information. A multitude of health indicators have been used in scientific studies of health and economic well-being drawing on data from both the developed and developing world. These have included mortality, reports of morbidities, health-related behaviors, self-assessments of overall health, assessments of physical functioning or activities of daily living, information on specific morbidities and a battery of physical assessments including biomarkers. In order to interpret the evidence on the relationships between health and development, it is critically important to understand what each of the indicators measures.

As noted above, health at a point in time combines the cumulative effects of phenotype factors including an individual's behavior through the life course as well as the health and socio-economic environments to which the individual has been exposed starting *in utero*. Health at any point in the life course also depends on genotype influences and, potentially, interactions between genotype and phenotype factors. Some measures of health can be thought of as stocks; attained height as an adult is an example which provides information about early life experiences. Other measures are flows and vary with high frequency; these include blood pressure or cortisol,[6] which respond to challenges; or the level of glucose in the blood which varies with food intake.

This section begins with a discussion of the relationship between life expectancy and development and then highlights key differences in cause of death between poor and better-off countries. We turn next to individual-level information and discuss the measurement of health of respondents in a socio-economic survey.

3.1. Mortality and life expectancy

Mortality, perhaps the ultimate measure of health, is the most widely-used indicator of the health of a population. At the population level, age-specific mortality rates are often converted to life expectancy. Figure 1 provides a visual summary of the relationship across countries between life expectancy at birth and GDP per capita for three years:

---

[6] Cortisol is a hormone produced by the adrenal cortex and is released in response to stress. The amount of cortisol present in serum follows a diurnal pattern being highest in the early morning and lowest in the evening after the onset of sleep. In addition, cortisol varies rapidly during the course of the day in response to challenges in the environment. In general, this variation is healthy, but consistently high levels of cortisol reactivity have been shown to be associated with elevated morbidity, reduced cognitive functioning and high risk of mortality. (See Seeman et al., 1997, 2004 for more information.)

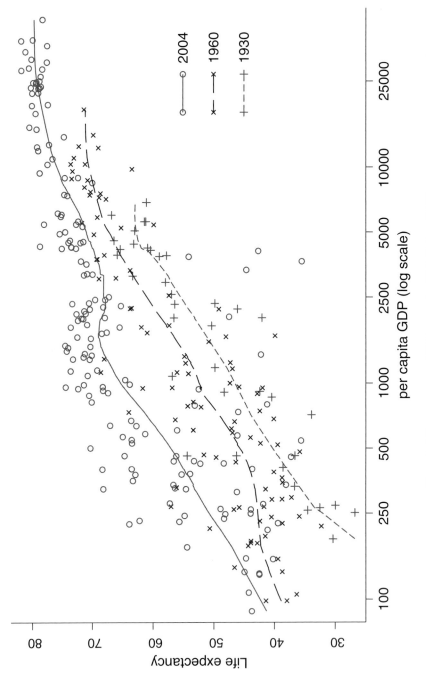

Figure 1. Life expectancy and GDP per capita: 1930, 1960 and 2004.

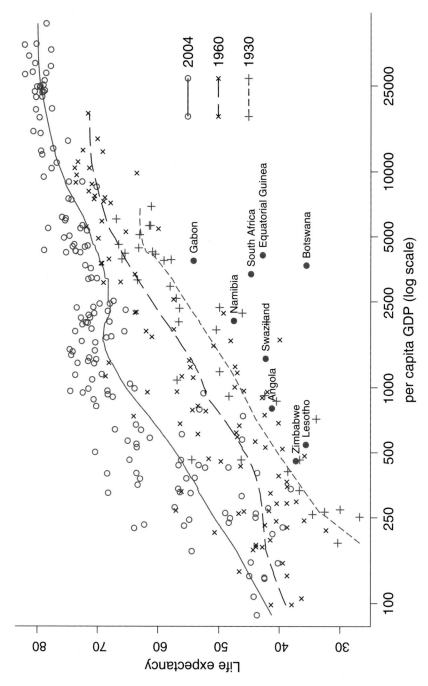

Figure 2. Life expectancy and GDP per capita: Highlighting outliers in 2004.

1930, 1960 and 2004.[7] It is important to recognize that mortality data are often incomplete in lower-income countries and so the estimates of life expectancy are likely to have large standard errors. Nonetheless, the "Preston Curves" (Preston, 1975) make three points very effectively.

First, people in richer countries can expect to live longer than those in poor countries. In 2004, a person born in a low-income country like Mali, where GDP per capita is $250, can expect to live to age 50, whereas someone born in the United States, where GDP per capita is over $35,000, can expect to live until 80. In the last half-century, diminishing marginal returns to income have set in. The Preston Curve remains steepest among the poorest countries, but the income level at which the curve flattens has declined over time.

Second, as indicated by the upward shift of the Preston Curve, there have been dramatic improvements in the health of populations over time.[8] These improvements have been greatest among the poorest. For example, in 2004, the average person born in a country where GDP per capita is about $250 (say, Mali) can expect to live about as long as someone born in a country with over twice that level of GDP in 1960 (say, Thailand) and five times the level of GDP in 1930 (say, Spain).

As Preston points out, if all the improvements in health were driven by aggregate income growth, countries would have merely moved along the Preston Curve over time. The upward shift of the curve, however, suggests that factors other than income are important, and Preston highlights the role of education, improved technology including the availability of vaccinations and oral rehydration therapy, expansion of public health services and nutrition. (See, also, Fogel, 2004 and Cutler, 2004.) Of course, as emphasized in the previous section, the positive association between income and health cannot be assigned a causal interpretation. Indeed part of the growth in income, itself, likely reflects technological progress.

Moreover, evidence suggests that all the benefits of improved technology and health services have not been fully realized by the poorest. For example, effective immunizations against measles have been available for over 40 years and childhood mortality associated with measles has essentially disappeared in richer countries. A WHO/UNICEF initiative, which began in 2000, targeted 45 low-income countries where measles was a leading cause of childhood mortality and provided immunizations. Wolfson et al. (2007)

---

[7] The data for 1930 are from Preston (1975); the data for 1960 and 2004 are from the World Bank's World Development Indicators (including the ex-Soviet bloc for 1960 and 2000). GDP per capita is measured in 2000 $US using official exchange rates, since purchasing power parity exchange rates are not available for 1930. It is important to underscore that the countries are not the same in each year with a larger sample of countries in the later years. This reflects an increase in the number of countries and improvements in the quality of data over time as more countries have estimates of life expectancy and GDP today than in 1930. The figure includes a non-parametric estimate of the association between life expectancy and per capita GDP for each of the three years. We use a locally weighted smoothed scatterplot estimator (Cleveland, 1979) with a 35% bandwidth for 1960 and 2000 and 70% bandwidth for 1930.

[8] Of course, this effect stretches back well before 1930. See, for example, Fogel (2004).

estimate the program resulted in an over 50% reduction of measles-related child mortality. Differences in the availability of treatments for HIV/AIDS in richer and poor countries is another of many examples

The third point that emerges clearly from Fig. 1 is that in 2004 there are several countries where life expectancy is substantially lower than its predicted level. For nine countries, highlighted in Fig. 2, life expectancy in 2004 is below the level that would have been predicted in 1930 given GDP per capita. Have the technological improvements of the last 70 years passed over these countries?

Six of the nine countries are in Southern Africa and it is HIV/AIDS that has resulted in substantially reduced life spans since the 1990s. Between 20 and 25% of 15–49 year-olds in those countries are thought to be infected with HIV/AIDS. The economies of Angola, Equatorial Guinea and Gabon are dominated by oil, and the benefits of rapid growth in recent years have not reached into population health.

Figure 3 presents time series of real GDP per capita and life expectancy for four countries from 1960 through 2004. Indonesia has seen a four-fold increase in per capita GDP and a 75% increase in life expectancy from around 40 to 70 years. In the United States, GDP has doubled and life expectancy has increased by about 10% to 78. The positive correlation between life expectancy tends to be larger in lower-income settings mimicking the cross-country evidence in Fig. 1.

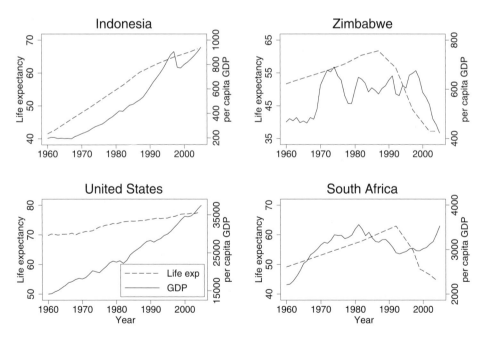

Figure 3. Life expectancy and GDP per capita.

Zimbabwe and South Africa are different: the effect of HIV/AIDS is clear. In Zimbabwe, life expectancy has plummeted from 60 in the late 1980s to 36 in 2004, among the lowest in the world. As in Indonesia and the United States, there is a positive correlation between life expectancy and aggregate income. Moreover, since the decline in life expectancy precedes the collapse of the economy, one might be tempted to conclude that health causes income. That conclusion would be premature.[9] In all the other southern African countries, there is little evidence that HIV/AIDS and GDP per capita are correlated. In South Africa, for example, income has grown substantially since the early 1990s but life expectancy has declined from 65 to 45 during the same period.[10]

Correlations between aggregate income and mortality within countries cannot be interpreted as uncovering causal relationships. Over and above the issues discussed above, it is far from clear that longevity and income should move in lock step even if they are related. Moreover, the literature has emphasized the potentially important role played by early life experiences on later life outcomes. Mortality reflects the cumulation of these experiences which further complicates the interpretation of cross-country and time series associations between life expectancy and current levels of income (or income growth).

Cutler, Deaton and Lleras-Muney (2006) provide an insightful discussion of the evidence on global mortality in considerably more depth. They conjecture that the preponderance of evidence suggests that it is science and technological innovation, including improved public health services, that have been the driving forces behind increased longevity of the world's population over the last century. Given the current state of knowledge, as they note themselves, their conclusions are tentative since key causal relationships underlying their argument have not been established.

3.2. Global burden of disease

Mortality is a very useful indicator of overall population health. However, health is far more than life or death and, as the southern African countries demonstrate, it is important also to understand the causes of death. That turns out to be complicated because the quality of data on cause of death varies dramatically across time and across countries and because in many cases only one cause of death is recorded, masking a far more complex reality. With these caveats in mind, Table 1, which is from Mathers, Lopez and Murray (2006), provides an overview of the global burden of disease.

Whereas, in the early twentieth century, infectious diseases accounted for a large fraction of deaths across the world, today they have essentially been eradicated in high-income countries. Nevertheless, they still account for almost one quarter of deaths in

---

[9] The collapse of the Zimbabwean economy can be traced to factors that are unrelated to the incidence of HIV/AIDS although arguably the severity of the health crisis is related to declining income in a complex way.
[10] Relying on the sort of cross-country evidence in Figs. 1 and 3, Pritchett and Summers (1996) conclude that it is income (or wealth) that drives health. That conclusion also seems premature.

Table 1
Causes of death in low/middle and high income countries (2001)

	1. Low and middle income countries		2. High income countries		3. All countries	
	# deaths (thousands)	% deaths	# deaths (thousands)	% deaths	# deaths (thousands)	% deaths
I. Communicable diseases, pregnancy outcomes, nutritional deficiencies	**17,622**	**36.4**	**552**	**7.0**	**18,174**	**32.3**
A Infectious and parasitic diseases	10,692	22.1	152	1.9	10,844	19.3
HIV/AIDS	*2554*	*5.3*	*22*	*0.3*	*2576*	*4.6*
Diarrheal diseases	*1778*	*3.7*	*6*	*0.1*	*1784*	*3.2*
Tuberculosis	*1590*	*3.3*	*16*	*0.2*	*1606*	*2.9*
Childhood diseases	*1363*	*2.8*	*2*	*0.0*	*1365*	*2.4*
Malaria	*1208*	*2.5*	*0*	*0.0*	*1208*	*2.1*
B Respiratory infections	3483	7.2	349	4.4	3832	6.8
C Perinatal conditions	2951	6.1	32	0.4	2983	5.4
D Nutritional deficiencies	451	0.9	18	0.2	469	0.8
II. Noncommunicable conditions	**26,037**	**53.8**	**6,868**	**86.5**	**32,905**	**58.5**
E Cardiovascular disease	13,362	27.6	3,039	38.3	16,401	29.1
F Malignant neoplasms	4957	10.2	2,066	26.0	7023	12.5
G Respiratory diseases	3127	6.5	477	6.0	3604	6.4
H Digestive diseases	1602	3.3	335	4.2	1937	3.4
I Diabetes mellitus	758	1.6	202	2.6	960	1.7
J Neuropsychiatric disorders	701	1.4	378	4.8	1079	1.9
K Congenital anomalies	477	1.0	30	0.4	507	0.9
III. Injuries	**4717**	**9.8**	**471**	**5.9**	**5188**	**9.2**
L Unintentional	3216	6.6	321	4.0	3537	6.3
M Intentional	1501	3.1	151	1.9	1652	2.9

Source: Mathers, Lopez and Murray (2006, Table 6.4).

low- and middle-income countries. In 2001, HIV/AIDS and tuberculosis, which often go hand in hand, accounted for over 8% of deaths (nearly 5 million people); diarrheal diseases and childhood diseases account for 6% of deaths in these countries. Many of these deaths would be prevented if the people benefited from the health services and technologies that are available in richer countries. That they have not reflects the combined effect of limited resources at the individual and family level, information, behavioral choices, and the health environment including lack of clean water, poor sanitation, nutrition and medical care as well as limited access to drugs.

Perinatal conditions account for another 5% of deaths in low- and middle-income countries but less than $\frac{1}{2}$% of deaths in high-income countries. The latter reflects spectacular technological innovations in the care of newborns and infants in richer countries.

The literature suggests that in many low-income countries, improved prenatal care, other health inputs and behavioral change during pregnancy are likely to significantly reduce infant mortality.

The vast majority of deaths in high-income countries are attributed to non-communicable diseases with cardiovascular disease and malignant neoplasms (cancers) accounting for nearly two thirds of all deaths. Many of the low- and middle-income countries are now passing through the epidemiological transition as infectious diseases diminish and non-communicable diseases emerge as major causes of death.[11] It is estimated that about 18 million people in low- and middle-income countries died from heart disease or cancers (over one third of all deaths). This number is over four times larger than the deaths from HIV/AIDS and tuberculosis combined. To be sure, heart disease and cancers are not only prevalent throughout the globe but will increase in prevalence as infectious diseases become better controlled.

Just under 5 million people (almost 1 in 10 deaths) died in 2001 in developing countries because of injuries, which is more people than died from HIV/AIDS or tuberculosis. The causes include traffic accidents, violence and abuse as well as injuries from natural events.

Interventions in high-income countries have demonstrated that deaths from traffic accidents can be avoided through enforcement of vehicle safety checks, driver education, seat-belt usage and speed control. In middle- and low-income countries, it is prime-age adults who are most likely to die in a traffic accident (World Health Organization, 2004). Bertrand et al. (2006) estimate that in a study of Indian driver license applicants (average age = 25), about two-thirds of those who obtained a license could not pass a basic driving test.

The December 2004 Indian Ocean tsunami killed approximately 250,000 people and the 2005 Pakistan earthquake killed nearly 75,000 people. Natural events tend to take a much larger toll in lower-income settings where the infrastructure is poorly suited to withstand the force of nature. In high-income countries, building codes, restrictions on development and early warning systems have proved effective mechanisms to minimize death and injury in these events.

Cause-of-death information provides insights only into the burden of disease at the end of life. In an effort to provide a richer summary measure of the health of a population at the aggregate level, estimates of healthy life expectancy (HALE) have been developed which include an adjustment for time in poor health. See Lopez et al. (2006) for a comprehensive discussion of these methods and description of changes in the global burden of disease in the last decade. We follow a complementary approach and focus on measurement of health of individuals in population surveys.

Before turning to that discussion, two points are worth emphasizing. First, the technology exists to avoid a substantial fraction of deaths in low- and middle-income countries. Identifying the impediments to bringing technologies and health services to these

---

[11] See Omran (1971) who was the first to describe this process.

populations is likely to have a high pay-off in terms of improving their well-being and contributing to scientific understanding of the determinants of population health.

Second, underlying the aggregate mortality estimates in Fig. 1 is considerable heterogeneity in the nature of the disease burden. As childhood diseases decline, life expectancy will increase and the burden of disease will shift towards more non-communicable diseases, many of which involve expensive treatments that can extend life for many years. The demographic transition with declining fertility and prolonged life spans will result in older people constituting a larger fraction of the population. The combination of aging populations and shifts in the burden of disease will have profound effects on the entire economy including the public and private health sectors, old age support and the distribution of resources between generations.

3.3. Physical health assessments: Anthropometry

Anthropometric measures, particularly height and weight, have been the workhorse in research on health in both the history and development literatures. Studies have also used such measurements as the circumference of the head, arm, waist and hip, among others, and skin-fold thickness in various body locations. They are all easy and inexpensive to measure in a field setting, can be measured accurately by a trained person and provide a wealth of information that can be compared across populations and over time.

Height (or length of babies and infants) reflects the combination of both genotype influences and phenotype influences *in utero* and during the first few years of life (Martorell and Habicht, 1986). Because attained height is fixed for adults (until shrinkage in older ages), it has provided important insights into differences in the early life health across cohorts. Moreover, height is positively correlated with cognitive achievement and schooling outcomes and predicts economic productivity and mortality, among others. These associations tend to be especially strong in lower-income settings.

Weight, a more contemporaneous indicator of general health and nutrition, reflects the combined effects of energy intake (food and diet) and energy output (physical activity). Weight is most easily interpreted when combined with height. Among young children, weight conditional on height along with growth in height are key markers for nutritional status and are typically compared with standard growth tables (see, for example, de Onis et al., 2006; CDC, 2000).

Body mass index (BMI), which is weight (in kg) divided by height (in m) squared, has proved to be a very convenient summary, particularly for adults. Extreme values of BMI (underweight BMI < 18.5 and overweight BMI > 25) have been shown to be associated with elevated morbidity and mortality (Waaler, 1984; Fogel, 2004). An overweight adult, and particularly an obese adult (BMI > 30), is at elevated risk of *inter alia* heart disease, dislipidemia, type II diabetes, stroke and some types of cancers. Many of these are the non-communicable diseases that are prevalent among older adults in high-income countries. This suggests that the epidemiological transition is likely to be accompanied by a nutrition transition (Popkin, 1994, 2003).

Figure 4 and Table 2 display the distribution of BMI for adult males and females (age 22 through 75) using survey data from six countries.[12] There are stark differences between the three poorer countries in the left panel of the figure and the three richer countries in the right panel: in general, the distribution of BMI tends to shift to the right as development proceeds.

In Bangladesh, the poorest of the six countries, over half the adult population is underweight and less than 5% are overweight. Moving up the GDP distribution to China, only about 10% of the population is underweight whereas about 15% is overweight. The distribution in Indonesia is similar although a smaller fraction of the population is in the healthy ranges of BMI. Obese people make up a very small fraction of the population in the three poorest countries.

In all six countries, women are more likely to be overweight and obese than men. These differences are nowhere greater than in South Africa. Whereas about 10% of South African males are underweight and 10% are obese; very few women are underweight and over one third of the women are obese. Continuing up the GDP ladder, in Mexico there is very little undernutrition but almost three quarters of the population is overweight and nearly a third are obese. The Mexican and United States distributions are very similar although GDP is about 5 times higher in the United States. The figures suggest that obesity rates rise with economic development which is troubling given the relationship between obesity and cardiovascular disease, stroke, diabetes and possibly cancer. The figures also suggest that growth in obesity is driven by more than income growth alone. Information and technology likely play a key role with physical activity at work and in leisure, food intake and the composition of the diet are all candidate proximate contributors to increased rates of obesity.

Figure 4 and Table 2 indicate that BMI rises with aggregate income. Does BMI increase with SES at the individual level? To answer this question, Fig. 5 uses individual-level data from the same six surveys and displays the relationship between BMI and education for males and females controlling age, in a regression framework.[13] The countries are ordered according to GDP.

In the five developing countries, BMI of males is positively correlated with education at all levels of education but in the United States BMI and education are not correlated among male high school dropouts and negatively correlated for better-educated males. Among females, there tends to be a positive correlation between BMI and education at

[12] Data are from Bangladesh, Indonesia, China, South Africa, Mexico and the United States. The South African, Mexican and United States surveys are nationally representative; the Indonesian survey is representative of about 80% of the Indonesian population; the Chinese survey is representative of 9 provinces and the Bangladesh survey is representative of one district. Figure 4 presents Epanechnikov kernel density estimates for males and females separately. The bandwidth is 0.7.

[13] The shapes in the figures are essentially identical if we relate the probability of being overweight to education. Education is specified as a spline with knots at 5 and 10 years of education; each regression includes splines for age (with knots at 10-year intervals). Separate regressions are estimated for males and females for each survey. Adults age 22 through 70 are included in the regressions.

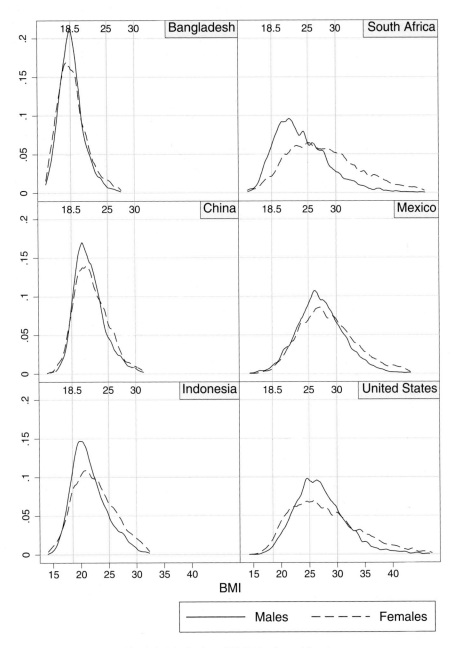

Figure 4. Distribution of BMI of males and females.

Table 2
Distribution of BMI in 6 countries

Indicator	Gender	Bangladesh	China	Indonesia	South Africa	Mexico	United States
All ages (25–70 yrs)							
BMI (Mean)	Male	18.7	21.8	21.5	24.0	27.2	27.1
	Female	18.7	22.2	22.5	28.2	28.7	28.1
% Underweight	Male	50.4	8.7	15.9	10.1	1.4	1.1
[BMI $\leqslant$ 18.5]	Female	52.7	10.3	14.7	4.7	0.9	2.4
% Overweight	Male	1.7	11.9	13.9	36.0	69.5	63.3
[BMI > 25]	Female	3.0	17.5	25.1	63.6	74.1	62.7
% Obese	Male	0.1	1.2	1.3	11.4	23.8	22.5
[BMI > 30]	Female	0.3	2.5	4.8	35.1	36.0	32.9
Prime age (25–44 yrs)							
% Underweight	Male	43.5	6.4	13.6	10.0	1.3	1.1
[BMI $\leqslant$ 18.5]	Female	45.2	8.3	10.5	5.0	0.8	2.7
% Overweight	Male	1.8	9.5	13.5	31.6	68.7	59.3
[BMI > 25]	Female	3.3	14.3	25.2	59.9	70.9	57.0
Older age (45–70 yrs)							
% Underweight	Male	57.3	12.0	19.7	10.2	1.6	1.2
[BMI $\leqslant$ 18.5]	Female	62.5	13.3	21.2	4.2	0.9	2.1
% Overweight	Male	1.6	15.2	14.8	42.1	70.6	67.8
[BMI > 25]	Female	2.6	22.3	25.0	68.1	79.4	69.9
Sample size	Male	3449	3257	7815	3547	4863	5636
	Female	4222	3457	8423	5242	6662	6431
Survey		MHSS	CHNS	IFLS	SADHS	MxFLS	NHANES III
Survey year		1996	1991	2000	1998	2002	1988–1994
GDP per capita ($US 2000)		310	421	800	2974	5852	27,833

Notes. MHSS is the 1996 Matlab Health and Socioeconomic Survey (Rahman et al., 1999). CHNS is the 1991 wave of the China Health and Nutrition Survey (Popkin, 1993). IFLS is the 2000 wave of the Indonesia Family Life Survey (Frankenberg and Karoly, 1995; Frankenberg and Thomas, 2000; Strauss et al., 2004). SADHS is the 1998 South African Demographic Health Survey (Demographic and Health Surveys, 2002). MxFLS is the 2002 wave of the Mexican Family Life Survey (Rubalcava and Teruel, 2004). NHANES III is the National Health and Nutrition Examination Survey Wave III (National Center for Health Statistics, 1994).

the bottom of the education distribution which turns negative at higher levels of schooling.

Recall that, on average, females have higher BMI than males. This is true at lower levels of education, but at the top of the education distribution in China, Mexico and the United States, males have higher BMI than females. Similarly, in South Africa the gap in BMI between males and females is very small among the best educated relative to those with no education.

Behind Figs. 3 and 4 there is substantial heterogeneity across age groups, some of which can be attributed to cohort differences. The lower panels in Table 2 display the fraction of prime-age adults and older adults who are underweight and overweight. In

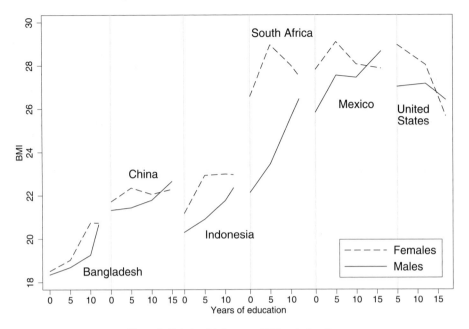

Figure 5. Relationship between BMI and education.

the three poorest countries, older adults are more likely to be underweight than prime-age adults indicating that in terms of improved nutrition, younger adults benefit more from economic growth. In contrast, in the richer countries, older adults are more likely to be overweight than prime-age adults suggesting that as populations move through the nutrition transition, it is the prime-age adults who are more responsive to the negative effects of being overweight. Notice also that in China (and among prime-age Indonesians) twice as many females are overweight as underweight suggesting rapid change in the nutrition profile is underway in these countries.

In fact, the evidence on differences across cohorts indicates that the rate of increase in obesity in many developing countries is far faster than it was in the more-developed countries. See, for example, Popkin (1993) and Monteiro et al. (2004) who discuss differences in BMI by SES, their causes and implications. The inverted U shape in Fig. 5 is consistent with evidence in the literature indicating that as a population moves through the nutrition transition, it is the most educated (and highest income) who are the first to exit under-nutrition. They are also the first to adjust their diet and physical activity to avoid the deleterious effects of being overweight, suggesting that behavioral changes have important impacts on health outcomes. Figure 5 also indicates that it is women who tend to lead this transition. The relative importance of information, resources, technology and other factors in these processes has not been established.

BMI cannot distinguish between lean tissue weight and weight due to body fat. Moreover, the location of fat on the body is predictive of elevated morbidity. For example, elevated levels of stress tend to result in body fat being deposited around the abdomen, elevated waist to hip circumference is a marker for elevated stress. However, higher waist to hip ratios can be caused by several other factors. More precise measures of fat and its distribution on the body are not as easy to assess although new technologies promise simple, non-invasive and rapid measurement of body composition in the future. At this point in time, a potential disadvantage of relying exclusively on anthropometric measures is that they provide information about general health and nutrition but little insight into the pathways through which health affects (or is affected by) life outcomes.

3.4. Physical health assessments and biomarkers

Several recent studies have attempted to measure more specific domains of health status through a wide array of physical assessments. These include simple physical activities that can be completed in a short period of time such as walking a specific distance, balance (standing on one leg for a specific time) or timed repeated stands from a sitting position. These assessments are easy to administer and can provide especially useful information when combined with self-assessed activities of daily living (ADLs).

Recent innovations in the development of non-invasive biomarker measures that can be implemented on a large scale in a field setting have had a major impact on the extent and quality of health measurement in socio-economic surveys. In the last decade, a large number of socio-economic surveys have included the collection of several biomarkers such as blood pressure, lung capacity, measures of strength, as well as measures of sight, hearing and oral health.

Some important indicators of health status can only be measured in biological samples. Studies have collected blood, cheek swabs, hair samples and urine which provide a host of genetic and non-genetic information about each respondent. In some cases, the biomarkers are measured in the home and are very straightforward to implement. For example, blood from a pin prick to the finger is sufficient to measure hemoglobin, glucose, a lipid profile, albumin and HIV status in a few minutes in the home. (Measurement of glucose and triglycerides requires fasting which complicates administration of the assessment.)

Technological innovation in health measurement promises to have a significant impact on empirical research in the area of health and development with less expensive, simpler and more robust methods for the collection, storage and assaying of biological materials being introduced at a rapid rate. One especially promising set of innovations involves the development of technology for the collection and analysis of dried blood spots (DBS). Blood from a finger prick is spotted on filter paper which is dried and stored for later analysis. It is typically feasible to collect several spots from a single finger prick and each spot can be used to measure a different marker. Protocols for over one hundred analytes have been validated for DBS (McDade, Williams and Snodgrass, 2006). These include markers for stress (such as antibodies to Epstein–Barr virus), inflammation (such as C-Reactive Protein, CRP), micronutrients (such as Transferrin Receptors, TfR, an indicator of iron stores), metabolic functioning (such as glycosylated hemoglobin, Hb_{A1c}, which has been implicated in type II diabetes) and reproductive health. Innovations in measurement of biomarkers using saliva, cheek swabs, hair and other minimally invasive methods that are easy to administer in a field setting are also likely to have a major impact on research in this area. (See Lindau and McDade, 2007, for an excellent summary of the state of the art.)

The inclusion of a broad array of biomarkers in population-based studies will not only provide a stronger biological foundation for research on health but also explore new hypotheses. For example, the metabolic syndrome highlights the cumulative effects of obesity, high blood pressure, high cholesterol and hyperglycemia on the risk of diabetes and heart disease (Haller, 1997). McEwen (1998) and his collaborators have highlighted the cumulative effects on health of multiple stress events, each of which triggers a biological response. Allostatic load is the wear and tear on the body due to the over-stimulation of these responses which either fail to shut down or fail to respond. Developing countries are ideal contexts for more fully exploring these constructs.

While innovations in health measurement are very exciting and promise to revolutionize the nature and quality of data on health that is collected in large-scale, population-based socio-economic surveys, to a large extent the benefits remain a promise. To date, only a relatively small number of studies have made effective use of biomarkers to provide new insights into the relationships between health over the life course and other indicators of well-being.

3.5. Self-assessed health

Many of the early studies of health in the social sciences relied on self-assessments of health and health behaviors. While these assessments provide important insights into the distribution of health and characteristics associated with better health, self-assessments do not only reflect intrinsic health. In many cases, these indicators also reflect perceptions of health and information about health, both of which are likely correlated with education, income and use of health services. This substantially complicates interpretation of the indicators.

The RAND Health Insurance Experiment (HIE) provides an example for General Health Status (GHS), a widely-used overall indicator of health which is very easy to administer in a survey and which has been shown to be predictive of future mortality (Ware and Sherbourne, 1992). In the RAND HIE, subjects were randomly assigned to receive free health care or to one of several programs that varied the price of care. Health care use rose the most among those who received free care and, among those who were in poor physical health at the beginning of the study, their physical health improved (Newhouse, 1996). However, the subjects who received free care reported their general health to be worse at the end of the study relative to other subjects, suggesting that GHS is influenced by exposure to health service providers who provide information about health problems which, in turn, affects the subject's own evaluation of his or her health. Similar results are reported for a health price experiment in Indonesia (Dow et al., 2004). This provides one explanation for why GHS tends to be lower for higher income respondents in many surveys from developing countries although mortality and physical health measures suggest that they are in better health than those with less income.

Similar issues arise with all self-reported health indicators to a greater or lesser extent. Many surveys include questions about whether the respondent suffered from one of several morbidities such as diarrhea, nausea, dizziness, fatigue, runny nose, flu, respiratory problems and so on. Not only is it likely that the meaning of "suffer from" varies across SES but the definition of a "runny nose" may well vary depending on what is "expected" health. Some studies ask about diagnosed conditions such as elevated cholesterol or blood pressure, and those reports will provide a distribution of population health that is selected on use of health services.

It has been suggested that ADLs, such as walking a specific distance or carrying a specific load for a specific distance, are less prone to these sorts of biases. It is unlikely, however, that these indicators are not also influenced by a respondent's perception of "good health" or "difficulty" conducting an activity. Moreover, in some cases, the activity might be outside the domain of the person's experience. A standard ADL is difficulty walking up stairs which is unlikely to be relevant in many rural settings. Since ADLs were originally developed to assess health of older adults, many of the standard questions such as difficulty getting up from the floor are not likely to provide much information about the health of prime-age adults.

Recent studies have attempted to develop vignettes which provide a mechanism to standardize each respondent's perception and information about "good health" (King et al., 2004). The value of the vignette approach remains an open question.

Some domains of health can only be assessed with self-reports. Psycho-social health is a good example. It has proved to be difficult to develop and validate instruments that can be fielded across cultural and social contexts. The WHO World Mental Health Surveys, which fielded an adaption of the Composite International Diagnostic Interview (CIDI) in 14 countries, provide an important baseline (WHO Mental Health Survey Consortium, 2004). There would seem to be substantial scope for important contributions to methods and measurement in this area in developing countries where poverty, uncertainty, death and disease likely take their toll.

3.6. Measurement error in health

The fact that health is multidimensional complicates interpretation of specific health markers as covariates in models if those markers are correlated with other health indicators that are not included in the model. In these cases, the health indicator included in the model will be correlated with unobserved indicators not in the model and the estimated "effect" will be biased. Since the included health measure proxies for other dimensions of health, it is not straightforward to interpret estimated "effects."

Health is also likely to be subject to random measurement error. For some physical assessments, such as height, error is attributable to poor measurement by enumerators and can be minimized with good training. Other sources of error affect physical assessments such as weight and blood pressure which vary over the course of the day. More of a concern are errors that depend on respondent performance such as timed chair stands; if more energetic and enthusiastic respondents complete the task more quickly, it is important to recognize these physical assessments capture more than, say, mobility and lower body strength.

Self-assessed indicators of health raise special concerns. In both developing and developed country contexts, interpretation of evidence that relies on self-reports will be complicated to the extent that those indicators reflect not only true health status but other influences that are systematically related to outcomes of interest in specific models, or to characteristics that are included in those models. For example, if individuals who earn higher wages are more likely to use health care services and, because of that use of care, tend to report their health as being worse than it would be if they did not use care, then it will be very difficult to interpret the relationship between wages and self-assessed health status. One approach to addressing this issue is to use instruments for self-reported health status. Given the non-classical nature of this type of measurement error, in general, it will be difficult to identify plausible instruments. This concern applies to all the self-assessed health indicators discussed above and needs to be born in mind when interpreting evidence in the literature.

4. Empirical evidence on health over the life course

We turn to a review of some of the key contributions in the literature, beginning with a body of new evidence that suggests that health in early life may have substantial effects on health and well-being throughout the entire life course. The origins of this work can be traced back to seminal work by Fogel and others in economic history and development as well as innovative lines of research in nutrition, epidemiology and the biomedical sciences. This is a rapidly developing line of inquiry and a very promising avenue for new research that brings together the best practices of these disciplines. It is also important from the perspective of the dynamic models. We begin with evidence on the impact of health *in utero* on mortality and later life health and then turn to economic outcomes in adulthood. This is followed by a brief review of the links between early life health and outcomes during adolescence. This is an area in which there is a substantial literature with contributions from many disciplines and is the subject of one of the chapters in this volume (Glewwe and Miguel, 2008).

We next examine health and socio-economic success in adulthood both from the perspective of the impact of health and health investments on economic productivity and the impact of income and resources on health. The dynamics underlying these relationships naturally leads to a discussion of the role that health may play in smoothing consumption which relates to a much broader literature in micro- and macro-economics. We end with a discussion of HIV/AIDS, arguably the most pressing public health crisis of our time.

4.1. Long-run impacts of early life health on later life outcomes

In recent years, a significant body of evidence has accumulated that establishes an association between health *in utero* or in very early childhood and later life outcomes including health status. Godfrey and Barker (2000) review the industrial country literature. Alderman and Behrman (2006) review studies of low birthweight impacts on later life outcomes in developing countries and provide estimates of the likely welfare costs of low-birthweight babies.

A leading explanation for the relationship between early and later life health has been that poor nutrition of the mother during pregnancy, or of the child during very early childhood, may induce adaptations in organ function or organ size, metabolism or cause gene expression to adapt to a new environment in order to raise survival probabilities through the early years but cause problems later in life (Barker et al., 1989; Fogel, 2004; Komlos, 1994).

Several biological mechanisms have been suggested for this relationship. Thinness at birth may result in slower than normal child growth as an adaptation to reduced nutrients. In the long run, it may lead to negative consequences such as a higher probability of elevated blood pressure, glucose intolerance, a poor lipid profile and elevated risk of type 2 diabetes and coronary heart disease. A corollary to the Barker hypothesis is the notion that a "thrifty phenotype" will develop as an adaption to adverse nutrition *in utero* which results in permanent metabolic and endocrine changes. These changes would be beneficial if food availability continued to be scarce after birth. However, if food is plentiful, the same metabolic changes are disadvantageous and they are associated with elevated risks of obesity, dyslipidemia and glucose intolerance in later life (Hales and Barker, 1992). Thus, in this model, it is those who are born small and thin but become overweight in adulthood that are at greatest risk of heart disease and type 2 diabetes in later life. Quantifying the extent of these effects seems crucial given the rapid rates of growth in obesity, heart disease and type 2 diabetes across the globe (Robinson, 2001).

The biomedical literature suggests that the timing of *in utero* nutrition insults matters. As an example, poor maternal nutrition during the period when arteries form in the fetus have been associated with elevated risk of hardened arteries when the individual reaches mid-life. Thus, it is not just those babies who are very small at birth that are at risk of suffering longer-term consequences of early life deprivation. Even normal birthweight babies are at risk and the extent of these effects depend on subsequent nutrition and other health inputs over the life course (Godfrey and Barker, 2000).

A second, possibly complementary, hypothesis is that inflammation caused by infections, even in very young children, can have deleterious long-run health consequences. The argument is that exposure to infectious disease results in inflammations that ultimately lead to the development of atherosclerosis, which is a major source of cardiovascular disease (Finch and Crimmins, 2004). Studies indicate that high levels of inflammations can promote atherogenesis, the process of forming plaques in the inner linings of arteries, even in the absence of high-fat diets. This process begins *in utero* and continues after birth, throughout life.

Experimental studies with rat models have provided support for both the nutrition and inflammation hypotheses (Godfrey and Barker, 2000; Finch and Crimmins, 2004). Although the nutrition literature is replete with randomized interventions that provide an array of supplements to pregnant women, the impact of those interventions beyond birth outcomes has been largely ignored. Long-term follow-up of those children have the potential to provide important new evidence. To date, therefore, most research on longer run effects of fetal health in humans has been limited to non-experimental designs. Elo and Preston (1992) provide a comprehensive and insightful review of the early literature.

4.1.1. Quasi-experimental studies on fetal health and health in later life

Perhaps some of the best empirical evidence comes from quasi-experimental studies. An important set of research exploits the fact that there was food rationing for 5 to 6 months during the winter of 1944–1945 in some Dutch cities and not in others (Stein et al., 1975). By using a difference-in-difference procedure, comparing birth cohorts exposed to the famine with cohorts not exposed and comparing those born in cities with rationing relative to those born in cities with no rationing, Stein et al. establish that exposure to the famine raised infant mortality, particularly in the first few months after birth, although there was little impact on mortality through age 18, conditional on surviving infancy.[14] Longer-term follow-up studies have mostly examined health at age 50, comparing cohorts exposed to the famine with cohorts not exposed (see Roseboom et al., 2001a, 2001b, for summaries). Mortality at age 50 is apparently unaffected by the famine, conditional on surviving infancy. However, exposure to the famine is associated with elevated risk of glucose intolerance among men and women, worse lipid profiles and elevated risk of coronary heart disease. Women exposed during the first trimester as a fetus tended to have higher BMI and waist circumference but not if the fetus was only exposed later in the pregnancy; there was no evidence of an impact on male body mass. Nor is there evidence that blood pressure is related to exposure to the famine (Ravelli et al., 1998, 1999).[15]

Luo, Mu and Zhang (2006) follow a similar approach and examine the long-run impact of the Great Chinese famine of 1959–1962 on body mass of men and women. The Chinese famine killed between 20 and 30 million people – far more than the Dutch Winter Famine – with deaths being concentrated in rural areas and distributed very unevenly across provinces. Using data from the China Health and Nutrition Survey (CHNS) Luo

---

[14] They also report no differences in an IQ-type test at age 18.

[15] An advantage of the study is that it is possible to draw on administrative data to identify those who have died and those who have emigrated. Although there are no detailed analyses of attrition in the literature, of 2400 individuals in the famine birth cohorts from Amsterdam, 90% were followed up when they were 50. One hundred and ninety-nine had emigrated and most of the rest had died.

et al. examine the BMI in adulthood comparing those born during the famine or soon afterwards and also drawing contrasts across regions of birth in a difference-in-difference framework. They find women born during the famine are more likely to be overweight 30–40 years later; they find no differences for men. Of course it is possible that other changes across time and across regions explain these differences. Perhaps more problematic in this case might be mortality selection. If more frail babies died during the famine, or were not brought to term, they might have been in worse health later in life, which would bias even a difference-in-difference estimator against finding significant effects.

Other studies are limited to comparing birth cohorts. While this has the disadvantage that all time-varying differences attributed to the cohort might in fact reflect confounding time or period effects, the long time series exploited in several important studies mitigates these concerns.

Crimmins and Finch (2006) estimate the impact of infant mortality on older-age mortality using aggregate data by birth cohort on age-specific mortality from different European countries in the 19th century. Specifically they regress mortality from age 70 to 74 years, q_{70-74}, on infant and child mortality rates for that same birth cohort.[16] They argue that infant and childhood mortality in 19th century Europe was a result largely of infectious disease, for which they have supporting evidence from death by cause data. Thus high infant and child mortality rates would be a proxy for high levels of infectious disease and thus inflammation. On the other hand, older-age mortality even in the 19th century was largely from chronic disease, of which heart disease was a major part. Again, they show some evidence in support of this claim. Of course, they have to assume that the only cohort-specific effect derives from different levels of childhood infection, and that period or time effects, possibly correlated with birth cohort effects, are not contaminating the results. Both are strong assumptions. Since they have no direct measures of infection or inflammation, this evidence is indirect.

In a similar study, Bengtsson and Lindstrom (2000) use vital records maintained by churches in four parishes in southern Sweden for the period 1760 to 1894. Using a Cox proportional hazard model they estimate how the probability a person dies, conditional on surviving to the prior period, varies with infant mortality in the year and area of birth as covariates, food prices and socio-economic background of the individual, controlling for cohort effects with a time trend. They find that both birth cohort and region-specific infant mortality are positively and significantly related to older-age mortality, similar to the findings of Crimmins and Finch (2006). However food prices at birth and child (0–5 years) mortality rates are not significantly related to subsequent mortality.

---

[16] They use q_{0-1}, q_{1-4}, q_{5-9} and q_{10-14} simultaneously. The pre-adolescent mortality rates tend to have the largest coefficients, but even controlling for cohort-specific later childhood mortality, infant mortality is significant for Sweden and Switzerland. On the other hand, results for France and England show a lack of significance or a negative coefficient for infant mortality, although later child mortality rates are significantly positive predictors of old-age mortality.

Using almost two decades of data from the Netherlands, van den Berg, Lindeboom and Portrait (2006) explore the relationship between being exposed to an economic recession during the first few years of life and later life mortality. They find that being born during a recession results in an 8 percent increase in the mortality rate after the first year of life and that exposure to reduced resources at the macro level during years 1 through 6 of a child's life have no longer-run implications. This can be interpreted as further evidence that conditions during the fetal period have long-lasting impacts on later life health.

In another historical cohort study, Kannisto, Christensen and Vaupel (1997) analyzed the impact of a large famine in Finland in 1866, 67 and 68, a period of three successive years of serious drought. (At the time, 92% of the Finnish population was rural.) Infant mortality rose to 40% (from 20%) in the last year of the famine, dropping back below 20% right after, so the famine's effect on infant mortality was large. Kannisto et al. compare cohorts born in the three famine years with cohorts born just before and just after. They find a large drop in survival to age 17 in the affected cohorts, consistent with the large period rise in infant mortality, but no impact on subsequent mortality from age 17 to older ages (40, 60 and 80). While later emigration out of Finland could cause biases, if the emigration were different for the different birth cohorts, data on emigration after age 17 shows roughly the same rates across birth cohorts. Of course, to the extent that the more frail died at young ages for cohorts exposed to the famine, this would reduce any observed mortality differences later in life. Unfortunately the data do not provide information on health conditions of the living when older. However, Kannisto et al. demonstrate that the impacts of these major health shocks *in utero* on adult health outcomes is not uniformly negative, as Barker and others hypothesize.

4.1.2. *Quasi-experimental studies on fetal health and economic prosperity in later life*

An innovative study by Almond (2006) explores the impact of impaired fetal health in the US on adult health, human capital accumulation and labor market outcomes. He compares people who were conceived during the Spanish flu pandemic in late 1918 (and born in 1919) with those born before the pandemic and those born at least nine months after the pandemic ended. By allowing for secular trend in the outcomes, he identifies the effect of being *in utero* during the flu pandemic by deviations from the trend. He also exploits variation in timing of the onset of the flu pandemic across the country. He finds large and significant effects of poor fetal health on disability in mid-life, educational attainment and income.

As he notes, Almond is not able to control for other factors that change abruptly because of the flu pandemic. A plausible candidate is food and other commodity prices since there was a positive spike in prices in 1918 associated with demands from World War I which may have affected women's health during pregnancy. Whatever the underlying reason, the evidence in the study suggests that insults to fetal health affect both health and economic prosperity well into adulthood.

Twin studies provide another type of quasi-experimental study. For example, Behrman and Rosenzweig (2004) uses data from a survey they conducted on a sample of same sex monozygotic twins from the Minnesota Twins Registry to estimate the impact of birthweight on adult height, body mass, schooling and wages. Since monozygotes share an identical genetic endowment, differences in their birthweights must reflect differences in their fetal health and nutrition. The average age of the sample is 45, so the impact of birthweight can be examined on outcomes in early and midlife adulthood.

Because the distribution of birthweight differences between twins is much smaller than that between two siblings or between two otherwise similar people in the general population, there may not be sufficient power to detect the impact of birthweight on these outcomes. In fact, examining differences in each outcome as a function of birthweight differences, Berhman and Rosenzweig find that the higher birthweight twin is taller, completed more education and has higher wages. In these data, BMI as an adult does not depend on birthweight. The literature suggests that birthweight may have a non-linear association with health and labor market outcomes. Behrman and Rosenzweig are not able to detect non-linear effects on any of the outcomes other than wages which may be a reflection of insufficient power.

4.1.3. Non-experimental evidence on early life health and later life outcomes

There is a very large literature that uses observational data to draw out the longer-term impacts of early life health. The historical and epidemiological literatures have documented the relationships between height and weight as adults, and subsequent adult mortality (Waaler, 1984; Fogel, 2004). To the extent that height as adults is positively conditioned by height attainment as a child, this evidence demonstrates links between childhood nutrition and health and health as an adult. Of course, if it could be that time persistent unobservables related to innate healthiness or lifetime resource constraints or preferences (perhaps correlated between parents and children) that are the underlying causes of these correlations.

One of the early epidemiological studies linking health as a young child and health when older is Barker and Osmond (1986) who show that in communities in England and Wales that had high neonatal and post-neonatal mortality in the early 1900s people had high adult death rates from coronary disease later in the century (Barker and Osmond, 1986). However, as Elo and Preston (1992) note, half of the population had migrated from its region of origin (and are therefore out of the sample) by the later survey dates, making the results less convincing. At the more micro level, death rates from coronary heart disease among British men and women born between 1911 and 1930 were higher among those persons with low birthweight (Godfrey and Barker, 2000). There is a real issue of how much of these simple correlations represent causal relationships. Many of these studies are bivariate only. Even multivariate studies in general can only control for a subset of potentially important influences. Hence, unobserved factors could easily result in these correlations, confounding the analyses. Still, these studies raise issues that cry out for further scientific investigation.

McDade et al. (2001) use multivariate methods with the Cebu Longitudinal Child Health and Nutrition Survey to examine the correlations between *in utero* health (that is intrauterine growth retardation as indicated by low birthweight for full-term babies) and antibody response to vaccination against typhoid when the same infants were adolescents. They chose a small, random sub-sample of 103 full-term babies of the Cebu study to participate in the vaccination study. Each child was vaccinated against typhoid, and antibody production was measured after vaccination. In their empirical analysis, McDade et al. estimate a health production function, including covariates for birthweight for gestational age, current (adolescent) body mass index, interactions between those two, whether the timing of maturation was early or late, weight gain in the first year of life, whether breastfeeding was long and interactions between those two covariates. They find that low birthweight is associated with a lower likelihood of exhibiting normal antibody responses to the typhoid vaccination, making the vaccination less effective. This negative effect of low birthweight is magnified if the adolescent also has low current body mass. The strength of this analysis is the rich set of health input variables spanning the entire lifetime of these adolescents available in the data. The weakness of the analysis is that these inputs might be determined jointly with the health outcomes. As discussed in Section 2, estimated effects will be biased if there are characteristics omitted from the antibody function that are correlated with the health inputs.

The McDade et al. (2001) study does not directly bear on very long-run health impacts of early childhood insults, as their Cebu sample uses data on adolescents. This issue is addressed by a recent study by Case, Fertig and Paxson (2005), who examine data from the National Child Development Study (NCDS) which collected information on a cohort of all children born in the UK during one week of March in 1958 and has reassessed those respondents periodically through 2004. Case et al. use data from birth through middle-age (42 years old). From the time of birth, they use birthweight and whether the mother smoked heavily during pregnancy. Heights at age 16 are available, as are certain household characteristics from that time period, such as family income. At age 42 and earlier adult ages, the health variable that is available is self-reported health: excellent, good, fair, poor. This is not ideal for the reasons explained above.

Using multivariate regression models, Case et al. examine the extent to which fetal and child health predict self-reported general health status at ages 23, 33 and 42 controlling socio-demographic characteristics. Low birthweight is associated with worse health, and taller children at age 16 report better health in later life although these effects are not always significant.[17] Conditional on these characteristics, whether the mother smoked during pregnancy is negatively associated with later life health which is interpreted as suggesting that *in utero* health affects health in middle age even after controlling birthweight. As Case et al. note, it is possible that these results are driven

---

[17] The mechanisms through which height at age 16 affects later life outcomes in not obvious given that height at this age is substantially affected by the timing of the puberty spurt and has not been shown to be associated with health and well-being in later life. A correlation between height at 16 and earnings at age 32 was reported by Persico, Postlewaite and Silverman (2004) using the same data.

by unobserved heterogeneity. In the context of the conceptual model discussed in Section 2, the estimated models are conditional demand functions with the conditioning variables being potentially correlated with factors that are not observed in the models. For example, a mother who smokes may also invest less in other dimensions of the health and human capital development of her children and so, controlling birthweight and genetic endowment, her children will perform less well in school, have more health problems and perform less well in the labor market in later life than similar children whose mother did not smoke.

More generally, studies that report correlations between early life health and later life outcomes are both suggestive and intriguing but do not establish causality. Finding that birthweight is predictive of health or human capital outcomes in later life may indicate that low birthweight is a marker for poverty or other sources of deprivation, broadly defined, while *in utero*. If that deprivation persists through life, it is not clear whether it is these other (unobserved and persistent) factors or low birthweight that causes poorer outcomes in later life. Distinguishing unobserved heterogeneity from state dependence is a problem that plagues many studies of behavioral choices and plays a central role in the literature on health.

The temporal nature of the measures rules out the possibility that later life outcomes cause early child health. There may well be unobserved heterogeneity that is correlated with both early life health and later life outcomes. Examples include unobserved factors that are associated with innate healthiness, tastes for investments in health, preferences towards good health and health behaviors.[18] Moreover, in the forward-looking model described above, it is possible that early life investments in health are made because of their implications for health in later life. Establishing that early life health has a causal impact on later life outcomes is not straightforward. In the absence of experimental or quasi-experimental variation in early life experiences, isolating the causal effect of, say, birthweight on later life outcomes, calls for measures of health input prices during the fetal period, that can be used as instruments in IV procedures. These might include the price, availability and quality of prenatal care, relative prices of foods that are rich in iron or other micronutrients that are critical during pregnancy.

4.1.4. Intergenerational transmission of health

Whereas there is a large literature on the inter-generational transmission of education and SES, there is substantially more limited evidence for health outside the biomedical and genetics literature. This is surprising given the fact that genetic endowments are transmitted across generations and, if fetal or infant health affects health and well-being in later life, it seems natural to assess the extent to which health is transmitted across generations.

---

[18] As discussed above, the same empirical issue arises in models of health and productivity. (See Behrman and Deolalikar, 1988 or Strauss, 1993, for early critiques.)

Animal studies have shown that fetal growth is retarded in offspring of mother rats that are fed protein-restricted diets over several generations. The offspring are born small relative to controls on a normal diet. However, when a later generation of those rats on the restricted diet were fed a normal diet, starting from conception, the rat is larger in size than controls. If these rats continue with the normal diet then within two generations, there are no differences in the size of the treatments and controls (Stewart et al., 1980).

Emanuel et al. (1992) show that in the NCDS, the 1958 British cohort study, there is a positive correlation between birthweights of mothers and children. This result has been replicated for the state of Washington by Emanuel et al. (1999). Historical data from a hospital in China shows that a higher BMI mother (greater than 26 compared to less than 23 in the 38th week of pregnancy) was more likely to give birth to a child who would have lower blood glucose and higher insulin concentrations when he/she reached age 60 (Barker, 2006). The same study demonstrates that maternal pelvic size is correlated with the odds of the child having a stroke or diagnosed hypertension as an adult.

An extensive literature in developmental psychology indicates that there are significant positive inter-generational correlations in health-related behaviors including smoking, drinking, substance abuse, diet and eating disorders as well as in psychosocial and emotional problems. (See Serbin and Karp, 2004 and Chapman and Scott, 2001, for reviews.) For example, the Concordia study (Serbin et al., 1991) indicates that children with mothers that had a history of aggression tend to have reduced cortisol reactivity when challenged by a verbal conflict task with the mother. Moreover, the same study reports a positive association between cortisol reactivity in the mothers and their children.

Using unique data from Denmark, Eriksson, Bratsberg and Raaum (2006) examine the inter-generational correlation in health of adults in their late forties with that of their parents focusing on a series of diagnosed conditions that include cancer, hypertension and heart disease, respiratory problems, allergies, migraines and psycho-social problems. Both own and parental reports are provided by the adult child. The adult child is at substantially higher risk of suffering from any of the ailments if either parent suffered from the same ailment. For example, if a father is reported to have had psycho-social problems, the child is eight times more likely to also report psycho-social problems; the risk is five times higher if the mother had psycho-social problems. Heart disease in either parent is associated with an elevated risk that is four times higher in the adult child. While some of these correlations may be driven by common measurement error (given the way the data were collected), they are large and consistent with evidence in the biomedical literature. Moreover, controlling own health status absorbs around a quarter of the inter-generational correlation in earnings.

Martorell et al. (1981) report a positive correlation between maternal height and the survival probabilities of their children in Guatemala. Thomas, Strauss and Henriques (1990) use multivariate models to demonstrate a positive association between a mother's height and the mortality of her children, for children from Brazil; controlling for factors such as mother's and father's schooling and household nonlabor income. These results may be driven by the impact of maternal pelvic size. However, Thomas, Strauss and Henriques (1990) also show a strong partial correlation between mother's and father's height and the age/sex standardized heights of children, again controlling for parental schooling and household income.[19]

In a clever and insightful study, Almond and Chay (2006) note that the health of blacks improved dramatically during the 1960s while the health of whites changed relatively little. This is indicated by the infant mortality rate of blacks declining from around 40 in the mid-1960s to below 30 in the mid-1970s; the absolute reduction in infant mortality rates was smaller for whites albeit about the same proportionate change. They argue that black women born in the late 1960s are substantially healthier than those born a decade before them. To examine the inter-generational transmission of health, they use data from the annual Natality Detail files and compare the health of babies born to black women born in these two cohorts and find that babies born to the later cohort are less likely to be low birthweight and have better APGAR scores. This is not driven by secular change in the broader society since there is no corresponding improvement in the health of babies born to white women from these two cohorts. As a further check on this, Almond and Chay compare the improvement of child outcomes across the cohorts of black mothers born in Mississippi, a state that had very large declines in black infant mortality, to black mothers born in Alabama, where mortality declines were smaller. These results reinforce their other results. Almond and Chay conclude that there is substantial and significant inter-generation transmission of health.

There are surely several mechanisms underlying observed correlations in health across generations. Part is likely to be attributable to inter-generational transmission of genetic endowment. Part of the correlation may reflect non-genetic dimensions of parental health being transmitted across generations. It is possible that parental health is a marker for unobserved ability in managing the inputs into the production of one's child's health (μ in the health production function) as well as tastes for health and other goods (ξ in the utility function) and that these are transmitted across generations. The work of Eriksson, Bratsberg and Raaum (2006) suggests that part of the unobserved factors that affect labor market success may be correlated with health. While the evidence at hand does not establish which of these mechanisms is important across contexts, it seems that this line of research has the potential to open new windows into the ways in which health investments and health outcomes affect the well-being of individuals and their progeny.

4.2. Child and adolescent health, human capital development and economic success

The previous subsection focused on the relationship between health *in utero* or during infancy and well-being, including health, in later life. Moving to the next stage in the life

---

[19] Also see Horton (1986) for an earlier study which uses mother's height to explain child's height.

course, in this section we explore the relationships among health and other indicators of human capital during childhood and adolescence. We also examine the longer-term effects on health in childhood on health and well-being during adulthood. Health in adulthood is discussed in the following subsection.

Studies of the links between child health, cognitive achievement and schooling outcomes are summarized by Behrman (1996) and discussed in detail in Glewwe and Miguel (2008). Therefore, we focus our discussion on relationships between different dimensions of health and human capital as a child including child growth. We then highlight the implications for well-being in later life.

Many of the early studies in this literature relied on non-experimental cross-sectional data and, by necessity, made strong assumptions. However, in recent years, a substantial body of research has developed which uses innovative experimental or quasi-experimental designs, in combination with longitudinal data, to provide new insights into the causal effect of child and adolescent health on well-being during childhood and as an adult.

4.2.1. Experimental studies

One of the most innovative studies in the field of health and development, and probably the best known large-scale treatment-control experimental study linking child health to cognitive development, is the INCAP longitudinal study (1969–1977) in rural Guatemala. Subsequent follow-ups in 1988–1989, 1997–1998 and 2002–2004 provide uniquely rich data spanning over three decades to examine the links between child health and well-being in adulthood. The motivation, study design and some of the key results are described in Martorell, Habicht and Rivera (1995), Grajeda et al. (2005a) and Martorell et al. (2005).

Four villages were chosen for the study. Pairs of villages were matched using fifteen village characteristics such as population, age distribution, nutritional status and health status. For each pair, one village was randomly assigned to treatment and the other to control. Using only four villages and randomizing at the village level limits the power of the experiment and also limits the extent to which matching yields a truly random design.

The study focused on young children, from birth to seven years in 1969–1977, and pregnant and lactating women. The treatment involved providing a daily nutritional supplement in the form of a fortified drink, Atole, which contained about 39 kilojoules of energy and 11.5 g of protein along with some micronutrients including iron and niacin. (This amounts to about 10% of recommended daily intake of energy and 20% of protein in a well-nourished population.) The placebo drink, Fresco, was provided in the control villages and contained around 14 kilojoules of energy from sugar.

Two years after the start of the intervention, both drinks were fortified with additional micronutrients so that Atole and Fresco contained the same amounts of iron, niacin, vitamin A, thiamine, fluorine and ascorbic acid. Health care services, including free curative care and immunizations, were provided in all four villages. To the extent that these health services, and the change in micro-nutrient content of the drinks, do not have the same impact on treatments and controls, then inferences about the impact of the protein/calorie supplement will be confounded.

The drinks were provided at centrally located venues in each village during the day. Participation was voluntary and about three quarters of all age-eligible children and pregnant or lactating women participated. Modeling participation is not straightforward and so most analyses have examined the intent to treat effect on all eligible villagers. There are two particularly troubling aspects of this dimension of the design. While participation rates are high relative to other, similar studies, in the treatment villages, lower-SES children were more likely to consume the drink; however no such difference is observed in the control villages. Second, since children older than 7 were not eligible for the drink, it is possible that families substituted food in favor of older children because younger children were receiving the supplement. In fact, children in larger families were more likely to participate in the program. These are additional factors that potentially confound interpretation of differences in outcomes between treatments and controls and between exposed cohorts and those cohorts not intended to be exposed.

The amount of the drink consumed by each subject in the study also differed. In the control villages, young children (age 0–3 years) drank far less of the drink than children in the treatment villages. Thus, the latter ingested more calories, protein and micro-nutrients. However, mothers in the control villages drank more than mothers in the treatment villages and so intakes of calories were roughly the same for all women and micro-nutrient intake was higher among the women in control villages. It is thus very difficult to interpret differences between treatment and control women. For example, a comparison of birthweight of children born to women in treatment relative to control villages yields no difference. However, birthweight is positively correlated with calorie intake from the drinks which, of course, reflects at least in part choices by the women. (See Martorell et al., 2005, for an excellent discussion of these issues.)

Baseline measurements of many health and nutrition factors were taken in this study and the children and mothers were followed up with measurements on breastfeeding, illness symptoms, solid food intakes, and anthropometry at intervals which depended on the child's age. Many other measurements were taken, particularly on cognitive development, starting during infancy, up to age 7 years during the 1969–1977 period. Taking the daily supplementation was closely monitored and records kept. While relatively little economic information was collected in the early phase of the study, the economic content of the follow-up surveys was substantially expanded in later waves.

The data from this study have been very extensively used, although only a subset of the studies exploit the experimental design. As a good example of the latter, Habicht, Martorell and Rivera (1995) use a difference-in-difference approach to measure the impact of supplementation on child growth. Comparing subjects from treatment villages with those from control villages and also comparing birth cohorts that were included in the study with those not included, they find that supplementation affects linear growth to around 36 months of age but not thereafter. This has been a very influential study and indicates that nutrition interventions in very early life are likely to have significant benefits in terms of improved health and well-being throughout life (see Martorell et al., 2005, for a summary).[20]

The experimental design has also been exploited to measure the impacts of nutrition on cognitive learning and schooling (Stein et al., 2005, has a summary). The first studies focused on children up to age three and reported very small, but significant, effects of the supplementation on a series of development markers. Subsequent studies on children when they were older found larger impacts on test scores, particularly among treated children from low-SES families (Pollitt et al., 1993). While the study exploits the experimental design, it also interacts the treatment group with an SES index at the time of the measurement and with years of schooling of the child, both of which are arguably related to unobserved characteristics that affect cognition and, therefore, are endogenous in the model. Moreover, recall that in treatment villages children of low-SES families were more likely to participate in the study which is, itself, another choice.

Maluccio et al. (2006) use the 2002–2004 follow-up data together with the original 1969–1977 data. The 2002–2004 follow-up data collected a lot of economic data, in addition to adding to the health data collected in prior waves. This round also administered achievement tests and Ravens' colored progression matrix tests to the survey respondents.

Maluccio et al. examine whether schooling attainment and test scores were affected by the supplementation given to treatments. Most respondents were in their 30s by 2002–2004 and thus had completed their schooling. Maluccio et al. estimate a reduced-form demand function for schooling attainment, test scores and other outcomes. To measure the intent to treat effect of the supplementation they use a difference-in-difference approach with all children in the study, irrespective of their participation status. They compare children exposed to the Atole treatment relative to those exposed to the Fresco control, drawing comparisons between children in birth cohorts that were exposed to the study from birth through 36 months of age with cohorts not fully exposed during those ages. Village fixed effects absorb the main effects of differences between villages. They find significant and positive effects of exposure to supplementation on a test for abstract reasoning, the Ravens' colored progression matrix test. Performance in school, however, was only enhanced among female subjects: they completed more grades of school by age 13, completed an extra year of schooling by early adulthood and they performed better on Spanish reading tests. It is not clear what drives these differences between males and females.

It is critical in any experiment that all subjects be followed. This is harder the longer-term the study. In the case of the INCAP surveys, the follow-up rates of children in the 1988–1989 survey were 70–75%, depending on the village and there is no evidence of differential attrition between the villages (Martorell, Habicht and Rivera, 1995). Whereas among those who did not move from the village, re-contact

---

[20] Several analyses which use these data but do not exploit the experimental design draw similar conclusions. These studies are plagued with potential confounds associated with unobserved heterogeneity.

was 86–90%; among migrants, 40–45% were re-interviewed (in part because tracking of movers was limited to the local district capital or Guatemala City). By the 2002–2004 wave, more of the study subjects had moved from the original village and attempts were made to re-contact all respondents no matter where they lived. They found about 60% of the original sample of children. Since 11% of the respondents had died, this amounts to a recontact rate of 70% among all eligible respondents (Maluccio et al., 2006). Their own analyses and those presented by Grajeda et al. (2005b) indicate that men, younger people and people who were not living with their parents in prior waves were less likely to be re-contacted. On the positive side, Maluccio et al. (2006) find insignificant effects of the exogenous intent to treat variables on individual attrition, which suggests attrition is unrelated to the treatment. They also use the method suggested by Fitzgerald, Gottschalk and Moffitt (1998) to reweight the sample and thereby control for attrition bias that can be attributed to selection on observed characteristics. The results are almost identical to those that ignore attrition, suggesting selective attrition that is correlated with treatment status is not important in this model.

A second important experimental study provides deworming treatments to school-age children in rural Kenya and examines the impact of reducing worm loads on school attendance and school performance (Miguel and Kremer, 2004). Intestinal helminth (worms) infections are prevalent in many parts of the developing world, and when worm burdens are high, they can result in iron deficient anemia, protein-energy deficiency and abdominal pain. Over one third of the children in the study suffered from moderate to heavy worm loads at the initiation of the study.

Most types of worms are readily treated with single-dose oral therapies. Seventy-five primary schools were randomly assigned to one of three groups. Children in schools in the first group received deworming treatments for two years starting at the initiation of the study. Children in schools in the second group received treatments in the second year only. Children in schools in the third group did not receive treatments until three years after the start of the study.

The treatments were administered in the schools and so children in treatment schools who were absent on the day of administration failed to get the treatment. About one-quarter of the children in the target schools did not receive the treatment with the compliance rate being lower in the second year.

After treatment, children in the treatment schools tended to be in better health than children in control schools. Deworming significantly increased school attendance in treatment schools by seven percentage points, which is a 25% reduction in school absenteeism. These gains are largest among the youngest children. Test scores are not affected by deworming.

The study demonstrates that health has a causal impact on school attendance although the evidence for benefits in terms of improved learning and cognitive development are less clear. The study also highlights the importance of externality benefits of deworming since reduced incidence of worms will lower infection rates for others in the school or community. For more discussion, see the chapter by Glewwe and Miguel (2008) in this volume.

Another set of important experimental studies exploits data from an evaluation sample of villages in Mexico that were randomly assigned to receive PROGRESA benefits immediately or with a delay. Those studies are discussed by Parker, Rubalcava and Teruel (2008) in this volume.

4.2.2. Quasi-experimental studies

Several quasi-experimental studies in low-income settings have used weather shocks to identify the effect of health shocks on subsequent health (weight gain) (Foster, 1995) and schooling outcomes (Jacoby and Skoufias, 1997). Strauss and Thomas (1998) survey that literature. Recent studies have examined the longer-term consequences of health shocks on health and schooling using the dynamic conditional demand function framework (15) discussed in Section 2.

A very useful set of studies uses data collected by Bill Kinsey from households living in rural land resettlement schemes in Zimbabwe. The project began in the early 1980s in rural Zimbabwe in an effort to assess the impact of a resettlement program initiated by the newly-elected majority-rule government. Households were surveyed in mid-1983 through early 1984, in 1987, 1992 and then annually through 2001.

Hoddinott and Kinsey (2001) use anthropometric data collected annually between 1993 and 1997 to examine growth in height among children age 12–24 months in 1993. They regress the change in child height (in cms) between adjacent years on lagged height (in cms), gender, age in 1993, time between measurements and time interacted with initial age, a series of mother's characteristics, including schooling and height, a series of household characteristics, including livestock and land holdings, and time dummies, including one for the drought year.

The OLS estimate of the coefficient on lagged height is −0.33 suggesting significant but incomplete catch-up in linear growth.[21] This is also consistent with reversion to the mean driven by measurement error.[22] As Hoddinott and Kinsey note, and as discussed in Section 2, it is not clear what to make of OLS estimates of this model. They adopt two different empirical strategies.

First, they apply an IV approach to account for the endogeneity of lagged height, using the child's birthweight and whether birthweight is known as instruments. There are two concerns. First, it is assumed that birthweight affects current height through height in the previous year. The limited evidence that exists suggests this is unlikely

---

[21] There was a severe drought in 1993–1994 which is associated with reduced linear growth, particularly among the youngest children (age 12–24 months).

[22] The authors were careful to take out some gross outliers based on height and that resulted in the −0.33 coefficient on lagged height. When they use all of the observations, the coefficient on lagged height falls to −0.59, which again is consistent with random measurement error imparting a negative bias to the growth equation estimate being a serious concern.

to be true at least for very young children. (See the discussion above of the INCAP results, in which birthweight is found to be negatively correlated with child growth up to 36 months, or the hypotheses on the impacts of early infections proposed by Crimmins and Finch, 2006.) The second and probably more important issue with the instruments is that birthweight is reported by the mother and known for only a fraction of the children. Putting aside recall issues, a mother will only know the birthweight if it was measured which, in Zimbabwe, typically means the birth took place in a clinic or hospital. Low-SES mothers are likely to give birth at home and so will not know the birthweight; if their children tend to grow less well than children of higher-SES mothers, the instrument will likely be correlated with unobserved characteristics in the model of linear growth.

As a second approach, Hoddinott and Kinsey estimate the growth in height model including mother fixed effects. The coefficient on lagged height is -0.81 suggesting almost complete catch-up growth. However, it is well known that in a model specified in terms of growth, random measurement error in the lagged dependent variable (lagged height in this case) will impart a negative bias in the estimates, apart from the usual bias towards zero. Comparing siblings (by including mother fixed effects) typically raises the noise to signal ratio and exacerbates the negative bias due to random measurement error. This is likely to at least partly explain the decline in the coefficient on lagged height from -0.33 to -0.81. Random measurement error in lagged height is likely to be exacerbated with the differencing involved with a mother's fixed effects estimator, then this negative bias may be enhanced, which would explain the drop in the lagged height coefficient from -0.33 to -0.81. In any event, mother fixed effects estimation will only control for correlations between birthweight and omitted variables if parents do not compensate for differences between children that are correlated with birthweight. (See Rosenzweig and Wolpin, 1988, for a classic treatment.)

Using data from Russia, Federov and Sahn (2005) estimate the impact of child health on later child health with the GMM method proposed by Arellano and Bond (1991). This amounts to taking first differences of individual child height to eliminate child-specific time invariant factors and then using instrumental variables to take into account correlations between lagged health and time-varying unobserved factors including measurement error. The assumption necessary for these estimates to be consistent is that there is no serial correlation in time-varying unobserved characteristics such as innate healthiness or ability. This is a strong assumption.

Recognizing this, Alderman, Hoddinott and Kinsey (2006) combine maternal fixed effects with instrumental variables to analyze the impact of pre-school height on later health and schooling using the Zimbabwean data. They examine three outcomes: adolescent height, age at which the child started school and the level of schooling completed by 2000. Pre-school height, which was measured in 1983, 1984 or 1987, was assumed to have been affected by two exogenous shocks: the 1982–1984 drought, the worst drought in living memory, and the 14-year civil war which ended with one-man one-vote elections in 1980. It is assumed that, controlling pre-school height, these shocks had no independent effect on subsequent height and schooling outcomes.[23]

In the first stage regressions, the drought and civil war are significant predictors of pre-school height. In the second stage, pre-school height has a positive and significant impact on adolescent height and years of attained schooling. Taller children also tend to start school earlier although this effect is not significant. The estimated effects are large. The drought resulted in adolescents being 2.3 cm shorter and completing 0.7 years less schooling. (By comparison, adult height increased by about 1 cm per decade in many developing countries in the last half of the twentieth century. See Strauss and Thomas, 1995.)

There was a substantial amount of attrition with around 60% of age-eligible respondents for this study being assessed in the 2000 wave (which is the wave when adolescent height and school attainment are measured). Attriters tend to be female, earlier birth cohorts and were taller prior to starting school. Conditional on age, sex and village controls, pre-school height is not a significant predictor of attrition suggesting that attrition bias is not related to unobserved characteristics correlated with pre-school height. Whether attrition is related to later height and schooling outcomes is, of course, an open question.

While the identifying assumptions in this paper are arguably weaker than those in most of the non-experimental literature on this topic, it is not clear that the 1982/1984 drought and civil war were "shocks" in the sense they were unanticipated and exogenous (to child human capital). The severity of the 1982–1984 drought might have been unexpected, droughts are common in southern Africa and the impact of the drought likely lasted several years through its impact on grain storage and prices and on livestock holdings and prices. This would likely affect human capital accumulation after the drought ended and so identification based on the years of the drought alone may not be appropriate beyond the drought. The civil war directly affected virtually every family in Zimbabwe and carried with it a tremendous amount of dislocation and destruction. Its end was not unanticipated and the impact of the subsequent rebuilding of infrastructure and civil society possibly affected adults and children for many years beyond the end of the war.

The impact of child health, as indicated by height, on later schooling outcomes is also examined by Alderman et al. (2001). Using 5 years of panel data from Pakistan, they exploit variation in prices, rather than weather variation and civil war, to identify pre-school height in a child schooling equation. Specifically, they model school enrollment at age 7 as a function of standardized height at age 5, controlling parental schooling, household composition and a three-year average of household per capita expenditure over three years (to represent long-run resources), and current prices of wheat, rice

---

[23] Specifically the 1982–1984 drought shock is an indicator variable for children who were born in 1981 or 1982 and so were age 12 to 36 months during the drought. The child's exposure to the civil war is measured by (the logarithm) of the age of the child (in days) when the war ended on August 18, 1980. These shock variables amount to cohort effects.

and milk. Village-level fixed effects are included in the models, so that the prices can be interpreted as deviations from village means which they interpret as current price shocks. The variation of price shocks over time is the source of the identification. Current prices enter the school enrollment probit, while lagged prices enter the pre-school height regression as identifying instruments. Village-level dummies, or fixed effects, capture expected prices. To obtain extra power in the first stage, the community-level price variables are interacted with household-level variables: mother's being schooled and gender of the child, as additional instruments.

The IV results indicate a strong, positive impact of height at age 5 on girls' enrollment at age 7, but not on boys' enrollment, an effect which is much larger than the OLS estimates. Paralleling the approach used in the Zimbabwe case (Alderman, Hoddinott and Kinsey, 2006), a key assumption is that price variation at age 5 affects height at that age but has no longer-lasting impacts on budget allocations, height and schooling when the child is older. If that assumption is not correct then other health variables belong in the second stage enrollment equations and if one does not include them, then lagged prices would affect the school enrollment decisions. In this case the price shocks would not be valid instruments. Given the discussion in the previous subsection, one might be concerned that since the initial measurement is at age 5, this may be too late for current prices to influence current height in a way that is likely to have a long-lasting impact on human capital. Alternatively, if we interpret these prices as being proxies for prices at age 2 (assuming that the prices are strongly serially correlated) then one can interpret the results more easily.

Rosenzweig and Zhang (2006) use an innovative sample of twins and non-twins, aged 7–18, taken in Kunming, China, to examine the impact of birthweight (and twins) on schooling and health of children. The researchers worked with one of the government's statistics bureaus and examined the 2000 Census data to identify likely twins in each household. These households were then surveyed, if found, in 2002, and a sample of non-twins were taken in the same areas. The twins were not necessarily monozygotic. Rosenzweig and Zhang (2006) use a within-twins fixed effects estimator to measure the impact of birthweight on non-required schooling expenditures per child (in China some expenditures, such as fees, would be required, while others, say for tutors, are not). The sample used in this exercise is from urban areas affected by the one-child policy, so that parents are constrained from having more than one child unless they had a twin. They are able to look at twins at first birth, which can be taken as exogenous in the China setting. They find a significant, positive impact on child educational expenditures, but one that is much lower than in a simple OLS estimate.

In a different set of regressions, they take the sample of urban children and regress measures of expected college completion (reported by the parents), scores on math and literature achievement tests, self-reported health being excellent or good, weight, height and BMI on whether the child is in a household with a first-born twin's birth and birthweight. Of interest here are the birthweight coefficients, which Rosenzweig and Zhang (2006) find to be significantly and positively related to all of the health variables, but not to the achievement test scores and only weakly to the parents' expectations of college enrollment.

One unknown in this study is how select the analysis sample is because of requiring data on birthweight. As explained above, birthweight data coming from self-reports, which these data presumably do, may suffer from selection issues related to who knows about birthweight.

4.2.3. Non-experimental studies

In a closely related paper to Maluccio et al. (2006), Behrman et al. (2006) estimate test score production functions for reading and cognitive skills, separately, for the INCAP 2002–2004 sample. The tests were given to the respondents in the latter survey period, when they were adults. Behrman et al. use variables measuring whether the respondent was stunted at age 7, years of schooling, age and age squared at the test, and tenure for having a skilled job, as covariates. The production functions do not use the experimental nature of the data, so non-experimental techniques are required for estimation. Behrman et al. treat all the covariates except age as endogenous and use instrumental variables to estimate the production function. For the instruments, however, the experimental nature of the data is used. As instruments for the variable stunting at age 7, being in a birth cohort fully exposed to either the supplementation or placebo, alone and interacted with a dummy for being in a treatment village, are used. These are the variables used by Maluccio et al. (2006) to measure intent to treat effects. Other instruments include household wealth when young, mother's and father's education, and variables measuring village teacher–student ratio at age 7 and whether a secondary school was available in the village at age 7. Behrman et al. find positive impacts of not being stunted at age 7 on these later adult test score outcomes.

There are two related issues with the interpretation of these estimates. First is whether the instruments are appropriately excluded from the achievement test production function. Take the intent to treat variables for instance. Excluding them assumes that the only nutrition variable that affects test outcomes is being stunted at age 7. But it is possible that the impact of height is not discrete, that weight-for-height at age 7 might matter or perhaps height at earlier ages might affect test outcomes. Indeed, the fetal programming hypothesis would suggest that birthweight may matter, after conditioning on height at age 7. Likewise, one can reasonably ask why school quality measures such as teacher–student ratios do not directly affect test score achievement. The second issue, which comes up in most attempts to estimate a human capital production function, is how completely and how well inputs are measured. The inputs used in this paper are rather sparse. As a result, it is likely that many of the instruments will proxy for those inputs and so should not be excluded from the second stage.

Glewwe, Jacoby and King (2001) use longitudinal data to also examine the impacts of early child health on later schooling outcomes. Using the Cebu Longitudinal Child and Nutrition Survey, they estimate an achievement production function in which lagged child height is one of the inputs. These data are, in principle, perfect for this purpose, since children are followed from birth to 11 years. Unfortunately Glewwe et al. do not use anthropometric data from the first two years of life, except as instruments. Rather they examine the impact of child height at the time of school enrollment (about age 7 in the Philippines) on school achievement test scores at age 11 or so. Other input variables are variables measuring gender, age at first enrollment, months in school in 1st and 2nd grades and in 3rd to 6th grades (as separate variables), months repeating these grades, months not in school and mother's years of schooling. The reason that heights before 2 years are not used in the test score equations is that family fixed effects are used in the estimation, together with IV. The family fixed effects involves taking the difference of covariates between children. To use height at age 2 years as a covariate would then require that both children have these data available. However, while the Cebu data has heights at birth and up to 24 months for index children, for younger siblings, height data are only available at sporadic ages, up to age 7, and in general not at age 2 years, so there is a missing data problem.

However, heights at age 7 are available for both index children and younger siblings. The family fixed effects controls for unobserved characteristics that are the same for both siblings. This may include parental preferences for schooling and health investments, for example. However, as long as parents observe innate ability of the individual children and act on that while making their investment decisions, there will still be omitted variables correlated with the sibling height difference, thus causing bias. To control for this, Glewwe et al. use instruments separately for the school inputs and the lagged height. The instruments for the schooling input variables are month of birth dummy variables for both siblings, age difference of testing of the siblings, and various interactions. For the lagged standardized height-for-age, the instrument is the height-for-age of the older sibling at birth, 12 and 24 months. The idea (from Rosenzweig and Wolpin, 1988) is that early childhood height of the older child is known when schooling investments are made in both children and should be correlated with the difference in sibling heights, but that this early height should be uncorrelated with later schooling outcomes conditional on later heights. A critical assumption being made is that time-invariant unobserved factors in a child's health production function are uncorrelated with unobserved factors that affect scores in a test score production function. The assumption is not tested. In addition, it may be that shocks to child health at birth or ages 12 and 24 months affect child cognitive development, even controlling child height at age 7. In this case, again, these variables belong in the achievement production function in addition to height at age 7.

Glewwe and King (2001) take advantage of the time-varying anthropometric measurements on the index children in the Cebu sample and estimate conditional demand functions for cognitive achievement, as indicated by a score on the Raven's colored progressive matrix assessment. Their covariates are birthweight, growth in height in 6 month intervals from 0–6 months, up to 24 months, and then growth from 24 months to 8 years; plus parental schooling and household wealth (which is time-varying). They use lagged rainfall and prices to instrument the lagged height growth variables, adding mother's height and arm circumference in some specifications. In the first stage estimates, few variables are individually significant, but Glewwe and King do not present *F*-statistics to test the identifying variables as a group. They find that while OLS results are positive and highly significant, IV estimates tend not to be significant, and when they are, are not consistent across different instrument sets.

While a number of studies have now appeared that examine impacts of exogenous shocks, rainfall or price, on health, few studies examine what can be done to counter these impacts. One exception is the Guatemala supplementation experiments. Another is a study by Yamano, Alderman and Christiaensen (2005) that examines whether food aid, given to households, results in enhanced child growth, using panel data from Ethiopia from 1995/1996. Yamano et al. have data on heights and weights of children six months apart. They know whether the household received food aid during this period, and how much. They estimate a dynamic conditional demand child growth equation, similar to the studies discussed previously, in which the change in child height is regressed on initial child height, age and a series of detailed household characteristics having to do with education and asset holdings within the household. Among the household variables is the amount of food aid received over the period. Community fixed effects are used to capture price, rainfall, and other community shocks. Yamano, Alderman and Christiaensen (2005) find that food aid is positively and significantly related to child growth in height, after controlling for a rich set of factors.

In their analysis, lagged height is treated as endogenous, but due to random measurement error. Lagged weight is used as the instrument, which requires the assumptions that measurement errors in height and weight are uncorrelated (which seems reasonable) and that lagged weight does not belong in the height growth equation conditional on lagged height (a stronger assumption, but one regularly made in this literature). This method does not correct for potential bias due to omitted variables; the authors argue that the bias due to measurement error may be the more important of these, but there is no way to know for certain.

Household (and community) receipt of food aid is also treated as endogenous, since it is the case that food aid was not distributed randomly across localities. Following a paper by Jayne et al. (2002) that used the same data, Yamano, Alderman and Christiaensen (2005) use the central government's assessment of each community's food aid needs during the famine period of 1984/1985 as an identifying instrument for household receipt of food aid, after conditioning in the second stage on measures of current year crop shocks at the household level. The idea is that it appears that the regional distribution of food aid in Ethiopia is quite similar to the distribution in the famine period, even ten years later. This is so controlling for many factors such as the current rainfall shock in each area, the coefficient of variation of long-run rainfall in each area and even larger area fixed effects. Hence, past central government assessments of food aid needs still strongly predicts whether the village (and households within the village) gets food aid and how much.

4.3. Adult health and SES

A large and growing literature documents a positive correlation between many dimensions of health as an adult and several indicators of socio-economic status.[24] As noted above, studies have demonstrated that early life health has important consequences for later life outcomes. This is manifest in one of the most robust findings in the literature relating health to socio-economic status in developing countries: in a wide variety of contexts, adult height is a powerful predictor of economic productivity as indicated, for example, by hourly earnings. In general, the association between height and economic success is substantially stronger in low-income countries than more developed economies. This likely reflects differentials in the returns to strength in the labor market, the incidence of poor nutrition in early life and differences in the extent of inter-generational transmission of human capital (Strauss and Thomas, 1998).

Pinning down the causal pathways that underlie the associations between health and socio-economic success has proved to be difficult. To date, experimental and quasi-experimental methods have provided the most compelling evidence on the impact of health on economic success.

Joshi and Schultz (2006) use "randomly-assigned" variation in access to contraceptives in rural Bangladesh to examine the impact on later female health, productivity, earnings and wealth. Using data from the 1996 Matlab Health and Socioeconomic Survey, Joshi and Schultz exploit the fact that starting in 1977, half the villages in Matlab were assigned to receive services from an intensive family planning and maternal-child health outreach program involving home visits every other week and encouragement to adopt modern contraceptives. While the selection of treatment and control areas was not strictly random, it is close for this analysis; an analysis by Joshi and Schultz (2006) shows that baseline fertility and schooling are uncorrelated with being in a treatment or control area. A comparison of completed fertility of women in treatment relative to control villages demonstrates the outreach program resulted in a large and significant decline in fertility. Joshi and Schultz investigate whether lowering the effective price of reproductive health services also affects other dimensions of the lives of women twenty years after the program was initiated. They report that female health, as indicated by BMI, is significantly improved and estimate that child mortality risks are reduced by about one-fifth. Better-educated women who lived in treatment villages reported higher earnings and total income and greater wealth.

Variation in the price of health care is also provided by the RAND Health Insurance Experiment (HIE) which randomly assigned subjects to different combinations of deductibles and co-payments. As noted above, those who received free care used more health care and were in better physical health at the end of the intervention. Dow et al. (2004) exploit the variation in price of health care to examine the short-run impact on labor supply. They report that females who received free care were more likely to

---

[24] Harris, Gruenewald and Seeman (2007) provide a recent review.

work than other females. A similar result is reported for males who had not completed high school. An experiment in Indonesia involved changes in the prices of health services. User fees at public health centers were raised in randomly selected "treatment" districts while prices were held constant (in real terms) in neighboring "control" districts. Two years after the intervention, relative to control areas, health care utilization and labor force participation had declined in treatment areas (where prices increased). Reductions in employment were particularly large (and significant) for men and women at the bottom of the education distribution, those whom we would expect to be the most vulnerable. The most plausible interpretation of both the HIE and Indonesian results is that the average treatment effects on labor supply indicate a causal role of improved health on the allocation of time to the labor market (Dow et al., 2004).

Experimental designs are well-suited to isolate the impact of specific nutrients on labor outcomes. Iron deficiency is prevalent throughout the developing world, particularly in south and southeast Asia. In addition, several studies have demonstrated there is a causal effect of iron deficiency on reduced work capacity suggesting there may be a direct link between iron deficiency and earnings (Haas and Brownlie, 2001). Iron plays an essential role in oxidative energy production. Iron deficient anemia affects physical activity through two main pathways. As hemoglobin levels decline, the maximum amount of oxygen the body can use (aerobic capacity) declines. As iron stores are depleted, the amount of oxygen available to muscles declines, reducing endurance and causing the heart to work harder for the same activity. Iron deficiency is also associated with, *inter alia*, greater susceptibility to disease, fatigue and reduced cognitive development.

Rigorous clinical trials with animals and humans demonstrate a causal relationship between iron deficiency and reduced maximum aerobic capacity (VO_2max) which changes by about 25–30% as subjects are made anemic or receive adequate iron supplementation. Iron deficiency is also associated with reduced endurance at below maximal work rates.

Demonstrating iron deficiency impedes maximal capacity and endurance does not reveal the economic consequences of iron deficiency in daily life. Those consequences may be more closely aligned with energy efficiency (the amount of physiological energy required to perform a given task). In fact, evidence from randomized treatment-control studies of Chinese female cotton mill workers and Sri Lankan female tea plantation workers suggest that elevated productivity resulted in changes in time allocation. Specifically, both studies found no evidence of greater productivity per hour among iron-deficient subjects who received iron supplements relative to subjects who were not supplemented. However, in both studies, treated women re-allocate time away from work and towards non-work activities (Li et al., 1994; Edgerton et al., 1979). Results from a random assignment treatment-control iron supplementation study of male rubber workers, however, indicates that treatments who were anemic at the initiation of the study were able to tap around 20% more rubber after supplementation, relative to anemic controls (Basta, Soekirman and Scrimshaw, 1979). Interpretation of this result is, however, complicated by the fact that attrition from the study exceeded 50%; if those subjects who did not benefit from the study were more likely to attrition, the estimated benefits will be biased upwards.

The Work and Iron Status Evaluation (WISE) is designed to examine the immediate and longer-term impact of providing iron supplements to older adults in Central Java, Indonesia (Thomas et al., 2006). In the population, about one-quarter of older men and a third of older women are iron deficient (as indicated by low hemoglobin). Older males are randomly assigned to receive a weekly iron supplement for slightly over a year or an identical appearing placebo. Everyone in the man's household was similarly assigned to treatment or control (in the small fraction of households with more than one older male, a random male was selected to determine assignment to treatment or control for the entire household).

Respondents who were iron deficient prior to the intervention and who were assigned to the treatment have higher levels of iron in the blood and are able to cycle for longer on an ergocycle at the end of the intervention, relative to comparable control subjects. Iron deficient treatments are better off in terms of physical health, psycho-social health and economic success. Relative to similar controls, treated subjects are more likely to be working, lose less work time to illness, are more energetic, more able to conduct physically arduous activities and their psycho-social health is better.

About half the male workers in the study are self-employed (primarily rice farmers) and the other half are paid a time wage. There is no evidence that hours of work responded to the treatment for time-wage workers or the self-employed. Among males who earned a time wage, there is no evidence of changes in productivity as indicated by their hourly earnings. Of course, if their wages are set by an employer, it is not obvious the worker will reap the benefits of greater productivity. This is not true for the self-employed. Males who were iron deficient and self-employed at baseline reported around 20% higher hourly earnings after six months of supplementation relative to similar controls. Since there was no change in their hours of work, this translates into 20% higher income from labor.

Wage workers who received the treatment reduced the amount of time spent sleeping by around 40 minutes and reallocated all of this time towards leisure. Self-employed workers made no such adjustments. A picture emerges of iron deficiency having a causal impact on work capacity and energy needed to complete tasks. The self-employed who benefited from the treatment allocate the additional energy to their fields and work harder, produce more and earn more per hour of work. In contrast, wage workers were able to channel the greater energy to reduced sleep and more time allocated to leisure. After twelve months of supplementation, there is evidence that some of the treated iron-deficient males who were working for a time wage at baseline had shifted to self-employment or taken up an additional job. While the study demonstrates iron deficiency has a causal impact on time allocation and economic productivity, it also highlights the importance of taking behavioral responses to the experiment itself in assessing the impact of the treatment.

4.4. Health and exogenous shocks

A literature has developed that explores the impacts of exogenous shocks, such as from weather, on health and other outcomes of interest. Most of this literature explores only short-run effects of shocks. Estimating longer-run effects is much more difficult, as explained in Section 4.1, because in part, other changes will occur after the shock, some because of the shock, and it will often be difficult to parse out the causality between the shock and other events.

Much of the earlier literature on health impacts of shocks focused on economic shocks such as unanticipated changes in the prices of staple foods. Alternative to using measured changes in prices or incomes, a number of papers compare health outcomes of birth cohorts (usually of young children) that were affected by the particular shock to adjacent birth cohorts, not so affected (for instance, Razzaque et al., 1990, short-run analysis of the 1974 famine in Bangladesh; Stein et al., 1975, long-run analysis of the Dutch winter famine; or Almond, 2006, long-run analysis of the 1919 flu pandemic). See the extended discussion of these historical and long-run studies of cohort "shocks" in Section 4.1. The one difficulty in these types of cohort studies is to ensure that there were not other factors changing over the same period that could confound the effects of the shock being measured. If regional variation is also present in exposure to the shock, this can help alleviate such potential biases (see Duflo, 2001, for such a modeling example using cohorts and regional differences in a different setting), as can appropriate interactions of the shocks with household-level variables. Interacting a community-level shock with a household-level variable can also greatly increase the power of test for the shock impact, but may suffer from endogeneity problems if the household variable is not exogenous. In practice, many studies use household assets because households with low assets may have more difficulty in obtaining loans, therefore the shocks may hit them harder. However, in a dynamic model many types of household assets will be endogenous. One asset that may be exogenous in some parts of the world is land owned. In south Asia, it is argued for example, that land sales markets are very thin and thus land rarely changes hands except for bequests (Rosenzweig and Wolpin, 1985).

A good example of a paper that uses rainfall shocks to investigate impacts on health is Rose (1999). She uses the NCAER ARIS national Indian household panel data from 1969–1971 and merges rainfall data at the district level. She examines the impact of rainfall shocks on the *relative* survival probability of girls to boys, by birth mother, finding that higher rainfall increases the odds that a surviving child is a girl. If households were perfectly able to smooth consumption in the face of shocks, then rainfall should have no impact on relative mortality, except through possible biological mechanisms. The fact that it does is consistent with the inability of households to perfectly smooth their consumption, since a positive rainfall shock should result in higher income. If there exists boy preference for any reason, then when incomes go down unexpectedly, it may be girls that suffer more than boys in terms of their allocations of health inputs. Then, when incomes improve, girls should benefit (see Alderman and Gertler, 1997, for a simple model in which this result emerges). Further, Rose finds that the rainfall shock effects on the relative survival of girls is stronger in landless households than households with land, consistent with a credit market constraint story affecting landless households more.

Jensen (2000) also uses historical rainfall data to form a measure of shock for areas in Cote d'Ivoire between 1986 and 1987, and using the World Bank's Living Standards Surveys, and relates the shock measures to income declines and then to investment in children, using a difference-in-difference approach. He categorizes regions into those affected by and not affected by rainfall shocks between 1986 and 1987 and then looks at differences in the fraction of standardized weight-for-height z-scores for children 0–10 years that are under -2 (wasted), and takes the difference-in-difference as his estimate of the shock. He finds significant, positive impacts of being in a rainfall shock region for boys' being stunted and positive, significant at 10%, for girls.

More recent papers that use the exposed and unexposed birth cohort comparison include Paxson and Schady (2005) and Rukumnuaykit (2003). Both papers examine the effects of economic crises on infant mortality: Paxson and Schady looking at the collapse of the Peruvian economy in the late 1980s and Rukumnuaykit at the impact of the financial crisis in Indonesia in the late 1990s. Paxson and Schady examine year-to-year changes in infant mortality rates using Demographic and Health Survey (DHS) data. Rukumnuaykit uses different waves of the Indonesia Family Life Survey (IFLS) and also constructs year-by-year changes in both neonatal and post-neonatal mortality. She also uses hazard analysis, allowing for trends in mortality, to estimate the change in mortality for exposed birth cohorts, relative to trend. Both find substantial impacts, increases of 1.4 percentage points in Indonesia and 2.5 percentage points in Peru.

In a slightly different, though related, study, Cutler et al. (2002) use a triple difference estimator to estimate the impacts of economic crisis in Mexico on age-specific mortality of children and the elderly. Cutler et al. look at changes in mortality rates for their "treatment" groups before and after each crisis, relative to changes in mortality for the same group in the years just prior to each crisis. Subtracting the latter change controls for trend changes in mortality before the crisis. They then use prime-aged male adults as a control group, arguing that mortality for this group should not have been much affected by an economic shock. They take difference-in-differences for this control group and subtract that from the difference-in-difference for each treatment group to arrive at their triple differences. They find that mortality during the 1995/1996 crisis did rise for both children under 5 and the elderly, relative to mortality changes for prime-aged men.

What is not clear from the Cutler et al. (2002) study is whether those young children and older persons who died were fragile in the first place and died a little earlier than they would have anyway. Results of McKenzie (2006) show that less-educated Mexican households during the 1995 Peso crisis cut back their expenditures on durables and semi-durables, and cut back by much less their expenditures on basic foods, possibly to better maintain their health.

Jensen and Richter (2003) investigate the impacts of the Russian economic crisis on health of adults. They note that in 1996 there was a major crisis in the pension system, that accompanied the overall economic collapse, the consequence of which was that many pensioners had their payments withheld (this was separate from the withholding of wage payments, which was even more common). They use a difference-in-difference regression strategy, defining dummy variables for whether the individual had pension arrears and another for the year 1996, when the pension arrears were binding, plus an interaction variable to identify the pension effect. Jensen and Richter (2003) find that calorie and protein intakes of men and women are lower if the person has pension arrears. Also they find that the probability of having a checkup in the last year is lowered, as is the likelihood of taking medication for a chronic health condition in the past week (conditional on the person having had the condition before the crisis). In terms of more chronic conditions, for men, the ADL index was worsened and men were more likely to report experiencing chest pains. Finally, Jensen and Richter look at the impact on subsequent mortality, but their regression is more like a health production function, including many health inputs, such as whether the person is obese, had experienced chest pains, drinks and smokes. Even holding constant all of these factors, having pension arrears is found to have a positive impact on subsequent mortality for men. However, one factor that reduces the impact on health is the coping mechanism reaction of these people. Jensen and Richter find that labor supply goes up and that assets are drawn down for those individuals whose pensions are in arrears.

Shocks other than economic have been examined for their impacts on health. For instance, in late 1997 there were a series of serious forest fires in Indonesia that greatly affected air pollutants in parts of Indonesia and neighboring countries. Frankenberg, McKee and Thomas (2005) use detailed data from the National Space and Aeronautical Administration's (NASA) Total Ozone Mapping Spectrometer (TOMS) data, which are daily, to measure haze from the fires, and matched those to the Indonesia Family Life Survey data from late 1997 and early 1998 using latitude and longitude data. They examine the short-run impacts of the haze on three health indicators of adults: difficulty in carrying a heavy load, whether coughing was reported in the past one month and whether general health was reported as poor; looking separately at prime-aged women, prime-aged men and the elderly (defined as over 55). Their empirical specification uses data from the 1993 and 1997 waves of IFLS. Many communities in the 1997 wave were not exposed to the haze, but many were. Frankenberg, McKee and Thomas (2005) look at the difference-in-difference between 1993 and 1997 health outcomes, between individuals in heavily exposed areas and individuals in not heavily exposed areas.

In their regression analysis they use individual fixed effects, together with exposure dummies that are timed as to whether exposure ended or started at the time of the survey or at least one month before. They find that exposure to the haze indeed did positively affect having difficulty in carrying a heavy load, and also affected coughing and being in poor health. From the time-dated exposure variables they discovered that people's health rebounded quite quickly to the end of haze exposure. The timing of exposure also helps to reassure one that one possible confounding variable, being exposed to cigarette smoke in the house, probably is not an issue. In studies of impacts of air pollution on health in the United States, it has been found (e.g., Mullahy and Portney, 1990) that areas that have greater air pollution are poorer areas, where cigarette smoking is more prevalent. In Indonesia, where 70% of men currently smoke (Witoelar, Strauss and Rukumnuaykit, 2006), the socio-economic gradients with smoking are weaker than in the US, but more to the point, do not vary over time much (Witoelar, Strauss and Rukumnuaykit, 2006). This implies that one should not expect to see rapid recovery in health impacts of haze, if they were really due to being exposed to cigarette smoke.

Another study, Sastry (2002), finds short-run impacts of haze from the Indonesian fires on mortality of infants and older persons 65–74 in Kuala Lumpur, and on older persons in Kuching. Sastry uses aggregate city mortality data by day from vital registration systems, merged with data on haze, that is more crude than the TOMS data that Frankenberg, McKee and Thomas (2005) use and estimates count models of mortality. Like the Cutler et al. study, it is not clear whether it was the frail old and very young who died, perhaps just a little before they would have anyway.

Jayachandran (2006) also uses smoke data for Indonesia and examines, by birth cohort, whether smoke during the prenatal or postnatal periods (separately) affected the size of the cohort in the Census year 2000. Size of cohort in 2000 is used as a proxy for infant mortality, which she does not observe in her data. Unfortunately there are many very strong assumptions that are required for birth cohort size in 2000 to be an unbiased proxy for infant mortality for past birth cohorts, so that the data are not the most suitable for testing of this hypothesis. Nevertheless, she finds a strong negative effect of smoke exposure on cohort size.

Pitt, Rosenzweig and Hassan (2005) examine the impacts of indoor smoke from cooking stoves on health of adult women, especially those who cook, and their children. In many poor countries cooking with wood stoves, or using fuels such as charcoal or kerosene, is common. Use of these fuels causes a lot of smoke, which may be quite harmful to health, especially respiratory health. They use survey data that contain detailed time allocation information, from which they can determine who in the household is cooking, and therefore most exposed to the smoke, and for how much time. They also are able to measure the permeability of the walls and roof, which will affect how well air circulation will spread. Unfortunately, they do not have any direct measures of smoke or particular matter in the air of the house (or kitchen of the house), nor do they have direct measures of how clean are the lungs of individuals living in the household.

They measure self-reported coughing, having difficulty breathing and having a fever, which they use as symptoms of respiratory problems. The discussion in Section 3.6 is relevant here. While there is likely to be real information in these self-reports, they may be biased in that higher-SES women may be more likely to have gone to the doctor and to have been properly diagnosed. Indeed, in Tables 2 and 4 of Pitt, Rosenzweig and Hassan (2005) the partial correlation of schooling with having respiratory or intestinal symptoms is positive and significant for women over 16 years.

Pitt, Rosenzweig and Hassan (2005) estimate a conditional health "demand" function for having one or more respiratory illness symptoms, as a function of time spent cooking, age, sex, schooling, per capita expenditure, having a permeable roof, walls, and whether the kitchen is outdoors. They use three different estimation techniques: household random effects, household fixed effects, and household fixed effects plus instrumental variables. As instruments they use variables that measure whether the woman is the spouse of the household head, or his daughter-in-law, the number of daughters-in-law in the household, and interactions between them. They argue that separate spheres of activities exist within the household, with the senior spouse being primarily responsible for the cooking. A key assumption is that this set of relationships with the household head affects the allocation of time to cooking but has no direct effect on health. While this assumption is plausible, it is not subjected to testing. There are also plausible conditions under which it will be violated. For example, if one's relationship with the household head affects spending on individual-specific health inputs, then there will be direct effects on individual health outcomes.

Pitt, Rosenzweig and Hassan (2005) do find that cooking time does significantly raise the likelihood of having respiratory symptoms, especially for women over 16 years. On the other hand, it does not affect intestinal symptoms, which is good for their argument, because if it had, one might have argued that the correlation with respiratory symptoms was spurious, based on omitted variables not controlled for by taking household fixed effects, or by the instruments. They also find that the permeability of walls and roofs has no effect in ameliorating the negative health impacts of smoke. Finally they find that among the determinants of time spent cooking, it is the inherent healthiness of the woman that matters, with less healthy women being more likely to work in the kitchen. If poor health has a bigger negative impact on agricultural productivity than productivity in cooking, then it would be sensible for the woman in the household who has the poorest health to spend the most time cooking in the kitchen.

4.5. Health and consumption smoothing

Since the work of Rosenzweig (1988) and Townsend (1994), empirical tests of consumption smoothing and the methods that households use to smooth their consumption have blossomed (see Dercon, 2004, for a recent compilation of papers). As an example, Foster (1995) uses data on flooding in an area in rural Bangladesh having a very good population surveillance system run by the International Centre for Diarrhoeal Disease Research, Bangladesh, to examine how young child standardized weights were affected. Foster has two periods of data available, one before the flood and one after, and looks at differences over time. The geographic area is small, so there is not regional variation in how hard the floods hit. However, households differ in ex ante assets, particularly land-owned, with some households being landless. Asset ownership arguably may condition how badly the flood affected children's weights. Foster builds a dynamic structural model of weight change under expected utility maximization and derives Euler equations that he estimates. The key point of the model is that changes in child weight may respond to household borrowing, and average (and variance of) village borrowing if interest rates vary within and across villages, perhaps because of segmented markets.[25] Indeed Foster finds that child weight gain after the flood is lower

---

[25] Foster uses borrowing, and not interest rates, because the latter are not observable in his data.

if the individual household borrows, conditional on mean village borrowing, but that this is true only for landless households. This result is consistent with many studies that find different interest rates for different households within a village, based on cost of lending to each household.

Foster's test is not specifically a test for income pooling within the village, certainly not like Townsend. However, of interest here is another covariate, the change in the proportion of days on which diarrheal illness was reported. While diarrheal disease incidence would normally be considered as measured with error, in these data it is likely measured much better. This variable may be a better measure of a health shock on child weight. Foster finds that when the proportion of diarrheal disease days is reduced, weight gain increases, as one would expect. The impact is greater for children from landless households, perhaps because they have a more frequent incidence of diarrheal disease days (and thus a higher marginal product of disease day reduction), or perhaps because they face more stringent credit market constraints.

Foster is cognizant of the potential endogeneity of changes in diarrheal disease days. Shocks which increase diarrheal disease days may also lower weight gains. Thus even though weight is specified in first differences, the diarrheal disease variable may be correlated with unobserved characteristics in the model. To correct for this, Foster uses initial-period diarrheal disease days as an instrumental variable for changes in diarrheal disease days. So long as diarrheal disease is not serially correlated, this IV is consistent. However, it seems likely that diarrheal disease might be serially correlated, in which case this strategy is not sufficient to obtain unbiased estimates.

Gertler and Gruber (2002) present a Townsend-type test of income pooling in response to a health shock, using Indonesian data. The nature of their test is simple; they regress change in variables that might be affected by a health shock (non-medical consumption, household head's labor supply, head's imputed earnings, imputed earnings of others in the household) on changes in household head's health, plus a series of other characteristics in the initial period (age, education, marital status). Thus the specification is a mix of a change and a growth equation.

Gertler and Gruber use three different measures of health shocks for the household head: illness symptoms, chronic symptoms, and an index of activities of daily living (ADLs). They find that positive changes in the ADL index are associated with positive, large changes in non-medical consumption and hours of work of the household head. Illness and chronic symptom changes, on the other hand, are not associated with changes in consumption or head's labor supply.

Of concern here is that both omitted variables may be causing changes in both variables, that there may be direct reverse causality, and measurement error. To explore this in more detail, it is useful to think about what we want to measure and then what we may be measuring in the first difference specification. We would like to measure an exogenous health shock when taking first difference of our health measure. There are likely to be differences in stocks and flows in this regard. For instance, reported health symptoms, one of the types of health measures used by Gertler and Gruber, are likely to be flow variables, whereas chronic disease symptoms and measures of activities of daily living (ADLs) are stocks. For a stock, first differencing will result in a health investment equation. The health investments will reflect choices of endogenous health inputs and behaviors, as well as exogenous unobserved healthiness. The endogenous health inputs and behaviors, in turn, will reflect income and price shocks, in addition to exogenous health shocks. Thus if the estimating equation does not have good proxies for price and income shocks, those are likely to be important omitted variables that would cause bias to the resulting estimates. Gertler and Gruber do include community fixed effects in their estimates. Since there are only two periods of data that they use, this will account for price and other community-level shocks. However, feedback effects from income shocks to health are not taken into account.

Gertler and Gruber are aware of these issues and test for omitted variables bias and feedback effects, but the tests are not very satisfactory. For instance they look at whether change in the head's ADL index matters differently for non-medical consumption if the head is a worker or not. The idea is that if the causation goes from health to consumption, then worker's ADLs should have a larger effect than non-workers. However, if, as Mirrlees (1975) pointed out long ago, workers get allocated nutrients on a favorable basis in order to make them more productive, then one might see a positive correlation between improvement in consumption and in health of workers that would bias upwards a health-consumption relationship even in changes.

Measurement error is acknowledged, but nothing is done about it. As we discuss, systematic measurement error may be differenced out by first differencing, but at the expense of random measurement error. The symptom data are likely to be more prone to both systematic and random measurement error.

Dercon and Krishnan (2000) write down a much more structural model than do Gertler and Gruber (2002) and estimate it using panel rural Ethiopian data. They relate changes in body mass index of adults to shocks of various kinds: regional rainfall shocks; household-level exogenous shocks, such as shocks to crops and livestock; recent household deaths (as a shock to labor supply), and the number of days a person was unable to work because of illness. The days a person could not work, Dercon and Krishnan view as a health shock variable; they are interested in examining its impact on own health as measured by BMI. Dercon and Krishnan treat own days lost to illness as endogenous, but not so whether an adult in the household died since the last interview, breastfeeding or pregnancy status. Thus they are not consistent in their treatment of health outcome and input variables, all of which can appropriately be considered as endogenous. This is a weakness in their approach. Change in lagged BMI is also used in the BMI change equation, and is treated as endogenous, identified by further lags in BMI, and the number of sick days taken in the last 5 years. This identification strategy, which is like the Arellano–Bond estimator in dynamic panel models, can work provided that the assumption is made that the time-varying error term in the BMI change equation is not serially correlated. If the change in adult BMI is related to early life events as suggested by the discussion in Section 4.1, this assumption may fail.

Days of lost work due to illness is recognized as being potentially correlated with omitted time-varying variables in the BMI change equation. Dercon and Krishnan include only non-gastrointestinal illnesses, because the latter might affect BMI directly. This is problematic, however, in that the severity of even non-gastrointestinal illnesses, such as measles for instance, may be affected by levels of nutrition.[26] Instead of using days of lost work due to illness, Dercon and Krishnan use the residual from an individual fixed effect regression of days of lost work on lagged BMI, lagged lost work days, individual and household characteristics and village/time dummies. The problem with this specification is that there may be other unobserved time-varying shock variables at the individual and household levels that are not controlled for that cause both nutrition and health shocks. While Dercon and Krishnan discount this, they have no evidence in support of their view, which does not seem convincing.

One other issue with the Dercon–Krishnan work is the health variable they use for shock: days of work lost to illness. This variable, as noted in Section 3, is just as much a labor supply variable as it is a health variable. Substitution effects would suggest that it is likely that persons with low values of time will be more likely to take off work from a given illness than someone with a higher value of time, while income effects would be reversed. The dominance of income effects may explain some of Dercon and Krishnan's results, specifically that it is for lower-income women in the south that the illness shock is most related to lowered BMI.

5. HIV/AIDS

In this section, the spotlight is placed on HIV/AIDS which has arguably posed the greatest global public health challenges over the last quarter century. It is estimated that in 2006 almost 40 million people were infected with HIV/AIDS and nearly 3 million died that year (UNAIDS/WHO, 2006; UNAIDS, 2006). The vast majority of the burden has fallen on developing countries, particularly sub-Saharan Africa, where it is estimated that 25 million people are infected with HIV/AIDS and over 2 million died in 2006.

We focus here on empirical evidence at the micro level which speaks to the impact of this major epidemic on the well-being of populations in developing countries. We have chosen to highlight HIV/AIDS because it is important, because there is a substantial literature on the economic impact of the disease and because the literature provides additional insights into understanding how poor health and reduced life expectancy affects the well-being of individuals and their family members.

The next subsection discusses measurement and methodological issues. It is important to note that much of the evidence on the impact of HIV/AIDS on economic outcomes has relied on information about the death of a prime-age adult to identify this effect. While many of these deaths in southern and eastern African populations are

---

[26] Scrimshaw, Taylor and Gordon (1968) showed that child death rates were much higher for children who had both diseases such as measles and were undernourished, compared to those who had measles only. The effects were found to be interactive.

likely to be associated with HIV/AIDS, the evidence should be interpreted as measuring the effect of the death of an adult. As more population-based socio-economic surveys include tests for HIV status, this literature is likely to yield substantially new insights into the links between HIV/AIDS and population well-being.

There is little experimental evidence on the impact of HIV/AIDS, which is unfortunate in view of the large number of treatment trials that have been conducted. We discuss the non-experimental evidence, focusing first on the impact of parental death on child schooling which has received much of the attention in the literature. The final subsection discusses the impact on other indicators of well-being. Our exploration of the micro evidence provides some suggestions for why forecasts in the macroeconomic and general equilibrium literatures of economic collapse because of HIV/AIDS have not been borne out. (See, for example, Bell, Devarajan and Gersbach, 2006.)

We do not attempt to review the literature on the epidemiology of HIV/AIDS or the development and availability of treatments and vaccines, but note several themes in common to that and the economics literatures. (See, for example, Bertozzi et al., 2006.) For example, the high prevalence of HIV/AIDS in sub-Saharan Africa reflects the influence of prior health, particularly untreated sexually transmitted diseases (STDs) which were identified as a key mechanism through which infections were transmitted as early as the late 1980s (Cates and Bowen, 1989). The combination of weak public health infrastructure and inadequate understanding of the risk factors, as well as potential consequences of HIV infections, has compounded the impact of the disease in sub-Saharan Africa. This contrasts sharply with the evidence of substantial behavioral change as well as broad availability of therapies that has occurred in the United States and developed countries (Ahitov, Hotz and Philipson, 1996).[27]

5.1. Methodological issues

Three methodological issues have limited progress in this field. First, most samples used in analyses are not random and span a short time horizon. Second, until recently, HIV/AIDS status was seldom recorded in survey data. Third, selectivity of those infected and those who die has often been ignored. We discuss each in turn.

5.1.1. Sampling

Many of the early studies of HIV/AIDS used samples drawn from "sentinel sites," which are often public ante-natal clinics, and samples were comprised of pregnant women.

---

[27] We could highlight other pernicious diseases such as malaria or an influenza pandemic which some predict will sweep through the world in the coming years. Many of the issues that arise in the examination of HIV/AIDS are relevant for these diseases including weak health infrastructure, inadequate adoption of relatively simple and well-understood technologies, co-morbidities and compromised immune systems associated with prior health insults.

Putting aside the difficulties of using pregnant women to infer population-level infection rates for all women, let alone men, this approach is likely to yield a selected sample which will potentially overstate the incidence of HIV. Specifically, in poor countries, many women give birth at home and are thus not counted in sentinel sites. These women tend to live in rural areas, are older, less well educated and poorer than the average woman. Early in the pandemic, these women tended to have lower rates of infection and so estimates based on sentinel site data overstated the prevalence of HIV/AIDS. Zambia provides an example. In 2001, using sentinel site data, it was estimated that 21.5% of the adult population was infected with HIV/AIDS (WHO and UNAIDS, 2003). The Zambia Demographic Health Survey (DHS) conducted in 2001 tested HIV status on a random sub-sample of the population and estimated prevalence to be 15.6% (Central Statistics Office et al., 2003). These estimates are also potentially biased because 20% of women and 25% of men refused to be tested. High refusal rates have been the norm in most household surveys that measures HIV status. Whether those who refused are more or less likely to be HIV positive is unknown, although the highest rate of refusal was among urban men suggesting there may be selection on HIV status. Similar evidence in several other sub-Saharan African countries has led the Population Division of the United Nations' Department of Economic and Social Affairs to lower prevalence estimates (WHO and UNAIDS, 2003).

In order to estimate behavioral relationships using sentinel data, it is necessary to assume that the probability a pregnant woman attended an antenatal clinic in the sentinel site is independent of her own HIV/AIDS status and that of her family members. This is a strong assumption. If higher-income women are more likely to attend antenatal clinics and if the incidence of HIV/AIDS is higher among those with more income, the assumption will be violated. Estimation of behavioral relationships using survey data suffers from similar problems if those who refuse to be tested are not random.

5.1.2. Measurement

Few socio-economic surveys have actually measured HIV status of respondents although this is changing rapidly with the availability of simple tests using mouth swabs. Many of the early studies followed the lead of the first Kagera Health and Development Survey (KHDS) and treat deaths of prime-aged adults as a proxy for HIV/AIDS (Ainsworth et al., 1992). During the first wave of the KHDS between 1991 and 1994, it was thought that the Kagera area in rural, northwest Tanzania had much higher rates of infection than the rest of Tanzania at that time, and it seemed plausible that the majority of prime-aged adult deaths were AIDS related. Proxy-reports on symptoms of those who died were consistent with AIDS being the major cause of these deaths (Ainsworth et al., 1992). A recent survey from South Africa that does collect HIV status suggests that relying only on adult deaths misses part of the reaction to HIV/AIDS because part of the behavioral reaction begins when the household recognizes that a member has HIV/AIDS, which can be well before death (Linnemayr, 2005).

The KHDS has one other feature that is very relevant to analysis. Because adult deaths are such a rare event, the sampling in KHDS was choice-based, with different probabilities of being in the sample depending on the 1988 Census estimates of adult deaths and depending on whether a village census showed there was a recent death in a particular household. The benefit of this sampling strategy is the power that comes with sufficient deaths to test hypotheses. The cost is that, with cross-sectional analyses, special estimation procedures are required to obtain unbiased estimates (Manski and Lerman, 1977).

5.1.3. Estimation

Many empirical models have related some indicator of well-being to whether a prime-age adult in a household has died or whether a child in the household is an orphan. These estimates cannot be given a causal interpretation since adult (or parental) death is not randomly assigned. Including a household fixed effect will yield unbiased estimates if there are time invariant household-level characteristics that underlie the death of the adult. However, if there are time-varying factors, such as variation in household structure, then these estimates will be biased.

As an example, an orphan may move into a new household. Including a household fixed effect in the destination household does not solve the problem of unobserved heterogeneity in parental death. Including a household fixed effect in the origin household raises a different source of selection bias – the selection of household to which an orphan moves, if the orphan does move. An alternative approach is to estimate models with child fixed effects in which case identification is based on time-varying exposure to the adult's death. These selection issues are complicated and the biases associated with them have not been fully explored in the literature. There is little guidance on the possible direction and magnitude of biases due to selectivity which are likely to vary depending on the context and period covered by a particular study.[28]

5.2. Parental death and child schooling

The issue that has received the most attention in the literature on the economic consequences of HIV/AIDS has been the impact of the death of a prime-age adult on child schooling. We start with an examination of that literature focusing on evidence based on

---

[28] Some studies report the association between SES and adult death is positive (Ainsworth and Semali, 1998); others indicate the association is zero (Chapoto and Jayne, 2005). De Walque (2006) reports no correlation between education and testing positively for HIV using DHS data from 5 sub-Saharan African countries (Burkina Faso, Cameroon, Ghana, Kenya and Tanzania) but notes that members of households with more assets are more likely to refuse to be tested. He also documents that the association between education and HIV status among young adults in southern rural Uganda switched from zero (or slightly positive) in 1990 to significantly negative in 2000 which he attributes to the impact of an anti-AIDS information campaign that had its biggest impact on young, better educated women (de Walque, 2004).

longitudinal data which are better suited to addressing concerns regarding unobserved heterogeneity and selection.

Ainsworth, Beegle and Kodi (2005) use the KHDS to examine the relationship between death of a parent and both attendance at school by 7 to 14-year-old children and the hours they spent at school in the previous week. They distinguish children who are paternal orphans (10%), maternal orphans (5%) and dual orphans (both parents are dead, 2.5%). They find a significant negative association between being a maternal orphan and school attendance for younger children (7–10 year-olds) but not for older children, suggesting the association works through delayed enrollment. Being a paternal orphan is not significantly associated with school attendance and dual orphanhood is no different from being a maternal orphan. Having any adult death in the last six months also has a negative association with attendance, again only for younger children.

The hours in school models are estimated conditional on being in school and are specified in terms of changes in hours over time. They find a negative association with maternal death but only for girls. They explore whether these changes precede, coincide with or follow the adult death and find that for both sons and daughters, hours in school decline during the period 4 to 6 months prior to a death and then return to prior levels after the mother's death. This indicates that the time of children is shifted away from school when the mother is very ill but this shift is only temporary.

Ainsworth, Beegle and Kodi (2005) measure the short-run relationships between school and parental death. Using a follow-up survey of the KHDS conducted in 2004, 13 years after the first wave, Beegle, De Weerdt and Dercon (2007) explore the longer-run relationship between orphanhood and attained schooling by age 19. Of the individuals who were children (aged 0–15 years) in the first wave, and alive in 2004, 80% were recontacted. Older children in the first wave, those from higher-income households, and those with better-educated parents were less likely to be recontacted if they were alive.

Beegle et al. restrict analysis to children who were not orphans in the 1992–1994 baseline and compare the educational attainment of those who become orphans with those who did not. They find children who were orphaned have significantly less schooling (0.9 years of schooling) than other children. The estimate can be interpreted as causal only if there are no unobserved characteristics that affect the probability a child becomes an orphan and the child's schooling. This is a strong assumption. Beegle et al. probe the assumption and report the height of 15-year-olds who became maternal orphans is 1.3% less than the height of other children not orphaned. Unless these differences are driven by the impact of maternal death that occurred during the first few years of life, the evidence suggests that children who were orphaned during the hiatus between the survey waves are not randomly selected from the population, but tend to have lower human capital than other children. It is not clear how much of the difference in schooling at age 19 should be attributed to this selection. (Beegle et al. also adopt a propensity score approach which, recall from above, assumes mortality selection is fully captured by observed characteristics.)

Two additional results are worth highlighting. First, the negative association between orphanhood and schooling is observed only among children who were not enrolled in school when the mother died. Second, there is no relationship between orphanhood and schooling among those children who moved away from the natal home. The first result does not appear to be driven by wealth although the second might be. Both results suggest that unobserved characteristics including parental preferences, short-term resource constraints and child ability might play a central role in explaining the estimated negative association between orphanhood and schooling.

Two related, important studies by Evans and Miguel (2007) and Case and Ardington (2006) use panel data from western Kenya and Kwa-Zulu Natal, South Africa, respectively. Both studies use a sample of children who are initially not orphans, with extensive information on the households prior to orphanhood. Both studies fully exploit their data to minimize the impact of potential biases due to selectivity of, for example, adult mortality and child mobility. Evans and Miguel use child-level fixed effects, and Case and Ardington use several different strategies, including both family and child fixed effects.

Evans and Miguel follow up children who were in the Miguel and Kremer (2004) worms study in western Kenya four years after the 1998 baseline. The sample is children age 5 to 18 years old, enrolled in primary school and not orphaned at baseline. Some of the analyses use sub-samples that have more baseline information, which requires that the child attended school on the day the worms study collected household-level information (which may impart some choice-based sampling bias). Around one quarter of the sample has missing or unreliable information on parental death or schooling.

Evans and Miguel find a significant, negative association between being an orphan and school attendance, with maternal deaths being associated with bigger reductions in schooling than paternal deaths. They report that declines in education begin one to two years before the parent's death and cumulate until three years after the death (which is the longest time period they can examine). There are no differences between sons and daughters, between younger and older children or between children from households with more or less assets. They do find that orphans who scored higher on school achievement tests in the 1998 baseline were more likely to be enrolled in school in the 2002 follow-up.

Building on prior work by Case, Paxson and Ableidinger (2004), Case and Ardington use very rich demographic surveillance data from the Africa Center in Kwa-Zulu Natal, South Africa, to which they added two rounds of a socio-economic survey they organized, in 2001 and 2004. They examine impacts of orphanhood on current school attendance, years of completed schooling and log of monthly educational expenditures. Orphanhood rates are high in these data, 9% of children are maternal and 15% are paternal orphans. Case and Ardington find strong, negative associations between mother's death and years of completed schooling, current enrollment, and education expenditures. They do not find significant associations with a father's death and the impact of being a double orphan are approximately equal to being a maternal orphan. Like Evans and Miguel, Case and Ardington find a cumulative impact of maternal death on child years of schooling, that is increasing in time since the mother died. They also find a significant interaction of the mother's death with whether a female pensioner lives in the household.

Case and Ardington conduct several analyses in order to determine whether the results are driven by unobserved heterogeneity. In some models, they include destination household fixed effects; in others, they include extensive household characteristics to control for potential omitted variables bias. They report that completed schooling at baseline, in 2001, is negatively associated with whether the mother was dead in 2001, but also knowing whether the mother was dead in 2004 does not help predict schooling in 2001. This is reassuring since it suggests that the estimates are not contaminated by time-invariant omitted variables. They proceed to use first differences (which is equivalent to including a child fixed effect) and report that maternal death between 2001 and 2004 is negatively related to the change in years of completed schooling as well as changes in enrollment between the waves. There is no association between paternal death between the waves and changes in the school outcomes of the child.

In a different study, Yamano and Jayne (2005) use three waves of a nationwide panel of rural households in Kenya. The first wave, fielded in 1997, was a farm household survey that did not collect any child schooling information, but they went back in 2000 and 2002 and did add child schooling information, as well as information on adult deaths and timing of those deaths. Importantly, they have information on schooling of children even if they left the household, so that potential biases from migration of children are avoided. The disadvantage of these data is that parental identification is not available except for children of the household head, so they use as their adult death variable a marker for any prime-aged adult in the household who died, hence the children in households with adult deaths are not necessarily orphans. Although households that moved are not followed, household attrition is low suggesting that selection biases associated with migration are not likely to be large. Yamano and Jayne (2005) use both household and child fixed effects estimators in their analyses, as well as models with household and individual controls, to control for mortality selection.

They find that without using any fixed effects, children from households with low initial wealth in 1997 and a subsequent household death experience lower enrollment. The impact starts before the death for girls, while for boys the largest impact comes right after the death. When adding household fixed effects, the impact for girls of a future death remains, but the impact on boys disappears. They also find that lagged regional HIV prevalence rates of pregnant women (from sentinel sites) are negatively associated with enrollment for boys, although the estimates become imprecise after taking household fixed effects, and no other community covariates are included in the model making omitted community variables a potential issue.

Several common threads emerge from these studies. First, there appears to be a negative impact of being orphaned on child schooling, particularly if the child's mother died. These effects tend to be larger for daughters, especially during the period prior to the death. This may be because the daughters are caring for the ill household members, or substituting for the mother in home production, rather than going to school. The evidence on whether these effects are larger or smaller for children in poorer households is ambiguous.[29]

5.3. Parental death and health of other household members

This subsection discusses the relationship between death of an adult and health of other family members. The next subsection explores the relationship with indicators of economic well-being at the individual and household level.

The elderly in a household may bear much of the brunt of an adult child having HIV and dying of AIDS. Knodel (2008) shows that in Thailand and Cambodia over 60% of adult children who died of AIDS lived with an elderly parent before death and that for over 90% of these adult children, a parent supplied at least some care during the last days of illness, and for over 70% the parent was the main care giver. Such care by the elderly for their adult children may well have health consequences on the elderly through creating greater stress for the older parents, not having enough younger members to care for the parents, or other causes.

Ainsworth and Dayton (2003) use the KHDS to examine the impact of the death of a prime-age adult on health, as measured by BMI, of other elderly household members (age 50 years or more). They relate changes in BMI to whether a death occurred before the survey, around the time of the survey or after the survey, controlling change in demographic characteristics, household composition and assets as well as community health infrastructure. They find very little evidence of an association between BMI of the elderly and an adult death although there is a suggestion that, among better-off households, BMI of the elderly tends to decline slightly prior to the adult's death and rise after the death. Overall, the health of the elderly does not appear to be related to the death of a prime-age household member.

Ainsworth and Semali (2000) examine the short-run impacts of adult deaths in the KHDS on child health measured by height-for-age, weight-for-height and proxy reported illness of young children (under 60 months). They report negative, significant associations between both mother's and father's death and child height, but the associations are not significant when child-level fixed effects are included in the models. There is some evidence that a recent adult death (not necessarily of a parent) in the

---

[29] The longer-run implications of being an orphan are investigated by Yamano (2006). He uses data on adults living in rural Kenya to examine whether completed schooling is associated with being an orphan by age 15. Orphanhood is measured retrospectively. While the models include respondent characteristics and community fixed effects, the estimates need to be interpreted cautiously since they are likely to be contaminated by unobserved characteristics including time-invariant parental characteristics and mortality selection. He reports that cohorts who went to school in the pre- and immediate post-colonial periods lost an average of one year of schooling if they were maternal orphans by age 15. These were cohorts whose maternal deaths came *before* HIV/AIDS was prevalent. Among younger cohorts, whose mothers were exposed to HIV/AIDS, there are much smaller schooling gaps between orphans and other adults. These differences across cohorts might indicate differences in selection, differences in period effects, or they may indicate that some families and communities are more resilient than others in the face of parental death.

last six months is associated with reduced height-for-age among children from poor households. As Ainsworth and Semali point out, in the fixed effects specification, the adult death indicates whether a child became an orphan between the survey rounds and very few children in the KHDS were orphaned during the first wave of field-work.

5.4. Parental death and household resources

A central issue regarding HIV/AIDS is the effect on both the household economy and the economy in aggregate. Although much has been written about the topic, there have been rather few reliable studies at the micro level.

In an important study, World Bank (1997) documents that households in the KHDS reporting a prime-aged adult death in the last year had 7.5% lower expenditures per adult equivalent (including durables) than households without an adult death. Households with a death had much higher funeral and health care expenditures just before and at the time of the death. This, together with the lower overall expenditures meant that other expenditures had to be lower. Of course this does not control for mortality selection, which in this case could result in an underestimate since the Kagera households having adult deaths tended to be higher-income households.

Other studies have examined the impacts of adult deaths on per capita consumption (Beegle, De Weerdt and Dercon, 2008, and Case and Ardington, 2006); on incomes (Yamano and Jayne, 2004; Chapoto and Jayne, 2008); on assets (Yamano and Jayne, 2004; Case and Ardington, 2006; Chapoto and Jayne, 2008) and on labor productiv-ity (Fox et al., 2004). As for the child schooling-orphan studies, there are differences in the controls that are available for mortality selection and in the magnitudes of the results, but most studies report a negative impact of an adult death on these out-comes.

Beegle, De Weerdt and Dercon (2008) use the first and second waves of the Kagera data to estimate the impact of a prime-aged adult death in a household between the 1991 and 2004 waves on the growth of household per capita expenditures, from the ini-tial interview (usually in 1991) to 2004. The adult deaths are categorized into dummy variables showing male or female deaths in one of three five-year intervals: 1991–1995, 1996–2000 and 2000–2004. They are set to one if the individual was living with that person at the time of death. This specification amounts to a difference-in-difference esti-mator. While unobserved factors related to the *level* of consumption are removed in this way, there might be omitted variables that are correlated with *changes*, particularly with the death of an adult member. To control for some of these omitted factors, Beegle et al. control for initial period household fixed effects. If subsequent adult deaths are cor-related with characteristics of the initial household, then this procedure will control for the selectivity of households that had an adult death. This procedure induces a different problem since comparisons will be drawn between members of the original household who stay and those who move. To address the possibility that other shocks may be correlated with consumption changes, they also control for self-reported agricultural shocks that affected each household.

Beegle, De Weerdt and Dercon (2008) find that recent deaths are associated with 7% lower consumption growth during the first five years after the death, but that consumption seems to recover after that, albeit not to the pre-death level. A 7% decline in consumption is not trivial, but is small in comparison with changes in consumption associated with large economic shocks such as the 1998 financial crisis in Indonesia (Frankenberg, Thomas and Beegle, 1999) or the large depression in Peru in the late 1980s (Glewwe and Hall, 1994). The consumption response to adult death does not appear to be related to whether the household is initially poor or how long the adult was ill prior to death. The evidence is suggestive that families respond to minimize the impact of an adult death on consumption, although what mechanisms are used is not explored.

Case and Ardington (2006) look at the impact of adult deaths in their South African sample, on log per capita expenditures and on assets owned, using the same specifications as they used to analyze orphan schooling. They find a significant negative impact of a father's, but not mother's death on both outcomes before they first difference. For assets, they are able to take first differences (regressing the change in assets on whether there was a death between the survey rounds), thereby eliminating time-invariant omitted variables, which might confound the estimates. The coefficient on assets is negative but halved in magnitude and not significant, suggesting the omitted variables bias is substantial in the models specified in levels.

The relationship between adult death and income is explored in Yamano and Jayne (2004) and Chapoto and Jayne (2008). Yamano and Jayne (2004) measure the impacts of adult deaths in a rural panel in Kenya on a number of farm income and input variables. The data were collected in 1997 and again in 2000 on a sample of 1500 farms throughout Kenya. Because the sample is random, deaths are very uncommon. Only 46 of the households reported a male adult death. Of those, only 27 of the deaths occurred between 1997 and 2000 – the time frame examined by Yamano and Jayne. (There were 37 female deaths reported in the survey.) The small number of "treated" households raises questions about the power of the tests.

Yamano and Jayne (2004) use a difference-in-difference estimator to estimate the impacts of adult deaths from 1997 to 2000. They have "baseline" information in 1997 and can split the sample into treatment and control groups based on whether an adult death occurred, or not. They regress the change in a dependent variable on whether a death occurred in the 3-year period, plus a set of village dummy variables, to absorb variation in prices, weather and other village-level characteristics. Fixed household characteristics are differenced out.

They find no effect of an adult death on the area cultivated for cereals or root crops. Evidently food crop areas are considered inviolate by these Kenyan farmers. However there is a significant decline of almost an acre in crops with high potential returns, such as coffee, tea, sugarcane, fruits and vegetables, when a male head of household dies (though not for deaths of other family members). When they examine the impact on gross and net farm output, they find that a death of a male head is associated with a decline in both gross and net farm output, but not on output per acre. Apparently households are choosing to reduce the land that is cropped, particularly for non-cereal crops, but there is no change in the intensity of input use and hence no change in yields. Neither, apparently are farmers choosing to reduce lower-productivity land, which would have resulted in a rise in yields. Again, however, the very small sample size of households with an adult death is likely to be affecting the possibility to observe such subtle impacts.

Yamano and Jayne also look at what happens to assets of different types and to off-farm income. They find that off-farm income does respond negatively to the death of a male head, while the value of small ruminants declines with the death of women who are not spouses of the head. This might be because such woman may take responsibility for the oversight of such animals. Finally, they find that the impacts of death of male heads of households are not uniform, but occur primarily among households in the bottom half of the initial 1997 asset distribution.

In a related study, Chapoto and Jayne (2008) look at a panel of nationally representative, rural Zambian households in 2001 and 2004. They report a high correlation of 0.84 between a household indicator of adult death and a community indicator of HIV prevalence, reported from sentinel sites, thus verifying the usefulness of reported adult mortality as an indicator of HIV exposure. Chapoto and Jayne also have a relatively small number of households that had adult deaths, but a substantially larger number than in the Yamano and Jayne (2004) study. In this case there were 90 households that had death of a male household head, and substantially more with any adult death (over 170 with a male death and over 220 with a female death).

Chapoto and Jayne (2008) estimate their models in household first differences, which will take out household time-invariant unobserved characteristics that may cause mortality selection. However, they go further. They have data on area rainfall, which they convert to rainfall deviations. In 1994/1995 there was a major drought that affected Zambia. Chapoto and Jayne argue that that shock might have helped induce migration which could affect mortality by 2004. They interact these rainfall shocks with age cohort, since the 1994 drought would have affected different age cohorts differently. These are the instruments that they use to predict adult deaths from 2001 to 2004. They find that the rainfall deviations interacted with age cohort are highly significant predictors of adult mortality in the household. Having instruments, they compute Wu–Hausman test statistics and find that adult mortality is not endogenous when the models are estimated in first differences. Hence using household first differences seems to "solve" the mortality selection issue in this study. They also use Wooldridge's (2002) inverse probability weighting estimator to try to correct for attrition (using interviewing team dummies for identification), but like Yamano and Jayne (2005) find the results to be very robust to this.

Chapoto and Jayne (2008) find that adult deaths do result in declines in household size, but less than one for one. They find that death of a male head is associated with a decline in total area cultivated, including a decline of area in cereals and in crops with high potential returns (in Zambia, these are cotton, coffee, tobacco, sunflower, vegetables and fruits). Death of a woman who is not a spouse is associated with less land in root crops. This makes sense because the main root crop is cassava, which is intensive in female labor for processing and is highly perishable once harvested; hence less available female labor will make it more difficult to grow. Unlike in Kenya, the gross value of production, either total or per hectare, is invariant to adult deaths, even of the male head. The value of livestock, however, especially small animals, but also cattle, are sensitive to the death of the male head and females for small animals. Off-farm income, however, is not sensitive to adult deaths. When they interact adult deaths with a measure of poverty status (being in the bottom half of the distribution of assets at baseline in 2000), Chapoto and Jayne (2008) find that the poor are more likely to reduce land area upon death of the male head, but gross output per cultivated hectare rises, particularly for the poor. This suggests that the poor are intensifying their agriculture with the death of a male head. A different measure of poverty in Zambia is land size. Chapoto and Jayne (2008) find that households with more land reduce their land area by more upon death of a household head, while these households do not intensify their input use, which results in lower output per hectare.

In sum, the results in both the Yamano and Jayne (2004) and Chapoto and Jayne (2008) studies suggest there is a large decline in income or output when an adult dies. This is in contrast with the early claims of HIV/AIDS resulting in economic collapse. However, family responses to the death of an adult differs across contexts. Yamano and Jayne indicate there is a decline in the area allocated to non-cereals but no change in yields in Kenya. Chapoto and Jayne (2008) demonstrate a small decline in area planted, but no decline in total output, in Zambia.

Fox et al. (2004) use unusually detailed data on daily tea picking by workers on a tea estate in Kenya to examine the impact of being near the end of life with HIV/AIDS on productivity. The tea workers on this estate are paid piece rate for plucking tea leaves and the company provided detailed individual records on worker output over several years. The company also owns a local hospital which cares for sick workers and their family members. From the hospital records, Fox et al. obtained names of workers who had died from HIV/AIDS as diagnosed by a medical practitioner or who were hospitalized and close to dying, again from diagnosed AIDS. The sample size is small: only 51 workers who had died. If workers went home to die of AIDS, as documented by studies such as Ainsworth, Ghosh and Semali (1995) and Chapoto and Jayne (2008), they would not be included in the sample as the hospital would not have their records. This could result in some (unknown) biases in terms of who is in the sample. Fox et al. obtained daily work records, both days worked and daily kilograms plucked, for these workers for the four years prior to death. They then matched workers who were working in the same field as the worker who died and obtained historical productivity records for the matched workers. The matching had to be done manually because of limited access to the company records. The matched sample is not perfect: there are more males, older workers and more experienced workers.

Fox et al. (2004) find that around the time of death, those who died picked about 20% less than the matched sample who were not infected with HIV/AIDS. The productivity differences emerged as being significant about 1.5 years prior to the death when there was a 10% productivity gap. There was no productivity gap 3 years prior to the death. In addition to these productivity differences, there were important differences in days worked. In the two years before death, AIDS-infected workers had double the missed days of work as the matched comparison workers, reaching 70 days missed in the year before death.

Fox et al.'s study of piece-rate workers on plantations provides evidence on the effect of HIV/AIDS on the productivity of individuals rather than family responses on small-holder plots. This is important since, as noted by Pitt and Rosenzweig (1986), in a recursive farm household production model, illness of a family member will have no impact on farm output or productivity. Specifically, if family and hired labor are perfect substitutes and if farmers are price takers for piece rate wages (or wages per efficiency unit of labor), then when a household member falls ill, the household will hire in labor to replace the ill person and there will be no change in demand for farm inputs, supply of output or farm profits (since those choices are driven by prices and technology which does not change when a household member is ill). Full income will decline because the hired worker is paid. Clearly, the combination of studies that examine the impact of HIV/AIDS on piece rate work and on family farm (and non-farm) businesses provides important insights into the likely behavioral responses of family members to the death of an adult.

Another set of studies has examined the link between HIV/AIDS and labor supply of household members who are not sick. Using the first KHDS, Beegle (2005) distinguishes hours worked on the farm, on household chores, in wage employment and on non-farm self-employment, for both men and women. She uses dummy variables measuring a death in the 12 months prior to the death and 12 months after the death. Estimation uses individual fixed effects to try to capture mortality selection, plus control for other unobserved factors such as preferences for work, time and risk preferences. Time-varying individual characteristics are also included. Beegle finds essentially little or no effects of an adult death on labor supply to the farm, to wage work, non-farm self-employment or to chores. She finds limited evidence that participation in coffee farming is reduced after a male death. She suggests that new members join a household after an adult death and thereby replace the labor. Yamano and Jayne (2004) provide evidence in support of this result and report that household size falls by less than one after an adult death.

Thirumurthy, Zivin and Goldstein (2006) conducted a survey in western Kenya in early 2004 and 2005 which comprised two samples: a random sample of households and a sample of households from which individuals had used a local HIV clinic. From the clinic, Thiramurthy et al. obtained records of how long each patient had undergone ARV therapy, plus medical records on two key biomarkers: CD4 protein count and BMI. Thirumurthy et al. begin by analyzing whether the ARV treatment had effects on CD4 counts and BMI, which it should have. They estimate a patient fixed effects model using longitudinal data on each patient in the HIV clinic and find that being on ARV therapy for at least 3 months had a large impact, but the impact dropped being on ARV for longer. For BMI, they found an immediate impact of being on ARV for 1 month, and a larger jump if the patient had been on ARVs for 6–9 months.

To assess the impacts of improved health on labor supply, Thirumurthy et al. estimate "reduced form" models. In doing so, they pool the random sample with the HIV infected sample. These reduced form models take being HIV positive as exogenous but treat "health" as measured by CD4 count or BMI as endogenous. Individual fixed effects models are estimated with the two periods of data, 2004 and 2005, which may account for the potential selection effect of HIV status, provided the true model is additively linear, with no separate trends for the two groups. Since individuals from the random sample are included, this amounts to a difference-in-difference procedure, with the time differences among the random sample, not infected by HIV, picking up any macro time trends. In addition, models are estimated that allow differential impacts of being on ARV at different times before the survey.

Thirumurthy et al. find large inter-temporal impacts of ARV treatment on labor supply, participation rising 20 percent, relative to those not HIV infected, and hours rising by 35 percent. Increases in family businesses comprise the major form of labor force increase. They also find that labor supply of women and young boys declines after ARV treatment begins, implying that these groups were substituting for the labor of the HIV infected persons.

In sum, studies of the relationship between of HIV/AIDS and household socio-economic outcomes are mixed. While several studies report negative associations and some indicate no association, none reports a large negative effect of HIV/AIDS on household economic status. Some of the differences in estimated effects are due to differences in outcomes, differences in methodologies and differences in contexts. Studies that examine individual-specific differences (include individual fixed effects) tend to yield robust results, although for many outcomes that approach is not feasible. Above all, it is apparent that scientific evidence in this area remains limited and claims that HIV/AIDS will have a devastating impact on economic prosperity are at best premature.

6. Conclusions

Overall there have been dramatic improvements in population health across the globe in the last century as the poorest countries have emerged from high levels of infant and child mortality, infectious diseases have come under better control and the incidence of under-nutrition among young children has been substantially reduced. The advent of HIV/AIDS has been a significant setback, primarily in southern and eastern Africa. As longevity increases, the fraction of the population that is older will increase and the burden of disease will shift to non-communicable diseases. This will bring new challenges to the health systems and economies of developing countries. Indeed, already several low-income populations that are emerging from the nutrition transition are experiencing rapid rates of increase in obesity, diabetes, cardio-vascular disease and cancers.

In recent years, there have been significant advances in understanding of the complex relationship between the many different domains of health and economic progress. Studies have highlighted the importance of distinguishing stocks from flows of health. This has led to greater emphasis on the development of dynamic models of health and prosperity that incorporate the complex feedbacks between health and productivity, and *vice versa*, both contemporaneously and over time. Research has also established the important role that households and families play in providing insurance to mitigate the adverse consequences on an individual of his or her own poor health.

Several important studies in economics have been substantially enriched by reaching into the biological and biomedical literatures. Those literatures are a source of extremely useful insights into likely causal pathways as well as potential mechanisms through which specific dimensions of health might impact other life outcomes. New evidence on the biological foundations underlying associations between early-life health, including fetal health, and later life outcomes has powerful implications for the design of policy and has suggested substantially new lines of research. Understanding these links is all the more pressing if fetal and childhood nutrition contribute to the rapid increase in rates of adult obesity – and the associated health problems – in low-income settings. More generally, further integration of theory and evidence between the biological and social sciences has the potential to yield major breakthroughs in understanding the links between health and development.

The Copenhagen Consensus highlighted poor health and nutrition as a key constraint to economic development. The evidence reviewed here identifies several pathways through which improved health contributes to development. Good health in early life is correlated with better health in later life. Health is positively associated with other dimensions of human capital, including schooling. Better health is associated with economic success. Isolating causality in these relationships continues to be a challenge although significant progress has been made on this front in recent years.

There are developments on the horizon that suggest a very exciting future for scientific research in this area. The development of high quality, long-term longitudinal socio-economic surveys of individuals, households, families and communities that are guided by insights from theory will provide the foundation for the empirical implementation of improved models of behavioral choices over the life course. These data, coupled with remarkable innovations in health measurement that enable population-based surveys to collect substantial biomarker and genetic information at low cost, promise to revolutionize the field of population health. As researchers integrate these data with theoretical insights from both the biological and social sciences and draw on innovative experimental and non-experimental methods to pin down causal mechanisms, the opportunities for significant progress in the health and development fields seem unparalleled.

References

Adams, P., Hurd, M., McFadden, D., Merrill, A., Ribeiro, T. (2003). "Healthy, wealthy and wise: Tests for direct causal paths between health and socioeconomic status". Journal of Econometrics 112 (1), 3–56.

Adda, J., Chandola, T., Marmot, M. (2003). "Socio-economic status and health: causality and pathways". Journal of Econometrics 112 (1), 57–63.

Ahitov, A., Hotz, V.J., Philipson, T. (1996). "The responsiveness of the demand for condoms to the local prevalence of AIDS". Journal of Human Resources 21 (4), 869–897.

Ainsworth, M., Beegle, K., Kodi, G. (2005). "The impact of adult mortality on primary school enrollment in northwestern Tanzania". Journal of Development Studies 41 (3), 412–439.

Ainsworth, M., Dayton, J. (2003). "The impact of the AIDS epidemic on the health of older persons in northwestern Tanzania". World Development 31 (1), 131–148.

Ainsworth, M., Ghosh, S., Semali, I. (1995). "The impact of adult deaths on household composition in Kagera Region, Tanzania". Development Research Group, World Bank.

Ainsworth, M., Semali, I. (1998). "Who is most likely to die of AIDS? Socio-economic correlates of adult deaths in Kagera region, Tanzania". In: Ainsworth, M., Fransen, L., Over, M. (Eds.), Confronting AIDS: Evidence from the Developing World. European Union, Brussels.

Ainsworth, M., Semali, I. (2000). "The impact of adult deaths on children's health in Northwestern Tanzania". Working paper 2266. Policy Research, The World Bank, Washington, DC.

Ainsworth, M., Koda, G., Lwihula, G., Mujinja, P., Over, M., Semali, I. (1992). "Measuring the impact of fatal adult illness in sub-Saharan Africa". Working paper 90. Living Studies Measurement Study, The World Bank, Washington, DC.

Alderman, H., Behrman, J.R. (2006). "Reducing the incidence of low birth weight in low-income countries has substantial economic benefits". World Bank Research Observer 21 (1), 25–48.

Alderman, H., Gertler, P. (1997). "Family resources and gender differences in human capital investments: The demand for children's medical care in Pakistan". In: Haddad, L., Hoddinott, J., Alderman, H. (Eds.), Intrahousehold Resource Allocation in Developing Countries: Models, Methods and Policy. Johns Hopkins Univ. Press, Baltimore, pp. 231–248.

Alderman, H., Hoddinott, J., Kinsey, W. (2006). "Long-term consequences of early childhood malnutrition". Oxford Economic Papers 58 (3), 450–474.

Alderman, H., Behrman, J.R., Lavy, V., Menon, R. (2001). "Child health and school enrollment: A longitudinal analysis". Journal of Human Resources 31 (1), 185–205.

Almond, D. (2006). "Is the 1918 Influenza pandemic over? Long-term effects of *in utero* exposure in the post-1940 US population". Journal of Political Economy 114 (4), 672–712.

Almond, D., Chay, K. (2006). "The long-run intergenerational impact of poor infant health: Evidence from cohorts born during the Civil Rights era". Mimeo. Department of Economics, University of California, Berkeley.

Angrist, J., Krueger, A.B. (1999). "Empirical strategies in labor economics". In: Ashenfelter, O., Card, D. (Eds.), Handbook in Labor Economics. North-Holland, Amsterdam, pp. 1277–1366.

Arellano, M., Bond, S. (1991). "Some tests of specification for panel data: Monte Carlo evidence and an application to employment equations". Review of Economic Studies 58, 277–297.

Banerjee, A., Deaton, A., Duflo, E. (2004). "Wealth, health, and health services in rural Rajasthan". American Economic Review, Papers and Proceedings 94 (2), 326–333.

Barbarin, O., Richter, L. (2001). Mandela's Children: Growing up in Post-apartheid South Africa. Routledge, New York.

Barker, D.J.P. (1994). Mothers, Babies and Health in Later Life. BMJ Publishing Group, London.

Barker, D.J.P. (2006). "Esther and Isadore Kesten memorial lecture. Leonard Davis School of Gerontology." University of Southern California, November 2.

Barker, D.J.P., Osmond, C. (1986). "Infant mortality, childhood nutrition and ischaemic heart disease in England and Wales". Lancet 1, 1077–1081.

Barker, D.J.P., Winter, P.D., Osmond, C., Margetts, B., Simmonds, S.J. (1989). "Weight in infancy and death from ischaemic heart disease". Lancet 2, 577–580.

Basta, S., Soekirman, K., Scrimshaw, N. (1979). "Iron deficiency anemia and productivity of adult males in Indonesia". American Journal of Clinical Nutrition 32, 916–925.

Beegle, K. (2005). "Labor effects of adult mortality in Tanzanian households". Economic Development and Cultural Change 53 (3), 655–683.

Beegle, K., De Weerdt, J., Dercon, S. (2007). "Orphanhood and the long-run impact on children". Mimeo. World Bank, Washington, DC.

Beegle, K., De Weerdt, J., Dercon, S. (2008). "Adult mortality and consumption growth in the age of HIV/AIDS". Economic Development and Cultural Change, in press.

Behrman, J.R. (1996). "The impact of health and nutrition on education". World Bank Research Observer 11 (1), 23–38.

Behrman, J.R. (1997). "Intrahousehold distribution and the family". In: Rosenzweig, M.R., Stark, O. (Eds.), Handbook of Population and Family Economics, vol. 1A. North-Holland, Amsterdam, pp. 125–187.

Behrman, J.R., Alderman, H., Hoddinott, J. (2004). "Hunger and malnutrition". In: Lomborg, B. (Ed.), Global Crises, Global Solutions. Cambridge Univ. Press, pp. 363–420.

Behrman, J.R., Deolalikar, A. (1988). "Health and nutrition". In: Chenery, H., Srinivasan, T.N. (Eds.), Handbook of Development Economics, vol. 1. North-Holland, pp. 632–711.

Behrman, J.R., Pollak, R., Taubman, P. (1982). "Parental preferences and provision for progeny". Journal of Political Economy 90 (1), 52–73.

Behrman, J.R., Rosenzweig, M.R. (2004). "Returns to birthweight". Review of Economics and Statistics 86 (2), 586–601.

Behrman, J.R., Hoddinott, J., Maluccio, J., Soler-Hampejsek, E., Behrman, E.L., Martorell, R., Ramirez-Zea, M., Stein, A. (2006). "What determines adult cognitive skills? Impacts of pre-schooling, schooling and post-schooling experiences in Guatemala". Mimeo. Department of Economics, University of Pennsylvania.

Bell, C., Devarajan, S., Gersbach, H. (2006). "The long-run economics costs of AIDS: A model with an application to South Africa". World Bank Economic Review 20 (1), 55–90.

Bengtsson, T., Lindstrom, M. (2000). "Childhood misery and disease in later life: The effects on mortality in old age of hazards experienced in early life, southern Sweden, 1760–1894". Population Studies 54, 263–277.

Bertozzi, S., Padian, N.S., Wegbreit, J., DeMaria, L.M., Feldman, B., Gayle, H., Gold, J., Grant, R., Isbell, M.T. (2006). "HIV/AIDS prevention and treatment". In: Jamison, D.T., Breman, J.G., Measham, A.R., Alleyne, G., Claeson, M., Evans, D.B., Jha, P., Mills, A., Musgrove, P. (Eds.), Disease Control Priorities in Developing Countries, Chapter 18. World Health Organization, Geneva, pp. 331–369.

Bertrand, M., Djankov, S., Hanna, R., Mullainathan, S. (2006). "Obtaining a driving license in India: An experimental approach to studying corruption". Mimeo. Harvard University.

Blundell, R., Powell, J.L. (2003). "Endogeneity in nonparametric and semiparametric regression models". In: Dewatripont, M., Hansen, L.P., Turnovsky, S.J. (Eds.), Advances in Economics and Econometrics: Theory and Applications, Eighth World Congress. Cambridge Univ. Press, Cambridge.

Browning, M., Chiappori, P.-A., Weiss, Y. (2007). Economics of the Family. Cambridge Univ. Press, Cambridge.

Card, D. (1999). "The causal effect of education on earnings". In: Ashenfelter, O., Card, D. (Eds.), Handbook of Labor Economics, Chapter 30. North-Holland, Amsterdam, pp. 1801–1863.

Case, A., Ardington, C. (2006). "The impact of parental death on school enrollment and achievement: Longitudinal evidence from South Africa". Demography 43 (3), 401–420.

Case, A., Deaton, A. (1998). "Large cash transfers to the elderly in South Africa". Economic Journal 108 (450), 1330–1361.

Case, A., Fertig, A., Paxson, C. (2005). "The lasting impact of childhood health and circumstance". Journal of Health Economics 24, 365–389.

Case, A., Paxson, C., Ableidinger, J. (2004). "Orphans in Africa: Parental death, poverty and school enrollment". Demography 41 (3), 483–508.

Cates, W., Bowen, G.S. (1989). "Education for AIDS prevention: Not our only voluntary weapon". American Journal of Public Health 79 (7), 871–874.

Cebu Study Team (1992). "A child health production function estimated from longitudinal data". Journal of Development Economics 38 (2), 323–351.

Center for Disease Control (CDC) (2000). CDC 200 Growth Charts, United States. CDC, Atlanta.

Central Statistics Office (2003). Central Board of Health, ORC Macro. Zambia Demographic and Health Survey, 2001–2002. Calverton, MD.

Chapman, D.A., Scott, K.G. (2001). "Intergenerational Risk Factors and Child Development". Developmental Review 21, 305–325.

Chapoto, A., Jayne, T. (2005). "Characteristics of individuals affected by AIDS related mortality in Zambia." Working paper 14. Food Security Research Project Department of Agricultural Economics, Michigan State University.

Chapoto, A., Jayne, T. (2008). "Impacts of AIDS-related mortality on farm household welfare in Zambia". Economic Development and Cultural Change, in press.

Cleveland, W.S. (1979). "Robust locally weighted regression and smoothing scatterplots". Journal of the American Statistical Association 74, 829–836.

Crimmins, E., Finch, C. (2006). "Infection, inflammation, height and longevity". Proceedings of the National Academy of Science 103 (2), 498–503.

Crimmins, E., Frankenberg, E., McDade, T., Seeman, T., Thomas, D. (2007). "Inflammation and socio-economic status in a low income population". Mimeo. UCLA.

Cutler, D. (2004). Your Money or Your Life. Oxford Univ. Press, Oxford.

Cutler, D., Deaton, A., Lleras-Muney, A. (2006). "The determinants of mortality." Working paper 11963. NBER.

Cutler, D., Knaul, F., Lozano, R., Mendez, O., Zurita, B. (2002). "Financial crisis, health outcomes and aging: Mexico in the 1980s and 1990s". Journal of Public Economics 84 (2), 279–303.

de Onis, M., Garza, C., Onyango, A.W., Martorell, R. (Eds.) (2006). WHO Child Growth Standards. Acta Pædiatrica, vol. 95. Supplement 450.

de Walque, D. (2004). "How does the impact of an HIV/AIDS information campaign vary with educational attainment: Evidence from rural Uganda". Working paper 3289. World Bank.

de Walque, D. (2006). "Who gets AIDS and how? The determinants of HIV infection and sexual behaviors in Burkina Faso, Cameroon, Ghana, Kenya and Tanzania". Working paper 3844. World Bank.

Demographic and Health Surveys (2002). "South African DHS: 1998 – Final Report". Measure/DHS, Columbia, MD.

Deolalikar, A.B. (1988). "Nutrition and labor productivity in agriculture: Estimates for rural south India". Review of Economics and Statistics 70 (3), 406–413.

Dercon, S. (Ed.) (2004). Insurance Against Poverty. Oxford Univ. Press, Oxford.

Dercon, S., Krishnan, P. (2000). "In sickness and health: Risk sharing with households in rural Ethiopia". Journal of Political Economy 108 (4), 688–727.

Dow, W., Thomas, D., Gertler, P., Schoeni, R., Strauss, J. (2004). "Health prices, health outcomes and labor outcomes". Mimeo, UCLA.

Duflo, E. (2000). "Child health and household resources in South Africa: Evidence from the old age pension program". American Economic Review 90 (2), 393–398.

Duflo, E. (2001). "Schooling and labor market consequences of school construction in Indonesia: Evidence from an unusual policy experiment". American Economic Review 91 (4), 795–813.

Duflo, E., Glennerster, R., Kremer, M. (2008). "Using randomization in development economics research: A toolkit". In: Schultz, T.P., Strauss, J. (Eds.), Handbook of Development Economics, vol. 4. North-Holland, Amsterdam.

Eckstein, Z., Wolpin, K.I. (1989). "The specification and estimation of dynamic stochastic discrete choice models: A survey". Journal of Human Resources 24 (4), 562–598.

Edgerton, V., Gardner, G.W., Ohira, Y., Gunawardena, K.A., Senewiratne, B. (1979). "Iron-deficiency anemia and its effect on worker productivity and activity patterns". British Medical Journal 2, 1546–1549.

Elo, I., Preston, S. (1992). "Effects of early-life conditions on adult mortality". Population Index 58 (2), 186–211.

Emanuel, I., Filakti, H., Alberman, E., Evans, S. (1992). "Ingenerational studies of human birthweight from the 1958 birth cohort: Evidence for a multigenerational effect". British Journal of Obstetrics and Gynaecology 99 (1), 67–74.

Emanuel, I., Leisenring, W., Williams, W., Kimpo, C., Estee, S., O'Brien, W., Hale, C. (1999). "The Washington State intergenerational study of birth outcomes: Methodology and some comparisons of maternal birthweight and infant birthweight and gestation in four ethnic groups". Paediatric and Perinatal Epidemiolgy 13 (3), 352–371.

Eriksson, T., Bratsberg, B., Raaum, O. (2006). "Earnings persistence across generations: Transmission through health?". Mimeo, University of Oslo.

Evans, D., Miguel, E. (2007). "Orphans and schooling in Africa: A longitudinal analysis". Demography 44 (1), 35–58.

Federov, L., Sahn, D. (2005). "Socioeconomic determinants of children's health in Russia: A longitudinal study". Economic Development and Cultural Change 53 (2), 479–500.

Finch, C., Crimmins, E. (2004). "Inflammatory exposure and historical changes in human life spans". Science 305, 1736–1739.

Fitzgerald, J., Gottschalk, P., Moffitt, R. (1998). "An analysis of sample attrition in panel data". Journal of Human Resources 33 (2), 251–299.

Fogel, R.W. (2004). The Escape From Hunger and Premature Death, 1700–2100. Cambridge Univ. Press, Cambridge.

Foster, A. (1995). "Prices, credit markets and child growth in low-income rural areas". Economic Journal 105, 551–570.

Fox, M.P., Rosen, S., MacLeod, W.B., Wasunna, M., Bii, M., Foglia, G., Simon, J.L. (2004). "The impact of HIV/AIDS on labour productivity in Kenya". Tropical Medicine and International Health 9 (3), 318–324.

Frankenberg, E., Karoly, L. (1995). "The 1993 Indonesian Family Life Survey: Overview and Field Report". RAND DRU-1195/1-NICHD/AID.

Frankenberg, E., McKee, D., Thomas, D. (2005). "Health consequences of forest fires in Indonesia". Demography 42 (1), 109–129.

Frankenberg, E., Suriastini, W., Thomas, D. (2005). "Can expanding access to basic healthcare improve children's health status? Lessons from Indonesia's 'midwife in the village' program". Population Studies 59 (1), 5–19.

Frankenberg, E., Thomas, D. (2000). "The Indonesia Family Life Survey (IFLS): Study Design and Results from Waves 1 and 2". RAND DRU-2238/1-NIA/NICHD.

Frankenberg, E., Thomas, D., Beegle, K. (1999). "The real costs of Indonesia's economic crisis". Working paper 99-04. Labor and Population, RAND, Santa Monica, CA.

Gertler, P., Gruber, J. (2002). "Insuring consumption against illness". American Economic Review 92 (1), 51–70.

Glewwe, P., Hall, G. (1994). "Poverty, inequality and living standards during unorthodox adjustment". Economic Development and Cultural Change 42 (4), 689–718.

Glewwe, P., Jacoby, H., King, E. (2001). "Early childhood nutrition and academic achievement: A longitudinal analysis". Journal of Public Economics 81 (3), 345–368.

Glewwe, P., King, E. (2001). "The impact of early childhood nutritional status on cognitive development: Does the timing of malnutrition matter?" World Bank Economic Review 15 (1), 81–113.

Glewwe, P., Miguel, E. (2008). "The impact of child health and nutrition on education in less developed countries". In: Schultz, T.P., Strauss, J. (Eds.), Handbook of Development Economics, vol. 4. North-Holland Press, Amsterdam.

Godfrey, K., Barker, D. (2000). "Fetal nutrition and adult disease". American Journal of Clinical Nutrition 71 (suppl), 1344S–1352S.

Goldman, D., Smith, J.P. (2002). "Can patient self-management help explain the SES health gradient?". Proceedings of the National Academy of Sciences 99 (16), 10929–10934.

Grajeda, R., Behrman, J.R., Flores, R., Stein, A.D., Maluccio, J.A., Martorell, R. (2005a). "Design and implementation of the INCAP early nutrition, human capital and economic productivity follow-up study, 2002–2004". Food and Nutrition Bulletin 26 (2), S15–S24.

Grajeda, R., Behrman, J.R., Flores, R., Maluccio, J., Martorell, R., Stein, A. (2005b). "The human capital study 2002–2004: Tracking, data collection, coverage and attrition". Food and Nutrition Bulletin 26 (2, Supplement 1), S15–S24.

Granger, C. (1969). "Investigating causal relations by econometric models and cross-spectral methods". Econometrica 37, 424–438.

Griliches, Z., Hausman, J.A. (1985). "Errors in variables in panel data: A note with an example". Journal of Econometrics 31, 93–118.

Grossman, M. (1972). "On the concept of health capital and the demand for health". Journal of Political Economy 80 (2), 223–255.

Haas, J., Brownlie, T. (2001). "Iron deficiency and reduced work capacity: A critical review of the research to determine a causal relationship". Journal of Nutrition 131 (supplement), 676S–688S.

Habicht, J.-P., Martorell, R., Rivera, J. (1995). "Nutritional impact of supplementation in the INCAP longitudinal study: Analytic strategies and inferences". Journal of Nutrition 125 (4S), 1042S–1050S.

Hales, C.N., Barker, D.J. (1992). "Type 2 (non-insulin-dependent) diabetes mellitus: the thrifty phenotype hypothesis". Diabetologia 35, 595–601.

Haller, H. (1997). "Epidemiology and associated risk factors of hyperlipoproteinemia". Z. Gesamte Inn. Med. 32 (8), 124–128.

Hamoudi, A., Thomas, D. (2005). "Pension income and the well-being of children and grandchildren: New evidence from South Africa". Working paper 043-05, CCPR.

Hardle, W. (1992). Applied Nonparametric Regression. Cambridge Univ. Press, Cambridge.

Harris, J.R., Gruenewald, T.L., Seeman, T. (2007). "An overview of biomarker research from community and population-based studies on aging". Chapter 5 in: Weinstein, M., Vaupel, J.W., Wachter, K.W. (Eds.), Biosocial Surveys. National Academies Press, Washington, DC.

Hausman, J.A. (2003). "Triangular structural model specification and estimation with application to causality". Journal of Econometrics 112 (1), 107–113.

Hayami, Y., Ruttan, V.W. (1971). Agricultural Development: An International Perspective. Johns Hopkins Univ. Press, Baltimore.

Heckman, J. (1978). "Dummy endogenous variables in a simultaneous equation system". Econometrica 46 (4), 931–959.

Heckman, J. (2003). "Conditioning, causality and policy analysis". Journal of Econometrics 112 (1), 73–78.

Heckman, J., Navarro-Lozano, S. (2004). "Using matching, instrumental variables, and control functions to estimate economic choice models". Review of Economics and Statistics 86 (1), 30–57.

Heckman, J., Robb, R. (1985). "Alternative methods for evaluating the impact of interventions". In: Heckman, J., Singer, B. (Eds.), Longitudinal Analysis of Labor Market Data. Wiley, New York, pp. 156–245.

Heckman, J., Vytlacil, E. (2006). "Econometric evaluation of social programs". In: Heckman, J., Leamer, E. (Eds.), Handbook of Econometrics, vol. 6. North-Holland, Amsterdam.

Hoddinott, J., Kinsey, B. (2001). "Child growth in the time of drought". Oxford Bulletin of Economics and Statistics 63 (4), 409–436.

Horton, S. (1986). "Child nutrition and family size in the Philippines". Journal of Development Economics 23 (1), 161–176.

Jacoby, H., Skoufias, E. (1997). "Risk, financial markets and human capital in a developing country". Review of Economic Studies 64, 311–335.

Jamison, D.T., Breman, J.G., Measham, A.R., Alleyne, G., Claeson, M., Evans, D.B., Jha, P., Mills, A., Musgrove, P. (2006). Disease Control Priorities in Developing Countries. Oxford Univ. Press and World Health Organization.

Jayachandran, S. (2006). "Air quality and early life mortality: Evidence from Indonesia's wildfires". Mimeo. UCLA.

Jayne, T.S., Strauss, J., Yamano, T., Molla, D. (2002). "Targeting of food aid in rural Ethiopia: Chronic need or inertia?" Journal of Development Economics 68 (2), 247–288.

Jensen, R. (2000). "Agricultural volatility and investment in children". American Economic Review Papers and Proceedings 90 (2), 399–404.

Jensen, R., Richter, K. (2003). "The health implications of social security failure: Evidence from the Russian pension crisis". Journal of Public Economics 88 (1–2), 209–236.

Joshi, S., Schultz, T.P. (2006). "Family planning as an investment in development and female human capital: Evaluating the long-run consequences in Matlab, Bangladesh". Mimeo. Yale University.

Kannisto, V., Christensen, K., Vaupel, J. (1997). "No increased mortality in later life for cohorts born during famine". American Journal of Epidemiology 145, 987–994.

King, G., Murray, C., Salomon, J., Tandon, A. (2004). "Enhancing the validity and cross-cultural validity of measurement in survey research". American Political Science Review 98 (1), 191–207.

Knodel, J. (2008). "Poverty and the impact of AIDS on older persons: Evidence from Cambodia and Thailand". Economic Development and Cultural Change, in press.

Komlos, J. (Ed.) (1994). Stature, Living Standards and Economic Development: Essays in Anthropometric History. Univ. of Chicago Press, Chicago.

Li, R., et al. (1994). "Functional consequences of iron supplementation in iron-deficient female cotton workers in Beijing, China". American Journal of Clinical Nutrition 59, 908–913.

Lindau, S.T., McDade, T.W. (2007). "Minimally invasive and innovative methods for biomarker collection in population-based research". Chapter 13 in: Weinstein, M., Vaupel, J.W., Wachter, K.W. (Eds.), Biosocial Surveys. National Academies Press, Washington, DC.

Linnemayr, S. (2005). "Consumption smoothing and HIV/AIDS: The case of two communities in South Africa". Mimeo. Paris-Jourdan Sciences Economiques, Paris.

Lomborg, B. (Ed.) (2004). Global Crises, Global Solutions. Cambridge Univ. Press, Cambridge.

Lomborg, B. (Ed.) (2006). How to Spend $50 Billion to Make the World a Better Place. Cambridge Univ. Press, Cambridge.

Lopez, A.D., Mathers, C.D., Ezzati, M., Jamison, D., Murray, C. (2006). Global Burden of Disease and Risk Factors. Oxford Univ. Press, Oxford.

Luo, Z., Mu, R., Zhang, X. (2006). "Famine and overweight in China". Review of Agricultural Economics 28 (3), 296–304.

Maluccio, J., Hoddinott, J., Behrman, J.R., Quisumbing, A., Martorell, R., Stein, A.D. (2006). "The impact of nutrition during early childhood on education among Guatemalan adults". Mimeo. IFPRI, Washington, DC.

Manski, C., Lerman, S. (1977). "The estimation of choice probabilities from choice-based samples". Econometrica 45 (7), 1977–1988.

Martorell, R., Habicht, J.-P. (1986). "Growth in early childhood in developing countries". In: Falkner, F., Tanner, J.M. (Eds.), Human Growth, vol. 3, Methodology. Ecological, Genetic, and Nutritional Effects on Growth. second ed. Plenum, New York, pp. 241–262.

Martorell, R., Habicht, J.-P., Rivera, J. (1995). "History and design of the INCAP Longitudinal Study (1969–77) and its follow-up (1988–89)". Journal of Nutrition 125 (4S), 1027S–1041S.

Martorell, R., Delgado, H., Valverde, V., Klein, R. (1981). "Maternal stature, fertility and infant mortality". Human Biology 53, 303–312.

Martorell, R., Behrman, J.R., Flores, R., Stein, A. (2005). "Rationale for a follow-up study focusing on economic productivity". Food and Nutrition Bulletin 26 (2, supplement 1), S5–S14.

Mathers, C., Lopez, A., Murray, C. (2006). "The burden of disease and mortality by condition: Data, methods and results for 2001". In: Lopez, A., Mathews, C., Ezzati, M., Jamison, D., Murray, C. (Eds.), Global Burden of Disease and Risk Factors. Oxford Univ. Press, Oxford, pp. 45–235.

McDade, T.W., Williams, S.R., Snodgrass, J.J. (2006). "What a drop can do: Expanding options for the analysis of blood-based biomarkers in population-level health research". Mimeo. Northwestern University.

McDade, T.W., Beck, M.A., Kuzawa, C., Adair, L.S. (2001). "Prenatal undernutrition, postnatal environments, and antibody response to vaccination in adolescence". American Journal of Clinical Nutrition 74 (4), 543–548.

McEwen, B.S. (1998). "Protective and damaging effects of stress mediators". New England Journal of Medicine 338, 171–179.

McKee, D. (2006). "Forward thinking and family support: Explaining retirement and old age labor supply in Indonesia". Working paper 005-06. CCPR, UCLA.

McKenzie, D. (2006). "The consumer response to the Mexican Peso crisis". Economic Development and Cultural Change 55 (1), 139–172.

Miguel, E., Kremer, M. (2004). "Worms: Identifying impacts on education and health in the presence of treatment externalities". Econometrica 72 (1), 159–217.

Mills, A., Shillcutt, S. (2004). "Communicable diseases". In: Lomborg, B. (Ed.), Global Crises, Global Solutions. Cambridge Univ. Press, Cambridge, pp. 62–114.

Mirrlees, J. (1975). "A pure theory of underdevelopment". In: Reynolds, L.G. (Ed.), Agriculture in Development Theory. Yale Univ. Press, New Haven.

Monteiro, C.A., Moura, E.C., Conde, W.L., Popkin, B.M. (2004). "Socioeconomic status and obesity in adult populations of developing countries: A review". Bulletin of the World Health Organization 82 (12), 940–946.

Mullahy, J., Portney, P.R. (1990). "Air pollution, cigarette smoking and the production of respiratory health". Journal of Health Economics 9 (2), 193–205.

Mwabu, G. (2008). "Health economics for low-income countries". In: Schultz, T.P., Strauss, J. (Eds.), Handbook of Development Economics, vol. 4. North-Holland, Amsterdam.

National Center for Health Statistics (NCHS) (1994). National Health and Nutrition Examination Survey Data Wave III. US Department of Health and Human Services, Hyattsville, MD. Centers for Disease Control and Prevention, http://www.cdc.gov/nchs/about/major/nhanes/nh3data.htm.

Nelson, R. (1964). "Aggregate production function and medium-range growth projections". American Economic Review 53, 974–1004.

Newhouse, J. (1996). Free for All?: Lessons from the RAND Health Insurance Experiment. Harvard Univ. Press.

Omran, A.R. (1971). "The epidemiologic transition: A theory of the epidemiology of population change". Millbank Memorial Fund Quarterly 49 (4.1), 509–538.

Parker, S., Rubalcava, L., Teruel, G. (2008). "Evaluating conditional schooling and health programs". In: Schultz, T.P., Strauss, J. (Eds.), Handbook of Development Economics, vol. 4. North-Holland, Amsterdam.

Paxson, C., Schady, N. (2005). "Child health and economic crisis in Peru". World Bank Economic Review 19 (2), 203–224.

Persico, N., Postlewaite, A., Silverman, D. (2004). "The effect of adolescent experience on labor market outcomes: The case of height". Journal of Political Economy 112 (5), 1019–1053.

Pitt, M.M. (1997). "Specification and estimation of the demand for goods within the household". In: Haddad, L., Hoddinott, J., Alderman, H. (Eds.), Intrahousehold Resource Allocation in Developing Countries: Models, Methods and Policy. Johns Hopkins Univ. Press, Baltimore.

Pitt, M.M., Rosenzweig, M.R. (1986). "Agricultural prices, food consumption and the health and productivity of Indonesian farmers". In: Singh, I., Squire, L., Strauss, J. (Eds.), Agricultural Household Models: Extension, Application and Policy. Johns Hopkins Univ. Press, Baltimore.

Pitt, M.M., Rosenzweig, M.R., Hassan, M.N. (1990). "Productivity, health and inequality in the intrahousehold distribution of food in low-income countries". American Economic Review 80 (5), 1139–1156.

Pitt, M.M., Rosenzweig, M.R., Hassan, M.N. (2005). "Sharing the burden of disease: Gender, the household division of labor and the health effects of indoor pollution". Working paper No. 93, BREAD.

Pollitt, E., Gorman, K.S., Engel, P., Martorell, R., Rivera, J. (1993). Early supplementary feeding and cognition. Monographs of the Society for Research in Child Development, Serial, vol. 235, 58(7).

Popkin, B.M. (1993). China Economic, Population, Nutrition and Health Survey, 1991. Questionnaires and Interview Manual. Online at http://www.cpc.unc.edu/projects/china/data.

Popkin, B.M. (1994). "The nutrition transition in low-income countries: An emerging crisis". Nutrition Reviews 52 (9), 285–298.

Popkin, B.M. (2003). "The nutrition transition in the developing world". Development Policy Review 21, 581–597.

Preston, S.H. (1975). "The changing relation between mortality and level of economic development". Population Studies 29 (2), 231–248.

Pritchett, L., Summers, L.H. (1996). "Wealthier is healthier". Journal of Human Resources 31 (4), 841–868.

Rahman, O., Menken, J., Foster, A., Peterson, C.E., Khan, M.N., Kuhn, R., Gertler, P. (1999). The 1996 Matlab Health and Socio-economic Survey: Overview and User's Guide. RAND, DRU-2018/1.

Ravelli, A.C.J., van der Meulen, J.H.P., Michels, R.P.J., Osmond, C., Barker, D., Hales, C.N., Bleker, O.P. (1998). "Glucose tolerance in adults after prenatal exposure to famine". Lancet 351, 173–177.

Ravelli, A.C.J., van der Meulen, J.H.P., Osmond, C., Barker, D., Bleker, O.P. (1999). "Obesity at the age of 50 years in men and women exposed to famine prenatally". American Journal of Clinical Nutrition 70, 811–816.

Razzaque, A., Alam, N., Wai, L., Foster, A. (1990). "Sustained effects of the 1974–75 famine on infant and child mortality in a rural area of Bangladesh". Population Studies 44 (1), 145–154.

Robinson, R. (2001). "The fetal origins of adult disease. No longer just a hypothesis and may be critically important in south Asia". British Medical Journal 322, 375–376.

Rose, E. (1999). "Consumption smoothing and excess female mortality in rural India". Review of Economics and Statistics 81 (1), 41–49.

Roseboom, T.J., van der Meulen, J.H.P., Osmond, C., Barker, D.J., Blecker, O.P. (2001a). "Adult survival after prenatal exposure to the Dutch famine 1944–1945". Paedeatric and Perinatal Epidemiology 15, 220–225.

Roseboom, T.J., van der Meulen, J.H.P., Ravelli, A., Osmond, C., Barker, D.J., Blecker, O.P. (2001b). "Effects of prenatal exposure to the Dutch famine on adult disease in later life: An overview". Twin Research 4 (5), 293–298.

Rosenbaum, P.R., Rubin, D.B. (1983). "The central role of the propensity score in observational studies for causal effects". Biometrika 70, 41–55.

Rosenzweig, M.R. (1988). "Risk, implicit contracts and the family". Economic Journal 98, 1148–1170.

Rosenzweig, M.R., Wolpin, K.I. (1985). "Specific experience, household structure and intergenerational transfers: Farm family land and labor arrangements in developing countries". Quarterly Journal of Economics 100 (Supplement), 961–987.

Rosenzweig, M.R., Wolpin, K.I. (1988). "Heterogeneity, intrafamily distribution and child health". Journal of Human Resources 23 (4), 437–461.

Rosenzweig, M.R., Wolpin, K.I. (2000). "Natural 'natural experiments' in economics". Journal of Economic Literature 38 (4), 827–874.

Rosenzweig, M.R., Zhang, J. (2006). "Do population control policies induce more human capital investment? Twins, birthweight and China's 'One Child' policy". Working paper No. 933. Economic Growth Center, Yale University.

Rubalcava, L., Teruel, G. (2004). "The Mexican Family Life Survey: Overview and Study Description". CIDE/UIA.

Rukumnuaykit, P. (2003). "Economic crises and demographic outcomes: Evidence from Indonesia". PhD dissertation. Department of Economics, Michigan State University, East Lansing, MI.

Sastry, N. (2002). "Forest fires, air pollution and mortality in southeast Asia". Demography 39 (1), 1–23.

Schultz, T.P. (1984). "Studying the impact of household economic and community variables on child mortality". In: Moseley, W.H., Chen, L. (Eds.), Child Survival: Strategies for Research. Population and Development Review 10 (Supplement) 215–236.

Schultz, T.P. (2005). "Productive benefits of health: Evidence from low-income countries". In: Lopez-Casasnovas, G., Riveras, B., Currais, L. (Eds.), Health and Economic Growth: Findings and Policy Implications. MIT Press, Cambridge MA, pp. 257–286.

Schultz, T.P., Tansel, A. (1997). "Wage and labor supply effects of illness in Cote d'Ivoire and Ghana: Instrumental variable estimates for days disabled". Journal of Development Economics 53 (2), 251–286.

Scrimshaw, N.S., Taylor, C.E., Gordon, J.E. (1968). Interactions of Nutrition and Infection. World Health Organization, Geneva.

Seeman, T.E., McEwen, B., Singer, B., Albert, M., Rowe, J. (1997). "Increase in urinary cortisol excretion and declines in memory: MacArthur Studies of Successful Aging". Journal of Clinical Endocrinology and Metabolism 82, 2458–2465.

Seeman, T.E., Crimmins, E., Huang, M.H., Singer, B., Bucur, A., Gruenewald, T., et al. (2004). "Cumulative biological risk and socio-economic differences in mortality: MacArthur studies of successful aging". Social Science and Medicine 58 (10), 1985–1997.

Serbin, L.A., Karp, J. (2004). "The intergenerational transfer of psychosocial risk: Mediators of vulnerability and resilience". Annual Review of Psychology 55, 333–363.

Serbin, L.A., Schwartzman, A.E., Moskowitz, D.S., Ledingham, J.E. (1991). "Aggressive, withdrawn, and aggressive/withdrawn children in adolescence: Into the next generation". In: Pepler, D.J., Rubin, K.H. (Eds.), The Development and Treatment of Childhood Aggression. Erlbaum, Hillsdale, NJ, pp. 55–70.

Smith, J.P. (1999). "Healthy bodies and thick wallets: The dual relation between health and economic status". Journal of Economic Perspectives 13 (2), 145–167.

Smith, J.P. (2004). "The impact of health on SES". Mimeo, The RAND Corporation.

Stein, Z., Susser, M., Saenger, G., Marolla, F. (1975). Famine and human development: The Dutch hunger winter of 1944–45. Oxford Univ. Press, Oxford.

Stein, A., Behrman, J.R., DiGirolamo, A., Grajeda, R., Martorell, R., Quisumbing, A.R., Ramakrishnan, U. (2005). "Schooling, educational achievement and cognitive functioning among young Guatemalan adults". Food and Nutrition Bulletin 26 (2), S46–S54.

Stewart, R.J.C., Sheppard, H., Preece, R., Waterlow, J.C. (1980). "The effect of rehabilitation at different stages of development of rats marginally malnourished for ten to twelve generations". British Journal of Nutrition 43 (3), 403–412.

Strauss, J. (1986). "Does better nutrition raise farm productivity?" Journal of Political Economy 94 (2), 297–320.

Strauss, J. (1993). "The impact of improved nutrition on labor productivity and human resource development". In: Pinstrup-Andersen, P. (Ed.), The Political Economy of Food and Nutrition Policies. Johns Hopkins Univ. Press, Baltimore.

Strauss, J., Thomas, D. (1995). "Human resources: Empirical modeling of household and family decisions". In: Behrman, J.R., Srinivasan, T.N. (Eds.), Handbook of Development Economics, vol. 3A. North-Holland, Amsterdam, pp. 1185–2023.

Strauss, J., Thomas, D. (1998). "Health, nutrition and economic development". Journal of Economic Literature 36 (2), 766–817.

Strauss, J., Beegle, K., Sikoki, B., Dwiyanto, A., Witoelar, F., Herawati, Y. (2004). The Third Wave of the Indonesia Family Life Survey (IFLS3): Overview and Field Report. RAND, WR-144/1-NIA/NICHD.

Thirumurthy, H., Zivin, J.G., Goldstein, M. (2006). "The economic impact of AIDS treatment: Labor supply in western Kenya". Discussion paper 947. Economic Growth Center, Yale University.

Thomas, D., Frankenberg, E., Smith, J.P. (2001). "Lost but not forgotten: Attrition in the Indonesia Family life Survey". Journal of Human Resources 36 (2), 556–592.

Thomas, D., Strauss, J., Henriques, M.-H. (1990). "Child survival, height for age and household characteristics in Brazil". Journal of Development Economics 33 (2), 197–234.

Thomas, D., Frankenberg, E., Friedman, J., Habicht, J.-P., Ingwersen, N., McKelvey, C., Hakimi, M., Jaswadi, P., Jones, N., Sikoki, B., Pelto, G., Seeman, T., Smith, J.P., Sumantri, C., Suriastini, W., Wilopo, S. (2006). "Causal effect of health on labor market outcomes: Experimental evidence". Mimeo, UCLA.

Townsend, R. (1994). "Risk and insurance in village India". Econometrica 62 (3), 539–592.

UNAIDS (2006). "2006 Report on the Global AIDS Epidemic." New York.

UNAIDS/WHO (2006). AIDS epidemic update: December 2006. United Nations and World Health Organization, New York.

van den Berg, G., Lindeboom, M., Portrait, F. (2006). "Economic conditions early in life and individual mortality". American Economic Review 96 (1), 290–293.

Waaler, H. (1984). "Height, health and mortality: The Norwegian experience". Acta Medica Scandinavica Supplement 679, 1–51.

Ware, J.E., Sherbourne, C.D. (1992). "The MOS 36-item short-form health survey (SF-36): I. Conceptual Framework and item selection". Medical Care 30 (6), 473–483.

Watson, M. (1953). African Highway, The Battle for Health in Central Africa. Murray, London.

World Health Organization Mental Health Survey Consortium (2004). "Prevalence, severity, and unmet need for treatment of mental disorders in the World Health Organization World Mental Health Surveys". JAMA 291, 2581–2590.

Witoelar, F., Strauss, J., Rukumnuaykit, P. (2006). "Smoking behavior among youth in a developing country: The case of Indonesia". Mimeo, University of Southern California.

Wolfson, L.J., Strebel, P.M., Gacic-Dobo, M., Hoekstra, E.J., McFarland, J.W., Hersh, B.S. (2007). "Has the 2005 measles mortality reduction goal been achieved? A natural history modelling study". The Lancet 369 (9557), 191–200.

Wooldridge, J. (2002). Econometric Analysis of Cross Section and Panel Data. MIT Press, Cambridge.

World Bank (1997). Confronting AIDS: Public Priorities in a Global Epidemic, Oxford Univ. Press, Oxford.

World Health Organization (WHO) (2004). World Report on Road Traffic Injury Prevention.

World Health Organization (WHO) and UNAIDS (2003). "Reconciling antenatal clinic-based surveillance and population-based survey estimates of HIV prevalence in sub-Saharan Africa". Geneva.

Yamano, T. (2006). "Long-term impacts of orphanhood on education attainments and land inheritance and adults in rural Kenya". Mimeo. Foundation for the Advanced Study of International Development, Tokyo. Paper presented at the Population Association of America annual meetings, April 2006, Los Angeles.

Yamano, T., Alderman, H., Christiaensen, L. (2005). "Child growth, shocks and food aid in rural Ethiopia". American Journal of Agricultural Economics 87 (2), 273–288.

Yamano, T., Jayne, T.S. (2004). "Measuring the impacts of working-age adult mortality on small-scale farm households in Kenya". World Development 32 (1), 91–119.

Yamano, T., Jayne, T.S. (2005). "Working-age adult mortality and primary school enrollment in rural Kenya". Economic Development and Cultural Change 53 (3), 619–653.

Chapter 55

SCHOOLING IN DEVELOPING COUNTRIES: THE ROLES OF SUPPLY, DEMAND AND GOVERNMENT POLICY*

PETER F. ORAZEM

Department of Economics, Iowa State University, 267 Heady Hall, Ames, IA 50011-1070, USA

ELIZABETH M. KING

The World Bank, 1818 H Street, NW Washington, DC 20433, USA

Contents

* This document represents the opinions of the authors and does not represent the opinions of the World Bank or its Board of Directors. Orazem began work on this paper while serving as Koch Visiting Professor of Business Economics at the University of Kansas, School of Business. We are grateful to Suzanne Duryea at the Inter-American Development Bank for early discussions about measuring education returns, and to Caridad Araujo, Arjun Bedi, Victoria Gunnarsson, Claudio Montenegro, and Norbert Schady for providing access to unpublished data used in the review. Esther Duflo and T. Paul Schultz provided extensive comments on earlier drafts that greatly improved the paper.

Handbook of Development Economics, Volume 4
© *2008 Elsevier B.V. All rights reserved*
DOI: 10.1016/S1573-4471(07)04055-7

Abstract

In developing countries, rising incomes, increased demand for more skilled labor, and government investments of considerable resources on building and equipping schools and paying teachers have contributed to global convergence in enrollment rates and completed years of schooling. Nevertheless, in many countries substantial education gaps persist between rich and poor, between rural and urban households and between males and females. To address these gaps, some governments have introduced school vouchers or cash transfers programs that are targeted to disadvantaged children. Others have initiated programs to attract or retain students by expanding school access or by setting higher teacher eligibility requirements or increasing the number of textbooks per student. While enrollments have increased, there has not been a commensurate improvement in knowledge and skills of students. Establishing the impact of these policies and programs requires an understanding of the incentives and constraints faced by all parties involved, the school providers, the parents and the children.

The chapter reviews the economic literature on the determinants of schooling outcomes and schooling gaps with a focus on static and dynamic household responses to specific policy initiatives, perceived economic returns and other incentives. It discusses measurement and estimation issues involved with empirically testing these models and reviews findings.

Governments have increasingly adopted the practice of experimentation and evaluation before taking steps to expand new policies. Often pilot programs are initiated in settings that are atypically appropriate for the program, so that the results overstate the likely impact of expanding the program to other settings. Program expansion can also result in general equilibrium feedback effects that do not apply to isolated pilots. These behavioral models provide a useful context within which to frame the likely outcomes of such expansion.

Keywords

education, household demand for education, education policy

JEL classification: I20, I21, I28, D13

1. Introduction

Enrollment rates and years of schooling have risen in most countries, a result of successive generations of parents investing in children's education. Over time, these investments have narrowed the differences in schooling across and within cohorts of children, across and within countries, and between and within genders. In 1960, the average schooling of men aged 25 and over in advanced countries was 5.8 times that of men in developing countries; in 2000, this ratio was down to 2.4.[1] During the same period, in developing countries, women's average schooling level as a ratio of men's increased from 0.5 to 0.7. While increasing incomes, shifts in demand for more skilled labor, and more classrooms have contributed to some global convergence in education as measured by years of schooling, substantial education gaps persist, however, such as between rural and urban households and also between males and females, in some settings. These gaps lead to the questions, what are the sources of these gaps and can they be influenced by economic growth, government policy, or international pressure?

Governments devote widely different shares of their budgets to education, at a range of 6–25 percent in 2000 across African countries alone. Parents also devote considerable resources to investments in their children, but also with high variability – in 2001, from 6 percent of total (public and private) spending for primary and secondary education in India to 33 percent in the Philippines. For the poorest parents who send their children to school, such investments will be most, if not all, of the wealth they transfer to their children.

Despite this large variation in rates of human capital investment, estimated private rates of return to years of completed schooling are remarkably similar across countries and across sub-populations within countries. The estimated proportional increase in labor earnings per year of schooling across many developing countries averaged 8% with an interquartile range of 5–10%. In comparison, there is less agreement about the magnitude of social rates of return to schooling, perhaps due to less agreement about how to measure these returns. Nonetheless, there seems broad agreement that schooling benefits society in many ways – in terms of better infant, child and maternal health; reduced fertility; enhanced ability to adopt new technologies or to cope with economic shocks; and rising labor productivity and sustainable economic growth. Reflecting the large collective evidence on these returns, theoretical models have included investments in human capital as an important source of persistent economic growth.

Governments have invested considerable resources on education. Numerous initiatives have been attempted aimed at increasing the returns to those investments. Some initiatives have aimed at raising school quality such as setting higher eligibility requirements for teachers or increasing the number of textbooks in the hands of students. Remedial programs have tried to reduce dropout rates. More recently, initiatives have

---

[1] Data as given in http://www.worldbank.org/edstats; raw data for these years are based on UNESCO statistics.

attempted to increase attendance at existing schools through school vouchers or cash transfers conditioned on child enrollment. Relatively few studies have found empirical evidence compelling enough to merit continued support for these initiatives. Nevertheless, governments often implement policy initiatives on a national scale straight from concept. Alternatively, initiatives are introduced primarily in settings where they are expected to be atypically successful rather than testing how they might perform in more diverse and challenging areas. The practice of experimentation and evaluation before policy adoption is a welcome recent innovation in many settings.

This chapter examines the magnitude of schooling gaps between population groups, why gaps occur, why they persist or diminish over time, how they respond to economic shocks, and how they are transmitted from parent to child. Models can assist us in forecasting where policies are most likely to succeed and where they are likely to fail. Behavioral models help to explain why experimental outcomes may be favorable in some settings and unfavorable in others, and for identifying the most promising locations where experiments can be replicated. Finally, behavioral models help to structure the empirical measurement of responses to government policies and economic circumstances that guide our ability to forecast how households react to government human capital investments and to perceived economic returns.

The chapter opens with a review of patterns, trends, and explanations of urban, rural, male and female education levels in the developing world (Section 2). Next, the chapter presents a model of how government policies affect education levels (Section 3). Static and dynamic models used to guide empirical studies of educational choices follow (Sections 4–5). Estimating these models involve a host of measurement issues which are addressed in Section 6.

2. Costs, returns and schooling gaps

We have already mentioned that education trends in the past half-century have been characterized paradoxically by greater convergence and also by persistent gaps. With or without economic growth, the opening up of national borders, faster information and communication technology, and international social mandates coupled with aid have raised the demand for education, even in poor countries. Indeed, many poor countries do foster high enrollments, especially in their urban areas – but other poor countries do not. Within countries, some groups are faster than others to respond to improved school access, thus widening within-country variation in schooling. Before turning to the factors that produce or sustain education gaps even as global factors appear to support convergence, we illustrate the different across- and within-country patterns in education levels of developing countries using age-enrollment "pyramids" for two low-income countries (Ethiopia and Tanzania) and two lower middle-income countries (Morocco and Turkey). The pyramids show markedly different patterns in the proportion of children enrolled in school by age, sex, and urban or rural residence (Fig. 1).

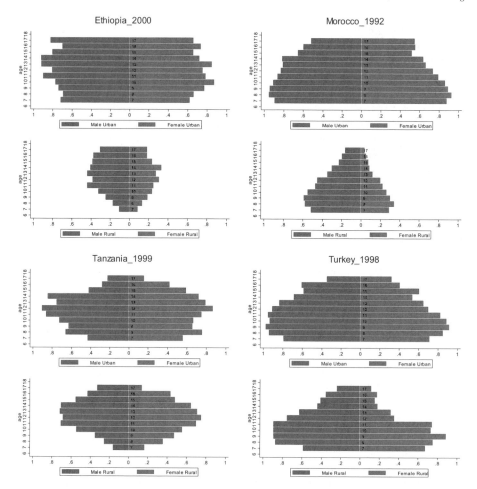

Figure 1. Age-enrollment bars, by gender and residence, selected countries.

Ethiopia is the poorest of the countries but has a remarkable proportion of its urban boys and girls enrolled in school and, through age 13, urban boys and girls attend school in equal proportions. In rural areas, however, enrollment rates never exceed 50 percent for any age or gender. Most urban children enter school at age 7, but rural children typically delay entry if they enter at all, leading to a large education gap between urban and rural children. Unlike urban areas, rural girls receive significantly less schooling than do rural boys.

Tanzania is only modestly wealthier than Ethiopia but has very different enrollment patterns. The gap between urban and rural schooling is much smaller, partly because rural children are much more likely to attend school and partly because urban children attend less. At the oldest ages, the rural children are more likely to be in school than in

Ethiopia, although this could be reflecting higher rates of grade repetition rather than more grades attained. There are no substantial schooling gaps between boys and girls except at these older ages.

Despite being much wealthier, Morocco looks more like Ethiopia than does Tanzania. The Moroccan age-enrollment pyramid is widest at its base, reflecting the more typical pattern of early entry into school and increasing dropout rates at older ages. Urban boys and girls receive similar schooling, but rural girls receive much less schooling than do boys. Turkey, the wealthiest of the four countries, share with the other three countries the pattern of enrollment rates dropping sharply once children reach 13 in both urban and rural areas, with a particularly pronounced dropout rate in rural areas. Girls and boys are treated similarly in urban areas, but rural girls drop out more rapidly after age 11.

2.1. A model of schooling length

Underlying the gaps within each country are individual household decisions of how long to send their children to school. Those decisions reflect trade-offs between schooling costs in the present against anticipated larger earnings capacity in the future. Building on Rosen's (1977) formulation, we model individual earnings as a function of the individual's stock of human capital upon leaving school, $q = q(E, z)$. Human capital production depends positively on E: years of schooling; and positively on z: a vector of exogenous factors that also raise school productivity such as ability or school quality so that $q_{Ez} > 0$. Ignoring the direct costs of schooling, the gross return per year of schooling is defined as $\rho = \frac{dq}{dE} \frac{1}{q} = \frac{q_E}{q}$. Schooling is subject to diminishing returns, and so ρ is assumed to diminish in E.

Schooling is not without cost, however. We assume that p is a constant cost per unit of schooling, and that this cost includes exogenous schooling tuition and other fees plus a fixed opportunity cost of time. Because costs are incurred and returns are earned over a period of time, we discount back to the initial period using an exogenous interest rate $r(y)$, $r'(y) < 0$, where y is a measure of household income. We assume that wealthier families have better access to credit markets and can command better credit terms; thus, interest rates are presumed to decrease in y.

The lifetime discounted value of income at birth net of schooling costs will be

$$
\begin{aligned}
V_0(E) &= \int_E^N q(E, z)e^{-rt}\, dt - \int_0^E pe^{-rt}\, dt \\
&= \frac{q}{r}\left(e^{-rE} - e^{-rN}\right) + \frac{p}{r}\left(e^{-rE} - 1\right)
\end{aligned}
\tag{2.1}
$$

where N is the anticipated retirement age. The formulation presumes that the student devotes full time to school for a period of length E and thereafter devotes full time to the labor market earning a wage $q(E, z)$ for a work career spanning from period E to N. At birth, N is very large, and so e^{-rN} approaches zero. Consequently, lifetime discounted income can be approximated by

$$V_0(E) = \frac{q}{r} e^{-rE} + \frac{p}{r} \left(e^{-rE} - 1 \right).$$ (2.2)

The optimal length of time to spend in school is selected so as to maximize discounted lifetime income at birth. Taking the derivative of $V_0(E)$ with respect to E and setting the result equal to zero, we obtain $V_0'(E) = -q e^{-rE} + \frac{q_E}{r} e^{-rE} - p e^{-rE} = 0$. Rearranging, this reduces to

$$r + r \frac{p}{q} = \frac{q_E}{q} = \rho.$$ (2.3)

The student will remain in school until the gross rate of return is equated with the interest rate plus a term that rises in the cost of schooling. If interest rates are higher in developing countries, we would expect returns to schooling to be higher and length of time in school to be lower in the poorest countries, other things constant.

The relationship (2.3) implicitly defines years of schooling as a function of the exogenous variables

$$E = E(y, p, z).$$ (2.4)

Years of schooling rise in household income (which lowers the interest rate) and fall as schooling becomes more costly, while the impact of z on years of schooling is uncertain.[2] The gross rate of return to schooling will also be endogenous, determined by the same factors so that $\rho = \rho(y, p, z)$.

In the typical Mincerian (1974) formulation, direct costs of schooling are assumed to be zero. In that case, the first-order condition simplifies to $r = \frac{q_E}{q} = \rho$. Inserting $q = \frac{q_E}{r}$ back into $V_0(E)$, and imposing $p = 0$ and $e^{-rN} = 0$, we get the relationship $r V_0(E) = (\frac{q_E}{r}) e^{-rE}$. Rearranging, this yields a log linear relationship between earnings and years of schooling, $\ln q = \ln(r V_0(E)) + rE$. The first-order condition implies that the coefficient of years of schooling E is equal to the gross rate of return ρ when $p = 0$. When costs are not zero, the relationship is the more unwieldy, $\ln(q + \frac{p}{r}) = \ln(r V_0(E) + \frac{p}{r}) + rE$. When $p > 0$, the first-order condition implies that the coefficient of years of schooling E will be $r < \rho$.

Thus far, we have equated human capital with the number of years of schooling that students spend in school. As we will discuss later in the chapter, due to grade repetition, student absences and variation in school quality, number of years of schooling is not a perfect measure of human capital accumulation. Other studies use an even simpler measure, enrollment in a particular grade or at a certain age. In settings where nearly a half of the population has never been to school or reports zero years of schooling, such as the case of rural Ethiopia, the most important schooling decision may indeed be whether a

---

[2] To derive the comparative static effects, it is convenient to rewrite (2.3) as $-q + \frac{q_E}{r} - p = 0$. Letting $A = (\frac{1}{r} q_{EE} - q_E) < 0$; $\frac{dE}{dp} = (1/A) < 0$; $\frac{dE}{dy} = r'(y)(\frac{q_E}{Ar^2}) > 0$; and $\frac{dE}{dz} = (q_z - \frac{q_{Ez}}{r})/A$ which has an ambiguous sign.

child ever attends school or not and so enrollment is the appropriate measure. In contexts where nearly all children of school age enter school, enrollment is an incomplete measure of the household's schooling decisions unless the focus of the study is on the timing of school entry. Yet other studies consider the quality, not just the quantity, of schooling as endogenous rather than exogenous, with households or individuals choosing which schools to attend and students deciding on their level of effort. Indeed, as data on measures of academic performance have become more available, more studies have turned to learning as measured by test scores as a better indicator of human capital.[3] We return to these measurement issues in Section 6.

The relationship in (2.3) suggests that two students of similar abilities facing identical interest rates, schooling costs and human capital production processes will choose the same length of time in school. However, gaps in schooling attainment exist between men and women in many developing countries, most often favoring men. Even larger gaps exist between urban and rural populations, nearly always favoring urban residents.

2.2. Male–female schooling gaps

Current enrollment rates for children and years of schooling completed for adults show gender gaps, but overall, women in developing countries have gained relative to men with respect to education.[4] These patterns emerge from information from the most recently available household surveys (e.g., country censuses, Living Standards Measurement Surveys, and Demographic and Health Surveys) for 70 developing countries; the data are weighted to produce country-wide averages. Figure 2(a) and 2(b) illustrates the range of gender enrollment gaps for two age groups 7–11 and 15–17 in urban and rural areas; the 12–14 year-old group had plot patterns lying between these two. By differentiating between urban and rural areas at the same time, we see an important aspect of the pattern in gender gaps.

Countries plotted in the northeast quadrant have enrollment gaps favoring boys in both urban and rural areas, while those in the southwest quadrant have gaps favoring girls. Countries in the southeast quadrant have gaps favoring girls in rural areas and boys in urban areas, whereas those in the northwest quadrant have gaps favoring girls in urban areas and boys in rural areas. Countries above the 45° line have more positive male–female gaps in urban areas while those below the 45° line have more positive male–female gaps in rural areas. A box centered on (0, 0) with sides of length 0.2 helps to illustrate which gaps are larger than 10% in either direction. Any point lying outside the box indicates at least one gap larger than 10%.

---

[3] In turn, several studies have estimated the return to the quality of schooling as separate from the return to years of schooling (e.g., Moffitt, 1996; Altonji and Dunn, 1996; Case and Yogo, 1999; Bedi and Edwards, 2002).

[4] The average years of schooling attained is defined as highest grade completed rather than the actual number of years enrolled in school. Due to grade repetition, the highest grade attained can imply fewer years of schooling than the number of years actually spent in school. We have no separate information on grade repetition from the surveys.

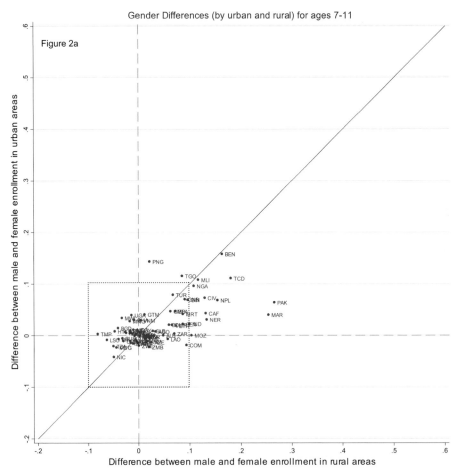

Source: Graphs computed from data from latest household surveys in 70 countries; database prepared for the World Bank, *World Development Report 2007*. All data, with few exceptions, are from year 2000 or later.

Figure 2. Combinations of male–female differences in enrollment rates, by urban and rural residence, age and country.

Several stylized facts emerge from the plots in panels 2a and 2b.

(1) In the youngest age group (7–11), male–female gaps tend to be small in both urban and rural areas. The gaps favor girls in many countries, but those differences tend to be small. The largest of gaps favor boys, most in rural areas.

(2) As children age, the variance in gaps increases. By ages 15–17, gender gaps exceed 10 percent in about half the countries. While the largest gaps favor boys, particularly in rural areas, gaps favor girls in urban and rural areas in one-third of the countries.

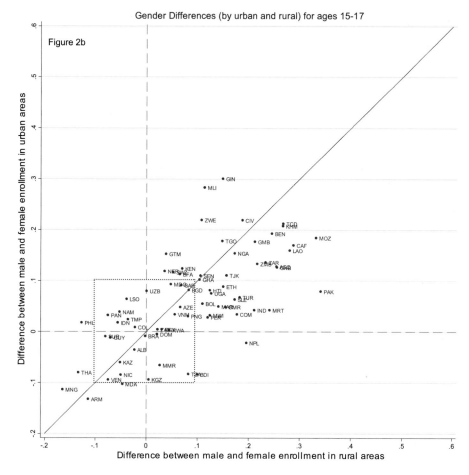

Figure 2. (*continued*)

(3) For ages 15–17, two thirds of the points lie below the 45° line, indicating larger male–female gaps in rural areas. It is in rural areas that girls' schooling mostly lags behind boys'.

(4) Girls face the greatest disadvantage in South Asian and African countries, whereas girls have higher enrollment rates than boys in both urban and rural areas in the former Soviet states which are atypically represented in the southwest quadrant.

Figure 3(a)–3(d) plots the differences in years of schooling attained by youth aged 15–24 and adults aged 25–60 for 70 developing countries. The age cutoff at 60 limits complications to our cross-country comparisons due to unequal life expectancy rates across countries. Comparing the older and younger cohorts allows us to infer changes in schooling investments across generations. In Fig. 3, panels 3a and 3b, the horizontal

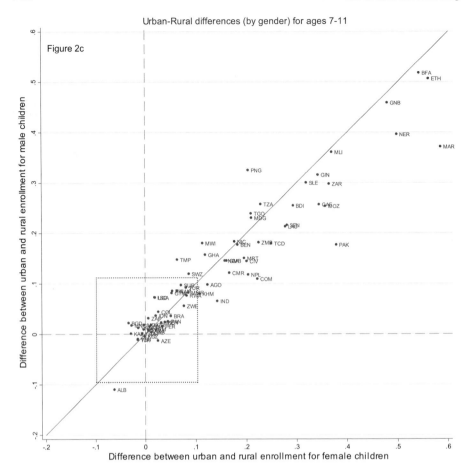

Figure 2. (*continued*)

axis shows the gender gap in years of schooling in rural areas, while the vertical axis presents the comparable indicator in urban areas. Points lying above the 45° line indicate a larger gender gap in urban areas; points below the line show larger gender gaps in rural areas. Points in the northeast quadrant imply that both gaps favor males, while points in the southwest quadrant indicate that both gaps favor females.

The graphs in 3a and 3b show several stylized facts:

(1) Women's schooling has been increasing relative to men's. In a few countries, women's gains are such that average schooling of women is now greater than that of men.

(a) Most schooling gaps for the younger cohort are less than two years in both urban and rural areas, while most gaps for the older cohort exceed two years of schooling in urban or rural areas.

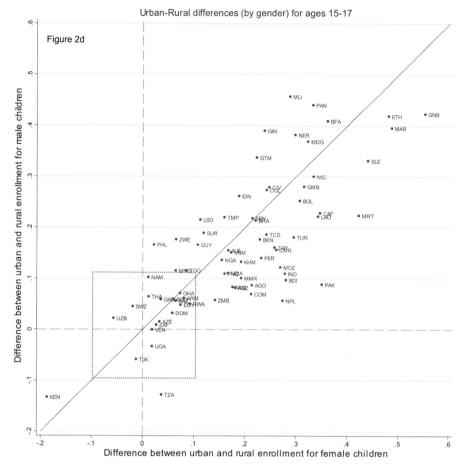

Figure 2. (*continued*)

(b) Many countries are in the southwest quadrant of the younger cohort plot but very few in the older cohort plot, indicating an increased likelihood that women attain more years of schooling than men in the younger cohorts. Correspondingly, there are fewer countries in the northeast quadrant for the younger than the older cohort, indicating a decreased probability that men's schooling exceeds women's in both urban and rural areas for the younger cohorts.

(2) In the plot of the older cohort, many countries lie above the 45° line, indicating that urban areas commonly have larger male–female gaps. In the younger-cohort plot, most countries fall below the 45° line, so the gender gaps are larger in rural areas.

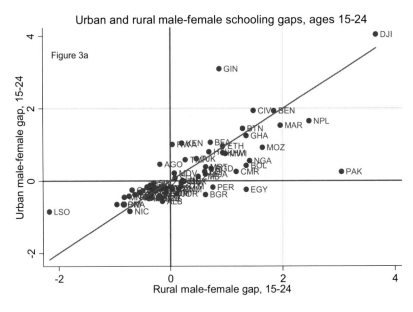

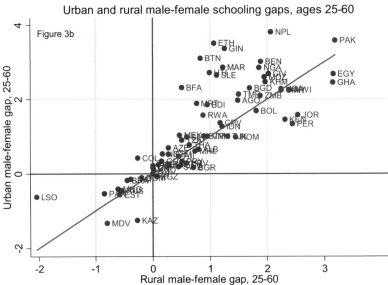

Source: Graphs computed from data from latest household surveys in 70 countries; database prepared for the World Bank, *World Development Report 2007*. All data, with few exceptions, are from year 2000 or later.

Figure 3. Urban–rural and gender gaps in years of completed schooling, ages 15–24 and 25–60.

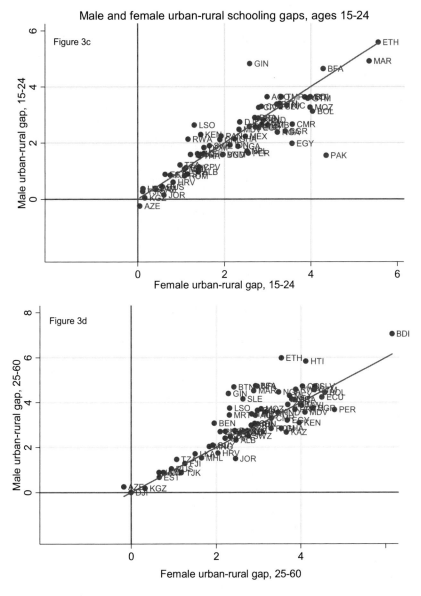

Figure 3. (*continued*)

(3) For the older cohort, the countries plotted in the extreme northeast are drawn from the Middle East, Africa and South Asia regions. Their absence from comparable positions in the younger-cohort plots suggests that it is in those areas that the most dramatic gains in women's relative to men's schooling have taken place.

Given the stopping rule for time in school implied by Eq. (2.3), it is not immediately apparent why boys and girls would spend different amounts of time in school. After all, boys and girls grow up in the same households and have equal household incomes and parent discount rates which affect schooling investment decisions. Gender differences in elements of z have ambiguous effects on boys and girls. For example, better nutrition for boys than for girls would raise the opportunity cost of schooling for boys because better-nourished boys would be more productive at work, but it would also make them more productive at school. Even improvements in the quality of schools have an ambiguous net effect because better schools imply that fewer years of schooling are needed to achieve a given level of learning.

Gender differences in work opportunities for educated labor also have an ambiguous effect because better opportunities raise both the opportunity cost of continuing in school and the potential returns to time in school. Differential returns to schooling merit some discussion here. Several recent reviews that have summarized the returns to schooling for men and women in developing countries have tended to find larger private returns to schooling for women than for men, although exceptions exist (Schultz, 1988, 2001, 2002).[5] An example of the pattern of estimated returns obtained from Mincerian earnings functions[6] is displayed in Fig. 4; the 45° line represents cases where estimated returns for men and women are identical. In only 5 of 71 cases is the return to schooling higher for men, and in 59 cases, the estimated returns were higher for women.[7] However, these estimates may be subject to measurement error and endogeneity biases; the higher average returns to schooling for women may be due to larger estimation biases in samples of women, but the existing literature lacks a systematic examination of the issue (Schultz, 1988).[8] Additional systematic investigation across countries is needed to assess whether the gap in private returns to schooling favoring women is a fiction of differential estimation bias between the sexes.

---

[5] Of 71 estimates each for men and women, education failed to raise earnings in only one case for women and in only 3 for men. As the consensus is that such estimates are likely lower-bound measures of true schooling returns, it seems safe to conclude that schooling generates positive private returns to both men and women.

[6] Using our earlier specification, these are estimates of the coefficient r from gender-specific regressions of the form $\ln q = \alpha_0 + rE + \alpha_x X + \varepsilon_q$, where X includes a quadratic in age, an urban dummy and marital status. Estimation is conducted separately for 71 harmonized household data sets from 48 developing countries. The data set is discussed in Fares, Montenegro and Orazem (2007).

[7] Duraisamy (2002) found higher returns for males at some education levels and for females at other education levels.

[8] Schultz (1988) finds only small differences between least squares and instrumented estimates of returns to schooling for both men and women. A more likely source of bias is differential nonrandom selection of men and women into wage work. Only 3% of women in Côte d'Ivoire and 7% in Ghana worked for wages compared to 19% and 26% of men in Côte d'Ivoire and Ghana, respectively (Schultz, 1988). It seems plausible that the more highly selected women in wage work would come atypically from the upper tail of the female ability distribution, creating a larger upward selection bias in female estimated returns. Schultz's results and those of Duraisamy (2002) suggest that selection biases for men and women are small and comparable across the sexes.

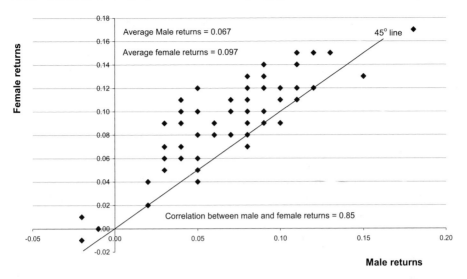

Figure 4. Paired least squares estimates of returns to schooling for males and females using household data sets from 49 developing countries, various years, 1991–2004.

Gender gaps may also reflect social norms about gender roles in familial relationships.[9] Some studies do contend that girls face higher opportunity costs of schooling due to their value in home production, although there is disagreement on how to measure the value of home time (Folbre, 2006; Hersch and Stratton, 1997; Parente, Rogerson and Wright, 2000; Smeeding and Weinberg, 2001). Indirect evidence of the impact of home production on schooling in Peru is presented by Jacoby (1993) who uses the age and sex composition of siblings (such as the presence of an older or younger sister). He finds that the number of children under five tends to raise the value of time of older children, increasing the probability of drop out.

In addition, there may be social taboos against allowing unmarried girls in public or traveling far from home but no such taboos for unmarried sons, making the cost of girls' schooling greater for girls than for boys. For example, in Pakistan special transportation or a chaperone must often be arranged for daughters in middle and secondary schools (Holmes, 2003). Social norms may also affect the returns to schooling, such as when norms specify that sons remain with their parents after marriage but that daughters move away, so parents might discount their daughters' schooling more heavily (Becker, 1985; Anderson, King and Wang, 2002; Connelly and Zheng, 2003; Quisumbing and Maluccio, 2000). If there are social taboos against allowing unmarried daughters in public or

[9] Munshi and Rosenzweig (2006), for example, examine how boys and girls respond to rapid changes in employment opportunities in urban areas in India and how caste-based networks interact with gender in determining school choice. They find that increased demand for skills can make it possible for girls from a low caste to have more schooling than boys.

being away from the family but no such taboos for unmarried sons, then the cost of girls' schooling will be greater than for boys.

In developed countries, schooling gaps between the sexes have largely disappeared as would be expected if the exogenous variables in (2.3) did not differ between boys and girls. If the source of the schooling gap in developing countries is differences in the value of child time outside of school, these differences will likely disappear as the country develops. If the source involves social norms or taboos that cause households to discount girls' schooling more heavily, the differences may persist. Also as countries impose and enforce legislative restrictions on child labor outside the home, boys would be likely to reduce their paid work while girls would continue with their responsibilities at home, thus increasing the relative cost of schooling for girls.

The public role for investing more in girls' schooling has been justified by the observed relationships between women's schooling and reduced fertility behavior, improved infant and child health, and higher cognitive attainment of children.[10] Studies have shown that mother's education improves child nutrition directly through the higher quality of care that more educated mothers can provide and through their greater ability to mitigate adverse shocks, such as food price changes, that might reduce food intake (Thomas and Strauss, 1992). In India, children of more literate mothers study nearly two hours more a day than children of illiterate mothers in similar households (Behrman et al., 1997). In Malaysia, while both the mother's and the father's education have significant positive effects on their children's schooling, the mother's education has a far greater effect than father's education on daughters' education, while the mother's and father's education have about equal, although lower, impact on sons' (Lillard and Willis, 1994). These findings underscore the gains that women's schooling can bring for improving the next generation's human capital, but are not necessarily considered by individual parents deciding how long to send their daughters to school.

2.3. Urban–rural schooling gaps

Returning to Fig. 2, panels (c) and (d) show the differences in urban–rural enrollment gaps for boys and girls of different ages. The interpretation of the urban–rural figures parallels that of the male–female plots. Points in the northeast quadrant represent countries with positive urban–rural gaps for both boys and girls, while those in the southwest represent countries with more favorable enrollment rate for rural children. Points below the 45° line imply larger urban–rural gaps for girls than boys. Among the conclusions:

(1) Urban–rural gaps are much larger than the male–female gaps. Even at the youngest ages of 7–11 years, there are many points outside the 10-percent box. The urban–rural gap exceeds 10% in half the countries. The gaps are generally of similar size for boys and girls, but the largest urban–rural gaps tend to be for girls.

---

[10] See Chapter 2 of King and Mason (2001) and Schultz in this Handbook for reviews of the literature in developing countries.

(2) As children age, the urban–rural gaps remain substantial with the largest gaps being for girls' enrollments. By ages 15–17, the urban–rural gap exceeds 10% in three quarters of the countries.

Figures 3(c) and 3(d) show urban–rural gaps in years of schooling for our young and old cohorts. The horizontal axis presents the urban–rural gap for females, while the vertical axis presents the urban–rural gap for males; as before, the 45° line shows combinations where the urban–rural gap is equal for males and females. Points lying above (below) the 45° line indicate a larger urban–rural gap for males (females). The plots reveal several stylized facts:

(1) Almost all countries lie in the northeast quadrant, suggesting nearly universal gaps favoring urban over rural years of schooling for both males and females. That pattern occurs for the plots for both older and younger cohorts.

(2) The range of gaps is as high as 6 years compared to about 3 in Figs. 3(a) and 3(b), and so urban–rural education gaps are larger, on average, than are male–female gaps.

(3) The countries align themselves closely to the 45° line, suggesting that urban–rural gaps are of similar size for males and females.

(4) There are more countries with gaps less than two years and fewer with gaps exceeding four years in the younger cohort plot than in the older cohort plot, suggesting that urban–rural gaps have been shrinking for some countries.

Several factors cause schooling levels in rural areas to lag behind those in urban areas. Comparisons of earnings from non-farm work between rural and urban markets generally find higher returns to schooling in urban areas (Agesa, 2001 for Kenya; de Brauw, Rozelle and Zhang, 2005 for China; and Schultz, 2004 for Mexico).[11] Indeed, Fig. 5 shows that the weight of previous empirical evidence suggests that returns to schooling are higher in urban than in rural markets. The data were derived from 66 of the household survey data sets used in Fig. 4 for which urban and rural residence was available. Results are quite consistent across countries.[12] In only three of 66 cases did schooling fail to raise earnings for both urban and rural residents of the country, although the estimated gains from schooling to rural residents are only marginally positive in ten percent

---

[11] Duraisamy (2002) found that returns to schooling were higher in rural areas for some education levels and higher in urban areas for others.

[12] Returns to schooling estimated from least squares may be subject to biases due to measurement error in the regressors and to unmeasured heterogeneity in ability. However, the consensus has been that these biases are of modest magnitudes (Schultz, 1988; Card, 1999; Krueger and Lindahl, 2001). However, there may be reasons why a comparison of estimated returns across urban and rural markets may yield misleading inferences. First, wages are only observed for those in wage work. Rural areas are likely to have a greater incidence of unpaid home production or self-employment, suggesting that there would be differences in the magnitude of selection bias across urban and rural markets. A second problem is that the most educated rural residents are most likely to migrate to urban markets or to be self-employed farmers, and so samples of urban workers include individuals educated in rural markets while the sample of rural workers is weighted toward the lower tail of those educated in rural schools. Schultz (1988) for Côte d'Ivoire and Ghana and Duraisamy (2002) for India found that estimated returns to schooling correcting for selection bias were very close to uncorrected measures, suggesting the bias may be modest, but the issue merits further investigation.

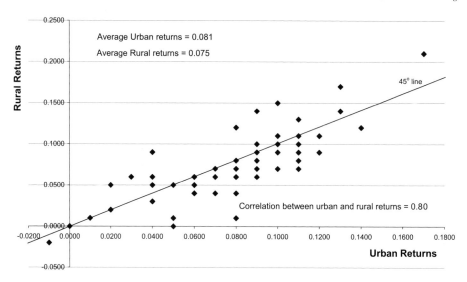

Figure 5. Paired least squares estimates of returns to schooling for urban and rural residents using household data sets from 46 developing countries, various years, 1991–2004.

of cases. Points plotted above the 45° line represents cases in which returns to schooling are higher in rural than in urban areas. In 30 of 66 pairs, the returns are equal or higher in rural than in urban areas, although urban returns are modestly higher on average.

The higher returns in urban areas provide a strong motivation for the educated to migrate from rural to urban areas. Assuming that urban and rural children have comparable latent abilities, the possibility of rural-to-urban migration means that those educated in rural areas face the same potential earnings as urban residents do. Schultz (1988) and Agesa (2001) conclude that increasing education levels in rural areas without improving employment opportunities is likely to lead to increased levels of migration: more educated youth in Latin American countries and in Kenya are likely to migrate to areas with better opportunities once they become adults.

A few other studies attempt to measure the effect of migration opportunities on schooling decisions. Kochar (2004) observes that education levels in rural areas in India are affected more by potential returns from jobs in nearby urban areas than by local wages. Schooling levels for rural males rose in areas where the wage differential between educated and less-educated male workers in urban was largest. Parents appear to pay greater attention to the employment prospects of more educated youth. Similarly, Boucher, Stark and Taylor (2007) find that rising returns to education in Mexico that can be attributed to the migration of educated rural workers to urban markets increased school attendance rates in rural areas beyond the compulsory level. In Turkey, Tansel (2002) finds that the distances to specific cities, variables that are expected to capture the effects of migration opportunities, have negative and statistically significant effects on schooling decisions, suggesting that schooling attainment is influenced by the higher education returns expected in an urban center than in a rural area. An alternative or additional interpretation is that proximity to cities could have modernizing effects on demand for schooling. Similarly, Godoy et al. (2005) find that in a sample of male household heads from four ethnic groups in rural Bolivia, the returns to education are higher among households who live close to market towns. The enhanced returns from schooling appear to be due to off-farm opportunities as there was no effect of schooling on agricultural productivity.

That higher rural schooling may lead to rural labor migrating to urban areas is a justification for a central government role in local provision of education. To the extent that education has external benefits, this out-migration of educated workers is a net transfer of schooling returns from rural to urban areas. The loss of educated labor from rural areas may cause an underinvestment in education in those areas relative to the socially optimal level. On the other hand, to the extent that rural households are anticipating, not fearing, their children's mobility, as seems to be the case in Bolivia, India, Mexico, and Turkey, the possibility of migration could help reduce schooling inequality between urban and rural areas.

In rural areas, the return to schooling depends on the pace of technological innovation in farming and on fluctuations in farm prices. A large literature has shown that more educated farmers are the first to adopt new seeds, tillage practices, fertilizers, and animal breeds (Welch, 1970; Huffman, 1977; Besley and Case, 1993; Foster and Rosenzweig, 1996, 2004; Abdulai and Huffman, 2005). Foster and Rosenzweig (1996) examine technological growth during the Green Revolution in India in the mid-1960s and 1970s, and conclude that the return to the completion of primary school as well as the attainment of primary completion increased in areas with higher rates of exogenous technological change. Returns to schooling were greater for landowners and particularly landowning sons, supporting the hypothesis that human capital is complementary with the new technologies. Similarly, Abdulai and Huffman (2005) find that more educated farmers were the earliest adopters of crossbred cattle in Tanzania, and that the technology diffused more rapidly in areas with higher average education. Huffman and Orazem (2006) argue that human capital is critical to the process of agricultural transformation whereby improvements in agricultural productivity are sufficiently great to generate both surplus food and surplus labor needed to jump start economic growth. As farmers adopt new technologies on-farm, the resulting rise in yields result in a decline of food prices which is equivalent to an increase in real urban wages. Rising urban real wages and declining food prices create a further incentive for rural-to-urban migration of those who cannot generate sufficient returns to their skills in rural markets.

Schultz (1975) famously argued that the returns to human capital come from being better able to deal with disequilibrium. Farms that purchase inputs and sell output on the market have to respond to price fluctuations, requiring skills in finance, input and output choices, and marketing that are less needed on subsistence farms. Farmers with better skills can make better decisions regarding needed resource reallocations when rules-of-thumb are no longer appropriate. The complexity of the chemical, genetic, finance and capital investment decisions required on modern farms explains, at least in part, why farmers and non-farmers in developed countries have more comparable schooling levels.

The return to human capital with respect to agricultural productivity is likely to be lower in farms that use traditional methods of production or where technical innovations are limited (Welch, 1970; Rosenzweig, 1980; Huffman, 1977). Hence, Schultz's (1964) observation that traditional farms are poor but efficient – historical rules-of-thumb will result in productive efficiency in environments where there are no new technological or price innovations. A large empirical literature also confirms this viewpoint. In China where it is common for household members to work in farm and non-farm activities, Yang (1997) finds that education does not enhance the labor productivity of routine farm tasks but it does increase wages from market work. Similarly, in Ghana Jolliffe (1998) concludes that returns to schooling are higher in non-farm than in farm activities, and in Pakistan Fafchamps and Quisumbing (1999) find that education has no significant effect on on-farm productivity but raises wages in non-farm work.

As a country develops, average household incomes rise, and the liquidity constraints on rural households will diminish. The agrarian sector will shrink, and labor market frictions between rural and urban markets will disappear. All of these factors will cause rural schooling attainment to rise toward the urban level, as has been observed in developed countries. For many poor countries, since income and interest rates are negatively related and since on average rural households are poorer than urban households, rural households are likely to discount the future earnings of their children more heavily. And given the preponderance of work open to children in farming activities, the opportunity cost of time in rural areas exceeds that in urban areas. These considerations result in lower rural education levels. Hence, the rationale for public subsidy of rural education is that household schooling investments based on these considerations yield less than socially optimal education levels. The external return from rural schooling may be related to the need for an educated population to react to new opportunities that arise from globalization, technological innovation, or changes in the composition of final demand for products. The rationale is even stronger if this underinvestment is due also to liquidity constraints or to parental ignorance of market opportunities for educated workers in urban markets.

3. How do government policies affect schooling gaps?

The previous section illustrates that urban–rural and male–female schooling gaps are commonly found in developing countries, and that those gaps have decreased at varying rates. This section develops a stylized model of the supply of and the demand for schooling in order to derive an equilibrium schooling investment rate first in the absence of government intervention. It then shows how alternative government policies can influence the equilibrium level of schooling. The model illustrates how differences in incomes, opportunity costs and direct costs of schooling can result in schooling gaps between urban and rural areas and how differences in the responses to those factors can predict the effectiveness of those policies. Similarly, differences in opportunity costs can lead to differences in enrollment rates between boys and girls.

The model also shows that the measured impact of a policy on educational investment will involve numerous behavioral parameters on both the demand side and the supply side. The same policy can have different effects depending on the magnitudes of those behavioral parameters. Even this simple formulation helps to illustrate why a policy may work in some settings and not others.

3.1. A local schooling market

In this model, we assume that there is a schooling market and that, given demand for schooling, the market yields an equilibrium human capital investment rate. (We use the term "market" here to emphasize the point that demand and supply factors are at work even when schooling is completely provided by government.) For our purposes, such a market is designated by location (an urban versus a rural district) and may also be differentiated by gender (boy or girl). Let each household have one unit of child time available which would be equal to the maximum amount of educational attainment possible. Let $0 \leqslant E^D \leqslant 1$ be the average level of schooling desired by households. Let $0 \leqslant E^S \leqslant 1$ be the average share of child time for which a school space exists. The stylized demand for schooling uses our result in (2.4) that $E = E(y, p, z)$. We abstract away from the role of complementary individual or household attributes z.[13] We presume that the supply of spaces in school responds positively to its price and negatively to costs. The market is summarized by

Demand: $\quad E^D = \eta\{(1 - V)p + (1 - B)w\} + \theta(1 + T)y,$

Supply: $\quad E^S = \varepsilon p + \varphi(1 - S)c.$ $\qquad\qquad$ (3.1)

The demand relationship relates market household demand for schooling to three factors commonly found to influence schooling demand, including p: the logarithm of the price of schooling; w: the logarithm of the wage a child can earn while of school age; and y: the logarithm of the income level per household.[14] The parameters reflect the associated schooling demand elasticities so that $\eta < 0$ is the price elasticity of demand for schooling and $\theta > 0$ is the income elasticity of demand for schooling. The signs reflect the implications of our schooling demand formulation that household demand for schooling is stronger in local markets with low costs of attending school, low opportunity costs of child time and higher household incomes.

---

[13] Note that z has an ambiguous effect on years of schooling because it serves to both raises schooling productivity and increases potential earnings upon leaving school.

[14] The demand relationship used by Card (1999, Eq. (4)) Also includes a term in exogenous expected returns to schooling which is endogenous in our formulation. Adding it as an additional exogenous factor positively influencing schooling demand did not affect the conclusions from the model. The three factors included in our demand formulation correspond to the second term in Card.

We also allow three alternative public policies to influence market demand for schooling. The subsidy $0 \leqslant V \leqslant 1$ lowers the price of schooling faced by households. This can be a voucher that pays a proportion of the schooling cost or a transfer payment given directly to the school (often called a capitation grant) that is tied to a child's enrollment cost. The transfer to the household $0 \leqslant B \leqslant 1$ is made conditional on the child attending school. The transfer (referred to here as a *bolsa* following the *Bolsa Escola* programs introduced in Brazil) lowers the opportunity cost of child time in school. We contrast the conditional transfer with an unconditional income transfer $0 \leqslant T \leqslant 1$ which changes the ability to pay for schooling but does not have an explicit tie to child time use.

The market supply reflects the aggregate number of spaces provided by local public and private schools as a fraction of the population of school-age children. Market supply of schooling is assumed to depend on p: the logarithm of the price households are willing to pay for schooling; and c: the logarithm of the cost of supplying schooling services to the market. The parameters include $\varepsilon > 0$: the price elasticity of supply for schooling, and $\varphi < 0$: the cost elasticity of supply for schooling. The signs reflect standard presumptions of how aggregate supply of schooling is influenced by costs and returns. We include one more potential government intervention in the form of a cost subsidy $0 \leqslant S \leqslant 1$ which lowers the expense of providing schooling services.

The equilibrium schooling price, P^*, and equilibrium school investment rate, E^*, are

$$P^* = \frac{\varphi(1 - S)c - \eta(1 - B)w - \theta(1 + T)y}{\eta(1 - V) - \varepsilon},$$

$$E^* = \frac{\eta\varphi c(1 - V)(1 - S) - \varepsilon\eta(1 - B)w - \varepsilon\theta(1 + T)y}{\eta(1 - V) - \varepsilon}. \tag{3.2}$$

3.2. Educational investments without government intervention

Virtually every government intervenes in the market for schooling in some way; in fact, school supply, especially at lower education levels, is presumed to be the purview of the government. Nevertheless, it is instructive to consider what educational investment rates would be if the government played no role in the provision of educational services so that $V = S = B = T = 0$. The equilibrium schooling price and education investments are

$$P^* = \frac{\varphi c - \eta w - \theta y}{\eta - \varepsilon},$$

$$E^* = \frac{\eta\varphi c - \varepsilon\eta w - \varepsilon\theta y}{\eta - \varepsilon}. \tag{3.3}$$

There is no guarantee that the equilibrium price is positive in the absence of government intervention. The denominator is negative, but only the first and third terms in the numerator are negative. As a consequence, private schools may not enter the market in the absence of government provision of educational services. Even with a positive equilibrium price, there is no guarantee that households will send children to school. The equilibrium level of education investments can be written as $E^* = \varepsilon P^* + \varphi c$. The first term is positive if $P^* > 0$, but the second term is negative, and so a positive equilibrium price is a necessary but not sufficient condition to ensure positive equilibrium education investments in the government's absence.

It is useful to consider what factors increase the likelihood that $E^* > 0$ without government intervention. Markets with low cost of school provision, low opportunity costs of child time, and high household incomes are more likely to have schools, even without public support. Such conditions are more likely to exist in urban areas. Relative to urban areas, rural areas typically have lower household incomes, higher demand for child labor, and higher costs of attracting teachers and of supplying school materials. Less densely populated areas may also be unable to take advantage of returns to scale in school provision.[15] Consequently, rural areas are less likely than urban areas to have schools without some form of government intervention.[16] Girls would also have lower schooling rates if, relative to boys, the demand for their education is less income elastic and more price elastic. Such differences in elasticities would reflect differences in parental tastes for girls' schooling versus boys' schooling. [17]

3.3. Modeling different interventions

Governments typically intervene in the market for schooling. The most common rationale for public schooling provision is that there is an expected public return to schooling above and beyond the private return captured by households, and so households will under-invest in schooling compared to the social optimum. Liquidity constraints that prevent households from borrowing against future earnings may further reduce the household's choice of schooling relative to the social optimum. The most common government intervention is through the direct provision of public schools, but in many countries, the government is not able to provide enough schools to meet demand at the public school price which may not be zero but is typically much lower than cost. As a result, both developed and developing countries have experimented with other mechanisms to raise enrollment rates. We model the factors that influence the likelihood of success of these interventions within our stylized supply-demand model for schooling. While we can predict how these mechanisms might work differently in urban and rural settings, how they differ in impact on boys and girls is less clear.

---

[15] See Alderman, Kim and Orazem (2003) for a comparison of school costs in urban and rural Pakistan.

[16] Estimated returns to schooling are typically lower in rural areas compared to urban areas, particularly in areas characterized by traditional agriculture and low rates of rural to urban migration. If treated as exogenous, low expected returns are another factor limiting rural schooling demand.

[17] Estimated returns to schooling for women are typically higher than for men, and so exogenous anticipated returns are not likely to explain gender differences in schooling unless parents receive benefits from their boys' schooling but not from their girls' schooling.

3.3.1. Subsidies of schooling costs

In the context of the stylized model, an entirely public school system would be equivalent to setting $S = 1$, while $V = B = T = 0$ in Eq. (3.2). In this case the government fully subsidizes schooling; more generally, however, the subsidy would be partial $(0 < S < 1)$ such that public schools meet additional costs by charging tuition and other fees, or public school spaces are limited and so some students have to enroll in private schools.

The effect of the school subsidy on the schooling investment is

$$\frac{\partial E^*}{\partial S} = \frac{-\eta \varphi c}{\eta - \varepsilon} > 0. \tag{3.4}$$

This means that equilibrium education rises unambiguously with the subsidy. The effectiveness of the subsidy is greatest in areas with high schooling costs, highly elastic supply responses to costs, price elastic demand for schooling and price inelastic schooling supply. Such subsidies are likely to be effective in rural areas that are characterized by high schooling costs and price elastic demand for schooling.

It is interesting to examine how government intervention in the supply of schooling services affects private provision of services. The equilibrium price falls as the government subsidy increases, as shown by

$$\frac{\partial P^*}{\partial S} = \frac{-\varphi c}{\eta - \varepsilon} < 0. \tag{3.5}$$

Consequently, if the government raises its subsidy of schooling costs by increasing direct provision of government schools with no coincident change in support for already existing private schools, it will displace some of the private school supply by lowering the equilibrium price. For example, the reduction or removal of public school fees may lead primarily to a transfer of students from private schools to public schools rather than to a net increase in enrollment. Such a crowding out effect was reported by Jimenez and Sawada (2001) in the Philippines. James (1993) found strong evidence of trade-offs between public and private school provision in developing countries.

3.3.2. Vouchers

The government may decide to allow students to use the public subsidy either in a public school or a private school. Some countries have initiated programs that give poor households vouchers that can be used to pay all or part of the tuition at a private school, while others have adopted capitation grants that transfer income directly to the school.[18] Indeed, evidence shows that private schools (though not necessarily private

---

[18] Evaluations of voucher or capitation grant programs in developing countries include King, Orazem and Wohlgemuth (1999) and Angrist et al. (2002) for Colombia; Kim, Alderman and Orazem (1999) for Pakistan; and Hsieh and Urquiola (2006) for Chile.

financing) is used extensively in many countries. In low-income countries, the 2003 average enrollment share of private schools was 15 percent at the primary level and 40 percent at the secondary level; in high-income countries, the corresponding shares were lower at 12 percent and 22 percent, respectively.[19]

Vouchers are often viewed as "demand-side" interventions and capitation grants as "supply-side" interventions, but they are the same policy in that they both lower the cost of schooling faced by the household. In practice, they differ in the number of transactions required to implement the policy: capitation grants require one transaction between the government and the school, while a voucher plan requires two transactions, one between the government and the household and a second between the household and the school. It is also possible that the two policies would have different effects because a voucher plan requires more involvement by the household in the transaction than a capitation grant, and thus may elicit more attention from parents on their children's schooling. In the context of our stylized model, we assume that the two policies have identical equilibrium effects on enrollment.[20]

Setting $V > 0$ and $S = B = T = 0$ in (3.2), the effect of a voucher or capitation grant on equilibrium schooling investment is

$$\frac{\partial E^*}{\partial V} = \frac{\eta \varepsilon (\varphi c - \eta w - \theta y)}{(\eta (1 - V) - \varepsilon)^2} = \frac{\eta \varepsilon (\eta - \varepsilon) P^*}{(\eta (1 - V) - \varepsilon)^2} \tag{3.6}$$

where P^* is the equilibrium price obtained without any government intervention in equation (3.3). The partial derivative is only positive if $P^* > 0$, or in other words, if economic conditions have induced private school entry even without government support. This implies that vouchers will not be effective in the absence of private schools, and so vouchers are more likely effective in urban rather than rural markets.

Conditional on $P^* > 0$, the effectiveness of the program in raising E^* rises as V rises. However, the second derivative is negative, and so the marginal increase in educational investment gets smaller as V increases. The schooling response to vouchers also increases as the equilibrium price of schooling increases. Consequently, it is possible that relatively modest vouchers may have positive effects on educational investment rates, even in areas with high-priced private schools.

The effectiveness of the voucher also increases as school supply responds more elastically to price. School supply is almost surely more elastic in urban areas, but will be particularly elastic in areas with excess school capacity (King, Orazem and Wohlgemuth, 1999). To the extent that additional space can be added at low cost to accommodate additional students, vouchers and conditional transfer programs will be most effective in markets characterized by excess private school capacity. Again, this favors the effectiveness of vouchers in urban rather than rural markets.

---

[19] These data on enrollment shares in private schools were obtained from the World Bank education database, available on http://sima.worldbank.org/edstats. Private schools pertain to church schools, private non-sectarian schools, and community schools, whether for-profit or not-for-profit.

[20] In our model, we treat the voucher as a payment to the household. It could also be treated as a payment to the school.

3.3.3. Unconditional income transfers

The relationship between household income and schooling investment has long been established. On this basis, policy analysts have suggested that income transfers or safety net programs will raise enrollment rates even without explicit conditions on school attendance. We can evaluate such a program by setting $S = V = B = 0$ in (3.2) and allowing $T > 0$.

$$\frac{\partial E^*}{\partial T} = \frac{-\varepsilon\theta y}{\eta - \varepsilon} > 0. \tag{3.7}$$

The income transfer program is most effective when schooling demand is income elastic but not price elastic and when schooling supply is price elastic so that additional space can be added without raising schooling prices rapidly. The best case for such transfers can be made as part of an income support program for low-income households that face periodic income shocks from unstable employment. Several recent studies (discussed in more detail in Section 5) have found that when poor households experience a sudden income loss due to business cycle shocks, national currency crises, or crop failures, child time is reallocated from school to work. Even temporary income shocks could cause permanent loss of potential human capital to the extent that children fall behind their peers in school and are more likely to drop out. Programs that help such households absorb transitory income shocks may allow them to keep their children in school. Nevertheless, most recently instituted income transfer programs have opted to place conditions on how child time is allocated rather than relying solely on the income effect of the transfer on child time in school.

3.3.4. Conditional income transfers

In Latin America, there has been an explosion of interventions that transfer income to poor households in exchange for a commitment to send children to school and/or to reduce child labor. Examples are Mexico's PROGRESA/*Oportunidades* program and Brazil's *Bolsa Escola* program.[21] Such a program implies setting $B > 0$ and $S = V = T = 0$. The predicted effect of a conditional transfer that exactly replaces the income previously generated by the child at work is

$$\frac{\partial E^*}{\partial B} = \frac{\eta\varepsilon w}{(\eta - \varepsilon)} > 0. \tag{3.8}$$

---

[21] For example, in the PROGRESA/Oportunidades program discussed by Parker, Rubalcava and Teruel in this Handbook, grants are awarded to mothers in households judged to be extremely poor every two months during the school calendar and all the children between 7 years and 18 years in these households are eligible. To receive the grant parents must enroll their children in school and ensure that children have a minimum attendance rate of 85%, monthly and annually.

The effect on schooling is unambiguously positive, reflecting a pure substitution effect toward increased schooling. More generally, for some households, the conditional transfer offers increased income while for others it will actually lower income because child time will be allocated away from labor and to school. Therefore, income is likely to change as a consequence of the conditional transfer so that $\frac{\partial y}{\partial B} \neq 0$. Incorporating the effect of the *bolsa* on income into the analysis, the impact on equilibrium education investment becomes

$$\frac{\partial E^*}{\partial B} = \frac{\eta \varepsilon w - \varepsilon \theta \frac{\partial y}{\partial B}}{(\eta - \varepsilon)}. \tag{3.9}$$

If household income rises as a consequence of the program, then $\frac{\partial y}{\partial B} > 0$ and both the substitution and income effects will raise enrollment. If $\frac{\partial y}{\partial B} < 0$, the income effect will work against the substitution effect. Nevertheless, even if household income falls in response to an income reduction, the derivative in Eq. (3.9) will be positive if the income effect is sufficiently small. Consequently, areas with income inelastic but price elastic demand for schooling can still increase enrollments through a conditional transfer, even if households lose income as a result of the program.

Conditional transfers will also be more effective in areas with high opportunity costs of child's time. This suggests that they may be particularly effective in rural areas where child labor is more prevalent. Indeed, this is the justification for Mexico's conditional transfer program which is targeted to rural areas. In addition, the program allocates larger transfers to girls than to boys on the presumption that girls' time is more valuable to the household than boys' time.[22] The factual basis for this assumption is uncertain at best because most child work is not priced by the labor market. Admittedly noisy information on actual child wages in Mexico (Schultz, 2004) and some unpublished data from Pakistan do not find large differences in market pay between boys and girls. However, if the presumption is true, then we might expect that the conditional transfers would have a larger effect on girls than on boys.

A natural question is whether unconditional or conditional transfers would raise enrollments more. An unconditional transfer has only an income effect, so its clearest advantage is in areas with price-inelastic but income-elastic schooling demand. Because the poor are likely to have a more price-elastic schooling demand, it is doubtful that unconditional income transfers would dominate conditional transfers in the low-income populations that would be targeted by such government programs. The conditional transfers also have an advantage in that there is less leakage – households only participate if they plan to meet the enrollment obligation, and these programs usually monitor this. Households that do not send their children to school receive no transfers under the rules of a conditional transfer program, in contrast to an unconditional transfer program

---

[22] In this program, grants at the secondary education level are higher for females, and this premium rises with the grade attended. The level of the grants was set with the aim of compensating for the opportunity cost of children's school attendance.

in which the government ends up subsidizing some households whose children are not enrolled.

The most plausible role for unconditional transfers is as a temporary income safety net that insures households from adverse income shocks. A temporary subsidy to an otherwise price inelastic household that has suffered an income shock may prove more cost effective in maintaining enrollment relative to a conditional transfer program that implies a longer-term contractual obligation.[23]

3.4. Endogenous program placement and participation

The model discussed in this section demonstrates that the impact of a government policy depends on household responses to the policy. It also shows that policies hold more promise in some settings than others. For example, school vouchers have the largest effects on educational investments in settings where private schools already exist as might be true in urban areas, while in rural areas, school construction and conditional transfers may have larger impacts on schooling demand. These decisions regarding where to locate a policy intervention and how to respond to those interventions complicate evaluation. Rosenzweig and Wolpin (1988) argue that mobile populations will migrate toward areas receiving geographically targeted benefits so that the estimated returns to the program will be subject to a selection bias: the parameters will reflect the population most likely to want the benefits rather than the true population average. Even with immobile populations, programs are likely to be placed in areas where they are expected to be most useful (Rosenzweig and Wolpin, 1986), and so the estimated impact of the program will reflect the policymakers' placement choices.

Even carefully designed pilot programs yield results that are relevant only for comparable areas and the results cannot be directly extended to dissimilar areas. If pilots are placed in areas atypically expected to prove successful, the evaluation cannot predict accurately how universal application of the policy would perform.

3.4.1. Application: Evaluating voucher programs in Latin America

Studies of the voucher programs in Chile and Colombia illustrate the difficulties in estimating the impact of government policies or programs. In 1980, Chile transferred public schools to municipalities, and teachers became municipal employees. At the same time, households were given the freedom to choose from three school types: free municipally

---

[23] Martinelli and Parker (2003) show that child welfare rises more from conditional than unconditional transfers when the household is bequest constrained, as would be the case for the poorest households. Households wealthy enough to be planning bequests to their children would prefer unconditional bequests. The logic follows the impact of positive income shocks in the context of the Becker–Tomes model of intergenerational transfers discussed in Section 5. Parker, Rubalcava and Teruel in this Handbook provide a general review of conditional transfer programs.

managed schools, free subsidized private schools called voucher schools, or unsubsidized private schools that charged fees. Subsidized municipal and voucher schools
receive one School Subsidy Unit for every attending child. Municipal and voucher
schools receive the same per-student capitation grant (Mizala and Romaguera, 2000).
The subsidized schools have to admit students up to a maximum class size, while the
unsubsidized private schools can select from a pool of applicants based on household
and child attributes such as income or ability.

Unlike Chile's nationwide program, Colombia's PACES program which began in
1992 gave vouchers only to eligible urban youths in poor neighborhoods. Not all municipalities agreed to participate since participation required cost-sharing between the
central government and the municipal government. Compared to the municipalities that
did not participate, the municipalities which opted to participate were the ones that had
excess capacity in their existing private schools, had apparent excess demand for available public schools, and were in better fiscal shape (King, Orazem and Wohlgemuth,
1999). Participation by municipalities, schools and households was voluntary, and so
any evaluation needs to address these endogenous choices.

Evaluations of Chile's reform have yielded mixed results,[24] in part because of differences in whether or how studies control appropriately for school choices. Hsieh
and Urquiola (2006) discount findings that the Chile reform has improved average test
scores, repetition rates and years of schooling because the "best" public school students
transferred to private schools. However, Contreras (2002) concludes that when one corrects for school choice, the evidence of improved outcomes in voucher schools becomes
stronger, not weaker. Hoxby (2003) contends that studies of Chile's reform cannot yield
convincing results because they rely entirely on post-program data due to the lack of
baseline data pre-dating the program. Without knowing which students chose public or
private schools before the program, it is hard to properly control for sorting after the
program is put in place.

In Colombia, endogenous household program participation can be addressed by the
fact that a few municipal governments conducted a lottery as a mechanism for allocating
the vouchers for which demand exceeded supply. Angrist et al. (2002) take advantage
of this lottery to identify an appropriate counterfactual group for the voucher recipients.
They compare several measures of education outcomes between lottery winners and lottery losers, and find that lottery winners completed 0.12–0.16 more years of schooling,
a large enough increase to raise the future annual incomes of the winners by $36–48 per
year. An achievement test given to a subset of lottery participants showed higher test

---

[24] Examples are Mizala and Romaguera (2000) and McEwan (2001) who investigated which type of school
has performed better. They approach the issue of selection bias differently. Mizala and Romaguera admitted
that school choice makes a difference and found that student characteristics differ across the types of schools;
they did not address this issue and so their results are biased. McEwan (2001) addressed this selection bias by
using the density of schools of each school type in the municipality to identify students' school choices; by
doing so, he assumed that this density variable does not belong in the achievement production function.

scores (0.2 of a standard deviation) equivalent to about one additional year of school-ing. Moreover, a follow-up study (Angrist, Bettinger and Kremer, 2006) finds that the program increased secondary school completion by 15–20 percent.[25] Note, however, that these impact estimates are derived from a particular universe of students – those who lived in municipalities that had more students interested in the voucher than there were vouchers available and who met the program eligibility criteria and applied to the program and thus participated in the lottery.[26] While it seems likely that for these pop-ulations vouchers improve student performance, it does not follow that vouchers will improve student performance in other municipalities that have less interest in private schools, or that vouchers will improve the schooling of less qualified students.

There is no strong *a priori* difference in policy effects on the enrollment rates of boys versus girls, but in Colombia's program, voucher status produced higher gains for girls than for boys: a statistically significant 0.12 more years of schooling for girls, primarily through reduced grade repetition and additional time in school, and statistically signif-icant higher test scores (0.26 higher test score), versus not statistically significant and smaller effects (0.06 more years and 0.17 higher score) for boys (Angrist et al., 2002). Since girls were not targeted by the program, these differences in impact between the sexes may depend more on demand elasticities (i.e. household tastes) than differences in public policy.[27]

Capitation grants are the supply-side variant of the voucher. A pilot project in the province of Balochistan, Pakistan subsidized the establishment of private girls' schools in ten randomly selected neighborhoods. Parents in each neighborhood were given re-sources to contract a school operator to open a neighborhood private school, with the level of support being tied to the number of neighborhood girls the new school could attract. This strategy was chosen over a voucher program because of the absence of pre-existing schools. Kim, Alderman and Orazem (1999) compared the enrollment growth

---

[25] After correcting for the greater percentage of lottery winners taking college admissions tests, the program impact on test score was the same as the finding from the earlier study: test scores increased by two-tenths of a standard deviation in the distribution of potential test scores. The authors conclude that the program was very cost effective given the low cost to the government and the benefits arising from the increase in winners' earnings due to greater educational attainment.

[26] In addition, as Angrist et al. (2002) point out, voucher status and scholarship use are not deterministic: about 10 percent of the lottery winners did not use the voucher, and 24 percent of the lottery losers used some other scholarship. However, the lottery outcome could be used as an instrument for scholarship use in a 2SLS model, and when the authors do so, they find effects that are 50 percent larger than a reduced-form effect of winning the lottery. Even with this method, however, the results still apply only to the particular universe of children that were exposed to the voucher.

[27] A few studies have estimated demand elasticities with respect to school availability for boys and girls. In Ghana, using cross-section data, Lavy (1996) finds that girls' schooling is more responsive to the distances to primary and secondary school (coefficients of −0.111 and −0.020, respectively) than boys' schooling (0.009 and −0.017), although the coefficient of distance to middle school is the same (Lavy, 1996). Tansel (1997) finds essentially the same results in Ghana – that distance in the middle school has a larger deterrent effect on girls' than on boys' schooling; however, in Cote d'Ivoire, the opposite seems to be the case, at least at the primary level.

in the program neighborhoods to enrollment growth in 10 otherwise similar neighborhoods that were not chosen in the drawing. The program increased girls' enrollments by around 33 percentage points. Boys' enrollments rose as well – though at a lower rate – partly because boys were also allowed to attend the new schools, and partly because parents would not send their girls to school and not also educate their boys.[28] A similar program attempted in rural areas of Balochistan could not sustain the schools because the rural communities were too poor to generate the revenues needed to allow a school to break even (Alderman, Kim and Orazem, 2003), consistent with our discussion above that suggested vouchers would have difficulty succeeding in less densely populated markets.

4. Static model

In order to establish *ex ante* projections of the likely success or failure of alternative government interventions in the market for schooling, we need to have a model of household behavior. In Section 2, we presented a model of how long a student stays in school, based on the relative present values of the stream of costs and of expected returns to schooling. In this section, we present a model to evaluate why an intervention had the impact it did, or to project what types of households or areas would be most suitable for expanding the intervention if it proves successful. The model shows why households might invest differently in the education of daughters versus sons or why otherwise comparable households might make different allocations of child time to school in urban versus rural areas. It also shows how various government policies enter the household's decisions. Even a simple static model of the household's schooling decisions demonstrates the salient issues we wish to explore.[29]

4.1. A household model

Households are assumed to have parents, a daughter, f, and a son, m. Parents decide how to allocate their children's time between work and school, with H_f and H_m representing the proportion of time in school. Parents are assumed to derive utility from their household's consumption of goods, C; and from their daughter's and son's human capital production, q_f and q_m. The treatment of schooling as a pure consumption good ignores the potential impact of schooling on the child's future labor productivity, but such issues can only be sensibly modeled in a life-cycle setting. Nevertheless, the utility parents derive from their child's schooling can also include expected future child earnings, so the static model can easily accommodate expected returns to human capital

---

[28] Private primary schools in Pakistan are generally coeducational, even though government schools are more typically single sex schools. Cultural taboos against mixing the sexes are more evident as girls age.

[29] See Becker (1993) and Singh et al. (1986) for more complete models.

investments. This model ignores leisure consumption, although adding leisure into the model does not change the model's implications for schooling choices or the implied reduced form schooling demand equations.

The productivity of child time spent in human capital production depends on the availability of local technologies that improve the productivity of child time spent in school, Z. Elements of Z include the quality of local schools, teachers and curriculum; the abilities of other children in the school, and the attributes of the school management including whether it is public or private and whether it is responsive to local parents. Child learning also depends on academic ability, μ_f and μ_m, which may affect child time in school or work.

Even if the son and daughter have identical abilities and face identical school supply, parents may value the outcomes of their time in school differently. Although there may be cases where boys' education is devalued, more common are cultural prohibitions against educating girls, exposing girls to the public, or placing women in the labor market may cause parents to derive less utility from their daughter's time in school. Applying Becker's (1971) innovation of a taste for discrimination, let parents discount the utility they get from their daughter's education relative to their son's by d_f.[30] The typical case will be $0 < d_f < 1$; if parents discount boys' schooling, then $d_f > 1$, while $d_f = 1$ indicates no discounting for either child.

Incorporating these various elements into the parents' concave utility function yields

$$U = U\big(C, d_f q(H_f, \mu_f, Z), q(H_m, \mu_m, Z)\big). \tag{4.1}$$

Parents face a budget constraint that depends on the time allocations of the household members. Because the great majority of children perform household chores or work in unpaid labor for a household enterprise rather than in the formal labor market, we use the marginal product of child time in household production as the relevant opportunity cost of child time in school. Let each household member be given one unit of time. Parents allocate full time to household production activities while children can either work in the home or go to school. The concave household production function is given by $Q = Q(1, 1 - H_f, 1 - H_m; \tau)$, where τ is the technology and fixed inputs that the household has at its disposal. The proceeds of the household's production are used to purchase consumption goods at price P_C, and to purchase schooling services that are priced at P_f and P_m per unit of the girl's time and the boy's time respectively. The budget constraint is

$$Q(1, 1 - H_f, 1 - H_m; \tau) + A - P_C C - P_f H_f - P_m H_m \tag{4.2}$$

---

[30] The discrimination coefficient could also be rationalized as the parents' relative expected return from the girl's human capital versus the boy's human capital. d_f might also reflect parents expectations that girls are more likely than boys to leave the household as adults, or that girls are less likely to remit earnings back to the household.

where A is non-labor income from assets. Parents maximize (4.1) with respect to (4.2), and using λ as the Lagrange multiplier, the first-order conditions are

$$U_C - \lambda P_C \geqslant 0, \tag{4.3a}$$

$$d_f U_q q_{Hf} - \lambda(Q_{Hf} + P_f) \gtreqless 0, \tag{4.3b}$$

$$U_q q_{Hm} - \lambda(Q_{Hm} + P_m) \gtreqless 0, \tag{4.3c}$$

$$Q(1, 1 - H_f, 1 - H_m; \tau) + A - P_C C - P_f H_f - P_m H_m \geqslant 0. \tag{4.3d}$$

When the inequality in (4.3b) or (4.3c) is strictly greater than zero, the girl or boy spends full time in school and does no household work. Similarly, when the inequality is in the opposite direction, the girl or boy spends full time in household work. When (4.3b) or (4.3c) holds with equality, the child allocates time for both school and household work. The child is more likely to spend full time in household work when the parents' marginal utility from child time in school is low, when the child's marginal product in home production is large, and when the price of schooling is high. A girl is also more likely to devote full time to household work when her parents discount more heavily her time in school.

Assuming all first-order conditions hold with equality, the trade-off between household consumption and educational investments in a boy (or a girl) is described by

$$\frac{U_C}{U_{H_m}} = \frac{P_C}{(Q_{H_m} + P_m)}. \tag{4.4}$$

The first-order conditions have useful insights also for why educational investments and outcomes for rural children typically lag behind those of urban children. Because rural households are poorer, on average, the marginal utility of consumption will tend to be large. Child time has many productive uses in agricultural households, raising the marginal product of child time. And inequality in school provision tends to mean that school supply is lower in rural areas and/or schools are of lower quality, thus increasing the cost of schooling as well as depressing the marginal utility of child time in school. In addition, as discussed in Section 2, human capital may have greater returns off-farm than on-farm, or in urban than in rural areas, thus lowering the utility rural parents derive from their children's schooling. Taken as a whole, the ratio of relative prices of consumption to schooling will tend to be lower in rural than urban areas, while the ratio of marginal utilities of consumption relative to school time will tend to be larger in rural than in urban areas. To bring the marginal utilities in line with relative prices, rural households must raise consumption and/or reduce child time in school relative to their urban counterparts.

The first-order conditions also have useful insights for why educational investments and outcomes may differ between boys and girls. The trade-off between investments in a daughter's versus a son's schooling is described by

$$\frac{U_q q_{Hm}}{U_q q_{Hf}} = \frac{d_f(Q_{Hm} + P_m)}{(Q_{Hf} + P_f)}. \tag{4.5}$$

Absent differences in school quality or availability, differences in productivity of time in the household or in school, or differences in the price of schooling, and if $d_f = 1$, parents should invest equally in the education of their daughters and sons. If $d_f < 1$, parents will view boys schooling as less expensive, even if boy's and girl's time is equally productive in the household and if the schooling prices are identical. Parents will invest more of the boy's time in schooling, even if the two children are equally productive in school. There is considerable evidence that parents in parts of South Asia, the Middle East and Africa discount their daughters' human capital relative to their sons', particularly in rural areas. However, there may also be circumstances when $d_f > 1$, particularly in societies where educated girls generate a higher bride price that goes to the parents.[31] The tendency to invest less in girls may be further reinforced if boys and girls schools are separated, and if boys' schools are of higher quality and closer proximity.

In some settings and cultures, boys are more likely than girls to work outside the home, and in most countries, girls spend more time in household work (cooking, cleaning, child care) than boys. These time allocations do not necessarily imply that girls are favored over boys to attend school, or vice versa. It is very common for children to combine school and work in developing countries, in part because the school session lasts only a few hours per day. While child work in the home or in the market may not reduce school enrollment directly, it may affect education investments by lowering the productivity of child time in school. One might expect market work to be more damaging to child schooling than is home work. Children engaged in market work are more likely to be exposed to hazards that would cause injuries or illnesses that would disrupt school time. Work outside the home may also be more intense in terms of time or physical demands, leaving the child too tired to perform well in school.

Efforts to measure the relative impact of child home or market work on human capital production, perhaps with an interest in gauging the relative effect of girls' and boys' work on schooling attainment, face a major hurdle: almost all children do work in the home. For example, virtually all third- and fourth-grade children in a sample of Latin American countries do household chores (Table 1). There is no correlation between household work and average language test scores, whether for boys or girls or urban or rural children, but that may be due to the lack of variation in household work and not to the absence of an effect. In contrast, those children who work outside the home perform worse by 14–19 percent in language tests than those who do not work outside the home, a pattern that holds for boys and girls and for urban and rural children. These correlations do not imply causality, and the inverse relationship between test scores and market work may as easily imply that poor students are more likely to work as that child workers will be weaker students. Our point is that any effort to assess the impact of household work on schooling will fail unless there is meaningful variation in the incidence of household work.

---

[31] Bommier and Lambert (2000) find that in Tanzania, households send their daughters to school at a younger age and that they leave school at a younger age than their sons. They argue that the pattern of behavior is consistent with maximizing the present value of the bride price.

Table 1

Incidence of child work and average language test scores, by location and type of work

	Girls		Boys		Rural		Urban	
	No	Yes	No	Yes	No	Yes	No	Yes
Home Work Incidence (%)	3.7	97.2	5.1	95.8	4.4	96.5	4.5	96.4
Language Test Score	10.5	11.0	10.2	10.4	8.8	9.4	10.8	11.1
Market Work Incidence (%)	44.7	46.2	35.9	55.1	29.5	61.4	43.6	47.3
Language Test	12.1	10.1	11.4	9.9	10.1	8.9	12.0	10.5

Notes: Countries include Argentina, Bolivia, Brazil, Chile, Colombia, Honduras, Mexico, Paraguay, Peru, the Dominican Republic and Venezuela. Home work incidence based on child responses to the question "Do you help in household chores?" Market work incidence based on child responses to the question "Do you work outside the home?" Test scores are average number correct of 19 possible from a common test of Spanish or Portuguese skills administered in all countries in 1998.

Source: Author's calculations based on data provided by Gunnarsson, Orazem and Sanchez (2006).

Equation (4.5) suggests an avenue by which policy can equalize investments across genders if other factors conspire to induce parents to treat their boys and girls differently. If, for example, girls receive less schooling than boys, the government could lower the relative price or the relative opportunity cost of schooling for girls. The use of conditional transfers to households if they send their daughters to school will lower the opportunity cost of girls' schooling, Q_{H_f}, while vouchers would lower the direct price of schooling, P_f. Improving the relative quality or proximity of girls' schools would also tend to reduce the gender gap in schooling. Of course, if the government wished to increase parental investments in education for both children, such policies could be applied equally for both boys and girls.

4.2. Estimating the static model

Assuming an interior solution to the system of Eqs. (4.3a)–(4.3d), the reduced form equations for boy's and girl's schooling will have the functional forms:

$$H_f = H_f(P_C, P_f, P_m, Q_{H_f}, Q_{H_m}, A, Z, \tau, d_f, \mu_f),$$
$$H_m = H_m(P_C, P_f, P_m, Q_{H_f}, Q_{H_m}, A, Z, \tau, d_f, \mu_m). \tag{4.6}$$

First-order approximations to these unknown functional forms are commonly used in studies of child time in school. P_m and P_f are measured by school tuition, fees and distance to the nearest school. Measures of the marginal product of child labor, Q_{H_f} and Q_{H_m}, can be estimated using a household production function or by measures of variables expected to shift the marginal product of child time but not time in school. Alternatively, researchers may use average local child wages as the value of child time, subject to the caveat that average wages are subject to considerable selection bias as most children who work do not work for wages. Furthermore, those who work may not be representative of all children who are confronted by the choice of going to school.

Measures of Z typically include the quality of the nearest school, but also the quality of household inputs that are viewed as complementary with schooling such as parental education and the availability of books or other reading materials in the home. Measures of household assets include various measures of non-labor income. Alternatively, researchers may compute the full income of the household, taken as the income that would be generated if all time were allocated solely to income generation.[32] Measures of technology typically include fixed productive assets in rural areas such as land, livestock, and farm tools and machinery. We will comment on these various measures in more detail in the next section.

The d_f is typically unobserved and will be part of the error term. However, if all the exogenous variables are available, a test of parental discriminatory preferences is to reject the null hypothesis that differences in educational investments between boys and girls can be completely explained by differences between genders in measured P_C, P_f, P_m, Q_{H_f}, Q_{H_m}, μ_f, μ_m, A, Z, and τ. Most of these measures will not differ between boys and girls, however, and those that do (presumably Q_{H_f}, Q_{H_m}, μ_f, and μ_m) are often unmeasured or unmeasurable. Of particular controversy is when the ability measures μ_f and μ_m are excluded from the analysis. Differences in observed human capital investments, H_f and H_m, or differences in observed schooling outcomes q_f and q_m may be interpreted alternatively as reflecting differences in parental or societal preferences for boys' or girls' education or as differences in underlying abilities μ_f and μ_m.[33] These interpretations invariably involve trading off potential cultural insensitivity in asserting parental favoritism with gender insensitivity in asserting differences in abilities between the sexes.

The problem of omitted variables bias is a general problem and not exclusively related to the issue of explaining differences between boys and girls. Writing the linearized reduced-form schooling demand equation for child i in household j as

$$H_{ij} = \alpha_0 + \alpha_1 A_i + \alpha_2 Z_j + \alpha_3 P_j + \alpha_4 X_j + (\gamma \mu_{ij} + \varepsilon_{ij}) \tag{4.7}$$

where the α's are unbiased regression parameters, A_i and Z_j are defined as before, P_j is a vector of child opportunity costs, and X_j is a vector of all the other household and community variables. Were ability observed, γ would be the true impact of μ_{ij} on child time in school. If instead ability were not observed, then the regression would be[34]

$$H_{ij} = (\alpha_0 + \gamma \beta_0) + (\alpha_1 + \gamma \beta_1) A_i + (\alpha_2 + \gamma \beta_2) Z_j + (\alpha_3 + \gamma \beta_3) P_j$$
$$+ (\alpha_4 + \gamma \beta_4) X_j + (\gamma \xi_{ij} + \varepsilon_{ij}) \tag{4.8}$$

where the β's are hypothetical coefficients one would obtain from an auxiliary regression of μ_{ij} on A_i, Z_j, P_j, and X_j, and ξ_{ij} is the error term in that regression. The

---

[32] In our application, that would be $Q(1, (1 - (H_f = 0)), (1 - (H_m = 0)); \tau) + A$.

[33] As an example, it is common for girls to outperform boys in language tests while boys outperform girls in mathematics, even when the children are in the same schools and have families with similar socioeconomic status.

[34] See Wooldridge (2002) for an excellent review of the omitted variable bias problem.

difference between the true parameter in (4.7) and the estimate derived from (4.8) depends on the magnitude of the effect of ability on observed time allocations, γ, and on the covariance between ability and the regressor, β_k.

It is plausible that the bias associated with unobserved ability, as measured by the auxiliary parameter γ in (4.8), grows with the accumulation of human capital. Parents may not know μ_{ij} until after the child has been in school long enough to allow recognition of native ability. If true, omitted variables bias should increase in magnitude the longer the child has been in school.

4.2.1. Application: The role of missing ability in evaluations of nutrition on cognitive attainment

Ability can be interpreted as the initial "school-readiness" of children. It is partially endogenous to the extent that it responds to the same variables that determine demand for schooling. Problems seen in schooling – for example, late entry, high repetition, early dropout, frequent absences, inattention and poor learning, as well as poor health of youths and adults – have been traced to malnutrition, disease, and neglect very early in the lives of children (Strauss and Thomas in this Handbook). Other studies have shown that behavioral problems in early childhood are strong predictors of high school dropout and delinquency. Children who are appropriately socialized develop the cognitive and various non-cognitive skills, including motivation, enthusiasm, cooperation, and teamwork, that allow them to develop into well-adjusted and productive adults (Carneiro and Heckman, 2003; Heckman and Rubinstein, 2001).

Several studies have examined the association between early nutritional and health status and cognitive and psychosocial skills and later educational attainment, earnings, and employment outcomes.[35] Malnutrition tends to be most common and severe during periods of greatest vulnerability, at pregnancy and the first two to three years of life. Glewwe and King (2001) conclude that malnutrition that persists into the second year of life is most critical for cognitive development, and that malnutrition in the first six months among Filipino children does not have the greatest adverse effects on child cognitive development, as argued by some observers, because it can be reversed. One estimation challenge for these studies is spurious correlation that arises due to unobserved family heterogeneity: some family or child endowment (ability) that explains a child's poor early nutritional status could explain also that child's poor cognitive development. Ignoring the ability factor attributes a causal relationship to an observed association between nutritional status and cognitive development. In principle, the problem could be

---

[35] For example, iodine deficiency and anemia cause poor cognitive development, particularly in children under two, and poor school performance later. In a sample of Costa Rican children, those with moderate to severe anemia had lower scores in cognitive and motor tests (Lozoff et al., 2000). See Currie (2001), Currie and Thomas (2000) and Karoly et al. (1998) for the United States; and Grantham-McGregor et al. (1997); Alderman et al. (2001), Glewwe and King (2001), Glewwe (2002), Martorell (1999), and Behrman, Cheng and Todd (2004) for developing countries. On links to adult productivities, see Strauss and Thomas (1995, 1998) for reviews.

addressed using experimental data from treatment and control groups of infants who are randomly selected, and the treatment group is provided an improved diet during the first few years of life and some years later both groups are given a test of cognitive development. One could then estimate the relationship between measures of early childhood nutrition and cognitive development, using treatment status as an instrumental variable for the latter. In the absence of an experimental intervention, Glewwe and King (2001) used community-level variables (e.g., local rainfall and prices associated with food supply) as instruments for early nutritional status, and the score in an IQ test applied before most children had entered school as a measure of cognitive achievement.

Using the same non-experimental data, Glewwe et al. (2004) examined the causal impact of early nutritional status on later schooling and academic achievement,[36] and concluded that children who were malnourished early in their lives enter school later and perform more poorly on cognitive achievement tests.[37] Using a measure of early nutritional status from longitudinal data is an improvement over using current nutritional status,[38] but it does not solve the problem of spurious correlation since parental inputs into a child's nutritional status and academic achievement are likely to be correlated and determined by unobserved (physical and cognitive) ability. To address the problem due to unobserved ability, the authors used within-family (sibling pairs) differences in IQ test scores. This controls for observed and unobserved family heterogeneity in cognitive ability, academic inputs, and nutritional inputs. The coefficient estimates of nutritional status may still be biased towards zero by measurement error so they instrument the sibling difference in heights using the older siblings' height-for-age (at birth, 12 months and 24 months) for identification.

Alderman et al. (2001) used a different approach to estimate a causal relationship between nutrition and schooling in rural Pakistan. They use the serendipitous availability of data on price shocks when the children were five years old to identify early parental inputs in child health from later inputs in schooling. Assuming that these early price shocks are uncorrelated with price shocks at later ages when schooling decisions were being made, they estimated that nutritional status is three times more important for de-

---

[36] Earlier studies that used cross-sectional non-experimental data found positive associations between preschool nutritional status and school achievements, but did not present persuasive evidence regarding causality. Without adequate longitudinal data, it is difficult to account for the fact that preschool nutrition reflects behavioral decisions in the presence of unobserved factors such as genetic endowments. See reviews of such studies by Pollitt (2000), Behrman (1996), and Strauss and Thomas (1995, 1998).

[37] They found that a one standard deviation increase in child height increases achievement test scores by about one-third of a standard deviation of that score or about the equivalent of spending eight more months in school.

[38] Cross-sectional data are limited in that direct measurements of preschool child health are usually not available and so this has to be inferred from current health. For example, Glewwe and Jacoby (1995) use cross-sectional data on Ghana to examine the relationship between *current* nutritional status and *current* cognitive achievement and the likelihood of delayed primary school enrollment, respectively. They find that the impact of child health on schooling is highly sensitive to the underlying behavioral assumptions and the nature of unobserved variables.

terminating school enrollment than had been found in studies that treated child health as exogenous.

4.3. Estimating schooling demand

The problem of bias in estimating the true relationship between observed earnings and years of schooling has been widely studied (Card, 1999). The consensus is that omitted ability biases downward the least-squares estimate of returns to schooling, but that the bias is modest in size. There is no comparable consensus regarding the role of omitted ability on parental investments in their children's education. In part, this is due to a lack of consistency in measured child time in school, whereas there is broad consensus in the use of log earnings as the dependent variable in regressions estimating returns to schooling. The value of γ will invariably differ depending on how H_{ij} is measured.

Even if γ is nonzero, missing ability will only bias the coefficient estimates if β_k is nonzero. To the extent that parental ability is correlated with wealth and child ability is inherited from parents, household assets and child ability will be correlated, and so $\beta_1 \neq 0$. The same problem holds for parental education: if children inherit ability from their parents, then parental education will be correlated with both parents' and child's missing ability measures. For school quality, if households select schools on the basis of their children's ability, then $\beta_2 \neq 0$. This is unlikely to be a problem in rural areas where there is only one school, and so we would expect better estimates of the impact of school quality on child time in school in samples of rural children. If ability changes the value of time, then $\beta_3 \neq 0$. Evidence suggests that for young children, labor productivity is more a function of stature than cognitive development, and so β_3 is likely to be small. Community level measures are unlikely to be correlated with unobserved individual ability, and so β_4 is also likely to be small. Unfortunately, most of the policy interest is in the role of household assets and school quality on child time allocation, the variables for which the bias is likely greatest.

4.3.1. Application: Using variation in school supply to identify years of schooling completed and returns to schooling

Duflo (2001) uses a large program aimed at expanding primary school availability to generate an exogenous change in the price of schooling. The resulting change in realized years of schooling for children exposed to the program is used to identify the impact of time in school on the wages the children received in adulthood. In 1973, Indonesia used oil revenues to fund the largest primary school building project in the history of the world. Within six years, 61,807 schools were built, doubling the number of primary schools in the country and adding about 1 school per 500 school aged children. The placement of schools was aimed at meeting the greatest need as indicated by the proportion of school aged children not in school, an aim that seems to have been at least partially met.

Duflo argues that this large change in the availability of schools could be viewed as an exogenous reduction in the cost of schooling for children reaching primary school age in 1974 (the first year that the new schools were available) relative to older cohorts. This exogenous reduction in schooling costs would shift outward the demand for schooling, and that in turn can be used to identify the impact of years of schooling on earnings. Duflo uses a 1995 sample of Indonesian men that included information on where the men were born, matching birth region with information on the number of schools built between 1973 and 1978. Men born after 1967 would have had the benefit of the school construction program for their entire primary experience. Men born before 1962 would have completed primary schooling before the building project began. Duflo compares the completed schooling and wages of the first beneficiaries (men born between 1968 and 1972) with those of the last non-beneficiaries (men born between 1957 and 1961). Because the number of schools built varied by region of the country, Duflo was able to also utilize cross-sectional comparisons of the magnitude of the effect on education and wages in regions that had large versus small increases in the number of schools.

The results are listed in Table 2. Regions are divided into two groups, high and low intensity of school construction, as measured by newly constructed schools per 1000 school-aged children. The nonrandom placement of schools clearly favors less educated areas, as the average years of schooling for the 1957–1961 birth cohort is 8.9 years in the high intensity regions and 10.4 years in the low intensity regions. Years of schooling grew faster in the high intensity school construction regions, rising by 0.5 years versus 0.4 years in the low intensity regions. Overall, the difference in education improvement in the high versus low intensity school construction regions was 0.13 years of schooling from one additional school per 1000 children. A comparable exercise relating wages to school construction finds that wages grew 3% faster for adults educated in regions with more school construction. As a check, Duflo conducts a similar exercise comparing education and wage growth between two cohorts (1952–1956 and 1957–1961), both of whom were not exposed to the school building program. The estimated changes in years of schooling and wages were much smaller and not statistically significant.

The difference in differences estimates of the impact of the school construction program on education and wages can be used to derive an estimate of the returns to schooling. Letting Z represent the intensity of school construction, H represent years of schooling and y represent the logarithm of wages, the Wald estimator for the returns to schooling would be $\frac{\partial y}{\partial H} = \frac{\text{Cov}(y,Z)}{\text{Cov}(H,Z)}$. In this case, a simple regression of H on Z would yield a parameter estimate $\frac{\partial H}{\partial Z} = \frac{\text{Cov}(H,Z)}{\text{Var}(Z)} = 0.13$ and a regression of y on Z would yield $\frac{\partial y}{\partial Z} = \frac{\text{Cov}(y,Z)}{\text{Var}(Z)} = 0.03$.

Missing ability means that direct estimates of $\frac{\partial y}{\partial H}$ will be biased. But because Z is an exogenous shock to both years of schooling and to earnings, the estimated derivatives of $\frac{\partial H}{\partial Z}$ and $\frac{\partial y}{\partial Z}$ are unbiased. The comparative static effect of H on y can be computed using the Wald estimator as $\frac{\partial y}{\partial H} = \frac{\partial y/\partial Z}{\partial H/\partial Z} = \frac{0.03}{0.13} = 0.23.$[39]

---

[39] Angrist and Krueger (1999) have an excellent review of methods to analyze labor market data including the methods reviewed in this section.

Table 2
Difference-in-differences measures of the impact of the Indonesian school building program on years of schooling and adult wages

	Years of education			Log(Wages)		
	New schools per 1000 children			New schools per 1000 children		
	Low	High	Difference	Low	High	Difference
1968–1972	10.84[a]	9.43[a]	−1.41[a]	7.48[a]	7.34[a]	−0.14[a]
1957–1961	10.44[a]	8.91[a]	−1.54[a]	7.8[a]	7.63[a]	−0.17[a]
Difference	0.40[a]	0.52[a]	0.13	−0.32[a]	−0.29[a]	0.03[b]
1957–1961	10.44[a]	8.91[a]	−1.54[a]	7.8[a]	7.63[a]	−0.17[a]
1952–1956	10.13[a]	8.56[a]	−1.58[a]	7.87[a]	7.69[a]	−0.18[a]
Difference	0.31[a]	0.35[a]	0.04	0.07[a]	0.06[a]	0.01

Source: Duflo (2001). Numbers adjusted to represent an average difference of 1 more school built per 1000 school aged children in the "High" regions versus the "Low" regions.
[a] Significant at the 0.05 level.
[b] Significant at the 0.10 level.

This is an unusually large estimate of the returns to schooling. The Wald estimate is likely influenced by other factors that affected schooling incentives that are contemporaneous with the school building program. For example, over the same time period there was at least one other major program to improve water and sanitation systems that targeted some of the same areas that received additional schools. It is plausible that improved sanitation or other contemporaneous changes may have improved child health that could also affect both schooling and wages in the same direction as the improved access to schools. To control for those factors, Duflo proposes a simplified variant of the reduced form regression (4.7) to explain years of schooling and wages (interpretable as the marginal product of schooling)

$$
H_{ijk} = \alpha_0 + \sum_{j=1}^{J-1} \alpha_{1j} R_{ij} + \sum_{k=1}^{K-1} \alpha_{2k} B_{ik} + \sum_{j=1}^{J} \sum_{k=1}^{K-1} \gamma_k^H Z_{ij} B_{ik}
$$

$$
+ \sum_{j=1}^{J} \sum_{k=1}^{K-1} \sum_{m=1}^{M} \delta_{mk}^H C_{ijm} B_{ik} + \varepsilon_{ijk}^H,
$$

$$
y_{ijk} = \beta_0 + \sum_{j=1}^{J-1} \beta_{1j} R_{ij} + \sum_{k=1}^{K-1} \beta_{2k} B_{ik} + \sum_{j=1}^{J} \sum_{k=1}^{K-1} \gamma_k^y Z_{ij} B_{ik}
$$

$$
+ \sum_{j=1}^{J} \sum_{k=1}^{K-1} \sum_{m=1}^{M} \delta_{mk}^y C_{ijm} B_{ik} + \varepsilon_{ijk}^y \tag{4.9}
$$

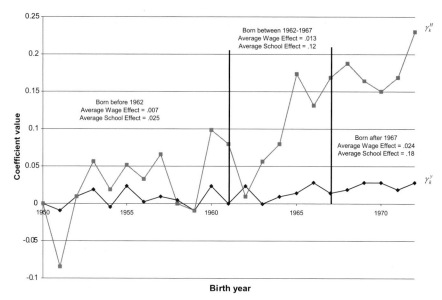

Source: Authors' compilations based on information provided in Duflo (2001).

Figure 6. Estimates of γ_k^H and γ_k^y.

for individual i in region j and birth cohort k. In this specification, birth cohort-specific effects of the regional intensity of the school building program are estimated controlling for region dummies, R_{ij}; birth cohort dummies, B_{ik}; and M region-specific variables whose impacts are allowed to vary by birth cohort. Our primary interest is in the time path of the estimates of γ_k^H and γ_k^y that are birth cohort specific estimates of the building program on years of schooling and wages.

Because of the timing of the school construction, cohorts born between 1962 and 1967 should have partial effects, and those born after 1968 should have total effects. The values of γ_k^H and γ_k^y are plotted by cohort in Fig. 6. The results are striking. Average values of the coefficients before 1962 are near zero, those in the intermediate period somewhat larger, and larger still for those born after 1967. Using the average values of the coefficients in the post 1967 period, the implied estimate of the returns to schooling is $(0.024/0.18) = 0.13$, much closer to standard estimates.

One can also use the first equation in (4.9) to identify H_{ijk} in an equation that explicitly measures the returns to schooling as in

$$y_{ijk} = \beta_0 + \sum_{j=1}^{J-1} \beta_{1j} R_{ij} + \sum_{k=1}^{K-1} \beta_{2k} B_{ik} + \beta_3 H_{ijk}$$

$$+ \sum_{j=1}^{J} \sum_{k=1}^{K-1} \sum_{m=1}^{M} \delta_{mk}^y C_{ijm} B_{ik} + \varepsilon_{ijk}^y. \tag{4.10}$$

Treating H_{ijk} as exogenous, the least squares estimate of β_3 is 0.077. Using Z_{ij} as an instrument for H_{ijk}, the two-stage least squares estimate of β_3 is 0.106. The finding that the OLS estimate is smaller than the 2SLS estimate is consistent with the results reported in Card's (1999) review of returns to schooling.[40]

While Duflo's estimates appear plausible, one cannot infer from the results that in general, building schools will raise enrollment or increase earnings. The schools were built where they were most needed, suggesting that the enrollment response would be atypically large. In addition, if the population can move to where the new schools are placed, the enrollment response cannot be identified by the building program as school distance becomes endogenous. The identification depends on an immobile population responding to an inflexible building rule. If the building rule flexibly responds to local demands, or if the local population changes in response to the existence or absence of the schools, then the identification breaks down.

Duflo finds that the impact of the school building project on educational attainment was greatest in less densely populated areas and in areas of greater poverty, suggesting that the price elasticity of demand for schooling is greater for the poor for rural residents. Applying a similar strategy to the case of a junior high school building project, also in Indonesia, Maliki (2005) finds that reducing the average distance to school increased school enrollment and lowered labor supply for both boys and girls, with the biggest effects in rural areas. The finding of larger impacts of school provision on rural enrollment is consistent with the implications of our stylized supply and demand model.[41]

Several recent papers have exploited the variation in school access as a plausible instrument for human capital time investments (Bedi and Gaston, 1999; Bedi and Marshall, 2002; Handa, 2002; Duflo, 2004; Foster and Rosenzweig, 2004; Glick and Sahn, 2006; and Emerson and Souza, 2006). School availability is measured alternatively by the number of schools per child or by average distance to school. School availability appears to function well as an instrument even in settings without massive new school building construction as in Indonesia, presumably because households do not relocate in response to school availability. The measure appears to be most useful in rural areas where there is more variation in school supply and where the cost of household relocation for schooling purposes is high relative to urban areas. In urban areas, variation in neighborhood school prices may be the better choice, particularly if it is difficult for households to move easily across neighborhoods.

---

[40] The commonly used regression specification using log earnings as a function of linear years of schooling in (4.10) to generate an estimate of the return per year of schooling β_3 is justified by the result from Section 2 that $\ln q = \ln(r V_0(E)) + r E$ where q is earnings, E is years of schooling, and $r = \beta_3$.

[41] Although these papers do not focus on private school provision, at least part of the reason that greater supply of government schools would have a smaller effect in urban areas is the possible reduction in urban private school supply. Because rural areas have fewer private schools, public provision would displace fewer rural private schools.

4.4. Discussion

Evaluations of schooling demand equations such as (4.7) should provide the key elasticities of interest for evaluating the potential values of government policies aimed at
raising schooling outcomes for boys and girls in urban and rural markets. Unfortunately,
despite many studies that evaluate schooling demand in different settings, conclusions
regarding the relative magnitudes of these elasticities between genders and across geographic areas must be viewed as tentative. It is tempting to argue that the problem of
identifying the true behavioral schooling demand parameters can be convincingly resolved only through controlled experiments. If children were randomly assigned into
environments with different household incomes, schooling prices, or child wages, one
could use the observed differences in human capital outcomes to derive the elasticities
needed to inform policy analysis. However, there are several reasons why we may not
be able to rely on social experiments alone to resolve the identification problem.

First, even the most complex social experiments discussed in this volume involve
relatively small variation in the magnitude of the income transfer, school voucher, or
conditional transfer that would alter the income, school price or child opportunity cost.
Therefore, there is little cross sectional variation in the exogenous prices or incomes
that would be needed to identify relevant elasticities.[42]

This problem is compounded by the simultaneous implementation of other social interventions in nutrition, parental education, health, sanitation, or other social services
that are outside the experiment and could affect schooling decisions. As a consequence,
even a rigorous evaluation that correctly identifies the overall change in schooling decisions resulting from the installation of a social program may not be able to isolate
the individual impacts of income changes, versus wage changes, versus price changes
on schooling demand. They may not even be able to identify the impact of the transfer from the impact of the health, sanitation, or parental education components of the
intervention.[43]

Third, evaluations are best aimed at new pilot programs rather than ongoing programs
(Heckman, La Londe and Smith, 1999). These pilot programs are likely to be installed

---

[42] This is illustrated by Jalan and Glinskaya (2003) who conclude that a large-scale school construction
program in India during the period 1993–1999 had only a limited impact on enrollment. The authors compared
changes in enrollment for individuals in districts that received an education program with enrollment changes
of a control group of matched individuals in nonrecipient districts. Simple estimators comparing enrollment
before and after the program could overstate the program's impact because enrollment increases could reflect
coincident changes occurring in both program and nonprogram areas. For example, enrollment of children
aged 6–10 in the program districts increased by 5.4 percentage points, only 1.3 percentage points higher
than the increase in comparable non-program districts. This limited impact was attributed to the fact that the
average distance to school before the program was implemented was already small.

[43] Schultz (2004) attempted to estimate an implied wage elasticity on schooling demand using schooling
responses to conditional transfers in the PROGRESA/Oportunidades program. He found an elasticity of −0.2
which he concluded was unreasonably small, perhaps a consequence of the possible contamination from
additional schooling responses to the various additional health and nutrition programs installed at the same
time in the same places.

in areas that atypically can benefit from them. As a consequence, the responses may not reflect population averages, but only the averages for similarly suitable areas. This is not an indictment of experimental evaluation methods, only a reminder that the results of these methods cannot easily be generalized to the population as a whole. In order to generalize to other populations, one must make use of a behavioral model that can predict how dissimilar households in alternative markets will react to the same policy.

Behavioral responses to pilot programs may not be the same as responses to those same programs were they to be maintained over a long period of time and entrenched in public expectations. Non-experimental methods will still need to be used to derive many of the behavioral parameters of interest to policy makers. The most compelling non-experimental studies are ones that more closely mimic the experimental objective of randomized exposure to changes in income, wages, school prices, or school quality.[44]

One problem in summarizing the findings from studies of schooling demand is that studies do not use the same measures of schooling demand. Some (enrollment, attendance) are short-term measures while others (grade for age, years of schooling attained, measured cognitive skills) reflect decisions made over several years. We return to these measurement issues in Section 6. Nevertheless, there are sufficient empirical analyses that allow comparisons for us to advance the following conclusions about urban–rural and male–female differences in schooling:

- Schooling demand in rural areas is more income elastic and also appears to be more elastic with respect to distance to the school.
- In places where girls receive less schooling than boys (South Asia and the Middle East, rural areas of many countries), the elasticities of girls' schooling with respect to income and prices are higher than for boys.
- Income elasticities of schooling demand are generally larger in developing countries than in developed countries. Following Becker and Tomes (1986), poorer households are likely to concentrate their wealth transfers from parent to child in the form of human capital transfers. This suggests that there will be more persistence of poverty and wealth across generations in developing countries than has been observed in developed countries, a possibility that has not been subject to many empirical tests. We discuss this more completely in the next section.

These conclusions must be viewed as tentative until more systematic studies are undertaken that allow us to compare results using similar data and methods across urban and rural areas and across countries.

5. Dynamic models

Our discussion of schooling demand elasticities indicated large responses to income shocks, perhaps larger than the schooling variation caused by normally occurring cross-sectional variation in household income. Such income shocks do not fit naturally into

---

[44] Ravallion in this Handbook provides an extensive discussion of nonexperimental evaluation methods.

the static household production environment. To capture how unforeseen changes in prices or income affect the child schooling decision, we can embed the human capital production function into a household life-time utility maximizing model. This variant is a simplification of the model advanced by Jacoby and Skoufias (1997). The jth household is assumed to have a utility function that is time separable in its arguments. We assume that parents can only work and have one unit of time available per period. Each household has one child that also has one unit of time per period, but child time can be divided between school and work. Adult and child leisure time is assumed fixed and not subject to choice.

We assume that parents are making the decision regarding child time allocation for a schooling phase that lasts until period T. Thereafter, the child begins to work full time and to form its own household and the parents die. During each period of the schooling phase, the investment of child time produces human capital according to the concave production function $q_j^c(t+1) = q(q_j^c(t), H_j(t); q_j^P, Z_j(t))$. The child's stock of human capital depends on past acquired human capital, time spent in school in the current period, their parents' human capital endowment and an exogenous vector of local schooling inputs that complement child time in school, $Z_j(t)$. The parents' decision involves choosing a sequence of household consumption, $\{C_j(t)\}$; and a sequence of child schooling time investments, $\{H_j(t)\}$. Lifetime expected utility at time t is specified as

$$U(C_j(t), q_j^c(t+1)) + \rho_j E_t\{V(A_j(t+1)), \phi(q_j^c(T+1)), G(T+1), t+1\}$$

(5.1)

where ρ_j is a discount factor; $E_t\{\cdot\}$ is the expectation operator conditional on information available at time t, and $V(\cdot)$ is a value function reflecting the maximum expected lifetime utility as of the start of period $t+1$. Underlying $V(\cdot)$ is the optimal future planned sequences of $\{C_j(t)\}$ and $\{H_j(t)\}$ through period T and a planned gift of human and physical capital $G(T+1)$ that will be turned over to the child at $T+1$.

The term $A_j(t+1)$ reflects the assets available at the start of period $t+1$ if the optimal sequence of household consumption and schooling decisions were followed, and so $V(\cdot)$ can be viewed as the present value of lifetime indirect utility evaluated at time $t+1$. Because time $t+1$ decisions incorporate information unavailable at period t, we need to take the expectation conditional on information available at the start of period t in making optimal period t decisions.[45]

Assets are accumulated from income net of consumption. Household income in any period t is determined by the concave household production function $Q(\cdot)$. The intertemporal budget constraint can be written

$$A_j^*(t) - A_j(t) = Q(q_j^P, (1 - H_j(t)); K_j(t)) - P_C(t)C_j(t)$$

(5.2)

---

[45] A detailed formulation of the lifetime utility maximization model is provided by MaCurdy (1985).

where q_j^P is the human capital of the parents endowed to them by their parents; $K_j(t)$ is a vector of productive capital assets that are potentially time varying but exogenous to the household[46]; and the price of consumer goods is $P_C(t)$.

The production function presumes that better educated parents can produce more household output, but the marginal product of the child is assumed to be solely dependent on child time and is unrelated to accumulated child human capital. This assumption greatly simplifies the analysis in that it keeps the opportunity cost of child time exogenous to household decisions.[47] $A_j^*(t)$ is the value of assets at the end of period t which determines the level of assets carried into the beginning of the next period by applying the known rate of interest r. The law of motion determining asset accumulation is

$$A_j(t+1) = \left(1 + r(t+1)\right)A_j^*(t). \tag{5.3}$$

Maximizing (5.1) subject to conditions (5.2) and (5.3) and the production functions for human capital and household output we get the first-order conditions

$$U_{C_j}(t) = \lambda_j(t)P_C(t),$$
$$U_{q_j^c}(t+1)q_{H_j}^c(t) = \lambda_j(t)Q_{Hj}(t),$$
$$\lambda_j(t) = \left(1 + r_j(t+1)\right)\rho_j E_t\{\lambda_j(t+1)\}. \tag{5.4}$$

The first two conditions are comparable to the ones derived from the static model of household consumption and schooling investments (4.3a)–(4.3c). The first condition equates the period t marginal utility of consumption with the marginal utility of wealth sacrificed to pay for that consumption. The second condition equates the marginal utility from allocating the child's human capital to further schooling to the marginal product of allocating child time to home production.

The difference between the first two conditions in (5.4) and the earlier static formulation is the inclusion of a time condition on $\lambda_j(t)$ which summarizes all of the past and anticipated future changes to household wealth. If there were no uncertainty, $\lambda_j(t)$ would be a known sequence over the lifetime of the household, reflecting known changes in interest rates, labor productivity, prices, or any other factors that would change asset accumulation. That distinction suggests that anticipated components of non-labor asset income such as savings, investments, and debt payments are endogenous and cannot be properly included as explanatory variables in reduced form equations explaining child time use.

The third condition in (5.4) relates the marginal utility of wealth in period (t) to that in period $(t + 1)$. As the other first-order conditions all relate solely to period (t), the

---

[46] Assets such as land, fixed buildings, or capital equipment may appreciate or depreciate at a known rate or may change productivity due to geoclimatic factors or market prices. Variable capital assets would have to be modeled jointly with decisions on time allocations.

[47] This may not be too heroic an assumption. Rosenzweig (1980) found that agricultural day wages in India did not rise with education. Alderman, Orazem and Paterno (2001) report that urban wages for children did not vary by age and presumably accumulated schooling.

third condition summarizes the dynamics of the model. To illustrate, combining the
second and third conditions and substituting in for $\lambda(t)$ and $\lambda(t+1)$, we get

$$E_t\left(\frac{U_{q^c}(t+1)q_H^c(t)}{U_{q^c}(t+2)q_H^c(t+1)}\right) = \rho\big(1+r(t+1)\big)E_t\left(\frac{Q_H(t)}{Q_H(t+1)}\right) \quad (5.5)$$

where the subscript j has been suppressed. In periods where child labor productivity
is relatively high, the household will optimally increase the marginal utility from time
allocated to schooling, but that requires decreasing child time in school.

5.1. Application: Structural estimation of the dynamic model: Mexico's PROGRESA Program

One estimation strategy is to specify a functional form for the objective function (5.1)
along with any associated restrictions and solve the lifetime maximization problem numerically. A recent example of this strategy is by Todd and Wolpin (2006) who estimate
an even more complex variant of the structural dynamic model described above. Their
model includes three annual decisions regarding child time use, including school, wage
work, and home production. They also incorporate an additional household choice of
whether to add another child to the household. They solve the dynamic programming
problem for each couple in their data set through backward induction from the last
period which is assumed to be the year the woman reaches age 59. The maximization involves estimating each household's expected utility from all possible sequences
of fertility choices and decisions regarding child schooling, work and home time. The
household is then assumed to select among these alternative time paths as in a multinomial logit formulation. The estimation also includes equations that yield the wages
offered to children, the income that parents receive, and the likelihood that a child succeeds in school. Readers interested in further estimation details will have to consult the
paper.

The model is applied to data on Mexican rural households. In 1998, Mexico initiated
PROGRESA (now Oportunidades), a program of several simultaneous interventions
aimed at improving the educational, health and nutritional status of poor rural families. PROGRESA provides cash transfers linked to youth's enrollment, regular school
attendance and health clinic visits. The program also includes in-kind health benefits
and nutritional supplements for children up to age five and for pregnant and lactating
women. By the end of 1999, PROGRESA covered approximately 2.6 million families
or about 40 percent of all rural families in Mexico. The installation of the program was
randomized so that 320 villages were assigned to receive the treatment in 1998 and 186
villages were scheduled for later program installation.

Todd and Wolpin use household data collected in 1997 on all 506 villages before
the program was begun. They first validate their model by examining whether it could
generate within-sample enrollment and child labor rates that matched the actual distribution of child time allocations in 1997. They further validate the model by predicting
how enrollment would respond to a change in the opportunity cost of schooling such

as would have occurred with the conditional transfer. The predicted changes are then compared to the actual change as reported from experimental evaluations of the PRO-GRESA. The model performs reasonably well for girls, predicting about an 8 percentage point increase in enrollment compared to a 10 percentage point increase from the experimental evaluations. For boys, the model predicts a 9.5 percentage point increase but the actual change was less than 5 percentage points. Note the projections only include responses to the conditional transfer. Any changes in enrollment due to the nutrition, health or other elements of the PROGRESA intervention would not be factored into the Todd–Wolpin projections and could cause their projections to deviate from the observed outcomes.

The importance of the behavioral model is that it allows Todd and Wolpin to contrast the outcomes from the conditional transfer program with other possible interventions that were not used. For example, they are able to demonstrate that unconditional income transfers would have raised enrollment by only 20% of the conditional transfer, consistent with the theoretical model that suggested the conditional transfer would have both income and substitution effects raising enrollment. They also are able to examine the sensitivity of parental schooling decisions to alternative timing and magnitude of the transfer. For example, a policy that restricts the subsidy to grades 6–9 rather than grades 3–9 but that increases the subsidy amount per child would have cost roughly the same amount but would have increased by 25% the gain in average years of schooling. Such counterfactual experiments would not be possible from the experimental evaluation alone.

It is unclear from the Todd–Wolpin exercise whether such a complex structural model is needed to generate the types of results they report. It would be useful to examine how alternative and perhaps more parsimonious behavioral models would perform in replicating the results from experimental evaluations. An additional concern is the reliance on child wages in the estimation when so few children work for wages. Only 8% of the children aged 12–15 work for wages with very few observations for the youngest children. While the authors make an accommodation for the use of such highly selected wages in their modeling, it may be that alternative strategies that would approximate the value of time in nonmarket production could generate very different results. The use of such a complicated structure makes it very costly to experiment with alternative measures of the value of time.[48]

In the end, the most promising lesson from the Todd–Wolpin study is that behavioral models can be fitted to data collected as a result of social experiments. If behavioral models can be validated by their ability to replicate the outcomes from experimental evaluations, there should be increased confidence in the counterfactual policy simulations that are based on those models.

---

[48] Parker, Rubalcava and Teruel in this Handbook review other examples of structural models applied to the PROGRESA case.

5.2. Dynamic labor supply equations

Interior solutions to the three first-order conditions in (5.4) result in reduced form equations for household consumption and child time in school[49]:

$$C_j(t) = C_j\big(\lambda_j(t), \overline{Q_j}(t), Q_{H_j}(t), q_{H_j}^C(t), P_C(t), q_j^P, K_j(t), Z_j(t)\big), \qquad (5.6a)$$

$$H_j(t) = H_j\big(\lambda_j(t), \overline{Q_j}(t), Q_{H_j}(t), q_{H_j}^C(t), P_C(t), q_j^P, K_j(t), Z_j(t)\big). \qquad (5.6b)$$

Household choices on consumption and time allocation will depend on the productivity of child time in home and school activities, on the price of consumer goods, on productive human and capital assets, and on the quality of local schools and other schooling inputs. They also depend on household full income (the amount the household could produce if all child time were allocated to home production, $\overline{Q_j}(t) = Q(q_j^P, 1; K_j(t))$) and on the marginal utility of wealth, $\lambda_j(t)$.

The sequence of $\lambda_j(t)$ is unobservable and will change over time due to new information on tastes, prices, interest rates, productivity and income. Before proceeding to the empirical specification, it is useful to illustrate how shocks to $\lambda_j(t)$ will affect $H_j(t)$. Consider a permanent, positive shock to household income caused by a permanent increase in average prices of household output. $\lambda_j(t)$ will fall because of diminishing marginal utility of wealth, as will all future $\lambda_j(t')$, $t' > t$. Rising wealth increases the household's ability to consume goods and schooling. However, $Q_{H_j}(t)$ will also increase, raising the opportunity cost of child time in school. The income and substitution effects conflict, and so the impact on child schooling is ambiguous.[50] If instead there is an increase in the productivity of adult labor in home production with no coincident change in the marginal productivity of child time, there will only be an increase in wealth and a decrease in current and future values of $\lambda_j(t)$. By the second equation in (4.4), the household would increase child time in school.

A temporary shock to household income caused by weather or price shocks that do not affect the expectation of future weather or prices will have similar but weaker predicted effects on time in school. If the household can insure itself against such transitory shocks by borrowing, saving, or taking advantage of formal or informal risk pooling mechanisms, then there may be no impact on household time allocation at all.[51]

---

[49] These are known as Frisch functions. See Blundell and MaCurdy (1999) for a review of the use of Frisch functions in labor supply estimation.

[50] For example, Bhalotra and Heady (2003) find an inverse relationship between land holdings and child time in school in Pakistan and Ghana, although the correlation is sensitive to covariates.

[51] Neri et al. (2006) found that households with more educated heads and higher initial incomes were best able to absorb shocks to parental employment without sacrificing their children's education. Glewwe and Hall (1998) also found that households with more educated heads were best able to maintain consumption in the face of adverse exogenous shocks related to the Peruvian business cycle.

5.2.1. Application: Jacoby and Skoufias: Enrollment responses to anticipated and unanticipated income shocks

Much of the research on household time allocation in a life-cycle setting has concentrated on household responses to permanent and transitory shocks to household income. As in many agrarian economies, rural Indian households experience unanticipated temporary increases or decreases in farm income depending on the timing and quantity of the annual monsoon rains. Jacoby and Skoufias (1997) use monthly longitudinal data from six agrarian villages from June 1975 through December 1978 to examine the extent to which child schooling can be insulated from exogenous income shocks. They further consider whether households have greater difficulty absorbing income shocks that encompass the entire community or those that hit an individual household uniquely. Their analysis is based on a variant of Eq. (5.6b). They set the child value of time equal to the local wage for market r, $W_r(t)$. They subsume all household productive attributes into the full income term $\overline{Q}_{jr}(t)$. The remaining elements are incorporated into a term representing the productivity of child time in school, $\overline{Z}_{jr}(t)$. When we first difference (5.6b), the resulting equation is of the form

$$\frac{\ln(H_j(t+1))}{\ln(H_j(t))} = \alpha_1 \Delta \ln \overline{Q}_{jr}(t) + \beta \ln W_{jr}(t) + \xi_{jr}(t) \tag{5.7}$$

where changes in the $\overline{Z}_{jr}(t)$ are assumed to make up a random error $\xi_{jr}(t)$.

Innovations in the full income term are decomposed into various common and idiosyncratic elements defined by the regression

$$\Delta \ln \overline{Q}_{jr}(t) = \gamma_{0r}(t) + \Phi'_{jr}(t-1)\gamma_1 + \left\{ \Phi_{jr}(t-1) \otimes (R_r(t) - R_r) \right\}' \gamma_2$$
$$+ \upsilon_{jr}(t) \tag{5.8}$$

where $\Phi_{jr}(t-1)$ is a vector of predetermined human and physical capital assets of farm j in village r; $(R_r(t) - R_r)$ is the year t deviation in rainfall from long-term village averages which is interacted with the household characteristics; and $\upsilon_{jr}(t)$ is a random error that represents remaining idiosyncratic changes in household j's full income. The Kronecker product generates a vector of interaction terms. The decomposition includes a village-specific constant $\gamma_{0r}(t)$ which provides a common unanticipated innovation to income for all households in village r. Jacoby and Skoufias argue that these aggregate shocks would be the most difficult for households to insure against. The next term, $\Phi'_{jr}\gamma_1$, is the permanent anticipated change in household full income that is forecastable based on known household attributes, which can be written as $\varepsilon^P_{jr}(t)$. The final term, $\{\Phi_{jr} \otimes (R_r(t) - R_r)\}'\gamma_2$, reflects the unanticipated idiosyncratic changes in household income due to the interaction between weather surprises and exogenous household attributes, which can be represented as $\varepsilon^T_{jr}(t)$. These changes are transitory to the extent that weather shocks do not persist across crop years.

Substituting into (5.8) yields

$$\frac{\ln(H_{jr}(t+1))}{\ln(H_{jr}(t))} = \alpha_{1r}\gamma_{0r} + \alpha_{1P}\varepsilon^P(t) + \alpha_{1T}\varepsilon^T(t) + \beta \ln W_{jr}(t) + \xi'(t+1)$$

(5.9)

where the various income innovation terms are allowed different parameters. If the household is fully insured against income shocks, all of these parameters will be zero. If the household cannot use formal or informal credit to smooth time allocations in response to income shocks, the coefficients will be positive and statistically significant.

There are several important issues regarding the empirical strategy for measuring permanent and transitory incomes. First, the use of full income measures is important because actual income may reflect the time allocation responses to the weather or price shocks. In that case, the measure of the transitory shock will be confounded with the consumption response to that shock. Second, it is important that the village means be taken over a long time period. Paxson (1992) argues that in short panels, it would be difficult to distinguish between permanent and transitory components of income, particularly if there is some persistence in weather levels across years. Third, the use of villages is important to allow transitory effects to be distinguished from common temporal effects across all households that confound transitory and permanent effects. As an example, a national change in tax policy could be fully anticipated and could affect all households similarly. Use of multiple villages enables such national income shocks to be controlled. Finally, the use of interactions between the rainfall shocks and household attributes allows the transitory shock to differ across households. This is the only way to test for the existence of credit relationships within villages or communities.

In the Jacoby–Skoufias sample, anticipated income fluctuations did not have much impact on child enrollments. In only one village was there substantial evidence that the anticipated aggregate shock mattered for schooling, and that was in the village with the greatest income variability over time. There was more consistent evidence that household idiosyncratic transitory shocks affected school enrollments. This was particularly true for the poorest households in the sample. The implication is that these poor agrarian households use child labor and reduced school time to help smooth consumption in the face of adverse income shocks.

If parents withdraw their children from school in the face of unexpected transitory income losses, are children permanently disadvantaged? The answer appears to be no as far as aggregate time spent in school is concerned. The simulations for India showed that even though poor households used child labor to smooth income fluctuations, the lost time in school was within 2% of the predicted school time of children in households that are perfectly insured against income fluctuations.

Much of the research on the permanent income hypothesis has concentrated on the consumption response to permanent and transitory income shocks. A common finding for farm households in the United States (Reid, 1952; Friedman, 1957; Langemeier and Patrick, 1990, 1993) and in developing countries (Wolpin, 1982; Paxson, 1993; Jacoby and Skoufias, 1998) is that consumption elasticities with respect to permanent income are near unity and that the propensity to save out of transitory income is much larger than the propensity to save out of permanent income. These findings have led authors to conclude that farm households can insure themselves against income shocks using government safety nets, financial intermediaries, household savings or community risk pooling arrangements. And if these insurance markets immunize the farm household from transitory shocks, then there should be no labor supply response to these shocks either. Jacoby and Skoufias have shown that an important mechanism agrarian households use to attain consumption smoothing is by adjusting child time in school and work. The next section examines this question as one element of the decision of parents to transfer wealth to their children.

5.2.2. Intergenerational wealth transfers

Consider a household with one parent and one child. The parent can transfer wealth to the child by investing in the child's human capital and/or by giving financial bequests. Becker and Tomes (1986) provide a structure to evaluate the relative importance of these two wealth transfer mechanisms. Our simplification of their model can be viewed as a two-period variant of the dynamic optimization framework. The parents' utility function in (5.1) is reconfigured as $U(C^P, W^c)$ where the utility depends on parental consumption C^P in the first period and the children's wealth W^C in the second period. The parent can allocate own lifetime wealth, W^P, to own consumption, to human capital transfers to the child valued at G_q^P, and to financial transfers or gifts, G^P. The human capital transfers can be purchased directly through school inputs Z or by devoting time to the child

$$G_q^P = Z + sw^P q^P \qquad (5.10)$$

where s is the proportion of parental time spent with children. Parental time is enhanced by the parent's stock of human capital which is valued at w^P per unit. These inputs are translated into the child's human capital by a production function $q^c = q(Z, sq^P)$. The human capital production process is subject to positive but diminishing returns and the marginal products get infinitely large as either Z or s approach zero. The child's human capital has expected value w^c.

The parent's decision is then

$$\max_{C^P, Z, s, G^P} U\left(C^P, w^c q(Z, sq^P) + (1+r)G^P\right)$$
$$+ \lambda\left(W^P - C^P - Z - sw^P q^P - G^P\right). \qquad (5.11)$$

All the current period decisions are in numeraire terms to reduce unneeded prices. The interest rate on financial bequests is r. The first-order conditions are

$$U_1 - \lambda \leqslant 0,$$
$$U_2 w^c q_Z - \lambda \leqslant 0,$$
$$U_2 w^c q^P q_s - \lambda w^P q^P \leqslant 0,$$
$$U_2(1+r) - \lambda \leqslant 0. \qquad (5.12)$$

5.2.3. Unconstrained households

If the household is unconstrained so that all first-order conditions are set equal to zero, the first-order conditions imply that

$$w^c q_Z = \frac{w^c}{w^P} q_s = (1+r) = \frac{U_1}{U_2}.$$

The first two conditions tell us that the parent will equate the marginal productivities of expenditures on school inputs and parental time. These marginal returns to investments in child human capital are equated with the return to financial assets which is also equated to the marginal rate of substitution between parental consumption and child wealth.

The marginal returns to human capital are declining at the equilibrium while the returns to financial assets are constant at the market rate of return. Consequently, if parental wealth increases, the implied reduction in the marginal utility of income λ will result in an increase in parental consumption and in their aggregate bequest to their children. However, all of the increased bequest will be in G^P as any additional human capital transfer would have a return below $(1+r)$.

Increases in expected returns to human capital would result in higher human capital investments. However, some of the anticipated increase in child's wealth will go toward increasing the parent's consumption. Consequently, parents can use financial instruments to smooth income fluctuations across generations. Increases in returns to financial wealth would cause parents to reduce the human capital transfer and increase the financial bequest.

5.2.4. Constrained households

If the household is liquidity constrained, as might be expected of poorer households, the last condition does not hold so that

$$(1+r) < \frac{\lambda}{U_2} = w^c q_Z = \frac{w^c}{w^P} q_s = \frac{U_1}{U_2}. \tag{5.13}$$

As a result, the entire parental bequest will be in the form of human capital whose return will exceed $(1+r)$. The level of investment will be inefficient in that the parent would prefer to borrow money at the market interest rate in order to finance additional schooling for the child. The child could then pay back the parent at the market rate. Constraints on such loans prevent poor households from making efficient human capital investments in their children.

Changes in the parent's income would result in an increase in the human capital transfer without any change in the financial transfer. Changes in returns to human capital investments would result in an increase in parental consumption as well as an increase in human capital transfers. On the other hand, a change in the return to financial assets would have no impact at all.

The first-order conditions for credit constrained parents show that the marginal rate of substitution between parent consumption and child wealth is higher than for unconstrained parents for whom $U_1/U_2 = (1 + r)$. This means that for parents with like preferences, the poorer (constrained) parents will devote a greater share of income to their investments in children than would their wealthier (unconstrained) counterparts.

Poor parents under-invest in their child's human capital because of the constraints on borrowing. Wealthy parents invest efficiently in their child's human capital, and that optimal level of human capital is not sensitive to marginal changes in income. Therefore, there can be a role for public transfers of human capital to poor households (through public schools or vouchers) that are funded by redistributive taxes on wealthy households.

5.2.5. *Implications for studies of intergenerational transfers for poor and wealthy households*

In wealthier, unconstrained households, marginal increases in parental income will have no impact on the child's human capital and hence on child's earnings. In poorer, liquidity constrained households, all of the transfer is in the form of human capital investments which will increase with marginal increases in parental income. Therefore, we would expect that human capital investments will be more sensitive to income changes in poor than in rich households. There will also be a larger correlation between parent and child earnings in poor than in rich households. Finally, there should be a larger correlation between parent and child wealth in poor than in wealthy households.

These hypotheses should form a strong foundation for an exploration of intergenerational transfers of human and financial capital in developing countries. As reviewed by Solon (2002) there are several studies of intergenerational wealth transfers in developed country settings with typical intergenerational wealth transfer elasticities of around 0.4. Typically these studies have not investigated the relative importance of human capital versus financial bequests, in part because they concentrate on comparisons of parent and child earnings rather than total human and financial assets. Comparable studies in developing country settings have been lacking. The model above suggests that the wealth transfer elasticities should be larger in poorer countries with more prevalent liquidity constraints than in developed countries.[52]

Another possible use of the model is to frame analyses of the link between parental income and child schooling. The model predicts that liquidity constraints should result in the largest correlations between parental income and child schooling occurring among the poorest households or countries. Indeed, estimated schooling demand elasticities with respect to household income or expenditure can be quite large in developing

---

[52] One study that examines intergenerational wealth transfers in developing country settings is by Dunn (2004) who finds intergenerational income elasticities of 0.69 in Brazil, much larger than those reported in Solon's (2002) review of comparable elasticities for developed countries.

countries compared to estimates for developed countries. Elasticities reported by (or derived from reported estimates) by Alderman, Orazem and Paterno (2001) and Bhalotra and Heady (2003) for Pakistan and Handa (2002) for Mozambique are near or greater than 1. The schooling response to income received as remittances from abroad also imply income elasticities greater than 1 in El Salvador (Cox-Edwards and Ureta, 2003). Edmonds, Mammen and Miller (2005) find substantial positive effects of increased cash transfers on child schooling in South Africa, with the income elasticity being greatest for the poorest households. These large income elasticities are not universal however. Glick and Sahn (2000) in Guinea, Bhalotra and Heady (2003) in Ghana, and Glewwe and Jacoby (2004) in Vietnam find income elasticities between 0 and 0.4. For perspective, Haveman and Wolfe's (1995) review of schooling demand in developed countries reports income elasticities that are all below 0.2. Their best assessment that the income elasticity is 0.1.

5.2.6. Genetic transfers of human capital

Virtually every study of schooling demand includes measures of parents' education and a measure of the full-income, non-labor income or consumption expenditures of the household. Typically, all three will have a positive and significant effect on child time in school. Some researchers have placed significance on the relative size of the coefficient on mother's versus father's schooling as reflecting the relative time each spend with the children, or their relative taste for schooling. This practice is ill-advised in that the father's education is potentially more closely tied to household income than the mother's, and so some of the impact of the father's schooling may be captured by the income variable. Even so, it is not uncommon for the coefficient on father's education to be larger than the mother's (Schultz, 2002), a result which often prompts the writer to express surprise. In fact, the transmission of parental human capital to children is undoubtedly much more complex than can be captured by the relative magnitude of reduced form coefficients.[53]

A few studies have attempted to assess if the positive linkage between parents' and children's human capital is driven by genetics or by parental attitudes toward education. Plug and Vijverberg (2003) compare the education acquired by adopted versus biological siblings to examine whether both benefit equally from the abilities of their parents. They find that the positive effect of parental IQ on their children's schooling is greater for their genetically linked children than for their adopted children. They conclude that at least 55% of the parental ability is transferred genetically.

---

[53] See the papers by Behrman and Rosenzweig (2002, 2005) and Antonovics and Goldberger (2005) for an example of how conclusions regarding the relative magnitude of the coefficient on mother's and father's schooling on child's schooling can vary due to seemingly innocuous decisions regarding coding years of schooling and sample inclusion. The first two papers argue that the correlation between mother's and child's schooling reflects a spurious correlation due to genetic endowments, but that father's education retains a significant positive effect even after controlling for genetic endowments. The latter concluded that there was no significant difference in the role of father's or mother's education on child education.

While the Plug and Vijverberg empirical design is plausible, an equally plausible comparison would be between the children who remain with their birth mothers and children who are placed for adoption. Because adopted children tend to be placed in households with two parents of higher than average education and wealth, it is likely that adopted children will have education levels that dominate the education received by their biological siblings who are not placed for adoption. Were such an empirical study possible, it is likely that the role of parental genetic ability (nature) would be dominated by the nurture offered by the adoptive parents. Evidence supporting this premise is provided by Zimmerman (2003) who finds that, in South Africa, fostered-in children receive the same education as children living with their own parents.[54]

5.2.7. Application: The 1998 Indonesia Currency Crisis

In January 1998, the Indonesian rupiah lost two-thirds of its value. The accompanying economic shock resulted in a 12% decline in GDP. Urban wages fell by 40% while rural wages fell by 15–20%. Such a large, widespread and apparently unforeseen shock provides an opportunity to observe how or whether different households can insulate themselves against large cyclical downturns.

Frankenberg, Smith and Thomas (2003) and Thomas et al. (2004) compare time allocation and consumption decisions of Indonesian households using two national household surveys conducted in 1997 before the crisis and in 1998 in the midst of the crisis. The methodology is largely descriptive but provides several interesting comparisons. Most important for us, they compare the responses of wealthier against poorer households, of urban against rural households, of older against younger children, and of boys against girls. Several notable results were apparent.

First, the proportional decline in per capita consumption expenditure was only half as large as the proportional decline in real wage rates. Households made up for part of the lost wages by increasing aggregate hours of work by over 40% in both rural and urban areas. Households also appeared to cope by some moving away from the heavier hit urban areas to rural areas.

Thomas et al. (2004) concentrate on how school enrollment changed across the income distribution. Wealthier households were more likely to have suffered financial losses because they owned rupiah denominated assets, while poorer households were more proportionately harmed by the decline in real wages. Note that the theory suggests that liquidity constrained households would substitute away from schooling as household incomes fall, while wealthier households may be able to borrow or consume out of assets in order to smooth consumption during the crisis. Furthermore, the decline in return to financial assets would actually induce a shift toward human capital investments

---

[54] Zimmerman (2003) also finds that households are more likely to accept foster children if they have no school-aged children, suggesting that the foster relationship may be based in part on household chores traded for educational access.

for wealthier households, while liquidity constrained households would be unaffected by the decline in returns to financial assets.

The pattern of enrollment changes is striking. Averaging across children aged 7–19, in both rural and urban areas, the largest enrollment declines are for households at the bottom of the distribution of per capita expenditures. For rural areas, the effect is confined to the lowest 25% of the expenditure distribution. In urban areas, the enrollment decline gradually gets smaller as household per capita expenditure rises, but only the top quintile did not experience some decline. Nevertheless, the strong prediction that enrollment of the poorest households should be most adversely affected by income changes is consistent with the Indonesian experience.

Differences in household responses to the income shock between urban and rural households are also interesting. The decrease in per capita expenditure averaged 22% in urban areas and only 6% in rural areas. However, the decline in educational expenditure per student was only 10% in urban areas but 19% in rural areas, suggesting that the larger income elasticity of schooling demand is in rural areas.

Thomas et al. (2004) also report that in poor households, enrollments declined for the youngest children most, while the enrollment of older children did not change. They argue that households are protecting the investments in their older children at the expense of younger siblings. An alternative explanation is that the poor households whose older children were still in school in 1997 were atypical of poor households generally. Most poor children aged 16–19 were already out of school before the crisis, as opposed to the near universal enrollment for children aged 8–11. That these poor households kept their children in school may reflect their atypically strong taste for schooling and not a pattern of households favoring older children over their younger siblings.

The findings that the enrollment decisions of rural households are most sensitive to cyclical shocks to household income are also found by Funkhouser (1999) for the Costa Rican recession of 1981–1983. Neri et al. (2006) found that schooling decisions of households in the lowest two income quintiles were most sensitive to job loss of the household head. None of these studies follow the children for a sufficiently long period to see if the increased child time in work during the crisis was made up later. However, aggregate enrollment statistics for Indonesia appear to have recovered by 2000, presumably reflecting both the increased ability of households to adapt over time and the gradual recovery of the Indonesian economy. There is evidence from Brazil supporting the presumption that at least some of the schooling investment lost to temporary income shocks may be regained later. Duryea et al. (2006) found that the average length of a spell of child labor in urban areas of Brazil is about four months. Combined with the evidence from Jacoby and Skoufias discussed above, it appears that transitory spells of child labor often disrupt a child's education without necessarily changing the aggregate amount of time spent in school. Nevertheless, it may be that these temporary spells out of school cause permanent loss of human capital compared to more continuous enrollment, an important question for future study.[55]

---

[55] Strauss and Thomas in this Handbook discuss the health consequences of income shocks.

6. Measurement matters

This section discusses the schooling input and output measurement issues one faces in estimating a static or dynamic model of schooling.

6.1. Measurement of time in school

The studies we have reviewed in this chapter have used a variety of measures of educational investments, including enrollment status, current grade or school cycle attended, and years of schooling completed. Frequently, researchers do not have a choice of which variable to use, having to rely on whatever measures are included in available survey data. However, not all measures will adequately represent the conceptual variables of interest.

Even subtle differences in the design of survey questions can yield significantly different information. The following three surveys illustrate how different series of questions can establish length of schooling:

- *Demographic and Health Survey (DHS) current core questionnaire*: Has (name) ever attended school? What is the highest level of school (name) has attended? Did (name) attend school at any time during the (xxxx) school year? During this/that school year, what level and grade [is/was] (name) attending? Did (name) attend school at any time during the previous school year, that is, (xxxx)? During that school year, what level and grade did (name) attend?

- *Living Standards Measurement Survey (LSMS)* household questionnaire (Ghana): Has (name) ever attended school? What was the highest level completed? What was the highest educational qualification attained? Did (name) attend school/college at any time during the past 12 months? How much time does (name) spend going to and from school daily? Has (name) left school now? Has (name) ever attended technical and/or vocational school? How many course-years did (name) complete? What was the highest certificate (name) achieved? Has (name) ever attended a tertiary educational institution (that is a university or college)? How many years did (name) attend? What was the last institution attended?

- *Indonesia's National Socioeconomic Household Survey, 2000 (IFLS)*, a nationally representative household budget survey conducted by the Indonesian central statistical bureau in February of each year). Of household members five years and older, the questions asked were: Is (name) in school, out of school, or has dropped out? If (name) has dropped out, what month and year did (name) drop out? What is the highest level and type of schooling (name) ever attended or is attending? What is the highest grade ever attended or being attended? What is the highest certificate earned?

It is clear from these sample questionnaires that some surveys provide data on highest grade attended but does not make clear if that grade was also completed. The LSMS and IFLS questionnaires contain questions about completion, but the DHS core questionnaire does not. The LSMS and IFLS give specific information on certificate earned but the DHS does not. Of the three, only the IFLS contains detailed information on the timing of school leaving. Comparisons across countries are complicated by this lack of consistency in measures of schooling investment across surveys, making it more difficult to establish a better frame of reference for the magnitude and distribution of the income and price elasticities needed for policy analysis. The exchange between Behrman–Rosenzweig (2002, 2005) and Antonovics–Goldberger (2005) on whether and how parental education is transferred to children demonstrates that even when using the same data set, imprecision in questions can modify or even reverse research results.

6.1.1. Enrollment status

Many studies of child schooling use enrollment status (that is, whether or not the child is enrolled during the current or specified school year) as the dependent variable. This measure collapses the schooling decision into a dichotomous variable, and a logit or probit model is used to estimate the schooling function (e.g., Jacoby, 1993; Kim, Alderman and Orazem, 1999; Anh et al., 1998; Case, Paxson and Ableidinger, 2004). Enrollment is a noisy measure for several reasons: First, depending on when the questionnaire is applied, enrollment may or may not mean that the child will complete the current school year. Education officials in developing countries recommend taking the count of enrollees after the first month of the school year in order to get a more reliable count of the number of students for the year. Secondly, the reference period for the enrollment question may not capture information accurately. For example, Jacoby (1993) warns against using "the past 12 months" as a reference period: "The twelve month reference period may span two years, so that it is possible that the child has already dropped out of school completely by the interview date." We agree that it would be better to mention a specific school year as the reference period in surveys.

Third, being a dichotomous measure, enrollment does not reflect the actual amount of time a child spends in school; one child can be registered and attend school daily while another may also be enrolled but attend only infrequently. Consequently, children who have identical observed enrollment can have dramatically different time allocated to school. We turn to attendance measures later in the section.

Fourth, two children of the same age who are both enrolled could be in different grades because one may have started school later or may have dropped out temporarily or may have repeated a grade. Current enrollment status by itself does not capture these important differences, nor does it capture total schooling investments. Some studies attempt to deal with these limitations by defining enrollment status with respect to a particular grade level and age. For example, Anh et al. (1998) predict enrollment status for a sample of children divided into three age groups (10–12, 13–18, and 19–24); they control for age, in each age group regression as well. In Vietnam, there is a very high correlation between age and grade, so controlling for age in the enrollment regression indicates whether or not a child is enrolled in a grade as expected. They also estimate a set of logit regressions for a series of schooling outcomes (i.e., any schooling, finished primary school, has some secondary schooling, finished upper secondary school). Censoring bias is a potential problem for these estimations; we turn to this issue in the next section.

Like Anh et al. (1998), Connelly and Zheng (2003) estimate a sequence of probit or logit models corresponding to enrollment in progressively higher education levels (i.e., entering primary school, graduating from primary school, entering middle school, graduating from middle school, and entering high school), with each logit equation being estimated on a sample conditioned on having finished the previous schooling cycle. By not linking the sequential decisions econometrically, however, the authors introduce a selection bias in which the sample of children who successfully complete each level may be different in ability or motivation from the group left behind.[56]

6.1.2. Years of schooling

The number of years of schooling completed is usually computed from data on the highest grade attended or completed by an individual, with enrollment in or completion of the grade being used interchangeably. Our sample questionnaires above illustrate why studies are forced to equate enrollment with completion and to ignore repeated grades and partial years of schooling completed. Specifically, unlike the LSMS or the IFLS questionnaires, the DHS core questionnaire asks only for the highest grade attended, not highest grade completed. The presumption is that the highest grade attended was, in fact, completed. If a student dropped out in the middle of the year, say, after the survey was conducted, then the highest grade completed is really one year less than the highest grade attended. This is not to say that a partial year of attendance, though not reflected in the reported highest grade completed, did not contribute at all to the accumulation of human capital.[57]

Questions eliciting information on the current grade attended will overestimate years of schooling attained for children who drop out before the year ends. For students still enrolled, current grade attended will underestimate years of schooling if they plan to continue in school. In fact, even youths who are not currently enrolled could return to school the following year, so their currently observed highest grade attended could potentially underestimate final schooling attained.[58] These considerations imply that

---

[56] If μ_{ij} is a common element across several equations, it is possible that its influence can be controlled through joint estimation of the equations. This requires imposing some structure on the problem, either exclusion restrictions on some equations so that the same regressors do not appear in every equation or to exploit nonlinearities in the regression equations due to the use of limited dependent variables as in Bommier and Lambert (2000).

[57] In some cases, even this is not available. Some surveys ask a respondent whether he or she has ever attended the primary or secondary cycle, so the discrete measure of schooling pertains to a range of years rather than a single year.

[58] In countries where grade repetition is very high, highest grade completed significantly underestimates the level of investment made by the student, the family, and the community. Most survey data, however, do not contain information on grade repetition.

the number of years of schooling is best used as a measure when the study population is older, such that further schooling is unlikely. However, excluding the younger population in predicting demand for schooling could miss some important changes in household decision-making and policy. Indeed, in settings where educational development is progressing rapidly, focusing only on the completed years of schooling of adults will fail to capture the dynamics of the rising educational attainment of youths. If school-age children are included in an analysis of schooling outcomes, then ordinary least squares is an inadequate estimation method and empirical methods that can utilize censored data on years of schooling will need to be considered.

Various empirical approaches have been proposed to deal with these problems. One estimation strategy that addresses these issues is the censored ordered probit model used by Lillard and King (1984), King and Lillard (1987), Glewwe and Jacoby (1995), Lavy (1996), Behrman et al. (1997), Bommier and Lambert (2000), Glick and Sahn (2000) and Holmes (2003). This approach explicitly takes into account that the reported years of schooling is the outcome of an ordered series of discrete choices about enrollment and completion. By combining information on a child's enrollment status, this method allows for enrollees to be treated differently than the non-enrollees and thus is able to differentiate between highest grade attended and highest grade completed. This is accomplished by specifying different likelihood functions for the two groups which makes it possible to estimate unbiased estimates of predicted completed schooling for a given child.

There is an implied assumption that older children who have never attended school will not enroll in the future. Data from many developing countries belie this assumption. Although the official entry age for the primary grades in most countries is six or seven years, the age-enrollment profiles of the four countries in Fig. 1 show that in rural Ethiopia and Tanzania, many children enter school for the first time at age twelve or thirteen.[59] In these settings, researchers will likely incorrectly treat late entrants as never enrolling and thus underestimate the years of education completed by children who enter later. Researchers have attempted to address this by limiting their samples to children closer to the age when most enter school. For Malaysia and the Philippines, on the basis of age of entry data, King and Lillard (1987) used eight years as the cut-off age for their sample; for Guinea-Conakry, Glick and Sahn (2000) used nine years as the cut-off age; for Vietnam, Anh et al. (1998) used 10 years. Clearly, there is a trade-off between trimming off too many young children from the sample and thus losing the information from those for whom the observed schooling data are legitimate, and attributing zero years of schooling to those who will eventually enter school three or four years late.

6.1.3. Grade-for-age

A simple grade-age ratio, used during early attempts to eliminate the (right) censoring bias discussed above, is predicated on an expected or "official grade-for-age" and does

---

[59] Bommier and Lambert (2000) observe that a child has only a 50 percent probability of entering school before age nine in their Tanzania sample of 5000 households.

not recognize the cumulative nature of falling behind as a child ages, such as we have seen in the age-enrollment pyramids in Section 2. An alternative measure that explicitly uses median schooling levels as a benchmark for assessing individual schooling attainment has been proposed by Joshi and Schultz (2005). This normalized Z-score measure of years of education completed is similar to that in the nutrition field. In nutrition, the weight-for-height Z-score is used as a measure of long-term malnutrition, and height-for-age Z-scores as a measure of stunting. In like manner, a schooling Z-score measures the deviation from the median years of schooling for children of that age (and sex) in the population, and this difference is then divided by the standard deviation of the years of schooling of the children of the same age (and sex). This strategy recognizes the growing dispersion in years of schooling completed as a cohort ages, and converts all the deviations to more equivalent units of standard deviations.[60] It collapses the information about an individual child's schooling relative to a reference population into one number, providing a useful measure for interpreting censored information.

Not surprisingly, the usefulness of this measure depends on the choice of the reference population. For single-country analysis, should one choose a single reference population and thus be able to compare how any child in one part of the country does relative to others? Or should one use separate reference populations by urban–rural residence or by gender, in order to have a better fit between the censored schooling attainment and the reference grade-for-age curve? Again returning to Fig. 1, we see that there are clear differences between the urban and rural populations and between the male and female populations in at least three of the countries, and so using four reference populations for each country, instead of one, to compute the Z-scores would lead to different interpretations of schooling levels. For example, borrowing the language of the nutrition literature, the Z-scores might suggest that a rural girl is not "educationally stunted" relative to other rural girls but is severely "stunted" relative to urban girls or urban boys. It would also be difficult to compare the elasticities of policy variables computed from the relationships estimated using these Z-scores.

This method also does not lend itself easily to comparisons across time and across countries. While in nutrition the height-for-age curve can be expected to remain stable for at least a few years once a reference population has been chosen, the same is not true for the grade-for-age curve. In fact, given the rapid changes in educational attainment that might follow, say, a large expansion of school supply, it is possible to observe notable shifts in the reference grade-for-age curve within just two to three years. This would be likely in areas where a large proportion of children previously never attended school. During a period of school construction, observed changes in the Z-score could be due either to changes in an individual child's schooling or to shifts in the distribution of the reference population (in terms of its mean or variance), or to both, and the

---

[60] Even with this Z-score measure there may still be some systematic variations in outcomes by the child's age (arising in part from other groupings), but this can be dealt with by including the child's age in years as an additional control variable in the regressions.

estimated model of demand for schooling would not be able to distinguish among these sources of change.

Similarly, comparisons across countries using this measure are difficult because one has to choose one reference population in order to be able to interpret the Z-scores. In the nutrition field, cross-country comparisons are made easier by the international community agreeing to use a single reference population. In schooling, the choice is complicated by the fact that countries have different official age of entries and enforcement, and different lengths of the education cycles, and so different "natural" grade-for-age curves.

6.1.4. Attendance: Days or hours of school

School attendance or absence during the year adds another dimension to time spent in school which might be termed "intensity." Unfortunately, answers to the survey question "Does your child attend school?" are more likely to reflect enrollment decisions and not how regularly the child actually attends. Surveys that elicit how often the child attended school the previous week are better but will still measure annual attendance with error. Parents' impressions of their child's attendance record are likely fraught with error, and students' responses to those questions may be even less reliable. Memory lapses are one reason; another is that parents and students may not be aware of which absences from school are authorized free days and which are not. The latter is not surprising when teachers themselves take many unofficial leave days.[61]

Bedi and Marshall (2002) model schooling decisions one day at a time, but takes as given that a child is enrolled for the school year. Daily attendance is computed by subtracting the number of days a child is absent from the number of days the school was open during the school year, and this estimate is used as an input in a production function of student achievement. Information about attendance is taken from school administrative records. It would have been better to combine official attendance records from the school with household survey data, but this has not been done frequently in practice. An exception is King et al. (2002) who compare school attendance records with household survey data and find that spot checks of student attendance corroborate official school records, even in schools where spot checks of teacher attendance are at considerable variance with the teacher attendance registry. Perhaps there is less incentive for teachers to misreport student attendance than their own attendance.

School attendance or absences can be a critical measure of child's actual exposure to schooling especially in settings where child work is common. In these contexts, whether a child is enrolled or not is a poor signal of how much time a child spends in school since work and schooling are not likely to be mutually exclusive (Ravallion and Wodon, 2000; Patrinos and Psacharopoulos, 1997; Gunnarsson et al., 2006; Rosati and Rossi, 2003;

---

[61] A study of teacher absences in six developing countries found high teacher absenteeism – 19 percent of days, on average, of which only approximately one-tenth were authorized leave days (Chaudhury et al., 2006).

and the review by Edmonds in this Handbook). In places where the school day may be as short as four hours, the time constraint does not prevent the child from being enrolled while also working. For example, Angrist et al. (2002) observe that Colombia's voucher program led to a decrease in child labor for the beneficiaries, as well as to an increase in years attained and test scores. Some children work too many hours which can decrease their school attendance, limit their ability to do homework, and lower their school performance. Longer school days and school terms may influence a child's learning, as well as reduce child labor. Yap et al. (2006) find that Brazil's after-school program in rural areas greatly reduced child labor. Differences in the length of the school term between black and white schools in the United States in the segregated era explain differences in school achievement (Orazem, 1987) and earnings (Card and Krueger, 1992) between blacks and whites.

In general, the length of the school term and the number of school hours each day are often standardized within countries, so they may not prove useful in explaining variation in academic success within a single country. Exceptions are when shortages of school spaces justify multiple shifts during the school day which shorten the school day for some students. In decentralized systems, local governments tend to have the authority to specify these durations for their schools as long as the minimum set by the central authority is met.

6.2. Measurement of school outcomes

Time spent in school is an input into the educational production process and not a measure of schooling outcomes. Almost any public policy related to education aims to raise human capital and not just enrollment or attendance. In fact, the few studies that have included both measures of cognitive achievement and years of schooling find it is the former that best explains variation in adult earnings (Glewwe, 2002). Therefore, it is extremely important to understand how to produce literacy and numeracy most efficiently in order to foster human capital development in poor countries. To that end, many researchers have estimated equations explaining schooling outcomes as a function of school attributes that are special cases of

$$q_k = q(Z_k, \bar{Z}, H_k, A_k, \mu_k) \tag{6.1}$$

where q_k is a measure of average cognitive attainment in school k, Z_k is a vector of variable school inputs $(Z_{1k}, Z_{2k}, \ldots, Z_{nk})$ that could include teaching personnel, materials, equipment, and methods; $\bar{Z}$ are fixed inputs that cannot be influenced by the school manager; H_k is a measure of the intensity of child time allocations to the school; A_k is a measure of the socioeconomic status of the parents; and μ_k is a measure of academic ability. Consistent with equation (4.6), parents will decide how much child time to devote to the school so that $H_k = H(Z_k, \bar{Z}, A_k, \mu_k, W_k)$ where the last term is a vector of other factors. Suppose that the school administrator decides on the mix of school inputs Z_k so as to maximize child attainment (6.1), given knowledge of child abilities and community wealth, given the parent's child time allocation decision, and given a budget constraint $B_k = \sum_n p_i Z_{ik}$ with attached Lagrange multiplier λ. The school's first-order conditions will be

$$\frac{\partial q}{\partial H_k}\frac{\partial H_k}{\partial Z_{ik}} + \frac{\partial q}{\partial Z_{ik}} - \lambda p_i \leqslant 0. \tag{6.2}$$

The school's reduced form input allocation decisions will be of the form $Z_{ik} = Z_i(B, p_1, p_2, \ldots, p_n, \bar{Z}, A_k, \mu_k)$. Schools will decide on the mix of inputs incorporating how those decisions will affect parents' decisions on whether or how much to send their children to school. Note that some school inputs may have no direct effect on child attainment but will still be productive if they make children attend more regularly. Other potential school inputs will not be used if they are deemed unproductive, particularly if they lower school attendance. This is true even if the input is available at no cost to the school, as would be the case if the school receives a fixed set of materials from a central authority. The inputs actually used in practice will reflect the decisions of the local school administrator.[62]

Even this simple description of the human capital production process illustrates the complications from interpreting an empirical approximation to Eq. (6.1). Data sets will typically not include information on student ability, and so μ_k will be part of the error term. Because school inputs will be selected to complement student abilities, $\text{Cov}(\mu_k, Z_k) \neq 0$ which will bias the coefficients on school inputs. As an example, suppose that schools that assign more independent projects do so only if their students have superior levels of ability, μ_k. The estimated effect of independent study on cognitive attainment will be positive, but one cannot infer that all schools should assign independent work.

Parents will send their children to the school more or less intensively depending on the mix of school inputs. Information on student cognitive attainment will only be available for children who attend on the day of the test, and they will presumably be the children whose abilities are most complementary with the mix of school inputs used. This nonrandom sorting into the school will further bias the estimates. Suppose, for example, that better schools retain a high fraction of their students while weaker schools retain only students from the upper tail of the ability distribution. The distribution of average test scores across schools will understate the true productivity of the superior schools.

Measures of the school inputs Z_k will typically include budgeted personnel, materials, and equipment, but the actual utilization of these inputs will reflect the decisions of the teachers and the school administration. Textbooks may be assigned but not used. Teaching methods may be prescribed but not followed. Teachers may be paid but not present. Severe measurement errors will exist because of the deviation between inputs allocated and used.

---

[62] The prices could be viewed as shadow prices of time if inputs require the administrator to provide training in their application. For example, the price of applying a new teaching method would include the cost of the in-service training as well as any associated materials.

Equation (6.2) suggests that schools will use inputs more intensively if they complement household assets or child abilities. Some combinations of inputs may be used in wealthier communities and others in poorer communities; other combinations with high ability children and still others with low ability populations. Natural complementarities among inputs imply that they will not be selected independent of one another but are selected in combination. If inputs are selected in groups and not independently, the frequent practice of using a very large number of highly intercorrelated school attributes in estimating educational production functions will not reliably measure the independent productivity of the included inputs.

Our model of input choice presumes that the local school manager wishes to maximize students' cognitive attainment. This may well be the case in schools with considerable parent involvement so that the school manager is acting as an agent for the parents. However, the principal may not serve as an agent for the parents. Politically or economically prominent local individuals may influence the school to misapply inputs to meet other ends, resulting in resources being diverted to unneeded school construction or hiring relatives. In other settings, the objective may be to maximize the utility of the teachers, resulting in frequent absenteeism. If the school administrator's objective function differs across schools, the observed pattern of inputs and cognitive attainment cannot be described by a single production function that assumes inputs are being allocated to maximize cognitive attainment subject to the mix of inputs.

Use of longitudinal data on test scores has been proposed as a possible correction for unobserved ability. If the growth in cognitive achievement is proportional to the initial test score, a regression of the change in test scores on the initial test score plus measures of A_i and Z_j may correct for the unobserved ability. However, μ_k would be expected to affect child time in school during the year, and so unobserved ability will still affect how intensively school inputs are used during the school year. Consequently, differencing will not purge the regression of ability bias. Furthermore, test scores measure cognitive ability with error, so taking the difference between two test scores may result in a high ratio of noise to the actual change in cognitive ability, and the use of the first test score as a regressor creates measurement error bias.[63]

Household surveys provide information on siblings and other members of the household. Various studies have used this feature of household data to generate household fixed effects to control for unobserved health or ability endowments and other unobserved household variables.[64] Data on twins, for example, are thought to be ideal for

---

[63] For more detail on these and other problems related to estimation of education production functions, see the careful review by Todd and Wolpin (2003).

[64] Household surveys usually collect detailed information only on the children residing in the household, ignoring the schooling of children who have been fostered out or who have left the household. The resulting selection bias can be large, but in an uncertain direction. Children who stay in school longest may have to leave the household for secondary schooling in larger towns. Alternatively, children who quit school and enter the labor market at early ages may leave the household first. The decision to leave the household might also be conditoned on unobserved abilities, but it is unclear whether the most able would leave at younger or older ages.

controlling for differences in natural ability (e.g., Behrman and Rosenzweig, 2002). Absent twins data, other studies include data on all children per household but estimate their models with household fixed effects (Lillard and Willis, 1994; Glewwe, Jacoby and King, 2001, and Section 4.2 of Strauss and Thomas in this Handbook). Such methods have the potential of correcting for ability bias on cognitive development, but they still leave an uncomfortable presumption that remaining differences in schooling intensity across children are not a result of child-specific attributes (Todd and Wolpin, 2003).

Randomized input assignments of the type reviewed by Duflo, Glennerster and Kremer in this Handbook may be a mechanism to avoid the endogenous school input problem. Of course, Eq. (6.2) suggests that the local school authority will decide whether or how the inputs are used, and parents may alter the child's time in school as well, and so there will be variation in input utilization across schools receiving the inputs. In addition, the productivity of the input (say, a new English language textbook) will depend on the other inputs available to the school (e.g., trained teachers, English medium instruction). An experimental infusion of certain inputs, but not others, may succeed in some settings, complicating the applicability of the lessons to other schools and contexts. As an example, Glewwe, Kremer and Moulin (2003) find that making textbooks more available in Kenya benefited students in the upper tail of the ability distribution who were prepared for the English medium texts, but the texts had no impact on below-average students who could not understand English. It is plausible that the textbooks encouraged more able students to attend school more regularly while discouraging weaker students from attending.

Studies that compare the productivity of school types, such as public versus private schools or religious versus secular schools, face similar challenges. If parents can choose where to send their children to school as well as how intensively to invest in schooling, then parents will select the school inputs Z_k and $\bar{Z}$ jointly with the type of school. These inputs will be correlated with all of the households assets and child ability endowments, and so differences in average school outcomes across school types will reflect the nonrandom sorting of children across school types. It is possible to measure how the availability of new choices affects schooling outcomes as in the Angrist et al. studies discussed in Section 3.4. However, this is the joint effect of attending the school and the application of home and school inputs, and not a means of establishing how individual inputs affect student outcomes.

No study has been able to address all of the difficulties outlined above, and problems of selection, measurement error, and differential objective functions are likely to be larger in developing than developed country settings. The many studies of the educational production process in developing countries have failed to generate consistent findings.[65] Teacher or school attributes that appear critically important for student performance in one study prove unimportant or even a detriment in another. This lack of

---

[65] For reviews of the results of educational production function estimation, see Hanushek (1997), Glewwe (2002), and Hanushek and Luque (2003).

consistency stands in marked contrast to the high degree of consistency across studies of estimated private returns to schooling which has been used to validate the use of log earnings equations in studies of returns to human capital. We conclude that the various misspecification problems that arise when estimating equations such as (6.1) are so pervasive as to render the coefficient estimates unreliable.

6.2.1. School quality

In many studies of schooling demand, one or more measures of the relative quality of local schools prove to be significant in explaining cross-sectional variation in attendance or enrollment, controlling for other household, school and community factors.[66] This contrasts with the lack of consensus regarding the impact of school quality on student achievement. This may suggest that the way school quality matters for learning is more in attracting and retaining children in school than in changing the pace of learning across children in different schools. Equally plausible is that the biases inherent in estimating the total derivative $\frac{\partial q}{\partial Z_{ik}}$ in (6.2) have led to the lack of consensus regarding the impact of school quality on student achievement, but that estimates of the impact of school quality on child time use ($\frac{\partial H_k}{\partial Z_{ik}}$ in (6.2)) are more reliable.

Before pressing this conclusion harder, it should be noted that the typical study of school quality on test scores uses numerous measures of school quality while the typical study of school quality on schooling demand uses only one or two measures of school quality. It may be that the perception that school quality is more important for child time in school than for cognitive development is due to more selective concentration on school quality measures that yield expected results in the schooling demand literature. Again, there is not a sufficiently well-developed literature on the relative importance of school quality on attendance versus school achievement to assess the reliability of the common finding that school quality affects child time in school. A particularly fruitful area for future research would be to evaluate whether variation in school quality matters more for explaining variation in attendance than for test scores, using a single data set appropriate for both questions.

6.2.2. Promotion, repetition and dropping out

In the absence of student test scores, some researchers and policymakers refer to repetition, promotion and dropping out as measures of student success or failure. This view is wrong because repetition and promotion rates reflect a confluence of factors, including academic standards and how strictly they are enforced, student performance and motivation, and household demand. Some schools and school systems practice social

---

[66] See for examples Case and Deaton (1999), Alderman, Orazem and Paterno (2001), Bedi and Marshall (2002), and Glick and Sahn (2006).

promotion in which all children are promoted to the next grade regardless of academic performance.[67] The belief underlying this practice is that children who are not promoted become discouraged and withdraw from school. The counter argument is that ill-prepared children fall further and further behind their peers and become discouraged, whereas holding them back until they are ready to progress allows time for remediation and eventual academic progress.

Obtaining measures of grade repetition and dropping out behavior is also difficult both at the individual and cohort levels. Of the three sample survey questionnaires we cited above, only one (the IFLS questionnaire) contains an attempt to determine the timing of school leaving so that it is possible to reconstruct the period when a child who is no longer enrolled was a student. By using the reported highest grade completed together with the child's current age, it is possible to get a rough estimate of age of entry in school; but, without direct questions about age of entry in school, number of grades repeated and which grades were repeated, whether a child who is currently in school had ever stopped for a year, and when a child who is no longer enrolled dropped out of school, it is not possible to characterize accurately the schooling histories of children in different settings and how these have changed across cohorts. Surveys such as the Malaysia Family Life Surveys, the Indonesia Family Life Surveys, and the Cebu Longitudinal Health and Nutrition Study (Philippines) have collected detailed life history data that contain these pieces of information. Even considering problems with the recall ability of the respondent and the availability of supporting documents which determine the reliability of the elicited information, such histories provide better data for understanding the schooling process.

6.3. Measurement of exogenous variables

Empirical tests of the theoretical static model of child schooling require data on child time allocations, household, school and community attributes, measures of the value of child time, and measures of schooling outcomes. This subsection discusses alternative empirical measures for the variables needed to estimate (4.8).[68]

6.3.1. Direct price of schooling

The direct costs faced by a household in sending a child to school include expenditures for tuition, required books and educational materials, transportation, uniform, exams,

---

[67] King, Orazem and Paterno (2002) examine whether social promotion increased the probability that a child continued in school in the Northwest Frontier Province of Pakistan. They find that promotions based on attendance and performance on tests increased the probability of continuation, but that promotions that were unrelated to school performance had virtually no effect on continuation. Consequently, continuation may be a better indicator of school performance than is promotion.

[68] Behrman and Rosenzweig (1994) discuss the implications of uneven data quality across developing countries for cross-country macroeconomic analyses of human capital and growth.

and admission fees required to gain access to the school. These costs usually vary by type of school. Private schools typically charge more than government schools, but there may be cost variation across private schools and across government schools as well. As noted in the previous subsection, variation in school distance (and thus in the cost of transportation) has proved to be a useful shifter of child time in school in several different settings, but distance to the nearest school for any one household or child is endogenous for at least two reasons – school choice which may be accompanied by a household relocating closer to a school, and endogenous school placement which is presumably aimed to reduce average distance to a school, so these observed marginal effects of school distance are likely biased downward.[69]

Market measures of the price of schools have typically included the average or median distance or cost across the schools that are available to the household (Gertler and Glewwe, 1990; Lavy, 1996; Alderman, Orazem and Paterno, 2001; Bedi and Marshall, 2002; Glick and Sahn, 2006). It is critically important that the price of schooling is not the price actually paid by the household but is a market-level measure of the variation in the price of schools (such as the average price in the village), since the actual price of the school selected is endogenous. This can lead to counterintuitive results if parents choose a more costly school that is a better school over nearer schools that are not as good. For example, Brown and Park (2002) found that increasing distance to school and the school price lowered the probability of dropout. An alternative approach suggested by Lavy (1996) is to estimate school price using as instruments area-specific characteristics that affect school placement but are not correlated with the demand for schooling. For Ghana, he uses distance to a public telephone and the post office to help identify the distance to a middle school in a given community; but assuming that community-specific attributes do not affect both the demand for schooling and its supply in the community is likely to be contested by some.

Average school price elasticities tend to be small, ranging from 0 to −0.4 in the studies mentioned above. They are of larger magnitude for private schools than for government schools. Poorer households are more responsive to price than richer households in all of the studies. The one study we found with comparable urban and rural estimates (Bedi and Marshall, 2002) did not find significant differences in price elasticities between urban and rural areas of Honduras, but it would be difficult to generalize from that study. More recently, several African countries have dispensed with school fees.

---

[69] Filmer (2004) provides a summary look at the availability of schools in several developing countries, as measured by the average distance to the nearest school reported in Demographic and Health Surveys. The data show large variation in average distance to school for households across the countries – from just 0.2 kilometers in Bangladesh to over seven kilometers in Chad – but the median average distance among 21 countries is only 1.4 km. The range in average distance to secondary schools is much greater – from 1.8 kilometers in Bangladesh to over 71 kilometers in Mali. Filmer (2004) finds that the distance to the nearest school is statistically significantly negatively related to school enrollment in 11 out of the 21 countries at the primary level (at the 5 percent significance level), and in six out of 21 countries at the secondary level. These results do not provide an overwhelming case for new school construction programs.

Deininger (2003) reports substantial increases in school enrollments in Uganda follow-ing the fee reduction. Ignoring the possibility that the fee reduction was anticipated ahead of its adoption, he nonetheless finds a substantial reduction in enrollment gaps between boys and girls, between urban and rural areas, and between rich and poor that suggest more price elastic demand for girls, for rural residents and for the poor.

6.3.2. Opportunity cost of child time

Most child labor occurs in the context of a family enterprise without pay, and so most of child labor occurs in the informal sector. This complicates the measurement of the opportunity cost of child time in school. One option (Orazem, 1987; Jacoby, 1993; Glewwe and Jacoby, 2004) is to estimate a production function and compute the mar-ginal product of child labor. This method, however, has an added complexity in that the marginal product of time is a function of time spent in home production, and is consequently a function also of time spent in school. The endogeneity of the marginal product of time is a difficult problem to solve in that the general solution to the house-hold's optimization problem makes child time in school a function of all the exogenous variables in the system. A tractable alternative is to approximate the child time equa-tions (4.6) by assuming that factors such as household productive assets or technologies shift the child's marginal product of time. If, for example, we assume that child mar-ginal productivity takes the form $Q_{H_i} = Q(A, \tau, \zeta)$ where ζ is a random error, then the reduced-form time use can be approximated by $H_i = H_i(P_C, P_f, P_m, A, Z, \tau, d_f, \mu_i)$ without having to impose the structural relationship among Q_{H_i}, A, and τ. For most applications, the reduced-form relationship will be sufficient.

  An alternative is to use measures of local child market wages. However, in households where children work at home in the face of an active local child labor market, it must be true that the marginal product of child time in the home enterprise exceeds the market child wage, and so the average wage would be a lower bound measure of the value of child time. More problematic is that even where child labor markets are active, the majority of children do not work for a wage and so the observed average wage is subject to serious selection bias problems that may outweigh any benefit of using wages as a measure of child time.

  It is plausible that the value of child time varies with age and physical maturity and not with what the child is learning in school, at least for the primary cycle. Several pieces of evidence suggest this conclusion. Rosenzweig (1980) finds that agricultural day wages in India did not rise with education. Fafchamps and Quisumbing (1999) observe that even adult returns to agricultural production in Pakistan rose with measures of the health and physical stature of both the husband and the wife in farm families, but not with their education. This suggests that age could be used as a proxy for the value of time, except that capacity for human capital accumulation will also rise with age, and so using age to distinguish between opportunity costs of schooling and capacity for learning can be problematic. Nevertheless, exogenous variation in age due to local policies concerning when a child can start or leave school or when a child can legally initiate work can create exogenous variation in the opportunity costs of schooling across markets due to factors outside the household control.[70]

7. Conclusions

Compared to developed countries, developing countries have large gaps in schooling attainment between men and women and between urban and rural residents. As countries develop and education levels rise, these gaps have tended to close. Most notable has been the reduction in educational gaps between males and females in many countries. Nevertheless, large gaps within countries remain. Comparisons across countries show that such gaps can be substantially different even among countries at similar income levels.

Certainly, governments believe policies and interventions matter, as they invest considerable resources in providing or financing education for their citizens. The potential private returns of education to citizens and the potential social returns to the state require that these investments pay off in terms of more academic achievement and higher productivity. This is not always assured, in part because time spent in school may not lead to a commensurate increase in knowledge and skills. For this reason, governments, international agencies and individual researchers are devoting more attention to examining which policies and programs are most cost-effective. Establishing the impact of these policies and programs requires an understanding of the incentives and constraints faced by all parties involved, the school providers, the parents and the children.

Increasingly, assessments are making use of experimental methods to estimate the impact of policy changes and programs on educational attainment. Such methods provide counterfactual populations for treated groups. This chapter argues that in order to generalize from individual experimental evidence to other settings, it is important to frame the experimental outcomes in the context of a behavioral model that can help explain why a particular pilot project generates the outcomes that it does. In addition, behavioral models are needed to guide nonexperimental evaluations in contexts where experimental evaluations are infeasible.

Behavioral models can also help to frame the magnitude of experimental results. Knowing that pilots are likely to be placed in settings where they will be atypically successful suggests that experimental outcomes derived from such settings will overstate the outcomes for the population as a whole.[71] Understanding that income surprises will

---

[70] Angrist and Krueger (1991), Tyler (2003), and Gunnarsson et al. (2006) use variation in child labor and truancy laws to create a source of exogenous variation in child ages in their estimates of schooling demand.

[71] For example, Miguel and Kremer's (2004) analysis of deworming medicine discussed extensively in the chapters written by Miguel and Glewwe and by Mwabu in this Handbook found large impacts on child health and school attendance in areas where 92% of the children were infected. One would expect more modest results if the program were to be expanded to areas with more modest infection rates. See also the discussion of vouchers in Section 3.

have atypically large impacts on credit constrained households suggests that the income elasticities derived by measuring short-term schooling demand responses to transitory income shocks will exaggerate the schooling demand responses to permanent income changes.

There are several important avenues for future research:

(a) A common, albeit not universal finding, is that the elasticity of child schooling with respect to household income is larger in developing than in developed countries. According to the Becker–Tomes framework, credit-constrained households will concentrate their transfers of wealth to their children in the form of human capital, but the investments will be below the efficient levels. Public provision of schooling should reduce the degree of under-investment and help to decrease the intergenerational transmission of poverty. Future research could evaluate schooling demand in developing countries in light of the Becker–Tomes model: Is it true that the tie between parent's income and child schooling is indeed greater in developing countries, and does the current allocation of schooling reduce or perpetuate income inequality in developing countries?

(b) Studies that examine household reactions to income shocks have followed behaviors for a limited time after the shock. Studies also tend to look only at consumption responses or time allocation responses in isolation rather than examine them as simultaneous decisions as implied by Eqs. (5.6a) and (5.6b). Longer time-series data with more complete model specifications would help to disentangle the short- from long-run schooling effects and time allocation from consumption responses. The same plea for future research applies with respect to household reactions to permanent and transitory price shocks.

(c) Longitudinal analysis of cognitive attainment is needed to establish whether lost human capital from transitory increases in child labor or school absences due to adverse income shocks is reversible or permanent.

(d) Because many of the interesting decisions regarding schooling investments do not lend themselves easily to experimental methods, more studies are needed that use convincing instruments to correct for the likely endogeneity of child time or of measurement error in explanatory variables used in evaluating schooling outcomes.

(e) Despite the large differences in schooling attainment between urban and rural residents, there are very few studies that use similar methods to compare schooling demand across urban and rural areas. As rural to urban migration becomes more important, rural migrants will need skills more similar to those of their urban contemporaries. Returns to rural education should not be undervalued because we fail to include the consequences of rural schooling on rural-urban migration and the resulting increases in lifetime earnings that result.

(f) There are no studies that evaluate the impact of urban–rural schooling gaps on economic development, or whether there are important external benefits to raising schooling outcomes in rural areas. Improved schooling in rural areas has been shown to increase outmigration from rural to urban markets, to supply skilled labor needed to fuel industrialization, to increase the pace of technological adoption and yield gain by farmers, and to reduce earnings inequality between urban and rural markets. If, as we suspect, these returns to schooling are large and of critical importance to a country's transition from an agrarian to an industrialized economy, we should find that improved rural schooling is tied to economic growth.

(g) Most of the studies reviewed in this chapter have focused on years of schooling and enrollment rates as measures of educational achievement. The economics research using measures of learning achievement, such as standardized test scores, has been on the rise, but this is generally still a nascent area. The growth of this body of research depends greatly on more countries having test score data that are linked to household and child characteristics and that are available for more than one year.

(h) As data and evidence from experimental evaluations in different settings become more available, there will be two important roles linking experiments to behavioral models:

1. Behavioral models can be tested using experimental methods to examine the extent to which econometric models can replicate the results from the experiments. Suitably calibrated behavioral models can then be used to conduct simulated counterfactual policy exercises as demonstrated by Todd and Wolpin (2006).

2. Behavioral models can be used to aggregate the results of various experiments to predict how similar interventions will perform in alternative environments.

(i) In many countries, girls receive less schooling than boys. In virtually all of those countries, least squares estimates of private returns to schooling are lower for boys than for girls. This could be a consequence of parents applying a larger discount to girls' future earnings. It could also reflect a higher opportunity cost of schooling for girls than boys. However, it may also be a consequence of greater selection bias in estimated returns to girls' schooling if the women who ultimately enter wage labor are disproportionately able compared to the average male wage worker. If girls' schooling also has greater external social benefits from reduced fertility or improved family health as many have argued, then there is a *prima facie* case that these developing countries under-invest in girls' education. However, except for Schultz (1988), economists have not conducted a systematic evaluation of the relative size of possible biases in estimated returns to schooling between males and females in developing countries. Countries such as Mexico have implemented conditional transfer programs that allocate slightly larger grants to girls than to boys on the presumption that girls' schooling responds less elastically to transfers and that returns to the investment are greater. The very limited evidence available does not refute that assumption, but much more work needs to be done.

(j) Average returns to schooling for rural nonmigrant residents are lower than for urban residents. On-farm returns to schooling are lower than off-farm returns to schooling in areas using traditional agricultural methods. However, it is a mistake to conclude that rural investments in schooling are unimportant. More educated rural residents migrate in greater numbers to urban markets, suggesting that observed rural returns to schooling are understated. We need studies that establish the returns to rural education for migrants versus nonmigrants.

Appendix Table 1
Country household data sets used to estimate returns to schooling in Figs. 4 and 5

Country	Years
Albania (ALB)	2002
Argentina (ARG)[a]	1994, 2001
Bangladesh (BNG)	2000
Bolivia (BOL)	2002
Brazil (BRA)	1995, 2001
Burkina Faso (BFA)	1994, 2003
Bulgaria (BUL)	2001
Burundi (BUR)	1998
Cambodia (KHM)	1997, 2004
Chile (CHL)	1990, 1996
Colombia (COL)	1995, 2000
Costa Rica (CRI)	1995, 2000
Croatia (HRV)	2004
Dominican Republic (DOM)	1997, 2004
East Timor (TMP)	20 01
Ecuador (ECU)	1995, 2004
Egypt (EGY)	1998
El Salvador (SLV)	1 995, 2002
Estonia (EST)	2000
Ghana (GHA)	1991
Guatemala (GUA)	1989, 2002
Guyana (GUY)	1992
Haiti (HTI)	2001
Honduras (HON)	1995, 2003
Indonesia (IDN)	2002
Jamaica (JAM)	1996, 2002
Jordan (JOR)	2002
Kyrgyzstan (KGZ)	1996
Maldives (MDV)	1998
Mauritania (MRT)	2000
Mexico (MEX)	1994, 2002
Mongolia (MON)	2002
Morocco (MAR)	1991
Mozambique (MOZ)	1996
Nicaragua (NIC)	1993, 2001
Nigeria (NGA)	2003
Pakistan (PAK)	1999, 2001
Palau (PLW)[a]	2000
Panama (PAN)	1995, 2003
Paraguaqy (PGY)	1995, 2001
Peru (PER)	1994, 2002
Romania (ROM)	1994
Sao Tome and Principe (STP)	2000
Sierra Leone (SLE)	2003
Tajikistan (TJK)	2003
Thailand (THA)	1990, 1994, 2002

(*continued on next page*)

Appendix Table 1
(*continued*)

Country	Years
Uganda (UGA)	2002
Uruguay (URY)[a]	1995, 2003
Vietnam (VNM)	1992

Source: Fares, Montenegro and Orazem (2007). Country three-letter codes used in Figs. 2 and 3 are reported in parentheses.
[a]Data not available for separate estimates for urban and rural areas.

References

Abdulai, A., Huffman, W.E. (2005). "The diffusion of new agricultural technologies: The case of crossbreeding technology in Tanzania". American Journal of Agricultural Economics 87, 645–659.

Agesa, R.U. (2001). "Migration and the urban to rural earnings difference: A sample selection approach". Economic Development and Cultural Change 49 (4), 847–865.

Alderman, H., Kim, J., Orazem, P.F. (2003). "Design, evaluation, and sustainability of private schools for the poor: The Pakistan urban and rural fellowship school experiments". Economics of Education Review 22, 265–274.

Alderman, H., Orazem, P.F., Paterno, E.M. (2001). "School quality, school cost and the public/private school choices of low-income households in Pakistan". Journal of Human Resources 36, 304–326.

Alderman, H., Behrman, J.R., Lavy, V., Menon, R. (2001). "Child health and school enrollment: A longitudinal analysis". Journal of Human Resources 36 (1), 185–205.

Altonji, J.G., Dunn, T.A. (1996). "Using siblings to estimate the effect of school quality on wages". Review of Economics and Statistics 78 (4), 665–671.

Anderson, K.H., King, E.M., Wang, Y. (2002). "Market wages, transfers, and demand for schooling in Malaysia, 1976–1989". Journal of Development Studies 39 (3), 1–28.

Angrist, J.D., Bettinger, E., Kremer, M. (2006). "Long-term educational consequences of secondary school vouchers: Evidence from administrative records in Colombia". American Economic Review 96, 847–862.

Angrist, J.D., Krueger, A.B. (1991). "Does compulsory school attendance affect schooling and earnings?" Quarterly Journal of Economics 106, 979–1014.

Angrist, J.D., Krueger, A.B. (1999). "Empirical strategies in labor economics". In: Ashenfelter, O., Card, D. (Eds.), Handbook of Labor Economics, vol. 3A. Elsevier Science B.V., Amsterdam.

Angrist, J.D., Bettinger, E., Bloom, E., King, E., Kremer, M. (2002). "Vouchers for private schooling in Colombia: Evidence from a randomized natural experiment". American Economic Review 92 (5), 1535–1559.

Anh, T.S., Knodel, J.E., Lam, D., Friedman, J. (1998). "Family size and children's education in Vietnam". Demography 35 (1), 57–70.

Antonovics, K.L., Goldberger, A.S. (2005). "Does increasing women's schooling raise the schooling of the next generation? Comment". American Economic Review 95, 1738–1744.

Becker, G.S. (1971). The Economics of Discrimination, second ed. The Univ. of Chicago Press, Chicago.

Becker, G.S. (1985). "Human capital, effort, and the sexual division of labor". Journal of Labor Economics 3 (1–2), S33–S58.

Becker, G.S. (1993). Human Capital, third ed. The Univ. of Chicago Press, Chicago.

Becker, G.S., Tomes, N. (1986). "Human capital and the rise and fall of families". Journal of Labor Economics 4, S12–S37.

Bedi, A.S., Edwards, J.H.Y. (2002). "The impact of school quality on earnings and educational returns–evidence from a low-income country". Journal of Development Economics 68 (1), 157–185.

Bedi, A.S., Gaston, N. (1999). "Using variation in schooling availability to estimate educational returns for Honduras". Economics of Education Review 18, 107–116.

Bedi, A.S., Marshall, J.H. (2002). "Primary school attendance in Honduras". Journal of Development Economics 69 (1), 129–153.

Behrman, J.R. (1996). Human Resources in Latin America and the Caribbean. The Johns Hopkins Univ. Press for the Inter-American Development Bank, Baltimore.

Behrman, J.R., Cheng, Y., Todd, P. (2004). "Evaluating pre-school programs when length of exposure to the program varies: A nonparametric approach". Review of Economics and Statistics 86 (1), 108–132.

Behrman, J.R., Rosenzweig, M.R. (1994). "Caveat emptor: Cross-country data on education and the labor force". Journal of Development Economics 44, 147–171.

Behrman, J.R., Rosenzweig, M.R. (2002). "Does increasing women's schooling raise the schooling of the next generation?" American Economic Review 92, 323–334.

Behrman, J.R., Rosenzweig, M.R. (2005). "Does increasing women's schooling raise the schooling of the next generation? Reply". American Economic Review 95, 1745–1751.

Behrman, J.R., Khan, S., Ross, D., Sabot, R. (1997). "School quality and cognitive achievement production: A case study for rural Pakistan". Economics of Education Review 16 (2), 127–142.

Besley, T., Case, A. (1993). "Modeling technology adoption in developing countries". American Economic Review 83, 396–402.

Bhalotra, S., Heady, C. (2003). "Child farm labor: The wealth paradox". World Bank Economic Review 17, 197–227.

Blundell, R., MaCurdy, T.E. (1999). "Labor supply: A review of alternative approaches". In: Ashenfelter, O., Card, D. (Eds.), Handbook of Labor Economics, vol. 3. Elsevier Science B.V., Amsterdam.

Bommier, A., Lambert, S. (2000). "Education demand and age at school enrollment in Tanzania". Journal of Human Resources 35, 177–203.

Boucher, S., Stark, O., Taylor, J.E. (2007). "A gain with a drain? Evidence from rural Mexico on the New Economics of the brain drain". In press.

Brown, P.H., Park, A. (2002). "Education and poverty in rural China". Economics of Education Review 21 (6), 523–541.

Card, D. (1999). "The causal effect of education on earnings". In: Ashenfelter, O., Card, D. (Eds.), In: Handbook of Labor Economics, vol. 3A. Elsevier Science B.V., Amsterdam.

Card, D., Krueger, A.B. (1992). "Does school quality matter? Returns to education and the characteristics of public schools in the United States". Journal of Political Economy 100, 1–40.

Carneiro, P., Heckman, J. (2003). "Human capital policy". In: Heckman, J.J., Krueger, A.J. (Eds.), Inequality in America: What Role for Human Capital Policies?. MIT Press, Cambridge, MA.

Case, A., Deaton, A. (1999). "School inputs and educational outcomes in South Africa". Quarterly Journal of Economics 114 (3), 1047–1084.

Case, A., Paxson, C.H., Ableidinger, J. (2004). "Orphans in Africa: Parental death, poverty, and school enrollment". Demography 41 (3), 483–508.

Case, A., Yogo, M. (1999). "Does school quality matter? Returns to education and the characteristics of schools in South Africa". Working paper 7399. National Bureau of Economic Research.

Chaudhury, N., Hammer, J., Kremer, M., Muralidharan, K., Rogers, F.H. (2006). "Missing in action: Teacher and health worker absence in developing countries". Journal of Economic Perspectives 20, 91–116.

Connelly, R., Zheng, Z. (2003). "Determinants of school enrollment and completion of 10 to 18 year-olds in China". Economics of Education Review 22 (4), 379–388.

Contreras, D. (2002). "Vouchers, school choice and the access to higher education". Discussion paper No. 845. Economic Growth Center, Yale University, June. Processed.

Cox-Edwards, A., Ureta, M. (2003). "International migration, remittances, and schooling: Evidence from El Salvador". Journal of Development Economics 72, 429–461.

Currie, J. (2001). "Early childhood education programs". Journal of Economic Perspectives 15 (2), 213–238.

Currie, J., Thomas, D. (2000). "School quality and the longer-term effects of head start". The Journal of Human Resources 35 (4), 755–774.

de Brauw, A., Rozelle, S., Zhang, L. (2005). "Labor market emergence and returns to education in rural China". Review of Agricultural Economics 27 (September), 418–424.

Deininger, K. (2003). "Does cost of schooling affect enrollment by the poor? Universal primary education in Uganda". Economics of Education Review 22, 291–305.

Duflo, E. (2001). "Schooling and labor market consequences of school construction in Indonesia: Evidence from an unusual policy experiment". American Economic Review 91, 795–813.

Duflo, E. (2004). "The medium run effects of educational expansion: Evidence from a large school construction program in Indonesia". Journal of Development Economics 74 (1), 163–197.

Dunn, C.S. (2004). "Intergenerational transmission of lifetime earnings: New evidence from Brazil". University of Michigan, PhD dissertation.

Duraisamy, P. (2002). "Changes in returns to education in India, 1983–94, by gender, age cohort and location". Economics of Education Review 21 (6), 609–622.

Duryea, S., Hoek, J., Lam, D., Levison, D. (2006). "Dynamics of child labor: Labor force entry and exit in urban Brazil". In: Orazem, P.F., Sedlacek, G., Zafiris Tzannatos, P. (Eds.), Child Labor and Education in Latin America. Inter-American Development Bank, Washington, DC. In press.

Edmonds, E.V., Mammen, K., Miller, D.L. (2005). "Rearranging the family? Household composition responses to large pension receipts". Journal of Human Resources 40, 186–207.

Emerson, P.M., Souza, A.P. (2006). "Is child labor harmful? The impact of starting to work as a child on adult earnings". University of Colorado at Denver. Processed.

Fafchamps, M., Quisumbing, A. (1999). "Human capital, productivity, and labor allocation in rural Pakistan". Journal of Human Resources 34, 369–406.

Fares, J., Montenegro, C.E., Orazem, P.F. (2007). Variations in the Returns to Schooling Across and Within Developing Economies. The World Bank. Processed.

Filmer, D. (2004). "If you build it, will they come? School availability and school enrollment in 21 poor countries". Working paper 3340. World Bank Policy Research, June.

Folbre, N. (2006). "Measuring care: Gender, empowerment, and the care economy". Journal of Human Development 7 (2), 183–199.

Foster, A.D., Rosenzweig, M.R. (1996). "Technical change and human-capital returns and investments: Evidence from the green revolution". American Economic Review 86 (4), 931–953.

Foster, A.D., Rosenzweig, M.R. (2004). "Agricultural productivity growth, rural economic diversity, and economic reforms: India, 1970–2000". Economic Development and Cultural Change 52, 509–542.

Frankenberg, E., Smith, J.P., Thomas, D. (2003). "Economic shocks, wealth and welfare". Journal of Human Resources 38 (2), 280–321.

Friedman, M. (1957). A Theory of the Consumption Function. Princeton Univ. Press, Princeton, NJ.

Funkhouser, E. (1999). "Cyclical economic conditions and school attendance in Costa Rica". Economics of Education Review 18, 31–50.

Gertler, P., Glewwe, P. (1990). "The willingness to pay for education in developing countries: Evidence from rural Peru". Journal of Public Economics 42, 251–275.

Glewwe, P. (2002). "Schools and skills in developing countries: Education policies and socioeconomic outcomes". Journal of Economic Literature 40 (2), 436–483.

Glewwe, P., Hall, G. (1998). "Are some groups more vulnerable to macroeconomic shocks than others? Hypothesis tests based on panel data from Peru". Journal of Development Economics 56, 181–206.

Glewwe, P., Jacoby, H. (1995). "An economic analysis of delayed primary school enrollment in a low income country: The role of early childhood nutrition". Review of Economics and Statistics 77, 156–169.

Glewwe, P., Jacoby, H. (2004). "Economic growth and the demand for education: Is there a wealth effect?" Journal of Development Economics 74 (1), 33–51.

Glewwe, P., Jacoby, H., King, E. (2001). "Early childhood nutrition and academic achievement: A longitudinal analysis". Journal of Public Economics 81 (3), 345–368.

Glewwe, P., King, E.M. (2001). "The impact of early childhood nutritional status on cognitive development: Does the timing of malnutrition matter?". World Bank Economic Review 15 (1), 81–113.

Glewwe, P., Kremer, M., Moulin, S. (2003). "Textbooks and test scores: Evidence from a randomized evaluation in Kenya". Development Research Group. World Bank, Washington, DC.

Glewwe, P., Kremer, M., Moulin, S., Zitzewitz, E. (2004). "Retrospective vs. prospective analyses of school inputs: The case of flip charts in Kenya". Journal of Development Economics 74, 251–268.

Glick, P., Sahn, D.E. (2000). "Schooling of girls and boys in a West African country: The effects of parental education, income, and household structure". Economics of Education Review 19 (1), 63–87.

Glick, P., Sahn, D.E. (2006). "The demand for primary schooling in Madagascar: Price, quality, and the choice between public and private providers". Journal of Development Economics 79 (1), 118–145.

Godoy, R., Karlan, D.S., Rabindran, S., Huanca, T. (2005). "Do modern forms of human capital matter in primitive economies? Comparative evidence from Bolivia". Economics of Education Review 24, 45–53.

Grantham-McGregor, S.M., Walker, S.P., Chang, S.M., Powell, C.A. (1997). "Effects of early childhood supplementation with and without stimulation on later development in stunted Jamaican children". American Journal of Clinical Nutrition 66, 247–253.

Gunnarsson, V., Orazem, P.F., Sanchez, M.A. (2006). "Child labor and school achievement in Latin America". World Bank Economic Review 20, 31–54.

Handa, S. (2002). "Raising primary school enrollment in developing countries: The relative importance of supply and demand". Journal of Development Economics 69, 103–128.

Hanushek, E.A. (1997). "Assessing the effects of school resources on student performance: An update". Education Evaluation and Policy Analysis 19, 141–164.

Hanushek, E.A., Luque, J.A. (2003). "Efficiency and equity in schools around the world". Economics of Education Review 22, 481–502.

Haveman, R., Wolfe, B. (1995). "The determinants of children's attainments: A review of methods and findings". Journal of Economic Literature 23, 1829–1878.

Heckman, J.J., La Londe, R.J., Smith, J.A. (1999). "The economics and econometrics of active labor market programs". In: Ashenfelter, O., Card, D. (Eds.), Handbook of Labor Economics, vol. 3. Elsevier, Amsterdam.

Heckman, J.J., Rubinstein, Y. (2001). "The importance of noncognitive skills: Lessons from the GED testing program". American Economic Review 91 (2), 145–149.

Hersch, J., Stratton, L.S. (1997). "Housework, fixed effects, and wages of married workers". Journal of Human Resources 32 (2), 285–307.

Holmes, J. (2003). "Measuring the determinants of school completion in Pakistan: Analysis of censoring and selection bias". Economics of Education Review 22, 249–264.

Hoxby, C.M. (2003). "School choice and school competition: Evidence from the United States". Swedish Economic Policy Review 10, 13–67.

Hsieh, C., Urquiola, M. (2006). "The effects of generalized school choice on achievement and stratification: Evidence from Chile's school voucher program". Journal of Public Economics 90, 1477–1503.

Huffman, W.E. (1977). "Allocative efficiency: The role of human capital". Quarterly Journal of Economics 91, 59–79.

Huffman, W.E., Orazem, P.F. (2006). "Agriculture and human capital in economic growth: Farmers, schooling and health". In: Evenson, R.E., Schultz, T.P., Pingali, P. (Eds.), Handbook of Agricultural Economics, vol. 3. North-Holland, Amsterdam.

Jacoby, H.G. (1993). "Shadow wages and peasant family labor supply: An econometric application to the Peruvian Sierra". Review of Economic Studies 60, 903–921.

Jacoby, H.G., Skoufias, E. (1997). "Risk, financial markets, and human capital in a developing country". Review of Economic Studies 64, 311–335.

Jacoby, H.G., Skoufias, E. (1998). "Testing theories of consumption behavior using information on aggregate shocks: Income seasonality and rainfall in rural India". American Journal of Agricultural Economics 80, 1–14.

Jalan, J., Glinskaya, E. (2003). "Improving primary school education in India: An impact assessment of DPEP-phase I". Indian Statistical Institute (New Delhi) and The World Bank. Processed.

James, E. (1993). "Why do different countries choose a different public-private mix of educational services?" Journal of Human Resources 28, 571–592.

Jimenez, E., Sawada, Y. (2001). "Public for private: The relationship between public and private school enrollment in the Philippines". Economics of Education Review 20, 389–399.

Jolliffe, D. (1998). "Skills, schooling, and household income in Ghana". World Bank Economic Review 12 (1), 81–104.

Joshi, S., Schultz, T.P. (2005). "Family planning as an investment in female human capital: Evaluating the long term consequences in Matlab, Bangladesh". Yale University. Processed.

Karoly, L.A., Greenwood, P.W., Everingham, S.S., Hoube, J., Kilburn, M.R, Rydell, C.P., Sanders, M., Chiesa, J. (1998). Investing in Our Children: What We Know and Don't Know About the Costs and Benefits of Early Childhood Interventions. RAND Corporation, Santa Monica, CA.

Kim, J., Alderman, H., Orazem, P.F. (1999). "Can private school subsidies increase enrollment for the poor? The Quetta urban fellowship program". World Bank Economic Review 13, 443–465.

King, E.M., Lillard, L.A. (1987). "Education policy and schooling attainment in Malaysia and the Philippines". Economics of Education Review 6 (2), 167–181.

King, E.M., Mason, A.D. (2001). Engendering Development through Gender Equality in Rights, Resources and Voice. Oxford Univ. Press, New York.

King, E.M., Orazem, P.F., Paterno, E.M. (2002). "Promotion with and without learning: Effects on student dropout". Iowa State University. Processed.

King, E.M., Orazem, P.F., Wohlgemuth, D. (1999). "Central mandates and local incentives: The Colombia education voucher program". World Bank Economic Review 13, 467–491.

Kochar, A. (2004). "Urban influences on rural schooling in India". Journal of Development Economics 74, 113–136.

Krueger, A.B., Lindahl, M. (2001). "Education for growth: Why and for whom?". Journal of Economic Literature 39, 1101–1136.

Langemeier, M.R., Patrick, G.F. (1990). "Farmers' marginal propensity to consume: An application to Illinois grain farms". American Journal of Agricultural Economics 72, 309–316.

Langemeier, M.R., Patrick, G.F. (1993). "Farm consumption and liquidity constraints". American Journal of Agricultural Economics 75, 479–484.

Lavy, V. (1996). "School supply constraints and children's educational outcomes in rural Ghana". Journal of Development Economics 51, 291–314.

Lillard, L.A., King, E.M. (1984). "Methods for analyzing schooling choice with household survey data". Report N-1963-AID. The RAND Corporation, Santa Monica, CA.

Lillard, L.A., Willis, R.J. (1994). "Intergenerational educational mobility: Effects of family and state in Malaysia". Journal of Human Resources 29 (4), 1126–1166.

Lozoff, B., Jimenez, E., Hagen, J., Mollen, E., Wolf, A.W. (2000). "Treatment for iron deficiency in infancy poorer behavioral and developmental outcome more than 10 years after". Pediatrics 105 (4), 51–62.

MaCurdy, T.E. (1985). "Interpreting empirical models of labor supply in an intertemporal framework with uncertainty". In: Heckman, J., Singer, B. (Eds.), Longitudinal Analysis of Labor Market Data. Cambridge Univ. Press, Cambridge.

Maliki, O. (2005). "Education policy and intergenerational transfers in Indonesia". PhD dissertation. University of Hawaii, Unpublished.

Martinelli, C., Parker, S.W. (2003). "Should transfers to poor families be conditional on school attendance". International Economic Review 44 (2), 523–544.

Martorell, R. (1999). "The nature of child malnutrition and its long-term implications". Food and Nutrition Bulletin 20 (3), 288–292.

McEwan, P.J. (2001). "The effectiveness of public, catholic, and non-religious private schools in Chile's voucher system". Education Economics 9 (2), 103–128.

Miguel, E., Kremer, M. (2004). "Worms: Identifying impacts on education and health in the presence of treatment externalities". Econometrica 72 (1), 159–217.

Mincer, J. (1974). Schooling, Experience and Earnings. Columbia Univ. Press, New York.

Mizala, A., Romaguera, P. (2000). "School performance and choice: The Chilean experience". Journal of Human Resources 35 (2), 392–417.

Moffitt, R. (1996). "Symposium on school quality and educational outcomes". Review of Economics and Statistics 78, 559–561.

Munshi, K., Rosenzweig, M. (2006). "Traditional institutions meet the modern world: Caste, gender, and schooling choice in a globalizing economy". American Economic Review 96 (4), 1225–1252.

Neri, M.C., Gustafsson-Wright, E., Sedlacek, G., Orazem, P.F. (2006). "The responses of child labor, school enrollment, and grade repetition to the loss of parental earnings in Brazil, 1982–1999". In: Orazem, P.F., Sedlacek, G., Zafiris Tzannatos, P. (Eds.), Child Labor and Education in Latin America. Inter-American Development Bank, Washington, DC. In press.

Orazem, P.F. (1987). "Black–white difference in schooling investment and human capital production in segregated schools". American Economic Review 77, 714–723.

Parente, S.L., Rogerson, R., Wright, R. (2000). "Homework in development economics: Household production and the wealth of nations". Journal of Political Economy 108, 680–687.

Patrinos, H.A., Psacharopoulos, G. (1997). "Family size, schooling and child labor in Peru – An empirical analysis". Journal of Population Economics 10, 387–405.

Paxson, C.H. (1992). "Using weather variability to estimate the response of savings to transitory income in Thailand". American Economic Review 82, 15–33.

Paxson, C.H. (1993). "Consumption and income seasonality in Thailand". Journal of Political Economy 99, 39–72.

Plug, E., Vijverberg, W. (2003). "Schooling, family background, and adoption: Is it nature or is it nurture?" Journal of Political Economy 111, 611–641.

Pollitt, E. (2000). "Developmental sequel from early nutritional deficiencies: Conclusive and probability judgments". Journal of Nutrition 130 (2), 350S–353S.

Quisumbing, A.R., Maluccio, J.A. (2000). "Intrahousehold allocation and gender relations: New empirical evidence from four developing countries". Discussion paper No. 84. International Food Policy Research Institute, FCND (April).

Ravallion, M., Wodon, Q. (2000). "Does child labor displace schooling? Evidence on behavioral responses to an enrollment subsidy". Economic Journal 110, 158–175.

Reid, M.G. (1952). "Effect of income concept upon expenditure curves of farm families". In: Studies in Income and Wealth, vol. 15. National Bureau of Economic Research, New York.

Rosati, F.C., Rossi, M. (2003). "Children's working hours and school enrollment: Evidence from Pakistan and Nicaragua". World Bank Economic Review 17, 283–295.

Rosen, S. (1977). "Human capital: A survey of empirical research". In: Ehrenberg, R.G. (Ed.), Research in Labor Economics, vol. I. JAI Press, Greenwich, CT.

Rosenzweig, M.R. (1980). "Neoclassical theory and the optimizing peasant: An econometric analysis of market family labor supply in a developing country". Quarterly Journal of Economics 94, 31–55.

Rosenzweig, M.R., Wolpin, K.I. (1986). "Evaluating the effects of optimally distributed public programs: Child health and family planning interventions". American Economic Review 76, 470–482.

Rosenzweig, M.R., Wolpin, K.I. (1988). "Migration selectivity and the effects of public programs". Journal of Public Economics 37, 265–289.

Schulz, T.P. (1988). "Education investments and returns". In: Chenery, H., Srinivasan, T.N. (Eds.), Handbook of Development Economics, vol. 1. North-Holland, Amsterdam.

Schultz, T.P. (2001). "Women's roles in the agricultural household: Bargaining and human capital investments". In: Gardner, B.L., Rausser, G.C. (Eds.), Handbook of Agricultural Economics. North-Holland, Amsterdam.

Schultz, T.P. (2002). "Why governments should invest more to educate girls". World Development 30, 207–225.

Schultz, T.P. (2004). "School subsidies for the poor: Evaluating the Mexican Progresa poverty program". Journal of Development Economics 74, 199–250.

Schultz, T.W. (1964). Transforming Traditional Agriculture. Yale Univ. Press, New Haven, CT.

Schultz, T.W. (1975). "The value of the ability to deal with disequilibria". Journal of Economic Literature 13, 827–846.

Singh, I., Squire, L., Strauss, J. (Eds.) (1986). Agricultural household models. The Johns Hopkins Univ. Press, Baltimore, MD.

Smeeding, T., Weinberg, D. (2001). "Toward a uniform definition of household income". Review of Income and Wealth 47, 1–24.

Solon, G.R. (2002). "Cross-country differences in intergenerational earnings mobility". Journal of Economic Perspectives 16, 59–66.

Strauss, J., Thomas, D. (1995). "Human resources: Empirical modeling of household and family decisions". In: Srinivasan, T.N., Behrman, J.R. (Eds.), Handbook of Development Economics, vol. 3A. North-Holland, Amsterdam, pp. 1883–2023.

Strauss, J., Thomas, D. (1998). "Health, nutrition, and economic development". Journal of Economic Literature 36 (June), 436–482.

Tansel, A. (1997). "Schooling attainment, parental education, and gender in Cote d'Ivoire and Ghana". Economic Development and Cultural Change 45 (4), 825–856.

Tansel, A. (2002). "Determinants of school attainment of boys and girls in Turkey: Individual, household and community factors". Economics of Education Review 21, 455–470.

Thomas, D., Strauss, J. (1992). "Prices, infrastructure, household characteristics and child height". Journal of Development Economics 39 (2), 301–331.

Thomas, D., Beegle, K., Frankenberg, E., Sikoki, B., Strauss, J., Teruel, G. (2004). "Education in a crisis". Journal of Development Economics 74, 53–85.

Todd, P., Wolpin, K.I. (2003). "On the specification and estimation of the production function for cognitive achievement". Economic Journal 113 (1), F3–F33.

Todd, P., Wolpin, K.I. (2006). "Assessing the impact of a school subsidy program in Mexico: Using a social experiment to validate a dynamic behavioral model of child schooling and fertility". American Economic Review 96 (5), 1384–1417.

Tyler, J.H. (2003). "Using state child labor laws to identify the effect of school-to-work on high school achievement". Journal of Labor Economics 21, 381–408.

Welch, F. (1970). "Education in production". Journal of Political Economy 78, 35–59.

Wolpin, K.I. (1982). "A new test of the permanent income hypothesis: The impact of weather on the income and consumption of farm households in India". International Economic Review 23, 583–594.

Wooldridge, J.M. (2002). Econometric Analyses of Cross Section and Panel Data. The MIT Press, Cambridge, MA.

Yang, D. (1997). "Education and off-farm work". Economic Development and Cultural Change 45, 613–632.

Yap, Y.-T., Orazem, P.F., Sedlacek, G. (2006). "Limiting child labor through behavior-based income transfers: An experimental evaluation of the PETI program in rural Brazil". In: Orazem, P.F., Sedlacek, G., Zafiris Tzannatos, P. (Eds.), Child Labor and Education in Latin America. Inter-American Development Bank, Washington, DC. In press.

Zimmerman, F.J. (2003). "Cinderella goes to school". Journal of Human Resources 38, 557–591.

Chapter 56

THE IMPACT OF CHILD HEALTH AND NUTRITION ON EDUCATION IN LESS DEVELOPED COUNTRIES*

PAUL GLEWWE

Department of Applied Economics, University of Minnesota, 337A Classroom Office Building, 1994 Buford Avenue, St. Paul, MN 55108, USA

EDWARD A. MIGUEL

Department of Economics, University of California, Berkeley, 549 Evans Hall # 3880, Berkeley, CA 94720-3880, USA

Contents

* We would like to thank Gustavo Bobonis, Mark Rosenzweig, John Strauss and T. Paul Schultz for comments on earlier versions of this chapter.

Handbook of Development Economics, Volume 4
DOI: 10.1016/S1573-4471(07)04056-9

Abstract

Hundreds of millions of children in less developed countries suffer from poor health and nutrition. Children in most less developed countries also complete far fewer years of schooling, and learn less per year of schooling, than do children in developed countries. Recent research has shown that poor health and nutrition among children reduces their time in school and their learning during that time. This implies that programs or policies that increase children's health status could also improve their education outcomes. Given the importance of education for economic development, this link could be a key mechanism to improve the quality of life in less developed countries. Many researchers have attempted to estimate the impact of child health on education outcomes, but there are formidable obstacles to obtaining credible estimates. Data are often scarce, although much less scarce than in previous decades. Even more importantly, there are many possible sources of bias when attempting to estimate relationships between child health and education. This Chapter provides an overview of what has been learned thus far. Although significant progress has been made, much more research is still needed – especially in estimating the long term impact of child health status on living standards. The chapter first reviews some basic facts about child health and education in less developed countries. It then provides a framework for analyzing the impact of health and nutrition on education, describes estimation problems and potential solutions, and summarizes recent empirical evidence, including both non-experimental and experimental studies. It concludes with suggestions for future research directions.

Keywords

child health, child nutrition, education, human capital

JEL classification: I12, I21, O12, O15

1. Introduction

Many children in less developed countries suffer from poor health and nutrition. The United Nations estimates that one third of preschool age children in less developed countries – a total of 180 million children under age 5 – experience growth stunting relative to international norms (United Nations, 2000), while hundreds of millions more suffer from tropical diseases, including malaria and intestinal parasites (WHO, 2000). To the extent that poor health and nutrition among children has a negative impact on their education, programs or policies that increase children's health status will also improve their education outcomes. Given the importance of education for economic development (World Bank, 2001), this link could be a key mechanism to improve the quality of life for people in less developed countries.

Many researchers have attempted to estimate the impact of child health on education outcomes, but there are formidable obstacles to obtaining credible estimates. Data are often scarce (although they are much less scarce than in previous decades), but even more importantly there are many possible sources of bias when attempting to estimate relationships between child health and education. This paper provides an overview of what has been learned thus far, building on earlier reviews in Behrman (1996) and Glewwe (2005). Although significant progress has been made, much more research is still needed – especially in estimating the long term impact of child health status on living standards.

It is also important to mention at the outset what this chapter does not aim to do. It does not survey the extensive literature on the effects of child birth weight, or other dimensions of intrauterine nutrition and health, on later life outcomes. While many estimation issues are common across these two literatures, the existing birth weight literature focuses almost exclusively on US or other OECD country data, and we thus leave a review of that literature to another forum. For recent work in this area, see Behrman and Rosenzweig (2004) and Almond, Chay, and Lee (2006). Finally, the chapter does not provide a general discussion of education in developing countries; two recent and very thorough general discussions are Glewwe and Kremer (2006) and Orazem and King (2008, in this book).

The following sections of this chapter first review some basic facts about child health and education in less developed countries, then provide a framework for analyzing the impact of health and nutrition on education, describe estimation problems and potential solutions, summarize recent empirical evidence, and, finally, make suggestions for future research directions.

2. Some basic facts on health, nutrition and education in less developed countries

Children in less developed countries usually have worse health and education outcomes than children in wealthy countries. This reflects the lower incomes of households in these countries, as well as lower quality and less accessible health and education services (relative to wealthy countries). This section sets the stage for the rest of the chapter by presenting some basic patterns on the health, nutrition and education outcomes of children in less developed countries.

2.1. Health and nutrition

Data on child health and nutrition that are comparable across a wide number of less developed countries are somewhat scarce. The most common data are on nutritional status (based on height and weight) and on mortality. Table 1 provides information on malnutrition (specifically low weight for age) and child mortality. Around the year 2000 (the exact date varies by country), about 27% of children in less developed countries were underweight in the sense that their weight was more than two standard deviations below the median weight of a population of healthy children of the same age. This figure varies widely by region within the less developed world, ranging from 9% in Latin America to 48% in South Asia (note that no figure is available for Sub-Saharan Africa because data are missing for many of the countries in that region). The consensus is that this poor performance in child growth reflects two main factors: inadequate intake of food and repeated episodes of diarrhea.

The mortality figures in Table 1 are sobering. In 1990, 10.3% of children born in less developed countries died before they reached the age of five. There is only modest improvement in this figure by 2003; under-five mortality had dropped to 8.7%. There is also wide variation in child mortality across regions. In Latin America the 2003 figure was relatively low at only 3.3%, while it was 9.2% in South Asia and a staggering 17.1% in Sub-Saharan Africa, a figure that is almost unchanged since 1990.

There are many different causes of child morbidity and mortality in less developed countries. A recent study by the World Bank (Lopez et al., 2006) presents estimates of the overall "burden of disease" in terms of "disability adjusted life years", which ac-

Table 1
Child health and nutrition in developing countries

Region	Underweight (%) (children < 5 years) 1995–2003	Under-five mortality rate (per 1000) 1990	Under-five mortality rate (per 1000) 2003
East Asia and Pacific	15	59	41
Latin America	9	53	33
Middle East/N. Africa	15	77	53
South Asia	48	130	92
Sub-Saharan Africa	–	187	171
All developing countries	27	103	87

Source: World Bank (2005).

Table 2
Estimated burden of disease for children in developing countries, 2001 (all data in percents)

	All less developed countries	East Asia and Pacific	Latin America and Caribbean	Middle East and North Africa	South Asia	Sub-Saharan Africa
Children Age 0–4 Years						
Communicable diseases, of which:	52.4	30.8	23.6	35.1	48.7	72.6
AIDS	2.5	0.3	0.8	0.1	0.3	6.0
Diarrhea	12.6	10.8	8.0	11.1	14.5	12.8
Pertussis	2.7	0.9	1.5	1.5	2.7	3.8
Measles	4.0	2.1	0.0	1.4	3.1	6.6
Tetanus	1.3	0.7	0.1	0.5	1.8	1.6
Malaria	8.5	1.4	0.3	2.7	1.3	20.2
Respiratory infections	14.8	10.5	7.5	7.5	18.7	14.7
Perinatal	21.1	28.8	26.7	19.8	26.3	12.4
Nutrition problems	4.4	4.5	3.7	5.8	4.3	4.1
Noncommunicable illnesses	18.6	30.3	41.8	33.4	17.3	8.4
Injuries	3.6	5.5	4.1	5.9	3.3	2.5
Percent of healthy years lost	**15.1**	**8.4**	**8.6**	**11.3**	**16.8**	**28.6**
Children Age 5–14 Years						
Communicable diseases, of which:	36.9	23.0	16.6	15.0	38.2	56.4
Tuberculosis	1.5	1.4	0.7	0.5	1.7	1.9
AIDS	3.7	0.1	1.4	0.0	0.4	11.3
Diarrhea	1.6	2.1	3.7	1.7	1.2	1.2
Measles	6.5	4.7	0.0	2.9	6.5	10.4
Tetanus	1.3	0.8	0.0	0.2	2.0	1.4
Malaria	1.2	0.5	0.3	0.8	0.9	2.3
Intestinal helminths	2.7	3.3	1.7	1.7	1.5	4.4
Respiratory infections	6.6	5.6	4.2	4.1	6.0	9.1
Nutrition problems	4.1	4.9	2.1	7.1	4.4	2.8
Noncommunicable illnesses	30.3	38.4	58.4	40.9	29.1	15.5
Injuries	28.5	33.6	22.6	36.7	28.1	25.0
Percent of healthy years lost	**0.8**	**0.5**	**0.5**	**0.6**	**0.9**	**1.4**

Source: Lopez et al. (2006, Table 3C).

counts for both illnesses and premature mortality, under a set of assumptions about the relative burden of different diseases. This information is given in Table 2, by region and separately for both young (0–4 years) and older (5–14 years) children. Among children aged 0–4 in less developed countries, about 15% of total "healthy years of life" are lost either due to mortality or to morbidity. About one half of this overall burden of disease is due to communicable diseases, the most prominent of which are (in descending order of importance) respiratory infections, diarrhea, malaria and measles (the last of which is easily prevented by vaccination). About one fifth of the burden of disease for children aged 0 to 4 is from perinatal problems (primarily low birthweight and difficulties during childbirth). Another one fifth reflects non-communicable diseases, which include mental retardation, congenital abnormalities and problems with internal organs. Nutrition problems (other than diarrhea) and injuries (primarily accidents) each account for about 4% of the burden of disease.

The burden of disease for children in the first five years of life shows substantial variation across geographic regions. In East Asia, Latin America and the Middle East, which primarily consist of middle income countries, only about one third (one fourth in the case of Latin America) of the burden of disease is due to communicable diseases, and the percent of healthy years of life lost is about 10%, while in the low income countries of South Asia and Sub-Saharan Africa the burden of disease due to communicable diseases is about one half and three fourths, and the percent of health years lost is 17% and 29%, respectively. AIDS and malaria play only a very small role in all regions expect Sub-Saharan Africa, where the combined impact of these two disease accounts for about one fourth of the burden of disease for young children. Finally, three diseases for which children can easily be vaccinated against (pertussis, measles and tetanus) contribute little to the burden of disease in the three regions dominated by middle income countries, while they account for about 8% of the burden of disease in South Asia and about 12% in Sub-Saharan Africa.

The burden of disease is somewhat different for children aged 5–14. First, in all regions only about 1 percent of healthy years of life are lost; in each region this percentage is about one twentieth of the respective figures for children aged 0–4. This suggests that illnesses of preschool age children that have permanent effects on children's mental development may have much stronger effects on education outcomes than illnesses children experience with they are of school age. Second, only about one third (37%) of the burden of disease is due to communicable diseases, of which respiratory infections and measles are the most prominent. Another one third (30%) is due to non-communicable diseases, and a little less than one third (29%) is due to injuries (again mainly accidents). Again, only about 4% of the burden of disease is due to nutritional problems.

As with younger children, there is wide variation in the burden of disease across geographic regions. In South Asia and Sub-Saharan Africa, which primarily consist of low income countries, communicable diseases contribute more to the overall burden of disease (38 and 56%, respectively). AIDS again plays a big role in Sub-Saharan Africa but a very small role elsewhere, and the role of measles and respiratory infections varies widely.

2.2. Education

Poor health may reduce learning for a variety of reasons, including fewer years enrolled, lower daily attendance, and less efficient learning per day spent in school. This subsection examines recent trends in enrollment and recent data on learning.

School enrollment rates have increased dramatically in almost all less developed countries since 1960 (the earliest year with reliable data), but there is still room for

Table 3
Primary school gross enrollment rates (percent of students of primary school age)

Area	1960	1970	1980	1990	2000
Country group					
Low-income	65	77	94	102	102
Middle-income	83	103	101	103	110
High-income	109	100	101	102	102
Region					
Sub-Saharan Africa	40	51	80	74	77
Middle East/North Africa	59	79	89	96	97
Latin America	91	107	105	106	127
South Asia	41	71	77	90	98
East Asia	87	90	111	120	111
East Europe/Former Soviet Union (FSU)	103	104	100	98	100
OECD[a]	109	100	102	103	102

Note. Countries with populations of less than 1 million are excluded.
Sources: Barro and Lee data set; UNESCO (2002); World Bank (2003).
[a]Organization for Economic Cooperation and Development.

improvement. The most widely available indicator of progress in education is the *gross enrollment rate*, the number of children enrolled in a particular level of education, regardless of age, as a percentage of the population in the age range associated with that level. The age range for primary school is usually 6 to 11 years. In 1960, primary school gross enrollment rate were 65% in low-income countries, 83% in middle-income countries, and over 100% in high-income countries, as seen in Table 3.[1] By 2000, enrollment rates had reached or exceeded 100% in both low and middle income countries, and in all regions except Sub-Saharan Africa, where gross enrollment rate peaked at 80% in 1980 and has declined slightly since, a troubling pattern for the world's poorest region.

Gross enrollment rates above 100% do *not* imply that all school-age children are in school. Both overreporting and grade repetition can cause reported gross enrollment rates to reach or exceed 100% even when some children never enroll in school. An alternative measure of progress toward universal primary education is *net enrollment rates*, the number of children enrolled in a particular level of schooling who are of the age associated with that level of schooling, divided by all children of the age associated with that level of schooling. Net enrollment rates can never exceed 100 percent, and they remove the upward bias in gross enrollment rates caused by the enrollment of "overage" children in a given level (due to repetition or delayed enrollment). They do

---

[1] This classification of countries is defined by per capita income in 1960. *Low-income countries* are those with a per capita income below $200 per year, *middle-income countries* are those with an income between $200 and $450, and *high-income countries* are those with an income greater than $450. These cut-off points, while arbitrary, yield about the same number of countries in each group.

Table 4
Primary school enrollment, repetition, and grade 4 survival rates (percents)

Areas	Gross enrollment 2000	Net enrollment 2000	Repetition 2000	On-time enrollment 2000
Country group				
Low-income	102	85	4	55
Middle-income	110	88	10	61
High-income	102	95	2[a]	73[b]
Region				
Sub-Saharan Africa	77	56	13	30
Middle East/North Africa	97	84	8	64
Latin America	127	97	12	74
South Asia	98	83	5	–
East Asia	111	93	2	56
East Europe/FSU	100	88	1	67[a]
OECD	102	97	2[a]	91[a]

Notes: Countries with populations of less than 1 million are excluded.
Source: UNESCO (2003).
[a]Data are based on between 25–50% of the total population of the country group or region.
[b]Idem, 10–25%.

not, however, address overreporting in official data. Table 4 shows that net enrollment rates are much lower than gross enrollment rates for low- and middle-income countries, and net enrollment rates for Sub-Saharan Africa are particularly low at only 56%.

Over the past 40 years, enrollment has increased dramatically at both the primary and secondary levels, as seen in Tables 3 and 5. However, progress in secondary enrollment has slowed in the past two decades. In both low- and middle-income countries the secondary gross enrollment rate increased by about 150% from 1960 to 1980, while the increase from 1980 to 2000 was 59% in low-income countries and about 51% in middle-income countries. Another way to see this is to note that from 1970 to 1980 middle-income countries increased their secondary enrollment ratio from 33 to 51% in only one decade, while low-income countries took 20 years (1980 to 2000) to increase from 34 to 54%. Middle-income countries' progress slowed down sharply in the 1980s, increasing by only eight percentage points (51 to 59%) in that decade, although the increase was stronger in the 1990s (from 59 to 77%).

Trends in secondary gross enrollment rates from 1960 to 2000 differ substantially by region. The secondary school rates in South Asia, Latin America and the Middle East and North Africa were similar in 1960 (10, 14, and 13%, respectively), but by 2000 the rate in Latin America (86%) was much higher than in South Asia (47%) and the Middle East and North Africa (66%). Sub-Saharan Africa's performance over time has been slower than that of other regions. A final interesting comparison is between Latin

Table 5
Secondary school gross enrollment rates (percent of students of secondary school age)

Area	1960	1970	1980	1990	2000
Country group					
Low-income	14	21	34	41	54
Middle-income	21	33	51	59	77
High-income	63	74	87	92	101
Region					
Sub-Saharan Africa	5	6	15	23	27
Middle East/North Africa	13	25	42	56	66
Latin America	14	28	42	49	86
South Asia	10	23	27	39	47
East Asia	20	24	44	48	67
East Europe/FSU	55	64	93	90	88
OECD	65	77	87	95	107

Notes: Countries with populations of less than 1 million are excluded.
Source: Barro and Lee data set; UNESCO (2003); World Bank (2003).

America and East Asia. East Asia had a higher secondary enrollment rate than Latin America in 1960 (20 vs. 14%), but the rates in Latin American countries surged in the 1990s, so that the average rate in 2000 was 86%, compared to 67% in East Asia.

In many countries, there are moderate gender disparities in access to education. Slightly more than half, about 56%, of the 113 million school-aged children not in school are girls (UNESCO, 2002). As shown in Table 6, primary gross enrollment rate in low-income countries is 107% for boys and 98% for girls; this gender gap is somewhat wider at the secondary level, 60% for boys and 47% for girls. In middle-income countries, the primary-school enrollment gap between boys and girls is very small (only 4 percentage points), and in secondary school girls actually have a slightly higher rate than boys. In high-income countries, there is almost no difference in primary enrollment rates, and girls have a slightly higher rate at the secondary level.

Important differences in gender gaps emerge across different regions of the world. In Latin America, East Asia, and Eastern Europe/Former Soviet Union and in the countries in the Organization for Economic Cooperation and Development (OECD), there is almost no gender gap at the primary level, although East Asian countries have a gender gap at the secondary level (Table 6). In contrast, in Sub-Saharan Africa and Middle East/North Africa, gender gaps are sizable at both the primary and secondary levels. The largest gender gaps at both the primary and the secondary levels are in South Asia.

The figures presented thus far have been on the *quantity* of education; however, the *quality* of education in many less developed countries is low in the sense that children learn much less in school than the curriculum states they should learn. This low quality is not entirely surprising because the rapid expansion of primary and secondary education in less developed countries in recent decades has strained those countries' financial

Table 6
Gender disparities in gross primary and secondary enrollment rates, 2000

Area	Primary		Secondary	
	Boys	Girls	Boys	Girls
Country group				
Low-income	107	98	60	47
Middle-income	112	108	77	78
High-income	102	101	100	102
Region				
Sub-Saharan Africa	83	71	29	24
Middle East/North Africa	101	92	71	61
Latin America	129	125	83	89
South Asia	107	90	53	39
East Asia	112	111	73	60
East Europe/FSU	100	99	88	89
OECD	102	102	106	108

Notes: Countries with populations of less than 1 million are excluded.
Source: World Bank (2003).

and human resources. Comparisons of education quality across countries require internationally comparable data on academic performance. Two important sources of such data are the Third International Mathematics and Science Study (TIMSS) and Progress in International Reading Literacy Study (PIRLS) projects administered by the International Association for the Evaluation of Educational Achievement (IAEEA).[2]

The scores of students in grades 7 and 8 on the 1999 TIMSS mathematics test are shown in the first two columns of Table 7. The two developed countries, Japan and the United States, have scores of 579 and 502, respectively. South Korean students scored even higher (587), and Malaysian students also performed very well (519). Scores were generally considerably lower in other less developed countries, ranging from 275 in South Africa to 467 in Thailand. Reading results for grade 4 students in 2001 are shown in the last column of Table 7. All seven of the participating less developed countries (Argentina, Belize, Colombia, Iran, Kuwait, Morocco and Turkey) have much lower performance than the three developed countries shown (France, the United Kingdom, and the United States). Note that this pattern occurs despite any sample selection effects caused by lower school enrollment in less developed countries, which if anything is likely to lead more of the poor performers there to miss the exam, thus partially dampening differences across less developed and wealthy countries.

---

[2] The first and second studies that were precursors to TIMSS were undertaken between 1964 and 1984. The results are not comparable with those of the TIMSS, and very few developing countries were included.

Table 7
Mean mathematics and reading achievement, TIMSS and PIRLS studies

| Country | Mathematics (TIMSS) 1999 | | Reading (PIRLS) 2001 |
	Grade 7	Grade 8	Grade 4
France	–	–	525
Japan	–	579	–
UK (England)	–	–	553
US	–	502	542
Argentina	–	–	420
Belize	–	–	327
Chile	–	392	–
Colombia	–	–	422
Indonesia	–	403	–
Iran	–	422	414
Jordan	–	428	–
Korea (South)	–	587	–
Kuwait	–	–	396
Malaysia	–	519	–
Morocco	337	–	350
Philippines	345	–	–
South Africa	–	275	–
Thailand	–	467	–
Tunisia	–	448	–
Turkey	–	429	449

Source: IAEEA (2000, 2003).

In summary, the health, nutrition and education status of children in less developed countries is much lower than that of their counterparts in developed countries. To formulate policies to improve the status of children in low and middle income countries, a clear understanding of the determinants of health, nutrition and education, and of the impact of health and nutrition on schooling, is needed. The remainder of this chapter assesses what economists and other social scientists have learned in this regard, and provides suggestions for future research.

3. Analytical framework

This section provides an analytical framework for thinking about the relationships between child health, nutrition and education outcomes. The first subsection presents a simple model of the determinants of children's academic achievement that highlights the role of child health. This is followed by a discussion of the relationships in the model that are of greatest interest to policymakers. For a discussion of these issues that incorporates both child and adult health, but does not focus on the impact child health and nutrition on education outcomes, see chapters by Mwabu (2008) and Strauss and Thomas (2008) in this Volume.

3.1. A simple two-period model of child health and schooling outcomes

To demonstrate the issues that arise when attempting to estimate the impact of child health and nutrition status on schooling outcomes, it is useful to begin with a simple model. Assume that there are two time periods. Time period 1 begins with conception and ends when the child is 5–6 years, the time the child is eligible to enroll in primary school. Time period 2 is the years that the child is of primary school age, say from 6 to 11 years old. (Most research on the impact of health and nutrition on school performance has focused on student performance in primary school.) Although dividing a child's life from conception to age 11 into only two time periods is rather simplistic, a two-period model illustrates many key issues that must be addressed when attempting to estimate the impact of child health and nutrition on education outcomes.

A useful starting point is a production function for academic skills, as measured by test scores when the child is of primary school-age (time period 2). These skills can be denoted by T_2. A simple yet very useful specification is the following:

$$T_2 = T_{2,P}(H_1, H_2, EI_1, EI_2, \alpha, SC, YS) \tag{1}$$

where the subscript "P" indicates that this is a production function; H_t is child health in time period t; EI_t is parents' provision of educational inputs (e.g., school supplies, books, education toys, and – perhaps most importantly – time spent by parents with the child that has pedagogical value) in time period t; α is the child's innate intelligence (ability); SC is school (and teacher) characteristics; and YS is years of schooling attained in time period 2. All variables have positive impacts on T_2. For simplicity, school characteristics are assumed not to change over time. Allowing school characteristics ("quality") to vary over time is somewhat more realistic but would complicate the exposition without making any fundamental contribution to understanding the impact of child health on educational outcomes.

The production function in Eq. (1) emphasizes the role of child health in determining academic skills. It shows how – holding constant parental education inputs, school characteristics, child ability, and years of schooling – child health status in both time periods could affect learning. This is a *structural* relationship because all of the variables in the production function *directly* affect academic skills, and all the variables with direct effects are included. As will be seen below, *indirect* effects are also possible, but when discussing any effect it is important to distinguish between direct and indirect effects.

If one had accurate data on all the variables in Eq. (1) one could estimate it using relatively simple methods, such as ordinary least squares, and so obtain unbiased estimates of the direct impacts of all variables, including child health status in both time periods, on child academic skills. To see other relationships that may also be of interest, and to see how these relationships have different data requirements, consider an economic model in which parents maximize the following utility function:

$$U = U(C_1, C_2, H_1, H_2, T_2) \tag{2}$$

where C_t is *parental* consumption of an aggregate consumption good in time period t. Utility is increasing in all variables. For simplicity, this model ignores household utility in later time periods; accounting for later decisions does not change the fundamental insights provided by this model, and in some cases it may be unrealistic to assume that parents make firm plans far into the future. Another simplification is that the amount of leisure consumed is fixed; this implies that actions that use parents' time, such as providing any kind of instruction to their children or taking them to a health care provider, have a price: the wage of the parent whose time is used to carry out those actions.

Utility is maximized subject to a budget constraint, the production function for academic skills shown in Eq. (1) and two production functions for child health:

$$H_1 = H_{1,P}\left(C_1^C, M_1, HE_1, \eta\right), \tag{3}$$

$$H_2 = H_{2,P}\left(H_1; C_2^C, M_2, HE_2, \eta\right) \tag{4}$$

where the subscript "P" indicates that this is a production function; C_t^C is the child's consumption of the aggregate consumption good in period t; M_t is health inputs ("medicine" and "medical treatment"), broadly defined, in time period t; HE_t is the local health environment (incidence of infectious diseases, air and water quality, etc.) in time period t; and η is the innate healthiness of the child. All variables in Eqs. (3) and (4) have positive impacts on child health. Assume that both the local health environment and η are beyond the control of the parents. As in the production function for academic skills, these production function relationships include only variables that *directly* affect child health; variables that have only *indirect* effects, such as prices of health inputs or household wealth, are excluded.

The last constraint faced by parents is the intertemporal budget constraint. Let W_0 be the initial wealth of the household, and assume that it can borrow and lend between the two time periods at an interest rate r. The budget constraint (W_0) is:

$$W_0 = p_{C,1}\left(C_1 + C_1^C\right) + p_{C,2}\left(C_2 + C_2^C\right)/(1+r) + p_{M,1}M_1 + p_{EI}EI_1$$
$$+ \left(p_{M,2}M_2 + p_{EI}EI_2 + p_S YS\right)/(1+r) \tag{5}$$

where $p_{C,t}$ is the price of the consumption good in time period t; $p_{M,t}$ is the price of medicine in time period t (which can include the price of travel time, measured in terms of forgone wages, and thus can reflect distance to health facilities); EI_t is educational inputs purchased by parents in time period t; p_{EI} is the price of educational inputs (which is assumed constant over time); and p_S is the price of a year of schooling in time period 2.

Optimizing the utility in Eq. (2) with respect to the constraints in Eqs. (1), (3), (4) and (5) gives the following standard demand functions for the nine endogenous variables that can be purchased in the market[3]:

$$C_t = C_{t,D}(W_0; r, p_{C,1}, p_{C,2}, p_{M,1}, p_{M,2}, p_{EI}, p_S;$$
$$HE_1, HE_2, SC, PS; \alpha, \eta, \sigma, \tau) \quad t = 1, 2, \qquad \text{(6) and (7)}$$

$$C_t^C = C_{t,D}^C(W_0; r, p_{C,1}, p_{C,2}, p_{M,1}, p_{M,2}, p_{EI}, p_S;$$
$$HE_1, HE_2, SC, PS; \alpha, \eta, \sigma, \tau) \quad t = 1, 2, \qquad \text{(8) and (9)}$$

$$M_t = M_{t,D}(W_0; r, p_{C,1}, p_{C,2}, p_{M,1}, p_{M,2}, p_{EI}, p_S;$$
$$HE_1, HE_2, SC, PS; \alpha, \eta, \sigma, \tau) \quad t = 1, 2, \qquad \text{(10) and (11)}$$

$$EI_t = EI_{t,D}(W_0; r, p_{C,1}, p_{C,2}, p_{M,1}, p_{M,2}, p_{EI}, p_S;$$
$$HE_1, HE_2, SC, PS; \alpha, \eta, \sigma, \tau) \quad t = 1, 2, \qquad \text{(12) and (13)}$$

$$YS = YS_D(W_0; r, p_{C,1}, p_{C,2}, p_{M,1}, p_{M,2}, p_{EI}, p_S;$$
$$HE_1, HE_2, SC, PS; \alpha, \eta, \sigma, \tau) \qquad \text{(14)}$$

where the subscript "D" indicates that these are (standard) demand functions; PS is parents' level of schooling; σ is parental tastes for child education; and τ is parental tastes for child health. Parental schooling is added because parent time used to provide instruction to children is likely to be more effective for educated parents, which lowers the effective price (in terms of forgone wages) of providing that educational input. Parental tastes for education and child health reflect variation in the utility function across parents. Note that all of the variables on the right hand side of these demand functions are exogenous; that is, none of them are under the control of the parents.[4]

Another important relationship is the demand for the child's academic skills. This can be obtained by inserting Eqs. (12), (13), and (14) directly into (1), inserting Eqs. (8) and (10) into (3), then inserting Eqs. (3), (9) and (11) into (4) and finally inserting Eqs. (3) and (4) into (1):

$$T_2 = T_{2,D}(W_0; r, p_{C,1}, p_{C,2}, p_{M,1}, p_{M,2}, p_{EI}, p_S;$$
$$HE_1, HE_2, SC, PS; \alpha, \eta, \sigma, \tau) \qquad \text{(15)}$$

where the subscript "D" indicates that this is a demand equation, and as in the other demand equations all the variables on the right-hand side are exogenous in the sense discussed above.

A final important relationship between child health and educational outcomes is the *conditional demand function* for child academic skills. Suppose that child health in both

---

[3] The term "endogenous" is used here in terms of its meaning in an economic model: endogenous variables are variables that can be influenced by household behavior. Whether these variables are endogenous in an *econometric* sense, that is correlated with the error term in an equation to be estimated, is a separate question, which will be discussed in Section 4.

[4] Whether these variables are exogenous in the econometric sense of being uncorrelated with the error term in an equation to be estimated is a separate question; this is discussed in Section 4.

time periods (i.e. H_1 and H_2) were "fixed" at the utility maximizing levels by "fixing" child consumption and health inputs in both time periods (C_1^C, C_2^C, M_1 and M_2) at the utility maximizing levels (recall that η, HE_1 and HE_2 are exogenously fixed). With the remaining funds (parents are still required to pay for the items that are "fixed"), which can be denoted by W_{CD}, parents will still choose the optimal levels of all the other variables. This gives the following conditional demand function for educational inputs (in both time periods) and years of schooling:

$$EI_1 = EI_{1,CD}(H_1, H_2; W_{CD}, r, p_{C,1}, p_{C,2}, p_{EI}, p_S; SC, PS; \alpha, \eta, \sigma, \tau)$$
$$= EI_{1,CD}(H_1, H_2; W_{CD}, \boldsymbol{\omega}), \tag{16}$$

$$EI_2 = EI_{2,CD}(H_1, H_2; W_{CD}, r, p_{C,1}, p_{C,2}, p_{EI}, p_S; SC, PS; \alpha, \eta, \sigma, \tau)$$
$$= EI_{2,CD}(H_1, H_2; W_{CD}, \boldsymbol{\omega}), \tag{17}$$

$$YS = YS_{CD}(H_1, H_2; W_{CD}, r, p_{C,1}, p_{C,2}, p_{EI}, p_S; SC, PS; \alpha, \eta, \sigma, \tau)$$
$$= YS_{CD}(H_1, H_2; W_{CD}, \boldsymbol{\omega}) \tag{18}$$

where W_{CD}, household "non-health" expenditures, is defined as $W_0 - p_{C,1}C_1^C - p_{M,1}M_1 - (p_{C,2}C_2^C - p_{M,2}M_2)/(1+r)$ and the vector $\boldsymbol{\omega}$ denotes the vector $\{r, p_{C,1}, p_{C,2}, p_{EI}, p_S; SC, PS; \alpha, \eta, \sigma, \tau\}$.[5]

Inserting these conditional demand functions into the production function for academic skills yields the conditional demand function for those skills:

$$T_2 = T_{2,P}(H_1, H_2, EI_1, EI_2, \alpha, SC, YS)$$
$$= T_{2,P}\big(H_1, H_2, EI_{1,CD}(H_1, H_2; W_{CD}, \boldsymbol{\omega}), EI_{2,CD}(H_1, H_2; W_{CD}, \boldsymbol{\omega}),$$
$$\alpha, SC, YS_{CD}(H_1, H_2; W_{CD}, \boldsymbol{\omega})\big)$$
$$= T_{2,CD}(H_1, H_2; W_{CD}, \boldsymbol{\omega}, \alpha, SC). \tag{19}$$

This equation shows how, when child health in both time periods is fixed at their utility maximizing levels, small changes in those two variables (holding all exogenous variables constant) affect parents' choice of (demand for) T_2. Note that these impacts of child health on academic skills are *not* the same as the impacts of child health on academic skills in the production function given in Eq. (1), because the direct effects measured in Eq. (1) do not allow for behavioral adjustments to EI_1, EI_2 and YS, while Eq. (19) does allow for those adjustments.

Equation (19) can be used to show how small deviations in H_1 or H_2 from their optimal levels will affect the (conditional) demand for academic skills, allowing for behavioral responses by parents. To see how these impacts of child health on academic skills differ from those in Eq. (1), consider the impact of a small increase in H_2 caused

[5] The health environment in both time periods does not belong in the conditional demand functions because their only role is to affect health, which already appears in those functions.

by a "random shock"[6]:

$$
\begin{aligned}
\frac{\partial T_{2,CD}}{\partial H_2} &= \frac{\partial T_P}{\partial H_2} + \frac{\partial T_P}{\partial EI_1}\frac{\partial EI_{1,CD}}{\partial H_2} + \frac{\partial T_P}{\partial EI_2}\frac{\partial EI_{2,CD}}{\partial H_2} + \frac{\partial T_P}{\partial YS}\frac{\partial YS_{CD}}{\partial H_2} \\
&= \frac{\partial T_P}{\partial H_2} + \frac{\partial T_P}{\partial EI_2}\frac{\partial EI_{2,CD}}{\partial H_2} + \frac{\partial T_P}{\partial YS}\frac{\partial YS_{CD}}{\partial H_2}.
\end{aligned}
\tag{20}
$$

There are four distinct impacts of this small exogenous increase in H_2 on academic skills. First, the term $\partial T_P/\partial H_2$ shows that the production function for academic skills will *directly* (and "automatically") transform this increase in child health in time period 2 into an increase in academic skills. The second term shows how an increase in child health in the second time period, *if this increase is known when decisions are made in the first time period*, will lead to a change in the demand for education inputs in the first period. Yet the assumption that the increase in H_2 is due to a "shock" implies that this increase was not anticipated, so it is impossible for parents to go back in time to alter EI_1. Thus the second term equals zero because $\partial E_{1,CD}/\partial H_2$ equals zero.

The third impact works through changes in EI_2, educational inputs in the second time period, caused by a small exogenous increase in child health in that time period (H_2). The sign of this effect is ambiguous because the sign of $\partial EI_{2,CD}/\partial H_2$ is ambiguous, due to complex income and substitution effects. First, the "automatic" increase in T_2 from the increase in H_2, via the production function for academic skills, raises "full" income by expanding the household's consumption possibilities set for C_2 and T_2,[7] which leads to an increase in the demand for T_2 (assuming that T_2 is a normal good). Yet it is possible that the first term in Eq. (20) raises T_2 by more than this income effect alone warrants, in which case the household would cut back on EI_2 (and YS) to reduce T_2 to the desired level induced by this income effect. Indeed, if H_1, H_2 and C_1 are weakly separable from C_2 and T_2 in the parents' utility function, and C_2 and T_2 are normal goods, then parents will shift resources from T_2 to C_2 so that this income effect can be used to increase the consumption of both T_2 and C_2. Thus the (full) income effect of the exogenous increase in H_2 on $EI_{2,CD}$ (and YS) is likely to be negative, but unless some assumptions are made the impact is ambiguous, even though the impact of H_2 on T_2 is clearly positive.

In addition to the (full) income effect, there are price effects from an increase in H_2 on T_2 and EI_2. An increase in H_2 is likely to raise the marginal productivity of EI_2 (and of YS), reducing the shadow price of T_2 and thus increasing its demand, which can be satisfied only by an increase in EI_2 (and in YS). This is an (indirect) own-price effect. There are also (indirect) cross-price effects in that the increase in H_2 will reduce the marginal utility of T_2 if H_2 and T_2 are substitutes in consumption, and thus will reduce the demand for T_2 and consequently the demand for EI_2 and YS. On the other hand,

---

[6] By "random shock" we mean that the change in H_2 occurs without any change in the endogenous inputs in the health production function for H_2 (H_1, C_2^C and M_2), which are still held fixed, and without any change in HE_2 or η. Changes in H_2 or H_1 induced by changes in HE_1, HE_2, C_1, C_2, M_1 or M_2 are discussed below.

[7] The assumption that the change in H_2 is a shock that occurs after the time period 1 is over implies that the choice for C_1 cannot be altered, just as the choice for EI_1 could not be altered.

if H_2 and T_2 are complements in consumption, an increase in H_2 will tend to increase the demand for T_2 (and thus for EI_2 and YS). In general, the own-price effects usually outweigh the cross-price effects, so the overall price effect will probably generate an increase in the demand for EI_2. Yet the (full) income effect on the demand for EI_2 is likely to be negative, therefore the sign of $\partial EI_{2,CD}/\partial H_2$ is also ambiguous, and so the same holds for the sign of the third term in Eq. (20).

The final term in Eq. (20) is the impact of H_2 on T_2 via years of schooling. This impact is identical to that of the impact of H_2 via EI_2. Thus the (full) income effect of an increase in H_2 on YS is ambiguous, although it is likely to be negative. Similarly, the (indirect) own-price effect of an increase in H_2 on YS will be positive, and the sign of the (indirect) cross-price effects will depend on whether H_2 and T_2 are substitutes or compliments in the utility function. While the positive own-price effect is likely to outweigh any negative cross-price effect, so that the overall price effect will be positive, the (full) income effect is likely to be negative, therefore the sign of $\partial YS/\partial H_2$, and thus the overall effect of the fourth term on the demand for T_2, is ambiguous.

A final comment on the third and fourth terms is that the discussion thus far has assumed that the increase in H_2 occurs before most or all of the decisions regarding EI_2 have been made (or at least before the point is reached that past decisions cannot be reversed). Generally speaking, the later in time period 2 that H_2 is exogenously changed, the less scope there is for changing EI_2 and thus third term will become closer to zero. Yet in contrast to EI_2, parents will be able to change YS in response to any unexpected increase in H_2 that occurs before the child leaves school, and even if the shock comes after the child leaves school it may be possible for the child to return to school to increase YS. Thus years of schooling is more arguably flexible in its responses to exogenous changes in H_2 than is educational inputs in the second time period.

To summarize, the impact of an exogenous increase in H_2 on the *conditional demand* for T_2 is positive because it raises full income and it tends to reduce the shadow price for T_2. However, it is unclear whether this impact is larger or smaller than the direct impact through the production function for academic skills (the first term in Eq. (20)), because the income and price effects on the (conditional) demand for EI_2 and YS work in opposite directions; income effects increase the demand for C_2 and thus lead to a reduction in resources for T_2 (i.e. a reduction in EI_2 and YS), while price effects increase the demand for T_2. Therefore the net effect of H_2 on T_2 may be either smaller or larger than the direct effect that works through the production function.

Next, consider what happens to the conditional demand for T_2 from an exogenous "shock" that increases H_1.[8] Differentiating Eq. (19) with respect to H_1 yields a somewhat more complicated expression than that in Eq. (20), but the overall finding is the same. $\partial T_{CD}/\partial H_1$ is equal to the structural effect, $\partial T_p/\partial H_1 + (\partial T_p/\partial H_2)(\partial H_2/\partial H_1)$,

---

[8] As with the change in H_2 discussed above, assume that the change in H_1 is a "shock" that occurs with no change in the purchased or endogenous inputs in the health production function for H_1 or H_2 (C_1^C, M_1, C_2^C and M_2) and without any change in HE_1, HE_2 or η. Thus this change in H_1 and H_2 does not affect W_{CD}.

plus three terms that account for behavioral adjustments that alter EI_1, EI_2 and YS. Income effects suggest that parents will reduce all three of these variables, but price effects create incentives for parents to increase their expenditures on EI_1, EI_2 and YS. As in the case with an increase in H_2, the overall impact of an increase in H_1 on T_2 will be positive, but it is unclear whether this increase in the *conditional* demand for T_2 will be greater or smaller than the (aggregate) structural increase that operates via $\partial T_P/\partial H_1 + (\partial T_P/\partial H_2)(\partial H_{2,P}/\partial H_1)$.

It is also instructive to examine how changes in exogenous variables that are likely to increase child health ultimately affect children's academic skills. The net effect of changes in $p_{M,1}$, $p_{M,2}$, HE_1 and HE_2 (prices for health inputs and the overall health environment) on T_2 is obtained directly by differentiating Eq. (15), yet more can be learned by decomposing these effects to illuminate the pathways by which they take place. Consider first an improvement in the health environment in the second time period, which can be expressed as an increase in HE_2. Note that such a change has no effect on W_{CD}, since it does not enter the budget constraint.

Substituting (8) and (10) into (3), and (3), (9) and (11) into (4), and then (3) and (4) into (1), and finally (12), (13) and (14) into (1) gives a more detailed *unconditional* demand function for academic skills (T_2). Differentiating this expression with respect to HE_2 gives:

$$
\begin{aligned}
\frac{\partial T_{2,D}}{\partial HE_2} &= \frac{\partial T_P}{\partial H_2}\left[\frac{\partial H_{2,P}}{\partial HE_2} + \frac{\partial H_{2,P}}{\partial M_2}\frac{\partial M_{2,D}}{\partial HE_2} + \frac{\partial H_{2,P}}{\partial C_2^C}\frac{\partial C_{2,D}^C}{\partial HE_2}\right.\\
&\quad\left. + \frac{\partial H_{2,P}}{\partial H_1}\left(\frac{\partial H_{1,P}}{\partial M_1}\frac{\partial M_{1,D}}{\partial HE_2} + \frac{\partial H_{1,P}}{\partial C_1^C}\frac{\partial C_{1,D}^C}{\partial HE_2}\right)\right]\\
&\quad + \frac{\partial T_{CD}}{\partial H_1}\left[\frac{\partial H_{1,P}}{\partial M_1}\frac{\partial M_{1,D}}{\partial HE_2} + \frac{\partial H_{1,P}}{\partial C_1^C}\frac{\partial C_{1,D}^C}{\partial HE_2}\right] + \frac{\partial T_P}{\partial EI_1}\frac{\partial EI_{1,D}}{\partial HE_2}\\
&\quad + \frac{\partial T_P}{\partial EI_2}\frac{\partial EI_{2,D}}{\partial HE_2} + \frac{\partial T_P}{\partial YS}\frac{\partial YS_D}{\partial HE_2}\\
&= \frac{\partial T_P}{\partial H_2}\left[\frac{\partial H_{2,P}}{\partial HE_2} + \frac{\partial H_{2,P}}{\partial M_2}\frac{\partial M_{2,D}}{\partial HE_2} + \frac{\partial H_{2,P}}{\partial C_2^C}\frac{\partial C_{2,D}^C}{\partial HE_2}\right]\\
&\quad + \frac{\partial T_P}{\partial EI_2}\frac{\partial EI_{2,D}}{\partial HE_2} + \frac{\partial T_P}{\partial YS}\frac{\partial YS_D}{\partial HE_2}
\end{aligned}
\tag{21}
$$

where the last line indicates that a change in the health environment in time period 2 comes "too late" for parents to reverse decisions made in time period 1 (this is relaxed below). Intuitively, a government policy that changes the health environment changes both H_1 and H_2, but households who are already in time period 2 when the government policy changes cannot change M_1, C_1^C, C_1 or EI_1, so for these households there is only a "short-run" effect of the policy change: H_2 changes but not H_1. A "long-run" effect applies only to households who are still in their first time period when the policy is implemented, or who enter time period 1 after the policy is implemented; for these households both HE_1 and HE_2 change by the same amount, and the long-run impact of that change in the health environment incorporates households' decisions to change M_1, C_1^C, C_1 and EI_1.

Beginning with the short-run effect of an increase in HE_2 on T_2, the positive structural effect via $(\partial T_p/\partial H_2)(\partial H_{2,P}/\partial HE_2)$ raises the consumption possibilities set in time period 2, so in general there will be a positive income effect. Yet this increase in HE_2 could affect the marginal impacts of M_2 and C_2^C on health in time period 2 (H_2). For example, improvements in sanitation may reduce the incidence of diarrhea and thus render anti-diarrheal medicines less effective in improving health in time period 2, which implies that the demand for those medicines will decrease, so $\partial M_{2,D}/\partial HE_2 < 0$. On the other hand, in some settings improvements in sanitation could make some medicines more effective because such improvements could lower the exposure to infectious diseases and thus increase the duration of improved health from an application of such medicines. Yet even if the overall effect of an increase in HE_2 leads to a decrease in purchases of medicine (i.e. $\partial M_{2,D}/\partial HE_2 < 0$), improvements in sanitation may make addition food more effective in raising child health (for instance, if nutrients are better absorbed by children free of diarrheal disease) and thus will increase the demand for C_2^C, so $\partial C_{2,D}^C/\partial HE_2 > 0$. Overall, the sign of the term $(\partial H_{2,P}/\partial M_2)(\partial M_{2,D}/\partial HE_2) + (\partial H_{2,P}/\partial C_2^C)(\partial C_{2,D}^C/\partial HE_2)$ is ambiguous.

Turning to the last two short run terms, those in the fourth line of Eq. (21), the overall effect of HE_2 on the demand for E_2 and YS_D is also ambiguous because, as in the case of an exogenous shock to H_2, the income effects create an incentive to divert resources from producing T_p to increasing of C_2, while price effects (a reduction in the shadow price of T_2) generate an incentive to increase T_p, so the two variables that can be used to modify T_2, EI_2 and YS, could either increase or decrease in response to an exogenous increase in child health in the second time period (H_2). In summary, due to multiple ambiguities it is unclear whether the short-run impact of an increase in HE_2 on the demand for T_p will be larger or smaller than the structural impact measured by $(\partial T_p/\partial H_2)(\partial H_{2,P}/\partial HE_2)$.

Now consider the long-run impact of an improvement in the health environment, which amounts to an increase in HE_1 and HE_2 of the same magnitude. With little loss of generality set HE to be the same in both time periods. The long-run impact of an improvement in the health environment is:

$$
\begin{aligned}
\frac{\partial T_{2,D}}{\partial HE} ={}& \frac{\partial T_P}{\partial H_2}\left[\frac{\partial H_{2,P}}{\partial HE} + \frac{\partial H_{2,P}}{\partial M_2}\frac{\partial M_{2,D}}{\partial HE} + \frac{\partial H_{2,P}}{\partial C_2^C}\frac{\partial C_{2,D}^C}{\partial HE} \right. \\
& \left. + \frac{\partial H_{2,P}}{\partial H_1}\left(\frac{\partial H_{1,P}}{\partial HE} + \frac{\partial H_{1,P}}{\partial M_1}\frac{\partial M_{1,D}}{\partial HE} + \frac{\partial H_{1,P}}{\partial C_1^C}\frac{\partial C_{1,D}^C}{\partial HE} \right)\right] \\
& + \frac{\partial T_{CD}}{\partial H_1}\left[\frac{\partial H_{1,P}}{\partial M_1}\frac{\partial M_{1,D}}{\partial HE} + \frac{\partial H_{1,P}}{\partial C_1^C}\frac{\partial C_{1,D}^C}{\partial HE} \right] + \frac{\partial T_P}{\partial EI_1}\frac{\partial EI_{1,D}}{\partial HE} \\
& + \frac{\partial T_P}{\partial EI_2}\frac{\partial EI_{2,D}}{\partial HE} + \frac{\partial T_P}{\partial YS}\frac{\partial YS_D}{\partial HE}.
\end{aligned}
\tag{22}
$$

The intuition here is that, in the long run, the change in the health environment also allows the household to adjust child health, parental consumption and education inputs in time period 1. The overall income effect implies that the household will want to increase C_1, which may take resources away from actions that would otherwise increase T_2. Moreover, the structural impact of HE on H_1, on H_2 and on T_2 (via $\partial T_{2,P}/\partial H_1$, $\partial T_{2,P}/\partial H_2$ and $(\partial T_{2,P}/\partial H_2)(\partial H_{2,P}/\partial H_1)(\partial H_1/\partial HE)$) implies a larger income effect than in the short-run. The issue is whether reallocation of resources to raise C_1 (and perhaps to raise H_1 beyond the direct effect via $\partial H_1/\partial HE$) lowers T_2 (relative to the short-run impact) more than the structural impact via H_1 raises T_2 (relative to the short-run impact). More precisely, the question is whether the net effect of all the terms in the second and third lines of (22) is positive or negative. Using the same reasoning above for the short-run effect, it is difficult to ascertain the sign of $(\partial H_{1,P}/\partial M_1)(\partial M_{1,D}/\partial HE) + (\partial H_{1,P}/\partial C_1^C)(\partial C_{1,D}^C/\partial HE)$, although clearly the impact of $\partial H_1/\partial HE$ will be positive. Turning to the third line, the impact on T_2 of $(\partial H_{1,P}/\partial M_1)(\partial M_{1,D}/\partial HE) + (\partial H_{1,P}/\partial C_1^C)(\partial C_{1,D}^C/\partial HE)$ is equally ambiguous, as is $\partial E_{1,D}/\partial HE$. Thus in the long run as well as the short run, it is unclear whether a change in the health environment will lead to a change in the demand for T_2 that is greater or smaller than the structural impact, which is $(\partial T_p/H_2)(\partial H_{2,P}/\partial HE)$ in the short run and $(\partial T_p/H_2)[(\partial H_{2,P}/\partial HE) + (\partial H_{2,P}/\partial H_1)(\partial H_{1,P}/\partial HE)]$ in the long run.

Finally, briefly consider the impact of a government policy to decrease the prices for health inputs, via a reduction in $P_{M,2}$ and $P_{M,1}$. There is no structural effect from this change because prices do not enter directly into the production function for child health. As in the case of a change in the health environment, there are short run and long run effects, the former including only a drop in $P_{M,2}$ while the latter includes a drop in both prices. The overall effect of a drop in either price will be an increase in T_2, as long as academic skills are a normal good, because a drop in prices increases the effective budget set of the household and also reduces the shadow price of T_2 by reducing the shadow price of H_1 and/or H_2.

An interesting question is whether a reduction in health input prices in one or both time periods that brings about an improvement in child health equal to an improvement brought about by a change in the health environment in one or both time periods has a larger or smaller impact on T_2. In general, for a given improvement in child health in one or both periods, the increase in child academic skills (T_2) will be higher if the change is induced by a reduction in prices for health inputs. This is the case because the change in the health prices has an income effect that does not occur with a change in the health environment. This can be seen by inspection of the conditional demand relationship in Eq. (19). The increase in health in one or both time periods has identical effects on child academic skills whether it is brought about by a reduction in prices or an improvement in the health environment. Yet recall that $W_{CD} = W_0 - p_{C,1}C_1^C - p_{M,1}M_1 - (p_{C,2}C_2^C - p_{M,2}M_2)/(1 + r)$. W_{CD} will increase if either price of health inputs decreases, but there is no such effect for a change in the health environment. This income effect will unambiguously increase T_2, so the impact of a given improvement in child health on child academic skills varies depending on the type of policy that brought it about.

3.2. Relationships of interest

The previous subsection presented three equations that showed the factors that determine children's academic skills, namely Eqs. (1), (15), and (19). The first is a production function, the second is a standard demand function, and the third is a conditional demand function. Each of these equations depict different processes, and a key question is: Which equation is most useful for making policy decisions? To answer this question, this subsection presents the merits of each of these relationships as guides for policy.

As explained above, Eq. (1) measures the direct (structural) impact of all variables that have direct impacts, including health status in both time periods, on children's academic skills in time period 2. At first glance, this would appear to be precisely what policymakers would like to know. (Whether this equation can be estimated is a separate question, one that will be discussed in the next section.) Yet this relationship *does not necessarily imply* that whenever the government implements a policy that improves a child's health status in one or both of those time periods that the education outcome of that child will increase according to the relationship shown in Eq. (1). Such discrepancies can arise because changes in child health status may lead parents to change their demand for education inputs and years of schooling, as seen in Eqs. (16), (17), and (18). In particular, the expressions for the change in parents' conditional demand for the child's academic skills due to a change in child health in time period 2 (Eq. (20)) or in time period 1 (not shown) reveal that the change in those skills, after accounting for behavioral adjustments, could be greater or less than the structural effects obtained by differentiating Eq. (1) with respect to H_1 or H_2. Thus while Eq. (1) is very informative it does *not* necessarily depict what will happen to children's academic skills if a program or policy increases child health in either time period by a certain amount.[9]

The relationship in Eq. (15) shows how changes in the health environment or in the prices of health inputs (or changes in any other variables in that equation) lead to changes in (the demand for) children's academic skills. Unlike Eq. (1), this equation accounts for *all* changes in behavior that arise in response to changes in the health environment and in prices of health inputs. For policymakers working in health, Eq. (15) is precisely what is needed to assess the impact of health *policies*, as opposed to health *status*, on children's academic skills. It measures the overall effect of any health policy or program on children's education outcomes through all potential channels. Thus one need not estimate Eq. (1) to make policy choices based only on impacts on academic skills if one has already correctly estimated Eq. (15). A final caution when using Eq. (15) to assess the impacts of policy changes is that it is important to distinguish

---

[9] Despite the shortcomings of Eq. (1) in estimating the actual impact of a change in child health on children's academic skills, it may provide better estimates of the overall welfare benefits of an increase in health because it measures the full impact of that change before parents make reallocation decisions. Eqs. (15) and (19) do not capture the welfare benefits of increased parental consumption that comes from these reallocations, but Eq. (1) approximates it by an application of the envelope theorem. See Glewwe et al. (2004) for a more detailed explanation.

between short-run and long-run effects; these could be quite different if child health in the first time period has much stronger structural effects on educational outcomes than child health in the second period, since the short-run effect includes only the impact on health in the second time period while the long-run effect includes the impacts on both time periods.

Finally, consider the conditional demand relationship in Eq. (19). It is useful for assessing how "shocks" to health in either time period can affect children's acquisition of academic skills, at least initially before parents adjust child health by modifying the choices of C_t^C (child consumption) and M_t (health inputs). In principle, it can also be used to assess the likely impact of a proposed policy that has a known impact on health but has not yet been implemented; for many new policies, it may be impossible to estimate the reduced form relationship in Eq. (15) because the data available do not adequately describe the new policy. For example, if clinical trials show how some new type of medicine or health care treatment affects child health in one or both time periods, Eq. (19) approximates how that medicine or treatment would eventually affect children's academic skills in a way that accounts for some, but not all, behavioral choices; the behavioral choices not accounted for would be those associated with child consumption and purchases of health inputs in both time periods (and wealth effects if the policy changes the prices of health inputs). Even if the new policy is implemented, the disadvantage of estimating Eq. (15) is that it may take 6–8 years before that policy's effect on health in the first time period will have had time to affect children's academic skills in time period 2, so using the conditional demand relationship (or, if nothing else is available, the production function in Eq. (1)) one can approximate the impact of the policy on educational outcomes much more quickly.

In summary, in any analysis of the impact of child health and nutrition on education outcomes, it is important to clarify what relationship one is trying to estimate, and whether the impact is long-run or short-run. Different results in different empirical studies are not necessarily inconsistent; they may be estimates of different relationships, and some may measure long-run impacts while others measure only short-run impacts. In practice, some of these relationships are more difficult to estimate than others; the final choice of what to estimate is determined both by the relationships of interest and by the feasibility of estimating each of those relationships. This brings us to econometric estimation issues, which are reviewed in the next section.

4. Estimation strategies: Problems and possible solutions

While economists know less about education than do education researchers, and certainly know less about health than medical and public health researchers, they have ample experience with, and have rigorously debated, many estimation methods. Economists also know that the methods that can be applied and the relationships that can be estimated depend on the data at hand. This section reviews what can be done to estimate the relationship between child health and education with the three main types of data available: cross-sectional data (data collected from the "real world" at one point in time), panel data ("real world" data collected from households or individuals at several points in time, also known as "longitudinal data"), and data from randomized evaluations (data collected from an experiment in which one or more groups is randomly selected to receive a treatment while the non-selected group serves as a control).

4.1. Retrospective estimates from cross-sectional data

The easiest data to collect, and therefore the most common type of data available, are data collected on a large number of children at a single point in time. Such data are often referred to as cross-sectional data, and they usually come from a household survey or a survey of schools. For the purpose of estimating the impact of child health on education outcomes, the minimum requirement for such data is that they contain at least one variable that measures child health and at least on variable that measures a schooling outcome of interest (often either school enrollment or a score on an academic test). With these two variables alone one can measure correlation at one point in time, but of course correlation does not imply causation.

In fact, to estimate causal relationships that show the impact of child health and nutrition status (or the impact of health policies or programs) on one or more education outcomes – that is to estimate either of Eqs. (1), (15) or (19) – one needs many more variables. To see why, consider the structural equation (1). To avoid problems of omitted variable bias (this is discussed in more detail below) one needs all of the explanatory variables in that equation that affect education outcomes: health status in both time periods, parental education inputs in both time periods, the child's innate intellectual ability, a large number of school and teacher characteristics, and years of schooling attained.[10] Only the last of these is easy to collect. With cross-sectional data, the only possibility for obtaining child health status and parental education inputs in past years is to ask the children or their parents to recall events from many years ago, which is likely to lead to considerable recall error. Moreover, schools and teachers vary in so many ways that it requires great effort to collect all the relevant data on those variables. Indeed, some school and teacher characteristics are difficult to measure, such as teachers' motivation and principals' managerial ability. Finally, it is not trivial to obtain data on a child's innate ability; even defining that concept is difficult in practice.

Thus, in most cases cross-sectional data will be incomplete in the sense that not all of the variables in Eq. (1) that determine learning will be in the data set. This is very likely to lead to omitted variable bias in estimates of the impact of child health on education outcomes. For example, suppose that data are available only on the current health status of the primary school student (H_2), not on past health status (H_1). Assume also that the

[10] The assumption in the model of Section 3 that there are only two time periods in the child's life up to age 11 was imposed solely to simplify the exposition. More realistic models are likely to need more time periods, which implies that health status and parental educational inputs must be measured for three or more time periods over the child's life up to age 11.

true impact of current health status is small while the impact of past health status is quite large. For example, poor health and nutrition in the first few years of life could have a lasting effect on a child's cognitive development. Because current and past health status are likely to be positively correlated, regressing current test scores on current health status and the non-health variables in Eq. (1) is likely to produce a positive and statistically significant coefficient on current health status, overestimating the true impact of current health status. If not interpreted cautiously, this could persuade policymakers to put large resources into programs that attempt to improve the current health of school-age children even though programs that focus on infants and very young children may be much more effective.

Another example of possible omitted variable bias is bias due to endogenous program placement when estimating the impact of a health program as in Eq. (15), where the health program affects child health by altering the health environment or the price of health inputs. Suppose that one has incomplete data on aspects of the local health environment (HE) pertaining to the natural prevalence of childhood diseases. Governments may attempt to address this problem by implementing a program (which would also be an HE variable) to reduce the prevalence of one or more of those diseases. Assuming that the program works, the intervention will have a negative causal impact on the prevalence of the childhood disease(s), and thus a positive impact on child health and on subsequent education outcomes. But if one observes only the program variable, and not the incidence of childhood diseases the estimate of the impact of that variable on children's education outcomes will be biased downward. Intuitively, if the program is implemented primarily in areas with high disease prevalence, this produces a positive association between the program and the prevalence of that disease and thus a negative association between the program and children's academic performance.

Omitted variable bias can also occur when non-health variables are missing. Suppose that parents of some healthy children understand that their children will do relatively well in school without additional investments, and thus they decide to reduce their efforts, and expenditures, on education inputs. This would lead to underestimation of the impact of child health on education outcomes in the structural Eq. (1) if the data do not include important components of parents' education inputs.

Another plausible example is that parental tastes for child education and child health are correlated, for example some parents are more "responsible" than others, caring about both the health and the education of their children. These tastes are difficult to observe, which will result in positive correlations between child health and child education that are not directly causal. Stated more crudely, irresponsible parents are likely to have children who are both less healthy and do less well in school than the children of responsible parents, but much (perhaps even most) of the causality may be from parental tastes (more specifically, the actions those tastes produce) to child education outcomes, not only from the direct impact of poor child health on schooling.

In addition to omitted variable bias, another estimation problem can arise: random measurement errors in the explanatory variables can lead to underestimation of the impact of the poorly measured variables on education outcomes (attenuation bias). If cross-sectional data include any retrospective data on past health status and parental education inputs, these data are likely to be measured with a substantial amount of error and thus estimates based on them are likely to suffer from bias towards zero (if measurement error is classical) or bias in an unknown direction (if measurement is non-classical, which is plausible in the context of retrospective health and education reports). Even current health status and parental education inputs may be measured with error, as could current school quality variables.

The discussion thus far has focused primarily on the structural Eq. (1), but they same estimation problems apply to the demand relationship in Eq. (15) and the conditional demand relationship in Eq. (19). Equation (15) has the advantage that parental education inputs are replaced by variables that are probably easier to observe (and thus to collect data on), such as household wealth, parental education, and prices of health and education inputs. Yet other hard to observe factors also appear, such as parental tastes for child education and health (σ and τ) and the child's innate healthiness (η) and innate ability (α), so omitted variable bias remains a very real problem; indeed, it is not clear whether the potential for such bias is lower in Eq. (15) than in Eq. (1). Measurement error is also a potential problem, and it is likely to be serious for variables in Eq. (15) that are not in Eq. (1), such as household wealth, prices, and the health environment. On the other hand, one could argue that the impacts of the price of medical care and the health environment variables, and of τ and η, in Eq. (15) are likely to be small and thus these can be dropped from that equation. This may be correct in some settings but we know of no study that has attempted to test the plausibility of this conjecture.

Finally, the demand equation (15) may be easier to estimate than the conditional demand equation (19) because the child health variables need not be directly observed. Yet Eq. (19) does not include the health environment variables and prices of health inputs (since it conditions on child health), so the endogenous program placement bias problem can occur in estimates of the demand equation (15) but not in estimates of the conditional demand equation (19). Moreover, the health environment can vary in dozens if not hundreds of different ways, which could imply major data collection difficulties when the goal is to estimate Eq. (15).

The standard econometric tool for overcoming bias due to omitted variables (other than collecting data on virtually all variables, which may never be possible) and for removing bias due to random measurement error in the explanatory variables is instrumental variable (IV) estimation. The basic idea is that all unobserved variables and errors in measurement can be considered to be included in the error term (residual) of the regression model, and the bias is due to correlation of the observed variables with that error term. If one can find valid instrumental variables – that is, variables that are: (1) correlated with the observed variables that are likely to have bias problems (the relevance condition); (2) uncorrelated with the error term, that is uncorrelated with all unobserved variables and any measurement errors (the exogeneity condition); and (3) not already included as explanatory variables in the equation of interest (the exclusion restriction) – one can then obtain unbiased estimates by first regressing the observed endogenous variables on the instruments, and then using the predicted values of these observed variables (instead of their actual values) as regressors in the equation of interest.

While IV estimation works in theory, it is very hard to find plausible instrumental variables for use in cross-sectional estimation of the impact of child health on education. Suppose, for example, that one is trying to estimate the structural relationship between child health and education in Eq. (1), and there are data on child health in time period 2 but not for the earlier time period. As mentioned above, child health is likely to be positively correlated over time, which will lead to overestimation of the impact of child health in time period 2 on students' current academic skills if simple ordinary least squares (OLS) estimation is used. The IV method requires an instrument that predicts child health in time period 2 but is not correlated with child health in the earlier time period. At first glance, health prices in time period 2 seem to satisfy these criteria, but health prices may change little over time and thus those prices could be highly correlated with health prices, and thus with child health, in the first period. Other examples of problems finding valid instrumental variables will be discussed below. On the other hand, the analytical framework in Section 3 provides a theoretical argument for a set of instrumental variables to estimate the conditional demand relationship in Eq. (19); the health environment (HE_t) and health input price ($P_{M,t}$) variables clearly satisfy the exclusion restriction (they do not affect child academic skills after conditioning on child health) and should satisfy the relevance condition and thus can be used as instruments for child health (H) in both time periods (although the exogeneity condition must still be examined).

4.2. Retrospective estimates from panel data

Panel data are data collected on the same children for two or more time periods. Researchers interested in the impact of child health on education outcomes have an obvious reason for using such data to estimate Eqs. (1), (15), and (19), which is that all three equations include not only variables from the second time period but also variables from the first time period. As pointed out above, cross-sectional data can include such variables only if they are obtained from respondents' memories, which could often be quite inaccurate (imagine trying to remember your exact height in centimeters when you were ten years old). Panel data need not be based on respondents' likely flawed memories of past events.

There is another potential benefit of panel data, which is that some unobserved variables that do not change over time can be differenced out of the regression and thus need not be measured. Estimates of Eqs. (1), (15) and (19) using cross-sectional data can lead to biased estimates because many variables that do not change over time – such as child intellectual ability and innate healthiness, parental tastes for educated and healthy children, and some aspects of school quality – are not observed and could be correlated with observed child health outcomes, leading to omitted variable bias. Similarly, any such variables that are measured with error are likely to lead to attenuation bias. In principle, panel data allows one to difference out these unchanging variables and estimate relationships of interest between the variables that do change over time. In many cases, the variables that change over time may also be relatively easier to observe than fixed characteristics (e.g., innate child healthiness), so the omitted variable bias problem is likely to be reduced.

However, this method has its own limitations. It assumes that the troublesome unobserved variables do not change over time, and that they do not interact with variables that do change over time. If either of these assumptions is untrue, then those variables will remain (and will still be unobserved) in the equation being estimated, leading to bias. Another serious problem is that measurement error in observed explanatory variables could lead to greater attenuation bias in estimates based on differenced equations than in estimates based on the original equation, if the signal to noise ratio is smaller for the differenced variables than for the variables themselves. There is also the obvious disadvantage that panel data are more expensive to collect because they require collecting data at two or more points in time. Limiting sample attrition in panel data collection is often expensive – and challenging – in practice, since respondents who have moved need to be located and interviewed. Movers are often an interesting and highly selected group, and thus important for drawing valid econometric inference. In particular, sample attrition may lead to biased estimates if tracking success is correlated with the variables of interest in the estimation equation, for instance, if healthier individuals are more (or less) likely to migrate elsewhere for work.

For a detailed discussion of the benefits and limitations of panel data, as well as practical advice for collecting such data in less developed countries, see Glewwe and Jacoby (2000). Further examples of how panel data can be used to estimate the impact of child health on education outcomes are discussed in Section 5.

4.3. Randomized evaluations

In the vast majority of studies, both cross-sectional data and panel data are collected from observational settings, that is, settings in which no attempt is made by the researchers to alter the behavior of the people from whom the data are collected. Such data are often called retrospective data. Yet the problems of bias raised above are very likely, if not almost certain, when using data collected in this manner.

A very different approach to estimating the impact of policies and programs is a method that has long used in medical sciences: randomized evaluation. Randomized evaluations randomly divide a population under study into two groups, one of which participates in the program, called the treatment group (or program group), and the other of which does not participate in the program, the control group (or comparison group). In some cases the population is divided into more than two groups, one control group and several treatment groups, each with a different treatment. If the division of the population into these groups is truly random, then the *only* difference between the two groups (other than random variation) is that one participated in the program while the other did not. While randomized studies have long been used in health research, until recently they have been rare in social science research, including economic research.

Randomized evaluations provide particularly transparent and credible evidence to poli-cymakers on program impacts, and have the potential to exert considerable influence on actual policy choices, as argued recently by Kremer (2003) and by Duflo, Glennerster, and Kremer (2008).

To see how randomized evaluations can be used to estimate the impact of child health on education outcomes, consider the demand for the child's academic skills, as shown in Eq. (15). A large sample of households or schools can be randomly divided into two groups, a treatment group that receives the health intervention (which can be character-ized formally as a change in one or more of the health input price or health environment variables), and a control group that does not receive the intervention. The differences across these two groups in the variables that characterize the intervention are completely uncorrelated with all of the other explanatory variables because these differences are determined solely by random assignment. Thus the difference in the average education outcomes (T_2) of the two groups must be due to the health intervention, since there are no other systematic differences between the two groups. This same logic applies to subgroups of interest within the general population: one can estimate impacts sep-arately by sex, wealth level, or any other group that can be defined using exogenous variables, or using any endogenous variables that are measured before the intervention is implemented.

While this may appear to be the solution to the econometric problems that stymie attempts to estimate such impacts from cross-sectional or panel data, randomized eval-uations also have some limitations. First, they are limited to health interventions that do not violate regulations on human subjects research. In health studies this stricture often is interpreted to mean that anyone who is known to have a treatable health problem cannot be denied access to any treatment that is being made available to others. Second, random assignment to treatment and control groups is often violated in practice, as in-dividuals or households in the control group attempt to switch into the treatment group. Even if researchers exclude from the analysis children who were randomly assigned to the control group but were able to obtain the treatment (e.g., enrolled in a treatment school), such children could affect the impact of the treatment on the children who were randomly selected to receive the treatment (e.g., by increasing class size in the treatment schools). This problem can often be addressed in practice, however, by an application of the approach in Angrist, Imbens, and Rubin (1996), in which assignment to treatment is used as an instrumental variable for actual treatment, under fairly weak assumptions.

Third, as with studies based on panel data, randomized evaluations may suffer from attrition bias, and this could lead to bias if attrition is correlated with a child's treat-ment status. For instance, if the health intervention makes schooling more attractive, the dropout rate among the treatment group may decline. If the study is based on a sam-ple of schools, weaker students will be less likely to drop out of the treatment schools (and thus typically out of the sample) than weaker students in the control schools, and so over time the impact of the program on student academic skills will be underestimated because the average innate ability of students in the treatment schools gradually drops relative to the average ability in the control schools. This sort of differential attrition need not be fatal for estimation, however. Under certain assumptions, researchers can place bounds on the resulting treatment effect estimates using the nonparametric methods described in Manski (1995) and the trimming method in Lee (2005). Unfortunately, in some cases these bounds may be too wide to be useful in practice.

A final limitation of randomized trials is that they are typically designed to estimate only the demand relationship in Eq. (15), more specifically they estimate the net effect of changes in one or more of the health input price ($P_{M,t}$) and health environment (HE_t) variables. Even if additional data are collected, they usually cannot be used to estimate the structural (direct) impact of child health status on education in Eq. (1) because one cannot disaggregate the overall impact of the intervention into the effects that work through the various elements of child health status (H_t) and the effects that operate through parental educational inputs (EI_t) and years of schooling (YS). If data collection is extensive, however, one may be able to combine data from randomized trials with structural modeling to recover estimates of key theoretical parameters of interest (for an example of a related approach in another context, see Todd and Wolpin, 2006). An important consequence of this limitation is that there may be a long time lag between the start of the intervention and the evaluation of its impact, as seen in the example above concerning an intervention that occurs in early childhood and thus requires 6–8 years before one can evaluate its impact on learning in primary school.

One strength of randomized evaluations is that they can be conducted with only one round of data collection – that is, by collecting cross-sectional data after the health policy or program has been implemented for the treatment group (and after enough time has passed to allow the intervention to have some effect). Another approach, which may be more statistically efficient is to collect panel data that measure children's education outcomes for the treatment and the control groups both before and after the intervention has been implemented in the treatment group. This allows researchers to look at *changes* in the outcome variables over time, which in some cases will provide an estimate of the impact of the program that has a smaller standard error.

5. Empirical evidence

This section reviews recent studies that examine the impact of child health and/or nutritional status on education outcomes. This is done for all three estimation methods (using cross-sectional data, using panel data and using randomized evaluations). For each method, the studies examined are among the best analyses done in recent years.

5.1. Retrospective estimates using cross-sectional data

Over the past 20–30 years, many studies have attempted to estimate the impact of child health status on education outcomes using cross-sectional data. Yet, as noted by Behrman (1996), most of these studies, especially the earlier ones, paid little attention to the possible biases that can arise when using cross-sectional data, and Behrman concludes that "because associations in cross-sectional data may substantially over- or underestimate true causal effects, however, much less is known about the subject than is presumed" (p. 24).

This subsection examines a paper by Glewwe and Jacoby (1995) that carefully investigates the impact of child nutrition on age of school enrollment and years of completed schooling using cross-sectional data from Ghana. Although the paper did not examine the impact of child nutrition on academic skills, the estimation issues encountered in the paper are virtually identical to those discussed above. Thus this paper is instructive in that it shows what can be done, and what cannot be done, using cross-sectional data. This paper is also typical for this literature in focusing on school enrollment derived from household surveys as the main educational outcome measure; we discuss alternative education data below.

Glewwe and Jacoby investigate delayed enrollment and (ultimate) grade attainment using cross-sectional data on 1757 Ghanaian children aged 6–15 years in 1988–1989. They use child height-for-age as their indicator of child health status; in terms of the model in Section 3, this variable reflects health status in both time periods but is primarily influenced by child health in the first time period (more precisely, in the first two or three years of that time period). As explained above, one problem with using cross-sectional data is that parental tastes for child health and child education outcomes (τ and σ, respectively) may be positively correlated. Glewwe and Jacoby propose a simple way to avoid such bias: they use only variation *within* families, not across families, to estimate the impact of child health on education outcomes. In particular, there is evidence that child health varies within families, but since parental tastes for child health and education outcomes do not vary within the family, within family correlation of child health and education outcomes should not be caused by any such correlation in parental tastes. A family fixed effects estimation procedure can be used to provide estimates that are based solely on within-family variation in health and education outcomes. This is very similar to the differencing approach for panel data discussed above in Section 4.2, the only difference being that the differences are not over time for one child but instead are across two children in the same family at the same time. Since the two dependent variables, delayed school enrollment and eventual years of schooling, reflect preferences and optimizing behavior, all the relationships estimated in this paper are conditional demand relationships similar to Eq. (19) in Section 3, rather than structural estimates of education production functions or unconditional demand relationship (Eqs. (1) and (15), respectively).

Another approach used by Glewwe and Jacoby to avoid biased estimates of the impact of child health on education outcomes is to search for instrumental variables that affect child health status but should have no causal impact on education outcomes after conditioning on (controlling for) child health status. The instrumental variables used are distance to nearby medical facilities and maternal height. However, this method can be used only when analyzing variation across households, since these instruments do not vary across children in the same family, and thus this method complements the household fixed effect approach discussed above. Distance to nearby medical facilities, which can be thought of as one of the health input price variables ($P_{M,i}$), should have an effect on child height, while mother's height reflects the mother's, and thus the child's, innate (genetic) healthiness (η). The key assumption, which follows from the theory of conditional demand relationships, is that the price variable ($P_{M,i}$) and innate genetic healthiness (η) can be removed from the list of exogenous variables for those relationships because they affect child schooling only through their impact on child health status.

Yet both of these approaches are open to reasonable criticisms. The authors admit that the first approach (family fixed effects), has a serious problem: variation in innate child healthiness (η) or random shocks to health among children within the same family may lead to reallocation of (unobserved) education resources across different children within that family. For example, suppose that parents recognize that their children who are relatively sickly will do worse in school. In response, they may allocate more (unobserved) education resources to that child to compensate for the disadvantage the child has in terms of his or her health. Family fixed effects estimation will not control for this intra-household allocation and, in this case, will tend to underestimate the impact of child health on education outcomes. Alternatively, if families decide to neglect sickly children and allocate most education resources to healthier children, then the impact of child health on education outcomes would be overestimated. In the absence of detailed data on intra-household allocation of resources including parental time, it is impossible to account for this effect. This casts doubt on the main results in Glewwe and Jacoby (1995) and, more generally, illustrates the limitations of cross-sectional analysis.

Turning to the second approach (instrumental variables), consider the conditional demand relationship for years of schooling. (The following line of argument also applies to the conditional demand relationship for delayed school enrollment, which is simply another parental choice made in the second time period.) This is Eq. (18) in Section 3. The assumption that the height of the mother and the distance to the nearest medical facility affect only child health is doubtful. A mother's height is likely to influence the marginal productivity of her labor, which affects household income and could influence unobserved parental time devoted to the educational activities of her children. While the distance to the nearest medical facility may affect schooling only through its impact on child health, it could be correlated with many community characteristics that influence education decisions, such as unobserved components of school quality, Thus both instrumental variables are likely to be correlated with the error term when estimating Eq. (18).

After explaining the limitations of their empirical work, Glewwe and Jacoby estimate the impact of child health (as measured by height-for-age) on school enrollment and final school attainment. They find strong negative impacts of child health on delayed enrollment using both the instrumental variable and fixed effects estimators, and they find little evidence for alternative explanations for delayed enrollment (credit constraints or rationing of limited spaces in school by child age). However, they find no statistically significant evidence that child health increases school attainment – indeed, the point estimate has an unexpected negative sign, although only marginally significant – but this may reflect the small sample size, since only about 7% of the children in the sample had finished their schooling at the time of the survey.

The above caveats are not limited to estimates of the determinants of years of schooling or delayed enrollment. In general, all of the above discussion applies with very little modification if one were to use cross-sectional data to estimate the impact of child health and nutrition on children's academic skills as measured by test scores. Clearly, very strong and often untestable assumptions need to be made for inference using cross-sectional data.

5.2. Retrospective estimates using panel data

Three recent studies have used panel data to estimate the impact of child health on education outcomes. The first, by Alderman et al. (2001), uses panel data collected from 1986 to 1991 for about 800 households in rural Pakistan. To avoid biased estimates due to unobserved parental tastes and children's innate ability and healthiness, the paper uses food prices (more precisely, deviations in prices from long-term trends) during time period 1 as instrumental variables for child health status in that time period. Education decisions in the second time period are assumed to be made conditional on all outcomes at the end of time period 1, which reflect not only decisions made in the earlier time period but also various exogenous shocks that occurred after decisions were made in the first time period.

Alderman and his coauthors find that child health, as measured by height-for-age when 5 years old, has a strong positive effect on the probability of being enrolled in school at age 7, especially for girls. This finding is consistent with the Glewwe and Jacoby results from Ghana that better health reduces delayed enrollment, since part of the enrollment impact in Pakistan is likely to operate through reducing delayed enrollment. More generally, the results for the two countries are consistent in the sense that improved child health, as captured by height, appears to have a large positive causal impact on education outcomes.

The Pakistan study has several potential limitations. First, the relationship they estimate is a conditional demand function. Thus their use of food price shocks in the first time period as instrumental variables for health status in that time period is theoretically valid only if they include an initial wealth variable that excludes spending on child health in the first time period (i.e. the appropriate wealth variable in terms of the model in Section 3 is W_{CD}, not W_0). But their household wealth variable, household expenditures averaged over three years, does not exclude spending on child health. Moreover, food prices in the first time period determine not only child health but also adult food consumption and thus they belong in the conditional demand function even after controlling for child health ($p_{C,1}$ is part of the ω vector in Eq. (18)). More intuitively, food price shocks can affect household savings in the first time period and thus affect education choices in the second time period. Thus, the use of food price shocks as instruments for health outcomes in Eq. (18) potentially violates the exclusion restriction, the requirement that the instruments have no effect on years of schooling apart from the effect that operates via lagged health status (H_1). The direction of bias is toward overestimation of the health effects: unusually high prices in the first time period probably not only reduce child health but also reduce savings for education inputs, via an income effect.

Another potential concern is that the paper assumes that household wealth (as proxied by consumption expenditures) is measured without error. Yet it is very likely that at least some measurement error is present, which implies biased estimates of the impacts not only of the consumption variable but also potentially of all other variables. Addressing this issue would require finding a suitable instrumental variable for consumption expenditures.

A second recent paper using panel data is that of Glewwe, Jacoby, and King (2001), which uses panel data from more than 2000 households in the Philippines. Unlike the Ghana and Pakistan studies, this paper estimates the determinants of academic skills as measured by test scores, not school enrollment, and it attempts to estimate the structural educational production function in Eq. (1), as opposed to estimating a conditional demand function. By making certain assumptions the authors attempt to get around the problem that the instruments could be correlated with unobserved parental education inputs in the first time period.

The Philippines study, like the Ghana study, is based on sibling differences. As will be seen below, this differencing is useful because it removes family averages of innate academic ability (α) and all school quality variables (virtually all siblings in the sample attended the same primary school) from Eq. (1). Yet using household fixed effects does not remove bias due to possible differences in innate ability across different children in the same family. In particular, decisions regarding health investments throughout childhood (M_1, C_1^C, M_2 and C_2^C), as well as decisions on educational inputs (EI_1 and EI_2), could be influenced by differences in innate ability among siblings in the same family, which may lead to correlation between early childhood health investments and primary school test scores (T_2) that once again is not causal. The authors argue that health investments made from conception through 24 months of age cannot be correlated with innate child academic ability because parents do not observe children's intelligence until after the child reaches at least 24 months of age. To justify this assumption, the authors cite psychology studies that conclude that parents cannot observe children's innate academic ability until the child is older than 24 months. This is a novel conceptual point, and is central to the paper's identification approach. The Philippines study also relies on the identifying assumption that the largest effects of child health on primary school outcomes in Eq. (1) are early in the first time period, that is from conception until the child is 24 months old, and on the assumption that changes in child health from 24 months of age until the start of primary school are not correlated with child health up to the age of 24 months. Finally, two implicit assumptions are that the impacts of parental education inputs before the child reaches primary school age (EI_1) and the impacts of current child health status (H_2) on primary school academic scores in Eq. (1) are negligible and thus can be dropped from that equation. These are relatively strong assumptions, but they deliver the needed econometric identification.

Together, these assumptions allow the authors to write the structural equation (1) as[11]:

$$T_2 = T(H_1, EI_2, \alpha, SC, YS)$$
$$= \beta_0 + \beta_1 H_1 + \beta_2 EI_2 + \beta_3 \alpha + \beta_4 SC + \beta_5 YS$$
$$= \beta_0 + \beta_1 Height_1 + \beta_2 EI_2 + \beta_3 \alpha + \beta_4 SC + \beta_5 YS \qquad (1')$$

where the second line is a simple linear approximation of the first line, and the third line explicitly uses child growth (measured by height) as the health indicator. That is, if good health leads to fast growth and poor health leads to slow growth, then H_1 is summarized by $Height_1$ (growth from conception until primary school). Equation $(1')$ is for one child. Differencing across two siblings from the same family who attend the same school yields:

$$\Delta T_2 = \beta_1 \Delta Height_1 + \beta_2 \Delta EI_2 + \beta_3 \Delta \alpha + \beta_5 \Delta YS. \qquad (1'')$$

Equation $(1'')$ is difficult to estimate because α and virtually all aspects of EI_2 are not observed and are likely to be correlated with the endogenous observed variables, $\Delta Height_1$ and ΔYS. One needs instrumental variables for $\Delta Height_1$ and ΔYS that are uncorrelated with $\Delta \alpha$ and ΔEI_2, the differences in the innate intelligence and parental education inputs across the two siblings.

The authors use the differences in the dates of birth of the two siblings as the main instrument for ΔYS, which is arguably uncorrelated with $\Delta \alpha$ and ΔEI_2 (although the authors cannot completely rule out a story in which parents jointly plan birth spacing and the allocation of parental education inputs across siblings). Regarding $\Delta Height_1$, the paper argues that the height of the older sibling by age 24 months is a valid instrument because it is uncorrelated with the α's of both siblings (since neither is observed until after 24 months of age for the older sibling) and it has strong predictive power for $\Delta Height_1$. Note that using instrumental variables also addresses the potential problem of bias due to measurement error in the height variables, if the measurement error is completely random.

Despite the innovative method of finding instruments for $\Delta Height_1$ and ΔYS in Eq. $(1'')$, the estimation strategy remains open to several criticisms. The main problem with the estimation strategy is that it is not clear that the height of the older child at age 24 months, the instrument for $\Delta Height_1$, is uncorrelated with differences in parental education inputs in the second time period (ΔEI_2). By the second time period of the older sibling, parents may take their children's health (which is measured by height) into account when making education input decisions. One could also quarrel with the implicit assumption that EI_1 does not have any direct effect on cognitive achievement.

---

[11] The model in the paper has three time periods, from conception to 24 months (denoted in the paper as time period 0), from 24 months to 5 or 6 years (time period 1), and primary school age (time period 2), but the basic approach is the same as the description given here.

The existence of a multi-billion dollar industry in the US claiming to boost infant intelligence (through "Baby Einstein" and related toys) suggests that many parents believe that EI_1 is valuable in improving later cognitive performance. This will introduce more variables into Eq. (1) for which instruments will be hard to find. The assumption that H_2 has no effect on child academic skills in period 2 (T_2) in Eq. (1) is also questionable. Overall, the approach used in the Philippines paper can be faulted, but the solutions to the criticisms raised here are far from obvious given the data at hand.

Using the estimation strategy explained above (modified to account for delayed enrollment and grade repetition), the Philippines study finds strong causal impacts of children's health status in the first two years of life (as measured by height at age 8) on several schooling outcomes. More specifically, better health leads to reductions in delayed enrollment, reduced grade repetition, and greater learning per year of schooling as measured by test scores. The impacts appear to be large in that back of the envelope calculations based on the cost and impact (on child height) of an unrelated feeding program in India (Kielmann et al., 1983), together with the relationship between wages and education calculated from Philippines data, suggest that each dollar spent on a feeding program could provide a social return of at least three dollars, and perhaps much more.

The third recent panel study that examines the impact of child health and nutrition on education is Alderman, Hoddinott, and Kinsey (2006). This paper estimates the impact of preschool height on years of completed schooling in a sample of 665 Zimbabwean young adults surveyed in early 2000. The authors also estimate impacts on delayed enrollment. The 2000 survey was a follow-up to two earlier surveys of children carried out in 1983/1984 and 1987, and the authors appear to have had considerable tracking success: there is education data in the year 2000 for a remarkable 99% of the sample, including information obtained from relatives if the child had moved away from the study area. This is so in part because of the unusual nature of the sample: sample households all resided in resettlement communities, and these households had to renounce any land claims in other parts of Zimbabwe. Moreover, male adults were not allowed to out-migrate from the resettlement area. The high tracking rate is a noteworthy feature of these data and one that other studies should try to emulate.

The study uses a sibling comparison instrumental variables method related to that of Glewwe, Jacoby, and King (2001). However, the source of variation that Alderman, Hoddinott, and Kinsey (2006) employ for their instrumental variables estimates is more exogenous than, and arguably an improvement over, previous (non-experimental) panel studies. Thus this quasi-experimental estimation approach is quite similar in spirit to the randomized evaluation studies described below in Section 5.3.

Children in the sample were born between September 1978 and September 1986, an extremely volatile period both politically and in terms of living standards. In particular Zimbabwe in the late 1970s experienced the final years of a brutal civil war, and the country was later affected by back-to-back droughts in 1982–1983 and 1983–1984. The authors utilize variation in exposure to these large "shocks" across siblings while the children were 12 to 36 months of age to estimate the impact of preschool height on later outcomes, the underlying assumption being that children's height (and, more broadly, their biological development) during that age range is more sensitive to nutritional deficiencies than at other ages. The strong first stage relationships the authors estimate validate this view: exposure to these "shock" episodes during the key 12–36 month age range are strongly correlated with shorter child stature in earlier survey rounds (1983–1984 and 1987). Over-identification tests confirm that these instruments do not blatantly violate the exclusion restriction. One concern is that schooling quality, or other unobserved inputs into education, are also affected by these macro-shocks, but there is no obvious reason why these shocks would translate into worse schooling quality several years later (when sample children enter primary school) only for the cohorts directly hit by the shock but not for their older or younger siblings.

Using this approach, Alderman, Hoddinott, and Kinsey (2006) find that increased early childhood height is associated with significantly greater young adult height (in 2000) and more years of educational attainment. The effects are substantial: the increase from median child height in this sample to median height in the international reference (rich country) sample would lead to an additional 0.85 grades of completed schooling and over 3 cm in height. These fixed effects instrumental variable estimates are substantially larger than simple fixed effects estimates. The existence of data on schooling attainment, rather than just delayed school enrollment, makes it easier to translate these schooling effects into likely later impacts on income, using existing estimates of the returns to education. Note that estimated health effects for females and males are not significantly different from each other in the Zimbabwe study, a pattern also found in the experimental studies described below.

The estimates from Alderman, Hoddinott, and Kinsey (2006), which are estimates of the conditional demand function in Eq. (19), largely confirm the findings of earlier cross-sectional and other panel studies in highlighting the important effect of early childhood height on later schooling outcomes. In summary, panel data provide additional possibilities for overcoming the estimation problems that plague studies based on cross-sectional data, but some estimation problems often remain. Undoubtedly, further data collection and innovative thinking will lead to improved estimates, like those in the Alderman, Hoddinott, and Kinsey (2006) study that utilize an arguably more convincing source of exogenous variation in child health, but the extent to which the remaining estimation problems can be resolved is difficult to predict.

On the other hand, it is worth noting that worries about estimation bias due to behavioral responses to health programs and policies may be exaggerated. Evidence in favor of this more optimistic viewpoint is found in a recent paper by Jacoby (2002) based on the same Philippines data used by Glewwe, Jacoby, and King (2001). Jacoby found that parents did not reduce food given to their children at home in response to the availability of school feeding programs in Filipino primary schools. Even so, it would be imprudent to ignore the potentially serious estimation programs that arise in estimates based on non-experimental cross-sectional and panel data. Thus the next subsection considers another approach: randomized evaluations.

5.3. Estimates based on randomized evaluations

Nutritionists and public health researchers have a long history of examining the impact of health programs and policies on cognitive and education outcomes using randomized evaluations. More recently, the difficulties of estimating the relationship between education outcomes and child health and nutrition have led some economists to initiate and analyze randomized evaluations in less developed countries. This subsection examines recent studies by both types of researchers, although it mainly focuses on the work of economists. Note also that this subsection does not review several recent studies that have used data from the Mexico Progresa project, mainly because that work is discussed in Chapter 62 in this Volume by Parker, Rubalcalva, and Teruel. An additional reason it does not cover this work is that the multiple components of Progresa assistance, and especially the income transfer component, in addition to health and nutrition interventions, complicate the task of isolating the impact of child health status per se on educational outcomes.

Many of the earliest randomized studies by nutritionists and other public health researchers focused on the impacts of specific nutrients that were lacking in children's diets. Studies in India and Indonesia by Soemantri, Pollitt, and Kim (1989), Soewondo, Husaini, and Pollitt (1989), and Seshadri and Gopaldas (1989) found large and statistically significant impacts on cognitive development and school performance of iron supplementation among anemic children, but a study by Pollitt et al. (1989) found no such impact in Thailand. See Nokes, Bosch, and Bundy (1998) for a more complete survey of the iron supplementation literature.

Other studies have focused on parasitic infections, especially intestinal parasites. Kvalsig, Cooppan, and Connolly (1991) examined whipworms and other parasites in South Africa and found that drug treatments had some effect on cognitive and education outcomes, but some impacts were not statistically significant. Nokes et al. (1992) evaluated treatment for whipworms in Jamaica and concluded that some cognitive functions improved from the drug treatment, but others, particularly those related to academic performance in schools, appeared not to have changed substantially. Overall, the early experimental literature on the impact of treatment for intestinal parasites on child growth and cognition did not reach strong conclusions, as argued in the Dickson et al. (2000) survey.

Other studies have focused on general food supplementation to supply calories and protein. The most well known of these is the INCAP study (Pollitt et al., 1993; Martorell, Habicht, and Rivera, 1995) initiated in four Guatemalan villages in 1969, two of which were randomly selected to receive a porridge (*atole*) high in calories and protein while the other two villages received a drink (*fresco*) with less calories and no protein. Follow-up studies over the next two decades appear to show sizeable effects on later cognitive outcomes from providing the *atole* to mothers and young children.

These projects are arguably among the most convincing research to date showing long-term effects of childhood health and nutrition on later education, and on life outcomes more broadly.[12] Yet these studies are also subject to some criticisms. Many of these studies have relatively small sample sizes, such as 210 children in the South African study and 103 in the Jamaican study. Other studies (not reviewed here) include education interventions combined with health interventions, so the impact of the health intervention by itself cannot be credibly assessed.

The pioneering INCAP study is also open to some criticism. In one sense, it has a sample size of only four villages since the intervention did not vary within villages, and it is unclear if the existing studies fully account for the intracluster correlation of respondent outcomes in their statistical analyses, thus perhaps leading them to overstate the statistical significance of their findings. Second, strictly speaking, the control group also received an intervention, the *fresco* drink, albeit one with a relatively small benefit compared with what was received in the treatment group. Third, within each village receipt of the *atole* or *fresco* was voluntary, which implies that those who were treated were not a random sample of the population within each village. This means that the most convincing estimation strategy may be an intention to treat analysis, rather than direct estimation of the effect of child health on education. Finally, sample attrition is a major concern in the 1988–1989 follow-up, as more than one quarter of the original sample were apparently lost, in sharp contrast to the exceptionally high tracking rate in the Alderman, Hoddinott, and Kinsey (2006) study described above, or to very high tracking rates in other recent panel studies in less developed countries, most notably the Indonesia Family Life Survey (Thomas, Frankenberg, and Smith, 2002). (Note that in recent work, the INCAP researchers have begun to extend their evaluation through 2002–2003, see Maluccio et al., 2006, but the analysis of long-run impacts remains preliminary at the time of writing this Chapter.)

Three recent randomized evaluation studies by economists on the impact of health interventions on education outcomes are useful additions to this literature. These studies also evaluate actual interventions carried out by real-world non-governmental organizations (NGOs), and as such the findings of these studies may be of particular interest to policymakers in less developed countries. All three papers evaluate school-based health interventions which some have argued may be among the most cost-effective approaches for delivering health and nutrition services to children in less developed countries (Bundy and Guyatt, 1996).

The first is that of Miguel and Kremer (2004), which evaluates a randomized program in Kenyan schools of mass treatment for intestinal worms using inexpensive deworming drugs. The study is based on a sample of 75 primary schools with a total enrollment of nearly 30,000 children, a much larger sample size than most other studies in this literature. The sampled schools were drawn from areas where there is a high prevalence of intestinal parasites among children. Worm infections – including hookworm, roundworm, whipworm and schistosomiasis – are among the most widespread diseases in

---

[12] For a very recent summary of work done by nutritionists see the set of papers recently published in *Lancet* (Grantham-McGregor et al., 2007; Walker et al., 2007; and Engle et al., 2007).

less developed countries: recent studies estimate that 1.3 billion people worldwide are infected with roundworm, 1.3 billion with hookworm, 900 million with whipworm, and 200 million with schistosomiasis. Infection rates are particularly high in Sub-Saharan Africa (Bundy, 1998; World Health Organization, 1993; see also the burden of disease figures in Table 2), where education outcomes and education progress are particularly low, as explained in Section 2. Geohelminths – hookworm, roundworm, and whipworm – are transmitted through poor sanitation and hygiene, while schistosomiasis is acquired by bathing in infected freshwater. School-aged children typically exhibit the greatest prevalence of infection and the highest infection intensity, as well as the highest disease burden, since morbidity is related to infection intensity (Bundy, 1988). Recall from Table 2 that intestinal helminths are estimated to account for about 3% of the total burden of disease among children aged 5–14 in less developed countries, and 4–5% in Sub-Saharan Africa. In fact, the impact of worms on the quality of life in the burden of disease calculations may be underestimated because they do not account for the impact of helminths on education outcomes.

The educational impacts of deworming are considered a key issue in assessing whether the poorest countries should accord priority to deworming, but until recently research on these impacts has been inconclusive (see Dickson et al., 2000 for a survey). Indeed, earlier randomized evaluations on worms and education suffer from several important methodological shortcomings that may partially explain their weak results. Earlier studies randomized the provision of deworming treatment *within* schools to treatment and placebo groups, and then examine the impact of deworming on cognitive outcomes. However, the difference in educational outcomes between the treatment and placebo groups understates the actual impact of deworming if placebo group pupils also experience health gains due to local treatment externalities (due to breaking the disease transmission cycle). The earlier studies also failed to adequately address sample attrition, an important issue to the extent that deworming increases school enrollment.

The study by Miguel and Kremer finds that absenteeism in treatment schools was 25% (7 percentage points) lower than in comparison schools and that deworming increased schooling by 0.14 years per pupil treated (on average). This is a large effect given the low cost of deworming medicine; the study estimates an average cost of only US$3.50 per additional year of school participation. The finding on absenteeism does not reflect increased school attendance on the part of children who attend school only to receive deworming drugs, since drugs were provided at only two preannounced days per year, and attendance on those two days is not counted in the attendance analysis. There is no statistically significant difference in treatment effects between female and male students, echoing the finding discussed above in Alderman, Hoddinott, and Kinsey (2006).

Somewhat surprisingly, despite the reduction in absence no significant impacts were found on student performance on academic tests. It is unclear what exactly is causing this discrepancy, although one possibility is that the program led to more crowded classrooms and that this may have partially offset positive effects of deworming on learning in the treatment schools. In ongoing work, the authors of the Kenya study are collecting a new data set, the Kenya Life Panel Survey (KLPS), in order to document the long-run impacts of the deworming program on educational attainment, cognitive skills, labor market outcomes, fertility, marital choices, health, physical strength and personal happiness.

The schooling data in Miguel and Kremer (2004) are noteworthy. School attendance was collected at sample schools by survey enumerators on unannounced days four to five times per year, rather than relying on school registers (which are thought to be unreliable) or on parent reports in household surveys, as done in most of the previous literature. Efforts were also made to follow children who transferred to other schools in the same Kenyan district. This yields a more detailed and reliable measure of school participation than the data available from most other studies. The Bobonis, Miguel, and Sharma (2006) and Vermeersch and Kremer (2004) papers described below use similar measures of school attendance.

The authors found that child health and school participation – i.e., attendance, where dropouts are considered to have an attendance rate of zero – improved not only for treated students but also for untreated students at treatment schools (22% of pupils in treatment schools chose not to receive the deworming medicine) and for students at nearby primary schools located within 6 kilometers of treatment schools, with especially large impacts within 3 kilometers. The impacts on neighboring schools appear to be due to reduced disease transmission brought about by the intervention, an epidemiological externality. Econometric identification of the cross-school treatment spillovers on the worm infection rate relies on the randomized design of the project: conditional on the total local density of primary school pupils, there is random exogenous variation in the number of local pupils assigned to deworming treatment through the program. A key finding of the paper is that failure to take these externalities (or spillovers) into account would lead to substantial underestimation of the benefits of the intervention and the cost effectiveness of deworming treatment.

Bobonis, Miguel, and Sharma (2006) conducted a randomized evaluation in India of a health program that provided iron supplementation and deworming medicine to preschool children age 2–6 years in 200 preschools in poor urban areas of Delhi. Even though only 30% of the sampled children were found to have worm infections, 69% of children had moderate to severe anemia according to international standards. After 5 months of treatment, the authors found large weight gains and a reduction of one-fifth in absenteeism, a treatment effect similar to the estimated school participation effect in the Miguel and Kremer (2004) study in Kenyan primary schools. The authors attempted to obtain estimates after 2 years, but high sample attrition and apparently non-random enrollment of new children into the preschools complicated attempts to obtain unbiased longer term impact estimates.

One plausible channel through which preschool attendance gains in Bobonis, Miguel, and Sharma (2006) could have long-run impacts is an improvement in future primary school performance, and in fact, 71 percent of parents in the Indian study area claimed (in a baseline survey) that improved primary school preparedness was an important motivation for sending their own children to the preschools. There is some evidence linking preschool participation to later educational outcomes in both less developed and wealthy countries. Berlinski, Galiani, and Gertler (2006) find primary school test score improvements of 8 percent for children who had earlier participated in public preschool programs in Argentina. There is also evidence from the U.S. Head Start program that early childhood interventions reduce later grade repetition and increase educational attainment (Currie and Thomas, 1995; Garces, Thomas, and Currie, 2002). In terms of long-run evidence, Cascio (2007) finds 30 percent reductions in high school grade repetition among African-American and Latino children, and a 20 percent reduction among white children, who had earlier participated in public kindergarten programs in the US South. Magnuson, Ruhm, and Waldfogel (2007) find evidence of medium-term gains from pre-kindergarten participation on first grade mathematics and reading, especially for children whose parents have low education or low income. Currie (2001) surveys the related US literature and concludes that there is considerable evidence linking early childhood interventions to improvements in later educational attainment and cognitive development. It is possible that preschool attendance impacts could be even more persistent in less developed country contexts, where there are fewer school remedial programs and where households are poorer (consistent with the pattern in Magnuson, Ruhm, and Waldfogel, 2007).

Another randomized evaluation using a similar research design is Vermeersch and Kremer (2004). Vermeersch and Kremer estimate the impact of a preschool feeding program in 50 Kenyan preschools. The daily feeding, with a protein enriched porridge, led to 30% higher preschool participation rates, and significant cognitive test score gains in schools with relatively experienced preschool teachers, although no significant cognitive gains in schools with less experienced teachers. The authors also document how the program led to large inflows of pupils into the feeding schools, suggesting that households' school choices may be sensitive to such programs. However, note that this feeding program is an order of magnitude more expensive than deworming treatment or micronutrient supplement, which will greatly reduce the benefit–cost ratio.

Yet even these recent randomized evaluation studies have important limitations. The main puzzle with the Kenya deworming study is that increased school participation (primarily attendance, but also reduced dropping out) is not reflected in students' academic test scores or cognitive test scores. The authors present some cost–benefit analyses at the end of the paper that suggest that the intervention is cost-effective, but it is unclear exactly how to interpret these if the intervention does not increase learning of basic skills. Finally, since deworming treatment was found to affect child health in multiple ways – including lower intestinal worm load, reduced anemia, and (marginally) increased height-for-age – it is impossible to separately estimate the impact of each of these health improvements on education without imposing additional econometric structure.

The Bobonis, Miguel, and Sharma (2006) study encountered serious sample selection and attrition problems in the second year, which prevented a clear assessment of the long-term impact of the health intervention in India. It also does not present data on any type of child learning, and thus is limited to examining anthropometric outcomes and school enrollment and attendance. Finally, because all children received a combined treatment of iron supplements and deworming medicine, the India study cannot distinguish between the separate impacts of these two treatments. Vermeersch and Kremer (2004) are unable to distinguish between school attendance gains resulting from improved child nutrition per se versus a desire to receive food through the daily feeding program, which makes their estimates difficult to interpret relative to previous work (and a similar concern cannot be decisively ruled out in Bobonis, Miguel, and Sharma (2006) with regard to the desire to receive more iron supplementation). A second limitation of Vermeersch and Kremer (2004) is the lack of anthropometric data on sample children, which limits comparability with previous studies in the literature.

6. Summary and concluding comments

This chapter has reviewed the most important estimation issues that complicate attempts to measure the impact of child health and nutrition status on education outcomes. As explained in Sections 3 and 4, the relationships between child health and schooling are very complex, and indeed there are multiple distinct relationships that are of potential interest, including the production function for academic skills, standard demand functions, and conditional demand functions. Perhaps the main message of this chapter is that it is very difficult, though not impossible, to credibly estimate the relationship between child health and education. The two fundamental problems are the following:

(1) it is impossible to obtain data on all variables that belong in the equations of interest, which raises serious problems of omitted variable bias; and

(2) the variables that one does have data on are often measured with error, which can lead to problems of attenuation bias.

These problems are not easy to fix, despite much richer data and the use of more careful estimation methods during the past ten years or so. Moreover, differences in data – in terms of both the health and education measures employed – complicate comparison of the magnitude of estimated health effects across studies.

Yet, despite these difficulties, most of the best recent studies using cross-sectional data, panel data, or data from randomized evaluations have found sizeable and statistically significant positive impacts of child health on education outcomes. Thus there is growing evidence of a causal impact of child health on education. There is no obvious reason to think that the litany of estimation problems described above systematically tend to overestimate the impacts of interest across all the different methodological approaches, data, and settings. A second noteworthy pattern emerging from the recent research is that there is no clear evidence of large gender differences in the impact of child health on education.

We close with a few suggestions for future research. In our view, future research on the links between child health and education outcomes should focus on two fronts (perhaps not surprisingly): better data, and better econometric identification. First, further analysis of panel data is warranted in both observational and randomized evaluation studies. Fortunately, more panel data collection efforts are now being undertaken in less developed countries than ever before, which will set the stage for such research. Improving sample tracking efforts will be critical to the success of ongoing studies, and the recent tracking success of the Alderman, Hoddinott, and Kinsey (2006) and IFLS (Thomas, Frankenberg, and Smith, 2002) studies means that sample attrition is not an insurmountable problem. Better panel datasets will also allow economists to directly estimate the long run impact of child health gains on their wages and living standards as adults, presumably the ultimate goal of much of this literature. Another area in which data can improve is in terms of the measurement of educational outcomes beyond simple parent reports on child school enrollment – perhaps following the approach in Miguel and Kremer, 2004 – and of richer health outcomes. Health is multifaceted and it is unclear whether the height variables typically employed in this literature, while easy to measure, are really capturing the most critical dimensions of health. Indeed, most of the diseases and health problems faced by children in developing countries, measured in terms of their contribution to the burden of disease as shown in Table 2, are unlikely to have strong impacts on height (the main exception being diarrhea), and variation in diseases so much health problems across geographic regions is ignored by focusing on height.[13]

Second, more randomized evaluations should be conducted, especially by large international aid organizations. The results of these evaluations should be broadly disseminated, which will not be easy for these organizations because many studies will find that existing programs do not work as intended. Randomized studies should always compare their findings with standard cross-sectional or panel data estimates based on the control group data, making clear which of the three types of relationships discussed in Section 3 are being compared. This will create a large source of information of the likely bias of non-experimental methods. It may be that there are many situations in which non-experimental methods do not suffer from substantial bias, but this will not become clear until a track record of results has been assembled. Randomized evaluations should also be designed in advance to go beyond the basic program impact evaluation results, to address broader theoretical and policy issues. Efforts to use structural modeling techniques in tandem with data from randomized evaluations (as in Todd and Wolpin, 2006) are similarly a promising direction for this literature.

How large could the long-run effects of poor childhood health and nutrition on economic development really be? Unfortunately, the answer to this question remains elusive despite the recent research progress reviewed in this chapter. However, there is suggestive evidence from at least one once-developing country – the United States – that the long-run effects of public deworming investments could be very large indeed. Recent economic history research finds that the Rockefeller Sanitary Commission's deworming campaigns in the United States South in the 1910s had major impacts on

---

[13] Preliminary results from a recent randomized evaluation of the impact of providing eyeglasses to children with poor vision in a poor province in rural China (Glewwe, Park, and Zhao, 2006) suggest large impacts on learning, but this is completely missed by focusing on child height.

educational attainment and income (Bleakley, 2007) and on agricultural productivity (Brinkley, 1995). In fact, Bleakley (2007) estimates that each case of hookworm averted increased average school attendance by twenty percent. This historical evidence provides hope that current public health investments in children in less developed countries could be planting the seeds for increased skills and, ultimately, greater prosperity during their adult lives.

References

Alderman, H., Hoddinott, J., Kinsey, B. (2006). "Long term consequences of early childhood malnutrition". Oxford Economic Papers 58 (3), 450–474.

Alderman, H., Behrman, J., Lavy, V., Menon, R. (2001). "Child health and school enrollment". Journal of Human Resources 36 (1), 185–205.

Almond, D., Chay, K., Lee, D.S. (2006). "The cost of low birth weight". Quarterly Journal of Economics 120 (3), 1031–1083.

Angrist, J., Imbens, G., Rubin, D. (1996). "Identification of causal effects using instrumental variables". Journal of the American Statistical Association 91, 444–472.

Behrman, J.R. (1996). "The impact of health and nutrition on education". World Bank Research Observer 11 (1), 25–37.

Behrman, J.R., Rosenzweig, M.R. (2004). "Returns to birth weight". Review of Economics and Statistics 86 (2), 586–601.

Berlinski, S., Galiani, S., Gertler, P. (2006). "The effect of pre-primary on primary school performance." Unpublished manuscript. University of California, Berkeley.

Bleakley, H. (2007). "Disease and development: Evidence from hookworm eradication in the American South". Quarterly Journal of Economics 122 (1), 73–117.

Brinkley, G.L. (1995). "Summaries of doctoral dissertation: The economic impact of disease in the American South, 1860–1940". Journal of Economic History 55, 371–374.

Bobonis, G., Miguel, E., Sharma, C.P. (2006). "Iron deficiency, anemia and school participation". Journal of Human Resources 41 (4), 692–721.

Bundy, D.A.P. (1988). "Population ecology of intestinal helminth infections in human communities". Philosophical Transactions of the Royal Society of London Series B 321 (1207), 405–420.

Bundy, D.A.P., Guyatt, J. (1996). "Schools for health: Focus on health, education, and the school-age child". Parasitology Today 12, 1–16.

Bundy, D.A.P., Chan, M.-S., Medley, G.F., Jamison, D., Savioli, L. (1998). "Intestinal nematode infections". In: Health Priorities and Burden of Disease Analysis: Methods and Applications from Global, National and Sub-national Studies. Harvard Univ. Press for the World Health Organization and the World Bank, in press.

Cascio, E. (2007). "Maternal labor supply and the introduction of kindergartens into American public schools". Journal of Human Resources, in press.

Currie, J. (2001). "Early childhood education programs". Journal of Economic Perspectives 15 (2), 213–338.

Currie, J., Thomas, D. (1995). "Does head start make a difference?" American Economic Review 85 (3), 341–364.

Dickson, R., Awasthi, S., Williamson, P., Demelweek, C., Garner, P. (2000). "Effect of treatment for intestinal helminth infection on growth and cognitive performance in children: Systematic review of randomized trials". British Medical Journal 320, 1697–1701.

Duflo, E., Glennerster, R., Kremer, M. (2008). "Using randomization in development economics research: A toolkit". In: Schultz, T.P., Strauss, J. (Eds.), Handbook of Development Economics, vol. 4. Elsevier/North-Holland, Amsterdam. (Chapter 61 in this book.)

Engle, P., Black, M., Behrman, J., Cabral de Mello, M., Gertler, P., Capiriri, L., Martorell, R., Young, M. (2007). "Strategies to avoid the loss of developmental potential in more than 200 million children in the developing world". Lancet 369, 229–242.

Garces, E., Thomas, D., Currie, J. (2002). "Longer-term effects of head start". American Economic Review 92 (4), 999–1012.

Glewwe, P. (2005). "The impact of child health and nutrition on education in developing countries: Theory, econometric issues, and recent empirical evidence". Food and Nutrition Bulletin 26 (2), S235–S250.

Glewwe, P., Jacoby, H. (1995). "An economic analysis of delayed primary school enrollment in a low income country: The role of early childhood nutrition". Review of Economic Statistics 77 (1), 156–169.

Glewwe, P., Jacoby, H. (2000). "Panel data". In: Grosh, M., Glewwe, P. (Eds.), Designing Household Survey Questionnaires for Developing Countries: Lessons from 15 Years of the Living Standards Measurement Study. Oxford Univ. Press, New York.

Glewwe, P., Jacoby, H., King, E. (2001). "Early childhood nutrition and academic achievement: A longitudinal analysis". Journal of Public Economics 81 (3), 345–368.

Glewwe, P., Kremer, M. (2006). "Schools, teachers, and education outcomes in developing countries". In: Hanushek, E., Welch, F. (Eds.), In: Handbook of the Economics of Education, vol. 2. North-Holland, Amsterdam.

Glewwe, P., Kremer, M., Moulin, S., Zitzewitz, E. (2004). "Retrospective vs. prospective analyses of school inputs: The case of flip charts in Kenya". Journal of Development Economics 74 (1), 251–268.

Glewwe, P., Park, A., Zhao, M. (2006). "The impact of eyeglasses on the academic performance of primary school students: Evidence from a randomized trial in rural China". University of Minnesota and University of Michigan.

Grantham-McGregor, S., Cheung, Y.B., Cueto, S., Glewwe, P., Richter, L., Strupp, B. (2007). "Over two hundred million children fail to reach their development potential in the first five years in developing countries". Lancet 369, 60–70.

IAEEA (2000). TIMSS 1999: International Mathematics Report. International Study Center, Boston College.

IAEEA (2003). PIRLS 2001 International Report. International Study Center, Boston College.

Jacoby, H. (2002). "Is there an intrahousehold flypaper effect? Evidence from a school feeding program". Economic Journal 112 (476), 196–221.

Kielmann, A.A., et al. (1983). Child and Maternal Health Services in Rural India: The Narangwal Experiment. The Johns Hopkins Univ. Press, Baltimore, MD.

Kremer, M. (2003). "Randomized evaluations of educational programs in developing countries: Some lessons". American Economic Review: Papers and Proceedings 93 (2), 102–106.

Kvalsig, J.D., Cooppan, R.M., Connolly, K.J. (1991). "The effects of parasite infections on cognitive processes in children". Annals of Tropical Medicine and Parasitology 73, 501–506.

Lee, D.S. (2005). "Training, wages, and sample selection: Estimating sharp bounds on treatment effects". Working paper #11721, National Bureau of Economic Research, October.

Lopez, A., Mathers, C., Ezzati, M., Jamison, D., Murray, C. (2006). "Global burden of disease and risk factors". The World Bank, Washington, DC.

Maluccio, J.A., Hoddinott, J., Behrman, J.R., Martorell, R., Quisumbing, A.R., Stein, A.D. (2006). "The impact of nutrition during early childhood on education among Guatemalan adults". Working paper #06-026, University of Pennsylvania Institute for Economic Research.

Magnuson, K.A., Ruhm, C., Waldfogel, J. (2007). "Does prekindergarten improve school preparation and performance". Economics of Education Review 26 (1), 33–51.

Manski, C. (1995). Casual Inference in the Social Science. Harvard Univ. Press, Cambridge.

Martorell, R., Habicht, J.P., Rivera, J.A. (1995). "History and design of the INCAP longitudinal study (1969–1977) and its follow-up (1988–1989)". Journal of Nutrition 125, 1027S–1041S.

Miguel, E., Kremer, M. (2004). "Worms: Identifying impacts on education and health in the presence of treatment externalities". Econometrica 72 (1), 159–217.

Mwabu, G. (2008). "Health economics for low-income countries". In: Schultz, T.P., Strauss, J. (Eds.), Handbook of Development Economics, vol. 4. Elsevier/North-Holland, Amsterdam. (Chapter 53 in this book.)

Nokes, C., van den Bosch, C., Bundy, D. (1998). "The effects of iron deficiency and anemia on mental and motor performance, educational achievement, and behavior in children: A report of the international nutritional anemia consultative group". USAID, Washington, DC.

Nokes, C., Grantham-McGregor, S., Sawyer, A., Cooper, E., Bundy, D. (1992). "Parasitic helminth infection and cognitive function in school children". Biological Sciences, Proceedings 247 (1319), 77–81.

Orazem, P.F., King, E.M. (2008). "Schooling in developing countries: The roles of supply, demand and government policy". In: Schultz, T.P., Strauss, J. (Eds.), Handbook of Development Economics, vol. 4. Elsevier/North-Holland, Amsterdam. (Chapter 55 in this book.)

Pollitt, E., Hathirat, P., Kotchabhakadi, N., Missel, L., Valyasevi, A. (1989). "Iron deficiency and education achievement in Thailand". American Journal of Clinical Nutrition 50 (3), 687–697.

Pollitt, E., Gorman, K., Engle, P., Martorell, R., Rivera, J. (1993). Early Supplemental Feeding and Cognition. Monographs of the Society for Research in Child Development, vol. 235. Univ. of Chicago Press, Chicago.

Seshadri, S., Gopaldas, T. (1989). "Impact of iron supplementation on cognitive functions in preschool and school-aged children: the Indian experience". American Journal of Clinical Nutrition 50 (3), 675–686.

Soemantri, A.G., Pollitt, E., Kim, I. (1989). "Iron deficiency anemia and education achievement". American Journal of Clinical Nutrition 50 (3), 698–702.

Soewondo, S., Husaini, M., Pollitt, E. (1989). "Effects of iron deficiency on attention and learning processes of preschool children: Bandung, Indonesia". American Journal of Clinical Nutrition 50 (3), 667–674.

Strauss, J., Thomas, D. (2008). "Health over the life course". In: Schultz, T.P., Strauss, J. (Eds.), Handbook of Development Economics, vol. 4. Elsevier/North-Holland, Amsterdam. (Chapter 54 in this book.)

Thomas, D., Frankenberg, E., Smith, J. (2002). "Lost but not forgotten: Attrition and follow-up in the Indonesian family life survey". Journal of Human Resources 36, 556–592.

Todd, P., Wolpin, K.I. (2006). "Using experimental data to validate a dynamic behavioral model of child schooling: Assessing the impact of a school subsidy program in Mexico". American Economic Review 96 (5), 1384–1417.

UNESCO (2002). "Education for All: Is the World On Track?" UNESCO Publishing, Paris.

UNESCO (2003). "UNESCO Institute of Statistics Electronic Database". http://www.uis.unesco.org/ev.php?URL_ID=5187&URL_DO=DO_TOPIC&URL_SECTION=201.

United Nations (2000). IACC/SCN 4th Report on the World Nutrition Situation. Washington, DC (in collaboration with the International Food Policy Research Institute.)

Vermeersch, C., Kremer, M. (2004). "School meals, educational achievement and school competition: Evidence from a randomized evaluation". World Bank Policy Research Working Paper No. 3523.

Walker, S., Wachs, T., Meeks Gardener, J., Lozoff, B., Wasserman, G., Pollitt, E., Carter, J. (2007). "Child development: Risk factors for adverse outcomes in developing countries". Lancet 369, 145–157.

World Bank (2001). World Development Report 2000/2001: Attacking Poverty. Oxford Univ. Press, New York.

World Bank (2003). "World development indicators 2003". Washington, DC.

World Bank (2005). "World development indicators". Washington, DC.

World Health Organization (WHO) (1993). "The control of schistosomiasis". Second report of the WHO. Technical Report Series 830. Expert Committee, WHO, Geneva.

World Health Organization (WHO) (2000). "The world health report 2000". Geneva.

Chapter 57

CHILD LABOR*

ERIC V. EDMONDS

Department of Economics at Dartmouth College, 6106 Rockfeller Hall, Hanover, NH 03755, USA

Institute for the Study of Labor (IZA), Germany

and

The National Bureau of Economic Research, USA

Contents

* I appreciate the comments and helpful discussions with Kathleen Beegle, Debopam Bhattacharya, Patrick Emerson, Deborah Levison, Peter Orazem, Nina Pavcnik, Norbert Schady, T. Paul Schultz, Najib Shafiq, Furio Rosati, Ken Swinnerton, and participants at the Bellagio conference for this volume. I am grateful to John Bellows, Zakariah Lakel, Ariel Rodman, Smita Reddy, Salil Sharma, Mahesh Shrestha, and Jiawen Ye for research assistance.

Handbook of Development Economics, Volume 4
© 2008 Elsevier B.V.   All rights reserved
DOI: 10.1016/S1573-4471(07)04057-0

Abstract

In recent years, there has been an astonishing proliferation of empirical work on child labor. An Econlit search of keywords "child lab*r" reveals a total of 6 peer reviewed journal articles between 1980 and 1990, 65 between 1990 and 2000, and 143 in the first five years of the present decade. The purpose of this essay is to provide a detailed overview of the state of the recent empirical literature on why and how children work as well as the consequences of that work.

Keywords

time allocation, child labor, labor supply, human capital, investments in children

JEL classification: J13, J22, J82, O15

1. Introduction

Few issues in developing countries draw as much popular attention as does child labor. The purpose of this chapter is to provide a detailed overview of the state of the recent empirical literature on why and how children work as well as the consequences of that work. A less detailed overview of recent developments in the child labor literature can be found in Edmonds and Pavcnik (2005a), and an older review with a more theoretical focus is Basu (1999).

Child labor has received considerable attention in economics throughout the discipline's history. Early writings tended to focus on child labor solely through the lens of labor demand. Adam Smith emphasized the value of children in labor shortage societies as motives for fertility. Friedrich Engels wrote extensively on the conditions of working children in the early industrial revolution, and to Marx, child labor was created by the industrial revolution. In his view, machines replaced the need for muscle power, allowing children to do the work formerly performed by men. Though his views on labor supply are not transparent, in *Das Kapital* he seems to assume that parents and capitalists inevitably exploit all opportunities to employ children. Interestingly, one exception to this assumption that working parents will take all opportunities to have children work is in Malthus. He argues that the prevalence of child labor in the late 18th century is evidence that families were unable to meet their most basic needs.

Modern writings on child labor are largely based on the human capital theory as developed by T.W. Schultz, Gary Becker, and others. In thinking through the determinants of investments in education, Schultz (1960) emphasized the importance of foregone earnings in human capital accumulation. Investors (parents, children) weigh the return on additional education investments against the costs such investments entail which includes the foregone economic contribution of children. Becker (1965) extended this argument to emphasize that non-wage uses of time are apt to be an equally important influence on the opportunity cost of child time in school. Rosenzweig and Evenson (1977) appear to be the first published study to apply this framework explicitly to analyze child labor in a developing country context.

In recent years, there has been an astonishing proliferation of empirical work on child labor. An Econlit search of keywords "child lab*r" reveals a total of 6 peer reviewed journal articles between 1980 and 1990, 65 between 1990 and 2000, and 143 in the first five years of the present decade. This rise in interest appears driven by three factors. First, child labor has drawn considerable policy and public attention over the last decade. This public interest seems to be motivated by a concern about child labor as a human rights issue and its implication for long-run growth and development through its interaction with education. The rise in interest in recent years may owe to rising trade and globalization more broadly. They have both raised awareness about the pervasiveness of child labor and elevated concerns among rich country residents about their role in its perpetuation. Second, concurrent with this rise in public interest is a booming theoretical literature on why children work. Prominent theoretical publications such as Basu and Van (1998) and Baland and Robinson (2000) have spurred a large battery of empirical research. Third, large-scale, nationally representative household surveys from developing countries have become increasingly available over the last fifteen years. This has both lowered the costs of working on child time allocation and increased the complexity of the types of questions that can be addressed empirically.

Any study of child labor must begin with a definition of what the researcher means by child labor. The next section surveys different definitions used in the existing literature and discusses some examples from a variety of countries about how children work. The types of activities popularly viewed as child labor are not usually the focus of empirical studies labeled "child labor." Often, academic studies of child labor are better viewed as child time allocation studies, and it seems clear that research must consider as wide a scope of activities as data permits in order to understand the dynamics of child time allocation. Data sources and data problems such as children that are hard to observe with randomized surveys are also discussed.

Section 3 considers the case for attention to the types of work activities that are most common in low income countries. Historically, activists sought to move children out of work so that children could enjoy their childhood, and the Progressive Era's "sacralization" of childhood (to quote Zelizer, 1994) persists in contemporary, anti-child labor resolutions such as the 1989 UN Convention on the Rights of the Child. Part of the reason for viewing working child work as a moral issue is that parents may make decisions for children about whether and how children work without fully internalizing the costs of such activities. Research on child labor tends to avoid moral arguments about how children should spend their time by focusing on quantifying the costs of working. Human capital theory generally post-dates the anti-child labor movements in developed economies, but most of the academic interest in child labor today is because of its consequences for human capital accumulation. Many studies examine whether specific types of work or groupings of activities appear to affect education, physical and mental health, or the nutritional status of working children. This begs the question of why focus on child labor as anything other than something to explain schooling or health changes. Several answers to this question are posited in the literature, and they are discussed in Section 3.

Section 4 reviews the accumulating evidence on why children work. This literature is of academic interest in its own right for all the same reasons that adult labor supply is of interest to research. Moreover, studying the determinants of common forms of work also can be informative about the case for attention to common activities. That is, how the common forms of work are affected by changes in the family's broader economic and social environment can reveal how family decision-makers view the most common forms of work in low income countries. Policies aimed to influence how and where children work can be useful for understanding the causes and consequences of working, and Section 5 discusses the minimal evidence that exists on how policies influence child labor supply. Section 6 concludes with a summary of the critical issues that have yet to be addressed in the literature.

A simple analytical model helps fix ideas in this chapter and can illustrate most of the basic points that have been emphasized in existing research on child labor. This model is presented in the remainder of this introduction. This model is meant to be heuristic. Cigno and Rosati (2005) present a more general time allocation model that can incorporate most of the important recent theoretical contributions in the child labor literature.

Consider a household with one parent, one child, and two time periods: the child's youth when the parent decides how to allocate the child's time and the child's future (the parent has no future in this model). The parent's labor supply is inelastic and yields an exogenous income Y. Parental preferences are over the family's current standard of living, S, and the child's future welfare V_k. $u(S, V_k)$ is the utility representation of parental preferences. The child's time is allocated between education E, leisure and play P, work outside of the household M, and work inside of the household H: $E + P + M + H = 1$. Work inside the household can be in the production of goods or services that might be resold to the market (market work) or it can be in similar activities that are important for the family in converting purchased inputs into a standard of living (domestic work).

The standard of living is produced by a linear homogeneous production function and depends on purchased inputs c and the input of child time H, $S = F(c, H)$. The child's future welfare depends on the positive, diminishing marginal product production function, $V_k = R(E, P)$. Leisure and play is likely complementary to schooling in the production of child welfare, but such statements about cross-partial derivatives are not necessary for the present discussion. Importantly, time spent in education is not necessarily limited to time in the classroom. Also, beyond the opportunity costs of education inherent in the time constraint, schooling entails direct costs, e. Direct costs are assumed to be increasing in the time spent in education. Thus, direct schooling costs entail eE in foregone consumption today. Work outside of the household is freely available in the formal labor market and brings an exogenous wage w. This income combines with non-child income Y to purchase inputs used in the production of the standard of living: $c = Y + wM - eE$. In this setting, the parent's problem is:

$$\max_{E,P,M,H} u\big(F(Y + wM - eE, H), R(E, P)\big)$$
$$\text{subject to:} \quad E + P + M + H = 1, \quad E \geqslant 0, \ P \geqslant 0, \ M \geqslant 0, \ H \geqslant 0. \qquad (1.1)$$

This setup emphasizes several points that will be raised in Sections 2 and 3. First, the residual claimant on child time outside of work is not schooling, and there is a return to leisure that parents may value and could be important for the child's future welfare. Second, if one is interested in child labor because of its impact on schooling, there is no theoretical reason to focus on work outside of the home alone. Consider a child that does not attend school. What are the possible explanations for this?

$$E = 0 \quad \Rightarrow \quad \frac{\partial u}{\partial V_k} \frac{\partial R}{\partial E} \leqslant \lambda + \frac{\partial u}{\partial S} \frac{\partial F}{\partial c} e. \qquad (1.2)$$

The family's marginal utility from the foregone consumption caused by schooling costs plus the marginal utility of time λ is at least as large as the family's marginal utility that comes through improving child welfare from additional education. The marginal utility of time will depend on how the family values the contribution of play to child welfare, the marginal utility of the standard of living, and how time spent in the wage market and in household production affects the standard of living. There is no reason to presume that the wage contribution is more likely to dominate schooling than is the household production contribution. In fact, most children work at home rather than in the wage labor market. This implies that, for most children, the return to time in household production is at least as large as the value the family places on the child's wage contribution. The idea that studies of child time allocation should consider as broad a definition of child work as the data permits is a main theme in Section 2. Of course, there are many reasons to be interested in why children work beyond its implications for schooling. Section 3 reviews the literature on the short term and long term consequences of child work.

This framework also implies several key reasons why children work. First, poverty is a key influence on child labor supply. It influences the family's valuation of child time in household production and the formal labor market, and it may affect the production function for future child welfare. Some researchers have emphasized that the influence on child labor of exiting poverty may differ from the effects of additional income, and this will be discussed in Section 4.

Second, the relative return to child time in schooling may be an important factor. The relative return depends in part on the returns to education as well as the returns to play, the return to child time in home production, the return to formal labor income, and the direct costs of schooling. Schooling improvements, labor demand factors including trade, technological change, and labor regulations all potentially affect child labor through these mechanisms. Similarly, living arrangements, fertility, and market imperfections in credit, land, or goods markets may all influence child labor through their impact on the relative return to child time.

Third, parental preferences play a key role in child time allocation decisions. In this setup, preferences do not drive differences in the allocation of child time between the formal labor market and household production, but they affect the family's valuation of child time in work activities relative to non-work activities. For example, a child engages in wage work and does not attend school if:

$$\frac{\partial u}{\partial V_k}\frac{\partial R}{\partial E} \leqslant \frac{\partial u}{\partial S}\frac{\partial F}{\partial c}(w + e). \tag{1.3}$$

The marginal utility from the child's contribution to the production of the standard of living (through wage income and the lack of educational expenditure) is at least as large as the marginal utility from the return to education. To the extent that preferences are important, then questions of intrahousehold allocation such as how household decisions are made and who makes these decisions become important in understanding child labor supply.

With so many influences on child labor, what types of policies will be useful in reducing it? Section 5 concludes with a discussion of different policy options that have been used to influence the activities of children. There is very limited evidence to suggest that anything other than long-term poverty reduction and development is likely to substantially alter the child labor picture although some findings from conditional cash transfer programs are encouraging. However, it is important to note that the general lack of evidence reflects a lack of scientific research more than a failure of programs. Moreover, very little is known about why children participate in some of the worst forms of child labor, where human rights issues are most relevant, and very little formal analysis has been done on the policies being pursued to help these most vulnerable children.

2. What is child labor?

Any discussion of child labor must begin with a precise description of what the term means. The phrase "child labor" conjures images of children chained into factories, sold as slaves, or forced into prostitution. Fortunately, while many children work in the developing world, few experience such atrocities. The International Labor Organization ILO, 2006a is the international body charged with counting child labor, and it estimates that in 2004 there are 218 million child laborers in the world (ILO, 2006a). Most of these working children labeled "child laborers" are helping their family at home, on the family farm, or in the family business. Economics research on "child labor" tends to focus on these more commonplace activities, both because of their greater prevalence and the relative ease in collecting data on the typical types of activities children perform. There is controversy about whether the types of activities that children typically participate in are harmful or beneficial to children and others. That discussion is reviewed in section three.

The present section aims to describe the different definitions of child labor and child work that are prevalent in the literature and overview how children typically work in low income countries. It should be clear from the discussion in the introduction that if one is ultimately interested in influencing the allocation of child time to a particular activity such as some form of work or schooling then researchers need to consider as broad a set of activities as possible. Children do not typically participate in the formal wage labor market. When children do not participate in the formal wage labor market, the shadow value of child time (λ in the analytical model) is determined by the child's involvement in chores, the family business, schooling, etc. Hence, focusing on a limited set of activities can bias a researcher's understanding of the dynamics of child time allocation. Of course, a broad focus on child time allocation overall inevitably means that a paper on "child labor" will consider types of work that are very different than the popular use of the term.

2.1. Terminology

2.1.1. Market and domestic work

In both research and policy discussions, there is extraordinary heterogeneity in how child labor is defined and in what words are used to describe the different categories of work in which children participate. The purpose of this subsection is to review how words are typically defined in the literature. There is no consensus. There is currently work underway to define statistical standards and develop a fixed terminology (see Guarcello et al., 2005) that is the basis for much of this section, but that work is still in its infancy. Both producers and consumers of research need to be careful to define exactly what is being studied in a particular research paper.

Table 1 lists commonly used phrases describing aspects of how children work. Activities are organized by whether the activity involves the direct production of economic goods and services that fall under the United Nations System of National Accounts (SNA). According to the SNA, "the production of economic goods and services includes all production and processing of primary products whether for the market, for barter, or for own consumption, the production of all other goods and services for the market and, in the case of households which produce such goods and services for the market, the corresponding production for own consumption" (ILO, 2000 p. 1). The production of economic goods and services will include wage employment, self-employment, participation in agriculture, milling, handicrafts, construction as well as water and wood collection.

Aggregate statistics of child employment typically cover the economically active population. Economically active is defined as being involved in economic activity, and it includes wage workers, employers, own-account workers, members of producer cooperatives, unpaid family workers, apprentices, members of the armed forces, and the unemployed. Economic work or market work is used similarly to economically active individuals, except the unemployed are excluded. Participants in market work are sometimes separated by whether their work is for the consumption of others (market oriented work) or their own family (non-market oriented work). One can imagine how this distinction is important in national accounts, but there is no clear reason why this distinction is important in studying child time allocation. Wage work is a subcategory of market oriented work, and many authors focus on studying wage employment alone. One unique challenge in classifying children engaged in market work outside of their own household is that children are not always paid directly in wages. They either receive pay in-kind (goods and services) or their labor is contracted for a fixed fee. Typically, these children are grouped with those paid in cash under "wage work," but some studies separate them, labeling them unpaid out of household market or economic work.

Child involvement in non-SNA activities is studied infrequently in child labor studies. A February 2005 review of empirical papers on child labor indexed in Econlit and published in peer reviewed economics journals since 1995 found that all but two considered wage work, half additionally considered other forms of market work such as work in the family farm or business, and 10 percent considered work that would fall outside the SNA definition of economic activity. The phrase non-economic work is sometimes used to denote participation in the provision of goods and services to family members or other members of the community that fall outside of the scope of the official definition of economic goods and services. This includes for example community service work that helps build or maintain local schools. It also includes domestic chores such

Table 1
Commonly used terms

Class term	Definition
SNA Economic Activities	
Economically active	Participates in the production of economic goods and services or is unemployed and seeking such employment
Employed	Economically active, excluding the unemployed, but including those temporarily out of work with a formal connection to a job
Economic work	Economically active, excluding the unemployed and those temporarily out of work
Market oriented economic work	Economically active in the production of goods or services for the market or barter
Wage work	Receives cash or in-kind payments for economic work
Non-market economic work	Economically active in the production of goods or services for own consumption
	Subcategories:
	Own account production of goods and services
	Own account construction and substantial repair services by owners of dwellings
	Own account collection and gathering activities
Family work	Economic work in own or family business or farm
Market work	Economic work
	Subcategories:
	Inside household
	Outside household (sometimes separated into paid and unpaid)
Non-SNA Activities	
Non-economic work	Participates in productive activities that are outside of the SNA definition of economic activity
	Alternatives: Non-economic activity, non-market household activity, non-market household production
Community service and volunteer work	Non-economic work provided outside of own household
Domestic chores	Provides services to own family members
	Alternatives: Household chores, housework (sometimes excludes shopping)
	Subcategories:
	Child and elder care
	Cooking
	Cleaning
	Small repairs
	Shopping for household goods and services
Domestic work	Non-economic work excluding community service and volunteer work

The designation of an activity as SNA is based on its classification in the 1993 UN System of National Accounts. See Guarcello et al. (2005) for additional discussion. See text for definition of economic goods and services.

as caring for family members, cooking, cleaning, or shopping. The phrase "housework" is sometimes in place of domestic chores or it is used to refer to domestic chores excluding shopping. Finally, "domestic work" is used in reference to non-economic work exclusive of community service and volunteer work.

The use of the word "economic" in the SNA is confusing. Since the early 1960s, economists have emphasized how important these "non-economic" activities are to the household's standard of living. Moreover, non-economic can be interpreted to imply that the associated activities are inelastic with respect to economic factors, an assumption that is not born out by the data. Many writers avoid using the phrases "economic" and "non-economic" work. Instead, they classify work into market work and domestic work. The remaining classification of work, community service and volunteer work, is rarely studied and poorly understood. There are two obvious problem with using this market and domestic work lexicon. First, market work and market oriented economic work are apt to be confused. Second, domestic work performed for compensation outside of the child's own household is considered a type of market work and is often referred to as domestic service or domestic work. The safest solution is for researchers to be explicit in how they are defining the activities under study.

Two commonly used terms to be avoided are child work and household work. Child work is typically used synonymously with market work. However, asserting that a child who works in substantive hours in the provision of services to their home is not working is difficult to justify. One could make the case for defining child work as covering both domestic and market work, but simply using the phrase "work" to refer to these activities together is apt to generate the least confusion given child work's common use as market work. Household work is often used as a synonym for domestic work. However, this is confusing, because market work most often occurs within the household.

2.1.2.   Child labor

Researchers often avoid labeling any one activity as child labor. Official definitions of child labor vary. Some countries officially define child labor as wage work (e.g. Pakistan) or market work that is harmful to the future well-being of children (e.g. Vietnam). This later standard is based on the precedent of the International Labor Organization's (ILO) C138 (ILO, 1973). C138 on the Minimum Age for Admission to Employment was passed in 1973 and has been signed by 135 countries to date. Signatories agree to pursue a national policy to abolish "child labor" and to increase the minimum age of employment to "a level consistent with the fullest physical and mental development of young persons" (C138, Article 1). Neither "child labor" nor "employment" is defined in the convention, but the age appropriateness of various activities depends on consideration of their effects on the health and development of the young. In general, the minimum age of employment is the minimum age of completion of compulsory schooling or at least 15 years old, although 14 can be consistent with the convention in very poor countries. Light work that is deemed consistent with schooling attendance and unlikely to be harmful to health and development is consistent with the convention in children as young as 12.

For statistical purposes, defining whether an activity is harmful to a child's health or development is a challenge, because whether an activity is harmful depends on what the child would be doing in the absence of work. The ILO's Statistical Information and Monitoring Program on Child Labor (SIMPOC) is the international body charged with tracking child labor around the world. Their definition of what exactly is "child labor" varies over time, in part because of controversy over what can be considered harmful. At the time of writing, a child laborer is defined by SIMPOC as an economically active child under 12 that works 1 or more hours per week, an economically active child 14 and under that works at least 14 hours per week or 1 or more hours per week in activities that are "hazardous by nature or circumstance," and a child 17 and under that works in an "unconditional worst form of child labor" (trafficked children, children in bondage or forced labor, armed conflict, prostitution, pornography, illicit activities, ILO, 2002). The ILO (2006a) estimates that there were 218 million child laborers in the world in 2004 under this definition.

Some researchers that choose to define an activity status as child labor adopt this SIMPOC definition, but others are also present in the literature. By far, the most common thing to do is to define children in wage work as child laborers. Others define child labor as market work. A few researchers also define child labor by adding in domestic work. Typically, an arbitrary cutoff in hours is employed in classifying some domestic workers as child laborers and others as not just as the SIMPOC definition arbitrarily classifies as 13 year old working 14 hours per week as a child laborer while the 13 year old working 13 hours per week is not. Given that "child labor" carries a particular connotation in the popular imagination, the safest course is likely for researchers to avoid labeling any one class of activities child labor.

"Light work" is sometimes used to refer to market work that is not deemed child labor. That is, light work is market work which is for some reason viewed as unlikely to be harmful to health, development, and does not affect school attendance, participation in vocational training, or the child's ability to benefit from any instruction received. Of course, it is not obvious how would know whether work could be harmful in any of these senses without establishing the counterfactual of what children would be doing absent this light work.

2.1.3. Worst and hazardous forms of child labor

While the general phrase "child labor" is poorly defined, some specific activities are labeled as a "hazardous form of child labor" or a "worst form of child labor". The minimum age convention, C138, places special emphasis on activities that "jeopardise the health, safety, or morals of young persons" (Article 3, Section 1) and defines 18 as the minimum age of employment for activities that can be described as such. In 1999, C182 on the Worst Forms of Child Labor asks signatory countries to clarify what types of activities fall under this label and to develop specific plans for their eradication

(ILO, 1999a). C182 has proven less controversial than C138 on the minimum age of employment. To date, C182 has 151 signatories.

While it is up to the individual country to identify "worst forms" in their own country, Article 3 of C182 contains several guidelines for what types of activities are to be considered for persons under the age of 18. These include all forms of slavery and "practices similar to slavery." This later clause is noted to include the sale and trafficking of children, debt bondage, serfdom, and forced or compulsory labor including for the purposes of armed conflict. These children as well as children in prostitution, pornography, the production or processing of drugs are in "unconditional worst forms" of child labor. The ILO (2002) estimates 8.4 million children under 18 in unconditional worst forms of child labor.

Article 3(d) is the most ambiguous part of convention 182. It allows worst forms to include "work which, by its nature or the circumstances in which it is carried out, is likely to harm the health, safety, or morals of children." Article 4 of the convention is explicit that it is up to individual countries to define what types of work are considered "worst forms" of child labor under this clause. Activities labeled "worst forms" under Article 3(d) of C182 are often labeled as "Hazardous forms of child labor." The companion recommendation document for C182, R190 Worst Forms of Child Labor Recommendation, suggests that these hazardous forms of child labor include:

"(a) work which exposes children to physical, psychological, or sexual abuse; (b) work underground, under water, at dangerous heights, or in confined spaces; (c) work with dangerous machinery, equipment and tools, or which involves the handling or transport of heavy loads; (d) work in an unhealthy environment which may, for example, expose children to hazardous substances, agents or processes, or to temperature, noise levels, or vibrations damaging to their health; (e) work under particularly difficult conditions such as work for long hours or during the night or work where the child is unreasonably confined to the premises or the employer." (ILO, 1999b, Section II.3.a–e)

It is worth noting that, unlike the more general child labor definitions discussed above, these hazardous forms of child labor are defined based on the characteristics of the work rather than relying on understanding what the child might do in the absence of work. Hence, the labeling of specific activity as a worst or hazardous form does not carry the same assumptions about the impact of that work as does the phrase child labor, and a specific country's policy definition of hazardous work or worst forms of child labor can guide researchers in the use of those terms. 170.5 million children under 18 are in hazardous forms of child labor (ILO, 2002).

2.2. Sources of data

2.2.1. Available data

Sources of data on child labor are increasing almost daily, and with them, our understanding of child labor should continue to increase accordingly. Unfortunately, it does not appear that much work is being done to validate the types of surveys and data collection methods that are being used extensively. Hence, there is considerable scope for work on how to measure the activities in which children participate.

Many early studies of child labor relied on cross-country data. Cross-country estimates of economic active populations come from the ILO's LABORSTA database although the most recent release (fifth edition) omits the 10–14 age group.[1] These LABORSTA estimates of economically activity populations are generally believed to understate the extent of work, because data on work inside the household (even market work) are often not collected. Moreover, although the LABORSTA data are available over time, very few low-income countries have multiple data sources on child labor over time. Much of the intertemporal variation in child labor in the LABORSTA data must thus be driven by the imputations and adjustments done for LABORSTA rather than independent observations on child labor. As a result, the LABORSTA data is not reliably useful for analyzing changes in child labor over time.

When the ILO's Statistical Information and Monitoring Program on Child Labor (SIMPOC) computes global estimates of the incidence of child labor, it does not rely on the LABORSTA data. Instead, it works wherever possible off available household surveys that facilitate a more complete picture of how children work and are free from LABORSTA's imputations. Understanding Children's Work (UCW) is a joint effort of the World Bank, UNICEF, and the ILO to coordinate studies relevant to child labor, and they maintain a thorough listing of labor force, child labor, and multi-purpose household surveys with information useful for studying how and why children work. Many dedicated child labor surveys assisted by SIMPOC are freely available for download from their website, and there are a variety of multi-purpose household surveys that can be downloaded for research purposes.[2]

This chapter draws extensively from UNICEF's Multiple Indicator Cluster Surveys (MICS) from 2000 and 2001.[3] They include a child labor module which asks children 5–14 whether they work outside of their household in the last week and the last year as well as how many hours they worked outside the household in the last week. The surveys also collect hours in the last week for work in domestic chores and in the household business (separately). No information is available on industry of employment, type of employer, nor compensation. An appealing feature of the MICS data is that survey instruments are nearly identical in each country. That said, questions are likely to be interpreted in different ways based on local context.[4]

---

[1] http://laborsta.ilo.org/. The fourth edition data (used herein) is available from UNSTAT as well.

[2] At the time of writing: UCW's data archive can be found at http://www.ucw-project.org; SIMPOC's archives are http://www.ilo.org/public/english/standards/ipec/simpoc/microdata/index.htm; World Bank assisted multi-purpose household surveys are available from http://www.worldbank.org/lsms/. The most recent Indonesian family life survey contains rich detail on how children spend their time: http://www.rand.org/labor/FLS/IFLS/. Several of the Demographic and Health Surveys also contain information on child time allocation: http://www.measuredhs.com/.

[3] http://www.childinfo.org/MICS2/MICSDataSet.htm.

[4] For example, 38 percent of children 5–14 in Niger answer that they work in unpaid work outside of their family. The average across all countries is 6 percent. It could be that this labor arrangement is much more

2.2.2. *Limitations of household surveys and missing children*

Several issues arise in using household survey data to examine child labor supply. First, there is the general question about who to ask about the child's labor supply. A great deal of attention has been directed by agencies such as SIMPOC and UCW towards what types of activities should be monitored, but it is difficult to find detailed analysis of how this information should be collected. It seems likely that measurement error in hours worked is a first order problem with this data while participation is perhaps less difficult to gauge.

Second, measurement of compensation is particularly complicated. Most children do not work for wages, so strong modeling assumptions are required even in detailed data to gauge their compensation. Moreover, it is not obvious that even in wage work any one respondent will be fully aware of the child's compensation. For example, a parent may be paid an amount that the child is not aware of for the child's services, but an employer may also compensate the child to reduce moral hazard problems.

Third, estimates of the incidence of any type of work will be sensitive to the recall period used. It is not unusual for children to work intermittently, and it is not obvious what the "right" recall period is for any analysis. For example, in agricultural communities, one often observes high participation rates in market work during harvest seasons but little other than domestic work at other times of year. Systematic evidence on the dynamics of child labor is extremely rare. Levison et al. (2003) is an exception. Brazil's urban, monthly employment survey follows approximately 35,000 household for fourth months (the survey is set up as a rotating panel). Levison et al use this data to document the intermittent nature of market work participation in urban Brazil from 1982 to 1999. In their sample, they observe that the percent of children employed in any given month is roughly half the number of children employed in at least one of the four months. Moreover, depending on the city, between 20 and 40 percent of children 10–14 experienced 2 or more employment transitions in a four month period. Hence, child labor measures are sensitive to both the types of work considered and the recall periods used to assess employment status. This intermittency of employment raises particular problems for child labor measures based on the intensity of the child's work.

Fourth, some of the most vulnerable children may be impossible to capture with surveys. Either they do not reside in households or their situation is sufficiently rare that the probability that they are sampled in a randomized survey is effectively zero. Moreover, there is often little reason to assume that selection into these activities (relative to other more easily measured forms of work) is random. To get at these rare or hard to find groups of children, researchers often employ contaminated sampling procedures, but it is hard to draw inferences with this data when children outside of the activity are unobserved. This is an active avenue of research (for example: Edmonds, 2006c).

frequent in Niger, or it may be that respondents are interpreting the question in a different way than are respondents in other countries.

There are two approaches that can be taken to gauge the problem of missing children. Both have severe limitations. First, enumerators can collect complete fertility histories and then account for all of the children. In general, this approach may be biased by errors of omission if children in particular circumstances are also omitted from fertility histories. Alternatively, this fertility history based approach may overstate the extent of missing children, because children that set up independent households or that are fostered in to other households should appear in those household rosters and would not be excluded from any analysis using representative data.

Table 2 presents an example of this approach. A subset of the MICS countries include fertility histories for women 15–49, and Table 2 lists the mean total births, number dead, and number absent for women in these countries in this age range that report having given birth in the last 15 years. Unfortunately, the data do not identify the timing or age of each birth. It is impossible to decipher the extent to which differences in adult mobility rates are driving differences in the number of absent children or how many of the absent children would be captured in other households in a study of children 10–14 (for example). In many countries, a negligible number of children are missing from the mother's household: less than a percent in Vietnam, Uzbekistan, Tajikistan,

Table 2
Number of children by women who gave birth in the last 15 years

Country	Total births	# Dead	# Absent
Albania	2.06	0.06	0.01
Azerbaijan	2.44	0.25	0.01
Burundi	3.16	0.54	0.09
Cameroon	2.82	0.39	0.36
CAR	3.38	0.61	0.39
Chad	3.46	0.65	0.27
Comores	3.35	0.22	0.23
D.R. Congo	3.12	0.56	0.22
Gambia	3.24	0.48	0.48
Guinea Bissau	3.06	0.64	0.46
Guyana	2.62	0.20	0.14
Kenya	2.83	0.25	0.21
Lesotho	2.26	0.23	0.25
Madagascar	2.76	0.36	0.26
Niger	3.35	0.79	0.33
Saotome	2.57	0.30	0.25
Sierraleone	3.33	0.93	0.65
Swaziland	2.46	0.21	0.47
Tajikistan	3.01	0.36	0.02
Uzbekistan	2.52	0.17	0.02
Vietnam	2.24	0.10	0.02

Source: Author's calculation from the 2000 MICS microdata: http://www.childinfo.org/MICS2/MICSDataSet.htm.

Azerbaijan, and Albania. However, nearly 20 percent of living births are absent in Sierra Leone and Swaziland. 15 percent are absent in Gambia and Guinea Bissau. Altogether, 10 percent or more of births are absent in 9 of 22 countries. It is impossible to tell whether these missing children would be relevant for an analysis of child labor supply or schooling. It is also impossible to identify how many of these children would appear in other households in a nationally representative randomized survey. However, there seems to be ample potential for a substantive problem in some settings.

The problem of missing children is most acute in panel data, because children that exit a panel household who would be captured in a representative survey are unlikely to reappear in other panel households. However, panel data permits a second approach to evaluate the scale of missing children. Many household panels collect information on individuals, including missing individuals over time. This data can be tabulated to gauge the scale of missing children for work. Extrapolating from this tabulation to representative data overstates the problem of missing children as many children that exit panel households would be captured in a survey of non-panel households, but it is an accurate reflection of the incidence of missing children in panel households.

Table 3 contains counts of missing and recaptured children in two household level panel data sets from Nepal and Vietnam. A comparison of missing children in the two panels is illustrative, because the questionnaires regarding attrition are very similar, both data sets are World Bank assisted Living Standards Measurement Surveys (LSMS), and at the start of each panel, the two countries have similar living standards as measured by GDP per capita. The counts in Table 3 are only for recaptured household and are not relevant for assessing child attrition in households that are not in the panel for each country. In the Vietnam data, 93 percent of boys and girls are recaptured. Of the missing children, 7 percent of boys and 8 percent of girls are potentially missing from the Vietnam data because of work or schooling (this includes children whose absence is not

Table 3
Missing children 6–14 in selected panel data

Country Round 1 Round 2	Nepal 1996 2001		Vietnam 1993 1998	
Gender	Boys	Girls	Boys	Girls
# Children in household in R1 that should be 6–14 in R2	704	675	2515	2410
# Present	546	503	2354	2241
Why Missing? Counts:				
Dead	5	19	19	13
Married or household split	83	131	130	142
Work	38	5	1	4
Schooling	24	12	5	6

Source: Author's calculations from the Nepal Living Standards Surveys (Central Bureau of Statistics, 1998, 2005) and the Vietnam Living Standards Surveys (General Statistical Office, 1994, 1999).

explained). This corresponds to less than a percent of the boys and girls that would be expected to appear in the second round of the panel in the Vietnamese data.

While out-migration for work or school is then unlikely to be a significant source of bias in the Vietnamese data (at least for recaptured households), it appears to be a much more substantive issue in the Nepali data. 78 percent of boys and 75 percent of girls are recaptured in panel households in the Nepali panel. Of the missing, 44 percent of boys and 13 percent of girls are potentially missing for work or school. These missing children constitute 10 percent of the boys and 3 percent of the girls expected to be in the household for the second round of the panel. Hence, while the data from Vietnam suggest that missing children is unlikely to be a substantive problem in that data, there is considerably more scope for problems in the Nepali data. Specific country contexts must be considered in discussing biases owing to missing children.

2.2.3. Idle children

Most household surveys of children capture a large number of children that neither work nor attend school. For example, the 2000 Indian National Sample Survey classifies 13 percent of rural children 10–14 in India as neither working nor attending school. These children are typically labeled "idle," and the exact interpretation of their status is controversial. Biggeri et al. (2003) discuss the interpretation of idle status in household surveys from six different countries. They argue that measurement error in activities (especially mismeasurement of domestic work), unemployment, and unobserved health issues are responsible for a significant part of the "idleness" status. Measurement issues may be particularly important in cross-country comparisons as understandings of "work" may vary from country to country.

Idleness is not necessarily simply measurement error in work. Idleness can be fully rational in a time allocation model with schooling costs such as that of Section 1. Equation (1.2) specifies that a child does not attend school when the marginal utility associated with the returns to education is less than the foregone utility caused by schooling costs and the shadow value of child time. When children also do not work ($H = 0$, $M = 0$), the shadow value of child time is simply the marginal utility associated with the return on leisure for the child's future welfare. Thus, idle status occurs when:

$$\{E = 0, \ M = 0, \ H = 0, \ P > 0\} \quad \Rightarrow \quad \frac{\partial u}{\partial V_k} \frac{\partial R}{\partial E} \leqslant \frac{\partial u}{\partial V_k} \frac{\partial R}{\partial P} + \frac{\partial u}{\partial S} \frac{\partial F}{\partial c} e,$$

$$\frac{\partial u}{\partial S_k} \frac{\partial F}{\partial c} \leqslant \frac{\partial u}{\partial V_k} \frac{\partial R}{\partial P},$$

$$\frac{\partial u}{\partial S_k} \frac{\partial F}{\partial H} \leqslant \frac{\partial u}{\partial V_k} \frac{\partial R}{\partial P}. \tag{2.1}$$

That is, true idleness occurs when the marginal utility associated with additional leisure is at least as large as that of the contribution of the child's work to household welfare. Is this ever plausible unless the parents put substantive weight on child leisure? There is no empirical evidence to inform this question, but it could occur when there are not wage employment options open to children ($M = 0$), and the shape of the home production function $F(-)$ is such that the marginal product of child labor can become non-positive. For example, there may be a limited amount of helpful tasks young children can do in a family business. Once completed, children may be more destructive to output (perhaps distractive to adult labor) than helpful. Whether the prevalence of idle children reflects the economic reality of the country or problems in how child time allocation data is collected is not yet answered. Interestingly, Edmonds, Pavcnik, and Topalova (2007) find that the poverty elasticity of idleness in Indian data is greater than is the poverty elasticity of market or domestic work. Hence, even if idleness reflects measurement error, it might not be classical measurement error.

2.3. Background on the activities of working children

2.3.1. Types of activities

Table 4 presents participation rates in various categories of activity for 34 countries included in UNICEF's MICS project. The questionnaires are nearly identical in all the countries in Table 4. The data present a unique opportunity to examine child labor across countries in as comparable a manner as possible (little can be done for cultural differences in the interpretation of the questions). Participation rates in schooling, market work, market work for wages, other market work outside of the household, market work inside the household, domestic work, any work, work without schooling, and no work and no schooling are reported in Table 4. Note that while there is considerable variation in schooling, schooling rates are surprisingly high. This reflects the structure of the questionnaire. It asks whether a child has attended school in the last year while the labor questions refer to the last week.

Several important properties of how children work are apparent in Table 4. First, work outside of the household is the least prevalent work category in every country except Azerbaijan, Kenya, and Venezuela. In these three countries participation rates in market work inside and outside of the household are similar. Altogether, 8 percent of children in the MICS data work outside of their household, and only 2 percent work in paid work outside of the household. It is unclear what the 6 percent of children who work outside their house without pay are doing in the MICS data, but in other data sets, they are often observed working in labor exchanges on neighboring farms, working in schools in exchange for materials or a reduction in fees, helping a relative with their work, etc. Domestic work is the most prevalent type of work. Across countries, 65 percent of children 5–14 report working in domestic work, compared to 23 percent in market work.

Second, the countries with the lowest school attendance rates have the highest incidence of "idle" children that neither work nor attend schooling. Work is not the residual claimant on child time outside of school. Moreover, work is not especially prevalent in these countries with high rates of idleness. They do not have the highest rates of work

Table 4
Participation rates in various activities by country for children 5–14

	Schooling	Market work			Domestic work	Any work	Any work, no school	No work, no school
		Any	Inside hh	Outside hh				
Sampled countries	89.2	22.7	18.2	8.4	64.6	68.0	6.4	4.4
Albania	54.7	31.3	29.5	3.5	56.1	62.7	32.6	12.7
Angola	93.2	25.7	20.4	8.8	77.0	78.2	5.9	1.0
Azerbaijan	99.1	8.6	4.0	5.3	61.4	63.3	0.7	0.2
Burundi	88.1	31.2	27.6	6.9	84.3	87.3	11.2	0.7
Cameroon	94.5	55.0	42.7	30.8	81.1	85.2	5.0	0.4
Central African Republic	85.5	62.2	50.3	37.3	85.0	88.9	13.6	0.8
Chad	95.0	62.6	55.2	26.7	82.5	88.3	4.6	0.3
Comores	77.1	38.1	32.2	16.3	61.1	66.8	15.9	6.3
Cote d'Ivoire	93.2	37.7	35.3	6.2	68.6	76.7	5.5	1.2
Democratic Republic of the Congo	53.5	19.2	12.9	10.4	50.3	52.3	17.4	29.1
Equatorial Guinea	94.9	33.7	31.0	5.4	84.9	85.8	3.1	0.6
Gambia	93.1	25.1	20.6	6.1	49.4	57.6	4.6	2.3
Guininea-Bissau	93.0	65.5	62.4	15.3	77.3	87.2	6.3	0.6
Guyana	97.4	26.3	15.9	14.7	72.8	75.2	2.3	0.3
Kenya	95.9	2.8	1.0	2.2	66.3	66.8	2.8	1.0
Laos	93.1	31.1	29.3	3.9	69.7	71.3	6.3	0.5
Lesotho	96.6	20.4	17.1	6.1	70.2	72.7	2.6	0.8
Madagascar	88.9	12.0	8.8	3.8	20.5	29.2	5.8	5.3
Moldova	97.3	30.5	23.2	11.8	86.3	88.0	2.1	0.6
Mongolia	95.2	21.4	20.6	1.4	91.2	91.7	4.6	0.2
Niger	88.1	67.1	44.4	42.9	88.7	93.7	11.4	0.4
North Sudan	86.0	16.4	14.2	4.1	52.8	56.7	10.1	4.0
Philippines	95.4	15.5	12.1	4.7	80.9	81.8	4.3	0.2
Rwanda	86.5	27.4	22.7	7.9	82.1	84.3	12.3	1.2
Sao Tome	88.7	15.5	10.0	7.8	80.0	81.3	9.5	1.7
Senegal	89.6	33.7	20.6	17.9	86.9	91.1	9.7	0.4
Sierra Leone	93.5	72.1	59.0	51.4	86.3	89.8	5.9	0.4
South Sudan	95.9	13.1	11.2	3.8	35.2	39.8	2.3	3.2
Swaziland	93.7	10.2	7.9	2.7	83.3	81.7	4.9	1.1
Tajikistan	97.2	12.4	10.0	3.4	72.5	74.6	2.6	0.3
Trinidad	98.0	3.2	2.3	1.1	56.3	56.6	1.1	0.8
Uzbekistan	96.4	15.2	10.6	5.8	78.1	79.8	3.4	0.3
Venezuela	92.0	8.1	3.9	4.5	62.4	64.6	3.8	4.2
Vietnam	95.1	24.4	23.4	1.9	51.7	57.8	4.3	0.6

Source: Author's calculation from the 2000 MICS microdata: http://www.childinfo.org/MICS2/MICSDataSet.
htm.

outside of the household or work in market work. This is consistent with the idea that no single indicator of activity will give a particularly complete idea of child time allocation, and research needs to take a comprehensive view of child time in order to understand how it is influenced.

Third, countries with the highest prevalence of work outside the household also have the highest prevalence of work inside the household. Sierra Leone has the highest rate of work outside the household, and the second highest rate of work inside the household. Niger is second with 43 percent of children working outside the household, while it has the fifth highest rate of market work inside the household. In Section 4.1 below, we discuss the weak nature of the evidence linking child's market work status and employment opportunities outside of the household, and the high correlation between work inside and outside the household are consistent with the idea that children are not working solely because wage labor market factors draw children away from their homes.

Fourth, participation in market work is highest in countries where domestic work is most prevalent. This positive correlation in participation rates for market and domestic work also appears in hours worked. However, the positive correlations between hours in various categories of work mask a more nuanced view—that participation in various activities is positively correlated when children work a small number of hours in each activity (as is typical) but not with extreme hours. This is evident in Fig. 1 which presents the joint distribution of hours worked in market and domestic work for all children 10–14 in the MICS data. Figure 1 is a contour map of the joint density of hours in market work and hours in domestic work for children 10–14 in the pooled MICS data. Each contour on the map is a given density. Thus each point on a given contour is equally likely. Density is increasing in color intensity.

Several key points are evident in Fig. 1. First, at the peak of the density, children work more hours per week in domestic work than market work. Ignoring domestic work would frequently understate total hours worked by a child by a factor slightly greater than 2. Second, children working a large number of hours in market work are more likely than not to spend additional time in domestic work. This is evidence by the humps in the market work direction. No such humps are evident with hours in domestic work. Third, as hours per week in domestic work increase, it becomes less likely to observe the child doing significant time in market work. This is evident in the increasing slope of contours as one heads up the domestic hours worked distribution.

The joint distribution of hours worked in Fig. 1 illustrates the problem with "child labor" definitions that focus on market work alone, especially definitions based on the intensity of hours worked. For example, suppose a researcher decided to be concerned about children that worked more than 20 or more hours per week. If only work outside the household was considered, this would be 8 percent of the MICS 10–14 sample. If market work inside the household is also included, 23 percent of children work more than 20 or more hours per week. When domestic work is also considered, 38 percent work 20 or more hours per week and 17 percent work 40 or more hours per week. Hence,

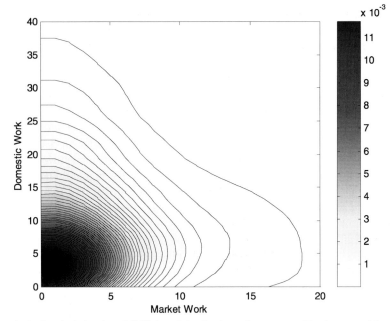

Source: Author's calculation from MICS data. Joint density estimates use a bivariate normal kernel with bandwidth chosen following Silverman (1986, p. 20). Each child in the MICS countries is weighted to reflect the number of individuals they represent. Hence, the picture is representative for the pooled populations of the MICS countries.

Figure 1. Joint density of hours worked in domestic and market work for children 10–14.

ignoring domestic work may seriously understate estimates of total hours worked and thereby the incidence of child labor if hours worked is used to define the concept.

2.3.2. *Occupation and industry of economically active children*

In Table 4, it is clear that most working children participate in domestic work. Among children engaged in market work, most of that work is inside the child's household. The industrial and occupational composition of employment in market work is not available in the MICS data. Comparable cross-country estimates of the industrial and occupational composition of child involvement in market work do not appear to exist. One possible source of this information is that most SIMPOC child labor surveys use similar questionnaires, and they tend to collect information on occupation and industry. In this section, we tabulate available information on industry and occupation for economically active children as reported in downloadable, English language SIMPOC reports.

Table 5 shows the industrial composition of economically active populations for available countries.[5] In almost every listed country, a majority of children economically active children are involved with agriculture, forestry, or fishing industries. The exceptions are the 5–17 populations of Costa Rica, Panama, and the Ukraine where these industries are still the largest employers of children. In most countries, the combination of hotel and restaurants and wholesale and retail trade are the next most important industrial sectors for economically active children. When they can be disaggregated, wholesale and retail trade tends to have a larger share of economically active children than does the hotel and restaurant sector. Manufacturing tends to be small relative to agriculture related and wholesale and retail trade sectors, but manufacturing employs a larger share of children than does mining or construction in every country in the table. Interestingly, private households are large employers of economically active children in Kenya, Tanzania, and Zambia. Many of these children are child domestic workers, and the phenomena of child domestic workers in Africa and elsewhere is infrequently studied in detail within economics.

The comparability of industry classifications in the SIMPOC surveys across countries is not as complete as one would like. Nor are the classifications particularly detailed. The 2002/03 Bangladesh Child Labor Survey is unusual in the incredible detail it provides on the industrial classification of economically active children. Table 6 tabulates the 4 digit industrial distribution of the economically active populations of children 5–17 in Bangladesh. Only sectors with at least 0.5 percent of economically active children in either rural or urban areas are reported in Table 6. In examining the detailed industrial composition of employment in Bangladesh, it is important to remember that there is no reason to believe that Bangladesh is representative of other low-income countries. There are an estimate 7.5 million economically active children 5–17 in Bangladesh. This corresponds to 18 percent of children 5–17.

The detailed classifications of Table 6 are useful to see what children are doing within the aggregate sectors. Children involved in agriculture and related industries are involved in the growing of cereals, vegetables, poultry farming, and inland fishing. Cereal cultivation is the largest single sector with 39 percent of all economically active children directly involved. In the retail trade industries, groceries and general stores are the largest employer of children. In manufacturing, wooden furniture and fixtures stand out. For construction, site preparation is relatively more important.

The disaggregated occupational composition of economically active children can provide further insight into what children do. Information at the 3 digit level is available

---

[5] Of the MICS countries from Table 4, only Kenya and the Philippines also have child labor surveys. It is interesting to note, that MICS estimates of participation rates in market work differ from estimates of the economically active population in the SIMPOC surveys for these two countries. The difference in the Philippine data is small. 16 percent of children are involved in market work in the MICS data, 11 percent in the SIMPOC survey. However, the differences in the Kenyan data are large. Three percent of Kenyan children 5–14 are involved in market work in the MICS surveys, but the SIMPOC surveys report an economic activity rate for this population of 15 percent. It is not clear why these estimates differ.

Table 5
Industrial composition of economically active children

Country	Age group	Agr. Forestry Fishing	Mining & Quarry	Manufact.	Construct.	Hotel Rest. Trade	Transport, Storage, Comm.	Social & Community Service	Private House	Other
Bangladesh	5–17	16.4	0.2	14.4	3.1	16.4	4.5	4.4		0.4
Cambodia	5–17	16.0	0.5	6.3	1.0	16.0	0.7	2.3		0.4
Costa Rica	5–17	26.5		9.0	7.0	26.5			5.9	8.0
Costa Rica	5–14	24.4		7.3	4.8	24.4			2.8	4.1
El Salvador	5–17	23.0	0.3	16.0	2.4	23.0	2.1	2.1	4.8	2.2
Ethiopia	5–9	1.0		0.4	0.1	1.0	0.0	0.3	0.3	0.2
Ethiopia	10–14	4.7		2.0	0.3	4.7	0.1	1.0	1.0	0.3
Ethiopia	15–17	9.6		4.3	0.7	9.6	0.2	2.0	2.0	0.5
Ghana	5–9	20.9	0.4	4.3		20.9	0.3	0.5	0.3	0.3
Ghana	10–14	28.3	0.5	5.9		28.3	0.2	0.3	0.3	0.2
Ghana	15–17	26.1	0.5	8.7		26.1	0.9	1.5	1.0	1.2
Honduras	5–9	35.5	0.0	8.5	1.5	35.5	0.2	0.0		0.0
Honduras	10–14	27.3	0.0	6.9	1.4	27.3	0.6	3.9		0.1
Honduras	15–17	21.0	0.3	9.3	4.5	21.0	1.4	9.5		0.4
Kenya	5–9	0.8	0.5	1.1	0.0	0.8	0.3	5.9	2.4	0.0
Kenya	10–14	2.6	0.5	1.8	0.4	2.6	0.1	6.1	8.8	0.7
Kenya	15–17	3.5	0.5	1.4	0.5	3.5	1.3	4.7	16.7	0.6
Namibia	6–10	0.1	0.0	0.1	0.0	0.1	0.9	5.2		13.0
Namibia	11–15	0.4	0.1	0.7	0.0	0.4	0.8	4.8		14.0
Namibia	16–18	4.9	0.1	1.3	0.7	4.9	1.5	7.5		12.1
Nicaragua	5–9	24.8		8.4		24.8		4.3		2.1
Nicaragua	10–14	23.0		9.7		23.0		7.0		2.0
Nicaragua	15–17	16.5		13.1		16.5		11.4		7.5
Pakistan	5–14	8.7		10.8	1.8	8.7	3.7	8.0		0.0
Panama	5–17	18.9	0.2	3.5	3.1	18.9	3.7	11.1	7.8	2.4
Phillippines	5–9	24.2	0.0	3.6	0.0	24.2	2.0	2.0	3.6	3.6
Phillippines	10–14	22.1	0.5	4.2	0.5	22.1	1.3	1.4	3.3	2.6
Phillippines	15–17	19.4	0.5	5.3	2.7	19.4	3.9	2.2	8.6	5.1
Phillippines	5–17	21.0	0.4	4.6	1.4	21.0	2.5	1.8	5.7	3.7
Sri Lanka	5–17	10.8	1.3	14.8	2.0	10.8	0.9	5.4		1.1
Tanzania	5–17	2.2	0.1	0.3	0.0	2.2	0.0		17.4	0.0
Tanzania	5–9	0.8	0.0	0.1	0.0	0.8			27.8	0.0
Tanzania	10–14	1.9	0.0	0.2	0.0	1.9	0.0		16.8	0.0
Tanzania	15–17	4.2	0.2	0.7	0.1	4.2	0.1		7.8	0.0
Turkey	6–17	10.2	*	21.8*	*	10.2		10.4		0.0
Ukraine	5–17	21.0	**	8**	9.0	21.0		19.0		0.0
Zambia	5–9	2.2	0.0	0.2	0.2	2.2	0.0		3.8	1.5
Zambia	10–14	3.4	0.0	0.4	0.1	3.4	0.0		2.1	0.7
Zambia	15–17	11.2	0.1	2.0	0.4	11.2	1.0		8.7	1.4
Zimbabwe	5–17	2.1	0.3	1.9	1.7	2.1	0.2		10.8	0.6

Age categories determined by availability in report. Industry groupings determined by availability in report. A missing reflects that industry was not available in report.

Sources: Bangladesh – Bangladesh Bureau of Statistics (2003); Cambodia – National Institute of Statistics (2002); Costa Rica – Trejos and Pisoni (2003); El Salvador – ILO-IPEC (2004); Ethiopia – Central Statistical Authority (2003); Ghana – Ghana Statistical Service (2003); Honduras – Cruz (2002); Kenya – Central Bureau of Statistics (2001); Namibia – Ministry of Labour (2000); Nicaragua – Silva (2003); Pakistan – Federal Bureau of Statistics (1996); Panama – Cornejo et al. (2003); Philippines – National Statistics Office (2003); Sri Lanka – Department of Census and Statistics (1999); Tanzania – National Bureau of Statistics (2001); Turkey – State Institute of Statistics (1999); Ukraine – State Statistics Committee (2001); Zambia – Central Statistical Office (1999); Zimbabwe – Ministry of Public Service, Labour and Social Welfare (1999).

*Turkey combines mining, quarrying, manufacturing, and construction.

**Ukraine combines Manufacturing, mining, and quarrying.

Table 6
4-Digit industrial composition of working children 5–17 in Bangladesh, 2002–2003

Industry description	Bangladesh (%)			Urban (%)		Rural (%)	
	Total	Boys	Girls	Boys	Girls	Boys	Girls
Growing of cereal crops (paddy, barley, jowar, etc.)	38.9	44.4	23.6	15.0	7.6	51.3	27.4
Growing of vegetable (potato, patal, tomato, etc.)	5.4	1.7	15.7	0.4	3.0	2.0	18.6
Growing of tea, coffee and other beverage crops	0.7	0.5	1.1	0.0	0.0	0.6	1.4
Farming of cattle, sheep, goats, horses areas, etc.	1.1	0.9	1.7	0.5	1.6	1.0	1.7
Poultry farming	4.3	1.0	13.6	0.4	11.0	1.2	14.2
Felling of frees and rough shaping of timber	0.6	0.6	0.8	0.4	0.3	0.6	0.9
Inland fishing (excluding shrimp farming)	2.7	3.2	1.2	2.0	0.6	3.5	1.3
Processing and preserving of fish and fish products	0.5	0.0	1.7	0.0	1.3	0.0	1.8
Rice milling	0.7	0.7	0.7	1.0	1.1	0.6	0.6
Manufacture of bidies	0.8	0.4	1.9	1.2	5.0	0.3	1.2
Cotton textiles except handlooms	0.5	0.5	0.4	1.1	1.6	0.4	0.2
Handloom textiles	1.5	1.2	2.1	1.3	2.4	1.2	2.0
Wearing apparel except fur apparel	1.3	0.9	2.3	2.0	8.4	0.7	0.9
Manufacture of corrugated paper and paper board containers	0.1	0.1	0.2	0.1	1.1	0.1	0.0
Manufacture of structural metal products	0.9	1.1	0.1	2.0	0.3	0.9	0.1
Manufacture of wooden furniture and fixtures	2.2	2.8	0.3	4.9	0.5	2.3	0.3
Manufacture of cane and bamboo furniture	0.4	0.2	0.9	0.2	1.5	0.1	0.8
Wood, cane and bamboo decorative handicrafts	0.8	0.4	2.0	0.3	1.6	0.4	2.1
Textile and sewing decorative handicrafts	1.2	0.0	4.2	0.2	12.6	0.0	2.3
Manufacture of jewellery and related articles	0.4	0.5	0.0	1.6	0.3	0.2	0.0
Site preparation	2.0	2.6	0.2	3.9	0.6	2.2	0.2
Building of complete construction or parts there of civil engineering	1.0	0.6	1.9	1.4	4.9	0.5	1.2
Maintenance and repair of motor vehicles	0.5	0.7	0.1	1.3	0.1	0.5	0.1
Retail trade of pan, cigarettes, biddies, betelnuts and tobacco	0.8	0.9	0.3	1.6	0.6	0.8	0.2
Retail trade of rice, pulse, wheat and flour	0.6	0.7	0.3	0.8	0.3	0.6	0.3
Retail trade of fish and sea food	0.5	0.6	0.2	1.3	0.1	0.4	0.2
Retail trade of grocery and general store	4.1	5.1	1.5	9.3	1.4	4.1	1.5
Retail sale of vegetables	1.1	1.0	1.2	1.8	1.5	0.8	1.2
Retail sale of textiles clothing, hosiery, foot ware and leather goods	0.7	0.8	0.7	2.0	1.1	0.5	0.6
Retail sale in specialized stores N.E.C.	0.9	1.0	0.6	1.8	1.0	0.8	0.6
Other non-store retail sale	1.0	1.2	0.4	2.1	1.3	1.0	0.3
Restaurants and non-residential hotels	0.8	0.9	0.4	1.7	0.5	0.7	0.4
Tea stalls	1.7	1.9	1.0	2.8	1.3	1.7	0.9
Land transport of scheduled passenger (bus, railway, etc.)	0.6	0.8	0.1	1.7	0.4	0.6	0.0
Land transport of non-scheduled passengers	1.8	2.4	0.1	4.5	0.4	1.9	0.1
All trade transport operation by road, whether scheduled or not	1.7	2.2	0.3	2.0	0.8	2.2	0.2
Activities of pre-primary school (kindergarten, coaching center, etc.)	0.3	0.2	0.6	0.4	1.3	0.1	0.5
Hairdressing and other beauty treatment	0.6	0.8	0.2	1.1	0.6	0.7	0.1
Tailoring services	1.7	1.4	2.5	2.2	3.3	1.2	2.3
Private household with employed persons (maids, cooks, etc.)	1.3	0.3	4.0	0.4	6.4	0.3	3.5
Other industries N.E.C.	11.7	12.8	8.5	21.1	10.3	10.9	8.1

N.E.C. – Not elsewhere classified. Only industries with at least 0.5 percent of economically active children in urban or rural Bangladesh are listed.

Source: Table C52 of the Report on National Child Labor Survey (Bangladesh Bureau of Statistics, 2003).

in the Bangladesh child labor force survey, and these data are tabulated in Table 7. 46 percent of children 5–17 are farm crop workers. The next largest occupations are salesmen and shop assistants (7 percent), poultry farmers (5 percent), sales supervisors (4 percent), fisherman (3 percent), and non-motorized road vehicle drivers (3 percent).

2.3.3. Gender differences

Gender differences in activities can be considerable in some countries. Compared to girls, boys generally have higher participation rates in market work and lower participation rates in domestic work. For example, in the MICS countries, girls are 18 percent more likely to be involved in domestic work and nearly 30 percent less likely to participate in paid market work. Estimates of gender differences tend to be extremely sensitive to what types of activities are considered in a study. Studies such as Assaad, Levison, and Zibani (2003) for Egypt, Levison and Moe (1998) for Peru, Levison, Moe, and Knaul (2001) for Mexico have documented the misleading picture that omitting domestic work can create for analysis of the determinants of child work.

In both market and domestic work, boys and girls often participate in different tasks. This is evident in the large gender differences in the industrial composition of economically active children in Bangladesh (Table 6). Boys are involved in a wider variety of industries. Boys are more likely to be engaged in the growing of cereal crops. Girls are more involved in growing vegetables and poultry farming. 14 percent of economically active girls are in poultry and 16 percent in vegetables while less than 2 percent of economically active boys are in each industry. Children involved in textile and sewing handicrafts and private household services are almost entirely female whereas boys are more involved in fishing, wooden furniture manufacture, construction site preparation, retail trade of grocery and general stores (as sales assistants and sales supervisors, Table 7), and transport (non-motorized vehicles, Table 7). We should not extrapolate from Bangladesh to assume such distinct gender differences in other countries, but its example shows that these gender differences can be large.

Large gender differences in types of tasks can complicate researcher decisions about how to treat gender. Do differences in activities reflect a fundamental difference in how girl time allocation decisions will be made with respect to the household's economic environment? If so, this would suggest that boys and girls should be considered separately in research. Qualitative evidence from specific country contexts can help inform where girls should be considered separately from boys, but bifurcating data by gender seems a reasonable default position.

Substantive gender differences in tasks and determinants of work can be especially challenging for studies that rely on within household comparisons (household fixed effects) of children. Assume average birth spacing is two years, the probability an observed child is a girl is 0.5, and that gender draws are independent within parents. This implies that a household fixed effects study of working children 10–14 will rely on gender differences in activities and tasks for half its variation.

Table 7
3-Digit occupational composition of economically active children 5–17 in Bangladesh, 2002–2003

Occupation description	Bangladesh (%)			Urban (%)		Rural (%)	
	Total	Boys	Girls	Boys	Girls	Boys	Girls
Teachers N.E.C. (religious/physical education)	0.3	0.2	0.6	0.4	1.3	0.1	0.5
Transport conductors (bus or train conductor, helper)	0.6	0.8	0.1	2.0	0.4	0.5	0.1
Working proprietors (wholesale and retail trade)	1.0	1.3	0.2	1.9	0.1	1.2	0.3
Sales supervisors (wholesale & retail trade)	4.1	4.1	4.0	7.4	6.4	3.3	3.5
Salesmen, shop assistants and related workers	7.4	9.1	2.7	17.2	3.4	7.2	2.5
Street vendors & door-to-door salesman	1.4	1.5	1.2	2.4	2.0	1.3	1.0
Waiters, bartenders and related workers	1.4	1.6	0.6	2.8	0.8	1.4	0.6
Maids and related housekeeping service workers N.E.C.	1.4	0.4	4.2	0.6	6.3	0.3	3.7
Hairdressers, barbers, beauticians and related workers	0.6	0.8	0.2	1.0	0.6	0.7	0.1
Agricultural crop farmers	0.6	0.6	0.7	0.1	0.0	0.7	0.8
Farm crop workers	45.6	47.3	40.9	16.0	11.0	54.6	47.9
Livestock workers	0.5	0.6	0.3	0.3	0.0	0.7	0.3
Dairy farm workers	0.7	0.4	1.3	0.4	1.6	0.4	1.2
Poultry farm workers	4.5	1.2	13.7	0.6	11.1	1.3	14.4
Loggers	0.5	0.5	0.7	0.2	0.1	0.5	0.9
Fisherman	3.2	3.7	1.6	2.6	0.8	4.0	1.9
Spinners and winders (textile)	0.8	0.7	1.1	1.3	2.5	0.5	0.8
Weavers and related workers	1.2	1.2	1.4	1.6	2.1	1.1	1.2
Knitters	0.8	0.5	1.5	0.8	4.4	0.5	0.8
Spinners, Weavers, knitters, dyers and related N.E.C.	1.1	0.2	3.6	0.2	12.6	0.1	1.5
Grain millers and related workers	0.7	0.7	0.8	1.0	1.3	0.6	0.7
Food preservers	0.4	0.0	1.7	0.0	1.1	0.0	1.8
Cigar makers	0.2	0.1	0.4	0.5	2.1	0.0	0.0
Tobacco preparers and tobacco product makers N.E.C.	0.7	0.4	1.5	0.8	2.9	0.3	1.2
Tailors and dressmakers	1.7	1.4	2.4	2.1	3.1	1.2	2.3
Sewers and embroiderers	0.9	0.4	2.3	0.8	4.2	0.3	1.9
Cabinetmakers	1.1	1.3	0.3	1.9	0.3	1.2	0.3
Cabinetmakers and related wood workers N.E.C.	1.0	1.3	0.1	2.7	0.5	1.0	0.0
Motor vehicle mechanics	0.6	0.8	0.1	1.6	0.1	0.6	0.1
Structural metal workers	0.3	0.4	0.0	1.1	0.1	0.2	0.0
Jewellery and precious metal workers	0.5	0.7	0.1	1.8	0.4	0.5	0.0
Basketry weavers and brush makers	1.4	0.6	3.4	0.5	3.7	0.6	3.4
Reinforced concretes and related workers	0.8	1.1	0.0	2.2	0.1	0.8	0.0
Construction carpenters	0.5	0.6	0.2	1.1	0.0	0.5	0.2
Other construction workers N.E.C.	0.9	0.6	1.8	1.2	4.4	0.5	1.2
Road non-motorised vehicles drivers	3.3	4.3	0.4	5.6	1.0	4.0	0.3
Laborers N.E.C.	7.5	8.9	3.8	15.3	7.2	7.3	3.1

N.E.C. – Not elsewhere classified. Only occupations with at least 0.5 percent of economically active children in urban or rural Bangladesh are listed.
Source: Table C50 of the Report on National Child Labor Survey (Bangladesh Bureau of Statistics, 2003).

2.3.4. Urban–rural differences

The research challenges associated with gender also arise with urban–rural data. Children tend to work more and for longer hours in rural than urban areas. For example, Edmonds and Pavcnik (2005a) tabulate urban–rural differences in the MICS data used in Fig. 1 and Table 4. 31 percent of rural children 5–14 are engaged in market work in rural areas compared to 19 percent in urban areas. Domestic work also has a higher prevalence in rural areas although the difference is smaller (68 percent compared to 61 percent). 26 percent of children work 20 or more hours per week in rural areas compared to 14 percent in urban, and 9 percent work 40 or more hours in rural areas compared to 4 percent in urban.

If children only worked more intensely in rural areas, then researchers could pool urban and rural children in their analysis, but children also tend to work in different types of activities. For example, in the MICS countries, the prevalence of unpaid market work is nearly double in rural areas, and paid employment accounts for 50 percent larger share of all market work in urban areas. A careful look at the urban–rural differences in the detailed Bangladesh data is illustrative for why researcher's default assumption should be to treat urban and rural child labor decisions distinctly.

In general, employment is more concentrated in rural areas in Bangladesh. For boys, urban–rural differences in employment are similar to what one would expect with rural areas more weighted to agriculture. A majority of economically active boys in rural areas are farm crop workers (Table 7) with most being involved in cereals (Table 6). Salesman and shop assistants, fisherman, and non-motorized vehicle drivers are the next most prevalent occupations among rural boys. In urban areas, boys are most active in sales. 27 percent of economically active boys in urban areas are working as sales supervisors, salesmen, shop assistants, and street vendors (Table 7). Much of this appears to be in retail grocery and general stores (Table 6) as well as tea stalls. However, farm crop workers in cereals, fisherman, and non-motorized vehicle operators are also prevalent in urban areas.

Urban–rural differences in occupation and industry of the economically active population in Bangladesh are more pronounced for girls. A majority of girls in rural areas are involved in cereals, vegetables, or poultry farming. While poultry is the second largest industry of employment for urban girls, together these agricultural industries are less than a quarter of urban employment for girls (Table 6). Spinners, weavers, knitters, etc., are unusual in rural areas, but 13 percent of economically active urban girls are in these occupations (Table 7). Employment of girls in the manufacture of bidies or in private households is also much more prevalent in urban areas (Table 6).

A difficulty in bifurcating data into urban and rural segments is that it presumes the two area types are segmented. In some contexts, there is no clear line either defining or separating urban and rural. In fact, there is an interesting literature that documents how household specialization changes with proximity to major urban areas (Fafchamps and Shilpi, 2004) and that this in turn affects schooling and both market and domestic work (Fafchamps and Wahba, 2006). Thus, it is difficult to draw generalities with regards to how and whether urban and rural areas should be treated differently by empirical researchers. Moreover, the example of Bangladesh illustrates that the extent to which urban and rural activities are comparable may differ by gender as well (Amin, Quayes, and Rives, 2006) also make this point in data from Bangladesh).

2.3.5. Age patterns

C138 established the idea that whether an activity is viewed negatively for a child depends on the child's age, and this has been codified into SIMPOC's definition of child labor. The idea behind this is that what may be appropriate for a 14 year old might not for a seven year old. This is logical, but implicit in this discussion is that 7-year olds tend do the same sorts of activities as a 14-year old. This does not appear to be the case in the limited available evidence.

Figure 2 pools the MICS countries and plots participation rates in various activities separately by age and gender. The four pictured categories are market work outside of one's own household, market work, any work (the difference between any and market work is children who only work in domestic work), and any work without also attending school. Participation rates in each of these categories looks smooth in age for boys until age 10 when there is a sizeable increase in participation rates in market and domestic

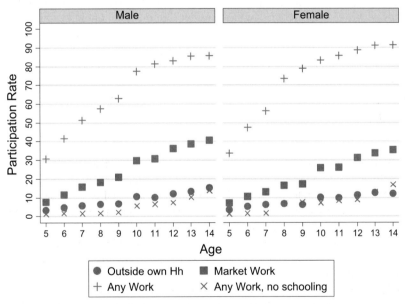

Source: Author's calculations from the pooled MICS data. Each child in the MICS countries is weighted to reflect the number of individuals they represent. Hence, the picture is representative for the pooled populations of the MICS countries.

Figure 2. Participation rates by age, gender, and type of work.

work and again for age 12. Girls appear to experience discrete jumps at age 8, 10, and 12. The increase at age 8 for girls appears to be most dramatic in domestic work whereas most of the increase at age 10 and 12 for girls is in market work. Overall "any work" patterns for girls look smooth at ages 10 and 12, suggesting that the increase in market work and 10 and 12 for girls complements the domestic work that began increased substantively starting around age 8.

Moreover, within market work, there are changes by age in the types of industries in which children are employed. This is evident in the SIMPOC data tabulated in Table 5. When available, the industrial composition of employment is also broken down by age. There are some interesting differences across age. For example, in Tanzania, the fraction of economically active children employed in private households is decreasing in age whereas the fraction in agriculture and related industries is increasing in age. However, the opposite is true for Kenya. Declining shares in agriculture and related industries with age is also present in Ethiopia, Ghana, Namibia, and Nicaragua. But the age patterns are ambiguous in Zambia and the Philippines. Hence, while there is no clear age pattern across countries in the industrial composition of employment, there appear to be patterns within countries that highlight how important age can be in the analysis of child labor.

The evidence in Fig. 2 and Table 5 implies that researchers should be as flexible as possible in how they treat age in their analysis. A full set of gender interacted age effects seems reasonable for regression work, especially for market work. A related issue concerns what ages researchers should consider. International organizations interested in child labor typically focus on children 6–14 for most activities but the under 18 are often considered in worst forms. However, C182 is careful to allow each country to set appropriated ages for different types of work, and individual country policies regarding work and schooling are useful for researchers in deciding what ages to consider and how to group those ages. While work laws tend not to be enforced in most current developing countries (more on this later), they are useful at providing insight into country specific views on the ages at which work is a concern. Researchers have to be careful, however, not to let subjective policy statements about "harmful" work drive what types of ages they consider as whether work is harmful ultimately depends on understanding why a child participates in it.

Research needs to be particularly concerned about schooling ages, and grouping children based on the category of schooling they would normally attend for their age can be prudent (especially when drop out rates at schooling transitions are high). For example, observing a seven year old who worked without attending school in a country where schooling typically begins at age 8 might reflect something very different than if the child were at a country where schooling begins at 5. Likewise observing a thirteen year old out of school in a country where thirteen year olds are usually in primary school may imply something different than in a country where thirteen year olds are in secondary school. Moreover, in many settings, the elasticity of child time allocation to factors in the environment appears to be increasing in age at young ages, and explaining child time allocation at pre-school ages is a challenge. Hence, country specific attention to the appropriate age grouping of the data seems merited.

2.3.6. Worst forms of child labor

The ILO's SIMPOC estimates that a total of 8.4 million children are involved in child trafficking, in forced or bonded labor, are soldiers, are prostitutes or involved in pornography, or participate in illicit activities (ILO, 2002). 68 percent of these children are in bonded or forced labor. An additional 170.5 million children are in hazardous activities. The definition of a hazardous activity varies from country to country. In implementing C182, the ILO has been active in assisting countries in assessing the prevalence of worst and hazardous forms of child labor as well as in developing plans for the eradication of these activities. Nepal was one of the first countries to initiate one of these "Time Bound Programs," and the findings from the baseline work for this program are illustrative of the types of activities that governments label as hazardous and the prevalence of worst forms in a very poor country.

Estimates of the extent and incidence of worst forms of child labor in Nepal are in Table 8. These estimates are from ILO (2001). There are approximately 8 million children below the age of 16 in Nepal, and approximately 1.5 percent of these children work in these worst forms of child labor. Child porters and domestic works are the two most common types of "worst forms" of child labor. Among child porters, there are two main types: short distance porters that work in urban markets and bus parks and long distance that work in the countryside. The ILO estimates that typically long distance porters stay and work with their families while short distance porters have often migrated to find work. Estimates are that there are about 42,204 long distance porters and 3825 short distance porters. 88 percent are boys. Domestic workers are most prevalent in high status urban households, though domestics typically come from rural areas. In Kathmandu, 1 out of 5 households employ children. The ILO estimates that 43 percent of employers of child domestics are government or non-government service holders. Domestics are believed to be evenly split between paid (to parents) and unpaid (more correctly, paid in a lump sum) workers. The other children included in Table 8

Table 8
Prevalence rates of worst forms of child labor in Nepal

	Number	(%)
Children in bonded labor	17,152	13.5
Child ragpickers	3965	3.1
Child porters	46,029	36.2
Child domestic workers (urban only)	55,655	43.8
Children in mines	115	0.1
Children in the carpet sector	4227	3.3
TOTAL	127,143	100

Source: ILO (2001).

because of the nature of their employment are children in mines, in the carpet sector, and ragpickers, who pick recyclables and other rubbish out of garbage dumps for resale.

Bonded laborers and trafficked children both fall under worst forms of child labor as well. Bonded children in Nepal are in bondage either because parents took out debts against the child's future earnings or because they were used as collateral on loans. The ILO estimates that some 17,152 children in bondage in Nepal, although this estimate is controversial because it does not include children whose parents are bonded in a system of bonded labor that pervades western Nepal (Sharma, Basynyat and Ganesh, 2001). Child trafficking is particularly hard to measure and evaluate. According to the ILO (2001), 12,000 girls are trafficked into the commercial sex industry each year in Nepal. By and large, these girls work in brothels in India. Unfortunately, because of the relative rarity of these activities and the challenges of capturing them in randomized surveys, little research exists on whether these activities are rightly viewed as a type of child work (where human rights is more obviously an issue) or whether they should be viewed as some other type of activity altogether.

One difficulty with classifying some activities as hazardous and including them as a worst form of child labor is that children can face hazards in the most common kinds of labor, too. Especially as children get older, they become active in all aspects of agriculture, and it is not unusual to see reports of injuries in operating farm machinery in child labor surveys. The self-reported injury rate from child labor surveys of children working in agriculture is actually higher, at 12 percent, than the 9 percent injury rate in manufacturing (Ashagrie, 1997). Agriculture can also be hazardous for children because of exposure to dangerous chemicals such as chemical herbicides or pesticides, exposure to heat or weather, repetitive work injuries, and threats posed by animals, reptiles, insects, parasites, and some plants. Hence, even though in principal, the distinction between hazardous child labor and other types of activities seems less vague than the distinctions some draw between child labor and light work (where "child labor" is labeled as work that is somehow known to be harmful to the child), in reality, a case can be made for looking at some of the more common forms of child labor even if one is only interested in activities that might fall under C182. The next section discusses the case for attention to child activities further.

2.3.7. Are worst forms different?

In the following sections, this chapter reviews evidence on why children work. This evidence is culled almost entirely from work that would not be considered hazardous or a worst form of child labor under C182, because the relatively rare worst forms of child labor are difficult to capture with randomized surveys. Hence, before turning to that evidence it is worth reviewing theories as to why selection into worst forms might be different.

Three views about differences in the selection process into common forms and worst forms of child labor seem to dominate the academic literature. In one view, worst forms are no different than other types of work from the parent or child's perspective, and factors that drive children to select into worst forms are the same factors that drive them to work in the first place. A variation on this view notes that the work may be more unpleasant but this unpleasantness may be fully compensated through higher wages. In this case, the link between worst forms and income will be the same as that of more common forms of child labor, and the resulting policy prescriptions will be the same. In a second view, worst forms of child labor are partially compensated so that they pay more (Dessy and Pallage, 2005). Thus, the entry process is similar to other types of work except that poorer households are more likely to select into worst forms, because the marginal utility for the additional income exceeds the disutility coming from the particular type of work. In a third view, children in worst forms of child labor enter because of poor information about what the work entails (Rogers and Swinnerton, 2007). Thus, ex ante children select into the work under the assumption that it is similar to other types of work, and there are barriers to exiting. This explanation is most often voiced to explain selection into prostitution, but it may be equally substantive for other worst forms of child labor. In reality, because of inference problems with rare events, research on why children select into worst forms and whether selection is driven by characteristics that differ from those discussed below is in its infancy (Edmonds, 2007 is a start).

3. The case for attention to working children

Few issues in developing countries draw more attention in rich countries than child labor. This attention is typically motivated by human rights concerns. Horrific newspaper issues of children burned to death while chained to their job in garment factories in Bangladesh or forced into prostitution in Thailand drives much of this concern. These human rights concerns are well grounded, but, as most working children are from poor families and are helping in their family's activities, the typical working child is not in a situation where the human rights issues are obvious. As such, much of child labor related policy is not directed at worst forms of child labor but instead at the more prevalent forms of child labor in developing countries. This section considers the academic case for attention to the more prevalent forms of work.

3.1. Child labor in international policy

Researchers for years have studied adult labor supply with great interest, but the research interest in child labor is augmented by policy's interest in the topic. Consumer boycotts and student protests against products with some child labor component during production are relatively frequent occurrences. One often reads of protests in American universities over the involvement of children in the production of athletic clothing. Outrage over the involvement of children in producing soccer balls hit a fever pitch in the late 1990s when it was learned that FIFA licensed products contained a considerable child labor component. Beyond boycotts, labeling campaigns such as the Rugmark campaign to label hand-knit carpets as "child labor free" garner considerable popular support.

This consumer activism has been matched by legislative interest. For example, the US Congress has repeatedly considered legislation that would prohibit imports into the United States of all products made with child labor. Under threat of such sanctions, export oriented garment factories in Bangladesh released more that 10,000 child workers under the age of 14 in the mid 1990s. More recently, the US House of Representatives has deliberated the "Child Labor Elimination Act" that would impose general trade sanctions, deny all financial assistance, and mandate US opposition to multilateral credits to 62 developing countries with a high incidence of child labor. This threat is implicit in a 2002 act of the US Congress that mandated a study by the Department of Labor's Bureau of International Labor Affairs about the relationship between military and education spending in countries with a high incidence of child labor. Under current law, the US can withdraw a poor country's eligibility for trade preferences under the Generalized System of Preferences (GSP) based on a country's poor record on child labor. Moreover, the 2000 Trade and Development Act restricts eligibility for trade benefits to countries that the Secretary of Labor certifies as showing progress towards eliminating the worst forms of child labor. This policy interest in child labor in developing countries is a relatively recent issue, and corresponding to it is growth in the academic literature that seeks to understand why children work and measure the short and long term consequences of work.

3.2. Work and schooling

3.2.1. Is schooling attendance lower for working children?

There are fixed number of hours in a day. As such, time spent working necessarily trades off with other uses of child time such as play, study time, or time in school. Despite their importance for child development, especially at young ages, very few researchers consider play and leisure in efforts to measure the opportunity costs of working. Concerns about play were at the forefront of concerns about child labor in early 20th century US (Fuller, 1922; Pangburn, 1929). In contrast, the extent to which work affects schooling attendance, performance, and attainment is perhaps the second most researched question in the child labor literature (second, to the income elasticity of child labor supply). The Minimum Working Age Convention (C138) in part necessitates this interest in that it permits light work in children as young as 12 provided it does not interfere with schooling. When and how does work interfere with schooling?

The main challenge in this literature is that schooling and child labor decisions are joint outcomes out of a single time allocation problem. Hence, the interpretation of any found correlation between labor status and schooling is controversial. Do children work because they are not attending school? Do children not attend school because they are working? Do other economic or cultural factors simultaneously influence both schooling and work decisions? Before turning to the problem of establishing causation, a simple description of the association between schooling attendance and work in the MICS countries will be useful.

Figure 3 shows school participation rates by gender and activity for children 10–14 in the MICS data (all countries are pooled and the data are weighted by population). Several points stand-out in Fig. 3. First, children can work and attend school. In fact, in the under 10 population, working children have slightly higher schooling rates than non-working children although this reflects age trends in both the start of schooling and work. Second, of different categories of activity, schooling attendance rates are lowest among children in market work outside of their household. Third, children who work only in market work without any domestic work tend to have lower schooling rates than children who work in domestic and market work. These two pieces of evidence are often cited as justification for only looking at wage work or market work respectively, but they may proxy hours worked and have little further implication. Children who only work in market work without any domestic work are typically working substantive hours, and children that work outside the household tend to spend more time working than those who help in the family business.

Figure 4 shows average total hours worked in the last week by type of activity and gender for the same population as Fig. 3. Total hours worked are highest among children that work outside their household in market work and lowest among children that only perform domestic work. In general, girls work more than boys (despite having similar school attendance rates), except among children that participate in market work only.

If the lower schooling attendance rates of children who work in market work alone or work outside the household reflects hours worked, this would imply that the decline in schooling attendance with total hours worked should be steepest in the neighborhood of 30 hours worked as is typical for those who only work outside the household. Figure 5 plots gross school attendance rates for children 10–14 in the MICS data against total hours worked (market plus domestic) in the last week. 95 percent confidence intervals are also pictured. School attendance rates appear relatively flat with respect to total hours worked until about 8 hours worked. The probability of observing a working child attend school declines gradually between 8 and 29 hours, then the rate of decline increases dramatically starting around 30 hours per week. The derivate of the curve in Fig. 5 is greatest between 35 and 45 hours worked per week. This is not surprising as it implies that it becomes most difficult to work and attend school simultaneously when the child is working full time. Non-linearities similar to that of Fig. 5 are also apparent in Ray and Lancaster's (2003) study of child labor and schooling attendance in 7 countries with child labor surveys administered by the ILO's SIMPOC.

One clear difficulty in assessing the tradeoff between hours worked and schooling attendance is that the tradeoff depends on how one defines work. Hours worked are largest and schooling attendance rates are lowest for children working outside of their home. However, a failure to consider work within the household or work in domestic work can create a misleading picture of the tradeoff between schooling and work, especially for girls. Assaad, Levison, and Zibani (2003) observes that the low attendance of Egyptian girls relative to boys appears to be associated with a substantial domestic work burden

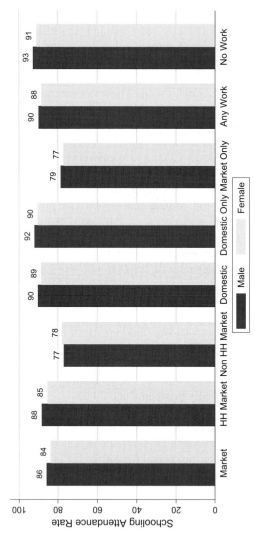

Source: Author's calculations from the pooled MICS data. Each child in the MICS countries is weighted to reflect the number of individuals they represent. Hence, the picture is representative for the pooled populations of the MICS countries.

Figure 3. School attendance rates (in last year) by category of work and gender, children 10–14.

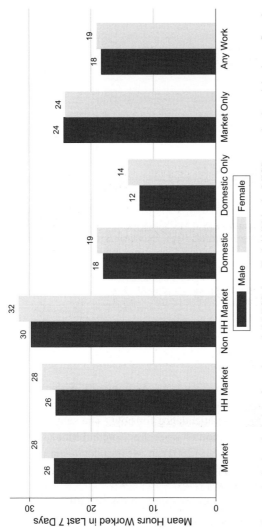

Source: Author's calculations from the pooled MICS data. Each child in the MICS countries is weighted to reflect the number of individuals they represent. Hence, the picture is representative for the pooled populations of the MICS countries.

Figure 4. Hours worked in the last week by type of activity and gender, children 10–14.

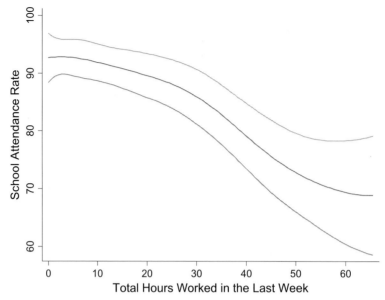

Source: Author's calculations from the pooled MICS data. Each child in the MICS countries is weighted to reflect the number of individuals they represent. Hence, the picture is representative for the pooled populations of the MICS countries. The pictured curve is from a nonparametric regression: an indicator for whether a child attends school is regressed on total hours, total hours squared, and a series of the form $\sin(j * \text{total hours})$ and $\cos(j * \text{total hours})$ $j = 1, 2, 3$ where total hours is transformed to range between 0 and $2 * \pi$. Fitted values ($* 100$) and the 95 percent confidence interval are pictured. Only fitted values between 0 and 2.5 standard deviations above the mean are pictured.

Figure 5. School attendance and total hours worked, children 10–14.

of girls. Because boys do not face the same work burden within the home, they face fewer barriers to schooling such that in the Egyptian data, they do not observe a tradeoff between working and schooling attendance for boys. The sensitivity of attainment to work also depends on the definition of work. Levison and Moe (1998) using Peruvian data and Levison, Moe, and Knaul (2001) in Mexico document that whether there is a tradeoff between schooling attainment and work depends on whether work includes domestic work, especially for girls.

In fact, school attendance rates do not appear to vary significantly with whether hours worked are in market or domestic work. Figure 6 plots school attendance rates by hours worked in market and domestic work separately using the MICS data. 95 percent confidence intervals are also pictured, and there is significant overlap in the confidence intervals. Beyond 10 hours of work, the school attendance rates associated with time in market work are slightly below that of time in domestic work. However, the differences are never statistically significant, and the shape of both curves looks as would

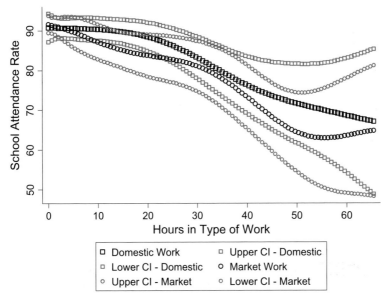

Figure 6. School attendance and hours worked in market and domestic work, children 10–14.

be expected from Fig. 5 given that work in one type of activity (e.g. market work) is associated typically with some work in the other activity (e.g. domestic work).

In contrast to market and domestic work, schooling attendance rates associated with hours worked inside and outside of the household appear very different. Figure 7 contains a plot of school attendance rates by hours worked inside and (separately) outside the household. Between 12 and 53 hours per week, a child who is working a given number of hours outside of their household is less likely to attend school than is a child who is spending the same amount of the time inside of the household. A large part of the reason for this apparent difference between work inside and outside of the household is that children working outside of the household typically also work significantly more hours inside the household. In the MICS data, each hour in work outside of the household is associated with an additional nine tenths of an hour work inside the household on average. In contrast, each hour in work inside the household is associated with one tenth of an hour work outside the household. Hence, the total hours worked for a child working 20 hours a week outside of the household is 38 hours. In Fig. 5, a child working 38 hours has a school attendance rate of slightly above 80 percent, within the confidence interval of the observed schooling attendance for a child working 20 hours a week outside the household. Thus, the difference between schooling attendance rates for children working inside and outside of the household appears to owe more to differences in the

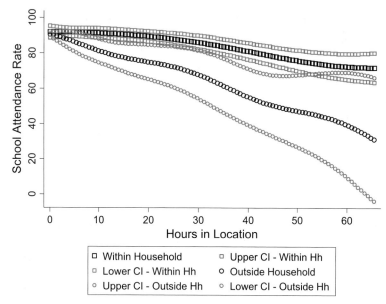

Source: See Fig. 5.

Figure 7. School attendance and hours worked inside and outside of the household, children 10–14.

resulting total hours worked by the child rather than something else intrinsic to work outside of home.

3.2.2. Is schooling achievement and attainment lower for working children?

If lower attendance is meaningful for human capital accumulation, it should translate into lower schooling attainment. Moreover, beyond attendance, work may undermine human capital accumulation by interfering with learning as evident in test scores or schooling completion rates. Panel data on child labor histories is rarely available, so studies typically compare current labor supply to current attainment. This is hard, because current work status necessarily depends on past education and work histories as these affect the value of child time and whether it's optimal for the child to work. This makes interpretation difficult, but studies typically find that attainment is lower for working children. Ray (2003) observes that an additional hour of wage work in Ghana is associated with more than a year's less completed educational attainment. Psacharopoulos (1997) notes that children in wage work in Bolivia have nearly a year less completed schooling than non working children and that working children in Venezuela have almost 2 years less attainment.

Beyond the obvious challenges of inferring causation from these correlations, another difficulty in interpreting evidence on attainment is that standards for advancement vary across schools and may be correlated with factors of interest. For example, it is not difficult to imagine that passing in a poor quality school in a poor area might reflect a different knowledge level than passing in a very good school in a rich area. However, work is also correlated with worse performance in other measures of academic achievement. For example, Akabayashi and Psacharopoulos (1999) note that working children spend less time studying which is reflected in both math and reading test scores in their Tanzanian data. Heady (2003), using the same Ghana data as Ray, notes that reading and mathematics test scores are substantially lower among wage working children than non working children.

3.2.3. *Is there a causal relationship between work and schooling achievement and attainment?*

Causal studies of the impact of child labor on schooling face the challenge of isolating some factor that affects child labor without simultaneously affecting schooling. This is difficult, because child labor, schooling, and leisure decisions are jointly determined; it is hard to imagine how one can be affected without all other decisions being affected. Consider the analytical model of Eq. (1.1). Choices of schooling, leisure, and all types of work depend on the shadow value of child time which is, in turn, a function of choices of schooling, leisure, and all types of work. Hence, without directly observing the shadow value of child time, there is no way to identify a causal impact of one type of activity on another without additional assumptions.

Studies typically rely on either modeling assumptions or on legal variation in child labor or schooling regulations (see Orazem and Gunnarsson, 2004 for a review). A common modeling assumption is that some factor only effects whether a child works without otherwise effecting how the family values other uses of the child time. Legal variation is typically assumed to be one such factor. These studies face two difficulties. It is typically hard to imagine the exclusion restriction of how factors that influence work decisions would not simultaneously influence other household decisions, and variation in the value of child time or regulation is apt to be correlated with latent socio-economic characteristics of the child's environment. Hence, authors estimating the causal impact of work on schooling face a considerable challenge.

Instrumental variables estimates of the effect of child labor on schooling tend to produce a stronger association between child labor and schooling than in the raw data (for examples: Boozer and Suri, 2001; Rosati and Rossi, 2003; Ray and Lancaster, 2003; Gunnarsson, Orazem, and Sanchez, 2006). This is not surprising as the instruments typically capture variation in the child labor-schooling relationship that is more variable than the full variation in the data. For example, instruments that work through the value of child time are then using variation in child labor that owes to the families need for the child's contribution or the relative return to work rather than school. It is not surprising to learn that this variation leads to a greater elasticity of schooling with respect to child labor relative to alternative reasons for child labor such as social norms about working, the absence of accessible quality schooling, etc. Legal variation is likely correlated with institutional quality and thereby living standards. Hence, for similar reasons, as the value of child time, these instruments, when valid, might be capturing variation in child labor which is inherently more apt to trade off with schooling.

3.2.4. Do changes in the price of schooling affect child labor supply?

Several studies implicitly consider the link between schooling and child labor by examining how child labor and schooling reply to a change in the relative price of schooling. In general, they find that cash or in kind transfers that are conditioned on school attendance increase schooling but have a much smaller effect on child labor. For example, Ravallion and Wodon (2000) consider market work participation and schooling attendance responses to the Food for Education Program (FFE) in Bangaldesh in which families receive food rations as long as they send their children to primary school. They observe that households who participate in this program have higher school attendance. Market work participation declines with this school attendance although the decline in market work is about a third of the increase in schooling. A similar finding is in Cardoso and Souza (2004) who compare market work and schooling attendance in families that receive cash transfers as a part of Brazil's Bosca Escola program to similar families that do not receive the payment. Bosca Escola conditions cash transfers on school attendance, and Cardosa and Souza find larger increases in schooling than declines in market work. Endogenous program participation is a concern in any study that compares program participants to non-participants. Ravallion and Wodon address this by instrumenting for program participation with whether the program is present in a child's village, and Cardosa and Souza use propensity score matching to create a control group with similar observable characteristics to program participants.

There is a debate about the implications of the finding that changes in the price of schooling lead to larger changes in school participation than in work *participation*. Some argue that this implies the absence of a connection between either schooling and child labor or poverty and child labor. There are several reasons to doubt this interpretation. First, if one observed changes in the consumption of two goods (leisure and schooling in this case) with a price change in one of the goods, but the quantity of one good changed more than another, would one conclude that there is no budget constraint? Second, this finding might reflect that there is more of an intensive margin with work than school. School attendance is a rather discrete thing. That is, when a child attends school, that typically means they attend a full days of classes (which is often in the neighborhood of 4 or 5 hours a day). However, market and domestic work are much more flexible. In response to attending school for 4 hours a day, a child could have a precisely corresponding change in total hours worked (indicating a 1 for 1 trade-off) but yet still work. In fact, in a much smaller sample with detailed time use data, Arends-Kuenning and Amin (2004) document that the decline in hours worked among FFE participants is similar in magnitude to the increase in time in school. Third, if children are working because of poverty, schooling subsidies may induce a substitution away from play and leisure to schooling, rather than work. In fact, Arends-Kuenning and Amin (2004) argue that before the FFE program arose in Bangladesh, children on average were not working so many hours that their labor burdens prohibited schooling. The idea that children work because of the family's poverty does not imply that children can have no leisure, especially in a setting where parents care about their child's welfare. Hence, it seems difficult to argue that a movement into schooling without a corresponding change in participation in market work can be interpreted as evidence against a child labor-schooling connection.

3.2.5. *Modeling the joint determination of schooling and other time allocation decisions*

Most researchers generally treat the analysis of schooling and work separately. That is, they estimate some limited dependent variable model (linear probability, logit, probit) for schooling and work separately. This is attractive for several reasons. First, it is transparent and the properties of these estimators are well understood. Second, it will lead to results that are consistent and comparable to studies that only consider schooling or only consider types of child work. However, because schooling and time allocation decisions are joint, studies frequently adopt empirical methods designed to model the correlation between schooling and work decisions.

The bivariate probit is probably the most common alternative to the single variable models. Conventionally, it is similar to a SUR regression in that it allows for correlations in errors between the schooling and child labor regressions. It can be efficient when bivariate normality of errors is correct, although this is not universally true when the same covariates are included in each regression. If there were viable exclusion restrictions, the model can be used to infer the effect of change in one endogenous variable on the other (that is, a type of work's effect on schooling), although there is still the difficulty of finding plausible exclusion restrictions. Moreover, there are several limitations that researchers need to consider. The bivariate probit has the standard probit problems (need to evaluate the cdf to compute a marginal effect that will vary with covariates, need for large samples per fixed effect to recover fixed effects, inconsistency under heteroskedasticity), and two important additional issues. First, when there are two outcomes of interest (child labor and schooling), computing the effect of a change in any covariate on child labor and schooling requires evaluating the joint density rather than the univariate density as in the standard probit. Second, when children are classified as either working or in school, the error distribution will become degenerate. Thus, the bivariate probit is not appropriate for data where most children either work or are in school so that the product of the two is zero in expectation. Hence, application of the bivariate probit approach requires some caution on the part of researchers.

Another frequent approach to modeling child labor and schooling is a multinomial choice model such as the multinomial logit (MNL) or probit (MNP). These models are especially attractive for structural models of time allocation. They are, however, inherently difficult for evaluating causal effects, because computing marginal effects of some covariate on the choice of schooling and work combination is not straightforward.

Typically, the different choices in a multinomial model are different activities that children may perform, and this approach seems broadly consistent with the simultaneous nature of decisions about time allocation. The computational simplicity of the MNL and the ease with which one can estimate fixed effects make it the more popular than the MNP. However, the MNL relies on the assumption of the independence of irrelevant alternatives (IIA). What does IIA mean in the case where children can participate in multiple tasks? Consider a setting where a child chooses between wage employment and the family farm. IIA implies that if a third choice is added (schooling or work in a family business), the third choice should not affect the probability the child chooses wage work over work on the family farm. IIA would be violated if the third choice drew children disproportionately out of either wage work or work on the farm. For example, a family business might draw more from the family farm than wage work. Schooling might draw more from wage work than working in the family farm.

Alternatives to the MNL that do not rely on IIA are available. If choices could be ranked and ordered, a nested logit might be feasible. However, given the joint nature of time allocation decisions, this seems problematic. Perhaps it might be feasible in cultural settings where there is strong qualitative evidence to support a particular nesting in familial decisions. The multinomial probit (MNP) does not require a hierarchy of choices, nor does it require IIA. However, it is used less frequently for several reasons. First, the model needs to estimate the entire covariance structure. Hence, the number of parameters that need to be estimated can be extreme. This requires large sample sizes and the model often has difficulty converging. Second, the MNP is flat near its optimum, and this can lead to parameter estimates that are arbitrary but within the tolerance of the optimization routine and hence difficult to detect.

A hierarchical choice model such as the sequential probit (SEQP) is also popular. Modeling typically proceeds by first modeling the choice of whether to attend school or work, then proceeding to model the choice of different types of work, conditional on surviving the previous choice of types of work. That is, the SEQP is essentially a selection model where the researcher uses the results of lower sequenced choices as corrections for selection into higher sequenced choices. When the same covariates are used in each step of the sequence, the SEQP should be identical to the MNP (assuming no misspecification). Hence, the purpose of the SEQP is to allow different variables to affect different choices. The logic behind this approach is not obvious. The shadow value of time for the child reflects the opportunities open to the child, and hence it seems impossible to imagine a sensible exclusion restriction. Moreover, when the included variables differ in the sequence of choices of activities, estimates will depend on the order of the sequence in addition to the exclusion restrictions and functional form of the selection correction. Perhaps qualitative evidence can make the case for some ordering and a set of exclusion restrictions in a particular country context. Overall, though, given the difficulties with all of the alternatives, it is not surprising that univariate models are the predominant tools for examining work and schooling choices.

3.2.6. Are there future consequences of working?

Because of the conceptual difficulty in isolating some exogenous factor that affects either schooling or child labor, most studies of child labor and schooling tend to focus on economic factors that influence both child labor and schooling without explicitly trying to parameterize the path through which participation in one activity affects participation in the other. However, another alternative is to exploit timing differences in when the adult or older child is observed and when child labor occurred. Factors that have changed over time but were correlated with whether the individual worked as a child can be used as instruments.

Much of the work on the effects of child labor in childhood on adult labor market outcomes comes from Brazil, where the 1996 large-scale PNAD household survey asks individuals at what age they entered the workforce (which is likely interpreted as beginning fulltime market work), Ilahi, Orazem and Sedlacek (2000) observe that adults age 18 and older who started fulltime work before age 13 have adult wages that are 13–17 percent lower than adults who entered the workforce later. Emerson and Souza (2004) extend the analysis of Ilahi et al by addressing the endogeneity of the age at which an adult started working as a child with state-time variation in the number of schools. Does the finding of lower adult wages for child laborers reflect anything more than lower educational attainment? It appears to. Early entry into the labor force lowers the return to a year of education by roughly 20 percent in Ilahi et al's data. Interestingly, in individuals with no education, they observe slightly higher wages for children that start working earlier, conditional on the adult's age. This might reflect an experience premium as without any education and conditional on age, earlier entry means more time to accumulate experience. Alternatively, starting work at an early age requires having employment opportunities, typically with the child's own family. Hence, this relationship could also reflect something about family background. Emerson and Souza (2004) speculate that the tradeoff between returns to experience and education depends on what sector the individual works in as an adult and child.

The tradeoff between additional experience and education is considered explicitly in Beegle, Dehejia, and Gatti (2005). Using panel data from Vietnam, they evaluate how the labor status of children influences their education, wages, and health five years after they are observed working. In their analysis, they focus on children who are enrolled in school and compare enrolled in school and participating in market work children to children enrolled in school without market work. They impose this sample selection rule in order to isolate the effects of market work itself without confounding the effects of working with the effects of not being in school. Thus, their attention is only on the effects of working per se; they do not capture how the future of children who work exclusively is affected by their work. When they correct for the endogeneity of market work participation as a child with economic conditions in the base year of their data, they find that each additional hour of work as a child while attending school is associated with a nearly 3 percentage point decline in the probability the child is in school 5 years out and a 0.06 year decline in grade attainment. The mean hours worked for a working child in the base year of their data is 24 hours per week in market work. Hence, going from 0 hours to the average is associated with a more than 90 percent decline in the probability the child attends school and a nearly 20 percent decline in completed schooling five years after the child is observed working while in school. They also observe that the probability the child engages in wage work and the child's wage earnings conditional on participating in wage work are increasing in the child's hours worked. Beegle et al calculate that over a relatively short horizon (as might be appropriate in poor, credit constrained families), the value of increased earnings and the return to experience will outweigh the opportunity cost of foregone education.

3.3. Work and health

3.3.1. Is the health status of working children worse?

The consequence of child labor may extend beyond schooling attendance and attainment. Woodhead (2004) surveys the psychological ramifications of work as a child, and it is not obvious how one should view the psychosocial impacts of child work. Research has focused more on the effects of child labor on child health. Much of the literature focuses on the injury and morbidity risks associated with the child's work environment. For example, Graitcer and Lerer (1998) list morbidity, injury, and hazard risks faced by children in different occupations and industries. While manufacturing draws a lot of popular attention, family work, including work on the farm, also poses risks. Moreover, Forastieri (2002) points out that the increased nutritional needs associated with arduous work may exacerbate malnutrition, leaving the child stunted and impairing the child's productivity into adulthood, and Parker (1997) emphasizes that children who start work at a young age will be exposed to environmental hazards in the work place for longer, perhaps at a time when the effects of these hazards on development are more substantive.

   However, working does not necessarily impair a child's health. To the extent that child labor brings additional resources to the child, this may improve health and nutrition (especially in the destitute populations where work is most prevalent). The benefit of this additional income to the child may be greater than other sources of family income as the child may retain greater control over her own earnings. Further, the fact that the child is a productive, contributing member to the household may affect the child's ability to capture other family resources or influence how they are spent in ways that benefit the child. These types of gains to the child must be balanced against any lost education (and its returns to health) as well as the consequences for malnutrition, morbidity, and injury.

   Several studies attempt to gauge the net effect of child labor on child health. Evidence that working children have worse health at the time of their work is generally absent from the literature. O'Donnell, Doorslaer, and Rosati (2002) look at data from 18 developing countries and observe that across these 18 countries self-reported health status looks unrelated to whether the child participates in market work, is in school, both, or neither. Francavilla (2003) look at data from 6 developing countries and find no evidence of a connection between domestic work and self-reported morbidity or BMI either. It is unclear whether the absence of evidence reflects a lack of any relationship, the countervailing factors discussed above, measurement problems, or heterogeneity in the effect of working on health. For example, children working outside, in the family farm in the summer might be no worse off because of their work while children working 12 hours a day in a tannery might be substantially worse off. However, because the former is much more common that the later, there is no apparent relationship on average in the data.

3.3.2. Does child labor affect future adult health?

There are two basic classes of mechanisms through which a child's labor status may influence adult health. First, physical injury at work may lead to health problems that survive into adulthood. Second, psychological stress or trauma at work in childhood may lead to health problems in adulthood. Speculation about this second mechanism owes to the psychology literature which shows a strong correlation between stress in childhood and the persistence of mental disorders such as depression, anxiety and panic disorders, and schizophrenia or even health problems such as diabetes, heart disease, and immune disorders (see Heim and Nemeroff, 2001 for a review). There is a debate over the interpretation of this evidence as there is a strong correlation between severe stress in childhood and stressful life events in adulthood (Horwitz et al., 2001), but some argue this association reflects that childhood traumas induces a vulnerability to the effects of stress later in life. Most of this research focuses on stresses like the loss of a parent and severe physical abuse at very young ages, so whether this evidence is relevant for typical child labor is an open question. Blattman (2006), for example, considers the psychological impacts of forced abduction into the military among children from northern Uganda, and he finds little evidence of sustained psychological distress after the end of conflict in child combatants relative to non-combatants.

Three recent studies consider whether child labor impacts future adult health. Kassouf, McKee, and Mossialos (2001) observes in Brazilian data that individuals who start work earlier have worse self-reported health status as adults. They observe that the younger a person starts working, the greater the probability that the individual reports being ill as an adult. This finding may reflect something about the impact of child labor on child health and how that persists into adulthood, the impact of education on adult health, the impact of income on adult health, or something about the child or adult's environment associated with both youthful work and adult health.

Two papers using Vietnamese panel data employ instrumental variable strategies to consider the effect of working as a child on young adult health outcomes five years later. O'Donnell, Doorslaer, and Rosati (2005) compare the BMI, self-reported morbidity, and height in 1998 of children who worked in agriculture in 1993 to those that did not. They instrument for a child's participation in agriculture in 1993 with labor market and education conditions in the child's community in 1993. They find that children working in 1993 have higher self-reported morbidity rates in 1998. Using the same data but a different identification strategy and a subset of the sample, Beegle, Dehejia, and Gatti (2005) observe similar patterns to O'Donnell et al. but the patterns are not statistically significant in Beegle et al. While O'Donnell et al. looks at rural children 6–15 in 1993, Beegle et al. considers rural children 8–13 who attend school in 1993. Beegle et al. also relates self-reported health status to variation in total hours worked, using a different source of variation. While the two papers are not directly comparable because of data and identification differences, it is not surprising that there do not appear to be detectable marginal effects of working one additional hour while working vs. not appears to have more substance for long-term health. Evidence on specific mechanisms through which child labor might propagate through to adulthood seems to be largely speculative.

3.4. Child labor externalities and general equilibrium considerations

The ramifications of a child's working status may extend well beyond the child. First, as the working child is supporting the family and its members, there may benefits to siblings of having a working child. Second, there may be intergenerational implications of a child's labor status, a so-called child labor trap. Third, they may be general equilibrium ramifications of a high prevalence of child labor that merit attention.

3.4.1. Do working children support their siblings?

When most working children are helping in their family, it is very difficult to quantify the economic contribution of working children to the household as their compensation is often not in monetary terms. Further, concerns about surplus labor or training aspects of the child's contribution to the household complicate distinguishing the child's marginal product from her average product. Nevertheless, efforts to value the child's contribution to family income typically guess it to be substantial. Psacharopoulos (1997) observes that income earned by working Bolivian 13 year olds amounted to 13 percent of total household income on average. Menon, Pareli, and Rosati (2005) attempt to compute the value of child's own farm labor to largely subsistence farm households in rural Nepal. They estimate that children contribute roughly 11 percent of the value of total agriculture production in Nepal or about 9 percent of GDP.

To what extent do siblings benefit from the economic contribution of their siblings? There are several possible mechanisms. In poor households additional income or output, may help maintain the consumption of family members. A number of studies, discussed below, document a role for child labor in how households cope with shocks. Beyond shifting out the budget constraint, working older siblings may provide money that is directed explicitly towards younger siblings. Alternatively, working older siblings may provide additional labor services to the household which lower the productivity of younger siblings, thereby encouraging their education.

Direct evidence on the influence of a child's income on the activities of siblings is rare. One often hears assertions, especially in the South and East Asian context, of older sisters working to support their sibling. Parish and Willis (1993) discuss this literature in detail, although they find little support for this hypothesis in Taiwanese data. Instead, they argue that early marriage is a more important channel through which older girls help their siblings. In contrast, Edmonds (2006b) finds some evidence that older siblings help their siblings through their work. He argues that one possible channel for this support owes to older siblings comparative advantage in working in both market and domestic work. In data from Nepal, he documents that older siblings are more likely to work than younger siblings, and their time allocation depends on the sex composition of younger siblings. In particular, time spent in market working is increasing in the number of younger boys in the household. Edmonds speculates that this additional market work is to help afford schooling and other investment expenditures that younger boys are more apt to command, but he lacks direct evidence of this.

Perhaps the most direct evidence of older siblings working to support younger siblings is in Manacorda (2006) who finds strong evidence of externalities towards siblings in early twentieth century US. He considers the relationship between a child's school attendance and participation in wage work and the fraction of co-resident children that are active in wage work. To address the obvious endogeneity concerns in correlating siblings' labor supplies, he uses state variation in the minimum age of employment laws and the age at which work permits become available. That is, consider a 10 year old child with siblings age 14 and 15. Across US states in 1920, there is variation in whether 1, both, or neither sibling can work in the formal wage labor market. Thus, whether the older sibling is able to bring in wage income to the household will vary with the sibling's age and the state of residence. He finds considerable sharing of resources across children. The greater the fraction of siblings who works, the lower the child's own labor supply. Moreover, Manacorda observes a rise in schooling with the fraction of siblings who can work that is about equal to the decline in work and no substantive change in idleness. However, the benefits of having children work appear to largely accrue to children. He does not observe any substantive change in either the labor supply of mothers or fathers as the fraction of working children increases. One important note is that his identification strategy works off variation in wage work that is constrained by child labor laws. Hence, affected families are apt to be those where child income is most needed to support siblings. As such, it might be isolating variation where externalities are largest.

3.4.2. Does child labor perpetuate across generations?

Are working children more likely to have working children? The most obvious mechanisms for intergenerational persistence of child labor are through child labor's impact on education. Barham et al. (1995) develop a model where financing for education is obtained from within the family. Hence, low educational attainment leads to lower income leads to lower educational investments in the next generation, an educational poverty trap. Beyond the effects of income, lower parental education might affect child health and nutrition which in turn feeds back to the relative productivity of schooling and work. Another option is that a parent's own experience growing up affects their attitudes about child labor. In turn, then, work experience at a young age might cause a parent to feel that such work is appropriate.

As discussed earlier, several studies document an effect of child labor status on future adult income. Using the same Brazilian data as Ilahi, Orazem and Sedlacek (2000) used to examine the effects of child labor on adult income, Emerson and Souza (2003) look at whether the child labor status of a parent affects the child labor status of the child. 17 percent of children whose father began working before age 14 are employed. 6 percent of children are working whose father did not. Mother's child labor status shows similar patterns with differences that are slightly larger in magnitude. Further, this intergenerational correlation in child labor persists even when they control for the educational attainment of both parents and family income. Possible explanations for this include measurement error in both parental education and family income that is correlated with parental child labor status or omitted socio-economic factors that persist over time that would be correlated with past and current child labor supply. These factors might include local or family labor market conditions, school quality, latent relative talent for work or school, or social norms/parental attitudes that are correlated with child labor status. Lillard and Willis (1994) try to disentangle the reasons why educational attainment is correlated across co-resident generations in Malaysians. They estimate that about two thirds of the impact of parental education on children's educational attainment is through direct and indirect effects of parental schooling. Omitted factors appear to account for the remaining third. However, more research is necessary to disentangle the mechanisms behind the observed intergenerational transmission of child labor.

3.4.3. Does child labor promote high fertility?

While the long-run implications of high population growth are often debated, a relatively common view is that high fertility rates are a source of long-run poverty traps. Emerson and Knabb (2003) for example is formal theoretical treatment of the idea that higher fertility can create a poverty trap, in their case through child labor: because families expect children to have to work, they have lots of children. Then because families have lots of children, they need them to work.

Do poor families have children in order to put them to work? The "wealth flows" theory of fertility posits that families have children, because they expect positive net transfers from the child, while the "evolutionary" view posits motives such as altruism, genetic survival, the consumption value of children, etc. (Kaplan, 1994). A necessary condition for the "wealth flows" view is that the net flows from child to parent are positive.

A number of studies find a connection between child employment opportunities and fertility. Rosenzweig and Evenson (1977), using data from rural India, find evidence of a connection between the economic contribution of children and fertility, child labor, and schooling decisions. Family attributes positively associated with the pecuniary returns to market work (size of landholdings, farm productivity, child wage rates) are negatively related to schooling and positively related to fertility and market work. Examining data from the US, Rosenzweig (1977) argues that the declining value of children as assets in agriculture is an important factor in declining farm birth rates for post-war US.

A number of accounting studies attempt to directly compute whether the net return to children is large enough to motivate fertility. The most cited evidence from this is from Mead Cain (1977). In a village in north central Bangladesh, he estimates that male children become net producers as early as age 12 and compensate for their own cumulative consumption by age 15. However, whether his findings generalize is an open question. In subsequent work in other Asian countries, Cain (1982) found that the individual earnings of boys exceeded consumption at far older ages, and Kaplan (1994) in data from a forager-horticulturist group in Peru, finds that Cain's observation is not robust to considering a larger basket of consumption goods than Cain examined. In fact, a more common finding is that it seems unlikely that parents are repaid all of the costs associated with children (Mueller, 1976; Lee and Bulatao, 1983; Stecklov, 1999; Lee, Kaplan, and Kramer, 2002). Stecklov (1999) for example finds that the annual rates of return on children in Cote d'Ivoire are between -6 and -10 percent. Two challenges throughout this work, however, are what discount rates to consider and whether and how to value the insurance value of children both as potential laborers in their youth and as sources of old-age security. Together, there appears to be little compelling evidence that variation in child labor opportunities can explain a large portion of the high fertility rates in developing countries.

3.4.4. Does child labor affect local labor markets?

In their seminal study, Basu and Van (1998) point out that if children and adults are substitutes in production (the "substitution axiom "), the prevalence of child labor depresses adult wages. Basu and Van focus on the implications of this depressive effect of child labor on the prevalence of child labor. In particular, they posit what they term the "luxury axiom": children only work when parental income is below subsistence levels. With the combination of the luxury and substitution axioms, Basu and Van argue that child labor depresses adult wages which in turn makes child labor necessary. Multiple equilibriums in the labor market are then possible (see Basu, 2001 for a general equilibrium treatment).

Because of this study's importance, a slightly more formal presentation is useful. A number of additional assumptions are necessary to keep the present exposition transparent. First, assume that the household consists of one parent and one child. The parent chooses whether the child works. Second, there are N one-parent, one-child households that may differ in what they perceive as their subsistence needs (s varies between $\{s_L, s_H\}$). Third, parental labor supply is perfectly inelastic. The adult daily wage from working is m. Fourth, when children work, they earn a daily wage of w. Define an indicator c that is 1 if the child works. Household income can then be written $m + wc$.

Finally, all household consumption is financed by adult and child labor. Households do not have assets that may contribute to household income and do not have access to credit markets.[6]

Define s as the subsistence level of expenditure, above which parents no longer have children work. The luxury axiom implies that if $m > s$, children do not work and household income is m. Effective labor supply for a household is 1 when children do not work. If parental income does not cover subsistence ($m \leqslant s$), children work and household income is $m + w$. The substitution axiom implies a strong relationship between child and adult wages. Namely, if one child's labor is equivalent to a ($a < 1$) units of adult labor, then the wage children are paid is $w = am$. Similarly, then, when children work, effective labor supply for a household is $1 + a$. Market labor supply is then $N * (1 + a)$.

Figure 8 depicts the resulting market labor supply function written in terms of adult labor income and effective units of adult labor. Market labor supply is the sum of all individual household labor supply functions and is marked ABCD. When daily wages are above the highest subsistence level s_H, no children work, and the market labor supply function is defined by the segment AB. If wages are below the lowest subsistence level s_L, all children work. The segment BC is drawn to be downward sloping (rather than the discontinuous horizontal line that each household perceives) to acknowledge that

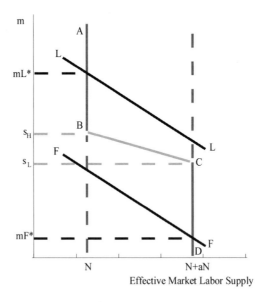

Figure 8. Wage determination and market equilibrium for child labor.

[6] Swinnerton and Rogers (1999) also emphasize a distributional axiom. In an economy where child labor persists despite the country being sufficiently rich so as to eliminate child labor (the multiple equilibria case discussed below), the existence of child labor is the result of inequality in the distribution of assets.

the subsistence level of expenditure *s* may vary across households based on household and community attributes as discussed below.

Market equilibrium adult (and thus child) wages are given by the price at which the supply of effective units of labor equals the demand for effective units of child labor. One possible labor demand curve is pictured in Fig. 8 and labeled LL. In the depicted equilibrium, labor demand is sufficiently high, that there is no child labor in the economy. Because adult wages are high, no children work. The effective employment in the economy is N and adult wages are indicated by $m*$. Note that if labor demand is very low (so it intersects labor supply along the CD segment but not along the AB segment), the economy is very poor and all children work.

Does the prevalence of child labor depress adult wages? Evidence which is broadly consistent with the luxury axiom (Edmonds, 2005) and the substitution axiom (Levison et al., 1998) will be discussed in greater detail below. However, while this is a critical question in the child labor literature, direct evidence on whether child labor affects adult labor markets is scarce. The reason for a lack of evidence is the joint determination of adult and child wages, especially when the substitution axiom holds. However, it is reasonable to ask how plausible it is that child labor, which is mostly outside of the formal labor wage market, can suppress adult wages. In countries where children form a substantial share of the active labor force, this effect seems more plausible than countries where it does not. Figure 9 contains the plot of the share of the economically active population that is 10–14 against the fraction of children 10–14 that are economically active for countries where at least 1 percent of the population 10–14 is economically active using the LABORSTAT data (ILO, 2000, see Section 2.2). All numbers are in

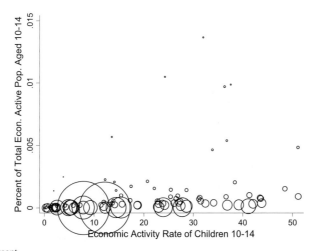

Note: 1 = 1 percent.
Source: Economic Activity for 2000 from LABORSTA (http://laborsta.ilo.org) and Population aged 10–14 weights (circle size) from UNSTAT.

Figure 9. Children's share of employment and the economic activity of children.

percentages: 0.01 is one hundredth of a percent. The size of the circles in the figure represents the 10–14 population in the country.

Two important issues are evident in Fig. 9. First, children are a larger share of the economically active population when their economic activity rates are higher. This could be mechanical if population is independent of economic activity rates. That said, the positive gradient in Fig. 9 is not particularly steep – going from 0 children working to the largest observed economic activity rate of children is associated with a two thousandths of a percentage point rise in the share of the economically active population that is children. Second, children constitute a very small share of the total economically active population, even in countries where economic activity rates of children are very high. There are only two countries in the world where children are more than a hundredth of a percent of the economically active population. Is it possible that variation in the activities of less than a hundredth of a percent of the economically active population can influence equilibrium wages in the labor market? Questions such as this are largely unanswered in the literature.

If child labor depresses adult wages in the local labor market, then the implications of child labor may extend much further than the working child. Ljungqvist (1992) for example develops a model where the prevalence of unskilled labor suppresses the wage of the uneducated workers relative to the educated. This causes the cost of education to be high relative to the labor earnings of an unskilled worker. Unskilled workers with few assets then choose not to obtain an education, because the marginal utility of foregone consumption during education is greater than the family's valuation of the return to education. Banerjee and Newman (1993) emphasize that depressed wages coupled with capital market imperfections can constrain entrepreneurship, leading to a stagnant, low wage economy. Thus, to the extent that child labor suppresses adult wages, this may have long run implications for growth and development.

4. Determinants of child time allocation

The framework in Eq. (1.1) highlights several influences on child time allocation including the marginal utility of income, the parent's valuation of the child's future welfare, how education and play affect the child's future welfare, the productivity of the child in family activities, the costs of schooling, and the earnings opportunities available to the child. Academic research on the determinants of child time allocation is often categorized as either labor demand or labor supply. Loosely defined, labor demand is typically concerned with the availability of employment whereas labor supply focuses more on questions related to willingness or ability to work. The distinction between the two is often difficult in the context of adult labor in high income economies. Despite the absence of formal tests of the separation hypothesis (e.g. Benjamin, 1992) for child labor, the general assumption among researchers is that distinguishing between demand and supply is especially arbitrary for children in low income countries where most children work with their parents in a family activity. Take for example, the literature on how household composition influences child labor. On one hand, the presence of younger children may raise the return on child time in domestic activities (labor demand), but on the other hand, younger children may also raise the marginal utility of income and thereby change labor supply. Should this research be classified as labor supply or demand?

Nevertheless, this section is organized by mimicking the labor demand and supply dichotomy. Section 4.1 focuses on what might be considered labor demand. What direct influence do local labor markets have on the activities of children? This includes evidence on how production technology, environmental factors, the industrial composition of local labor markets, the employer composition of local labor markets, and internal and international trade affects the employment opportunities open to children. Section 4.2 considers research on family factors that influence the activities of children. This includes research on agency problems, adult and child labor supply interactions, and the interaction of siblings. These factors are easily viewed as both labor demand and supply, and hence merit their own section.

Sections 4.3 and 4.4 consider issues that are typically considered as labor supply. Modern researchers tend to focus on returns to schooling as the main opportunity cost of work, and Section 4.3 surveys the literature on how returns and costs of schooling affect on decisions about how children work. No topic has garnered more attention that the relationship between child labor and poverty, and Section 4.4 considers this literature.

4.1. Local labor markets and child time allocation

Most of the work on why children work focuses on why families send their children to work. Comparatively few papers consider child productivity in the family or the wage market. This lack of research reflects that very few children are employed in the formal labor market and that suitable data for examining labor demand in the formal labor market is extremely limited. Most researchers work with household surveys which are generally not suited to modeling the formal employment sector and which will rarely have power to analyze the comparatively rare event of wage employment. Establishment surveys with detailed data on child labor appear to be non-existent.

4.1.1. Production technology

How is child labor influenced by the technology used in production? Put another way, are there certain types of production that are especially apt to draw in working children? Marx argues that a supply of children and women is critical for the early stages of industrialization, because they are both cheap and suited to affine tasks that require little fingers. A similar argument is in Goldin and Sokoloff (1982). With data from early 19th century US, they emphasize that comparative advantage appears to be the explanation for high female and child labor participation rates in early industrialization. The proportion of the northeastern manufacturing labor force composed of females and young males seems to have grown from about 10 percent at the start of the 19th century to 40 percent by 1932. The low relative productivity of women and children in the North's agriculture sector (hay, dairy, grains) kept the opportunity cost of their labor low relative to that in the South. In fact, Goldin and Sokoloff (1984) argue that this may partially account for why manufacturing industries were disproportionate in the northeast.

Because most working children are by their parent's side in the family farm or business, an emphasis on industrialization to explain the high rates of working children around the world is clearly unsatisfactory. Moreover, in a contemporary setting, very few studies even document a link between changes in the activities of children and either the industrial composition of local labor market or the types of employer in a community. Edmonds (2003) is one exception. Using both cross-section and a household panel in Vietnam, he considers both the association between the activities of children and the types of industries and employers in the child's community. He observes that domestic work is more prevalent and market work less prevalent in locations where handicraft industries are located but observes very little association between the activities of children and variation in other types of industries (over time or between locations) including manufacturing. For type of employer, Edmonds observes that children are less likely to be engaged in market and wage work in locations where state or large private employers are more prevalent, while hours worked is slightly larger in communities with significant small employer presence. However, the endogenous placement of industries and employers is a serious concern and it is not addressed, and his findings cannot be taken as more than suggestive of future avenues for research.

Are there tasks that might be important in industrialization that require children for anything other than cheap labor? The literature on child development suggests possible ways in which children might have an advantage in several activities. Sloutsky and Fisher (2004) showed color pictures of animals for memorization to a small number children around age 5 and young adults around 20. Children appear more effective at memorization of details because of differences in their approach to memorization. The young adults memorized by categorizing the animals whereas the children appeared to memorize by comparing each new animal to a reference animal. When the experimenters asked the young children to categorize animals for memorization, their performance deteriorated. Other work has found that children perform better than young adults in comparing visual objects and in drawing spatial analogies (Gentner, 1977). Studies that compare young adults to older individuals suggest that the tendency towards categorization and thereby false analogy grows stronger with age (Koutstaal and Schacter, 1997). Research like this might imply that children would have an advantage at detailed work requiring pattern memorization such as carpet weaving or knitting.

The most detailed case-study we have on child productivity in manufacturing focuses explicitly on an industry where these developmental advantages should be most important: the hand-knitted carpet industry. Levison et al. (1998) find little empirical support for the "nimble fingers" view. Adults and children tend to work on the same types of carpets and that children are 21 percent less productive in hand-knitting than adults (productivity is measured in square inches knit per hour). This case seems consistent with the overwhelming empirical fact about child labor in today's developing countries: formal sector wage employment of children is extremely rare. If children were critical for the early stage of industrialization, then its low prevalence would be a surprise. That said, our understanding of labor demand would clearly benefit from additional work like Levison et al. (1998).

While it is unclear whether there are activities for which children have an absolute advantage in, there must be activities in which children have a comparative advantage. It is this comparative advantage that Goldin and Sokoloff appeal to in order to explain north-south differences in the employment of women. When the return to these activities in which children have comparative advantage is high relative to other uses of child time, we expect children to work everything else equal. Interestingly, Galbi (1997) argues that the nature of the child's comparative advantage in early English cotton mills was that adult laborers did not know how to be factory workers. In fact, he argues, that children were replaced in English cotton mills when the children became adults, trained and socialized for factory work.

Collection activities are often mentioned as activities where children will have comparative advantage. For example, Nankhuni and Findeis (2004) note that children in deforested areas of Malawi spend significantly more time collecting wood for fuel than do children in less deforested areas, and this collection time is associated with reduced schooling participation. Several studies document a connection between variation in access to water facilities and child schooling. For example, Psacharopoulos and Arriagada (1989) find that schooling is higher in Brazilian households with piped water; Cockburn and Dostie (2007) note that work time is lower and schooling higher in Ethiopian households with better access to water; and Guarcello and Lyon (2003) observe in Yemen that households connected to a water network are more likely to send their children to school and less likely to report their children as idle. While these studies do not address the non-random nature of water access, they are suggestive of how important the return to child time in activities other than schooling can be for child time allocation.

Several recent studies note that children work more in households with more self-employment activities (Edmonds and Turk, 2004 for Vietnam, Parikh and Sadoulet, 2005 in Brazil), and Wydick (1999) notes a correlation between work and household involvement in a microcredit program. For example, using detailed time use data from Botswana, Mueller (1984) documents that the more productive capital the household has, the more productive work its children perform. Using Mueller's data from Botswana, Chernichovsky (1985) observes that this association between market work inside the household and the presence of productive capital varies depending on whether substitutes for child labor are present in the household. Cockburn and Dostie (2007) go into further detail in Ethiopian data. He notes that small livestock and land appear to be market work increasing whereas oxen, bulls, ploughs, land quality, and again, proximity to water are child labor decreasing. Shafiq (2006b) points out that, while greater assets may lead children to report working more because of the availability of employment opportunities, the human capital ramifications of this are unclear. In his data from

Bangladesh, children work more in the presence of productive assets, but they are also more likely to attend school.

Some closely related evidence also illustrates how technology changes that replace the types of activities typically done by children can alter schooling and the activities of children. For example, Brown, Christiansen, and Philips (1992) documents technological changes in the US Fruit and Vegetable canning industry that lead to a shift to adult labor. Levy (1985) shows a relationship between the mechanization of Egyptian agriculture and the decline of child labor in cotton. Two important technologies he emphasizes are the spread of tractors and irrigation pumps. Dessy and Pallage (2005) emphasize the importance of technology in child labor formally in arguing that one way to view child labor is as the result of a coordination failure between parents and firms investing in skill intensive technologies. Technology changes can also affect child time outside of the formal wage labor market. Fafchamps and Shilpi (2004) observe that in Nepali data, there appears to be greater household specialization as proximity to urban areas increases, and Fafchamps and Wahba (2006) argue that children are more likely to attend school and not work as specialization increases with urban proximity. Interestingly, they note that while work in the household is reduced with urban proximity, there is a rise in child labor outside of the household although it is not enough to offset the total decline in hours worked.

4.1.2. Trade

One frequently reads popular anecdotes about children working in export industries, and it is often asserted that the ability to trade with high income countries causes children in developing countries to work. Put another way, this argument implies that trade creates work opportunities for children that would otherwise not be present. Maskus (1997) is a formal presentation of this idea. In his model, the poor country produces an export good that is labor intensive and an import-competing, capital intensive good. The export sector subcontracts to the informal sector which employs children. The demand for child labor then depends on product demand for the export good. An expansion of the export sector then increases child labor through higher equilibrium child wages.

A number of studies have examined data on cross-country trade flows to consider whether there is any evidence of a link between trade and child labor in aggregate statistics. They typically document a negative correlation between child labor and openness which is defined as the sum of exports and imports as a share of GDP. Edmonds and Pavcnik (2006a) is one such study that explicitly attempts to account for the endogeneity of openness. They instrument for openness with trade based on geography. The main identification assumption in this approach is that trade which is driven by geography does not affect working children except in its impact on total trade flows. They also observe that economic activity rates for children are lower in countries that trade more. Moreover, addressing the endogeneity of trade nearly doubles the magnitude of the elasticity of child economic activity rates with respect to openness.

What explains why children work less in countries that trade more? Edmonds and Pavcnik find that the negative association between openness and economic activity rates mostly reflects the well documented positive link between trade and income. Once they condition on a country's income, they find a very small and statistically insignificant relationship between trade and child labor. This result holds in the full sample, when they split the sample into different country groups, consider only trade between high and low income countries, or focus on exports of unskilled-labor intensive products from low income countries. Thus, the cross-country data provide no support for the claim that trade perpetuates high levels of child labor in poor countries via the labor demand channel.

Given that most children work in agriculture and family businesses, it is perhaps unsurprising that there is no evidence of a labor demand effect on economic activity rates through trade in the cross-country data. More detailed industry or within country data on changes in industrial employment with growing trade is promising for shedding more light on how international markets might affect the activities of children.

Edmonds and Pavcnik (2005b) examine the relationship between market work, domestic work, and trade using panel data on rural Vietnamese households. Vietnam liberalized its rice export quota during the 1990s and lifted restrictions on trade in rice across Vietnamese regions. Subsequently, from 1993 to 1998 the price of rice increased on average by almost 30 percent relative to the consumer price index, and rice price changes varied widely across communities of Vietnam. Edmonds and Pavcnik relate market work participation to regional and intertemporal variation in rice prices. Despite the growth in labor demand associated with a booming rice sector, they find that market work and domestic work decrease by more in communities that experience greater increases in rice prices. The declines in working children are greatest in households that were net rice producers prior to market reform. Part of this decline in work owes to an income effect, but part also owes to a rise in household specialization that Edmonds and Pavcnik (2006b) document in the context of these rice trade liberalizations.

Land and labor are the two primary inputs into rice production, and overall both are sufficiently equally distributed in Vietnam that most overall both are sufficiently equally distributed in Vietnam that most households are well positioned to enjoy the additional income stemming from this trade liberalization. Of course, it is possible that a growth in trade could have opposite effects when the income gains are not distributed to those whose employment opportunities are rising. For example, Kruger (2004) observes that during the coffee boom of the mid-1990s in Nicaragua, there is an overall increase in market work that is especially large in poor households in coffee producing areas. Her findings mirrors what Alessie et al. (1992) observed with cash crop price increases in Cote d'Ivoire: increases in cash crop prices are associated with more children working in the cultivation of those crops. One explanation for Kruger's findings is that because of the concentration of land in coffee (and the resulting market power in local labor markets), poor laborers have received increases in income that are minor compared to the growth in labor demand, and hence market work has increased. Another interpretation of these findings is emphasized in Kruger's (2007) study of the coffee boom's effects on working children in Brazil. In that context, she emphasizes that when booms are expected to be transitory, households should seize temporary employment opportunities, especially if it is easy to make up for lost schooling time in the future. Her findings are then consistent with evidence of delaying schooling or temporary withdrawals from school in response to macroeconomic crisis as discussed in Section 4.4 below.

In the Vietnam rice price case, much of the affected population is exiting poverty while such improvements in living standards are not evident in Kruger's coffee data. Edmonds, Pavcnik, and Topalova (2007) look at the connection between trade policy, child labor, and poverty directly in their study of schooling and child labor responses to India's trade reform in 1991. They observe that children who were in areas with a concentration of heavily protected industries prior to liberalization are more impacted by tariff cuts. They do not experience the same increases in schooling and declines in work without schooling evident elsewhere in India over the 1990s. This pattern of rising work without schooling and declining schooling relative to the national trend does not appear to be explainable with falling returns to schooling (they appear to be increasing) or rising unskilled wages (which appear to be falling). Rather, they reflect the relative rise in poverty in areas that experience a larger decline in protection. Further, they argue that the avoidance of schooling costs lies behind this trade policy – child labor-schooling connection. This combination of micro-studies emphasizes how multidimensional the interaction of trade and child labor can be and that the effects of international trade on the working status of children will be context specific.

4.2. Child labor and the family

4.2.1. Who makes child labor decisions?

Unitary models of the household are typically used in the child labor literature. The model of Section 1 is one example with its single decision-maker. Implicit within these is an assumption of either unanimity of preferences within the family or a dictatorial household. Typically, parents are viewed as the primary decision-makers for child labor supply and schooling. This raises the classic parental agency problem. While parents may make child labor decisions, they do not fully internalize the costs of these decisions. Moreover, this assumption that parents make child labor decisions has led many to assert that child labor supply is evidence of parental callousness and indifference to their children. Specifically, if parents make decisions about child labor supply and do not consider either the current or future welfare in so-doing, then they will select higher levels of child labor than the child would choose or than governments would consider socially optimal. "Nimble Fingers" theories of child labor take this parental agency problem to an extreme. They posit that parents always take advantage of employment opportunities open to children and therefore that labor demand is the dominant determinant of whether and how children work.

In recent years, more attention has been paid to the fact that there is typically not one decision-maker in the household, and empirical studies uniformly reject the unitary household model. Decisions about child time allocation will be influenced by mothers, fathers, extended family, and perhaps even children themselves. Edmonds and Sharma (2006) consider an extreme example of how child time allocation can be affected by multiple decision-makers. In studying a population in Western Nepal with a high intrinsic risk of bondage, they argue that child labor is increased and schooling reduced in part, because neither parents, children, or bondholders have security over the returns to investments in children. They argue their case can be read as an extreme representation of the classic parental agency problem.

Several recent studies examine deviations from the unitary household model in more conventional situations. A common question is how parental characteristics affect the activities of children. Emerson and Souza (2007) for example observe that the elasticity of child labor supply with respect to parental education is greater for fathers than mothers and that it is more important for the son's labor supply than the daughter's. Whether this reflects something intrinsic to education, relative earnings ability, actual incomes, type of occupation, or some omitted geographic characteristic correlated with child labor and schooling decisions is outside the scope of the study. A perennial difficulty in tests of the unitary household model is to find characteristics that are associated with variation in the influence of different family members but that do not simultaneously affect child labor and schooling decisions, but Emerson and Souza's findings are suggestive that researchers may observe patterns in child labor that is consistent with what other studies of intrahousehold allocation have found. Similar findings for education are surveyed in Strauss and Thomas (1995), and they argue that the evidence strongly supports effects of parental education that go beyond the effect of education on income.

Basu (2006) considers how the status of women in the household affects child labor supply. In his model, both mothers and fathers dislike sending their children to work, but they differ in their preferences over consumption goods. As female status improves, the family opts for less child labor, because it becomes increasingly difficult to agree on other decisions over which there is disagreement. However, as women's status improves and she becomes dominant in the household, child labor may rise as she can exert more influence over consumption choices in other goods. For example, suppose that utility depends on the child's labor status and consumption of two different goods. Additional consumption of good 1 does not improve the woman's utility, and additional consumption of good 2 does not benefit the man (but it does the woman). Thus, as female power increases in the household, first the family shifts to less child labor, then it shifts to more good 2 consumption and more child labor. Thus, the relationship between child labor and female power in the household is predicted to be a U-shape. Basu and Ray (2002) examine this in household survey data from Nepal. The maximal female education in the household as a share of the sum of the maximal female and male education in the household proxies female power. The Nepali data are consistent with this inverted U-shape hypothesis.

Comparatively little attention has been directed to the child's own role in child time allocation decisions. The focus on parents is driven by the observation that parents have comparatively more power within the household than do children. The fact that most working children are employed within the household in activities that are apt to confer little in the way of status or economic independence seems consistent with this view. Moreover, work is typically considered in tandem with schooling, and schooling is expensive in ways that may require the parents to finance it. If children cannot pay for alternatives to work, then parents necessarily influence child labor supply. However, there is some evidence that suggests that when opportunities outside of the household are open to children, they may be able to influence household decision making.

Moehling (2005) is perhaps the most compelling direct evidence on the ability of working children to influence household decision-making. She examines data from the US collected between 1917 and 1919. She observes that the share of total household expenditures on child goods is increasing in the children's contribution to household income. Unless the child's work demands this expenditure, it is hard to understand why more income to children increases spending on child goods more so than other types of income without some impact of child's income on family decision-making. Interestingly, Moehling (2006) notes that despite the fact that young children typically turned over their entire pay envelope to their parents, it still seems to be treated differently than other sources of income although her results for younger children may reflect something about the younger children's requirements for work. Basu (2006) also points out that there may be a cycle of power in the household. As children work, their ability to influence household activities increases, and thus they may choose to work more.

How important is the child's role in deciding her own labor supply? If she can influence household decision-making by working, it seems the potential is large. However, very little research has considered the child's own role in deciding her own labor supply or schooling. One suggestive piece of evidence is from Iversen (2002). He interviews child migrants in one location in a rural South Indian district about why they migrated and the extent to which they have contact with parents. He reports that the labor supply of young children and girl migrants seem to be largely determined by parents. However, boys who start working at ages 13 and above, report little contact with parents which may reflect that they are working by their own choice. Iverson speculates that autonomy is an important motivation for this group's migration decision; these early teen migrants may have migrated and work in order to have greater control over their lives.

The implications of some child influence over their time allocation can be very important for interpreting evidence that purports to show a link between the labor market opportunities of children and child labor supply. This evidence is often interpreted as parental callousness about the welfare of their children or indifference to education. However, it may reflect more about the child's own valuation of their time. In particular, if children are myopic relative to adults, they may respond more to changes in their employment opportunities than parents. If this is the case, there may be relatively little scope for anti-poverty policies, etc., to affect the labor supply of this group. Future research understanding the child's own role in her time allocation is perhaps the most pressing need in the child labor literature.

4.2.2. Parental attitudes towards work and schooling

One of the key reasons why child labor is viewed as a human rights issue is that parents likely have considerable influence over child time allocation. They may capture many of the benefits of child work while not personally bearing the costs (except in as much as they internalize the child's welfare). As discussed above, it is unclear how important child and parental agency are in child time allocation, but to the extent that parents have influence (especially over young children), then parental attitudes towards work are of potentially great importance.

Accusations of parental callousness towards their children and disregard of the costs of work abound in the policy debate and in the academic literature. The focus of the anti-child labor campaigns in the Progressive Era of the United States was largely on changing parental attitudes towards work. Zelizer (1994) emphasizes the important role changing attitudes towards children played in the changes in schooling and work in the US during the later half of the nineteenth, first part of the twentieth century. Analogous campaigns to stigmatize work for children are pervasive in many developing countries today.

There is ample basis for this focus on norms in the treatment of children in qualitative work on child labor and schooling decisions. For example, the Public Report on Basic Education in India (1999) found that 37 percent of parents listed a lack of parental interest in educating their children as an explanation for why boys had never enrolled in school. However, it is very difficult to disentangle cause and effect in studies of child labor and parental attitudes towards work and school, and statements about motives are often a challenge to interpret.

There are a few approaches taken in the econometrics literature to study the influence of parental attitudes on work decisions. One approach is to look at correlations between the parent's background and the child's activities. This evidence has already arisen in Section 3.4 and obviously attitudes towards work are only one component of how parental background can influence child time allocation. A second approach is to look at some measure of parental attitudes or gender bias within the household and correlate these with child time allocation. These studies are surprisingly rare, perhaps because of the challenge of capturing variation in attitudes or gender bias that is not simultaneous with other factors influencing child work. A third approach is to correlate community average behaviors with an individual household's schooling or work decisions. The hope is that the community mean reflects local values and not anything else about the community. In reality, the econometric challenges presented by this approach are insurmountable.

Several studies assert that regression residuals capture social norms or parental attitudes for child labor decisions. This is strange. By construction, in linear regressions, residuals are mean zero and orthogonal to included covariates. However, it seems unlikely that norms and attitudes towards work have no influence on work decisions on average or that these beliefs would be orthogonal to observable household characteristics. Moreover, regression residuals will be influenced by misspecification of the model, mismeasurement of any included covariates, and the researcher's subjective choice about what covariates to include in the estimated models.

Perhaps the most frequently cited evidence directly on parental attitudes towards child labor is Parsons and Goldin (1989). They consider the association between savings and child wage labor supply among industrial families in the US in the late nineteenth century. They note that the marginal propensity to save out of child income is significantly less than 1 and that there is a positive correlation between asset levels and child labor income. In both cases, child income appears to be treated like adult income in the household. Moreover, Parsons and Goldin observe that child income appears to have little effect on total family income. Each dollar of child income implies a 9/10 reduction in male household head income. They hypothesize that this reflects family migration toward areas with better child labor opportunities that comes at the expense of adult income. Indeed, Parson and Goldin paint a bleak picture of how parents allocate the time of their children. They write: "These working-class families apparently sold the schooling and potential future earnings of their offspring very cheaply" (p. 655).

There are, however, several difficulties with this interpretation of the patterns observed by Parsons and Goldin. In particular, the source of variation in child income is unclear in their data. Suppose, for example, that parents are altruistic towards their children and only have children work when it is critical to meet basic needs (as assumed in Basu and Van, 1998, Section 3.4). In that case, we would expect to observe lower adult earnings as child labor earnings are higher, but the causality runs from adult earnings to child earnings. In this case, child income is compensating for the loss of adult income, so the marginal propensity to save or spend should be similar for each. With imperfect insurance markets, part of the family's basic needs must include a saving component to help cope with future shocks. Hence, the marginal propensity to save out of income is likely to be above 0. The positive correlation between child income and asset accumulation is more of a puzzle, albeit one that can be explained in several ways. It may reflect the same concerns as savings (and may be the instrument for savings); it may reflect the indivisibility of fixed schooling costs (school costs tend to need to be paid on irregular intervals like the start of the school year); or it may reflect a latent correlation between the degree of economic activity in an area and the activities of children. Recall, that even perfectly altruistic parents send their children to work when the relative returns are highest. Hence, it is very difficult to draw concrete conclusions about the callousness of parents in this data.

Future studies of norms or attitudes towards child labor and schooling would be better served in trying to codify or measure such attributes directly. In general, the role attitudes and norms play in child labor is poorly understood. It is clear that child time allocation is in general elastic with respect to the household's economic environment, but it is not clear whether this elasticity is bounded by social attitudes towards work, whether there are some children who are especially vulnerable in this regard, and whether this elasticity reflects changing norms or if norms are just one component of how child time allocation decisions are made. Ultimately, the interest in parental norms is most acute for its implications for the design of policy, and it is unfortunate that so little work has been done to study how policy efforts to change attitudes towards work have influenced child time allocation decisions.

4.2.3. Child and adult labor supply interactions

Most working children work inside their home. There are several explanations for this. Parents may prefer to have children at home to better monitor their working conditions or simply, because they enjoy their proximity. There may be strong norms against child work outside of the household which lowers the perceived return from having a child work outside of their home. Children may also be more productive workers at home. Parents may be more effective at monitoring or disciplining children. Moral hazard problems may be especially acute with children who may not perceive or care about threats of social sanction outside of the household.

There is a literature on the activities of children in family run businesses in developed economies that emphasizes the productivity of children relative to hired in labor. Sanders and Nee (1996) for example consider the role of children within the self-employed immigrant families in the US. They emphasize the importance of child labor within these families because it is both very reliable and continuous over time in comparison to other sources of labor. In her study of Chinese take-out businesses, Song (1999) emphasizes the work of children as translators and mediators in these businesses. Parents rely on their English language skills for assistance and guidance, often freeing the parent for oversight duties of hired in help. Song also emphasizes that parents often prefer family labor, because typically there is not much privacy in the work environment that often starts in the family home (p. 71). For children to work within their own household, there must be a sufficient amount of economic activity and working capital within the household. Hence, many observers emphasize a positive correlation between family asset holdings and work inside the household. This is discussed in detail in Section 4.4.

When children work outside of their household, there appears to be a strong association between the types of work they do and that of their parents. Parents may prefer their children to work with them, be more effective at affecting high levels of effort, have better information about job opportunities open to children, and there may be geographic clustering in the types of activities performed. Genicot (2005) also emphasizes nutritional spillovers to children from adult earnings as an explanation for the association between child and adult work. She considers (theoretically) a setting were an employer elects to pay a higher wage to enhance his employee's nutritional status. The worker spends a portion of this higher wage on his child, enhancing the child's productivity. The employer then prefers to hire the child in addition to the parent in order to capture all of this externality.

Some of the strongest evidence of complementarities between parent and child in the type of wage work performed comes from US history. For example, Goldin and Parsons (1981) find that the median schooling of males whose fathers were employed in textiles (where child labor was also prevalent) was 3.3 years less than those whose fathers were not, even controlling for parental income differences. Goldin (1979) observes positive elasticities of male and female child labor supply with respect to the father's wage in nineteenth century Philadelphia, but she does not see this pattern in mother's labor supply. From this, she infers that children (rather than wives) were the most common source of labor income apart from the male head of household.

However, in a contemporary setting, there is much more evidence of same sex substitution patterns with respect to adult female labor supply. For example, Skoufias (1993) observes a negative correlation between adult female wages and wage child labor. He theorizes that this connection is driven by children filling in for absent mothers in the households and thereby reducing their work outside of the household (although an income effect is hard to rule out in his case). Wahba (2006) observes that wage work is less frequent for boys in the parts of Egypt where unskilled wages are greater. She emphasizes an income effect explanation. Further, Katz (1995) and Hazarika and Sarangi (2005) observe increases in girl domestic work as mothers become more involved in home enterprises or microcredit programs. Katz (1995) speculates that the availability of an older girl to substitute for the mother in domestic work could act as a binding constraint on female labor supply in her data from Guatemala.

Adult–child substitution patterns can be affected by changes in the returns to activities in which adults or children have comparative advantage. For example, Field (2003) examines how patterns of child and adult time allocation change when Peruvian squatters receive secure titles to their land. She finds that children work less outside of their household when titled and that adults work more outside of the household. Her evidence does not seem to suggest that this is an income effect as their does not appear to be an identifiable income effect of titling. Instead, she argues that adults have comparative advantage in providing security for their property. Hence with insecure property rights, children work away from home, but adults are freed to work away with titling. Thus, there is support in the empirical literature for both complementarities in wage labor supply and substitution possibilities between child and adult labor depending on the economic environment.

4.2.4. Does parental co-residence influence child labor?

There are many ways that parents might influence child labor supply aside from either complementarities or substitution patterns in child labor. The absence of a parent might either attenuate the employment options open to children or accentuate the need for children to fill in for the parent's work. It is worth noting that these two issues work in opposite directions and are most likely to affect different types of work. Thus, the relationship between child and adult work can be very sensitive to the types of activities considered. Beyond substitution patterns, the absence of a parent is likely associated with variation in family income (although the direction of this variation is unclear). There is a separate concern from biology that parents might have differential investment incentives in their genetic offspring. This can be modeled by allowing child investment incentives to vary with the biological relationship.

Moehling (2004) considers the association between family structure and child labor and schooling in the American South at the start of the twentieth century. Living apart from one or both parents is associated with lower school attendance and greater market work participation, especially for black children. She is careful to note that the variation in child labor and schooling for American blacks that is attributable to variation in living arrangements is small compared to parental literacy, household resources, and school characteristics.

Interest in the relationship between parental co-residence and investments in children has risen significantly in recent years, because of the AIDS crisis in Sub-Saharan Africa. Most existing studies find that orphanhood is associated with reduced schooling enrollment. Two approaches are common in the literature. First, many studies compare children living within the same household who differ in whether they have had a parent die. Case, Paxson, and Ableidinger (2004) exemplify this household fixed effects approach in their study of orphanhood and school enrollment in 10 Sub-Saharan Africa countries using data from demographic and health surveys. They find that orphans are less likely to attend school than the non-orphans with whom they live. These within household (household fixed effects) comparisons are complicated by the fact that the orphans and non-orphans likely come from different backgrounds and certainly differ in one important experience: the loss of a parent.

A second approach to study the relationship between schooling and parental death is to use individual level panel data that follow children over time. Evans and Miguel (2005) is one such study. In a panel of 20,000 rural Kenyan children, they find a substantial decrease in participation in school following a parental death and some decline prior to the death. Beegle, De Weerdt, and Dercon (2006) follow a smaller sample of children from the Kagera region of Tanzania for over 10 years, and find substantive, sustained declines in educational attainment and height associated with parental mortality.

The effects of parental death on child work are less clear. There does not appear to be any individual level panel studies on orphanhood with detail on child work. Guarcello et al. (2004) use some of the same demographic and health survey data as Case, Paxson, and Ableidinger (2004) from Sub-Saharan Africa and cannot draw generalities about correlations between parental death and various forms of work. Throughout this literature, a chronic problem is how to separate different mechanisms for the impact of parental death from the non-random nature of deaths. Are children withdrawing from school to work to substitute for lost parental wages, to fill in for the parent's role in the household? Alternatively, is withdrawal a trauma effect of the loss of a parent? Studying child time allocation seems to be a promising way to better understand the schooling–orphanhood connection, and it is likely to be of interest in its own right.

4.2.5. How does sibling composition affect child labor?

A number of studies document a positive correlation between family size and child labor. This correlation is generally viewed as suggestive of resource and credit constraints on child time allocation (e.g. Knodel and Wongsith, 1991; Patrinos and Psacharopoulos,

1997). Family size may also influence the shadow value of child time when there are tasks for which it is difficult to hire in help. Many researchers have attempted to better understand why children work by looking inside the household to see how sibling composition affects child labor and schooling. The reason for this attention is that by looking at differences in how parents treat children, many believe it might be possible to infer the influence of parental preferences in child labor and schooling decisions, although it is not obvious how we can learn about preferences from sibling differences in child labor.

Studies typically look at birth order, sibling sex composition, or birth spacing. There are a variety of mechanisms through which birth order may affect investments in children. They can be roughly categorized as mechanisms owing to parent's age, socialization, or resource constraints. Higher birth order children will have older parents who may be wealthier, more experienced at raising children, or feel more altruistic but they also face a higher risk of birth defects and twinning. Lower birth order children grow up in a more adult environment, have the experience of teaching their siblings, but have comparative advantage to younger siblings in the wage labor market and in household production. Higher birth order children grow up in households with more competition for scarce resources such as income and parental time, the present value of returns on investment may be lower because of longer time horizons until the market realization of these returns, or they may benefit from sibling transfers. Ejrnaes and Portner (2004) argue that birth order (conditional on household size) reveals something about the child's latent genetic talent, because they argue that the probability the family stops having children is increasing in the child's ability relative to the family's expectation.

While a number of studies document an association between birth order and child labor or schooling, few studies attempt to distinguish a mechanism. Emerson and Souza (2002) observe in Brazil that older boys and girls are more likely to work and less likely to attend school than their younger siblings. They point out that this could be of credit constraints—older children might be working because poor families are unable to borrow to finance education. Edmonds (2006b) observes similar patterns in Nepal and argues that they may also owe to differences in comparative advantage in household production. He cannot exclude a preference or credit constraints based explanation, but he observes that sibling differences in total hours worked are largest in household production, and that the oldest girls especially spend more time working in domestic work when there are more younger siblings. Parish and Willis (1993) emphasize a similar supportive role of the oldest girl in Taiwanese households. She helps with the schooling outcomes of their younger children by caring for younger children and by bringing in income through wage employment that helps with school fees and allows later entry into the labor force for younger siblings. However, Parish and Willis argue that her most important contribution to the household comes through leaving early and marrying.

Two studies stand out in their ability to identify specific mechanisms through which birth order is correlated with child labor and schooling. First, Manacorda (2006) finds that children are less likely to work when they have older siblings and are in US states where those older siblings can work (see Section 3.4 for more detail on this paper).

Second, Birdsall (1991) emphasizes the importance of constraints on time in generating birth order effects. In data from urban Columbia, she shows that education is lower for later born children. She argues that this is inconsistent with what would expect to see with credit constraints where older children should support younger children. Moreover, she observes that birth order effects are less likely among working mothers in urban Columbia. She argues that this reflects that time can be traded for money in the market so that working mothers can shift in and out of the labor force to keep the shadow value of time equal in all periods.

The sibling sex composition literature tends to emphasize sibling rivalry, peer effects, or sex-typing to explain sibling sex composition effects on child labor and schooling. The sibling rivalry idea is that everything else equal, the child is better off with more siblings who are comparatively less valued in terms of preferences, market opportunities, social status, etc. For this to hold there needs to be some type of a constraint on credit, transfers, labor markets, or household production that cause household investment decisions to depend on the sex composition of children in the household or parental preferences have to vary across children. Peer effects work through the influence of the sex composition of siblings on the family environment. A more masculine environment, for example, may influence a girl's social interactions in the world. Sex-typing occurs when there are certain tasks that are stereotypically male or female but a child goes against type because of the absence of an appropriately gendered individual to carry out the task in the household. For example, a boy raised in a household without girls may engage in tasks that are more typically female in a household.

Peer effects and sex-typing of tasks have drawn the most attention in the developed economy context, but for developing economies, many writers have emphasized sibling rivalry. Parish and Willis (1993) for example emphasize in Taiwan that it is the support available from having an older sister that is critical for schooling. While Parish and Willis focus on the oldest sister, Edmonds (2006b) observes in Nepali data that the probability younger boys and girls work is declining in the number of older sisters. Morduch (2000) finds that moving from all brothers to all sisters raises completed schooling by nearly half a year in Tanzania. Similar patterns are documented in Garg and Morduch (1998) for Ghana, but the result is not as general as Morduch (2000) observes no such pattern in South Africa. Whether sibling rivalry is more intense between sexes or within sex groups may vary across cultures. In Malaysian data, for example, Lillard and Willis (1994) observe that siblings of the same sex appear to be rivals in attracting investment of resources from their parents in the sense that female education is reduced by more girls present, boys by more boys.

Much of the attention in the child labor literature has been on sibling sex composition or birth order. Comparatively little attention has been devoted to issues of birth-spacing. Implicitly, many of the mechanisms for birth order effects on child labor are actually working through spacing. For example, two children close in age are more apt to be seen as substitutes in household production, work, or schooling opportunities. Likewise, the probability of receiving substantive support from an older sibling is likely to increase with the age gap between siblings. While there is some suggestive evidence in Edmonds

(2006b) that sibling sex differences in activities are more pronounced when age gaps are small, more research on the implication of birth spacing for child labor and schooling is needed.

Several empirical problems plague most of the research into how sibling structure effects investments in children. First, births are typically unobserved. Rather, only co-resident children are observed. This could easily be resolved by surveys that collect complete fertility histories or details about non-resident siblings, but in practice, this appears rare in surveys with detailed child labor data. Second, household composition is typically endogenous to the household's economic environment (and thereby labor supply) through fostering, mortality, marriage, migration, etc. Akresh (2004), for example, emphasizes how important fostering can be to a family's risk management strategy. Third, when households include extended families or when polygamy is prevalent, it may be impossible to even establish resident sibling relationships. Fourth, fertility is endogenous to factors influencing child labor supply. Sex composition may reflect parental preferences about the type of children they would like to have. Birth order, for example, cannot be separated from factors influencing fertility or from household size as higher order birth orders can only be observed in larger households. Several authors address this later problem with specifications that compares birth order effects within household size groupings. However, the empirical challenges dealing with these issues are considerable.

An additional issue is whether to include household fixed effects in the analysis. On the positive side, this controls for common household factors such as current employment opportunities inside and outside the household, parental attitudes that may be correlated with sibling size, and other child invariant characteristics. However, this approach will limit the analysis to children with siblings, exaggerate sibling differences when they are relatively small, and may not address most omitted variable concerns as the effects of factors such as local labor market opportunities or household endowments may vary with age and thereby birth order, age spacing, or sibling sex composition. To the extent controlling for household fixed effects expands within sibling differences, they may make controlling for differences in factors associated with age more difficult. Similarly, within household differences in sibling composition owe to differences in the sex of the child or differences in parents. Both of which create estimation problems. Hence, while household fixed effects can be useful, they are often viewed incorrectly as a solution to most of the empirical problems that plague the empirical analysis of sibling differences in child labor.

4.3. Child labor and the (net) return to schooling

In the developed country context, a number of authors have emphasized that work is not the main opportunity cost of schooling; rather, foregone leisure is (e.g. Parsons, 1975). In the developing country context, researchers tend to view work as the main opportunity cost of schooling. If so, there should be a close connection between work and the relative return to schooling. This section surveys the evidence on a link between the measured or proxied return to schooling and child labor. Note that in the model of Section 1, it is the relative return to education that matters for child labor supply. For example, for a child that engages in wage work and schooling, the allocation between schooling and wage work requires:

$$\frac{\partial u}{\partial V_k}\frac{\partial R}{\partial E} - \frac{\partial u}{\partial S}\frac{\partial F}{\partial c}e = \frac{\partial u}{\partial S}\frac{\partial F}{\partial c}w. \tag{4.1}$$

Thus, time allocation between wage work and school depends on the local wage, the marginal utility of income (in the model of Section 1 where credit constraints are implicit), and the net return to schooling. The net return to schooling is the difference between the marginal utility associated with any future returns to education and the foregone consumption schooling costs require. A major consideration in the literature on the returns to schooling and child labor is what factors could lead to a situation where the returns to schooling do not affect child labor. A lack of parental altruism or credit constraints are the two most frequently cited explanations. We have considered altruism in the previous section. Here, we discuss credit constraints.

4.3.1. Credit constraints and child labor

Most recent studies of credit constraints and child labor are based on the theoretical work of Baland and Robinson (2000).[7] Baland and Robinson is a variant on the Ben-Porath (1967) model that emphasizes child labor explicitly. Baland and Robinson has a single household decision-maker (a parent) who decides child labor and schooling decisions after making other household income decisions. The parent lives two periods. In the first period, the parent chooses savings s and the fraction of child time spent working, h. The household's income each period is m. Wages from working are normalized to 1. Thus, consumption in the first period is: $c_1 = m + h - s$. In the second period, in addition to the parent's income m, the parent receives the savings income and gives a bequest b to the child: $c_2 = m + s - b$. Parental utility comes from consumption in period 1, period 2, and the well being of the child: $U_p(c_1, c_2, U_c(w_c))$. Child well-being depends on the return to the time spent not working, $z(1 - h)$, and income from bequests: $w_c = z(1 - h) + b$.

Baland and Robinson (2000) show that if savings and bequests are not zero, then the household chooses child labor so that the cost in terms of foregone consumption today of decreasing child labor exactly equals the return to the child of foregoing child labor: $z'(1 - h) = 1$. They argue then that child labor is privately efficient, although Bommier

---

[7] Ranjan (2001) is a similar model to Baland and Robinson although Ranjan's model is explicitly dynamic and focuses on household heterogeneity. Adding household heterogeneity allows Ranjan to examine how income inequality interacts with credit constraints in influencing the prevalence of child labor in the economy. A comparison of his discussion with that of Swinnerton and Rogers (1999) who add household heterogeneity to the Basu and Van (1998) model is useful to see the similar underpinnings of the Baland–Robinson and Basu–Van models.

and Dubois (2004) show that this efficiency is not the case even with complete markets if children have a disutility of labor. However, if bequests are zero, then the return to not-working is greater than the household's cost of not having the child work, and child labor is inefficiently high. Without bequests, children cannot compensate parents for the foregone consumption that comes from decreasing child labor. Likewise, if savings are zero, then, the household's marginal utility of consumption in the first period is greater than the marginal utility the household attains from increasing child well-being, and child labor is inefficiently high.[8]

Evidence directly on whether credit constraints influence child labor and schooling is relatively rare, because of the difficulty of disentangling credit constraints from other market imperfections. For example, a number of studies that will be discussed below consider the association between child labor and crop shocks, but they cannot in general separate insurance failures from changes in the relative returns to work or from credit constraints.

There is some suggestive evidence at the cross-country level. Jafarey and Lahiri (2002) emphasize that borrowing constraints in the aggregate should decline as access to international credit markets increase and that this in turn should mitigate the need for children to work. Dehejia and Gatti (2002) consider the link between formal financial development and child labor in aggregate cross-country data. They measure credit constraints by the ratio of private credit issued by deposit-money banks to GDP, and call this "financial development." They find that financial development is negatively correlated with economic activity rates. In particular, a move from the 25th to 75th percentile of financial development among low income countries is associated with a 17 percent decline in the economic activity rates of children 10–14.

The BR model and other theoretical writings on child labor and credit constraints tend to emphasize the inability of families to borrow against the future returns to child education. Testing for constraints on intergenerational transfers or long-term borrowing is generally not feasible in existing data sets. However, if households are not able to move resources over relatively short (and potentially measurable) time horizons, then it seems unlikely that they should be able to move resources over the long term. Micro-studies of household responses to crop-shocks have attempted to look at credit constraints to see whether there is a correlation between household assets and responses to shocks. Unfortunately, isolating the credit channel in this way seems infeasible given the correlation between household assets and the value of child time in a setting when most children work at home.

An alternative approach is to consider household responses to anticipated changes in their economic environment. For example, Edmonds (2006a) examines the response of schooling and market work to the timing of anticipated income in the context of the social pension program in South Africa. The end of apartheid in South Africa brought the

---

[8] Baland and Robinson (2000) show that these results for savings and bequests also hold under reciprocal altruism when children value the well-being of their parents.

extension of the white social pension program to black South Africans. The pensions are large (125 percent of median black per capita income in 1999), highly anticipated, and primarily determined by age in the elder black population. Edmonds compares market work and schooling in families about to receive a fully anticipatable social pension income to market work and schooling in families already receiving the income. The average rural South African child living with an elder that is not yet pension eligible spends 3 hours per day working. In the data, pension income to an elder male is associated with over an hour less work per day. These declines in hours worked occur simultaneously with increases in school attendance (to nearly 100 percent for rural boys). These changes in hours worked and schooling with male pension eligibility lead to levels of work and schooling that are similar to what the data report for nearly eligible elder women. Hence, his results suggest a role for credit constraints, but only for elder men. Moreover, unlike the data above that tend to emphasize the economic contribution of children, the South African data suggest that an inability to afford schooling is the primary reason why children are not in school prior to receipt of anticipated income.

One interesting appendum to the empirical work on credit constraints and child labor is the theoretical paper by Rogers and Swinnerton (2004) who point out that with credit constraints and an agency problem, rising incomes can increase child labor. In their model, each child is altruistic toward his parent and the savings strategy of a very poor parent includes investing in her child's education in part to induce a voluntary repayment when the child grows up. To induce repayment, the poor parent realizes that her consumption decisions must be consistent the child's preferences, and as a result she provides more education for her child than she would if not for the "child preference" constraint. As parental income rises, there comes a point when the parent can optimally circumvent the "child preference constraint" by doing her all of her saving directly, rather than in part through the child's education, so that the education meant to induce voluntary repayment stops. At this point, child labor goes up. The interesting dynamics between incomes and intergenerational transfers is a fertile area for further study.

4.3.2. Does child labor respond to the return to schooling?

The presence of credit constraints within a population does not exclude the possibility of the relative returns to education influencing child labor. The major challenge in isolating the returns to education as a causal influence on child labor is that it is very difficult to measure perceptions about the returns to education.

Typically, researchers rely on the assumption that the expected returns to education at the time child labor decisions are made depends on the current return to education or literacy. While likely imprecise, even this approximation is difficult to estimate for two reasons. First, it is difficult to separate variation in the returns to education from confounding factors influencing income in the local community. Hence, an apparent response to the returns to education may just reflect parental income differences. Second, it is often very difficult to measure the returns to education, because child labor is most prevent in locations where wage work is rare. Most production occurs in family enterprises, and there is little specialization. Hence, it is extremely difficult to assign income to individuals in places where child labor tends to be most prevalent, and analysis based only on wage workers may suffer from severe selection bias that is likely to be correlated with child work status.

How does one identify returns to education in populations where few individuals work for wages? One option is to measure the returns to education data at some aggregate level. Chamarbagwala (2006) is one example. She observes that Indian children in regions with higher returns to education are more likely to attend school and less likely to work. In addition to the problems of confounding factors and selection mentioned above, an additional difficulty inherent in this aggregate approach is that estimates of the returns to education are essentially a common effect to the level of aggregation with a functional form assumption and the more aggregate the study is, the less variation researchers have to work with. Hence, Chamarbagwala is one of the few published studies using this approach.

A second option is to examine whether there are changes in the returns to education and schooling for a common factor rather than directly measuring the link between the two. Foster and Rosenzweig (1996) approach this by estimating a conditional profit function from the adoption of HYV rice in India and capturing the additional profit associated with more schooling in areas where HYV has diffused. They report changes in schooling which are consistent with improvements in the return to schooling (and school construction) by finding the same variables linked to increased schooling.

A related approach is to infer movements in returns to education through observing other behaviors that depend on the returns to education. For example, Edmonds, Pavcnik, and Topalova (2007) infer movements in returns to education in two ways. First, they compare differences in per capita expenditure by head's literacy or schooling completion. Second, they examine changes in adult employment by education status. They assume that adult labor supply is upward sloping and that expectations about the returns to education are based on differences in the wages of literate and illiterate populations with a given geographic area (the district in India in their case). They infer what must be occurring then to returns to education in the labor market by comparing changes in employment of the literate and illiterate populations.

A novel set of studies considers how the schooling activities of rural children are influenced by urban labor markets to which they could migrate. In addition to being a realistic description of how expectations of returns to education are formed, this approach minimizes the problem of a confounding between returns to education and adult income effects and is more apt to be measurable. Kochar (2004) for example finds that urban rates of return influence rural schooling in India, especially among landless who are most apt to migrate to urban areas. De Brauw and Giles (2005) observe that the education of rural migrants does not appear to be rewarded in the city in China. They make use of geographic and time variation in the implementation of national identity cards which make legal migration possible, and find that schooling enrollment declines with the opportunity to migrate. Of course, unlike the above studies that seek to isolate a returns to education effect, these two studies consider more the relative returns to schooling in the rural sector. While limited, it may not be possible to isolate returns to education from changes in labor market opportunities.

An alternative approach to studying the link between returns to schooling and child labor and schooling is to look at whether improvements in school quality affect child labor. Causal evidence on a link between school quality and child labor that would meet modern standards of evidence does not appear in the literature. However, descriptive studies such as those by Lloyd et al. (2003) suggest a connection, and evidence on the link between some measures of school quality such as pupil–teacher ratios and schooling attainment is well documented. For example, Case and Yogo (1999) use variation in school quality for blacks in apartheid South Africa to study the link between pupil–teacher ratio, the returns to schooling, and school attendance. Their findings are dramatic. A decline in the pupil–teacher ratio by 10 students is associated with a 2 percent increase in the return to education and an additional 0.6 years of completed schooling. Hence, while the problems with looking at the return to education are considerable, there is some suggestive evidence of a connection between returns to education and schooling which might also be reflected in child labor data provided that the marginal utility of income today is not the dominant causal factor in the decision to have a child work.

4.3.3. School costs and child labor

Further, the relevant return to schooling is the return net of direct costs, and like with school quality, direct evidence on a link between schooling costs and child labor is rare. Several studies document an association between the mitigation of school costs and schooling (for example, Duflo et al., 2006), and Foster and Rosenzweig (2004) argue that school construction accompanying the green revolution in India facilitated increased schooling and decreased child labor in both landed and landless households although they do not directly observe a measure of child labor in their data.

Slightly more direct evidence of a link between child labor and schooling costs also exists. Several studies find a link between measured schooling costs and child labor. In rural Pakistan, Hazarika and Bedi (2003) observe that children are more apt to work outside the household in communities where schooling costs are higher. Shafiq (2006b) observes that boys are more likely to work and less likely to attend school in Bangladesh in communities where schooling costs are higher. Edmonds, Pavcnik, and Topalova (2007) argue that the avoidance of schooling costs explains the child labor-schooling-poverty association observed in their study of rural India, and they find that the relative declines in schooling and increases in work associated with India's tariff reforms are smaller in areas where schooling is less expensive. Edmonds (2006a) study of credit constraints in South Africa reports some qualitative evidence suggesting that schooling costs are an important part of why there is a link between credit constraints and child labor and schooling. Kondylis, and Manacorda (2006) study one dimension of schooling costs, travel time, in rural Tanzania. They observe that children longer travel times induce children to specialize in either schooling without work or work without schooling.

The interpretation of all of these studies is complicated by the fact that the source of variation in schooling costs is not well understood, and it is difficult to separate whether these findings reflect support of other siblings or the child's own schooling, however, as higher costs for one child likely imply higher costs for siblings in the same. Nevertheless, these studies provide some support for the idea that the relationship between child labor and schooling costs and quality is a fertile area for future research.

One important interpretation point often emphasized in the literature (e.g. Shafiq, 2006a; Das and Deb, 2006) is that the relevant return on education for family decision-making is the present discounted value of the future return to education. Thus, differences in discount rates across households can lead to differences in the family's valuation of education or the marginal utility of income and thereby differences in child labor and schooling. Why might discount rates vary across households? Das and Deb model this explicitly as a function of the family's current consumption, the subject to which we now turn.

4.4. Child labor and poverty

4.4.1. The link between child labor and living standards

Theoretically, there are many reasons why there might be a negative connection between family incomes and child labor. First, child labor may be a bad in parental preferences so that as incomes improve, the family chooses to have children work less. In fact, in the seminal child labor paper by Basu and Van (1998), they posit the "luxury axiom": children only work when the family is unable to meet its basic needs. Beyond subsistence, the luxury axiom posits, families always opt to keep children out of work. In the model of Section 1, the idea that work might be a bad is captured by families receiving positive utility from child leisure. The luxury axiom is just a particular characterization of preferences. Second, with diminishing marginal utility of income, the value of the marginal contribution of the child's income decreases. Note that an important part of the child's economic contribution to the family might be through not attending school if direct and indirect schooling costs are high. That said, the economic contribution of working children can be substantial. Psacharopoulos (1997) observes that income earned by working Bolivian children of age 13 amounted to 13 percent of total household income on average. Menon, Pareli, and Rosati (2005) attempt to compute the value of child's own farm labor to largely subsistence farm households in rural Nepal. They estimate that children contribute roughly 11 percent of the value of total agriculture production in Nepal or about 9 percent of GDP.

Third, higher family incomes may facilitate the purchase of substitutes for child labor that lower the return to child labor within the household. For example, a washboard, fertilizer spreader, or a combine harvester may replace child labor within the home. In the model of Section 1, this would be a downward shift in productivity in household work, $F(-)$, and would only reduce work when work outside the household is at a corner solution. Fourth, the child's productivity in other activities such as schooling might improve because the family might be able to afford better inputs to schooling such as nutrition, textbooks, or uniforms. In addition, market imperfections and other aspects of the family's economic environment (including discount rates) might be correlated with family economic status and also affect child labor supply.

The important question for policy is to what extent a family's standard of living is the dominant determinant of whether children work. Are returns to education or leisure sufficiently high or employment opportunities sufficiently unproductive that children can be expected to transition away from work as incomes improve without additional policy changes? If child labor is an outgrowth of poverty and nothing else, then it is difficult to make an argument for attention to child labor without attention to the factors that create a need for the child to work. On the other hand, if child labor is independent of the family's economic status and if it has long term consequences for child welfare, then there exists a much stronger case for policy attention specific to child labor. The answer to the question of living standard's role in child labor is obviously context specific and can be expected to vary both between and within countries as well as over time. It is not surprising that there are a wide variety of findings evident within the empirical literature.

4.4.2. The empirical evidence

The cross-country data on living standards and child labor suggests a strong connection between economic status and economic activity rates. Figure 10 plots the ILO's

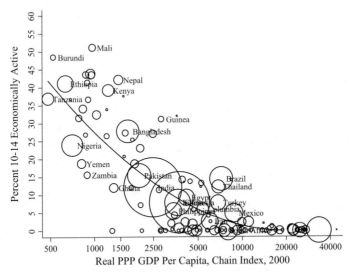

Source: Economic Activity for 2000 from LABORSTA (http://laborsta.ilo.org), GDP per capita from Penn World Tables 6.1, and Population aged 10–14 weights from UNSTAT.

Figure 10. The relationship between economic status and economic activity, 2000.

E.V. Edmonds

LABORSTA estimates of economic activity rates for children 10–14 against estimates of real GDP per capita (using purchasing power parity exchange rates) from the Penn World Tables 6.1. Each country observation is pictured as a circle where the size of the circle represents the size of the country's population between ages 10 and 14. While child labor is pervasive in poor economies such as Ethiopia and Nepal, child labor is unusual in a country wealthier than Gabon with a GDP per capita of $8400. The curve in Fig. 10 is from the regression of a country's economic activity rate for children on a third order polynomial in GDP per capita (to allow a non-linear relationship). The regression curve shown here is weighted by the population of children aged 10–14 in each country, but the unweighted regression curve is nearly identical. With this specification, variation in GDP per capita explains 73 percent of the variation in the economic activity rates of children.

Countries differ in many ways that may be associated with economic activity rates and GDP per capita. Hence, the relationship in Fig. 10 cannot be interpreted as causal. Attempts to address the endogeneity of income as in Edmonds and Pavcnik (2006a) do little to affect the strong correlation between national income and economic activity rates of children.

Most within country studies of the link between income and child labor are cross-sectional. They specify a linear relationship between some measure of work and family income, and test the hypothesis that the marginal effect of family income on work is different from zero on average. In general, researchers that compare poor households to rich households at a single point in time in a country find mixed evidence of a link between poverty and child labor. Comparative studies implement the same empirical approach in multiple countries, and the different results observed between countries in comparative studies such as Bhalotra and Heady (2003) (for Pakistan and Ghana), Ersado (2005) (for Nepal, Peru, and Zimbabwe), Maitra and Ray (2002) (for Peru, Pakistan, and Ghana), Psacharopoulos (1997) (for Bolivia and Venezuela), and Ray (2000) (for Pakistan and Peru) illustrate how varied the cross-sectional relationship between economic status and child labor can be.

An intrinsic problem in studies of the link between economic status and child labor is that poor households differ from rich households in many ways that might be associated with child labor. Disentangling these omitted factors from the underlying causal relationship is difficult. Despite the great challenge, there are two basic approaches researchers use to address the endogeneity of living standards. First, many studies address part of the problem by relating child labor to variation in income that excludes the child's income (Dammert, 2005; Duryea and Arends-Kuenning 2003; Ray, 2000). While this addresses a mechanical source of endogeneity, it does not deal with the joint nature of child time allocation and family living standards. The second approach focuses on the broader endogeneity problem and argues that certain factors affect family income without also affecting the time allocation of children except through family income. Examples include Bhalotra (2007), Bhalotra and Heady (2003), and Ersado (2005). Note that the assumptions required for identification are often quite strong in these studies, as almost anything that affects the family's economic environment should also influence the value of child time in one activity (schooling, work outside the home, market work in the home, domestic chores). Glewwe and Jacoby (2004) focus on education rather than child labor, but they emphasize the types of structural assumptions necessary to accept many of the common IV strategies.

Another approach to address the intrinsic differences that exist between poor and rich families is to track children in the same household (or cohort) over time. Of course, using panel data only replaces the problem of cross-sectional heterogeneity with the problem of explaining differential changes over time. That said, studies tracking families over time almost universally find large increases in child labor with substantive declines in family incomes. For example, in tracking children over a three-year period in rural Tanzania, Beegle, Dehejia, and Gatti (2006) find that children tend to work when households experience unexpectedly poor harvest, and that children stop working when households recover from the bad harvest. Duryea, Lam, and Levison (2007) find that children transition in and out of employment with adult unemployment spells in urban Brazil. Dammert (2006) observes that market work increases in coca growing states of Peru after coca production (and its associated income) shifts out of Peru for Columbia.

Beyond endogeneity, another methodological issue is important in the child labor – living standards literature. There are strong theoretical reasons to expect the relationship between child labor and families to be non-linear. In the Basu and Van (1998) model, children no longer work when families can meet their subsistence needs with adult earnings. Hence, variation in income below subsistence should have no effect on child labor, nor should variation in income above subsistence. It is only over the range of incomes that corresponds to the existing heterogeneity in perceived subsistence needs in which Basu and Van would expect to see changes in child labor that are correlated with improvement in living standards. Edmonds (2005) finds support for this idea directly with panel data collected during Vietnam's economic boom in the 1990s.

Figure 11 plots market work participation rates for children 6–15 in Vietnam in 1993 and 1998 against household per capita expenditures in 1993. The data for this figure comes from the 1993 and 1998 Vietnam Living Standards Survey where information on the activities of children is collected in over 3000 rural households that are interviewed first in 1993 and again in 1998. The top curve in Fig. 11, which compares households at different levels of per capita expenditure in 1993, suggests a strong negative correlation between household living standards and child labor. For households below the 1993 poverty line, participation of children in market work exceeds 30 percent. From 1993 to 1998, real expenditure per capita increased by more than 50 percent for the poorest 10 percent of the population. For Vietnam overall, the incidence of poverty declined 36 percent. The bottom curve in Fig. 11 pictures the relationship between participation in market work in 1998 and household's per capita expenditure in 1993. Thus, for each point on the per capita expenditure distribution in 1993 (the x-axis), market work participation rates are pictured for the same households in 1993 and 1998. Participation rates drop substantially over time, with the largest declines in market work occurring in households in the neighborhood of the poverty line in 1993.

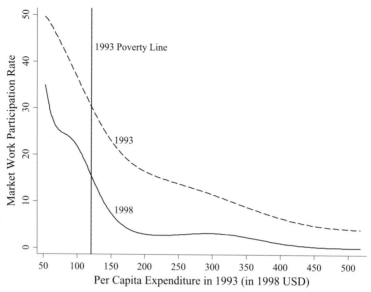

Source: General Statistical Office (1994, 1999): Vietnam Living Standards Survey, Rural Panel, 1993 & 1998.

Figure 11. Living standard improvements and market work among children 6–15 in Vietnam in the 1990s.

Edmonds (2005) uses the market work–per capita expenditure relationship in 1993 to recover the implied distribution of subsistence levels across households. He then projects the changes in market work that would be expected in the Basu and Van framework based on the observed improvements in per capita expenditures between 1993 and 1998. He finds that improvements in per capita expenditure and the implied distribution of subsistence levels across households can explain 80 percent of the decline in child labor that occurs in households whose expenditures improve enough to move out of poverty. The strong structure of the Basu and Van model is not the only model that could generate these findings (a simple Engel curve in preferences would as would variable discount rates that depend on living standards). Moreover, factors other than preferences can generate important non-linearity in the child labor–economic status relationship. For example, one can imagine non-linearity in the household production function that would lead to discrete changes in the value of child time within the household. A family might opt to change its production technology to replace the labor of a child, and this type of shift could generate results as in Edmonds if changes in household production techniques are correlated with exiting poverty. Nonetheless, non-linearity in the child labor–economic status relationship appears very important, as does the correlation between improvements in living standards and declines in child labor.

4.4.3. Can the effect of rising incomes differ from that of declining poverty?

The empirical literature on child labor and living standards largely attempts to estimate whether there is a link, but it might serve policy more by considering why there is a link. Indeed, one suspects that a more nuanced view of the determinants and definition of child labor might resolve some of the apparent inconsistencies observed across cross-sectional studies. For example, in the Basu and Van model and in Edmonds' data, child labor declines rapidly in the neighborhood of the poverty line, but appears relatively income inelastic elsewhere. Hence, depending on the distribution of variation in income in a population, standard approaches may miss the importance of poverty in child labor decisions.

Moreover, depending on the definition of child labor and local economic conditions, it may be that child labor appears to increase with family incomes. Rising incomes might be associated with changes in the types of activities in which children participate. Edmonds and Pavcnik (2006b) for example find that growing trade inside Vietnam is associated with a rise in household specialization which in turn may explain some of the decline in work in the family farm and business that they observe in Edmonds and Pavcnik (2005b). Fafchamps and Wahba (2006) observe a positive correlation between household specialization and wage work in Nepal as well. Consequently, if child labor is defined as wage work, then it might appear to grow with rising incomes even if the total time spent working when one includes work within the household declines. This might explain the rise in wage employment among children with economic growth that Swaminathan (1998) documents in Gujarat, India or that Kambahampati and Rajan (2005) have observed across Indian states.

Moreover, in a setting where the lack of employment opportunities is relevant, child labor may actually increase with rising incomes if they are associated with expanding economic activity or increased employment opportunities for children within their households. This is obvious in the model of Eq. (1.1) as it should be clear that the shadow value of child time depends on the wages in the local market and the household's production opportunities. Several studies discussed in Section 4.1 note a connection between market work participation and household assets. Bhalotra and Heady (2003) label the positive correlation between market work participation and household assets or employment opportunities in the household a "wealth paradox." Ganglmair (2005) shows that this "paradox" occurs in Ugandan data when one fails to control for variation in the employment opportunities open to children and when one only considers types of work directly engaged with the asset. Shafiq (2006b) points out that, while greater assets may lead children to report working more because of the availability of employment opportunities, the human capital ramifications of this are unclear. In his data from Bangladesh, children work more in the presence of productive assets, but they are also more likely to attend school.

In fact, several studies find a negative correlation between child wages and child employment and a positive correlation between child wages and schooling. This may be, because children are often substitutes for adults. Rising child wages imply higher adult wages, and child work appears more elastic with respect to adult income than child wages. The finding in Edmonds and Pavcnik's (2005b) study of rice price changes in Vietnam is suggestive of this. Children are actively involved in rice cultivation, the returns to that cultivation increase, but market work declines. Wahba (2006) is more direct evidence. She finds in Egyptian data from 1988 that a 10 percent increase in the illiterate male market wage *lowers* the probability that a child engages in wage work by 22 percent for boys and 13 percent for girls.

In fact, the academic literature on how households respond to macroeconomic shocks tends to emphasize declining child labor with declining income. Thomas et al. (2004) examine education responses to the Indonesian financial crisis. They find that poor households coped with the shock in part by reducing educational expenditures and educational enrollment. These declines in education were particularly large for younger children as households appeared to triage to protect the schooling of older children. Interestingly, Cameron (2004) notes that in Indonesia, declines in schooling do not appear to be accompanied by a rise in formal employment amongst children. This is consistent with Thomas et al.'s observation that young children were withheld from school to cope with the crisis. In fact, Schady (2004) suggests that as a result of the decline in employment options for children during Peru's 1988–1992 macroeconomic crisis, schooling attainment for affected cohorts has increased substantially. This discussion highlights the potential importance of labor demand related factors in child labor as discussed above in Section 4.1.

Thus, even if poverty is a key reason children work, it is possible to find child labor rising with incomes. More attention to the reasons why there might be a link between family incomes and child labor can then be important in understanding how child labor will evolve, as countries grow richer.

4.4.4. Economic shocks, credit constraints, poverty, and child labor

Poor households are more apt to be credit constrained, because their poverty typically means they lack collateral with which to access credit and they often live in locations with poor credit institutions. In Section 4.3, we have discussed how an inability to access credit can lead to higher levels of child labor than is privately efficient from the parent's perspective (Baland and Robinson, 2000). The poor also are less likely to have access to formal insurance and more likely to face uninsured credit risks. Pouliot (2006) adds uncertainty to the Baland and Robinson model, showing that incomplete insurance markets can lead to inefficiently high levels of child labor even with functioning credit markets. Several studies document a relationship between child labor and schooling and an inability of the household to cope with income shocks that extend beyond any effect the potential for uncertainty has on schooling and work decisions.

The adult labor supply literature in developing countries tends to emphasize how individual labor supply is used to buffer income shocks. Kochar (1999) for example observes that Indian men increase their market hours of work in response to unanticipated (weather related) variation in crop profits and that this rise in labor supply explains reduced form results that fail to find a significant effect of crop shocks on consumption. Does child labor supply also act to help cope with shocks? Using the same ICRISAT data as Kochar (1999), Jacoby and Skoufias (1996) find that market work and variation in school attendance is an important part of family self-insurance. They observe declines in schooling and increases in market work in households that experience both idiosyncratic and aggregate shocks. Moreover, they decompose variation in income using rainfall data to estimate predictable seasonal variation in income and unpredictable variation in income. They find that small farm households adjust schooling and work in response to both predictable and unpredictable variation in income. Hence, they argue that small farms are not well insured ex ante, and they do not have access to seasonal borrowing and lending. A similar study in Tanzania is Beegle, Dehejia, and Gatti (2006). They correlate self-reported crop shocks with changes in child labor. They observe a significant increase in market work in households that report experiencing a crop shock, and that this shock is larger among households with few assets. One important point in Jacoby and Skoufias is that, despite variation in work and schooling with both predictable and unpredictable income variation, the overall effect of this on schooling attainment appears very modest. De Janvry et al. (2006) note that the conditional cash transfers in Mexico's Progresa program were sufficient to protect school enrollment in the presence of agricultural shocks, but conditional transfers appeared to have little effect on the rise in market work associated with the shocks. As they point out, this is to be expected if child labor supply is part of the household's self-insurance strategy.

Insurance failures and child labor are not just interconnected in rural agrarian societies. Using a longitudinal employment survey from urban Brazil, Duryea, Lam, and Levison (2007) compare households in which the male head becomes employed during a four month period to household where the head is continuously employed. They find that an unemployment shock significantly increases the probability that a child enters the labor force (by as much as 60 percent) and decreases the probability the child attends school. They do not observe changes in labor supply in anticipation of shocks. Hence, they conclude that the child's labor supply in part compensates for the lack of unemployment insurance. Moreover, unlike the evidence in Jacoby and Skoufias, Duryea et al observe substantial declines in schooling completion with these adult unemployment spells. For girls in particular, it seems that the loss of employment for the male household head often triggers a complete and permanent withdrawal from school.

The idea that child labor is part of the household's self-insurance strategy seems broadly supported in the literature. Yang's (2006) study of how Philippine households with overseas members were affected by the 1997 Asian financial crisis is especially useful for framing how to think about the insurance component of child labor supply. Migrants from the Philippines work in dozens of countries. Thus, the financial crisis was broadly felt in the Philippines, but there is a great deal of heterogeneity in how families were impacted by the crisis depending on what country their migrant members lived. Yang observes that a 10 percent appreciation in the Philippine/foreign exchange rate is associated with a 6 percent increase in remittance flows. Schooling increases, schooling expenditures increase, and work declines in households that benefited from the appreciation. This behavior is similar to classical permanent income behavior. Schooling is an investment, and families seem to be "saving" transitory income through increased schooling and less work. Likewise, the temporary (as in Jacoby and Skoufias) or permanent (as in Duryea, Lam, and Levison) declines in schooling and increases in work may reflect similar permanent income behavior. It is striking that decisions about schooling and work might reflect how households manage transitory income. These findings illustrate the complex set of interactions and response to market imperfections and market failures that are important in understanding the determinants of child time allocation.

5. Policy

Given the diverse array of social and economic factors that affect child time allocation decisions, most development related policies can influence child time allocation. In discussing the determinants of child time allocation, we have already reviewed research from microcredit programs, public infrastructure and school construction projects, school quality interventions, and programs to mitigate schooling costs. Risk reduction and management policies, health interventions, and production technology projects all could have large impacts on child time allocation. However, in this section, we consider policies that aim to directly affect how children spend their time.

Empirical research on child labor related policies that meets modern scientific standards is extremely limited. This does not owe to a lack of policy attention. Policies towards child labor can be grouped loosely into six categories: information campaigns, income replacement programs, flexible schooling programs, reintegration projects, restrictions on employment, and conditional cash transfers. Only legislative restrictions and conditional cash transfers have a sizeable academic literature. This research is described below. First, we describe the other four categories of child labor policies.

5.1. Child labor specific programs

An incredible variety of policies and programs have been directed towards working children, and there are a considerable number of policy documents that describe these activities. ILO (2006b) for example reviews several ILO affiliated programs. This section briefly discusses these types of programs. However, causal evidence that has survived peer review within economics does not appear to exist for any of these programs at the time of writing.

Information or awareness campaigns attempt to educate parents, employers, and children that children should not work or should attend school. The mechanisms for delivery of information vary as does the precise content of information conveyed. Mass media campaigns are frequent, employing radio or TV programs, news reports, or billboards. Community mobilization is also common where activists or community leaders reach out personally to individuals involved with working or out of school children. Another frequent community mobilization approach is to organize community events that draw attention to whatever type of activity is being targeted. In practice, information and awareness campaigns seem to be the most common type of policy directed at working children, and they seem to be motivated in part by assumptions that parents do not know what is best for their children.

Income replacement programs attempt to compensate families for the loss of the child's income in the event that the child stops working. Some programs aim to provide alternative sources of income to the household, often to the mother, by providing working capital and training. Implicit in these programs is that parents make decisions about whether children work and that the direct economic contribution of the child's work is a main reason why children work. Other programs, attempt to redirect children towards work activities that are more compatible with schooling. For example, one program in Brazil gave working children goats, because it is easy to care for goats outside of school hours. These child income replacement programs address the child's agency in work decisions in addition to economic motives for work. Often, income replacements programs contain some conditionality component. For example, conditional cash transfers typically require that children attend school in order receive transfers. Conditional cash transfers are the one type of child labor related program that have received rigorous evaluation, and we discuss these in detail in Section 5.4.

Flexible schooling programs attempt to make schooling and work more compatible. That is, they typically do nothing to influence whether the child works, but instead aim to make schooling compatible with work. In this way, flexible schooling programs mitigate the costs of working. Many different types of programs are prevalent. School hours can be modified to accommodate work schedules. Academic calendars can be adjusted to reflect local conditions. Additional school shifts could be added during off-work times. Independent study modules might allow students to progress through schooling at their own pace. The assumption behind these programs is that the timing of school causes conflict between work and school. The actual time spent working is not enough in itself to impair human capital accumulation. Some flexible schooling programs also modify the curriculum to increase child interest in the program. Other flexible schooling programs extend the hours in which school or related facilities are available to children. They programs are analogous to daycare programs. For some children, work is just a way to occupy the child's time, and the extended schooling hours provide an alternative, educational way to occupy the child's time. Moreover, this may benefit older siblings who, absent the extend hours available to younger siblings, would have to care for younger siblings.

It is straightforward to imagine how programs designed to prevent children from starting to work can influence child schooling, but children who are already working full time need help to reenter school. Reintegration projects aim to help students return to regular school when students have missed school or lag behind in school because of work. Working children may be unfamiliar with the school environment, be poorly socialized for schooling, and may be significantly older than nonworking children with the same educational background. This makes returning working children to school a challenge. Most reintegration projects include some counseling directed at formerly working children, some remedial education to catch working children up to age in skills, and some bridge program to gradually introduce working children back into the class-room. This emphasis on how to get working children back into school is often neglected in economics discussions, because most theoretical models such as that of Section 1 treat child time allocation as seamless between different sectors of work, schooling, and leisure.

Unfortunately, while these policies are pervasive, scientific evaluation of them is not. This absence of policy research severely limits our ability to design or improve existing policy. To be effective, scientific evaluation needs to be designed into a project from its inception, with control populations selected to be comparable, ideally through random-ization. This is rare. It is telling that of the 35 final program evaluations included in ILO (2006b), none of the publicly available research has been peer reviewed by indepen-dent researchers. Moreover, while detailed information is hard to come by, it appears that most of the reviews are process evaluations (did the project do what it is supposed to?) rather than impact evaluations (was the project effective? did it improve the well-being of impacted children?). The typical objection to formal evaluation is expense, but the growing body of randomized evaluation of education related initiatives shows that careful, informative, and scientific evaluations can be conducted on modest bud-gets. Moreover, considerable money is being spent on evaluation. That research is just not being held to the standards of peer review that are commonplace in other sciences. Hopefully, future scientific research on how these projects influence time allocation can both improve the design of policy and build our understanding of the determinants of work.

5.2. Restrictions and prohibitions on employment

Prohibitions on employment typically target children in specific activities. Often prohi-bitions are intended as symbolic gestures, but at times, they may be enforced by industry groups or the governments, Programs of identification and removal of working children from specific activities have occurred throughout the world. Anecdotes abound about what happens to children upon removal from targeted activities, but rigorous statistical research does not appear available at the time of writing. The case for targeting one activity at a time is that it is more manageable to implement and enforce. However, it can lead to some inconsistencies that lead some to question the motives for targeting a particular activity.

General prohibitions on work or restrictions on working conditions are also common in low income countries. ILO Convention C138 on the minimum age of employment has been ratified by 141 countries, and nearly every developing country has some formal restriction on the age of employment for certain types of employment. Similarly, most countries have compulsory school ages as well. Beyond these aggregate laws, many countries have committed to pursue aggressive policies to eliminate child labor from certain sectors and 156 countries have committed to identify and eliminate worst forms of child labor under C182. Yet, despite all this policy discussion, there does not appear to be any study of the effectiveness of restrictions on work that would meet current standards of evidence. Part of the reason for this might be that bans are often not passed with the intention of enforcement. Instead, the motivation for such legislation can be that it helps outreach and education programs change social views about working children. However, there is a theoretical case that can be made for the enforcement of general bans on child labor.

The Basu and Van (1998, Section 3.4) model is the most common framework used to illustrate the conditions under which enforced prohibitions on child labor may be welfare improving. Basu and Van give multiple equilibriums as such, it allows a role for policy in the elimination of child labor. One frequently advocated policy is an enforced prohibition on child labor. Consider the labor market equilibriums that arise when demand function is given by a line marked GG in Fig. 12. In this instance, there are two possible stable equilibriums marked E1 and E2.[9] In E2, children work. The presence of child labor depresses wages and hence creates a need for children to work. The equilibrium E1 creates an opportunity for policy to affect child labor supply. If policy can prevent children from working, the equilibrium in the economy can switch to E1. That is, by preventing children from working (i.e. eliminating CD and BC segment of labor

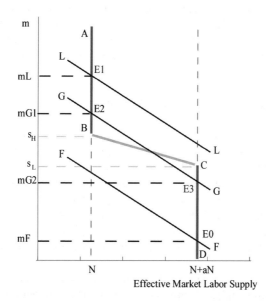

Figure 12. Labor demand and the potential for policy interventions.

[9] The middle intersection of supply and demand is an unstable equilibrium and is neglected in the present discussion.

supply), market wages increase, eliminating the household's need to send children to work.

Obviously, the potential existence of multiple equilibriums is not a sufficient condition for policy aimed at prohibiting child labor. For example, when labor demand is represented by FF, there is little that a ban can do to curtail child labor without improving labor demand (i.e. shifting FF up). Similarly, policy aimed at curtailing the demand for child labor could have the unintended consequence of moving households from the equilibrium defined by mG2 to the equilibrium indicated by mF if policy lowers labor demand for child labor without the commensurate increase in demand for adult labor (Dessy and Pallage, 2005 suggest a different model with the same result). This might occur for example if a consumer boycott drove an industry out of business in a community.[10] Figure 12 clarifies that whether any case can be made for policy actions against child labor depends on the characteristics of the local labor market.

Empirical evidence from contemporary low income countries on either the effectiveness of general bans or restrictions on employment is not available. The case that a ban could be welfare improving even for those with working children relies on the existence of multiple equilibria in the labor market. As discussed in Section 3.4, this seems hard to imagine as a general proposition given that children are such a small share of total employment in general. While there is no evidence of the existence of multiple equilibria owing to child labor supply, Doran (2006) finds evidence in Mexico of a depressive effect of child labor on adult wages. The problem with identifying an effect of child labor on adult wages is that one needs something to affect child labor without separately impacting the adult labor market. Doran argues that the conditional cash transfer program in rural Mexico discussed below (Progresa) withdraws children from work without otherwise effecting local labor market characteristics (see Parker, Rubalcava, and Teruel, 2008, for related work). Doran observes that in randomly selected Progresa treatment communities less children work during the corn harvest and there is an associated increase in adult wages and adult employment relative to control communities. This raises the possibility that some of the foregone child labor earnings can be replaced by increasing adult wages although Doran does not observe full replacement.

The most compelling evidence on the effects of general prohibitions on child labor come from the historical experiences of developed countries. Several careful empirical studies exploit variation in the implementation of the child labor and compulsory schooling laws across the US states to examine whether these legislative measures were the *driving* force behind the drastic declines in child labor at the turn of the last century and increases in secondary school enrollment and educational attainment between 1910 and 1940. Moehling (1999), for example, finds little evidence that minimum age laws for manufacturing employment implemented between 1880 and 1910 contributed to the decline in child labor during this period. She compares differences in participation

---

[10] See Davies (2004) for a theory on the consumer boycotts of products that are not child labor-free and why firms might select to produce their product child-free when their competitors do not do so.

rates of 13 and 14 year olds across states with and without a minimum working age of 14 before and after the enactment of laws. This difference-in-differences-in-differences strategy can distinguish the effects of the law from differential pre-existing trends in child labor across states with and without minimum age limits that could have influenced the implementation of the law. While the participation rates of children covered by the law declined in states that enacted the laws, boys in control groups experienced similar declines. The results for girls suggest that declines in child labor might be driven by endogenous child labor law implementation: states were more likely to implement the minimum age legislation if other labor demand and supply factors reduced their reliance on child labor prior to the reforms. Doepke and Zilibotti (2005) formalize this idea in a model with endogenous adoption of child labor laws.

While the overall contribution of child labor laws to child labor declines may have been small in the US, there appears to have been some marginal contribution. A number of studies have emphasized this. For example, Lleras-Muney (2002) documents an association between schooling completion rates and increases in the age at which children can apply for a work permit or reductions in the school entrance age in the US in the early twentieth century. She finds some evidence of an effect of school continuation laws among white males but no other demographic group. Manacorda (2006) uses this variation in education owing to work permit ages to look at spillovers to siblings from child labor supply, and a number of studies have used this variation in educational attainment to evaluate the returns to education (Acemoglu and Angrist 1999; Oreopoulos, Page, and Stevens, 2006). Overall, however, Goldin and Katz (2003) emphasize that all these legislative measures combined can explain at most 5 percent of the increase in high school enrollment and subsequent educational attainment between 1910 and 1939.

5.3. Trade sanctions and labor standards

Popular discontent in developed economies about child labor in developing countries have lead to numerous calls for harmonized labor standards, trade sanctions against countries with high levels of child labor, and consumer boycotts of products made with child labor. While empirical evidence directly on any of these issues is non-existent, it is worth reviewing the issues raised in the theoretical literature. More rigorous surveys of the theoretical work in this area are in Maskus (1997), Basu (1999), and Brown (2001).

Calls for harmonized labor standards typically envision a regime where some international arbitrator would oversee adherence to certain core labor standards. One common argument is to incorporate labor standards into the WTO. Either the WTO or ILO would monitor compliance with these standards. Violators would be punished via trade sanctions.[11] In fact, the idea of core labor standards is already enshrined in the ILO, and the

---

[11] Abolition of child labor is one of the ILO's four core labor standards that some view should be respected by all nations regardless of their level of economic development. Discussion of international labor standards is beyond the scope of this paper and is covered in Maskus (1997), Basu (1999), and Brown (2001).

abolition of child labor is one of the ILO's core four labor standards that many argued should be followed independent of level of development. Moreover, harmonization is argued to be necessary to avoid a race to the bottom, where governments lower their standards to attract business and gain competitive advantage. In fact, one can theoretically show that coordinated bans on child labor *might* be more effective in reducing child labor than a national ban when capital can easily move across countries (Basu, 1999), but one cannot show that this outcome is necessarily the case.

Others have suggested the use of unilateral trade sanctions by the rich countries as a stick to fight child labor. Such policies have often been debated in the US. For example, the Child Labor Deterrence Act (the Harkin Bill) aimed to prohibit imports of products into the US that are manufactured by child labor. While this legislation has yet to pass, the Sander's Amendment to the 1930 Tariff Act passed in 1997. It prohibits imports of goods produced by forced or indentured child labor. The 2000 Trade and Development Act restricts eligibility for trade benefits to countries that the Secretary of Labor certifies as showing progress to eliminate the worst forms of child labor.

Consumer boycotts of products produced by child labor have become popular in rich countries. Consumers who do not wish to consume goods produced by child labor can do so by purchasing products labeled as "child labor free" at a premium. Visible examples of such policies include RUGMARK-approved hand knotted rugs and "FIFA approved" soccer balls. Davies (2004) considers consumer boycotts in the context of a model or Bertrand competition with product differentiation. The threat of boycott allows for the creation of a profitable niche for adult-labor firms which in turn implies the creation of an analogous niche for child-labor firms. Moreover, he shows that even in the case of monopoly, a monopolist can segment the market by offering different product lines and then price-discriminate to increase profits. It is very difficult to show that this sort of product line specialization will be welfare improving for children. Basu and Zarghamee (2005) think about product boycotts with a focus on labor supply rather than demand. They emphasize that when wages are set locally, a product boycott can depress child wages. When children work only to help families meet subsistence needs, a decline in child wages can cause more children to need to work. Boycotts can increase child labor. Brown (2006) argues that donation labels where monitoring agencies denote some fraction of the purchase price to child welfare would be a more efficient way to reduce child labor. That said, empirical scientific evidence on the impact of boycotts on children is entirely absent.

The potential for unintended consequence is not limited to consumer boycotts. In general, it is not clear what types of policies these sanctions, threats, or boycotts are trying to affect, and it is hard to distinguish whether they reflect a genuine interest in the wellbeing of children in poor countries or are forms of hidden protectionism with all of these policies. When policies aim to restrict the employment options open to children, they can in turn have a depressive effect on child wages. If bans are not completely successful in eliminating or affecting enforced policies to prevent child labor, they may make child labor worse in two ways. More children may need to work to compensate for lost income, or children may be reallocated to sectors where monitoring is more difficult (see Basu, 2005 for a formal discussion). It is not obvious that children are better off working in non-export sectors or underground. Scientific evidence on what happens to children displaced from export sectors is essentially nonexistent even in the most publicized prohibitions on the employment of children owing to the threat of sanctions involving Bangladeshi Garment industry and Pakistani soccer balls (see Elliott and Freeman, 2003 for a description of both cases, pp. 112–115). In the case of Bangladesh, some suggest that most displaced child laborers went to work for lower wages in garment factories that did not produce for export while others describe children displaced into prostitution and stone crushing. However, it is unclear on what scale these diversions occur and whether they might be offset by improvements in other children's lives.

5.4. Conditional cash transfers

A number of countries have adopted policies designed to discourage child labor and increase schooling by lowering the cost of schooling via educational subsidies. Examples include PETI and Bolsa Escola in Brazil, the Mid-day Meals program in India, and the Progresa program in Mexico. The idea of these programs is to condition transfers on household's taking certain desirable actions such as attending school. Consequently, they both lower the relative costs of schooling while raising family incomes. PETI appears to be the only conditional cash transfer program at present that explicitly targets working children, and it is novel in that it requires after school activities for children as a way of mitigating the number of children who work and attend school. Most other conditional cash transfers only affect work as a by product of the cash transfers or as a result of the schooling requirement embedded in the program.

The Progresa program is particularly important, because it embedded scientific evaluation into the design of the program at the start. Consequently, it is the most researched of the conditional cash transfer program, and it is the most emulated. Schooling incentives in Progresa increase with the age of the child in order to compensate the household for the older child's greater opportunity cost of schooling. In addition, at secondary school ages, girls receive larger cash payments for attending school than do boys. Because of the conditionality of the program, it is not possible to separate the effects of changing household income from changes in schooling costs. Nevertheless, the evaluation data on Progresa is extremely encouraging. Schultz (2004) finds a significant reduction in wage and market work associated with eligibility for Progresa. Skoufias and Parker (2001) also document declines in domestic work for girls. Similar findings have been found in other countries as well. Schady and Araujo (2006) for example document declines in market work in Ecuador's program. Interestingly, grants in Ecuador's cash transfer program were not conditioned on schooling, but it appears that a significant number of recipients believed them to be.

The advantage of this type of positive program that indirectly discourages child labor through increasing schooling is that it also addresses the agency problems, credit market imperfections, and difficulty in monitoring most forms of child labor that may interfere with the efficacy of other child labor related interventions such as child labor bans, compulsory schooling laws, etc. Of course, the effect of these schooling incentives on child labor may be small relative to their effects on schooling, as Ravallion and Wodon (2000) found in their evaluation of Bangladesh's Food for Education program which pays students in rice for attending school.

It is also worth emphasizing that the idea that conditional cash transfer are in some (imprecise) way the optimal policy tool to combat child labor or encourage schooling is largely without formal justification. Moreover, it assumes that it is worthwhile to encourage schooling. That is, it presumes the availability of quality schools that are advantageous to the child relative to work. This point is emphasized in Jafarey and Lahiri (2005) who point out that improvement in education quality may be more effective relative to (unconditional) cash or in-kind transfers when credit markets operate. Conditional cash transfer programs are discussed at length in other chapters of this handbook.

6. Conclusion

The recent boom in empirical work on child labor has substantially improved our understanding of why children work and what the consequences of that work might be. This survey aims to assess what we currently know about child labor and to highlight what important questions still require attention.

Child labor research needs to carefully define exactly what measures of time allocation are being considered. Studies that consider too narrow a scope of activities are apt to generate misleading conclusions. Children are active in a wide variety of tasks and appear to substitute between them easily. Thus, if a child is observed working less in one task (like wage work), one cannot assume that she is working less. Moreover, though wage work appears less likely to be associated with simultaneous schooling, differences in schooling associated with variation in hours worked are much greater than those associated with location of work. Work is typically classified as market work or domestic work. Domestic work (often labeled "chores") is too often ignored in child time allocation studies. For a given number of hours worked, domestic work appears as likely as work in the farm or family business to trade off with school. Hence, studies of child labor need to consider as wide a range of activities as the data permit. There is considerable scope for learning about total labor supply or schooling changes by looking at changes in participation in various disaggregate activities.

Policy interest in child labor in today's rich countries arose during the late 19th century because of what Zelizer (1994) terms the "sacralization" of children's lives. She writes: "The term sacralization is used in the sense of objects being invested with sentimental or religious meaning" (p. 11). This view is behind much of policy's and the public's interest in child labor in developing countries today. This issue arises within economics because of concern about whether child labor is driven by agency problems – do parents fully consider the tradeoffs and costs of work when sending their children to work? However, despite some suggestive evidence, the primacy of agency problems in determining child labor supply has yet to be established.

Instead, most contemporary research in economics on child labor is interested because of the impact of work on human capital accumulation. There are a finite number of hours in a day, so at some margin, there must be a tradeoff between work and schooling. However, work and schooling are simultaneous outcomes of a single decision-making process. Identifying a causal relationship between the two seems likely to be an uninformative exercise. Moreover, work is not the residual claimant on child time outside of school, and the incidence of children who neither work nor attend school appears highest where schooling is the lowest. Consequently, it is somewhat problematic to motivate interest in commons forms of work out of a concern for schooling. Studies of schooling should consider child labor supply in attempts to understand schooling variation, but the existing evidence is insufficient to motivate studying of child labor alone without considering schooling if human capital is the researcher's only concern. Researchers have considered several other consequences of working that might go beyond the child's time constraint and agency problems such as whether there are health consequences, externalities, effects on attitudes and values, occupation choice, fertility, or local labor markets. Much of this work is in its infancy.

The interconnection of child labor and poverty seems intuitive, but evidence has been more difficult to establish. This is because the assertion that child labor stems from poverty is often taken to imply that the only reason children work is because of high marginal utility of income. The data are inconsistent with this extreme view in general.

In fact, a more general description of the child labor problem is that the child works when the utility from working today is greater than the utility associated with not working. This raises several issues that the literature has considered about why children work. Perhaps the most important issue is the least researched: who makes child labor decisions – that is, whose marginal utility matters?

There is some evidence that child time allocation is influenced by the net return to schooling. While estimating the return to schooling is a challenge, there is suggestive evidence that it influence child time allocation. Several studies document a correlation between the employment opportunities open to children inside and outside their household and child time allocation. Hence, there should be situations when work is the most efficient use of child time, and there is nothing in the literature which precludes this.

The fact that work can be optimal does not exclude the possibility that child labor's prevalence owes less to its efficiency but more to the family's need for the child's contribution to the household. There appears to be a fairly broad consensus that credit constraints force families to make child labor decisions without fully considering future returns to education, and several studies document that declining poverty is associated with rapid declines in the fraction of children who are working, especially in market work. For this to be true, there needs to be both credit constraints among the very poor and substantive changes in the marginal utility of the child's contribution as the family exits poverty. However, while transitioning out of poverty may be associated with declining economic activity levels, higher income households are apt to have more employment opportunities both outside and inside the household. This creates a difficult econometric problem for researchers if both labor supply and labor demand change in opposite ways with rising income. A failure to understand this has caused many to assert that there is little link between poverty and child labor. Fortunately, as research progresses, there has been increasing attention to all of the different factors that can influence child time allocation.

While the quantity and quality of research on child labor has been increasing dramatically in recent years, there are several omissions in the literature that need to be resolved (beyond the agency issues we have already mentioned). Policy appears to be largely operating in a vacuum from research. Namely, rhetoric is increasingly directed against "worst forms of child labor," but I am not aware of any current empirical work on why children select into worst forms that has survived peer review in a contemporary mainstream economics journal. Moreover, outside of conditional cash transfer programs, policies targeted at these worst forms and more common forms of child labor are not being evaluated in a scientific way as far as I can find. This is unfortunate. Not only could more effective policies be designed but fundamental questions about why children work could be answered in the process. Hopefully, future work on child labor will aim to combine rigorous research on these unanswered questions with formal evaluation of child labor policy.

References

Acemoglu, D., Angrist, J. (1999). "How large are the social returns to education: Evidence from compulsory schooling laws". Working paper No. 7444. National Bureau of Economic Research, USA.

Akabayashi, H., Psacharopoulos, G. (1999). "The trade-off between child labour and human capital formation: A Tanzanian case study". Journal of Development Studies 35, 120–140.

Akresh, R. (2004). "Adjusting household structure: School enrollment impacts on child fostering in Burkina Faso". Unpublished paper, University of Urbana-Champaign.

Alessie, R., Baker, P., Blundell, R., Heady, C., Meghir, C. (1992). "The working behavior of young people in rural Cote d'Ivoire". World Bank Economic Review 6, 139–154.

Amin, S., Quayes, S., Rives, J. (2006). "Market work and household work as deterrents to schooling in Bangladesh". World Development 34, 1271–1286.

Arends-Kuenning, M., Amin, S. (2004). "School incentive programs and children's activities: The case of Bangladesh". Comparative Education Review 48, 295–317.

Ashagrie, K. (1997). Statistics on Working Children and Hazardous Child Labour in Brief. International Labor Office, Geneva.

Assaad, R., Levison, D., Zibani, N. (2003). "The effect of child work on schooling in Egypt". Unpublished paper. University of Minnesota.

Baland, J., Robinson, J.A. (2000). "Is child labor inefficient?" Journal of Political Economy 108, 663–679.

Banerjee, A., Newman, A. (1993). "Occupational choice and the process of development". Journal of Political Economy 101, 274–298.

Bangladesh Bureau of Statistics (2003). Report on National Child Labour Survey 2002–2003. Government of the People's Republic of Bangladesh, Parishankhan Bhaban, Dhaka, Bangladesh.

Barham, V., Boadway, R., Marchand, M., Pestieau, P. (1995). "Education and the poverty trap". European Economic Review 39, 1257–1275.

Basu, K. (1999). "Child labor: Cause, consequence, and cure, with remarks on international labor standards". Journal of Economic Literature 37, 1083–1119.

Basu, K. (2001). "A note on the multiple general equilibria with child labor". Economics Letters 74, 301–308.

Basu, K. (2005). "Child labor and the law: Notes on possible pathologies". Economics Letters 87, 169–174.

Basu, K. (2006). "Gender and say: A model of household behavior with endogenously determined balance of power". Economic Journal 116, 558–580.

Basu, K., Ray, R. (2002). "The collective model of the household and an unexpected implication for child labor: Hypothesis and an empirical test". Working paper series: 2813. The World Bank, Policy Research.

Basu, K., Van, P. (1998). "The economics of child labor". American Economic Review 88, 412–427.

Basu, K., Zarghamee, H. (2005). "Is product boycott a good idea for controlling child labor?" Unpublished paper. Cornell University, Ithaca, NY.

Becker, G. (1965). "A theory of the allocation of time". Economic Journal 75, 493–517.

Beegle, K., Dehejia, R., Gatti R. (2005). "Why should we care about child labor? The education, labor market, and health consequences of child labor". Working paper No. 347, World Bank Policy Research.

Beegle, K., Dehejia, R., Gatti, R. (2006). "Child labor and agricultural shocks". Journal of Development Economics 81, 80–96.

Beegle, K., De Weerdt, J., Dercon, S. (2006). "Orphanhood and the long-run impact on children". American Journal of Agricultural Economics 88, 1266–1272.

Ben-Porath, Y. (1967). "The production of human capital and the life cycle of earnings". Journal of Political Economy 75, 352–365.

Benjamin, D. (1992). "Household composition, labor markets, and labor demand: Testing for separation in agricultural household models". Econometrica 60, 287–322.

Bhalotra, S. (2007). "Is child work necessary?" Oxford Bulletin of Economics and Statistics 69, 29–55.

Bhalotra, S., Heady, C. (2003). "Child farm labor: The wealth paradox". World Bank Economic Review 17, 197–227.

Biggeri, M., Guarcello, L., Lyon, S., Rosati, F. (2003). "The puzzle of 'idle' children: Neither in school nor performing economic activity: Evidence from six countries". Working paper. "Understanding Children's Work".

Birdsall, N. (1991). "Birth order effects and time allocation". In: Schultz, T. (Ed.), Research in Population Economics. JAI press, Greenwich, Connecticut and London, pp. 191–213.

Blattman, C. (2006). "The consequences of child soldiering". Working paper No. 22. "Household in Conflict Network".

Bommier, A., Dubois, P. (2004). "Rotten parents and child labor". Journal of Political Economy 112, 240–248.

Boozer, M., Suri, T. (2001). "Child labor and schooling decisions in Ghana". Unpublished paper, Yale University.

Brown, D. (2001). "Labor standards: Where do they belong on the international trade agenda?" Journal of Economic Perspectives 15, 89–112.

Brown, D. (2006). "Consumer product labels, child labor, and educational attainment". Contributions to Economic Analysis and Policy 5, 1372.

Brown, M., Christiansen, J., Philips, P. (1992). "The decline of child labor in the US fruit and vegetable canning industry: Law or economics?" Business History Review 66, 723–770.

Cain, M. (1977). "The economic activities of children in a village in Bangladesh". Population and Development Review 3, 201–227.

Cain, M. (1982). "Perspectives on family and fertility in developing countries". Population Studies 36, 159–175.

Cameron, L. (2004). "Can a public scholarship program successfully reduce school drop-outs in a time of economic crisis? Evidence from Indonesia". Unpublished paper. University of Melbourne, Melbourne, Australia.

Cardoso, E., Souza, A. (2004). "The impact of cash transfers on child labour and school attendance in Brazil". Working paper No. 407. Department of Economics, Vanderbilt University.

Case, A., Yogo, M. (1999). "Does school quality matter? Returns to education and the characteristics of schools in South Africa". Working paper No. 7399, National Bureau of Economic Research.

Case, A., Paxson, C., Ableidinger, J. (2004). "Orphans in Africa: Parental death, poverty and school enrollment". Demography 41, 483–508.

Central Bureau of Statistics (1998). The Nepal Living Standards Survey 1. National Planning Commission, Kathmandu.

Central Bureau of Statistics (2001). The 1998/99 Child Labour Report. Central Bureau of Statistics, Ministry of Finanace and Planning Republic of Kenya.

Central Bureau of Statistics (2005). The Nepal Living Standards Survey 2. National Planning Commission, Kathmandu.

Central Statistical Authority (2003). Ethiopia Child Labour Survey Report 2001. Ministry of Labour and Social Affairs and ILO, Federal Democratic Republic.

Central Statistical Office (1999). Child Labour Survey: Country Report. Central Statistical Office, Zambia and ILO-IPEC.

Chamarbagwala, R. (2006). "Regional returns to education, child labor, and schooling in India". Journal of Development Studies, in press.

Chernichovsky, D. (1985). "Socioeconomic and demographic aspects of school enrollment and attendance in rural Botswana". Economic Development and Cultural Change 33, 319–332.

Cigno, A., Rosati, F. (2005). The Economics of Child Labour. Oxford Univ. Press, Cambridge.

Cockburn, J., Dostie, B. (2007). "Child work and schooling: The role of household asset profiles and poverty in rural Ethiopia". Journal of African Economics 16, 519–563.

Cornejo M., Rodriguez A., Adames Y., Castillo R. (2003). National Report on the Results of the Child Labour Survey in Panama. ILO/IPEC/SIMPOC.

Cruz, R. (2002). National Report on the Result of the Child Labour Survey in Honduras. ILO, San Jose, Costa Rica.

Dammert,A. (2005). "Does child labor decline with household income? A non-parametric approach". Unpublished paper, Syracuse University.

Dammert, A. (2006). "Child labor response to changes in coca production: Evidence from rural Peru". Unpublished paper, Syracuse University.

Das, S., Deb, R. (2006). "A dynamic analysis of child labor with a variable rate of discount: Some policy implications". Contributions to Economic Analysis and Policy 5, 1562.

Davies, R. (2004). "Abstinence from child labor and profit seeking". Journal of Development Economics 76, 251–263.

de Brauw, A., Giles, J. (2005). "Migrant opportunity and the educational attainment of youth in rural China". Discussion paper No. 2326, Institute for the Study of Labor.

de Janvry, A., Finan, F., Sadoulet, E., Vakis, R. (2006). "Can conditional cash transfers serve as safety nets in keeping children at school and from working when exposed to shocks?" Journal of Development Economics 79, 349–373.

Dehejia, R., Gatti, R. (2002). "Child labor: The role of income variability and credit constraints across countries". Working paper No. 9018. National Bureau of Economic Research, Cambridge, MA.

Department of Census and Statistics (1999). Child Activity Survey: Sri Lanka 1999. Ministry of Finance and Planning, Sri Lanka.

Dessy, S., Pallage, S. (2005). "A theory of the worst forms of child labour". Economic Journal 115, 68–87.

Doepke, M., Zilibotti, F. (2005). "The macroeconomics of child labor regulation". American Economic Review 95, 1492–1524.

Doran, K. (2006). "Can we ban child labor without harming household welfare? An answer from schooling experiments". Unpublished paper. Princeton University, Princeton, NJ.

Duflo, E., Dupas, P., Kremer, M., Sinei, S. (2006). "Education and HIV/AIDS Prevention: Evidence from a randomized evaluation in Western Kenya". Working paper No. 4024. World Bank Policy Research, World Bank, Washington, DC, October.

Duryea, S., Arends-Kuenning, M. (2003). "School attendance, child labor and local labor market fluctuations in urban Brazil". World Development 31, 1165–1178.

Duryea, S., Lam, D., Levison, D. (2007). "Effects of economic shocks on children's employment and schooling in Brazil". Journal of Development Economics 84, 188–214.

Edmonds, E. (2003). "Child labor in South Asia". Working paper No. 5. OECD Social, Employment and Migration.

Edmonds, E. (2005). "Does child labor decline with improving economic status?" Journal of Human Resources 40, 77–99.

Edmonds, E. (2006a). "Child labor and schooling responses to anticipated income in South Africa". Journal of Development Economics 81, 386–414.

Edmonds, E. (2006b). "Understanding sibling differences in child labor". Journal of Population Economics 19, 795–821.

Edmonds, E. (2006c). "Alternative income generation and entry into worst forms of child labor". In: Linking Theory and Practice to Eliminate the Worst Forms of Child Labor. Department of Labor, Washington, DC.

Edmonds, E. (2007). "Selection into worst forms of child labor: Child domestics, porters, and ragpickers in Nepal". Unpublished paper. Dartmouth College, Hanover, NH.

Edmonds, E., Pavcnik, N. (2005a). "Child labor in the global economy". Journal of Economic Perspectives 19, 199–220.

Edmonds, E., Pavcnik, N. (2005b). "The effect of trade liberalization on child labor". Journal of International Economics 65, 401–419.

Edmonds, E., Pavcnik, N. (2006a). "International trade and child labor: Cross-country evidence". Journal of International Economics 68, 115–140.

Edmonds, E., Pavcnik, N. (2006b). "Trade liberalization and the allocation of labor between households and markets in a poor country". Journal of International Economics 69, 272–295.

Edmonds, E., Pavcnik, N., Topalova, P. (2007). "Trade adjustment and human capital investments: Evidence from Indian tariff reform". Working paper No. 12884. National Bureau of Economic Research, USA.

Edmonds, E., Sharma, S. (2006). "Investments in children vulnerable to bondage". Unpublished paper. Dartmouth College, Hanover, NH.

Edmonds, E., Turk, C. (2004). "Child labor in transition in Vietnam". In: Glewwe, P., Agrawal, N., Dollar, D. (Eds.), Economic Growth, Poverty and Household Welfare in Vietnam. World Bank, Washington, DC, pp. 505–550.

Ejrnaes, M., Portner, C. (2004). "Birth order and the intrahousehold allocation of time and education". Review of Economics and Statistics 86, 1008–1019.

Elliot, K., Freeman, R. (2003). Can Labor Standards Improve Under Globalization? Institute for International Economics, Washington, DC.

Emerson, P., Knabb, S. (2003). "Self-fulfilling expectations, child labor, and economic development". Unpublished paper, Oregon State University.

Emerson, P., Souza, A. (2002). "Birth order, child labor, and school attendance in Brazil". Working paper No. 212, Vanderbilt University.

Emerson, P., Souza, A. (2003). "Is there a child labor trap? Intergenerational persistence of child labor in Brazil". Economic Development and Cultural Change 51, 375–398.

Emerson, P., Souza, A. (2004). "Is child labor harmful? The impact of working as a child on adult earnings". Unpublished paper, University of Colorado at Denver.

Emerson, P., Souza, A. (2007). "Child labor, school attendance and intra-household gender bias in Brazil". World Bank Economic Review 21, 301–316.

Ersado, L. (2005). "Child labor and school decisions in urban and rural areas: Comparative evidence from Nepal, Peru, and Zimbabwe". World Development 33, 455–480.

Evans, D., Miguel, E. (2005). "Orphans and schooling in Africa: A longitudinal analysis". Working paper No. 143. Center for International and Development Economics Research, University of California, Berkeley.

Fafchamps, M., Shilpi, F. (2004). "Cities and specialization: Evidence from South Asia". Working paper No. 139, University of Oxford.

Fafchamps, M., Wahba, J. (2006). "Child labor, urban proximity, and household composition". Journal of Development Economics 79, 374–397.

Federal Bureau of Statistics (1996). Summary Results of Child Labour Survey in Pakistan. Federal Bureau of Statistics, Statistics Division, Ministry of Labour, Manpower and Overseas Pakistanis, ILO and IPEC, Islamabad, Pakistan.

Field, E. (2003). "Entitled to work: Urban property rights and labor supply in Peru". Working paper No. 220. Research Program in Development Studies, Princeton University.

Forastieri, V. (2002). Children at Work: Health and Safety Risks. International Labor Office, Geneva.

Foster, A., Rosenzweig, M. (1996). "Technical change and human capital returns and investments: Evidence from the green revolution". American Economic Review 86, 931–953.

Foster, A., Rosenzweig, M. (2004). "Technological change and the distribution of schooling: Evidence from green-revolution India". Journal of Development Economics 74, 87–111.

Francavilla, F. (2003). "Household chores and child health: Preliminary evidence from six countries". Working paper. "Understanding Children's Work".

Fuller, R. (1922). "Child labor and child nature". Pedagogical Seminary 29, 44–63.

Galbi, D. (1997). "Child labor and the division of labor in the early English cotton mills". Journal of Population Economics 10, 357–375.

Ganglmair, B. (2005). "A note on the effects of income and property on child labor in rural Uganda". Unpublished paper. Bonn Graduate School of Economics, Bonn, Germany.

Garg, A., Morduch, J. (1998). "Sibling rivalry and the gender gap: Evidence from child health outcomes in Ghana". Journal of Population Economics 11, 471–493.

General Statistical Office (1994). Vietnam Living Standards Survey 1992–93. Government of Vietnam, Hanoi, Vietnam.

General Statistical Office (1999). Vietnam Living Standards Survey, 1998. Government of Vietnam, Hanoi, Vietnam.

Genicot, G. (2005). "Malnutrition and child labor". Scandinavian Journal of Economics 107, 83–102.

Gentner, D. (1977). "Children's performance on a spatial analogies task". Child Development 48, 1034–1039.

Ghana Statistical Service (2003). Ghana Child Labour Survey.

Glewwe, P., Jacoby, H. (2004). "Economic Growth and the demand for education: Is there a wealth effect?" Journal of Development Economics 74, 33–51.

Goldin, C. (1979). "Household and market production of families in a late nineteenth century city". Explorations in Economic History 16, 111–131.

Goldin, C., Katz, L. (2003). "Mass secondary schooling and the state: The role of state compulsion in the high school movement". Working paper No. 10075. National Bureau of Economic Research, Cambridge, MA.

Goldin, C., Parsons, D. (1981). "Economic well-being and child labor: The interaction of family and industry". Working paper No. 707. National Bureau of Economic Research, Cambridge, MA.

Goldin, C., Sokoloff, K. (1982). "Women, children, and industrialization in the early republic: Evidence from the manufacturing censuses". Journal of Economic History 42, 741–774.

Goldin, C., Sokoloff, K. (1984). "The relative productivity hypothesis of industrialization: The American case, 1820 to 1850". Quarterly Journal of Economics 99, 461–488.

Graitcer, P., Lerer, L. (1998). "Child labor and health: Quantifying the global health impacts of child labor". Manuscript. The World Bank, Atlanta.

Guarcello, L., Lyon, S. (2003). "Children's work and water access in Yemen". Working paper. "Understanding Children's Work", Rome, Italy, April.

Guarcello, L., Lyon, S., Rosati, F., Valdivia, C. (2004). "The influence of orphanhood on children's schooling and labour: Evidence from Sub-Saharan Africa". Working paper No. 13. "Understanding Children's Work", Rome, Italy.

Guarcello, L., Lyon, S., Rosati, F., Valdivia, C. (2005). "Towards statistical standards for children's non economic work: A discussion based on household survey data". Working paper No. 16. "Understanding Children's Work", Rome, Italy.

Gunnarsson, V., Orazem, P., Sanchez, M. (2006). "Child labor and school achievement in Latin America". World Bank Economic Review 20, 31–54.

Hazarika, G., Bedi, A. (2003). "Schooling costs and child work in rural Pakistan". Journal of Development Studies 39, 29–64.

Hazarika, G., Sarangi, S. (2005). "Household access to microcredit and child work in rural Malawi". Discussion paper No. 1567, Institute for the Study of Labor.

Heady, C. (2003). "The effect of child labor on learning achievement". World Development 31, 385–398.

Heim, C., Nemeroff, C. (2001). "The role of childhhod trauma in the neurobiology of mood and anxiety disorders: Preclinical and clinical studies". Biological Psychiatry 49, 1023–1039.

Horwitz, W., Widom, C., McLaughlin, J., White, H. (2001). "The impact of childhood abuse and neglect on adult mental health: A prospective study". Journal of Health and Social Behavior 42, 184–201.

Ilahi, N., Orazem, P., Sedlacek, G. (2000). "The implications of child labor for adult wages, income and poverty: Retrospective evidence from Brazil". Manuscript, International Monetary Fund.

ILO-IPEC (2004). Understanding Children's Work in El Salvador. ILO, San Jose, Costa Rica.

International Labour Organization (ILO) (1973). C138 Minimum Age Convention, 1973. ILO, Geneva.

International Labour Organization (ILO) (1999a). C182 Worst Forms of Child Labour Convention, 1999. ILO, Geneva.

International Labour Organization (ILO) (1999b). R190 Worst Forms of Child Labour Recommendation, 1999. ILO, Geneva.

International Labour Organization (ILO) (2000). "Estimates and projections of the economically active population". In: Sources and Methods: Labor Statistics 10. ILO, Geneva.

International Labour Organization (ILO) (2001). The Time Bound Program in Nepal. ILO, Kathmandu.

International Labour Organization (ILO) (2002). Every Child Counts: New Global Estimates on Child Labour. ILO, Geneva.

International Labour Organization (ILO) (2006a). The End of Child Labor: Within Reach. ILO, Geneva.

International Labour Organization (ILO) (2006b). IPEC action against child labour: Highlights 2006. ILO, Geneva.

Iversen, V. (2002). "Autonomy in child labor migrants". World Development 30, 817–834.

Jacoby, H., Skoufias, E. (1996). "Risk, financial markets, and human capital in a developing country". Review of Economic Studies 64, 311–335.

Jafarey, S., Lahiri, S. (2002). "Will trade sanctions reduce child labour? The role of credit markets". Journal of Development Economics 68, 137–156.

Jafarey, S., Lahiri, S. (2005). "Food for education versus school quality: A comparison of policy options to reduce child labour". Canadian Journal of Economics 38, 394–419.

Kambhampati, U., Rajan, R. (2005). "Economic growth: A panacea for child labor". World Development 34, 426–445.

Kaplan, H. (1994). "Evolutionary and wealth flows theories of fertility: Empirical tests and new models". Population and Development Review 20, 753–791.

Kassouf, A., McKee, M., Mossialos, E. (2001). "Early entrance to the job market and its effects on adult health". Journal of Health Policy and Planning 16, 2–20.

Katz, E. (1995). "Gender and trade within the household: Observations from rural Guatemala". World Development 23, 327–342.

Knodel, J., Wongsith, M. (1991). "Family size and children's education in Thailand: Evidence from a national sample". Demography 28, 119–131.

Kochar, A. (1999). "Smoothing consumption by smoothing income: Hours-of-work responses to idiosyncratic agricultural shocks in rural India". Review of Economics and Statistics 81, 50–61.

Kochar, A. (2004). "Urban influences on rural schooling in India". Journal of Development Economics 74, 113–136.

Kondylis, F., Manacorda, M. (2006). "School proximity and child labor: Evidence from rural Tanzania". Unpublished paper. London School of Economics, London, England.

Koutstaal, W., Schacter, D. (1997). "Gist-based false recognition of pictures in older and younger adults". Journal of Memory and Language 37, 555–583.

Kruger, D. (2004). "Child labor and schooling during a coffee sector boom: Nicaragua 1993–1998". In: Lopez Calva, L.F., (Ed.), Trabjo Infantil: Teoría y Evidencia desde Latinoamerica, Fondo de Cultura Económica de México, Mexico, DF, in press.

Kruger, D. (2007). "Coffee production effects on child labor and schooling in rural Brazil". Journal of Development Economics 82, 448–463.

Lee, D., Kaplan, H., Kramer, K. (2002). "Children and the elderly in the economic cycle of household: A comparative study of three groups of horticulturalists and hunter-gatherers". Unpublished paper, UC Berkeley.

Lee, R., Bulatao, R. (1983). "The demand for children: A critical essay". In: Lee, R., Bulatao, R. (Eds.), Determinants of Fertility Change in Developing Countries: A Summary of Knowledge. National Academy of Sciences Press, Washington, DC.

Levison, D., Moe, K. (1998). "Household work as a deterrent to schooling: An analysis of adolescent girls in Peru". Journal of Developing Areas 32, 339–356.

Levison, D., Moe, K., Knaul, F. (2001). "Youth education and work in Mexico". World Development 29, 167–188.

Levison, D., Anker, R., Ashraf, S., Barge, S. (1998). "Is child labor really necessary in India's carpet industry?" In: Anker, R., Barge, S., Rajagopal, S., Joseph, M.P. (Eds.), Economics of Child Labor in Hazardous Industries of India. Hindustan Publishing, New Delhi, India, pp. 95–133.

Levison, D., Hoek, J., Lam, D., Duryea S. (2003). "Implications of intermittent employment for child labor estimates". Research report No. 03-539. Population Studies Center, University of Michigan.

Levy, V. (1985). "Cropping patterns, mechanization, child labor, and fertility behavior in a farming economy: Rural Egypt". Economic Development and Culture Change 33, 777–791.

Lillard, L., Willis, R. (1994). "Intergenerational educational mobility: Effects of family and state in Malaysia". Journal of Human Resources 29, 1126–1166.

Ljungqvist, L. (1992). "Economic underdevelopment: The case of a missing market for human capital". Journal of Development Economics 40, 219–239.

Lleras-Muney, A. (2002). "Were compulsory attendance and child labor laws effective? An analysis from 1915 to 1939". Journal of Law and Economics 45, 401–435.

Lloyd, C., El Tawali, S., Clark, W., Mensch, B. (2003). "The impact of educational quality on school exit in Egypt". Comparative Education Review 47, 444–467.

Maitra, P., Ray, R. (2002). "The joint estimation of child participation in schooling and employment: Comparative evidence from three continents". Oxford Development Studies 30, 41–62.

Manacorda, M. (2006). "Child labor and the labor supply of other household members: Evidence from 1920 America". American Economic Review 96, 1788–1800.

Maskus, K. (1997). "Core labor standards: Trade impacts and implications for international trade policy". Working paper. International Trade Division, The World Bank.

Menon, M., Pareli, F., Rosati, F. (2005). "Estimation of the contribution of child labour to the formation of rural incomes: An application to Nepal". Working paper No. 10. Centre for Household Income, Labour, and Demographic Economics, Rome, Italy.

Ministry of Labour (2000). Namibia Child Activities Survey 1999: Report of Analysis. Ministry of Labour, Windhoek.

Ministry of Public Service, Labour and Social Welfare (1999). National Child Labour Survey: Country Report. Zimbabwe.

Moehling, C. (1999). "State child labor laws and the decline of child labor". Explorations in Economic History 36, 72–106.

Moehling, C. (2004). "Family structure, school attendance, and child labor in American south in 1900 and 1910". Explorations in Economic History 41, 73–100.

Moehling, C. (2005). "She has suddenly become powerful: Youth employment and household decision making in the early twentieth century". Journal of Economic History 65, 414–438.

Moehling, C. (2006). "Children's pay envelopes and the family purse: The impact of children's income on household expenditures". Unpublished paper. Rutgers University, New Brunswick, NJ.

Morduch, J. (2000). "Sibling rivalry in Africa". American Economic Review 90, 405–409.

Mueller, E. (1976). "The economic value of children in peasant agriculture". In: Ridker, R. (Ed.), Population and Development: The Search for Selective Interventions. Johns Hopkins Univ. Press, Baltimore, MD, pp. 98–153.

Mueller, E. (1984). "The value and allocation of time in rural Botswana". Journal of Development Economics 15, 329–360.

Nankhuni, F., Findeis, J. (2004). "Natural resource-collection work and children's schooling in Malawi". Agricultural Economics 31, 123–134.

National Bureau of Statistics (2001). Child Labour in Tanzania: Country Report 2000/2001. Integrated Labour Force and Child Labour Survey. Ministry of Labour, Youth Development and Sports,Tanzania, ILO-IPEC.

National Institute of Statistics (2002). Cambodia Child Labour Survey 2001. Ministry of Planning, Phnom Penh, Cambodia.

National Statistics Office (2003). 2001 Survey of Children 5–17 Years Old: Final Report. National Statistics Office, Philippines and ILO-IPEC.

O'Donnell, O., Doorslaer, E., Rosati, F. (2002). "Child labour and health: Evidence and research issues". Working paper No. 1. "Understanding Child's Work".

O'Donnell, O., Doorslaer, E., Rosati, F. (2005). "Health effects of child work: Evidence from rural Vietnam". Journal of Population Economics, in press.

Orazem, P. , Gunnarsson, L. (2004). "Child labour, school attendance, and performance: A review". Working paper No. 11177. Department of Economics, Iowa State University.

Oreopoulos, P., Page, M., Huff Stevens, A. (2006). "Does human capital transfer from parent to child? The intergenerational effects of compulsory schooling". Journal of Labor Economics 24, 729–760.

Pangburn, W. (1929). "Play, the business of childhood". American Child, 29–31.

Parikh, A., Sadoulet, E. (2005). "The effect of parents' occupation on child labor and school attendance in Brazil". Working paper No. 1000, UC Berkeley.

Parish, W., Willis, R. (1993). "Daughters, education, and family budgets: Taiwan experiences". Journal of Human Resources 28, 862–898.

Parker, D. (1997). "Health effects of child labour". The Lancet 350, 1395–1396.

Parker, S., Rubalcava, L., Teruel, G. (2008). "Evaluating conditional schooling and health programs". In: Schultz, T., Strauss, J. (Eds.), Handbook of Development Economics, vol. 4. Elsevier. (Chapter 62 in the book.)

Parsons, D. (1975). "The cost of school time, foregone earnings, and human capital formation". Journal of Political Economy 83, 251–266.

Parsons, D., Goldin, C. (1989). "Parental altruism and self interest: Child labor among late nineteeth-century American families". Economic Inquiry 27, 637–659.

Patrinos, H., Psacharopoulos, G. (1997). "Family size, schooling and child labor in Peru – An empirical analysis". Journal of Population Economics 10, 387–405.

Pouliot, W. (2006). "Introducing uncertainty into Baland and Robinson's model of child labour". Journal of Development Economics 79, 264–272.

Psacharopoulos, G. (1997). "Child labour versus educational attainment: Some evidence from Latin America". Journal of Population Economics 10, 377–386.

Psacharopoulos, G., Arriagada, A. (1989). "The determinants of early age human capital formation: Evidence from Brazil". Economic Development and Cultural Change 37, 683–708.

Ranjan, P. (2001). "Credit constraints and the phenomenon of child labor". Journal of Development Economics 64, 81–102.

Ravallion, M., Wodon, Q. (2000). "Does child labor displace schooling? Evidence on behavioural responses to an enrollment subsidy". Economic Journal 110, C158–C175.

Ray, R. (2000). "Analysis of child labour in Peru and Pakistan: A comparative study". Journal of Population Economics 13, 3–19.

Ray, R. (2003). "The determinants of child labour and child schooling in Ghana". Journal of African Economics 11, 561–590.

Ray, R., Lancaster, G. (2003). "Does child labour affect school attendance and school performance? Multi-country evidence on SIMPOC data". Unpublished paper, University of Tasmania.

Rogers, C., Swinnerton, K. (2004). "Does child labor decrease when parental incomes rise". Journal of Political Economy 112, 939–968.

Rogers, C., Swinnerton, K. (2007). "A theory of exploitative child labor". Oxford Economic Papers, in press.

Rosati, F., Rossi, M. (2003). "Children's working hours and school enrollment: Evidence from Pakistan and Nicaragua". World Bank Economic Review 17, 283–295.

Rosenzweig, M. (1977). "Farm-family schooling decisions: Determinants of the quantity and quality of education in agricultural populations". Journal of Human Resources 12, 71–91.

Rosenzweig, M., Evenson, R. (1977). "Fertility, schooling, and the economic contribution of children in the rural India: An econometric analysis". Econometrica 45, 1065–1079.

Sanders, J., Nee, V. (1996). "Immigrant self-employment: The family as social capital and the value of human capital". American Sociological Review 61, 231–249.

Schady, N. (2004). "Do macroeconomic crisis always slow human capital accumulation". World Bank Economic Review 18, 131–154.

Schady, N., Araujo, M. (2006). "Cash transfers, conditions, school enrollment, and child work: Evidence from a randomized experiment in Ecuador". Working paper No. 3930. Policy Research, The World Bank, Washington, DC.

Schultz, T.W. (1960). "Capital formation by education". Journal of Political Economy 68, 571–583.

Schultz, T.W. (2004). "School subsidies for the poor: Evaluating the Mexican Progresa poverty program". Journal of Development Economics 74, 199–250.

Shafiq, M. (2006a). "Household rates of return to education for boys in rural Bangladesh: Accounting for direct costs, child labor, and option value". Unpublished paper, Washington and Lee University.

Shafiq, M. (2006b). "Household schooling and child labor decisions in rural Bangladesh". Unpublished paper, Washington and Lee University.

Sharma, S., Basynyat, B., Ganesh, G. (2001). "Bonded labour amoung child workers of the Kamaiya system: A rapid assessment". Working paper. National Labor Academy, ILO/IPEC, Kathmandu.

Silva, M. (2003). National Report on the Results of the Child and Adolescent Labour Survey in Nicaragua. ILO/IPEC/SIMPOC.

Skoufias, E. (1993). "Labor market opportunities and intrafamily time allocation in rural households in South Asia". Journal of Development Economics 40, 277–310.

Skoufias, E., Parker, S. (2001). "Conditional cash transfers and their impact on child work and schooling: Evidence from the PROGRESA program in Mexica". Economia 2, 45–96.

Sloutsky, V., Fisher, A. (2004). "When development and learning decrease memory: Evidence against category-based induction in children". Psychological Science 15, 553–558.

Song, M. (1999). Helping Out: Children's Labor in Ethnic Businesses. Temple Univ. Press, Philadelphia.

State Institute of Statistics (1999). Child Labour in Turkey 1999. Prime Ministry, Turkey and ILO.

State Statistics Committee (2001). Child Labour in Ukraine 1999. State Statistics Committe, Ukraine and International Labour Organization.

Stecklov, G. (1999). "Evaluating the economic returns to childbearing in Côte d'Ivoire". Population Studies 53, 1–17.

Strauss, J., Thomas, D. (1995). "Human resources: Empirical modeling of household and family decisions". In: Behrman, J., Srinivasan, T. (Eds.), Handbook of Development Economics. Elsevier Science, Amsterdam, pp. 1883–2023.

Swaminathan, M. (1998). "Economic growth and the persistence of child labor: Evidence from an Indian city". World Development 26, 1513–1528.

Swinnerton, K., Rogers, C. (1999). "The economics of child labor: Comment". American Economic Review 89, 1382–1385.

Thomas, D., Beegle, K., Frankenberg, E., Sikoki, B., Strauss, J., Teruel, G. (2004). "Education during a crisis". Journal of Development Economics 74, 55–86.

Trejos, C., Pisoni, R. (2003). National Report on the Results of the Child and Adolescent Labour Survey in Costa Rica. ILO-IPEC, San Jose, Costa Rica.

Wahba, J. (2006). "The influence of market wages and parental history on child labour and schooling in Egypt". Journal of Population Economics 19, 823–852.

Woodhead, M. (2004). "Psychosocial impacts of child work: A framework for research, monitoring, and intervention". Working paper. "Understanding Children's Work", Florence, Italy.

Wydick, B. (1999). "The effect of microenterprise lending on child schooling in Guatemala". Economic Development and Cultural Change 47, 853–869.

Yang, D. (2006). "International migration, remittances, and household investment: Evidence from Philippine migrants' exchange rate schocks". Economic Journal, in press.

Zelizer, V. (1994). Pricing the Priceless Child. Princeton Univ. Press, Princeton, NJ.

Chapter 58

EXTENDED FAMILY AND KINSHIP NETWORKS: ECONOMIC INSIGHTS AND EVOLUTIONARY DIRECTIONS[*]

DONALD COX

Department of Economics, Boston College, Chestnut Hill, MA 02167, USA

MARCEL FAFCHAMPS

Department of Economics, University of Oxford, Manor Road, Oxford OX1 3UQ, UK

Contents

[*] We wish to thank Paul Schultz for helpful advice and comments on previous drafts. We have also benefited from the comments of Ingela Alger, Megan Way, Kwok Ho Chan, and numerous seminar participants. Cox acknowledges financial support from the National Institute on Child Health and Human Development (R01-HD045637). Fafchamps thanks the Economics and Social Research Council (UK) for their financial support. The work is part of the program of the ESRC Global Poverty Research Group. The findings, interpretations and conclusions expressed in this paper are entirely those of the authors. They do not necessarily represent the views, opinions, or policy of the National Institutes of Health, the World Bank, or of any other government agency.

Handbook of Development Economics, Volume 4
© *2008 Elsevier B.V. All rights reserved*
DOI: 10.1016/S1573-4471(07)04058-2

Abstract

What do we know about the role of extended families and kinship networks for redistributing resources? What gaps in our knowledge most need to be filled? How can we best organize current work and identify priorities for future research? These questions are important for several reasons: households in developing countries depend on friends and relatives for their livelihood and sometimes their survival; help exchanged within extended families and kin networks affects the distribution of economic well-being, and this private assistance and exchange can interact with public income redistribution. Yet despite rapid recent progress there remain significant deficiencies in our understanding of the economics of extended families. Researchers confront a large and sometimes bewildering array of findings. We review and assess this literature by starting with an emphasis on standard economic concerns, most notably the possible interaction between government-provided social insurance and private kinship networks. Our review of the evidence suggests that the specter of complete "crowding out," whereby introduction or expansion of public transfers merely supplants private transfers, appears quite remote, though not impossible. However, numerous studies do suggest partial – but nonetheless substantial – crowding out, on the order of a 20-to-30-cent reduction in private transfers per dollar increase in public transfers. But the range of estimated effects is exceedingly wide, with many studies suggesting little private transfer response at all. Reconciling and explaining these disparate findings is a priority for future research. Theorizing about the economics of families should move beyond its concentration on income effects. The empirical literature indeed indicates that non-economic variables, such as age and gender, can have a powerful association with private transfers. We suggest that economists tap into the extensive non-economic literature that takes an evolutionary approach to the family. We show that this literature provides valuable guidance for modeling the effects of age, sex and relatedness in the interactions among extended family members. The evolutionary literature has much to offer economists interested in family behavior by proposing novel interpretations of existing findings and pointing out new and fruitful directions for future research. We encourage economists to pay more attention to this approach when studying kinship networks.

Keywords

extended family, kinship network, private transfers, remittances, inter-household transfers, crowding out, risk sharing, Hamilton's rule, cultural norms

JEL classification: A12, D10, H42, I30, J13, J10, J43, J61, O17, Q12, Z13

1. Introduction

What do we know about kinship networks and extended families in developing countries? What do we wish we knew? This chapter organizes the rapidly growing, and sometimes unwieldy, economics literature on private transfers and risk sharing between households. We start by "viewing the glass as half full," by assessing the many contributions that economic research has made in recent years to our understanding of the behavior of kin networks and extended families. We end by "viewing the glass as half empty," by pointing out how research in this sub-discipline might be improved and expanded. We note in particular the potential for evolutionary thinking to inform future economic research on family behavior.

Extended families are important just about everywhere, but especially so in poor countries, where social safety nets are incomplete or nonexistent and households must cope with an unforgiving environment of severe poverty and shocks to economic and physical well-being. Autonomy is not a likely option for a household struggling to make ends meet in the face of looming disasters such as drought, flooding, pestilence or infectious disease – especially against a backdrop of inadequate formal credit and insurance markets and a minimal welfare state. In poor, laissez-faire economies ties to communities, friends and relatives – both near and far – can make the difference between surviving and perishing.

We begin the Chapter by documenting the various economic roles that kinship networks and extended family have been shown to play – but also their limitations. Two questions arise from the literature:

(1) What are the reasons for the limited effectiveness of kinship networks?
(2) Are the services provided by kinship replaced by public provision?

The answer to the first question takes us to review succinctly the now extensive literature on limited commitment and asymmetric information. The answer to the second takes us back to the debate on crowding out. For over three decades economists have been intrigued by the interplay between kinship ties and public-sector efforts to alleviate poverty and mitigate risk. Public safety net interventions can dilute incentives to maintain a private, informal coping network. Economists have long been cognizant of the specter of such "crowding out," an unintended consequence of public income redistribution that could, at least in principle, render the distribution of economic well-being impervious to the most ambitious plans for fighting poverty.

While the logic of crowding out was first proposed long ago (Becker, 1974) and has gone through numerous variations and refinements, pertinent evidence was comparatively lacking at first. But nowadays, thanks to advances in data collection and econometrics, lower costs of computing and burgeoning interest among empirical researchers, there exists a large and rapidly growing empirical literature on inter-household transfers and risk sharing. This corpus of work enables us to take an initial stab at assessing the economic importance of crowding out and other issues connected to networks of extended kin.

At the same time, our summary of the literature reveals a patchwork of disparate methods and focus. While the empirical literature has grown, it has not yet matured to the point of providing a consistent picture of extended families, and much work needs to be done to reconcile conflicting findings. For instance, though we have much more evidence about crowding out than we did 15 years ago, it is sometimes diffuse and often contradictory; estimates range from "extremely important" to "negligible," and compelling explanations for these disparities are frequently lacking. The literature is ripe for consolidation and reconciliation – much like, we believe, the empirical labor supply literature in the early 1980s. We are reassured to find that work in this vein has recently begun, and we discuss it at the end of our survey.

After our assessment of what is *in* today's literature, we turn to a discussion of what remains *missing* from it. Much of the existing literature on private transfers and risk sharing between households is concerned, one way or another, with income effects: how private transfers respond to pre-transfer household incomes, the extent to which risk sharing networks buffer consumption from income shocks, and the like. But our reading of the empirical literature suggests that demographic variables, such as age, gender and relatedness, also figure importantly in kinship networks. Yet economics provides little theoretical guidance for understanding these effects *per se*.

We contend that evolutionary biology represents a fruitful avenue for addressing this gap. In the latter part of this chapter, we explain how insights from evolutionary biology inform and complement economic research on extended families by providing a framework for understanding, among other things, age patterns in inter-household transfers, differences in the behavior of fathers and mothers, and differences in the treatment of sons versus daughters. We conclude that a biologically based approach has the potential to expand the economic literature on kinship in novel and useful directions.

1.1. The role of kinship networks in informal exchange and public good provision

We begin by providing a brief overview of the evidence regarding the role that kinship and extended families play in various forms of exchange and provision of public goods. There is a large literature documenting the exchange of services and the provision of public goods between households in informal, non-market ways. In fact, this literature is so large that it is impossible to do it justice in a few pages. Here we limit ourselves to a few salient examples. We first illustrate the many roles that kinship networks play before pulling some common threads upon which we focus in the rest of the Chapter.

Much of the recent economic literature on kinship has focused on risk sharing. This follows a decade in which risk sharing between households attracted a lot of attention from economists (e.g. Mace, 1991; Cochrane, 1991; Townsend, 1994). Empirical investigation of gifts and transfers between households has brought to light their role as risk sharing mechanisms (e.g. Rosenzweig, 1988; Rosenzweig and Stark, 1989; Fafchamps and Lund, 2003). Researchers have also noted that most transfers between households take place between close relatives (e.g. Lucas and Stark, 1985; Ellsworth, 1989; Lund, 1996; Fafchamps and Gubert, 2007a). Most papers, however, reject the hypothesis of "full" risk sharing in favor of "partial" risk sharing. A close look at the numbers also reveals that, while the signs of the coefficients are consistent with risk sharing, the magnitudes themselves can be quite tiny, as in Rosenzweig (1988) for instance. Why this may be the case is discussed in Section 2.

Households do not just pool risk. Labor pooling is an institution commonly found in many developing countries. It takes many different forms, such as rotating arrangements and labor gangs. One of its purposes is to provide protection against health risk. Farming operations must be done in a timely manner. If a farmer is ill and cannot complete a critical task on time, the work of a whole season may be lost. Labor pooling enables farmers to seek assistance from their neighbors. In their discussion of labor pooling groups in rural Ethiopia, Krishnan and Sciubba (2004) point out the role that extended families and kinship play in facilitating the formation of these groups.

Fostering children from another family is a very common practice in many poor countries, and is often used to enable children to attend a distant school (e.g. Akresh 2004, 2005). Child fostering also takes place in response to shocks, such as the death of one or both parents. Evans (2005) illustrates the role that child fostering plays in caring for AIDS orphans in Africa (see also Evans and Miguel, 2005 and Ksoll, 2007). In all studies, child fostering takes place primarily between close relatives. In their work on South African pensioners, Case and Deaton (1998) document how frequent it is for children to live with their grandparents. Evans (2005) finds the same for AIDS orphans. Not all children in need enjoy the benefits of fostering, however. A small minority end up as street children. Many others remain in the care of parents who do not have the resources or wherewithal to provide them with the nutrition and schooling they need.

The extended family and kinship networks provide many forms of insurance and protection against external events. Those who flee drought and famine or roving bandits and lawless armies seek shelter among relatives and kin whenever possible. Migrants provide shelter and assistance to freshly arrived migrants, creating tightly knit migration networks linking village of origin and place of destination (e.g. Munshi, 2003; Granovetter, 1995a). Funeral societies are another illustration of insurance institutions that transcend the household. Dercon et al. (2004) document the importance of funeral societies in rural Ethiopia and Tanzania as a way of dealing with funeral costs. While the funeral society is in many ways a formal institution with clearly defined regular contributions, the enforcement of contractual obligations often rests on extended family and kinship ties.

Other public goods require the pooling of resources to protect productive assets, such as the cleaning of irrigation canals or the preservation of communal resources. In these cases too, informal institutions play a paramount role (e.g. Wade, 1988; Baland and Platteau, 2000). But the form that collaboration must take depends on the distribution of occupations and assets, not on family and kinship ties. For instance, farmers must maintain the irrigation canal they share, whether they are related to each other or not. This makes collaboration more difficult, which probably explains why irrigation maintenance and the preservation of common property resources have received more attention in the literature than forms of collaboration in which households can choose each other freely. Indeed, when they can choose with whom to collaborate, households tend to se-lect individuals related by blood or kin, probably because they anticipate things to go more smoothly.

Networks of blood and kin also serve to relay important information, such as informa-tion about job or business opportunities. Granovetter (1995b), for instance, documents the role that networks play in matching workers and employers. Montgomery (1991) proposes a model in which employed workers help their employer identify suitable re-cruits. In practice, these new recruits often are relatives and kin members (Barr and Oduro, 2002). Munshi (2003) and Granovetter (1995a) provide evidence of how infor-mation about business opportunities circulates in family and ethnic networks.

Sometimes cooperation goes beyond the exchange of useful information, as when individuals pool resources together to create a new business. At the heart of many busi-nesses a partnership can be found, and many partnerships are grounded in family and kin ties. In agricultural communities, relatives may pool their efforts in order to maintain a larger farm, using vertically or horizontally integrated households (Binswanger and McIntire, 1987). Individuals can also pool their savings by creating rotating savings and credit associations (ROSCAs) (e.g. van den Brink and Chavas, 1997; Besley, Coate and Loury 1993). These associations often transcend family relationships, as, for example, when market traders form a ROSCA to reconstitute their working capital. This probably explains why ROSCAs are rather formal, with clearly defined rules and obligations (e.g. Aryeetey and Udry, 1997; Anderson and Baland, 2002).

It has been argued that family and kin networks play a role in markets themselves, implying that market transactions often take place between relatives and kin. Fisman (2001b), for instance, interprets evidence that supplier credit is preferentially given to members of the same ethnic group as evidence of family ties. Fafchamps (2001) argues that this is not in general the case: because they are embedded in long-term relation-ships, exchanges between close relatives seldom take the form of a well-defined market transaction. It is, however, possible to find examples of preferential hiring and of higher wages paid to employed relatives (Barr and Oduro, 2002). There is also evidence, how-ever, that entrepreneurs are reluctant to employ relatives because they are difficult to discipline. A much more common form of family involvement in the business is as unpaid help or partners. This ensures that profits are shared and is consistent with the long-term risk sharing relationship that typically binds extended family members.

Fafchamps and Lund (2003) demonstrate that risk is shared via gifts, transfers and informal loans. They show that risk sharing takes place primarily within relative and kin-based networks. They also point out that while close relatives provide gifts, more distant relatives make informal loans. These loans are hybrid debt contracts, whereby money is lent at zero interest in exchange for the promise of future repayment. As Udry (1994) and Fafchamps and Gubert (2007a) show, repayment of such loans is contingent on shocks affecting both parties. They further show that contingent repayment takes place by letting borrowers in difficulty delay repayment and pay off part of the debt in labor.

As we have illustrated, family relations can be used for good things. They can also be used for bad. Fisman (2001a), for instance, provides empirical evidence that Indonesian businesses headed by relatives of the Suharto family benefited from preferential treatment. Family and kin ties can be used for collusion and price fixing, or to cement efforts to exclude outsiders from jobs and market opportunities: the Ku Klux Klan is perhaps the most despicable illustration of this type of network effect. Family ties can be used to attract and divert development aid, as discussed by Platteau and Gaspart (2003). Ensminger (2004) provides a chilling account of how development aid directed at poor Kenyan herders was diverted by a family ring. Family ties can also be harnessed to ensure collaboration and enforce a law of silence among criminals and terrorists. Gambetta (1993) illustrates this in the case of the mafia. Others have discussed it in the case of terrorism (Krueger and Maleckova, 2003).

What this brief overview of the literature shows is that family and kinship networks often fulfill roles that economists normally attribute to other entities. They can provide insurance, facilitate transactions and support the exchange of goods and services, which are roles commonly assumed to be fulfilled by markets. Unlike markets, however, in these roles they do not rely on legal contracts.[1] Kinship networks can also help organize the provision of public goods, a role that normally falls upon the government. But they do so without the power to tax or mobilize resources. Rather, the provision of public goods is organized as a form of exchange of favors between individuals and households.

In the absence of formal contracts, exchange typically takes the form of a sequence of unilateral transfers. There may be an implicit understanding that the exchange of favors is embedded in a long-term relationship between individuals. But what cements this relationship is not entirely clear: Is it quid pro quo? Is it altruism, and if so, where does altruism come from? The answers to these questions are important because they determine what we can reasonably expect the limitations to kinship networks to be, and how we should expect these networks of interact with markets and with government provisioning of public goods. To these issues we now turn.

2. The logic of private inter-household transfers

What is the economic logic that governs private transfers of money and other forms of assistance between households? What relationships in the data would we expect if donors were motivated by unvarnished altruism? How about if they gave in expectation of some *quid pro quo* or in response to pressure from potential recipients? Are the decisions of donor households best envisioned as unilaterally determined or as part of a bargaining process?

---

[1] Within households, patrimonial issues are often regulated by law – e.g., inheritance, child support, alimony. But relations between households typically fall outside the purview of patrimonial law.

2.1. Why theory is important and what makes for good theory

Examining the logic of inter-household transfers and kinship ties among extended family members is important for several reasons. First, we seek *parsimony*: without some logic to narrow down the list of conceivable hypotheses, empirical investigations of inter-household transfers could veer toward disorganization and vagueness. To say without further elaboration that private transfers are governed by, say, "human nature" or "norms," for example, opens to door to haphazard, torturous empirical inquiry, exacerbated by the availability of ever-more-complex household surveys containing hundreds if not thousands of questions. Empirical work unmoored by parsimonious theory risks falling prey to a "curse of dimensionality," whereby partial correlations are ground out in conceivably limitless fashion. Such insidious combinatorics create fertile ground for any number of Type I errors.

Second, we seek the *counter-intuitive*: ideally, the logic of private transfer behavior should not just narrow the field of empirical relationships deemed interesting, it should illuminate non-obvious behavioral pathways. (Why bother theorizing if it just produces answers anyone could have guessed *ex ante?*) Not all theories fare equally well on this front. For instance, a theory might posit that feelings of affection and closeness lead to transfers and assistance among family members. An empirical "test" might constitute correlating self-reported subjective feelings of closeness and actual assistance given. It would be surprising if such correlations did not turn out positive, yet such putative "theory" does little to impel us to think about family behavior in new and different ways.

Third, we seek the *falsifiable*: we want our theories to be bold enough that they dare empirical researchers to shoot them down. Non-testable assertions are devoid of predictive power.

Economic theories of inter-household transfers and kinship have done well in some respects but not in others. The successes have mostly to do with explaining the income effects of private inter-household transfers. The prominent approaches provide succinct, falsifiable and sometimes even surprisingly provocative hypotheses about the interplay between income endowments and private transfers. The remaining deficiencies have mostly to do with how influences such as age and gender are conceptualized in the economics of family behavior. We suggest how these deficiencies might be remedied later. First, we point out where economic theory has succeeded to date.

We now discuss three major categories of explanations for the existence of private transfers along kinship or extended family networks: altruism, quid pro quo, and bargaining.

2.2. The logic of family behavior begins with Becker's model of altruism

Without question, Becker's (1974) model of altruistic transfers provides the central conceptual benchmark for analyzing the behavior of extended families, and not just because it marks the beginning of modern economic analyses of the family. Becker's simple framework contains a prediction of manifest significance for both the understanding of family behavior and for income redistribution policy – namely, the possibility that public transfers of income, instead of shuffling resources from rich to poor, might merely supplant private transfers, leaving the distribution of economic well-being unchanged.

The argument is simple. Imagine two people, an altruistic donor, d, and a recipient, r, endowed with incomes I_d and I_r. "Altruistic" here means utility interdependence; the donor's utility, U, depends on her own consumption, c_p, and the recipient's utility, V, which in turn depends on recipient consumption, c_k:

$$U = U\big(c_p, V(c_k)\big). \tag{1}$$

The donor implicitly decides individual consumption levels by adding a private transfer, T, to the recipient's endowment of income I_r, in order to achieve a consumption pair $\{c_p, c_k\}$ that is most desirable from the donor's perspective. Joint consumption possibilities are determined by aggregate income, $I_d + I_r$; the donor's preferences in (1) pin down the optimal transfer T^*.

Now imagine a forced income transfer (a tax or subsidy, say) of $\tau < T^*$ from donor to recipient. Joint consumption possibilities remain unchanged, as do donor preferences. Hence each person's optimal consumption is likewise unchanged. What *does* change, then, is the private transfer, which must fall enough to exactly offset the public transfer τ.

The thought experiment of the forced transfer has become known as the "transfer derivative" (see, e.g., Cox and Rank, 1992; Altonji, Hayashi and Kotlikoff, 1997), expressed as $\partial T/\partial I_r - \partial T/\partial I_d = \partial T/\partial \tau$. Assuming pre-redistribution private transfers match or exceed τ, the Beckerian transfer derivative is -1; public transfers completely "crowd out" private ones. Adding administrative costs to public income redistribution generates a perverse outcome: by shrinking joint consumption possibilities, it hurts those it is presumably trying to help!

It is no exaggeration that the specter of crowding out served as a primary catalyst for the burgeoning literature on private transfer behavior. Not that it is the only reason to be interested in private transfers, which have been implicated in such diverse economic phenomena as: capital formation (Kotlikoff and Summers, 1981); human capital investment, inequality and intergenerational mobility (Becker and Tomes, 1979); insurance against income risk (e.g., Rosenzweig, 1988); migration (e.g., Lucas and Stark, 1985); and the alleviation of capital market imperfections (Ishikawa, 1974; Cox, 1990). Nonetheless, crowding out is still routinely cited as a leading impetus for investigations of private transfers, and the measurement of transfer derivatives continues to figure prominently in empirical work.

Despite the simplicity of the model, some misconceptions about the logic of crowding out and altruism arise repeatedly in the applied literature. The most common one is this:

- *Misconception* – Testing for evidence consistent with altruistic preferences entails checking that the *sign* of the estimated value $\partial T/\partial I_r$ is negative.

Wrong: the *magnitude* of $\partial T/\partial I_r$ matters too. For the sake of the argument, imagine a regression equation – free from any specification problems – that produces a precisely estimated value of -0.02 for $\partial T/\partial I_r$. For the value of the transfer derivative

$\partial T / \partial I_r - \partial T / \partial I_d$ to be consistent with altruistic preferences (i.e., equal to -1) would require an implausibly large estimated value for $\partial T / \partial I_d$.[2] To be consistent with altruistic preferences, the empirical value of $\partial T / \partial I_r$ must generally be not just negative, but *negative and large in absolute value*. For instance, an altruist with Cobb–Douglas preferences who places equal weight on her own consumption and that of the recipient would respond to a shortfall in recipient income by raising her transfers 50 cents per dollar shortfall – a far cry from the meager 2-cent response above.[3]

Moreover, while large transfer derivatives are necessary for the presence of altruistic transfer motives, they are not sufficient:

- *Caveat* – Finding large transfer derivatives does not necessarily imply altruistic preferences.

For instance, it is possible, at least in principle, for two completely selfish people to enter into a mutually beneficial co-insurance arrangement. They might decide, for example, to pool their incomes, setting each person's consumption equal to, say, half of their combined income. Such an arrangement can yield transfer derivatives that are identical to those implied by altruism. The reason has to do with the logic of shared budget constraints: as in the altruism case, any redistribution that keeps joint income constant must prompt equal and offsetting adjustments in private transfers in order to maintain the agreed upon allocation rule for consumption.

But tweak the rather implausible scenario above with just a bit of realism – say, the addition of moral hazard – and one can get vastly smaller transfer derivatives, as we will see in more detail in our discussion of non-altruistic transfer motives. The intuition is simple: like a market insurance company, I am concerned that if I protect a huge fraction of your income shortfalls, you will take less care to guard against preventable trouble. I act on this concern by requiring you to bear part of the consequence of any shortfall; hence, transfer derivatives would be smaller with moral hazard.[4]

A further observation about the logic of altruism and transfer derivatives with possible consequences for empirical work is this:

---

[2] For more extensive discussions of tests for intergenerational altruism, see Cox and Rank (1992) and Altonji, Hayashi and Kotlikoff (1997).

[3] Can the 2-cent response ever be consistent with altruism? Yes, as we will see below, but for this to happen requires stepping outside of a single-period framework.

[4] A bit of logic associated with the altruism model that is rarely discussed, but potentially important for empirical work is this:

- *An overlooked attribute of the altruism model* – Altruism generates a *linear* relationship between private transfers and income.

The transfer derivative emanates from movement along a linear family budget constraint: taxing the donor and giving the proceeds to the recipient and the corresponding adjustment in private transfers are each movements along a linear constraint. All of the action in these comparative statics emanates from the budget constraint; the preferences themselves do not matter except to insure an interior solution for transfers.

Why is this linearity relevant for empirical work? Because an empirical test of altruism that regresses (say) the log of transfer receipts on the log of donor and recipient incomes may be getting the specification wrong from the very start. Altruism imposes a linear structure that comes straight out of the logic of the model. Whatever its other putative merits, a log–log specification is logically inconsistent with shared budget constraints.

- *Life-cycle considerations can matter* – The pronounced transfer derivatives predicted by the altruism model could well be a good deal *weaker* once life-cycle
  considerations are taken into account.

Here is a simple illustration: suppose that donor and recipient live for 50 periods.
Suppose also – and this is crucial – that each has access to perfect capital markets. For
simplicity, abstract away from subjective rates of time preference or interest rates; each
is zero, and desired consumption profiles are flat. Imagine a forced transfer that occurs
in the first period only: the donor is taxed $100 to finance a one-shot subsidy for the
recipient. The logic of crowding out still applies; the donor will reduce his transfers to
the recipient by the same amount. Only now the *timing* of this reduction is no longer
pinned down. The donor could reduce his private transfers immediately and all at once,
but he could also spread out the reduction in $2 installments over 50 periods. If we were
to observe only the first period, it would appear that transfer derivatives were rather
tepid; when in fact over the life-cycle they still attain the full value of -1 predicted by
altruism.

Relax the perfect capital markets assumption and it is possible to restore the full
value of the transfer derivative in the first period. Suppose that the recipient is credit
constrained in the first period, and that the altruistic donor is currently transferring $150
to alleviate this constraint. The same $100 forced redistribution would now prompt an
immediate $100 reduction in private transfers. Thus, life-cycle considerations and bor-
rowing constraints can figure importantly into the logic of transfer derivatives in the
altruism model.[5]

An empirical exigency that sometimes gets glossed over is that private transfers are
rarely so widespread that all households participate: hence, prior to coming to grips
with the relationship of primary interest – namely, the transfer derivative – researchers
must first grapple with the problem of the *occurrence* of a transfer. While most empirical work scrupulously attends to the potential selection bias inherent in estimation
of income effects conditional on a transfer taking place, many find it tempting to interpret the income effects pertaining to transfer events (income coefficients in a probit
estimation for transfer receipt, for instance) in light of the altruism hypothesis. While
finding, for example, that private transfers tend to be targeted to low-income households
might be consistent with the altruism hypothesis, it does not necessarily rule out other,
non-altruistically motivated explanations, such as exchange (Cox, 1987).

A final observation about altruism and transfer derivatives pertains to whether the
donor values the act of giving *per se*:

- *The "purity" of altruism matters* – If an altruistic donor cares not just about the
  recipient but also about the act of giving, transfer derivatives will be weaker and
  crowding out less than complete.

---

[5] For a detailed discussion, see Cox (1990). One obviously important empirical issue is the extent to which
poor households in developing countries face capital market imperfections. See Conning and Udry (2007) for
a recent review of the myriad imperfections that beset rural credit markets in developing countries.

In Becker's model altruism is "pure"; as long as the recipient is happy, the donor is happy, regardless of *how* the recipient's consumption is financed: be it a result of the donor's own largesse or someone else's. In contrast, if for some reason the donor also cares separately about his or her own giving – the so-called the "warm glow" or "impurely altruistic" model of Andreoni (1989) – then in the donor's eyes private and public transfers are no longer perfect substitutes. Returning to our example of income redistribution and crowding out, the impurely altruistic donor would respond by cutting private transfers T by less than the forced transfer τ. The donor's reluctance to sacrifice "warm glow" generates this less than dollar-for-dollar response.

We have assigned a central role to transfer derivatives and crowding out in our discussion of the altruism hypothesis. It is the possibility of crowding out that, in our view, makes altruism the model to consider first and foremost, and the hub around which the rest of the theoretical literature on the extended family revolves. Because most of that other literature, with its emphasis on alternative motives for private inter-household transfers, refutes the prediction of crowding out, we think it makes sense at first pass to divide the logic of familial transfers into altruistic and non-altruistic approaches.

2.3. Quid pro quo

Despite its pre-eminence as a conceptual benchmark for family behavior, it is easy to imagine motivations for inter-household transfers that do not, at the margin, operate according to the altruistic framework pioneered by Becker. For instance:
- Private transfers might be given in *exchange* for goods or services provided by the recipient: a migrant remits to his sister to compensate her for taking care of his property while he is gone; a parent lends money to his young adult child in exchange for old-age support later in life; a landowner conditions a bequest on the appropriate behavior of children.
- Private transfers might be part of an *informal insurance contract* among self-interested people.

A primary reason to care about these and other non-altruistic motives for private transfers is that they likely entail transfer derivatives that differ markedly from those implied by Beckerian altruism.

2.3.1. Exchange

For instance, it is unlikely that public transfers would crowd out private transfers if the latter were not altruistically motivated but instead part of a two-way *exchange* (Bernheim, Shleifer, and Summers, 1985; Cox, 1987).[6] Suppose that the donor uses private transfers, T, to compensate the recipient for the latter's provision of services, s.

---

[6] While altruistic feelings might be intermingled as well – as in, for example, Lucas and Stark's (1985) eclectic approach – let us focus strictly upon exchange for the moment.

These "services" can be just about anything with less-than-perfect market substitutes, such as hours of care a wife provides to her mother-in-law. Suppose that providing services is costly and requires compensation. One can think of an implicit price that translates services into financial compensation[7]:

$$T = ps. \tag{2}$$

Exchange-related transfer derivatives can differ dramatically from altruistic transfer derivatives. For instance, a rise in recipient income, I_r, would reduce the supply of services, raising p and reducing s. To a first approximation, T would rise or fall with I_r depending on whether the donor's demand for services were price inelastic or not. This result is obviously quite different from that of Beckerian altruism, where $\partial T/\partial I_r$ is unambiguously negative and plausibly large.

2.3.2. Mutual insurance

The value of $\partial T/\partial I_r$ can likewise be markedly weaker than the "Beckerian benchmark" if private transfers are part of a self-interested system of mutual insurance (Kotlikoff and Spivak, 1981; Kimball, 1988; Coate and Ravallion, 1993). To illustrate, consider an example from Coate and Ravallion (1993): two self-interested parties play a non-cooperative 'insurance game' over an infinite horizon. What should be the rule for how transfers respond to income shocks, seeing how such a game can only be sustained if players do not have an incentive to defect? Coate and Ravallion show that the solution to this "implementability constraint" places a floor on transfers from the more fortunate to the less fortunate party. The floor serves to limit the more fortunate party's liability in order to prevent him from ducking an especially onerous transfer obligation through defection. Once this floor is reached, $\partial T/\partial I_r = 0$. This simple example can be extended to many forms of informal exchange based on quid pro quo. To this we now turn.

2.3.3. A theory of informal agreements with limited commitment

The theory of informal exchange with limited commitment starts from the observation that the enforcement of contracts by courts is not always feasible. Courts may be absent or unreliable, or the arrangement may be illegal or simply unprotected by law. In mutual insurance arrangements, writing a complete contract allowing for all contingencies may be too time consuming or simply impossible. Many transactions are too small to justify court action, or the parties too poor to recover anything in case of victory in court. This is particularly true in developing countries where many firms and market transactions are small and many people are too poor to be sued. In all these circumstances legal enforcement of contracts is problematic even though gains from exchange and public good provision may be relatively large. Informal enforcement mechanisms become necessary

---

[7] Implicit because few families would likely be so mercenary as to even use the "p"-word.

to enforce contracts, ensure contribution to public goods, and coordinate individual actions.

The literature has identified a variety of enforcement mechanisms that do not rely directly on legal institutions (e.g. Platteau, 1994a, 1994b; Greif, 1993; Fafchamps, 1996). Economists have paid most attention to mechanisms that rely on rational self-interest. Borrowing from Evans-Pritchard's (1940) observation that it is scarcity not prosperity that makes the Nuer (in Southern Sudan) generous, Posner (1980) pointed out that informal arrangements can be built upon *quid pro quo*: I help you today because I expect you to help me tomorrow. Behavioral evidence supports the quid pro quo idea: individuals in experimental situations conditionally cooperate even in finitely repeated games. This point was made most forcefully by Axelrod (1984), who described tit-for-tat behavior in such experiments as 'brave reciprocity'. Axelrod's interpretation is that, when faced with somebody new, people often give them the benefit of the doubt and start by playing cooperatively. They continue playing cooperatively as long as the other person does. But if they are cheated, they retaliate. The emergence of this human trait can be given an evolutionary interpretation, arguing that brave reciprocity makes it possible for human societies to achieve cooperation in a rapid and decentralized manner (see the economics literature on evolutionary games).

These insights were subsequently formalized with the help of repeated game theory to explain how contracts can be enforced in the absence of legal recourse. Early applications of this principle can be found in the literature on sovereign debt (e.g. Eaton and Gersovitz, 1981; Eaton, Gersovitz, and Stiglitz, 1986; Kletzer, 1984; Grossman and Van Huyck, 1987). The successful application of repeated game theory to risk sharing by Kimball (1988), Fafchamps (1992) and Coate and Ravallion (1993) has been able to explain many empirical puzzles, notably the failure of informal risk sharing during times of great stress, the emphasis on quasi-credit rather than gifts, and asymmetric risk pooling between rich and poor – often referred to as patronage. Further extensions by Ligon, Thomas, and Worrall (2001), Foster and Rosenzweig (2001) and Fafchamps (1999) have bridged the gap between gift exchange and quasi-credit of the kind described by Platteau and Abraham (1987), Udry (1994), and Fafchamps and Gubert (2007b).

In a repeated prisoner's dilemma, the threat of exclusion is the cornerstone of the enforcement strategy: breach of contract is deterred by threatening exclusion from future exchange. The cost of exclusion rises if an informal arrangement is embedded within a long-term multifaceted relationship: breaching an informal arrangement not only leads to the loss of further exchange within the arrangement, but possibly leads to the loss of other benefits associated with this relationship, such as socialization, participation in religious and social rituals, access to potential mates. This point was made by Basu (1986) and many anthropologists. Blood relations are long lasting and generate multifaceted relations between individuals, from physical exchange to moral support and camaraderie. Consequently, they provide the perfect environment for enforcing informal arrangements.

Repeated game theory has also found multiple uses in explaining market institutions (e.g. Greif, 1993; Fafchamps, 2004). In particular, it has brought to light the importance of information sharing for informal enforcement. Such contract enforcement processes are typically called reputation mechanisms or reputational contracts. Drawing inspiration from the way credit reference agencies operate, Kandori (1992) illustrates how sharing simple information about past behavior – e.g., a credit report – can be used to deter cheating in a repeated game setting. This point has been further expanded on by Taylor (2000) and Raub and Weesie (1990) to information sharing within networks. Market efficiency in general depends on the type and extent to which accurate information is shared, and on the inference economic agents draw from past action, a point made by Fafchamps (2002).

It follows that information-sharing networks play an important role in market efficiency, even when they do not directly enforce contracts, because they circulate information that is relevant to reputation mechanisms. Fafchamps (2000, 2003), for instance, provides evidence that networks facilitate market exchange. Empirical evidence on the role of networks in enforcing contracts is provided by Fafchamps and Minten (1999, 2002), among others. We have seen that family and kinship networks often circulate market relevant information, such as information about jobs, business opportunities, prices, goods for sale, house rentals and the quality of products and services. So doing, they may be instrumental to market exchange. This point has been emphasized by authors including Granovetter (1985), who argues that all market transactions are embedded in a social context.

2.3.4. Emotions

Repeated game theory is not the only possible enforcement mechanism in informal arrangements. Emotions can also be enlisted to help enforce contracts, a point that has often been overlooked by economists.

The first emotion that is instrumental in enforcing contracts is guilt: that is, the capacity for an individual to feel bad for failing to fulfill a promise. Guilt has been studied by psychologists who have demonstrated that it critically depends on upbringing. Individuals who have been repeatedly abused during childhood tend to have a guilt deficit, psychopaths representing the extreme case. As a result, the capacity to feel guilty or not tends to be inherited across generations, at least in the statistical sense, because abused parents tend to abuse their own children. It is also likely that guilt is shaped by identity and religion and, as we will discuss more in detail later in this chapter, by family ties.

Another important emotion that can be harnessed to enforce informal arrangements is shame. Unlike guilt, shame is triggered by public exposure and disapproval and thus requires the sharing of information about one's actions. As Barr (2001) has illustrated, the capacity to resent shame varies from person to person. It may also vary across cultures. Identification with a group plays an important role in shaming. Individuals who choose to exclude themselves from the rest of the community often feel little or no shame transgressing community rules – or may even derive pride from it (Blume, 2002).

Other emotions also play an enforcement role. In many circumstances, it is not rational to retaliate after having been cheated. This means that the threat of retaliation is not subgame perfect and hence not credible. In practice, human beings often become angry and irrational as a result of being cheated. Out of a sense of outrage, they often lash out at the culprit in ways that are self-damaging. Or they decide to sue simply to make a point, to be righted, in spite of the fact that suing costs them money. Anger brings an element of irrationality into the situation that makes the threat of retaliation credible or, at least, possible. In his book Passions within Reason, Frank (1988) makes arguments based on evolutionary games that traits like hard-wired vindictiveness can survive precisely because they allow for credible enforcement.

Altruistic sentiments represent another set of potentially strong emotions that can be harnessed for the enforcement of informal arrangements (e.g. Cox, 1987; Cox, Hansen, and Jimenez, 2004; Ravallion and Dearden, 1988). Such sentiments provide an emotional reward for doing the right thing, for helping others. As pointed out by Durlauf and Fafchamps (2005), a bit of altruism is often sufficient to eliminate free riding in prisoner's dilemma situations. Voluntary contribution to public goods is thus easier to achieve if parties are altruistic towards each other.

2.3.5. Identification with a group

We have already discussed how family and kinship ties can be harnessed to circulate information pertinent to reputation mechanisms and to increase the cost of exclusion. We now discuss briefly the relationship between emotions, family and kinship. Altruism has been found to be stronger among genetically related individuals. This may explain why family and kin ties facilitate the enforcement of informal arrangements. Shared genes thus raise the incentive power of altruism. Identification with the family or kinship group also facilitates guilt and shame. Given this, it is not surprising to find that extended family and kinship networks play a fundamental role in most non-market exchange – and in some forms of market exchange as well.

Identification with a group can also be created artificially by providing bonding experiences such as initiation ceremonies and other kinship activities. We suspect that bonding is strongest if it is accomplished at a young age, probably around puberty and in teenage years. This tends to bond people of the same age together. Once the kin group has been socially engineered, it can serve many of the same functions as the extended family.

Other social phenomena, such as religious sects, gangs and brotherhoods can also be used to generate strong bonds and engineer a family feel. Churches often seek to tap into the emotions triggered by family relationships by using titles such as "father," "brother," and "sister." The use of such titles demonstrates a desire to trigger the same emotional attachment as is found within an extended family.

2.4. Bargaining and other models of collective action

Useful insights on exchange within family networks have also been gained from the literature on household bargaining. Indeed:

- Private transfers might be determined by a *bargaining* process. Even if they are partly altruistic, the logic of bargaining conceivably takes us far afield from the Becker framework and its attendant crowding out.
- Private transfers might be the result of *misanthropy* rather than altruism; perhaps a powerful relative extorts money from a less powerful one.

2.4.1. Nash bargaining

A key assumption of Becker's altruism model is that the donor does the maximizing while the recipient passively reacts. One alternative to this "donor dominates" framework is cooperative bargaining between donor and recipient, pioneered in the models of Manser and Brown (1980) and McElroy and Horney (1981). Though these models have been used mainly to analyze *intra*-household allocation, they can just as well be applied to *inter*-household transfers as well. The key aspect of bargaining, as it affects crowding out, is this:

- With bargaining, transfer derivatives are no longer minus one; crowding out is not complete.

Recall that in Becker's model the donor dominates the decision making. But with cooperative bargaining, both donor and recipient arrive at the transfer decision jointly, usually according to the model proposed by Nash (1950, 1953).

The easiest way to see how bargaining affects transfer derivatives is to consider a variant of a very simple model by Kotlikoff, Razin and Rosenthal (1990), in which private transfers are the outcome of Nash bargaining between donor and recipient. Formally, the optimal transfer, T, is the value that maximizes

$$N = \left[U\big(c_d, V(c_r)\big) - U_0 \right] \times \left[V(c_r) - V_o \right], \tag{3}$$

where $U_0 = U(I_d, V(I_r))$ and $V_0 = V(I_r)$ are the respective "threat point" utilities of donor and recipient.[8] The solution to (3) has the following comparative statics properties: $\partial c_r / \partial I_r - \partial c_r / \partial I_d > 0$; $\partial c_d / \partial I_r - \partial c_r / \partial I_r < 0$. In this model, even though transfers are motivated by altruism, a forced redistribution from donor to recipient does not leave individual consumption unchanged, as in Becker's model. The reason has to do with Nash bargaining; the redistribution strengthens the recipient's bargaining position

---

[8] We think that the simplicity of Kotlikoff, Razin and Rosenthal's application of Nash bargaining makes it the easiest way to illustrate how bargaining affects transfer derivatives. Pedagogy aside, however, one might question its relevance for actual family behavior. The authors argue that their approach accounts for the recipient's option to refuse any transfer offered by the donor. Fair enough, and we suppose that recent evidence from ultimatum games – where subjects opt for nothing rather than accept an unfair division of money (see, e.g., Fehr and Gachter, 2000) might be taken as supporting evidence. But it is one thing to turn down a 15 percent share of $100; it is quite another to walk away from a parcel of the family farm. Part of the problem is endemic to Nash bargaining; "threat points" notwithstanding, no threat is ever carried out in equilibrium. For an excellent, intuitive introduction to Nash bargaining and its drawbacks, see Kennan (1986); see also Chiappori (1988) for a critical perspective on Nash bargaining.

relative to the donor, thus raising the relative consumption of the recipient. It follows that the transfer derivative $\partial T / \partial I_r - \partial T / \partial I_d$ is less than unity in absolute value: Nash bargaining renders crowding out less than complete.

An alternative to Nash bargaining is the "separate spheres" bargaining model proposed by Lundberg and Pollak (1993). Their model, which like Nash bargaining models was designed to analyze intra-household allocation, can, like their Nash-bargaining counterparts, be applied to inter-household transfers. The key innovation of Lundberg and Pollak is to imagine that the alternative to cooperation is not complete estrangement but a non-cooperative equilibrium in which individuals revert to traditional roles that entail less-than-ideal contributions to the family. The Lundberg–Pollak approach re-defines the "threat point" utility that accrues to individuals if the cooperation falls apart. Applied to the generic "donor–recipient" framework above, the separate spheres model states that the recipient's threat-point need not be $V_0 = V(I_r)$ (which implies severed relations between donor and recipient) but the utility that accrues from a non-cooperative, perhaps dysfunctional, relationship with the donor. Despite the different characterization of threat points, the bottom line with respect to crowding out is unchanged: bargaining renders crowding out less than complete.

2.4.2. The collective model

Crowding out is likewise incomplete within the more general, "collective" model of household behavior proposed by Chiappori (1988, 1992). Though the model is primarily intended to describe within-household behavior, its logic can be applied to between-household transfers. Chiappori's model boils down to a consumption "sharing rule" that depends upon, among other things, individual endowment incomes. The workings of the rule itself and the variables that influence it are left unspecified; all that is assumed is that the equilibrium allocations be efficient.

In the context of our simple example, we can specify the sharing rule $\mu = \mu(I_r, I_d)$, where μ denotes the fraction of total household expenditures allocated to the recipient. Such a rule implies that, in general, $\partial c_r / \partial I_r - \partial c_r / \partial I_d \neq 0$ and $\partial c_d / \partial I_r - \partial c_r / \partial I_r \neq 0$. While there are variants of the collective model that imply transfer derivatives consistent with income pooling – and therefore outcomes that are observationally equivalent to the crowding out implied by Becker's model – these transfer derivatives are not a *necessary* implication of the collective model (Browning, Chiappori, and Lechene, 2004).

2.4.3. Mixed motives

Obviously, donors' behavior can be governed by more than a single motive, a point forcefully underscored, for example, by Lucas and Stark (1985) who propose an eclectic model of "tempered altruism," or "enlightened self-interest," which ". . . views remittances as part of, or one clause in, a self-enforcing contractual arrangement between migrant and family. The underlying idea is that for the household as a whole it may be a Pareto-superior strategy to have members migrate elsewhere, either as a means of risk sharing or as an investment in access to higher earnings streams. Remittances may then be seen as a device for redistributing gains, with relative shares determined in an implicit arrangement struck between the migrant and the remaining family. The migrant adheres to the contractual arrangement so long as it is in his or her interest to do so. This interest may be either altruistic or more self-seeking, such as concern for inheritance or for the right to return home ultimately in dignity" (p. 902).

To return to our central theme: How might mixed motives affect transfer derivatives? The short answer is "in myriad ways," since there is no end to the variety of eclectic, mixed-motives models that can be specified. Accordingly, and more pointedly, let us recast the question: "Is there a mixed-motives approach that encompasses Beckerian altruism and its predictions for crowding out?" This narrower question is not only tractable but more pertinent, in light of the importance of crowding out as a conceptual benchmark. What follows is a synopsis of the "mixed motives" analysis put forth by Cox, Hansen, and Jimenez (2004).

Before getting to the analytics, we provide the intuition for a particular "mixed motives" model, and a summary of its implications for empirical work. Imagine that, in addition to being motivated by Beckerian altruism given by Eq. (1), that the donor is also motivated by another, non-altruistic, consideration. For simplicity, and without losing anything essential, let us assume that this other motive is exchange. But before getting to exchange, consider the following example of unmitigated altruism.

Imagine that the recipient is victim of a flood. The donor, spared from the flood, provides transfers to the recipient in order to keep him alive: in technical terms, the altruist responds to the recipient's enormous, post-flood marginal utility of consumption.

To continue: the donor hears news of an impending food shipment from a relief agency. If the shipment gets through to feed the recipient, the donor will be happy and relieved. Should the shipment not arrive, the donor stands ready with large financial transfers. In the parlance of the altruism model, $\partial T / \partial I_r$ is negative and large in absolute value, where I_r includes the value of the food shipment. There is no exchange motive at the margin; in this matter of life and death, consideration of repayment is decidedly beside the point.

Fast-forward: The recipient has recovered fully from the flood, now long past. In terms of the model, I_r is at its pre-crisis level – a value too large, say, for the donor's altruistic transfer motive to be operative. Nevertheless, the donor still makes transfers to the recipient, but they now are given in exchange for in-kind services that the recipient provides to the donor. The transfer derivatives associated with these are much less pronounced than the large negative one associated with altruism. Indeed, as we saw above, $\partial T / \partial I_r$ might even be positive over some values of I_r.

The upshot is that with mixed motives the relationship between I_r and T need not be linear, even though Beckerian altruism is part of the mix. Indeed, the relationship need not even be monotonic. An illustration is provided in Fig. 1, drawn for a fixed value of I_d. When recipient incomes fall below the cutoff $\bar{I}_r$, the donor's motive is altruistic; transfer derivatives are governed by Beckerian altruism and crowding out is complete. But with $I_r \geqslant \bar{I}_r$, the altruistic transfer motive is no longer operative. Transfers still take

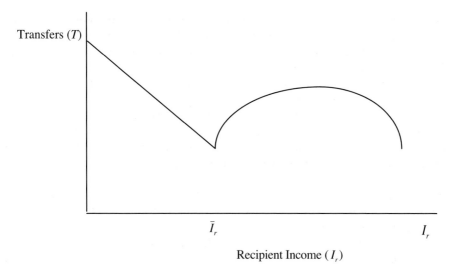

Figure 1. The non-linear relationship between private transfers and recipient income that can arise in a model with a mixture of altruistic and other motives for private transfers.

place but are now exchange motivated, with different transfer derivatives (Cox, Hansen, and Jimenez, 2004). The primary empirical motivation of the mixed motives approach is that the estimation of transfer derivatives entails rather complex functional forms; the simple linear transfer function implied by Beckerian altruism alone is misspecified. Cox, Hansen, and Jimenez (2004) find evidence supportive of the mixed-motives approach; a detailed discussion of their findings is deferred to Section 3.

2.4.4. Coercion

Private transfers have thus far been characterized either as altruistic *giving* or as part of a two-way *exchange*. But how about *taking* as an alternative to giving or exchange? Udry (1996) cites the practice of domestic violence in West Africa as *prima facie* evidence against Pareto Optimality in household allocations; and Bloch and Rao (2002) present direct evidence of the role violence plays in such allocations in their case study of a potter community in South India.

Becker (1993) has worked out a simple model of coercion[9] that captures much of the essence of the problem. Consider the canonical donor–recipient framework. Imagine that despite being altruistic toward the recipient, the donor's transfer motive is *inoperative*, so that his intended transfers, T, are zero. Suppose that this "donor" – the word is now in quotes since private transfers will flow in the opposite direction – has the ability

---

[9] Which he calls "preference formation."

to extort a gift, g, from the "recipient" by spending resources, x, in order to make the latter feel guilty or fearful. Extortion works if these unpleasant feelings, which Becker appends to the recipient's utility function as $-G(x, g)$, are assuaged by increases in g, (i.e., $G_g < 0$) and if extortion intensifies this effect ($G_{xg} > 0$).

As one might guess, the income effect in this model is different from altruistic crowding out. For instance, an increase in I_r can act like a red flag in front of a bull for the extortionist, prompting an increase in x.[10] Of all the possible motivations for familial transfers, coercion is by far the least studied, likely because of the scarcity of information on things like violence or other forms of familial pressure; thus family conflict represents a potentially valuable area for further research.

2.4.5. Village-level risk-sharing

More than just two people can pool their resources, obviously; plus, there are many ways other than private transfers for people to cope with the vicissitudes of economic life. The so-called "village risk sharing" or "perfect markets" approach pioneered by Townsend (1994) adds these considerations to analyses of networks of family and friends.

What are the implications of the group-risk-sharing perspective with regard to crowding out? How do they relate to our starting point, the Beckerian altruism model? The two approaches share an important prediction, which is that *individual consumption depends not on individual income but on aggregate income* – only now the aggregation is over more than just two people – it is over all households in the village. But the approaches part ways when it comes to *transfer derivatives*, because private transfers are not the only means of redistributing incomes or coping with idiosyncratic income risk, that is household-specific shocks that affect its current resources. The perfect markets approach embodies the myriad ways that households can adjust to income fluctuations, including but not limited to private transfers: the use of formal and informal credit, adjustments to savings, changes in labor supply, the timing of durable purchases and asset sales, reliance on formal safety nets, and so forth.

As in the collective model, and unlike Becker's model, no single member of the group dominates decision-making: given the aggregate income of the group, individual consumption is determined by a "Pareto weight" analogous to the sharing rule in the collective model. The addition of degrees of freedom – more households, more ways to finance consumption – breaks the strict relationship between private and public transfers predicted in Becker's model. Consequently, much of the empirical attention in the risk-sharing literature has been focused not on private transfers but on the connection between individual consumption, individual income and the aggregate income of the risk sharing pool. The model's key prediction is that only income of the risk sharing pool, not individual income, should matter for individual household consumption.

---

[10] Bloch and Rao indeed find that domestic violence against wives is fueled by the perpetrator's desire to extort money from his in-laws.

The result is a cross-sectional analogue of the implication of the life-cycle/permanent income hypothesis that permanent income – not current income – determines current consumption.

3. Empirical evidence on private inter-household transfers and risk sharing

3.1. Crowding out

So much for theories of crowding out; what is the available evidence? There has been a boom in the number of empirical articles on private inter-household transfers in the past 15 years or so. Much available evidence is consistent with partial crowding out – that is, transfer derivatives that are substantial enough that they probably should merit the concern of policymakers – but the typical study does not produce estimates large enough to be consistent with complete crowding out as predicted by Becker's model. Several studies estimate transfer derivatives in the range of 20 or 25 cents on the dollar. Empirical transfer derivatives, however, cover a wide range: a few are close to being consistent with complete crowding out while others suggest hardly any effect at all.

A complete accounting for differences in estimated transfer derivatives would be a daunting task, because so many things differ from one study to the next, for instance: the details of how private transfer information is collected, how private transfers are defined, how transfer functions are specified, how much detail is available on the characteristics of potential recipient and donor households, the priorities given to the various econometric issues, and the institutional settings of the individual countries. Nonetheless, the surge of empirical work on private transfers in developing countries during the past decade and a half has contributed much to our understanding of crowding out, most importantly by demonstrating how seldom complete crowding out has appeared in the data. Additionally, this work has afforded us a much clearer picture of future research directions and needs.

So what does the recent empirical literature tell us about crowding out? Most of the work indicates that the necessary *background conditions* for crowding out to be a *possibility* are indeed in place in most developing countries. One necessary condition is that private inter-household transfers be widespread and large, for the simple reason that, were this not the case, there would be little to be crowded out. Another necessary condition is that private transfers function like means-tested public income redistribution by flowing from better off to worse-off households. Recent work suggests that, in most places, both conditions hold.

3.1.1. The prevalence of private inter-household transfers

How widespread are private transfers between households? While there is no single number that captures the idea succinctly, we do our best to summarize, with caveats to follow. It is a safe bet that, across the spectrum of developing countries that have been studied, the modal percentage of households involved in private transfers in a given year (either as recipients, donors, or both) is somewhere around 40 percent. Some countries report much lower *involvement rates* (i.e. the fraction of households giving or receiving or both) and some report much higher rates: the minimum is perhaps around 10 percent, and the maximum at least 90 percent. So these numbers indeed suggest a great deal of private-transfer activity across households.

But having stuck our necks out by providing such a summary, we are compelled to qualify the above statement along several lines:

- There is no generally accepted, standardized way to collect information about private transfers. Hence, many of the conclusions about the prevalence of transfers (as we will see below) may merely be the consequence of how the data are collected. For instance, the more questions about private transfers a survey contains, the higher the survey's reported involvement rates.

- There is no generally accepted definition of what constitutes a private inter-household transfer. For instance, some surveys count informal loans between households as private transfers, others do not. Whether such loans should indeed be counted – and indeed how to distinguish a loan from a gift – entails subtle judgment calls that are not so easily resolved.

- There is no generally accepted definition of what "inter-household" means. Suppose someone who ordinarily lives in the household temporarily resides elsewhere, and remits a sum of money to that household. Typically this transfer is treated as an inter-household transfer, but one could imagine that in cases of extremely short absences it might be more appropriately categorized as an intra-household transfer.

- Even if the above problems were to someday be solved, there would no doubt remain further difficulties on several fronts, including cognition, culture and stigma. It is not clear what the optimal time frame would be for efficient recall of private transfers, for example. Definitions of what constitutes a loan versus a gift would surely vary from one culture to the next. In some cultures there may be stigma attached to (for instance) receiving money from one's children; in others, there may be stigma attached to *not* receiving money from one's children!

- Nearly all surveys and studies of private transfers deal with *realized*, rather than *potential*, private transfers. But it is actually the latter that determines, in the language of Barro (1974), whether the transfer motive is *operative*. Perhaps I have a brother who stands ready to help me in case of emergency, but that emergency never happens. Nonetheless I am insured. Such potential transfers are likely crucial, but are missed by standard surveys.

Cox, Galasso, and Jimenez (2006) studied private inter-household transfers in a diverse cross section of developing countries for which nationally representative surveys with requisite information was available, in roughly comparable form (all surveys were from the World Bank's Living Standards Measurement Surveys (LSMS)). The cross section contains information reported between 1994 and 1998 from 11 countries from around the world: Albania, Bulgaria, Jamaica, Kazakhstan, the Kyrgyz Republic, Nepal, Nicaragua, Panama, Peru, Russia and Vietnam. Private transfers are defined as monetary gifts and the money value of in-kind transfers given and received by households (inter-household loans were excluded). Per LSMS definition, individuals absent from the household longer than three months during the past year were not counted as household members, nor were boarders or lodgers. Most countries (seven) queried respondents about transfers during the past 12 months, three asked about transfers during the last month, and one asked about transfers from the past three years.[11]

Five of the 11 countries had involvement rates of 40 percent in private transfers; 7 of the 11 had involvement rates ranging between 30 and 50 percent. But the definition of private transfers makes a difference in these calculations. For instance, Vietnam's private-transfer involvement rate based on gifts, calculated from that country's LSMS for 1998 was 37 percent, but the comparable figure adding in inter-household loans was 52 percent (Cox, 2004).

Further, it is not clear whether what a household calls a "loan" does not contain at least some element of a gift if, for example, it is given interest free. Conversely, what is reported as a gift might in fact be given in expectation of some future reciprocal help, in which case it might be more aptly conceptualized as a loan.

Several other recent studies of private transfers for which involvement rates are readily available indicate significant proportions of households involved with private transfers. These include: Amelina, Chirbuca, and Knack (2004) for Romania; Cox and Jimenez (1998) for urban poor in Cartagena, Colombia; Cox, Jimenez, and Okrasa (1997) for Poland; Cox, Hansen, and Jimenez (2004) for the Philippines; de la Briere et al. (2002) for the Dominican Sierra, Dominican Republic; Frankenberg, Lillard, and Willis (2002) for Indonesia; Hoddinott (1992) for elderly households in Western Kenya; Jensen (2004) for South African "homelands"; Kazianga (2006) for Burkina Faso; Kuhn and Stillman (2004) for Russia; LaFerrara (2003) for Ghana; Lee, Parish, and Willis (1994) for Taiwan; Lillard and Willis (1997) for Malaysia; Maitra and Ray (2003) for South Africa; McKernan, Pitt, and Moskowitz (2005) for Bangladesh; Miller and Paulson (2000) for Thailand; Raut and Tran (2005) for Indonesia and Udry (1994) for Nigeria.

In a few cases, however, the incidence of private transfers between households appears low. For instance, Cox, Galasso, and Jimenez (2006) found only an 11 percent involvement rate for Albania, despite the fact that respondents there were asked to report any transfers received or given during the past three years. Albarran and Attanasio (2002) found that only 11 percent of their Mexican sample reported receiving transfers, and conjectured that the low percentages were due to the short reporting window of 30 days. Secondi (1997) found that only 6 percent of a sample of rural Chinese households reported receiving transfers in 1989, but "transfers" carried the connotation of "financial support." When information about receipts of gifts is added, the rate of

---

[11] The World Bank's Living Standards Measurement Surveys gather a wide range of data from households in developing countries in an attempt to better understand and assess the well-being of those households and the effect of public policies on living conditions in those countries. More information can be found at http://www.worldbank.org/LSMS/.

transfer inflows rises to 30 percent. These findings underscore the earlier points about the relevance of transfer definitions for assessing the pervasiveness of private transfer networks.

How about the actual money value of the transfers? Available evidence indicates that, in the modal case, there is indeed much in private transfers that could be crowded out. For instance, consider the modal four countries in terms of private transfer involvement rates (Kazakhstan, the Kyrgyz Republic, Russia and Vietnam) from the 11-country study of Cox, Galasso, and Jimenez (2006). For these countries, the percentage of private transfer receipts in total household income ranges from 6 to 8 percent for all households, including non-recipients. Among sub-samples of recipient households, the percentage of private transfers in total household income range from one-quarter to one-third. So both the prevalence and size of private transfers can indeed be substantial.

Despite advances in knowledge about the scope of private transfer networks that recent data collection and analysis has provided, there remains a conceptual flaw (which we believe could be easily remedied) in how information about transfers is gathered. Nearly all surveys tend to focus on *realized* rather than *potential* transfers. Yet the latter are what might guide the household's behavior. Knowing that my brother stands ready to bail me out of a jam can affect my savings and investment decisions, and though it may turn out that trouble never finds me, nonetheless I can depend on an operative transfer motive. Such potential transfers might function like precautionary savings, yet they may be invisible to researchers using standard survey tools.

Not that questions about potential transfers are entirely absent from existing surveys. For instance, the survey of urban poor in Cartagena, Colombia undertaken by Bamberger et al. (1992) and used in Cox and Jimenez (1998) asked respondents to report the number and financial status of network members, where a network was defined as "a set of individuals or households who regularly assist each other through the provision of money, goods, services or the provision of accommodation."[12] Such information is useful for identifying households who might rely on networks even if they have not received help of late.

Much more could be done, probably at low cost, to obtain higher quality information concerning the scope of operative inter-household transfers in developing countries. Consider the following simple survey question from the first wave of the United States Health and Retirement Survey (HRS), a household survey of persons approaching retirement age. Respondents were asked the following:

> Suppose you (and your (husband/wife/partner)) ran into severe financial problems in the future. Do you have relatives or friends who would be both willing and able to help you out over a long period of time?

A significant fraction of households *not* currently receiving private transfers nonetheless answered "yes" to this question, suggesting that a possibly large gap might exist

---

[12] Bamberger et al. (1992, p. 2-1).

between realized and potential transfers. So, the question conceivably conveys valuable information about the extent of operative transfers. Further, the question is simple and direct; it would seem rather straightforward and inexpensive to graft it onto, for instance, an LSMS survey module dealing with inter-household transfers.

Further, researchers could do more to explore innovative questions that are already available in existing surveys. For instance, the second and third waves of the Indonesian Family Life Survey (IFLS) contain innovative questions concerning decision-making power regarding familial transfers. Specifically, respondents were asked:

> In your household, who makes decisions about: giving money to your parents/family ... [and] ... giving money to your spouse's parents/family.

In addition, the community questionnaires contain similar questions asked of community leaders regarding traditions and practices concerning which family members make decisions about private transfers.

3.1.2. Evidence on transfer derivatives and crowding out

While the existence of widespread private transfers is *necessary* for crowding out, it is far from *sufficient*. To cite a trivial example: if transfers were determined by strict cultural rules that specified fixed monetary amounts to be given irrespective of income or other events, crowding out would be nil even with ubiquitous private transfers. So we turn to empirical evidence on transfer derivatives. As noted above, the modal transfer derivative – around 20 to 25 cents on the dollar – is large enough that policymakers and academics should probably sit up and take notice, but findings of complete crowding out, while noteworthy, are nonetheless rare. (We discuss them later on, and we also summarize much of the recent empirical findings in Table 1.)

Before getting to details, and to continue our broad-brush summary of the empirical literature on private transfers, we note that in many ways it is analogous to the empirical literature on United States labor supply in the late 1970s and early 1980s. Back then, empirical researchers contributing to that literature took diverse theoretical and empirical approaches to the data, and (perhaps not surprisingly) produced a spate of sometimes dramatically divergent estimates. Labor economists then turned their attention to unifying and resolving conflicting estimates in the literature, as in Killingsworth's (1983) classic early study, which addressed a variety of modeling and econometric issues in order to understand what was driving divergent estimates. The empirical private transfers literature awaits such a full-scale unification. At the end of this section, we point out a recent paper that is noteworthy for attempting this for private transfers, and encourage further work along these lines. For now, though, we note that the findings summarized below are generated from a variety of methods, and that some papers pay much more attention to certain econometric issues (e.g., endogeneity of income, selection bias, potential non-linearities) than others.

Since this section is primarily about income effects, we need to settle on convenient terminology. We will use the word "income" to denote "pre-private-transfer income," or

Table 1

Country and segment of population	Year	GDP per capita (2000 USD)	Percentage of households		Mean transfer amt. as a percentage of mean income		Transfer responsiveness to income	Source
			Receiving	Giving	Receiving	Giving		
Albania	1996	983	8.8	2.5	70.4*	15.4*	–	Cox, Galasso, and Jimenez (2006)
Bangladesh	1998–1999	346*						McKernan, Pitt, and Moskowitz (2005)
Gifts			14.6	1.7	48.3*	–	–0.25 (women)*	
Informal loans			12.7	5.0	57.6*	–	–0.31 (men)	
Botswana (*remittances*)	1978–1979	918*	–	–	–	–	0.011 (elasticity)*	Lucas and Stark (1985)
Bulgaria	1995	1567	16.3	14.4	20.9*	19.0*	–	Cox, Galasso, and Jimenez (2006)
Burkina Faso								Kazianga (2006)
Rural	1994	211	29.9	15.3	20.4*	33.3*	–0.153*	
	1998	225	33.6	15.0	14.1	27.0	–0.132*	
Urban	1994		18.6	17.9	9.7	8.2	–0.194*	
	1998		22.7	26.5	10.3	9.0	–0.244*	
China (*rural hh cross-China*)	1988	347	29.9	–	9.3	–	0.011*	Secondi (1997)
Colombia (*Cartagena's poor*)	?		46	52	9.1	6.3	–	Cox and Jimenez (1998)
Dominican Republic (*receipt of remittances by farm households in Dominican Sierra*)	1994	1712	49	–	–	–	0.09*	de la Briere et al. (2002)

(continued on next page)

Table 1
(continued)

Country and segment of population	Year	GDP per capita (2000 USD)	Percentage of households		Mean transfer amt. as a percentage of mean income		Transfer responsiveness to income	Source
			Receiving	Giving	Receiving	Giving		
El Salvador *(remittances)*	1997	2028						Cox, Edwards and Ureta (2003)
Rural			14	—	49*	—	—	
Urban			15	—	37*	—	—	
Ghana *(rural and semi-urban informal borrowing)*	1988–1989	212*	32	33	4.4*	—	—	LaFerrara (2003)
India *(six villages in semi-arid tropics)*	1977–1983	234*	—	—	—	—	−0.0209*	Rosenzweig (1988)
India *(rural informal borrowing in Northern Uttar Pradesh)*	1981–1982	234*	17	—	—	—	—	Kochar (1997)
Indonesia*	1993	730						Frankenberg, Lillard, and Willis (2002)
Exchange with children			55.2	43.5	3.0	3.0	0.132 (elasticity)*	
Exchange with parents			27.9	53.5	0.5–2.0	1.0–3.0		
Indonesia *(parents receiving from non-cores children)*	1993	730	34.5	—	20.3*	—	−0.494*	Raut and Tran (2005)

(continued on next page)

Table 1
(continued)

Country and segment of population	Year	GDP per capita (2000 USD)	Percentage of households		Mean transfer amt. as a percentage of mean income		Transfer responsiveness to income	Source
			Receiving	Giving	Receiving	Giving		
Jamaica (remittances post-Hurricane Gilbert)	1989	2894	36	–	–	–	–0.25*	Clarke and Wallsten (2003)
Jamaica	1997	3140	52.9	17.5	17.7*	11.1*	–	Cox, Galasso, and Jimenez (2006)
Kazakhstan	1996	1021	27.2	20.3	29.9*	20.2*	–	Cox, Galasso, and Jimenez (2006)
Kenya (Western)* (transfers from children)	1988	442						Hoddinott (1992)
to elderly			87.8	–	34.0*	–	–	
to non-elderly			22.1	–	4.7*	–	–	
Kyrgyz Republic	1996	240	33.2	15.6	32.2*	23.3*	–	Cox, Galasso, and Jimenez (2006)
Malaysia (parent/child transfers)	1988	2230						Lillard and Willis (1997)
Parents			61.5	23.6	7.8*	–	–	
Children			18.5	54.3	–	9.2*	–	
Mexico (poor, rural areas)	1998	5513	10.6*	0.80*	28.9*		Between –0.23 and –1.59*	Albarran and Attanasio (2002)
Nepal	1996	218	23.4	10.1	38.2*	17.6*	–	Cox, Galasso, and Jimenez (2006)
Nicaragua	1998	736	20.3	1.1	29.7	7.8	–	Cox, Galasso, and Jimenez (2006)

(continued on next page)

Table 1
(continued)

Country and segment of population	Year	GDP per capita (2000 USD)	Percentage of households		Mean transfer amt. as a percentage of mean income		Transfer responsiveness to income	Source
			Receiving	Giving	Receiving	Giving		
Nigeria (rural villages informal borrowing)	1988–1989	320*	65	75	8.5*	–	–	Udry (1994)
Panama	1997	3726	38.2	17.1	9.8*	4.5*	–	Cox, Galasso, and Jimenez (2006)
Peru	1985–1986	2188*	25	–	4	–	Low inc. 0.140* High inc. −0.013	Cox, Eser, and Jimenez (1998)
Peru	1994	1852	35.4	13.5	14.1*	8.5*	–	Cox, Galasso, and Jimenez (2006)
Philippines (remittances)	1993	877	17	–	8*	–	–	Rodriguez (1996)
Philippines (rural villages)	1994–1995	916*	100*	100*	23.4*	11.1*	–	Fafchamps and Lund (2003)
Philippines Rural	1988	882	89	50	13.0	1.1	Low inc. −0.4* High inc. −0.03	Cox, Hansen, and Jimenez (2004)
Urban			82	44	14.3	0.8	Low inc. −0.39 High inc. −0.01	
Poland (worker households)	1987	3053*	49	29	9.4	2.7	−0.054*	Cox, Jimenez, and Okrasa (1997)
	1992	2894	53	28	4.2	2.8	−0.031	
Romania (gifts, loans, other informal transactions)	2003	1963	37.2*	59.6*	8.5	12.4	negligible*	Amelina, Chirbuca, and Knack (2004)

(continued on next page)

Table 1
(continued)

Country and segment of population	Year	GDP per capita (2000 USD)	Percentage of households		Mean transfer amt. as a percentage of mean income		Transfer responsiveness to income	Source
			Receiving	Giving	Receiving	Giving		
Russia*	1994–2000	1591*					−0.1 (elderly hh only)*	Kuhn and Stillman (2004)
Rural			18	22	10*	9*		
Urban			25	24	9	6		
Russian Federation	1996	1564	24.4	23.4	40.9*	30.3*	–	Cox, Galasso, and Jimenez (2006)
South Africa*	1994	2846	21.9	3.5	–	–	Earned Income: Above poverty level: 0.00 Below poverty level: −0.07* Public Pensions: Above poverty level: 0.04 Below poverty level: −0.09*	Maitra and Ray (2003)
South Africa (remittances going to pensioners in Venda province – low income)	1989 1992	3131 2842	68 70	– –	25 12	– –	Women: −0.30* Men: −0.26 (responsiveness of remittances to pension increase between 1989 and 1992)	Jensen (2004)
Taiwan (exchanges of support between sons, daughters and parents > 50 years)	1989	–	Sons: 14 Daughters: 21	Sons: 79 Daughters: 70	– –	– –	– –	Lee, Parish, and Willis (1994)

(continued on next page)

Table 1
(*continued*)

Country and segment of population	Year	GDP per capita (2000 USD)	Percentage of households		Mean transfer amt. as a percentage of mean income		Transfer responsiveness to income	Source
			Receiving	Giving	Receiving	Giving		
Thailand (*remittances*)	1988	1185	21.6	15.6	33.2*	16.4*	–	Miller and Paulson (2000)
United States	1988	27362	20.2	13.3	5.7	6.2	−0.013*	Schoeni (1997)
United States	1989	28062						Glick (1999)
Mexican-Americans			4.8	10.1–13.3*	–	–	–	
Mexican immigrants (*support to/from relatives only*)			3.1	14.5–24.7	–	–	–	
Vietnam	1997–1998	364*	25.9	18.9	31.6*	14.7*	–	Cox, Galasso, and Jimenez (2006)
Vietnam	1993	265	20.3	16.5	32.0*	–	–	Cox (2004)
	1998	364	23.2	18.8	25.3*			
			37.3*	24.2*	32.7*			

– Percentage of households receiving or giving transfers *in the past year*, unless otherwise noted.
– Mean transfer amounts as percentage of mean income are calculated using mean transfer amount for those who are recipients/donors divided by mean post-transfer income for total sample, unless otherwise noted.
– Transfer Responsiveness to Income: Answers the question, if income increases by 1 unit, by how many units do private transfer inflows increase or decrease?
– GDP per capita from World Bank World Development Indicators, 2000 USD.

Albania
• *May include loans, as loans are not asked about explicitly.
• *Mean transfer amounts as percentage of mean income are calculated as noted above for **net** recipients and **net** givers only.

(*continued on next page*)

Table 1
(continued)

Bangladesh
- *GDP per capita for 1999.
- *Mean of gift or loan as percentage of total household income is calculated using mean post-transfer household income for recipients only, not mean income overall.
- *TRI is responsiveness of combination of gifts and informal loans.

Botswana
- *GDP per capita for 1978.
- *TRI is an elasticity – a 1% increase in income would result in a 0.011% increase in remittance.

Bulgaria
- *May include loans, as loans are not asked about explicitly.
- *Mean transfer amounts as percentage of mean income are calculated as noted above for **net** recipients and **net** givers only.

Burkina Faso
- *Mean gift as percentage of total household income calculated for those who are givers and receivers ONLY. Mean income amounts calculated separately for rural and urban areas.
- *TRI calculated using splines and instrumenting for income. Results for rural areas reported for the 2nd income quartile, and results for urban areas reported for the 3rd income quartile. (Inconsistency due to lack of significance of some of the results.)

China
- *TRI calculated by OLS for those families reporting a transfer. Includes transfers from families and gifts from non-relatives. Transfers from family members alone has a responsiveness of 0.033.

Dominican Republic
- *TRI depends upon specification of regression, ranging from −0.01 for the OLS estimates (not significant), to 0.09 for the "Censored Least Absolute Deviations" estimate.

El Salvador
- *Transfer amount as percentage of income uses mean **pre-remittance** household income.

Ghana
- *GDP per capita from 1989.
- *Informal loan amount as percentage of mean household **expenditure**, not income.

India (Rosenzweig, 1988)
- *GDP per capita from 1980.
- *TRI is transfer responsiveness to deviations in "household full-income," coefficient from specification (1) in Table 4. Other specifications result in much lower coefficients.

(continued on next page)

Table 1
(*continued*)

India (Kochar, 1997)
- *GDP per capita from 1982.

Indonesia (Frankenberg, Lillard, and Willis, 2002)
- *Nationally representative sample of married couples with at least one non-coresident child and/or one non-coresident parent.
- *TRI is an elasticity: 1% increase in father's wages results in 0.132% increase in transfers from children to parents.

Indonesia (Raut and Tran, 2005)
- *Transfer as percentage of income is calculated as mean amount received/mean parental income.
- *TRI is the part of the total transfer derivative attributable to change in the recipient's income. When the total transfer derivative is calculated, TRI $= -0.956$.

Jamaica (Clarke and Wallsten, 2003)
- *TRI in this case is transfer responsiveness to a dollar's worth of hurricane damage (comparable to a decrease in income).

Jamaica (Cox, Galasso, and Jimenez, 2006)
- *Mean transfer amounts as percentage of mean income are calculated as noted above for **net** recipients and **net** givers only.

Kazakhstan
- *May include loans as loans are not asked about explicitly.
- *Mean transfer amounts as percentage of mean income are calculated as noted above for **net** recipients and **net** givers only.

Kenya
- *Sample of 160 households in Western Kenya sublocation of Karateng (76 elderly, defined as age 60 or older, and 84 non-elderly).
- *Mean transfer amounts as percentage of mean income calculated for recipients only. Timeframe not explicitly given, but assumed over the past year.

Kyrgyz Republic
- *Mean transfer amounts as percentage of mean income are calculated as noted above for **net** recipients and **net** givers only.

Malaysia
- *Receiving figure is mean percentage of parents' hh post-transfer income received as a gift from children, for **entire** sample of parents (not just recipients).
- *Giving figure is percentage of children's hh income given to parents when both husbands' and wives' parents are alive, for the **entire** sample of children (not just donors).

Mexico
- *Percentage having received or given a transfer from friends, relatives or migrants in last **month** only.
- *Mean transfer amounts as percentage of mean income calculated as noted above, but only for prior month.
- *TRI calculated using the effect on transfers at mean PROGRESA grant size (250 pesos) from migrants (-0.2228) and friends/relatives (-1.588).

Nepal
- *Mean transfer amounts as percentage of mean income are calculated as noted above for **net** recipients and **net** givers only.

Nicaragua
- *Mean transfer amounts as percentage of mean income are calculated as noted above for **net** recipients and **net** givers only.

(*continued on next page*)

Table 1
(*continued*)

Nigeria
- *GDP per capita from 1989.
- *Amount borrowed reported as percentage of household **wealth**, not income.

Panama
- *May include loans, as loans are not asked about explicitly.
- *Mean transfer amounts as percentage of mean income are calculated as noted above for **net** recipients and **net** givers only.

Peru (Cox, Eser, and Jimenez, 1998)
- *GDP per capita from 1986.
- *TRI based on splines approach dividing sample into low income and high income households.

Peru (Cox, Galasso, and Jimenez, 2006)
- *Mean transfer amounts as percentage of mean income are calculated as noted above for **net** recipients and **net** givers only.

Philippines (Rodriguez, 1996)
- *Represents 8% of total Philippine household income, according to National Statistics Office.

Philippines (Fafchamps and Lund, 2003)
- *GDP per capita from 1995.
- *Percentage of households receiving/giving transfers includes gifts and loans.
- *For mean transfer amount, transfers include gifts only (not gifts and loans) and the percentage is calculated as the percentage of **pre-transfer** income.

Philippines (Cox, Hansen, and Jimenez, 2004)
- *TRI based on splines estimation with estimated cutoff points.

Poland
- *GDP per capita from 1990 (1987 not available).
- *TRI is calculated at sample means (see p. 203).

Romania
- *Percentages are of **net** recipients and donors, calculated on pre-transfer income, not gross.
- *TRI based on tobit analysis reported in Table B1, evaluated at the mean.

Russia
- *All values are for the month prior to the interview.
- *GDP per capita for 1997.
- *Transfers as percentage of mean income are overall mean transfer/overall mean income for each urban/rural category.
- *TRI results from OLS regression that only includes income from elder pensions, so responsiveness of transfers to income only given for single-generation elderly households.

(*continued on next page*)

Table 1
(continued)

Russian Federation
- *May include loans as loans are not asked about explicitly.
- *Mean transfer amounts as percentage of mean income are calculated as noted above for **net** recipients and **net** givers only.

South Africa (Maitra and Ray, 2003)
- *South African time period covers last 30 days, not last year.

South Africa (Jensen, 2004)
- *TRI figured in a differences in differences estimation, where men and women were estimated separately.

Thailand
- *Remittances as percentage of income recorded for previous month, not previous year.

United States
- *TRI from the tobit estimates of transfers received.

United States (Mexican American and Mexican Immigrant populations)
- *The ranges for giving are based on the numbers reporting giving to different categories of relatives.

Vietnam (Cox, Galasso, and Jimenez, 2006)
- *GDP per capita from 1998.
- *Mean transfer amounts as percentage of mean income are calculated as noted above for **net** recipients and **net** givers only.

Vietnam (Cox, 2004)
- *Mean transfer amount as percentage of mean income for recipients only.
- *Loans included in addition to gifts.

what is sometimes referred to as "endowment income," that is, the value of household resources. Unless otherwise noted, "income" refers to *current* household pre-private-transfer income.

One rather coarse stylized fact about inter-household private transfers is that there is evidence that they act like means-tested public transfers, in the following sense: private transfers appear to flow from high- to low-income households in nearly every country for which such information is available. For instance, in their 11-country study of LSMS data, Cox, Galasso, and Jimenez (2006) find that for 10 out of the 11 countries, the average incomes of private-transfer donors exceeds that of recipients – and usually by a wide margin.[13] And in most of the countries in their sample, the share of income accruing to the lowest quintile increases markedly in percentage terms after private transfers are figured into total household income.

So what does the recent literature tell us about the responsiveness of private transfers to a one-dollar increase in public transfers? One approach is to take the dozen papers for which it is straightforward to obtain the estimated value of the transfer derivative $\partial T/\partial I_r - \partial T/\partial I_d$ or the estimated partial derivative $\partial T/\partial I_r$.[14] A ranking of those estimates puts both the median and mode at the -0.25 to -0.30 range. Consider three studies from the middle of the distribution: Clarke and Wallsten (2003), Jensen (2004) and McKernan, Pitt, and Moskowitz (2005).

Clarke and Wallsten (2003) avail themselves of a natural experiment – Hurricane Gilbert, which struck Jamaica in 1988 – to estimate the impact of exogenous damage-related income shocks on inflows of remittances. Using panel data created from the Jamaican Survey of Living Conditions (an LSMS-style survey), they found that remittances increased 25 cents for every dollar's worth of damage inflicted by the hurricane. A potential problem with this episode is that the estimates might not provide much information about crowding out if private donors respond differently to hurricane-related shocks than they would to income changes from tax and public-transfer policies.

Jensen (2004) exploits a natural experiment generated from public policy – South Africa's dramatic post-apartheid expansion in public pension benefits – to estimate the response of private transfers to changes in public transfers, and finds that a one-rand increase in pensions is associated with a 0.26–0.30 rand reduction in remittances received from children living away from home.

The last "modal" study, by McKernan, Pitt, and Moskowitz (2005) also uses policy-generated income variation – this time from credit programs targeted to the poor in Bangladesh – to investigate trade-offs between program-provided credit versus informal credit-plus-private-transfers. They find that a 100 Taka increase in female program

---

[13] The only country in their sample that did not conform to this pattern was Albania.

[14] These are Albarran and Attanasio (2002), Clarke and Wallsten (2003), Cox, Eser, and Jimenez (1998), Cox and Jimenez (1992), Cox, Jimenez, and Okrasa (1997), Cox, Hansen, and Jimenez (2004), Jensen (2004), Kazianga (2006), Lucas and Stark (1985), McKernan, Pitt, and Moskowitz (2005), Raut and Tran (2005) and Secondi (1997).

credit reduces net private transfers and informal loans by 25 Taka; the equivalent figure for men is 31 Taka.

It would be misleading to conclude from these papers that any sort of consensus exists concerning crowding out; the actual range of estimates in the literature is exceedingly wide. For instance, a few of the dozen studies cited above (Cox, Eser, and Jimenez, 1998; Lucas and Stark, 1985; and Secondi, 1997) estimate *positive* values for $\partial T/\partial I_r$. At the other end of the spectrum, some of the estimates of the transfer derivative $\partial T/\partial I_r - \partial T/\partial I_d$ estimated in Raut and Tran (2005) are exceedingly close to the value of -1 predicted by Becker (1974).

Nor is the current state of the art sufficiently developed to easily reconcile such differences (though recent developments suggest that the literature might be headed in this direction). For instance, Frankenberg, Lillard, and Willis (2002) use the same data set as Raut and Tran (2005) (the 1993 IFLS) but obtain estimated income effects nowhere near as large as the latter. A possible reason is that Raut and Tran use the Altonji–Ichimura method for controlling for sample selection bias (Altonji and Ichimura, 2000; Altonji, Hayashi, and Kotlikoff, 1997). This estimator accounts for the inherent nonseparability between incomes and preferences in the altruism model of transfers. Failing to account for such nonseparability can bias estimated transfer derivatives away from the strong effects implied by altruism. Intuitively, imagine that parents vary in their (unobservable) altruism toward their children. A child whose income is large relative to that of his parents but nonetheless *still* receives a transfer is more likely to have especially generous parents, who accordingly would be prone to give especially large transfers. Failing to account for this non-linear, nonseparable source of selection bias generates estimated values of $\partial T/\partial I_r - \partial T/\partial I_d$ that are biased toward zero, because they fail to control for the spurious effects generated by the interplay between unobserved heterogeneity in parental altruism, on the one hand, and past and current transfers and incomes, on the other.[15]

Another source of non-linearity, referred to in the earlier discussion of theory, is the possibility that more than one motive might govern private transfer behavior, and that large transfer derivatives might prevail only for households whose incomes are low enough to prompt assistance motivated by unvarnished altruistic sentiments (as opposed to, say, a desire for reciprocal assistance). Such a model implies, for example, that $\partial T/\partial I_r$ would be negative and large in absolute value for low values of I_r, but might well be negligible for higher values of I_r. Cox, Hansen, and Jimenez (2004) estimate such a non-linear model for the Philippines, and find rather pronounced non-linearities consistent with a mixed-motives approach to private transfers. The non-linear transfer function takes the form of a spline, where the knot point of the spline is itself a parameter to be estimated. They find striking differences in the estimated values of $\partial T/\partial I_r$

---

[15] The authors generalize the maximum likelihood expression for Tobit taking into account the fact that explanatory variables implicated in the calculation of transfer derivatives – notably, donor and recipient incomes – and donor altruism are not additively separable (see Altonji, Hayashi and Kotlikoff, (1997, pp. 1127–1131; and Altonji and Ichimura, 2000).

by I_r: about -0.40 for poorer households (29th percentile and below for urban households, 20th percentile and below for rural households) and negligible estimated values of $\partial T/\partial I_r$ for the others. They also show that failing to account for non-linearities can generate misleadingly tepid estimates of $\partial T/\partial I_r$; a linear transfer function generates values between -0.02 and -0.03.

Maitra and Ray (2003) find corroborating evidence for South Africa, namely, that public pensions appear to crowd out private transfers among poor households, whereas the two forms of transfer appear to complement each other for the non-poor.

One problem with the study of Cox, Hansen, and Jimenez (2004) and several related studies of inter-household private transfers is that no matched information on transfer donors and recipients is available. This data deficiency can lead to potentially serious problems of omitted variable bias, which tend to stack the cards against finding evidence for crowding out. For instance, in the case of altruistically motivated intergenerational transfers, positive correlation of incomes of parents and children would tend to bias estimated values of $\partial T/\partial I_r$ toward zero. In the case of the Cox, Hansen, and Jimenez (2004) paper, the possibility of such bias makes the estimates that much more noteworthy, and the authors suggest that Becker's (1974) crowding out conjecture, so many times rejected empirically, should not yet be ruled out of court. Further, they argue that, paradoxically, the most appropriate testing ground for crowding out might well be laissez-faire economies such as the Philippines, whose low rates of social spending have (perhaps) not yet rendered crowding out a *fait accompli*.

Another piece of evidence to suggest that income effects of private transfers might not be reduced to a single number comes from simple descriptive panel evidence for Vietnam, using LSMS data that initially surveyed households in 1993 and then re-surveyed them in 1998 (Cox, 2004). Indeed, there is evidence of extreme household-specific heterogeneity in transfer derivatives. The panel data were used to construct a simple, household-specific transfer derivative, $\Delta T/\Delta I$, where ΔT denotes the change in net transfer receipts (excess of inflows over outflows) between 1993 and 1998, and ΔI denotes the change in per capita household income. The empirical distribution of $\Delta T/\Delta I$ spanned an exceedingly wide range, from -0.75 at the 10th percentile to 0.29 at the 90th percentile. The first figure is in line with received wisdom about private transfers, since changes in transfers act to offset changes in income. But the latter figure is at odds with that story, and indeed indicates that private transfers can have a destabilizing effect on total household income.

So while we have learned much about crowding out in the past 15 years or so, mounting evidence points to disparities in estimated private-transfer income effects that need explanation – disparities between households within a country, disparities between countries, disparities between studies using the same data set for the same country, and so on.

With this thought in mind, we single out two papers in the literature that we think are exemplary for pushing the frontier of research on crowding out. The first is a study of private transfers in Burkina Faso by Kazianga (2006). He finds little evidence for crowding out in this country, but what is noteworthy here is not so much the findings themselves but the approach. What is attractive about this paper is that it takes rather standard data (surveys similar to the World Bank's LSMS) and applies a painstaking econometric approach that seeks to address a variety of estimation issues at once, including selection bias (making use of the Altonji–Ichimura estimator), potential endogeneity of income, and non-linearities in income effects. As such, the paper comes closest to embarking on what Killingsworth (1983) did for the empirical labor supply literature, which is to establish some benchmarks for econometric "best practice." As the literature on private transfers moves ahead, such benchmarks will prove increasingly valuable, so that researchers and policymakers wishing to see the big picture will be able to focus on differences in estimated crowding out attributable to fundamentals (such as country differences in social safety nets) as opposed to those due to modeling issues (such as the failure to properly model selection bias).

A second exemplary paper – a Romanian case study by Amelina, Chirbuca and Knack (2004) – pushes a distinctly different edge of the research frontier on crowding out by undertaking truly innovative and path-breaking data collection. This effort, undertaken under the auspices of the World Bank in 2002, produced the Romanian Public/Private Transfers and Social Capital Survey. What this study – and survey – does that is different and valuable is that it goes beyond a narrow focus on private inter-household transfers to seek detailed information about so-called "social capital" and civic life: that is, involvement in formal private associations and clubs, and participation in collective action and local government decision making. In a nutshell, the study expands the purview of private transfers from the extended family into the neighborhood, and, from there, into local politics and beyond. The survey attempts to measure perceived corruption and trust in local government, for instance. Further, the survey supplements standard questionnaires by engaging in open-ended discussions with respondents in order to obtain more in-depth information about causes and consequences of private transfers and other coping mechanisms.

A basic insight that emerges from this work is that the canonical model of crowding out – whereby public transfers are exogenously bestowed like manna from heaven – needs to be rethought. The next generation of models of interactions between the public and private sectors should pay more attention to the subtle realities of how public transfers are allocated. How, for instance, interest groups must organize in order to elbow their way into the public trough. Amelina, Chirbuca and Knack find that the Romanian poor are disadvantaged on many margins. They tend to be shut off from sources of formal private transfers such as clubs and associations. They tend to have a low level of trust in neighbors, strangers, and institutions, and in contrast to their richer counterparts they have trouble reaping gains from social capital. Further, the authors find that, in the case of Romania, private familial transfers are of little help, since the poorest give about as much as they get, so that private transfers affect their economic position very little.

We hope that similar survey instruments and analyses will be implemented for other countries, and that the entrenched dichotomous view of public versus private transfers in the crowding out literature will be replaced with a more nuanced approach that recognizes a continuous spectrum of social safety nets that are not necessarily so easily pigeonholed. For instance, the Becker (1974) model demonstrates how endogenously determined private transfers respond to exogenous changes in public transfers. Yet it is just as easy to imagine that one might want to analyze a world in which public transfers are determined endogenously by private, grassroots networks that are partly familial, partly neighborhood-like and partly related to civic organizations. More cohesive private networks could be more adept at steering public benefits their way – "crowding in," rather than crowding out.

3.2. Demographic and other variables in empirical studies of private transfers

There can be little doubt that the specter of crowding out has been one of the largest – if not *the* largest – galvanizing force motivating empirical work on private transfers. Hence researchers have devoted considerable attention to both the logic and evidence associated with income effects and private transfers. But it is equally obvious that other variables – such as demographic influences like age and gender – are also important determinants of private transfers.

One thing that distinguishes age effects from income effects is that the latter tend, at least roughly, to be the same from one country to the next, in the sense that the trend is almost always for private transfers to flow from high- to low-income households (e.g., as noted earlier in reference to the study of Cox, Galasso, and Jimenez, 2006). In contrast, age patterns often differ dramatically between countries. For instance, Cox, Galasso, and Jimenez (2006) find that transfers from young to old exceed those going from old to young in both the Latin American countries in their sample (Jamaica, Panama, Peru and Nicaragua) and in Vietnam and Nepal as well, whereas the opposite is true for Russia and Bulgaria. While some of these effects are no doubt attributable to differences in public pensions and crowding out, the inter-country differences in age patterns nonetheless persist even after controlling for household resources.

Why the differences? One researcher who has devoted a large part of his career to pondering this issue is economic demographer Ronald Lee. He, along with anthropologist Hillard Kaplan, have proposed that age patterns in intergenerational transfers could be affected by the stage of economic development, as appreciated against a backdrop of evolutionary considerations. We will consider the latter in more detail in the next section, but for now, suffice it to say that our species has weathered the vicissitudes of the past 150,000 years or so (and, indeed, has flourished) in no small part due to our ingrained proclivity to nurture and support our young. The evolutionary baseline is that older generation members care about, and provide support for, younger relatives more than *vice versa*. Kaplan's (1994) review of evidence from traditional (i.e. hunter-gatherer, or pre-agricultural) societies – which are thought to best reflect the evolutionary baseline – indeed supports this view: transfers from old to young predominate. The same pattern tends to hold for advanced industrial and post-industrial societies (Lee, 1997).

What then, are we to make of countries like Vietnam, where transfers from young to old, rather than old to young, tend to predominate? First, note that, in most of the developing world, social security consists of private old-age support from adult children. But probing more deeply beneath this proximate influence, Lee (1997) advances an intriguing hypothesis concerning agriculture; namely, support of elder farmers can indirectly redound to the benefit of young children. How? Consider, as emphasized by Rosenzweig and Wolpin (1985), that idiosyncratic farm characteristics might exercise a heavy influence on agricultural productivity, lending primacy to the role of intergenerationally transmitted, farm-specific knowledge. Intergenerational transfers from adult children to their elderly parents can benefit grandchildren and their forebears if they serve to perpetuate the valuable farm-specific human capital embodied in the elderly. There are, by now, a sufficient number of LSMS surveys from a diverse enough set of countries to test this hypothesis.

Unlike age patterns, which vary by country, patterns by gender do not: private transfers tend to be targeted to female-headed households. For instance, in each of the 11 countries studied by Cox, Galasso, and Jimenez (2006), female-headed households were more likely to receive private transfers than male-headed households. Further, nearly all single-country studies of private transfers, be they developing or advanced economies, uncover this pattern: e.g., Lucas and Stark (1985) for Botswana; Kaufmann and Lindauer (1986) for El Salvador; Cox, Hansen, and Jimenez (2004) for the Philippines; Guiso and Japelli (1991) for Italy; and Cox (1987) for United States.

One obvious potential explanation for the pattern has to do with migration, with wives receiving remittances from husbands temporarily absent from home. But Cox, Galasso, and Jimenez (2006) find that the pattern holds up even if households with temporary migrants are removed from the samples. Another explanation is sex differentials in life expectancy, with old age support disproportionately targeted to widows. But again, the pattern holds up even controlling for age.

A different, and perhaps complementary, explanation advanced by Cox (1987) has to do with the exchange motivation for private transfers. There is abundant evidence from sociology and social psychology that women are more heavily involved in the provision of inter-familial services (e.g., caring for extended family members) that are predicted, under the exchange hypothesis, to be compensated for by inter-household transfers.

As with gender, several other of the covariates typically entered into the standard empirical transfer function are subject to multiple interpretations. Take education, for instance. It is correlated with lifetime resources. It may be correlated with past transfers, and hence be picking up the strength of parental altruism. It also might be proxying the recipient's ability to reciprocate transfers they receive. Interpretations can differ with respect to hypothesized sign for the partial correlation of education and private transfers: for instance, the first story would predict a negative sign for educational attainment, the second and third predict a positive sign.

Even in a simpler world in which the latter two considerations were wiped away, the hypothesized sign of education need not be pinned down so simply. For instance, imagine a model in which private transfers are used to alleviate liquidity constraints, as in Cox (1990). Further, suppose in a regression of transfer receipts on education, that current income is being controlled for, and imagine that education, then, is picking up the permanent income of the potential recipient. With current income constant, more education implies higher permanent income and hence higher desired consumption. With current income constant then, more education implies a bigger gap between desired consumption and current resources. If private transfers alleviate liquidity constraints (and hence are used to fill this gap) predicted transfers should rise with education. On the other hand, however, if liquidity constraints were not important, so that private transfers were used to equalize, say, lifetime earning capacity, then education would be expected to enter the transfer function with a negative sign.

Indeed, the education effects produced in the empirical literature reflect these cross currents; some studies produce positive education effects, others produce negative ones, and usually there is little attempt to explicate the exact rationale for education's role in the transfer function. The same is true for other "controls" that are typically included in empirical studies of inter-household transfers, such as household size, number and ages of children, ethnicity, and so forth.[16]

Indeed, there exists a kind of double standard in the transfers literature with respect to the relationship between theory and empirics. Usually there is a painstaking discussion of the logic of income effects, often stemming from concerns about crowding out and a desire to understand underlying motivations for private transfers. Accordingly, the ensuing empirical work rests on a foundation that facilitates the interpretation of income effects. In sharp contrast, however, demographic and other variables are often merely entered as controls, and frequently they are given short shrift in the discussion – either described in an *ad hoc* manner or sometimes the results are suppressed altogether.

Yet these other influences are at least as important as income for explaining variation in private transfers, and a major piece of unfinished business in the literature – something that we return to in the last section – is subjecting these influences to the same exacting theoretical scrutiny that has been directed toward income effects. Before venturing into those uncharted waters, however, we complete our survey of inter-household relationships by discussing the remaining major sub-discipline in the field – inter-household risk-sharing.

3.3. Risk sharing

As a segue into our discussion of the risk sharing literature, we begin by noting a couple of additional findings from the private transfers literature not yet discussed. There is abundant evidence (perhaps not surprisingly) that private transfers appear responsive to adverse shocks experienced by households. For instance, in each of the countries studied by Cox, Galasso, and Jimenez (2006) samples of households with someone sick enough to have to miss work or limit daily activities received transfers in greater numbers than

---

[16] The use of controls such as number and age composition of children, for instance, can be clearly problematic for attempting to understand familial resource allocation via inter-household transfers, since fertility and household composition are themselves endogenous and likely to be correlated with unobservables in estimations of private transfers.

healthy households. Fafchamps and Lund (2003) found, for a sample of Filipino households, that gifts and informal loans were highly responsive to certain shocks to income and expenditures, such as the unemployment of the household head or spouse, or the onset of funeral expenses. These findings are consistent with a central premise of the so-called "risk sharing" literature, which is that households provide mutual insurance to one another in order to smooth their consumption in the face of risk.

But in some key aspects, the approach of the risk sharing literature is different from that of the private transfers literature. Most importantly, the variable that gets placed front and center in this literature – both conceptually and empirically – is not private transfers but consumption. The key question – first posed by Robert Townsend in his seminal 1994 paper – is this: as a rural household in a small village, facing risks of drought, pestilence, illness, and the like, what is it that determines my consumption in a given year? If I get sick or lose my job or my crops, will my family and I go hungry? Or might the appropriate "consuming entity" extend beyond the walls of my home? Suppose that households in my village act as an extended family, pooling resources and consuming, as it were, from a common village pot. Such pooling would serve to lessen the sensitivity of my own consumption to fluctuations in my income; what would matter is the resources of the entire village.

To a first approximation, the risk-sharing hypothesis can be thought of as a cross-sectional analogue of the life-cycle/permanent income (LC/PIH) hypothesis. (The analogy is not exact since there are time subscripts in the risk sharing model, but it is pedagogically useful nonetheless.) Hall's (1978) pioneering test of the LC/PIH hinged in part upon the irrelevance of current income for consumption once permanent income had been controlled for. Townsend's test parallels that of Hall's, in that with risk sharing, an individual household's current income should play only a minor role in determining its consumption.

Another attractive aspect of the risk sharing approach (and here is where we leave the cross section analogy behind) is that, by focusing on consumption smoothing, the theoretical and empirical models can come to grips with *all* of the means by which households might cope with shocks in order to smooth consumption: not just through private transfer networks, but by using capital and credit markets, availing themselves of public transfers, private insurance, adjustments in the timing of discretionary durable purchases, and just about any other conceivable means of controlling consumption flows. Households, for instance, might adjust their labor supply in order to smooth consumption (Kochar, 1999; Rose, 2001). Rather than seeking to parse out the individual mechanisms for smoothing, risk sharing studies focus on the bottom line: if consumption got smoothed, *some* combination of factors must have been at work to make it happen.[17]

---

[17] Because kin-based and other inter-household transfers are but one element of the array of means by which households smooth consumption in the risk sharing framework, our treatment of this sub-literature in this Chapter is not as detailed as that of private transfers in earlier sections. For more detailed surveys, we refer readers to a variety of excellent papers, including Alderman and Paxson (1994), Morduch (1995, 1999), Townsend (1995), Fafchamps (1999), Dercon (2002) and Attanasio and Rios Rull (2003).

In addition, the cost of collecting consumption data in developing countries – relative to advanced economies – is low. Accordingly, there exist many data sets amenable for testing the predictions of the risk sharing hypothesis, and, since the appearance of Townsend's (1994) paper, the literature has burgeoned considerably.

A consensus has emerged from this literature that parallels the literature on inter-household transfers, which is that, while there is evidence that households can mitigate the effects of shocks to their economic well-being via risk sharing, such insurance is only partial, not complete. An early generation of tests, beginning with Townsend's (1994) own classic paper, followed by others such as Ravallion and Chaudhuri (1997), Townsend (1995) and many others, reported the extent to which the household's propensity to consume depended upon its own income after controlling for community resources. (To return to an earlier analogy: this parallels the "excess sensitivity" tests of the LC/PIH in the macro consumption literature.) The estimated propensities are never zero, though some estimates are surprisingly low. (Again, the heterogeneity in estimates mirrors what has been found in the inter-household transfers literature for transfer derivatives: a range of estimates, with pronounced neutralization of income fluctuations the exception rather than the norm.)

A second generation of risk sharing tests, based upon variances rather than means, reinforces these earlier findings. Inspired by an early suggestion of Deaton and Paxson (1994), Attanasio (2002) and others have pioneered tests of risk sharing based upon comparisons of the variance of consumption versus the variance of income. The intuition for the test is rather straightforward: if households can avail themselves of various mechanisms for smoothing consumption, the variance of consumption should be less than that of income. An example of such a test is Attanasio and Szekely (2004), who find that Mexican households have difficulty insuring against wage shocks, and that negative shocks can cause cutbacks in purchases of goods related to human capital investment, thus possibly jeopardizing a household's future earning capacity.

The concept of income variances enters the risk sharing literature's perspective on crowding out, which is a bit different from that of the private transfers literature. The argument, as explicated by Attanasio and Rios Rull (2000), goes like this: public transfers reduce income variability, and the good news is that this can allow households to do a better job of consumption smoothing. A possible downside, however, is that, with incomes thus smoothed, households may no longer have sufficient incentive to band with others to form private risk sharing arrangements. Attanasio and Rios Rull (2000) go on to find supporting evidence: benefits from Mexico's Progresa program do indeed appear to partially crowd out private transfers. Dercon and Krishnan (2003) find similar results for publicly provided food aid in rural Ethiopia.

The risk sharing literature has matured rapidly, both conceptually and empirically, in the sense that it is now accepted that problems such as commitment and enforceability should be incorporated as standard fixtures in the modeling landscape. For instance, Foster and Rosenzweig (2001) propose a creative way of inferring problems of commitment (as well as the advantages of familial altruism) by examining how past transfers affect current giving. The idea is that, all else equal (and with little altruism to impel continued generosity) having a long history of giving transfers should reduce a household's propensity to make an additional transfer. The authors indeed find evidence to this effect, and they also find that problems of imperfect commitment do not appear so pressing in the presence of familial altruism. Ligon, Thomas, and Worrall (2001) explicitly incorporate limited commitment into a model of household risk sharing, and find that this model empirically outperforms the simpler risk sharing model originally proposed by Townsend.

Another practical problem with inter-household risk sharing is that some risks will obviously be much easier to insure than others, and there is emerging evidence to support this idea. For instance, Gertler and Gruber (2002) find that Indonesian risk sharing networks can cope rather effectively with costs of ordinary illnesses, but not with severe ones that impair long-term health. Likewise, Fafchamps and Lund (2003) find that certain risks appear more insurable than others.

Townsend's original insight was to focus on the village as the unit of aggregation for the pooling of risk. This idea has much to recommend it, seeing how, for example, propinquity may be necessary for forming the bonds of trust needed to seal an implicit risk sharing agreement. People who live in close proximity have more opportunity to get to know one another and also have an easier time monitoring one another in order to police and mitigate moral hazard problems. But proximity entails problems too, not least of which is covariate risk. As Rosenzweig and Stark (1989) emphasize, one way to mitigate the problem of correlated risks is to forge links with far flung friends and relatives.

Recent work has attempted to move beyond the village-based risk sharing format. For instance, Grimard (1997) emphasizes how ethnic ties might play a role in the formation of risk sharing networks in Cote d'Ivoire; likewise, Munshi and Rosenzweig (2006) focus on the role of castes for risk sharing in India. Murgai et al. (2002) examine the role of transactions costs in determining the (endogenous) size and localization of the risk sharing group. Suri (2005) considers a multi-level approach whereby households share risk within villages, which in turn can pool their fortunes amongst other villages within districts. This is an important issue to cultivate in future research on risk sharing. Too often, the literature takes a rather casual approach to the potential size of the risk sharing group, and does not pay enough attention to problems of constraints on group size. We return to this issue in the next section.

4. Moving forward in an evolutionary direction

So much for what we have *learned* in recent years: What *gaps* in the economic literature on extended families and kinship networks would we like to see filled? And how might researchers go about filling them? The considerable progress that economists have made in the past 15 years has largely been concentrated in improving our understanding of forces that are central to the discipline: income effects, price effects, shared budget constraints, and the like. True, we have learned about other things along the way – demographic, cultural and geographic effects, for instance – but such influences are usually cast as adjuncts to economic issues or conceptualized in an *ad hoc*, purely descriptive manner.

Consider a typical regression from the empirical literature on private transfers: On the left-hand side, a measure of private transfer receipts; on the right-hand side, the household's income and/or wealth, including – data permitting – resources of potential donors. Education variables would likely be included, perhaps as indicators of permanent income. This canonical regression would likely also contain demographic variables, such as female headship, age, and marital status, number of children, household size, and the like. But as our discussion earlier in this chapter makes clear, while economists can draw upon a considerable body of theory for interpreting *income*-related variables, they have little guidance for thinking about the *demographic* variables – age and gender, in particular – which often are just included as "controls."

We suspect that this is because economists lack a cogent framework for thinking about age or sex-related influences *per se*. We contend that well-established insights from evolutionary biology can complement economic approaches to produce a more powerful model for understanding a fuller array of influences on family networks. Further, we argue that the approach is straightforward, easy to learn and parsimonious. It ties together diverse facets of behavior with just a few basic premises. And it is likely to look appealingly familiar to economists, entailing, as it does, maximization subject to constraints.

Before getting to details, and by way of motivation, we preview a sampling of predictions and insights that an evolutionary approach can provide:

- Mothers are expected to be more altruistic toward children than fathers. Relatedly, it may be highly useful to distinguish between *maternal* versus *paternal* grandmothers as sources of private inter-household transfers.
- Investigations of whether *sons* versus *daughters* tend to be favored with familial transfers might well pay attention to the parental family's wealth ranking in the relevant marriage market (and whether that market veers at least somewhat toward polygyny).
- Attention to biological basics helps to explain age patterns in the provision of assistance between extended family members and predicts that altruism of parents toward children should be stronger than that of children toward parents.
- Evolutionary theory predicts conflicts of interest can arise within families: children, for instance, will tend to want more than parents are willing to give to them, and interests of relatives from the husband's versus the wife's side of the family will not necessarily coincide.
- The theory advances clear-cut hypotheses regarding nepotistic behavior and transfers contingent upon biological relatedness. Stepchildren, adopted children and foster children, for example, are expected to gain less from familial transfer networks than biological children.

The evolutionary approach unifies diverse phenomena in kinship networks, such as: fetal development, health of the elderly, conflict between siblings over what constitutes fair treatment by parents, conflict between husbands and wives concerning quantity versus quality of children, conflict between in-laws, and the use of gifts versus loans in risk sharing networks (*gifts* are predicted to go to kin, *loans* to non-kin). To see how the approach works, we begin with its foundation, what is commonly referred to as "Hamilton's Rule."

4.1. Hamilton's rule: The evolutionary cornerstone of familial altruism

Which should we expect to be stronger, a mother's altruism toward her young son, or an adult son's altruism toward his elderly mother? Might we expect mothers to be more solicitous toward their children than fathers? How about maternal versus paternal grandmothers? How much might we expect sons to be treated differently than daughters, purely because of their sex? Should we expect siblings to be natural allies, or rivals who vie for scarce parental resources? Or perhaps we should expect they might be a bit of each?

Note that these questions are concerned with demographic effects *per se:* mothers versus fathers, sons versus daughters, old versus young. What is now known as Hamilton's rule was proposed by biologist William D. Hamilton over 40 years ago (Hamilton, 1964), and related theories, primarily those of Robert Trivers and his collaborators, form the basis for understanding the evolutionary impetus for familial altruism. These theories make clear predictions about demographic influences within kinship networks. In addition to being falsifiable, the logic of Hamilton's rule is exceedingly compact, and its implications are sometimes far from intuitively obvious. As such, the biologically based approach shares strengths in common with the best of economic theory; it is parsimonious, counter-intuitive and falsifiable.

4.1.1. What is Hamilton's rule?

Hamilton's rule is a simple but far-reaching system of logic that contains the biological foundations for familial altruism. Acts of altruism, such as the honeybee's suicidal defense of its hive, seemed to contradict the Darwinian dictum of "survive and reproduce," the evolution-based objective of all living things including humans. Hamilton solved the problem of altruism by focusing on the *gene* rather than the *individual*. The honeybee's altruistic act could be optimal from the "gene's eye view": though the genetic code of the individual altruist is lost, even more of that code, no longer imperiled, gets to prevail within the bee's rescued relatives. Richard Dawkins (1976) calls organisms 'survival machines,' *disposable* devices for protecting and disseminating *long-lived* genetic code.

Imagine a hypothetical construct called a "helping gene," something that impels the individual to make sacrifices to help others. Hamilton asked: "What sort of helping genes might spread in the population?" Hamilton contended that altruistic behavior among kin was governed by the implicit calculation based upon expected costs and benefits measured in terms of *inclusive fitness. Fitness* represents reproductive success, usually cast as the expected number of progeny; *inclusive fitness* is one's *own* fitness plus the weighted sum of *relatives'* fitness, where the weights are the probabilities that a relative and I share the same helping gene.

Consider an illustration adapted from Cox (2007): My brother and I are soldiers, and an enemy sniper has him in his sights. Suppose I could either cry out a warning to save him, thus drawing the sniper's deadly fire toward myself, or remain silent. If I call out, I lose my own helping gene with certainty. What do I gain? Since my brother is a genetic relative, there is a 50–50 chance we share the same helping gene (that is, the 0.25 probability that we both inherit the gene from our mother plus the 0.25 probability we inherit it from our father). Thus, in expected value terms, the benefit from calling out is half the value of my helping gene. From the "gene's eye view," then, the optimal policy is to remain silent. But suppose there were three brothers in the sniper's sights rather than one. Now there are net gains to being altruistic, since 1.5 helping genes (in expected value) are saved, a net gain of one half. Thus, a gene that impelled an organism to issue a risky, even suicidal, warning cry could spread if such cries saved enough close relatives.

In more general terms, Hamilton's rule can be expressed as follows. Denote the *cost* of the altruistic act to the *donor* by C, and *benefits* of the act to the *recipients* by B. Let r denote the *coefficient of relatedness*, i.e., the chances that donor and recipient share the identical helping gene.[18] Hamilton's rule stipulates that the donor provides help if

$$rB > C. \tag{4}$$

In our example, B and C are counted in terms of lives saved. Return to the warfare example and imagine that I am, and will continue to be, childless, but that my brother is expected to have three children (for simplicity let us stop at the second generation). My brother's fitness is his helping gene plus the expected value of his helping gene in the children, or $1 + 0.5 + 0.5 + 0.5$. The value of rB is therefore 1.25, so Hamilton's rule predicts that my inclusive fitness would be enhanced by sacrificing my life in order to save my brother. This example illustrates how Hamilton solved Darwin's dilemma of altruistic behavior among social insects, which are often sterile.

Sterility occurs in humans as well, with menopause, and therein lies a prediction related to Hamilton's rule: its onset should, all else equal, spur increased altruistic behavior toward kin. Menopause is but one illustration of the built-in age-specific imbalances in altruistic sentiments that emanate from Hamilton's rule. Human relatedness is reflexive (r between grandmother and granddaughter is 0.25 no matter whose point of view is taken) but fitness need not be, as in the case where the granddaughter – but not the grandmother – is fertile. Family elders, therefore, would in general be expected to be more altruistic toward their younger kin than *vice versa*. Note that we have said nothing about income endowments; Hamilton's rule pertains to the sentiments embodied in the grandmother's utility function, not the money in her bank account. Another

---

[18] Another common (and mathematically equivalent) way to express relatedness is by the fraction of genes shared by dint of having the same parents (i.e., common descent). (See Cox, 2007.)

way to express this is that Hamilton's rule predicts that, between a granddaughter and grandmother, each of whom has $100 to her name, one would expect it more likely for the grandmother to make transfers to the granddaughter than other way around.[19]

4.2. Hamilton's rule and conflict in the family

Hamilton's rule predicts several avenues for familial conflict: between parents and off-spring, among siblings, between husbands and wives, and among in-laws. It is perhaps in this respect that the evolutionary approach differs most dramatically from the economic approach; until very recently, economists focused almost exclusively on Pareto Optimal solutions to economic problems in the family. For instance, Becker's (1974) "Rotten Kid" theorem implied that altruistic transfers from parent to child would obviate conflict, since no child would choose to bite the hand that feeds him. Likewise, and as we saw in earlier sections, bargaining and collective models retain Pareto Optimal solutions.

In contrast, Trivers' (1974) model of parent-offspring conflict delineates conditions where a child might harm his mother, his siblings, or even himself to increase his share of parental transfers. Imagine a mother with two sons, Andy and Ben. Her relatedness to each is one-half, so if they are otherwise identical she would treat each equally according to Hamilton's rule. But neither son would be inclined to go along with this. While Andy's relatedness to Ben is one-half, his relatedness to *himself* is higher, namely, unity. Hence from Andy's perspective equal treatment does not go far enough; he would prefer to get more than Ben, and *vice versa*.

4.2.1. Sibling rivalry – A case study

Consider the following East African case study of sibling rivalry and parent-offspring conflict from the 1950s. P.H. Gulliver (1961) studied the transition to cash farming among a group of subsistence farmers in Northern Tanzania (then Tanganyika). Traditional systems of inheritance were founded upon land abundance; a man's land typically was inherited by distant kin such as cousins or half brothers. Sons preferred to acquire land outside their natal village. But once land became scarce and valuable, inheritance laws quickly changed, so that land now passed from a father to his children (an outcome, by the way, predicted by Hamilton's rule, since parental altruism is stronger for sons than for more distant kin). The new system gave the eldest brother authority to allocate land between himself and among his younger siblings, with predictable results:

At first, and as land grew scarcer and more valuable, the eldest brother took the larger portion of the dead father's land, leaving his juniors to seek elsewhere as

---

[19] Nor do such considerations of inclusive fitness always skew investments toward the youngest. A mother's altruism toward an unhealthy infant with slim chances of surviving to reproduce are predicted to be less than her altruism toward a healthy and mature child.

they could. But younger brothers quickly came to demand more nearly equal shares and a share for each, and in this they were supported by the local Nyakyusa courts (Gulliver, p. 18).

Consistent with Trivers' hypothesis, the increase in land values fostered not only sibling rivalry but father-son conflict. Again, in Gulliver's words:

> A second locus of conflict is in the father-son relationship. Whereas formerly a son was not dependent on his father for agricultural or residential land (for he easily acquired land in the new village of his contemporaries), now he is primarily dependent on his father ... (Sons) allege that a father expects too much work and subordination and gives too small shares in the joint enterprise. Fathers allege the exact reverse (Gulliver, p. 19).

4.3. Conflict between fathers and mothers

The male-female difference in reproductive biology – the enormous costs that reproduction imposes on a woman relative to a man, for instance – implies that mothers and fathers would disagree about quality/quantity trade-offs in fertility: mothers favor quality; fathers, quantity. Males and females differ in the size and number of sex cells (gametes) they produce. Indeed gamete size is what defines males and females. The lifetime production of the male gamete (sperm) numbers in the billions, while that of the female gamete (eggs) numbers in the hundreds. More importantly, female mammals invest more in offspring than do males, and this is especially true for humans. Owing to our outsized brains, childbirth is far more traumatic for women than for other female primates. While a man can at least in principle "go forth and multiply," a woman can only "go forth and add" – and with great cost.

Trivers (1972) argued that this sex imbalance in minimal requirements for parental investment creates a backdrop for mother-father conflict over child quality versus quantity. Total reproductive effort consists of investing in existing children and producing new ones – including effort to attract new mates. Men benefit relatively more than women from the latter reproductive pursuit.

Further, except in unusual circumstances, a mother is always certain her offspring is a genetic relative, whereas a putative father could in principle harbor doubt. A straightforward adjustment of Hamilton's rule to reflect this uncertainty implies a lower value of paternal relative to maternal altruism.[20]

While prominent in biological analyses, these basic facts frequently get glossed over in economic models. While some early models of the economics of the family, notably Becker's (1981) analyses of the sexual division of labor, paid explicit attention to biological differences between men and women, later economic models of household

---

[20] For further discussion of theory and evidence pertaining to paternity uncertainty, see, e.g., Hrdy (1981) and Cox (2003).

behavior usually ascribed nothing special to being a father versus a mother; each may have well been "persons 1 and 2," and indeed are often referred to as such.

Such agnosticism about sex differences needlessly ties economists' hands, for each of these "biological basics" – sex differences in investment costs and paternity uncertainty – imply that mothers would be expected to behave more altruistically toward children than fathers. Had these off-the-shelf "bio-foundations" been incorporated in a vintage model of household allocation, such a framework would have turned out to have tremendous predictive power. Indeed, maternal favoritism has been found in dozens of studies of intra-household allocation (for instance see surveys by Strauss and Thomas, 1995 and Haddad, Hoddinott, and Alderman, 1997). What is rather astonishing is how the results are usually presented; there is generally little discussion about how it is always the mother who invests more. Instead, and in keeping with the standard "person 1–person 2" approach, economists merely note that the "preferences" of the spouses appear to "differ," and that the "unitary" model of household decision-making can be rejected. From a biological perspective, such verbiage is unduly circuitous, to say the least. But more important, economists could generate useful extensions of their approach to household bargaining by paying attention to biological traits, which relate the strength of mother-father conflict to things like cultural practices connected with paternity confidence, marriage and mating markets and a host of other variables pertinent to biology.

4.4. Marriage and 'mate guarding'

A biologically based view of marriage differs markedly from most economics-based analyses, which emphasize gains from trade between husbands and wives, utility gains from pair bonding, the sharing of public goods, and the like. In contrast, and in raw form, the biological view is that marriage is a system of "mate guarding" arranged by mutually suspicious spouses (especially husbands) and their relatives, to monitor the fidelity of each spouse. (For a discussion of this view for various species, see, e.g., Birkhead, 2000.) Since paternity is uncertain, husbands have an incentive to monitor their wives' activities to insure that they are investing in children that are indeed biological relatives. In addition, since ovulation is hidden, husbands (so the theory goes) have to be more vigilant than, say, male chimpanzees, who are only interested in guarding females when they are in estrus, that is, the days when they display outward signs of being fertile.

Wives have an incentive to monitor husbands too, but for a different reason. Husbands who seek outside mating opportunities divert resources from their wife's offspring, toward individuals who are not her genetic relatives. Further, the fitness costs associated with a spouse's infidelity are generally different for husbands versus wives. From the husband's perspective, cuckoldry, i.e., raising an unrelated child thought to be a genetic relative, entails potentially enormous fitness costs. From the wife's perspective, a husband's philandering need not entail such an extreme downside in terms of fitness costs. Hence, the infamous "double standard" pertaining to sexual fidelity that prevails in nearly all cultures, where female infidelity is punished more heavily and more strenuously guarded against than male infidelity. Such mate guarding takes the form of onerous restrictions in women's rights, sequestering, chaperoning, regulations on women's market work, and so forth. In extreme form, such guarding can be injurious to health and well-being or even life threatening. For instance, female circumcision can be interpreted as an attempt to discourage female infidelity by reducing capacity for sexual pleasure, and domestic violence a weapon wielded by husbands for controlling the social lives of their spouses. Thus mate guarding is implicated in extensive, worldwide public health problems. The World Health Organization (2000), for example, estimates that between 100 and 140 million women and girls in 28 countries have experienced some form of genital mutilation, including clitoridectomy (removal of the entire clitoris) and infibulation (sewing the vagina shut in order to insure virginity).

Evolutionary psychologists argue that jealousy is an emotion intimately related to mate guarding, and sex differences in mate guarding concerns have been found to play out with respect to corresponding differences in how jealousy is experienced. Buss et al. (1992) find that male jealousy tends to be triggered by the prospect of sexual infidelity on the part of their mate, whereas female jealousy tends to be ignited by emotional infidelity, that is, the prospect that their mate is cultivating serious romantic involvement elsewhere. This accords with sex differences in the costs of infidelity: while the worst-case scenario for the male is cuckoldry, the worst-case scenario for the female is desertion.

4.5. In-laws and support for grandchildren

Seldom do in-laws get mentioned in economic models of marital matching and gains from trade. Nor is there much concern about whether such matches occur ceremoniously or not. In contrast, a mate guarding perspective places in-laws and ceremony front and center. The public nature of marriage helps enlist extended kin, friends, and gossip networks of all description in the task of enforcing fidelity of the spouses. In all cultures, marriage is an exceedingly public event; elopement is generally quite rare.

One prediction about in-law altruism that emanates from considerations of mate guarding and paternity uncertainty is that relatives from the husband's side of the family might be expected to be more prone to condition their gifts and help upon their ability to monitor their child's spouse. Maternal grandmothers, for instance, are always certain that their grandchildren are biologically related to them, whereas paternal grandmothers might not be. So financial transfers from a maternal grandmother might be less sensitive to her grandchild's geographic distance than financial transfers from a paternal grandmother, since paternal grandmothers who live close by would presumably face lower costs of monitoring their daughters-in-law.

Duflo (2003) finds empirical evidence consistent with differential altruism between maternal and paternal grandmothers in the context of an interesting natural experiment, South African pension reform. After the end of apartheid, in an attempt to address racial imbalances in pensions, the South African government increased cash transfers to the elderly (Case and Deaton, 1998). Many South African households are multigenerational, with grandparents and grandchildren living under one roof. Duflo examined the impact of pension changes on nutrition indicators for grandchildren (weight for height and height for age) and found positive and significant effects in but one case – where grandchildren co-resided with their maternal grandmother.

Related evidence in a different context was found by Sear et al. (2002), who examined the relationship between the availability of kin and child mortality in rural Gambia. As in Duflo (2003), the maternal grandmother was the only grandparent whose presence mattered for child outcomes. In contrast (and despite the villages being patrilocal) loss of kin from the father's side of the family had no significant effect on child mortality.

By no means do these case studies comprise any sort of consensus evidence for maternal versus paternal grandmotherly largesse. Indeed, a recent study by Hamoudi and Thomas (2005) shows that, once living arrangements are treated as endogenous, it turns out that, for one component of consumption (girls' clothing), the altruism of grand*fathers* toward granddaughters appears stronger than that of grandmothers.

What the Duflo and Hamoudi–Thomas papers *do* illustrate are the both the key strengths of the economic approach and the potential for further progress by integration of biological considerations. First, with respect to the strength of the economic approach: each paper gives exacting attention to the distinction between correlation and causality and lays out clearly the assumptions necessary to identify the effects of pension income. Further, Duflo in particular derives rather ingenious methods for dealing with various endogeneity problems (for instance, by focusing on child height-for-weight outcomes within households and comparing how siblings born before pension reform fared relative to their post-pension-reform counterparts).

Second, with respect to how evolutionary biology can contribute: neither Duflo nor Hamoudi–Thomas provide detailed discussion of why splitting grandparents along maternal/paternal lines might matter in and of itself. Indeed, the former paper incorporates such a split and the latter does not. Nor does economics provide much guidance for specification, since what matters most is pension eligibility. It is here that considerations of evolutionary biology can pick up where economics leaves off, by providing exacting logic as to why and how a maternal-paternal split among grandparents could matter for the specification.

4.6. The Trivers–Willard hypothesis

Duflo's (2003) study of grandparental transfers and South African pension reform reveals another intriguing demographic pattern, which is that grandmotherly largesse is directed at granddaughters not grandsons. Such a finding is arguably consistent with another biology-based theory of family behavior, the so-called Trivers–Willard hypothesis, named after Trivers and his mathematician co-author, Dan Willard, from a 1973 paper of theirs (Trivers and Willard, 1973).

The Trivers–Willard hypothesis has to do with how parents might favor the production of, and investment in, sons versus daughters, and how such favoritism might vary with parental socioeconomic status. Consider a marriage market that is somewhat polygynous (perhaps socially sanctioned, perhaps only *de facto*), with high-status males having opportunities for garnering multiple mates and low-status ones at risk of not mating at all. Extremely poor parents concerned with their reproductive legacy would favor daughters, on the grounds that sons might not produce any grandchildren, while even poor daughters could reproduce (either in a monogamous or polygynous marriage) and perhaps advance their status via marriage as well. Conversely, the sons of extremely rich parents have the wherewithal to attract multiple spouses and thus produce several grandchildren.

The Trivers–Willard hypothesis was formulated for analyzing sex ratios at birth, but the approach can also be used to analyze boy–girl disparities in parental investments in children, as noted, for example, by Edlund (1999).

An illustration of how low-status families might bias investments toward daughters is provided in Cronk's (1989) anthropological study of East African pastoralists, the Mukugodo of Kenya. The Mukugodo occupy the very lowest rung of the status hierarchy in the regional – and somewhat polygynous – marriage market, and they intermarry with their richer neighbors.

Cronk finds a pronounced pro-female bias in sex ratios at birth and among children aged 0–4; among the latter, daughters outnumber sons 3 to 2. Moreover, daughters have higher reproductive success than sons; nearly all daughters reproduce, but many sons do not, and completed fertility is 25 percent higher for daughters compared to sons. Further, Cronk finds evidence of pro-daughter biased parental investments. Among children aged 0–4 taken to a nearby Catholic health clinic, Mukugodo daughters are over-represented relative to their proportion in the population (58 percent of the population but 64 percent of the visits). Among the non-Mukugodo children, the figures are reversed (daughters make up 49 percent of the population but only 45 percent of the visits to the clinic).

Similar patterns were found in a study of Hungarian Gypsies (Bereczkei and Dunbar, 1997) who, like the Mukugodo, had opportunities to intermarry with wealthier neighbors (the Hungarian population). Gypsies were found to invest more heavily in daughters than sons compared to their Hungarian counterparts. Bereczkei and Dunbar found pro-daughter bias in several indicators of production and investment: sex ratio at birth, frequency of abortion, duration of breastfeeding and years of education.

What about bias toward sons among the relatively wealthy? A case study from nineteenth-century northern India reported in Hrdy (1999) represents a possible example:

> Selective elimination of daughters first attracted attention in the West during the years of the British Raj. Nineteenth-century travelers visiting Rajasthan and Uttar Pradesh in northern India remarked on the rarity of seeing girls among any of the elite clans. It was assumed that as part of purdah the daughters of these proud descendants of warrior-kings were kept in seclusion. "I have been nearly four years in India and never beheld any women but those in attendance as servants in European families, the low caste wives of petty shopkeepers and (dancing) women," wrote Fanny Parks in her 1850 travelogue through northern India. It did not occur to the observer that *there were no daughters...* Among the most elite clans such as

the Jhareja Rajputs and the Bedi Sikhs – known locally as the "daughter destroyers" – censuses confirmed the near total absence of daughters; lesser elites killed only later born daughters. Overall, including lower-ranking clans who kept some or all daughters, sex ratios in the region were as high as 400 little boys surviving for every 100 girls (p. 326).

Hrdy prefaces this account with an explanation along the lines of the Trivers–Willard hypothesis:

In patriarchal social systems, a wealthy son finds himself in control of productive resources that women need. He will be in a position to attract multiple mates. In a stratified society such as Rajasthan's, families seeking social advancement compete among themselves to amass a dowry large enough to secure a place for their daughter in an elite household. This brings a prestigious alliance for parents along with the prospect of well-endowed grandsons. Should calamity strike, it is the only prospect for descendants surviving at all. Thus does son preference among elites lead to hypergamy, the custom by which women marry men of higher status. At the top of the hierarchy, however, hypergamy dooms daughters. There is no higher-ranking family for them to marry into (p. 325).

We hasten to add that there are several other (arguably dominant) factors that can lead to favoritism of sons over daughters (or *vice versa*), which have little to do with Trivers–Willard effects. For instance, support from adult children is the predominant form of old-age support in the developing world (Nugent, 1985) and for a farm family, investment in sons may have higher returns than investment in daughters (see e.g. Cain, 1977).[21]

Further, the Trivers–Willard hypothesis is not uncontroversial. For instance, Freese and Powell (1999) find little support for Trivers–Willard effects in data on parental investments in adolescents in the United States. In contrast, Norberg (2004) found a slight but precisely measured difference in sex ratios at birth favoring the production of boys when the mother was living with a spouse or partner at the time of conception or birth. This is consistent with the Trivers–Willard hypothesis since, all else equal, fathers' presence would be correlated with resources for investment in the child.

One possible reason for disparities across studies could be that sample sizes in typical household surveys are too small to shed much light on possible Trivers–Willard effects. Recently, Almond and Edlund (2006) examined US natality data for 1983–2001 for 48 million births. Like Norberg, they find evidence consistent with the Trivers–Willard hypothesis. For instance, they find that married mothers (as well as better educated mothers) are more likely to give birth to male offspring.

Another conceivable reason for mixed results with United States data is that the Trivers–Willard hypothesis is one of extremes, derived within the context of at least

---

[21] A recent crosscurrent in the sex ratio debate is the possible role of Hepatitis B in affecting sex ratios at birth (Oster, 2005), a controversial hypothesis that has been challenged by Das Gupta (2005).

a somewhat polygynous marriage market. Accordingly, it is not clear that a developed economy is the most appropriate testing ground. There is definitely more potential for exploring further the possibility of Trivers–Willard effects in developing countries.

Sex ratio at birth is but one component of the Trivers–Willard hypothesis, since parents can and do make decisions about how much to invest in children once they are born. (Almond and Edlund, for example, found that, in addition to contributing to the chances of bearing a son, a mother's being married reduced the risk of infant mortality for male children.) Parents in some places nowadays can also practice sex-specific abortion, and infanticide and neglect were always available as a means to control the sex composition of families. The famous problem of the "100 million missing women," actively publicized by Amartya Sen, is evidence of the leeway that parents have for influencing sex ratios. While much of this bias is no doubt caused by preference for the old-age support that sons provide in patrilineal, agrarian societies, Sen (2001) notes that sex preference is not always biased toward boys. Pondering the significant variation in sex ratios and sex-specific child mortality across individual Indian regions and states, he also expresses puzzlement that high income is not necessarily associated with absence of anti-female bias. Yet such patterns suggest it might be worthwhile considering the Trivers–Willard hypothesis, though Sen makes no mention of it.

Nor does Esther Duflo mention Trivers–Willard in her (2003) study discussed above, though her finding of favoritism toward girls might be interpreted in light of such effects. From the perspective of poor families, the ending of Apartheid, and possibilities for decreased social stratification could open up new opportunities for female hypergamy.

In one of the few papers in economics that explicitly refers to Trivers–Willard effects, Edlund (1999) illuminates the possibility for pernicious dynamics – via household bargaining effects – that would serve to perpetuate the low status of women. Assuming, as much evidence indicates, that a wife's power within marriage is influenced by parental wealth, female hypergamy implies lower bargaining power of wives relative to their husbands. If such imbalance stifles a mother's capacity to provision daughters (as, for example, the empirical work of Thomas (1994) appears to indicate) then Trivers–Willard effects could contribute to intergenerational hysteresis in the lowered status of women.

The economic development literature has a long tradition of investigating the treatment of sons versus daughters in the family (for examples of careful and thorough reviews, see Behrman, 1997 and Strauss and Thomas, 1995). But there is little work on how such favoritism could interact with the constellation of variables pertinent to the Trivers–Willard hypothesis, including familial socioeconomic status within the marriage market, the inherent polygynousness of that market, and sex-specific patterns in exogamy and inheritance of status. The interplay between Trivers–Willard effects and household bargaining as explicated by Edlund (1999) would have obvious implications for extended family and kin networks, since they would affect, among other things, the relative incomes of the kin from the wives' versus husbands' side of the family and the scarcity of marriageable daughters relative to sons.

4.7. Evolutionary perspectives on interactions with non-kin, boundedness of human groups and risk sharing

As we have seen, when it comes to the analysis of *kin* relations, economics and evolutionary biology have often been like two ships passing in the night. Cross-fertilization of ideas has been lacking, to the detriment of the economics of the family especially, and we hope that this chapter will help speed the bridging of the two disciplines. In contrast, however, when it comes to analysis of *non-kin* relations there has already been profitable trade between the two fields, with biologists borrowing useful concepts from economics and *vice versa*. (For a recent review of this lively and productive literature, see Fehr and Fischbacher, 2003.)

Analyses of problems of cooperation between non-kin (or between, say, firms or nations) was already well underway in economics and political science before biologists broached the subject. Economists had been using insights from game theory – the prisoner's dilemma in particular – long before biologist Robert Trivers published his seminal work on reciprocal altruism in 1971. Trivers posed a question similar to Hamilton's (1964) query, but with a twist: "Can a gene that impels someone to assist a non-relative prevail under natural selection?" The answer, at least in principle, is of course a qualified "yes," as long as some form of fitness-enhancing payback is prompted by such altruistic acts. Ten years later, the interdisciplinary efforts of a biologist (Hamilton, again) and a political scientist (Robert Axelrod) produced a landmark study of the problem of cooperation among non-relatives using a repeated prisoner's dilemma framework (Axelrod and Hamilton, 1981).

Biologist John Maynard Smith borrowed insights from game theory starting in the early 1970s (e.g., Maynard Smith, 1974), added to the theory, then economists, starting with Daniel Friedman (1991), began borrowing and adding to Maynard Smith's framework. The result of this cross-fertilization, evolutionary game theory, has of course become a vibrant discipline all its own.

Early analyses of prisoner's dilemma games concentrated on individual choice of strategies, where homogeneous players decided whether to cooperate with one another or not. An insight added by Maynard Smith was to imagine heterogeneous, fixed "types," say, "hawks" and "doves," who were born to defect or cooperate, respectively. Consider random pairings, where two doves enjoy the fruits of cooperation, two hawks muddle through with mutual defection, and hawk–dove pairings generate plunder for hawks and crumbs for doves. Imagine too that hawks and doves leave descendants who tend to inherit their traits, and that the richer the parent, the more offspring it leaves.

Since defection is the dominant strategy in a prisoner's dilemma, hawks would eventually drive doves to extinction. But suppose there were some marking that honestly signaled whether someone was a hawk or dove. No sane dove would pair off with a hawk; they would seek out each other to enjoy the cooperative life. That would leave hawks the relatively meager rewards of mutual defection and eventually it would be hawks who would be driven extinct, leaving a society of doves living in cooperative peace.

Imagine, though, that one day a mutant appears who shatters the idyll: a hawk disguised as a dove. He and his descendants would go marauding through the population of doves until no true dove were left – only hawks in dove's clothing, living the Hobbesian life of mutual defection. An alternative to this scenario, however, might be that, though every bird looks the same, for a price one could get a glimpse into its soul to verify whether it was truly hawk or dove. Such conditions could support a heterogeneous population of hawks and doves, with equilibrium proportions determined by the costs versus benefits of screening. To mix metaphors, this cat-and-mouse game involving signaling, screening, and concerns about cheating provided fertile ground for the work of evolutionary psychologists Leda Cosmides and John Tooby, who argue that human mental modules have evolved with the express purpose of detecting cheaters and signaling cooperativeness (Cosmides and Tooby, 1992). Cosmides and Tooby argue that the ubiquity of prisoners' dilemma problems and the high stakes associated with success or failure with them, would have led, over the many thousands of years of human evolution, to dedicated, and finely honed, cognitive tools designed for navigating the potentially treacherous waters of social life. Their "mental module" approach can be likened to the dedicated language acquisition modules in the brains of toddlers. Linguist and evolutionary psychologist Steven Pinker argues that language is just too important an adaptation to be relegated to learning from scratch; hard-wired language acquisition modules that facilitate the absorption of complex grammatical and syntactical processes give individuals an advantage for surviving and reproducing (Pinker, 1994).

Likewise, Cosmides and Tooby argue that similar mental modules exist for solving problems of social exchange, such as the detection of cheaters. Perhaps their best known experiment involves the effects of content on the ability to comprehend the nuances of logical problems. Their idea is that people are a lot smarter at solving problems expressed in the very concrete and pressing terms of detecting cheaters than they are at solving logically identical problems that are expressed without the cheater-detection backdrop. These results indicate, in their view, that though human minds are somewhat poorly equipped to handle abstract problems concerning necessary and sufficient conditions, they are in contrast naturally adept at solving problems concerning the social contract.

Indeed, some evolutionary psychologists have advanced the hypothesis that possessing the cognitive wherewithal to succeed in the practice of social intrigue conferred distinct adaptive advantages and that intelligence and language are human adaptations for social exchange. This proposition is known as the "Machiavellian intelligence" hypothesis (Humphrey, 1988). Why might these ideas from evolutionary psychology matter for networks of mutual support? A key reason has to do with the subtleties of "cheater detection" modules. Presumably, since these adaptations are likely to have evolved in small groups, cues obtained from face-to-face contact are likely to have played a significant role in social exchange among non-kin. Casual acquaintance "A" proposes a cooperative venture with non-relative "B." "B" listens and watches intently for cues connected with dishonesty: sweating, failure to maintain eye contact, dryness of mouth and hoarseness of voice, excessive blinking, etc. If detection of cheating matters, the formation of far-flung support networks with non-kin is predicted to be far dicier than the formation of support networks with kin (since the dictates of Hamilton's rule can at least partially facilitate the latter). Accordingly, we would expect that geographic propinquity (and perhaps middlemen) would play a more significant role in non-kin support networks. We would also expect to see a higher prevalence of non-kin support (relative to kin support) in places with higher population densities.

4.7.1. Human groups for risk sharing and production

A key function of cooperation among rural households is the sharing of idiosyncratic risks that can befall families. The response of private transfers to income fluctuations and calamities caused by things like droughts and pestilence has occupied much of the literature dealing with support networks. How large might we expect the typical risk-sharing network to be? Might there be limits on the size of networks? How might opportunities for increased division of labor in production affect risk-sharing networks? We argue below that evolutionary considerations can provide fresh insight into comparatively neglected problems in economic analyses of group behavior.

Much of the existing empirical literature on risk-sharing in economics pays little attention to the size of informal risk-sharing groups. For example, these groups have been alternately envisioned as: the extended family (Altonji, Hayashi, and Kotlikoff, 1992); the village (Townsend, 1994); subsets of states in the United States (Asdrubali, Sorensen, and Yosha, 1996); the entire United States (Mace, 1991); even the whole world (Lewis, 1996). The lack of attention to group size in this literature stems from its emphasis on the complete set of possible means by which households deal with risk – not just the use of informal groups, but borrowing, drawing from savings, sales of durable goods, and so forth. The tide is beginning to change, however, and economists are beginning to give increased attention to inherent limits in network and group size (see, for example, Fafchamps and Quisumbing, this volume). Still, economists can avail themselves of useful evolutionary insights on the limitations of network size. We begin by recognizing that many activities besides risk-sharing – including work, leisure, defense and governance – take place within groups. Second, we start with a motivating example of a natural experiment that illustrates how limitations on group size can conceivably constrain production.

One problem in determining the effectiveness of group size in production is that all we can usually observe are endogenously determined, equilibrium values. Lin's (1990) study of collectivization in China and agricultural output is less prone to this problem because group size was, to a large extent, exogenously determined. After the communist takeover in 1949, small, family-run farms were liberated from their corrupt landlords and family farm work was consolidated in various forms of cooperatives, where labor and other inputs were pooled among households. Cooperative schemes ran the gamut from the "mutual aid team" (4 or 5 households), the "elementary cooperative" (20–30 households), to the "advanced cooperative" (150–200 households). Collectives were allowed to coalesce voluntarily. Later on we will discuss the potential evolutionary significance of the maximum values 150–200.

Lin reports that the early stages of collectivization, from 1952 through 1958, saw a substantial gain – over 25 percent – in agricultural output. Further consolidation was mandated by the Great Leap Forward, initiated in 1958, and the average commune size ballooned to 5000 households, and agricultural output collapsed. The sharp reduction in productivity is consistent with a binding network constraint, in which the cohesiveness of the production group is destroyed.[22] On the risk-sharing front as well, too large a group can thwart the objective of harmonious consumption from a common pot. Witness the failed Utopian societies of the nineteenth century, or the spate of defunct hippie communes from the 1960s. Usually, effective risk-sharing requires a small group. For example, Lomnitz's ethnography of reciprocal networks in a Mexico City shantytown indicates a maximum size of 6 households, with an average size of 3.65 families per network. In their study of risk-sharing in the Philippines, Fafchamps and Lund (2003) find that mutual insurance, primarily provided in the form of informal loans between households, takes place not at the village level, but instead among much smaller groups of friends and relatives. The costs of maintaining group cohesiveness is likely to increase with the size of the group. In the realm of both risk-sharing and teamwork, groups can be beset with the problem of free-riding. What can be done to mitigate the problem? There are basically three options:

(1) the group can try to screen out those likely to cheat,
(2) it can attempt to alter individual preferences to make them less prone to moral hazard, or
(3) the group can invent incentives and systems of monitoring that make cheating less likely.

Economists have devoted the most attention to the third option. For example, Kimball (1988) and Coate and Ravallion (1993) investigate trigger strategies that can help keep reciprocal relationships together. Coate and Ravallion consider an infinite horizon, repeated, non-cooperative game in which two individuals attempt to insure one another from random shocks to income. As discussed in earlier sections of this Chapter, they emphasize the implementability constraint – a condition that insures that utility from immediate defection is always less than utility from continued cooperation. The prediction from the Coate and Ravallion model is that mutual aid will only be responsive to income shortfalls up to a point, since the requirements of extremely large contributions would violate the implementability constraint. As discussed earlier, private transfers follow a non-linear relationship with the earnings of the potential recipient. They are at first responsive to income shortfalls, then flatten out.

---

[22] Lin argues that the unwieldy size of the communes was not the root cause of the output collapse, however. He points to a rule change implemented during the Great Leap Forward that eradicated previous rights to withdraw from a commune. Lin argues that this rule change ruined work incentives, and points to evidence that agricultural productivity did not recover once communes returned to their smaller size but retained their compulsory membership rules.

Kimball limits his investigation to full, rather than partial, risk-sharing, but considers the possibility of more than just two risk-sharers and the implications of increased group size. The larger the risk-sharing group, the bigger the gains from cooperation and the larger the penalties from defection. But once formed, larger groups are harder to maintain, since defection would be relatively attractive for those with lucky group members, who would otherwise have to share their windfalls with too many others. Fafchamps (1992) presents a detailed treatment of a variety of features of mutual insurance systems in pre-industrial society in a unified framework that emphasizes findings from the theory of repeated games. He and others have also applied game theoretic considerations to incentive problems in work teams. For example, a partnership in which output is split among n workers would be expected to be beset with free-rider problems, since each worker would reap only one-nth of the fruits of his or her efforts. Fafchamps shows how subsistence insurance can generate better incentives than full income pooling. Repeated games can lead to self-enforcing agreements and help overcome the moral hazard problem (Telser, 1980; Radner, 1986). Becker (1992) has argued that the problems of commitment emphasized in game-theoretic approaches to strategic interactions, such as those described above, are exaggerated because they ignore the possibility that habits of commitment and loyalty can be deliberately inculcated.

If we recognize the prospect that risk-sharers and teammates can engage in "bonding," that is, activity that enhances the functionality and cohesiveness of a small group, then the relationship between group size constraints and functionality becomes more transparent. Rotemberg (1994) pursues the idea that bonding can affect performance in the workplace. He cites evidence from the "Hawthorne experiments," a classic study in organizational behavior from the 1930s, which investigated worker behavior in Western Electric's Hawthorne plant. In one group of experiments, increased time for worker socializing was linked to increased productivity. Increased friendliness among workers was cited as the reason for the increased output. If there are costs to cultivating feelings of altruism toward an individual, as envisioned by Mulligan (1997) and Rotemberg, then the costs of developing a cohesive group will increase with its size.[23] Platteau (1991) cites a different example of bonding, in the context of risk-sharing, among the !Kung San, hunter-gatherers who live in the Kalahari. The !Kung San practice *hxaro*, a system of hunger insurance that is characterized by sharing with far-flung kin, both fictive and real. The initiation of a hxaro relationship is highly ritualized and time-consuming, involving a staggered gift exchange between two persons for a year or longer. The ceremonial gifts are intended to inculcate bonds of friendship. Stack's (1970) ethnography of low-income Blacks living outside Chicago documents the same principle, called "swapping": "Since an object is offered with the intent of obligating the receiver over a period of time, two individuals rarely simultaneously exchange things. Little or no premium

---

[23] A countervailing argument is advanced by Kandel and Lazear (1992), however. They argue that peer pressure might be more effective in larger groups, because shirking can potentially arouse the ire of more persons. They do acknowledge though, that after some point increases in group size would undermine the quality of interpersonal relationships and the strength of peer pressure.

is placed upon immediate compensation; time has to pass before a counter-gift or a series of gifts can be repaid. While waiting for repayments, participants in exchange are compelled to trust one another" (p. 41). Similar patterns have been documented in Lomnitz's (1977) study of networks in a Mexican shantytown and in Mauss' (1950 (1990)) comparative study of gift giving and exchange.

4.7.2. Group size constraints can create trade-offs between risk-sharing and specialization in production

Carol Stack's (1970) ethnography documents the demands that risk-sharing networks make on their participants, increasing the costs of participating in other social spheres, such as work life. Resources devoted to the maintenance of ties within the sharing network leave little room for relationships outside of the network, making it difficult for network members to straddle the demands of the network and those of a life outside the network:

> Marriage and its accompanying expectations of a home, a job, and a family built around the husband and wife have come to stand for an individual's desire to break out of poverty. It implies the willingness of an individual to remove himself from the daily obligations of his kin network. People in The Flats recognize that one cannot simultaneously meet kin obligations and the expectations of a spouse (Stack, p. 113).

Horne (1918) and Jevons (1918) discuss the difficulty that family networks posed for Indian industrial development in the early twentieth century. Horne notes that a leading cause of labor scarcity in urban jute mills was the return of workers to their homes to look after their "domestic affairs." Much more recent analysis of this problem is provided by Munshi and Rosenzweig (2006) who find that the prospect of losing the risk-mitigating services of caste networks can impede migration and mobility.

In a completely different context, a study by Berman (2000) documents the tremendous influence of participation in religious schooling (Yeshiva) among Ultra-Orthodox Jews in Israel. Ultra-Orthodox communities practice mutual insurance to an extreme degree. They also have pathologically low rates of rates of labor force participation of prime-aged males, which is indicative of a trade-off between risk-sharing and production. Berman argues that the poverty is a sacrifice used to insure that those with insufficient commitment to the religious community are screened out, following the logic of the model of religious behavior proposed by Iannaccone (1992). This example highlights the potential trade-off between the size of a production team and the size of a risk-sharing clan.

Considerations of limitations of group size and possible trade-offs between producing and risk-sharing have novel implications for the impact of public income distribution on productivity. The standard argument is that public safety nets are antithetical to productivity, since, for example, income guarantees can sap incentives to work. In contrast, the considerations of group size above suggest that these safety nets, by obviating the need to form risk-sharing networks, can allow people to concentrate their limited group management resources on the problem of team production. If the production technology exhibits increasing returns in the number of workers, and public safety nets make it possible to field larger work teams, production and incomes rise. Group size limitations could play a significant role in the transition from agriculture to manufacturing. The number of workers per establishment is an order of magnitude larger in manufacturing than in either agriculture or services. Seen in this light, public safety nets might help facilitate industrialization. For example, Mokyr (1985) conjectures that the early existence of public safety nets in England may have contributed to its industrialization:

> Indeed, it could be maintained that the Poor Laws, despite their obvious flaws (in particular their non-uniformity), may have had some overall positive effects on the Industrial Revolution. A comparison of Ireland, which had no formal system of poor relief prior to 1838, bears this out... The social safety net provided by the Poor Laws allowed English individuals to take risks that would have been imprudent in Ireland where starvation was still very much a possibility. In societies without such laws, self-insurance in the form of large families and liquid assets were widely held (p. 14).

The approach also provides an explanation for the policy focus on state-provided redistribution during the process of rapid transition from agriculture to manufacturing, as that which occurred in the Soviet Union during the middle part of the twentieth century. The state usurps the duties of the clan, so that limited capacity for group formation can be concentrated within the realm of the work team.

4.7.3. Group size constraints and group lending

Group lending schemes, such as the Grameen Bank, could be modeled in a similar manner to that of risk-sharing. The key idea is that the emotional and intellectual resources necessary to sustain a viable group loan compete with other activities, such as production, which also require these resources. One puzzle in the literature is the nearly exclusive targeting of group lending to women. Typical explanations are usually concerned with the incidence of poverty and liquidity constraints, but these indicators cannot explain the pronounced gender divide in group lending that is usually observed. For example, 94 percent of Grameen Bank borrowers are women (Pitt and Khandker, 1998). Group lending started in rural Bangladesh, where female work for wages is rare and women tend to be secluded in accordance with Islamic law. Such seclusion could contribute to the success of group lending since in such isolated settings constraints on network size are unlikely to be binding.

5. Conclusion

A survey is supposed to take stock of a literature and point out fruitful future directions. All along in writing this Chapter we have assumed (perhaps pretended is a better word) that our reader is a novice in the sub-discipline – a graduate student, perhaps, or someone who has just switched into the field. What would we recommend to such a person in order to make the most of his or her research efforts? We will now go out on a limb and attempt to give some advice to such readers, with the proviso that all research prospects are at least somewhat risky, and that our advice may not be suitable for all and accordingly that other opinions should be sought out.

With those caveats in mind, we think that research on income effects in inter-household transfers is beginning to hit sharply diminishing returns. The specter of complete crowding out, which energized the empirical literature during the past few decades, appears to be fading as a policy concern and an intellectual problem. Not that private behavioral responses of transfer networks can be safely ignored by policymakers; far from it. It is just that the marginal value of an additional case study of income effects from a standard data set, such as the LSMS, is likely to be relatively low.

Instead, the current focus on income effects should give way to an intensified scrutiny of all of the other variables that researchers typically consider – but rarely think very hard about – in studies of inter-household transfers, particularly the effects of age, gender and kin-relationship. For instance, we need to understand better why it is that in some countries intergenerational transfers are used primarily for old-age support, whereas in others, they are targeted primarily to younger households. The question matters, for example, for reasons of economic growth: the more resources are directed toward the young, in the form of human capital investments, the better are the prospects for growth.

We also need to have a better understanding of gender differences in kinship relations and support. Too often, economic models are gender blind, populated with generic parents and children and "spouses 1 and 2," rather than husbands, wives, fathers, mothers, sons and daughters. This modeling choice is in part a legacy of the nature of economics, which has little to say about gender in and of itself – such as the nature of motherhood versus fatherhood. But as we argue in Section 4, evolutionary biology *does* have a lot to say about these things, and that combining insights from that discipline, in order to refine our notions of familial utility functions, could open new doors for understanding demographic influences in inter-household transfers. Likewise, evolutionary biology has a lot to say about human cooperation among non-kin, and researchers can now avail themselves of an exceedingly well-developed literature that has enormous potential for shedding new light on problems of mutual assistance and cooperation that extends beyond strictly familial ties.

References

Akresh, R. (2004). "Adjusting household structure: School enrollment impacts of child fostering in Burkina Faso." Working paper No. 89. BREAD, Washington, DC.

Akresh, R. (2005). "Risk, network quality, and family structure: Child fostering decisions in Burkina Faso." Discussion paper No. 902. Economic Growth Center, Yale University.

Albarran, P., Attanasio, O.P. (2002). "Do public transfers crowd out private transfers? Evidence from a randomized experiment in Mexico." Discussion paper No. 2002-6. World Institute for Development Economics, Helsinki, Finland.

Alderman, H., Paxson, C. (1994). "Do the poor insure? A synthesis of the literature on risk and consumption in developing countries". In: Bacha, D. (Ed.), Economics in a Changing World. vol. 4: Development, Trade and the Environment. Macmillan, London.

Almond, D., Edlund, L. (2006). Trivers–Willard at birth and one year: Evidence from US natality data 1983–2001." Working paper No. 2006-09. Institute for Social and Economic Research and Policy, Columbia University.

Altonji, J.G., Ichimura, H. (2000). "Estimating derivatives in nonseparable models with limited dependent variables." Mimeo. Yale University, New Haven, CT.

Altonji, J.G., Hayashi, F., Kotlikoff, L.J. (1992). "Is the extended family altruistically linked? Direct tests using micro data". American Economic Review 82, 1177–1198.

Altonji, J.G., Hayashi, F., Kotlikoff, L.J. (1997). "Parental altruism and inter-vivos transfers: Theory and evidence". Journal of Political Economy 105, 1121–1166.

Amelina, M., Chirbuca, D., Knack, S. (2004). "Mapped in or mapped out? The Romanian poor in interhousehold and community networks." Working paper No. 34. The World Bank, Washington, DC.

Anderson, S., Baland, J.M. (2002). "The economics of ROSCAs and intrahousehold resource allocation". Quarterly Journal of Economics 117, 963–995.

Andreoni, J. (1989). "Giving with impure altruism: Applications to charity and Ricardian equivalence". Journal of Political Economy 97, 1447–1468.

Aryeetey, E., Udry, C. (1997). "The characteristics of informal financial markets in sub-Saharan Africa". Journal of African Economies 6, 161–203.

Asdrubali, P., Sorensen, B.E., Yosha, O. (1996). "Channels of interstate risk sharing: United States 1963–1990". Quarterly Journal of Economics 111, 1081–1110.

Attanasio, O.P. (2002). "Consumption and income inequality: What we know and what we can learn from it." Mimeo. University College London. Presented to the Society of Economic Dynamics, New York.

Attanasio, O.P., Rios Rull, J.-V. (2000). "Consumption smoothing in island economies: Can public insurance reduce welfare?" European Economic Review 44, 1225–1258.

Attanasio, O.P., Rios Rull, J.-V. (2003). "Consumption smoothing and extended families". In: Dewatripont, M., Hansen, L., Turnovsky, S. (Eds.), Advances in economics and econometrics: Theory and Applications, Eighth World Congress. In: Econometric Society Monographs, vol. 37. Cambridge Univ. Press, Cambridge, UK.

Attanasio, O.P., Szekely, M. (2004). "Wage shocks and consumption variability in Mexico during the 1990s". Journal of Development Economics 73, 1–25.

Axelrod, R. (1984). The Evolution of Cooperation. Basic Books, New York.

Axelrod, R., Hamilton, W. (1981). "The evolution of cooperation". Science 211, 1390–1396.

Baland, J.-M., Platteau, J.-P. (2000). Halting Degradation of Natural Resources: Is there a Role for Rural Communities? Oxford Univ. Press, Oxford.

Bamberger, M., Kaufmann, D., Velez, E., Parris, S. (1992). "Interhousehold transfers and survival strategies of low-income households: Experiences from Latin America, Asia, and Africa." Mimeo. The World Bank, Washington, DC.

Barr, A. (2001). "Cooperation and shame." Working paper WPS/2002-05. Centre for the Study of African Economies, Department of Economics, University of Oxford.

Barr, A., Oduro, A. (2002). "Ethnic fractionalization in an African labor market". Journal of Development Economics 68, 355–379.

Barro, R.J. (1974). "Are government bonds net wealth?" Journal of Political Economy 82, 1095–1117.

Basu, K. (1986). "One kind of power". Oxford Economic Papers 38, 259–282.

Becker, G.S. (1974). "A theory of social interactions". Journal of Political Economy 82, 1063–1093.

Becker, G.S. (1981). A Treatise on the Family. Harvard Univ. Press, Cambridge, MA.

Becker, G.S. (1992). "Habits, addictions, and traditions". Kyklos 45, 327–346.

Becker, G.S. (1993). "Nobel lecture: The economic way of looking at behavior". Journal of Political Economy 101, 385–409.

Becker, G.S., Tomes, N. (1979). "An equilibrium theory of the distribution of income and intergenerational mobility". Journal of Political Economy 87, 1153–1189.

Behrman, J.R. (1997). "Intrahousehold distribution and the family". In: Stark, O., Rosenzweig, M. (Eds.), Handbook of Population and Family Economics. Elsevier, New York.

Bereczkei, T., Dunbar, R.I.M. (1997). "Female-biased reproductive strategies in a Hungarian Gypsy population". Proceedings: Biological Sciences 264, 17–22.

Berman, E. (2000). "Sect, subsidy and sacrifice: An economist's view of ultra-orthodox Jews". Quarterly Journal of Economics 115, 905–953.

Bernheim, B.D., Shleifer, A., Summers, L.H. (1985). "The strategic bequest motive". Journal of Political Economy 93, 1045–1076.

Besley, T., Coate, S., Loury, G. (1993). "The economics of rotating savings and credit associations". American Economic Review 83, 792–810.

Binswanger, H.P., McIntire, J. (1987). "Behavioral and material determinants of production relations in land-abundant tropical agriculture". Economic Development and Cultural Change 36, 73–99.

Birkhead, T. (2000). Promiscuity. Harvard Univ. Press, Cambridge, MA.

Bloch, F., Rao, V. (2002). "Terror as a bargaining instrument: A case study of dowry violence in rural India". American Economic Review 92, 1029–1043.

Blume, L.E. (2002). Stigma and Social Control: The Dynamics of Social Norms. Cornell Univ. Press, Ithaca, NY.

Browning, M., Chiappori, P.-A., Lechene, V. (2004). "Collective and unitary models: A clarification." Working paper 2004-15. Centre for Applied Microeconometrics, University of Copenhagen.

Buss, D.M., Larsen, R.J., Westen, D., Semmelroth, J. (1992). "Sex differences in jealousy: Evolution, physiology and psychology". Psychological Science 3, 251–255.

Cain, M. (1977). "The economic activities of children in a village in Bangladesh". Population and Development Review 13, 201–227.

Case, A., Deaton, A. (1998). "Large cash transfers to the elderly in South Africa". Economic Journal 108, 1330–1361.

Chiappori, P.-A. (1988). "Rational household labor supply". Econometrica 56, 63–90.

Chiappori, P.-A. (1992). "Collective labor supply and welfare". Journal of Political Economy 100, 437–467.

Clarke, G., Wallsten, S.J. (2003). "Do remittances act like insurance? Evidence from a natural disaster in Jamaica." Mimeo. Development Research Group, The World Bank.

Coate, S., Ravallion, M. (1993). "Reciprocity without commitment: Characterization and performance of informal insurance arrangements". Journal of Development Economics 40, 1–24.

Cochrane, J.H. (1991). "A simple test of consumption insurance". Journal of Political Economy 99, 957–976.

Conning, J., Udry, C. (2007). "Rural financial markets in developing countries". In: Evenson, R., Pingali, P., Schultz, T.P. (Eds.), The Handbook of Agricultural Economics, vol. 3. Elsevier, New York.

Cosmides, L., Tooby, J. (1992). "Cognitive adaptations for social exchange". In: Barkow, J., Cosmides, L., Tooby, J. (Eds.), The Adapted Mind. Oxford Univ. Press, New York.

Cox, D. (1987). "Motives for private income transfers". Journal of Political Economy 95, 508–546.

Cox, D. (1990). "Intergenerational transfers and liquidity constraints". Quarterly Journal of Economics 105, 187–217.

Cox, D. (2003). "Private transfers within the family: Mothers, fathers, sons and daughters". In: Munnell, A., Sunden, A. (Eds.), Death and Dollars: The Role of Gifts and Bequests in America. Brookings Institution Press, Washington, DC.

Cox, D. (2004). "Private interhousehold transfers in Vietnam in the early and late 1990s". In: Glewwe, P., Dollar, D. (Eds.), Economic Growth and Household Welfare: Policy Lessons from Vietnam. The World Bank, Washington, DC.

Cox, D. (2007). "Biological basics and the economics of the family". Journal of Economic Perspectives 21, 91–208.

Cox, D., Edwards, A., Ureta, M. (2003). "International migration, remittances, and schooling: Evidence from El Salvador". Journal of Development Economics 72, 429–461.

Cox, D., Eser, Z., Jimenez, E. (1998). "Motives for private transfers over the life-cycle: An analytical framework and evidence for Peru". Journal of Development Economics 55, 57–80.

Cox, D., Galasso, E., Jimenez, E. (2006). "Private transfers in a cross section of developing countries." WP 2006-2. Center for Retirement Research, Boston College, Chestnut Hill, MA.

Cox, D., Hansen, B.E., Jimenez, E. (2004). "How responsive are private transfers to income? Evidence from a laissez-faire economy". Journal of Public Economics 88, 2193–2219.

Cox, D., Jimenez, E. (1992). "Social security and private transfers in developing countries: The case of Peru". World Bank Economic Review 6, 155–169.

Cox, D., Jimenez, E. (1998). "Risk sharing and private transfers: What about urban households?" Economic Development and Cultural Change 46, 621–637.

Cox, D., Jimenez, E., Okrasa, W. (1997). "Family safety nets and economic transition: A study of worker households in Poland". Review of Income and Wealth 43, 191–209.

Cox, D., Rank, M.R. (1992). "Inter-vivos transfers and intergenerational exchange". Review of Economics and Statistics 74, 305–314.

Cronk, L. (1989). "Low socioeconomic status and female-biased parental investment: The Mukogodo example". American Anthropologist 91, 414–429.

Das Gupta, M. (2005). "Explaining Asia's 'missing women': A new look at the data". Population and Development Review 31, 529–535.

Dawkins, R. (1976). The Selfish Gene. Oxford Univ. Press, Oxford.

de la Briere, B., Sadoulet, E., de Janvry, A., Lambert, S. (2002). "The roles of destination, gender, and household composition in explaining remittances: An analysis for the Dominican Sierra". Journal of Development Economics 68, 309–328.

Deaton, A., Paxson, C. (1994). "Intertemporal choice and inequality". Journal of Political Economy 102, 384–394.

Dercon, S. (2002). "Income risk, coping strategies, and safety nets". World Bank Research Observer 17, 141–166.

Dercon, S., Krishnan, P. (2003). "Risk sharing and public transfers". Economic Journal 113, C86–C94.

Dercon, S., Bold, T., DeWeerdt, J., Pankhurst, A. (2004). "Group-based funeral insurance in Ethiopia and Tanzania." Working paper 227. The Centre for the Study of African Economies, Oxford University, Oxford, UK.

Duflo, E.C. (2003). "Grandmothers and granddaughters: Old age pension and intra-household allocation in South Africa". World Bank Economic Review 17, 1–25.

Durlauf, S.N., Fafchamps, M. (2005). "Social capital". In: Durlauf, S.N., Aghion, P. (Eds.), Handbook of Economic Growth. Elsevier, Amsterdam.

Eaton, J., Gersovitz, M. (1981). "Debt with potential repudiation: Theoretical and empirical analysis". Review of Economic Studies XLVIII, 289–309.

Eaton, J., Gersovitz, M., Stiglitz, J.E. (1986). "The pure theory of country risk". European Economic Review 30, 481–513.

Edlund, L. (1999). "Son preference, sex ratios, and marriage patterns". Journal of Political Economy 107, 1275–1304.

Ellsworth, L. (1989). "Mutual insurance and non-market transactions among farmers in Burkina Faso." Unpublished PhD thesis. University of Wisconsin, Madison, WI.

Ensminger, J. (2004). "Social network analysis in an African ethnographic setting: Implications for economic experiments and the study of corruption." Presented at the CSAE Conference on Networks, Behavior, and Poverty, Oxford University, Oxford.

Evans, D. (2005). "The spillover impacts of Africa's orphan crisis." Presented at CSAE Conference 2006, Oxford University, Oxford.

Evans, D., Miguel, E.A. (2005). "Orphans and schooling in Africa: A longitudinal analysis." Paper C05-143. Center for International Development and Economics Research, University of California, Berkeley, CA.

Evans-Pritchard, E.E. (1940). The Nuer. Clarendon Press, Oxford.

Fafchamps, M. (1992). "Solidarity networks in pre-industrial societies: Rational peasants with a moral economy". Economic Development and Cultural Change 41, 147–174.

Fafchamps, M. (1996). "The enforcement of commercial contracts in Ghana". World Development 24, 427–448.

Fafchamps, M. (1999). "Risk sharing and quasi-credit". Journal of International Trade and Economic Development 8, 257–278.

Fafchamps, M. (2000). "Ethnicity and credit in African manufacturing". Journal of Development Economics 61, 205–235.

Fafchamps, M. (2001). "Networks, communities, and markets in Sub-Saharan Africa: Implications for firm growth and investment". Journal of African Economies 10, 109–142.

Fafchamps, M. (2002). "Spontaneous market emergence". Topics in Theoretical Economics 2 (1): article 2. Berkeley Electronic Press at http://www.bepress.com.

Fafchamps, M. (2003). "Ethnicity and networks in African trade". Contributions to Economic Analysis and Policy 2 (1): article 14. Berkeley Electronic Press at http://www.bepress.com.

Fafchamps, M. (2004). Market Institutions in Sub-Saharan Africa. MIT Press, Cambridge, MA.

Fafchamps, M., Gubert, F. (2007a). "The formation of risk sharing networks". Journal of Development Economics 83, 326–350.

Fafchamps, M., Gubert, F. (2007b). "Contingent loan repayment in the Philippines." Economic Development and Cultural Change, in press.

Fafchamps, M., Lund, S. (2003). "Risk sharing networks in rural Philippines". Journal of Development Economics 71, 261–287.

Fafchamps, M., Minten, B. (1999). "Relationships and traders in Madagascar". Journal of Development Studies 35, 1–35.

Fafchamps, M., Minten, B. (2002). "Returns to social network capital among traders". Oxford Economic Papers 54, 173–206.

Fehr, E., Fischbacher, U. (2003). "The nature of human altruism". Nature 425, 785–791.

Fehr, E., Gachter, S. (2000). "Fairness and retaliation: The economics of reciprocity". Journal of Economic Perspectives 14, 159–181.

Fisman, R. (2001a). "Estimating the value of political connections". American Economic Review 91, 1095–1102.

Fisman, R. (2001b). "Trade credit and productive efficiency in developing economies". World Development 29, 311–321.

Foster, A.D., Rosenzweig, M.R. (2001). "Imperfect commitment, altruism and the family: Evidence from transfer behavior in low-income rural areas". Review of Economics and Statistics 83, 389–407.

Frank, R.H. (1988). Passions within Reason: The Strategic Role of the Emotions. W.W. Norton, New York.

Frankenberg, E., Lillard, L., Willis, R.J. (2002). "Patterns of intergenerational transfers in southeast Asia". Journal of Marriage and the Family 64, 627–641.

Freese, J., Powell, B. (1999). "Sociobiology, status, and parental investment in sons and daughters: Testing the Trivers–Willard hypothesis". American Journal of Sociology 106, 1704–1743.

Friedman, D. (1991). "Evolutionary games in economics". Econometrica 59, 637–666.

Gambetta, D. (1993). The Sicilian Mafia: The Business of Private Protection. Harvard Univ. Press, Cambridge, MA.

Gertler, P., Gruber, J. (2002). "Insuring consumption against illness". American Economic Review 92, 51–70.

Glick, J.E. (1999). "Economic support from and to extended kin: A comparison of Mexican Americans and Mexican immigrants". International Migration Review 33, 745–765.

Granovetter, M.S. (1985). "Economic action and social structure: The problem of embeddedness". American Journal of Sociology 91, 481–510.

Granovetter, M.S. (1995a). "The economic sociology of firms and entrepreneurs". In: Portes, A. (Ed.), The Economic Sociology of Immigration: Essays on Networks, Ethnicity, and Entrepreneurship. Russell Sage Foundation, New York, pp. 128–165.

Granovetter, M.S. (1995b). Getting a Job: A Study of Contacts and Careers, second ed. Univ. of Chicago Press, Chicago, IL.

Greif, A. (1993). "Contract enforceability and economic institutions in early trade: The Maghribi traders' coalition". American Economic Review 83, 525–548.

Grimard, F. (1997). "Household consumption smoothing through ethnic ties: Evidence from Cote d'Ivoire". Journal of Development Economics 53, 391–422.

Grossman, H.I., Van Huyck, J.B. (1987). "Nominally denominated sovereign debt, risk shifting, and reputation." Working paper No. 2259. NBER, Cambridge, MA.

Guiso, L., Japelli, T. (1991). "Intergenerational transfers and capital market imperfections: Evidence from a cross section of Italian households". European Economic Review 35, 103–120.

Gulliver, P.H. (1961). "Land shortage, social change, and social conflict in East Africa". Journal of Conflict Resolution 5, 16–26.

Haddad, L., Hoddinott, J., Alderman, H. (Eds.) (1997). Intrahousehold Resource Allocation in Developing Countries. Johns Hopkins Univ. Press, Baltimore, MD.

Hall, R.E. (1978). "Stochastic implications of the life cycle-permanent income hypothesis: Theory and evidence". Journal of Political Economy 86, 971–987.

Hamilton, W.D. (1964). "The genetical evolution of social behavior, I and II". Journal of Theoretical Biology 7, 1–52.

Hamoudi, A., Thomas, D. (2005). "Pension income and the well-being of children and grandchildren: New evidence from South Africa." Working paper No. CCPR-043-05. California Center for Population Research, UCLA.

Hoddinott, J. (1992). "Rotten kids or manipulative parents: Are children old age security in western Kenya?" Economic Development and Cultural Change 40, 545–565.

Horne, E.A. (1918). "Industrial development and the labour question". Bengal Economic Journal 2, 181–193.

Hrdy, S.B. (1981). The Woman that Never Evolved. Harvard Univ. Press, Cambridge, MA.

Hrdy, S.B. (1999). Mother Nature. Ballantine Books, New York.

Humphrey, N.K. (1988). "The social function of intellect". In: Byrne, R.W., Whiten, A. (Eds.), Machiavellian Intelligence: Social Expertise and the Evolution of Intellect in Monkeys, Apes and Humans. Clarendon Press, Oxford.

Iannaccone, L.R. (1992). "Sacrifice and stigma: Reducing free-riding in cults, communes, and other collectives". Journal of Political Economy 100, 271–291.

Ishikawa, T. (1974). "Imperfection in the capital market and the institutional arrangement of inheritance". Review of Economic Studies 41, 383–404.

Jensen, R.T. (2004). "Do private transfers 'displace' the benefits of public transfers? Evidence from South Africa". Journal of Public Economics 88, 89–112.

Jevons, H.S. (1918). "The labor question as affecting industrial development in India". Bengal Economic Journal 2, 194–204.

Kandel, E., Lazear, E. (1992). "Peer pressure and partnerships". Journal of Political Economy 100, 801–817.

Kandori, M. (1992). "Social norms and community enforcement". Review of Economic Studies 59, 63–80.

Kaplan, H. (1994). "Evolutionary and wealth flows among the elderly: Empirical tests and new models". Population and Development Review 20, 753–791.

Kaufmann, D., Lindauer, D. (1986). "A model of income transfers for the urban poor". Journal of Development Economics 22, 337–350.

Kazianga, H. (2006). "Motives for household private transfers in Burkina Faso". Journal of Development Economics 79, 73–117.

Kennan, J. (1986). "The economics of strikes". In: Ashenfelter, O., Layard, R. (Eds.), Handbook of Labor Economics, vol. II. Elsevier Science, New York.

Killingsworth, M. (1983). Labor Supply. Cambridge Univ. Press, New York.

Kimball, M. (1988). "Farmers' cooperatives as behavior toward risk". American Economic Review 78, 224–232.

Kletzer, K.M. (1984). "Asymmetries of information and LDC borrowing with sovereign risk". Economic Journal 94, 287–307.

Kochar, A. (1997). "An empirical investigation of rationing constraints in rural credit markets in India". Journal of Development Economics 53, 339–371.

Kochar, A. (1999). "Smoothing consumption by smoothing income: Hours-of-work responses to idiosyncratic agricultural shocks in rural India". Review of Economics and Statistics 81, 50–61.

Kotlikoff, L.J., Razin, A., Rosenthal, R.W. (1990). "A strategic altruism model in which Ricardian equivalence does not hold". Economic Journal 100, 1261–1268.

Kotlikoff, L.J., Spivak, A. (1981). "The family as an incomplete annuities market". Journal of Political Economy 89, 372–391.

Kotlikoff, L.J., Summers, L.H. (1981). "The role of intergenerational transfers in aggregate capital accumulation". Journal of Political Economy 89, 706–732.

Krishnan, P., Sciubba, E. (2004). "Endogenous network formation and informal institutions in village economies." Working paper in economics No. 462. University of Cambridge, UK.

Krueger, A.B., Maleckova, J. (2003). "Education, poverty and terrorism: Is there a causal connection?" Journal of Economic Perspectives 17, 119–144.

Ksoll, C. (2007). "Family networks and orphan caretaking in Tanzania." Mimeo. Economic Growth Center, Yale University, New Haven.

Kuhn, R., Stillman, S. (2004). "Understanding interhousehold transfers in a transition economy: Evidence from Russia". Economic Development and Cultural Change 53, 131–156.

LaFerrara, E. (2003). "Kin groups and reciprocity: A model of credit transactions in Ghana". American Economic Review 93, 1730–1751.

Lee, R. (1997). "Intergenerational relations and the elderly". In: Wachter, K.W., Finch, C.E. (Eds.), Between Zeus and the Salmon: The Biodemography of Longevity. National Academy Press, Washington, DC.

Lee, Y.-J., Parish, W.L., Willis, R.J. (1994). "Sons, daughters, and intergenerational support in Taiwan". American Journal of Sociology 99, 1010–1041.

Lewis, K.K. (1996). "What can explain the apparent lack of international risk-sharing?" Journal of Political Economy 104, 267–297.

Ligon, E., Thomas, J.P., Worrall, T. (2001). "Informal insurance arrangements with limited commitment: Theory and evidence in village economies". Review of Economic Studies 69, 209–244.

Lillard, L.A., Willis, R.J. (1997). "Motives for intergenerational transfers: Evidence from Malaysia". Demography 34, 115–134.

Lin, J.Y. (1990). "Collectivization and China's agricultural crisis in 1959–1961". Journal of Political Economy 98, 1228–1252.

Lomnitz, L.A. (1977). Networks and Marginality: Life in a Mexican shantytown. Academic Press, New York.

Lucas, R.E., Stark, O. (1985). "Motivations to remit: Evidence from Botswana". Journal of Political Economy 93, 901–918.

Lund, S. (1996). "Credit and risk-sharing networks in the rural Philippines." Unpublished PhD thesis. Food Research Institute, Stanford University, Stanford, CA.

Lundberg, S., Pollak, R. (1993). "Separate spheres and the marriage market". Journal of Political Economy 101, 988–1010.

Mace, B. (1991). "Full insurance in the presence of aggregate uncertainty". Journal of Political Economy 99, 928–956.

Maitra, P., Ray, R. (2003). "The effect of transfers on household expenditure patterns and poverty in South Africa". Journal of Development Economics 71, 23–49.

Manser, M., Brown, M. (1980). "Marriage and household decision-making: A bargaining analysis". International Economic Review 21, 31–44.

Mauss, M. (1950). The Gift. W.W. Norton, New York (reprinted 1990).

Maynard Smith, J. (1974). "The theory of games and the evolution of animal conflicts". Journal of Theoretical Biology 47, 209–221.

McElroy, M., Horney, M. (1981). "Nash-bargained household decisions: Toward a generalization of the theory of demand". International Economic Review 22, 333–349.

McKernan, S.-M., Pitt, M.M., Moskowitz, D. (2005). "Use of the formal and informal financial sectors: Does gender matter? Empirical evidence from rural Bangladesh." Working paper 3491. Policy Research, The World Bank, Washington, DC.

Miller, D., Paulson, A. (2000). "Informal insurance and moral hazard: Gambling and remittances in Thailand." Contributed paper No. 1463, Econometric Society World Congress.

Mokyr, J. (1985). Why Ireland Starved: Quantitative and Analytical History of the Irish Economy, 1800–1850. Harper Collins, New York.

Montgomery, J.D. (1991). "Social networks and labor-market outcomes: Toward an economic analysis". American Economic Review 81, 1408–1418.

Morduch, J. (1995). "Income smoothing and consumption smoothing". Journal of Economic Perspectives 9, 103–114.

Morduch, J. (1999). "Between the state and the market: Can informal insurance patch the safety net?" World Bank Research Observer 14, 187–207.

Mulligan, C. (1997). Parental Priorities and Economic Inequality. Univ. of Chicago Press, Chicago.

Munshi, K. (2003). "Networks in the modern economy: Mexican migrants in the US labor market". Quarterly Journal of Economics 118, 549–599.

Munshi, K., Rosenzweig, M. (2006). "Why is mobility in India so low? Social insurance, inequality, and growth." Discussion paper, Yale University.

Murgai, R., Winters, P., Sadoulet, E., de Janvry, A. (2002). "Localized and incomplete mutual insurance". Journal of Development Economics 67, 245–274.

Nash, J.F. (1950). "The bargaining problem". Econometrica 18, 155–162.

Nash, J.F. (1953). "Two-person cooperative games". Econometrica 21, 128–140.

Norberg, K. (2004). "Partnership status and the human sex ratio at birth". Proceedings of the Royal Society: Biological Sciences 271, 2403–2410.

Nugent, J. (1985). "The old-age security motive for fertility". Population and Development Review 11, 75–97.

Oster, E. (2005). "Hepatitis B and the case of the missing women". Journal of Political Economy 113, 1163–1216.

Pinker, S. (1994). The Language Instinct. Harper Collins, New York.

Pitt, M.M., Khandker, S.R. (1998). "The impact of group-based credit programs on poor households: Does the gender of participants matter?" Journal of Political Economy 106, 958–996.

Platteau, J.-P. (1991). "Mutual insurance as an elusive concept in traditional rural communities". Journal of Development Studies 33, 764–796.

Platteau, J.-P. (1994a). "Behind the market stage where real societies exist: Part I. The role of public and private order institutions". Journal of Development Studies 30, 533–577.

Platteau, J.-P. (1994b). "Behind the market stage where real societies exist: Part II. The role of moral norms". Journal of Development Studies 30, 753–815.

Platteau, J.-P., Abraham, A. (1987). "An inquiry into quasi-credit contracts: The role of reciprocal credit and interlinked deals in small-scale fishing communities". Journal of Development Studies 23, 461–490.

Platteau, J.-P., Gaspart, F. (2003). "The risk of resource misappropriation in community-driven development". World Development 31, 1687–1703.

Posner, R.A. (1980). "A theory of primitive society, with special reference to law". Journal of Law and Economics XXIII, 1–53.

Radner, R. (1986). "Repeated partnership games with imperfect monitoring and no discounting". Review of Economic Studies 53, 43–57.

Raub, W., Weesie, J. (1990). "Reputation and efficiency in social interactions: An example of network effects". American Journal of Sociology 96, 626–654.

Raut, L.K., Tran, L.H. (2005). "Parental human capital investment and old-age transfers from children: Is it a loan contract or reciprocity for Indonesian families?" Journal of Development Economics 77, 389–414.

Ravallion, M., Chaudhuri, S. (1997). "Risk and insurance in village India: Comment". Econometrica 65, 171–184.

Ravallion, M., Dearden, L. (1988). "Social security in a moral economy: An empirical analysis for Java". Review of Economics and Statistics 70, 36–44.

Rodriguez, E.R. (1996). "International migrants' remittances in the Philippines". Canadian Journal of Economics 29, S427–S432.

Rose, E. (2001). "Ex ante and ex post labor supply response to risk in a low-income area". Journal of Development Economics 64, 371–388.

Rosenzweig, M.R. (1988). "Risk, implicit contracts and the family in rural areas of low-income countries". Economic Journal 98, 1148–1170.

Rosenzweig, M.R., Stark, O. (1989). "Consumption smoothing, migration, and marriage: Evidence from rural India". Journal of Political Economy 97, 905–926.

Rosenzweig, M.R., Wolpin, K.I. (1985). "Specific experience, household structure, and intergenerational transfers: Farm family land and labor arrangements in developing countries". Quarterly Journal of Economics 100, 961–987.

Rotemberg, J. (1994). "Human relations in the workplace". Journal of Political Economy 102, 684–717.

Schoeni, R.F. (1997). "Private interhousehold transfers of money and time: New empirical evidence". Review of Income and Wealth 43, 423–448.

Sear, R., Steele, F., McGregor, I., Mace, R. (2002). "The effects of kin on child mortality in rural Gambia". Demography 39, 43–63.

Secondi, F. (1997). "Private monetary transfers in rural China: Are families altruistic?" Journal of Development Studies 33, 487–511.

Sen, A. (2001). "The many faces of misogyny". The New Republic 225, 35–40.

Stack, C.B. (1970). All Our Kin. Harper and Row, New York.

Strauss, J., Thomas, D. (1995). "Human resources: Empirical modeling of household and family decisions". In: Behrman, J., Srinivasan, T.N. (Eds.), Handbook of Development Economics. Elsevier Science, Amsterdam.

Suri, T. (2005). "Spillovers in village consumption: Testing the extent of partial insurance." Discussion paper, Yale University.

Taylor, C.R. (2000). "The old-boy network and the young-gun effect". International Economic Review 41, 871–891.

Telser, L.G. (1980). "A theory of self-enforcing agreements". Journal of Business 53, 27–44.

Thomas, D. (1994). "Like father, like son, like mother, like daughter: Parental resources and child height". Journal of Human Resources 29, 950–988.

Townsend, R.M. (1994). "Risk and insurance in village India". Econometrica 62, 539–591.

Townsend, R.M. (1995). "Consumption insurance: An evaluation of risk-bearing systems in low-income economies". Journal of Economic Perspectives 9, 83–102.

Trivers, R.L. (1972). "Parental investment and sexual selection". In: Campbell, B. (Ed.), Sexual Selection and the Descent of Man. Aldine, Chicago, IL.

Trivers, R.L. (1974). "Parent-offspring conflict". American Zoologist 14, 249–264.

Trivers, R.L., Willard, D.E. (1973). "Natural selection of parental ability to vary sex ratios of offspring". Science 179, 90–92.

Udry, C. (1994). "Risk and insurance in a rural credit market: An empirical investigation in northern Nigeria". Review of Economic Studies 61, 495–526.

Udry, C. (1996). "Gender, agricultural production, and the theory of the household". Journal of Political Economy 104, 1010–1046.

van den Brink, R., Chavas, J.-P. (1997). "The microeconomics of an indigenous African institution: The rotating savings and credit association". Economic Development and Cultural Change 45, 745–772.

Wade, R. (1988). "The management of irrigation systems: How to evoke trust and avoid prisoners' dilemma". World Development 16, 489–500.

World Health Organization (2000). "Female genital mutilation." Fact sheet No. 241.

PART 13

PROGRAM EVALUATION: METHODS AND APPLICATIONS

Chapter 59

EVALUATING ANTI-POVERTY PROGRAMS*

MARTIN RAVALLION

Development Research Group, The World Bank, 1818 H Street, NW, Washington, DC 20433, USA

Contents

* These are the views of the author, and should not be attributed to the World Bank or any affiliated organization. For their comments the author is grateful to Pedro Carneiro, Aline Coudouel, Jishnu Das, Jed Friedman, Emanuela Galasso, Markus Goldstein, Jose Garcia-Montalvo, David McKenzie, Alice Mesnard, Ren Mu, Norbert Schady, Paul Schultz, John Strauss, Emmanuel Skoufias, Petra Todd, Dominique van de Walle and participants at a number of presentations at the World Bank and at an authors' workshop at the Rockefeller Foundation Center at Bellagio, Italy, May 2005.

Handbook of Development Economics, Volume 4
© *2008 Elsevier B.V. All rights reserved*
DOI: 10.1016/S1573-4471(07)04059-4

Abstract

The chapter critically reviews the methods available for the *ex post* counterfactual analysis of programs that are assigned exclusively to individuals, households or locations. The emphasis is on the problems encountered in applying these methods to anti-poverty programs in developing countries, drawing on examples from actual evaluations. Two main lessons emerge. Firstly, despite the claims of advocates, no single method dominates; rigorous, policy-relevant evaluations should be open-minded about methodology, adapting to the problem, setting and data constraints. Secondly, future efforts to draw useful lessons from evaluations call for more policy-relevant data and methods than used in the classic assessment of mean impact for those assigned to the program.

Keywords

impact evaluation, antipoverty programs, selection bias, experimental methods, randomization, nonexperimental methods, instrumental variables, external validity

JEL classification: H43, I38, O22

1. Introduction

Governments, aid donors and the development community at large are increasingly asking for hard evidence on the impacts of public programs claiming to reduce poverty. Do we know if such interventions really work? How much impact do they have? Past "evaluations" that only provide qualitative insights into processes and do not assess outcomes against explicit and policy-relevant counterfactuals are now widely seen as unsatisfactory.

This chapter critically reviews the main methods available for the counterfactual analysis of programs that are assigned exclusively to certain observational units. These may be people, households, villages or larger geographic areas. The key characteristic is that some units get the program and others do not. For example, a social fund might ask for proposals from communities, with preference for those from poor areas; some areas do not apply, and some do, but are rejected.[1] Or a workfare program (that requires welfare recipients to work for their benefits) entails extra earnings for participating workers, and gains to the residents of the areas in which the work is done; but others receive nothing. Or cash transfers are targeted exclusively to households deemed eligible by certain criteria.

After an overview of the archetypal formulation of the evaluation problem for such assigned programs in the following section, the bulk of the chapter examines the strengths and weaknesses of the main methods found in practice; examples are given throughout, mainly from developing countries. The penultimate section attempts to look forward – to see how future evaluations might be made more useful for knowledge building and policy making, including in "scaling-up" development initiatives. The concluding section suggests some lessons for evaluation practice.

2. The archetypal evaluation problem

An "impact evaluation" assesses a program's performance in attaining well-defined objectives against an explicit counterfactual, such as the absence of the program. An observable outcome indicator, Y, is identified as relevant to the program and time-period over which impacts are expected. "Impact" is the change in Y that can be causally attributed to the program. The data include an observation of Y_i for each unit i in a sample of size n. Treatment status, T_i, is observed, with $T_i = 1$ when unit i receives the program (is "treated") and $T_i = 0$ when not.[2]

The archetypal formulation of the evaluation problem postulates two potential outcomes for each i: the value of Y_i under treatment is denoted Y_i^T while it is Y_i^C under

---

[1] Social funds provide financial support to a potentially wide range of community-based projects, with strong emphasis given to local participation in proposing and implementing the specific projects.

[2] The biomedical connotations of the word "treatment" are unfortunate in the context of social policy, but the near-universal usage of this term in the evaluation literature makes it hard to avoid.

the counterfactual of not receiving treatment.[3] Then unit i gains $G_i \equiv Y_i^T - Y_i^C$. In the literature, G_i is variously termed the "gain," "impact" or the "causal effect" of the program for unit i.

In keeping with the bulk of the literature, this chapter will be mainly concerned with estimating average impacts. The most widely-used measure of average impact is the *average treatment effect on the treated*: $TT \equiv E(G \mid T = 1)$. In the context of an anti-poverty program, TT is the mean impact on poverty amongst those who actually receive the program. One might also be interested in the average treatment effect on the untreated, $TU \equiv E(G \mid T = 0)$ and the combined average treatment effect (ATE):

$$ATE \equiv E(G) = TT \Pr(T = 1) + TU \Pr(T = 0).$$

We often want to know the *conditional* mean impacts, $TT(X) \equiv E(G \mid X, T = 1)$, $TU(X) \equiv E(G \mid X, T = 0)$ and $ATE(X) \equiv E(G \mid X)$, for a vector of covariates X (including unity as one element). The most common method of introducing X assumes that outcomes are linear in its parameters and the error terms (μ^T and μ^C), giving:

$$Y_i^T = X_i \beta^T + \mu_i^T \quad (i = 1, \ldots, n), \tag{1.1}$$
$$Y_i^C = X_i \beta^C + \mu_i^C \quad (i = 1, \ldots, n). \tag{1.2}$$

We define the parameters β^T and β^C such that X is exogenous ($E(\mu^T \mid X) = E(\mu^C \mid X) = 0$).[4] The conditional mean impacts are then:

$$TT(X) = ATE(X) + E(\mu^T - \mu^C \mid X, T = 1),$$
$$TU(X) = ATE(X) + E(\mu^T - \mu^C \mid X, T = 0),$$
$$ATE(X) = X(\beta^T - \beta^C).$$

How can we estimate these impact parameters from the available data? The literature has long recognized that impact evaluation is essentially a problem of *missing data*, given that it is physically impossible to measure outcomes for someone in two states of nature at the same time (participating in a program and not participating). It is as-sumed that we can observe T_i, Y_i^T for $T_i = 1$ and Y_i^C for $T_i = 0$. But then G_i is not directly observable for any i since we are missing the data on Y_i^T for $T_i = 0$ and Y_i^C for $T_i = 1$. Nor are the mean impacts identified without further assumptions; neither $E(Y^C \mid T = 1)$ (as required for calculating TT and ATE) nor $E(Y^T \mid T = 0)$ (as needed for TU and ATE) is directly estimable from the data. Nor do Eqs. (1.1) and (1.2) constitute an estimable model, given the missing data.

---

[3] This formulation of the evaluation problem in terms of potential outcomes in two possible states was proposed by Rubin (1974) (although with an antecedent in Roy, 1951). In the literature, Y_1 or $Y(1)$ and Y_0 or $Y(0)$ are more commonly used for Y^T and Y^C. My notation (following Holland, 1986) makes it easier to recall which group is which, particularly when I introduce time subscripts later.

[4] This is possible since we do not need to isolate the direct effects of X from those operating through omitted variables correlated with X.

With the data that are likely to be available, an obvious place to start is the *single difference* (D) in mean outcomes between the participants and non-participants:

$$D(X) \equiv E\left[Y^T \mid X, T = 1\right] - E\left[Y^C \mid X, T = 0\right]. \tag{2}$$

This can be estimated by the difference in the sample means or (equivalently) the Ordinary Least Squares (OLS) regression of Y on T. For the parametric model with controls, one would estimate (1.1) on the sub-sample of participants and (1.2) on the rest of the sample, giving:

$$Y_i^T = X_i \beta^T + \mu_i^T \quad \text{if } T_i = 1, \tag{3.1}$$

$$Y_i^C = X_i \beta^C + \mu_i^C \quad \text{if } T_i = 0. \tag{3.2}$$

Equivalently, one can follow the more common practice in applied work of estimating a single ("switching") regression for the observed outcome measure on the pooled sample, giving a "random coefficients" specification[5]:

$$Y_i = X_i\left(\beta^T - \beta^C\right)T_i + X_i \beta^C + \varepsilon_i \quad (i = 1, \ldots, n) \tag{4}$$

where $\varepsilon_i = T_i(\mu_i^T - \mu_i^C) + \mu_i^C$. A popular special case in practice is the *common-impact model*, which assumes that $G_i = ATE = TT = TU$ for all i, so that (4) collapses to[6]:

$$Y_i = ATE \cdot T_i + X_i \beta^C + \mu_i^C. \tag{5}$$

A less restrictive version only imposes the condition that the latent effects are the same for the two groups (i.e., $\mu_i^T = \mu_i^C$), so that interaction effects with X remain.

While these are all reasonable starting points for an evaluation, and of obvious descriptive interest, further assumptions are needed to assure unbiased estimates of the impact parameters. To see why, consider the difference in mean outcomes between participants and non-participants (Eq. (2)). This can be written as:

$$D(X) = TT(X) + B^{TT}(X) \tag{6}$$

where[7]:

$$B^{TT}(X) \equiv E\left[Y^C \mid X, T = 1\right] - E\left[Y^C \mid X, T = 0\right] \tag{7}$$

is the bias in using $D(X)$ to estimate $TT(X)$; B^{TT} is termed *selection bias* in much of the evaluation literature. Plainly, the difference in means (or OLS regression coefficient on T) only delivers the average treatment effect on the treated if counterfactual mean outcomes do not vary with treatment, i.e., $B^{TT} = 0$. In terms of the above parametric

---

[5] Equation (4) is derived from (3.1) and (3.2) using the identity: $Y_i = T_i Y_i^T + (1 - T_i)Y_i^C$.

[6] The justification for this specialization of (4) is rarely obvious and (as we will see) some popular estimation methods for Eq. (5) are not robust to allowing for heterogeneity in impacts.

[7] Similarly $B^{TU}(X) \equiv E(Y^T \mid X, T = 1) - E(Y^T \mid X, T = 0)$; $B^{ATE}(X) = B^{TT}(X) \Pr(T = 1) + B^{TU}(X) \Pr(T = 0)$ in obvious notation.

model, this is equivalent to assuming that $E[\mu^C \mid X, T = 1] = E[\mu^C \mid X, T = 0] = 0$, which assures that OLS gives consistent estimates of (5). If this also holds for μ^T then OLS will give consistent estimates of (4). I shall refer to the assumption that $E(\mu^C \mid X, T = t) = E(\mu^T \mid X, T = t) = 0$ for $t = 0, 1$ as "conditional exogeneity of placement." In the evaluation literature, this is also variously called "selection on observables," "unconfounded assignment" or "ignorable assignment," although the latter two terms usually refer to the stronger assumption that Y^T and Y^C are independent of T given X.

The rest of this chapter examines the estimation methods found in practice. One way to assure that $B^{TT} = 0$ is to randomize placement. Then we are dealing with an *experimental evaluation*, to be considered in Section 4. By contrast, in a *nonexperimental (NX) evaluation* (also called an "observational study" or "quasi-experimental evaluation") the program is non-randomly placed.[8] NX methods fall into two groups, depending on which of two (non-nested) identifying assumptions is made. The first group assumes conditional exogeneity of placement, or the weaker assumption of exogeneity of changes in placement with respect to changes in outcomes. Sections 5 and 6 look at single-difference methods while Section 7 turns to double- or triple-difference methods, which exploit data on changes in outcomes and placement, such as when we observe outcomes for both groups before and after program commencement.

The second set of NX methods does not assume conditional exogeneity (either in single-difference or higher-order differences). To remove selection bias based on unobserved factors these methods require some potentially strong assumptions. The main assumption found in applied work is that there exists an *instrumental variable* that does not alter outcomes conditional on participation (and other covariates of outcomes) but is nonetheless a covariate of participation. The instrumental variable thus isolates a part of the variation in program placement that can be treated as exogenous. This method is discussed in Section 8.

Some evaluators prefer to make one of these two identifying assumptions over the other. However, there is no sound *a priori* basis for having a fixed preference in this choice, which should be made on a case-by-case basis, depending on what we know about the program and its setting, what one wants to know about its impacts and (crucially) what data are available.

3. Generic issues in practice

The first problem often encountered in practice is getting the key stakeholders to agree to doing an impact evaluation. There may be vested interests that feel threatened, possibly including project staff. And there may be ethical objections. The most commonly

---

[8] As we will see later, experimental and NX methods are sometimes combined in practice, although the distinction is still useful for expository purposes.

heard objection to an impact evaluation says that if one finds a valid comparison group then this must include equally needy people to the participants, in which case the only ethically acceptable option is to help them, rather than just observe them passively for the purposes of an evaluation. Versions of this argument have stalled many evaluations in practice. Often, some kind of "top-down" political or bureaucratic force is needed; for example, state-level randomized trials of welfare reforms in the US in the 1980s and 1990s were mandated by the federal government.

The ethical objections to impact evaluations are clearly more persuasive if eligible people have been knowingly denied the program for the purpose of the evaluation *and* the knowledge from that evaluation does not benefit them. However, the main reason in practice why valid comparison groups are possible is typically that fiscal resources are inadequate to cover everyone in need. While one might object to that fact, it is not an objection to the evaluation *per se*. Furthermore, knowledge about impacts can have great bearing on the resources available for fighting poverty. Poor people benefit from good evaluations, which weed out defective anti-poverty programs and identify good programs.

Having (hopefully) secured agreement to do the evaluation, a number of problems must then be addressed at the design stage, which this section reviews.

3.1. Is there selection bias?

The assignment of an anti-poverty program typically involves purposive placement, reflecting the choices made by those eligible and the administrative assignment of opportunities to participate. It is likely that many of the factors that influence placement also influence counterfactual outcomes. Thus there must be a general presumption of selection bias when comparing outcomes between participants and non-participants.

In addressing this issue, it is important to consider both observable and unobservable factors. If the X's in the data capture the "non-ignorable" determinants of placement (i.e., those correlated with outcomes) then it can be treated as exogenous conditional on X. To assess the validity of that assumption one must know a lot about the specific program; conditional exogeneity should not be accepted, or rejected, without knowing how the program works in practice and what data are available.

In Eqs. (3) and (4), the X's enter in a linear-in-parameters form. This is commonly assumed in applied work, but it is an *ad hoc* assumption, which is rarely justified by anything more than computational convenience (which is rather lame these days). Under the conditional exogeneity assumption, removing the selection bias is a matter of assuring that the X's are adequately balanced between treatment and comparison observations. When program placement is independent of outcomes given the observables (implying conditional exogeneity) then the relevant summary statistic to be balanced between the two groups is the conditional probability of participation, called the *propensity score*. The propensity score plays an important role in a number of NX methods, as we will see in Section 5.

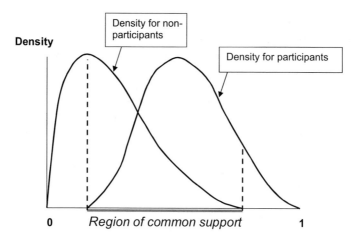

Figure 1. Region of common support.

The region of the propensity scores for which a valid comparison group can be found is termed the *region of common support*, as in Fig. 1. Plainly, when this region is small it will be hard to identify the average treatment effect. This is a potentially serious problem in evaluating certain anti-poverty programs. To see why, suppose that placement is determined by a "proxy-means test" (PMT), as often used for targeting programs in developing countries. The PMT assigns a score to all potential participants as a function of observed characteristics. When strictly applied, the program is assigned if and only if a unit's score is below some critical level, as determined by the budget allocation to the scheme. (The PMT pass-score is non-decreasing in the budget under plausible conditions.) With 100% take-up, there is no value of the score for which we can observe *both* participants and non-participants in a sample of any size. This is an example of what is sometimes called "failure of common support" in the evaluation literature.

This example is a rather extreme. In practice, there is usually some degree of fuzziness in the application of the PMT and incomplete coverage of those who pass the test. There is at least some overlap, but whether it is sufficient to infer impacts must be judged in each case.

Typically, we will have to truncate the sample of non-participants to assure common support; beyond the inefficiency of collecting unnecessary data, this is not a concern. More worrying is that a non-random sub-sample of participants may have to be dropped for lack of sufficiently similar comparators. This points to a trade-off between two sources of bias. On the one hand, there is the need to assure comparability in terms of initial characteristics. On the other hand, this creates a possible sampling bias in inferences about impact, to the extent that we find that we have to drop treatment units to achieve comparability.

All is not lost when there is too little common support to credibly infer impacts on those treated. Indeed, knowing only the local impact in a neighborhood of the cut-off point may well be sufficient. Consider the policy choice of whether to increase a program's budget by raising the "pass mark" in the PMT. In this case, we only need know the impacts in a neighborhood of the pass-mark. Section 6 further discusses "discontinuity designs" for such cases.

So far we have focused on selection bias due to observable heterogeneity. However, it is almost never the case that the evaluator knows and measures all the relevant variables. Even controlling optimally for the X's by nicely balancing their values between treatment and comparison units will leave latent non-ignorable factors – unobserved by the evaluator but known to those deciding participation. Then we cannot attribute to the program the observed $D(X)$ (Eq. (2)). The differences in conditional means could just be due to the fact that the program participants were purposely selected by a process that we do not fully observe. The impact estimator is biased in the amount given by Eq. (7). For example, suppose that the latent selection process discriminates against the poor, i.e., $E[Y^C \mid X, T = 1] > E[Y^C \mid X, T = 0]$ where Y is income relative to the poverty line. Then $D(X)$ will overestimate the impact of the program. A latent selection process favoring the poor will have the opposite effect. In terms of the classic parametric formulation of the evaluation problem in Section 2, if participants have latent attributes that yield higher outcomes than non-participants (at given X) then the error terms in the equation for participants (3.1) will be centered to the right relative to those for non-participants (3.2). The error term in (4) will not vanish in expectation and OLS will give biased and inconsistent estimates. (Again, concerns about this source of bias cannot be separated from the question as to how well we have controlled for *observable* heterogeneity.)

A worrying possibility for applied work is that the two types of selection biases discussed above (one due to observables, the other due to unobservables) need not have the same sign. So eliminating selection bias due to one source need not reduce the total bias, which is what we care about. I do not know of an example from practice, but this theoretical possibility does point to the need to think about the likely *directions of the biases* in specific contexts, drawing on other evidence or theoretical models of the choices underlying program placement.

3.2. Is selection bias a serious concern in practice?

La Londe (1986) and Fraker and Maynard (1987) found large biases in various NX methods when compared to randomized evaluations of a US training program. (Different NX methods also gave quite different results, but that is hardly surprising since they make different assumptions.) Similarly, Glewwe et al. (2004) found that NX methods give a larger estimated impact of "flip charts" on the test scores of Kenyan school children than implied by an experiment; they argue that biases in their NX methods account for the difference. In a meta-study, Glazerman, Levy and Myers (2003) review 12 replication studies of the impacts of training and employment programs on earnings; each study compared NX estimates of impacts with results from a social experiment on the same program. They found large discrepancies in some cases, which they interpreted as being due to biases in the NX estimates.

Using a different approach to testing NX methods, van de Walle (2002) gives an example for rural road evaluation in which a naïve comparison of the incomes of villages that have a rural road with those that do not indicates large income gains when in fact there are none. Van de Walle used simulation methods in which the data were constructed from a model in which the true benefits were known with certainty and the roads were placed in part as a function of the average incomes of villages. Only a seemingly small weight on village income in determining road placement was enough to severely bias the mean impact estimate.

Of course, one cannot reject NX methods in other applications on the basis of such studies; arguably the lesson is that better data and methods are needed, informed by past knowledge of how such programs work. In the presence of severe data problems it cannot be too surprising that observational studies perform poorly in correcting for selection bias. For example, in a persuasive critique of the La Londe study, Heckman and Smith (1995) point out that (amongst other things) the data used contained too little information relevant to eligibility for the program studied, that the methods used had limited power for addressing selection bias and did not include adequate specification tests.[9] Heckman and Hotz (1989) argue that suitable specification tests can reveal the problematic NX methods in the La Londe study, and that the methods that survive their tests give results quite close to those of the social experiment.

The 12 studies used by Glazerman et al. Glazerman, Levy and Myers (2003) provided them with over 1100 observations of paired estimates of impacts – one experimental and one NX. The authors then regressed the estimated biases on regressors describing the NX methods. They found that NX methods performed better (meaning that they came closer to the experimental result) when comparison groups were chosen carefully on the basis of observable differences (using regression, matching or a combination of the two). However, they also found that standard econometric methods for addressing selection bias due to unobservables using a control function and/or instrumental variable tended to *increase* the divergence between the two estimates.

These findings warn against presuming that more ambitious and seemingly sophisticated NX methods will perform better in reducing the total bias. The literature also points to the importance of specification tests and critical scrutiny of the assumptions made by each estimator. This chapter will return to this point in the context of specific estimators.

3.3. Are there hidden impacts for "non-participants"?

The classic formulation of the evaluation problem outlined in Section 2 assumes no interference with the comparison units, which allows us to locate a program's impacts

---

[9] Also see the discussion in Heckman, La Londe and Smith (1999).

amongst only its direct participants. We observe the outcomes under treatment (Y_i^T) for participants $(T_i = 1)$ and the counterfactual outcome (Y_i^C) for non-participants $(T_i = 0)$. The comparison group is unaffected by the program.[10]

This can be a strong assumption in practice. Spillover effects to the comparison group are have been a prominent concern in evaluating large public programs, for which contamination of the control group can be hard to avoid due to the responses of markets and governments, and in drawing lessons for scaling up ("external validity") based on randomized trials (Moffitt, 2003).

To give a rather striking example in the context of anti-poverty programs in developing countries, suppose that we are evaluating a workfare program whereby the government commits to give work to anyone who wants it at a stipulated wage rate; this was the aim of the famous *Employment Guarantee Scheme* (EGS) in the Indian state of Maharashtra and in 2006 the Government of India implemented a national version of this scheme. The attractions of an EGS as a safety net stem from the fact that access to the program is universal (anyone who wants help can get it) but that all participants must work to obtain benefits and at a wage rate that is considered low in the specific context. The universality of access means that the scheme can provide effective insurance against risk. The work requirement at a low wage rate is taken by proponents to imply that the scheme will be self-targeting to the income poor.

This can be thought of as an assigned program, in that there are well-defined "participants" and "non-participants." And at first glance it might seem appropriate to collect data on both groups and compare their outcomes (after cleaning out observable heterogeneity). However, this classic evaluation design could give a severely biased result. The gains from such a program are very likely to spillover into the private labor market. If the employment guarantee is effective then the scheme will establish a firm lower bound to the entire wage distribution – assuming that no able-bodied worker would accept non-EGS work at any wage rate below the EGS wage. So even if one picks the observationally perfect comparison group, one will conclude that the scheme has no impact, since wages will be the same for participants and non-participants. But that would entirely miss the impact, which could be large for both groups.

To give another example, in assessing treatments for intestinal worms in children, Miguel and Kremer (2004) argue that a randomized design, in which some children are treated and some are retained as controls, would seriously underestimate the gains from treatment by ignoring the externalities between treated and "control" children. The design for the authors' own experiment neatly avoided this problem by using mass treatment at the school level instead of individual treatment (using control schools at sufficient distance from treatment schools).

Spillover effects can also arise from the behavior of governments. Indeed, whether the resources made available actually financed the identified project is often unclear. To some degree, all external aid is fungible. Yes, it can be verified in supervision that the

---

[10] Rubin (1980) dubbed it the stable unit treatment value assumption (SUTVA).

proposed sub-project was actually completed, but one cannot rule out the possibility that it would have been done under the counterfactual and that there is some other (infra-marginal) expenditure that is actually being financed by the external aid. Similarly, there is no way of ruling out the possibility that non-project villages benefited through a re-assignment of public spending by local authorities, thus lowering the measured impact of program participation.

This problem is studied by van de Walle and Mu (2007) in the context of a World Bank financed rural-roads project in Vietnam. Relative to the original plans, the project had only modest impact on its immediate objective, namely to rehabilitate existing roads. This stemmed in part from the fungibility of aid, although it turns out that there was a "flypaper effect" in that the aid stuck to the roads sector as a whole. Chen, Mu and Ravallion (2006) also find evidence of a "geographic flypaper effect" for a poor-area development project in China.

3.4. How are outcomes for the poor to be measured?

For anti-poverty programs the objective is typically defined in terms of household income or expenditure normalized by a household-specific poverty line (reflecting dif-ferences in the prices faced and in household size and composition). If we want to know the program's impact on poverty then we can set $Y = 1$ for the "poor" versus $Y = 0$ for the "non-poor."[11] That assessment will typically be based on a set of poverty lines, which aim to give the minimum income necessary for unit i to achieve a given reference utility, interpretable as the minimum "standard of living" needed to be judged non-poor. The normative reference utility level is typically anchored to the ability to achieve cer-tain functionings, such as being adequately nourished, clothed and housed for normal physical activity and participation in society.[12]

With this interpretation of the outcome variable, ATE and TT give the program's impacts on the headcount index of poverty (% below the poverty line). By repeating the impact calculations for multiple "poverty lines" one can then trace out the impact on the cumulative distribution of income. Higher order poverty measures (that penalize inequality amongst the poor) can also be accommodated as long as they are members of the (broad) class of additive measures, by which the aggregate poverty measure can be written as the population-weighed mean of all individual poverty measures in that population.[13]

However, focusing on poverty impacts does not imply that we should use the con-structed binary variable as the dependent variable (in regression equations such as (4)

---

[11] Collapsing the information on living standards into a binary variable need not be the most efficient ap-proach to measuring impacts on poverty; we return to this point.

[12] Note that the poverty lines will (in general) vary by location and according to the size and demographic composition of the household, and possibly other factors. On the theory and methods of setting poverty lines see Ravallion (2005).

[13] See Atkinson (1987) on the general form of these measures and examples in the literature.

or (5), or nonlinear specifications such as a probit model). That entails an unnecessary loss of information relevant to explaining why some people are poor and others are not. Rather than collapsing the continuous welfare indicator (as given by income or expenditure normalized by the poverty line) into a binary variable at the outset it is probably better to exploit all the information available on the continuous variable, drawing out implications for poverty after the main analysis.[14]

3.5. What data are required?

When embarking on any impact evaluation, it is obviously important to know the programs' objectives. More than one outcome indicator will often be identified. Consider, for example, a scheme that makes transfers targeted to poor families conditional on parents making human resource investments in their children.[15] The relevant outcomes comprise a measure of current poverty and measures of child schooling and health status, interpretable as indicators of future poverty.

It is also important to know the salient administrative/institutional details of the program. For NX evaluations, such information is key to designing a survey that collects the right data to control for the selection process. Knowledge of the program's context and design features can also help in dealing with selection on unobservables, since it can sometimes generate plausible identifying restrictions, as discussed further in Sections 6 and 8.

The data on outcomes and their determinants, including program participation, typically come from *sample surveys*. The observation unit could be the individual, household, geographic area or facility (school or health clinic) depending on the type of program. Clearly the data collection must span the time period over which impacts are expected. The sample design is invariably important to both the precision of the impact estimates and how much can be learnt from the survey data about the determinants of impacts. Section 9 returns to this point.

Survey data can often be supplemented with useful other data on the program (such as from the project monitoring data base) or setting (such as from geographic data bases).[16] Integrating multiple data sources (such by unified geographic codes) can be highly desirable.

---

[14] I have heard it argued a number of times that transforming the outcome measure into the binary variable and then using a logit or probit allows for a different model determining the living standards of the poor versus non-poor. This is not correct, since the underlying model in terms of the latent continuous variable is the same. Logit and probit are only appropriate estimators for that model if the continuous variable is unobserved, which is not the case here.

[15] The earliest program of this sort in a developing country appears to have been the *Food-for-Education* program (now called *Cash-for-Education*) introduced by the Government of Bangladesh in 1993. A famous example of this type of program is the *Program for Education, Health and Nutrition* (*PROGRESA*) (now called *Opportunidadas*) introduced by the Government of Mexico in 1997.

[16] For an excellent overview of the generic issues in the collection and analysis of household survey data in developing countries see Deaton (1997).

An important concern is the comparability of the data on participants and non-participants. Differences in survey design can entail differences in outcome measures. Heckman, La Londe and Smith (1999, Section 5.33) show how differences in data sources and data processing assumptions can make large differences in the results obtained for evaluating US training programs. Diaz and Handa (2004) come to a similar conclusion with respect to Mexico's *PROGRESA* program; they find that differences in the survey instrument generate significant biases in a propensity-score matching estimator (discussed further in Section 5), although good approximations to the experimental results are achieved using the same survey instrument.

There are concerns about how well surveys measure the outcomes typically used in evaluating anti-poverty programs. Survey-based consumption and income aggregates for nationally representative samples typically do not match the aggregates obtained from national accounts (NA). This is to be expected for GDP, which includes non-household sources of domestic absorption. Possibly more surprising are the discrepancies found with both the levels and growth rates of private consumption in the NA aggregates (Ravallion, 2003b).[17] Yet here too it should be noted that (as measured in practice) private consumption in the NA includes sizeable and rapidly growing components that are typically missing from surveys (Deaton, 2005). However, aside from differences in what is being measured, surveys encounter problems of under-reporting (particularly for incomes; the problem appears to be less serious for consumptions) and selective non-response (whereby the rich are less likely to respond).[18]

Survey measurement errors can to some extent be dealt with by the same methods used for addressing selection bias. For example, if the measurement problem affects the outcomes for treatment and comparison units identically (and additively) and is uncorrelated with the control variables then it will not be a problem for estimating *ATE*. This again points to the importance of the controls. But even if there are obvious omitted variables correlated with the measurement error, more reliable estimates may be possible using the double-difference estimators discussed further in Section 7. This still requires that the measurement problem can be treated as a common (additive) error component, affecting measured outcomes for treatment and comparison units identically. These may, however, be overly strong assumptions in some applications.

It is sometimes desirable to collect *panel data* (also called longitudinal data), in which both participants and non-participants are surveyed repeatedly over time, spanning a period of expansion in program coverage and over which impacts are expected. Panel data raise new problems, including respondent attrition (another form of selection bias). Some of the methods described in Section 7 do not strictly require panel data, but only observations of both outcomes and treatment status over multiple time periods, but not

---

[17] The extent of the discrepancy depends crucially on the type of survey (notably whether it collects consumption expenditures or incomes) and the region; see Ravallion (2003b).

[18] On the implications of such selective survey compliance for measures of poverty and inequality and some evidence (for the US) see Korinek, Mistiaen and Ravallion (2006).

necessarily for the same observation units; these methods are thus more robust to the problems in collecting panel data.

As the above comments suggest, NX evaluations can be data demanding as well as methodologically difficult. One might be tempted to rely instead on "short cuts" including less formal, unstructured, interviews with participants. The problem in practice is that it is quite difficult to ask counter-factual questions in interviews or focus groups; try asking someone participating in a program: "what would you be doing now if this program did not exist?" Talking to participants (and non-participants) can be a valuable complement to quantitative surveys data, but it is unlikely to provide a credible impact evaluation on its own.

Sometimes it is also possible to obtain sufficiently accurate information on the past outcomes and program participation using *respondent recall*, although this can become quite unreliable, particularly over relatively long periods, depending on the variable and whether there are important memory "markers." Chen, Mu and Ravallion (2006) demonstrate that 10-year recall by survey respondents in an impact evaluation is heavily biased toward more recent events.

4. Social experiments

A social experiment aims to randomize placement, such that all units (within some well-defined set) have the same chance *ex ante* of receiving the program. Unconditional randomization is virtually inconceivable for anti-poverty programs, which policy makers are generally keen to target on the basis of observed characteristics, such as households with many dependents living in poor areas. However, it is sometimes feasible a program assignment that is *partially randomized*, conditional on some observed variables, X. The key implication for the evaluation is that all other (observed or unobserved) attributes prior to the intervention are then independent of whether or not a unit actually receives the program. By implication, $B^{TT}(X) = 0$, and so the observed *ex post* difference in mean outcomes between the treatment and control groups is attributable to the program.[19] In terms of the parametric formulation of the evaluation problem in Section 2, randomization guarantees that there is no sample selection bias in estimating (3.1) and (3.2) or (equivalently) that the error term in Eq. (4) is orthogonal to all regressors. The non-participants are then a valid control group for identifying the counterfactual, and mean impact is consistently estimated (nonparametrically) by the difference between the sample means of the observed values of Y_i^T and Y_i^C at given values of X_i.

---

[19] However, the simple difference in means is not necessarily the most efficient estimator; see Hirano, Imbens and Ridder (2003).

4.1. Issues with social experiments

There has been much debate about whether randomization is the ideal method in practice.[20] Social experiments have often raised ethical objections and generated political sensitivities, particularly for governmental programs. (It is easier to do social experiments with NGOs, though for small interventions.) There is a perception that social experiments treat people like "guinea pigs," deliberately denying program access for some of those who need it (to form the control group) in favor of some who do not (since a random assignment undoubtedly picks up some people who would not normally participate). In the case of anti-poverty programs, one ends up assessing impacts for types of people for whom the program is not intended and/or denying the program to poor people who need it – in both cases running counter to the aim of fighting poverty.

These ethical and political concerns have stalled experiments or undermined their continued implementation. This appears to be why randomized trials for welfare reforms went out of favor with state governments in the US after the mid-1990s (Moffitt, 2003) and why subsequent evaluations of Mexico's *PROGRESA* program have turned to NX methods.

Are these legitimate concerns? As noted in Section 3, the evaluation itself is rarely the reason for incomplete coverage of the poor in an anti-poverty program; rather it is that too few resources are available. When there are poor people who cannot get on the program given the resources available, it has been argued that the ethical concerns favor social experiments; by this view, the fairest solution to rationing is to assign the program randomly, so that everyone has an equal opportunity of getting the limited resources available.[21]

However, it is hard to appreciate the "fairness" of an anti-poverty program that ignores available information on differences in the extent of deprivation. A key, but poorly understood, issue is what constitutes the "available information." As already noted, social experiments typically assign participation conditional on certain observables. But the things that are observable to the evaluator are generally a subset of those available to key stakeholders. The ethical concerns with experiments persist when it is known to *at least some* observers that the program is being withheld from those who clearly need it, and given to those who do not.

Other concerns have been raised about social experiments. Internal validity can be questionable when there is selective compliance with the theoretical randomized assignment. People are (typically) free agents. They do not have to comply with the evaluator's assignment. And their choices will undoubtedly be influenced by latent factors deter-

---

[20] On the arguments for and against social experiments see (*inter alia*) Heckman and Smith (1995), Burtless (1995), Moffitt (2003) and Keane (2006).

[21] From the description of the Newman et al. (2002) study it appears that this is how randomization was defended to the relevant authorities in their case.

mining the returns to participation.[22] The extent of this problem depends on the specific program and setting; selective compliance is more likely for a training program (say) than a cash transfer program. Sections 7 and 8 will return to this issue and discuss how NX methods can help address the problem.

The generic point is that the identification of impacts using social experiments is rarely "assumption-free." It is important to make explicit all the assumptions that are required, including about behavioral responses to the experiment; see, for example, the interesting discussion in Keane (2006) comparing experiments with structural modeling.

Recall that the responses of third parties can generate confounding spillovers (Section 3). A higher level of government might adjust its own spending, counteracting the assignment. This is a potential problem whether the program is randomized or not, but it may well be a bigger problem for randomized evaluations. The higher level of government may not feel the need to compensate units that did not get the program when this was based on credible and observable factors that are agreed to be relevant. On the other hand, the authorities may feel obliged to compensate for the "bad luck" of units being assigned randomly to a control group. Randomization can induce spillovers that do not happen with selection on observables.

This is an instance of a more general and fundamental problem with randomized designs for anti-poverty programs, namely that the very process of randomization can alter the way a program works in practice. There may well be systematic differences between the characteristics of people normally attracted to a program and those randomly assigned the program from the same population. (This is sometimes called "randomization bias.") Heckman and Smith (1995) discuss an example from the evaluation of the JTPA, whereby substantial changes in the program's recruiting procedures were required to form the control group. The evaluated pilot program is not then the same as the program that gets implemented – casting doubt on the validity of the inferences drawn from the evaluation.

The JTPA illustrates a further potential problem, namely that institutional or political factors may delay the randomized assignment. This promotes selective attrition and adds to the cost, as more is spent on applicants who end up in the control group (Heckman and Smith, 1995).

A further critique points out that, even with randomized assignment, we only know mean outcomes for the counterfactual, so we cannot infer the joint distribution of outcomes as would be required to say something about (for example) the proportion of gainers versus losers amongst those receiving a program (Heckman and Smith, 1995). Section 9 returns to this topic.

---

[22] The fact that people can select out of the randomized assignment goes some way toward alleviating the aforementioned ethical concerns about social experiments. But selective compliance clouds inferences about impact.

4.2. Examples

Randomized trials for welfare programs and reforms were common in the US in the 1980s and early 1990s and much has been learnt from such trials (Moffitt, 2003). In the case of active labor market programs, two examples are the Job Training Partnership Act (JTPA) (see, for example, Heckman, Ichimura and Todd, 1997), and the US National Supported Work Demonstration (studied by La Londe, 1986, and Dehejia and Wahba, 1999). For targeted wage subsidy programs in the US, randomized evaluations have been studied by Burtless (1985), Woodbury and Spiegelman (1987) and Dubin and Rivers (1993).

Another (rather different) example is the Moving to Opportunity (MTO) experiment, in which randomly chosen public-housing occupants in poor inner-city areas of five US cities were offered vouchers for buying housing elsewhere (Katz, Kling and Liebman, 2001; Moffitt, 2001). This was motivated by the hypothesis that attributes of the area of residence matter to individual prospects of escaping poverty. The randomized assignment of MTO vouchers helps address some long-standing concerns about past NX tests for neighborhood effects (Manski, 1993).[23]

There have also been a number of social experiments in developing countries. A well-known example is Mexico's *PROGRESA* program, which provided cash transfers targeted to poor families conditional on their children attending school and obtaining health care and nutrition supplementation. The longevity of this program (surviving changes of government) and its influence in the development community clearly stem in part from the substantial, and public, effort that went into its evaluation. One third of the sampled communities deemed eligible for the program were chosen randomly to form a control group that did not get the program for an initial period during which the other two thirds received the program. Public access to the evaluation data has facilitated a number of valuable studies, indicating significant gains to health (Gertler, 2004), schooling (Schultz, 2004; Behrman, Sengupta and Todd, 2002) and food consumption (Hoddinott and Skoufias, 2004). A comprehensive overview of the design, implementation and results of the *PROGRESA* evaluation can be found in Skoufias (2005).

In another example for a developing country, Newman et al. (2002) were able to randomize eligibility to a World Bank supported social fund for a region of Bolivia. The fund-supported investments in education were found to have had significant impacts on school infrastructure but not on education outcomes within the evaluation period.

Randomization was also used by Angrist et al. (2002) to evaluate a Colombian program that allocated schooling vouchers by a lottery. Three years later, the lottery winners had significantly lower incidence of grade repetition and higher test scores.

Another example is Argentina's *Proempleo* experiment (Galasso, Ravallion and Salvia, 2004). This was a randomized evaluation of a pilot wage subsidy and training

[23] Note that the design of the MTO experiment does not identify neighborhood effects at the origin, given that attributes of the destination also matter to outcomes (Moffitt, 2001).

program for assisting workfare participants in Argentina to find regular, private-sector jobs. Eighteen months later, recipients of the voucher for a wage subsidy had a higher probability of employment than the control group. (We will return later in this chapter to examine some lessons from this evaluation more closely.)

It has been argued that the World Bank should make greater use of social experiments. While the Bank has supported a number of experiments (including most of the examples for developing countries above), that is not so of the Bank's Operations Evaluation Department (the semi-independent unit for the *ex post* evaluation of its own lending operations). In the 78 evaluations by OED surveyed by Kapoor (2002), only one used randomization[24]; indeed, only 21 used any form of counterfactual analysis. Cook (2001) and Duflo and Kremer (2005) have advocated that OED should do many more social experiments.[25] Before accepting that advice one should be aware of some of the concerns raised by experiments.

A well-crafted social experiment will eliminate selection bias, but that leaves many other concerns about both their internal and external validity. The rest of this chapter turns to the main nonexperimental methods found in practice.

5. Propensity-score methods

As Section 3 emphasized, selection bias is to be expected in comparing a random sample from the population of participants with a random sample of non-participants (as in estimating $D(X)$ in Eq. (2)). There must be a general presumption that such comparisons misinform policy. How much so is an empirical question. On *a priori* grounds it is worrying that many NX evaluations in practice provide too little information to assess whether the "comparison group" is likely to be sufficiently similar to the participants in the absence of the intervention.

In trying to find a comparison group it is natural to search for non-participants with similar pre-intervention characteristics to the participants. However, there are potentially many characteristics that one might use to match. How should they be weighted in choosing the comparison group? This section begins by reviewing the theory and practice of matching using propensity scores and then turns to other uses of propensity scores in evaluation.

5.1. Propensity-score matching (PMS)

This method aims to select comparators according to their propensity scores, as given by $P(Z) = \Pr(T = 1 \mid Z)$ $(0 < P(Z) < 1)$, where Z is a vector of pre-exposure con-

---

[24] From Kapoor's description it is not clear that even this evaluation was a genuine experiment.

[25] OED only assesses Bank projects after they are completed, which makes it hard to do proper impact evaluations. Note that other units in the Bank that do evaluations besides OED, including in the research department invariably use counterfactual analysis and sometimes randomization.

trol variables (which can include pretreatment values of the outcome indicator).[26] The values taken by Z are assumed to be unaffected by whether unit i actually receives the program. PSM uses $P(Z)$ (or a monotone function of $P(Z)$) to select comparison units. An important paper by Rosenbaum and Rubin (1983) showed that if outcomes are independent of participation given Z, then outcomes are also independent of participation given $P(Z_i)$.[27] The independence condition implies conditional exogeneity of placement ($B^{TT}(X) = 0$), so that the (unobserved) $E(Y^C \mid X, T = 1)$ can be replaced by the (observed) $E(Y^C \mid X, T = 0)$. Thus, as in a social experiment, TT is non-parametrically identified by the difference in the sample mean outcomes between treated units and the matched comparison group ($D(X)$). Under the independence assumption, exact matching on $P(Z)$ eliminates selection bias, although it is not necessarily the most efficient impact estimator (Hahn, 1998; Angrist and Hahn, 2004).

Thus PSM essentially assumes away the problem of endogenous placement, leaving only the need to balance the conditional probability, i.e., the propensity score. An implication of this difference is that (unlike a social experiment) the impact estimates obtained by PSM must always depend on the variables used for matching and (hence) the quantity and quality of available data.

There is an important (often implicit) assumption in PSM and other NX methods that eliminating selection bias based on observables will reduce the aggregate bias. That will only be the case if the two sources of bias – that associated with observables and that due to unobserved factors – go in the same direction, which cannot be assured on *a priori* grounds (as noted in Section 3). If the selection bias based on unobservables counteracts that based on observables then eliminating only the latter bias will increase aggregate bias. While this is possible in theory, replication studies (comparing NX evaluations with experiments for the same programs) do not appear to have found an example in practice; I review lessons from replication studies below.

The variables in Z may well differ from the covariates of outcomes (X in Section 2); this distinction plays an important role in the methods discussed in Section 8. But what should be included in Z?[28] The choice should be based on knowledge about the program and setting, as relevant to understanding the economic, social or political factors influencing program assignment that are correlated with counterfactual outcomes. Qualitative field work can help; for example, the specification choices made in Jalan and Ravallion (2003b) reflected interviews with participants and local administrators in Argentina's *Trabajar* program (a combination of workfare and social fund). Similarly Godtland et al. (2004) validated their choice of covariates for participation in an agricultural extension program in Peru through interviews with farmers.

---

[26] The present discussion is confined to a binary treatment. In generalizing to the case of multi-valued or continuous treatments one defines the generalized propensity score given by the conditional probability of a specific level of treatment (Imbens, 2000; Lechner, 2001; Hirano and Imbens, 2004).

[27] The result also requires that the T_i's are independent over all i. For a clear exposition and proof of the Rosenbaum–Rubin theorem see Imbens (2004).

[28] For guidance on this and the many other issues that arise when implementing PSM see the useful paper by Caliendo and Kopeinig (2005).

Clearly if the available data do not include a determinant of participation relevant to outcomes then PSM will not have removed the selection bias (in other words it will not be able to reproduce the results of a social experiment). Knowledge of how the specific program works and theoretical considerations on likely behavioral responses can often reveal likely candidates for such an omitted variable. Under certain conditions, bounds can be established to a matching estimator, allowing for an omitted covariate of program placement (Rosenbaum, 1995; for an example see Aakvik, 2001). Later in this chapter we will consider alternative estimators that can be more robust to such an omitted variable (although requiring further assumptions).

Common practice in implementing PSM is to use the predicted values from a logit or probit as the propensity score for each observation in the participant and the non-participant samples, although non-parametric binary-response models can be used.[29] The comparison group can be formed by picking the "nearest neighbor" for each participant, defined as the non-participant that minimizes $|\hat{P}(Z_i) - \hat{P}(Z_j)|$ as long as this does not exceed some reasonable bound.[30] Given measurement errors, more robust estimates take the mean of the nearest (say) five neighbors, although this does not necessarily reduce bias.[31]

It is a good idea to test for systematic differences in the covariates between the treatment and comparison groups constructed by PSM; Smith and Todd (2005a) describe a useful "balancing test" for this purpose.

The typical PSM estimator for mean impact takes the form $\sum_{j=1}^{NT}(Y_j^T - \sum_{i=1}^{NC} W_{ij}Y_{ij}^C)/NT$ where NT is the number receiving the program, NC is the number of non-participants and the W_{ij}'s are the weights. There are several weighting schemes that have been used in the literature (see the overview in Caliendo and Kopeinig, 2005). These range from nearest-neighbor weights to non-parametric weights based on kernel functions of the differences in scores whereby all the comparison units are used in forming the counterfactual for each participating unit, but with a weight that reaches its maximum for the nearest neighbor but declines as the absolute difference in propensity scores increases; Heckman, Ichimura and Todd (1997) discuss this weighting scheme.[32]

The statistical properties of matching estimators (in particular their asymptotic properties) are not as yet well understood. In practice, standard errors are typically derived by a bootstrapping method, although the appropriateness of this method is not evident in all cases. Abadie and Imbens (2006) examine the formal properties in large samples of nearest-k neighbor matching estimators (for which the standard bootstrapping

---

[29] The participation regression is of interest in its own right, as it provides insights into the targeting performance of the program; see, for example, the discussion in Jalan and Ravallion (2003b).

[30] When treated units have been over-sampled (giving a "choice-based sample") and the weights are unknown one should instead match on the odds ratio, $P(Z)/(1 - P(Z))$ (Heckman and Todd, 1995).

[31] Rubin and Thomas (2000) use simulations to compare the bias in using the nearest five neighbors to just the nearest neighbor; no clear pattern emerges.

[32] Frölich (2004) compares the finite-sample properties of various estimators and finds that a local linear ridge regression method is more efficient and robust than alternatives.

method does not give valid standard errors) and provide a consistent estimator for the asymptotic standard error.

Mean impacts can also be calculated conditional on observed characteristics. For anti-poverty programs one is interested in comparing the conditional mean impact across different pre-intervention incomes. For each sampled participant, one estimates the income gain from the program by comparing that participant's income with the income for matched non-participants. Subtracting the estimated gain from observed post-intervention income, it is then possible to estimate where each participant would have been in the distribution of income without the program. On averaging this across different strata defined by pre-intervention incomes one can assess the incidence of impacts. In doing so, it is a good idea to test if propensity-scores (and even the Z's themselves) are adequately balanced *within* strata (as well as in the aggregate), since there is a risk that one may be confusing matching errors with real effects.

Similarly one can construct the empirical and counter-factual cumulative distribution functions or their empirical integrals, and test for dominance over a relevant range of poverty lines and measures. This is illustrated in Fig. 2, for Argentina's *Trabajar* program. The figure gives the cumulative distribution function (CDF) (or "poverty incidence curve") showing how the headcount index of poverty (% below the poverty line) varies across a wide range of possible poverty lines (when that range covers all incomes we have the standard cumulative distribution function). The vertical line is a widely-used poverty line for Argentina. The figure also gives the estimated counter-factual

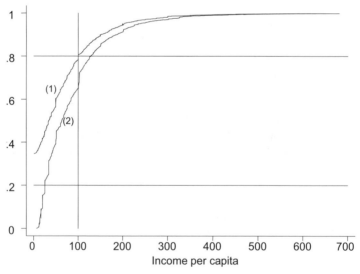

(1) Participant sample pre-intervention (estimated)
(2) Participant sample post-intervention (observed)
Source: Jalan and Ravallion (2003b).

Figure 2. Poverty impacts of disbursements under Argentina's Trabajar program.

CDF, after deducting the imputed income gains from the observed (post-intervention) incomes of all the sampled participants. Using a poverty line of $100 per month (for which about 20% of the national population is deemed poor) we see a 15 percentage point drop in the incidence of poverty amongst participants due to the program; this rises to 30 percentage points using poverty lines nearer the bottom of the distribution. We can also see the gain at each percentile of the distribution (looking horizontally) or the impact on the incidence of poverty at any given poverty line (looking vertically).[33]

In evaluating anti-poverty programs in developing countries, single-difference comparisons using PSM have the advantage that they do not require either randomization or baseline (pre-intervention) data. While this can be a huge advantage in practice, it comes at a cost. To accept the exogeneity assumption one must be confident that one has controlled for the factors that jointly influence program placement and outcomes. In practice, one must always consider the possibility that there is a latent variable that jointly influences placement and outcomes, such that the mean of the latent influences on outcomes is different between treated and untreated units. This invalidates the key conditional independence assumption made by PSM. Whether this is a concern or not must be judged in the context of the application at hand; how much one is concerned about unobservables must depend, of course, on what data one has on the relevant observables. Section 7 will give an example of how far wrong the method can go with inadequate data on the joint covariates of participation and outcomes.

5.2. How does PSM differ from other methods?

In a social experiment (at least in its pure form), the propensity score is a constant, since everyone has the same probability of receiving treatment. Intuitively, what PSM tries to do is create the observational analogue of such an experiment in which everyone has the same probability of participation. The difference is that in PSM it is the conditional probability $(P(Z))$ that is intended to be uniform between participants and matched comparators, while randomization assures that the participant and comparison groups are identical in terms of the distribution of all characteristics whether observed or not. Hence there are always concerns about remaining selection bias in PSM estimates.

A natural comparison is between PSM and an OLS regression of the outcome indicators on dummy variables for program placement, allowing for the observable covariates entering as linear controls (as in Eqs. (4) and (5)). OLS requires essentially the same conditional independence (exogeneity) assumption as PSM, but also imposes arbitrary functional form assumptions concerning the treatment effects and the control variables. By contrast, PSM (in common with experimental methods) does not require a parametric model linking outcomes to program participation. Thus PSM allows estimation of mean impacts without arbitrary assumptions about functional forms and error distributions. This can also facilitate testing for the presence of potentially complex interaction

---

[33] On how the results of an impact assessment by PSM can be used to assess impacts on poverty measures robustly to the choice of those measures and the poverty line see Ravallion (2003a).

effects. For example, Jalan and Ravallion (2003a) use PSM to study how the interaction effects between income and education influence the child-health gains from access to piped water in rural India. The authors find a complex pattern of interaction effects; for example, poverty attenuates the child-health gains from piped water, but less so the higher the level of maternal education.

PSM also differs from standard regression methods with respect to the sample. In PSM one confines attention to the region of common support (Fig. 1). Non-participants with a score lower than any participant are excluded. One may also want to restrict potential matches in other ways, depending on the setting. For example, one may want to restrict matches to being within the same geographic area, to help assure that the comparison units come from the same economic environment. By contrast, the regression methods commonly found in the literature use the full sample. The simulations in Rubin and Thomas (2000) indicate that impact estimates based on full (unmatched) samples are generally more biased, and less robust to miss-specification of the regression function, than those based on matched samples.

A further difference relates to the choice of control variables. In the standard regression method one looks for predictors of outcomes, and preference is given to variables that one can argue to be exogenous to outcomes. In PSM one is looking instead for covariates of participation. It is clearly important that these include those variables that also matter to outcomes. However, variables with seemingly weak predictive ability for outcomes can still help reduce bias in estimating causal effects using PSM (Rubin and Thomas, 2000).

It is an empirical question as to how much difference it would make to mean-impact estimates by using PSM rather than OLS. Comparative methodological studies have been rare. In one exception, Godtland et al. (2004) use both an outcome regression and PSM for assessing the impacts of field schools on farmers' knowledge of good practices for pest management in potato cultivation. They report that their results were robust to changing the method used. However, other studies have reported large differences between OLS with controls for Z and PSM based on $P(Z)$ (Jalan and Ravallion, 2003a; van de Walle and Mu, 2007).

5.3. How well does PSM perform?

Returning to the same data set used by the La Londe (1986) study (described in Section 3), Dehejia and Wahba (1999) found that PSM achieved a fairly good approximation – much better than the NX methods studied by La Londe. It appears that the poor performance of the NX methods used by La Londe stemmed in large part from the use of observational units outside the region of common support. However, the robustness of the Dehejia–Wahba findings to sample selection and the specification chosen for calculating the propensity scores has been questioned by Smith and Todd (2005a), who argue that PSM does not solve the selection problem in the program studied by La Londe.[34]

---

[34] Dehejia (2005) replies to Smith and Todd (2005a), who offer a rejoinder in Smith and Todd (2005b). Also see Smith and Todd (2001).

Similar attempts to test PSM against randomized evaluations have shown mixed results. Agodini and Dynarski (2004) find no consistent evidence that PSM can replicate experimental results from evaluations of school dropout programs in the US. Using the *PROGRESA* data base, Diaz and Handa (2004) find that PSM performs well as long as the same survey instrument is used for measuring outcomes for the treatment and comparison groups. The importance of using the same survey instrument in PSM is also emphasized by Heckman, Smith and Clements (1997) and Heckman et al. (1998) in the context of their evaluation of a US training program. The latter study also points to the importance of both participants and non-participants coming from the same local labor markets, and of being able to control for employment history. The meta-study by Glazerman, Levy and Myers (2003) finds that PSM is one of the NX methods that can significantly reduce bias, particularly when used in combination with other methods.

5.4. Other uses of propensity scores in evaluation

There are other evaluation methods that make use of the propensity score. These methods can have advantages over PSM although there have as yet been very few applications in developing countries.

While matching on propensity scores eliminates bias (under the conditional exogeneity assumption) this need not be the most efficient estimation method (Hahn, 1998). Rather than matching by estimated propensity scores, an alternative impact estimator has been proposed by Hirano, Imbens and Ridder (2003). This method weights observation units by the inverses of a nonparametric estimate of the propensity scores. Hirano et al. show that this practice yields a fully efficient estimator for average treatment effects. Chen, Mu and Ravallion (2006) and van de Walle and Mu (2007) provide examples in the context of evaluating the impacts on poverty of development projects.

Propensity scores can also be used in the context of more standard regression-based estimators. Suppose one simply added the estimated propensity score $\hat{P}(Z)$ to an OLS regression of the outcome variable on the treatment dummy variable, T. (One can also include an interaction effect between $\hat{P}(Z_i)$ and T_i.) Under the assumptions of PSM this will eliminate any omitted variable bias in having excluded Z from that regression, given that Z is independent of treatment given $P(Z)$.[35] However, this method does not have the non-parametric flexibility of PSM. Adding a suitable function of $\hat{P}(Z)$ to the outcome regression is an example of the "control function" (CF) approach, whereby under standard conditions (including exogeneity of X and Z) the selection bias term can be written as a function of $\hat{P}(Z)$.[36] Identification rests either on the nonlinearity of the CF in Z or the existence of one or more covariates of participation (the vector Z)

---

[35] This provides a further intuition as to how PSM works; see the discussion in Imbens (2004).

[36] Heckman and Robb (1985) provide a thorough discussion of this approach; also see the discussion in Heckman and Hotz (1989). On the relationship between CF and PSM see Heckman and Navarro-Lozano (2004) and Todd (2008). On the relationship between CF approaches and instrumental variables estimators (discussed further in Section 8) see Vella and Verbeek (1999).

that only affect outcomes *via* participation. Subject to essentially the same identification conditions, another option is to use $\hat{P}(Z)$ as the instrumental variable for program placement, as discussed further in Section 8.

6. Exploiting program design

Nonexperimental estimators can sometimes usefully exploit features of program design for identification. Discontinuities generated by program eligibility criteria can help identify impacts in a neighborhood of the cut-off points for eligibility. Or delays in the implementation of a program can also facilitate forming comparison groups, which can also help pick up some sources of latent heterogeneity. This section discusses these methods and some examples.

6.1. Discontinuity designs

Under certain conditions one can infer impacts from the differences in mean outcomes between units on either side of a critical cut-off point determining program eligibility. To see more clearly what this method involves, let M_i denote the score received by unit i in a proxy-means test (say) and let m denote the cut-off point for eligibility, such that $T_i = 1$ for $M_i \leqslant m$ and $T_i = 0$ otherwise. Examples include a proxy-means test that sets a maximum score for eligibility (Section 3) and programs that confine eligibility within geographic boundaries. The impact estimator is $E(Y^T \mid M = m - \varepsilon) - E(Y^C \mid M = m + \varepsilon)$ for some arbitrarily small $\varepsilon > 0$. In practice, there is inevitably a degree of fuzziness in the application of eligibility tests. So instead of assuming strict enforcement and compliance, one can follow Hahn, Todd and Van der Klaauw (2001) in postulating a probability of program participation, $P(M) = E(T \mid M)$, which is an increasing function of M with a discontinuity at m. The essential idea remains the same, in that impacts are measured by the difference in mean outcomes in a neighborhood of m.

The key identifying assumption is that the discontinuity at m is in outcomes under treatment *not* outcomes under the counterfactual.[37] The existence of strict eligibility rules does not mean that this is a plausible assumption. For example, the geographic boundaries for program eligibility will often coincide with local political jurisdictions, entailing current or past geographic differences in (say) local fiscal policies and institutions that cloud identification. The plausibility of the continuity assumption for counterfactual outcomes must be judged in each application.

In a test of how well discontinuity designs perform in reducing selection bias, Buddlemeyer and Skoufias (2004) use the cut-offs in *PROGRESA*'s eligibility rules

---

[37] Hahn, Todd and Van der Klaauw (2001) provide a formal analysis of identification and estimation of impacts for discontinuity designs under this assumption. For a useful overwiew of this topic see Imbens and Lemieux (2007).

to measure impacts and compare the results to those obtained by exploiting the program's randomized design. The authors find that the discontinuity design gives good approximations for almost all outcome indicators.

The method is not without its drawbacks. It is assumed that the evaluator knows M_i and (hence) eligibility for the program. That will not always be the case. Consider (again) a means-tested transfer whereby the income of the participants is supposed to be below some predetermined cut-off point. In a single cross section survey, we observe post-program incomes for participants and incomes for non-participants, but typically we do not know income at the time the means test was actually applied. And if we were to estimate eligibility by subtracting the transfer payment from the observed income then we would be assuming (implicitly) exactly what we want to test: whether there was a behavioral response to the program. Retrospective questions on income at the time of the means test will help (though recognizing the possible biases), as would a baseline survey at or near the time of the test. A baseline survey can also help clean out any pre-intervention differences in outcomes either side of the discontinuity, in which case one is combining the discontinuity design with the double difference method discussed further in Section 7.

Note also that a discontinuity design gives mean impact for a selected sample of the participants, while most other methods (such as social experiments and PSM) aim to give mean impact for the treatment group as a whole. However, the aforementioned common-support problem that is sometimes generated by eligibility criteria can mean that other evaluations are also confined to a highly selected sub-sample; the question is then whether that is an interesting sub-sample. The truncation of treatment group samples to assure common support will most likely tend to exclude those with the highest probability of participating (for which non-participating comparators are hardest to find), while discontinuity designs will tend to include only those with the lowest probability. The latter sub-sample can, nonetheless, be relevant for deciding about program expansion; Section 9 returns to this point.

Although impacts in a neighborhood of the cut-off point are non-parametrically identified for discontinuity designs, the applied literature has more often used an alternative parametric method in which the discontinuity in the eligibility criterion is used as an instrumental variable for program placement; we will return to give examples in Section 8.

6.2. Pipeline comparisons

The idea here is to use as the comparison group people who have applied for a program but not yet received it.[38] *PROGRESA* is an example; one third of eligible participants did not receive the program for 18 months, during which they formed the control group. In

---

[38] This is sometimes called "pipeline matching" in the literature, although this term is less than ideal given that no matching is actually done.

the case of *PROGRESA*, the pipeline comparison was randomized. NX pipeline comparisons have also been used in developing countries. An example can be found in Chase (2002) who used communities that had applied for a social fund (in Armenia) as the source of the comparison group in estimating the fund's impacts on communities that received its support. In another example, Galasso and Ravallion (2004) evaluated a large social protection program in Argentina, namely the Government's *Plan Jefes y Jefas*, which was the main social policy response to the severe economic crisis of 2002. To form a comparison group for participants they used those individuals who had successfully applied for the program, but had not yet received it. Notice that this method does to some extent address the problem of latent heterogeneity in other single-difference estimators, such as PSM; the prior selection process will tend to mean that successful applicants will tend to have similar unobserved characteristics, whether or not they have actually received the treatment.

The key assumption here is that the timing of treatment is random given application. In practice, one must anticipate a potential bias arising from selective treatment amongst the applicants or behavioral responses by applicants awaiting treatment. This is a greater concern in some settings than others. For example, Galasso and Ravallion argued that it was not a serious concern in their case given that they assessed the program during a period of rapid scaling up, during the 2002 financial crisis in Argentina when it was physically impossible to immediately help everyone who needed help. The authors also tested for observable differences between the two subsets of applicants, and found that observables (including idiosyncratic income shocks during the crisis) were well balanced between the two groups, alleviating concerns about bias. Using longitudinal observations also helped; we return to this example in the next section.

When feasible, pipeline comparisons offer a single-difference impact estimator that is likely to be more robust to latent heterogeneity. The estimates should, however, be tested for bias due to poorly balanced observables and (if need be) a method such as PSM can be used to deal with this prior to making the pipeline comparison (Galasso and Ravallion, 2004).

Pipeline comparisons might also be combined with discontinuity designs. Although I have not seen it used in practice, a possible identification strategy for projects that expand along a well-defined route is to measure outcomes on either side of the project's current frontier. Examples might include projects that progressively connect houses to an existing water, sanitation, transport or communications network, as well as projects that expand that network in discrete increments. New facilities (such as electrification or telecommunications) often expand along pre-existing infrastructure networks (such as roads, to lay cables along their right-of-way). Clearly one would also want to allow for observable heterogeneity and time effects. There may also be concerns about spillover effects; the behavior of non-participants may change, in anticipation of being hooked up to the expanding network.

7. Higher-order differences

So far the discussion has focused on single-difference estimators that only require a single survey. More can be learnt if we track outcomes for both participants and non-participants over time. A pre-intervention "baseline survey" in which one knows who eventually participates and who does not, can reveal specification problems in a single-difference estimator. If the outcome regression (such as Eqs. (4) or (5)) is correctly specified then running that regression on the baseline data should indicate an estimate of mean impact that is not significantly different from zero (Heckman and Hotz, 1989).

With baseline data one can go a step further and allow some of the latent determinants of outcomes to be correlated with program placement given the observables. This section begins with the *double-difference* (DD) method, which relaxes the conditional exogeneity assumption of single-difference NX estimators by exploiting a baseline and at least one follow-up survey post-intervention. The discussion then turns to situations – common for safety-net programs set-up to address a crisis – in which a baseline survey is impossible, but we can track ex-participants; this illustrates the *triple-difference* estimator.

7.1. The double-difference estimator

The essential idea is to compare samples of participants and non-participants before and after the intervention. After the initial baseline survey of both non-participants and (subsequent) participants, one does a follow-up survey of both groups after the intervention. Finally one calculates the difference between the "after" and "before" values of the mean outcomes for each of the treatment and comparison groups. The difference between these two mean differences (hence the label "double difference" or "difference-in-difference") is the impact estimate.

To see what is involved, let Y_{it} denote the outcome measure for the ith observation unit observed at two dates, $t = 0, 1$. By definition $Y_{it} = Y_{it}^C + T_{it} G_{it}$ and (as in the archetypal evaluation problem described in Section 2), it is assumed that we can observe T_{it}, Y_{it}^T when $T_{it} = 1$, Y_{it}^C for $T_{it} = 0$, but that $G_{it} = Y_{it}^T - Y_{it}^C$ is not directly observable for any i (or in expectation) since we are missing the data on Y_{it}^T for $T_{it} = 0$ and Y_{it}^C for $T_{it} = 1$. To solve the missing-data problem, the DD estimator assumes that the selection bias (the unobserved difference in mean counterfactual outcomes between treated and untreated units) is time invariant, in which case the outcome changes for non-participants reveal the counterfactual outcome changes, i.e.:

$$E(Y_1^C - Y_0^C \mid T_1 = 1) = E(Y_1^C - Y_0^C \mid T_1 = 0). \tag{8}$$

This is clearly a weaker assumption than conditional exogeneity in single-difference estimates; $B_t^{TT} = 0$ for all t implies (8) but is not necessary for (8). Since period 0 is a baseline, with $T_{0i} = 0$ for all i (by definition), $Y_{0i} = Y_{0i}^C$ for all i. Then it is plain that the double-difference estimator gives the mean treatment effect on the treated for period 1:

$$DD = E\left(Y_1^T - Y_0^C \mid T_1 = 1\right) - E\left(Y_1^C - Y_0^C \mid T_1 = 0\right) = E(G_1 \mid T_1 = 1). \qquad (9)$$

Notice that panel data are not necessary for calculating DD. All one needs is the set of four means that make up DD; the means need not be calculated for the same sample over time.

When the counterfactual means are time-invariant ($E[Y_1^C - Y_0^C \mid T_1 = 1] = 0$), Eqs. (8) and (9) collapse to a *reflexive comparison* in which one only monitors outcomes for the treatment units. Unchanging mean outcomes for the counterfactual is an implausible assumption in most applications. However, with enough observations over time, methods of testing for structural breaks in the times series of outcomes for participants can offer some hope of identifying impacts; see for example Piehl et al. (2003).

For calculating standard errors and implementing weighted estimators it is convenient to use a regression estimator for DD. The data over both time periods and across treatment status are pooled and one runs the regression:

$$Y_{it} = \alpha + \beta T_{i1} t + \gamma T_{i1} + \delta t + \varepsilon_i \qquad (t = 0, 1; \ i = 1, \ldots, n). \qquad (10)$$

The single-difference estimator is $SD_t \equiv E[(Y_{it} \mid T_{i1} = 1) - (Y_{it} \mid T_{i1} = 0)] = \beta t + \gamma$ while the DD estimator is $DD_1 \equiv SD_1 - SD_0 = \beta$. Thus the regression coefficient on the interaction effect between the participation dummy variable and time in Eq. (10) identifies the impact.

Notice that Eq. (10) does not require a balanced panel; for example, the interviews do not all have to be done at the same time. This property can be useful in survey design, by allowing "rolling survey" approach, whereby the survey teams move from one primary sampling unit to another over time; this has advantages in supervision and likely data quality. Another advantage of the fact that (10) does not require a balanced panel is that the results will be robust to selective attrition. In the case of a balanced panel, we can instead estimate the equivalent regression in the more familiar "fixed-effects" form:

$$Y_{it} = \alpha^* + \beta T_{i1} t + \delta_t + \eta_i + \nu_{it}. \qquad (11)$$

Here the fixed effect is $\eta_i = \gamma T_{i1} + \bar{\eta}^C + \mu_i$.[39]

Note that the term γT_{i1} in Eq. (10) picks up differences in the mean of the *latent* individual effects, such as would arise from initial selection into the program. The single-difference estimate will be biased unless the means of the latent effects are balanced between treated and non-treated units ($\bar{\eta}^T = \bar{\eta}^C$, i.e., $\gamma = 0$). This is implausible in general, as emphasized in Section 2. The double-difference estimator removes this source of bias.

This approach can be readily generalized to multiple time periods; DD is then estimated by the regression of Y_{it} on the (individual and date-specific) participation dummy

---

[39] Note that $\eta_i = \eta_i^T T_{i1} + \eta_i^C (1 - T_{i1}) = \gamma T_{i1} + \bar{\eta}^C + \mu_i (E(\eta_i \mid T_{i1}) \neq 0)$ where $\gamma = \bar{\eta}^T - \bar{\eta}^C$, $\mu_i = (\eta_i^T - \bar{\eta}^T) T_{i1} + (\eta_i^C - \bar{\eta}^C)(1 - T_{i1})$, $E(\mu_i) = 0$, $\varepsilon_{it} = \nu_{it} + \mu_i$ and $\alpha = \alpha^* + \bar{\eta}^C$.

variable T_{it} interacted with time, and with individual and time effects. Or one can use a differenced specification in which the changes over time are regressed on T_{it} with time fixed effects.[40]

7.2. Examples of DD evaluations

In an early example, Binswanger, Khandker and Rosenzweig (1993) used this method to estimate the impacts of rural infrastructure on agricultural productivity in India, using district-level data. Their key identifying assumption was that the endogeneity problem – whereby infrastructure placement reflects omitted determinants of productivity – arose entirely through latent agro-climatic factors that could be captured by district-level fixed effects. They found significant productivity gains from rural infrastructure.

In another example, Duflo (2001) estimated the impact on schooling and earnings in Indonesia of building schools. A feature of the assignment mechanism was known, namely that more schools were built in locations with low enrollment rates. Also, the age cohorts that participated in the program could be easily identified. The fact that the gains in schooling attainments of the first cohorts exposed to the program were greater in areas that received more schools was taken to indicate that building schools promoted better education. Frankenberg, Suriastini and Thomas (2005) use a similar method to assess the impacts of providing basic health care services through midwives on children's nutritional status (height-for-age), also in Indonesia.

Galiani, Gertler and Schargrodsky (2005) used a *DD* design to study the impact of privatizing water services on child mortality in Argentina, exploiting the joint geographic (across municipalities) and inter-temporal variation in both child mortality and ownership of water services. Their results suggest that privatization of water services reduced child mortality.

A *DD* design can also be used to address possible biases in a social experiment, whereby there is some form of selective compliance or other distortion to the randomized assignment (as discussed in Section 4). An example can be found in Thomas et al. (2003) who randomized assignment of iron-supplementation pills in Indonesia, with a randomized-out group receiving a placebo. By also collecting pre-intervention baseline data on both groups, the authors were able to address concerns about compliance bias.

While the classic design for a *DD* estimator tracks the differences *over time* between participants and non-participants, that is not the only possibility. Jacoby (2002) used a *DD* design to test whether intra-household resource allocation shifted in response to a school-feeding program, to neutralize the latter's effect on child nutrition. Some schools had the feeding program and some did not, and some children attended school

---

[40] As is well known, when the differenced error term is serially correlated one must take account of this fact in calculating the standard errors of the DD estimator; Bertrand, Duflo and Mullainathan (2004) demonstrate the possibility for large biases in the uncorrected (OLS) standard errors for DD estimators.

and some did not. The author's *DD* estimate of impact was then the difference between the mean food-energy intake of children who attended a school (on the previous day) that had a feeding program and the mean of those who did not attend such schools, *less* the corresponding difference between attending and non-attending children found in schools that did not have the program.

Another example can be found in Pitt and Khandker (1998) who assessed the impact of participation in Bangladesh's Grameen Bank (GB) on various indicators relevant to current and future living standards. GB credit is targeted to landless households in poor villages. Some of their sampled villages were not eligible for the program and within the eligible villages, some households were not eligible, namely those with land (though it is not clear how well this was enforced). The authors implicitly use an unusual *DD* design to estimate impact.[41] Naturally, the returns to having land are higher in villages that do not have access to GB credit (given that access to GB raises the returns to being landless). Comparing the returns to having land between two otherwise identical sets of villages – one eligible for GB and one not – reveals the impact of GB credit. So the Pitt–Khandker estimate of the impact of GB is actually the impact on the returns to land of *taking away* village-level access to the GB.[42] By interpretation, the "pre-intervention baseline" in the Pitt–Khandker study is provided by the villages that *have* the GB, and the "program" being evaluated is not GB but rather having land and hence becoming ineligible for GB. (I return to this example below.)

The use of different methods and data sets on the same program can be revealing. As compared to the study by Jalan and Ravallion (2002) on the same program (Argentina's *Trabajar* program), Ravallion et al. (2005) used a lighter survey instrument, with far fewer questions on relevant characteristics of participants and non-participants. These data did not deliver plausible single-difference estimates using PSM when compared to the Jalan–Ravallion estimates for the same program on richer data. The likely explanation is that using the lighter survey instrument meant that there were many unobservable differences; in other words the conditional independence assumption of PSM was not valid. Given the sequence of the two evaluations, the key omitted variables in the later study were known – they mainly related to local level connections (as evident in memberships of various neighborhood associations and length of time living in the same barrio). However, the lighter survey instrument used by Ravallion et al. (2005) had the advantage that the same households were followed up over time to form a panel data set. It would appear that Ravallion et al. were able to satisfactorily address the problem of bias in the lighter survey instrument by tracking households over time, which allowed them to difference-out the mismatching errors arising from incomplete data.

---

[41] This is my interpretation; Pitt and Khandker (1998) do not mention the *DD* interpretation of their design. However, it is readily verified that the impact estimator implied by solving Eqs. (4)(a)–(d) in their paper is the *DD* estimator described here. (Note that the resulting *DD* must be normalized by the proportion of landless households in eligible villages to obtain the impact parameter for GB.)

[42] Equivalently, they measure impact by the mean gain amongst households who are landless from living in a village that is eligible for GB, less the corresponding gain amongst those with land.

This illustrates the trade-off between collecting cross-sectional data for the purpose of single-difference matching, versus collecting longitudinal data with a lighter survey instrument. An important factor in deciding which method to use is how much we know *ex ante* about the determinants of program placement. If a single survey can convincingly capture these determinants then PSM will work well; if not then one is well advised to do at least two rounds of data collection and use *DD*, possibly combined with PSM, as discussed below.

While panel data are not essential for estimating *DD*, household-level panel data open up further options for the counterfactual analysis of the joint distribution of outcomes over time for the purpose of understanding the impacts on *poverty dynamics*. This approach is developed in Ravallion, van de Walle and Gaurtam (1995) for the purpose of measuring the impacts of changes in social spending on the inter-temporal joint distribution of income. Instead of only measuring the impact on poverty (the marginal distribution of income) the authors distinguish impacts on the number of people who escape poverty over time (the "promotion" role of a safety net) from impacts on the number who fall into poverty (the "protection" role). Ravallion et al. apply this approach to an assessment of the impact on poverty transitions of reforms in Hungary's social safety net. Other examples can be found in Lokshin and Ravallion (2000) (on the impacts of changes in Russia's safety net during an economy-wide financial crisis), Gaiha and Imai (2002) (on the Employment Guarantee Scheme in the Indian state of Maharashtra) and van de Walle (2004) (on assessing the performance of Vietnam's safety net in dealing with income shocks).

Panel data also facilitate the use of dynamic regression estimators for the *DD*. An example of this approach can be found in Jalan and Ravallion (2002), who identified the effects of lagged infrastructure endowments in a dynamic model of consumption growth using a six-year household panel data set. Their econometric specification is an example of the non-stationary fixed-effects model proposed by Holtz-Eakin, Newey and Rosen (1988), which allows for latent individual and geographic effects and can be estimated using the Generalized Method of Moments, treating lagged consumption growth and the time-varying regressors as endogenous (using sufficiently long lags as instrumental variables). The authors found significant longer-term consumption gains from improved infrastructure, such as better rural roads.

7.3. *Concerns about DD designs*

Two key problems have plagued *DD* estimators. The first is that, in practice, one sometimes does not know at the time the baseline survey is implemented who will participate in the program. One must make an informed guess in designing the sampling for the baseline survey; knowledge of the program design and setting can provide clues. Types of observation units with characteristics making them more likely to participate will often have to be over-sampled, to help assure adequate coverage of the population treatment group and to provide a sufficiently large pool of similar comparators to draw upon. Problems can arise later if one does not predict well enough *ex ante* who will participate. For example, Ravallion and Chen (2005) had designed their survey so that the comparison group would be drawn from randomly sampled villages in the same poor counties of rural China in which it was known that the treatment villages were to be found (for a poor-area development program). However, the authors subsequently discovered that there was sufficient heterogeneity within poor counties to mean that many of the selected comparison villages had to be dropped to assure common support. With the benefit of hindsight, greater effort should have been made to over-sample relatively poor villages within poor countries.

The second source of concern is the *DD* assumption of time-invariant selection bias. Infrastructure improvements may well be attracted to places with rising productivity, leading a geographic fixed-effects specification to overestimate the economic returns to new development projects. The opposite bias is also possible. Poor-area development programs are often targeted to places that lack infrastructure and other conditions conducive to economic growth. Again the endogeneity problem cannot be dealt with properly by positing a simple additive fixed effect. The selection bias is not constant over time and the *DD* will then be a biased impact estimator.

Figure 3 illustrates the point. Mean outcomes are plotted over time, before and after the intervention. The lightly-shaded circles represent the observed means for the treatment units, while the hatched circle is the counterfactual at date $t = 1$. Panel (a) shows the initial selection bias, arising from the fact that the program targeted poorer areas than the comparison units (dark-shaded). This is not a problem as long as the bias is time invariant, as in panel (b). However, when the attributes on which targeting is based also influence subsequent growth prospects we get a downward bias in the *DD* estimator, as in panel (c).

Two examples from actual evaluations illustrate the problem. Jalan and Ravallion (1998) show that poor-area development projects in rural China have been targeted to areas with poor infrastructure *and* that these same characteristics resulted in lower growth rates; presumably, areas with poor infrastructure were less able to participate in the opportunities created by China's growing economy. Jalan and Ravallion show that there is a large bias in *DD* estimators in this case, since the changes over time are a function of initial conditions (through an endogenous growth model) that also influence program placement. On correcting for this bias by controlling for the area characteristics that initially attracted the development projects, the authors found significant longer-term impacts while none had been evident in the standard *DD* estimator.

The second example is the Pitt and Khandker (1998) study of Grameen Bank. Following my interpretation above of their method of assessing the impacts of GB credit, it is clear that the key assumption is that the returns to having land are independent of village-level GB eligibility. A bias will arise if GB tends to select villages that have either unusually high or low returns to land. It seems plausible that the returns to land are lower in villages selected for GB (which may be why they are poor in the first place) and low returns to land would also suggest that such villages have a comparative advantage in the non-farm activities facilitated by GB credit. Then the Pitt–Khandker method will overestimate GB's impact.

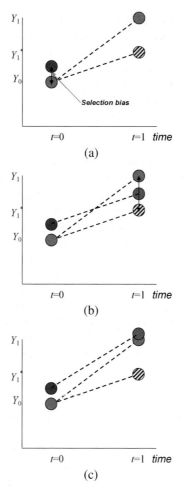

Figure 3. Bias in double-difference estimates for a targeted anti-poverty program.

The upshot of these observations is that controlling for initial heterogeneity is crucial to the credibility of *DD* estimates. Using PSM for selecting the initial comparison group is an obvious corrective, and this will almost certainly reduce the bias in *DD* estimates. In an example in the context of poor-area development programs, Ravallion and Chen (2005) first used PSM to clean out the initial heterogeneity between targeted villages and comparison villages, before applying *DD* using longitudinal observations for both sets of villages. When relevant, pipeline comparison groups can also help to reduce bias in *DD* studies (Galasso and Ravallion, 2004). The *DD* method can also be combined with a discontinuity design (Jacob and Lefgren, 2004).

These observations point to important synergies between better data and methods for making single difference comparisons (on the one hand) and double-difference (on the other). Longitudinal observations can help reduce bias in single difference comparisons (eliminating the additive time-invariant component of selection bias). And successful efforts to clean out the heterogeneity in baseline data such as by PSM can reduce the bias in *DD* estimators.

7.4. What if baseline data are unavailable?

Anti-poverty programs in developing countries often have to be set up quickly in response to a macroeconomic or agro-climatic crisis; it is not feasible to delay the operation to do a baseline survey. (Needless to say, nor is randomization an option.) Even so, under certain conditions, impacts can still be identified by observing participants' outcomes in the absence of the program *after* the program rather than before it. To see what is involved, recall that the key identifying assumption in all double-difference studies is that the selection bias into the program is additively separable from outcomes and time invariant. In the standard set-up described earlier in this section, date 0 precedes the intervention and *DD* gives the mean current gain to participants in date 1. However, suppose now that the program is in operation at date 0. The scope for identification arises from the fact that some participants at date 0 subsequently drop out of the program. The *triple-difference* (*DDD*) estimator proposed by Ravallion et al. (2005) is the difference between the double differences for stayers and leavers. Ravallion et al. show that their *DDD* estimator consistently identifies the mean gain to participants at date 1 (*TT*) if two conditions hold: (i) there is no selection bias in terms of who leaves the program and (ii) there are no current gains to non-participants. They also show that a third survey round allows a joint test of these two conditions. If these conditions hold and there is no selection bias in period 2, then there should be no difference in the estimate of gains to participants in period 1 according to whether or not they drop out in period 2.

In applying the above approach, Ravallion et al. (2005) examine what happens to participants' incomes when they leave Argentina's *Trabajar* program as compared to the incomes of continuing participants, after netting out economy-wide changes, as revealed by a matched comparison group of non-participants. The authors find partial income replacement, amounting to one-quarter of the *Trabajar* wage within six months of leaving the program, though rising to one half in 12 months. Thus they find evidence of a post-program "Ashenfelter's dip," namely when earnings drop sharply at retrenchment, but then recover.[43]

Suppose instead that we do not have a comparison group of nonparticipants; we calculate the *DD* for stayers versus leavers (that is, the gain over time for stayers less that for leavers). It is evident that this will only deliver an estimate of the current gain to participants if the counter-factual changes over time are the same for leavers as for stayers.

---

[43] "Ashenfelter's dip" refers to the bias in using *DD* for inferring long-term impacts of training programs that can arise when there is a pre-program earnings dip (as was found in Ashenfelter, 1978).

More plausibly, one might expect stayers to be people who tend to have lower prospects for gains over time than leavers in the absence of the program. Then the simple *DD* for stayers versus leavers will underestimate the impact of the program. In their specific setting, Ravallion et al. find that the *DD* for stayers relative to leavers (ignoring those who never participated) turned out to give a quite good approximation to the *DDD* estimator. However, this may not hold in other applications.

8. Instrumental variables

The nonexperimental estimators discussed so far require some form of (conditional) exogeneity assumption for program placement. The single-difference methods assume that placement is uncorrelated with the latent determinants of outcome *levels* while the double-difference assumes that changes in placement are uncorrelated with the changes in these latent factors. We now turn to a popular method that relaxes these assumptions, but adds new ones.

8.1. The instrumental variables estimator (IVE)

Returning to the archetypal model in Section 2, the standard linear IVE makes two extra assumptions. The first is that there exists an *instrumental variable* (IV), denoted Z, which influences program placement independently of X:

$$T_i = \gamma Z_i + X_i \delta + v_i \quad (\gamma \neq 0). \tag{11}$$

(Z is exogenous, as is X.) The second assumption is that impacts are *homogeneous*, in that outcomes respond identically across all units at given X ($\mu_i^T = \mu_i^C$ for all i in the archetypal model of Section 2); a common special case in practice is the *common-impact model*:

$$Y_i = ATE \cdot T_i + X_i \beta^C + \mu_i^C. \tag{5}$$

We do not, however, assume conditional exogeneity of placement. Thus v_i and μ_i^C are potentially correlated, inducing selection bias ($E(\mu^C \mid X, T) \neq 0$). But now there is a solution. Substituting (11) into (5) we obtain the reduced form equation for outcomes:

$$Y_i = \pi Z_i + X_i (\beta^C + ATE \cdot \delta) + \mu_i \tag{12}$$

where $\pi = ATE\gamma$ and $\mu_i = ATEv_i + \mu_i^C$. Since OLS gives consistent estimates of both (11) and (12), the Instrumental Variables Estimator (IVE), $\hat{\pi}_{OLS}/\hat{\gamma}_{OLS}$, consistently estimates ATE.[44] The assumption that Z_i is not an element of X_i allows us to identify π in (12) separately from β^C. This is called the "*exclusion restriction*" (in that Z_i is excluded from (5)).

---

[44] A variation is to rewrite (11) as a nonlinear binary response model (such as a probit or logit) and use the predicted propensity score as the IV for program placement (Wooldridge, 2002, Chapter 18).

8.2. Strengths and weaknesses of the IVE method

The standard (linear) IVE method described above shares some of the weaknesses of other NX methods. As with OLS, the validity of causal inferences typically rests on *ad hoc* assumptions about the outcome regression, including its functional form. PSM, by contrast, is non-parametric in the outcome space.

However, when a valid IV is available, the real strength of IVE over most other NX estimators is its robustness to the existence of unobserved variables that jointly influence program placement and outcomes.[45] This also means that (under its assumptions) IVE is less demanding of our ability to model the program's assignment than PSM. IVE gives a consistent estimate of *ATE* in the presence of omitted determinants of program placement. And if one has a valid IV then one can use this to test the exogeneity assumption of PSM or OLS.

This strength of IVE rests on the validity of its assumptions, and large biases in IVE can arise if they do not hold.[46] The best work in the IVE tradition gives close scrutiny to those assumptions. It is easy to test if $\gamma \neq 0$ in (11). The exclusion restriction is more difficult. If one has more than one valid IV then (under the other assumptions of IVE) one can do the standard over-identification test. However, one must still have at least one IV and so the exclusion restriction is fundamentally untestable within the confines of the data available. Nonetheless, appeals to theoretical arguments or other evidence (external to the data used for the evaluation) can often leave one reasonably confident in accepting, or rejecting, a postulated exclusion restriction in the specific context.

Note that the exclusion restriction is not strictly required when a *nonlinear* binary response model is used for the first stage, instead of the linear model in (11). Then the impact is identified off the nonlinearity of the first stage regression. However, it is widely considered preferable to have an identification strategy that is robust to using a linear first stage regression. This is really a matter of judgment; identification off nonlinearity is still identification. Nonetheless, it is worrying when identification rests on an *ad hoc* assumption about functional form and the distribution of an error term.

---

[45] IVE is not the only NX method that relaxes conditional exogeneity. The control-function approach mentioned in Section 5 also provides a method of addressing endogeneity; by adding a suitable control function (or "generalized residual") to the outcome regression one can eliminate the selection bias. Todd (2008) provides a useful overview of these approaches. In general, the CF approach should give similar results to IVE. Indeed, the two estimates are formally identical for a linear first-stage regression (as in Eq. (11)), since then the control function approach amounts to running OLS on (5) augmented to include $\hat{v}_i = T_i - \hat{\gamma} Z_i$ as an additional regressor (Hausman, 1978). This CF removes the source of selection bias, arising from the fact that $\text{Cov}(v_i, \mu_i^C) \neq 0$.

[46] Recall that Glazerman, Levy and Myers (2003) found that this type of method of correcting for selection bias tended in fact to be bias-increasing, when compared to experimental results on the same programs; they point to invalid exclusion restrictions as the likely culprit.

8.3. Heterogeneity in impacts

The common-impact assumption in (5) is not a harmless simplification, but is crucial to identifying mean impact using IVE (Heckman, 1997). To see why, return to the more general model in Section 2, in which impact heterogeneity arises from differences between the *latent* factors in outcomes under treatment versus those under the counterfactual; write this as: $G_i = ATE + \mu_i^T - \mu_i^C$. Then (5) becomes:

$$Y_i = ATE \cdot T_i + X_i \beta^C + \left[\mu_i^C + \left(\mu_i^T - \mu_i^C \right) T_i \right] \tag{13}$$

where the term in [·] is the new error term. For IVE to consistently estimate *ATE* we now require that $\mathrm{Cov}[Z, (\mu^T - \mu^C)T] = 0$ (on top of $\gamma \neq 0$ and $\mathrm{Cov}(Z, \mu^C) = 0$). This will fail to hold if selection into the program is informed by the idiosyncratic differences in impact ($\mu^T - \mu^C$); likely "winners" will no doubt be attracted to a program, or be favored by the implementing agency. This is what Heckman, Urzua and Vytlacil (2006) call "essential heterogeneity." (Note that this is no less of a concern in social experiments with randomized assignment but selective compliance.) To interpret the IVE as an estimate of ATE, we must assume that the relevant agents do not know μ^T or μ^C, or do not act on that information. These are strong assumptions.

  With heterogeneous impacts, IVE identifies impact for a specific population subgroup, namely those induced to take up the program by the exogenous variation attributable to the IV.[47] This sub-group is rarely identified explicitly in IVE studies, so it remains worryingly unclear how one should interpret the estimated IVE. It is presumably the impact for someone, but who?

  The *local instrumental variables* (LIV) estimator of Heckman and Vytlacil (2005) directly addresses this issue. LIV entails a nonparametric regression of outcomes Y on the propensity score, $P(X, Z)$.[48] Intuitively, the slope of this regression function gives the impact at the specific values of X and Z; in fact this slope is the *marginal treatment effect* introduced by Björklund and Moffitt (1987), from which any of the standard impact parameters can be calculated using appropriate weights (Heckman and Vytlacil, 2005). To see whether impact heterogeneity is an issue in practice, Heckman, Urzua and Vytlacil (2006) recommend that one should first test for linearity of Y in the propensity score. (A standard functional form test, such as RESET, would be appropriate.) If nonlinearity is indicated then LIV is the appropriate estimator; but if not then the standard IVE is justified; indeed, the OLS regression coefficient of Y on the propensity score $P(X, Z)$ directly gives *ATE* in this case (Heckman, 1997).

---

[47] The outcome gain for this sub-group is sometimes called the "local average treatment effect" (LATE) (Imbens and Angrist, 1994). Also see the discussion of LATE in Heckman (1997).

[48] Linear controls X can be included, making this a "partial linear model"(for a continuous propensity score); see Yatchew (1998) on partial linear models and other topics in nonparametric regression analysis.

8.4. Bounds on impact

In practice, IVE sometimes gives seemingly implausible impact estimates (either too small or too large). One might suspect that a violation of the exclusion restriction is the reason. But how can we form judgments about this issue in a more scientific way? If it is possible to rule out certain values for Y on *a priori* grounds then this can allow us to establish plausible bounds to the impact estimates (following an approach introduced by Manski, 1990). This is easily done if the outcome variable is being "poor" versus "non-poor" (or some other binary outcome). Then $0 \leqslant TT \leqslant E(Y^T \mid T = 1)(\leqslant 1)$ and[49]:

$$\left(E\left[Y^T \mid T = 1\right] - 1\right) \Pr(T = 1) - E\left[Y^C \mid T = 0\right] \Pr(T = 0)$$
$$\leqslant ATE \leqslant \left(1 - E\left[Y^C \mid T = 0\right]\right) \Pr(T = 0) + E\left[Y^T \mid T = 1\right] \Pr(T = 1).$$

The width of these bounds will (of course) depend on the specifics of the setting. The bounds may not be of much use in the (common) case of continuous outcome variables.

Another approach to setting bounds has been proposed by Altonji, Elder and Taber (2005a, 2005b) (AET). The authors recognize the likely bias in OLS for the relationship of interest (in their case probably overestimating the true impact), but they also question the exclusion restrictions used in past IV estimates. Recall that OLS assumes that the unobservables affecting outcomes are uncorrelated with program placement. AET study the implications of the extreme alternative assumption: that the unobservables in outcomes have the same effect on placement as does the index of the observables (the term $X_i \beta^C$ in (5)); in other words, the selection on unobservables is assumed to be as great as that for the observables.[50] Implementing this assumption requires constraining the correlation coefficient between the error terms of the equations for outcomes and participation (μ^C in (5) and ν in (11)) to a value given by the regression coefficient of the score function for observables in the participation equation ($X_i \delta$ in Eq. (11) with $\gamma = 0$) on the corresponding score function for outcomes ($X_i \beta^C$).

AET argue that their estimator is a lower bound to the true impact when the latter is positive; this rests on the (*a priori* reasonable) presumption that the error term in the outcomes equation includes at least some factors that are truly uncorrelated with participation. OLS provides an upper bound. Thus, the AET estimator gives a useful indication of how sensitive OLS is to any selection bias based on unobservables. Altonji, Elder and Taber (2005b) also show how their method can be used to assess the potential bias in IVE due to an invalid exclusion restriction. One would question an IVE that was outside the interval spanning the AET and OLS estimators.

[49] The lower bound for *ATE* is found by setting $E[Y^T \mid T = 0] = 0$ and $E[Y^C \mid T = 1] = 1$ while the upper bound is found at $E[Y^T \mid T = 0] = 1$, $E[Y^C \mid T = 1] = 0$.
[50] Altonji, Elder and Taber (2005a) gives conditions under which this will hold. However (as they note) these conditions are not expected to hold in practice; their estimator provides a bound to the true estimate, rather than an alternative point estimate.

8.5. Examples if IVE in practice

There are two main sources of IVs, namely experimental design features and *a priori* arguments about the determinants of program placement and outcomes. The following discussion considers examples of each.

As noted in Section 4, it is often the case in social experiments that some of those randomly selected for the program do not want to participate. So there is a problem that actual participation is endogenous. However, the randomized assignment provides a natural IV in this case (Dubin and Rivers, 1993; Angrist, Imbens and Rubin, 1996; the latter paper provides a formal justification for using IVE for this problem). The exclusion restriction is that being randomly assigned to the program only affects outcomes via actual program participation.

An example is found in the aforementioned MTO experiment, in which randomly-selected inner-city families in US cities were given vouchers to buy housing in better-off areas. Not everyone offered a voucher took up the opportunity. The difference in outcomes (such as school drop-out rates) only reveal the extent of the external (neighborhood) effect if one corrects for the endogenous take-up using the randomized assignment as the IV (Katz, Kling and Liebman, 2001).

An example for a developing country is the *Proempleo* experiment. Recall that this included a randomly-assigned training component. Under the assumption of perfect take-up or random non-compliance, neither the employment nor incomes of those receiving the training were significantly different to those of the control group 18 months after the experiment began.[51] However, some of those assigned the training component did not want it, and this selection process was correlated with the outcomes from training. An impact of training was revealed for those with secondary schooling, but only when the authors corrected for compliance bias using assignment as the IV for treatment (Galasso, Ravallion and Salvia, 2004).

Randomized outreach (often called an "encouragement design") can also provide a valid IV.[52] The idea is that, for the purpose of the evaluation, one disseminates extra information/publicity on the (non-randomly placed) program to a random sample. One expects this to be correlated with program take-up and the exclusion restriction is also plausible.

The above discussion has focused on the use of randomized assignment as an IV for treatment, given selective compliance. This idea can be generalized to the use of randomization in identifying economic models of outcomes, or of behaviors instrumental to determining outcomes. We return to this topic in Section 9.

---

[51] The wage subsidy included in the *Proempleo* experiment did have a significant impact on employment, but not current incomes, though it is plausible that expected future incomes were higher; see Galasso, Ravallion and Salvia (2004) for further discussion.

[52] Useful discussions of encouragement designs can be found in Bradlow (1998) and Hirano et al. (2000). I do not know of any examples for anti-poverty programs in developing countries.

The bulk of the applications of IVE have used nonexperimental IVs. In the literature in labor economics, wage regressions often allow for endogenous labor-force participation (and hence selection of those observed to have wages). A common source of IVs is found in modeling the choice problem, whereby it is postulated that there are variables that influence the costs and benefits of labor-force participation but do not affect earnings given that choice; there is a large literature on such applications of IVE and related control function estimators.[53]

The validity of such exclusion restrictions can be questioned. For example, consider the problem of identifying the impact of an individually-assigned training program on wages. Following past literature in labor economics one might use characteristics of the household to which each individual belongs as IVs for program participation. These characteristics influence take-up of the program but are unlikely to be directly observable to employers; on this basis it is argued that they should not affect wages conditional on program participation (and other observable control variables, such as age and education of the individual worker). However, for at least some of these potential IVs, this exclusion restriction is questionable when there are productivity-relevant spillover effects within households. For example, in developing-country settings it has been argued that the presence of a literate person in the household can exercise a strong effect on an illiterate worker's productivity; this is argued in theory and with supporting evidence (for Bangladesh) in Basu, Narayan and Ravallion (2002).

In evaluating anti-poverty programs in developing countries, three popular sources of instrumental variables have been the geographic placement of programs, political variables and discontinuities created by program design.[54] I consider examples of each.

The *geography of program placement* has been used for identification in a number of studies. I discuss three examples. Ravallion and Wodon (2000) test the widely heard claim that child labor displaces schooling and so perpetuates poverty in the longer term. They used the presence of a targeted school enrollment-subsidy in rural Bangladesh (the Food-for-Education Program) as the source of a change in the price of schooling in their model of schooling and child labor. To address the endogeneity of placement at the individual level they used prior placement at the village level as the IV. The worry here is the possibility that village placement is correlated with geographic factors relevant to outcomes. Drawing on external information on the administrative assignment rules, Ravallion and Wodon provide exogeneity tests that offer some support their identification strategy, although this ultimately rests on an untestable exclusion restriction and/or nonlinearity for identification. Their results indicate that the subsidy increased schooling by far more than it reduced child labor. Substitution effects appear to have helped protect current incomes from the higher school attendance induced by the subsidy.

---

[53] For an excellent overview see Heckman, La Londe and Smith (1999).

[54] Natural events (twins, birth dates, rainfall) have also been used as IVs in a number of studies (for an excellent review see Rosenzweig and Wolpin, 2000). These are less common as IVs for poverty programs, although we consider one example (for infrastructure).

A second example of this approach can be found in Attanasio and Vera-Hernandez (2004) who study the impacts of a large nutrition program in rural Colombia that provided food and child care through local community centers. Some people used these facilities while some did not, and there must be a strong presumption that usage is endogenous to outcomes in this setting. To deal with this problem, Attanasio and Vera-Hernandez used the distance of a household to the community center as the IV for attending the community center. These authors also address the objections that can be raised against the exclusion restriction.[55] Distance could itself be endogenous through the location choices made by either households or the community centers. Amongst the justifications they give for their choice of IV, the authors note that survey respondents who have moved recently never identified the desire to move closer to a community center as one of the reasons for choosing their location (even though this was one of the options). They also note that if their results were in fact driven by endogeneity of their IV then they would find (spurious) effects on variables that should not be affected, such as child birth weight. However, they do not find such effects, supporting the choice of IV.

The geography of program placement sometimes involves natural, topographic or agro-climatic, features that can aid identification. An example is provided by the Duflo and Pande (2007) study of the district-level poverty impacts of dam construction in India. To address the likely endogeneity of dam placement they exploit the fact that the distribution of land by gradient affects the suitability of a district for dams (with more positive gradients making a dam less costly).[56] Their key identifying assumption is that gradient does not have an independent effect on outcomes. To assess whether that is a plausible assumption one needs to know more about other possible implications of differences in land gradient; for example, for most crops land gradient matters to productivity (positively for some negatively for others), which would invalidate the IV. The authors find that a dam increases poverty in its vicinity but helps the poor downstream; on balance their results suggest that dams are poverty increasing.

Political characteristics of geographic areas have been another source of instruments. Understanding the political economy of program placement can aid in identifying impacts. For example, Besley and Case (2000) use the presence of women in state parliaments (in the US) as the IV for workers' compensation insurance when estimating the impacts of compensation on wages and employment. The authors assume that female law makers favor workers' compensation but that this does not have an independent effect on the labor market. The latter condition would fail to hold if a higher incidence of women in parliament in a given state reflected latent social factors that lead to higher

---

[55] As in the Ravallion–Wodon example, the other main requirement of a valid IV, namely that it is correlated with treatment, is more easily satisfied in this case.

[56] Note that what the authors refer to as "river gradient" is actually based on the distribution of land gradients in an area that includes a river. (See Duflo and Pande, 2007, Appendix, p. 641.)

female labor force participation generally, with implications for aggregate labor market outcomes of both men and women.

To give another example, Paxson and Schady (2002) used the extent to which recent elections had seen a switch against the government as the IV for the geographic allocation of social fund spending in Peru, when modeling schooling outcomes. Their idea was that the geographic allocation of spending would be used in part to "buy back" voters that had switched against the government in the last election. (Their first stage regression was consistent with this hypothesis.) It must also be assumed that the fact that an area turned against the government in the last election is not correlated with latent factors influencing schooling. The variation in spending attributed to this IV was found to significantly increase school attendance rates.

The third set of examples exploit *discontinuities in program design*, as discussed in Section 6.[57] Here the impact estimator is in the neighborhood of a cut-off for program eligibility. An example of this approach can be found in Angrist and Lavy (1999) who assessed the impact on school attainments in Israel of class size. For identification they exploited the fact that an extra teacher was assigned when the class size went above 40. Yet there is no plausible reason why this cut-off point in class size would have an independent effect on attainments, thus justifying the exclusion restriction. The authors find sizeable gains from smaller class sizes, which were not evident using OLS.

Another example is found in Duflo's (2003) study of the impacts of old-age pensions in South Africa on child anthropometric indicators. Women only become eligible for a pension at age 60, while for men it is 65. It is implausible that there would be a discontinuity in outcomes (conditional on treatment) at these critical ages. Following Case and Deaton (1998), Duflo used eligibility as the IV for receipt of a pension in her regressions for anthropometric outcome variables. Duflo found that pensions going to women improve girls' nutritional status but not boys', while pensions going to men have no effect on outcomes for either boys or girls.

Again, this assumes we know eligibility, which is not always the case. Furthermore, eligibility for anti-poverty programs is often based on poverty criteria, which are also the relevant outcome variables. Then one must be careful not to make assumptions in estimating who is eligible (for constructing the IV) that pre-judge the impacts of the program.

The use of the discontinuity in the eligibility rule as an IV for actual program placement can also address concerns about selective compliance with those rules; this is discussed further in Battistin and Rettore (2002).

As these examples illustrate, the justification of an IVE must ultimately rest on sources of information outside the confines of the quantitative analysis. Those sources

---

[57] Using discontinuities in IVE will not in general give the same results as the discontinuity designs discussed in Section 6. Specific conditions for equivalence of the two methods are derived in Hahn, Todd and Van der Klaauw (2001); the main conditions for equivalence are that the means used in the single-difference comparison are calculated using appropriate kernel weights and that the IVE estimator is applied to a specific sub-sample, in a neighborhood of the eligibility cut-off point.

might include theoretical arguments, common sense, or empirical arguments based on different types of data, including qualitative data, such as based on knowledge of how the program operates in practice. While the exclusion restriction is ultimately untestable, some studies do a better job than others of justifying in their specific case. Almost all applied work has assumed homogeneous impacts, despite the repeated warnings of Heckman and others. Relaxing this assumption in specific applications appears to be a fertile ground for future research.

9. Learning from evaluations

So far we have focused on the "internal validity" question: does the evaluation design allow us to obtain a reliable estimate of the counterfactual outcomes in the specific context? This has been the main focus of the literature to date. However, there are equally important concerns related to what can be learnt from an impact evaluation beyond its specific setting. This section turns to the "external validity" question as to whether the results from specific evaluations can be applied in other settings (places and/or dates) and what lessons can be drawn for development knowledge and future policy from evaluative research.

9.1. Do publishing biases inhibit learning from evaluations?

Development policy-making draws on accumulated knowledge built up from published evaluations. Thus publication processes and the incentives facing researchers are relevant to our success against poverty and in achieving other development goals. It would not be too surprising to find that it is harder to publish a paper that reports unexpected or ambiguous impacts, when judged against received theories and/or past evidence. Reviewers and editors may well apply different standards in judging data and methods according to whether they believe the results on *a priori* grounds. To the extent that impacts are generally expected from anti-poverty programs (for that is presumably the main reason why the programs exist) this will mean that our knowledge is biased in favor of positive impacts. In exploring a new type of program, the results of the early studies will set the priors against which later work is judged. An initial bad draw from the true distribution of impacts may then distort knowledge for some time after. Such biases would no doubt affect the production of evaluative research as well as publications; researchers may well work harder to obtain positive findings to improve their chances of getting their work published. No doubt, extreme biases (in either direction) will be eventually exposed, but this may take some time.

These are largely conjectures on my part. Rigorous testing requires some way of inferring the counterfactual distribution of impacts, in the absence of publication biases. Clearly this is difficult. However, there is at least one strand of evaluative research where publication bias is unlikely, namely replication studies that have compared NX results with experimental findings for the same programs (as in the meta-study for labor programs in developed countries by Glazerman, Levy and Myers, 2003). Comparing the distribution of *published* impact estimates from (non-replication) NX studies with a counterfactual drawn from replication studies of the same type of programs could throw useful light on the extent of publication bias.

9.2. Can the lessons from an evaluation be scaled up?

The context of an intervention often matters to its outcomes, thus confounding inferences for "scaling up" from an impact evaluation. Such "site effects" arise whenever aspects of a program's setting (geographic or institutional) interact with the treatment. The same program works well in one village but fail hopelessly in another. For example, in studying Bangladesh's *Food-for-Education* Program, Galasso and Ravallion (2005) found that the program worked well in reaching the poor in some villages but not in others, even in relatively close proximity. Site effects clearly make it difficult to draw valid inferences for scaling up and replication based on trials.

The local institutional context of an intervention is likely to be relevant to its impact. External validity concerns about impact evaluations can arise when certain institutions need to be present to even facilitate the experiments. For example, when randomized trials are tied to the activities of specific Non-Governmental Organizations (NGOs) as the facilitators, there is a concern that the same intervention at national scale may have a very different impact in places without the NGO. Making sure that the control group areas also have the NGO can help, but even then we cannot rule out interaction effects between the NGO's activities and the intervention. In other words, the effect of the NGO may not be "additive" but "multiplicative," such that the difference between measured outcomes for the treatment and control groups does not reveal the impact in the absence of the NGO.

A further external-validity concern is that, while partial equilibrium assumptions may be fine for a pilot, *general equilibrium effects* (sometimes called "feedback" or "macro" effects in the evaluation literature) can be important when it is scaled up nationally. For example, an estimate of the impact on schooling of a tuition subsidy based on a randomized trial may be deceptive when scaled up, given that the structure of returns to schooling will alter.[58] To give another example, a small pilot wage subsidy program such as implemented in the *Proempleo* experiment may be unlikely to have much impact on the market wage rate, but that will change when the program is scaled up. Here again the external validity concern stems from the context-specificity of trials; outcomes in the context of the trial may differ appreciably (in either direction) once the intervention is scaled up and prices and wages respond.

---

[58] Heckman, Lochner and Taber (1998) demonstrate that partial equilibrium analysis can greatly overestimate the impact of a tuition subsidy once relative wages adjust; Lee (2005) finds a much smaller difference between the general and partial equilibrium effects of a tuition subsidy in a slightly different model.

Contextual factors are clearly crucial to policy and program performance; at the risk of overstating the point, in certain contexts anything will work, and in others everything will fail. A key factor in program success is often adapting properly to the institutional and socio-economic context in which you have to work. That is what good project staff do all the time. They might draw on the body of knowledge from past evaluations, but these can almost never be conclusive and may even be highly deceptive if used mechanically.

The realized impacts on scaling up can also differ from the trial results (whether randomized or not) because the socio-economic composition of program participation varies with scale. Ravallion (2004) discusses how this can happen, and presents results from a series of country case studies, all of which suggest that the incidence of program benefits becomes more pro-poor with scaling up. Trial results may well underestimate how pro-poor a program is likely to be after scaling up because the political economy entails that the initial benefits tend to be captured more by the non-poor (Lanjouw and Ravallion, 1999).

9.3. What determines impact?

These external validity concerns point to the need to supplement the evaluation tools described above by other sources of information that can throw light on the *processes* that influence the measured outcomes.

One approach is to repeat the evaluation in different contexts, as proposed by Duflo and Kremer (2005). An example can be found in the aforementioned study by Galasso and Ravallion in which the impact of Bangladesh's *Food-for-Education* program was assessed across each of 100 villages in Bangladesh and the results were correlated with characteristics of those villages. The authors found that the revealed differences in program performance were partly explicable in terms of observable village characteristics, such as the extent of intra-village inequality (with more unequal villages being less effective in reaching their poor through the program).

Repeating evaluations across different settings and at different scales can help address these concerns, although it will not always be feasible to do a sufficient number of trials to span the relevant domain of variation found in reality. The scale of a randomized trial needed to test a large national program could be prohibitive. Nonetheless, varying contexts for trials is clearly a good idea, subject to feasibility. The failure to systematically plan locational variation into their design has been identified as a serious weakness in the randomized field trials that have been done of welfare reforms in the US (Moffitt, 2003).

Important clues to understanding impacts can often be found in the geographic differences in impacts and how this relates to the characteristics of locations, such as the extent of local inequality, "social capital" and the effectiveness of local public agencies; again, see the example in Galasso and Ravallion (2005). This calls for adequate samples at (say) village level. However, this leads to a further problem. For a given aggregate sample size, larger samples at local level will increase the design effect on the standard error of the overall impact estimate.[59] Evaluations can thus face a serious trade-off between the need for precision in estimating overall impacts and the ability to measure and explain the underlying heterogeneity in impacts. Small-area estimation methods can sometimes improve the trade-off by exploiting Census (or larger sample survey) data on covariates of the relevant outcomes and/or explanatory variables at local level; a good example in the present context can be found in Caridad et al. (2006).

Another lens for understanding impacts is to study what can be called "intermediate" outcome measures. The typical evaluation design identifies a small number of "final outcome" indicators, and aims to assess the program's impact on those indicators. Instead of using only final outcome indicators, one may choose to also study impacts on certain intermediate indicators of behavior. For example, the inter-temporal behavioral responses of participants in anti-poverty programs are of obvious relevance to understanding their impacts. An impact evaluation of a program of compensatory cash transfers to Mexican farmers found that the transfers were partly invested, with second-round effects on future incomes (Sadoulet, de Janvry and Davis, 2001). Similarly, Ravallion and Chen (2005) found that participants in a poor-area development program in China saved a large share of the income gains from the program (as estimated using the matched double-difference method described in Section 7). Identifying responses through savings and investment provides a clue to understanding current impacts on living standards and the possible future welfare gains beyond the project's current lifespan. Instead of focusing solely on the agreed welfare indicator, one collects and analyzes data on a potentially wide range of intermediate indicators relevant to understanding the processes determining impacts.

This also illustrates a common concern in evaluation studies, given behavioral responses, namely that the study period is rarely much longer than the period of the program's disbursements. However, a share of the impact on peoples' living standards may occur beyond the life of the project. This does not necessarily mean that credible evaluations will need to track welfare impacts over much longer periods than is typically the case – raising concerns about feasibility. But it does suggest that evaluations need to look carefully at impacts on partial intermediate indicators of longer-term impacts even when good measures of the welfare objective are available within the project cycle. The choice of such indicators will need to be informed by an understanding of participants' behavioral responses to the program.

In learning from an evaluation, one often needs to draw on information external to the evaluation. Qualitative research (intensive interviews with participants and administrators) can be a useful source of information on the underlying processes determining outcomes.[60] One approach is to use such methods to test the assumptions made by an intervention; this has been called "theory-based evaluation," although that is hardly an

---

[59] The design effect (*DE*) is the ratio of the actual variance (for a given variable in the specific survey design) to the variance in a simple random sample; this is given by $DE = 1 + \rho(B - 1)$ where ρ is the intra-cluster correlation coefficient and B is the cluster sample size (Kish, 1965, Chapter 5).
[60] See the discussion on "mixed methods" in Rao and Woolcock (2003).

ideal term given that NX identification strategies for mean impacts are often theory-based (as discussed in the last section). Weiss (2001) illustrates this approach in the abstract in the context of evaluating the impacts of community-based anti-poverty programs. An example is found in an evaluation of social funds (SFs) by the World Bank's Operations Evaluation Department, as summarized in Carvalho and White (2004). While the overall aim of a SF is typically to reduce poverty, the OED study was interested in seeing whether SFs worked the way that was intended by their designers. For example, did local communities participate? Who participated? Was there "capture" of the SF by local elites (as some critics have argued)? Building on Weiss (2001), the OED evaluation identified a series of key hypothesized links connecting the intervention to outcomes and tested whether each one worked. For example, in one of the country studies for the OED evaluation of SFs, Rao and Ibanez (2005) tested the assumption that a SF works by local communities collectively proposing the sub-projects that they want; for a SF in Jamaica, the authors found that the process was often dominated by local elites.

In practice, it is very unlikely that all the relevant assumptions are testable (including alternative assumptions made by different theories that might yield similar impacts). Nor is it clear that the process determining the impact of a program can always be decomposed into a neat series of testable links within a unique causal chain; there may be more complex forms of interaction and simultaneity that do not lend themselves to this type of analysis. For these reasons, the so-called "theory-based evaluation" approach cannot be considered a serious substitute for assessing impacts on final outcomes by credible (experimental or NX) methods, although it can still be a useful complement to such evaluations, to better understanding measured impacts.

Project monitoring data bases are an important, under-utilized, source of information. Too often the project monitoring data and the information system have negligible evaluative content. This is not inevitably the case. For example, the idea of combining spending maps with poverty maps for rapid assessments of the targeting performance of a decentralized anti-poverty program is a promising illustration of how, at modest cost, standard monitoring data can be made more useful for providing information on how the program is working and in a way that provides sufficiently rapid feedback to a project to allow corrections along the way (Ravallion, 2000).

The *Proempleo* experiment provides an example of how information external to the evaluation can carry important lessons for scaling up. Recall that *Proempleo* randomly assigned vouchers for a wage subsidy across (typically poor) people currently in a workfare program and tracked their subsequent success in getting regular work. A randomized control group located the counterfactual. The results did indicate a significant impact of the wage-subsidy voucher on employment. But when cross-checks were made against central administrative data, supplemented by informal interviews with the hiring firms, it was found that there was very low take-up of the wage subsidy by firms (Galasso, Ravallion and Salvia, 2004). The scheme was highly cost effective; the government saved 5% of its workfare wage bill for an outlay on subsidies that represented only 10% of that saving.

However, the supplementary cross-checks against other data revealed that *Proempleo* did not work the way its design had intended. The bulk of the gain in employment for participants was not through higher demand for their labor induced by the wage subsidy. Rather the impact arose from supply side effects; the voucher had credential value to workers – it acted like a "letter of introduction" that few people had (and how it was allocated was a secret locally). This could not be revealed by the (randomized) evaluation, but required supplementary data. The extra insight obtained about how *Proempleo* actually worked in the context of its trial setting also carried implications for scaling up, which put emphasis on providing better information for poor workers about how to get a job rather than providing wage subsidies.

Spillover effects also point to the importance of a deeper understanding of how a program operates. Indirect (or "second-round") impacts on non-participants are common. A workfare program may lead to higher earnings for non-participants. Or a road improvement project in one area might improve accessibility elsewhere. Depending on how important these indirect effects are thought to be in the specific application, the "program" may need to be redefined to embrace the spillover effects. Or one might need to combine the type of evaluation discussed here with other tools, such as a model of the labor market to pick up other benefits.

The extreme form of a spillover effect is an economy-wide program. The evaluation tools discussed in this chapter are for assigned programs, but have little obvious role for economy-wide programs in which no explicit assignment process is evident, or if it is, the spillover effects are likely to be pervasive. When some countries get the economy-wide program but some do not, cross-country comparative work (such as growth regressions) can reveal impacts. That identification task is often difficult, because there are typically latent factors at country level that simultaneously influence outcomes and whether a country adopts the policy in question. And even when the identification strategy is accepted, carrying the generalized lessons from cross-country regressions to inform policy-making in any one country can be highly problematic. There are also a number of promising examples of how simulation tools for economy wide policies such as Computable General Equilibrium models can be combined with household-level survey data to assess impacts on poverty and inequality.[61] These simulation methods make it far easier to attribute impacts to the policy change, although this advantage comes at the cost of the need to make many more assumptions about how the economy works.

9.4. Is the evaluation answering the relevant policy questions?

Arguably the most important things we want to learn from any evaluation relate to its lessons for future policies. Here standard evaluation practices can start to look disappointingly uninformative on closer inspection.

---

[61] See, for example, Bourguignon, Robilliard and Robinson (2003) and Chen and Ravallion (2004).

One issue is the choice of counterfactual. The classic formulation of the evaluation problem assesses mean impacts on those who receive the program, relative to counterfactual outcomes in the absence of the program. However, this may fall well short of addressing the concerns of policy makers. While common practice is to use outcomes in the absence of the program as the counterfactual, the alternative of interest to policy makers is often to spend the same resources on some other program (possibly a different version of the same program), rather than to do nothing. The evaluation problem is formally unchanged if we think of some alternative program as the counterfactual. Or, in principle, we might repeat the analysis relative to the "do nothing counterfactual" for each possible alternative and compare them, though this is rare in practice. A specific program may appear to perform well against the option of doing nothing, but poorly against some feasible alternative.

For example, drawing on their impact evaluation of a workfare program in India, Ravallion and Datt (1995) show that the program substantially reduced poverty amongst the participants relative to the counterfactual of no program. Yet, once the costs of the program were factored in (including the foregone income of workfare participants), the authors found that the alternative counterfactual of a uniform (un-targeted) allocation of the same budget outlay would have had more impact on poverty.[62]

A further issue, with greater bearing on the methods used for evaluation, is whether we have identified the most relevant impact parameters from the point of view of the policy question at hand. The classic formulation of the evaluation problem focuses on mean outcomes, such as mean income or consumption. This is hardly appropriate for programs that have as their (more or less) explicit objective to reduce poverty, rather than to promote economic growth *per se*. However, as noted in Section 3, there is nothing to stop us re-interpreting the outcome measure such that Eq. (2) gives the program's impact on the headcount index of poverty (% below the poverty line). By repeating the impact calculation for multiple "poverty lines" one can then trace out the impact on the cumulative distribution of income. This is feasible with the same tools, though evaluation practice has been rather narrow in its focus.

There is often interest in better understanding the *horizontal impacts* of program, meaning the differences in impacts at a given level of counterfactual outcomes, as revealed by the joint distribution of Y^T and Y^C. We cannot know this from a social experiment, which only reveals net counterfactual mean outcomes for those treated; *TT* gives the mean gain net of losses amongst participants. Instead of focusing solely on the net gains to the poor (say) we may ask how many losers there are amongst the poor, and how many gainers. We already discussed an example in Section 7, namely the use of panel data in studying impacts of an anti-poverty program on poverty dynamics. Some interventions may yield losers even though mean impact is positive and policy makers will understandably want to know about those losers, as well as the gainers. (This can

---

[62] For another example of the same result see Murgai and Ravallion (2005).

be true at any given poverty line.) Thus one can relax the "anonymity" or "veil of igno-rance" assumption of traditional welfare analysis, whereby outcomes are judged solely by changes in the marginal distribution (Carneiro, Hansen and Heckman, 2001).

Heterogeneity in the impacts of anti-poverty programs can be expected. Eligibility criteria impose differential costs on participants. For example, the foregone labor earn-ings incurred by participants in workfare or conditional cash transfer schemes (via the loss of earnings from child labor) will vary according to skills and local labor-market conditions. Knowing more about this heterogeneity is relevant to the political economy of anti-poverty policies, and may also point to the need for supplementary policies for better protecting the losers.

Heterogeneity of impacts in terms of observables is readily allowed for by adding interaction effects with the treatment dummy variable, as in Eq. (4), though this is still surprisingly far from universal practice. One can also allow for latent heterogeneity, using a random coefficients estimator in which the impact estimate (the coefficient on the treatment dummy variable) contains a stochastic component (i.e., $\mu_i^T \neq \mu_i^C$ in the error term of Eq. (4)). Applying this type of estimator to the evaluation data for *PRO-GRESA*, Djebbari and Smith (2005) find that they can convincingly reject the common effects assumption in past evaluations. When there is such heterogeneity, one will of-ten want to distinguish marginal impacts from average impacts. Following Björklund and Moffitt (1987), the marginal treatment effect can be defined as the mean gain to units that are indifferent between participating and not. This requires that we model ex-plicitly the choice problem facing participants (Björklund and Moffitt, 1987; Heckman and Navarro-Lozano, 2004). We may also want to estimate the joint distribution of Y^T and Y^C, and a method for doing so is outlined in Heckman, Smith and Clements (1997).

However, it is questionable how relevant the choice models found in this literature are to the present setting. The models have stemmed mainly from the literature on evaluat-ing training and other programs in developed countries, in which selection is seen as a largely a matter of individual choice, amongst those eligible. This approach does not sit easily with what we know about many anti-poverty programs in developing countries, in which the choices made by politicians and administrators appear to be at least as important to the selection process as the choices made by those eligible to participate.

This speaks to the need for a richer theoretical characterization of the selection prob-lem in future work. An example of one effort in this direction can be found in the Galasso and Ravallion (2005) model of the assignment of a decentralized anti-poverty program; their model focuses on the public-choice problem facing the central gov-ernment and the local collective action problem facing communities, with individual participation choices treated as a trivial problem. Such models can also point to instru-mental variables for identifying impacts and studying their heterogeneity.

When the policy issue is whether to expand a given program at the margin, the classic estimator of mean-impact on the treated is actually of rather little interest. The problem of estimating the marginal impact of a greater duration of exposure to the program on those treated was considered in Section 7, using the example of comparing "leavers" and "stayers" in a workfare program (Ravallion et al., 2005). Another example can be found in the study by Behrman, Cheng and Todd (2004) of the impacts on children's cognitive skills and health status of longer exposure to a preschool program in Bolivia. The authors provide an estimate of the marginal impact of higher program duration by comparing the cumulative effects of different durations using a matching estimator. In such cases, selection into the program is not an issue, and we do not even need data on units who never participated. The discontinuity design method discussed in Section 6 (in its non-parametric form) and Section 8 (in its parametric IV form) is also delivering an estimate of the marginal gain from a program, namely the gain when the program is expanded (or contracted) by a small change in the eligibility cut-off point.

A deeper understanding of the factors determining outcomes in *ex post* evaluations can also help in simulating the likely impacts of changes in program or policy design *ex ante*. Naturally, *ex ante* simulations require many more assumptions about how an economy works.[63] As far as possible one would like to see those assumptions anchored to past knowledge built up from rigorous *ex post* evaluations. For example, by combining a randomized evaluation design with a structural model of education choices and exploiting the randomized design for identification, one can greatly expand the set of policy-relevant questions about the design of *PROGRESA* that a conventional evaluation can answer (Todd and Wolpin, 2002; Attanasio, Meghir and Santiago, 2004, and de Janvry and Sadoulet, 2006). This strand of the literature has revealed that a budget-neutral switch of the enrollment subsidy from primary to secondary school would have delivered a net gain in school attainments, by increasing the proportion of children who continue onto secondary school. While *PROGRESA* had an impact on schooling, it could have had a larger impact. However, it should be recalled that this type of program has two objectives: increasing schooling (reducing future poverty) and reducing current poverty, through the targeted transfers. To the extent that refocusing the subsidies on secondary schooling would reduce the impact on current income poverty (by increasing the forgone income from children's employment), the case for this change in the program's design would need further analysis.

10. Conclusions

Two main lessons for future evaluations of anti-poverty programs emerge from this survey. Firstly, no single evaluation tool can claim to be ideal in all circumstances. While randomization can be a powerful tool for assessing mean impact, it is neither necessary nor sufficient for a good evaluation, and nor is it always feasible, notably for large public programs. While economists have sometimes been too uncritical of their non-experimental identification strategies, credible means of isolating at least a share of the exogenous variation in an endogenously placed program can still be found in practice. Good evaluations draw pragmatically from the full range of tools available. This

---

[63] For a useful overview of *ex ante* methods see Bourguignon and Ferreira (2003). Todd and Wolpin (2006) provide a number of examples, including for a schooling subsidy program, using the PROGRESA data.

may involve randomizing some aspects and using econometric methods to deal with the non-random elements, or by using randomized elements of a program as a source of instrumental variables. Likely biases in specific nonexperimental methods can also be reduced by combining with other methods. For example, depending on the application at hand (including the data available and its quality), single-difference matching methods can be vulnerable to biases stemming from latent non-ignorable factors, while standard double-difference estimators are vulnerable to biases arising from the way differing initial conditions can influence the subsequent outcome changes over time (creating a time-varying selection bias). With adequate data, combining matching (or weighting) using propensity scores with double-difference methods can reduce the biases in each method. (In other words, conditional exogeneity of placement with respect to *changes* in outcomes will often be a more plausible assumption than conditional exogeneity in levels.) Data quality is key to all these methods, as is knowledge of the program and context. Good evaluations typically require that the evaluator is involved from the program's inception and is very well informed about how the program works on the ground; the features of program design and implementation can sometimes provide important clues for assessing impact by nonexperimental means.

Secondly, the standard tools of counter-factual analysis for mean impacts can be seen to have some severe limitations for informing development policy making. We have learnt that the context in which a program is placed and the characteristics of the participants can exercise a powerful influence on outcomes. And not all of this heterogeneity in impacts can readily be attributed to observables, which greatly clouds the policy interpretation of standard methods. We need a deeper understanding of this heterogeneity in impacts; this can be helped by systematic replications across differing contexts and the new econometric tools that are available for identifying local impacts. The assumptions made in a program's design also need close scrutiny, such as by tracking intermediate variables of relevance or by drawing on supplementary theories or evidence external to the evaluation. In drawing lessons for anti-poverty policy, we also need a richer set of impact parameters than has been traditional in evaluation practice, including distinguishing the gainers from the losers at any given level of living. The choice of parameters to be estimated in an evaluation must ultimately depend on the policy question to be answered; for policy makers this is a mundane point, but for evaluators it seems to be ignored too often.

References

Aakvik, A. (2001). "Bounding a matching estimator: The case of a Norwegian training program". Oxford Bulletin of Economics and Statistics 639 (1), 115–143.

Abadie, A., Imbens, G. (2006). "Large sample properties of matching estimators for average treatment effects". Econometrica 74 (1), 235–267.

Agodini, R., Dynarski, M. (2004). "Are experiments the only option? A look at dropout prevention programs". Review of Economics and Statistics 86 (1), 180–194.

Altonji, J., Elder, T.E., Taber, C.R. (2005a). "Selection on observed and unobserved variables: Assessing the effectiveness of catholic schools". Journal of Political Economy 113 (1), 151–183.

Altonji, J., Elder, T.E., Taber, C.R. (2005b). "An evaluation of instrumental variable strategies for estimating the effects of catholic schools". Journal of Human Resources 40 (4), 791–821.

Angrist, J., Hahn, J. (2004). "When to control for covariates? Panel asymptotics for estimates of treatment effects". Review of Economics and Statistics 86 (1), 58–72.

Angrist, J., Imbens, G., Rubin, D. (1996). "Identification of causal effects using instrumental variables". Journal of the American Statistical Association XCI, 444–455.

Angrist, J., Lavy, V. (1999). "Using Maimonides' rule to estimate the effect of class size on scholastic achievement". Quarterly Journal of Economics 114 (2), 533–575.

Angrist, J., Bettinger, E., Bloom, E., King, E., Kremer, M. (2002). "Vouchers for private schooling in Colombia: Evidence from a randomized natural experiment". American Economic Review 92 (5), 1535–1558.

Ashenfelter, O. (1978). "Estimating the effect of training programs on earnings". Review of Economic Studies 60, 47–57.

Atkinson, A. (1987). "On the measurement of poverty". Econometrica 55, 749–764.

Attanasio, O., Meghir, C., Santiago, A. (2004). "Education choices in Mexico: Using a structural model and a randomized experiment to evaluate PROGRESA". Working paper EWP04/04. Institute of Fiscal Studies, London.

Attanasio, O., Vera-Hernandez, A.M. (2004). "Medium and long run effects of nutrition and child care: Evaluation of a community nursery programme in rural Colombia". Working paper EWP04/06. Centre for the Evaluation of Development Policies, Institute of Fiscal Studies, London.

Basu, K., Narayan, A., Ravallion, M. (2002). "Is literacy shared within households?" Labor Economics 8, 649–665.

Battistin, E., Rettore, E. (2002). "Testing for programme effects in a regression discontinuity design with imperfect compliance". Journal of the Royal Statistical Society A 165 (1), 39–57.

Behrman, J., Cheng, Y., Todd, P. (2004). "Evaluating preschool programs when length of exposure to the program varies: A nonparametric approach". Review of Economics and Statistics 86 (1), 108–132.

Behrman, J., Sengupta, P., Todd, P. (2002). "Progressing through PROGESA: An impact assessment of a school subsidy experiment in Mexico". Mimeo, University of Pennsylvania.

Bertrand, M., Duflo, E., Mullainathan, S. (2004). "How much should we trust differences-in-differences estimates?" Quarterly Journal of Economics 119 (1), 249 275.

Besley, T., Case, A. (2000). "Unnatural experiments? Estimating the incidence of endogenous policies". Economic Journal 110 (November), F672–F694.

Binswanger, H., Khandker, S.R., Rosenzweig, M. (1993). "How infrastructure and financial institutions affect agricultural output and investment in India". Journal of Development Economics 41, 337–366.

Björklund, A., Moffitt, R. (1987). "The estimation of wage gains and welfare gains in self-selection". Review of Economics and Statistics 69 (1), 42–49.

Bourguignon, F., Ferreira, F. (2003). "Ex ante evaluation of policy reforms using behavioural models". In: Bourguignon, F., Pereira da Silva, L. (Eds.), The Impact of Economic Policies on Poverty and Income Distribution. Oxford Univ. Press, New York.

Bourguignon, F., Robilliard, A.-S., Robinson, S. (2003). "Representative versus real households in the macroeconomic modeling of inequality". Working paper 2003-05. DELTA, Paris.

Bradlow, E. (1998). "Encouragement designs: An approach to self-selected samples in an experimental design". Marketing Letters 9 (4), 383–391.

Buddlemeyer, H., Skoufias, E. (2004). "An evaluation of the performance of regression discontinuity design on PROGRESA". Working paper 3386. Policy Research, The World Bank, Washington, DC.

Burtless, G. (1985). "Are targeted wage subsidies harmful? Evidence from a wage voucher experiment". Industrial and Labor Relations Review 39, 105–115.

Burtless, G. (1995). "The case for randomized field trials in economic and policy research". Journal of Economic Perspectives 9 (2), 63–84.

Caliendo, M., Kopeinig, S. (2005). "Some practical guidance for the implementation of propensity score matching". Paper 1588. Institute for the Study of Labor, IZA.

Caridad, A., Ferreira, F., Lanjouw, P., Ozler, B. (2006). "Local inequality and project choice: Theory and evidence from Ecuador". Working paper 3997. Policy Research, The World Bank, Washington, DC.

Carneiro, P., Hansen, K., Heckman, J. (2001). "Removing the veil of ignorance in assessing the distributional impacts of social policies". Swedish Economic Policy Review 8, 273–301.

Carvalho, S., White, H. (2004). "Theory-based evaluation: The case of social funds". American Journal of Evaluation 25 (2), 141–160.

Case, A., Deaton, A. (1998). "Large cash transfers to the elderly in South Africa". Economic Journal 108, 1330–1361.

Chase, R. (2002). "Supporting communities in transition: The impact of the Armenian social investment fund". World Bank Economic Review 16 (2), 219–240.

Chen, S., Mu, R., Ravallion, M. (2006). "Are there lasting impacts of aid to poor areas? Evidence from rural China. Working paper 4084. Policy Research, The World Bank, Washington, DC.

Chen, S., Ravallion, M. (2004). "Household welfare impacts of WTO accession in China". World Bank Economic Review 18 (1), 29–58.

Cook, T. (2001). "Comments: Impact evaluation, concepts and methods". In: Feinstein, O., Piccioto, R. (Eds.), Evaluation and Poverty Reduction. Transaction Publications, New Brunswick, NJ.

Deaton, A. (1997). The Analysis of Household Surveys, a Microeconometric Approach to Development Policy. Johns Hopkins Univ. Press, Baltimore, for the World Bank.

Deaton, A. (2005). "Measuring poverty in a growing world (or measuring growth in a poor world)". Review of Economics and Statistics 87 (1), 1–19.

Dehejia, R. (2005). "Practical propensity score matching: A reply to Smith and Todd". Journal of Econometrics 125 (1–2), 355–364.

Dehejia, R., Wahba, S. (1999). "Causal effects in non-experimental studies: Re-evaluating the evaluation of training programs". Journal of the American Statistical Association 94, 1053–1062.

de Janvry, A., Sadoulet, E. (2006). "Making conditional cash transfer programs more efficient: Designing for maximum effect of the conditionality". World Bank Economic Review 20 (1), 1–29.

Diaz, J.J., Handa, S. (2004). "An assessment of propensity score matching as a non-experimental impact estimator: Evidence from a Mexican poverty program". Mimeo. University of North Carolina, Chapel Hill.

Djebbari, H., Smith, J. (2005). "Heterogeneous program impacts of PROGRESA". Mimeo, Laval University and University of Michigan.

Dubin, J.A., Rivers, D. (1993). "Experimental estimates of the impact of wage subsidies". Journal of Econometrics 56 (1/2), 219–242.

Duflo, E. (2001). "Schooling and labor market consequences of school construction in Indonesia: Evidence from an unusual policy experiment". American Economic Review 91 (4), 795–813.

Duflo, E. (2003). "Grandmothers and granddaughters: Old age pension and intrahousehold allocation in South Africa". World Bank Economic Review 17 (1), 1–26.

Duflo, E., Kremer, M. (2005). "Use of randomization in the evaluation of development effectiveness". In: Pitman, G., Feinstein, O., Ingram, G. (Eds.), Evaluating Development Effectiveness. Transaction Publishers, New Brunswick, NJ.

Duflo, E., Pande, R. (2007). "Dams". Quarterly Journal of Economics 122 (2), 601–646.

Fraker, T., Maynard, R. (1987). "The adequacy of comparison group designs for evaluations of employment-related programs". Journal of Human Resources 22 (2), 194–227.

Frankenberg, E., Suriastini, W., Thomas, D. (2005). "Can expanding access to basic healthcare improve children's health status? Lessons from Indonesia's 'Midwife in the Village' program". Population Studies 59 (1), 5–19.

Frölich, M. (2004). "Finite-sample properties of propensity-score matching and weighting estimators". Review of Economics and Statistics 86 (1), 77–90.

Gaiha, R., Imai, K. (2002). "Rural public works and poverty alleviation: The case of the employment guarantee scheme in Maharashtra". International Review of Applied Economics 16 (2), 131–151.

Galasso, E., Ravallion, M. (2004). "Social protection in a crisis: Argentina's plan Jefes y Jefas". World Bank Economic Review 18 (3), 367–399.

Galasso, E., Ravallion, M. (2005). "Decentralized targeting of an anti-poverty program". Journal of Public Economics 85, 705–727.

Galasso, E., Ravallion, M., Salvia, A. (2004). "Assisting the transition from workfare to work: Argentina's Proempleo experiment". Industrial and Labor Relations Review 57 (5), 128–142.

Galiani, S., Gertler, P., Schargrodsky, E. (2005). "Water for life: The impact of the privatization of water services on child mortality". Journal of Political Economy 113 (1), 83–119.

Gertler, P. (2004). "Do conditional cash transfers improve child health? Evidence from PROGRESA's control randomized experiment". American Economic Review, Papers and Proceedings 94 (2), 336–341.

Glazerman, S., Levy, D., Myers, D. (2003). "Non-experimental versus experimental estimates of earnings impacts". Annals of the American Academy of Political and Social Sciences 589, 63–93.

Glewwe, P., Kremer, M., Moulin, S., Zitzewitz, E. (2004). "Retrospective vs. prospective analysis of school inputs: The case of flip charts in Kenya". Journal of Development Economics 74, 251–268.

Godtland, E., Sadoulet, E., de Janvry, A., Murgai, R., Ortiz, O. (2004). "The impact of farmer field schools on knowledge and productivity: A study of potato farmers in the Peruvian Andes". Economic Development and Cultural Change 53 (1), 63–92.

Hahn, J. (1998). "On the role of the propensity score in efficient semiparametric estimation of average treatment effects". Econometrica 66, 315–331.

Hahn, J., Todd, P., Van der Klaauw, W. (2001). "Identification and estimation of treatment effects with a regression-discontinuity design". Econometrica 69 (1), 201–209.

Hausman, J. (1978). "Specification tests in econometrics". Econometrica 46, 1251–1271.

Heckman, J. (1997). "Instrumental variables: A study of implicit behavioral assumptions used in making program evaluations". Journal of Human Resources 32 (3), 441–462.

Heckman, J., Hotz, J. (1989). "Choosing among alternative NX methods for estimating the impact of social programs: The case of manpower training". Journal of the American Statistical Association 84, 862–874.

Heckman, J., Ichimura, H., Todd, P. (1997). "Matching as an econometric evaluation estimator: Evidence from evaluating a job training programme". Review of Economic Studies 64 (4), 605–654.

Heckman, J., La Londe, R., Smith, J. (1999). "The economics and econometrics of active labor market programs". In: Ashenfelter, A., Card, D. (Eds.), Handbook of Labor Economics, vol. 3. Elsevier Science, Amsterdam.

Heckman, J., Lochner, L., Taber, C. (1998). "General equilibrium treatment effects". American Economic Review, Papers and Proceedings 88, 381–386.

Heckman, J., Navarro-Lozano, S. (2004). "Using matching, instrumental variables and control functions to estimate economic choice models". Review of Economics and Statistics 86 (1), 30–57.

Heckman, J., Robb, R. (1985). "Alternative methods of evaluating the impact of interventions". In: Heckman, J., Singer, B. (Eds.), Longitudinal Analysis of Labor Market Data. Cambridge Univ. Press, Cambridge.

Heckman, J., Smith, J. (1995). "Assessing the case for social experiments". Journal of Economic Perspectives 9 (2), 85–110.

Heckman, J., Smith, J., Clements, N. (1997). "Making the most out of programme evaluations and social experiments: Accounting for heterogeneity in programme impacts". Review of Economic Studies 64 (4), 487–535.

Heckman, J., Todd, P. (1995). "Adapting propensity score matching and selection model to choice-based samples". Working paper. Department of Economics, University of Chicago.

Heckman, J., Urzua, S., Vytlacil, E. (2006). "Understanding instrumental variables in models with essential heterogeneity". Review of Economics and Statistics 88 (3), 389–432.

Heckman, J., Vytlacil, E. (2005). "Structural equations, treatment effects and econometric policy evaluation". Econometrica 73 (3), 669–738.

Heckman, J., Ichimura, H., Smith, J., Todd, P. (1998). "Characterizing selection bias using experimental data". Econometrica 66, 1017–1099.

Hirano, K., Imbens, G. (2004). "The propensity score with continuous treatments". In: Missing Data and Bayesian Methods in Practice. Wiley, in press.

Hirano, K., Imbens, G., Ridder, G. (2003). "Efficient estimation of average treatment effects using the estimated propensity score". Econometrica 71, 1161–1189.

Hirano, K., Imbens, G.W., Ruben, D.B., Zhou, X.-H. (2000). "Assessing the effect of an influenza vaccine in an encouragement design". Biostatistics 1 (1), 69–88.

Hoddinott, J., Skoufias, E. (2004). "The impact of PROGRESA on food consumption". Economic Development and Cultural Change 53 (1), 37–61.

Holland, P. (1986). "Statistics and causal inference". Journal of the American Statistical Association 81, 945–960.

Holtz-Eakin, D., Newey, W., Rosen, H. (1988). "Estimating vector autoregressions with panel data". Econometrica 56, 1371–1395.

Imbens, G. (2000). "The role of the propensity score in estimating dose-response functions". Biometrika 83, 706–710.

Imbens, G. (2004). "Nonparametric estimation of average treatment effects under exogeneity: A review". Review of Economics and Statistics 86 (1), 4–29.

Imbens, G., Angrist, J. (1994). "Identification and estimation of local average treatment effects". Econometrica 62 (2), 467–475.

Imbens, G., Lemieux, T., (2007). "Regression discontinuity designs: A guide to practie". Journal of Econometrics, in press.

Jacob, B., Lefgren, L. (2004). "Remedial education and student achievement: A regression-discontinuity analysis". Review of Economics and Statistics 86 (1), 226–244.

Jacoby, H.G. (2002). "Is there an intrahousehold 'flypaper effect'? Evidence from a school feeding programme". Economic Journal 112 (476), 196–221.

Jalan, J., Ravallion, M. (1998). "Are there dynamic gains from a poor-area development program?" Journal of Public Economics 67 (1), 65–86.

Jalan, J., Ravallion, M. (2002). "Geographic poverty traps? A micro model of consumption growth in rural China". Journal of Applied Econometrics 17 (4), 329–346.

Jalan, J., Ravallion, M. (2003a). "Does piped water reduce diarrhea for children in rural India?" Journal of Econometrics 112, 153–173.

Jalan, J., Ravallion, M. (2003b). "Estimating benefit incidence for an anti-poverty program using propensity score matching". Journal of Business and Economic Statistics 21 (1), 19–30.

Kapoor, A.G. (2002). "Review of impact evaluation methodologies used by the operations evaluation department over 25 years". Operations Evaluation Department, The World Bank.

Katz, L.F., Kling, J.R., Liebman, J.B. (2001). "Moving to opportunity in Boston: Early results of a randomized mobility experiment". Quarterly Journal of Economics 116 (2), 607–654.

Keane, M. (2006). "Structural vs. atheoretical approaches to econometrics." Mimeo, Yale University.

Kish, L. (1965). Survey Sampling. John Wiley, New York.

Korinek, A., Mistiaen, J., Ravallion, M. (2006). "Survey nonresponse and the distribution of income". Journal of Economic Inequality 4 (2), 33–55.

La Londe, R. (1986). "Evaluating the econometric evaluations of training programs". American Economic Review 76, 604–620.

Lanjouw, P., Ravallion, M. (1999). "Benefit incidence and the timing of program capture". World Bank Economic Review 13 (2), 257–274.

Lechner, M. (2001). "Identification and estimation of causal effects of multiple treatments under the conditional independence assumption". In: Lechner, M., Pfeiffer, F. (Eds.), Econometric Evaluations of Labour Market Policies. Physica-Verlag, Heidelberg.

Lee, D. (2005). "An estimable dynamic general equilibrium model of work, schooling, and occupational choice". International Economic Review 46 (1), 1–34.

Lokshin, M., Ravallion, M. (2000). "Welfare impacts of Russia's 1998 financial crisis and the response of the public safety net". Economics of Transition 8 (2), 269–295.

Manski, C. (1990). "Nonparametric bounds on treatment effects". American Economic Review, Papers and Proceedings 80, 319–323.

Manski, C. (1993). "Identification of endogenous social effects: The reflection problem". Review of Economic Studies 60, 531–542.

Miguel, E., Kremer, M. (2004). "Worms: Identifying impacts on education and health in the presence of treatment externalities". Econometrica 72 (1), 159–217.

Moffitt, R. (2001). "Policy interventions, low-level equilibria and social interactions". In: Durlauf, S., Peyton Young, H. (Eds.), Social Dynamics. MIT Press, Cambridge MA.

Moffitt, R. (2003). "The role of randomized field trials in social science research: A perspective from evaluations of reforms of social welfare programs". Working paper CWP23/02. CEMMAP, Department of Economics, University College London.

Murgai, R., Ravallion, M. (2005). "Is a guaranteed living wage a good anti-poverty policy?" Working paper. Policy Research, The World Bank, Washington, DC.

Newman, J., Pradhan, M., Rawlings, L.B., Ridder, G., Coa, R., Evia, J.L. (2002). "An impact evaluation of education, health, and water supply investments by the Bolivian social investment fund". World Bank Economic Review 16, 241–274.

Paxson, C., Schady, N.R. (2002). "The allocation and impact of social funds: Spending on school infrastructure in Peru". World Bank Economic Review 16, 297–319.

Piehl, A., Cooper, S., Braga, A., Kennedy, D. (2003). "Testing for structural breaks in the evaluation of programs". Review of Economics and Statistics 85 (3), 550–558.

Pitt, M., Khandker, S. (1998). "The impact of group-based credit programs on poor households in Bangladesh: Does the gender of participants matter?" Journal of Political Economy 106, 958–998.

Rao, V., Ibanez, A.M. (2005). "The social impact of social funds in Jamaica: A mixed methods analysis of participation, targeting and collective action in community driven development". Journal of Development Studies 41 (5), 788–838.

Rao, V., Woolcock, M. (2003). "Integrating qualitative and quantitative approaches in program evaluation". In: Bourguignon, F., Pereira da Silva, L. (Eds.), The Impact of Economic Policies on Poverty and Income Distribution. Oxford Univ. Press, New York.

Ravallion, M. (2000). "Monitoring targeting performance when decentralized allocations to the poor are unobserved". World Bank Economic Review 14 (2), 331–345.

Ravallion, M. (2003a). "Assessing the poverty impact of an assigned program". In: Bourguignon, F., Pereira da Silva, L. (Eds.), The Impact of Economic Policies on Poverty and Income Distribution. Oxford Univ. Press, New York.

Ravallion, M. (2003b). "Measuring aggregate economic welfare in developing countries: How well do national accounts and surveys agree?" Review of Economics and Statistics 85, 645–652.

Ravallion, M. (2004). "Who is protected from budget cuts?" Journal of Policy Reform 7 (2), 109–122.

Ravallion, M. (2005). "Poverty lines". In: Blume, L., Durlauf, S. (Eds.), New Palgrave Dictionary of Economics, second ed. Palgrave Macmillan, London.

Ravallion, M., Chen, S. (2005). "Hidden impact: Household saving in response to a poor-area development project". Journal of Public Economics 89, 2183–2204.

Ravallion, M., Datt, G. (1995). "Is targeting through a work requirement efficient? Some evidence for rural India". In: van de Walle, D., Nead, K. (Eds.), Public Spending and the Poor: Theory and Evidence. Johns Hopkins Univ. Press, Baltimore.

Ravallion, M., van de Walle, D., Gaurtam, M. (1995). "Testing a social safety net". Journal of Public Economics 57 (2), 175–199.

Ravallion, M., Wodon, Q. (2000). "Does child labor displace schooling? Evidence on behavioral responses to an enrollment subsidy". Economic Journal 110, C158–C176.

Ravallion, M., Galasso, E., Lazo, T., Philipp, E. (2005). "What can ex-participants reveal about a program's impact?" Journal of Human Resources 40 (Winter), 208–230.

Rosenbaum, P. (1995). Observational Studies. Springer-Verlag, New York.

Rosenbaum, P., Rubin, D. (1983). "The central role of the propensity score in observational studies for causal effects". Biometrika (70), 41–55.

Rosenzweig, M., Wolpin, K. (2000). "Natural experiments in economics". Journal of Economic Literature 38 (4), 827–874.

Roy, A. (1951). "Some thoughts on the distribution of earnings". Oxford Economic Papers 3, 135–145.

Rubin, D.B. (1974). "Estimating causal effects of treatments in randomized and nonrandomized studies". Journal of Education Psychology 66, 688–701.

Rubin, D.B. (1980). "Discussion of the paper by D. Basu". Journal of the American Statistical Association 75, 591–593.

Rubin, D.B., Thomas, N. (2000). "Combining propensity score matching with additional adjustments for prognostic covariates". Journal of the American Statistical Association 95, 573–585.

Sadoulet, E., de Janvry, A., Davis, B. (2001). "Cash transfer programs with income multipliers: PROCAMPO in Mexico". World Development 29 (6), 1043–1056.

Schultz, T.P. (2004). "School subsidies for the poor: Evaluating the Mexican PROGRESA poverty program". Journal of Development Economics 74 (1), 199–250.

Skoufias, E. (2005). "PROGRESA and its impact on the welfare of rural households in Mexico". Research report 139. International Food Research Institute, Washington, DC.

Smith, J., Todd, P. (2001). "Reconciling conflicting evidence on the performance of propensity-score matching methods". American Economic Review 91 (2), 112–118.

Smith, J., Todd, P. (2005a). "Does matching overcome La Londe's critique of NX estimators?" Journal of Econometrics 125 (1–2), 305–353.

Smith, J., Todd, P. (2005b). "Rejoinder". Journal of Econometrics 125 (1–2), 365–375.

Thomas, D., Frankenberg, E., Friedman, J. et al. (2003). "Iron deficiency and the well-being of older adults: Early results from a randomized nutrition intervention". Paper Presented at the Population Association of America Annual Meetings, Minneapolis.

Todd, P. (2008). "Evaluating social programs with endogenous program placement and selection of the treated". In: Schultz, T.P., Strauss, J. (Eds.), Handbook of Development Economics, vol. 4. Elsevier/North-Holland, Amsterdam. (Chapter 60 in this book.)

Todd, P., Wolpin, K. (2002). "Using a social experiment to validate a dynamic behavioral model of child schooling and fertility: Assessing the impact of a school subsidy program in Mexico." Working paper 03-022. Penn Institute for Economic Research, Department of Economics, University of Pennsylvania.

Todd, P., Wolpin, K. (2006). "Ex-ante evaluation of social programs". Mimeo. Department of Economics, University of Pennsylvania.

van de Walle, D. (2002). "Choosing rural road investments to help reduce poverty". World Development 30 (4).

van de Walle, D. (2004). "Testing Vietnam's safety net". Journal of Comparative Economics 32 (4), 661–679.

van de Walle, D., Mu, R. (2007). "Fungibility and the flypaper effect of project aid: Micro-evidence for Vietnam". Journal of Development Economics 84 (2), 667–685.

Vella, F., Verbeek, M. (1999). "Estimating and interpreting models with endogenous treatment effects". Journal of Business and Economic Statistics 17 (4), 473–478.

Weiss, C. (2001). "Theory-based evaluation: Theories of change for poverty reduction programs". In: Feinstein, O., Piccioto, R. (Eds.), Evaluation and Poverty Reduction. Transaction Publications, New Brunswick, NJ.

Woodbury, S., Spiegelman, R. (1987). "Bonuses to workers and employers to reduce unemployment". American Economic Review (77), 513–530.

Wooldridge, J. (2002). Econometric Analysis of Cross Section and Panel Data. MIT Press, Cambridge, MA.

Yatchew, A. (1998). "Nonparametric regression techniques in economics". Journal of Economic Literature 36 (June), 669–721.

Chapter 60

EVALUATING SOCIAL PROGRAMS WITH ENDOGENOUS PROGRAM PLACEMENT AND SELECTION OF THE TREATED*

PETRA E. TODD

Department of Economics, University of Pennsylvania, McNeil 520, 3718 Locust Walk, Philadelphia, PA 19104, USA

Contents

* This chapter was presented at a Conference at the Rockefeller Center in Bellagio, Italy, organized by the editors. I am grateful to T. Paul Schultz, John Strauss, Andrew Foster and other conference participants for very helpful comments. I also benefitted greatly from collaborations with James J. Heckman, Hidehiko Ichimura and Ken Wolpin. This chapter summarizes some results from that research.

Handbook of Development Economics, Volume 4
DOI: 10.1016/S1573-4471(07)04060-0

Abstract

This chapter considers methods for evaluating the impact of social programs in the presence of nonrandom program placement or program selection. It first presents the evaluation problem as a missing data problem and then considers various solutions proposed in the statistics and econometrics literature. For ex post evaluation, the following estimation methods are discussed: traditional regression methods, matching, control function methods, instrumental variable and local instrumental variable (LIV) methods, and regression-discontinuity. Alternative estimators are described along with their identifying assumptions, the behavioral implications of those assumptions, and the data requirements for implementation. The chapter also considers methods for ex ante evaluation, which can be used to assess the effects of programs prior to their implementation, for example, in trying to design a program that achieves some desired outcomes for a given cost. Throughout the chapter, numerous examples from the development literature illustrate applications of the different estimation methods and highlight factors affecting estimator performance.

Keywords

program evaluation, self-selection, treatment effects, matching, control function, regression-discontinuity, instrumental variables

JEL classification: C21, C53, I38

1. Introduction

This chapter considers econometric methods for evaluating effects of social programs when the programs are nonrandomly placed and/or the program participants are non-randomly selected. For example, family planning programs are often targeted at high fertility regions and individuals typically self-select into the programs. Similarly, health, education and nutrition interventions are often targeted at high poverty areas and eligibility for such programs is usually restricted to individuals or families who meet some criteria. The focus of this chapter is on estimating the effects of program interventions using nonexperimental data. Some of the estimation methods can also be adapted to experimental settings, to address related problems of nonrandom program attrition or dropout.

Two questions that are often of interest in evaluating effects of programs are (1) Do participants in programs benefit from them? and (2) How would program impacts and costs differ if the features of the program were changed? This chapter considers alternative approaches to answering these questions, recognizing that how individuals respond to treatment is potentially heterogeneous.

We distinguish two types of evaluations, *ex post* evaluations, which analyze effects of existing programs, and *ex ante* evaluations, which analyze effects of programs that have not yet been implemented, often termed *counterfactual* programs. Most of this chapter considers methods for ex post evaluation, which is the most common and preoccupies most of the evaluation literature. Section four takes up the problem of evaluating programs prior their implementation, which is useful for designing new programs or for comparing existing programs to alternative ones. For example, if the program includes either conditional or unconditional subsidies, it could be of interest to assess program impacts for a range of subsidy levels.

The goals of this chapter are (i) to describe the identifying assumptions needed to justify the application of different kinds of estimators, (ii) to discuss the behavioral implications of these assumptions, (iii) to illustrate how different kinds of estimators are related to one another, (iv) to summarize the data requirements of the estimators and (v) to provide examples of how these evaluation methods have been applied in the development literature.

2. The evaluation problem

We begin by defining some notation for describing the evaluation problem and key parameters of interest. For simplicity, suppose there are only two states of the world, corresponding to the state of being with and without some treatment intervention. For example, the outcome of interest could be a health indicator and the treatment could be participating in a health or nutrition program.

Let $D = 1$ for persons who receive the intervention and $D = 0$ for persons who do not receive it. Associated with each state is a potential outcome. Y_0 denotes the potential outcome in the untreated state and Y_1 the potential outcome in the treated state. Each person has associated a (Y_0, Y_1) pair that represents the outcomes that would be realized in the two states. Because the person can only be in one state at a time, at most one of the two potential outcomes is observed at any given point in time. The observed outcome is

$$Y = DY_1 + (1 - D)Y_0.$$

The gain from moving an individual from the state "without treatment" to the state "with treatment" is

$$\Delta = Y_1 - Y_0.$$

Because only one state is observed at any given time, the gain from treatment is not directly observed for anyone. Inferring gains from treatment therefore requires solving a missing data problem, and the evaluation literature has developed a variety of approaches to solve this problem.

2.1. Parameters of interest

In evaluating the effects of a social program, there may be many questions of interest, such as the benefits accruing to participants, spillover effects on nonparticipants, and program costs, which may include tax receipts used to finance the program. For example, consider the effects of a school subsidy program that provides incentive payments to parents to send their children to school. If the subsidies are sufficiently large, we would expect such a program to have direct effects on the families participating in it. The program may also have indirect effects on nonparticipating families, perhaps through program-induced changes in the schools attended by nonparticipating children.[1] If the program is financed from general taxes, the indirect effects might include any disincentives to work due to higher taxes. Thus, we distinguish between

direct effects: effects of the program on outcomes of program participants; and

indirect effects: effects of the program that are not directly related to program participation.

The program evaluation literature has focused mainly on estimating direct effects of the program and also on investigating program effects if the program offer were extended to individuals not currently participating. Nonparticipants are often used as a source of control group data, under the assumption that the indirect effects on nonparticipants are negligible, an assumption that is also maintained throughout this chapter.

Because program impacts are not directly observed for any individual, researchers usually aim to uncover only some features of the treatment impact distribution, such as its mean or median. Typical parameters of interest considered in the evaluation literature are the following:

---

[1] For example, the program might induce changes in school quality measures, such as pupil–teacher ratios.

(a) the proportion of program participants that benefit from the program

$$\Pr(Y_1 > Y_0 \mid D = 1) = \Pr(\Delta > 0 \mid D = 1);$$

(b) the proportion of the total population benefitting from the program:

$$\Pr(\Delta > 0 \mid D = 1)\Pr(D = 1);$$

(c) quantiles of the impact distribution (such as the median), where q is the selected quantile

$$\inf_{\Delta}\{\Delta: F(\Delta \mid D = 1) > q\};$$

(d) the distribution of gains for individuals with some characteristics X_0

$$F(\Delta \mid D = 1, X = X_0),$$

where X represents some individual characteristics that are not affected by the program, such as age, education, race, or poverty level prior to the program intervention.

Much of the program evaluation literature develops methods for estimating two key parameters of interest[2]:

(e) the average gain from the program for persons with characteristics X

$$E(Y_1 - Y_0 \mid X) = E(\Delta \mid X);$$

(f) the average gain from the program for program participants with characteristics X:

$$E(Y_1 - Y_0 \mid D = 1, X) = E(\Delta \mid D = 1, X).$$

The parameter (e) is commonly referred to as the *average impact of treatment (ATE)* and parameter (f) is known as the *average impact of treatment on the treated (TT)*. The *ATE* parameter is the gain from the program that would be experienced on average if a randomly chosen person with characteristics X were assigned to the participate in the program. The *TT* parameter is the average gain experienced for the subset of individuals who actually participated in the program (for whom $D = 1$). If the individuals who take the program tend to be the ones that receive the greatest benefit from it, then one would expect $TT(X) > ATE(X)$.

---

[2] See, e.g., Rosenbaum and Rubin (1985), Heckman and Robb (1985), or Heckman, La Londe and Smith (1999).

2.2. What is the distinction between average program gain and average program gain for participants?

We will next consider further the distinction between the *ATE* and the *TT* parameters and the conditions under which the two are the same. Suppose the outcomes in the treated and untreated states can be written as an additively separable function of observables (X) and unobservables (U_0 and U_1):

$$Y_1 = \varphi_1(X) + U_1,$$
$$Y_0 = \varphi_0(X) + U_0.$$

The observed outcome $Y = DY_1 + (1 - D)Y_0$ can thus be written as:

$$Y = \varphi_0(X) + D\big(\varphi_1(X) - \varphi_0(X)\big) + \big\{U_0 + D(U_1 - U_0)\big\}.$$

Assume that $E(U_0 \mid X) = E(U_1 \mid X) = 0$. The gain to an individual from participating in the program is $\Delta = D(\varphi_1(X) - \varphi_0(X)) + D(U_1 - U_0)$. Individuals may or may not know their values of U_1 and U_0 at the time of deciding whether to participate in a program. If people self-select into the program based on their anticipated gains from the program, then we would expect that $E(U_0 \mid X, D) \neq 0$ and $E(U_1 \mid X, D) \neq 0$. That is, if the gain from the program depends on U_1 and U_0 and if people know their future values of U_1 and U_0, or can to some extent forecast the values, then we would expect people to make use of this information when they decide whether to select into the program.

In the notation of the above statistical model for outcomes, the *average impact of treatment (ATE)* for a person with characteristics X is

$$E(\Delta \mid X) = \varphi_1(X) - \varphi_0(X) + E(U_1 \mid X) - E(U_0 \mid X)$$
$$= \varphi_1(X) - \varphi_0(X).$$

The *average impact of treatment on the treated (TT)* is

$$E(\Delta \mid X) = \varphi_1(X) - \varphi_0(X) + E(U_1 - U_0 \mid X, D = 1).$$

As discussed in Heckman (2000), the average effect of treatment on the treated in unconventional in the sense that it combines the "structural parameters" (the parameters of the functions $\varphi_0(X)$ and $\varphi_1(X)$) with means of the unobservables.

For completeness, we can also define the *average impact of treatment on the untreated (UT)* as

$$E(\Delta \mid X) = \varphi_1(X) - \varphi_0(X) + E(U_1 - U_0 \mid X, D = 0),$$

which gives the impact of a program or intervention on the group that currently does not participate in it. This parameter may be of interest if there are plans to expand the scope of the program to include those currently nonparticipating. The relationship between

TT, ATE and *UT* is:

$$ATE = \Pr(D = 1 \mid X)TT + \Pr(D = 0 \mid X)UT.$$

Observe that if $U_1 = U_0$, then the *TT, ATE* and *UT* parameters are the same. The advantage of allowing the residual term to differ in treated and untreated states is that it allows the potential for unobserved heterogeneity in how people respond to treatment. Under a special case, the parameters may be equal even if $U_1 \neq U_0$. That case arises when

$$E(U_1 - U_0 \mid X, D) = 0.$$

This restriction implies the participation decision (D) is uninformative on $U_1 - U_0$, so that $U_1 - U_0$ could not have been a factor in the decision to participation. The restriction might be satisfied if the agents making the participation decisions (e.g. individuals, program administrators or others) do not act on $U_1 - U_0$, perhaps because agents do not know the idiosyncractic gain from participating in the program (and cannot forecast it) at the time of deciding whether to participate. In this special case, there is said to be *ex post* heterogeneity in how people respond to treatment, which is not acted upon *ex ante*.

As discussed in Heckman, La Londe and Smith (1999), there are three different types of assumptions that can be made in the evaluation model that vary in their level of generality. In order of increasing generality, they are:

(A.1) conditional on X, the program effect is the same for everyone $(U_1 = U_0)$;

(A.2) conditional on X, the program effect varies across individuals but $U_1 - U_0$ does not help predict program participation;

(A.3) conditional on X, the program effect varies across individuals and $U_1 - U_0$ does predict who participates in the program.

We will consider ways of estimating the *TT* and *ATE* parameters of interest under these three different sets of assumptions.

2.3. Sources of bias in estimating $E(\Delta \mid X, D = 1)$ and $E(\Delta \mid X)$

Consider again the model of the previous section

$$Y = \varphi_0(X) + D\big(\varphi_1(X) - \varphi_0(X)\big) + \big\{U_0 + D(U_1 - U_0)\big\}.$$

In terms of the two parameters of interest, $(ATE = E(\Delta \mid X)$ and $TT = E(\Delta \mid X, D = 1))$, the model can be written as:

$$Y = \varphi_0(X) + DE(\Delta \mid X) + \big\{U_0 + D(U_1 - U_0)\big\} \tag{*}$$

or

$$\begin{aligned} Y = \varphi_0(X) &+ DE(\Delta \mid X, D = 1) \\ &+ \big\{U_0 + D\big[U_1 - U_0 - E(U_1 - U_0 \mid X, D = 1)\big]\big\}. \end{aligned}$$

For simplicity, suppose the X variables are discrete and that we estimate the effects of the intervention (D) by the coefficients $\hat{b}_x$ from an ordinary least squares regression[3]:

$$Y = aX + b_x XD + v.$$

This model is known as the *common effect* model and is popular in applied work. A special case of the model assumes that b_x is constant across X:

$$Y = aX + bD + v.$$

In light of the true model, bias for the *ATE* parameter $(E(\Delta \mid X))$ arises if the mean of the error term does not have conditional mean zero, i.e.

$$E\big(U_0 + D\big((U_1 - U_0) \mid X, D\big)\big) \neq 0.$$

Under assumptions (A.1) and (A.2), bias arises only from $E(U_0 \mid X, D) \neq 0$, but under the more general assumption (A.3), there is also the potential of bias from $E(U_1 - U_0 \mid D, X) \neq 0$. For estimating the *TT* parameter $E(\Delta \mid X, D = 1)$, under assumptions (A.1)–(A.3), bias arises if $E(U_0 \mid X, D) \neq 0$.

3. Solutions to the evaluation problem

3.1. Traditional regression estimators

Nonexperimental estimators of program impacts typically use two types of data to impute the missing counterfactual (Y_0) outcomes for program participants: data on participants at a point in time prior to entering the program and data on nonparticipants. We next consider three widely used methods for estimating the (TT) parameter, $E(\Delta \mid X, D = 1)$, using nonexperimental data: (a) the *before–after* estimator, (b) the *cross-sectional* estimator, and (c) the *difference-in-difference* estimator. In each case, we illustrate the assumptions required to justify application of the estimator. Extensions to estimating the *ATE* parameter are straightforward.

To describe the estimators and their assumptions, we introduce a panel data regression framework. Using the same notation as previously, denote the outcome measures by Y_{1it} and Y_{0it}, where i denotes the individual and t the time period of observation,

$$Y_{1it} = \varphi_1(X_{it}) + U_{1it},$$
$$Y_{0it} = \varphi_0(X_{it}) + U_{0it}. \tag{1}$$

U_{1it} and U_{0it} are assumed to be distributed independently across persons and to satisfy $E(U_{1it} \mid X_{it}) = 0$ and $E(U_{0it} \mid X_{it}) = 0$. Here, X_{it} represents conditioning variables that may either be fixed or time-varying (such as gender or age), but whose distributions

---

[3] Here, we allow the effects of treatment to differ by the observed X, as reflected in the X subscript on b.

are assumed to be unaffected by whether an individual participates in the program.[4] The observed outcome at time t can be written as

$$Y_{it} = \varphi_0(X_{it}) + D_{it}\alpha^*(X_{it}) + U_{0it}, \tag{2}$$

where D_{it} denotes being a program participant in the program and $\alpha^*(X_{it}) = \varphi_1(X_{it}) - \varphi_0(X_{it}) + U_{1it} - U_{0it}$ is the treatment impact for an individual. Prior to the program intervention, we observe $Y_{0it} = \varphi_0(X_{it}) + U_{0it}$ for everyone. After the intervention we observe $Y_{1it} = \varphi_1(X_{it}) + U_{1it}$ for those who received the intervention (for whom $D_{it} = 1$, for $t > t_0$, the time of the intervention) and $Y_{0it} = \varphi_0(X_{it}) + U_{0it}$ for those who did not receive it (for whom $D_{it} = 0$ in all time periods).

This model is a random coefficient model, because the treatment impact can vary across persons even after conditioning on X_{it}. Assuming that $U_{0it} = U_{1it} = U_{it}$, so that the unobservable is the same in both the treated and untreated states, yields the fixed coefficient or *common effect* version of the model. In this model, the *TT* parameter is given by:

$$\alpha^*_{TT}(X_{it}) = E\big(\alpha^*(X_{it}) \mid D_{it} = 1, D_{it'} = 0, X_{it}\big),$$

where the conditioning on $D_{it} = 1$, $D_{it'} = 0$ denotes that the person was not in the program at time t' but did participate by time t.

3.1.1. Before–after estimators

As noted above, the evaluation problem can be viewed as a missing data problem, because each person is only observed in one of two potential states at any point in time. The before–after estimator addresses the missing data problem by using pre-program data to impute the missing counterfactual outcomes for program participants.

Let t' and t denote two time periods, one before and one after the program intervention. In a regression model, the before–after estimator is the least squares solution for the *TT* parameter $(\alpha^*_{TT}(X_{it}) = E(\alpha^*(X_{it}) \mid D_{it} = 1, D_{it'} = 0, X_{it}))$ is obtained by

$$Y_{it} - Y_{it'} = \varphi_0(X_{it}) - \varphi_0(X_{it'}) + \alpha^*_{TT}(X_{it}) + \varepsilon_{it}$$

where

$$\varepsilon_{it} = \big[U_{1it} - U_{0it} - E(U_{1it} - U_{0it} \mid D_{it} = 1, D_{it'} = 0, X_{it})\big]$$
$$+ U_{0it} - U_{0it'}.$$

Consistency of the estimator for $\alpha^*_{TT}(X_{it})$ requires that $E(\varepsilon_{it} \mid D_{it} = 1, D_{it'} = 0, X_{it}) = 0$. The term in brackets has conditional mean zero by construction, so the assumption required to justify application of this estimator is $E(U_{0it} - U_{0it'} \mid D_{it} = 1$,

---

[4] For example, if the set of conditioning variables X_{it} includes marital status and the program intervention is a job training program, we need to assume that the job training program does not affect marital status.

$D_{it'} = 0, X_{it}) = 0$. A special case where this assumption would be satisfied is if U_{0it} can be decomposed into a fixed effect error structure, $U_{0it} = f_i + v_{it}$, where f_i does not vary over time and v_{it} is a i.i.d. random error that satisfies $E(v_{it} - v_{it'} \mid D_i = 1, D_{it'} = 0, X_{it}) = 0$. Note that this assumption allows selection into the program to be based on f_i, so the estimation strategy admits to person-specific permanent unobservables that may affecting the program participation decision.

One drawback of a before–after estimation strategy is that identification breaks down in the presence of time-specific intercepts, making it impossible to separate effects of the program from other general time effects on outcomes.[5] Before–after estimates can also be sensitive to the choice of time periods used to construct the estimator.

Many studies of employment and training programs in the US and in other countries have noted that earnings and employment of training program participants dip down in the time period just prior to entering the program, a pattern now known as *Ashenfelter's Dip*. (See Ashenfelter, 1978; Heckman and Smith, 1999, and Heckman, La Londe and Smith, 1999.) The dip pattern can arise from serially correlated transitory downward shocks to earnings that may have been the impetus for the person applying to the training program.[6] Another potential explanation for the observed dip pattern are the program eligibility criteria that are often imposed that tend to select out the most disadvantaged persons for participation in programs. These criteria will select into the program persons with low transitory earnings shocks. A simple before–after estimation strategy that includes the pre-program "dip" period typically gives an upward biased estimate of the effect of the program if the estimator is based on a pre-program period that occurs during the "dip".

An advantage of the before–after estimator relative to other classes of estimators is that it is implementable even when data are available only on program participants. At a minimum, two cross sections of data are required, one pre-program and post-program.

3.1.2. Cross-sectional estimators

A *cross-sectional* estimator uses data on a comparison group of nonparticipants to impute counterfactual outcomes for program participants. The data requirements of this estimator are minimal, only post-program data on $D_{it} = 1$ and $D_{it} = 0$ persons. Define $\hat{\alpha}_{CS}(X_{it})$ as the ordinary least squares solution to

$$Y_{it} = \varphi_0(X_{it}) + D_{it}\alpha^*_{TT}(X_{it}) + \varepsilon_{it},$$

where

$$\varepsilon_{it} = U_{0it} + D_{it}\big[(U_{1it} - U_{0it}) - E(U_{0it} - U_{1it} \mid D_{it} = 1, X_{it})\big]$$

---

[5] Such a common time effect may arise, e.g., from life-cycle wage growth over time or from shocks to the economy.

[6] A fixed effect error structure would not generate a dip pattern.

where the regression is estimated on $D_{it} = 1$ and $D_{it} = 0$ persons observed at time t. Consistency of the cross-sectional estimator requires that $E(\varepsilon_{it} \mid D_{it}, X_{it}) = 0$. This restriction rules out the possibility that people select into the program based on expectations about their idiosyncratic gain from the program, which could violate the assumption that $E(U_{0it} \mid X_{it}, D_{it}) = 0$. Importantly, the cross-sectional estimator does not admit to unobservable variables affecting outcomes and the decision to participate in the program, which is a strong assumption.

3.1.3. Difference-in-differences estimators

The *difference-in-differences* (DID) estimator is commonly used in evaluation work, as in the numerous applications of it described below. This estimator measures the impact of the program intervention by the difference in the before–after change in outcomes between participants and nonparticipants.

Define an indicator that equals 1 for participants (for whom $D_{it'} = 0$ and $D_{it} = 1$), denoted by I_i^D and zero otherwise. The difference-in-differences treatment effect estimator is the least squares solution for $\alpha_{TT}^*(X_{it})$ in

$$Y_{it} - Y_{it'} = \varphi_0(X_{it}) - \varphi_0(X_{it'}) + I_i^D \alpha_{TT}(X_{it}) + \varepsilon_{it},$$
$$\varepsilon_{it} = D_{it}\big[U_{1it} - U_{0it} - E(U_{1it} - U_{0it} \mid D_{it} = 1, D_{it'} = 0, X_{it})\big]$$
$$+ U_{0it} - U_{0it'}.$$

This regression is similar to a before–after regression, except that now the model is estimated using both participant and nonparticipant observations.

The DID estimator addresses the main shortcoming of the before–after estimator in that it allows for time-specific intercepts that are common across groups (which can be included in $\varphi_0(X_{it})$). The time effects are separately identified from the nonparticipant observations. The estimator is consistent if $E(\varepsilon_{it} \mid D_{it}, X_{it}) = 0$, which would be satisfied under a fixed effect error structure (see the discussion above for the before–after estimator). The data requirements to implement the DID estimator are either longitudinal or repeated cross section data on program participants and nonparticipants.[7]

Alternatively, the DID estimator can be implemented from a regression

$$Y_{it} = \varphi_0(X_{it}) + I_i^D \gamma + D_{it}\alpha_{TT}^*(X_{it}) + \tilde{\varepsilon}_{it} \quad \text{for } t = t', \dots, t,$$
$$\tilde{\varepsilon}_{it} = U_{0it} + D_{it}\big[U_{1it} - U_{0it} - E(U_{1it} - U_{0it} \mid D_{it} = 1, X_{it})\big].$$

The main advantage of longitudinal estimators (before–after or difference-in-difference) over cross-sectional methods are that they allow there to be unobservable

---

[7] For discussion of how repeated cross-sectional data can be used to implement difference-in-difference estimators, see Heckman and Robb (1985).

determinants of program participation decisions and outcomes. However, the fixed effect error structure that is usually assumed to justify application of these estimators only incorporates the potential influence of time-invariant unobservables.[8]

3.1.4. Within estimators

Within estimators identify program impacts from changes in outcomes within some unit, such as within a family, a school or a village. The previously described before–after and DID estimators fall within the class of within estimators, where the variation exploited is for a given individual over time. We next describe other kinds of within estimators where the unit of observation is broader than a single individual, representing, for example, a family or village.

Let Y_{0ijt} and Y_{1ijt} denote the outcomes for individual i, from unit j, observed at time t, and for simplicity at first assume that $U_{1it} = U_{0it}$. Write the model for outcomes as:

$$Y_{ijt} = \varphi_0(X_{ijt}) + I_{ij}^D \gamma + D_{ijt}\alpha_{TT}(X_{ijt}) + \varepsilon_{ijt}$$

and assume that the error term ε_{ijt} ($= U_{0it}$) can be decomposed as: $\varepsilon_{ijt} = \theta_j + v_{ijt}$, where θ_j represents the effects of unobservables that vary across units but are constant for individuals within the same unit and v_{ijt} are i.i.d.

Taking differences between two individuals from the same unit observed in the same time period gives

$$Y_{ijt} - Y_{i'jt} = \varphi_0(X_{ijt}) - \varphi_0(X_{i'jt}) + \left(I_{ij}^D - I_{i'j}^D\right)\gamma + (D_{ijt} - D_{i'jt})\alpha_{TT}(X_{ijt})$$
$$+ (v_{ijt} - v_{i'jt}).$$

Consistency of the OLS estimator of $\alpha_{TT}(X_{ijt})$ requires that $E(v_{ijt} - v_{i'jt} \mid X_{ijt}, X_{i'jt}, D_{ijt}, D_{i'jt}) = 0$. This assumption implies that within a particular unit, which individual receives the treatment is random with respect to the error term v_{ijt}. In the more general random coefficients version of the model, it has to be assumed that within a particular unit, which individual receives the treatment is random with respect to that individual's idiosyncratic gain from the program. That is, the program may be targeted at specific units (e.g. families or villages), but within those units, for a within estimation strategy to be valid, it is necessary to assume that which individuals participated in the program is unrelated to the idiosyncratic gain from the program. Also, because the estimator relies on comparisons between the outcomes of treated and untreated persons, the approach requires assuming that there be no spillover effects from treating one individual on other individuals within the same unit. As with the before–after and difference-in-differences estimation approaches, the within estimator allows treatment to be selective across units.

---

[8] For example, an unobservable attribute such as an individual's "motivation" could affect the outcome measure and also influence the program participation decision.

Namely, it allows $E(\varepsilon_{ijt} \mid D_{ijt}, X_{ijt}) \neq 0$, because treatment selection can be based on the unobserved heterogeneity term θ_j.

When the variation being exploited for identification of the treatment effect is variation within a family, village, or school at a single point in time, then the within estimator can be implemented with as little as a single cross section of data.

Sometimes it happens that all individuals within a unit receive treatment at the same time, in which case $D_{ijt} = D_{i'jt}$ for all i in j and the above approach is not feasible. In that situation, a within-estimation strategy may still be feasible if pre-program data (t') are available by taking differences across individuals in the same unit observed at different time periods:

$$Y_{ijt} - Y_{i'jt'} = \varphi_0(X_{ijt}) - \varphi_0(X_{i'jt'}) + \left(I_{ij}^D - I_{i'j}^D\right)\gamma + (D_{ijt} - D_{i'jt'})\alpha^*$$
$$+ (v_{ijt} - v_{i'jt'}),$$

where $D_{i'jt'} = 0$. Consistency requires that $E(v_{ijt} - v_{i'jt'} \mid D_{ijt}, D_{i'jt'}, X_{ijt}, X_{i'jt'}) = 0$. When $I_{ij}^D = 1$ for all i, j, the estimation method is analogous to a before–after estimator, except that comparisons are between different individuals within the same unit across time.[9]

3.1.5. Applications

The above described estimators are widely used in empirical evaluation research in development. One of the earliest applications of the within estimator is by Rosenzweig and Wolpin (1986), which assesses the impact of a family planning and health counseling program on child outcomes in the Philippines. Their study provides an early discussion of the statistical problems created by nonrandom program placement, in particular, when the placement of a program potentially depends on the outcome variable of interest. For example, family planning programs are often placed in areas where the need is considered to be the greatest. Not accounting for nonrandom placement would lead to the erroneous conclusion that family planning programs cause fertility.

Rosenzweig and Wolpin's (1986) empirical analysis adopts the following statistical model:

$$H_{ijt}^a = \rho_{ij}^a \beta + \mu_i + \mu_j + \varepsilon_{ijt},$$

where H_{ijt}^a is a child health measure (height, weight) for child i observed at age a, living in locality j at time t. ρ_{ij}^a represents the length of time that child was exposed to the program intervention. μ_i is a time invariant, child-specific unobserved health endowment and μ_j is an unobserved locality level effect. The estimation approach compares changes in health outcomes for children who were exposed to the program to changes for children who were not exposed to it.[10] This evaluation method allows

---

[9] In that case, the estimator suffers from the same drawback as the before–after estimator of not being able to separately identify time effects.

[10] Locality level effects are separately identified from individual effects using observations on families that migrated across localities. Without migration, they would not be separately identified.

the allocation of the program to be selective on unobservables, namely locality level or individual level unobserved characteristics. A subsequent study by Rosenzweig and Wolpin (1988a, 1988b) adopts a similar within child estimation strategy to evaluate the effects of a Colombian child health intervention.

A more recent evaluation that adopts a similar identification and estimation strategy is that of Duflo (2001), in which a within estimator is used to evaluate the effects of a school construction program in Indonesia on education and wages. The paper notes that the new schools were in part locally financed, which led to nonrandom placement of schools into more affluent communities. Because individuals from those communities usually experience better outcomes even in the absence of the intervention, it is difficult to draw reliable inferences from cross-sectional comparisons of localities with and without the new schools. Duflo observed that exposure to the school construction program varied by region and year. For this reason, the education of individuals who were young when the program began would be more affected by the school building program than that of older individuals. Also, individuals in regions where a larger numbers of schools were built are more likely to have been affected by the programs. Essentially, her identification strategy draws comparisons between outcomes of older and younger individuals in regions where the school construction program was very active with those of similar individuals in regions where the school construction program was less active.

A recent paper by Glewwe et al. (2004) questions the reliability of a difference-in-difference estimation approach in an application that evaluates the effectiveness of an educational intervention in Kenya. The program intervention provided schools with flip-charts to use as teaching aids in certain subjects. One of the goals of their study is to compare the estimates obtained by a nonexperimental DID estimation approach to those obtained from a randomized social experiment. Their DID estimator compares changes over time in test scores in flip-chart and non-flip-chart subjects within the schools that received the intervention. The experiment randomly allocated the schooling intervention (flip-charts) to a subset of schools and compares the schools that did and did not receive the intervention. When Glewwe et al. (2004) compare the nonexperimental to the experimental estimates, they find substantial differences. The experimental results indicate that flip-charts had little effect on test scores, while the DID estimates are statistically significantly different from zero at conventional levels. The authors conclude that the difference-in-difference estimator is unreliable.[11] Glewwe, Kremer, and Moulin (2000, 2003) carry out a similar comparison between a nonexperimental DID estimator and an experimental estimator, in which they evaluate other schooling interventions.

---

[11] In their application, an implicit assumption of the DID estimator is that having flip-charts in certain subjects does not affect students' achievements in other subjects. For example, the DID estimator could be invalid if teachers spent more time teaching flip-chart subjects as a result of the intervention and less time on other subjects. This may account for the deviation between the experimental and the nonexperimental DID estimates.

3.2. Matching methods

Matching is a widely-used method of evaluation that compares the outcomes of program participants with the outcomes of similar, matched nonparticipants. Their use in evaluating the effects of program interventions in developing country settings is relatively new. Some of the earliest applications of matching to evaluate economic development programs were World Bank evaluations of anti-poverty programs.[12]

One of the main advantages of matching estimators over other kinds of evaluation estimators is that they do not require specifying the functional form of the outcome equation and are therefore not susceptible to bias due to misspecification along that dimension. For example, they do not require specifying that outcomes are linear in observables. Traditional matching estimators pair each program participant with an observably similar nonparticipant and interpret the difference in their outcomes as the effect of the program intervention (see, e.g., Rosenbaum and Rubin, 1983). More recently developed methods pair program participants with more than one nonparticipant observation, using statistical methods to estimate the matched outcome. In this discussion, we focus on a class of matching estimators called *propensity score matching* estimators, because these methods are the most commonly used and have been shown in some studies to be reliable, under the conditions described below.[13]

There are two different variants of matching estimators, cross-sectional matching and difference-in-difference matching. Cross-sectional matching estimators allow for selection on unobservables only in a very limited sense, as described below. For the most part, these estimators are only applicable in contexts where the researcher is relatively certain that the major determinants of program participation are accounted for and that any remaining variation in who participates is due to random factors. Difference-in-difference matching estimators identify treatment effects by comparing the change in outcomes for treated persons to the change in outcomes for matched, untreated persons. Difference-in-difference matching estimators allow for selection into the program to be based on unobserved time-invariant characteristics of individuals. Below, we first describe cross-sectional matching estimators, which are the type considered in most of the statistical literature on matching and are the most widely used. Then we discuss difference-in-difference matching, which is a more recent variant introduced in the econometrics literature.

Cross-sectional matching estimators assume that there exist a set of observed characteristics Z such that outcomes are independent of program participation conditional on Z. That is, it is assumed that the outcomes (Y_0, Y_1) are independent of participation status D conditional on Z,[14]

$$(Y_0, Y_1) \perp\!\!\!\perp \mid Z. \tag{3}$$

---

[12] See the applications discussed below.

[13] For discussions of other kinds of matching estimators, see e.g. Cochran and Rubin (1973), Rubin (1980, 1984).

[14] In the terminology of Rosenbaum and Rubin (1983) treatment assignment is "strictly ignorable" given Z.

It is also assumed that for all Z there is a positive probability of either participating ($D = 1$) or not participating ($D = 0$) in the program, i.e.,

$$0 < \Pr(D = 1 \mid Z) < 1. \tag{4}$$

This second assumption is required so that a matches for $D = 0$ and $D = 1$ observations can be found. If assumptions (3) and (4) are satisfied, then the problem of determining mean program impacts can be solved by simply substituting the Y_0 distribution observed for the matched nonparticipant group for the missing Y_0 distribution for program participants.

Heckman, Ichimura and Todd (1998) show that the above assumptions are overly strong if the parameter of interest is the mean impact of treatment on the treated (TT), in which case a weaker conditional mean independence assumption on Y_0 suffices:

$$E(Y_0 \mid Z, D = 1) = E(Y_0 \mid Z, D = 0) = E(Y_0 \mid Z). \tag{5}$$

Furthermore, when TT is the parameter of interest, the condition $0 < \Pr(D = 1 \mid Z)$ is also not required, because that condition only guarantees the possibility of a participant analogue for each nonparticipant. The TT parameter requires only

$$\Pr(D = 1 \mid Z) < 1. \tag{6}$$

Under these assumptions, the mean impact of the program on program participants can be written as

$$\begin{aligned}
\Delta &= E(Y_1 - Y_0 \mid D = 1) \\
&= E(Y_1 \mid D = 1) - E_{Z|D=1}\{E_Y(Y \mid D = 1, Z)\} \\
&= E(Y_1 \mid D = 1) - E_{Z|D=1}\{E_Y(Y \mid D = 0, Z)\},
\end{aligned}$$

where the second term can be estimated from the mean outcomes of the matched (on Z) comparison group.[15] Assumption (5) implies that D does not help predict values of Y_0 conditional on Z. Thus, selection into the program cannot be based directly on anticipated values of Y_0. However, no restriction is imposed on Y_1, so the method does allow individuals who expect high levels of Y_1 to be selecting into the program. Thus, the estimator accommodates selection on unobservables (assumption (A-3) discussed in Section 1.3), but only in a very limited sense, because there is a strong restriction on the nature of the selection process.

With nonexperimental data, there may or may not exist a set of observed conditioning variables for which (3) and (4) hold. A finding of Heckman, Ichimura and Todd (1997) and Heckman, Ichimura, Smith and Todd (1996, 1998) in their application of matching methods to JTPA data is that (4) was not satisfied, meaning that for a fraction of program participants no match could be found. If there are regions where the support of Z does

---

[15] The notation $E_{Z|D=1}$ denotes that the expectation is taken with respect to the $f(Z \mid D = 1)$ density. $E_{Z|D=1}\{E_Y(Y \mid D = 0, Z)\} = \int_z \int_y y f(y \mid D = 0, z) f(z \mid D = 1) \, dy \, dz$.

not overlap for the $D = 1$ and $D = 0$ groups, then matching is only justified when performed over the *region of common support*.[16] The estimated treatment effect must then be defined conditionally on the region of overlap. Empirical methods for determining the region of overlap are described below.

3.2.1. Reducing the dimensionality of the conditioning problem

Matching can be difficult to implement when the set of conditioning variables Z is large.[17] Rosenbaum and Rubin (1983) provide a theorem that is useful in reducing the dimension of the conditioning problem. They show that for random variables Y and Z and a discrete random variable D

$$E(D \mid Y, P(D = 1 \mid Z)) = E(E(D|Y, Z) \mid Y, \Pr(D = 1 \mid Z)),$$

so that

$$E(D \mid Y, Z) = E(D \mid Z)$$
$$\implies E(D \mid Y, \Pr(D = 1 \mid Z)) = E(D \mid \Pr(D = 1 \mid Z)).$$

This result implies that when Y_0 outcomes are independent of program participation conditional on Z, they are also independent of participation conditional on the probability of participation, $P(Z) = \Pr(D = 1 \mid Z)$. Thus, when matching on Z is valid, matching on the summary statistic $\Pr(D = 1 \mid Z)$ (the *propensity score*) is also valid. Provided that $P(Z)$ can be estimated parametrically (or semiparametrically at a rate faster than the nonparametric rate), matching on the propensity score reduces the dimensionality of the matching problem to that of a univariate problem. Because they are much easier to implement, much of the literature on matching focuses on propensity score matching methods.[18]

Using the Rosenbaum and Rubin (1983) theorem, the matching procedure can be broken down into two stages. In the first stage, the propensity score $\Pr(D = 1 \mid Z)$ is estimated, using a binary discrete choice model such as a logit or probit.[19] In the second stage, individuals are matched on the basis of their first stage estimated probabilities of participation.

The literature has developed a variety of matching estimators. The next section describes some of the leading examples.

---

[16] An advantage of randomized experiments noted by Heckman (1997), as well as Heckman, Ichimura and Todd (1997) and Heckman et al. (1998), is that they guarantee that the supports are equal across treatments and controls, so that the mean impact of the program can always be estimated over the entire support.

[17] If Z is discrete, small cell problems may arise. If Z is continuous and the conditional mean $E(Y_0 \mid D = 0, Z)$ is estimated nonparametrically, then convergence rates will be slow due to the "curse of dimensionality" problem.

[18] Heckman, Ichimura and Todd (1998) and Hahn (1998) consider whether it is better in terms of efficiency to match on $P(X)$ or on X directly. For the TT parameter, they show that neither is necessarily more efficient than the other. If the treatment effect is constant, then it is more efficient to condition on the propensity score.

[19] Semiparametric estimation methods, such as Ichimura's (1993) semiparametric least squares (SLS) method can also be used.

3.2.2. Alternative matching estimators

For notational simplicity, let $P = P(Z)$. A typical cross-sectional matching estimator takes the form

$$\hat{\alpha}_M = \frac{1}{n_1} \sum_{i \in I_1 \cap S_P} \left[Y_{1i} - \hat{E}(Y_{0i} \mid D = 1, P_i) \right],$$

$$\hat{E}(Y_{0i} \mid D = 1, P_i) = \sum_{j \in I_0} W(i, j) Y_{0j}, \tag{8}$$

where I_1 denotes the set of program participants, I_0 the set of non-participants, S_P the region of common support (see below for ways of constructing this set). n_1 denotes the number of persons in the set $I_1 \cap S_P$. The match for each participant $i \in I_1 \cap S_P$ is constructed as a weighted average over the outcomes of non-participants, where the weights $W(i, j)$ depend on the distance between P_i and P_j.

Define a neighborhood $C(P_i)$ for each i in the participant sample. Neighbors for i are non-participants $j \in I_0$ for whom $P_j \in C(P_i)$. The persons matched to i are those people in set A_i where $A_i = \{j \in I_0 \mid P_j \in C(P_i)\}$. Alternative matching estimators (discussed below) differ in how the neighborhood is defined and in how the weights $W(i, j)$ are constructed.

3.2.2.1. Nearest neighbor matching   Traditional, pairwise matching, also called *nearest-neighbor matching*, sets

$$C(P_i) = \min_j \| P_i - P_j \|, \quad j \in I_0.$$

That is, the non-participant with the value of P_j that is closest to P_i is selected as the match and A_i is a singleton set. The estimator can be implemented either matching with or without replacement. When matching is performed with replacement, the same comparison group observation can be used repeatedly as a match. A drawback of matching without replacement is that the final estimate will likely depend on the initial ordering of the treated observations for which the matches were selected. The nearest neighbor matching estimator is often used in practice, in part due to ease of implementation.

3.2.2.2. Caliper matching   *Caliper matching* (Cochran and Rubin, 1973) is a variation of nearest neighbor matching that attempts to avoid "bad" matches (those for which P_j is far from P_i) by imposing a tolerance on the maximum distance $\| P_i - P_j \|$ allowed. That is, a match for person i is selected only if $\| P_i - P_j \| < \varepsilon$, $j \in I_0$, where ε is a prespecified tolerance. For caliper matching, the neighborhood is $C(P_i) = \{P_j \mid \| P_i - P_j \| < \varepsilon\}$. Treated persons for whom no matches can be found (within the caliper) are excluded from the analysis. Thus, caliper matching is one way of imposing a common support condition. A drawback of caliper matching is that it is difficult to know a priori what is a reasonable choice for the tolerance level.

3.2.2.3. Stratification or interval matching   In this variant of matching, the common support of P is partitioned into a set of intervals. Within each interval, a separate impact is calculated by taking the mean difference in outcomes between the $D = 1$ and $D = 0$ observations within the interval. A weighted average of the interval impact estimates, using the fraction of the $D = 1$ population in each interval for the weights, provides an overall impact estimate. Implementing this method requires a decision on how wide the intervals should be. Dehejia and Wahba (1999) implement interval matching using intervals that are selected such that the mean values of the estimated P_i's and P_j's are not statistically different from each other within intervals.

3.2.2.4. Kernel and local linear matching   More recently developed matching estimators construct a match for each program participant using a weighted average over multiple persons in the comparison group. Consider, for example, the nonparametric *kernel matching estimator*, given by

$$\hat{\alpha}_{KM} = \frac{1}{n_1} \sum_{i \in I_1} \left\{ Y_{1i} - \frac{\sum_{j \in I_0} Y_{0j} G(\frac{P_j - P_i}{a_n})}{\sum_{k \in I_0} G(\frac{P_k - P_i}{a_n})} \right\},$$

where $G(\cdot)$ is a kernel function and a_n is a bandwidth parameter.[20] In terms of Eq. (8), the weighting function, $W(i, j)$, is equal to $\dfrac{G(\frac{P_j - P_i}{a_n})}{\sum_{k \in I_0} G(\frac{P_k - P_i}{a_n})}$. For a kernel function bounded between -1 and 1, the neighborhood is $C(P_i) = \{|\frac{P_i - P_j}{a_n}| \leqslant 1\}, j \in I_0$. Under standard conditions on the bandwidth and kernel, $\dfrac{\sum_{j \in I_0} Y_{0j} G(\frac{P_j - P_i}{a_n})}{\sum_{k \in I_0} G(\frac{P_k - P_i}{a_n})}$ is a consistent estimator of $E(Y_0 \mid D = 1, P_i)$.[21]

Heckman, Ichimura and Todd (1997) also propose a generalized version of kernel matching, called local linear matching.[22] The local linear weighting function is given by

$$W(i, j) = \frac{G_{ij} \sum_{k \in I_0} G_{ik}(P_k - P_i)^2 - [G_{ij}(P_j - P_i)][\sum_{k \in I_0} G_{ik}(P_k - P_i)]}{\sum_{j \in I_0} G_{ij} \sum_{k \in I_0} G_{ij}(P_k - P_i)^2 - (\sum_{k \in I_0} G_{ik}(P_k - P_i))^2}.$$
$$\tag{9}$$

As demonstrated in research by Fan (1992a, 1992b), local linear estimation has some advantages over standard kernel estimation. These advantages include a faster rate of

---

[20] See Heckman, Ichimura and Todd (1997, 1998) and Heckman et al. (1998).

[21] Specifically, we require that $G(\cdot)$ integrates to one, has mean zero and that $a_n \to 0$ as $n \to \infty$ and $na_n \to \infty$.

[22] Recent research by Fan (1992a, 1992b) demonstrated advantages of local linear estimation over more standard kernel estimation methods. These advantages include a faster rate of convergence near boundary points and greater robustness to different data design densities. See Fan (1992a, 1992b).

convergence near boundary points and greater robustness to different data design densities. (See Fan, 1992a, 1992b.) Thus, local linear regression would be expected to perform better than kernel estimation in cases where the nonparticipant observations on P fall on one side of the participant observations.

To implement the matching estimator given by Eq. (8), the region of common support S_P needs to be determined. To determine the support region, Heckman, Ichimura and Todd (1997) use kernel density estimation methods. The common support region can be estimated by

$$\hat{S}_P = \big\{P\colon \hat{f}(P \mid D = 1) > 0 \quad \text{and} \quad \hat{f}(P \mid D = 0) > 0\big\},$$

where $\hat{f}(P \mid D = d), d \in \{0, 1\}$ are nonparametric density estimators given by

$$\hat{f}(P \mid D = d) = \sum_{k \in I_d} G\left(\frac{P_k - P}{a_n}\right),$$

and a_n is the bandwidth parameter. To ensure that the densities are strictly greater than zero, it is required that the densities be strictly positive (i.e. exceed zero by a certain amount), determined using a "trimming level" q. That is, after excluding any P points for which the estimated density is zero, we exclude an additional small percentage of the remaining P points for which the estimated density is positive but very low. The set of eligible matches is therefore given by

$$\hat{S}_q = \big\{P \in \hat{S}_P\colon \hat{f}(P \mid D = 1) > c_q \text{ and } \hat{f}(P \mid D = 0) > c_q\big\},$$

where c_q is the density cut-off level that satisfies:

$$\sup_{c_q} \frac{1}{2J} \sum_{\{i \in I_1 \cap \hat{S}_P\}} \big\{1\big(\hat{f}(P \mid D = 1)\big) < c_q + 1\big(1\big(\hat{f}(P \mid D = 0)\big)\big) < c_q\big\} \leqslant q.$$

Here, J is the cardinality of the set of observed values of P that lie in $I_1 \cap \hat{S}_P$. That is, matches are constructed only for the program participants for which the propensity scores lie in $\hat{S}_q$.

The above estimators are straightforward representations of matching estimators and are commonly used. The recent literature has developed some alternative, more efficient estimators. See, for example, Hahn (1998) and Hirano, Imbens and Ridder (2000). In addition, Heckman, Ichimura and Todd (1998) propose a regression-adjusted matching estimator that replaces Y_{0j} as the dependent variable with the residual from a regression of Y_{0j} on a vector of exogenous covariates. The estimator explicitly incorporates exclusion restrictions, i.e. that some of the conditioning variables in the outcome equation do not enter into the participation equation or vice versa. In principal, imposing exclusions restrictions can increase efficiency. In practice, though, researchers have not observed much gain from using the regression-adjusted matching estimator.

3.2.2.5. Difference-in-difference matching The cross-sectional estimators described above assume that after conditioning on a set of observable characteristics, mean outcomes are conditionally mean independent of program participation. However, for a variety of reasons there may be systematic differences between participant and non-participant outcomes, even after conditioning on observables, which could lead to a violation of the above maintained assumptions. Such differences may arise, for example, because of program selectivity on unmeasured characteristics, or because of levels differences in outcomes across different labor markets in which the participants and nonparticipants reside.

A difference-in-difference (DID) matching strategy, as defined in Heckman, Ichimura and Todd (1997) and Heckman et al. (1998), better accommodates the potential for selection on unobservables by allowing for temporally invariant differences in outcomes between participants and nonparticipants. This type of estimator is analogous to the standard differences-in-differences regression estimator defined in Section 3.1, but it reweights the observations according to the weighting functions implied by matching estimators (defined above). The DID matching estimator requires that

$$E(Y_{0t} - Y_{0t'} \mid P, D = 1) = E(Y_{0t} - Y_{0t'} \mid P, D = 0),$$

where t and t' are time periods after and before the program enrollment date. This estimator also requires the support condition given in (7), which must now hold in both periods t and t'. The local linear difference-in-difference estimator is given by

$$\hat{\alpha}_{DID} = \frac{1}{n_1} \sum_{i \in I_1 \cap \hat{S}_q} \left\{ (Y_{1ti} - Y_{0t'i}) - \sum_{j \in I_0 \cap \hat{S}_q} W(i, j)(Y_{0tj} - Y_{0t'j}) \right\},$$

where the weights correspond to the local linear weights defined above. If repeated cross section data are available, instead of longitudinal data, the estimator can be implemented as

$$\hat{\alpha}_{DID} = \frac{1}{n_{1t}} \sum_{i \in I_{1t} \cap \hat{S}_q} \left\{ Y_{1ti} - \sum_{j \in I_{0t} \cap \hat{S}_q} W(i, j) Y_{0tj} \right\}$$
$$- \frac{1}{n_{1t'}} \sum_{i \in I_{1t'} \cap \hat{S}_q} \left\{ Y_{1t'i} - \sum_{j \in I_{0t'} \cap \hat{S}_q} W(i, j) Y_{0t'j} \right\},$$

where $I_{1t}, I_{1t'}, I_{0t}, I_{0t'}$ denote the treatment and comparison group datasets in each time period.

Finally, the DID matching estimator also allows selectivity into the program to be based on anticipated gains from the program, in the sense of assumption (A.2) described in Section 2.2. That is, D can help predict the value of Y_1 given P. However, a maintained assumption is that D does not help predict changes in the value of Y_0 (i.e. $Y_{0t} - Y_{0t'}$) conditional on P. Thus, individuals who participate in the program may be the ones who expect the highest values of Y_1, but they may not be systematically different in terms of their changes in Y_0.

3.2.3. Matching with choice-based sampled data

The samples used in evaluating the impacts of programs are often choice-based, with program participants being oversampled relative to their frequency in the population. Under choice-based sampling, weights are required to consistently estimate the probabilities of program participation, where the weights correspond to the ratio of the proportion of program participants in the population relative to the proportion in the sample.[23] The true population proportions usually are not obtainable from the sample and have to be derived from some other sources. When the weights are known, the Manski and Lerman (1977) procedure can be implement to consistently estimate propensity scores. However, oftentimes the population weights are unknown. Heckman and Todd (1995) show that in the case where the weights are unknown, with a slight modification, matching methods can still be applied, because the odds ratio $(P/(1-P))$ estimated using a logistic model with incorrect weights (i.e., ignoring the fact that samples are choice-based) is a scalar multiple of the true odds ratio, which is itself a monotonic transformation of the propensity scores. Therefore, matching can proceed on the (misweighted) estimate of the odds ratio (or of the log odds ratio).[24]

3.2.4. When does bias arise in matching?

The success of a matching estimator depends on the availability of observable data to construct the conditioning set Z, such that (5) and (6) are satisfied. Suppose only a subset $Z_0 \subset Z$ of the variables required for matching is observed. The propensity score matching estimator based on Z_0 then converges to

$$\alpha'_M = E_{P(Z_0)|D=1}\big(E\big(Y_1 \mid P(Z_0), D=1\big) - E\big(Y_0 \mid P(Z_0), D=0\big)\big). \tag{7}$$

The bias for the parameter of interest, $E(Y_1 - Y_0 \mid D = 1)$, is

$$bias_M = E(Y_0 \mid D=1) - E_{P(Z_0)|D=1}\big\{E\big(Y_0 \mid P(Z_0), D=0\big)\big\}.$$

3.2.5. Some additional considerations in applying matching methods

3.2.5.1. Choosing the set of matching variables   As described earlier, the propensity score matching estimator requires that the outcome variable be mean independent of the treatment indicator conditional on the propensity score, $P(Z)$. An important consideration in implementation is how to choose the set of conditioning variables used in

---

[23] See, e.g., Manski and Lerman (1977) for discussion of weighting for logistic regressions.

[24] With nearest neighbor matching, it does not matter whether matching is performed on the odds ratio or on the propensity scores (estimated using the wrong weights), because the ranking of the observations is the same and the same neighbors will be selected either way. Thus, failure to account for choice-based sampling will not affect nearest-neighbor point estimates. However, it will matter for kernel or local linear matching methods, because these methods take into account the absolute distance between the P observations.

estimating the propensity score. Unfortunately, there is no theoretical basis for how to choose a particular set Z to satisfy the identifying assumptions. Moreover, the set Z that satisfies the matching conditions is not necessarily the one the most inclusive one, as augmenting a set that satisfies the conditions for matching could lead to a violation of the conditions. Using too many conditioning variables could also exacerbate a common support problem.

To guide in the selection of Z, there is some accumulated empirical evidence on how bias estimates of matching estimators depended on the choice of Z in particular applications. For example, Heckman, Ichimura and Todd (1997) and Lechner (2002) show that which variables are included in the estimation of the propensity score can make a substantial difference to the estimator's performance. These papers found that biases tended to be more substantial when cruder sets of conditioning variables where used. These papers selected the set Z to maximize the percent of people correctly classified by treatment status under the model.

3.2.5.2. Other determinants of the performance of matching estimators Empirical explorations have shown that matching estimators perform best when the treatment and control groups are located in the same geographic area, so that regional effects on outcomes are held constant across groups. Lastly, a few papers have studied the performance of matching estimators when a different survey instrument is used to collect the comparison group data from that used to collect the treatment group data.[25] Smith and Todd (2005) and Heckman, Ichimura and Todd (1997) found that matching estimators performed poorly when the survey instrument is not the same and concluded from that evidence that matching estimators do not compensate for biases caused by differences in how variables are measured across surveys, a purpose for which they were not designed. The results also indicated that difference-in-difference matching methods are more reliable than cross-sectional matching methods, particularly when treatments and controls are mismatching geographically or in terms of the survey instrument. In general, the success of matching approaches to evaluation depends strongly on the data being of relatively high quality.

3.2.5.3. Using balancing tests to check the propensity score specification Rosenbaum and Rubin (1983) present a theorem that does not aid in choosing which variables to include in Z, but which can help in determining which interactions and higher order terms to include in the propensity score model for a given set of Z variables. The theorem states that

$$Z \perp\!\!\!\perp D \mid \Pr(D = 1 \mid Z),$$

or equivalently

$$E\big(D \mid Z, \Pr(D = 1 \mid Z)\big) = E\big(D \mid \Pr(D = 1 \mid Z)\big).$$

---

[25] It is often the case in evaluation work that the comparison group data are collected using a different survey instrument. (See La Londe, 1986; Dehejia and Wahba, 1998, 1999; and Smith and Todd, 2005.)

The basic intuition is that after conditioning on $\Pr(D = 1 \mid Z)$, additional conditioning on Z should not provide new information about D. Thus, if after conditioning on the estimated values of $P(D = 1 \mid Z)$ there is still dependence on Z, this suggests mis-specification in the model used to estimate $\Pr(D = 1 \mid Z)$. Note that the theorem holds for any Z, including sets Z that do not satisfy the conditional independence condition required to justify matching. As such, the theorem is not informative about what set of variables to include in Z.

This result motivates a specification test for $\Pr(D = 1 \mid Z)$, which tests whether or not there are differences in Z between the $D = 1$ and $D = 0$ groups after conditioning on $P(Z)$. Various testing approaches have been proposed in the literature. Eichler and Lechner (2001) use a variant of a test suggested in Rosenbaum and Rubin (1985) that is based on standardized differences between the treatment and matched comparison group samples in terms of means of each variable in Z, squares of each variable in Z and first-order interaction terms between each pair of variables in Z. An alternative approach used in Dehejia and Wahba (1998, 1999) divides the observations into strata based on the estimated propensity scores. These strata are chosen so that there is not a statistically significant difference in the mean of the estimated propensity scores between the experimental and comparison group observations within each strata, though how the initial strata are chosen and how they are refined if statistically signif-icant differences are found is not made precise. The problem of choosing the strata in implementing the balancing test is analogous to the problem of choosing the strata in implementing the interval matching estimator, described earlier. A common practice is to use five strata (e.g. quintiles of the propensity score). Within each stratum, t-tests are used to test for mean differences in each Z variable between the experimental and comparison group observations.

Another way of implementing the balancing test estimates a regression of each ele-ment of the set Z, Z_k on D interacted with a power series expansion in $P(Z)$:

$$
\begin{aligned}
Z_k = {}& \alpha + \beta_1 P(Z) + \beta_2 P(Z)^2 + \beta_3 P(Z)^3 + \cdots + \beta_j P(Z)^j \\
& + \gamma_1 P(Z)D + \gamma_2 P(Z)^2 D + \gamma_3 P(Z)^3 D + \cdots + \gamma_j P(Z)^j D + \upsilon,
\end{aligned}
$$

and then tests whether the estimated γ coefficients are jointly insignificantly different from zero.

When significant differences are found for particular variables, higher order and inter-action terms in those variables are added to the logistic model and the testing procedure is repeated, until such differences no longer emerge. In this way, the specification for the propensity score is iteratively refined.

3.2.6. Assessing the variability of matching estimators

Distribution theory for cross-sectional and difference-in-difference kernel and local lin-ear matching estimators is derived in Heckman, Ichimura and Todd (1998). However, implementing the asymptotic standard error formulae can be cumbersome, so standard errors for matching estimators are often instead generating using bootstrap resampling methods.[26] A recent paper by Imbens and Abadie (2004a) shows that standard bootstrap resampling methods are not valid for assessing the variability of nearest neighbor estimators. Their criticism does not, however, apply for kernel or local linear matching estimators, for which bootstrap methods are valid. Imbens and Abadie (2004b) present alternative standard error formulae for assessing the variability of nearest neighbor matching estimators.

3.2.7. Applications

Matching estimators have only recently been applied in evaluating the impacts of program interventions in developing countries. In one of the early applications, Jalan and Ravallion (2003) use propensity score matching techniques to assess the impact of a workfare program in Argentina (the *Trabajar* program) on the wages of individuals who took part in the program. Their study finds sizable average wage gains due to the program. In another application, Jalan and Ravallion (2001) use propensity score matching methods to study the effects of public investments in piped water in rural India on child health outcomes, where the matching estimators are used to control for nonrandomness in which households have access to piped water. Their study finds statistically significant impacts of having piped water on reducing the prevalence and duration of diarrhea among children under five.[27]

Handa and Maluccio (2006) study the performance of matching estimators by comparing nonexperimental estimates obtained by matching to estimates obtained from a randomized social experiment. They find that the matching estimators perform well in replicating the experiment only for outcomes that are relatively easily measured, such as schooling attainment, but perform less well for more complex outcomes such as expenditures. They find that stringently imposing common support and choosing highly comparable comparison groups from which to draw the matched outcomes improves the performance of their propensity score matching estimators.

Matching methods were also used in the large-scale evaluation of the urban *Oportunidades* program in Mexico that was carried out in 2005. The program is described in detail in Chapter 62 of this handbook. Briefly, the *Oportunidades* program provides monetary subsidies to families for sending their children to school and for attending health clinics. The rural version of the program was evaluated using a place-based randomized experiment, which randomized a set of 506 villages in or out of the program. Because of high cost and out of ethical concerns, this type of randomization was deemed infeasible in high density urban areas. The alternative evaluation design adopted was a

---

[26] See Efron and Tibshirani (1993) for an introduction to bootstrap methods, and Horowitz (2001) for a recent survey of bootstrapping in econometrics.

[27] Upon more detailed examination of the distribution of treatment effects, however, Jalan and Ravallion (2003) also observe that the observed health gains largely bypass children from the poorest families, particularly those where the mother is poorly educated.

matched comparison group study. Matches for treatment group households were drawn from two data sources: families living in intervention areas who did not sign up for the program but who otherwise met the eligibility criteria, and families who met the eligibility criteria for the program but who were living in areas where the program was not yet available.[28] The propensity score model was estimated using data on program participants and nonparticipants living in intervention areas, and then used to impute propensity scores for the families living in nonintervention areas. The scores represent the probability that these families would participate in the program if it were offered to them. Program impact estimates were obtained using kernel and local linear regression matching estimators with bootstrapped standard errors. When longitudinal variation in the outcome of interest was available, difference-in-difference matching estimators were applied. The analysis of children and youth age 6–20 indicated statistically significant program impacts on school enrollment, educational attainment, dropout rates, employment and earnings of youth, and on the numbers of hours spent doing homework.[29]

In another recent application of difference-in-difference matching methods, Galiani, Gertler and Schargrodsky (2005) analyze effects of privatization of water services on child mortality in Argentina. Temporal variation of ownership in water provision provides a source of variation for identifying the effects of privatization, although which municipalities privatized first was nonrandom. To take into account unobserved municipality characteristics that may affect the decision to privatize and may affect child health outcomes, Galiani, Gertler and Schargrodsky (2005) use a difference-in-difference kernel matching. Their study finds that privatization of water services significantly reduced child mortality and that the effects were most pronounced in the poorest areas. Godtland et al. (2004) apply cross-sectional propensity score matching estimators to evaluate the effectiveness of a farmer field school that provided agricultural extension services to farmers in Peru. They find a statistically significantly positive effect of the program on measures of farmer knowledge.

Behrman, Cheng and Todd (2000) use matching methods to evaluate the effects of a preschool program in Bolivia on child heath and cognitive outcomes. Their approach identifies program effects by comparing children with different lengths of duration in the program. Instead of controlling for selectivity in program participation, as is usually done, their method controls for selectivity into alternative program participation durations, conditional on having chosen to participate. The estimator matches on the hazard rate and is used to nonparametrically recover the relationship between program duration and magnitude of treatment impact.

Other applications of matching methods in the recent economic development literature are Gertler, Levine and Ames (2004), in a study of the effects of parental death on

---

[28] To participate in the program, families had to attend sign-up modules during a time period when the modules were open.

[29] See, for example, Behrman et al. (2005), which analyzes the impact of *Oportunidades* on education outcomes.

child outcomes, Lavy (2004), in a study of the effects of a teacher incentive program in Israel on student performance, Angrist and Lavy (2001), in a study of the effects of teacher training on children's test scores in Israel, and Chen and Ravallion (2003), in a study of a poverty reduction project in China. There are numerous applications of matching estimators in the job training literature, many of which are reviewed in Heckman, La Londe and Smith (1999).

3.3. Control function methods

As noted in the previous section, matching estimators do not require specifying functional form assumptions for the outcome equation, but they make strong assumptions about how unobservables are allowed to affect program participation decisions. The most general variant of matching, difference-in-difference matching, allows individuals to select into programs based on time-invariant unobservable characteristics. It does not allow time-varying unobservables to affect participation decisions.

Another class of evaluation estimators are *control function methods*, also known as *generalized residual methods*. These methods were proposed as a solution to the evaluation problem in Heckman and Robb (1985), but they are closely related to the earlier selection bias correction methods developed in Heckman (1979). Like the regression estimators discussed in Section 3.1, they are usually defined within the context of an econometric model for the outcome process. Control function estimators explicitly recognize that nonrandom selection into the program gives rise to an endogeneity problem and aim to obtain unbiased parameter estimates by explicitly modeling the source of the endogeneity. They allow selection into the program to be based on time varying unobservable variables at the expense of stronger functional form assumptions needed to secure identification.

To see how the generalized residual method applies to the evaluation problem, write the model for outcomes as

$$Y = \varphi_0(X) + D\alpha_{TT}^*(X) + \tilde{\varepsilon},$$

where

$$\alpha_{TT}^*(X) = E(Y_1 - Y_0 \mid X, D = 1) = \varphi_1(X) - \varphi_0(X) + E(U_1 - U_0 \mid X, D = 1)$$

is the parameter of interest ($TT(X)$) and

$$\tilde{\varepsilon} = U_0 + D\big(U_1 - U_0 - E(U_1 - U_0 \mid X, D = 1)\big).$$

Because the decision to participate may be endogenous with respect to the outcomes, we expect that $E(U_0 \mid X, D) \neq 0, i = 0, 1$.

Heckman (1979) showed that the endogeneity problem can be viewed as an error in model specification analogous to the problem of omitted variables. By adding and subtracting $E(U_0 \mid X, D) = DE(U_0 \mid D = 1, X) + (1 - D)E(U \mid D = 0, X)$, we can rewrite the outcome model as

$$Y = \varphi_0(X) + D\alpha^*_{TT}(X) + E(U \mid D = 0, X)$$
$$+ D\big[E(U_0 \mid D = 1, X) - E(U_0 \mid D = 0, X)\big] + \varepsilon$$
$$= \varphi_0(X) + D\alpha^*_{TT}(X) + K_0(X) + D\big[K_1(X) - K_0(X)\big] + \varepsilon \qquad (8)$$

where

$$K_0(X) = E(U_0 \mid D = 0, X),$$
$$K_1(X) = E(U_0 \mid D = 1, X),$$
$$\varepsilon = D\{U_0 - E(U_0 \mid D = 1, X)\} + (1 - D)\{U_0 - E(U_0 \mid D = 0, X)\}$$
$$+ D\{U_1 - E(U_1 \mid D = 1, X)\}.$$

By construction, ε has conditional mean equal to 0. The functions $K_1(X)$ and $K_0(X)$ are termed *control functions*. When these functions are known up to some finite number of parameters, they can be included in the model to control for the endogeneity and regression methods (either linear or nonlinear) applied to consistently estimate program.

3.3.1. Methods for estimating control functions

If no restrictions where placed on either $\alpha^*(X)$, $K_1(X)$, or $K_0(X)$, then the treatment impact parameter $(\alpha^*_{TT}(X))$ could not be separately identified from the control functions. For example, suppose $K_1(X) - K_0(X) = \rho_0 + \rho_1 X + \rho_2 X^2$. Clearly, $\alpha^*_{TT}(X)$ could not be separately identified from the difference in the control functions. Some identifying restrictions are necessary, and different implementations of control function estimators proposed in the literature impose different kinds of restrictions. Usually, the restrictions consist of functional form restrictions and/or exclusion restrictions. In this context, exclusion restrictions are requirements that some variables that determine the participation process (i.e. the choice of D) be excluded from the outcome equation. These excluded variables generate variation in $K_1(X)$ and $K_0(X)$ that is independent from $\alpha^*_{TT}(X)$. The following types of restrictions could be imposed: (1) functional form restrictions on $\alpha^*_{TT}(X)$ and on $K_1(X)$ and $K_0(X)$ without exclusion restrictions; (2) Exclusion restrictions without functional form assumptions (for example, if all the regressors in the outcome and participation equations were mutually exclusive and linearly independent); and (3) a combination of functional form and exclusion restrictions.

One interesting approach to identification considered in the econometric evaluation literature is called *identification at infinity*. (See Heckman, 1990; Andrews and Schafgans, 1998.) This approach is feasible only when there is a subgroup in the data for which $\Pr(D = 1 \mid Z) = 1$ for some set Z, meaning that individuals with that set of characteristics always select into the program and there is no selection problem for them. This subgroup can be used to identify some of the model parameters that are not otherwise identified, under the requirement that there is at least one continuous variable included in Z but not contained in X (termed an exclusion restriction).

Heckman and Robb (1985) motivate particular functional form restrictions on $K_d(X)$, $d \in \{0, 1\}$, through an economic model of the participation process. Participation is assumed to depend on a set of characteristics Z through an index $h(Z\gamma)$ and on unobservable characteristics V as follows:

$$D = \begin{cases} 1 & \text{if } h(Z\gamma) + V > 0, \\ 0 & \text{if } h(Z\gamma) + V \leqslant 0. \end{cases}$$

In a random utility framework, $h(Z\gamma) + V$ represents the net utility from participating in a program. (McFadden, 1984, and Manski and McFadden, 1981.)

Under this model, the function $K_0(X) = E(U_0 \mid D = 1, X)$ can be written as

$$E(U_0 \mid D = 1, X) = E\big(U_0 \mid h(Z\gamma) + V > 0, X\big)$$
$$= \frac{\int_{-h(Z\gamma)}^{\infty} \int_{-\infty}^{\infty} u f(u, v \mid X) \, du \, dv}{\int_{-h(Z\gamma)}^{\infty} \int_{-\infty}^{\infty} f(u, v \mid X) \, du \, dv}.$$

If $F(u, v \mid X)$ is assumed to be continuous with full support in R^2 and $F_V(\cdot)$ is invertible, then the index $Z\gamma$ can be written as a function of the conditional probability of participation[30]:

$$\Pr(D = 1 \mid Z) = \Pr\big(V > -h(Z; \gamma)\big)$$
$$= 1 - F_V\big(-h(Z; \gamma)\big)$$
$$\implies \quad h(Z; \gamma) = -F_v^{-1}\big(-\Pr(D = 1 \mid Z)\big).$$

Heckman and Robb (1985) note that with the additional assumption that the joint distribution of the unobservables, does not depend on X, except possibly though the index, $h(Z; \gamma)$:

$$f(u, v \mid X) = f\big(u, v \mid h(Z; \gamma)\big),$$

then $E(U_0 \mid D = 1, X)$ can be written solely as a function of the probability of participating in the program, $\Pr(D = 1 \mid Z)$:

$$E(U_0 \mid D = 1, X) = E\big(U_0 \mid D = 1, P(Z)\big) = K_1\big(P(Z)\big),$$
$$E(U_0 \mid D = 0, X) = E\big(U_0 \mid D = 0, P(Z)\big) = K_0\big(P(Z)\big).[31]$$

Assuming that a linear index is sufficient to represent the bias control function (so-called *index sufficiency*) greatly simplifies the problem of estimating the $K_d(X)$, $d \in \{0, 1\}$ functions. It also aids in the identification problem. For example, suppose $\varphi_0(X)$ and $h(Z\gamma)$ were both linear in the regressors. Under the index assumption and

---

[30] From the above expression, it can be seen that as $h(Z\gamma)$ approaches infinity, $E(U_0 \mid D = 1, Z)$ approaches $0 \,(= E(U_0 \mid Z))$. For this reason, subgroups with a high probability of participating in the program can be used to secure identification of model parameters. (See Heckman, 1990.)

[31] A stronger assumption that would all imply index sufficiency is independence, $f(u, v \mid X) = f(u, v)$.

with one continuous variable included in Z but excluded from X, we can allow for overlap between X and Z and even for the case where X are fully contained in Z.[32]

In the original formulation of the control function method in Heckman (1979), it was assumed that U_0 and V were jointly normal which implies a parametric form for $K_1(P(Z))$ and $K_0(P(Z))$. In Heckman et al. (1998), the index sufficiency assumption is invoked and the $K(\cdot)$ functions are estimated nonparametrically as a function of the probability of participating in the program.[33]

3.3.2. A comparison of control function and matching methods

Control function and matching methods were developed largely in separate literatures in econometrics and statistics, but the two methods both make use of propensity scores in implementation and are related. Conventional matching estimators can in some cases be viewed as a restricted form of a control function estimator. Recall that traditional cross-sectional matching methods assume that selection is on observables, whereas control function methods explicitly allow selection into programs to be on the basis of observables Z or unobservables V. Assume the model for outcomes given in (1). The assumption that justifies matching outcomes on the basis of Z characteristics is

$$E(Y_0 \mid D = 1, Z) = E(Y_0 \mid D = 0, Z).$$

If $X \subset Z$, then, in the notation of the previous model for outcomes, this assumption is implies that[34]

$$E(U_0 \mid D = 1, Z) = E(U_0 \mid D = 0, Z).$$

Under the control function approach, this assumption is equivalent to assuming that the control functions are equal for both the $D = 0$ and $D = 1$ groups

$$K_1(P(Z)) - K_0(P(Z)) = 0, \tag{9}$$

in which case the model for outcomes can be written as

$$Y_0 = \varphi_0(X) + D\alpha^*(X) + K_0(P(Z)) + D\{U_1 - U_0 - E(U_1 - U_0 \mid D = 1, X)\}.$$

[32] If the control functions are estimated nonparametrically, separately distinguishing the treatment effect from the control function requires the application of identification at infinity methods. These approaches have been criticized in the literature, because they base identification of a subset of model parameters on a typically small sample of individuals with a probability of participating close to 1.

[33] In that study, estimates of the probabilities of participating in the program (the propensity scores) are first obtained by a discrete choice model and then control functions are estimated nonparametrically using the predicted probabilities. That paper also develops a test for index sufficiency and finds that it cannot be rejected for a data sample of adult male applicants to the US JTPA (Job Training and Partnership Act) program.

[34] See Heckman, Ichimura and Todd (1997, 1998) for the more general case where Z contains variables not in X.

In the literature, assumption (9) is referred as the special case of *selection on observables* (see Heckman and Robb, 1985; Heckman et al., 1996; and Barnow, Cain and Goldberger, 1980).

When selection is of this form, many of the identification problems that arise in trying to separate the treatment impact $\alpha^*(X)$ from the bias function $K_1(X)$ go away. That is, $\alpha^*(X)$ could be estimated without imposing functional form restrictions or exclusion restrictions. The functions $\varphi_0(X)$ and $K_0(P(Z))$ cannot be separately identified without additional restrictions, but if the goal of the estimation is to recover treatment impacts then there may be no need to separately identify these functions. As seen in the previous section, matching estimators recover $E(Y_0 \mid D, X)$ directly with any attempt to separate the different components and without restrictions on the functional form of the conditional mean of the outcome equation.

In traditional implementations of the control function method, it was common to assume that (U_0, V) are joint normally distributed. Under the normal model, the restriction that $K_0(P(Z)) = K_1(P(Z))$ will, in general, not be satisfied unless the errors have zero covariance, $\sigma_{U_0 V} = 0$. To see why that is the case, note that under joint normality

$$E(U_0 \mid D = 1, Z) = K_1\big(P(Z)\big) = \frac{\sigma_{U_0 V}}{\sigma_{V^2}} \frac{\phi(-h(Z\gamma))}{1 - \Phi(-h(Z\gamma))},$$

$$E(U_0 \mid D = 0, Z) = K_0\big(P(Z)\big) = \frac{\sigma_{U_0 V}}{\sigma_{V^2}} \frac{-\phi(-h(Z\gamma))}{\Phi(-h(Z\gamma))}.$$

$K_1(P(Z))$ equals $K_0(P(Z))$ if $\sigma_{U_0 V} = 0$.

3.3.3. Applications

Control function methods have not yet been widely used in the context of evaluating development programs. For discussion of many applications to evaluating job training programs, see Heckman, La Londe and Smith (1999).

3.4. Instrumental variables, local average treatment effects (LATE), and LIV estimation

Instrumental variables methods provide another approach to estimating program effects in the presence of nonrandom self-selection. In this section, we consider both traditional instrumental variables estimators as well as more recently developed local instrumental variable (*LIV*) methods.

3.4.1. The Wald estimator

Consider again the treatment effect model of the previous section:

$$Y = \varphi_0(X) + D\alpha^*_{TT}(X) + \tilde{\varepsilon},$$

where

$$\alpha_{TT}^*(X) = E(Y_1 - Y_0 \mid X, D = 1) = \alpha(X) + E(U_1 - U_0 \mid X, D = 1)$$

is the parameter of interest (*TT*) and

$$\tilde{\varepsilon} = U_0 + D\big(U_1 - U_0 - E(U_1 - U_0 \mid X, D = 1)\big).$$

Suppose that there is an exclusion restriction, namely a variable Z that affects the program participation decision but does not enter into the outcome equation. Also, for ease of exposition, assume that the conditioning variables X and the instrument Z are binary variables and that the instrument takes on the values Z_1 and Z_2. We first partition the dataset by X and then use the instrument to estimate the program effect using the method of instrumental variables within X subsamples. The identifying assumption is that

$$E(U_0 \mid X, Z) = E(U_0 \mid X).$$

The so-called Wald estimator (applied within X strata) is given by

$$
\begin{aligned}
\hat{\alpha}_{IV}^*(X) &= \frac{\hat{E}(Y \mid Z = Z_1, X) - \hat{E}(Y \mid Z = Z_2, X)}{\hat{E}(D \mid Z = Z_1, X) - \hat{E}(D \mid Z = Z_2, X)} \\
&= \frac{\hat{E}(Y \mid Z = Z_1, X) - \hat{E}(Y \mid Z = Z_2, X)}{\widehat{\Pr}(D = 1 \mid Z = Z_1, X) - \widehat{\Pr}(D = 1 \mid Z = Z_2, X)},
\end{aligned}
$$

where the denominator is the difference in the probability of participating in the program under the two different values of the instrument. As noted in Heckman (1992), the estimator $\hat{\alpha}_{IV}^*(X)$ recovers the average impact of treatment on the treated (the *TT* parameter) only under one of two alternative assumptions on the error term:

Case I: $U_1 = U_0$

or

Case II: $U_1 \neq U_0$ and $E(U_1 - U_0 \mid X, Z, D = 1) = E(U_1 - U_0 \mid X, D = 1)$.

Either of these assumptions would give $E(D(U_1 - U_0 - E(U_1 - U_0 \mid X, D = 1))) = 0$. In the first case, the average impact of treatment on the treated (*TT*) is assumed to be the same as the average treated effect (*ATE*). Under the second case, the *ATE* and *TT* parameters differ, but the instrument does not forecast the idiosyncratic gain from the program.[35] Heckman (1992) provides several examples where the assumption that the instrument does not help forecast the program gain can be problematic. Whether such an assumption is tenable or not will depend on the particular application at hand.

---

[35] Note that $E(D(U_1 - U_0 - E(U_1 - U_0 \mid X, D = 1)) \mid X, Z) = \Pr(D = 1 \mid X)E(U_1 - U_0 - E(U_1 - U_0 \mid X, D = 1)) \mid X, Z, D = 1)$, so the required assumption is that $E(U_1 - U_0 \mid X, Z, D = 1) = E(U_1 - U_0 \mid X, D = 1)$. For this reason, as shown in Heckman (1992), the required assumption to apply the IV estimator for the purpose of estimating the treatment on the treated parameter is that the instrument not help forecast the gain from the program.

If assumptions I or II are not satisfied, then the Wald estimator no longer recovers the average impact of treatment on the treated. Nonetheless, it has a meaningful alternative interpretation as a *Local Average Treatment Effect* (see Imbens and Angrist, 1994), which is the average effect of treatment for the subset of persons induced by a change in the value of the instrument from Z_1 to Z_2 to receive the treatment. In the above example, the *LATE* estimator gives the average treatment impact for the subset of individuals who would not get treatment if $Z = Z_2$ but do get treatment if $Z = Z_1$. The *LATE* parameter is discussed further below.

3.4.2. Marginal treatment effects (MTE) and local instrumental variables (LIV) estimation and its relationship to TT, ATE, LATE

Recent advances in the program evaluation literature have led to a better understanding of the relationship between the *TT*, *ATE* and *LATE* parameters and of new ways to estimate them. Heckman and Vytlacil (2005) develop a unifying theory of how the parameters relate to one another using a new concept, called a *marginal treatment effect* (MTE). Here, we provide an overview of the major results of the paper. Consider the treatment effect model of the previous sections, written in slightly more general form, where there is again an outcome equation and a participation equation:

$$Y = DY_1 + (1 - D)Y_0,$$
$$Y_1 = \mu_1(X, U_1),$$
$$Y_0 = \mu_0(X, U_0),$$
$$D = 1 \quad \text{if } \mu_0(Z) - U_D \geqslant 0.$$

It is assumed that $\mu_0(Z_i)$ is nondegenerate conditional on X_i, so that there is variation in who participates in the program holding X_i constant (i.e. that there is an exclusion restriction). The error terms are assumed to be independent of Z_i conditional on X_i.[36] As before, denote the propensity score as $P(Z) = \Pr(D = 1 \mid Z = z) = F_{U_D}(\mu_0(Z_i))$ and assume that there is full support ($0 < \Pr(D = 1 \mid Z) < 1$). Heckman and Vytlacil (2005) show that without loss of generality, one can assume U_{D_i} distributed uniformly. To see why, suppose that

$$D = 1 \quad \text{if } \varphi(Z) - v \geqslant 0$$

so that

$$\Pr(v < c) = F_V(c).$$

Because $F_V(\cdot)$ is a monotone transformation of the random variable v, we have

$$\Pr\big(F_V(v) < F_V(c)\big) = F_V(c).$$

---

[36] See Heckman and Vytlacil (2005) for other technical conditions that are not central to the argument here.

Define $U_D = F_V(v)$ and note that $\Pr(U_D < t) = t$. Thus, U_D is uniformly distributed between 0 and 1.

Next, note that when U_D is uniformly distributed,

$$E(D \mid Z) = \Pr(D = 1 \mid Z) = F_{U_D}(\mu_0(Z)) = \mu_0(Z).$$

Let Z and Z' be two values of the instrument such that $\Pr(D = 1 \mid Z) < \Pr(D = 1 \mid Z')$. The threshold crossing model of program participation implies that some individuals who would have chosen $D = 0$ with $Z = Z$ will instead choose $D = 1$ when $Z = Z'$, but no individual with $D = 1$ when $Z = Z$ would choose $D = 0$ when $Z = Z'$.[37]

Using this framework, we can define different parameters of interest:
  (i) The average treatment effect (*ATE*) is given by $\Delta^{ATE}(X) = E(\Delta \mid X = x)$.
  (ii) The average effect of treatment on the treated, conditional on a value of $P(Z)$, is given by $\Delta^{TT}(X, P(Z), D = 1) = E(\Delta \mid X = x, P(z) = P(Z), D = 1)$.
  (iii) The marginal treatment effect (MTE) conditions on a value of the unobservable: $MTE = \Delta_{MTE}(X) = E(\Delta \mid X = x, U_D = u)$.
  (iv) The local average treatment effect (*LATE*) parameter is given by

$$
\begin{aligned}
LATE &= \Delta_{LATE}(X, P(Z), P(Z')) \\
&= \frac{E(Y \mid P(Z) = P(Z), X) - E(Y \mid P(Z) = P(Z'), X)}{P(Z) - P(Z')}.
\end{aligned}
$$

The MTE is a new concept. If $U_D = P(Z)$, then the index $\mu_0(Z_i) - U_{D_i} = 0$ (by the above reasoning, $\mu_0(Z_i) = P(Z)$ when U_{D_i} is uniformly distributed). People with the index equal to zero have unobservables that make them just indifferent between participating or not participating in the program. People with $U_{D_i} = 0$ have unobservables that make then most inclined to participate, while people with $U_{D_i} = 1$ have unobservables that make them the least inclined to participate.

Heckman and Vytlacil (2005) show that all the parameters of interest can be written in terms of the marginal treatment effect $\Delta_{MTE}(X)$:

$$\Delta_{TT}(X) = \frac{\int_0^{P(Z)} E(\Delta \mid X = x, U_D = u) \, dU_D}{P(Z)},$$

$$\Delta_{TT}(X) = \int_0^1 E(\Delta \mid X = x, U_D = u) \, dU_D,$$

$$\Delta_{LATE}(X, P(Z), P(Z')) = \frac{\int_{P(Z')}^{P(Z)} E(\Delta \mid X = x, U_D = u) \, dU_D}{P(Z) - P(Z')}.$$

---

[37] As shown in Vytlacil (2002), the assumptions required to justify a threshold crossing model are the same as the monotonicity conditions typically assumed to justify application of *LATE* estimators, proposed in Imbens and Angrist (1994).

That is, each of the parameters of interest can be written as an average of $\Delta_{MTE}(X)$ for values of U_D lying in different intervals. Knowledge of the MTE function therefore enables computation of all the other parameters of interest.

The MTE function depends on a value of an unobservables, raising the question of how to estimate the MTE function. Heckman and Vytlacil (2000) propose the following estimation strategy that is implementable when the researcher has access to a continuous instrumental variable, Z, that enters into the participation equation but not the outcome equation. First, define a *local instrumental variables* estimator as

$$
\begin{aligned}
\Delta_{LIV}&\left(X, P(Z)\right) \\
&= \frac{\partial E(Y \mid P(Z) = P(Z), X)}{\partial P(Z)} \\
&= \lim_{P(Z') \to P(Z)} \frac{E(Y \mid P(z) = P(Z), x = X) - E(Y \mid P(z) = P(Z'), x = X)}{P(Z) - P(Z')} \\
&= MTE\left(X, U_D = P(Z)\right).
\end{aligned}
$$

The $\Delta_{LIV}(X, P(Z))$ parameter can be obtained by first estimating the program partic-ipation (propensity score) model to get $\hat{P}(Z)$, and then estimating $\frac{\partial E(Y \mid \hat{P}(z) = \hat{P}(Z), X)}{\partial P(Z)}$ nonparametrically (which can be done by local linear regression). The first step can be carried out using a parametric, semiparametric or nonparametric estimator for the bi-nary choice model. The second step can be performed by local linear regression of the outcome ($Y = DY_1 + (1 - D)Y_0$) on the estimated $\hat{P}(Z)$.[38] Evaluating this function for different values of $P(Z)$ traces out the MTE function. The different estimates *TT*, *ATE*, *LATE* can then be obtained by integrating under different regions of the MTE function.

3.4.3. Applications

LIV estimators have only been recently developed, and there are so far no applications to evaluating effects of program interventions in developing country settings. For a recent application to estimating returns to education using US data, see Carneiro, Heckman and Vytlacil (2001).

3.5. Regression-discontinuity methods

Sometimes, in evaluating effects of a program intervention, there is information avail-able on the rule generating assignment of individuals into treatment. For example, suppose that individuals who apply to the program are assigned a program eligibility score (based on their characteristics) and that only individuals with a score below a

---

[38] If the data are choice-based sampled, the choice-based sampling will have to be taken into account in both steps.

threshold are allowed to enter the program. This type of data design was first considered in Thistlethwaite and Campbell (1960) in an application in which they estimated the effect of receiving a National Merit Scholarship Award has on students' success in obtaining additional college scholarships and on their career aspirations. They observed that the awards are given on the basis of whether a test score exceeds a threshold, so one can take advantage of knowing the cut-off point to learn about treatment effects for persons near the cut-off.[39] The defining characteristic of regression discontinuity (RD) data designs is that the treatment variable changes discontinuously as a function of one or more underlying variables.

In the evaluation literature, there are several papers considering identification of treatment effects under a RD data design along with different kinds of assumptions on the processing governing the outcome variables and on the distribution of treatment effects. Trochim (1984) discusses alternative parametric and semiparametric RD estimators that have been proposed in the statistics literature. Van der Klaauw (1996) considers identification and estimation in a semiparametric model under a constant treatment effect assumption. Hahn, Todd and Van der Klaauw (2001) consider a more general case that allows for variable treatment effects and that imposes weak assumptions on the distribution (or conditional mean function) of the outcome variables. The discussion below follows along the lines of the Hahn, Todd and Van der Klaauw (2001).

Suppose that the goal of the evaluation is to determine the effect that some binary treatment variable D_i has on an outcome Y_i. The model for the observed outcome can be written as

$$Y_i = Y_{0i} + D_i \cdot \Delta_i. \tag{10}$$

If the data are purely observational (or nonexperimental), then little may be known a priori about the process by which individuals are selected into treatment. With data from a RD design, the analyst has some information about the treatment assignment mechanism.

There are two main types of discontinuity designs considered in the literature – the *sharp design* and the so-called *fuzzy design* (see e.g. Trochim, 1984). With a sharp design, treatment D_i is known to depend in a deterministic way on some observable variable Z_i, $D_i = f(Z_i)$, where Z takes on a continuum of values and the point z_0 where the function $f(Z)$ is discontinuous is assumed to be known.

With a fuzzy design, D_i is a random variable given Z_i, but the conditional probability $f(Z) \equiv E[D_i \mid Z_i = z] = \Pr[D_i = 1 \mid Z_i = z]$ is known to be discontinuous at z_0.[40] Next we consider formally why knowing that the probability of receiving treatment

---

[39] Other more recent applications of the regression-discontinuity methods include Van der Klaauw (1996), Angrist and Lavy (1999), and Black (1999).

[40] For example, in the application of Van der Klaauw (1996), the probability that a student receives financial aid changes discontinuously as a function of a known index of the student's GPA and SAT scores. However, there are other factors, some of which are unobserved, which affect the financial aid decision, so the data fits a fuzzy rather than a sharp design.

changes discontinuously as a function of an underlying variable is a valuable source of identifying information.

3.5.1. Identification of treatment effects under sharp and fuzzy data designs

3.5.1.1. Sharp design To simplify the exposition, consider the special case of a sharp discontinuity design. Treatment is assigned based on whether Z_i crosses a threshold value z_0:

$$D_i = \begin{cases} 1 & \text{if } Z_i > z_0, \\ 0 & \text{if } Z_i \leqslant z_0. \end{cases}$$

As z may be correlated with the outcome variable, the assignment mechanism is clearly not random and a comparison of outcomes between persons who received and did not receive treatment will generally be a biased estimator of treatment impacts. However, we may have reason to believe that persons close to the threshold z_0 are similar. If so, we may view the design as almost experimental near z_0.

To make ideas concrete, let $e > 0$ denote an arbitrary small number. Comparing conditional means for persons who received and did not receive treatment gives

$$E[Y_i \mid Z_i = z_0 + e] - E[Y_i \mid Z_i = z_0 - e]$$
$$= E[\Delta_i \mid Z_i = z_0 + e] + E[Y_{0i} \mid Z_i = z_0 + e] - E[Y_{0i} \mid Z_i = z_0 - e].$$

When persons near the threshold are similar, we would expect $E[Y_{0i} \mid Z_i = z_0 + e] \cong E[Y_{0i} \mid Z_i = z_0 - e]$. This intuition motivates the following assumptions:

RD-1: $E[Y_{0i} \mid z_i = z]$ is continuous in Z at z_0.[41]

RD-2: The limit $\lim_{e \to 0^+}[\Delta_i \mid Z_i = z_0 + e]$ is well-defined.

Under conditions (RD-1) and (RD-2),

$$\lim_{e \to 0^+} \{ E[Y_i \mid Z_i = z_0 + e] - E[Y_i \mid Z_i = z_0 - e] \} = E[\Delta_i \mid z_0]. \tag{11}$$

By comparing persons arbitrarily close to the point z_0 who did and did not receive treatment, we can in the limit identify $E[\Delta_i \mid z_i = z_0]$, which is the average treatment effect for people with values of Z_i at the point of discontinuity z_0. Conditions (RD-1) and (RD-2) are all that is required for identification.

It is a limitation of a RD design that we can only learn about treatment effects for persons with z values near the point of discontinuity. Sometimes, however, the treatment effects near the boundary are of particular interest, for example, if the policy change being considered were that of expanding the cut-off.

---

[41] It is assumed that the density of Z_i is positive in the neighborhood containing z_0.

3.5.1.2. Fuzzy design The fuzzy design differs from the sharp design in that the treatment assignment is not a deterministic function of z_i, because there are additional unobserved variables that determine assignment to treatment. The common feature it shares with the sharp design is that the probability of receiving treatment (the propensity score), $\Pr[D_i = 1 \mid Z_i]$, viewed as a function of z_i, is discontinuous at z_0. As shown in Hahn, Todd and Van der Klaauw (2001), mean treatment effects can be identified even under a fuzzy design under different some assumptions on the heterogeneity of impacts.

3.5.1.3. Common treatment effects Suppose that the treatment effect is constant across different individuals and is equal to Δ. The mean difference in outcomes for persons above and below the discontinuity point z_0 is

$$\Delta \cdot \{E[D_i \mid Z_i = z_0 + e] - E[D_i \mid Z_i = z_0 - e]\}$$
$$+ E[Y_{0i} \mid Z_i = z_0 + e] - E[Y_{0i} \mid Z_i = z_0 - e].$$

Under (RD-1), we have

$$\lim_{e \to 0^+} E[Y_i \mid Z_i = z_0 + e] - E[Y_i \mid Z_i = z_0 - e]$$
$$= \Delta \cdot \lim_{e \to 0^+} \{E[D_i \mid Z_i = z_0 + e] - E[D_i \mid Z_i = z_0 - e]\}.$$

Thus, we can identify Δ by the ratio

$$\frac{\lim_{e \to 0^+} E[y_i \mid z_i = z_0 + e] - \lim_{e \to 0^+} E[y_i \mid z_i = z_0 - e]}{\lim_{e \to 0^+} E[x_i \mid z_i = z_0 + e] - \lim_{e \to 0^+} E[x_i \mid z_i = z_0 - e]}. \tag{12}$$

The denominator is nonzero because the fuzzy RD design guarantees that $\Pr[D_i = 1 \mid z_i = z]$ (the propensity score) is discontinuous at z_0.

3.5.1.4. Variable treatment effects Now suppose treatment effects are heterogeneous, and in addition to assumptions (RD-1) and (RD-2), we assume

RD-3: D_i is independent of Δ_i conditional on Z_i near z_0: $D_i \perp \Delta_i \mid Z_i = z_0$.

Then the same ratio identifies $E(\Delta_i \mid Z_i = z_0)$. In addition to the cases considered above, Hahn, Todd and Van der Klaauw (2001) also consider an alternative local average treatment effect (*LATE*) interpretation of the same ratio.[42]

---

[42] Extending the idea of Imbens and Angrist (1994) or Angrist, Imbens and Rubin (1994) to the RD design, the ratio gives the average impact for people induced to receive treatment by whether the instrument is above or below the cut-off z_0.

3.5.2. Estimation

We next describe an estimation approach proposed in Hahn, Todd and Van der Klaauw (2001).[43] For both the sharp design and fuzzy design, (12) identifies the treatment effect at $z = z_0$. Thus, given consistent estimators of the four one-sided limits in (12), the treatment effect can be consistently estimated. One simple nonparametric estimator would estimate the limits by averages over the Y_i values and the D_i values within a specified distance of the boundary points (the bandwidth). Let $\hat{\Delta}$ denote an estimator for the treatment impact

$$\hat{\Delta} = \frac{\hat{y}^+ - \hat{y}^-}{\hat{x}^+ - \hat{x}^-},$$

where $\hat{y}^+$, $\hat{y}^-$, $\hat{x}^+$, and $\hat{x}^-$ are estimators for each of the limit expressions. Given appropriate bandwidths h_+ and h_-, we would estimate the limits by

$$\hat{y}^+ = \frac{\sum_i Y_i \cdot 1(z_0 < Z_i < z_0 + h_+)}{\sum_i 1(z_0 < Z_i < z_0 + h_+)}, \qquad \hat{y}^- = \frac{\sum_i Y_i \cdot 1(z_0 - h_- < Z_i < z_0)}{\sum_i 1(z_0 - h_- < Z_i < z_0)},$$

and

$$\hat{x}^+ = \frac{\sum_i D_i \cdot 1(z_0 < Z_i < z_0 + h_+)}{\sum_i 1(z_0 < Z_i < z_0 + h_+)}, \qquad \hat{x}^- = \frac{\sum_i D_i \cdot 1(z_0 - h_- < Z_i < z_0)}{\sum_i 1(z_0 - h_- < Z_i < z_0)}.$$

The RD estimator can also be implemented using local linear regression methods, as proposed in Hahn, Todd and Van der Klaauw (2001), which have better performance than simple averaging methods or kernel methods at boundary points. (See Fan, 1992a.)[44] For this problem, all the estimation points are boundary points.

3.5.3. Applications of RD methods

Regression-discontinuity methods have only occasionally been used in evaluating social programs in developing country settings. Buddlemeier and Skoufias (2004) study the performance of RD methods using data from the Mexican PROGRESA experiment.[45] As discussed in Section 3.2.7, the PROGRESA program was a school and health subsidy program introduced by the Mexican government. The PROGRESA experiment randomized villages in and out of the program. Within each village, only families who

---

[43] One estimation approach proposed by Van der Klaauw (1996) for the sharp design is to assume (in addition to continuity) a flexible parametric specification for $g(Z) = E[Y_{0i} \mid z_i]$ and add this as a 'control function' to the regression of Y_i on D_i. For the fuzzy design he proposes a similar approach but where D_i in the control function-augmented regression equation is now replaced by a first stage estimate of $E[D_i \mid Z_i]$. This estimation approach is consistent under correct specification but can be sensitive to misspecification.

[44] Boundary points are points within one bandwidth of the boundary. See Härdle (1990) or Härdle and Linton (1994) for discussion of the boundary bias problem.

[45] This experiment is described in detail in Chapter 62 of this handbook.

were eligible for the program according to an eligibility index were allowed to participate in it, where the index was derived from poverty criteria, such as whether the family had a dirt floor or a bathroom in their home. Most families deemed eligible for the program decided to participate in it to some extent.

Buddlemeier and Skoufias (2004) observe that families with eligibility index values just above the cut-off who received the program are highly similar to families with eligible values just below the cut-off. The criteria for eligibility were not made public, alleviating concerns that households could have manipulated their poverty status to become eligible for the program.[46] Using a RD estimation approach, Buddlemeier and Skoufias (2004) calculate program impacts for the households near the eligibility cut-off by comparing households living in treated communities with scores just above and below the cut-off. They find that the estimates based on the RD method are close to those derived from the experiment, lending credibility to the RD approach. Moreover, most of the households in their sample have eligibility scores near the cut-off values, making the sample near the cut-off an interesting subsample to study.

In another application of RD methods, Lavy (2004) uses an RD estimator to evaluate the effects of a teacher incentive program on student performance. The program introduced a rank-order tournament (among teachers of English, Hebrew, and mathematics in Israel) that rewarded teachers with cash bonuses for improving their students' performance on high-school matriculation exams. The regression discontinuity method of Lavy (2004) exploits both a natural experiment stemming from measurement error in the assignment variable and a sharp discontinuity in the assignment-to-treatment variable. The results show that performance incentives significantly affect students in the treatment group, with some minor spillover effects on untreated subjects. A recent study by Chay, McEwan and Urquiola (2005) similarly evaluates the effects of an incentive program using a RD design. The program is a school resource program in Chile that awards resources to schools based on cut-offs in the school's test scores. Their results indicate that the program had statistically significant effects on child test scores.

4. Ex ante program evaluation

Thus far, we have considered the problem of how to evaluate effects of existing programs, and all of the methods described in the previous sections assumed access to data on program participants. However, policy makers are sometimes interested in evaluating effects of hypothetical programs before deciding which type of program to implement. Some of the desired goals may be (i) to optimally design a social program to achieve some desired effects, (ii) to forecast the take-up rates and costs of alternative programs, or (iii) to study the effectiveness of alternatives to an existing program. Evaluating the effects of programs that do not yet exist requires an evaluation method that makes use

---

[46] If households were selecting nonrandomly into the program around the cut-off, then this could invalidate the assumption RD-1.

only of data on people who have never participated in the program. Answering question (iii) requires a way of extrapolating from experience with an existing program to alternative programs.

The problem of forecasting the effects of social programs is part of the more general problem of assessing the effects of policy changes prior to their implementation that was considered in the early work of Marshak (1953). He described it as one of the most challenging problems facing empirical economists. In the early discrete choice literature, the problem was cast as the "forecast problem," whereby researchers were trying to predict the demand for a good prior to its being introduced into the choice set. For example, McFadden and Talvitie (1977) used a discrete choice random utility model to forecast the demand for the San Francisco BART subway system prior to its being built.

There are a few empirical studies that study the performance of economic models for forecasting program effects by comparing models' forecasts to program effects that are estimated using experimental data. For example, Wise (1985) develops and estimates a model of housing demand that he uses to forecast the effects of a housing subsidy. The housing subsidy program was actually implemented as a randomized experiment, and Wise (1985) is able to compare forecasts he obtains from alternative models to the subsidy effects estimated experimentally.

More recently, Todd and Wolpin (2006) develop and estimate a dynamic behavioral model of family decision making about child schooling and fertility that they use to forecast the effects the PROGRESA program (see discussion of this program in Section 3.2.7) on choices about children's schooling and work and on family fertility.[47] The PROGRESA program was evaluated by an experiment that randomly assigned 506 villages to treatment and control groups. To assess the efficacy of the economic model for ex ante evaluation purposes, Todd and Wolpin (2006) estimate the model using data only on untreated individuals and then compare the model's predictions about program impacts to those observed under the experiment. They find that the model provides relatively accurate ex ante forecasts of program effects on school enrollment and child work patterns. They then use the model to evaluate take-up rates, costs and program effects of a variety of counterfactual programs, such as changes to the subsidy schedule (how the subsidy varies by gender and grade). Lastly, they use the model to evaluate effects of some radically different programs, such as an income subsidy program that removes the school attendance requirement.

To illustrate how a behavioral model can be used to predict the impacts of a program that has not been implemented, the next section presents a simple model of schooling choice and shows how the effects of a school subsidy program can potentially be identified, even when none of the families in the data actually receive a subsidy. This example is drawn from Todd and Wolpin (2005).

---

[47] The PROGRESA program is described in detail in Chapter 62 of this handbook.

4.1. An illustrative model of identification of subsidy effects

Consider a household making a single period decision about whether to send a child to school or to work. Let the utility of the household be separable in consumption (C) and school attendance (s), namely $u = C + (\alpha + \varepsilon)s$, where $s = 1$ if the child attends school, $= 0$ otherwise and ε is a preference shock. Assume that the cost of attending school depends on distance to the school, denoted k. Children who work contribute to family income, so the family's income is $y + w(1 - s) - \delta ks$, where y is parent's income, w is the child's earnings, and δks is the cost that is only incurred if the child attends school. Under utility maximization, the family chooses to have the child attend school if $\varepsilon > w - \alpha + \delta k$.

Suppose that wages are only on-served for children who work and specify a child wage offer equation:

$$w = z\gamma + v$$

where z are characteristics (such as age or sex) that are determinants of wage offers and are observed for all children. The equation governing whether a family sends a child to school or work is

$$s = 1 \quad \text{if } \alpha - \delta k + \varepsilon > z\gamma + v, \quad \text{else } s = 0.$$

The probability that a child attends school can be written as

$$\Pr(s = 1 \mid z) = \Pr(z\gamma - \alpha + \delta k < \varepsilon - v)$$
$$= F_{\varepsilon - v}(z\gamma - \alpha + \delta k),$$

where $F_{\varepsilon - v}(\cdot)$ is the cdf of $\varepsilon - v$. Under an assumption that the median of $\varepsilon - v$ is 0 conditional on z, the parameters γ, α and δ can be identified up to scale and estimated by either a parametric or semiparametric discrete choice estimation method.[48]

Next, consider estimation of the child wage offer equation using data on children who work $(s = 0)$ for whom wages are observed. We can write the wage equation as

$$y = z\gamma + E(v \mid z, s = 0) + \{v - E(v \mid z, s = 0)\},$$

where the error term in brackets $(\eta = v - E(v \mid z, s = 0))$ has conditional mean zero by construction.

As described in Section 3.3, the parameter γ can be consistently estimated by including a control function $E(v \mid z, s = 0)$.[49] Under the assumption that (i) v and ε are jointly distributed with density $f(v, \varepsilon)$ and (ii) the conditional density equals the unconditional density, $f(v, \varepsilon \mid z, k) = f(v, \varepsilon)$, as described along in Section 3.3, we

[48] See Manski (1975, 1988).
[49] See Heckman (1979).

obtain

$$w = z\gamma + K(P) + \eta,$$

where P is the probability of working. If there is a continuous exclusion restriction that affects the work decision but not the wage offer equation (in this case, the distance variable k), then the parameter γ can be nonparametrically identified under very weak assumptions on the K function.[50] To see why, note that an exclusion restriction allows us to hold constant z at some value and vary P, thereby tracing out the shape of the K function. Then, fixing K at some value, we can estimate γ.[51] Once the scale of γ is identified, we can use the results of the discrete choice estimation to obtain α and δ.[52]

Next, consider how the estimated model can be used for ex ante evaluation. Suppose that the government is contemplating a program to increase school attendance of children though a subsidy to parents in the amount b if they send their child to school. Under such a program, the probability that a child attends school will increase by $F_{\varepsilon-v}(z\gamma - \alpha - b + \delta k) - F_{\varepsilon-v}(z\gamma - \alpha + \delta k)$. The function $F_{\varepsilon-v}(s)$ can be estimated nonparametrically by a nonparametric regression of the school attendance indicator, s, on $z\hat{\gamma} - \hat{\alpha} + \hat{\delta}k$.[53] To assess the effect of the subsidy on the probability of attending school, we simply evaluate the $F_{\varepsilon-v}(s)$ function at the point $z\hat{\gamma} - \hat{\alpha} - b + \hat{\delta}k$.

The above described approach is semiparametric and does not require specifying the distribution, for example, of $\varepsilon - v$ or the specification of the K function. Of course, a fully parametric approach would also be feasible.

5. Conclusions

This chapter has considered traditional and new approaches to evaluating the effects of treatment interventions using nonexperimental data. The major challenge to the evaluator is how to take account both observable and potentially nonobservable preexisting differences between program participants and nonparticipants in drawing inferences about the program's causal effect. Differences between participants and nonparticipants may arise either because programs are nonrandomly placed, are targeted at certain groups, or because of individual nonrandom self-selected into the program. All three of these factors may occur simultaneously.

Each of the econometric evaluation estimators discussed in this chapter invokes a different set of assumptions to justify its application. The question of which method to

---

[50] Assumptions on the continuity of the K function are required.

[51] The intercept of the wage offer equation will, in general, not be separately identified from the K function unless there is a subset of the data for which $\Pr(s = 0 \mid z, k) = 1$. See Heckman (1990) and Andrews and Schafgans (1998).

[52] Given an estimate of γ, the scaling factor in the discrete choice problem can also be obtained.

[53] Here, we can use the fact that the conditional expectation of s, $E(s \mid z\hat{\gamma} - \hat{\alpha} + \hat{\delta}k = \tau) = \Pr(s = 1 \mid z\hat{\gamma} - \hat{\alpha} + \hat{\delta}k = \tau)$.

adopt in any particular circumstance will generally be context-specific and will also depend on the quality of the available data. For example, matching methods impose weak assumptions on the form of the conditional mean of the outcome equation, but make the strong assumptions that which unit receives treatment is ignorable after conditioning on a set of observed covariates. Such a method should only be adopted only in situations where the available conditioning variables are rich enough to make the required assumption plausible. Difference-in-difference matching estimators overcome this strong assumption to a degree by allowing permanent, time-invariant unobservables to affect participation decisions. Control function estimators are the most general class of estimators in that they explicitly allow possibly time-varying unobservables to affect program participation decisions. The implementation of parametric control function estimators is relatively straightforward, but a drawback to them is that they usually assume that error terms are normally distributed. Semiparametric control function estimators are more flexible, but usually require additional assumptions to achieve identification.

Regression-discontinuity estimators can be applied in situations where there is a known discontinuity in the treatment assignment rule as a function of some underlying variable, such as a score determining who is eligible for the treatment. These estimators invoke weak assumptions, but can only provide information on treatment effects at the points of discontinuity, which may not be sufficient to evaluate the efficacy of a program.

Lastly, the evaluator also has access to a class of instrumental variables estimators, that can be applied in situations where there is a variable that affects the program participation decision but does not affect outcomes. When there is an exclusion restriction, one option is to apply the Wald IV estimator, which recovers the local average treatment effect (LATE) parameter (see Imbens and Angrist, 1994). A potential drawback of LATE is that it is instrument dependent and therefore may not correspond to the main parameter of interest The most recent of the evaluation methods considered in this chapter are Local Instrumental Variable (LIV) estimators of Heckman and Vytlacil (2005) that can be applied in situations where there is a continuous instrumental variable (or at least one that is continuous over a range). LIV estimators provide a means of learning about the full distribution of treatment effects and of building up the various other parameters of interest, including LATE, treatment on the treated (TT), and average treatment effect (ATE).

The many recent developments in the evaluation literature have greatly increased the set of tools available for empirical evaluation researcher and have furthered the understanding of how different estimation methods relate to one another. It is hoped that by discussing the assumptions, data requirements, and implementation issues, this chapter has made the relative strengths and weaknesses of various approaches more transparent and thereby made the choice among estimators in any particular context easier.

References

Abadie, A., Imbens, G. (2004a). "On the failure of the bootstrap for matching estimators". Manuscript, Harvard University.

Abadie, A., Imbens, G. (2004b). "Large sample properties of matching estimators for average treatment effects". Manuscript, Harvard University.

Andrews, D., Schafgans, O. (1998). "Semiparametric estimation of the intercept of a sample selection model". Review of Economic Studies 65, 497–518.

Angrist, J., Imbens, G., Rubin D. (1994). "Identification of causal effects using instrumental variables". Journal of the American Statistical Association.

Angrist, J., Lavy, V. (1999). "Using Maimonides rule to estimate the effect of class size on scholastic achievement". Quarterly Journal of Economics, May.

Angrist, J., Lavy, V. (2001). "Does teacher training affect pupil learning? Evidence from matched comparisons in Jerusalem public schools". Journal of Labor Economics 19 (2), 343–369.

Ashenfelter, O. (1978). "Estimating the effect of training programs on earnings". Review of Economics and Statistics 60, 47–57.

Barnow, B., Cain, G., Goldberger, A. (1980). "Issues in the analysis of selectivity bias". In: Stromsdorfer, E., Farkas, G. (Eds.), In: Evaluation Studies Review Annual, vol. 5. Sage, San Fransisco, pp. 290–317.

Behrman, J., Cheng, Y., Todd, P. (2000). "Evaluating preschool programs when length of exposure to the program varies: A nonparametric approach". Review of Economics and Statistics 86 (1), 108–132.

Behrman, J., Garcia-Gallardo, J., Parker, S., Todd, P., Vélez-Grajales, V. (2005). "How conditional cash transfers impact school and working behavior of children and youth in urban Mexico". Manuscript.

Black, S.E. (1999). "Do better shools matter? Parental valuation of elementary education". Quaterly Journal of Economics 114 (2), 577–599.

Buddlemeyer, H., Skoufias, E. (2004). "An evaluation of the performance of regression discontinuity design on PROGRESA". Working paper series 3386. Policy Research, The World Bank.

Carneiro, P., Heckman, J.J., Vytlacil, E. (2001). "Understanding what instrumental variables estimate: Estimating marginal and average returns to education". Manuscript, University of Chicago.

Chay, K.Y., McEqan, P.J., Urquiola, M. (2005). "The central role of noise in evaluating interventions that use test scores to rank schools". American Economic Review.

Chen, S., Ravallion, M. (2003). "Hidden impact? Ex post evaluation of an anti-poverty program". Journal of Public Economics.

Cochran, W., Rubin, D. (1973). "Controlling bias in observational studies". Sankyha 35, 417–446.

Dehejia, R., Wahba, S. (1998). "Propensity score matching methods for nonexperimental causal studies". Working paper No. 6829, NBER.

Dehejia, R., Wahba, S. (1999). "Causal effects in nonexperimental studies: Reevaluating the evaluation of training programs". Journal of the American Statistical Association 94 (448), 1053–1062.

Duflo, E. (2001). "Schooling and labor market consequences of school construction in Indonesia: Evidence from an unusual policy experiment". American Economic Review.

Efron, B., Tibshirani, R. (1993). An Introduction to the Bootstrap. Chapman & Hall, New York.

Eichler, M., Lechner, M. (2001). "An evaluation of public employment programmes in the East German state of Sachsen-Anhalt". Labour Economics, in press.

Fan, J. (1992a). "Design adaptive nonparametric regression". Journal of the American Statistical Association 87, 998–1004.

Fan, J. (1992b). "Local linear regression smoothers and their minimax efficiencies". The Annals of Statistics 21, 196–216.

Galiani, S., Gertler, P., Schargrodsky E. (2005). "Water for life: The impact of the privatization of water services on child mortality in Argentina". Journal of Political Economy.

Gertler, P., Levine, D., Ames, M. (2004). "Schooling and parental death". Review of Economics and Statistics 86 (1).

Glewwe, P., Kremer, M., Moulin, S. (2000). "Textbooks and test scores. Evidence from a prospective evaluation in Kenya". Manuscript.

Glewwe, P., Kremer, M., Moulin, S. (2003). "Teacher incentives". Working paper #9671, NBER.

Glewwe, P., Kremer, M., Moulin, S., Zitzewitz, E. (2004). "Retrospective vs. prospective analyses of school inputs: The case of flip charts in Kenya". Journal of Development Economics 74, 251–268.

Godtland, E.M., Sadoulet, E., deJanvry, A., Murgai, R., Ortiz, O. (2004). "The impact of farmer field schools on knowledge and productivity: A study of potato farmers in the Peruvian Andes". Educational Development and Cultural Change, vol. 53, pp. 63–92.

Hahn, J. (1998). " On the role of the propensity score in efficient estimation of average treatment effects". Econometrica 66 (2), 315–331.

Hahn, J., Todd, P., Van der Klaauw, W. (2001). "Identification of treatment effects by regression-discontinuity design" Econometrica, February, 201–209.

Handa, S., Maluccio, J.A. (2006). "Matching the gold standard: Evidence from a social experiment in Nicaragua". Working paper. Department of Public policy, University of North Carolina.

Härdle, W. (1990). Applied Nonparametric Regression. Cambridge Univ. Press, New York.

Härdle, W., Linton, O. (1994). "Applied nonparametric methods". In: McFadden, D.F., Engle, R.F. (Eds.), Handbook of Econometrics, vol. 4. North-Holland, Amsterdam, pp. 2295–2339.

Heckman, J. (1979). "Sample selection bias as a specification error". Econometrica 47 (1), 153–161.

Heckman, J. (1990). " Varieties of selection bias". American Economic Review 80, 313–318.

Heckman, J. (1992). "Randomization and social policy evaluation". In: Manski, C., Garfinkle, I. (Eds.), Evaluating Welfare and Training Programs. Harvard Univ. Press, Cambridge, MA, pp. 201–230.

Heckman, J. (1997). "Randomization as an instrumental variables estimator: A study of implicit behavioral assumptions in one widely-used estimator". Journal of Human Resources 32, 442–462.

Heckman, J. (2000). "Causal parameters and policy analysis in economics: A twentieth century retrospective". Quarterly Journal of Economics 115, 45–97.

Heckman, J., Ichimura, H., Todd, P. (1997). "Matching as an econometric evaluation estimator: Evidence from evaluating a job training program". Review of Economic Studies 64 (4), 605–654.

Heckman, J., Ichimura, H., Todd, P. (1998). "Matching as an econometric evaluation estimator". Review of Economic Studies 65 (2), 261–294.

Heckman, J., La Londe, R., Smith, J. (1999). "The economics and econometrics of active labor market programs". In: Ashenfelter, O., Card, D. (Eds.), Handbook of Labor Economics, vol. 3. North-Holland, Amsterdam, pp. 1865–2097.

Heckman, J., Robb, R. (1985). "Alternative methods for evaluating the impact of interventions". In: Heckman, J., Singer, B. (Eds.), Longitudinal Analysis of Labor Market Data. Cambridge Univ. Press, Cambridge, UK, pp. 156–246.

Heckman, J., Smith, J. (1999). "The pre-program earnings dip and the determinants of participation in a social program: Implications for simple program evaluation strategies". Economic Journal 109 (457), 313–348.

Heckman, J., Todd, P. (1995). "Adapting propensity score matching and selection models to choice-based samples". Manuscript, University of Chicago.

Heckman, J., Vytlacil, E. (2000). "Causal parameters, structural equations, treatment effects and randomized evaluations of social programs". Manuscript, University of Chicago.

Heckman, J., Vytlacil, E. (2005). "Structural equations, treatment effects, and econometric policy evaluation". Econometrica.

Heckman, J., Ichimura, H., Smith, J., Todd, P. (1996). "Sources of selection bias in evaluating social programs: An interpretation of conventional measures and evidence on the effectiveness of matching as a program evaluation method". Proceedings of the National Academy of Sciences 93 (23), 13416–13420.

Heckman, J., Ichimura, H., Smith, J., Todd, P. (1998). "Characterizing selection bias using experimental data". Econometrica 66 (5), 1017–1098.

Hirano, K., Imbens, G., Ridder, G. (2000). "Efficient estimation of average treatment effects using the estimated propensity score". Manuscript, UCLA.

Horowitz, J. (2001). "The bootstrap". Chapter 52 in: Heckman, J.J., Leamer, E.E. (Eds.), Handbook of Econometrics, vol. 5. Elsevier Science, pp. 3159–3228.

Ichimura, H. (1993). "Semiparametric least squares (SLS) and weighted SLS estimation of single-index models". Journal of Econometrics 58, 71–120.

Imbens, G., Angrist, J. (1994). "Identification of local average treatment effects". Econometrica 62, 467–475.

Jalan, J., Ravallion, M. (2001). "Does piped water reduce diarrhea for children in rural India". Journal of Econometrics 112, 153–173.

Jalan, J., Ravallion, M. (2003). "Estimating the benefit incidence of an antipoverty program by propensity score matching". Journal of Business and Economic Statistics, February.

La Londe, R. (1986). "Evaluating the econometric evaluations of training programs with experimental data". American Economic Review 76, 604–620.

Lavy, V., (2004). "Performance pay and teachers' effort, productivity and grading ethics". Working paper #10622, National Bureau of Economic Research.

Lechner, M. (2002). "Some practical issues in the evaluation of heterogeneous labour market programmes by matching methods". Journal of the Royal Statistical Society Series A 165 (Part 1), 59–82.

Manski, C.F. (1975). "The maximum score estimation of the stochastic utility model of choice". Journal of Econometrics 27, 313–333.

Manski, C.F. (1988). "Identification of binary response models". Journal of the American Statistical Association 83 (403), 729–737.

Manski, C., Lerman, S. (1977). " The estimation of choice probabilities from choice-based samples". Econometrica 45 (8), 1977–1988.

Manski, C., McFadden, D. (1981). "Alternative estimators and sample designs for discrete choice analysis". In: Manski, C.F., McFadden, D. (Eds.), Structural Analysis of Discrete Data with Economic Applications. MIT Press, Cambridge, MA, pp. 1–50.

Marschak, J. (1953). "Economic measurements for policy and prediction". In: Hood, W., Koopmans, T. (Eds.), Studies in Econometric Method. Wiley, New York, pp. 1–26.

McFadden, D. (1984). "Econometric analysis of qualitative response models". Griliches, Z., Intriligator, M.D. (Eds.), Handbook of Econometrics, vol. II.

McFadden, D., Talvitie, A.P. (1977). "Validation of disaggregate travel demand models: Some tests". In: Urban Demand Forecasting Project, Final Report, vol. V. Institute of Transportation Studies, University of California, Berkeley.

Rosenbaum, P., Rubin, D. (1983). "The central role of the propensity score in observational studies for causal effects". Biometrika 70, 41–55.

Rosenbaum, P., Rubin, D. (1985). "Constructing a control group using multivariate matched sampling methods that incorporate the propensity score". American Statistician 39, 33–38.

Rosenzweig, M.R., Wolpin, K.I. (1986). "Evaluating the effects of optimally distributed public programs: Child health and family planning". American Economic Review 76 (3), 470–482.

Rubin, D.B. (1980). "Bias reduction using Mahalanobis' metric matching". Biometrics 36 (2), 295–298.

Rubin, D.B. (1984). "Reducing bias in observational studies using subclassification on the propensity score". Journal of the American Statistical Association 79, 516–524.

Smith, J., Todd, P. (2005). "Does matching address La Londe's critique of nonexperimental estimators?" Journal of Econometrics 125 (1–2), 305–353.

Thistlethwaite, D., Campbell, D. (1960). "Regression-discontinuity analysis: An alternative to the ex post facto experiment". Journal of Educational Psychology 51, 309–317.

Todd, P.E., Wolpin, K.I. (2006). "Assessing the impact of a school subsidy program in Mexico". American Economic Review 96 (5), 1384–1417.

Todd, P., Wolpin, K.I. (2005). "Ex ante evaluation of social programs". Manuscript, University of Pennsylvania.

Trochim, W. (1984). Research Design for Program Evaluation: The Regression-Discontinuity Approach. Sage Publications, Beverly Hills.

Van der Klaauw, W. (1996). "A regression-discontinuity evaluation of the effect of financial aid offers on college enrollment". International Economic Review.

Vytlacil, E. (2002). "Independence, monotonicity and latent index models: An equivalence result". Econometrica 70 (1), 331–341.

Wise, D.A. (1985). "A behavioral model versus experimentation: The effects of housing subsidies on rent". In: Methods of Operations Research, vol. 50. Verlag Anton Hain.

Wolpin, K.I., Rosenzweig, M.R. (1988a). "Evaluating the effects of optimally distributed programs: Child health and family planning programs". American Economic Review 76 (3), 470–482.

Wolpin, K.I., Rosenzweig, M.R. (1988b). "Migration selectivity and effects of public programs". Journal of Public Economics 37, 265–289.

Chapter 61

USING RANDOMIZATION IN DEVELOPMENT ECONOMICS RESEARCH: A TOOLKIT*

ESTHER DUFLO

MIT Department of Economics and Abdul Latif Jameel Poverty Action Lab, E52-252g, 50 Memorial Drive, Cambridge, MA 02142-1347, USA

RACHEL GLENNERSTER

MIT Department of Economics and Abdul Latif Jameel Poverty Action Lab, E60-275, 30 Memorial Drive, Cambridge, MA 02142, USA

MICHAEL KREMER

Department of Economics, Harvard University and Abdul Latif Jameel Poverty Action Lab, Littauer Center M-20, Cambridge, MA 02138, USA

Contents

* We thank the editor T.Paul Schultz, as well Abhijit Banerjee, Guido Imbens and Jeffrey Kling for extensive discussions, David Clingingsmith, Greg Fischer, Trang Nguyen and Heidi Williams for outstanding research assistance, and Paul Glewwe and Emmanuel Saez, whose previous collaboration with us inspired parts of this chapter.

Handbook of Development Economics, Volume 4
© *2008 Elsevier B.V.   All rights reserved*
DOI: 10.1016/S1573-4471(07)04061-2

Abstract

This paper is a practical guide (a toolkit) for researchers, students and practitioners wishing to introduce randomization as part of a research design in the field. It first covers the rationale for the use of randomization, as a solution to selection bias and a partial solution to publication biases. Second, it discusses various ways in which randomization can be practically introduced in a field settings. Third, it discusses designs issues such as sample size requirements, stratification, level of randomization and data collection methods. Fourth, it discusses how to analyze data from randomized evaluations when there are departures from the basic framework. It reviews in particular how to handle imperfect compliance and externalities. Finally, it discusses some of the issues involved in drawing general conclusions from randomized evaluations, including the necessary use of theory as a guide when designing evaluations and interpreting results.

Keywords

randomized evaluations, experiments, development, program evaluation

JEL classification: I0, J0, O0, C93

1. Introduction

Randomization is now an integral part of a development economist's toolbox. Over the last ten years, a growing number of randomized evaluations have been conducted by economists or with their input. These evaluations, on topics as diverse as the effect of school inputs on learning (Glewwe and Kremer, 2006), the adoption of new technologies in agriculture (Duflo, Kremer and Robinson, 2006), corruption in driving licenses administration (Bertrand et al., 2006), or moral hazard and adverse selection in consumer credit markets (Karlan and Zinman, 2005b), have attempted to answer important policy questions and have also been used by economists as a testing ground for their theories.

Unlike the early "social experiments" conducted in the United States – with their large budgets, large teams, and complex implementations – many of the randomized evaluations that have been conducted in recent years in developing countries have had fairly small budgets, making them affordable for development economists. Working with local partners on a smaller scale has also given more flexibility to researchers, who can often influence program design. As a result, randomized evaluation has become a powerful research tool.

While research involving randomization still represents a small proportion of work in development economics, there is now a considerable body of theoretical knowledge and practical experience on how to run these projects. In this chapter, we attempt to draw together in one place the main lessons of this experience and provide a reference for researchers planning to conduct such projects. The chapter thus provides practical guidance on how to conduct, analyze, and interpret randomized evaluations in developing countries and on how to use such evaluations to answer questions about economic behavior.

This chapter is not a review of research using randomization in development economics.[1] Nor is its main purpose to justify the use of randomization as a complement or substitute to other research methods, although we touch upon these issues along the way.[2] Rather, it is a practical guide, a "toolkit," which we hope will be useful to those interested in including randomization as part of their research design.

The outline to the chapter is as follows. In Section 2, we use the now standard "potential outcome" framework to discuss how randomized evaluations overcome a number of the problems endemic to retrospective evaluation. We focus on the issue of selection bias, which arises when individuals or groups are selected for treatment based on characteristics that may also affect their outcomes and makes it difficult to disentangle the

---

[1] Kremer (2003) and Glewwe and Kremer (2006) provide a review of randomized evaluations in education; Banerjee and Duflo (2006) review the results from randomized evaluations on ways to improve teacher's and nurse's attendance in developing countries; Duflo (2006) reviews the lessons on incentives, social learning, and hyperbolic discounting.

[2] We have provided such arguments elsewhere, see Duflo (2004) and Duflo and Kremer (2005).

impact of the treatment from the factors that drove selection. This problem is compounded by a natural publication bias towards retrospective studies that support prior beliefs and present statistically significant results. We discuss how carefully constructed randomized evaluations address these issues.

In Section 3, we discuss how can randomization be introduced in the field. Which partners to work with? How can pilot projects be used? What are the various ways in which randomization can be introduced in an ethically and politically acceptable manner?

In Section 4, we discuss how researchers can affect the *power* of the design, or the chance to arrive at statistically significant conclusions. How should sample sizes be chosen? How does the level of randomization, the availability of control variables, and the possibility to stratify, affect power?

In Section 5, we discuss practical design choices researchers will face when conducting randomized evaluation: At what level to randomize? What are the pros and cons of factorial designs? When and what data to collect?

In Section 6 we discuss how to analyze data from randomized evaluations when there are departures from the simplest basic framework. We review how to handle different probability of selection in different groups, imperfect compliance and externalities.

In Section 7 we discuss how to accurately estimate the precision of estimated treatment effects when the data is grouped and when multiple outcomes or subgroups are being considered. Finally in Section 8 we conclude by discussing some of the issues involved in drawing general conclusions from randomized evaluations, including the necessary use of theory as a guide when designing evaluations and interpreting results.

2. Why randomize?

2.1. The problem of causal inference

Any attempt at drawing a causal inference question such as "What is the causal effect of education on fertility?" or "What is the causal effect of class size on learning?" requires answering essentially counterfactual questions: How would individuals who participated in a program have fared in the absence of the program? How would those who were not exposed to the program have fared in the presence of the program? The difficulty with these questions is immediate. At a given point in time, an individual is either exposed to the program or not. Comparing the same individual over time will not, in most cases, give a reliable estimate of the program's impact since other factors that affect outcomes may have changed since the program was introduced. We cannot, therefore, obtain an estimate of the impact of the program on a given individual. We can, however, obtain the average impact of a program, policy, or variable (we will refer to this as a treatment, below) on a group of individuals by comparing them to a similar group of individuals who were not exposed to the program.

To do this, we need a comparison group. This is a group of people who, in the absence of the treatment, would have had outcomes similar to those who received the treatment. In reality, however, those individuals who are exposed to a treatment generally differ from those who are not. Programs are placed in specific areas (for example, poorer or richer areas), individuals are screened for participation (for example, on the basis of poverty or motivation), and the decision to participate in a program is often voluntary, creating self-selection. Families chose whether to send girls to school. Different regions chose to have women teachers, and different countries chose to have the rule of law. For all of these reasons, those who were not exposed to a treatment are often a poor comparison group for those who were. Any difference between the groups can be attributed to both the impact of the program or pre-existing differences (the "selection bias"). Without a reliable way to estimate the size of this selection bias, one cannot decompose the overall difference into a treatment effect and a bias term.

To fix ideas it is useful to introduce the notion of a *potential outcome*, introduced by Rubin (1974). Suppose we are interested in measuring the impact of textbooks on learning. Let us call Y_i^T the average test score of children in a given school i if the school has textbooks and Y_i^C the test scores of children in the same school i if the school has no textbooks. Further, define Y_i as outcome that is actually observed for school i. We are interested in the difference $Y_i^T - Y_i^C$, which is the effect of having textbooks for school i. As we explained above, we will not be able to observe a school i both with and without books at the same time, and we will therefore not be able to estimate individual treatment effects. While every school has two potential outcomes, only one is observed for each school.

However, we may hope to learn the expected average effect that textbooks have on the schools in a population:

$$E[Y_i^T - Y_i^C]. \tag{1}$$

Imagine we have access to data on a large number of schools in one region. Some schools have textbooks and others do not. One approach is to take the average of both groups and examine the difference between average test scores in schools with textbooks and in those without. In a large sample, this will converge to

$$
\begin{aligned}
D &= E[Y_i^T | \text{School has textbooks}] - E[Y_i^C | \text{School has no textbooks}] \\
&= E[Y_i^T | T] - E[Y_i^C | C].
\end{aligned}
$$

Subtracting and adding $E[Y_i^C|T]$, i.e., the expected outcome for a subject in the treatment group had she not been treated (a quantity that cannot be observed but is logically well defined) we obtain,

$$
\begin{aligned}
D &= E[Y_i^T | T] - E[Y_i^C | T] - E[Y_i^C | C] + E[Y_i^C | T] \\
&= E[Y_i^T - Y_i^C | T] + E[Y_i^C | T] - E[Y_i^C | C].
\end{aligned}
$$

The first term, $E[Y_i^T - Y_i^C | T]$, is the *treatment effect* that we are trying to isolate (i.e., the effect of treatment on the treated). In our textbook example, it is the answer to the question: on average, in the treatment schools, what difference did the books make?

The second term, $E[Y_i^C | T] - E[Y_i^C | C]$, is the *selection bias*. It captures the difference in potential untreated outcomes between the treatment and the comparison schools; treatment schools may have had different test scores on average even if they had not been treated. This would be true if schools that received textbooks were schools where parents consider education a particularly high priority and, for example, are more likely to encourage their children to do homework and prepare for tests. In this case, $E[Y_i^C | T]$ would be larger than $E[Y_i^C | C]$. The bias could also work in the other direction. If, for example, textbooks had been provided by a non-governmental organization to schools in particularly disadvantaged communities, $E[Y_i^C | T]$ would likely be smaller than $E[Y_i^C | C]$. It could also be the case that textbooks were part of a more general policy intervention (for example, all schools that receive textbooks also receive blackboards); the effect of the other interventions would be embedded in our measure D. The more general point is that in addition to any effect of the textbooks there may be systematic differences between schools with textbooks and those without.

Since $E[Y_i^C | T]$ is not observed, it is in general impossible to assess the magnitude (or even the sign) of the selection bias and, therefore, the extent to which selection bias explains the difference in outcomes between the treatment and the comparison groups. An essential objective of much empirical work is to identify situations where we can assume that the selection bias does not exist or find ways to correct for it.

2.2. Randomization solves the selection bias

One setting in which the selection bias can be entirely removed is when individuals or groups of individuals are randomly assigned to the treatment and comparison groups. In a randomized evaluation, a sample of N individuals is selected from the population of interest. Note that the "population" may not be a random sample of the entire population and may be selected according to observables; therefore, we will learn the effect of the treatment on the particular sub-population from which the sample is drawn. We will return to this issue. This experimental sample is then divided *randomly* into two groups: the *treatment* group (N_T individuals) and the *comparison* (or control) group (N_C individuals).

The treatment group then is exposed to the "treatment" (their treatment status is T) while the comparison group (treatment status C) is not. Then the outcome Y is observed and compared for both treatment and comparison groups. For example, out of 100 schools, 50 are randomly chosen to receive textbooks, and 50 do not receive textbooks. The average treatment effect can then be estimated as the difference in empirical means of Y between the two groups,

$$\hat{D} = \hat{E}[Y_i | T] - \hat{E}[Y_i | C],$$

where $\hat{E}$ denotes the sample average. As the sample size increases, this difference converges to

$$D = E[Y_i^T | T] - E[Y_i^C | C].$$

Since the treatment has been randomly assigned, individuals assigned to the treatment and control groups differ in expectation only through their exposure to the treatment. Had neither received the treatment, their outcomes would have been in expectation the same. This implies that the selection bias, $E[Y_i^C | T] - E[Y_i^C | C]$, is equal to zero. If, in addition, the potential outcomes of an individual are unrelated to the treatment status of any other individual (this is the "Stable Unit Treatment Value Assumption" (SUTVA) described in Angrist, Imbens and Rubin (1996)),[3] we have

$$E[Y_i | T] - E[Y_i | C] = E[Y_i^T - Y_i^C | T] = E[Y_i^T - Y_i^C],$$

the causal parameter of interest for treatment T.

The regression counterpart to obtain $\hat{D}$ is

$$Y_i = \alpha + \beta T + \epsilon_i, \tag{2}$$

where T is a dummy for assignment to the treatment group. Equation (2) can be estimated with ordinary least squares, and it can easily be shown that $\hat{\beta}_{OLS} = \hat{E}(Y_i | T) - \hat{E}(Y_i | C)$.[4]

This result tells us that when a randomized evaluation is correctly designed and implemented, it provides an unbiased estimate of the impact of the program in the sample under study – this estimate is internally valid. There are of course many ways in which the assumptions in this simple set up may fail when randomized evaluations are implemented in the field in developing countries. This chapter describes how to correctly implement randomized evaluations so as to minimize such failures and how to correctly analyze and interpret the results of such evaluations, including in cases that depart from this basic set up.

Before proceeding further, it is important to keep in mind what expression (1) means. What is being estimated is the *overall impact* of a particular program on an outcome, such as test scores, allowing other inputs to change in response to the program. It may be different from the impact of textbooks on test scores *keeping everything else constant*.

To see this, assume that the production function for the outcome of interest Y is of the form $Y = f(I)$, where I is a vector of inputs, some of which can be directly varied using policy tools, others of which depend on household or firm responses. This relationship is

---

[3] This rules out externalities–the possibility that treatment of one individual affects the outcomes of another. We address this issue in Section 6.3.

[4] Note that estimating Eq. (2) with OLS does not require us to assume a constant treatment effect. The estimated coefficient is simply the average treatment effect.

structural; it holds regardless of the actions of individuals or institutions affected by the policy changes. The impact of any given input in the vector I on academic achievement that is embedded in this relationship is a structural parameter.

Consider a change in one element of the vector I, call it t. One estimate of interest is how changes in t affect Y when all other explanatory variables are held constant, i.e., the partial derivative of Y with respect to t. A second estimate of interest is the total derivative of Y with respect to t, which includes changes in other inputs in response to the change in t. In general, if other inputs are complements to or substitutes for t, then exogenous changes in I will lead to changes in other inputs j. For example, parents may respond to an educational program by increasing their provision of home-supplied educational inputs. Alternatively, parents may consider the program a substitute for home-supplied inputs and decrease their supply. For example, Das et al. (2004) and others suggest that household educational expenditures and governmental non-salary cash grants to schools are substitutes, and that households cut back on expenditures when the government provides grants to schools.

In general, the partial and total derivatives could be quite different, and both may be of interest to policymakers. The total derivative is of interest because it shows what will happen to outcome measures after an input is exogenously provided and agents re-optimize. In effect it tells us the "real" impact of the policy on the outcomes of interest. But the total derivative may not provide a measure of overall welfare effects. Again consider a policy of providing textbooks to students where parents may respond to the policy by reducing home purchases of textbooks in favor of some consumer good that is not in the educational production function. The total derivative of test scores or other educational outcome variables will not capture the benefits of this re-optimization. Under some assumptions, however, the partial derivative will provide an appropriate guide to the welfare impact of the input.

Results from randomized evaluations (and from other internally valid program evaluations) provide reduced form estimates of the impacts of the treatment, and these reduced form parameters are total derivatives. Partial derivatives can only be obtained if researchers specify the model that links various inputs to the outcomes of interest and collect data on these intermediate inputs. This underscores that to estimate welfare impact of a policy, randomization needs to be combined with theory, a topic to which we return in Section 8.

2.3. Other methods to control for selection bias

Aside from randomization, other methods can be used to address the issue of selection bias. The objective of any of these methods is to create comparison groups that are valid under a set of identifying assumptions. The identifying assumptions are not directly testable, and the validity of any particular study depends instead on how convincing the assumptions appear. While it is not the objective of this chapter to review these methods in detail,[5] in this section we discuss them briefly in relation to randomized evaluations.[6]

2.3.1. Controlling for selection bias by controlling for observables

The first possibility is that, conditional on a set of observable variables X, the treatment can be considered to be as good as randomly assigned. That is, there exists a vector X such that

$$E\big[Y_i^C | X, T\big] - E\big[Y_i^C | X, C\big] = 0. \tag{3}$$

A case where this is obviously true is when the treatment status is randomly assigned conditional on a set of observable variables X. In other words, the allocation of observations to treatment or comparison is not unconditionally randomized, but within each strata defined by the interactions of the variables in the set X, the allocation was done randomly. In this case, after conditioning on X, the selection bias disappears. We will discuss in Section 6.1 how to analyze the data arising from such a setup. In most observational settings, however, there is no explicit randomization at any point, and one must *assume* that appropriately controlling for the observable variables is sufficient to eliminate selection bias.

There are different approaches to control for the set of variables X. A first approach, when the dimension of X is not too large, is to compute the difference between the outcomes of the treatment and comparison groups within each cell formed by the various possible values of X. The treatment effect is then the weighted average of these within-cell effects (see Angrist, 1998 for an application of this method to the impact of military service). This approach (fully non-parametric matching) is not practical if X has many variables or includes continuous variables. In this case, methods have been designed to implement matching based on the "propensity score," or the probability of being assigned to the treatment conditional on the variables X.[7] A third approach is to control for X, parametrically or non-parametrically, in a regression framework. As described in the references cited, matching and regression techniques make different assumptions and estimate somewhat different parameters. Both, however, are only valid on the underlying assumption that, conditional on the observable variables that are controlled for, there is no difference in potential outcomes between treated and untreated individuals. For this to be true, the set of variables X must contain all the relevant differences between the treatment and control groups. This assumption is not testable and

---

[5] Much fuller treatments of these subjects can be found, notably in this and other handbooks (Angrist and Imbens, 1994; Card, 1999; Imbens, 2004; Todd, 2008; Ravallion, 2008).

[6] We do not discuss instrumental variables estimation in this section, since its uses in the context of randomized evaluation will be discussed in Section 6.2, and the general principle discussed there will apply to the use of instruments that are not randomly assigned.

[7] The results that controlling for the propensity score leads to unbiased estimate of the treatment effect under assumption (3) is due to Rosenbaum and Rubin (1983) see chapters by Todd (2008) and Ravallion (2008) in this volume for a discussion of matching).

its plausibility must be evaluated on a case-by-case basis. In many situations, the variables that are controlled for are just those that happen to be available in the data set, and selection (or "omitted variable") bias remains an issue, regardless of how flexibly the control variables are introduced.

2.3.2. Regression discontinuity design estimates

A very interesting special case of controlling for an observable variable occurs in circumstances where the probability of assignment to the treatment group is a discontinuous function of one or more observable variables. For example, a microcredit organization may limit eligibility for loans to women living in household with less than one acre of land; students may pass an exam if their grade is at least 50%; or class size may not be allowed to exceed 25 students. If the impact of any unobservable variable correlated with the variable used to assign treatment is smooth, the following assumption is reasonable for a small ϵ:

$$ E\left[Y_i^C | T, X < \overline{X} + \epsilon, X > \overline{X} - \epsilon\right] = E\left[Y_i^C | C, X < \overline{X} + \epsilon, X > \overline{X} - \epsilon\right], \quad (4) $$

where X is the underlying variable and $\overline{X}$ is the threshold for assignment. This assumption implies that within some ε-range of $\bar{X}$, the selection bias is zero and is the basis of "regression discontinuity design estimates" (Campbell, 1969); see Todd (2008) chapter in this volume for further details and references). The idea is to estimate the treatment effect using individuals just below the threshold as a control for those just above.

This design has become very popular with researchers working on program evaluation in developed countries, and many argue that it removes selection bias when assignment rules are indeed implemented. It has been less frequently applied by development economists, perhaps because it faces two obstacles that are prevalent in developing countries. First, assignment rules are not always implemented very strictly. For example, Morduch (1998) criticizes the approach of Pitt and Khandker (1998), who make implicit use of a regression discontinuity design argument for the evaluation of Grameen Bank clients. Morduch shows that despite the official rule of not lending to household owning more than one acre of land, credit officers exercise their discretion. There is no discontinuity in the probability of borrowing at the one acre threshold. The second problem is the officials implementing a program may be able to manipulate the level of the underlying variable that determines eligibility, which makes an individual's position above or below the threshold endogenous. In this case, it cannot be argued that individuals on either side of the cutoff have similar potential outcomes and Eq. (4) fails to hold.

2.3.3. Difference-in-differences and fixed effects

Difference-in-difference estimates use pre-period differences in outcomes between treatment and control group for control for pre-existing differences between the groups, when data exists both before and after the treatment. Denote by Y_1^T (Y_1^C) the potential outcome "if treated" ("if untreated") in period 1, after the treatment occurs, and Y_0^T (Y_0^C) the potential outcome "if treated" ("if untreated") in period 0, before the treatment occurs. Individuals belong to group T or group C. Group T is treated in period 1 and untreated in period 0. Group C is never treated.

The difference-in-differences estimator is

$$\widehat{DD} = \left[\hat{E}[Y_1^T|T] - \hat{E}[Y_0^C|T]\right] - \left[\hat{E}[Y_1^C|C] - \hat{E}[Y_0^C|C]\right]$$

and provides an unbiased estimate of the treatment effect under the assumption that $[\hat{E}(Y_1^C|T) - \hat{E}(Y_0^C|T)] = [\hat{E}(Y_1^C|C) - \hat{E}(Y_0^C|C)]$, i.e., that absent the treatment the outcomes in the two groups would have followed parallel trends.

Fixed effects generalizes difference-in-differences estimates when there is more than one time period or more than one treatment group. The fixed effects estimates are obtained by regressing the outcome on the control variable, after controlling for year and group dummies. Both difference-in-differences and fixed effect estimates are very common in applied work. Whether or not they are convincing depends on whether the assumption of parallel evolution of the outcomes in the absence of the treatment is convincing. Note in particular that if the two groups have very different outcomes before the treatment, the functional form chosen for how outcomes evolved over time will have an important influence on the results.

2.4. Comparing experimental and non-experimental estimates

A growing literature is taking advantage of randomized evaluation to estimate a program's impact using both experimental and non-experimental methods and then test whether the non-experimental estimates are biased in this particular case. La Londe's seminal study found that many of the econometric procedures and comparison groups used in program evaluations did not yield accurate or precise estimates and that such econometric estimates often differ significantly from experimental results (La Londe, 1986). A number of subsequent studies have conducted such analysis focusing on the performance of propensity score matching (Heckman, Ichimura and Todd, 1997; Heckman et al., 1998; Heckman, Ichimura and Todd, 1998; Dehejia and Wahba, 1999; Smith and Todd, 2005). Results are mixed, with some studies finding that non-experimental methods can replicate experimental results quite well and others being more negative. A more comprehensive review by Glazerman, Levy and Myers (2003) compared experimental non-experimental methods in studies of welfare, job training, and employment service programs in the United States. Synthesizing the results of twelve design replication studies, they found that retrospective estimators often produce results dramatically different from randomized evaluations and that the bias is often large. They were unable to identify any strategy that could consistently remove bias and still answer a well-defined question.

Cook, Shadish and Wong (2006) conducts a comparison of randomized and non-randomized studies, most of which were implemented in educational settings, and arrives at a more nuanced conclusion. He finds that experimental and non-experimental results are similar when the non-experiment technique is a regression discontinuity or "interrupted time series" design (difference-in-differences with long series of pre-data), but that matching or other ways to control for observables does not produce similar results. He concludes that well designed quasi-experiments (regression discontinuity designs in particular) may produce results that are as convincing as those of a well-implemented randomized evaluation but that "You cannot put right by statistics what you have done wrong by design." While Cook's findings are extremely interesting, the level of control achieved by the quasi-experiments he reviews (in terms, for example, of strictly following threshold rules) is such that for developing countries these designs may actually be less practical than randomized evaluations.

We are not aware of any systematic review of similar studies in developing countries, but a number of comparative studies have been conducted. Some suggest omitted variables bias is a significant problem; others find that non-experimental estimators may perform well in certain contexts. Buddlemeyer and Skofias (2003) and Diaz and Handa (2006) both focus on Progresa, a poverty alleviation program implemented in Mexico in the late 1990s with a randomized design. Buddlemeyer and Skofias (2003) use randomized evaluation results as the benchmark to examine the performance of regression discontinuity design. They find the performance of such a design to be good, suggesting that if policy discontinuities are rigorously enforced, regression discontinuity design frameworks can be useful. Diaz and Handa (2006) compare experimental estimates to propensity score matching estimates, again using the Progresa data. Their results suggest that propensity score matching does well when a large number of control variables is available.

In contrast, several studies in Kenya find that estimates from prospective randomized evaluations can often be quite different from those obtained using a retrospective evaluation in the same sample, suggesting that omitted variable bias is a serious concern. Glewwe et al. (2004) study an NGO program that randomly provided educational flip charts to primary schools in Western Kenya. Their analysis suggests that retrospective estimates seriously overestimate the charts' impact on student test scores. They found that a difference-in-differences approach reduced but did not eliminate this problem.

Miguel and Kremer (2003) and Duflo, Kremer and Robinson (2006) compare experimental and non-experimental estimate of peer effects in the case of the take up of deworming drug and fertilizer adoption, respectively. Both studies found that the individual's decision is correlated with the decisions of their contacts. However, as Manski (1993) has argued, this could be due to many factors other than peer effects, in particular, to the fact that these individuals share the same environment. In both cases, randomization provided exogenous variation in the chance that some members of a particular network adopted the innovation (deworming or fertilizer, respectively). The presence of peer effect can then be tested by comparing whether others in the network were then more likely to adopt as well (we will come back to this specific method of evaluating peer effects in Section 6.3). Both studies find markedly different results from the non-experimental results: Duflo, Kremer and Robinson (2006) find no learning effect, while Miguel and Kremer (2003) find *negative* peer effects. Furthermore, Miguel and Kremer (2003) run on the non-experimental data a number of specifications checks that have been suggested in the peer effects literature, and all these checks support the conclusion that peer effects are in fact positive, suggestive that such checks may not be sufficient to erase the specification bias.

Future research along these lines would be valuable, since comparative studies can be used to assess the size and prevalence of biases in retrospective estimates and provide more guidance which methodologies are the most robust. However, as discussed below, these types of studies have to be done with care in order to provide an accurate comparison between different methods. If the retrospective portions of these comparative studies are done with knowledge of the experimental results, there is a natural tendency to select from plausible comparison groups and methodologies in order to match experimental estimates. To address these concerns, future researchers should conduct retrospective evaluations before the results of randomized evaluations are released or conduct blind retrospective evaluations without knowledge of the results of randomized evaluations or other retrospective studies.

2.5. Publication bias

2.5.1. Publication bias in non-experimental studies

Uncertainty over bias in the reported results from non-experimental studies is compounded by publication bias, which occurs when editors, reviewers, researchers, or policymakers have a preference for results that are statistically significant or support a certain view. In many cases, as we just reviewed, researchers will have many possible choices of how to specify empirical models, and many of these might still be subject to remaining omitted variable bias.

Consider an example in which the true treatment effect is zero, but each non-experimental technique yields an estimated treatment effect equal to the true effect plus an omitted variable bias term that is itself a normally distributed random variable with mean zero. Unfortunately, what appears in the published literature may not reflect typical results from plausible specifications, which would be centered on zero, but may instead be systematically biased.

In any study, a number of choices will need to be made about how the analysis would most appropriately be conducted, which method should be used, which control variable should be introduced, which instrumental variable to use. There will often be legitimate arguments for a variety of different alternatives. Researchers focus their time and effort on completing studies that seem to produce statistically significant results, those that do not end up in the "file drawer."

Some researchers may inappropriately mine various regression specifications for one that produces statistically significant results. Even researchers who do not deliberately search among specifications for those that yield significant results may do so inadvertently. Consider a researcher undertaking a retrospective study for which there are several potentially appropriate specifications, not all of which are known to the researcher before beginning the analysis. The researcher thinks of one specification and runs a series of regressions. If the results are statistically significant and confirm what the researcher expected to find, it is perhaps likely that he or she will assume the specification is appropriate and not spend much time considering possible alternatives. However, if the regression results are not statistically significant or go against what the researcher expected to find, he or she is perhaps more likely to spend substantial amounts of time considering other possible specifications. In addition to generating too many false positives in published papers, this type of specification searching probably leads to under-rejection of commonly held views.

Even if a researcher introduces no bias of this kind, the selection by journals of papers with significant results introduces another level of publication bias. Moreover, citation of papers with extreme results by advocates on one side or another of policy debates is likely to compound publication bias with citation bias. The cumulative result of this process is that even in cases when a program has no effect, strongly positive and/or strongly negative estimates are likely to be published and widely cited.

A growing body of available evidence suggests publication bias is a serious problem within the economics literature. DeLong and Lang (1992) devise a test to determine the fraction of un-rejected null hypotheses that are false. They note that under the null, the distribution of test statistics is known; their cumulative distributions are given by the marginal significance levels associated with them. For example, any test statistic has a 5% chance of falling below the value of the 0.05-significance level. They use this observation to examine whether the distribution of these test statistics conform to what would be expected if a pre-specified fraction of the null hypotheses were in fact true. Using data from articles published in major economics journals, the authors find they can reject at the 0.05 level the null hypothesis that more than about one third of un-rejected null hypotheses were true. Although the authors acknowledge several potential explanations for their findings, they argue publication bias provides the most important explanation.

Statisticians have developed a meta-analysis framework to examine whether inferences are sensitive to publication bias. Hedges (1992) proposed a formal model of publication bias where tests that yield lower p-values are more likely to be observed. Ashenfelter, Harmon and Oosterbeek (1999) apply Hedges' analytic framework to the literature on rates of return to education and find strong evidence that publication bias exists for instrumental variables (IV) estimates on the rate of return to education, which suggests that the often cited results that IV estimates of returns to education are larger than OLS estimates may just be an artifact of publication bias. Likewise, Card and Krueger (1995) find evidence of significant publication bias in the time-series minimum wage literature, leading to an over-reporting of significant results.

2.5.2. Randomization and publication bias

Some, though not all, of the problems of publication bias can be addressed by randomized evaluations. First, if a randomized evaluation is correctly implemented, there can be no question that the results, whatever they are, give us the impact of the particular intervention that was tested (subject to a known degree of sampling error). This implies that if results are unexpected, they have less chance of being considered the result of specification error and discarded. Miguel and Kremer (2003) evaluation of the impact of network and peer effects on the take up of deworming medicine, which we discussed above, provides an interesting example. Ex ante, the researchers probably expected children with more links to students in treatment schools to increase their uptake of deworming treatment in subsequent rounds of the program as they learned about the medicine's benefits. Instead, their experimental findings showed a significant effect in the opposite direction. Had they obtained these results in a retrospective study, most researchers would have assumed there was a problem with their data or specification and explored alternative specifications. The experimental design leaves little doubt that peer effects are in fact negative.

Second, in randomized evaluation the treatment and comparison groups are determined before a researcher knows how these choices will affect the results, limiting room for ex post discretion. There is usually still some flexibility ex post – including what variables to control for, how to handle subgroups, and how to deal with large numbers of possible outcome variables – which may lead to "cherry-picking" among the results. However, unlike omitted variable bias which can become arbitrarily large, this ex post discretion is bounded by the ex ante design choices.

Nevertheless, "cherry-picking" particular outcomes, sites, or subgroups where the evaluation concluded that the program is effective provides a window through which publication biases can appear in randomized evaluations. This is why the FDA does not consider results from subgroup analysis in medical trials valid evidence for the effectiveness of a drug. Below, we discuss how to handle these issues.

Third, randomized evaluations can also partially overcome the file drawer and journal publication biases as their results are usually documented even if they suggest insignificant effects. Even when unpublished, they are typically circulated and often discussed in systematic reviews. This is because researchers discover whether the results are significant at a much later stage and are much less likely to simply abandon the results of an evaluation that has taken several years to conduct than they are to abandon the results of a quick dip into existing data to check out an idea. In addition, funding agencies typically require a report of how their money was spent regardless of outcomes.

Despite this, it would still be extremely useful to put institutions in place to ensure that negative as well as positive results of randomized evaluations are disseminated. Such a system is in place for medical trial results, and creating a similar system for documenting evaluations of social programs would help to alleviate the problem of publication bias. One way to help maintain such a system would be for grant-awarding institutionsJ>T require researchers to submit results from all evaluations to a centralized database. To avoid problems due to specification searching ex post, such a database should also include the salient features of the ex ante design (outcome variables to be examined, subgroups to be considered, etc.) and researchers should have to report results arising from this main design. While researchers could still report results other than those that they initially had included in their proposal, they should be clearly sign-posted such that users should be able to distinguish between them. This information would be useful from a decision-theoretic perspective – several positive, unbiased estimates that are individually statistically insignificant can produce significant meta-estimates – and be available to policymakers and those seeking to understand the body of experimental knowledge regarding the effectiveness of certain policies.

3. Incorporating randomized evaluation in a research design

In the rest of this chapter, we discuss how randomized evaluations can be carried out in practice. In this section, we focus on how researchers can introduce randomization in field research in developing countries. Perhaps the most widely used model of randomized research is that of clinical trials conducted by researchers working in laboratory conditions or with close supervision. While there are examples of research following similar templates in developing countries,[8] most of the projects involving randomization differ from this model in several important ways. They are in general conducted with implementation partners (governments, NGOs, or private companies) who are implementing real-world programs and are interested in finding out whether they work or how to improve them. In some cases, randomization can then be included during pilot projects, in which one or several version of a program are tried out. There are also cases where randomization can be included outside pilot projects, with minimal disruption to how the program is run, allowing the evaluation of on-going projects.

Section 3.1 discusses the possible partners for evaluation. Section 3.2 discusses how randomization can be introduced in the context of pilot projects and how these pilot projects have the potential to go beyond estimating only program effects to test specific economic hypotheses. Section 3.3 discuses how randomization can be introduced outside pilot projects.

3.1. Partners

Unlike conducting laboratory experiments, which economists can do on their own, introducing randomization in real-world programs almost always requires working with a partner who is in charge of actually implementing the program.

Governments are possible partners. While government programs are meant to serve the entire eligible population, pilots programs are some times run before the programs are scaled-up. These programs are limited in scope and can sometimes be evaluated using a randomized design. Some of the most well-known early social experiments in

---

[8] The best example is probably the "Work and Iron Supplementation Experiment" (see Thomas et al., 2003), where households were randomly assigned to receive either iron supplementation or a placebo for a year, and where compliance with the treatment was strictly enforced.

the US – for example the Job Partnership Training Act and the Negative Income Tax –
were conducted following this model.

There are also a few examples from developing countries. Progresa (now called
Oportunidades) (also discussed in Todd, 2008 and Parker, Rubalcava and Teruel, 2008
chapters in this volume) is probably the best known example of a randomized evaluation conducted by a government. The program offers grants, distributed to women,
conditional on children's school attendance and preventative health measures (nutrition
supplementation, health care visits, and participation in health education programs). In
1998, when the program was launched, officials in the Mexican government made a
conscious decision to take advantage of the fact that budgetary constraints made it impossible to reach the 50,000 potential beneficiary communities of Progresa all at once,
and instead started with a randomized pilot program in 506 communities. Half of those
were randomly selected to receive the program, and baseline and subsequent data were
collected in the remaining communities.

The task of evaluating the program was given to academic researchers through the
International Food Policy Research Institute. The data was made accessible to many
different people, and a number of papers have been written on its impact (most of them
are accessible on the IFPRI Web site). The evaluations showed that it was effective in
improving health and education. (see in particular Gertler and Boyce, 2001 and Schultz,
2004).

The Progresa pilot had an impressive demonstration effect. The program was continued and expanded in Mexico despite the subsequent change in government, and
expanded in many other Latin American countries, often including a randomized pilot
component. Some examples are the Family Allowance Program (PRAF) in Honduras
(International Food Policy Research, 2000), a conditional cash transfer program in
Nicaragua (Maluccio and Flores, 2005), a conditional cash transfer program in Ecuador
(Schady and Araujo, 2006), and the Bolsa Alimentação program in Brazil.

These types of government-sponsored (or organized) pilots are becoming more frequent in developing countries than they once were. For example, such government pilot
programs have been conducted in Cambodia (Bloom et al., 2006), where the impact of
public-private partnership on the quality of health care was evaluated in a randomized
evaluation performed at the district levels. In some cases, governments and researchers
have worked closely on the designs of such pilot. In Indonesia, Olken (2005) collabo-
rated with the World Bank and the government to design an experiment where different
ways to fight corruption in locally administered development projects were tried in different villages. In Rajasthan, India, the police department is working with researchers
to pilot a number of reforms to improve police performance and limit corruption across
randomly selected police stations in nine districts.

Randomized evaluations conducted in collaboration with governments are still relatively rare. They require cooperation at high political levels, and it is often difficult to
generate the consensus required for successful implementation. The recent spread of
randomized evaluations in development owes much to a move towards working with
non-governmental organizations (NGOs). Unlike governments, NGOs are not expected

to serve entire populations, and even small organizations can substantially affect budgets for households, schools, or health clinics in developing countries. Many development-focused NGOs frequently seek out new, innovative projects and are eager to work with researchers to test new programs or to assess the effectiveness of existing operations. In recent years, numerous randomized evaluations have been conducted with such NGOs, often with evaluation-specific sponsorship from research organizations or foundations. A number of examples are covered throughout this chapter.

Finally, for-profit firms have also started getting interested in randomized evaluations, often with the goal of understanding better how their businesses work and thus to serve their clients better and increase their profits. For example, Karlan and Zinman (2005a, 2006a, 2006b) and Bertrand et al. (2005) worked with a private consumer lender in South Africa. Many micro-finance organizations are now working with researchers to understand the impact of the salient features of their products or to design products that serve their clients better.[9]

What are the advantages of different partners? As mentioned, NGOs are more willing to want to partner on an evaluation, so they are often the only partner of choice. When possible, working with governments offers several advantages. First, it can allow for much wider geographic scope. Second, the results may be more likely to feed into the policy process. Third, there will be less concern about whether the results are dependent on a particular (and impossible to replicate) organizational culture. However, NGOs and firms offer a much more flexible environment, where it can be easier for the researchers to monitor the implementation of the research design. One of the main benefits of the move to working with NGOs has been an increased scope for testing a wider range of questions, implementing innovative programs, and allowing for greater input from researchers into the design of programs, especially in the pilot stage.

3.2. Pilot projects: From program evaluations to field experiments

A natural window to introduce randomization is before the program is scaled up, during the pilot phase. This is an occasion for the implementation partner to rigorously assess test the effectiveness of the program and can also be a chance to improve its design.

Many early field randomized studies (both in the US and in developing countries) simply sought to test the effectiveness of particular programs. For example, the Progresa pilot program implemented the program in the treatment villages and did not introduce it in the comparison villages. The evaluation is only able to say whether, taken together, all the components of Progresa are effective in increasing health and education outcomes. They cannot disentangle the various mechanisms at play without further assumptions.

Such evaluations are still very useful in measuring the impact of policies or programs before they are scaled up, but increasingly, researchers have been using such pilot programs to go beyond the simple question of whether a particular program works or not.

---

[9] See the research coordinated by the Centre for Micro Finance in India, for many examples.

They have helped their partners design programs or interventions with specific theories in mind. The programs are designed to help solve the partner's practical problems but they also serve as the test for the theories. A parallel movement has also happened in developed countries, fueled by the concerns on the external validity of laboratory experiments (see Harrison and List, 2004 for a review of this literature).

These pilot programs allow standard "program evaluation" to transform itself into "field experiments," in the sense that both the implementing agency and the researchers are experimenting together to find the best solution to a problem (Duflo, 2006). There is an explosion of such work in development economics.[10] In practice, the distinction between "simple" program evaluation and field experiment is of course too stark: there is a wide spectrum of work ranging from the most straightforward comparison between one treatment and one comparison group for a program, to evaluation involving a large number of groups allowing researchers to test very subtle hypotheses in the field.

Here we mention only two examples which illustrate well the power of creative designs. Ashraf, Karlan and Yin (2006) set out to test the importance of time-inconsistent ("hyperbolic") preferences. To this end they designed a commitment savings product for a small rural bank in the Philippines. The rural bank was interested in participating in a program that had the potential to increase savings. Individuals could restrict the access to the funds they deposited in the accounts until either a given maturity or a given amount of money was saved. Relative to standard accounts, the accounts carried no advantage other than this feature. The product was offered to a randomly selected half of 1700 former clients of the bank. The other half of the individuals were assigned either to a pure comparison group or to a group who was visited and given a speech reminding them of the importance of savings. This group allowed them to test whether the simple fact of discussing savings is what encourages clients to save, rather than the availability of a time-commitment device. Having these two separate groups was possible only in the context of a pilot with a relatively flexible organization.

Duflo, Kremer and Robinson (2006) evaluated a series of different interventions to understand the determinants of the adoption of fertilizer in Western Kenya. The design of the interventions made it possible to test some of the standard hypotheses of the hindrance to the adoption of new technology. Field demonstrations with treatment and control plots were conducted to evaluate the profitability of fertilizer in the local conditions. Because the farmers were randomly selected, those field trials also allowed them to study the impact of information provision and the channels of information transmission; other ways to provide information (starter kits, school based demonstrations) were also examined; finally, financing constraints and difficulties in saving were also explored, with interventions helping farmers to buy fertilizer at the time when they have most money in the field.

---

[10] Many of these very recent or on going studies are reviewed in the review articles mentioned in the Introduction.

3.3. Alternative methods of randomization

The examples we have looked at so far are in one respect similar to classic clinical trials: in all cases the randomized study was introduced concurrent with a new program and where the sample was randomly allocated into one or more treatment groups and a comparison group that never received the treatment. However, one of the innovations of recent work is to realize that there are many different ways to introduce an element of randomization into programs. It is often possible to introduce randomization into existing programs with minimal disruption. This has spurred rapid growth in the use of randomized studies by development economists over the last ten years. In this section we run through the four key methods – oversubscription, phase-in, within-group randomization, and encouragement design – for introducing randomization into new and existing programs.

3.3.1. Oversubscription method

A natural opportunity for introducing randomization occurs when there are limited resources or implementation capacity and demand for a program or service exceeds supply. In this case, a natural and fair way to ration resources is to select those who will receive the program by lottery among eligible candidates.

Such a method was used to ration the allocations of school vouchers in Colombia and the resulting randomization of treatment and comparison groups allowed for a study to accurately assess the impact of the voucher program (Angrist et al., 2002) evaluated the impact of expanded consumer credit in South Africa by working with a lender who randomly approved some marginal loan applications that would normally have been rejected. All applicants who would normally have been approved received loans, and those who were well below the cutoff were rejected. Such an evaluation was only possible because the experimental design caused minimal disruption to the bank's normal business activities. When interpreting these results, one must be careful to keep in mind that they only apply to those "marginal" borrowers or, more generally, to the population over which assignment to the treatment group was truly random.

3.3.2. Randomized order of phase-in

Financial and administrative constraints often lead NGOs to phase-in programs over time, and randomization will often be the fairest way of determining the order of phase-in. Randomizing the order of phase-in can allow evaluation of program effects in contexts where it is not acceptable for some groups or individuals to receive no support. In practical terms, it can facilitate continued cooperation by groups or individuals that have randomly been selected as the comparison group. As such, where logistics permit, randomization of phase-in may be preferable to a pure lottery because the expectation of future benefits provides subjects an incentive to maintain contact with researchers and thus alleviates issues associated with attrition (see Section 6.4).

The Primary School Deworming Project provides an example of this type of randomized phase-in trial (Miguel and Kremer, 2004). This program provided medical treatment for intestinal worms (helminths) and schistosomiasis as well as worm-prevention health education lessons to children in 75 primary schools in rural Busia district, Kenya during 1998–2002. The program randomly divided the schools into three groups, each consisting of 25 primary schools. Treatment in the schools was done as follows: 25 Group 1 schools began receiving treatment in 1998; 25 Group 2 schools began receiving treatment in 1999; and 25 Group 3 schools began receiving treatment in 2000. The impact of the program on the health, nutrition, and education of the children was evaluated by comparing the results from Group 1 schools in 1998 with Group 2 and 3 acting as comparisons and the results of Group 1 and 2 schools in 1999 with Group 3 schools acting as a comparison. The researchers found that deworming led to improved health and increased school participation.

One drawback of randomized phase-in designs is that they often prevent researchers from estimating a program's long-run effects; however, when a program targets well-identified cohorts, this is still possible. In the deworming program, for example, children were not eligible for treatment after they left school. Taking advantage of this, Miguel and Kremer are following the cohorts who "missed out" on the program because they were too old to receive treatment when it was phased-in to their school. These cohorts provide a valid control group to study the long-run effects of the program on the equivalent cohorts from treated schools.

In contrast, if a randomized phase-in is too rapid relative to the time it takes for program effects to materialize, it will be impossible to detect treatment effects at all. For example, one would be unlikely to detect the effect of a microcredit program that was phased-in to control villages only six months after it was introduced to the treatment group. When planning a phase-in design, the time between phases should be sufficient to encompass any treatment lag.

Randomized phase-in becomes problematic when the comparison group is affected by the expectation of future treatment. For example, in the case of a phased in microcredit program, individuals in the comparison groups may delay investing in anticipation of cheaper credit once they have access to the program. In this case, the comparison group is also affected by its participation in the experiment and does not provide a valid counterfactual. Some have argued that this may have been at play in the case of the Progresa experiment.

3.3.3. Within-group randomization

Even a randomized phase-in may not spread the benefits sufficiently smoothly across the whole group to ensure good cooperation with the study. For example, schools may refuse to let researchers collect test scores on their students while the schools do not benefit from participating in the study. In this case, it is still possible to introduce an element of randomization by providing the program to some subgroups in each area.

The evaluation of the balsakhi program, a remedial education assistance in poor urban schools in India provided by Pratham, an Indian education NGO (Banerjee et al., 2007) provides an example. The program was designed to provide those children falling behind in school the basic skills they need to learn effectively. Pratham hires and trains tutors, referred to as *balsakhi* or "child's friend," to give remedial math and reading comprehension instruction to children. To ensure cooperation from school authorities, every school in the study received a balsakhi in every year. However, based on random assignment, some schools were asked to use the balsakhi in grade 3 and others in grade 4.[11]

This design was deemed fair by school teachers, since all schools received the same assistance. Further more, since the NGO could make a credible case that they could not provide more than one balsakhi per school, there was no expectation that all children in a school should benefit from the program.

The drawback of such designs is that they increase the likelihood that the comparison group is contaminated. For example, in the balsakhi program, one may have been worried that headmasters reallocated resources from grade 3 to grade 4 if grade 3 got a balsakhi but grade 4 did not. In this particular application, such contamination was unlikely because schools have a fixed number of teachers per grade and few other resources to reallocate. But this risk needs to be considered when deciding whether or not to adopt such a design.

3.3.4. Encouragement designs

Encouragement designs allow researchers to evaluate the impact of a program that is available in the entire study area but whose take up is not universal. They are particularly useful for evaluating programs over which randomization of access is not feasible for ethical or practical reasons. Rather than randomize over the treatment itself, researchers randomly assign subjects an encouragement to receive the treatment. One of the early encouragement designs was a study of whether studying for the GRE could lead to an increase in test scores (Holland, 1988). While studying is available to everyone, researchers increased the number of students who studied for it by mailing out free materials to a randomly selected set of GRE candidates. More recently, Duflo and Saez (2003) studied the impact of receiving information about tax deferred accounts (TDA) by providing financial incentives to university employees to attend the session organized by their university (to which everybody is invited). The incentive increased the fraction of people who chose to attend the session in the group where it was sent, and the TDA adoption of those individuals can then be followed over time and compared to that of groups that did not receive the incentive.

In Kenya, Duflo, Kremer and Robinson (2006) evaluated the impact of witnessing fertilizer demonstration on another farmer's plot on future adoption of fertilizer by farmers.

---

[11] Glewwe, Kremer, and Moulin (2004) used a similar approach in their study of a program to give textbooks to schools in Kenya.

To do so, they set up fertilizer demonstrations on randomly selected farmers' plots and then explicitly invited a randomly selected subset of the farmers' friends to view the demonstration. While a farmer's other friends were also welcome to come, the fraction who attended was much larger among those "invited" than "not invited." Since the invitation was randomly assigned, it provides a natural instrumental variable with which to evaluate the impact of the treatment.

Because they only *increase* the probability that a treatment is received without changing it from zero to one, encouragement designs pose specific analytical challenges. We discuss the analytical requirements of this approach in Section 6.2.

4. Sample size, design, and the power of experiments

The power of the design is the probability that, for a given effect size and a given statistical significance level, we will be able to reject the hypothesis of zero effect. Sample sizes, as well as other design choices, will affect the power of an experiment.

This section does not intend to provide a full treatment of the question of statistical power or the theory of the design of experiment.[12] Rather, its objective is to draw attention on the key factors that influence the statistical power of randomized evaluations. It presumes a basic knowledge of statistics and ignores some of the more complicated or subtle issues. We first review basic principles of power calculations. We then discuss the influence of design factors such as multiple treatment groups, randomization at the group level, partial compliance, control variables, and stratification. Finally, we discuss the practical steps involved in making power calculations, and the roles they should be given when planning evaluations.

4.1. Basic principles

The basic principles of power calculation can be illustrated in a simple regression framework. As we discussed above, the difference in sample means for two groups (our estimate of the average treatment effect) is the OLS coefficient of β in the regression

$$Y_i = \alpha + \beta T + \epsilon_i. \tag{5}$$

Assume that there is only one possible treatment, and that a proportion P of the sample is treated. Assume for now that each individual was randomly sampled from an identical population, so that observations can be assumed to be i.i.d., with variance σ^2. The variance of $\hat{\beta}$, the OLS estimator of β, is given by

$$\frac{1}{P(1-P)} \frac{\sigma^2}{N}. \tag{6}$$

---

[12] A good reference for power calculations is Bloom (1995). An good reference on the theory of design of experiments is Cox and Reid (2000).

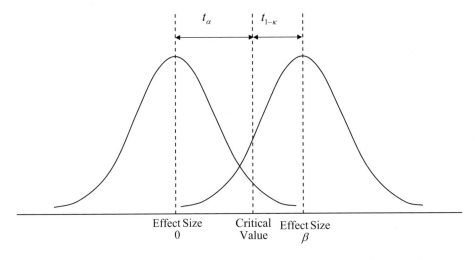

Figure 1.

We are generally interested in testing the hypothesis, H_0, that the effect of the program is equal to zero against the alternative that it is not.[13] The *significance level*, or size, of a test represents the probability of a type I error, i.e., the probability we reject the hypothesis when it is in fact true.

The bell shape picture on the left in Fig. 1 is the distribution of $\hat{\beta}$ under the null hypothesis of no effect.[14] For a given significance level, H_0 will be rejected if $\hat{\beta}$ falls to the right of the critical level, that is if $|\hat{\beta}| > t_\alpha * SE_{\hat{\beta}}$, where t_α depends on the significance level ($t_{\alpha/2}$ for a two-sided test) and is obtained from a standard t-distribution.

In Fig. 1, the curve to the right shows the distribution of $\hat{\beta}$ if the true impact is β. The *power* of the test for a true effect size β is the fraction of the area under this curve that falls to the right of the critical value t_α, i.e., the probability that we reject H_0 when it is in fact false.

To achieve a power κ, it must therefore be that

$$\beta > (t_{1-\kappa} + t_\alpha) SE(\hat{\beta})$$

where $t_{1-\kappa}$ is again given by a t-table. For example, for a power of 80%, $t_{1-\kappa} = 0.84$.

The *minimum detectable effect size* for a given power (κ), significance level (α), sample size (N), and portion of subjects allocated to treatment group (P) is therefore

---

[13] Note that in some cases, it may be interesting and important to evaluate programs that researchers *do not expect* will have a large effect (for example to counteract a policy fad). The power calculation should then be run not to test $H_0 = 0$ (since failing to reject that a program has zero effect does not mean "accepting" that the program has zero effect), but to test that the effect of the program is no larger than some number.

[14] The exposition here follows Bloom (1995).

given by

$$MDE = (t_{(1-\kappa)} + t_\alpha) * \sqrt{\frac{1}{P(1-P)}} \sqrt{\frac{\sigma^2}{N}} \qquad (7)$$

for a single sided test (t_α is replaced by $t_{\alpha/2}$ for a two-sided test). Alternatively, Eq. (7) implicitly defines the sample size N required to achieve a given power, given the effect size that is posited and the level of significance chosen.

Equation (7) shows that there is a trade-off between power and size. When the size decreases, t_α increases, so that the minimum effect size increases for a given level of power. Thus there is trade-off between the probability of falsely concluding that the program has an effect when it does not and the probability of falsely concluding that it has no effect when it does. The other parameters that are relevant for this basic power calculation are the minimum effect size the researcher wants to be able to detect, the standard deviation of ϵ, the proportion of the sample that is allocated to the treatment and comparison groups, and the sample size.

Equation (7) also provides some guidance on how to divide the sample between the treatment and the comparison group. With one treatment, if the main cost of the evaluation is data collection, it shows that an equal division between treatment and comparison group is optimal, since the equation is minimized at $P = 0.5$. However, when the treatment is expensive and data collection is cheap (for example, when administrative data on the outcome is available for both the treatment and the comparison group), the optimal sample size will have a larger comparison group. More generally the optimal proportion of treated observations can be obtained by minimizing Eq. (7) under the budget constraint $Nc_d + NPc_t \leqslant B$, where N is the total sample size, c_c is the unit cost per comparison subject, and c_t is the unit cost per treatment subject (including both data collection and the treatment cost). This gives the following optimal allocation rule:

$$\frac{P}{1-P} = \sqrt{\frac{c_c}{c_t}},$$

that is, the ratio of subjects in the treatment group to those in the comparison should be proportional to the inverse of the square root of their costs.

The logic of Eq. (7) can be extended to apply to sample size calculations when more than one treatment is evaluated. Suppose an experiment involves two treatments (for example, the evaluation of the SEED commitment savings product program described above had a comparison group, a social marketing group, and a "commitment savings" group). A first possibility is that the researchers are only interested in the contrast between the comparison group and the marketing group on the one hand and the comparison and the commitment savings group on the other hand. In this case, if the researcher puts equal weight on these estimates, he wants to minimize the sum of the minimum detectable effect (MDE) for the two treatments. The optimal allocation thus requires twice as many observations in the comparison than in each treatment group. Of course, the researcher may want to be able to detect a smaller effect in one intervention than in the other, which can be translated by a higher weight put on one MDE than the other. The main point that remains is that the sample size of the comparison group should be larger.[15]

If, on the other hand, a researcher interested in the contrast between the two treatments (which was the case in the SEED evaluation) they will need a sample size sufficient to be able to detect a difference between the two groups. If the difference between the two treatments is not very large, this may require a larger sample size than the evaluation of either treatment separately would.

4.2. Grouped errors

Many of the designs we discussed above involve randomizing over groups rather than individuals. In such cases, researchers nevertheless often have access to individual data. For example, in the Progresa program, the village was the unit of randomization, but individual data were available.

When analyzing individual data from programs randomized at a group level, it is important to take into account that the error term may not be independent across individuals. People in the same group may be subject to common shocks, which means their outcomes may be correlated. Because treatment status is also uniform within groups, this correlation in the outcomes of interest may be mistakenly be interpreted as an effect of the program. For example, consider a case where among two districts with large populations, all individuals in one district are given a nutritional supplement program, and those in the other district are assigned to comparison group. Now assume that the comparison district suffers a drought. It will not be possible to distinguish the effect of the drought from the effect of the program.

Formally, consider a modified version of equation 4.5 (this treatment follows Bloom, 2005):

$$Y_{ij} = \alpha + \beta T + \upsilon_j + \omega_{ij} \qquad (8)$$

where j indexes the group and ij the individual. For simplicity of exposition, assume there are J clusters of identical size n, υ_j is i.i.d. with variance τ^2, and ω_{ij} is i.i.d. with variance σ^2. The OLS estimator of $\hat{\beta}$ is still unbiased, and its standard error is

$$\sqrt{\frac{1}{P(1-P)}}\sqrt{\frac{n\tau^2 + \sigma^2}{nJ}}. \qquad (9)$$

---

[15] The optimal allocation is given by

$$\frac{N_i}{N_j} = \frac{\sum_{H_I} \omega_h}{\sum_{H_J} \omega_h}\sqrt{\frac{c_j}{c_i}}$$

where ω_h is the weight placed on testing hypothesis h, and H_I is the set of all hypotheses including group I.

If the randomization had been conducted at the level of the individual, the standard error of $\hat{\beta}$ would have been

$$\sqrt{\frac{1}{P(1-P)}}\sqrt{\frac{\tau^2+\sigma^2}{nJ}}. \tag{10}$$

Equations (9) and (10) imply that the ratio between the standard errors for group level randomization and for individual level randomization given a fixed number of members per group, the *design effect*, is equal to

$$D = \sqrt{1+(n-1)\rho} \tag{11}$$

where n is the number of individuals in each group and $\rho = \tau^2/(\tau^2+\sigma^2)$ is the intracluster correlation, i.e., the proportion of the overall variance explained by within group variance. As Eq. (11) shows, the design effect increases with both the intracluster correlation and the number of individuals per group. This effect can be quite large, even for modest values of the intraclass correlation. The standard error will more than double, for example, with group size of 50 and intraclass correlation of 0.06.

This increase in variance has obvious implication for sample sizes calculations. Specifically, Bloom (2005) shows that the MDE with J groups of size n each is given by

$$MDE = \frac{M_{J-2}}{\sqrt{P(1-P)J}}\sqrt{\rho+\frac{1-\rho}{n}}\sigma \tag{12}$$

where $M_{J-2} = t_{\alpha/2}+t_{1-\kappa}$, for a two sided test.

Equation (12) shows that, ignoring the effect of J on the critical values of the t distribution, the MDE varies roughly proportionally as a function of the number of groups J. On the other hand, the number of observations per group affects precision much less, especially when ρ is relatively large. This implies that, for a given sample size, an increase in the number of individuals sampled per cluster increases the precision much less than increasing the number of clusters being randomized. Intuitively, when group outcomes are correlated, data from another individual in an existing group provides less information than data from the first individual in a new cluster. Finally, the equation shows that both the total number of clusters to be sampled and the number of people to sample per cluster are very dependent on ρ.

Note that all these calculations were carried out under the assumption of common variances, which may not be the case, though the assumption simplifies the power calculation. In Section 7 we will discuss how to compute standard errors with grouped data without making this assumption.

4.3. Imperfect compliance

We saw a number of cases where the randomized design only influences the *probability* that someone receives a treatment. In Section 6.2 we will discuss in detail how to analyze and interpret data arising from such experiments.

What is important to note here is that the possibility that compliance may not be perfect should be taken into account when determining the optimal sample size. In Section 6.2 we will show that the ratio of the difference between the initial treatment and control groups to the difference in the probability of being treated in the two groups is an estimate of the causal effect of the treatment among the compliers (those induced by the randomization to receive the treatment).

The power of the design is therefore going to arise from the difference between the outcomes in those who were *initially* assigned to the treatment and those who were not, irrespective of whether they were treated or not (this is the reduced form effect of the initial assignment). Denote by c the share of subjects initially assigned to the treatment group who actually receive the treatment and by s the share of subjects initially assigned to the comparison group who receive the treatment. The reduced form effect is going to be the actual treatment effect multiplied by $c - s$.

Hence, the minimum detectable treatment effect size accounting for partial compliance is now given by

$$MDE = (t_{(1-\kappa)} + t_\alpha) * \sqrt{\frac{1}{P(1-P)}} \sqrt{\frac{\sigma^2}{N} \frac{1}{c-s}}. \tag{13}$$

Partial compliance thus strongly affects the power of a design, since the MDE increases *linearly* with the compliance rate, while it increases proportionally to the square root of the number of observations. Thus, if there is only an 80% difference in take up between the treatment and control group, the sample size would have to be 56% larger to achieve the same minimum detectable effect. Alternatively, at the same sample size, the minimum detectable effect would be 25% larger.

This (in addition to the interpretation issues that arise when compliance is imperfect which we discuss in details below) underscores the importance of compliance in experiments. This implies that if a researcher has the choice between two designs with different level of compliance, choosing one which will have the highest compliance can have important implication on sample size. This is useful to think about when to introduce randomization. Suppose for example that one wants to evaluate a voluntary business training program for microcredit clients. A first approach would be an encouragement design, where randomly selected clients would be asked whether they want to participate in the program, and they could choose whether or not to do it. The evaluation would then compare those invited to those who were not invited. A second approach would be an oversubscription design, where the clients would be asked to apply, and the program would be randomized among applicants. The take-up of the program in the second design would presumably be much larger than that in first design. The MDE for the effect of the training on those who choose to participate when offered the option will decrease in proportion.[16]

---

[16] One may worry that the evaluation would be less "representative" in the second sample since the evaluation is carried out in a sample of applicants. This is, however, not quite correct: as we will see below, the

4.4. Control variables

In a simple randomized experiment, controlling for baseline values of covariates likely
to influence or predict the outcome does not affect the expected value of an estimator
of β, but it can reduce its variance. Note that controlling for covariates affected by
the treatment would bias the estimate of the treatment effect by capturing part of its
impact. Information on covariates should therefore be collected in the baseline surveys.
A special case of a covariate of interest is the pre-treatment value of the outcome.
   Consider the equation:

$$Y_{ij} = \alpha + \beta T + X_{ij}\gamma + \tilde{\upsilon}_j + \tilde{\omega}_{ij}, \tag{14}$$

where X_{ij} is a set of control variables, which can be the group- or individual-levels. $\tilde{\upsilon}_j$
and $\tilde{\omega}_{ij}$ now represent the unexplained variance after controlling for X_{ij}. Ignoring the
effect of adding covariates on degrees of freedom, controlling for covariates has three
effects on variance estimates. First, it reduces the (true) residual variance and thereby
tends to reduce the variance of parameter estimates. Second, in a completely randomized experiment, it *may* increase $(W'W)^{-1}$, where W is the matrix of all covariates
including the treatment indicator, and thereby increase the variance of $\hat{\beta}$. Note that this
effect is not present with stratification (see below) because stratification ensures that
the treatment indicator is orthogonal to the other covariates in practice, whereas in a
completely randomized experiment this is only true in expectation. Finally, the estimated variance of $\hat{\beta}$ is noisier than without controlling for covariates. It can be larger or
smaller, but it is unbiased.
   In general, controlling for variables that have a large effect on the outcome can help
reduce standard errors of the estimates and thus the sample size needed. This is a reason
why baseline surveys can greatly reduce sample size requirement when the outcome
variables are persistent. For example, controlling for baseline test scores in evaluations
of education interventions greatly improves the precision of estimates, which reduces
the cost of these evaluations when a baseline test can be conducted. Note, however, that
controlling for variables that explain little or none of the variation in the outcome will
increase standard errors by reducing degrees of freedom.[17] Choosing which variables
to control for is therefore a difficult exercise. Note that this choice must in principle be
specified in advance to avoid the risk of specification searching.

---

right interpretation of the treatment effect in the first design is that it is the effect of the intervention among
compliers, that is those who get the training if they are selected for it, and not otherwise. Therefore, even in the
first design, we will evaluate the effect of the training on those who are interested in getting it. The population
that will be affected is not necessarily exactly the same in the two designs: it is of course possible that some
people would not think of applying by themselves but would accept to be trained if offered an option. But the
difference may not be that large.

[17] Even controlling for the pre-treatment value of the outcome may reduce precision if the outcome is not
highly persistent and it is measured with error.

4.5. Stratification

Since the covariates to be used must be chosen in advance in order to avoid specification searching and data mining, they can be used to stratify (or *block*) the sample in order to improve the precision of estimates. This technique (first proposed by Fisher, 1926) involves dividing the sample into groups sharing the same or similar values of certain observable characteristics. The randomization ensures that treatment and control groups will be similar *in expectation*. But stratification is used to ensure that along important observable dimensions this is also true *in practice* in the sample. For example, in the balsakhi program, described in Section 3.3.3, researchers stratified according to class size, language of instruction, and school gender (boys, girls, or coed) as well as according to pre-test scores for schools in the Mumbai area. A block is constituted of all the schools that share the same language of instruction, the same school gender, and fall in the same "bin" of pre-test scores. By doing so, they ensured that the treatment and comparison groups would be balanced by gender and language of instruction and that pre-test score would be similar. An extreme version of blocked design is the pairwise matched design where pairs of units are constituted, and in each pair, one unit is randomly assigned to the treatment and one unit is randomly assigned to the control.

When the same proportion of observations are assigned to the treatment and the comparison groups in each block, the average treatment effect is equal to the difference between the outcomes of all treated and all untreated units or, equivalently, to the weighted average of the difference between treated and untreated units in each group (with the number of observations in each group as weight).

Very much like controlling for baseline variables ex post, blocking according to variables will improve precision to the extent the variables used for blocking explain the variation in the treatment of interest (Cox and Reid, 2000). However, blocking is more efficient than controlling ex post for these variables, since it ensures an equal proportion of treated and untreated unit within each block and therefore minimizes variance. An easy way to see this is to observe that, at the extreme, a completely randomized design could lead to a situation where, in some blocks, there are only treatment or only control units. These blocks would not contribute anything to the analysis of difference between treatment and comparison groups when we control for the variables ex post, thus reducing the effective sample size and the precision of the treatment effect estimate.

More generally, Imbens, King and Ridder (2006) show that when the proportion of treated and control units is the same in all strata (and equal to that in a completely randomized experiment) the variance of the treatment effect estimate is always weakly lower in the stratified design, with or without ex post controls. The same logic also implies that if several binary variables are available for stratification, it is a good idea to use all of them, even if some of them may not end up having large explanatory power for the final outcome. The fact that the blocks within which the randomization will be performed may end up being very small is not a concern, since the estimate will be computed as an average over all these blocks.

When one or several of the possible stratification variables are continuous, so that one could form pairs on the basis of just one continuous variable, it will be necessary to make choices about which variables to use for stratification. For example, if one stratifies first according to gender and then by income, the treatment and comparison group's average incomes will be less similar than if one stratified only according to income. This choice is made taking into consideration the extent to which the candidate stratification variables are likely to explain the outcome variable and the treatment effect.

An estimate of the treatment effect and its variance that takes into account stratification can be obtained by estimating

$$Y_{ij} = \alpha + \beta T + M_{ij} + \tilde{\upsilon}_j + \tilde{\omega}_{ij}, \tag{15}$$

by OLS, where M is a set of dummy variables indicating the observation's block, by least squares using either the standard or robust estimates of least squares variance and taking into account the reduction in degrees of freedom due to stratification. Alternatively, one could ignore the stratification and estimate (5), which is simply (15) without the block dummies.

Both methods are acceptable: With equal proportion of treatment and comparison units within each strata, ignoring stratification and estimating (15) without the block dummies leads to the exact same point estimates for β but a higher residual variance. The standard OLS variance based on that regression is a conservative estimator for the variance of $\hat{\beta}$. Although, *in expectation* the variance estimator based on (15) is less than or equal to that of the regression ignoring the block dummies, it is also noisier and, in a given sample, could be higher (Imbens, King and Ridder, 2006).

Apart from reducing variance, an important reason to adopt a stratified design is when the researchers are interested in the effect of the program on specific subgroups. If one is interested in the effect of the program on a subgroup, the experiment must have enough power for this subgroup (each subgroup constitutes in some sense a distinct experiment). Stratification according to those subgroups then ensure that the ratio between treatment and control units is determined by the experimenter in each subgroup, and can therefore be chosen optimally. It is also an assurance for the reader that the subgroup analysis was planned in advance.

4.6. Power calculations in practice

This section reviewed the basic theoretical principles behind the calculation of power in an experiment. But how should power calculations be carried out by researchers in practice when planning an experiment, and for what purpose should they be used?

A first comment is that, despite all the precision of these formulas, power calculations involve substantial guess work in practice. To carry out power calculations, one must first have an idea of the mean and the variance of the outcome in the absence of the experiment, after controlling for possible covariates and/or stratification. For grouped designs, one must also have a sense of what the correlation in the outcomes of interest between different group members is likely to be. The best way to obtain guesses about

Table 1
Intra-class correlation, primary schools

Location	Subject	Estimate	Reference
Madagascar	Math + language	0.5	AGEPA data base
Busia, Kenya	Math + language	0.22	Miguel and Kremer (2004)
Udaipur, India	Math + language	0.23	Duflo and Hanna (2006)
Mumbai, India	Math + language	0.29	Banerjee et al. (2007)
Vadodara, India	Math + language	0.28	Banerjee et al. (2007)
Busia, Kenya	Math	0.62	Glewwe et al. (2004)
Busia, Kenya	Language	0.43	Glewwe et al. (2004)
Busia, Kenya	Science	0.35	Glewwe et al. (2004)

these parameters is in general to use previously collected data, ideally from the same country or region. Sometimes such data are not available, and it is necessary to conduct a baseline survey to get a sense of the magnitude of these variables. But it may be difficult and time consuming, particularly when one of the variables one plans to control for is the baseline value of the outcome variable (this would require two surveys separated by some length of time). For clustered designs, finding reliable estimates for ρ can prove to be a challenge in practical applications. Table 1 displays a range of intraclass correlation for test scores (where the "class" corresponds to a grade level within a school. It shows that the intraclass correlation is high for test scores, ranging from 0.2 to 0.6. It is often smaller in other applications. It is worth performing power calculations with a variety of levels for ρ to get a range of required sample sizes.

One must then chose a level for the test. This is conventionally set at 5% or 10%, since this is the probability of a type-I error generally accepted as significant in published papers. Finally, one must specify the effect size that one wishes to be able to detect. As a rule of thumb for a policy intervention evaluation, this should be the smallest effect size that is large enough such that the intervention would be cost effective if it were to be scaled up. Cheap interventions should therefore be evaluated using larger samples. This, however, ignores the cost of the experiment itself. Moreover, for economists interested in getting insights about structural parameters, this rule of thumb may not apply. It may be of intrinsic interest from an economics point of view to answer the question of whether a given intervention can have even a small effect on an outcome, irrespective of the immediate policy implications.

A shortcut when data on mean and standard deviation of the outcomes are not available is to directly specify the effect size one wishes to detect in multiples of the standard deviation of the outcome. Cohen (1988) proposes that an effect of 0.2 standard deviation is "small," 0.5 is "medium" and 0.8 is "large." Unfortunately, without a sense of what the standard deviation is, it is not clear that the distinction between large, medium and small has much practical meaning. But it can at least provide some idea to the researcher on whether the design will have power to perform a given design. This information can then be plugged into software which computes power under different scenarios.[18]

The final question is the level of power for which a researcher should aim and, more generally, how to use power calculations. A first view of power calculations is that they should be conducted ex ante to determine the necessary sample to obtain a given power – many funding agency consider 80% to 90% an appropriate target. However, sample size is often determined in large part by budget or implementation constraints. In this case, a second view of power calculations is that they can help evaluate the power of a specific design, and thus help the researcher decide whether to embark on the project at all. Here, a question that naturally arises is therefore whether or not a researcher should accept to conduct a low-powered study. The answer is not obvious. Some argue that since the study has little chance to deliver conclusive results, it is not worthwhile to conduct it. From a social point of view (in particular if one adopt a Bayesian or decision theoretic point of view), however, this is forgetting that any particular study is only one of many that may be conducted on the topic. The greatest incremental precision on a given question comes from the first few observations. Moreover, results from several low power studies can be combined in a meta-analysis which will have more power. It remains that, from a purely private point of view, and taking into account the fact that each experiment involves fixed costs (in designing the experiments, the questionnaires, etc.), low-powered designs are probably best avoided in most cases by individual researchers.

A third use of power calculations is to help make decisions about how to design the experiment to achieve the maximum power within a given budget. For example, is it worth conducting a baseline? In clustered designs, how many clusters should be sampled and how many units per cluster, given the fixed cost of surveying each cluster and the intra-class correlation within each cluster? How should many should individuals be allocated to different treatment groups? How many treatments can be reliably evaluated given the available sample size? Of course, these designs issues choices are not determined only by the need for precision. In the next section, we discuss them in more details.

5. Practical design and implementation issues

This section discusses various design and implementation issues faced by those conducting randomized evaluations. We begin with the choice of randomization level. Should one randomize over individuals or some larger group? We then discuss crosscutting designs that test multiple treatments simultaneously within the same sample. Finally, we address some data collection issues.

---

[18] "Optimal Design" is a free tool that performs such power calculations (see Raudenbush et al., 2005).

5.1. Level of randomization

An important practical design choice is whether to randomize the intervention at the level of the individual, the family, the village, the district, etc. While early social experiments in the US were all randomized at the individual level, many evaluations in developing countries are randomized across groups.[19] For some interventions, such as those seeking to influence an entire community, the choice does not arise. For example, Chattopadhyay and Duflo (2004) study the reservation for women of leadership positions in village councils. The randomization necessarily takes place at the level of the *gram panchayat*, a local council encompassing several villages. All villages in a given *gram panchayat* are therefore either treatment or comparison; there is no room for randomization at the village level.

But for many interventions, it is possible to choose whether to randomize at the individual or the group level, and this choice is not always evident. For example, early randomization of deworming medicines were carried out at the individual level within schools (Dickson et al., 2000), while Miguel and Kremer (2004) look at similar programs by randomly phasing-in the program at the school level. Interventions such as input provisions in classrooms could be carried out at the school level (for example, schools get selected to receive textbooks or flip charts) or at the level of individuals students (in the Tennessee Star experiment, students within schools were randomly assigned to either a large class, a small class, or a class with a teacher aid (Krueger and Whitmore, 2002)

When there is flexibility in the level at which to randomize, several factors need to be taken into account. First, as discussed in Section 4.2, the larger the groups that are randomized, the larger the total sample size needed to achieve a given power. The level of randomization thus has a potentially large effect on the budget and administrative burden of the evaluation, making individual-level randomization attractive when possible.

Second, however, spillovers from treatment to comparison groups can bias the estimation of treatment effects. In such case, the randomization should occur at a level that captures these effects. For example, Miguel and Kremer (2004) found much larger effects of deworming drugs than did earlier evaluations that randomized across individuals. They argue that because worm infections spread easily among children, the comparison group in individual-level randomizations also benefited from treatment, reducing the difference between the outcomes of treated and control children. While such spillovers are not necessarily absent when randomizing at larger levels (for example, Miguel and Kremer do show spillover across schools in their samples), they are typically much smaller. This can be an argument for randomizing at a level that captures any large spillover effects. Another form of externality that can occur is that individuals in the comparison group may change their behavior in anticipation of being treated in the

---

[19] See Bloom (2005) for discussion of clustered randomized trials in the US context.

future. It may be easier in a village-level randomization to leave the comparison group unaware of the existence of a treated group.

Third, randomization at the group level may some times be much easier from the implementation point of view, even if it requires larger sample sizes. There are various reasons for this. In interventions that have a strong fixed cost element in each location, it is cost-efficient to allow as many people as possible to take advantage of the interventions. For example, Banerjee, Duflo, and Glennerster are currently evaluating a community based iron fortification method. A local NGO trains the village miller to fortify flour with iron and supplies the fortification compound to him. Not allowing everyone in the community to take advantage of the trained miller would imply that the initial set up costs are not fully leveraged.

Another reason why group-level randomization may be preferred is that individual-level randomization of a program perceived as desirable in a village or a neighborhood may create resentment towards the implementation organization. Organizations may simply refuse to participate in such evaluations and, even if they agree, may be less likely to implement the experiment as designed. There may be slippage from the comparison to the treatment group (for example, some students assigned to large classes in the Tennessee Star Experiment found their way into small classes), either because the comparison individuals manage to get treated after a while, or because the field staff, intentionally or not, do not treat the right individuals based on the initial random assignment. It is much easier for a research team to ensure that villages are being treated according to an initial random assignment than to monitor individuals.

The choice of the level at which to randomize is therefore very context specific. It depends on the nature of the intervention as well as the nature of the interactions between the individuals to be treated.

5.2. Cross-cutting designs

One of the institutional innovations that led to a large increase in the number of randomized evaluations is the increased use of cross-cutting (or factorial) designs. In cross-cutting designs several different treatments are tested simultaneously with randomizations being conducted so that treatments are orthogonal to each other. Kremer (2003) describes many of those experiments conducted in education in Western Kenya.

There are two ways to think about cross-cutting designs. First, they can be used to test various interventions and combinations of interventions relative to a comparison groups and relative to each other. They can also establish whether treatments have important interaction effects. Policymakers are often interested in using a variety of strategies to change an outcome. For example, the Progresa program we discussed above is a combination of several programs: a cash transfer, a redistribution of resources towards women, and an incentive component. From a policy perspective, the evaluation of the "full Progresa" package may be sufficient for the Mexican government when deciding whether or not to continue with Progresa. But in order to learn about behavior and, for policy purposes, to understand which components of Progresa should be scaled up, one might want to know whether the incentive part of the scheme is necessary, whether distributing the money to women rather than to men matters, etc. In principle, a cross cutting design could have been used in order to disentangle the various component of Progresa.

If a researcher is cross-cutting interventions A and B, each of which has a comparison group, she obtains four groups: no interventions (*pure control*); A only; B only; and A and B together (*full intervention*). If a researcher wants to test whether B has a different effect when combined with A than alone, the sample sizes must be sufficient to allow her to statistically distinguish A versus A and B, as well as B versus A and B. As we discussed in Section 4, one may consider making the *full intervention* and *pure control* groups larger than the *A only* and *B only* groups.

When such cross-cutting designs are too costly or require too large a sample size, a practical question that often arises is whether to evaluate a combined program (A and B) or to separately evaluate the two components. Policymakers may have a preference to evaluate the A and B combination as long it has the potential to be scaled up, since the A and B combination is more likely to have an effect than either A or B separately.

From an economist's perspective, the drawback of evaluating packages of interventions is that it makes it difficult to understand what drove the response and thus to extract lessons more general than just "this particular package worked." The advantage is that a more intensive intervention is more likely to have an impact and thus to show that outcomes can indeed be affected. If there is substantial uncertainty about the fact that either component may make a big difference to the outcomes of interest, it may make sense to first evaluate the combined package and then follow up with later studies designed to disentangle the various potential mechanisms at work. In the initial study, intermediate variables likely to be affected by one intervention but not the other can be used to shed light on which part of the intervention was effective. For example, in the deworming pilot mentioned above (Miguel and Kremer, 2004), two programs were combined: deworming pills were distributed, and children were given advice about preventive behavior (wearing shoes, washing hands, etc.). Researchers collected variables on behavior which suggested that no behavior changed in the treatment schools. This strongly suggests that the component of the intervention that made the difference was the provision of the deworming pill.

Even when there is no interest in potential interactions between programs, cross-cutting designs can also be useful for testing multiple hypotheses rather than one, with little increase in cost, since the main cost of randomized evaluations typically consists of conducting the surveys to establish baseline conditions and to measure outcome variables. In this case, the overall sample size need only be large enough to have sufficient power for the intervention that is expected to have the smaller effect. For example, Banerjee et al. (2007) tested in the same sample (the municipal schools in Vadodara, India) the effect of remedial education and the effects of Computer Assisted Learning. As we saw above, half the schools received the remedial education program for grade 4. Half the schools received the computer assisted learning program, also for grade 4 students. The randomization for the computer assisted learning was stratified according to treatment status for the remedial education program. The same test scores were used to look at the effect of both programs.

In this case, the effect of remedial education we obtain is that of remedial education conditional on half the school getting computer assisted learning as well. This may have been problematic if computer assisted learning had little chance to be scaled up and if the effect of remedial education turned out to be very different in schools with and without computers. In this case, the two programs did not seem to interact with each other at all, so that the existence of two treatments did not diminish the external validity of the evaluation of each of them.

Because they significantly reduce costs, cross-cutting different treatments has proved very important in allowing for the recent wave of randomized evaluations in development economics.[20] They may also provide a window for graduate students or others who have limited access to resources to implement randomized research projects as additional treatments as part of larger projects. For example, using a cross-cutting design, Duflo et al. (2006) evaluate the effect on risky sexual behavior of Kenya's teacher training for HIV/AIDS education and that of helping children stay in school longer by reducing the cost of education. As part of her dissertation, Dupas (2006) evaluated an additional intervention which she designed and implemented with the help of the NGO that was facilitating the initial project: the program was an information intervention where teenagers were informed of the relative prevalence of HIV/AIDS in different age groups. The intervention itself is very cheap and could be added to the program at minimal costs. Collecting the data would have been extremely expensive, but the necessary data was collected as part of the initial project. It turns out that this intervention proved to be much more effective in reducing pregnancy rates (the marker of risky sexual behavior) than the regular teacher training program. This suggests that adding this component to the regular program has the potential to make it much more effective in reducing risky sexual behavior.

A final advantage of cross-cutting designs, evident in this example, is that, while a full welfare analysis is, as we discussed earlier, difficult, it is possible to compare the effectiveness of several different techniques for achieving a specific outcome. That is at least a second best.

5.3. Data collection

We do not discuss specific survey design issues here as they are already covered by a substantial literature (see for example Deaton, 1997). Our main focus here is on the choice of what type of data to collect, the value of a baseline survey, and the use of administrative data.

---

[20] Many of the experiments on education in Kenya described in Kremer (2003) were cross-cutting designs.

5.3.1. Conducting baseline surveys

One of the first data collection questions that a researcher must address is whether or not to conduct a baseline survey. In principle, randomization renders baseline surveys unnecessary, since it ensures the treatment and comparison groups are similar in expectation. However, there are several reasons why researchers may want to conduct a baseline survey.

First, as we have discussed, a baseline survey generates control variables that will reduce the variability in final outcomes and therefore reduces sample size requirements. In terms of the cost of the evaluation, the trade-off between conducting a baseline survey and not conducting one boils down to comparing the cost of the intervention, the cost of data collection, and the impact that variables for which data can be collected in a baseline survey may have on the final outcome. When the intervention is expensive and data collection is relatively cheap, conducting a baseline will save money. When the intervention is cheap but data collection is expensive, it may be more cost effective to run a larger experiment without conducting a baseline.

Cost is not the only consideration, however. There are several other advantages of conducting baseline surveys. First, they make it possible to examine interactions between initial conditions and the impact of the program. In many cases this will be of considerable importance for assessing external validity. Second, a baseline survey provides an opportunity to check that the randomization was conducted appropriately. Third, collecting baseline data offers an opportunity to test and refine data collection procedures.

The alternative strategy of collecting "pre-intervention data" retrospectively in the post-survey will usually be unacceptable, because even if the program does not affect those variables it may well affect recall of those variables. Sometimes sufficient administrative data is already available and can substitute for a baseline to gauge the validity of randomization and provide control variable for looking at the significance of interventions.

5.3.2. Using administrative data

Using administrative data (data collected by the implementing organization as part of their normal functioning) linked to information on treatment can greatly reduce the cost of data collection and reduce attrition. Use of administrative data is more common in developed countries, but even in developing countries researchers can have access to such data. For example, Angrist, Bettinger and Kremer (2006) examine the medium-run impact of the Colombia voucher program by linking data on the voucher lottery with data on registration for Colombia's school completion/college entrance exam.

It is, however, important in such cases to ensure that data is comparable between treatment and comparison groups. For example, it may be that outcome variables of interest are collected as part of a program but only in program areas. It might be tempting to reduce data collection costs by only putting in place a new survey in comparison areas and relying on program data to get outcome variables in treatment areas. However, this could introduce biases as a difference in measured outcomes between treatment and comparison areas could reflect different data collection methodologies. For example, Duflo and Hanna (2006) study the impact of providing incentives based on teacher attendance in informal schools. In treatment schools, attendance is measured every day using date and time-stamped photographs. In comparison schools, attendance needs to be measured by through unannounced visits to the schools. In order to ensure uniformity of data collection, the program is evaluated by comparing random visits in both types of schools. And indeed, the average absence rate measured through the daily camera data is different than that measured through the random visit.

Another issue to be aware of is that a program may impact the *measurement* of an underlying variable of interest more than the variable itself. Consider an evaluation for which the outcome of interest is some underlying latent variable (such as learning) that is imperfectly measured by some proxy (such as test scores). In many cases the relationship between the latent variable and the proxy is plausibly unaffected by the program. However, if the program itself creates incentives which are tied to the proxy, then it will be desirable to measure the effect of the intervention using another proxy variable which is also highly correlated with the latent variable but which is not linked to the incentives of the program. For example, in their evaluation of a teacher incentives program based on district test scores, Glewwe and Kremer (2003) collected data not only on the district test scores (on which the incentives was based) but also on a "low stakes" NGO-administered test, which provides an independent measure of learning.

6. Analysis with departures from perfect randomization

This section discusses potential threats to the internal validity of randomized evaluation designs, and ways to either eliminate them ex-ante, or handle them in the analysis ex post. Specifically, we discuss how to analyze data when the probability of selection depends on the strata; analysis of randomized evaluations with imperfect compliance; externalities; and attrition.

6.1. The probability of selection depends on the strata

A first departure from perfect randomization is when randomization is conditional on observable variables, with different probability of being selected depending on the value of the observable variables. In Section 4.5 we discussed designs where blocked designs (or stratification) were used to reduce the variance of the estimated treatment effect. The allocation of observations to treatment and comparison groups was the same in all blocks. It may also happen, however, that the probability of selection differs in different strata. Consider for example the Colombia voucher program already discussed. The randomization was done within each city, with a pre-fixed number of winners in each city. The ratio of lottery winners to total applicants was therefore different in each city. This implies that the lottery status is not random in the overall sample (for example, there may be more losers in Bogota than in Cali if Bogota had more applicants for a given number of places). However, it is still random within each city. In other words, the treatment status is random conditional of a set of observable variables (a stratum: in this case, a city).

Denote as T the treatment status, and X a set of dummy variables indicating the strata. Randomization conditional on observables implies that

$$E[Y_i^C|X, T] - E[Y_i^C|X, C] = 0,$$

so

$$E[Y_i|X, T] - E[Y_i|X, C] = E[Y_i^T|X, T] - E[Y_i^C|X, T].$$

Therefore

$$E_X\{E[Y_i^T|X, T] - E[Y_i^C|X, C]\} = E[Y_i^T - Y_i^C|T],$$

our parameter of interest. Finally,

$$E_X\{E[Y_i^T|X, T] - E[Y_i^C|X, T]\}$$
$$= \int \{E[Y_i^T|x, T] - E[Y_i^C|x, C]\} P(X = x|T)\, dx.$$

This means that, if X takes discrete values, we can compare treatment and comparison observations in each strata and then take a weighted average over these strata, using as weights the proportion of treated units in the cells (this is the sample analog of the above expression). This gives the average effect of the treatment on the treated. The cells where everybody is treated or nobody is are dropped. This method can be applied whenever the randomization is conditional on a set of pre-determined characteristics. An alternative is simply to control for X in an OLS regression of the outcome Y on T. One must, however, be sure to include all the relevant dummies in the regression. Suppose for example that the probability to receive a program depends both on city and income (with two income categories: rich and poor). Then X must include dummy variables for each city, for each income categories, and all their interactions.

6.2. Partial compliance

In some cases, an evaluation is designed to reach all individuals assigned to the treatment group and great care is taken to ensure that compliance is near perfect. This was the case in the Indonesian iron supplementation experiment discussed in the introduction of Section 3, where compliance rates exceeded 92% (Thomas et al., 2003). There are many other cases, however, where compliance is not expected to be perfect. Sometimes only a fraction of the individuals who are offered the treatment take it up. Conversely, some members of the comparison group may receive the treatment. This is referred to as "partial (or imperfect) compliance."

A common reason for partial compliance is that researchers rarely have perfect control over what the comparison group chooses to do. To go back to the example of the iron supplementation study, some individuals in both experimental groups may have already been taking iron supplements, and may have continued to do so even after the evaluation started, since they knew they had one chance in two to be part of the placebo group. Even though nearly all individuals in the treatment groups were treated, since some individuals in the comparison group may have been treated as well, the difference in treatment probability between the treatment and comparison groups was not one. In some instances, members of the comparison group are treated directly by the program. For example, when randomization is at the school level for example, some students may decide to transfer from the comparison group to treatment group in order to benefit from the program offered to the treatment group. In the well-known Tennessee STAR class size evaluation, some children initially assigned to a large class also moved to a small class (Krueger and Whitmore, 2002).

There are also cases where it is not possible to enforce compliance in the treatment group. For example, in the deworming program, only children present on the day of the deworming received the deworming pills. Tracking the children at home to administer the pills would have been prohibitively expensive. Thus not every child in the treated schools was treated.

In many cases, experiments do not intend to treat everybody in the treatment group. This is always the case in encouragement designs. For example, in the evaluation of the effect of information sessions on tax deferred account take up discussed previously (Duflo and Saez, 2003), treatment individuals were offered financial incentives to attend an information session. Individuals in the treatment and the comparison groups were, however, both free to attend. The probability of attending the session among those who received the letter was 19% and only 6% among those who did not. While the difference in the probability to attend was fairly large (13 percentage points) and very statistically significant, it was far from being one.

In this case, the manipulation that the experimenters performed was to send a letter informing the employee of the benefit. However, the benefits office is more concerned about the impact of the information session itself. More generally, we are often interested in the effect of a given treatment, but the randomization only affects the *probability* that the individual is exposed to the treatment, rather than the treatment itself.

To be valid and to prevent the reintroduction of selection bias, an analysis needs to focus on groups created by the initial randomization. One must compare *all* those initially allocated to the treatment group to *all* those initially randomized to the comparison group, whatever their actual behavior and their actual treatment status. The analysis cannot exclude subjects or cut the sample according to behavior that may have been affected by the random assignment. Doing so can lead to erroneous results. This was the case in several early studies examining a program in Cambodia that contracted out government health services to NGOs (Keller and Schwartz, 2001; Bhushan, Keller, and Schwartz, 2002; Schwartz and Bhushan, 2004). Using a 1997 baseline survey and 2001 midterm survey, these studies found that outcomes improved more in the districts with contracting than in comparison districts; however, the 2001 midterm survey did not collect data in three of the eight districts initially assigned to treatment, but where acceptable bids were not received. Thus any estimates would be biased if districts that received acceptable bids differed from those that did not in unobserved variables that influence outcomes. For example, if potential contractors were more likely to bid on districts in which it appeared easiest to reach the contract targets, program effects could be overestimated. Bloom et al. (2006) corrected the problem by collecting data on all districts that were randomly assigned to either the treatment or comparison groups and by comparing all districts initially assigned to the treatment group with all those assigned to the comparison group, regardless of their final assignment.

In cases where the actual treatment is distinct from the variable that is randomly manipulated, call Z the variable that is randomly assigned (for example, the letter inviting the university employees to the fair and offering them \$20 to attend), while T remains the treatment of interest (for example, attending the fair). Denote $Y_i(0)$ the potential outcome for an individual if $Z = 0$, and $Y_i(1)$ the potential outcome for an individual if $Z = 1$.

Because of random assignment, we know that $E[Y_i(0)|Z = 1] - E[Y_i(0)|Z = 0]$ is equal to zero, and that the difference $E[Y_i|Z = 1] - E[Y_i|Z = 0]$ is equal to the causal effect of Z. However, this is not equal to the effect of the treatment, T, since Z is not equal to T. Because Z has been chosen to at least influence the treatment, this difference is called the *Intention to Treat estimate* (ITT).

In many contexts, the intention-to-treat estimate is actually a parameter of interest. For example, in the case of the deworming program, if policymakers are interested in the cost effectiveness of a universal school based deworming treatment, and tracking children at home is not practical, any estimate of the effectiveness of the program needs to take into account the fact that not all children will be present at school on the day of the treatment. In this case, the parameter of interest is the intention-to-treat.

There are, however, many circumstances where researchers are interested in the effect of the intervention (T) itself, rather than that of the instrument. This is particularly true when the evaluation is not designed to be scaled up as a policy but rather to understand the impact of a treatment that could potentially be delivered in many other ways. This was the case in the iron supplementation experiment. A policy that delivers iron pills and carefully monitors compliance is not a practical policy option. There are much cheaper ways to deliver iron, for example by investing in supplementation of food. Policymakers and researchers are therefore interested in the impact of a diet rich in iron, which only individuals who complied with the treatment are getting.

We now investigate what can be learned about the causal effect of the treatment T when compliance is imperfect, so that the randomization generates an instrument Z for the treatment of interest T. This is discussed in Angrist and Imbens (1994, 1995) and related work, and the analysis here follows their treatment.

6.2.1. From intention to treat to average treatment effects

Consider the Wald estimate, which is the ratio of the intention-to-treat estimate and the fraction of individuals who were treated in the treatment and the comparison group.

$$\beta_W = \frac{E[Y_i|Z_i = 1] - E[Y_i|Z_i = 0]}{E[T_i|Z_i = 1] - E[T_i|Z_i = 0]}. \tag{16}$$

Note that the Wald estimate is the IV estimate of β in Eq. (2), using the dummy Z as an instrument. Imbens and Angrist show that, under two assumptions below, this ratio can be interpreted as the average treatment effect for a well-defined group of individuals, namely those who are induced by the instrument Z to take advantage of the treatment.

The two identification assumptions are the following:

1. Independence: $(Y_i^C, Y_i^T, T_i(1), T_i(0))$ is independent of Z; and
2. Monotonicity: Either $T_i(1) \geqslant T_i(0)$ for all i or $T_i(1) \leqslant T_i(0)$ for all i.

The independence assumption subsumes two requirements. First, the fact that the comparison between outcomes for individuals exposed to different values of the instrument identify the causal impact of the instrument. This will be true by construction in the case of randomized evaluation, since the instrument is randomly assigned. Second, that potential outcomes are not directly affected by the instrument. This assumption does not necessarily hold in randomized evaluations and will need to be examined carefully.

The monotonicity assumption requires that the instrument makes *every person* either weakly more or less likely to actually participate in the treatment. For example, every person in the treatment group for the iron study is no less likely to get iron than had they been in the comparison group. This assumption needs to be examined on a case by case basis, but in most cases it will be reasonable.

We can manipulate the numerator of expression (16).

$$\begin{aligned}
E[Y_i|Z_i = 1] &- E[Y_i|Z_i = 0] \\
&= E\left[T_i(1)Y_i^T + \left(1 - T_i(1)\right)Y_i^C|Z_i = 1\right] \\
&\quad - E\left[T_i(0)Y_i^T + \left(1 - T_i(0)\right)Y_i^C|Z_i = 0\right] \\
&= E\left[\left(T_i(1) - T_i(0)\right)\left(Y_i^T - Y_i^C\right)\right] + E\left[Y_i^C|Z_i = 1\right] - E\left[Y_i^C|Z_i = 0\right],
\end{aligned}$$

which, by the independence assumption, is equal to $E[(T_i(1) - T_i(0))(Y_i^T - Y_i^C)]$. This can be expanded to

$$\begin{aligned}
E\Big[-&\left(Y_i^T - Y_i^C\right)|T_i(1) - T_i(0) = -1\Big]P\left[T_i(1) - T_i(0) = -1\right] \\
&+ E\left[\left(Y_i^T - Y_i^C\right) * 0|T_i(1) - T_i(0) = 0\right]P\left[T_i(1) - T_i(0) = 0\right] \\
&+ E\left[Y_i^T - Y_i^C|T_i(1) - T_i(0) = 1\right]P\left[T_i(1) - T_i(0) = 1\right].
\end{aligned}$$

The first term cancels out due to the monotonicity assumption. The second term cancels out since the difference is pre-multiplied by zero. This expressions therefore simplifies to

$$E\left[Y_i^T - Y_i^C|(T_i(1) - T_i(0) = 1\right]P\left[T_i(1) - T_i(0) = 1\right].$$

Meanwhile,

$$\begin{aligned}
P\left[T_i(1) - T_i(0) = 1\right] &= P\left[T_i(1) = 1, T_i(0) = 0\right]\mathbf{1}\left[T_i(1) = 1, T_i(0) = 0\right] \\
&= \mathbf{1}\left[T_i(1) = 1\right] - \mathbf{1}\left[T_i(0) = 1\right].
\end{aligned}$$

Taking expectations,

$$P[T_i(1) - T_i(0) = 1] = E[T_i(1)] - E[T_i(0)]$$
$$= E[T_i|Z = 1] - E[T_i|Z = 0].$$

Hence

$$\hat{\beta}_W = \frac{E[Y_i|Z_i = 1] - E[Y_i|Z_i = 0]}{E[T_i|Z_i = 1] - E[T_i|Z_i = 0]}$$
$$= E[Y_i^T - Y_i^C|(T_i(1) - T_i(0)) = 1].$$

Under the monotonicity and the independence assumptions, the Wald estimator gives us the effect of the treatment *on those whose treatment status was affected by the instrument*, which is known as the local average treatment effect (LATE) (Angrist and Imbens, 1994). These are those who, in the absence of the randomly assigned instrument, would not have been treated but are induced to receive treatment by the assigned instrument. They are often referred to as the *compliers*.

A special case is when nobody in the comparison group is treated, $T_i(0) = 0$. In this case, the Wald estimate is the *effect of the treatment on the treated*. For example, in the second year of the balsakhi study, some schools that had been assigned a balsakhi did not get one. The difference between the average test score of all children in the initial, randomly-assigned treatment group and all children in the initial, randomly-assigned comparison group, divided by the probability that a school receives a balsakhi conditional on having been assigned to the treatment group is an estimate of the average effect of the balsakhi program on children in schools that were actually treated. To the extent that the treatment schools that did not get a balsakhi are different from those that did, the estimated effect may not be representative of the programs impact on the average school.

Another special case is when everybody in the treatment group is treated, $T_i(1) = 1$. This will often be true in "oversubscription" designs, where successful applicants are selected from a list, and offered the treatment. In this case (subject to the caveats we discuss below), the Wald estimate identifies the effect of the treatment on those who would not be treated without inducement.

When the randomization only induces imperfect assignment to the treatment and the comparison groups, it is therefore still possible to make meaningful causal statements. However, the average causal effect that is estimated is not necessarily representative of the average causal effect for the entire population. Depending on circumstances, it may or may not be representative of a sub-population of interest. Those who are induced by the evaluation to take up a particular treatment may be different than those who were already taking it up or who would be likely to be induced to take it up by another policy intervention. In other words, another selection effect appears in this case, although it does not bias the estimation of the causal effect for compliers.[21]

---

[21] See Heckman and Vytlacil (2005) for a more extensive discussion of marginal treatment effects.

In some cases, the group of compliers is exactly the group of interest, precisely because they are the ones that are likely to be affected by a policy. In some cases, policymakers are really interested in the impact of average impact of the policy in as representative a group as possible.

In this case, there may be a trade-off between the benefits of a less tightly controlled evaluation, where the initial random assignment is used as an instrument for the policy and that of an evaluation where the initial randomization is very closely respected. The first evaluation may be much easier to implement, and can be conducted in a larger area and on a larger sample, but the group of compliers may be small and the treatment effects may not be representative of what would be obtained in the population at large. The second evaluation is more difficult to carry out, and requires much larger budgets or a smaller sample size.

This analysis also helps us compare prospective randomized evaluations and natural experiments. Some non-experimental studies take advantage of "natural experiments," where assignment to a treatment or a policy is in part due to a randomly assigned variable that can be used as instrument for the treatment. For example, Angrist (1990) studies the impact veteran status on civilian earnings by taking advantage of the Vietnam draft lottery, where draft assignment to service was in part based on a random number. Because in many cases the random factor only explains part of the variation in the actual treatment, such studies often have a first-stage that is small in magnitude (even if it is very statistically significant), which implies that compliers represent only small share of the population. Even when a natural experiment utilizes very large samples that may be representative of a country's entire population, the resulting estimate may not have more external validity (that is, be less applicable in other contexts) than those of a randomized evaluation conducted in a smaller sample, but carefully controlled such that the first stage is much larger, because identification comes from a very narrow and non-random group of the population.[22]

6.2.2. When is IV not appropriate

In order for the IV estimate to be interpreted as the causal effect of a treatment on the compliers, both the monotonicity and the independence assumptions must hold. Randomized evaluations make it likely that both assumptions are satisfied, but they do not necessarily ensure it. Recall that the independence assumption discussed above requires that potential outcomes of any treatment state, (Y_i^T, Y_i^C), are independent of Z, the instrument. In some case, this assumption fails to hold.

First, the instrument may affect non-compliers in the treatment group. Return to the balsakhi example, and consider only the first year of the evaluation where compliance was perfect at the school level (Banerjee et al., 2007). Because schools were

---

[22] As an example, Card (1999) discusses the interpretation of natural experiment estimates of returns to education and shows that many of them can be interpreted as the returns to education for individuals with high discount rates or credit constrained individuals. This may explain why they tend to be larger than OLS estimates.

randomly assigned to the treatment and comparison groups, the comparison between the test scores of *all* children in the treatment groups and *all* children in the comparison groups provides an unbiased estimate of the average effect of the program on all children, or the intention-to-treat estimate. Noting that only 20% of the children in treatment schools were actually assigned to work with the balsakhi – recall that this is a remedial education program – it is tempting to divide the *ITT* estimate by the probability of being sent to the balsakhi in the treatment group in order to obtain the effect of working with the balsakhi on the children who actually received the remedial education. This, however, is inappropriate, because children in treatment schools who were not sent to the balsakhi may have benefited from the fact that their class is now smaller for most of the day, and their weakest peers have left the classrooms. At the extreme, it could have been the case that the entire effect on the average class was due to an improvement in the learning level of top scoring children who were not sent to the balsakhi and now enjoy better learning conditions. By using the fact that the school was assigned to the program as an instrument for the fact that the child actually received the remedial education, one would, possibly erroneously, force all the impact of the treatment to work through the remedial education classes. If these effects are positive (as we may expect in this case), the IV will be an overestimate of the impact of the treatment on compliers.

The same situation occurred in the deworming program (Miguel and Kremer, 2004). Since not all children in treatment schools were treated, it may again be tempting to divide the intention-to-treat estimate by the fraction of children treated to estimate an average treatment effect. However, as Miguel and Kremer show (and we discuss in more detail below), non-treated children in treatment schools actually benefited from the treatment, since they were exposed to fewer worm-carrying children. Once again, the Wald estimator would overestimate the effect of treatment on the treated, while the intention-to-treat estimate is a valid estimate of the effect of the program on the entire school.

It is important to note that, even if these externalities are small, the bias will be magnified because the ITT estimate is divided by a number smaller than one. While this is less of a concern when the first stage is very powerful, when it is weak the bias can become extremely large.

6.3. Externalities

Experimental interventions can create spillover effects such that untreated individuals are affected by the treatment. Spillovers may be physical – substantial disease reduction externalities were found in the evaluation of a Kenyan primary school deworming program for example (Miguel and Kremer, 2004). They may also result from price changes – Vermeersch and Kremer (2004) found that the provision of school meals to preschoolers at some schools in Kenya led nearby schools to reduce school fees. Spillovers can also occur in the form of learning and imitation effects (see Duflo and Saez, 2003; Miguel and Kremer, 2004).

To see how spillovers can lead to biased estimates of treatment effects, consider the simple situation in which a treatment is randomly allocated across a population of individuals and compliance is perfect. Using the potential outcome framework, the intention-to-treat estimate is ITT $= E[Y_i^T | T = 1] - E[Y_i^C | T = 0]$. In order to interpret this difference as the effect of the treatment, the standard unit treatment value assumption (SUTVA) must hold. It says that the potential outcomes for each individual are independent of his treatment status, as well as the treatment group status of any other individual (Angrist, Imbens and Rubin, 1996). If this is violated, $\hat{E}[Y_i^C | T = 0]$ in the sample is not equal to $E[Y_i^C | T = 0]$ in the population, since the sample contains both treated and untreated individuals. The potential outcome for each individual (and therefore the ITT) now depends on the entire vector of allocations to treatment and comparison groups. If the spillover effects on untreated individuals are generally positive, then the intention-to-treat estimate ITT will generally be smaller than it would have been without spillovers.

It is easy to see that this assumption will be violated when externalities are present. Consider once again the deworming program in Kenya. Those children who received the treatment were directly protected against worms; however, the untreated children with whom they have contact and against whom they are compared will experience fewer infections as well since treated individuals no longer transmit worms. Miguel and Kremer (2004) note that previous work on deworming programs may have underestimated treatment effects because it randomized treatment among individuals in the presence of positive spillovers. If spillovers are negative, the estimate would be upward biased.

If spillovers are global (e.g., changes in world prices), identification of program effects will be problematic with any methodology. If they are local, randomization at the group level can allow for estimation of the total program effect on the group. If externalities do not operate across groups, group-level randomization is sufficient to identify overall treatment effects. It cannot, however, decompose the direct and spillover effects.

Where spillovers are likely to be important, experiments can be specifically designed to estimate their extent and magnitude. A first technique is to purposefully vary the level of exposure to a treatment within a group. For example, in their study of information and 401(k) participation, Duflo and Saez (2003) randomized the offer of getting an incentive to attend information session at two levels. First a set of university departments were randomly chosen for treatment, and then a random set of individuals within treatment departments were offered the prize. This allowed the authors to explore both the direct effect on attendance and plan enrollment of being offered an incentive and the spillover effect of being in a department in which others had been offered incentives.

A second technique is to exploit the variation in exposure across groups that naturally arises from randomization. For example, Duflo, Kremer and Robinson (2006) performed on-site agricultural trials in a randomly selected sample of farmers. They then asked all farmers the names of the three farmers they discuss agriculture with the most often (referred to below as friends). They then compare adoption of fertilizer among the "friends" of the treatment farmers to that of the "friends" of the comparison farmers. This allows them to estimate the extent of information externalities. Likewise,

Miguel and Kremer (2004) compare adoption of deworming pills among the friends of children who were in early treatment schools to that of the friends of children in the late treatment schools. Miguel and Kremer (2004) estimate cross-group externalities by exploiting the fact that randomization created local variation in the density of treatment schools and hence random variation in the likelihood that a student in a non-treated school would be exposed to spillovers. Specifically, they estimate regressions of the form $y_{ij} = \beta_0 + \beta_1 T_j + \sum_d \gamma_d N_{dj}^T + \sum_d \phi_d N_{dj} + \varepsilon_{ij}$, where y_{ij} is the outcome of interest for individual i in school j, T_j indicates whether school j is a treatment school, and N_{dj}^T and N_{dj} measure the number of pupils within distance d of school j in treatment schools and all schools, respectively. The independent effect of school density on the outcome is captured by ϕ_d. The average effect of treatment on the outcome in treatment schools is given by $\beta_1 + \sum_d \gamma_d \bar{N}_d^T$, where $\bar{N}_d^T$ is the average number of treatment pupils a student in a treatment school is exposed to within distance d. The first term represents the direct effect (including within-school externalities on any non-treated pupils) and the second term represents the cross-school externality.

A third technique to estimate spillover effects is to randomly assign individuals to different peer groups. For example, the *Moving to Opportunity* experiment in the US (Liebman, Katz and Kling, 2004) offered randomly selected individuals vouchers to move to lower poverty neighborhoods. The comparison between those who received vouchers and those who didn't provides an estimate of the importance of neighborhood effects.

6.4. Attrition

Attrition refers to the failure to collect outcome data from some individuals who were part of the original sample. Random attrition will only reduce a study's statistical power; however, attrition that is correlated with the treatment being evaluated may bias estimates. For example, if those who are benefiting least from a program tend to drop out of the sample, ignoring this fact will lead us to overestimate a program's effect. While randomization ensures independence of potential outcomes in the initial treatment and comparison groups, it does not hold after non-random attrition. This problem occurred in the first large-scale randomized evaluation in the US, the Negative Income Tax experiment, and produced a rich econometric literature of ways to address the issue (Hausman and Wise, 1979; Heckman, 1979).

Even if attrition rates are similar in treatment and comparison groups, it remains possible that the attritors were selected differently in the treatment and comparison groups. For example, in the evaluation of a medication, attrition due to death may be reduced in the treatment group, but attrition due to the fact that the subject feel healthier and stop complying with the experimental protocol may be increased in the treatment group.

This makes attrition a very difficult problem to solve ex post and that implies managing attrition during the data collection process is essential. Attrition can be limited by implementing systems to carefully track participants even after they leave the program. For example, in the balsakhi program (Banerjee et al., 2007) children were tested at home if they were not found in school after a number of visits, which resulted in low attrition rates. This requires good information on where to find participants even if they drop out of the program. If the goal is to follow participants for a long time after the end of the program, it is important to collect good information in the baseline on how to find them later on (for example the names of neighbors and relatives that can be interviewed if the respondent cannot be found). When following up with *all* attritors is too expensive, a random sample of the attritors can be selected for intensive follow-up. In the analysis, these observations need to be given a higher weight, reflecting their sampling probability.

A first step in the analysis of an evaluation must always be to report attrition levels in the treatment and comparison groups and to compare attritors with non-attritors using baseline data (when available) to see if they differ systematically, at least along observable dimensions. If attrition remains a problem, statistical techniques are available to identify and adjust for the bias. These techniques can be parametric (see Hausman and Wise, 1979; Wooldridge, 2002 or Grasdal, 2001) or nonparametric. We will focus on non-parametric techniques here because parametric methods are more well known. Moreover, non-parametric sample correction methods are interesting for randomized evaluation, because they do not require the functional form and distribution assumptions characteristic of parametric approaches. Important studies discussing non-parametric bounds include Manski (1989) and Lee (2002)

The idea of non-parametric Manski–Lee bounds is to use plausible assumptions about the monotonicity of potential outcomes and attrition along with relative rank restrictions on the distribution of potential outcomes to derive a bound on the treatment effect that can be estimated from available data. Ordinary treatment effect estimates will provide either upper or lower bounds on the true effect depending on the direction of attrition bias. When attrition bias is negative and the treatment effect is positive, the ordinary estimates provide a lower bound for the true effect, and the upper bound is estimated using the Manski–Lee approach.

Below we summarize the approach to attrition taken by Angrist, Bettinger and Kremer (2006) to evaluate the long term impact of a Colombian voucher program on latent learning. As we discussed above, secondary school vouchers were allocated by lottery among a set of applicants. The authors matched lottery winners and losers to records from Colombia's high school graduation/college entrance exam, finding that winners were more likely to take the exam. The differential high school completion rates, while interesting in their own right, make estimating the impact of the program on learning tricky. Let y_{1i} be the outcome for individual i if offered treatment and y_{0i} the outcome they would otherwise obtain. D_i is an indicator variable for random assignment to treatment. Let T_{1i} be an indicator variable for whether the individual would remain in the sample conditional being assigned to the treatment group, and T_{0i} similarly indicate whether they would remain in the sample if assigned to the comparison group. Assume that $y_{1i} \geqslant y_{0i}$ and $T_{1i} \geqslant T_{0i}$ for all i. These assumptions mean that treatment is never harmful and that those offered treatment at least as likely to remain in the sample as those who are not. Now define an outcome variable that is zero for attritors: $Y_{Xi} = T_{Xi}y_{Xi}$ for $X = \{0, 1\}$. Then we can write the following equation linking the actually observed outcome Y_i to potential outcomes, attrition status, and treatment group:

$$Y_i = Y_{0i} + (Y_{1i} - Y_{0i})D_i = T_{0i}y_{0i} + (T_{1i}y_{1i} - T_{0i}y_{0i})D_i.$$

Let $q_{i0}(\theta)$ be the θ-quantile of the distribution of Y_{i0} and let $q_{i1}(\theta)$ be the θ-quantile of the distribution of Y_{i1}. Now define a rank-preservation restriction: Y_{1i} is said to be a θ-quintile preserving transformation of the random variable Y_{0i} if $P(Y_{i1} \geqslant q_{i1}(\theta)|Y_{i0} \geqslant q_{i0}(\theta)) = 1$. In other words, the rank preservation restriction says that when the potential outcome in the comparison state is above a certain quantile in its own distribution, then the potential outcome in the treatment state is also above that quantile in its own distribution. Given the assumptions already outlined and a choice of θ such that $\theta \geqslant \theta_0$ where $q_{0i}(\theta_0) = 0$, Angrist, Bettinger and Kremer (2006) prove that

$$\begin{aligned}
&E\big[Y_i|D_i = 1, Y_i > q_{i1}(\theta)\big] - E\big[Y_i|D_i = 0, Y_i > q_{i0}(\theta)\big] \\
&\geqslant E\big[y_{i1} - y_{i0}|y_{i0} > q_{i0}(\theta), T_{i0} = 1\big] \\
&\geqslant E\big[Y_i|D_i = 1, Y_i > q_{i0}(\theta)\big] - E\big[Y_i|D_i = 0, Y_i > q_{i0}(\theta)\big].
\end{aligned}$$

One can then choose a quantile, θ_0, such that $q_{0i}(\theta_0) = 0$, and then drop the lower θ_0 percent of the Y_{i1} distribution to obtain an upper bound on $E[y_{i1} - y_{i0}|T_{i0} = 1]$ while the unadjusted treatment effect provides a lower bound. Note that the bound will be the tighter, the lower is the attrition. This underscores the need for limiting attrition bias as much as possible.

7. Inference issues

This section discusses a number of the key issues related to conducting valid inference from randomized evaluations. We begin by returning to the issue of group data addressing how to compute standard errors that account for the grouped structure. We then consider the situation when researchers are interested in assessing a program's impact on several (possibly related) outcome variables. We next turn to evaluating heterogeneous treatment effect across population subgroups, and finally discuss controlling for covariates in estimation.

7.1. Grouped data

As was introduced in Section 4.2, when the randomization takes place at the group level, standard errors need to take into account possible correlation in the outcome variables between members of the same group. Equation (11) gives us the inflation factor for the standard errors under the assumption of no heteroskedasticity and a common covariance structure across group (Moulton, 1990). In this case, Eq. (2) can also be estimated more efficiently by Generalized Least Squares, assuming a group random effect.

If one wants to avoid the assumption of a common covariance structure, one approach to computing standard errors with grouped data is to use the cluster-correlated Huber–White covariance matrix estimator. This approach is recommended when the number of groups randomized is large enough. However, Donald and Lang (2001) and Wooldridge (2004) have pointed out that asymptotic justification of this estimator assumes a large number of aggregate units. Simulations in Duflo, Mullainathan and Bertrand (2004) show the cluster-correlated Huber–White estimator performs poorly when the number of clusters is small (less than 50), leading to over-rejection of the null hypothesis of no effect.

When the number of clusters is small, hypothesis tests can also be generated using randomization inference (Rosenbaum, 2002). This approach involves generating placebo random assignments P_j and associated regression coefficients, denoted B_p. Denote the set of all possible assignments from the randomization process $\{P_j\}$. Now consider β_p in the regression equation

$$Y_{ij} = \delta + \beta_p P_j + \upsilon_{ij}.$$

Since P_j is a randomly generated placebo, $E(\beta_p) = 0$. Let $\hat{F}(\hat{\beta}_p)$ be the empirical c.d.f. of $\hat{\beta}_p$ for all elements of $\{P_j\}$. We can now perform a hypothesis test by checking if our measured treatment effect is in the tails of the distribution of placebo treatments. We can reject H_0: $\hat{\beta}_T = 0$ with a confidence level of $1 - \alpha$ if $\hat{\beta}_T \leqslant \hat{F}^{-1}(1 - \frac{\alpha}{2})$ or $\hat{\beta}_T \geqslant \hat{F}^{-1}(1 - \frac{\alpha}{2})$. Since the placebo assignments, P_j, only vary across clusters, this method takes intracluster correlations into account.

The advantage of randomization inference is that it is valid for any sample size, and can thus be used even when the number of sample is very small. Bloom et al. (2006) use this method to compute standard errors in their study of the impact of subcontracting the management of public health care center in Cambodia. Randomization was carried out at the district level, and only 12 districts participated in the study. Clustered standard errors could therefore be affected by fairly strong bias. Note, however, that while unbiased, randomization inference has low power relative to more parametric approaches when the true effect is large because it does not put even minimal structure on the error term (see the discussion in Bloom et al., 2006).

7.2. Multiple outcomes

Evaluations often affect many different outcomes that the experimenter subsequently measures. Testing hypotheses regarding multiple outcomes calls for special techniques. Standard hypothesis testing supposes that the experimenter is interested in each outcome separately. But when testing multiple outcomes, the probability of rejecting a true null hypothesis for at least one outcome is greater than the significance level used for each test (Kling and Liebman, 2004); a researcher testing ten independent hypotheses at the 5% level will reject at least one of them with a probability of approximately 40%.

Suppose that in our example, individual hypotheses test showed the estimated effect of the intervention was statistically significant for scores in math but for no other subjects. While a policymaker concerned only with math scores might focus on the point estimate of the effect on math, an experimenter reporting the results of the program would be wrong to draw the inference that the program worked in math but not in other subjects. In order to make a correct inference, the standard errors must be adjusted to account for the fact that the outcome is a member of a family of hypotheses. This is often referred to as the "family-wise" error.

Adjusted *p*-values for each outcome are to be constructed such that the probability is less than 0.05 that at least one of the tests in a family would exceed the critical value under the joint null hypothesis of no effects. The simplest and most conservative approach is Bonferroni adjustment, in which each *p*-value is multiplied by the number of tests in the family (Savin, 1984). This approach is too conservative, however, since it treats all the hypotheses as independent.[23]

An alternative approach with multiple related hypothesis (a family of hypotheses) is thus to test whether the *overall* effect of treatment on a family of outcomes is significantly different from zero. Following our example, a policy maker may be interested in the effect of their intervention on test scores in general, rather than on each subject separately. Measurement of such overall effects has its roots in the literature on clinical trials and on meta-analysis (see O'Brien, 1984; Logan and Tamhane, 2003; and Hedges and Olkin, 1985). A summary measure that captures this idea is the mean standardized treatment effect. Suppose that there are K different outcomes in the family of interest. Let the point estimate and standard error for each effect be given by and $\hat{\pi}_k$ and $\hat{\sigma}_k$. Following O'Brien (1984), Logan and Tamhane (2003), and Kling et al. (2004), the mean standardized treatment effect is given by $\bar{\pi} = \frac{1}{K} \sum_{k=1}^{K} \frac{\hat{\pi}_k}{\hat{\sigma}_k}$. The standard error of this mean effect needs to take into account the fact that all the outcomes are correlated: this can be done by running seemingly unrelated regressions (SUR) for all the standardized outcomes falling into a family. The mean standardized treatment effect is preferable to alternatives, such as a joint F-test across all the outcomes, since it is unidirectional and thus has more power to detect whether all effects go in the same direction.

These corrections help avoid the publication bias problems discussed above. Unlike a retrospective analysis which may draw data from a large data set with many potentially unrelated variables (like a census), all the variables collected in a prospective evaluation were, presumably, collected because they were considered potential outcome variables. All should therefore be reported whether they are significant or not. Where there are a large number of variables, it can also be useful for the researcher to set out ahead of time which variables fall into which families for family testing.

---

[23] Alternative approaches are the Bonferroni–Holm step-down adjustment (Holm, 1979) and the bootstrap method of Westfall and Young (1993) (see Kling and Liebman, 2004 for an example).

7.3. Subgroups

Interventions often have heterogeneous effects on the population they affect. For example, we might expect a remedial education program to have a greater effect on students who have low test scores than on those who have high test scores. If we randomly allocate an intervention across groups (such as classrooms) containing students of both types, then the effect of treatment will be an average of the effect on low and high scoring children. Researchers and policymakers may, however, be interested in testing the effect separately for low- and high-scoring children.

Ideally, researchers should know when designing the evaluation protocol, either through a priori reasoning or through knowledge gained from other studies, which of the possible subgroups should be investigated separately and make this decision clear ex ante. Theoretical restrictions may in fact give rise to additional testable hypotheses – for example, that the program has a significant impact on low-scoring children, but not on high-scoring children.

Note that in clustered designs evaluations may have almost as much power for such subgroup as it is for the entire sample. This is because the number of observations per cluster matter more for power than the number of clusters. Moreover, if one of the reason for the correlation within cluster was that the fraction of individuals belonging to each subgroups vary from a cluster to another, examining subgroups separately may reduce the within-group correlation enough to compensate for the loss in sample size (Bloom, 2005).

In some cases (though not when the randomization is carried out at the group level and each group contain members of different subgroups of interest) it is possible to stratify our randomization of individuals into treatment and comparison groups by the subgroups, and to estimate treatment effects in each subgroup. This makes the intention to looking at the effects for different subgroup explicit. Even when subgroups are determined in advance, standard errors need to be adjusted for the fact that there are several subgroups. The possible adjustments are very much like the adjustments for multiple outcomes just reviewed.

What if a researcher discovers after the randomization has been conducted and the evaluation begun that a particular subgroup seems to have a very different treatment effects? For example, Glewwe, Kremer, and Moulin (2004) find no evidence that providing textbooks to rural Kenyan primary schools increased scores for the typical student. However, there is evidence that the program increased test scores for students with initially higher academic achievement. While this "cut" was not intended in advance, it can be easily be rationalized: since the textbooks were in English, they were unlikely to help the weaker student. Should such evidence be reported? Likewise, evaluation results are often separately reported for different sites.[24] In Kenya, Kremer, Miguel and

---

[24] This is the case for most social experiments in the US. For example, the results of the *Moving to Opportunity* experiment were first reported for the city of Boston (Liebman, Katz and Kling, 2004), where it seemed to have bigger effects than in some other sites, at least in early years of the program.

Thornton (2004) separately report the result of an incentives program for two districts, one where it "worked" and the other where it was ineffective. One could argue that dividing the sample according to a variable that was not part of the original randomized design may lead to data mining. Because the universe of possible "cuts" of the data is not known, computing Bonferroni bounds or similar adjustments is not possible, and standard errors cannot be properly calculated.

The most stringent standard, which is applied by the FDA in clinical trials of new drug therapies, is that unless the subgroups are specified ex ante, results for specific subgroups will not be considered sufficient evidence for drug license. The FDA requires a new trial designed ex ante to measure the impact on any subgroups. The reason the FDA takes this approach is that if a researcher (or pharmaceutical company) has free reign to examine an arbitrary number of subgroups, it will typically be possible to choose subgroups such that the intervention appears effective within that group.

From a Bayesian point of view, however, a policymaker who trusts that the researcher has not data mined among many potential subgroups, and who believes there is a good a priori case to believe that effects might differ by subgroups would seem to have reason to take into account the results of subgroup analysis, even if done ex post. In this context it is also important to remember that randomized trials constrain researchers' options much more than in standard empirical economics, where, almost by construction, there are many more opportunities to engage in data mining, subgroup selection, and specification searching.

While every effort should be made to lay out the planned subgroup analysis in advance and typically to stratify the randomization by subgroup, we do believe that it may sometimes be worthwhile to report results from ex post grouping as well as those that were initially planned, since they can shed additional light on the first set of results. However, if results according to ex post grouping are reported, a researcher's report must make it very clear which subgroups were defined ex ante and which subgroup was defined ex post. From the point of view of a researcher, an evaluation that yields suggestive results *ex post* on groups that had not been designed *ex ante* should be thought of as the first step to a further evaluation focusing in particular on these effects.

7.4. Covariates

Another element of choice in the analysis of an experiment is the choice of what to control for. As we discussed above, controlling for variables not affected by the treatment may reduce the variance of the outcome, leading to more precise estimates (controlling for variables that are *affected* by the experiment would of course lead to biased estimates). But once again, those variables should be specified ex ante, to avoid specification searching. It is common practice to report both "raw" differences and as well as regression-adjusted results.

8. External validity and generalizing randomized evaluations

Up until now we have mainly focused on issues of internal validity, i.e., whether we can conclude that the measured impact is indeed caused by the intervention in the sample. In this section we discuss external validity – whether the impact we measure would carry over to other samples or populations. In other words, whether the results are generalizable and replicable. While internal validity is necessary for external validity, it is not sufficient. This question has received a lot of attention in the discussions surrounding the use of randomized evaluation. A very interesting overview of this debate is given by the papers of Bardhan, Basu, Mookherjee and Banerjee in a symposium on "new development economics" (Banerjee, 2006; Basu, 2005; Mookherjee, 2005; Bardhan, 2005; Banerjee et al., 2005). In this section, we discuss reasons why one may worry about the external validity of randomized evaluations, and what are the ways to ameliorate these concerns.

8.1. Partial and general equilibrium effects

Because randomized evaluations compare the difference between treatment and comparison populations in a given area, they are not able to pick up general equilibrium effects (Heckman, Lochner and Taber, 1998). Such effects may be particularly important for assessing the welfare implications of scaling up a program. For example, in the evaluation of the voucher program in Colombia, the researchers compared the outcomes for students who were given vouchers to attend private school with those of students who applied for but did not receive vouchers. This evaluation was able to identify the impact of winning a voucher given that there was a system of vouchers in place – in other words, it measured the partial or localized effect of the program on recipients. It was not, however, able to say what the overall impact of introducing a voucher system was on the education system in Colombia.

Both advocates and detractors of voucher systems point to potential general equilibrium effects of vouchers. Proponents suggest that the added competition introduced by vouchers increases the pressure on public schools and that these schools improve their performance as a result (Hoxby, 2003). Opponents argue that vouchers are likely to increase sorting of students by ability, preferences, and race and may undermine the role of education in creating a cohesive society with common identity and shared values (Hsieh and Urquiola, 2003). To the extent that vouchers pull the most motivated children and their parents out of public schools, they may reduce the pressure generated by articulate, motivated parents on public schools to perform well.

Neither of these effects can be measured in the study on Colombian vouchers. Increased competition could improve the quality of education in public schools (where more comparison children are educated) and so reduce the difference between treatment and comparison outcomes. This would reduce the measured effect of vouchers even though there was a positive impact of vouchers on the system. Increased sorting would impact both treatment and comparison schools, and so a comparison between the two would not be able to pick it up. A decline in performance in public schools due to the loss of the most committed students and parents would show up in a study of this kind as a larger gap between the performance of treatment and comparison students. In other words, the bigger the magnitude of this negative effect of vouchers, the better it would make the outcomes of vouchers appear.

General equilibrium effects of this kind can be thought of as another variety of externality. As with externalities, it would be possible to pick up some of these general equilibrium effects if the unit of observation were large enough – although this is not always practical. For example, the impact of vouchers on between school competition, on sorting, and on the children remaining in public schools, could be analyzed by randomizing vouchers at the community level (assuming a community was large enough to incorporate several schools, some public and some private). If most children stayed within this community to go to school, a comparison of communities that (on a random basis) introduced vouchers with those that did not would tell us something about these general equilibrium effects.

In other cases, the general equilibrium effects may work at the level of the country or even the world (if, for example, they impact wages or prices). It would be difficult to implement a randomized evaluation that picked these up as it would involve randomizing at the national or even international level.

8.2. Hawthorne and John Henry effects

Another limitation of prospective evaluations is that the evaluation itself may cause the treatment or comparison group to change its behavior. Changes in behavior among the treatment group are called Hawthorne effects, while changes in behavior among the comparison group are called John Henry effects.[25] The treatment group may be grateful to receive a treatment and conscious of being observed, which may induce them to alter their behavior for the duration of the experiment (for example, working harder to make it a success). The comparison group may feel offended to be a comparison group and react by also altering their behavior (for example, teachers in the comparison group for an evaluation may "compete" with the treatment teachers or, on the contrary, decide to slack off).

These behavioral responses are often discussed in the context of being specific concerns for randomized evaluations, although similar effects can occur in other settings. For example, provision of school inputs could temporarily increase morale among students and teachers, which could improve performance in the short run. Such effects would create problems for fixed-effects, difference-in-differences and regression discontinuity estimates as well as randomized evaluations. What makes an experiment

---

[25] The Hawthorne Effect refers to the Hawthorne works of the Western Electric Company in Chicago. During a series of studies regarding the effect of work conditions on worker productivity, researchers concluded that the knowledge they were being observed induced workers to exert additional effort. The John Henry effect refers to the rail worker of American folklore.

special is that individuals may know they are part of an evaluation and may thus re-act to the very fact of being evaluated, not only to the inputs received.

One way to disentangle Hawthorne or John Henry effects from long-run impacts of the program which would obtain outside of an evaluation is to collect longer run data. For example, Duflo and Hanna (2006) continued to monitor the impact of the camera program over a year after the official "experiment" was over (but the NGO decided to continue to implement the program as a permanent program). The fact that the results are similar when the program is not being officially evaluated any more and at the beginning of the evaluation period suggest that the initial results on presence where not due to Hawthorne effects.

Evaluations can also be designed to help disentangle the various channels and help ameliorate concerns of John Henry or Hawthorne effects. One example is the evaluation of the SEED program, mentioned above (Ashraf, Karlan and Yin, 2006). In this case, the authors were concerned that individuals may have saved more not because of the special SEED savings program but just because they were visited by a team that sug-gested saving. Their solution was to create an additional treatment group to which they marketed a "regular" savings program. That is, of the half of these individuals not as-signed to the SEED commitment treatment group, one fourth were assigned to the pure comparison group while one fourth were assigned to a third group – the "marketing treatment" group. Clients in this group were given virtually the same marketing cam-paign as received by clients in the SEED commitment treatment group, except that the marketing was strictly limited to conventional and existing savings products of the par-ticipating microfinance institution. By comparing savings levels of clients in the SEED commitment treatment and marketing treatment groups, the authors were able to isolate the direct effect of the SEED product from the effect of the marketing campaign.

While the coefficient on the indicator for the "marketing treatment" was insignificant in all regression specifications, it was also positive in every specification. This sug-gests that the marketing treatment may have had an impact on savings, though this was small in magnitude and the sample size did not provide sufficient statistical power to estimate it.

8.3. Generalizing beyond specific programs and samples

More generally, an issue that often comes up with randomized evaluations is the extent to which the results are replicable or generalizable to other contexts. Sure, a specific program worked in one community in Western Kenya, but can we extrapolate that it will work elsewhere? Was its success linked to a specific NGO? Would a similar program, but with minor variations, have the same impact?

Three major factors can affect the generalizability of randomized evaluation results: the ways in which the programs are implemented (are the programs implemented with special care in a way that makes it very difficult to replicate them?), the fact that the evaluation is conducted in a specific sample, and the fact that specific programs are implemented (would a slightly different program have the same results?). We consider these factors in turn.

The first question is whether the program is implemented with a level of care that makes it impossible to replicate it. Pilot programs are often run with particular care and with particularly high-quality program officials in a way that is impossible to replicate on a wider scale. When they are implemented by NGOs that are open to having programs tested, one may also worry that only these types of NGOs could implement them so effectively. As a program is expanded, the quality may deteriorate. While completely preventing this problem is difficult, it is important and possible to avoid "gold plating" programs. It is also important to clearly document the procedures followed in the program and to collect data on how well the program was implemented (in particular, the compliance rates and whether the procedures were followed) so that what is being evaluated is clearly understood.

A more difficult issue is whether we can conclude that because one population responded to a program in one way, another population will respond in the same way to a similar program. If a program worked for poor rural women in Africa, will it work for middle-income urban men in South Asia? This problem is of course not limited to randomized evaluations. Any empirical study informs us about the sample on which the research was performed, and can be generalized only under some assumptions. But for logistical reasons, randomized evaluations are often conducted in relatively small regions, which exacerbates the problem, while retrospective research can take advantage of nationally representative data sets.[26]

Given that implementation constraints require working in a small number of selected sites, the external validity of randomized evaluations for a given population (say, the population of a country) would be maximized by randomly selecting sites and, within these sites, by randomly selecting treatment and comparison groups. The former is almost never done. Randomized evaluations are typically performed in "convenience" samples, with specific populations. While these choices are often necessary to make an evaluation possible, they may also limit its external validity.

There are two responses to this dilemma. We should test and see whether a program or research result holds in different contexts. But as we cannot test every single permutation and combination of contexts, we must also rely on theories of behavior that can help us decide whether if the program worked in context A and B it is likely to work in C. We discuss these two responses below.

The third question is related: given that a specific version of a program had a given impact, what can we learn about similar, but not identical, programs. For example what

---

[26] It is nevertheless worth pointing out that in some cases, this trade-off between internal and external validity also occurs in non-experimental studies. For example, regression discontinuity designs solve internal validity issues with very mild identifying assumption by focusing on a very small subset of the population, those who are "marginal" for getting the treatment of interest; IV strategies identify the effect for a group of compliers that may be small and not representative of the general population.

would have been the response to the Progresa program if the slope of the transfer scheduled with respect to secondary school enrollment of children of different ages had been different? Here again, the same two responses hold: one would like to try various versions of programs to understand what versions matter. As the experience accumulate on a given programs, it may be possible to infer a "schedule" of responses to different transfer size for example. But the number of possible variations on a given program is potentially infinite, and a theoretical framework is definitely needed to understand which variations are important to replicate and which are not. Here again, it is a combination of replications and theory that can help generalize the lessons from a particular program.

8.4. Evidence on the generalizability of randomized evaluation results

Evidence on program replication is unfortunately limited at this point. The relatively limited experience of programs that have been tested in different environments suggest that (at least for these randomized trials) the results have generalized quite well. However, it will clearly be important to do more of this type of testing on different types of programs. There may be another kind of publication incentive at work here: researchers do not have strong incentives to replicate existing evaluations, and journals are also less interested in publishing such studies. Ideally, institutions should emerge that both carry out such evaluations and ensure the diffusion of the results to policymakers, even if academic publications are not the ideal forum.

Replication was built into the design of the randomized evaluations of the remedial education discussed above (Banerjee et al., 2007). The evaluation was simultaneously conducted in two large cities (Mumbai and Vadodara), with completely different implementation teams. Mumbai's team was experienced as the program had already been run in that city for some time; Vadodara's team was new. Mumbai and Vadodara are very different cities. Mumbai is a much richer city where initial learning levels were higher. The results were generally very similar in Mumbai and Vadodara with one interesting exception: in language, the effects in Mumbai were much smaller than in Vadodara, to the point of being insignificant. This is likely related to the fact that over 80% of the children in Mumbai had already mastered the basic language skills the program was covering, as the baseline tests demonstrated.

The deworming program discussed above was also replicated in a different context and produced similar results. The original deworming evaluation was run in rural primary schools in western Kenya. The program was then modified to meet the needs of preschool children in urban India, with iron supplementation added given the high level of anemia in that population (Bobonis, Miguel and Sharma, 2004). The program was also implemented by different organizations – Pratham in India and International Child Support Africa in Kenya. The results, however, were surprisingly similar. In Kenya, school participation increased by 7 percentage points, height-for-age z-score increased by 0.09, and weight-for-age did not change. In India, participation increased by 6 percentage points, there were no average gains in child height-for-age, and weight increased by 1.1 pounds.

One result that was different between the two studies was that externalities were much larger in Kenya than in India, possibly because of differences in the transmission mechanism of worms and because iron fortification does not produce externalities.

It is possible that medical interventions of this type are more likely to replicate than programs attempting to influence behavior. However, the limited evidence on the replicability of results from incentive programs is also encouraging. Progresa was initially introduced and tested in Mexico but it has since been replicated in several other Latin American countries (including Ecuador, Colombia and Brazil) as well as in other countries, such as Turkey. In several cases, these programs have also been tested using randomized evaluations. These additional trials have allowed researcher both to verify that the effect of conditional cash transfers replicate in countries other than Mexico – they generally do – and also to shed some light on the importance of particular points of program design. For example, Schady and Araujo (2006) studied the impact on school enrollment in Ecuador of a cash transfer that was *not* conditional on school enrollment. They found that the program nevertheless had large impact on school enrollment, but this was concentrated among households who believed (mistakenly) that the program was conditional on enrollment.

8.5. Field experiments and theoretical models

While it is necessary to replicate studies in different contexts, it will never be feasible to rigorously test the extent to which research results hold in all possible situations. However, experiments can deliver much more general lessons when they are combined with economic theories or models.

There are two main ways to combine theory and structure with randomized evaluations. First, economic modeling can be combined with variation coming from randomized evaluations to estimate a richer set of parameters. The cost is a set of additional assumptions, but the benefit is a richer set of parameters, which can be used to make prediction about how variation of the program would affect behavior. Attanasio, Meghir, and Santiago (2005) combine structural modeling with the variation coming from the experimental design in Progresa to estimate a flexible model of education choice, which allows them to estimate the possible effects of different variants of Progresa. A related use of randomized evaluation is an "out of sample" validation of the assumption made by structural models. Todd and Wolpin (2006) estimate a structural model of schooling and work decision for children in the Progresa control villages. They then simulate what effect Progresa would have if their model was right and compare it to the actual treatment effect.

A more ambitious use of theory and randomization in development economics is to set up experiments explicitly to test particular theories about economic behavior. Karlan and Zinman (2005a, 2005c) and Bertrand et al. (2005) are three related projects offering excellent examples of using field experiments to test theories. Both projects were conducted in collaboration with a South African lender, giving small loans to high-risk borrowers at high interest rates. In both cases, the main manipulation started by sending different direct mail solicitation to different people. Karlan and Zinman (2005c) set out to test the relative weights of ex post repayment burden and ex ante adverse selection in lending. In their set up, potential borrowers with the same observable risk are randomly offered a high or a low interest rate in an initial letter. Individuals then decide whether to borrow at the solicitation's "offer" rate. Of those that respond to the high rate, half are randomly given a new lower "contract" interest rate when they actually apply for the loan, while the remaining half continue to receive the rate at which they were offered the loan. Individuals do not know beforehand that the contract rate may differ from the offer rate. The researchers then compare repayment performance of the loans in all three groups. This design allows the researchers to separately identify adverse selection effects and ex post repayment burden effects (which could be due to moral hazard or sheer financial distress ex post). Adverse selection effects are identified by considering only the sample that eventually received the low contract rate, and comparing the repayment performance of those who responded to the high offer interest rate with those who responded to the low offer interest rate. Ex post repayment burden effects are identified by considering only those who responded to the high offer rates, and comparing those who ended up with the low offer to those who ended up with the high offer. The study found that men and women behave differently: while women exhibit adverse selection, men exhibit moral hazard. This experiment constitutes a significant methodological advance because it shows how simple predictions from theory can be rigorously tested.

Bertrand et al. (2005) apply the same principle to a broader set of hypotheses, most of them coming directly from psychology. The experiment is overlaid on the Karlan and Zinman basic experiment: the offer letters are made to vary along other dimensions, which should not matter economically, but have been hypothesized by psychologists to matter for decision-making, and have been shown to have large effects in laboratory settings. For example, the lender varied the description of the offer, either showing the monthly payment for one typical loan or for a variety of loan terms and sizes. Other randomizations include whether and how the offered interest rate is compared to a "market" benchmark, the expiration date of the offer, whether the offer is combined with a promotional giveaway, race and gender features introduced via the inclusion of a photo in the corner of the letter, and whether the offer letter mentions suggested uses for the loan. The analysis then compares the effect of all these manipulations. While not all of them make a difference, many do, and some of the effects are large and surprising. For example, for male customers, having a photo of a woman on top of the offer letter increases take-up as much as a 1% reduction in the monthly interest rate. In some sense, the juxtaposition of the two experiments may be the most surprising. On the one hand individuals react as *homo economicus* to information – they are sensitive to interest rates and poor-risk borrowers accept the highest interest rates (at least among women). On the other hand, these effects are present in the same setting where seemingly anodyne manipulations make a large difference.

The two experiments and many others already described in this chapter illustrate how development economists have gone much beyond "simple" program evaluations to use randomization as a research tool. Compared to retrospective evaluations (even perfectly identified ones), field experiments, when the collaboration with the partner is very close, offer much more flexibility and make it possible to give primacy to the hypothesis to test, rather than to the program that happens to have been implemented. With retrospective evaluations, theory is used instrumentally, as a way to provide a structure justifying the identifying assumptions (this is more or less explicit depending on the empirical tradition the researchers belong to). With prospective evaluations, it is the experimental design that is instrumental. This gives more power both to test the theory and to challenge it. A theoretical framework is necessary to suggest which experiments should be run and help give them a more general interpretation. Some of the most recent experimental results may not fit very well within the existing theories (this is what Banerjee, 2006 calls the "new challenge to theory"). They should prompt a back-and-forth between theoretical modeling and field experiments, with each new wave of results challenging existing theories and providing some direction about how to formulate new ones.

References

Angrist, J.D. (1990). "Lifetime earnings and the Vietnam era draft lottery: Evidence from social security administrative records". American Economic Review 80 (3), 313–336.

Angrist, J.D. (1998). "Estimating the labor market impact of voluntary military service using social security data on military applicants". Econometrica 66 (2), 249–288.

Angrist, J.D., Bettinger, E., Kremer, M. (2006). "Long-term educational consequences of secondary school vouchers: Evidence from administrative records in Colombia". American Economic Review 96 (3), 847–862.

Angrist, J.D., Imbens, G. (1994). "Identification and estimation of local average treatment effects". Econometrica 62 (2), 467–475.

Angrist, J.D., Imbens, G. (1995). "Two-stage least squares estimation of average causal effects in models with variable treatment intensity". Journal of the American Statistical Association 90 (430), 431–442.

Angrist, J.D., Imbens, G.W., Rubin, D.B. (1996). "Identification of causal effects using instrumental variables". Journal of the American Statistical Association 91, 444–455.

Angrist, J.D., Bettinger, E., Bloom, E., King, E., Kremer, M. (2002). "Vouchers for private schooling in Colombia: Evidence from a randomized natural experiment". American Economic Review 92 (5), 1535–1558.

Ashenfelter, O., Harmon, C.P., Oosterbeek, H. (1999). "A review of estimates of the schooling/earnings relationship". Labour Economics 6 (4), 453–470.

Ashraf, N., Karlan, D.S., Yin, W. (2006). "Tying Odysseus to the mast: Evidence from a commitment savings product in the Philippines". Quarterly Journal of Economics 121 (2), 635–672.

Attanasio, O., Meghir, C., Santiago, A. (2005). "Education choices in Mexico: Using a structural model and a randomised experiment to evaluate Progresa". Working paper EWP05/01. IFS.

Banerjee, A. (2006). "New development economics and the challenge to theory". Economic and Political Weekly 40, 4340–4344.

Banerjee, A., Duflo, E. (2006). "Addressing absence". Journal of Economic Perspectives 20 (1), 117–132.

Banerjee, A., Bardhan, P., Basu, K., Kanbur, R., Mookherjee, D. (2005). "New directions in development economics: Theory or empirics?". Working paper No. 106. BREAD, A Symposium in Economic and Political Weekly.

Banerjee, A., Duflo, E., Cole, S., Linden, L. (2007). "Remedying education: Evidence from two randomized experiments in India". Quarterly Journal of Economics 122 (3), 1235–1264.

Bardhan, P. (2005). "Theory or empirics in development economics". Mimeo. University of California at Berkeley.

Basu, K. (2005). "The new empirical development economics: Remarks on its philosophical foundations". Economic and Political Weekly.

Bertrand, M., Karlan, D.S., Mullainathan, S., Shafir, E., Zinman, J. (2005). "What's psychology worth? A field experiment in the consumer credit market". Working paper 918. Economic Growth Center, Yale University. Available at http://ideas.repec.org/p/egc/wpaper/918.html.

Bertrand, M., Djankov, S., Hanna, R., Mullainathan, S. (2006). "Does corruption produce unsafe drivers?" Working paper #12274. NBER.

Bhushan, I., Keller, S., Schwartz, B. (2002). "Achieving the twin objectives of efficiency and equity: Contracting health services in Cambodia". ERD Policy Brief Series. Asian Development Bank, vol. 6.

Bloom, E., Bhushan, I., Clingingsmith, D., Hung, R., King, E., Kremer, M., Loevinsohn, B., Schwartz, B. (2006). "Contracting for health: Evidence from Cambodia". Mimeo.

Bloom, H.S. (1995). "Minimum detectable effects: A simple way to report the statistical power of experimental designs". Evaluation Review 19, 547–556.

Bloom, H.S. (2005). "Learning more from social experiments". In: Randomizing Groups to Evaluate Place-Based Programs. Russell Sage Foundation, NY, pp. 115–172.

Bobonis, G.J., Miguel, E., Sharma, C.P. (2004). "Iron deficiency anemia and school participation". Paper No. 7. Poverty Action Lab.

Buddlemeyer, H., Skofias, E. (2003). "An evaluation on the performance of regression discontinuity design on progresa". Discussion paper No. 827. Institute for Study of Labor.

Campbell, D.T. (1969). "Reforms as experiments". American Psychologist 24, 407–429.

Card, D. (1999). "The causal effect of education on earnings". In: Ashenfelter, O., Card, D. (Eds.), Handbook of Labor Economics, vol. 3. North-Holland, pp. 1801–1863.

Card, D., Krueger, A.B. (1995). Myth and Measurement: The New Economics of the Minimum Wage. Princeton Univ. Press, Princeton, NJ.

Chattopadhyay, R., Duflo, E. (2004). "Women as policy makers: Evidence from a randomized policy experiment in India". Econometrica 72 (5), 1409–1443.

Cohen, J. (1988). Statistical Power Analysis for the Behavioral Science, second ed. Lawrence Erlbaum, Hillsdale, NJ.

Cook, T.D., Shadish, W.R., Wong, V.C. (2006). "Within study comparisons of experiments and non-experiments: Can they help decide on evaluation policy?" Mimeo. Northwestern University.

Cox, D., Reid, N. (2000). "Theory of the Design of Experiments". Chapman and Hall, London.

Das, J., Krishnan, P., Habyarimana, J., Dercon, S. (2004). "When can school inputs improve test scores?". Working paper No. WPS 3217. World Bank Policy Research.

Deaton, A. (1997). "The Analysis of Household Surveys". International Bank for Reconstruction and Development, World Bank.

Dehejia, R.H., Wahba, S. (1999). "Causal effects in nonexperimental studies: Reevaluating the evaluation of training programs". Journal of the American Statistical Association 94 (448), 1053–1062.

DeLong, J.B., Lang, K. (1992). "Are all economic hypotheses false?" Journal of Political Economy 100 (6), 1257–1272.

Diaz, J.J., Handa, S. (2006). "An assessment of propensity score matching as a non-experimental impact estimator: Evidence from Mexico's Progresa program". Journal of Human Resources 41 (2), 319–345.

Dickson, R., Awasthi, S., Williamson, P., Demelweek, C., Garner, P. (2000). "Effect of treatment for intestinal helminth infection on growth and cognitive performance in children: systematic review of randomized trials". British Medical Journal 320, 1697–1701.

Donald, S., Lang, K. (2001). "Inference with differences-in-differences and other panel data". Discussion paper. Boston University Department of Economics.

Duflo, E. (2004). "Accelerating development". In: Scaling Up and Evaluation. Oxford Univ. Press and World Bank.

Duflo, E. (2006). "Field experiments in development economics". Discussion paper.

Duflo, E., Hanna, R. (2006). "Monitoring works: Getting teachers to come to school". Working paper No. 11880. NBER.

Duflo, E., Kremer, M. (2005). "Use of randomization in the evaluation of development effectiveness". In: Feinstein, O., Ingram, G.K., Pitman, G.K. (Eds.), Evaluating Development Effectiveness. Transaction Publishers, vol. 7. New Brunswick, NJ and London, UK, pp. 205–232.

Duflo, E., Kremer, M., Robinson, J. (2006). "Understanding technology adoption: Fertilizer in western Kenya, preliminary results from field experiments". Mimeo.

Duflo, E., Mullainathan, S., Bertrand, M. (2004). "How much should we trust difference-in-differences estimates?" Quarterly Journal of Economics 119 (1), 249–275.

Duflo, E., Saez, E. (2003). "The role of information and social interactions in retirement plan decisions: Evidence from a randomized experiment". Quarterly Journal of Economics 118 (3), 815–842.

Duflo, E., Dupas, P., Kremer, M., Sinei, S. (2006). "Education and HIV/AIDS prevention: Evidence from a randomized evaluation in western Kenya". Mimeo. MIT.

Dupas P. (2006). "Relative risks and the market for sex: Teenagers, sugar daddies, and HIV in Kenya". Mimeo, Dartmouth College.

Fisher, R.A. (1926). "The arrangement of field experiments". Journal of the Ministry of Agriculture 33, 503–513.

Gertler, P.J., Boyce, S. (2001). "An experiment in incentive-based welfare: The impact of Progresa on health in Mexico". Mimeo, UC-Berkeley.

Glazerman, S., Levy, D., Myers, D. (2003). "Nonexperimental Replications of Social Experiments: A Systematic Review". Mathematica Policy Research, Inc., Princeton, NJ.

Glewwe, P., Kremer, M. (2003). "Teacher incentives". Working paper 9671. National Bureau of Economic Research.

Glewwe, P., Kremer, M. (2006). "Schools, teachers, and education outcomes in developing countries". Chapter 16 in: Handbook on the Economics of Education, vol. 2. North-Holland, pp. 945–1018.

Glewwe, P., Kremer, O., Moulin, S. (2004). "Textbooks and test scores: Evidence from a prospective evaluation in Kenya". Mimeo, Harvard University.

Glewwe, P., Kremer, M., Moulin, S., Zitzewitz, E. (2004). "Retrospective vs. prospective analyses of school inputs: The case of flip charts in Kenya". Journal of Development Economics 74, 251–268.

Grasdal, A. (2001). "The performance of sample selection estimators to control for attrition bias". Health Economics 10, 385–398.

Harrison, G., List, J.A. (2004). "Field experiments". Journal of Economic Literature XLII, 1013–1059.

Hausman, J.A., Wise, D.A. (1979). "Attrition bias in experimental and panel data: The Gary income maintenance experiment". Econometrica 47 (2), 455–473.

Heckman, J. (1979). "Sample selection bias as a specification error". Econometrica 47 (1), 153–161.

Heckman, J., Ichimura, H., Todd, P. (1997). "Matching as an econometric evaluation estimator: Evidence from evaluating a job training programme". Review of Economic Studies 64 (4), 605–654.

Heckman, J., Ichimura, H., Todd, P. (1998). "Matching as an econometric evaluation estimator". Review of Economic Studies 65 (2), 261–294.

Heckman, J., Lochner, L., Taber, C. (1998). "General equilibrium treatment effects: A study of tuition policy". Working paper 6426. National Bureau of Economic Research.

Heckman, J., Vytlacil, O. (2005). "Structural equations, treatment effects and econometric policy evaluation". Econometrica 73 (3), 669–738.

Heckman, J., Ichimura, H., Smith, J., Todd, P. (1998). "Characterizing selection bias using experimental data". Econometrica 66 (5), 1017–1098.

Hedges, L. (1992). "Modeling publication selection effects in meta-analysis". Statistical Science 7, 227–236.

Hedges, L.V., Olkin, I. (1985). "Statistical Methods for Meta-Analysis". Academic Press, San Diego, CA.

Holland, P.W. (1988). "Causal inference, path analysis, and recursive structural equations models". Sociological Methodology 18, 449–484.

Holm, O. (1979). "A simple sequentially rejective multiple test procedure". Scandinavian Journal of Statistics 6, 65–70.

Hoxby, C.M. (2003). "The economics of school choice". In: School Choice and School Productivity (or, Could School Choice be a Rising Tide that Lifts All Boats?). Univ. of Chicago Press, Chicago.

Hsieh, C.-T., Urquiola, M.S. (2003). "When schools compete, how do they compete? An assessment of Chile's nationwide school voucher program". Working paper No. W10008, NBER.

Imbens, G.W. (2004). "Nonparametric estimation of average treatment effects under exogeneity: A review". The Review of Economics and Statistics 86 (1), 4–29.

Imbens, G., King, G., Ridder, G. (2006). "On the benefits of stratification in randomized experiments". Mimeo, Harvard.

International Food Policy Research (2000). "Monitoring and evaluation system". Discussion paper. International Food Policy Research (IFPRI).

Karlan, D.S., Zinman, J. (2005a). "Elasticities of demand for consumer credit". Mimeo, Yale University.

Karlan, D.S., Zinman, J. (2005b). "Observing unobservables: Identifying information asymmetries with a consumer credit field experiment". Working paper 911. Economic Growth Center, Yale University. Available at http://ideas.repec.org/p/egc/wpaper/911.html.

Karlan, D.S., Zinman, J. (2005c). "Observing unobservables: Identifying information asymmetries with a consumer credit field experiment". Discussion paper. Available at http://ideas.repec.org/p/egc/wpaper/911.html.

Karlan, D.S., Zinman, J. (2006a). "Expanding credit access: Using randomized supply decisions to estimate the impacts". Mimeo. Yale University.

Karlan, D.S., Zinman, J. (2006b). "Observing unobservables: Identifying information asymmetries with a consumer credit field experiment". Mimeo.

Keller, S., Schwartz, B. (2001). "Final evaluation report: contracting for health services pilot project". Report No. 1447-CAM. Asian Development Bank on Loan, Unpublished.

Kling, J.R., Liebman, J.B. (2004). "Experimental analysis of neighborhood effects on youth". Working paper No. RWP04-034, KSG.

Kling, J.R., Liebman, J.B., Katz, L.F., Sanbonmatsu, L. (2004). "Moving to opportunity and tranquility: Neighborhood effects on adult economic self-sufficiency and health from a randomized housing voucher experiment". Working paper No. 481. Princeton University, Department of Economics, Industrial Relations Section.

Kremer, M. (2003). "Randomized evaluations of educational programs in developing countries: Some lessons". American Economic Review 93 (2), 102–106.

Kremer, M., Miguel, E., Thornton, R. (2004). "Incentives to learn". Mimeo, Harvard University.

Krueger, A., Whitmore, D. (2002). "Would smaller classes help close the black–white achievement gap?" In: Chubb, J., Loveless, T. (Eds.), Bridging the Achievement Gap. Brookings Institute Press, Washington, DC.

La Londe, R.J. (1986). "Evaluating the econometric evaluations of training programs using experimental data". American Economic Review 76 (4), 602–620.

Lee, D.S. (2002). "Trimming for bounds on treatment effects with missing outcomes". Working paper 51.

Liebman, J.B., Katz, L.F., Kling, J. (2004). "Beyond treatment effects: Estimating the relationship between neighborhood poverty and individual outcomes in the MTO experiment". Working paper 493. Princeton, IRS.

Logan, Tamhane (2003). "Accurate critical constants for the one-sided approximate likelihood ratio test of a normal mean vector when the covariance matrix is estimated". Biometrics 58, 650–656.

Maluccio, J.A., Flores, R. (2005). "Impact evaluation of a conditional cash transfer program". Discussion paper. International Food Policy Research Institute, Research Report No. 141.

Manski, C.F. (1989). "Schooling as experimentation: A reappraisal of the postsecondary dropout phenomenon". Economics of Education Review 8 (4), 305–312.

Manski, C.F. (1993). "Identification of exogenous social effects: The reflection problem". Review of Economic Studies 60, 531–542.

Miguel, E., Kremer, M. (2003). "Networks, social learning, and technology adoption: The case of deworming drugs in Kenya". Working paper 61.

Miguel, E., Kremer, M. (2004). "Worms: Identifying impacts on education and health in the presence of treatment externalities". Econometrica 72 (1), 159–218.

Mookherjee, D. (2005). "Is there too little theory in development economics?" Economic and Political Weekly 40 (40).

Morduch, J. (1998). "Does microfinance really help the poor? New evidence from flagship programs in Bangladesh". Mimeo, Princeton University.

Moulton, B.R. (1990). "An illustration of a pitfall in estimating the effects of aggregate variables on micro units". Review of Economics and Statistics 72 (2), 334–338.

O'Brien, P.C. (1984). "Procedures for comparing samples with multiple endpoints". Biometrics 40, 1079–1087.

Olken, B. (2005). "Monitoring corruption: Evidence from a field experiment in Indonesia". Mimeo, Harvard University.

Parker, S., Rubalcava, L., Teruel, G. (2008). "Evaluating conditional schooling and health transfer programs". In: Handbook of Development Economics, vol. 4. Elsevier/North-Holland, Amsterdam. (Chapter 62 in this book.)

Pitt, M., Khandker, S. (1998). "The impact of group-based credit programs on poor households in Bangladesh: Does the gender of participants matter?" Journal of Political Economy.

Raudenbush, S.W., Spybrook, J., Liu, X., Congdon, R. (2005). "Optimal design for longitudinal and multilevel research: Documentation for the optimal design software". Retrieved April 15, 2005 from http://sitemaker.umich.edu/group-based/optimal_design_software.

Ravallion, M. (2008). "Evaluating anti-poverty programs". In: Evenson, R.E., Schultz, T.P. (Eds.), Handbook of Development Economics, vol. 4. Elsevier/North-Holland, Amsterdam. (Chapter 59 in this book.)

Rosenbaum, P.R. (2002). "Covariance adjustment in randomized experiments and observational studies (with discussion)". Statistical Science 17, 286–327.

Rosenbaum, P.R., Rubin, D.B. (1983). "The central role of the propensity score in observational studies for causal effects". Biometrika 70, 41–55.

Rubin, D.B. (1974). "Estimating causal effects of treatments in randomized and non-randomized studies". Journal of Educational Psychology 66, 688–701.

Savin, N.E. (1984). "Multiple hypothesis testing". In: Handbook of Econometrics, vol. II. Elsevier, Amsterdam, pp. 827–879.

Schady, N.R., Araujo, M.C. (2006). "Cash, conditions, school enrollment and child work: Evidence from a randomized experiment in Ecuador". Unpublished manuscript.

Schultz, T.P. (2004). "School subsidies for the poor: Eevaluating the Mexican Progresa poverty program". Journal of Development Economics 74 (1), 199–250.

Schwartz, B., Bhushan, I. (2004). "Reducing inequity in the provision of primary health care services: Contracting in Cambodia". Mimeo.

Smith, J., Todd, P. (2005). "Does matching overcome Lalonde's critique of nonexperimental estimators?" Journal of Econometrics 125 (1–2), 305–353.

Thomas, D., Frankenberg, E., Friedman, J., Habicht, J.-P., Al E. (2003). "Iron deficiency and the well being of older adults: Early results from a randomized nutrition intervention". Mimeo, UCLA.

Todd, P. (2008). "Evaluating social programs with endogenous program placement and selection of the treated". In: Handbook of Development Economics, vol. 4. Elsevier/North-Holland, Amsterdam. (Chapter 60 in this book.)

Todd, P.E., Wolpin, K.I. (2006). "Ex ante evaluation of social programs". Mimeo, University of Pennsylvania.

Vermeersch, C., Kremer, M. (2004). "School meals, educational achievement, and school competition: Evidence from a randomized evaluation". Working paper No. 3523. World Bank Policy Research.

Westfall, P., Young, S. (1993). "Resampling-Based Multiple Testing: Examples and Methods for p-Value Adjustment". Wiley, New York.

Wooldridge, J.M. (2004). "Cluster-sample methods in applied econometrics". American Economic Review 93 (2), 133–138.

Wooldridge, J.M. (2002). "Inverse probability weighted M-estimators for sample selection, attrition, and stratification". Portuguese Economic Journal 1, 117–139.

Chapter 62

EVALUATING CONDITIONAL SCHOOLING AND HEALTH PROGRAMS*

SUSAN W. PARKER

División de Economía, Centro de Investigación y Docencia Económica (CIDE), Carretera Mexico-Toluca No. 3655, Col. Lomas de Santa Fe, 01210 México, DF Mexico

Spectron Desarrollo B. de Avraznos 61, Bosques de las Lomas, 11700 México, DF Mexico

LUIS RUBALCAVA

Spectron Desarrollo B. de Avraznos 61, Bosques de las Lomas, 11700 México, DF Mexico

Centro de Investigación y Docencia Económicas, A.C., Carretera Mexico-Toluca No. 3655, Col. Lomas de Santa Fe, 01210 México, DF Mexico

GRACIELA TERUEL

Universidad Iberoamericana, Departamento de Economia, Ubicación: Edificio I, Planta Baja, Prolongación Paseo de la Reforma 880, Lomas de Santa Fe, C.P. 01210, Ciudad de México, Mexico

Contents

* We gratefully acknowledge very helpful comments by T. Paul Schultz, Cesar Martinalli, and Edward Miguel as well as by conference participants at the Rockefeller Conference Center in Bellagio in May, 2005.

Handbook of Development Economics, Volume 4
© 2008 Elsevier B.V.   All rights reserved
DOI: 10.1016/S1573-4471(07)04062-4

Abstract

We analyze in this chapter the development and evaluation of a new genre of social
programs termed conditional cash transfer programs which have become widespread
across Latin America and are now extending outside the region. Conditional transfer programs typically link monetary transfers to human capital investment, generally
education, health or a combination of both. These transfer programs are considered innovative because they condition the receipt of monetary benefits on such behaviors as
regular school attendance and preventive clinic visits. Effectively they are a subsidy
to schooling and health, reducing the shadow price of human capital acquisition. We

focus here primarily on a case study of Progresa (the Education, Health and Nutrition Program), a Mexican anti-poverty program which has served as a model for the implementation of conditional programs in other countries, and on which most evidence exists on impacts. We also review results from the newer conditional cash transfer programs. The chapter thus analyzes what we know about the success of conditional cash transfer programs as a mechanism for reducing poverty and identifies what research which is still needed in order for broader conclusions to be drawn.

Keywords

conditional cash transfer programs, evaluation

JEL classification: O12, O15

1. Introduction

The design of social policies which encourage human capital accumulation among the poor, thus breaking the transmission of poverty from one generation to the next is a basic concern for development economists. Roughly speaking, these policies can be classified as either "supply side" interventions which improve the infrastructure or quality of education or "demand-side" interventions which provide incentives for poor parents to keep their children longer in school. We analyze in this chapter the development and evaluation of a new genre of social programs termed conditional cash transfer programs which have become widespread across Latin America. Conditional transfer programs typically link monetary transfers to human capital investment, generally education, health or a combination of both. They now represent a major instrument for combating poverty in Latin America, an area noted for high inequality and high rates of extreme poverty. Furthermore, their popularity is spreading outside the region. A number of other countries including Turkey and Cambodia now also have conditional programs, and others such as Indonesia are in the planning/implementation stages. The programs are also under consideration in Africa and a pilot program is underway in New York City.

These transfer programs are considered innovative because of their conditionality, e.g. they condition the receipt of monetary benefits on such behaviors as regular school attendance and preventive clinic visits. Effectively they are a subsidy to schooling and health, reducing the shadow price of human capital acquisition (Becker, 1999). The programs typically thus have a price or substitution effect due to the conditionality and an income effect from the increase in household income. While most research focuses on the conditionality aspect, the programs also are likely to have an important effect on alleviating current poverty. Most also give the cash directly to the mother and thus may have a bargaining effect as well. Note that from an economist's point of view, conditioning might not necessarily seem welfare enhancing, although there are economic arguments which would justify conditionality, which we discuss in more detail in the chapter. The popularity of conditional transfer programs may also reflect that governments find the programs more attractive politically than unconditional transfers; they may be less likely to be viewed as a "handout."

The programs have generally had little relation to supply or quality improvements in schools and health clinics, although some programs have provided money for supply side interventions in order to reduce potential reductions in quality due to crowding. While improving quality of public education and health institutions has traditionally been viewed to be outside the scope of conditional cash programs, the issues of how quality may limit or constrain the impacts of the programs is an area beginning to receive more attention.

We focus here primarily on a case study of Progresa (the Education, Health and Nutrition Program), a Mexican anti-poverty program which has served as a model for the implementation of conditional programs in other countries including Colombia, Nicaragua, Honduras, and Jamaica, and on which most evidence exists on impacts. Progresa conditions cash transfers on children's enrollment and regular school attendance as well as clinic attendance. Besides its design the program has become noteworthy because it was subject to a large scale rigorous evaluation effort in rural areas which included an experimental design (Krueger, 2002). While experimental designs to evaluate social programs have become more common within the United States, they are still relatively rare within the developing world. The Progresa evaluation has also become a model for the evaluation of other conditional programs in the region, some of which also have experimental designs. In the evaluation design of Progresa, a subset of eligible communities was randomly assigned to a treatment (320 communities) or control (186 communities) group to receive benefits about 18 months later. A number of impact studies were produced taking advantage of the experimental design which we review. We also review results from the newer conditional cash transfer programs.

The chapter analyzes what we know about the success or potential success of conditional cash transfer programs as a mechanism for reducing poverty. We discuss the limitations of conditional cash transfer programs and identify areas where additional research is needed. Note that because of the objective of reducing the poverty of the next generation, the evaluation of conditional cash programs would ideally be long-term, e.g. from early childhood through adulthood. Progresa, the oldest of the conditional cash transfer programs has impacts results based only on 6 years, clearly insufficient for measuring long term impacts. Thus, many questions as to the long term impacts of conditional cash transfer programs will necessarily need to be studied in the future.

The chapter is organized as follows. In Section 2, we present theory of the potential effects of conditional cash transfer programs. Sections 3, 4 and 5 present the design, evaluation and results of the Progresa program. Section 6 reviews the initial findings of conditional cash programs in other countries. Section 7 concludes with some lessons learned from the evaluation of conditional cash transfer programs and areas for future research.

2. Theoretical considerations of conditional programs

The main innovation of conditional cash transfer programs is the linking of benefits to human capital investment, particularly of children. The aim is thus to alleviate current poverty through monetary transfers as well as future poverty, by increasing human capital of children.[1] In this section, we discuss the main effects of conditional cash transfer programs from the point of view of economic theory. We focus the analysis on school subsidies, which constitute the largest fraction of the monetary benefits provided under these programs.

---

[1] An area of some debate, which we retake later on in the text, is the extent to which the program can fulfill both objectives e.g. of reducing both current and future poverty simultaneously.

2.1. Income and substitution effects

In order to discuss the income and substitution effects of conditional cash transfers, we present a two-period model extending Behrman, Parker and Todd (2007). In the first period of the model, individuals are children and can allocate their time between leisure, market work, home production, and school. In the second period, they are adults and can choose between leisure, market work, and home production. Market work in the second period has a wage that depends on the time spent in school in the first period, and work in home production in the second period has a productivity that depends on time spent in school in the first period. Let C_1 and C_2 denote consumption of the individual as a child and as an adult,[2] L_1 and L_2 denote leisure, h_1 and h_2 denote work in home production, S amount of schooling, T the time endowment, W_1 the child wage rate, $W_2(S)$ the adult wage rate, $M_1(h_1)$ the child labor contribution to house production, $M_2(h_2, S)$ the adult labor contribution to house production, and B transfers to the individual from parents and other family members. We assume that M_1 and M_2 are increasing in labor at a decreasing rate. Also, let t_1 denote the amount of time spent working in period 1 and t_2 the amount of time spent working in period 2. β denotes the discount rate and p_s the subsidy paid for amount of schooling attended. We assume diminishing marginal utility of consumption and of leisure in each period and diminishing marginal productivity of schooling on second period marginal product of labor in house production and on the second period wage. We also assume that consumption and leisure are normal goods in both periods. There is no direct utility from schooling, which solely provides a technology for increasing the second period income.

Individuals maximize the objective function

$$U_1(C_1, L_1) + \beta U_2(C_2, L_2),$$

subject to the constraints

$$S + t_1 + h_1 + L_1 \leqslant T,$$
$$t_2 + h_2 + L_2 \leqslant T,$$
$$C_1 + C_2/(1+r) = B + p_s S + t_1 W_1 + M_1(h_1) + t_2 W_2(S)/(1+r)$$
$$+ M_2(h_2, S)/(1+r).$$

An optimality condition that holds in any interior solution of the problem is

$$MU_{L1} - MU_{C1} p_s = \beta MU_{C2}\big(t_2 W_2'(S) + M_{2S}(h_2, S)\big),$$

or equivalently,

$$MU_{C1}(W_1 - p_s) = \beta MU_{C2}\big(t_2 W_2'(S) + M_{2S}(h_2, S)\big).$$

[2] Let $P_1 = P_2 = 1$.

The left-hand side is the cost of time spent in school, in term of monetary direct costs and foregone leisure (or equivalently, foregone earnings from work, since another optimality condition equates the marginal utility from leisure with the marginal utility in added consumption derived from work). The right-hand side is the marginal benefit of spending additional time in school, i.e. higher earnings as an adult.

The optimality condition discussed above shows that the subsidy affects the marginal costs of schooling in the same way as would a decrease in the child wage rate: the subsidy reduces the shadow wage (or relative value) of children's time in activities other than school.

The benefit to schooling depends on how much time the individual as an adult spends working either at the market or at home. Another optimality condition that holds in any solution to the problem above is

$$M_{2h}(h_2, S) = W_2(S).$$

If labor productivity in home production does not rise as rapidly as in the market with schooling, at least at the secondary school level and beyond, an implication of a school subsidy will be a reduction in the time spent in home production. If women dedicate more time to housework in the absence of subsidies, and if the marginal effect of schooling on labor productivity in housework is decreasing in the time devoted to housework, a result of school subsidies may be an increased participation of women relative to men in the labor market.[3]

A decrease in the direct costs of schooling, resulting from the subsidy, has both substitution and income effects. The substitution effect decreases the amount of time spent in leisure and working at home or in the market as a child and increases the amount of time spent in school. The income effect (an increase in life-time earnings) increases consumption of all normal goods, namely of leisure and consumption in the first and second periods. Thus, the net effect on childhood time spent in leisure in the first period is ambiguous. The net effect on time spent working and time spent in school is also, in principle, ambiguous. However, if the substitution effect on leisure dominates the income effect, then leisure in the first period will go down and time spent in nonleisure activities will go up. Because the subsidy increases the relative benefit of school relative to work, we expect that time spent in school will go up and time spent working will go down.

The optimality condition can be rewritten as a tangency condition

$$MU_{C1}/\beta MU_{C2} = \left(t_2 W_2'(S) + M_{2S}(h_2, S)\right)/(W_1 - p_s)$$

where the left-hand side gives us the slope of the indifference curves between present and future consumption for the child and the right-hand side gives us the slope of the frontier of the feasible consumption set. The model so far ignores the indivisibilities built in the program with respect to school subsidies. Consider a version of the model

---

[3] We thank T. Paul Schultz for bringing this point to our attention.

in which there is no proportional school subsidy (i.e. $p_s = 0$) but rather a subsidy p is paid to every child that obtains a level of education larger or equal than S_{min} and a subsidy of zero to every child that does not. Here S_{min} may represent the minimum mandatory attendance to receive the benefits of the program. The resource constraint of the individual is now

$$C_1 + C_2/(1+r) = B + pI(S) + t_1W_1 + M_1(h_1) + t_2W_2(S)/(1+r)$$
$$+ M_2(h_2)/(1+r),$$

where

$$I(S) = \begin{cases} 0 & \text{if } S < S_{min}, \\ 1 & \text{if } S = S_{min}. \end{cases}$$

There is a discontinuity now in the frontier of the feasible consumption set. This subsidy scheme will affect children differently according to the decisions regarding schooling before school subsidies were introduced. For children who were already receiving more than S_{min} units of education before the introduction of school subsidies, the program has only an income effect.[4] For children who were not receiving that level of education and who do not receive it either after the introduction of the subsidies, the program has neither an income nor a substitution effect. And for children who did not receive S_{min} units of education before the program but who do so after, there are both income and substitution effects. Given the heterogeneity of preferences and constraints, the extent to which the program has a significant impact on the human capital and work of children can only be determined through empirical analysis.

2.2. Bargaining effects

Note that it is not obvious why a government interested in increasing the welfare of the child would prefer school subsidies over unconditional transfers in the context of the simple model discussed above. Many might argue that conditionality requirements are paternalistic and therefore not necessarily welfare improving relative to unconditional transfers. One potential motivation for conditioning benefits is that there are some social returns to investing in education which are not reaped by the individual. A review of the literature, however, was unable to find empirical studies which demonstrated that social returns were significantly higher than private returns (see the discussion in Martinelli and Parker, 2003). An alternative motivation to condition transfers is the role of conditionality in implementing outcomes that are favorable to the child in the context of intrahousehold bargaining. For instance, unconditional transfers to the child may be counterweighed by a reduction in the resources transferred by family members to

---

[4] We are ignoring here for simplicity the fact that the frontier of the feasible consumption set may be non-linear.

the child. In fact, conditional cash transfer programs almost always specify the monetary benefits to be received by the mother of the household. This design feature was motivated by a growing social science literature which argues that resources under the control of women tend to have a greater impact on the well-being of children than resources under the control of men (see e.g. Thomas, 1990).

In order to discuss the bargaining effects of conditional cash transfers, we present in here a simple two-period model based on Martinelli and Parker (2003, 2004). We consider a family composed by a man, a woman and a child. There is a single consumption good. The man cares only about his own consumption and the consumption of the child; similarly, the woman cares only about her own consumption and that of the child. That is, from the point of view of the two adults, child's consumption is a public good. We have chosen this simple formulation as the paper focuses on the possibility of the adults disagreeing with respect to child consumption. Preferences of the man and the woman are given by the utility functions $U_m(C_m, C_k)$ and $U_f(C_f, C_k)$, respectively, where C_m, C_f and C_k are the (nonnegative) consumption levels of the man, the woman and the child.

In the first period, only the two adults consume. The man and the woman supply inelastically each T units of time in a labor market. The adults also decide how to allocate the child's time, T, between child labor and schooling, S. Finally, the adults decide how much to leave as a (nonnegative) bequest to the child, B. Wages for the three types of labor are equal to W_1, and the price of consumption goods is normalized to one. The first period budget constraint for the family is given by:

$$C_m + C_f + S + B \leqslant 3TW_1.$$

In the second period, only the child consumes. Besides any bequests from the parents, the child obtains a labor income given by $TW_2(S)$. The second period budget constraint is then:

$$C_k \leqslant B + TW_2(S).$$

Decisions about C_m, C_f, S and B are made by the two adults in the first period according to the Nash bargaining solution, that is maximizing

$$\left(U_f(C_f, C_k) - U_f^d\right)\left(U_m(C_m, C_k) - U_m^d\right),$$

where U_f^d and U_m^d represent the utilities the two adults would experience if they were unable to reach an agreement about household decisions. It may reflect what would happen if the marriage is dissolved or if the adults stay married but behave with respect to the household in a non-cooperative way (see e.g. Lundberg and Pollak, 1993).

Define S^* as the solution to $TW_2'(S) = 1$. This is the "efficient" level of schooling in terms of maximizing the family's lifetime income. From the first order conditions of the household problem, we obtain that any interior solution belongs to one of two cases. In the first case, $S < S^*$ and $C_k = TW_2(S)$. We refer to a family in this situation as bequest-constrained. In intuitive terms, a family in this situation would like to leave "negative bequests" to the child; since negative bequests are ruled out, the family instead sets schooling below the efficient level, or equivalently, sets child labor above the efficient level. In the second case, $S = S^*$ and $B \geqslant 0$. We refer to a family in this situation as bequest-unconstrained. In intuitive terms, adults leaving positive bequests are better off setting human capital investment at its efficient level as they can trade between bequests and investment (see the discussion in Becker and Murphy, 1988). We can expect the poorest families to be bequest-constrained, as a family is bequest-constrained if and only if $C_k \leqslant T W_2(S^*)$. It is immediate that, holding preferences constant, inefficiently low levels of human capital will be associated with poverty.

We now introduce in the model a government agency with a positive budget G. The agency has two available policies: it can either give G as an unconditional transfer to the adults, or it can provide a schooling subsidy p_s. In this last case, we assume that p_s is set so as to induce the family to choose schooling level of G/p_s. For a bequest-constrained family, the level of schooling corresponding to a conditional transfer is necessarily higher than that corresponding to an unconditional transfer since the former includes a substitution effect. Since for a bequest-constrained family $C_k = T W_2(S)$, we obtain that the child is better off with a conditional transfer. Indeed, under plausible conditions discussed by Martinelli and Parker (2003), the mother is also better off with conditional transfers. Intuitively, if the mother gives more weight than the father to the children's future consumption, conditioning transfers moves the solution to the family's bargaining problem in the direction of the mother's preferences. If the family is bequest-unconstrained, however, conditioning transfers makes every member of the family worse-off. Intuitively, in this case conditional transfers induce an inefficiently high level of schooling, which depresses the family's lifetime income.

2.3. Targeting effects

Gahvari and de Mattos (2007) argue that conditional cash transfer programs can be useful to implement redistribution without distortionary losses, using the combination of cash and in-kind transfers as a screening device. They consider a situation in which an indivisible good such as formal education can be provided in different qualities and people must decide which of the qualities to consume. In a similar situation, Besley and Coate (1991) have shown that some redistribution can be obtained if the state provides a low quality for free and charges a head tax, at the cost of some deadweight loss. Gahvari and de Mattos (2007) show that such deadweight loss can be avoided if the state can provide a tax rebate or conditional transfer to those consuming the lower quality good. Intuitively, without conditional transfers, the only instrument that the government has to achieve self-targeting is the quality of the publicly provided good, so the government is (generically) forced to provide a quality that is different from what would be optimal for the poor. Introducing conditional transfers provides the government one more instrument, so that in many cases there are combinations of good quality/conditional transfers that achieve self screening (in the sense of being undesirable for the non poor) and are efficient (in the sense that the poor would not be willing to accept an offer of increasing or decreasing the quality of the publicly provided good financed by a change in their net tax).

3. The Progresa program

3.1. Program description

Progresa began operating in 1997 and has grown quickly to become the principal anti-poverty strategy of the Mexican government, occupying about half the annual poverty budget. By the end of 2004, 5 million families were receiving benefits, corresponding to almost one fourth of the Mexican population (Appendix Table 1). Progresa conditions cash transfers on children's enrollment and regular school attendance as well as clinic attendance. The program also includes in-kind health benefits and nutritional supplements for children up to age five, and pregnant and lactating women.

The program thus provides benefits in education, health, and nutrition. Combining three different components e.g. education, health and nutrition in one program was aimed at creating synergies. For instance, children who suffer from malnutrition might be more likely to drop out of school or repeat years of school, which would imply that attempts to insure children go to school will be more effective if combined with adequate nutrition and health programs. There is, however, little direct evidence which has tested the hypothesis of synergies, nor was the evaluation or program design of Progresa designed to do so. Based on a review of the literature on the determinants of education, health and nutrition investments from around the world, Behrman (2000) suggests that synergies in Progresa might be substantial, particularly with regard to the impact of preschool nutrition on schooling outcomes.

3.1.1. Education

Under the education component, Progresa provides monthly educational grants; and monetary support or in-kind school supplies. Education grants are given for children under 22 years of age and enrolled in school between the third grade of primary and the third grade of senior high school (e.g. up until twelfth grade).[5] Originally, the program provided grants only for children between the third and ninth grade. In 2001, the grants were extended to senior high school. Table 1 shows the monthly grant levels available for children between the third grade and the twelfth grade in the first semester of 2006 (Appendix Table 2 provides the historical trends of benefits since the program initiated, grants are nominally adjusted for inflation every semester). Grants increase as children progress to higher grades and beginning at the junior high level, are slightly higher

---

[5] We refer to grades 1 through 6 as primary school (*primaria*), 7 through 9 as junior high school (*secundaria*) and 10 to 12 as senior high school (*media superior*) throughout the text.

Table 1
Cash benefits of Progresa (pesos per month, 2006)

	Boys	Girls
Primary School		
Grade 3	120	120
Grade 4	140	140
Grade 5	180	180
Grade 6	240	240
Middle School		
Grade 7	350	370
Grade 8	370	410
Grade 9	390	450
High School		
Grade 10	585	675
Grade 11	630	715
Grade 12	665	760
Fixed monthly nutrition grant per household		180 pesos
Support for adults aged 70 or more		250 pesos
Maximum household monthly transfer with no children in HS		1095 pesos
Maximum household monthly transfer with children in HS		1855 pesos

Note. Exchange rate: 11 pesos = $1US. Progresa also provides in-kind benefits including school supplies, medical consultations and nutritional supplements.

(by 10 to 15%) for girls than for boys. Higher grants for girls were originally motivated, according to Progresa, by the observation that in rural areas, girls tended to have a higher dropout rate than boys after finishing primary school. Thus, the higher grant levels were aimed at compensating for this lower achievement.[6]

In the first semester of 2006, the specific grant amounts range from $US11.00 (120 pesos) in the third grade of primary to about $US60 (665 pesos) for boys and $US69 (760 pesos) for girls in the third year of senior high school. For comparison, note that the minimum wage in Mexico was 48 pesos per day in 2006 (with some minor variations by region), corresponding to about 1060 pesos monthly for full time work (22 days). By senior high school then, the grant amounts represent about two thirds of a minimum wage. The grants are given every two months during the school calendar. To receive the grant parents must enroll their children in school and ensure regular attendance (i.e., students must have a minimum attendance rate of 85%, both monthly and annually). Failure to comply will lead to the loss of the benefit, at first temporarily, but eventually

[6] Nevertheless, as shown in Behrman, Sengupta and Todd (2000) and Parker and Pederzini (2001), actual attainment of girls in terms of years of completed schooling in rural areas is quite similar to that of boys. While girls tend to have lower enrollment, boys tend to have higher repetition rates than girls.

permanently. Program rules allow students to fail each grade once, but students are not allowed to repeat a grade twice, at that point education benefits are discontinued permanently for the youth. Note this allows a student theoretically to receive two years of grants for the same grade for each grade in which the student enrolls. Enrollment and attendance are verified before grants are paid.[7] All monetary grants are given to the mother of the family with the exception of scholarships for upper-secondary school, which can be received by the youth themselves.

3.1.2. Health and nutrition

The health care component provides basic health care for all members of the family, with some emphasis on preventive health care (Table 2). These services are provided by public health institutions in Mexico including the Secretary of Health and the Mexican Social Security Institute. The nutritional component includes a fixed monetary transfer equal to about $US16.50 (180 pesos) monthly (specified to be for "improved food consumption" although Progresa does not monitor the expenditures of beneficiaries), as well as nutritional supplements, which are principally targeted to children between the ages of four months and two years, and pregnant and lactating women. They are also given to children aged 2 to 4 if any signs of malnutrition are detected. Mothers

Table 2
Interventions in the basic health services package: Progresa

- Basic hygiene
- Family planning
- Prenatal, childbirth and post-natal care
- Supervision of nutrition and children's growth
- Vaccinations
- Prevention and treatment of outbreaks of diarrhea
- Anti-parasite treatment
- Prevention and treatment of respiratory infections
- Prevention and control of tuberculosis
- Prevention and control of high blood pressure and diabetes mellitus
- Accident prevention and first-aid for injuries
- Community training for health care self-help

Source: Oportunidades, 2004 (Program Operating Rules) http://www.oportunidades.gob.mx.

---

[7] Operationally, there are two basic forms which verify enrollment and regular attendance. The E1 form is given to parents, who take it to the specific school where each child is to be registered to be signed by a school teacher/director to certify enrollment at the beginning of each school year. The E2 form, for monthly attendance records, is sent directly to the schools with names of registered children taken from the E1 forms and then forwarded from the schools to the Progresa offices, which process the information before sending out the corresponding transfers.

Table 3
Annual frequency of health care visits required by Progresa

Age group	Frequency of check-ups
Children	
Less than 4 months	3 check-ups: 7 and 28 days, and at 2 months
4 months to 24 months	8 check-ups: 4, 6, 9, 12, 15, 18, 21 and 24 months with 1 additional monthly weight and height check-up
2 to 4 years old	3 check-ups a year: 1 every 4 months
5 to 16 years old	2 check-ups a year: 1 every 6 months
Women	
Pregnancy	5 check-ups: prenatal period
Post-pregnancy	2 check-ups: 1 immediately following birth and 1 during lactation
Adults and youths	
17 to 60 years old	One check-up per year
Over 60 years old	One check-up per year

Source: Oportunidades, 2004 (Program Operating Rules) http://www.oportunidades.gob.mx.

visit the clinic at least once a month (more if they are pregnant or have small children) and pick up nutritional supplements monthly. To receive the fixed health and nutrition transfer, all members of beneficiary families must adhere to a regular schedule of health clinic visits. The calendar of visits varies by the age and gender of each individual (Table 3).[8] Beneficiaries (generally mothers) are also required to attend monthly health and nutrition talks at the clinic on topics such as nutrition, hygiene, infectious diseases, immunization, family planning, and chronic diseases detection and prevention. Under the recent extension of education grants to the high school level, high school students are also required to attend (separate) talks on topics aimed towards adolescents.

3.1.3. Size of monetary transfers

Progresa has a maximum limit of monthly benefits for each family equivalent in 2006 to about $US100 for families with children in primary and junior high school and $US175 for those with (at least one) children in senior high school. The maximum amount of benefits is intended to reduce any incentive the program might provide to have additional children. Benefits are provided directly to the female beneficiary by wire transfer

---

[8] Like the E1 form in the case of education, the schedule of clinic visits is entered on an S1 form, which is brought to the clinic by the beneficiary, ensuring that a record of attendance by household members is kept at the clinic. Each clinic receives an S2 form every two months that contains the names of all individuals in beneficiary families. The S2 form registers compliance or non-compliance by the household and is filled out by a nurse or doctor at the health unit every two months, certifying whether family members visited the health units as required. This form is then sent back to Progresa and processed before receipt of the bimonthly health and nutrition transfer.

in offices and modules which are installed nearby the communities. In some urban areas, benefits are transferred directly to beneficiary bank accounts.

The average monthly transfers during the twelve-month period of 2003 (the last year of the rural evaluation survey) was 309 pesos monthly per beneficiary family or about $US27.50. Payments are higher during non-summer months when education grants are received in addition to the fixed nutrition transfer.

3.1.4. Targeting and continued program eligibility[9]

The program is means tested with an elaborate targeting mechanism, which varies somewhat between rural and urban areas. In both rural and urban areas, the first stage of targeting is geographic, using aggregate local indicators to select poor rural communities and urban blocks. To identify household level beneficiaries, in rural areas, Progresa carries out a survey of socio-economic conditions for all households denominated the ENCASEH, in the selected communities. With this data, discriminant analysis is used to identify eligible households from non-eligible households. In essence, the program makes an initial classification of poverty depending on a household's per capita income. Using this initial classification, a discriminant analysis is carried out relating this initial classification to a number of other household characteristics including dwelling characteristics in the household, dependency ratios, ownership of durable goods, animals and land, and the presence of disabled individuals. According to the predicted scores, a final classification of households as poor (eligible) or non-poor is made.[10] Individuals sign their acceptance as program beneficiaries and receive registration forms for schools and the family clinic. Nearly all selected families enrolled in the program in rural areas, so that self-selection in program participation is not a significant evaluation issue in the first years of the evaluation. However, Alvarez, Devoto and Winter (2006) analyze the dropout program in the first five years of Progresa and show that relatively poorer beneficiaries are less likely to dropout, which they attribute to program conditionality potentially acting as a screening device.

In urban areas, the targeting includes an element of self-selection where individuals are required to apply for the program at modules set up in poor urban areas throughout the country. As in rural areas, basic socio-economic levels are assessed, for those

---

[9] A number of add-ons to the program are occurring. *Jóvenes con Oportunidades* was added in 2003, which extends program benefits past the end of upper high school. In 2006, a pension for the elderly was added to the program, providing a monthly payment to each adult age 70 or over who is part of an *Oportunidades* family, equal in 2006 to 250 pesos monthly (about US$22). The impact of these new components have not yet been analyzed in the Progresa evaluations.

[10] Once beneficiary households have been identified, an assembly is arranged in the community where the list of selected families is made public. An interesting third stage in the targeting is that community leaders have the opportunity to express reservations about any of the families selected and potentially remove families from the list who are not deemed to be poor. While hard evidence is unavailable about the importance of this last stage, program officials claim that this last step rarely resulted in significant changes to the list of beneficiary families.

that pass this initial qualifying test at the module, a home visit is programmed to verify socio-economic information and based upon this information, a similar discriminant
analysis as in rural areas is used to decide whether the household is eligible for Progresa. The issue of self-selection is important from the beginning in the urban program
evaluation, as many eligible households do not apply. (See Coady and Parker, 2005 for
more description.)

Once families become beneficiaries, they remain in the program for three years
without further verification of their economic status. However, after three years, a re-
interview takes place, at which point, either their beneficiary status is renewed or they
are transitioned to a scheme of partial benefits (called EDA, Esquema Diferenciado de
Apoyos, which includes only secondary and high school educational grants but excludes
primary school scholarships and cash transfers for food).

3.2. Discussion

Section 2 illustrated that the general impact of conditional transfer programs is to increase time spent in school and reduce time spent in work, broadly defined. It is worth
elaborating however on other potential impacts.

While the conditionality of the program should unambiguously affect enrollment,
the potential impact on passing grades is more ambiguous. While children who fail
the same grade twice during the cycle of grants are permanently excluded from the
Program, Progresa does allows children to fail each grade once (e.g. for each grade
they can repeat the year and receive the grant). This taken at face value might imply
there are incentives to fail some (or each) grades, so as to increase the years receiving
grants. However, this incentive must be balanced against the point that passing a grade
leads to a higher grant received during the next grade, as well as that the opportunity
cost of attending school presumably increases with age. Clearer incentives might derive
from not permitting grants to be received in two years for the same grade, however,
the high failure rates in Mexico during primary school (as high as 30 percent in some
grades) suggest that this might be too harsh, and possibly in the longer term lead to
lower schooling impacts.

The maximum benefit of the program also presumably complicates the modeling
of the program. The maximum benefit was set as a disincentive for families to have
additional children, although note that children do not receive a grant until grade 3
(around age 8) and so the discount rate on these expected benefits would presumably
have to be low to motivate families to have additional children. Under the initial program
with grants offered only up until the 9th grade, about 10 percent of families would run
up against the maximum benefit, e.g. in these families if all children were enrolled
in school, at least 1 child would not receive the stipulated grant level. Relative to a
program with no maximum benefit, the maximum benefit might lead families to send

fewer children to school, since the marginal benefit for the last children sent would be less than the grant amount.[11]

This was further complicated by the introduction of grants at the senior high school level (10 to 12th grades) in 2001 where families with children enrolled at this level are subject to a higher maximum benefit than families with children only in primary or lower secondary school. Note that this endogenizes to some extent the maximum monetary benefit families are eligible to receive.

With respect to work, while, as indicated by the model, the program is likely to reduce time spent in work of children, the potential impacts on adult work are more ambiguous. An unconditional income transfer, through the income effect, would presumably as in other contexts reduce the incentives to work. Nevertheless, with children likely to spend less time in work, the conditionality effect could increase the time adults spend in work. The structure of program benefits, at least for the first three years of benefits, unlike traditional welfare benefits, does not penalize work. However, after three years, a re-interview takes place, at which point, either their beneficiary status is renewed or they are transitioned to a scheme of partial benefits which lasts for another three years before benefits are discontinued. Thus, particularly in the longer term, it remains possible that the program may reduce work incentives in beneficiary households in an effort to maintain beneficiary status.

4. The Progresa evaluation: Design, data and empirical issues

In this section we present the initial evaluation design in rural areas, based on the randomized design carried out where a subset of communities eligible to receive Progresa was randomly assigned to a treatment (320 communities) or control (186 communities) group. The control group under this design, however began to receive treatment about 18 months after the experiment began. A new comparison group of communities never receiving benefits was brought into the evaluation design in 2003. Throughout this chapter, we will refer to original treatment households as T1998 (e.g. in treatment communities eligible for benefits in 1998), original control households as T2000 (treatment communities eligible for benefits in 2000), and the new comparison group as C2003 (eligible communities never receiving benefits by 2003).

---

[11] When a family runs up against the maximum benefit in a particular bimester, the Program "reduces" the amount of each child's grant so that the sum is equal to the maximum benefit, (e.g. rather than indicating that one child is not receiving a grant). Some studies have used this program feature to argue that this provides variation in the amount of grants for students in the same age (de Janvry and Sadoulet, 2006; Dubois, de Janvry and Sadoulet, 2004) which might be used to estimate how program impacts vary with changes in grant amounts. However, a family might strategize by for instance by sending the "last" child to work and not to school, so that this sort of variation seems a bit suspect.

4.1. Design and data collection

The randomized trial evaluation of Progresa was carried out in the initial stages of its operation, which resulted in a couple of clear advantages. First, the small scale of the program in its initial phases implied the potential ethical issue of maintaining eligible households out of the program was less binding. E.g. given a limited budget, many eligible households (indeed, in the early program stages, millions of households were in this category) could not receive program benefits, so that randomization was arguably an equitable method of assigning benefits in the context of limited resources (although this argument was not made publicly in Mexico at the time). A second advantage is that the early evaluation allowed the quick production of a number of studies on the program, which in turn, made possible policy changes in the program while the program was still continuing to grow and evolve (Parker and Teruel, 2005).

There is unfortunately little written evidence on how precisely the randomization was done.[12] The available government documentation suggests that a universe of potential treatment communities and control communities was randomly selected from the overall universe of communities in high poverty eligible for Progresa. From these two "sample" universes, a treatment sample of 320 communities was selected and a sample of 186 control communities were randomly selected. The communities are from seven states which were among the first states to receive Progresa benefits. Larger communities were apparently given less weight in the sampling scheme.

The best evidence on the quality of the randomization derives from analyses based on the baseline data, for instance whether there are any significant differences in the distribution of characteristics between treatment and control groups, or regressions attempting to predict treatment or control status. Behrman and Todd (1999) compare characteristics in the treatment and control group for a wide variety of indicators, prior to program implementation. In general, they conclude that at the community level, the level at which the randomization was done, treatment and control groups appear to be random. Nevertheless, at the individual level, where most of the analysis was done due to the larger sample size, they find some generally small but significant differences in pre-program characteristics between the treatment and control group for a number of different characteristics.[13]

Treatment beneficiary household began to receive benefits in May of 1998, whereas control households began to receive benefits in December of 1999. However, prior to beginning to receive benefits, households were informed they had been deemed eligible

---

[12] The lack of documentation by government officials may reflect their perception of the controversial nature of carrying out an evaluation with an experimental design. In fact when the results of the initial evaluation studies were made public in 2000, a number of Mexico City newspapers ran articles criticizing the "unethical" nature of the evaluation.

[13] In fact, at the individual level, a much larger number of significant differences exist than would be expected by chance alone (32 percent of 187 characteristics studied). Behrman and Todd argue that this may in part reflect the large sample size at the individual level (e.g. 24,000 households and more than 100,000 individuals) and thus the "tendency to reject even minor differences."

by the Program, it is unfortunately not clear either for the T1998 or T2000 group the exact date they were informed. The duration of the experiment lasted approximately 18 months, as measured from the time the first families in T1998 began to receive benefits to when the first households in the T2000 group began to receive benefits. During this period, the program grew quite quickly, from less than 400,000 households in 1997, its first year of operation, to more than 2 million households in over 50,000 communities by the year 2000. This rapid growth created a scenario where many of the original control communities began literally to become "surrounded" by communities (presumably similar to themselves) receiving program benefits.

The evaluation entered a second stage in 2003, with the introduction to the evaluation sample of a new comparison group, composed of communities who had never received benefits. Households in 152 communities selected on the basis of matching to the original treatment communities were added to the sample for a new follow-up round carried out in 2003. The 152 matched localities were chosen from a pool of 14,000 potential matches that had not yet begun to receive benefits. Matching was based on locality-level information on the average characteristics of households in each locality from the 2000 Mexican Census data, including demographics of household residents, characteristics of the dwelling and community characteristics as well as distance to schools (see Todd, 2004 for more details). Given the communities are drawn from different geographic areas from the treatment group, they may experience different local area effects (labor market conditions, quality of schooling, quality of health clinics, prices) that may affect the evaluation outcomes of interest.

In an effort to have "pre-program" data on households in the new comparison group, the fieldwork included a retrospective questionnaire for those in the new comparison group on basic characteristics in 1997. This retrospective questionnaire was unfortunately not applied to the original evaluation group, so that comparisons of pre-program 1997 information between the original evaluation group and the new comparison group use actual 1997 information for the original evaluation (T1998 and T2000) and retrospective information for the new C2003 comparison group. Recall bias may thus unfortunately affect the estimated propensity scores as well as the impact estimations. An additional point is that differences in outcomes may suffer from sample selection if households in the comparison group who in 2003 answered the questionnaire retrospectively differ from those living there in 1997.

The new comparison communities were chosen based on a matching of community characteristics between the original evaluation communities and the set of communities not yet incorporated into the program. Not surprisingly then, comparisons based on community level characteristics show few significant differences (Attanasio and DiMaro, 2004). At the individual level, however, the story is different. Table 4 presents general characteristics based on data on 1997 characteristics between the groups T1998–T2000 and C2003 groups. (Comparisons between the groups based on the after program 2003 data are contaminated by program impacts.) Nearly all of the individual characteristics presented in the table show significant differences between the original evaluation group and the new comparison group. In particular, along a num-

Table 4

Differences between original treatment group and new comparison group in 1997

	T1998, T2000	C2003		
	Mean	Mean	Difference	p-value
HH, spouse characteristics				
Age of household head	46.90	43.28	3.63	0.00
Age of spouse	40.30	37.86	2.44	0.00
Gender of household head	0.89	0.86	0.03	0.00
Hh head indigenous	0.34	0.27	0.08	0.00
Spouse indigenous	0.28	0.21	0.07	0.00
Years schooling HH head	2.70	4.50	−1.80	0.00
Years schooling spouse	2.68	4.47	−1.79	0.00
Employed HH head	0.88	0.91	−0.03	0.00
Employed spouse	0.12	0.18	−0.07	0.00
Demographic				
Children 0 to 5	0.85	1.30	−0.44	0.00
Children 6 to 21	1.05	0.95	0.10	0.00
Women 20 to 39	0.65	0.63	0.02	0.05
Women 40 to 59	0.37	0.34	0.03	0.00
Women 60+	0.20	0.27	−0.07	0.00
Men 20 to 39	1.28	1.22	0.06	0.00
Men 40 to 59	0.37	0.35	0.02	0.05
Men 60+	0.21	0.27	−0.06	0.00
Dwelling charact.				
# Rooms	1.84	1.66	0.18	0.00
Electricity in HH	0.73	0.70	0.03	0.00
Water in HH	0.37	0.45	−0.08	0.00
Dirt floor	0.59	0.65	−0.06	0.00
Room material (inferior)	0.72	0.70	0.02	0.011
Wall material (inferior)	0.16	0.15	0.01	0.048
Own animals	0.38	0.26	0.12	0.00
Own land	0.63	0.45	0.17	0.00
Score	2.56	2.51	0.05	0.04
Total HH income	1146.86	2051.93	−905.06	0.00
Durable goods		0		
Blender	0.34	0.27	0.06	0.00
Refrigerator	0.15	0.14	0.02	0.01
Gas stove	0.31	0.31	0	0.877
Radio	0.63	0.52	0.12	0.00
Television	0.46	0.37	0.10	0.00
Washer	0.05	0.03	0.02	0.00
Car	0.02	0.03	−0.01	0.08
Truck	0.08	0.05	0.03	0.00

Source: ENCASEH for T1998 and T2000 and ENCEL 2003 retrospective questionnaire for C2003.

ber of dimensions, the new comparison group appears to be less poor than the original treatment group. The table makes clear the inappropriateness of simple comparisons between the original sample and this new 2003 comparison group for obtaining impacts and the need for some non-experimental approach to account for these differences.

We turn now to the data collection. The data collection carried out in the rural evaluation has been relatively extensive and now includes seven rounds of the evaluation survey. In each of the survey rounds, all households in each community were interviewed. The first data available for the original evaluation sample (T1998 and T2000) is the Survey of Socio-Economic Characteristics (ENCASEH), carried out in 1997, applied to households in eligible communities for the purpose of selecting households eligible for the Program. This data contains information on household demographics and composition, child schooling, labor force behavior, income, durable goods and assets including agricultural assets. This data has proved useful as a baseline survey, in part because it was carried out before any households might have been informed they would be beneficiaries.

The follow-up Evaluation Surveys ENCEL surveys were carried out approximately every 6 months between the fall of 1998 and the end of 2000, for a total of 5 after program rounds during the first phase of the evaluation. These household surveys focused mainly on socio-economic information, e.g. including demographic information, a schooling module, a labor module, a health module with self-reported health indicators and clinic/hospital attendance history, expenditures, income, and assets information. For most after program rounds, identical or similar modules were applied through the rounds, facilitating the comparison of impacts over time. For a small sub-sample, mainly children, some anthropometrics, e.g. weight and height were collected.[14]

A final ENCEL follow up round, which included the addition of the new comparison group to the sample, was carried out in the fall of 2003. This last round contains the most extensive information of the survey, with a number of biological and educational tests not previously applied, including cognitive and behavioral tests applied to young children and their mothers, as well as achievement tests applied to adolescents. Additionally, surveys of prices, school characteristics, and medical clinics were carried out. Appendix Table 3 provides a summary of the information available for the different rounds of the evaluation survey. Note that administrative information on who is a beneficiary and the amounts of benefits received are available from the beginning of the Program for those in the evaluation sample. Table 5 provides a time-line on the evaluation design and data collection.[15]

---

[14] Fieldwork for the collection of these anthropometric measures was done at different times and by different teams than the ENCEL survey, which appears to have complicated somewhat the use of the information (see Behrman and Hoddinott, 2005 for some discussion).

[15] The first generation of Progresa evaluation studies was coordinated by the International Food Policy Research Institute, lasting between 1998 and 2000. Since 2000, however, the Progresa evaluation has been coordinated by a Mexican institute, the Institute for Public Health (Instituto Nacional de Salud Publica – INSP) in Cuernavaca as well as an evaluation committee composed of national (Mexican) as well

Table 5
Time-line for Progresa rural evaluation and data sources

	Fall 1997	March 1998	May 1998	Nov. 1998	May 1999	Nov. 1999
(1) ENCASEH survey to determine program eligibility	X					
(2) Experimental design (randomization) 506 communities, 320 T1998, 186 T2000	X					
(4) Treatment (T1998) begins to receive benefits			X			
(5) Follow-up ENCEL		X		X	X	X

	Jan. 2000	May 2000	Nov. 2000	Oct. 2003
(5) Follow-up ENCEL		X	X	X
(6) Control group (T2000) begins to receive benefits	X			
(7) New comparison group added (C2003) to sample 152 new rural communities				X

Definitions: T1998 = original treatment communities under experimental design, began receiving benefits in May 1998.
T2000 = original control communities under experimental design, began receiving benefits in January 2000.
C2003 = new matched comparison communities never receiving benefits before 2003.
Source: Oportunidades, 2004. Nota metodologica de la muestra rural.

The collection of data on all households in all of the selected communities has the advantage of providing information on both eligible households and non-eligible households. This, in principal allows the use of non-eligible households as a potential control group under impact estimators such as regression discontinuity. However, the definition of who is eligible for the program has evolved over time. The initial eligibility criteria was established based on the ENCASEH information from 1997. Under this criteria, approximately 50 percent of all households in T1998 were declared eligible for the program in the original evaluation sample, informed and began to receive benefits by early 1998.[16] Nevertheless, shortly thereafter, the Program perceived that the selection mechanism was excluding elderly households with few children in school age, and an adjustment, called a "densification" was carried out. This densification increased the

as international researchers. All databases, questionnaire and other documentation are publicly available at http://evaluacion.oportunidades.gob.mx/evaluacion.

[16] Once households are declared eligible, there is an "incorporation ceremony" at which households are informed they have been selected as eligible and where they sign a form agreeing to be beneficiaries. The receipt of monetary benefits generally starts several months later, however, although arguably from the moment of incorporation, households become beneficiaries. Note that for some variables, such as school enrollment or attendance, given program rules, one would expect behavior to change once households are aware they are beneficiaries. For others, such as food expenditures, one might not expect behavior changes until actual transfers begin.

Table 6
Number of total households in evaluation sample, eligible households and beneficiary households in the Progresa evaluation

	Commu-nities	House-holds	Eligible house-holds (under 1997 eligibility criteria)	Eligible households under new densified criteria adopted in 1998	Households incorporated in 1998	Households incorporated by 2000	Households incorpo-rated by 2003
Treatment group (T1998)	320	14,856	7837	11,623	8009	8478	11,387
Control group (T2000)	186	9221	4682	7173	0	6134	7262
New control group (C2003)	152	6768	6218		0	0	0

Source: Author's calculations using 1997 ENCASEH and ENCEL surveys from 1998, 2000 and 2003.

percentage of eligible households in the selected communities to a total of 78 percent by the fall of 1998. (Because of operational errors, many of these "densified" house-holds did not actually begin to receive benefits until much later.) Additionally, after three years families are re-interviewed at which time non-poor households can solicit incorporation, providing an opportunity for additional households to be incorporated at that point. Table 6 shows the number and distribution of eligible households, as well as the percentage of those receiving benefits over time. Given the changes in eligibility and numbers of households receiving benefits, many of the evaluation studies concentrate on the comparison of households initially chosen to be eligible to receive benefits in 1997, which is a clean definition of program participation.

4.2. Estimators of the evaluation

In this subsection we present the main estimators used in the first and second generation studies of the impacts of Progresa. Beginning with some standard notation: Let Y_1 denote the outcome with treatment, and Y_0 denote the outcome for persons without treatment. The gain to the individual of moving from Y_0 to Y_1, we can denote as Δ. Let $D = 1$ if persons receive treatment, $D = 0$ if not. Let X denote other characteristics used as conditioning variables and let $P(X) = \Pr(D = 1 \mid X)$.

The typical parameter estimated in the literature is the impact of treatment on the treated, e.g.

$$TT = E(\Delta \mid X, D = 1)E(Y_1 - Y_0) \mid X, D = 1)$$
$$= E(Y_1 \mid X, D = 1) - E(Y_0) \mid X, D = 1).$$

Normally, one has data on Y_1 for those who participate in the program and data on Y_0 for those who do not participate but do not have Y_0 for participants. A randomized design solves the evaluation problem under the assumption that $E(Y_0 \mid D = 0)$ is a good approximation of $E(Y_0 \mid D = 1)$, that is the control group provides a good estimation of what would have happened to the treatment group in the absence of treatment.

To the extent possible, the initial Progresa evaluation papers use double difference methods, in order to control for any pre-program differences in the impact variables of interest (Behrman and Todd, 1999). When relevant impact variables were not available in the baseline, cross-sectional estimators are generally used to estimate program impacts. That is, the estimator is based on comparing differences between the treatment and control group after program implementation.

The *cross-sectional estimator* assumes:

$$E\big(Y_{0t} \mid P(X), D = 1\big) = E\big(Y_{0t} \mid P(X), D = 0\big) \tag{CS.1}$$

at some post program time period t and for some subset of characteristics X.

The *difference-in-difference estimator* requires longitudinal (or repeated cross section data) on program participants and nonparticipants. Let t and t' be two time periods, one before the program start date and one after. Y_{0t} is the outcome observed at time t. The main condition needed to justify the application of the estimator is:

$$E\big(Y_{0t} - Y_{0t'} \mid P(X), D = 1\big) = E\big(Y_{0t} - Y_{0t'} \mid P(X), D = 0\big) \tag{DID.1}$$

where t is a post-program time period and t' a pre-program time period.

The standard equation used to estimate double difference impact estimates in almost all of the initial reports is of the following type:

$$Y_{itc} = \alpha_0 + \alpha_1 R_t + \alpha_2 T_{ic} + \alpha_3^* T_{ic} R_t + \sum_{j=1}^{J} \beta_j X_{jitc} + \varepsilon_{itc}$$

where Y_{itc} reflects the impact variable of interest, R_t refers to the round of the EN-CEL; T_{ic} refers to whether the individual/household (i) lives in a treatment or control community (c); X_{jitc} refers to the vector of j control observed characteristics for individual/household i in period t in community c; ε_{itc} is an error term assumed to be equally distributed across individuals/households; The equation assumes only 2 rounds of the evaluation survey (before and after), although in practice additional rounds are often used.[17]

Note that this framework provides double difference estimators of the impact of Progresa. The coefficient α_2 is expected to be statistically insignificant from 0 and provides an indication of whether pre-program differences exist between the treatment

---

[17] Note that in specifications which use the amount of benefits households receive or other measures of program benefits which vary within households over time, an individual/household fixed effect can be added to the specification. See Rubalcava, Teruel and Thomas (2006) and Behrman and Hoddinott (2005).

group and the control group. The coefficient α_3^* provides an estimate of the differences between the treatment and control group in the relevant round after program implementation relative to α_2. This framework extends to allowing additional interaction terms between R and T to analyze how the estimated impacts might differ over time.

When only data after the program are available, as was the case for a number of indicators such as consumption, the regression equation simplifies with α_2 capturing the direct impact of the program in the following equation under the assumption that pre-program differences are not significantly different from zero (although this may be questionable given evidence by Behrman and Todd described above):

$$Y_{ic} = \alpha_0 + \alpha_2 T_{ic} + \sum_{j=1}^{J} \beta_j X_{jic} + \varepsilon_{ic}.$$

As the above discussion implies, the most frequent variable used to measure program impact is the simple treatment/control dummy, with most analyses restricting attention to the sample eligible for the program. This estimator provides an estimate of the "intent to treat" estimator. When using the initial eligibility definition, most households (96 percent) did in the beginning of the program participate, so that, for this eligibility definition there are few differences between an intent to treat estimator and a treatment on the treated estimator.[18]

With the original control group receiving benefits as of 2000 and the addition of the non-experimental comparison group, estimation of longer run program impacts rely on non-experimental estimators, which generally compare the original treatment group with the new comparison group, which provides an estimate of the impact of receiving benefits for 5.5 years versus never receiving benefits. The studies using this comparison we term "second generation" Progresa studies, because of the non-experimental nature of the selection of the new comparison group. Mainly matching estimators have been used (see Heckman, Ichimura and Todd, 1997).

The second generation studies concentrate on estimating the *mean impact of treatment on the treated* by using only those persons/households who actually participated in the program, although as in the first phase evaluation, one could estimate an intent to treat parameter by using all individuals potentially eligible for the program, as is done by Angelucci, Attanasio and Shaw (2004) in their study of the effects of urban Progresa on consumption, which we discuss further in Section 6. Analogous to the first stage studies, there are two types of matching estimators that have been used in the evaluations, the cross-sectional matching estimator and the difference in difference matching estimator.[19]

---

[18] Available data includes dates and amounts of program benefits for beneficiaries, thus facilitating the comparison of estimators based on eligibility versus actual program status. See Hoddinott and Skoufias (2004) for a description.

[19] Given that many of the second generation studies use the retrospective questionnaire on 1997 characteristics applied to the C2003 group to construct matching estimators (with 1997 data collected in 1997 for

This *cross-sectional matching estimator* assumes:

$$E(Y_{0t} \mid P(X), D = 1) = E(Y_{0t} \mid P(X), D = 0), \tag{CS.1}$$

$$0 < \Pr(D = 1 \mid X) < 1 \tag{CS.2}$$

at some post program time period t and for some subset of characteristics X. Under these conditions, an estimator for TT is

$$\Delta_{D=1} = (1/n_1) \sum_i Y_{1i}(P(X_i)) - E(Y_{0i} \mid P(X_i), D = 0)$$

where the sum is over n_1, the number of treated individuals with X values that satisfy (CS.2).[20] $E(Y_{0i} \mid P(X_i), D = 0)$ represents the matched outcome for each treated individual, which can be estimated nonparametrically by nearest neighbor, kernel or local linear regression.

The *difference-in-difference matching estimator* requires longitudinal (or repeated cross section data) on program participants and nonparticipants. Let t and t' be two time periods, one before the program start date and one after. Y_{0t} is the outcome observed at time t. Conditions needed to justify the application of the estimator are:

$$E(Y_{0t} - Y_{0t'} \mid P(X), D = 1) = E(Y_{0t} - Y_{0t'} \mid P(X), D = 0), \tag{DID.1}$$

$$0 < \Pr(D = 1 \mid X) < 1 \tag{DID.2}$$

where t is a pre-program time period and t' a post-program time period. The DID matching estimator, based on longitudinal data, is

$$\Delta_{D=1} = (1/n_{1t}) \sum_i [Y_{1i}(P(X_i)) - Y_{0it'}P(X_i) - E(Y_{0it} \mid P(X_i), D = 0)$$

$$- E(Y_{0it'} \mid P(X_i, D = 0))].$$

Here n_{1t} and $n_{1t'}$ are the number of treated observations in the two time periods.[21]

---

the T1998 sample), reporting bias may affect the estimated impacts. For instance, if the C2003 tended to underreport their economic conditions in 1997 relative to their actual values, the matching based on 1997 characteristics would systematically match the T1998 group to households with upwardly biased propensity scores. Ideally, the module on retrospective information in 1997 would also have been applied to the T1998 and T2000 groups, thus providing a direct way to estimate reporting bias by comparing actual characteristics in 1997 with information in 2003 on characteristics in 1997 for the original sample. Lacking such information, there are (at least) two alternatives exist to analyze possible reporting bias. One is to use for the propensity score matching only 2003 characteristics which are unlikely to have been altered by the program, so as to use questions asked in an identical manner during the same time period. Another alternative would be to explore alternative propensity score matching excluding and including variables which might be more or less theoretically subject to reporting bias.

[20] The (CS.2) condition that insures that matches can be found for the treated individuals. See Heckman et al. (1997), for a discussion of the relevance of common support restrictions for matching estimators.

[21] Note that at the baseline time period we observe $Y_{0it'}$ (no treatment outcomes) for the $D = 1$ and $D = 0$ groups.

The propensity score matching estimators are estimated in two stages. In the first stage, $P(X)$ is estimated using a probit or logit model and a set X consisting of pre-program (1997) household and locality level characteristics.[22] In the second stage, the matched outcomes are constructed, i.e. $E(Y_{0t} \mid P(X, D = 0))$ for the cross-sectional estimator and, additionally, $E(Y_{0t'} \mid P(X), D = 0)$ for the difference-in-difference estimator.

With regard to how matching performs relative to alternative estimators, this has been a matter of some recent debate, available research is mainly based on programs in the United States. Within the current context, difference and difference matching e.g. comparing say the T1998 group with the C2003 group can only be carried out for very limited indicators, at least until an additional follow up round of the ENCEL is carried out.

The early nature of the second generation studies implies there has been thus far limited explorations of how different matching estimators perform under varying dimensions or how matching compares to other non-experimental estimators. How the results vary with different estimators as well as the appropriateness of the estimators should be an important part of analyzing the robustness of program impacts in the second generation of studies, we elaborate further below.[23,24]

4.3. Attrition in Progresa

Attrition has turned out to be important in the ENCEL surveys. Fieldwork protocols throughout the evaluation of Progresa have been to revisit only the original dwellings. Households who move have not been followed. Individuals who leave households that remain are not followed although some limited demographic and schooling information was captured in the ENCEL2003 for individuals who left. Note, however, that households are never dropped entirely from the interview roster. Thus, a household which was

---

[22] The distribution of X should be unaffected by the receipt of treatment. Using preprogram characteristics makes likely that this requirement is satisfied, because, in 1997, none of the respondents had any knowledge of the program.

[23] Substitution bias is frequently mentioned as a potential limiting factor of evaluation design e.g. non-beneficiaries may look elsewhere for a substitute program (Heckman and Smith, 1995). In the rural areas where the program began, this seems fairly unlikely as there are few alternative programs available (or received) pre-program. It is however the case that Progresa specifically prohibits the receipt of programs considered to be "similar" to Progresa, these included school breakfast, subsidized milk, tortilla, and other education grant programs. If one compares the percentage of households receiving these benefits before and after Progresa, there are some declines in the percentage of treatment households reporting these benefits, compared with the controls. However, the percentage of households receiving benefits (in 1997) from other programs was quite low so that at least in the early stages of the Program, participation in other programs seem unlikely to substantially alter the estimated impacts. See Skoufias (2005) for a summary of participation in other social programs before and after the implementation of Oportunidades in the original treatment and control groups.

[24] Smith and Todd (2005) use evidence from the NSW (National Supported Work Demonstration) to analyze the performance of different non-experimental estimators and conclude that difference in difference matching is likely the best, in terms of obtaining impacts closest to those derived from an experimental evaluation, due to "eliminating potential sources of temporally-invariant bias, such as geographic mismatch."

Table 7
Presence of ENCASEH original households and individuals across waves

Round t	Households in 1997 and in wave t	Households in wave t and in all previous waves
1997	24,077	24,077
1998 (Oct.)	22,551	22,551
1999 (May)	20,857	20,192
1999 (Nov.)	20,908	18,632
2000 (May)	20,496	17,033
2000 (Nov.)	20,223	15,777
2003	20,067	14,495

Round t	Individuals in 1997 and in wave t	Individuals in wave t and in all previous waves
1997	125,669	125,669
1998 (Oct.)	111,886	111,886
1999 (May)	102,123	98,550
1999 (Nov.)	105,648	90,355
2000 (May)	94,979	75,978
2000 (Nov.)	97,426	67,984
2003	98,471	58,958

Source: ENCASEH 1997, ENCEL 1998o, ENCEL 1999m, ENCEL 2000m, ENCEL 2000n, ENCEL 2003.

not interviewed in a given round because of temporary absence, say, might reappear in the next ENCEL round. Table 7 illustrates this. Of the original 24,077 households of the evaluation sample, only 14,495 report information in every round of analysis. However, 20,067 households have information in both 2003 and 1997. Similarly for the case of individuals, of the original 125,669 individuals only 58,958 have information in all of the evaluation rounds whereas 98,471 have information in (at least) 1997 and 2003. Most of this attrition is caused by apparent changes of residence or migration (more than 80%) and the rest is related to non-response and deaths (Teruel and Rubalcava, 2007).[25]

If attrition differs between the T1998 and T2000 groups (e.g. treatment is a good predictor of attrition), this selective attrition may bias the estimated impacts of the program. Also, in the context of a program like Progresa which improves education in highly poor areas with few non-agricultural employment options, presumably larger or at least different impacts are likely to be obtained by those who migrate out of their communities after participating in the program. It is obviously of interest to know the impacts of the program not only on the population remaining in their home communities, but also the population that leaves.

---

[25] There have also been some reported problems with matching identifiers at the individual level across the different rounds. See Teruel and Rubalcava (2007) for some discussion.

In the first stage evaluation studies, none of the analysis considered the possible biasing effects of attrition/migration on estimated program impacts. Some more recent studies begin to look at the potential bias caused by non-random attrition. Teruel and Rubalcava (2007) analyze attrition during the first phase of the evaluation (1997–1999) and argue that households in the original treatment group (T1998) are more likely to leave the household than those in the original control group in 2000. This estimation in effect compares households with two years of receiving benefits with those who have received benefits for only about 6 months. Their results show that at the household level, poor treatment households are 4.2 percent more likely to have left the original 1997 sample by 2000, relative to control households. Young individuals below 18 and adults who were 51–65 in 1997 in T1998 are more likely to leave the sample. In that paper, Teruel and Rubalcava replicate Schultz's (2004) JDE schooling enrollment results (discussed below) controlling for attrition by instrumenting using interviewer fixed effects, and find that for the secondary school level, program impacts are significantly higher, particularly for women. Bobonis (2004) in his study of Progresa's impacts on marriage dissolution and spending patterns analyzes the probability of leaving the sample, and concludes for his sample of women in reproductive age, that while attrition rates are balanced across treatment groups, the likelihood of attrition is correlated with some observable characteristics. This is suggestive that program impacts, even when concentrated only on those who remain in the community, may be biased by differential attrition rates, although the potential magnitude of this bias has not yet been studied.

In the case of the second stage evaluations, Behrman, Parker and Todd (2005) show that for the original treatment and control group, out-migration rates were very high by the 2003 round for those aged 15 to 21 with approximately 40 percent no longer living in the household in 2003 compared with 1997. For a few variables of interest, though, including years of schooling and occupation, actual attrition is less than 20 percent, because information on outcomes is provided by the parents or other informants. Note, however, there are few significant differences between the original treatment and control group, estimates which effectively compare those with 5.5 years of benefits versus 4.0 years of benefits. (This does not necessarily mean that Progresa has no impact on attrition/migration for these age groups, rather that differential exposure in the program does not seem to have an impact.) As in Bobonis (2004), a number of individual and household characteristics can predict attrition.[26]

While the second stage studies use matching estimators primarily, with respect to attrition, the matching estimators provide unbiased impact estimates for those who remain in the community only under the assumption that attrition out of the program is on observables, e.g. that it can be taken into account by conditioning on observed child and family characteristics. If unobservables that are related to program impacts are determinants of who remains in the sample, this may potentially be addressed through

---

[26] Behrman, Parker and Todd (2005) use a difference-in-difference approach combined with a density reweighting method to take into account attrition occurring between the baseline and follow-up surveys.

difference in difference matching that allows for time-invariant unobservable differences in the outcomes between participants and non-participants. Of course, even if the attrition from the survey does not reflect differential sample selection between participants and non-participants, the matching estimators only estimate the impact of the program on those who remain in the survey.[27]

Some insight on how program impacts might differ between migrants and non-migrants is provided in Gandini and Parker (2007). They carry out a pilot study following and interviewing youth migrants originally from the ENCEL sample in the state of Queretaro to their new locations both within Mexico and the United States. Comparing evaluation impacts of the program after 6 years where migrants are included in the sample versus when they are excluded shows that including youth migrants actually reduces the estimated program impacts on education. An interpretation of these results is that impacts on migrants are lower precisely because of their choice to migrate, rather than remaining in the community to attend school, e.g. those youth migrating did not take advantage of the grants.

5. Progresa rural evaluation results

In this section we present the main results of the rural Progresa evaluation as of mid 2006. The evaluation remains relatively new and is ongoing, thus many of the papers cited are preliminary and/or have not yet been published, particularly those from what we term the "second" phase of the evaluation. Tables 8 and 9 provide a list of the main studies, we focus on those measuring principal indicators of program impacts.[28]

5.1. Short term results: Rural areas 1998 to 2000

5.1.1. Targeting and current poverty

Before turning to the program impact studies, a first obvious question to answer is the extent to which the program is well-targeted. Skoufias, Davis and de la Vega (2001)

---

[27] An alternative for assessing potential biases in impact estimates due to attrition is to place bounds on the treatment effects when there is differential attrition between treatment and control group. In general, the idea is to estimate bounds of treatment effects through assuming that missing observations are either (1) highest or (2) lowest. See Lee (2005) and Bobonis, Miguel and Sharma (2006) for applications. These methods have thus far not been attempted within the Progresa evaluation.

[28] A number of the initial studies we describe in this section were originally commissioned and coordinated by the International Food Policy Research Institute (IFPRI) between 1998 and 2000. IFPRI was hired by the Mexican Government in 1998 to carry out the initial evaluation reports on a wide variety of impact indicators, including education, health, nutrition, women's status, expenditure, and community outcomes, cost–benefit analysis as well as operations. The hiring of IFPRI represented a strategy on the part of the program to provide a credible evidence of the program's impacts, potentially affecting the probability the program would continue to exist under future governments.

Table 8
Selected impacts: Progresa evaluation: Short-run impacts rural 1997–1999

Impact indicator	Summary of principal impacts	Groups	Authors
EDUCATION			
Enrollment in secondary school	9 percentage point increase for girls and 5 to 6 percentage point increase for boys. Simulation of long-run impact of program: increase schooling by 0.6 years.	6 to 8 years of schooling pre-program	Schultz (2004)
Proportion of school days attended	No significant impacts.	6 to 8 years of schooling pre-program	Schultz (2000)
Failure, repetition, dropout and progression	Significant impact on reducing repetition, dropout, and increasing progression in primary and secondary. Simulation of short-run impacts implies increase of 0.7 years of schooling in the long run.	Age 6–14	Behrman, Sengupta and Todd (2005)
Child school achievement test scores	No significant impacts.	Grade 4 to 9	Behrman, Sengupta and Todd (2000)
School enrollment, years of schooling, completed fertility.	Increases of 10 to 12 percent of 12–15 year olds enrolled in school, long-run estimated increase of 0.5–0.6 years of schooling.	Age 6–14	Todd and Wolpin (2006)
CHILD HEALTH			
Child illness in previous four weeks	Reduction in 22 percentage points.	Age 0–3	Gertler (2004)
Child height	Increase of 1 cm.	Age 1–3	Behrman and Hoddinott (2005), Gertler (2004)
Days of illness in previous 4 weeks	Reduction of 0.3.	Adults age 18–50	Gertler and Boyce (2001)
POVERTY AND CONSUMPTION			
Calories consumption, four weeks	Increase of 6.4 percent.	Eligible HH	Hoddinott and Skoufias (2004)
Percentage below poverty line	Reduction of 17 percent.	Eligible HH	Skoufias, Davis and de la Vega (2001)
LABOR AND TIME USE			
Employment (measure excludes domestic activities)	Boys, aged 12–13, reductions from 2.8 to 4.1 percentage points; Boys, aged 14–15 reductions of 4–6.0 percentage points; Girls, aged 14 to 15 reductions of between 2.6 and 3.9 percentage points.	Age 8–17	Skoufias and Parker (2001)

(continued on next page)

Table 8
(*continued*)

Impact indicator	Summary of principal impacts	Groups	Authors
Time spent in a wide range of activities (including domestic activities) during previous day	Significant reductions in participation in domestic work, with impacts ranging from a reduction between 5 and 10 percent of pre-program levels.	Age 8–17	Skoufias and Parker (2001)
Time spent in a wide range of activities (including domestic activities) during previous day	No significant impacts on work or leisure.	Age 18 and above	Parker and Skoufias (2000)
MIGRATION			
Domestic and international migration	Program increases (individual) international migration, by 0.4 percentage points (from reference in control group of 0.7).	All ages	Angelucci (2004)
Domestic and international migration	Program reduces odds of international migration in 40 percent. No impact on domestic migration.	Household level analysis	Stecklov et al. (2005).

provide some fairly convincing evidence that the program in rural areas has been reasonably targeted. They analyze Progresa's accuracy in targeting at both the community level, and the household level by comparing Progresa's selection to an alternative selection of households based on per capita consumption. They also evaluate Progresa's targeting performance by comparing its potential impact on poverty alleviation relative to other targeting and transfer schemes with the same total budget. The overall undercoverage and leakage rates are relatively low (about 16 percent respectively). More convincing, however, are the Foster–Greer–Thorbecke (FGT) adjusted leakage and undercoverage rates which show that the targeting errors in the Program tend to be made around the cutoff point, e.g. the program is very good at including the extremely poor and very good at excluding the non-poor.

Similar conclusions derive from the simulations of poverty after Progresa transfers (assuming unchanged pre-program income). After Progresa's cash transfers, the headcount ratio, which simply measures the percentage of the population with income levels below the poverty level in a community, is reduced by about 10%. However, higher order α (= 1, = 2) show much greater reductions (30 percent and 45 percent respectively), almost as high as that achieved under the "perfect targeting" alternative based on household consumption.

Table 9
Selected impacts: Progresa evaluation: Medium-run impacts rural 1997–2003

Impact indicator	Summary of principal impacts	Groups	Authors
EDUCATION			
Years of schooling	Increases of about a year for youth aged 9 to 12 pre-program (15–18 in 2003). Slightly smaller effects for girls. Increase of 0.45 years for youth aged 0 to 8 pre-program.	Age 15–21 in 2003	Behrman, Parker and Todd (2006, 2007)
Grade progression	Increase of 13.5 percentage points for girls, 16 percentage points for boys.	Age 15–21 in 2003	Behrman, Parker and Todd (2006)
LABOR			
Employment (measure excludes domestic activities)	Reduction of work of boys 15–16 in 10 percentage points, increases work for 19–21 by 6 percentage points, increases work of girls 19–21 in 5 percentage points.	Age 15–21 in 2003	Behrman, Parker and Todd (2007)
CHILD DEVELOPMENT			
Woodcock Johnson cognitive achievement	No significant effects.	Age 3–6	Gertler and Fernald (2005)
Gross motor development (McCarthy scale)	Average increase of 15 percent in gross motor skills for boys and 10 percent for girls.	Age 3–6	Gertler and Fernald (2005)
Peabody Picture vocabulary test	Significant increase for boys, no significant effect for girls.	Age 3–6	Gertler and Fernald (2005)
Achenbach Child Behavior	No significant effects.	Age 3–6	Gertler and Fernald (2005)
DEMOGRAPHICS			
Migration, HH partition, attrition.	Significant outflow of young adults, and division of families into two families.	Eligible HH	Rubalcava and Teruel (2006), Teruel and Rubalcava (2007)

While the targeting is generally shown to be effective, a potential question arises about the merits of targeting in very small communities, e.g. less than 50 families, where more than 90 percent are typically declared eligible. In these particular communities, it is plausible that the costs of targeting and excluding such a small fraction of households are larger than the benefits of targeting.

We now turn to the program's impacts on current poverty. While an obvious hypothesis is that Progresa will reduce the income poverty of its beneficiaries, there are a number of possible incentive effects which might affect or crowd out transfer income. First, if by subsidizing schooling, Progresa reduces child labor, then children's income is likely to fall. Secondly, given the program has an income effect, adults might choose to work less and consume more leisure, reducing family labor income. Finally, the program might affect other income receipt, for instance, transfers from outside the household, in particular remittances to beneficiary households from the United States.

Skoufias (2005) uses difference in difference estimates to compare poverty and income trends over time between the original treatment (T1998) and control (T2000) groups. Using household income and a basic food basket as a poverty line, the results show that by the fall of 1999, Progresa had reduced the headcount poverty rate in 11.7 percentage points, a decline of 17 percent in poverty relative to poverty in the absence of the program. Reductions of higher order poverty terms show even larger proportional reductions, with the squared poverty gap showing reductions as high as 46 percent in poverty. Note these impact estimates are similar to those based on simulations assuming no changes in pre-program income described above, suggestive that crowding out effects do not appear to be overly large (although this could mask for instance reductions in income from child work and increases from other sources).[29]

Hoddinott and Skoufias (2004) examine the impacts of the program on food consumption, finding significant positive impacts on calorie consumption (increasing average consumption by 6.4 percent), with larger impacts on vegetable and animal products, suggesting that families are not just consuming more, but consuming a more diverse and presumably healthier diet. In an attempt to analyze whether the positive impacts on consumption reflect only the increased income of the families, Hoddinott and Skoufias control for total expenditures, finding that the increased income explains about 50 percent of the total consumption impact. Hoddinott and Skoufias interpret the remaining impacts as possibly reflective of the health talks attended by Progresa mothers whereas Rubalcava, Teruel and Thomas (2004) find that the consumption of a healthier diet can be to some extent explained by the fact that women receive the cash benefit. Note that information on consumption was only carried out after the program, so that the estimation is limited by the inability to control for pre-program differences. However, because of operational issues, few and irregular payments were received by households in the first months of operation, which Hoddinott and Skoufias exploit to estimate difference in difference regressions with household fixed effects in effect taking the first after program round as a pre-program baseline.

In summary, the program at least in the early years has, apparently sizably, reduced the poverty level and increased consumption and expenditures of the rural population. Large crowding out effects do not appear in this initial evidence. An important caveat is that these results are based on impacts from the first 18 months of the program and

---

[29] Attanasio and Rio-Rull (2001) and Albarran and Attanasio (2003) provide some evidence on the potential impacts of the program on crowding out, analyzing whether individuals in control villages, relative to treatment villages are more likely to receive transfers, or to receive higher amounts of transfers. Their results, based on cross-sectional probit and tobit models for transfers (excluding the program and remittances) finds some evidence consistent with a reduction in the size of monetary transfers to the household as a result of the program. They do not specifically focus on the impact of the program on remittances from abroad.

many of the issues discussed here of potential negative incentive effects warrant a re-examination of data in the medium and longer term. Recall that beneficiaries are re-evaluated after three years of benefits, and this additional means testing may increase the importance of potential negative disincentive effects of the program.

5.1.2. Education impacts

One of the first studies of the education impacts of Progresa comes from Schultz (2004), who focuses on school enrollment. Using difference in difference estimations which compare enrollment before and after the program for the treatment and control group, he finds that positive enrollment impacts are concentrated at the junior high level, and in particular at the transition between primary (elementary) and junior high school, where many children prior to the program tended to leave school. Limited impacts are observed on enrollment in primary, reflecting already very high enrollment rates (generally over 95 percent) in primary school prior to the program. The preferred point estimates based on double difference regression analysis translate to about a one percentage point increase in enrollment at the primary level. At the junior high level, the estimates are higher implying between a 7 and 9 percentage point increase for girls and between a 5 and 6 percentage point increase for boys overall. In another study, Schultz (2000) shows that the program has little impact on attendance rates, e.g. days attended per month, likely reflecting the very high (97 percent) number of days children enrolled in school report attending.[30]

Assuming these impacts do not change over time and assuming no program impacts on other related variables (e.g. grade failure and repetition), Schultz estimates the long-run increase on schooling attainment to be 0.72 years of schooling for girls and 0.64 years for boys, an increase of about 10 percent of completed years of schooling pre-program. Using actual returns to education on wages in urban areas of Mexico, Schultz compares the gain in earnings associated with additional schooling to the cost of the grants, finding an internal rate of return of about 8 percent.

Behrman, Sengupta and Todd (2005) use a different approach to estimate the education impacts of Progresa. Using a Markov schooling transition model, they compare transition matrixes between the treatment and control group, in this way looking at, for each age, program impacts on enrollment, repetition, dropout and re-entry. Unlike the case of enrollment, younger children (6 to 10) experience large reductions in grade repetition and better grade progression. At the junior high school level, the program reduces the dropout rate and also encourages re-entry among those who have dropped out. Using the transition matrixes from the first year of program operation (1997–1998), they then simulate the long-run impacts of the program, assuming the transition matrixes are stationary over time. They estimate that the average child, by age 14 will have accumulated

---

[30] Note that parents may have an incentive to over-report their children's enrollment and attendance, alternative evidence on attendance and enrollment would thus be highly useful, say through unannounced visits to schools (Duflo and Hanna, 2005).

0.68 additional years of schooling. These estimates are similar to those of Schultz described above, although one might expect Behrman et al.'s estimates to be larger, given their analysis takes into account the positive impacts of the program on reducing failure and other variables besides enrollment.

5.1.3. Health and nutrition

Behrman and Hoddinott (2005) provide the first study of the potential impacts of Progresa on child height. Unfortunately, the initial data collected on child outcomes in 1998–1999, by the National Institute of Public Health (INSP), have some important limitations. Only a subsample of the original ENCEL sample were applied child nutrition questionnaires and there are difficulties linking children back to the larger ENCEL data. Two rounds of nutritional data were carried out, in August–September 1998 and October–December of 1999. While overall sample sizes of the original sub-sample were large, very few children (663) originally interviewed in 1998 were re-interviewed in 1999. Furthermore, by the fall of 1998, many families had begun to receive program benefits, so that the "baseline" was technically carried out post-program.

Behrman and Hoddinott focus on impact results for those receiving nutritional supplements. They demonstrate, however, that only about two thirds of children actually report receiving and taking the nutritional supplements and furthermore, that those children taking the supplements have a greater degree of malnutrition than children not taking the supplements. Their impact results thus compare children taking supplements with children not taking supplements in the treatment communities over time, using child fixed effects to control for unobserved heterogeneity (e.g. factors correlated with the treatment variable and the outcome measure, in this case, height). Their analysis focuses on impact results for children aged 12 to 36 months in the first survey round in 1998, leaving out infants under 12 months who might be less likely to benefit from the nutritional supplements because of breastfeeding. They show that controlling for child fixed effects, rather than community fixed effects, results in the estimated impact coefficient changing from a negative sign to positive and significant, with the resulting magnitude implying an increase in height of 1 cm due to a year of benefits. This estimator is an impact of treatment on the treated although the issue of selection in who takes the supplements still remains. Estimates of the intent to treat parameter (e.g. using the entire sample of program eligible children rather than only those taking the supplement) show an overall positive but insignificant impact of the program.

Rivera et al. (2004) study program impacts on child height and on the prevalence of anemia. Their evidence is based on the same samples, with an extra round of analysis in 2000, although they make no attempt to link the data back to the ENCEL surveys, instead relying on more limited socio-economic surveys carried out at the time of the 1999 and 2000 to construct control variables. This is likely problematic, however, as these socio-economic surveys were applied post-program so that the reported households' characteristics had potentially been altered by the program and thus including post-program indicators as independent variables is likely to bias potential treatment impacts. The observed impacts on height compare children receiving 2 years of benefits to those receiving only one year of benefits, imply an increase in height of about 1 cm, for infants 12 months or younger in 1998.

A third study by Gertler (2004) reports results based on the original data from 1998 and 1999 for children aged 12 to 36 months in 1998 and reports similar results, finding a program impact of 1 cm. He also reports a program impact of a reduction in 25 percent in the probability of a newborn becoming ill (during 4 weeks previous to survey) and a corresponding reduction of 22 percent for those age 0 to 3 at baseline.

5.1.4. Work

Using double difference estimators, Skoufias and Parker (2001) study the schooling, work and time use decisions of beneficiary children in the early years of the program. The results strongly support the hypothesis that the program reduces work. Looking first at employment (e.g. excluding domestic work) boys aged 12 to 13 and aged 14 to 15 show significant reductions in working. For boys aged 12 to 13 pre-program, the reductions range from 2.8 to 4.1 percentage points and 5.4 to 6.0 percentage points for boys aged 14 to 15, corresponding to a reduction relative to pre-program levels of about 15 to 20 percent. Girls, age 14 to 15 who have very low pre-program labor force participation rates, show reductions of between 2.6 and 3.9 percentage points, corresponding to an overall reduction of between 15 to 25 percent in the probability of working. Note that for boys, the impact estimates are a majority (between 65 to 82 percent) of the size of the Program increase in school enrollment, implying that school and work operate as substitutes in *Progresa* communities. Using time use data carried out after the program (which permit only difference estimations to be carried out), Skoufias and Parker also analyze the impact of the program using a broader definition of work (e.g. to include market or paid work, home agricultural work and domestic work). This analysis confirms significant reductions in work of both boys and girls with Progresa. Interestingly, both boys and girls show reductions in participation in domestic work, with impacts ranging from a reduction between 5 and 10 percent of pre-program levels.

Parker and Skoufias (2000) analyze program impacts on adult labor supply using double difference estimators comparing participation and hours worked before and after the program. The results in general show no significant impacts of the program on participation or on hours worked. Furthermore, using after program information on time use, there also is no significant impact of Progresa on time spent in leisure. The evidence in the early years of the program then, is that adult beneficiaries do not use the benefits to work less and increase their leisure. These results may in part reflect the design of Progresa, where benefits are provided to families for three years, irrespective of family income, so that there is no (immediate) disincentive effect on work, as opposed to transfer programs in other countries which often reduce benefits with work income.

The work of Gertler, Martinez and Rubio-Codina (2006) also is consistent with evidence that the program has not reduced incentives to work. They analyze the impact of

Progresa on participation in micro-enterprises and agriculture and find significant impacts on the amount of land in use, the probability of having a micro-enterprise and the ownership of animals. In particular, program participation increase the probability of having a micro-enterprise in about 3 percentage points, a significant increase given the overall level in the control group of 5.8 percent.

5.1.5. Migration

How might Progresa affect the incentives to migrate? The higher income Progresa provides might, in a context of credit constraints, make migration more feasible. Nevertheless, the conditionality of the income might reduce migration, e.g. because those receiving the education grant must attend school and thus are presumably less likely to migrate. The woman head of the household furthermore is responsible for picking up benefits, which in rural areas would likely require her to at least be in the area. Thus, the potential incentives seem likely to vary by the household member. The topic of the potential impact of the program on international migration is particularly interesting, given the high fraction of Mexicans who migrate.

Two recent studies look at the effect of Progresa on migration in the early years of the program, focusing in particular on international migration. Unlike studies of most other topics of Progresa in the early years under the experimental design which tend to coincide in the estimated impacts, the two available studies find different impacts of Progresa on migration.

Angelucci (2004) argues that the net theoretical effect of the program on migration is ambiguous. Unconditional (to schooling) income can be expected to increase migration by reducing the financial constraints to migrating. Nevertheless, conditioning benefits (to schooling) is likely to reduce migration, at least for individuals eligible to enroll in school, by providing incentives to remain in the home village. Angelucci finds that overall international migration (to the US) is substantially (by about 60 percent) increased by the Program although the impacts only appear in 1998 and disappear by 1999, which is puzzling given that in 1998 much less money had been transferred to the Progresa households than in 1999 and presumably the transfers would affect migration by providing additional resources to finance migration. Domestic migration does not appear to be significantly affected on average by the Program. Angelucci attempts to separately identify the impact of an unconditional income transfer from that of the conditional income transfer. This is done by controlling for the conditionality effect through controlling for the proportion of the income grant thought to be "conditional" and attributing the rest of the impact to the unconditional income transfer. The results are suggestive that unconditional income increases migration whereas conditional income reduces it. Nevertheless, given other program aspects (for instance, a bargaining effect by giving women the transfers) and the high correlation of conditional income with the demographic structure of the household, it appears difficult to isolate the impact of "conditional" income.

It is plausible that migration might increase after completing schooling, if youth move out of the rural areas with likely limited non-agricultural employment to areas where they can expect the largest return to their schooling. To get some insight into this issue, Angelucci analyzes the impact on migration of those having some junior high/secondary school schooling at the end of the program and finds no significant impact on the probability of migrating for this group.[31]

Stecklov et al. (2005) also analyze the short-term program impact on migration, concluding that the Program reduces international migration, in contrast to Angelucci's work above, and in particular, reduces international migration by almost 40 percent. Their indicator of migration is based at the household, e.g. whether anyone from the household migrates. Stecklov et al. use both cross-sectional and double difference (comparing before and after program migration) which one might normally expect to give similar results, given the randomization. Results based on the after program cross-sectional results show an insignificant impact of the program on migration. Rather the main results emphasized by the authors are those based on the difference in difference estimates, which use pre-program trends in migration based on reported migration in the household during the five-year period previous to the program.

Given the use of the same data sources, it is difficult to understand the differences for such highly opposing results in the two studies. One potential reason might be use of a household measure as opposed to an individual measure of migration. Stecklov et al. do not address the presumably differing incentives to migrate that the program might induce between household members as well as the different program effects (e.g. conditional versus unconditional income). Nevertheless, Angelucci also analyzes a household level indicator of migration to the United States and continues to find a positive and significant effect in 1998, so that the level of analysis does not in principal explain the differences. Other potential explanations might be different definitions of who migrates. Also Angelucci claims that pre-program migration trends show no significant differences while Stecklov et al. claim to find some pre-program differences.

In summary, the theoretical work of Angelucci seems more complete in terms of addressing the different incentives to migrate according to different program components. However, neither set of empirical results is entirely convincing. This is clearly an issue where further work is needed, and is important both for understanding impacts of the program on well-being of beneficiaries as well as overall public policy initiatives as to whether social programs might affect Mexican migration to the United States.

5.1.6. Fertility

Although benefits are capped, a large fraction of transfers are related to the number of children through the educational grants. Should beneficiary households perceive the

---

[31] Nevertheless, it is not clear that comparisons of the treatment and control group for this purpose are valid. Individuals with some completed junior high school in 1999 in the treatment group have likely already been affected by the program, and thus may have different characteristics than their counterparts in the control group who achieved their schooling in the absence of program impacts.

program to be permanent that would presumably induce an increment in the desired number of children. Schultz (2004) analyzes the program effects on fertility in the first 18 months of the program, and finds no statistically significant impacts on fertility. Similarly, Stecklov et al. (2006) analyze the impact of Progresa on fertility in the initial years of program operation. Their overall analysis shows no effect of the program on fertility, marriage or use of contraceptives in the early years of the program for the group of women aged 15 to 49. Todd and Wolpin (2006) simulate the impact of Progresa on permanent fertility and conclude fertility effects are likely to be insignificant.

5.1.7. Impacts related to intra-household allocation

One of the distinctive design features of Progresa is that the monetary transfers were given directly to the woman, typically the mothers, who pick up the payment at the local post office. This design feature reflects research in the social sciences that indicates that men and women do not share the same preferences. In carefully controlled experimental settings, women have been shown to be more altruistic and more risk averse than men. (See Eckel and Grossman, 2005a, 2005b for reviews.) Non-experimental evidence, based on population surveys, suggests that in some contexts women allocate resources under their control towards goods they or their children consume (such as clothing, see Lundberg, Pollak and Wales, 1997) and also to investments that improve child health and well-being (Thomas, 1990; Duflo, 2000). Legitimate concerns, however have been raised regarding the extent to which this evidence against the unitary model of household behavior is contaminated by unobserved heterogeneity that is correlated with the distribution of resources within households. Therefore, a central stumbling block in the empirical literature has been identifying sources of "power" that vary exogenously to better understand household behavior.

In the case of Progresa, the randomization at the community level provides an instrument of the share of income under the control of woman. Nevertheless, the program, in addition to giving money to the woman, increases the total income to the family. Furthermore, this income is conditional on human capital investment and thus likely to alter these investments as well as others complementary or substitutes with human capital investment which may also affect the outcomes to be studied. In this sense, the randomization does not provide an ideal instrument for analyzing the relevance of the unitary model. (An ideal randomization design would randomly assign some households where the woman receives benefits and others where the man receives.)

Attanasio and Lechene (2002) use the Progresa data to test the common preferences household model using expenditure shares as outcome indicators. In their analysis, the Progresa treatment dummy instruments for the proportion of female income in the household. As they note, however, their approach requires valid instruments that induce variation not only in the income share, but also in total expenditures and schooling because of their endogeneity. Total expenditures are first instrumented by total income, but given total income is also likely endogenous in the current case, total expenditures are instrumented by the community agricultural wage. Community agricultural wages information in the Progresa data is however somewhat limited. Controlling for the endogeneity of schooling provides another challenge, Attanasio and Lechene include in their regression controls for schooling enrollment prior to the program in an effort to separately control for the conditionality program impact. Attanasio and Lechene estimate that the coefficient on the share of woman's income is positively and significantly related to spending on both boys' and girls' clothing. There are, however, no impacts on spending on other goods, even on those such as male and female adult clothing where one might expect to observe impacts of the female share of income. If the conditionality impacts are not fully controlled, however, it is plausible that the share of female income instrumented by Progresa would also be picking up conditionality impacts of the program.

Rubalcava, Teruel and Thomas (2006) use Progresa administrative records on actual payments that beneficiary household receive to analyze the effect of the Program on allocation patterns over time. The analysis is restricted to beneficiary households living in treatment communities with a married or cohabitating couple. To isolate the Program's "power effect" from income or other Program's effects, the authors examine the marginal effect of Progresa income on allocations, controlling for total household resources (including Progresa income). Their findings suggest that Progresa income increases the power of women towards investments in the future. Specifically, more money is spent on children, higher quality nutrient intake and there is investment in small livestock which, in the communities of study, are traditionally cared for by (and under the control of) women. The results are robust to household fixed effects, to variation in the timing of Progresa payments within treatment households and also to controlling for expected future benefits.[32] They find that in households headed by single females or single males, Progresa income is treated no differently from any other income. Direct evidence on inter-temporal preferences gathered in the Mexican Family Life Survey[33] indicates that women are more patient than males when thinking about the future. Taken together, the results suggest that Progresa income results in a shift in the balance of power within households and that women are more inclined to invest.[34]

Bobonis (2004) also finds evidence against the income pooling hypothesis, particularly for the indigenous population. He uses information from the Encaseh 1997 and the

---

[32] Results are shown to be robust to the inclusion of income variance. It is also possible that the expected payments (from the program's rules), as opposed to actual payments (from administrative records), are the underlying decision making variable. Models that include both expected and actual benefits show no significant change in the effects of actual benefits.

[33] http://www.mxfls.cide.edu.

[34] The evidence presented in these studies is in line with the qualitative evidence from interviews conducted with Progresa households that indicate that Progresa income was perceived as being under the control of women (Adato et al., 2000).

first four rounds of the evaluation survey and exploits the variation from the randomization in the program and variation attributable to localized rainfall shocks to instrument for the overall level of family spending. By showing that rainfall shocks are uncorrelated with observed time-variant and time-invariant characteristics of households and that the distribution of total spending is not significantly affected by the combination of program treatment and the shocks, his model identifies changes in the effective share of income in the household earned by women, while total household income is unchanged. He finds a 40 percent increase in the share of children's clothing among households where women received cash transfers and suffered a rainfall shock; this percentage increases to 60 percent among the indigenous. For this analysis, Bobonis uses a subsample of the evaluation survey since his identification strategy relies on the assumption that conditionality constraints are not likely to be binding for households with primary school children at baseline and that confounding factors with the program conditionality would be minimal in a sample of eligible households with children ages 9 years and younger at baseline and households with mothers between the ages of 16 and 55.

5.1.8. Spillover effects

A majority, but not all, of families within a community are eligible and receive Progresa benefits. In the evaluation surveys, all households within a community are interviewed so that four types of households can be identified, eligible households in treatment villages, ineligible households in treatment villages, eligible households in control villages and ineligible households in control villages. Thus, the evaluation data provides an opportunity to study potential spillover effects of Progresa on non-eligible households. Bobonis and Finan (2005) analyze Progresa schooling impacts on non-eligible children. They argue that significant spillover effects of enrollment exist for non-beneficiary children, which are primarily concentrated on ineligible children closer to the poverty cutoff. They estimate an "endogenous peers" parameter by using treatment in the program to instrument the effect of eligible school participation on ineligible children. The IV exclusion restriction is that an increase in school participation among ineligible children in treatment villages is the result of the exogenous increase in school participation among the eligible secondary-school children within the village and not the result of changes in contextual variables affected by the program. The reported estimates are quite high, the peer effects with the IV estimates imply a 0.72 percentage point increase in a child's probability of enrollment as a result of a 1 percentage point increase in the reference group's enrollment rate.

Angelucci and De Giorgi (2006) analyze the effects of Progresa on consumption, finding Progresa increases food consumption for non-beneficiary households in between 5 and 6 percent after 12 to 18 months of program benefits. They argue that the increased consumption is explained by higher loans/transfers to the non-beneficiary families and a reduction in savings of crops and animals, which they interpret as evidence that the program, seen as a positive income shock to beneficiary families, benefits non-beneficiary families through improving consumption smoothing.[35]

5.2. Other studies related to the evaluation

5.2.1. Can non-experimental estimators replicate experimental estimators?

Given the relative rarity of experimental evaluations as well as their generally low duration, an interesting issue is the extent to which non-experimental estimators can replicate the impact estimates based on the experimental evaluation. A large and recent literature on this topic exists in the United States, beginning with La Londe (1986) and more recently as demonstrated by Smith and Todd (2005). In the case of Progresa, two papers exist which use alternative estimators to estimate impacts and compare these with those based on the experimental design.

Skoufias and Buddlemeyer (2004) use regression discontinuity (RD) analysis to estimate program impacts on work and schooling and compare these impacts to those estimated using the experimental design of the program. Under RD design, comparing individuals within a very small range around the threshold score is equivalent to conducting a randomized experiment at the threshold score (see Hahn, Todd and van der Klaaus, 2001 for a formal elaboration). Because of the original eligibility criteria where those above or below a critical value were either selected or excluded from program benefits, Skoufias and Buddlemeyer are able to construct a "sharp" RD design.

The results in Skoufias and Buddlemeyer show that the RD estimator (using a variety of bandwidth and kernel functions), performs well in approximating the pre-program differences between treatments and control as well as the impacts in 1999. Nevertheless, in 1998, the RD design finds no significant impacts on child school enrollment whereas substantial impacts are reported based on the experimental design estimates although the RD estimates for 1999 are similar to those obtained from the experimental design. Skoufias and Buddlemeyer argue that these mixed findings can be explained by potential problems with the control group (on which the experimental estimates are based), for instance if the control anticipates receiving benefits in the future and alters behavior in the present.

Diaz and Handa (2006) attempt to replicate the estimates from Progresa's experimental design on expenditure shares, school enrollment and child work using non-experimental estimators, in their case matching. Diaz and Handa use the Survey of Income and Expenditures in Mexico (ENIGH), a nationally representative repeated cross section survey to construct a comparison group to be matched to beneficiary households in the ENCEL treatment group. Their work provides some supportive evidence to Heckman et al. (1997) and Smith and Todd (2005) who argue that obtaining

---

[35] However, when exploring possible mechanisms to explain program effects on non-beneficiary households, Bobonis and Finan find no significant effect of Progresa on the consumption of non-beneficiary households, inconsistent with the work of Angelucci and De Giorgi.

credible results for matching is greatly facilitated when survey instruments are similar for both the treatment group as well as the comparison group from which the matches are drawn. For the indicators where similar survey questions and structure are available (school enrollment and child work), Diaz and Handa are able to closely replicate the experimental design estimates using cross-sectional matching estimators, with insignificant differences between the experimental design estimates and those based on their matching analysis. For those based on expenditures, where the survey instruments vary substantially, the estimates are significantly different.

5.2.2. Structural estimation of program impacts

A number of studies have considered the estimation of program impacts and simulation of potential design changes through structural estimation (Todd and Wolpin, 2006; Attanasio, Meghir and Santiago, 2004). An advantage of the use of the Progresa data is that the experimental design provides the potential for validating the model's predictions by seeing how well the model predicts the experimental impact of the program, under the assumption that the behavior model for the control group should be the same as the model for the treatment group. Todd and Wolpin (2006) estimate a behavioral model of parental decisions of fertility and child schooling using the Progresa data, using information on child wages to identify the impact of changes in subsidies. They estimate an increase in average schooling for boys and girls of about 0.55 years, which is similar to those based on extrapolations of the experimental results carried out in Schultz (2004) and Behrman, Sengupta and Todd (2005).

An important point is how good is the model at predictions, and in general the model is adequate at predicting the level variables, e.g. the percentage of children enrolled in school. They remain good at approximating the experimental impact results for girls, but to a much lesser extent for boys. The reasons for this are not clear, but may relate to the selection of the sample which is restricted to landless households, which might increase the probability that children, particularly boys would be in the labor force. On the whole, the study is an interesting example of combining the use of detailed evaluation data from a randomized evaluation with structural estimation, allowing the comparison of experimental impacts with those generated from a behavioral model. Additionally, Todd and Wolpin simulate a number of potential policy changes in Progresa, including eliminating the conditionality, eliminating primary level grants, and doubling the size of secondary grants. According to their estimates, program impacts would be significantly lower if the conditionality is removed with schooling increasing by only 0.1 years compared with the current program estimate of 0.55 years. Reallocating primary grants to increase secondary school grants would increase impacts over the actual program in 0.15 additional years of schooling, with, by design, no increase in program costs.

Attanasio, Meghir and Santiago (2004) develop and structurally estimate impacts of Progresa on schooling, allowing income generated by working children to have a different effect on schooling decisions than income generated by the school subsidy and using post-program treatment data to estimate the model. They also allow for anticipatory effects, e.g. that the control group may have anticipated plans to bring them into the program at a future date. While the model is substantially different, the empirical estimates of Progresa are qualitatively similar to Todd and Wolpin, and no anticipatory effects are found.

5.3. Medium term results: Rural areas 1998–2003

The previous studies generally demonstrate significant impacts on indicators or inputs to human capital. By 2003, the original treatment group had received benefits for nearly 6 years, presumably sufficient time to begin to observe longer term impacts of the program and potentially provide some evidence on whether the objective of reducing the intergenerational transmission of poverty is likely to be achieved. We now discuss these "second generation" studies, all using non-experimental estimators, generally matching. While there is still experimental variation in the sense that comparing the treatment and control group provides "differential exposure" estimates of about 18 months, the main objective thus far has been to estimate the impacts of receiving the program for five to six years versus never having received benefits. The studies we review here use the follow up round of 2003 as well as the new comparison group (C2003) added in 2003 to generate medium term impacts of Progresa, e.g. after 5.5 years of program benefits. Note that this second generation studies are recent, most paper thus far produced represent unpublished drafts. (Table 9 provides a list.)

5.3.1. Infant development

A critical question relating to longer term impacts is the impact of the program on infant development. Gertler and Fernald (2005) analyze the impacts of the program on a number of different dimensions of infant development for children aged 3 to 6 in 2003. Their sample includes children born to mothers who were receiving/taking the Program's nutritional supplement as well as those who were already infants at the time their household became beneficiaries of the program, allowing some analysis of how impacts might vary if "participation" in the program began during the prenatal period. The indicators analyzed include: (1) cognitive development, as measured by Woodcock Johnson tests of short term, long term memory and visual integration, language development measured by the Peabody Picture vocabulary test for 3 to 6 year olds and the McArthur Communicative Development Inventories for 2 year olds; (2) physical development, measured by gross motor skills (McCarthy scale), fitness measured by the resting heart rate, growth measured by height for age, and stunting; and (3) socio-emotional development, measured by the Achenbach Child Behavior Checklist. Note that all of these tests were carried out for the first time in 2003, thus all estimations in Gertler and Fernald (2005) are based on cross-sectional matching.[36]

---

[36] For these age groups, longitudinal (difference-in-difference) matching would clearly not be possible as only those aged 6 in 2003 were born before 1997. It would have been useful to have information on a cohort

   The results based on the cross-sectional matching show some important impacts on the physical development of children of both boys and girls as well as some improvement in socio-emotional development for girls. For the 8 different gross motor skills tests (for instance, walking backwards, jumping, etc.), improvements of 15 percent for boys and 10 percent for girls on average in the proportion who can carry out each of the skills are observed. While these results would seem to be quite positive, they contrast sharply with those observed in the area of cognitive development, no significant effects were observed for any of the 6 different indicators used, which covered children from age 2 to 5. These results are disappointing, particularly given the overall low rates of cognitive development in the communities where Progresa operates. The authors speculate that a potential explanation might be the lack of stimulation within the household, a context where parents have very low levels of educational attainment, and few toys, books or other stimulation or educational tools.

5.3.2. Education and work

The early nutrition interventions motivating the impacts observed in Gertler and Fernald described above were also hoped to increase the educational performance of children once they began to enter school. Behrman, Parker and Todd (2007) analyze program impacts in the medium term on the early education of those aged 0 to 8 prior to the program, or 6 to 14 in 2003. A particular group of interest are children aged 0 to 2 in 1997 who, prior to 2003, were exposed directly only to the infant nutritional supplement and check-up components of the program (though they may have been affected indirectly by other aspects of the program, such as income transfers to other household members). The matching estimates based on comparisons of those receiving 5.5 years of benefits versus never having received benefits show some positive impacts of the program on these children, in particular showing a reduction in the age of entry to primary school for girls. Overall, both boys and girls aged 0 to 8 pre-program show an increase in completed years of schooling of about 0.45 years, with higher impacts as expected for those aged 6 to 8 (12 to 14 in 2003). Grade progression also show significant increases with the program, with impacts for children age 9 to 14 post-program increasing the probability of progressing on time (e.g. without failing any grade) by between 15 and 22 percentage points, for both boys and girls. This group, however is only recently entering school age, it thus is early for final conclusions on the eventual impacts of the early nutritional intervention to be drawn.
   Initial evaluations of Progresa showed the largest impacts on education of the program on enrollment in junior high school (Schultz, 2004), implying that the largest impacts thus far of the program may be seen by children at or near the transition to junior high school pre-program. Behrman, Parker and Todd (2007), focus on those plausibly

---

of children aged 0 to 6 in 1997 which would have allowed difference in difference matching using repeated cross sections and provided some perspective on possible pre-program difference between the T1998 and C2003 in these different child indicators.

close to or undergoing this transition, children aged 9 to 15 prior to the program (15 to 21 in 2003), examining a variety of indicators in education and work, including years of schooling, achievement test scores in reading, math, and writing, employment and wages. They carry out two types of estimators, differential exposure estimates, which are based on comparing the original treatment group T1998 (receiving 5.5 years of benefits by 2003) with the original control group T2000 (receiving 4.0 years of benefits) and matching estimates, based on comparing the new comparison group with the original treatment, thus estimating the impact of 5.5 years of benefits versus never having received benefits.

Overall, the difference in difference matching estimates show impacts of about a year of schooling for youth in households receiving benefits. In particular, boys aged 9 to 12 prior to the program (and thus close to the important transition from primary and junior high school) show an increase in schooling between 0.8 and 1.0 years and for girls between 0.7 and 0.8. The differential exposure estimates show an increase of about 0.2 years of schooling for boys and girls aged 9 to 12 prior to the program. These estimates, based on the original experimental design reflecting an additional 1.5 years of program benefits between the original treatment and control group, are consistent with the matching estimates based on 5.5 years of benefits.

The paper also considers the impact on achievement tests, which were for the first time applied in 2003 in the areas of reading, writing and mathematics (Woodcock Johnson) to youth aged 15 to 21 in 2003. The achievement tests were applied in the household to all youth in this age group, thus avoiding the problem of selection on those enrolled in school which typically arises in program evaluation of impacts on tests applied at school. Nevertheless, for this analysis, only difference matching estimates could be constructed, which is problematic. Behrman, Parker and Todd (2007) find some important pre-program differences in schooling between the treatment and new comparison groups favoring the new comparison group; it is probable that impacts based only on difference matching may underestimate potential impacts on test scores. The matching estimates show no significant impacts on achievement tests.

With regard to program impacts on labor, note first that the overall impact on employment and wages in the medium run is ambiguous. The schooling grants will presumably lead to delayed entry to the labor market for many of those in the sample whereas those completing their schooling (with higher grades of schooling due to the program) would presumably be more likely to be employed and at higher wage jobs. Behrman, Parker and Todd (2007) find for boys aged 15–16 in 2003, there is a negative and significant impact on the probability of employment, consistent with the point that at this age, many boys are still attending school and thus likely to postpone entry to the labor market. For girls aged 19–21 in 2003, a significant positive impact of the program is observed, equivalent to between 6 and 9 percentage points. These impacts overall confirm the model and hypotheses presented earlier, with school being a deterrent to work for younger youth and for older youth, greater years of completed schooling increasing work. Particularly for girls who tend to have lower labor force participation in the traditional rural communities studied here, the percentage increases in work are quite important.

5.3.3. Living arrangements

Rubalcava and Teruel (2006) study the impact of Progresa on living arrangements
and migration decisions in the medium term. They compare original households 1997
(T1998) to the new comparison group added in 2003 (C2003), and using double difference propensity score matching they find that households who benefited from the
Program reveal a higher rate of rotation of their members. The evidence suggests that
the program promotes young adults, sons and daughters of the household head with
their children to exit the household, suggesting a partition effect in which the Program
may provide greater independence to individuals that wish to form their own families.

   There also seems to be an inflow of new members, (e.g. not previously in the household prior to the Program's implementation), which supports the hypothesis of providing support to members of the extended family, such as parents and grandparents. The
implication of this is that members of the extended family – for which the program was
not directly intended – also benefit from the Program.

   In summary, some clearly positive impacts on longer term measures of completed
schooling and infant and child health are emerging as well as some interesting impacts
on migration and living arrangements. Nevertheless, few positive impacts in the areas
such as cognitive development and cognitive achievement have been found thus far.
There is some evidence that double difference matching provide higher estimates overall than cross-sectional matching, which might be expected given that the comparison
communities appear to be less poor in some ways than the original treatment areas. Unfortunately, for many of the indicators of interest, pre-program levels were not available
for the new comparison group. Much further research will be necessary to analyze how
robust the estimators used are, how they might vary with different types of matching
and with the use of other estimators. Additional data bases, such as the Mexican Family Life Survey (MXFLS) should also be considered for the estimation of long term
impacts.

6. Other conditional schooling-health programs around the world

A progressively growing number of other countries in Latin America and the developing
world have implemented conditional cash transfer programs with some similarities to
Progresa, and an important subset of these have also implemented rigorous evaluations.
It is useful to review the evidence of these other experiences, in order to gauge how
representative the impacts in Progresa might be and also to the extent possible evaluate
how different structure of benefits might affect impacts. The evidence, however, is more
preliminary than that of Progresa, all of these evaluations are still undergoing what we
have termed "first-stage" evaluations, with most studies still in report form, and none
published in academic journals. We also review the experience of the urban chapter of
Progresa, a non-experimental evaluation which began in 2002 and is also in the first
stage of evaluation studies. A summary of impacts is provided in Table 10.

Table 10
CCT around the world – Selected impacts

Program/Source	Education	Health	Other
RPS Nicaragua (Maluccio and Flores, 2004) Experimental design, *DD* estimator	grades 1–4, 23% increase in attendance, 6.5% improvement in retention rate	5% decrease in prevalence of stunting children under 5, 6% decrease in prevalence of underweight children under 5	4% increase in food share in household budget
PRAF Honduras (IFPRI, 2003) Experimental design, *DD* estimator	no significant impact on enrollment of children age 6–12, but increased attendance	15–21% increase in children's health services, 4–7% increase in vaccination	no impact on consumption
FA Colombia (Attanasio, Fitzsimons and Gomez, 2005) Non-experimental design, matching estimator	5–10% increase in enrollment children age 12–17	0.44 cm increase height infants under 24 mths, 23–33% rise in preventive care use	9–19% increase in expenditure
BA/PETI Brazil Non-experimental, matching estimator		no impact on height-for-age children ages 0–7, 31 g decrease in weight children under 3 (Morris et al., 2004)	4.5–18% decrease in child labor ages 7–14 (Yap, Sedlacek and Orazem, 2002)
BE Brazil (de Janvry et al., 2006) Non-experimental, *DD* estimator	7.8% decrease dropout children ages 6–15, 6% decrease grade retention		
BDH Ecuador (Schady and Araujo, 2006) Experimental, *DD* & IV estimator	10% increase enrollment children ages 6–17		17% decrease child labor ages 6–17
Bangladesh Khandker, Pitt and Fuwa (2003) Non-experimental, fixed effects estimator	Marginal effect: 12% increase probability of enrollment girls ages 11–18		
JFPR Cambodia (Filmer and Schady, 2006) Non-experimental, matching estimator	33–43% increase 8th grade enrollment girls		
Oportunidades Urban Mexico Non-experimental, matching estimator	two year impacts: Boys: increase of 0.25 in years of schooling for age 12 to 14 and 0.28 for aged 15 to 18. Girls: increase in years of schooling 0.15 to 0.17 for 12 to 14 and 0.15 to 0.19 for aged 15 to 18 (Behrman et al., 2006a)	reduction of 6.1% sick-days for children 6–15, 17% increase preventive care use (Gutierrez et al., 2004a, 2004b)	4% increase in total consumption, 9% increase in food (Angelucci, Attanasio and Shaw, 2004)

6.1. Urban Progresa

In 2001, Progresa was extended to urban areas of Mexico and renamed Oportunidades. The urban program retains the identical benefits of the rural program, although the targeting mechanism was changed to include an element of self-selection where individuals are required to apply for the program at modules set up in poor urban areas throughout the country. At the module, their basic socio-economic levels are assessed, for those that pass this initial qualifying test, a home visit is programmed to verify socio-economic information and based upon this information, a similar discriminant analysis as in rural areas is used to decide whether the household is eligible for Progresa. (See Coady and Parker, 2004 for a description.)[37]

The urban evaluation design is not experimental, but rather uses the method of matching to choose comparison groups. From urban localities eligible for the program, a sample of 149 poor blocks was selected.[38] All 20,859 households in these 149 treatment blocks were initially interviewed to gather information on the socio-economic characteristics used to calculate the proxy-means score. Using this information, a discriminant score was calculated using the same formula as *Progresa* for each household and households were classified into three groups: Poor, Quasi-Poor (i.e. those just above the cut-off), and Non-Poor. A stratified random sample, based on these classifications in addition to the self-reported beneficiary status was used to select the treatment urban households.

The sampling procedure used for selecting a comparison group (households living in areas planned to be incorporated to the Program until 2004) involved matching treatment blocks with non-participating localities using a logistic regression approach and data from the Census of 2000. In all, 388 control blocks (matched to the 149 treatment blocks) were selected for further sampling of households. A similar procedure to that followed in the treatment localities was used to sample control households, including a census tamizaje in selected blocks and probability-weighted sampling. Both in treatment and control areas, a socio-economic survey was applied the Urban Household Socio-Economic Characteristics Questionnaire, henceforth "ENCELURB"), beginning in 2002 (the baseline) with after program follow-ups in 2003 and 2004. The survey includes both socio-economic information as well as some anthropometric and biological measures and cognitive development and achievement tests.

---

[37] Martinelli and Parker (2006) take advantage of data on reported conditions at the module and actual household characteristics found in the verification visit to analyze the extent of mis-reporting. As might be expected, under-reporting is substantial. Surprisingly, over-reporting in some goods also occurs, but only in goods where most applicants have the good (e.g. toilet, concrete floor, running water), and thus where "embarrassment" of reporting, say, not having a toilet might be higher. This is important because while under-reporting can theoretically be corrected by the verification (assuming no hiding), households who over report, may over-report themselves out of the program.

[38] All blocks with poor populations greater than 50 households were selected and an additional 50 blocks were selected weighted by the inverse of their poor population. The blocks chosen represent a very heavily weighted sample towards urban blocks with the highest density of poor households, thus the impacts derived in the urban evaluation are only relevant for this population.

Most of the studies that have been carried out thus far use matching. There are several possible comparison groups including eligible households in control areas as well as eligible households in treatment areas who did not apply to the program. (See Parker, Todd and Wolpin, 2005 for some discussion in the context of education impacts on how results vary with the comparison group used.) Take up in the urban program was initially low, with less than half of eligible households taking up the program. This low take up has, however, provoked some debate, as to the appropriateness of using matching in a context with low program take up. Angelucci and Attanasio (2005) argue that the conditional independence assumption is inappropriate in such a context and thus that estimating the average treatment on the treated effect through matching is not appropriate. They suggest an estimator approximating this parameter, using the intent to treat parameter and adjusting by the program participation share. For the case of impacts on household consumption, more intuitive program impacts are obtained with their method relative to matching, however, note this is does not appear to be the case for education, as discussed below. Nevertheless, most available studies report impacts based only one estimation method.

There are two studies which analyze education impacts, both provide estimations of the program impacts after two years of operation. Beginning with the educational outcomes of the beneficiary population, Behrman et al. (2006c) provide estimates of the program impact on both school enrollment and years of completed schooling, based on difference in difference matching between eligible participants in treatment areas and eligibles in comparison areas. After two years, the findings indicate that the program has a significant impact on both variables for boys and girls, with the largest impacts generally for those aged 12 to 14 and 15 to 18 pre-program (2002). For boys, the estimated increase in years of schooling for the group age 12 to 14 is about 0.25 years of schooling and about 0.28 for those aged 15 to 18. For girls, the estimated impacts are slightly smaller, ranging from 0.15 to 0.17 for those aged 12 to 14 and 0.15 to 0.19 for those aged 15 to 18. For school enrollment, the program shows significant results for boys and girls aged 6–7, 8–11 and boys aged 15 to 18. School enrollment for those aged 6 to 7 (reflecting earlier enrollment as well as additional enrollment) is increased by almost 7 percentage points for girls and about 4.5 percentage points for boys. From age 8 to 11, the impacts show about a 2 percentage points increase for both sexes. For boys age 15 to 18, the program increase enrollment after one year by 8 percentage points although the effect becomes insignificant after two years (Behrman et al., 2006c).

Parker, Todd and Wolpin (2005) use a dynamic panel data model allowing for unobserved heterogeneity and sibling based estimation procedures to identify the program impact (intent to treat) for younger siblings on school enrollment and years of completed schooling in urban areas. The analysis takes advantage of data which collect a complete education history for all siblings. The preferred estimates, based on a sibling difference IV estimator show significant enrollment estimates, largely concentrated on youth age 12 to 17. For this age group, the impacts range between 9 and 12 percentage point increases for boys and 12.6 to 14.4 percentage point increases for girls.

However, the estimated impacts on grades completed show slightly higher impacts for boys, ranging from 0.1 to 0.15 for boys and 0.08 to 0.1 for girls. The authors also carry out simulations of long term exposure, e.g. if the program were able from age 6 to 17, estimating an increase of almost 0.6 years in overall schooling years. The estimates from this study are slightly lower than those of the Behrman et al. (2006c) study described above which may reflect that in the first study, average treatment effects are estimated, whereas intent to treat estimates are provided in Parker, Todd and Wolpin.[39]

Gutiérrez et al. (2004a) analyze program impacts after a year of program benefits on health status, morbidity and utilization of medical services of the beneficiary population. Methods based on difference in difference propensity score matching are presented, however, only one potential comparison group is used (based on households in control areas) so that it is difficult to assess how variable the estimates might be to different estimators. Limited impacts on health are however observed. The number of hospitalization in the past year is reduced in about 0.1 for both youth and adults. The reported estimates are a reduction of 0.27 sick-days in the last 30 days for children 6–15 years-old, and 0.23 for adults aged 16 to 49. There is some positive evidence on the capacity to perform activities of daily living for adults and the elderly.

With regard to nutrition and indicators, Neufeld et al. (2004a) analyze the impacts of the program on hemoglobin, anemia, height and weight and language development of small children. Only a small sample of the urban evaluation surveys (children age 6 to 23 months) were selected to receive the biomarker tests and the sample was not random, but rather chosen to minimize the number of geographic areas visited to reduce field costs, so it is not clear how representative the sample is of other areas. Control children were eligible children in treatment areas not receiving benefits. Estimates using this sub-sample indicate that the program reduced the prevalence of anemia in 46%. There is no effect on hemoglobin levels, weight-for-height and height-for-age.

One factor which may constrain nutritional impacts, as in the rural case, is the extent to which nutritional supplement provided by Progresa to children and women are actually consumed. Neufeld et al. (2004b) report that only one fourth of lactating mothers consumed the supplement, and only about 60% prepared the supplement according to the recommendations given. Only about half the children of 6–23 months-old take the nutritional supplement at least once a week. Among those taking the supplement, 66.4% consume the supplement regularly. The median of the supplement consumption, among those who reported consuming it, was about 20 g, significantly less than the 44 g recommended by the program.

---

[39] Note that the estimated education impacts in the short run in urban areas seem similar to those in the early years of the program in rural areas. Perhaps one would have expected significantly larger impacts priori, given that the urban program included high school grants from the beginning and thus would be expected to have larger impacts on enrollment than in rural areas. Further research is needed to study the differential impacts between rural and urban areas and whether the differing impacts might reflect higher opportunity costs in urban areas (recall the grants offered are identical in both rural and urban areas).

Finally, Angelucci, Attanasio and Shaw (2004) analyze the impact of Progresa on the level and composition of consumption in urban areas. Difference-in-difference estimates, measuring the intent-to-treat effect of the program based on baseline (2002) and first-year (2003) data from households in treatment and control areas show that the program increases total consumption by 4%. Furthermore, this increase is mainly captured by food consumption, which goes up by 9%. Additionally, as in rural areas, the areas where consumption increases the most are proteins, fruits and vegetables (Angelucci, Attanasio and Shaw, 2004). Matching program estimates, which estimate the average effect of the treatment on the treated show estimates of similar magnitude although they would presumably be expected to be larger, given the low participation rates in the urban Progresa program. These last findings, as discussed above, lead the authors to question whether propensity score matching in this context are adequate to control for the factors that are driving participation.

Overall, the initial short-run impacts in urban areas appear to be positive and relatively consistent with those estimated in the initial evaluation of Progresa in rural areas. Further follow up is obviously necessary. Additionally, given the non-experimental nature of the evaluation design and relatively low take up, alternative estimators and comparison groups should be used to explore the robustness of the impacts. Perhaps a lesson, as compared with the rural evaluation, is that the lack of the experimental design has resulted in some controversy over the appropriate estimators to be used, points which did not particularly arise in the rural evaluation. The issue of attrition has also not yet been addressed in the urban areas, but like rural areas is likely to be important.

6.2. Other programs in Latin America

6.2.1. Nicaragua

Nicaragua was among the first countries following Mexico to implement a cash transfer program. The *Red de Proteccion Social* (RPS) focuses on reducing school dropout in the first four years of primary school, improving the health and nutritional status of children under 5 years old, and improving consumption. The program began with a pilot phase subject to an experimental evaluation, and was then extended to other rural communities.

The RPS education component stipulates that households with children age 7–13 receive a cash transfer under the requirement that they enroll their children in school and that children comply with 85% attendance. Part of the education grant is fixed (US$8 per household per month), and part varies with the number of children (US$20 per child per year for school supplies).[40,41] The health and nutrition component includes a

---

[40] There is also a small transfer to the teachers per participant children, with the purpose of compensating teachers for the potential increase in class size that the program would cause.

[41] According to the 2000 RPS Census, 63% of the households had at least one child age 6–12.

cash transfer under the condition that mothers attend community workshops, and that they take their children under age 5 to periodical medical controls and immunization programs. As in Progresa, the nutrition transfer is fixed per household, equivalent to about US$17 per household/month. The money is given to the mother. Relative to total annual household expenditure, the nutrition transfer represents around 13% and the average education grant 18% of total household expenditure per year. This is closely comparable to Progresa, although unlike Progresa, the RPS transfer is not inflation adjusted.[42]

The pilot phase was implemented in six municipalities of two of the 17 country departments. Within these municipalities, 42 rural census communities (comarcas) were targeted based on a marginality index computed from a 1995 Census. Half the comarcas were randomized into the program, while the other half were incorporated after two years. The program's enrollment rate in the intervention areas turned out to be relatively high, with almost 90% of the eligible population participating, representing around 6000 households. A household panel data survey was collected with interviews in treatment and control areas in 2000 (baseline), 2001, and 2002, with about 1600 households. The randomization appeared to be adequate with no few significant differences in pre-program levels of program impact variables (Maluccio and Flores, 2004).

Maluccio and Flores (2004) use difference-in-difference estimates between the treatment and control areas to get measures of the intent-to-treat effect of RPS. After two years of the program, results show that RPS increased per capita household expenditure by 13%, and that most of that increase was allocated to food. In the context of education, enrollment in grades 1–4 rose by 17.7 percentage points, while attendance increased by 11 percentage points and the retention rate improved by 6.5%. Furthermore, the program had a significant effect on some health indicators. The use of primary care services increased significantly, although child vaccination rates are not differentially higher for the treatment group. Finally, RPS also had positive effects on the nutritional status of children, decreasing the prevalence of stunting prevalence in children under age 5 by 3 percentage points, and the prevalence of underweight by 6 percentage points.

6.2.2. Honduras

In 2000 Honduras began its conditional cash transfer program *Programa de Asignacion Familiar* (PRAF) with a similar focus on education, health and nutrition. The educational component was targeted to primary school enrollment, while the health component aimed at poor households with children age 0–3 and/or with pregnant women. PRAF had an innovative evaluation design, with communities randomized into one of

---

[42] The real value of the transfer fell by 8% after two years.

four groups: a group receiving demand incentives, one receiving supply incentives, another one with both supply and demand incentives, and one receiving no incentives (control group).

Eligible households were given an educational voucher of US$58 per child per year conditional on fulfilling requisites of school enrollment and not having more than 7 absences every 3-month period. They were given a health voucher equivalent to US$46 per year upon compliance with a certain frequency of health care visits. In the supply-side subsidy, health facilities and schools received a subsidy (US$6020 per health facility/year, US$4000 per school/year, on average) under the commitment that they guaranteed adequate supply and improved the quality of their services.

The program was implemented in the seventy poorest municipalities of the country – ten in the supply group and twenty in each of the rest. For the evaluation of PRAF, a household survey was conducted at baseline and then at year-one and year-two of implementation, covering around 6000 households. Impact measures after the first two years of the program (IFPRI, 2003) show that the distribution of demand side incentives generally reached the target population, with low leakage rates. On the other hand, the execution of supply subsidies was substantially below the planned target. Transfers to health facilities amounted to only 17% of the stipulated. In the field of education, supply incentives were partially implemented, teacher training schemes were executed at a 74% of planned budget but only 7 percent of school subsidies were spent.

Transfers focused on boosting demand were generally successful. Use of children's health services increased by 15 to 21% relative to the control group (Morris et al., 2004). A significant effect on increasing vaccination rates by 4–7% was also observed. Regarding education, the program caused an increase in attendance of about one day per month, but there does not seem to be a significant impact on enrollment of children age 6–12. There was no significant impact of the program on consumption patterns, interpreted by the authors as reflecting the low PRAF transfers, representing only 3.6% of total household expenditures (IFPRI, 2003). With the possible exception of health clinic visits, the overall impacts for Honduras are more limited, plausibly relating to the relatively low level of grants offered by the program. Supply-oriented grants show no significant impact on the health and educational status of children but given their very partial implementation described above, it is difficult to draw any conclusions on the efficacy of the supply-side interventions.

6.2.3. Colombia

Another example of a conditional transfer program with a rigorous, although non-experimental, evaluation is *Familias en Accion* (FA), implemented in Colombia in 2001. Also inspired by Progresa, FA has an education component targeted to poor households with children 6–17, and a health component for poor households with children in ages 0–5. The program delivers a subsidy of about US$6 per month for every child in primary school, and US$12 per month for each child in junior high school. The transfer is conditional on an 80% attendance requirement. The nutritional subsidy amounts to

US$20 per family/month, while requiring regular visits to health care centers for children's growth and development checks, and attendance of mothers to workshops for basic health education.

Targeting of the program was done first at the geographic and then at the household level. The selection was based on municipalities that, having less than 100,000 inhabitants, had adequate school and health facilities, a bank, and up to date household poverty information. Based on means testing in eligible municipalities, about 400,000 households became eligible, of which almost 90% enrolled in the program (Attanasio et al., 2005). In the case of the FA evaluation, the program was not randomly assigned between treatments and controls, but rather matching was done between treatment and control municipalities. Control communities were matched on the basis of population size, urbanization and quality of life indicators, and generally would have qualified for FA but were lacking bank facilities.

Attanasio et al. (2005) examine the impacts of the program on education, nutrition and consumption after one year of program benefits, using of difference-in-difference regressions. The authors find no impact on enrollment of children 8 to 11 (reflecting already high enrollment rates pre-program), but positive effects on enrollment for the 12–17 age group. Effects are sizable both for urban and rural areas (about 5 and 10 percentage points respectively).

Results also show that FA had a significant impact on household consumption, with increases in expenditure of 19% in rural areas and 9% in urban areas. Furthermore, in rural (urban) communities, 80% (90%) of the increase was allocated to food. Within food expenditures, the highest portion of the increase is concentrated in proteins and cereals. Most of the remaining share of total consumption is allocated to children's clothing and shoes while expenditures on alcohol and tobacco are not significantly affected (Attanasio et al., 2005).

Regarding child health and nutrition, the impact of FA appears to be encouraging as well. The percentage of children with preventive care increased 23% for children less than 24 months, and 33% for those between 24 and 48 months. The incidence of diarrhea was reduced by 10 percentage points in rural areas. Finally, FA increased the height of children under 24 months old by 0.44 centimeters (Attanasio et al., 2005).

6.2.4. Brazil

Brazil has a long history of CCT program dating back to the mid 1990s. The conditional cash transfer Programs *Programa de Eradicaçao de Trabalho Infantil* (PETI), *Bolsa Alimentação*, and *Bolsa Escola*, were unified into Bolsa Familia in 2003, becoming the largest CCT program in the developing world.

The Bolsa Alimentação (BA) program consists of a cash transfer to low income families with pregnant and lactating women and/or children under 7 years of age. Mothers must comply with prenatal care attendance, child growth checkups, and vaccination schedules. Household benefits depend on the quantity of eligible members, and range from US$6.25 to US$18.70, given monthly for a semester, and renewable conditional on remaining eligible.[43] The Bolsa Escola (BE) program was targeted to children in the ages 6 to 15, and set its conditionality on children's attendance to school. A particular characteristic that differentiates the Brazilian conditional cash transfer programs from other programs, such as Progresa, is that – they were administered in a decentralized fashion by municipalities, both for the selection of beneficiaries and receipt of the cash transfer itself. A study by de Janvry et al. (2005) of Bolsa Escola finds that there seemed to be considerable heterogeneity in the quality of implementation across local governments.

De Janvry, Finan and Sadoulet (2006) assess the impact of BE on dropout and failure rates. They use administrative data, choosing 2 schools randomly with a weight proportion to the number of Bolsa Escola beneficiaries, for each of 261 municipalities in four states in Northeast Brazil. School records including school enrollment and repetition were collected for all children in the school, on average 500 per school. The records included school enrollment and repetition for five years, two years prior and three years post-program.

Their analysis is based on a double difference method, using as a control group children that were not selected by the municipality and including individual fixed effects. The main findings of the study are that BE led to a decrease of 7.8 percentage points in the dropout rate of children 6–15 years of age, but increased failure rate by 0.8 percentage points. Nevertheless, methodological problems include the lack of information on children who transfer out of the school and the fact that treatment children appear significantly different pre-program in education indicators than control children so that it is not clear that fixed effects are adequate to resolving the selection problem.

6.2.5. Other countries

Conditional transfers have become popular not only in Latin America, but also in other developing countries around the globe. We elaborate on two programs, in Bangladesh and Cambodia. Both aim at fostering female education, given the sharp gender disparities typical of the region.

In the Bangladesh case, the program was introduced in the mid 1990s and was targeted to rural households with girls in secondary school age. Apart from a 75% attendance requirement, the transfer was conditional on satisfactory academic performance, and on the girl remaining unmarried. The transfer covers 100% of tuition costs and 50% of other direct expenses. In total, the subsidy is equivalent to around 6% of per capita income, and it benefits over 2 million girls.

---

[43] Bourguignon, Ferreira and Leite (2003) carry out a simulation of Bolsa Escola's impacts using a round of the annual PNAD (Pesquisa Nacional por Amostra de Domicilios), a nationally representative household survey. Their simulation results suggest that as many as 6 out of 10 children out of school in absence of the program would enroll in school with Bolsa Escola.

Even though the program included all rural areas of the country, it was launched at different times in different regions. Exploiting this variation in timing, Khandker, Pitt and Fuwa (2003) study the impact of the program using the 1991 and 1998 rounds of a cross-sectional household and school survey. Given that all the villages in the survey had the program in 1998, and none in 1991, the authors can estimate the marginal effect of the program, not the average effect. Results show that, after controlling for village-level unobserved heterogeneity, the program had a significant effect on the schooling of girls, and no impact on that of boys. An additional year of program duration increases the probability of enrollment by 12 percentage points for 11–18 year-old girls, large compared with the pre-program enrollment rate of 44%.

In the case of Cambodia, the program – Japan Fund for Poverty Reduction (JFPR) – targeted girls making the transition between primary and secondary school, given the context of extremely low secondary school enrollment of girls. Using data from program applications and surprise school visits and comparing girls receiving the scholarship with those who do not, Filmer and Schady (2006) conclude that JFPR had a large and positive effect on high school enrollment and attendance of girls. Results based on propensity score matching indicate that JFPR beneficiaries are 43% more likely to be enrolled and attending class at program schools, and 33% more likely to be enrolled and attending at any school.

In summary, the initial results of other conditional cash transfer programs, present a picture of fairly similar results in terms of increasing school enrollment, health clinic attendance, and consumption levels, particularly of food. The PRAF program in Honduras had the lowest impacts, but also is a program with the smallest size of benefits.

7. Analysis: Some lessons learned

In this section we analyze the evaluation experience of conditional cash transfer programs. We focus first on what we have learned from the evaluations of conditional cash transfer programs and what future research would be useful. We also comment on some lessons learned on carrying out evaluations of large scale programs with experimental designs in developing countries.

Unlike most cash transfer programs, which generally focus on alleviating the conditions of current poverty, conditional cash transfer programs aim to both alleviate current poverty and future poverty, by increasing human capital investment. The "first generation" of studies of the impact of Progresa focused on indicators likely to be correlated with this human capital investment. The diverse studies showed almost uniformly positive results on the short-term indicators measured. Among other impacts, better health, greater school attendance, less child work, and improved household consumption were reported. The evidence, although more preliminary, from other conditional cash transfer programs is also supportive of important impacts of conditional cash transfer programs on schooling and health outcomes.

Conditional cash transfer programs can be considered both anti-poverty programs and human capital investment programs. From a cost–benefit perspective then, the programs can presumably be evaluated in terms of how well they achieve these goals relative to other potential programs. For instance, one might judge conditional cash transfer programs merely on their merits as cash transfer programs, whereas indicators such as the reductions in poverty of its beneficiaries would be the main indicators of interest to be contrasted with potential costs of the program. If one takes the longer term view, that the program is primarily a human capital investment program, then the program can be evaluated as such, where the impacts on schooling/health are estimated as well as the potential value of these benefits and contrasted with the costs of the program to obtain a cost–benefit analysis of the program which can be compared to other education programs (Coady and Harris, 2004). However, given the program's significant impacts on current poverty, it is not clear that it is correct to judge the program simply as a human capital program, to be compared with other potential programs such as improving school quality which focus only on human capital outcomes.

Assuming the estimated short run effects of Progresa are stable over the longer term, Schultz (2004) estimates an internal rate of return of program grant expenditures on private labor market earnings for Progresa. The exercise is to compare program expenditures on education grants with estimated increases in labor market earnings based on the schooling increment generated by the Program. The returns to schooling are based on urban schooling returns, implying that beneficiaries are assumed to migrate after finishing their schooling, although Schultz assumes a 20 percent less than the estimated urban return (lower school quality in rural areas might imply a lower return to schooling for migrants than for urban dwellers). Under these assumptions, Schultz finds an internal rate of return on program expenditures of 8 percent. These findings are suggestive that even judged only as a human capital program, the program is obtaining a reasonable return on its expenditures, assuming the human capital returns are not far off those used here.[44]

Using the medium term program impact estimates on years of schooling described above, Behrman, Parker and Todd (2007) carry out cost–benefit estimates, under a variety of scenarios of the return to education and the discount rate. The benefits are, as in Schultz, the estimated increase in earnings due to having higher education. The costs include resource costs (administrative, private and distortionary costs from raising revenues). The benefits nearly always greatly exceed the costs, with the exception of a scenario of very low returns to education (6 percent) combined with a high discount rate (10 percent). Overall, then the results are suggestive that even if the program is

---

[44] It is difficult to estimate a rural return to schooling using the Progresa surveys given most workers are self-employed agricultural workers. This reiterates the difficulty of simulating the potential returns to increases in schooling through Progresa, so that the best way to estimate these returns is likely to be through direct assessment of wages in the future.

treated as only a human capital program, the benefits are substantially greater than the costs.[45]

Of course it is possible that other potential human capital programs might have higher benefit/cost ratios. In fact, in other contexts, there are a number of recent randomized interventions showing significant education impacts, including impacts on test scores, obtained at very low cost.[46,47] Nevertheless, most of these interventions have been carried out in much poorer contexts than the primarily middle income countries of Latin America. There is a clear need to extend impact evaluations in Latin America so as to potentially compare alternative human capital investment programs. In Latin America, there are relatively few education programs which have been evaluated.[48]

7.1. Unanswered questions

There are still many unanswered questions related to the longer term impacts of conditional cash transfer programs. The short term evaluations are an input into the longer term question of whether the central goal between the linking of the program to investment in human capital will be fulfilled. That is, are children who achieve more education today and a better health and nutrition, less likely to be poor in the future as a direct result of program benefits? The second generation of studies in the case of Progresa begins to examine these issues, showing significant accumulation of schooling for youth and some important positive effects on the gross motor development of toddlers. Many further studies and follow-up data will be necessary in order to provide more conclusive evidence of the extent to which conditional transfer programs can reduce the future poverty of the children in beneficiary families.

One of the most important outstanding questions on conditional cash transfer programs is the extent to which the additional schooling they achieve with the program will impact their lifelong earnings, as would be expected assuming significant returns to schooling. Substantial direct evidence on this is still lacking largely, in great part because of the relative recent development of conditional cash transfer programs and the point that the medium term impacts may take 15 or 20 years to observe if one is interested in evaluating the impacts into early adulthood.

The cognitive development and academic achievements of the Progresa beneficiaries appear to be limited and there is as yet no other evidence on this topic from

---

[45] Note that there are other potential effects of conditional programs which are perhaps relevant to weight in a cost–benefit type analysis. For instance, de Janvry et al. (2006) show that for families suffering income shocks such as natural disasters or illness, the potential negative effect on schooling is mitigated if the household is a beneficiary (although the same does not appear to be true for child labor).

[46] See Duflo (2006) and Duflo and Kremer (2003) for reviews.

[47] See Coady, 2000 for a description of Progresa program costs.

[48] An exception is Coady and Parker (2004) who compare the cost effectiveness of Progresa to a program of constructing additional secondary schools in rural areas, and find, that under all plausible scenarios of discount rates, Progresa grants are a far more cost effective intervention for increasing enrollment than building schools, even in rural areas where most communities do not have a secondary school in their community.

other conditional cash transfer programs (Gertler and Fernald, 2005). While conditional cash transfer programs were not explicitly designed to improve the cognitive and academic development of young children, some positive effects were presumably expected through better nutrition and school attendance and the limited effects thus far observed are quite worrying. In other contexts, some randomized evaluations show significant impacts of other education interventions on learning, including remedial education programs, incentives to reduce teacher absenteeism, and other incentives for learning such as linking benefits explicitly to performance (Duflo, 2006). Most conditional cash transfer valuations have not even included the collection of cognitive development and achievement tests. Such indicators of child development and learning should form part of conditional cash transfer evaluations, evidence of the impact of conditional transfer programs on these indicators is urgently needed.

In a sense, the design of conditional cash transfer programs as a demand program is neutral on the topic of available school quality.[49] The issue of school quality in the areas where conditional cash transfer programs are received is, however, a topic with an urgent need for analysis. Higher enrollment might induce crowding and lower school quality, unless education authorities react by compensating such crowding with additional school resources to schools with higher enrollment increases. And such effects might constraint the actual impacts of the program, particularly on learning indicators. There is little concrete evidence on the issue, however. Parker (2003) shows that student teacher ratios in Progresa remained approximately constant between 1997 and 2002, implying that the education ministry reacted by increasing the number of teachers at schools with large enrollment increases. Additionally, a recent study (Behrman et al., 2006b) suggests that schooling impacts of Progresa are higher when available school quality is higher. If school quality affects schooling returns, then this is potentially suggestive that higher labor market impacts of the program may be on those children fortunate to have access to higher quality schools. The impacts of school quality are thus clearly related with the long term impacts of the program on youth and the next generation.

Migration is clearly related to the long term impacts of the program by interacting with program impacts in at least two ways. First, conditional cash transfer programs may affect migration, and in fact, particularly in rural areas would be expected to, given the general lack of employment opportunities other than agricultural work. So, the possible impact of the program on migration is of interest. There are however, few studies of the topic and, at least for Progresa, conflicting findings on the existing studies. This is an area, thus, where the impact of conditional cash transfers programs is really not known. Furthermore, migration is plausibly a variable whose impacts might be less immediate than others such as school enrollment, so that additional follow-up studies are clearly needed.

---

[49] Although from a welfare point of view, in a context with extremely low school quality, unconditional cash transfers might increase welfare more than conditional cash transfers.

A second important reason for studying migration is the point that the impacts of conditional cash transfer programs thus far studied are based on individuals who remain in their communities of interest, and it is quite possible that different impacts will be seen on those who leave their communities. A pilot study following *Progresa* migrants (Parker and Gandini, 2007) points to the possibility of locating and interviewing migrants and shows that migrants effectively do have different program impacts than non-migrants. For the longer term, in order to provide a picture of the long-term impacts of the program, interviewing migrants as well as non-migrants will be crucial. Attrition is likely to worsen as the collection of data progresses over time. Careful preparation of protocols and fieldwork plans should be developed at the beginning of the evaluation (Thomas, Frankenburg and Smith, 2001).

A final issue for the medium term we mention here is that of program dependency. Research on welfare programs in developed countries have typically argued that cash transfer programs create negative incentive effects of work of transfer programs. Beneficiaries of conditional cash transfer programs have generally been promised benefits for a certain period of time (e.g. 2 or 3 years) without further means testing of the prospect of losing benefits, presumably work disincentives might be lower under such a design. In the context of Progresa, Parker and Skoufias (2000) find no impact of the program on adult labor force participation rates or on hours worked after a year of program benefits. Nevertheless, since eligibility is presumably not for life in conditional programs, at some point households will likely be reassessed so that program receipt in the longer term might affect work incentives differently than in the short run.

Note that while conditional cash transfer programs, have at least initially, be judged as successful, there is little evidence on what particular aspects are most relevant. E.g. is the most important aspect the conditionality (price effect), the income effect or the potential intra household allocation effect deriving from women receiving the transfer. A couple of studies have tried to isolate particular impacts of different components (e.g. Angelucci, 2004; Rubalcava, Teruel and Thomas, 2004; Hoddinott and Skoufias, 2004). Since there is no experimental variation within a particular conditional cash transfer program, this is of course inherently difficult. Todd and Wolpin (2006) simulate different "programs" and suggest that conditionality is responsible for most of the program impacts e.g. unconditional income transfers would have low impacts on schooling. Bourguignon, Ferreira and Leite (2003) suggest the same in the context of Brazil.

7.2. Lessons from experimental evaluations of conditional programs

We close with a few comments on the benefits/limitations of experimental evaluations of conditional cash transfer programs. As the first of the experimental evaluations of conditional cash transfer programs, the Progresa evaluation has played an important role in raising the visibility of conditional cash transfer programs and of experimental designs in their evaluation. The Program has clearly had quite a significant impact at the international level, as indicated by a number of Latin American countries adopting similar programs and evaluations after Progresa. It has also, however had an impact on public policy in Mexico. The evaluation likely played an important role in ensuring that the program was not eliminated with the change of government in 2000, as had been common in previous administrations, but rather was expanded.

Generally speaking, the experimental evaluations of conditional cash transfers have taken place in the initial phases of the program, thus ensuring the feasibility of having a control group, e.g. when there are a lot of eligible households who were not yet incorporated due to budget and operative limitations. With rapid program growth, it would have been much more difficult to incorporate an experimental design at a later date. For instance, in the case of Progresa, by the time the control group was treated, one in every three households in rural areas was a beneficiary. In a context of such rapid growth, it was difficult to continue to maintain the control group, indeed, the control group communities began to pressure for their inclusion, given they were literally becoming surrounded by communities being incorporated into the program.

Early evaluations also ensured that results were available at an early juncture in the program, when perhaps program changes are easier to carry out and when programs may be more susceptible to budget cuts. In Mexico, the experimental design played a critical role in increasing the impact and visibility of the evaluation, and by providing credible, easily understood results at a critical time when the program was under potential scrutiny.[50]

Most randomized experiments, particularly in the context of developing countries are however unlikely to survive a long period of time. Certainly, expecting a randomized experiment to survive more than 5 years is not very reasonable, particularly in the context of programs where coverage is expanding quickly, as was the case of Progresa. For programs where the immediate program impacts are the main interest, this is not particularly problematic. However, given the design of conditional cash transfer programs, there is a clear interest in measuring the medium to longer run impacts on the intergenerational transmission of poverty.

Thus, one obvious lesson for evaluations of conditional cash transfer programs or at least for new evaluation endeavors, is to anticipate that any experiment is likely to last only a short time, and thus contemplate alternative strategies for evaluating long term impacts from the initial stages of program evaluation. For instance, in the Progresa context, the new comparison communities, which were initially not eligible at the beginning of the Program, could have been incorporated into the evaluation sample

---

[50] A recent source of evaluations with experimental design have been the initiatives by MIT/Poverty Action Lab as well as Innovations for Poverty Action in New Haven. Note, however, these programs have a different focus, e.g. small scale interventions generally carried out by academics/NGOs rather than large scale government transfer programs, where the operational issues associated with evaluation are likely to be different.

from the beginning. This would at a minimum, have resulted in identical survey instruments from the beginning and allowed the non-experimental impact estimators to be constructed and directly compared with impacts derived from the original experimental design.

One might ask whether the experimental design is useful in the longer term, e.g. after the original control groups become treated. Presumably, the experimental design is generally still valid, but the interpretation of comparison changes from treated versus untreated to differential treatment exposure. We would argue that the experimental designs are still useful by comparing the effects of the program on families/individuals who received benefits for X years versus the control group of for instance, $X - 2$ years. These comparisons are also useful as a way to judge the extent to which the non-experimental impacts are reasonable.

With relatively short lengths of experimental design, the fundamental nature of the evaluation of longer term impacts of conditional cash transfer programs is likely to shift to non-experimental methods.[51] Given that most conditional programs use proxy means tests (which generally are define eligibility on a basis of a continuous variable based on a strict cut-off), the method of regression discontinuity continues to be another potential option, assuming that the definition of program eligibility does not change over time (as has happened in the case of Progresa). Another potential comparison group for the future includes older siblings who did not participate in the program alternatives (Parker, Todd and Wolpin, 2005).

Appendix Table 1
Growth of Progresa over time by area. By date and geographic area

Year	Rural	Urban	Total
1997	205,318	14,626	219,944
1998	1,474,972	143,564	1,618,536
1999	1,895,385	271,077	2,166,462
2000	1,915,747	273,973	2,189,720
2001	2,409,432	609,249	3,018,681
2002	2,922,911	1,114,185	4,037,096
2003	3,059,721	1,180,279	4,240,000
2004	3,453,872	1,546,128	5,000,000

Note: Urban area incorporation officially began in 2001, the vast majority of urban households prior to this date correspond to semi-urban areas (2500–50,000 inhabitants) or to areas previously defined as rural but whose classification changed in the 2000 census.
Source: Progresa administrative records.

[51] Note that, in the context of Progresa, the "long-run" impacts simulated by the short term evaluations in the area of education (Schultz, 2004; Behrman, Sengupta and Todd, 2005) look quite plausible in comparison with those beginning to emerge in the second generation studies based on non-experimental evaluations.

Appendix Table 2
Historical monthly amounts of Progresa benefits

	Jul.–Dec. 2004	Jan.–Jun. 2004	Jul.–Dec. 2003	Jan.–Jun. 2003	Jul.–Dec. 2002	Jan.–Jun. 2002	Jul.–Dec. 2001
Fixed grant from nutrition component (conditioned on attending scheduled visits to health centers)	165	160	155	155	150	145	145
Education grant per child (conditioned on child school enrollment and regular attendance)							
Primary							
3rd grade	110	110	105	105	100	95	95
4th grade	130	125	120	120	115	115	110
5th grade	165	160	155	155	150	145	145
6th grade	220	215	210	205	200	195	190
Junior High							
1st year							
Male	320	315	305	300	290	285	280
Female	340	330	320	315	310	300	295
2nd year							
Male	340	330	320	315	310	300	295
Female	375	370	355	350	340	330	325
3rd year							
Male	360	350	335	335	325	315	310
Female	415	405	390	385	375	365	360
Upper High School							
1st year							
Male	540	530	510	505	490	475	470
Female	620	610	585	580	565	545	540
2nd year							
Male	580	570	545	545	525	510	505
Female	660	645	625	620	600	585	575
3rd year							
Male	615	600	580	575	555	540	535
Female	700	685	660	655	635	620	610
Max. monthly benefit (with upper HS grants)	1010	985	950	945	915	890	880
Max. monthly benefit (w/o upper HS grants)	1710	1685	1635	1605	1570	1525	1500
School Supplies Support							
Primary:	220		210		200		195
First semester	145		140		135		130
Second semester	75		70		65		65
Junior high school	275		260		250		240
Upper high school	275		260		250		240

(*continued on next page*)

Appendix Table 2
(*continued*)

	Jan.–Jun. 2001	Jul.–Dec. 2000	Jan.–Jun. 2000	Jul.–Dec. 1999	Jan.–Jun. 1999	Jul.–Dec. 1998	Jan.–Jun. 1998
Fixed grant from nutrition component (conditioned on attending scheduled visits to health centers)	140	135	130	125	115.0	105.0	95.0
Education grant per child (conditioned on child school enrollment and regular attendance) *Primary*:							
3rd grade	95	90	85	80	75.0	70.0	65.0
4th grade	110	105	100	95	90.0	80.0	75.0
5th grade	140	135	130	125	115.0	105.0	95.0
6th grade	185	180	170	165	150.0	135.0	130.0
Junior High 1st year							
Male	275	260	250	240	220.0	200.0	185.0
Female	290	275	265	250	235.0	210.0	195.0
2nd year							
Male	290	275	265	250	235.0	210.0	195.0
Female	320	305	295	280	260.0	235.0	220.0
3rd year							
Male	305	290	280	265	245.0	225.0	205.0
Female	350	335	320	305	285.0	255.0	240.0
Upper High School 1st year							
Male							
Female							
2nd year							
Male							
Female							
3rd year							
Male							
Female							
Max. monthly benefit (with senior HS grants)							
Max. monthly benefit (w/o senior HS grants)	855	820	790	750	695.0	630.0	585.0
School Supplies Support Primary		180		165		135.0	
First semester		120		110		90.0	
Second semester		60		55		45.0	
Junior high school		225		205		170.0	

Note: Grants are adjusted every semester according to consumer price index (INCP). 11 pesos = $US 1 in January, 2005.

Source: http://www.oportunidades.gob.mx.

Appendix Table 3

Content of baseline and follow-up surveys in rural Progresa

Date of Survey	Baseline 10-1997	Baseline 3-1998	Follow-up 1 10-1998	Follow-up 2 5-1999	Follow-up 3 11-1999	Follow-up 4 5-2000	Follow-up 5 5-2003
Demographic Characteristics							
Age, sex, relation to head, schooling, language, marital status, etc.	X	X	X	X	X	X	X
Verification of ID, demographics, Δ in HH membership & reasons		X	X	X	X	X	X
Receipt of PROGRESA Benefits							
Nutrition cash transfer			X	X	X	X	X
Educational cash transfer			X	X	X	X	X
Nutrition supplement			X	X	X	X	X
Education of those 5 years & older							
Literacy, school enrollment, years completed schooling	X	X	X	X	X	X	X
Parental opinions of school quality & student achievement			X	X	X		
Age started school, grade repetition, drop out						X	X
School choice		X	X	X	X	X	X
Consumption							
Weekly consumption of food booth purchased & home produced		X	X	X	X	X	X
Weekly & monthly expenditures on non-food items			X	X	X	X	X
Health & Health Care							
Child > 5: Immunizations, ill in last 4 weeks, child was breastfed		X	X	X	X	X	X
Preventive/Curative care by provider type, contraceptive use			X	X	X	X	X
Work/school days lost & days in bed due to illness				X	X	X	X
Self-reported physical function measures				X	X	X	X
Maternal & child anthropometrics & blood tests		X				X	X
DHS-like fertility & child mortality histories						X	X
Cognitive Development & Achievement							
Woodcock Johnson of cognitive development (age 2 to 6)							X
MacArthur test of language development (age 2 to 3)							X
Peabody test (age 3 to 6)							X
McCarthy gross motor (age 2 to 5)							X
Woodcock Johnson of cognitive achievement (age 15 to 21)							X

(continued on next page)

Appendix Table 3
(continued)

Date of Survey	Baseline 10-1997	Baseline 3-1998	Follow-up 1 10-1998	Follow-up 2 5-1999	Follow-up 3 11-1999	Follow-up 4 5-2000	Follow-up 5 5-2003
Peabody vocabulary test (adults)							
Work and Earning							
Labor force participation, days & hours worked	X	X	X	X	X	X	X
Labor earnings from wage & farm/enterprise	X	X	X	X	X	X	X
Non-labor earnings, public & private transfers	X	X	X	X	X	X	X
Women's status & household decision making		X	X	X	X		
Migration							
Characteristics of child & adults not at home, 5 yr. History	X		X		X		X
Assets (level and change)							
House ownership & characteristics, household appliances	X	X	X	X	X	X	X
Housing improvements			X	X	X	X	X
Land ownership, land use, & crops produced	X	X	X	X	X	X	X
Animals	X		X	X		X	X
Community Questionnaire							
Transportation & public infrastructure and services	X	X	X	X	X	X	X
Health Facilities and School characteristics		X	X	X	X	X	X
Local labor market & wages		X	X	X	X	X	X
Private infrastructure & services		X	X	X	X	X	X
Biologicals							
Height, weight, pulse, blood pressure							X
Blood sample, glucose tests and cholesterol (adults)							X
Blood sample – anemia and herpes (age 15 to 21)							X
Urine sample clamydia and pregnancy (age 15 to 21)							X
Woodcock Johnson of cognitive achievement (age 15 to 21)							X
Other							
Fertility history							X
1997 Characteristics for new comparison group (like baseline 1997 info)							X

Source: ENCASEH and ENCEL questionnaires 1997–2003.

References

Adato, M., de la Brière, B., Mindek, D., Quisumbing, A. (2000). "Final report: The impact of PROGRESA on women's status and intrahousehold relations". International Food Policy Research Institute, Washington, DC.

Albarran, P., Attanasio, O. (2003). "Limited commitment and crowding out of private transfers: Evidence from a randomised experiment". Economic Journal 113, C77–C85.

Álvarez, C., Devoto, F., Winters, P. (2006). "Why do the poor leave the safety net in Mexico? A study of the effects of conditionality on dropouts". Working paper 2006-10. American University, Department of Economics.

Angelucci, M. (2004). "Aid and migration: An analysis of the impact of Progresa on the timing and size of labour migration". Discussion papers 1187, IZA.

Angelucci, M., Attanasio, O. (2005). "Estimating ATT effects with non-experimental data and low compliance". Mimeo.

Angelucci, M., Attanasio, O., Shaw, J. (2004). "The effect of Oportunidades on the level and composition of consumption in urban areas". Technical document #8, on the evaluation of Oportunidades. Instituto Nacional de Salud Pública, Mexico.

Angelucci, M., De Giorgi, G. (2006). "Indirect effects of an aid program: The case of Progresa and consumption". Mimeo.

Attanasio, O., Di Maro, V. (2004). "Medium run effects of Oportunidades on consumption in rural areas". Mimeo, Institute for Fiscal Studies.

Attanasio, O., Fitzsimons, E., Gomez, A. (2005). "The impact of a conditional education subsidy on school enrollment in Colombia". Institute for Fiscal Studies, London.

Attanasio, O., Lechene, V. (2002). "Tests of income pooling in household decisions". Review of Economic Dynamics 5, 720–748.

Attanasio, O., Meghir, C., Santiago, A. (2004). "Education choices in Mexico: Using a structural model and a randomized experiment to evaluate PROGRESA". Working paper EWP04/04, IFS.

Attanasio, O., Rios-Rull, J.V. (2001). "Consumption smoothing in island economies: Can public insurance reduce welfare?" European Economic Review 44, 1225–1258.

Attanasio, O., Battistin, E., Fitzsimons, E., Mesnard, A., Vera-Hernandez, M. (2005). "How effective are conditional cash transfers? Evidence from Colombia". The Institute for Fiscal Studies.

Becker, G.S. (1999). "'Bribe' third world parents to keep their kids in school". Business Week, November 22.

Becker, G., Murphy, K. (1988). "The family and the state". Journal of Law and Economics 31, 1–18.

Behrman, J.R. (2000). "Literature review on interactions between health, education and nutrition and the potential benefits of intervening simultaneously in all three". Mimeo, IFPRI.

Behrman, J.R., Hoddinott, J. (2005). "Program evaluation with unobserved heterogeneity and selective implementation: The Mexican Progresa impact on child nutrition". Oxford Bulletin of Economics and Statistics 67, 547–569.

Behrman, J.R., Parker, S.W., Todd, P.E. (2005). "Long-term impacts of the Oportunidades conditional cash transfer program on rural youth in Mexico". Discussion paper 122. Ibero–America Institute for Economic Research (IAI). Also in: Klasen, S., Nowak-Lehmann, F. (Eds.). Poverty, Inequality, and Policy in Latin America. MIT Press, Cambridge, MA, in press.

Behrman, J.R., Parker, S.W., Todd, P.E. (2006). "Medium-term effects of the Oportunidades program package on young children". Mimeo (Revised version).

Behrman, J.R., Parker, S.W., Todd, P.E. (2007). "Do school subsidy programs generate lasting benefits? A five-year follow-up of *Oportunidades* participants". Mimeo.

Behrman, J.R., Sengupta, P., Todd, P.E. (2000). "Final report: The impact of PROGRESA on achievement test scores in the first year". International Food Policy Research Institute. Washington, DC. September. Processed.

Behrman, J.R., Sengupta, P., Todd, P.E. (2005). "Progressing through PROGRESA: An impact assessment of a school subsidy experiment". Economic Development and Cultural Change 54, 237–276.

Behrman, J.R., Todd, P.E. (1999). "Randomness in the experimental samples of PROGRESA (Education, Health, and Nutrition Program)". February. Report submitted to PROGRESA, International Food Policy Research Institute, Washington, DC.

Behrman, J.R., Gallardo-García, J., Parker, S.W., Todd, P.E., Vélez-Grajales, V. (2006a). "How conditional cash transfers impact schooling and working behaviors of children and youth in urban Mexico". Mimeo, University of Pennsylvania.

Behrman, J.R., Parker, S.W., Todd, P.E., Gandini, L. (2006b). "Impacts of Oportunidades and available school supply in rural communities". Mimeo.

Behrman, J.R., Gallardo-García, J., Parker, S.W., Todd, P.E., Vélez-Grajales, V. (2006c). "How conditional cash transfers impact schooling and working behaviors of children and youth in urban Mexico". Mimeo. University of Pennsylvania.

Besley, T., Coate, S. (1991). "Public provision of private goods and the redistribution of income". American Economic Review 81, 979–984.

Bobonis, G.J. (2004). "Income transfers, marital dissolution, and intra-household resource allocation: Evidence from rural Mexico". Mimeo.

Bobonis, G.J., Finan, F. (2005). "Endogenous peer effects in school participation". University of Toronto, Ontario, Canada and UC-Berkeley, CA.

Bobonis, G.J., Miguel, E., Sharma, D.P. (2006). "Anemia and school participation". Journal of Human Resources 41 (4), 692–721.

Bourguignon, F., Ferreira, F.H., Leite, P.G. (2003). "Conditional cash transfers, schooling, and child labor: Micro-simulating Brazil's Bolsa Escola program". World Bank Economic Review 17, 229–254.

Coady, D.P. (2000). "Final report: The application of social cost–benefit analysis to the evaluation of PROGRESA". Report submitted to PROGRESA. International Food Policy Research Institute, Washington, DC, November.

Coady, D.P., Harris, R. (2004). "Evaluating transfer programmes within a general equilibrium framework". Economic Journal 114 (498), 778–799.

Coady, D.P., Parker, S.W. (2004). "A cost-effectiveness analysis of demand and supply side education interventions: The case of Progresa in Mexico". Review of Development Economics 8, 440–451.

Coady, D.P., Parker, S.W. (2005). "Program participation under means-testing and self-selection targeting methods". FCND discussion paper 191, International Food Policy Research Institute (IFPRI).

de Janvry, A., Finan, F., Sadoulet, E. (2006). "Evaluating Brazil's Bolsa Escola program: Impact on schooling and municipal roles". Mimeo, University of California at Berkeley.

de Janvry, A., Sadoulet, E. (2006). "Making conditional cash transfers more efficient: Designing for maximum effect of the conditionality". World Bank Economic Review 20, 1–29.

de Janvry, A., Finan, F., Sadoulet, E., Nelson, D., Lindert, K., de la Briére, B., Lanjouw, P. (2005). "Brazil's Bolsa Escola program: The role of local governance in decentralized implementation". Social Safety Nets Primer Series. The World Bank, Washington, DC.

de Janvry, A., Finan, F., Sadoulet, E., Vakis, R. (2006). "Can conditional cash transfers serve as safety nets to keep children out of school and out of the labor market". Journal of Development Economics 79, 349–373.

Diaz, J.J., Handa, S. (2006). "An assessment of propensity score matching as a nonexperimental impact estimator: Evidence from Mexico's PROGRESA program". Journal of Human Resources 41, 319–345.

Dubois, P., de Janvry, A., Sadoulet, E. (2004). "Effects on school enrollment and performance of a conditional transfer program in Mexico". Mimeo.

Duflo, E. (2000). "Child health and household resources in South Africa: Evidence from the old age pension program". American Economic Review 90, 393–398.

Duflo, E. (2006). "Field experiments in development economics". Mimeo.

Duflo, E., Hanna, R. (2005). "Monitoring works: Getting teachers to come to school". Mimeo, MIT.

Duflo, E., Kremer, M. (2003). "Use of randomization in the evaluation of development effectiveness". Paper prepared for the World Bank Operations Effectiveness Department Conference on Evaluation and Development Effectiveness.

Eckel, C.C., Grossman, P. (2005a). "Men, women and risk aversion: Experimental evidence". In: Plott, C., Smith, V. (Eds.), Handbook of Experimental Results. Elsevier, New York, in press.

Eckel, C.C., Grossman, P. (2005b). "Differences in economic decisions of men and women: Experimental evidence". In: Plott, C., Smith, V. (Eds.), Handbook of Experimental Results. Elsevier, New York, in press.

Filmer, D., Schady, N. (2006). "Getting girls into school: Evidence from a scholarship in Cambodia". Working paper 3910. World Bank Policy Research, Washington, DC.

Gahvari, F., de Mattos, E. (2007). "Conditional cash transfers, public provision of private goods, and income redistribution". American Economic Review 97, 491–502.

Gandini, L., Parker, S.W. (2007). "Migration and the evaluation of social programs: Evidence from Mexico". Mimeo.

Gertler, P.J. (2004). "Do conditional cash transfers improve child health? Evidence from PROGRESA's control randomized experiment". American Economic Review 94, 336–341.

Gertler, P.J., Boyce, S. (2001). "An experiment in incentive based welfare: The impact of Progresa on health in Mexico". Mimeo, University of California at Berkeley.

Gertler, P.J., Fernald, L. (2005). "The medium term impact of Oportunidades on child development in rural areas". Mimeo.

Gertler, P.J., Martinez, S., Rubio-Codina, M. (2006). "Investing cash transfers to raise long term living standards". Working paper series 3994. Policy Research, The World Bank.

Gutiérrez, J.P., Bautista, S., Gertler, P., Hernández, M., Bertozzi, S. (2004a). "Impacto de Oportunidades en el estado de salud, morbilidad y utilización de servicios de salud de la población beneficiaria: Resultados de corto plazo en zonas urbanas y de mediano plazo en zonas rurales". Documento Técnico #3 en la Evaluación de Oportunidades 2004, Evaluación Externa de Impacto del Programa de Desarrollo Humano Oportunidades, Instituto Nacional de Salud Pública, Mexico.

Gutiérrez, J.P., Gertler, P., Hernández, M., Bertozzi, S. (2004b). "Impacto de Oportunidades en comportamientos de riesgo de los adolescentes y en sus consecuencias inmediatas: Resultados de corto plazo en zonas urbanas y de mediano plazo en zonas rurales". Documento Técnico #12 en la Evaluación de Oportunidades 2004, Evaluación Externa de Impacto del Programa de Desarrollo Humano Oportunidades, Instituto Nacional de Salud Pública, Mexico.

Hahn, J., Todd, P.E., van der Klaaus, W. (2001). "Identification and estimation of treatment effects with a regression-discontinuity design". Econometrica 69, 201–209.

Heckman, J.J., Ichimura, H., Todd, P.E. (1997). "Matching as an econometric evaluation estimator". Review of Economic Studies 65, 261–290.

Heckman, J.J., Smith, J. (1995). "Assessing the case for social experiments". Journal of Economic Perspectives 9, 85–110.

Heckman, J.J., Ichimura, H., Smith, J., Todd, P.E. (1997). "Characterizing selection bias using experimental data". Econometrica 66, 1017–1089.

Hoddinott, J., Skoufias, E. (2004). "The impact of PROGRESA on consumption". Economic Development and Cultural Change 53, 37–63.

International Food Policy Research Institute (IFPRI) (2003). "Proyecto PRAF/BID fase II: Impacto intermedio". Sexto informe, Washington, DC.

Khandker, S., Pitt, M., Fuwa, N. (2003). "Subsidy to promote girls' secondary education: The female stipend program in Bangladesh". Mimeo.

Krueger, A.B. (2002). "Economic scene: A model for evaluating the use of development dollars, south of the border". New York Times, May 2.

La Londe, R. (1986). "Evaluating the econometric evaluations of training programs with experimental data". American Economic Review 76, 604–620.

Lee, D. (2005). "Training, wages, and sample selection: Estimating sharp bounds on treatment effects". Mimeo, University of California at Berkeley.

Lundberg, S., Pollak, R.A. (1993). "Separate spheres and the marriage market". Journal of Political Economy 101, 988–1010.

Lundberg, S.J., Pollak, R.A., Wales, T.J. (1997). "Do husbands and wives pool their resources? Evidence from the United Kingdom child benefit". Journal of Human Resources 32, 463–480.

Maluccio, J., Flores, R. (2004). "Impact evaluation of a conditional cash transfer program: The Nicaraguan Red de Proteccion Social". Discussion paper No. 184. FCND, IFPRI, Washington, DC.

Martinelli, C., Parker, S.W. (2003). "Should transfers to poor families be conditional on school attendance: A household bargaining approach". International Economic Review 44, 523–544.

Martinelli, C., Parker, S.W. (2004). "Do school subsidies promote human capital investment among the poor?" Mimeo.

Martinelli, C., Parker, S.W. (2006). "Deception and misreporting in a social program". Journal of the European Economic Association, in press.

Morris, S., Flores, R., Olinto, P., Medina, J.M. (2004). "Monetary incentives in primary health care and effects on use and coverage of preventive health care interventions in rural Honduras: Cluster randomised trial". Lancet 364 (9450), 2030–2037.

Neufeld, L., Sotres-Álvarez, D., Flores-López, L., Tolentino-Mayo, L., Jiménez-Ruiz, J., Rivera-Dommarco, J. (2004a). "Consumo del suplemento alimenticio nutrisano y nutrivida de niños y mujeres beneficiarios de Oportunidades en zonas urbanas". Documento Técnico #6 en la Evaluación de Oportunidades 2004, Evaluación Externa de Impacto del Programa de Desarrollo Humano Oportunidades, Instituto Nacional de Salud Pública, Mexico.

Neufeld, L., Sotres-Álvarez, R., García-Peregrino, A., García-Guerra, L., Tolentino-Mayo, L.F., Rivera-Dommarco, J. (2004b). "Evaluación del estado nutricional y adquisición de lenguaje en niños de localidades urbanas con y sin el programa Oportunidades". Documento Técnico #7 en la Evaluación de Oportunidades 2004, Evaluación Externa de Impacto del Programa de Desarrollo Humano Oportunidades, Instituto Nacional de Salud Pública, Mexico.

Parker, S.W. (2003). "Evaluación de impacto de Oportunidades sobre la inscripción escolar: Primaria, secundaria y media superior". Secretaría de Desarrollo Social, Mexico.

Parker, S.W., Gandini, L. (2007). "Migration and the evaluation of social programs: Evidence from Mexico". Mimeo.

Parker, S.W., Pederzini, C. (2001). "Gender differences by education in Mexico". In: Katz, E., Correia, M. (Eds.), The Economics of Gender in Mexico: Work, Family, State and Market. The World Bank, Washington, DC.

Parker, S.W., Skoufias, E. (2000). "The impact of PROGRESA on work, leisure and time allocation". Report submitted to PROGRESA. International Food Policy Research Institute, Washington, DC, October.

Parker, S.W., Teruel, G.M. (2005). "Randomization and social program evaluation: The case of Progresa". The ANNALS of the American Academy of Political and Social Science 599, 199–219.

Parker, S.W., Todd, P.E., Wolpin, K.I. (2005). "Within family treatment effect estimators: The impact of Oportunidades on schooling in Mexico". Mimeo, University of Pennsylvania.

Rivera, J.A., Sotres-Alvarez, D., Habicht, J.P., Shamah, T., Villalpando, S. (2004). "Impact of the Mexican program for education, health, and nutrition (Progresa) on rates of growth and anemia in infants and young children". Journal of the American Medical Association 291, 2563–2570.

Rubalcava, L., Teruel, G. (2006). "Conditional public transfers and living arrangements in rural Mexico evidence". Paper CCPR-006-06. California Center for Population Research, On-line working paper series.

Rubalcava, L., Teruel, G., Thomas, D. (2004). "Spending, saving and public transfers paid to women". Paper CCPR-024-04. California Center for Population Research. On-line working paper series.

Rubalcava, L., Teruel, G., Thomas, D. (2006). "Investments, time preferences and public transfers paid to women". Mimeo, California Center for Population Research.

Schady, N., Araujo, M. (2006). "Cash transfers, conditions, school enrollment, and child work: Evidence from a randomized experiment in Ecuador". Working paper 3930. The World Bank Policy Research, Washington, DC.

Schultz, T.P. (2000). "Impact of Progresa on school attendance rates in the sampled population". International Food Policy Research Institute, Washington, DC.

Schultz, T.P. (2004). "School subsidies for the poor: Evaluating a Mexican strategy for reducing poverty". Journal of Development Economic 74 (1), 199–250.

Skoufias, E. (2005). "PROGRESA and its impacts on the human capital and welfare of households in rural Mexico". Research report No. 139. International Food Policy Research Institute, Washington, DC.

Skoufias, E., Buddlemeyer, H. (2004). "An evaluation of the performance of regression discontinuity design on PROGRESA". Working paper series 3386. Policy Research, The World Bank.

Skoufias, E., Davis, B., de la Vega, S. (2001). "Targeting the poor in Mexico: Evaluation of the selection of beneficiary households into PROGRESA". World Development 29, 1969–1984.

Skoufias, E., Parker, S.W. (2001). "Conditional cash transfers and their impact on child work and schooling: Evidence from the PROGRESA program in Mexico". Economia 2, 45–96.

Smith, J., Todd, P. (2005). "Does matching overcome La Londe's critique of nonexperimental estimators?" Journal of Econometrics 125, 305–353.

Stecklov, G., Winters, P., Stampini, M., Davis, B. (2005). "Do conditional cash transfers influence migration? A study using experimental data from the Mexican PROGRESA program". Demography 42, 769–790.

Stecklov, G., Winters, P., Todd, J., Regalia, F. (2006). "Demographic externalities from poverty programs in developing countries: Experimental evidence from Latin America". Working paper 2006-01. American University, Department of Economics.

Teruel, G., Rubalcava, L. (2007). "Attrition in PROGRESA". Mimeo.

Thomas, D. (1990). "Intrahousehold resource allocation: An inferential approach". Journal of Human Resources 25, 635–664.

Thomas, D., Frankenberg, E., Smith, J.P. (2001). "Lost but not forgotten: Attrition in the Indonesian family life survey". Journal of Human Resources 36, 556–592.

Todd, P.E. (2004). "Technical note on using matching estimators to evaluate the Oportunidades program for six year follow-up evaluation of Oportunidades in rural areas". Mimeo. University of Pennsylvania, Philadelphia.

Todd, P.E., Wolpin, K.I. (2006). "Using a social experiment to validate a dynamic behavioral model of child schooling and fertility: Assessing the impact of a school subsidy program in Mexico". American Economics Review 96 (5), 1384–1417.

Yap, Y., Sedlacek, G., Orazem, P. (2002). "Limiting child labor through behavior-based income transfers: An experimental evaluation of the PETI program in rural Brazil". The World Bank, Washington, DC.

AUTHOR INDEX

n indicates citation in a footnote.

SUBJECT INDEX